S0-EPD-852

CAMBRIDGE STUDIES IN
INTERNATIONAL AND COMPARATIVE LAW
General Editors:
C. J. HAMSON AND R. Y. JENNINGS

VII

STATE SUCCESSION IN MUNICIPAL LAW
AND INTERNATIONAL LAW

VOLUME I

IN THIS SERIES

I Comparative Law: an Introduction to the Comparative Method of Legal Study and Research
by H. C. GUTTERIDGE

II Full Powers and Ratification: a Study in the Development of Treaty-making Procedure   *by* J. MERVYN JONES

III Recognition in International Law   *by* H. LAUTERPACHT

IV Governmental Liability: a Comparative Study
by H. STREET

V The Law of State Succession   *by* D. P. O'CONNELL

VI Expropriation in Public International Law
by B. A. WORTLEY

STATE SUCCESSION
IN MUNICIPAL LAW AND
INTERNATIONAL LAW

BY

D. P. O'CONNELL

B.A., LL.M. (N.Z.), PH.D. (CANTAB.)

Professor of International Law in the University of Adelaide

VOLUME I
INTERNAL RELATIONS

CAMBRIDGE
AT THE UNIVERSITY PRESS
1967

Published by the Syndics of the Cambridge University Press
Bentley House, 200 Euston Road, London, N.W. 1
American Branch: 32 East 57th Street, New York, N.Y. 10022

© Cambridge University Press 1967

Library of Congress Catalogue Card Number: 66-21072

Printed in Great Britain
at the University Printing House, Cambridge
(Brooke Crutchley, University Printer)

PREFACE

International law is not only an intellectual discipline whose roots are grounded in philosophy but also a practical adjunct of diplomacy. Its content necessarily varies according to diplomatic exigencies, so that while its systematic elaboration is a matter of juristic reasoning its practical content must correspond with the realities of international life and intercourse. For this reason a rule of international law, while it does not necessarily derive from State practice, must nonetheless be verified by reference to it, and there is in every branch of international law a complex interaction of the speculative and the empirical, the theoretical and the practical.

The topic of State succession illustrates this interaction perhaps more clearly than any other in the corpus of international law. The content of the rules of State succession has been influenced, not only by observation of what States have done in the past and by recognition of their present needs, but also by the systematic construction superimposed on the subject matter by theory. Necessarily those features of international law concerned with the birth, life and death of States are influenced by the notions of the State prevalent in any particular historical epoch; and those notions in their turn derive from current philosophies of human society: In the Age of Reason the approach to the problem of change in the form of government of a country necessarily derived from the notion of the social contract and the theory of natural rights: with the abstraction of sovereignty in the post-Hegelian period the problems posed by mutations in political authority over territory were resolved by reference to the concept of national identity and the all-embracing State. The concept of State succession is inconstant because theories of the State vary from age to age, and the doctrine enunciated in the past must constantly be verified by reference to the actualities of the present. Particular instances may call for particular solutions, and the theorist must avoid the temptation to resolve all problems arising from changes of sovereignty and government by reference to a single rubric and to a doctrine no longer viable in the political, economic and administrative environment of the moment.

The need to bring into focus the problem of State succession in all its aspects is obvious, yet the difficulties confronting the jurist who attempts to do so are profound. He must take into account, not only the precedents of the past, and distinguish them in the light of the circumstances of the present, but he must also distinguish between the numerous types and occasions of change. At the present time he is confronted by the fundamental obstacle of a distinction, derived from the post-Hegelian period, between change of sovereignty and change of government, between continuity of States and State succession. The line between these two types of change in some instances wears thin to the point of disappearance, and the placing of a particular instance of change within the one or the other category is often quite arbitrary. To permit the solution of complex political and economic problems to depend on this arbitrary cataloguing is to divorce the law from the actualities of international life. If there is any rubric, therefore, to which one could resort as a touchstone for the solution of all problems of political change over territory it might be this: that the consequences of such change should be measured according to the degree of political, economic and social disruption which occurs. There might, therefore, be a spectrum of solutions rather than a unique solution. If this is to introduce relativity into the law it is by no means to divorce it from philosophical considerations or from the need for theoretical elaboration, for, one's approach to any problem of State succession will depend upon one's approach to the philosophy and methodology of international law as a whole.

When I published my work, *The Law of State Succession*, in 1956, the most recent historic phase of State succession was that which occurred as a result of the upheavals of World Wars I and II. The problem of decolonization was just beginning, and its novelty was not obvious in the cases of the partition of India or the independence of Burma and Ceylon. Since that date the universe of international relations has fundamentally altered with the appearance of a large number of new States. The international community could not tolerate the notion that change of sovereignty in these circumstances could produce a collapse of existing economic and administrative relationships which existing rules of law sustain, even if it tolerated it in the case of particular and isolated instances in the past. Reflexion on the problems presented to the world by decolonization increased my insight into the problem of State succession as a whole; and while I believe that I have not departed fundamentally from the thesis expounded in that book, I have taken greater account of the diversity of situations and the variety of problems generated by them. For this reason it became obvious to the editors of the series in which the book appeared that a second edition would not be appropriate and that a new work was called for, which would take into account, not only my own more mature reflexions, but also the new form which contemporary problems has imposed on the subject matter of State succession. The present work, while it incorporates the material of the 1956 book, has a new and expanded content, and its primary aim is to draw into perspective the whole range of State succession problems which have arisen, and to see present issues as merely one phase in a long and complex historical movement.

It also became obvious to me that the problem of the relationship between international law and municipal law in the solution of the legal problems resulting from change of sovereignty was more complex than I had earlier conceded. Indeed the analysis of the matter discloses that international law plays a very restricted role in the matter except with respect to treaties, international claims and protection of foreign investment. For this reason it seemed logical to divide the subject matter into two volumes, the first dealing with problems arising primarily under municipal law and the second dealing with problems arising primarily under international law. Naturally this division is not entirely symmetrical because of the inter-relationship of international law and municipal law in the matter of protection of private rights; and also because certain questions of an internal character, such as succession in debt relationships, may also arise between sovereigns and be governed by international law. However, it is clear that the problem of succession to treaties can be a suitable subject of a separate monograph, and the division of this work into two volumes is a useful way of separating the material on treaties from other subject-matters.

This work could never have been brought to fruition has I not been fortunate enough to be elected the Rapporteur of the International Law Association's committee on State Succession. Supported generously by the Ford Foundation the Committee has been able, over a period of years, to study the problem of State succession and to provide me with the necessary support in the way of staff and travel without which the material could not have been collected or adequately processed. I have been enabled through the International Law Association and the facilities made available by the British Foreign Office to consult with most of the governments of the new States at the highest level. I have therefore not only been able to analyse the material, but also to gain an insight into the needs and attitudes of most of the new States and of a considerable number of the old ones as well. Naturally this insight is reflected in the conclusions which I offer. It remains only to acknowledge the inestimable debt which I owe to the International Law Association, and especially to the encouragement of Lord McNair, to the Ford Foundation, to the governments concerned, to the legal counsel of the large number of international organizations whom I have personally consulted and with whom I have corresponded, and to the Committee itself, than whom a more agreeable and helpful group could hardly be imagined. Considering the vast bulk of contemporary international law, and taking into account divergence in national outlook and philosophical opinions and the complexity of actual problems, it is doubtful if any scholar can adequately state the law in any chapter of international law without the type of international co-operation which I have been fortunate enough to enjoy.

The work would also be less comprehensive without the devoted help of my research assistants, in the first instance, Dr I. Shearer, now Senior Lecturer in Law in the University of Adelaide, Miss M. Broderick, his successor, and for a period Miss I. Pearson. I would like to mention Dr J. Varsanyi and Mr J. A. Neumann, both of Adelaide, whose help in the matter of East European materials and the bibliography has been important. The help which I have received from so many people in government, in international organizations, and in universities throughout the world, is so enormous that it is impossible to select those who might be specifically mentioned. I trust that this general acknowledgement will be taken as an expression not only of indebtedness, but also of gratitude.

The cut-off date of the information in this work is 31 December 1965, but during the process of proof correcting it has been possible to introduce the more important references for 1966. Congo (Léopoldville) became known as Congo (Kinshasa) after the work was in production, and references to Congo (L.) should be read accordingly. The Law Officers' Opinions in the Appendix to the 1956 book are not reproduced, and to this extent that book is not superseded.

D.P.O'C.

CONTENTS

Preface	page v
Table of Cases	xxi
A. International Cases	xxi
B. Municipal Cases	xxii
Table of United Kingdom Statutes	xxxiii
Table of United Kingdon Statutory Instruments	xxxvi
Table of Commonwealth and Other Statutes and Statutory Instruments	xxxviii
Table of Treaties	xlii
A. Multilateral Treaties	xlii
B. Bilateral Treaties	xlvi
Table of United Nations Documents Relating to State Succession	ci
Abbreviations	cii

PART I

THE THEORY AND PROCESS OF STATE SUCCESSION

CHAPTER I. THE NATURE AND THEORY OF STATE SUCCESSION

1	The Nature of State Succession	3
2	The Relationship between State Succession and Continuity of States	4
3	The Theory of State Succession	8
I	Theories of Continuity	9
(a)	The theory of universal succession	9
(b)	The theory of popular continuity	11
(c)	The theory of organic substitution	12
(d)	The theory of self-abnegation	14
II	Negative Theories	14
(a)	Imperative theories of law	15
(b)	Theories of a sceptical character	17

III	Theories Importing International Law	page 17
IV	Communist Theory of State Succession	19
V	Implications for State Succession of Theories of Territory	22
VI	Criticisms of these Theories	24
4	Conclusions	30

CHAPTER 2. EVOLUTION OF THE BRITISH EMPIRE AND COMMONWEALTH

1 Introduction — 36

2 Treaty-making Power and Autonomy of the Older Dominions — 38

   I The Situation prior to Dominion Status — 39
      (a) Reserved application of commercial treaties — 41
      (b) Power of separate denunciation — 42
      (c) Colonial participation in the negotiation of a treaty — 43
      (d) Non-commercial agreements — 44
      (e) The international law implications of colonial competence — 44

   II Dominion Status and Treaties — 46

   III The Statute of Westminster, 1931 — 47

3 The Evolution of the other Commonwealth Countries — 49

   I Pre-independence Autonomy — 49

   II The Technique of Granting Independence — 52
      (a) Grant of independence as a republic (or foreign monarchy) — 52
      (b) Grant of independence as a monarchy — 55

CHAPTER 3. EVOLUTION OF THE FRENCH COMMUNITY AND FRANCOPHONE STATES

1 The Pre-Independence Situation — 58

   I The French Union of 1946 — 58

   II The Loi-cadre of 23 June 1956 — 59

III	The Community of 4 October 1958	page 60
	(a) International unity	61
	(b) Centralization	62
2	The Conventional Community of 1960	64
3	The System of Co-operation	68
	I Agreements on Participation in the Community and the *Union Africaine et Malagache*	69
	II The Co-operation Agreements	71
	(a) The diplomatic, economic and defence agreements	71
	(b) The arbitration convention	72
	(c) The franc zone	72
	(d) Co-operation in the matter of justice	73
	(e) Agreement on fundamental rights and establishment	74
4	The Implications of Community Evolution in the Law of State Succession	75
	I The Legal Orders of the Overseas Territories	75
	II The Evolutionary Character of the Community and the Survival of the Legal Order	75
	III Application of French Treaties to the Overseas Territories	77
	IV Treaties in the French Internal Legal Order after 1946	80

Table 1. Multilateral co-operation agreements 82
Table 2. Bilateral co-operation agreements 83

CHAPTER 4. EVOLUTION OF THE CONGO

1 The Cession of the Congo to Belgium, 1907 89
2 The Independence of the Congo, 1960 93

CHAPTER 5. EVOLUTION OF THE NETHERLANDS INDIES 97

PART II

THE EFFECT OF CHANGE OF SOVEREIGNTY ON THE LEGAL AND ADMINISTRATIVE STRUCTURE OF THE AFFECTED TERRITORY

CHAPTER 6. THE EFFECT OF CHANGE OF SOVEREIGNTY ON THE LEGAL SYSTEM IN THE AFFECTED TERRITORY

1 The Basis of Legal Continuity *page* 101

2 The Distinction between Public Law and Private Law 104

3 Inconsistency between Laws of the Predecessor and Successor States 107

4 Continuity of Law in Ceded or Annexed Territory 108

British cessions and annexations (p. 108). United States cessions (p. 109). The *Anschluss* of Austria to the *Reich*, 1938 (p. 111). The acquisition of German territory by Poland, 1945 (p. 111). Other cases (p. 112). The cession of Newfoundland to Canada, 1949 (p. 112).

5 Continuity of Law upon the Formation and Dissolution of Composite States, and Dismemberment of States 112

The formation of the United Arab Republic, 1958 (p. 112). The formation of the Somali Republic, 1960 (p. 112). The formation of Malaysia, 1963 (p. 113). The formation of Tanzania, 1964 (p. 113). The dismemberment of Ruanda-Urundi, 1962 (p. 114). The dissolution of the Federation of the West Indies, 1962 (p. 114). The dissolution of the Federation of Rhodesia and Nyasaland, 1963 (p. 114). The partition of India, 1947 (p. 116): Taxation (p. 116). Companies (p. 117). Private contracts (p. 117). The separation of Singapore from Malaysia, 1965 (p. 118).

6 Continuity of Law in New States 118

Independence of British territories (p. 118). The definition of 'British possession' (p. 120). The definition of 'British ship' (p. 121). The Fugitive Offenders Act, 1881 (p. 122). The Copyright Acts (p. 124). English warrants in Ireland (p. 127). The Enforcement of Maintenance Orders Acts (p. 127). The Colonial Divorce Acts (p. 127). The effect of legislative repeal in United Kingdom Acts (p. 128). The independence of the Philippines, 1946 (p. 129). The independence of Indonesia, 1949 (p. 130). The independence of Burma, 1947 (p. 130). The independence of Israel, 1948 (p. 131). The continuity of law in the French Community (p. 132). The independence of the Congo (Léopoldville), 1960 (p. 133). The problem of continuity of law in Poland after 1919 (p. 134).

CHAPTER 7. THE EFFECT OF STATE SUCCESSION ON THE JUDICIAL SYSTEM

1 The Judicial Organization   *page* 142

2 The Judicial Jurisdiction   144

  I Civil Proceedings   144

    (*a*) Pending claims   144

Solution in the absence of legislation (p. 144). Solution provided by treaties and legislation (p. 145). State practice generally (p. 145). The partition of India, 1947 (p. 146). The dismemberment of Palestine, 1947 (p. 148). The independence of British territories (p. 149). The union of Tanganyika and Zanzibar, 1964 (p. 149). The independence of the Francophone States (p. 150). The independence of Algeria, 1962 (p. 151). The cession of the French Establishments in India, 1954 (p. 151). The independence of the Congo (Léopoldville), 1960 (p. 151). The dismemberment of Ruanda-Urundi, 1962 (p. 152).

    (*b*) Judgments   152

State practice generally (p. 152). The partition of India, 1947 (p. 155). The independence of the Francophone States (p. 157).

    (*c*) Appeals   158

Appeals to the Italian Court of Cassation and Council of State (p. 159). Appeals to the French *Cour de Cassation* and *Conseil d'État* (p. 159). Appeals to the Belgian *Cour de Cassation* and *Conseil d'État* (p. 162). The formation of Malaysia, 1963, and the separation of Singapore, 1965 (p. 163). Appeals to the Court of Appeal of Eastern Africa (p. 163). Appeals to the British Caribbean Court of Appeal (p. 164). Appeals to the Privy Council (p. 164). The dissolution of the Federation of Rhodesia and Nyasaland, 1963 (p. 167). Treaty provisions for pending appeals (p. 167). The partition of India, 1947 (p. 168).

    (*d*) Judicial precedent   168

  II Criminal Proceedings   169

Table of legislation of the Francophone States   173

CHAPTER 8. THE EFFECT OF CHANGE OF SOVEREIGNTY ON THE ADMINISTRATION OF ABSORBED TERRITORY

1 The Civil Service   177

2 The Armed Forces   181

3 Practice in the Matter of Civil Service Continuity   182

The partition of India, 1947 (p. 182). The independence of Burma and Ceylon, 1947 (p. 184). The independence of Israel, 1948 (p. 184). Independence within the

Commonwealth (p. 185). The dissolution of the Federation of Rhodesia and Nyasaland, 1963 (p. 185). The formation of Malaysia, 1963 (p. 186). The Francophone States (p. 186). The independence of the Congo (Léopoldville), 1960 (p. 188).

4   Continuity of Government Departments   page 189

5   The Right to Tax   190

6   The Currency   191

CHAPTER 9. THE EFFECT OF CHANGE OF SOVEREIGNTY ON THE PUBLIC PROPERTY OF THE STATE

1   The Public and Private Domains   199

    I   The distinction between the Public Domain and Private Domain, and the Factor of Territorial Identity   199

    II The National Exchequer   204

    III Incorporeal Rights   205

2   The Public and Private Domains situated outside the Affected Territory   207

3   Practice in the Matter of the Public and Private Domains   210

The abolition of the Crown in Commonwealth countries (p. 210). The independence of the Francophone States (p. 210). The dismemberment of Czechoslovakia, 1938–9 (p. 212). The *Anschluss* of Austria to the *Reich*, 1938 (p. 214). The absorption of the Baltic States in the Soviet Union, 1939 (p. 214). The cession of Roumanian territory, 1940 (p. 214). The dismemberment of Yugoslavia, 1942 (p. 214). The Italian Peace Treaty, 1947 (p. 215). The independence of Libya, 1951 (p. 217). The partition of India, 1947 (p. 220). The cession of the Indian Establishments, 1954 (p. 222). The independence of the Philippines, 1946 (p. 222). The independence of Syria and the Lebanon, 1946 (p. 222). The independence of Burma, 1948 (p. 223). The independence of Israel, 1948 (p. 223). The transfer of Newfoundland to Canada, 1949 (p. 225). The independence of Indonesia, 1949 (p. 226). The independence of Indochina, 1953 (p. 226). The formation of Somalia, 1960 (p. 227). The dismemberment of the Mali Federation, 1960 (p. 228). The independence of the Congo (Léopoldville), 1960 (p. 228). The independence of Algeria, 1962 (p. 229). The dissolution of the Federation of the West Indies, 1962 (p. 229). The dissolution of the Federation of Rhodesia and Nyasaland, 1963 (p. 230). The formation of Malaysia, 1963, and the separation of Singapore, 1965 (p. 232).

4   Archives   232

PART III

THE DOCTRINE OF ACQUIRED RIGHTS IN THE LAW OF STATE SUCCESSION

CHAPTER 10. STATE SUCCESSION AND THE DOCTRINE OF ACQUIRED RIGHTS

1   The Nature of the Municipal Law Obligations of the State   page 237

2   The History of the Doctrine of Acquired Rights   239

3   The Elements of the Doctrine of Acquired Rights   244

4   The Doctrine of Acquired Rights and the Doctrine of Act of State   250

   The doctrine of act of State in English law (p. 251). Recognition of rights by the successor sovereign in English law (p. 255). The date of an Act of State (p. 257). The distinction between property and contractual claims (p. 257). The act of State doctrine in the law of India (p. 258). The act of State doctrine in civil law systems (p. 262).

5   Expropriation of Acquired Rights and the Principle of Compensation   263

CHAPTER 11. DIPLOMATIC AND JUDICIAL PRACTICE IN THE MATTER OF ACQUIRED RIGHTS

I   Practice in Cases of Cession and Annexation   269

   The cession of Java by Great Britain to the Netherlands, 1830 (p. 270). The cession of Fiji to Great Britain, 1874 (p. 271). The establishment of British protectorate over the Gilbert Islands, 1892 (p. 272). The cession of German territory to Poland, 1919 (p. 272). General judicial practice (p. 277). The termination of the federal status of Eritrea, 1962 (p. 278). The cession of West New Guinea (West Irian) to Indonesia, 1962 (p. 278). The cession of the French Establishments in India, 1954 (p. 278). The formation of the United Arab Republic, 1958 (p. 279).

II   Practice in Cases of Independence   279

   Land tenure in West Africa (p. 280). The Ghana land concessions (p. 281). The expropriation of Netherlands property in Indonesia, 1957–9 (p. 284). The nationalization of Indian property in Burma, 1948–1955 (p. 286). German property in Israel: the Templar mediation (p. 287). Acquired rights in North Vietnam (p. 291). Acquired rights in the Philippines (p. 292). Acquired rights of French citizens in Morocco and Tunisia (p. 292). Rights of lawyers in Guinea (p. 294). Acquired rights of French citizens in Algeria (p. 294). Acquired rights of French citizens in the Francophone States (p. 296). Acquired rights in Zanzibar (p. 296). Acquired rights in Kenya (p. 296). Acquired rights in the Congo (Léopoldville) (p. 297).

CHAPTER 12. THE THEORY OF STATE SUCCESSION
RESPECTING GOVERNMENTAL CONTRACTS page 298

CHAPTER 13. THE DOCTRINE OF ACQUIRED RIGHTS
AND ECONOMIC CONCESSIONS

1 The Nature of a Concessionary Contract 304

2 Judicial and Diplomatic Practice in the Matter of Concessions 307
The cession of the Ionian Islands to Greece, 1864 (p. 307). The cession of Peruvian territory to Chile, 1883 (p. 308). The annexation of Madagascar by France, 1896 (p. 308). The cession of Cuba and the Philippines by Spain, 1898 (p. 311). The annexation of the Boer Republics, 1900 (316). The annexation of Korea by Japan, 1910 (p. 322). General practice, 1911–20 (p. 323). The dissolution of the Ottoman Empire, 1923: the Mavrommatis and Lighthouses Cases (p. 323). The Sopron-Köszeg Local Railway Company Arbitration, 1929 (p. 329). The Forests of Central Rhodope Case, 1934 (p. 331). The annexation of Ethiopia by Italy, 1935 (p. 332). The independence of Transjordan, 1946 (p. 334). The Peace Treaty with Italy, 1947 (p. 334). The Petsamo Nickel Concession Issue, 1947 (p. 335). Concessions in Indonesia (p. 335). Concessions in Mandated Territories (p. 335). Concessions in Israel (p. 336). Concessions in the Lebanon (p. 338). Concessions in the Congo (Léopoldville) (p. 342). Concessions in the United Arab Republic (p. 344). Concessions in Algeria, Malagasy Republic and Mali (p. 344). Mining Concessions in Zambia (p. 344).

3 Expropriation of Concessions and the Principles of Compensation 345

CHAPTER 14. THE DOCTRINE OF ACQUIRED RIGHTS
AND ADMINISTRATIVE CONTRACTS

1 Practice of States 355
General practice, 1797–1866 (p. 355). Judicial practice in Italian courts, 1877–86 (p. 356). Decision of the French *Conseil d'État*, 1876 (p. 357). The annexation of Burma by Great Britain, 1886 (p. 358). The annexation of the Boer Republics, 1900 (p. 360). Judicial practice in Polish courts, 1919 (p. 362). The partition of India, 1947 (p. 363). The independence of the Philippines, 1946 (p. 366). The independence of Libya, 1950 (p. 366). The independence of Somalia, 1960 (p. 366). The dissolution of the Federation of Rhodesia and Nyasaland, 1963 (p. 366). Abolition of the Crown in Commonwealth countries (p. 367).

2 Conclusion 367

CHAPTER 15. THE DOCTRINE OF ACQUIRED RIGHTS AND THE NATIONAL DEBT

1 Introduction   *page* 369

2 The Relationship between Creditor and Sovereign Debtor   371

3 Total Succession   373

    I   Annexation   373

British annexations, 1874–7 (p. 376). The annexation of Hawaii by the United States, 1898 (p. 377). French annexations, 1881–96 (p. 377). The British annexations of Burma, 1886, and the Boer Republics, 1900 (p. 378). The annexations of the Congo, 1907, and Korea, 1910 (p. 380). The annexation of Austria, 1938 (p. 380). The annexation of Danzig by Poland, 1945 (p. 384).

    II   Federation   384

The incorporation of Texas into the United States, 1845 (p. 384). The federation of British colonies (p. 386). The creation of the United Arab Republic, 1958 (p. 386). The incorporation of the Baltic States in the Soviet Union, 1940 (p. 386).

    III   Dismemberment   387

The dissolution of the United Netherlands, 1830 (p. 388). The dissolution of the Union of Colombia, 1829 (p. 388). The dismemberment of Czechoslovakia, 1939 (p. 389). The dismemberment of Yugoslavia, 1941 (p. 390). The dismemberment of Ruanda-Urundi, 1962 (p. 391). The dissolution of the Federation of Rhodesia and Nyasaland, 1963 (p. 392).

4 Partial Succession   394

    I   The Unsecured Debt   394

General practice, 1783–1825 (p. 396). The secession of Texas from Mexico, 1840 (p. 397). General practice, 1859–71 (p. 397). The Act of the Congress of Berlin, 1878 (p. 398). General practice, 1903–13 (p. 398). The Peace Treaties, 1919–23 (p. 399). The Mandate over Syria and the Lebanon (p. 402). General practice, 1920–46 (p. 404). The partition of British India, 1947 (p. 404). The independence of Libya, 1950 (p. 406).

    II   The Secured Debt   407

       (*a*) Pledged assets   408

The cession of the province of Tarapacá by Peru to Chile, 1883 (p. 409). Decision of the *Reichsgericht*, 1885 (p. 411). Secured debts in the Peace Treaties, 1919 (p. 411).

       (*b*) Pledged revenues   411

The incorporation of Texas in the United States, 1845: Texan Bonds Arbitration (p. 412). The projected transfer of a province by Mexico to the United States, 1866 (p. 412). The cession of Cuba by Spain, 1898: Cuban debt controversy (p. 412). The cession of Ottoman territory, 1913 (p. 413). Pledged revenues in the Peace Treaties, 1919–23 (p. 414). Pledged revenues in the Lighthouses Case, 1955 (p. 414).

CHAPTER 16. THE DOCTRINE OF ACQUIRED RIGHTS AND LOCAL DEBTS

1 Debts of a Fiscally Autonomous Region   *page* 416

General practice, 1648–1866 (p. 418). The secession of the Spanish-American colonies (p. 419). General practice, 1864–1905 (p. 419). The Peace Treaties, 1919–23 (p. 420). The debts of the German colonies after 1919 (p. 421). The independence of British dependencies (p. 423): Colonial Stock Act, 1877 (p. 424); Colonial Development Loans (p. 426). The transfer of Newfoundland to Canada, 1949 (p. 427). The independence of Ceylon, 1947 (p. 427). The independence of Burma, 1947 (p. 428). Loans, advances and investment of private capital in Mandated Territories (p. 430). The independence of Israel, 1948 (p. 431). The independence of the Philippines, 1946 (p. 433). The independence of Indochina, 1948–53 (p. 434). The cession of the French Establishments in India, 1954 (p. 435). The independence of Libya and Ethiopia (p. 435). The restoration of Austria's independence, 1945 (p. 435). The independence of Indonesia, 1949 (p. 437). The independence of the Congo (Léopoldville), 1960 (p. 439). The independence of the French African States (p. 444). The independence of Algeria, 1962 (p. 444).

2 World Bank Loans   446

3 Administrative Debts   448

Administrative debts of British India, 1947 (p. 450). Administrative debts of the Boer Republics, 1900 (p. 450). Administrative debts of Czechoslovakia, 1940 (p. 451). Administrative debts of the Federation of Rhodesia and Nyasaland, 1963 (p. 452).

4 Debts of Local Government Bodies   452

CHAPTER 17. THE DOCTRINE OF ACQUIRED RIGHTS AND THE REPARTITION OF DEBTS

1 The Basis of Repartition   454

2 The Rights of Creditors   456

3 Odious Debts   458

    I   Hostile Debts   459

The Cuban debt controversy, 1898 (p. 459). Odious debts in the Peace Treaties, 1919 (p. 460).

    II   War Debts   461

The annexation of the Boer Republics, 1900 (p. 461). War debts in the Peace Treaties, 1919 (p. 462).

4	Debts of a Bankrupt State	page 463
5	Arrears of Interest	464

CHAPTER 18. THE DOCTRINE OF ACQUIRED RIGHTS AND PENSIONS AND SALARIES

1 Service Pensions 465

   I Pensions Accruing before Change of Sovereignty 465
      (*a*) Total succession 466
      (*b*) Partial succession 467

   Where the central government was the employer (p. 468). Where a regional government was the employer (p. 469). The cession of the Ionian Islands, 1864 (p. 470). The partition of India, 1947 (p. 470). The independence of Burma, 1947 (p. 471). The independence of Ceylon, 1947 (p. 471). The independence of Indochina, 1949; cession of the French Establishments, 1954 (p. 472). The termination of the Palestine Mandate, 1948 (p. 472). The independence of Indonesia, 1949 (p. 472). The independence of Algeria, 1962 (p. 473).

   II Pensions Accruing after Change of Sovereignty 473

   III Public Officers' Agreements and Localization of the Civil Service 474

2 Superannuation 479

3 Non-Service Pensions 479

4 Salaries 480

CHAPTER 19. THE EFFECT OF STATE SUCCESSION UPON STATE RESPONSIBILITY FOR DELICTS

1 The Theoretical Problem of Succession 482

2 Practice in the Matter of Succession to Delicts 486

   The union of Belgium and the Netherlands, 1815 (p. 486). The dissolution of the Union of Colombia, 1831 (p. 486). The annexation of Burma, 1886 (p. 486). The annexation of the Boer Republics, 1900 (p. 487). The annexation of Hawaii, 1898: the Hawaiian claims (p. 490). Judicial practice in general (p. 492). The partition of India, 1947 (p. 493). Independence of Commonwealth and Francophone countries (p. 493).

PART IV
THE EFFECT OF CHANGE OF SOVEREIGNTY ON NATIONALITY

CHAPTER 20. THE EFFECT OF CHANGE OF SOVEREIGNTY ON NATIONALITY OF INHABITANTS OF THE AFFECTED TERRITORY

1 Introduction *page* 497

2 The Manner in which Change of Nationality is Effected 499

3 The Categories of Persons Subject to Change of Nationality 506

4 The Effect of Independence on Nationality 518
   The Commonwealth (p. 519). The Community and Associated States (p. 523). Somalia (p. 527). India and Pakistan (p. 527).

CHAPTER 21. OPTION FOR AN ALTERNATIVE NATIONALITY 529

CHAPTER 22. STATE SUCCESSION AND THE NATIONALITY OF CLAIMS

1 The Doctrine of Continuous Nationality 537

2 Diplomatic Protection of Companies of Alien Shareholding 541

Bibliography 543
   A. *Studies in the Law of State Succession* 543
   B. *Works Containing Material Relevant to the Law of State Succession* 549

Author Index to volumes I and II 563

General Index 570

TABLE OF CASES

A. INTERNATIONAL CASES

Aaland Islands Case, I, 4; II, 15, 16, 231
Agricultural Labour and Production Case, II, 301
Alsop Case, I, 541
Arbitration between Germany and Poland in 1924 concerning the interpretation of the Minorities Treaty, I, 499
Arbitration between Germany and Poland, I, 535, 536
Arbitration between Spain and Great Britain in 1924 (Consulate in Rio Martin), II, 43
Atellis, Case of Orazio de, *see* Santangelo

Barcs-Pakrac Railways *v.* Yugoslavia, I, 330
Benson Robert Henry Claim, I, 272
Brown, Robert E., Case, I, 16, 249, 449, 483, 485, 487, 488, 489, 490, 491
Burt Claim, I, 271

Chorzów Factory Case, I, 289
Clipperton Islands Arbitration, II, 278
Compagnie du Port, des Quais et des Entrepôts de Beyrouth and the Société Radio-Orient Case, I, 340-1

Delagoa Bay Railway Co. Case, I, 347, 353
Diverted Cargoes Case, I, 194

Electricité de Beyrouth Co. Case, I, 340
Exchange of Greek and Turkish Populations Case, I, 512

Forests of Central Rhodope Case, I, 245, 331-2, 538
Free Zones of Upper Savoy and the District of Gex Case, II, 14, 15, 231
Frontier (Local Authorities) Award, I, 216
Frystatzki *v.* Polish State, I, 180

Case Concerning Certain German Interests in Polish Upper Silesia, I, 274
German Settlers (Settlers of German Origin in Territories Ceded by Germany to Poland) Case, I, 203, 251, 273
Gleadell, Captain W. H. (G.B.) *v.* United Mexican States, I, 538
Goldbeck *v.* Mexico, I, 517
Grzesik *v.* Polish State, I, 466

Hausen *v.* Polish State, I, 179, 466
Hawaiian Claims, I, 463, 490
Heirs of John B. W. Williams Claim, I, 272

Isaac M. Brower Claim, I, 272

Jablonsky *v.* German Reich, I, 246

Koranyi *v.* Roumania, I, 417
Kügele *v.* Polish State, I, 246, 264

Ladislaus Chira Fils *v.* Czechoslovak State, I, 535
Levy *v.* German State, I, 355
Lighthouses Arbitration, I, 301, 327, 372, 414, 483, 484, 485, 486
Lighthouses Case, I, 325, 326, 492

Masson *v.* Mexico, I, 517
Mavrommatis Case, I, 324, 337, 346, 539
The Mechanic (U.S.-Equador), II, 92
Minnie Stevens Eschauzier (G.B.) *v.* United Mexican States, I, 538

National Bank of Egypt *v.* Austro-Hungarian Bank, I, 541
Nationality Decrees in Tunis and Morocco Case, I, 499; II, 52, 292
Niederstrasser *v.* Polish State, I, 251, 265, 348
Niger Co. Ltd. *v.* Germany, I, 423
North Atlantic Coast Fisheries Case, II, 17

xxii Table of Cases

Norwegian Shipowners' Claims, I, 353
Nottebohm Case, I, 502, 510

Oscar Chinn Case, I, 246
Ottoman Debt Arbitration, I, 372, 402

Panevezys–Saldutiskis Railway Co. Case, I, 539
Peinitsch v. German State, I, 511
Peter Pázmány University Case, I, 203
Polish Officials in Danzig Case, II, 20
Preah Vihear, Case Concerning Temple of, see Temple

Radziwill v. Germany, I, 541
Reservations to the Genocide Convention Case, II, 372
Rights of Nationals of the United States of America in Morocco Case, II, 146, 292
Rights of Passage Case, II, 128, 130

Santangelo Case, I, 537
Saudi Arabia v. Arabian American Oil Co. (Aramco), I, 347
Serbian & Brazilian Loans Case, I, 192, 371
Sicilian Sulphur Monopoly Case, I, 353

Sopron–Köszeg Local Railway Company Arbitration 1929, I, 330
International Status of South West Africa Case, II, 14, 263
South West Africa (Succession) Case, I, 422
Spanish Zones of Morocco Claims, II, 43, 52
Statute of the Memel Territory Case, II, 301

Temple of Preah Vihear Case (Thailand, Cambodia), II, 146–8
Texan Bonds Arbitration, I, 385

U.S.A. (International Fisheries Co.) v. United Mexican States, I, 353
U.S. v. Great Britain in the Matter of the North Atlantic Coast Fisheries, II, 17

Venezuelan Bond Cases, I, 353

William Webster Claim, I, 272
Wildermann v. Stinnes, I, 509
S.S. Wimbledon Case, 262

B. MUNICIPAL CASES

Australia

Bell v. Mansfield, I, 121
Bradley, in re, I, 123
Ffrost v. Stevenson, II, 63
N.S.W. v. Bardolph, I, 305
Quan Yuk v. Hinds, I, 37
Roche v. Kronheimer, II, 63
R. v. Burgess, ex parte Henry, II, 63, 82
R. v. Poole ex parte Henry, II, 63
R. v. Ross, I, 121
Wong Man On v. The Commonwealth, II, 9

Austria

A.F.v.Government of the Federal County (Landesregierung) of Vienna, I, 533
A.P. v. Federal Minister of the Interior, I, 533
G.M. v. (Austrian) Federal Minister for the Interior, I, 533
Kleihs v. Republic of Austria, I, 367
Kugler v. (Austrian) Federal Minister for the Interior, I, 533
Military Decoration Pension Case, I, 4
Paternity Suit (Austria) Case, I, 145
Post Office Official (Austrian Succession) Case, I, 180
Republic of Austria v. City of Vienna, I, 207
S. Ferdinand v. (Austrian) Federal Chancellery, I, 535

Belgium

Baugnet-Hock v. État Belge, I, 96, 441
Cortvriendt v. Wandewyver, II, 341
Creplet v. État Belge et Société des Forces Hydro-Electriques de la Colonie, I, 96, 442, 483
Deleers v. De Rosen de Borgharen, I, 193
Demol v. État Belge, Ministre des Finances, I, 442

Table of Cases

Dumont v. État Belge, I, 95, 96, 442
Dupret v. van den Hove, I, 193
Entreprises Fernand Gillion en Afrique 'Sogiarf' v. Banque Centrale du Congo Belge et du Ruanda-Urundi, I, 193
État Belge v. De Smet, I, 439
État Belge v. Dumont, I, 96, 189, 441
De Keer v. État Belge, I, 96, 441
Lipschutz v. Böhmische Esconto Bank and Credit Anstalt, I, 102
Mahamba Case, I, 163
Meert Case, I, 94, 95, 96, 134, 441, 483
Northern Assurance Co. Ltd v. Gouvernement du Congo Belge, I, 95, 441
Pittacos v. État Belge, I, 442
Pulenciks v. Augustovskis, I, 508
Sarrot v. Colonie du Congo Belge et État Belge, I, 440
Sidaf v. Cimenki, I, 193
Société Lebrun et Cie v. Dussy et Lucas, II, 379
Windey v. Fonds des Invalides des Employés du Congo et du Ruanda-Urundi, I, 193

Canada

Ex parte O'Dell & Griffen, II, 122
Francis v. The Queen, II, 122, 300

Congo (L.)

Subbe Case, II, 140

Cuba

Guzman and Latamble, In re, II, 260
Spanish Subjects in Cuba (Equality) Case, I, 533

Czechoslovakia

Austrian Officials (Succession) Case, I, 181
Czechoslovakia Succession in Taxes Case, I, 191
Hungarian Officials (Succession) Case, I, 180, 181
Hungarian Officials (Succession) Case No. II, I, 181
Option (Loss of Nationality Case), I, 529
Salary due by the former Government (Czechoslovakia) Case, I, 480

Succession in obligations (Fees paid in Error Case), I, 420
Succession in Obligations (Advance Payment of Duty) Case, I, 420

Danzig

Danzig Pension Case, I, 468

Denmark

Kaufmann v. Augustenborg Town Council, I, 518
Schwerdtfeger v. Danish Government, I, 250

East Africa

Sunderdass Hariram v. Bhupendra Shamjibhai, I, 164, 167

Egypt

Agapios v. Sanitary and Quarantine Council of Egypt, I, 513
Messih v. Minister of the Interior, I, 536
Pini v. Pini, I, 510
Psilas v. Egyptian Government, II, 109
Romano v. Comma, I, 509, 510, 529

France

A, Re, I, 502
Abdouloussen, Re, II, 49
Affaire Dame Ravero, I, 263
Affaire de Du-Ngoc-Truong, I, 79
Affaire Max Alkan, I, 515
Affaire Union des Populations du Cameroun, I, 161
Amar v. Soussan, II, 144
Anna Gueisse v. Nauche, I, 160
Association des Porteurs de Parts de Scripts Lombards v. Italian State and Comité des Obligataires de la Compagnie des Chemins de Fer Danube-Save-Adriatique, I, 262
Berutti v. P. & G. Aix-en-Provence, I, 515
Boch v. Tinchant, I, 79
Chaurand v. Agent Judiciaire du Trésor Public, I, 446
Chemin de Fer d'Alsace v. Levy, II, 221
Cie d'Assurances Rhin et Moselle, I, 106
Cied es Transports Régionaux de l'Est et du Centre Case, I, 150, 161

Table of Cases

Consorts Marteau *v.* Receveur des Finances de Saint Nazaire, I, 158
Cozzolino *v.* Cozzolino, I, 133
Davidson's Case, I, 80; II, 127
Des Bois Case, I, 517
Duvernoy Case, I, 161
Eccoffard *v.* Air France, II, 142, 215, 328, 363
Espagne *v.* Chemin de Fer d'Alsace-Lorraine, II, 379
Établissements Coullerez *v.* Maison Stein, II, 221, 348
État Independent du Congo Belge *v.* Montefiore, I, 90, 417, 440
Fédération des Syndicats des Travailleurs de la Fonction Publique de Madagascar Case, I, 161
Ghattas, Re, I, 515
Guyen *v.* Freink I, 142, 172
Hong Wang Wang Fat *v.* Procureur de la Républic, I, 524
Ickelheimer *v.* Richault, I, 515
Iconomidis *v.* Couve, Dugrip R. et Cie, I, 263
Iltis *v.* Procureur de la Républic, I, 516
In re Hospices Civil de Chambéry, I, 246
Kremer, In re, I, 179, 181
Leparc et Moise *v.* Air France, II, 215, 328
Levy *v.* Cie d'Assurances l'Equité et Cie d' Assurances la Paternelle Africaine, I, 142
Mante et Borelli de Régis *v.* État Français Ré, I, 263
Mayi-Matip Case, I, 161
Mbounya Case, I, 162
Mitjaville et Pena *v.* Chemin de Fer Paris à Orléans, II, 221
Pornot *v.* French State, I, 133
Société Comptoir Commercial Franco-Africain *v.* Carabibier, I, 142
Société Générale de Surveillance de Genève *v.* Banque de l'Indochine, I, 80
Trésor Public *v.* Cie Air Laos, II, 326
Union Régionale Algérienne de la C.F.T.C. Case, I, 151

Germany

Aix-La-Chappelle Railroad Co. *v.* Thewis and the Royal Dutch Government, Intervenor, II, 20
Baron A. *v.* Prussian Treasury, I, 168
Customs House (State Succession) Case, II, 180, 181, 216, 345
Extradition (Germany & Czechoslovakia Case), II, 179
Federal Government of Germany *v.* Lower Saxony, II, 84
German Railway Station at Basle Case, II, 20
The Indian Prince, II, 58
Pensions (Prussia) Case, I, 452
Polish Mining Corporation *v.* District of Ratibor, I, 452
R. and G. *v.* H. Hoch Bahn A. G., I, 111
Rural District Council of Guttentag *v.* P., I, 452
S. Th. *v.* German Treasury, I, 421, 422
Sch. *v.* Germany, I, 422
Slouzak Minority in Teschen (Nationality) Case, I, 515
State Succession (Windhuk in S.W. Africa) Case, I, 452
Tanganyika Succession Case, I, 421, 422
X *v.* German Reich, I, 422

Ghana

Ex parte Otchere, I, 123

Greece

Nisyros Mines Case, I, 326
Occupation of Crete Case, I, 103
Salonica Appeals Case, I, 158
Samos (Liability in Torts) Case, I, 492

Hungary

Kalmár *v.* Hungarian Treasury, I, 479

India

Ahidbar Ghose *v.* Jagabandhu Roy, I, 147, 155
Anand Balkrishna Behare *v.* Police Leshkar, I, 109
Antonius Raab, In re, I, 528
Ashalata Debi *v.* Sir Jadunath Roy, I, 168
Assam Suppliers *v.* Union of India, I, 365
Associated Hotels of India Ltd *v.* R.B. Jodha Mal Kothalia, I, 148, 156

Table of Cases

Ayub Ali v. Harinarayan Kanu, I, 147, 156
Babu Ram Saksena v. The State, II, 77
Babu S/O Kalu v. Parsham S/O Salam, I, 116, 171
Bapu and Bapu v. Central Provinces, I, 253
Batala Civil Engineering Co. Case, I, 117
Bhagwan Shankar v. Kojarum Bapu, I, 157
Bihar, State of, v. Santo Kumar Mitra, I, 109
Blackwood & Sons Ltd v. Parasuraman, I, 124
Brajmohan Bose Benimadhav Kishorilal Kishanlal, I, 157
Buland Sugar Co. Ltd v. Union of India, I, 260
Chaman Lal Loona & Co. v. Dominion of India, I, 365
Chintamoni Padham v. Paika Samal, I, 157
Chunilal Patua v. The State of Assam, I, 365
Collector of Sabakantha v. Shankarlal Kalidas Patel, I, 256
Dabrai v. Air India Ltd, II, 336, 338, 349
Dalmia Dadri Cement Co. v. Commissioner of Income Tax, I, 253, 257, 258, 260
Dawood Ali Arif v. Deputy Commissioner of Police, I, 528
Dominion of India v. Hiralal Bothra, I, 156
Elahi Bux v. Union of India, I, 365
Farid Ahmad v. Government of the United Provinces, I, 253, 256, 258
Francesco Corsi v. Gorakhram Gokalchand, II, 354
Gajjan Singh v. Union of India, I, 253, 259
Ganapatrao Shankarrao v. State of Bombay, I, 256
Ganguli Engineering Ltd v. Shrimata Sushila Bala Dasi, I, 148
Ghaurul Hasan v. The State of Rajasthan, I, 527
Hari Trading Co. v. Dominion of India, I, 365
Hiranand Dobey v. Jyoti Ram Goel, I, 156

H. M. Subbaraya Setty & Sons v. S. K. Palani Chetty & Sons, I, 157
Idumati v. State of Saurashtra, I, 253, 262
Iswar Madan Gopal Jiu v. Province of West Bengal, I, 406
Jagannath Agarwala v. State of Orissa, I, 257
Jalla Begum v. Ghulam Zohra, I, 528
Karnaphuli Jute Mills Ltd v. Union of India, I, 493
Khagendra Nath v. State of West Bengal, I, 493
Kishori Lal v. Shrimati Shanti Devi, I, 155, 172
Krishna Ranjan Basu Rey v. Union of India, I, 365
Kumar Jagadish Chandra Sinha v. Commissioner of Income Tax, I, 116
Lakhmi Chand v. Punjab State, I, 148
Lunaji Narayan v. Purshottam Charan, I, 157
Madhya Bharat, State of, v. Mohanlal Motilal, I, 109
Madras, State of, v. C. G. Menon, I, 123, 125
Madras, State of, v. Rajagopalan, I, 183, 259
Maharaj Umeg Singh v. State of Bombay, I, 253, 262
Maloyi Rao v. Sankar Saran, I, 157
Meherunnissa Begum v. Venkat Murli Manohar Rao, I, 157
Messrs Parmeshri Das Mehra & Sons v. Ramchand Om Prakesh, I, 117
Midnapore Zamindary v. Province of West Bengal, I, 148
Mithan Singh v. The Subdivisional Canal Officer, I, 109, 253, 256, 259
Naresh Chandler Bose v. Sachinder Nath, I, 156
Nazakat Ali Khan v. Bankey, I, 148
Naziranbai v. The State, I, 527, 528
Nisar Ahmed v. Union of India, I, 528
Noor Mohammed v. The State, I, 527
Orissa, The State of, v. Harichandan Babu, I, 257
Pannalal Mukherjee v. Union of India, I, 365

Table of Cases

Promod Chandra Deb. *v.* The State of Orissa, I, 256, 260, 262
Protap Kumar Sen *v.* Nagendra Nath Mazumdar, I, 156
Province of West Bengal *v.* Midnapore Zamindary Co., I, 406
Radheyshiam *v.* Firm Sawai Modi Basdeo Prasad, I, 157
Raja Rajinder Chand *v.* Mst. Sukhi, I, 259
Raj Kumar Narasingh Pratap Singh Deo *v.* State of Orissa, I, 256, 257
Rajvi Amar Singh *v.* State of Rajast han, I, 259
Ram Narain *v.* Central Bank of India Ltd, I, 172
Rama Nand Vijay Parkash *v.* Gokal Chand, I, 117
Ramesh Chandra *v.* State of West Bengal, I, 493
Said Ul-Hamid *v.* Federal Indian Assurance Co. Ltd, I, 156
Satyabrata Ghose *v.* Mugneeran Bangur & Co., I, 187
Saurashtra, The State of, *v.* Jamadar Mohammed Abdulla, I, 260
Shah Kantilal *v.* Dominion of India, I, 157
Shah Premchand *v.* Shah Danmel, I, 157
Shiva Jute Baling Ltd *v.* Hindley & Co. Ltd, II, 354
Shri Krishna Sharma *v.* State of West Bengal, II, 358
Sree Rajendra Mills Ltd. Gandhinagar Salem *v.* The Income Tax Officer, I, 117
State *v.* Abdul Hamid, I, 528
Surendra Nath Kolay *v.* Mila Mia Laskar, I, 156
Tirlok Nath *v.* Moti Ram, I, 168
State of Tripura *v.* Province of East Bengal, I, 148, 493
Union of India *v.* Balwant Singh Jaswant Singh, I, 365
Union of India *v.* Chaman Lal Loona & Co., I, 365
Union of India *v.* Chinubhai Jeshingbhai, I, 365
Union of India *v.* Loke Nath Saha, I, 365
Union of India *v.* Manmull Jain, I, 258
Vinayak Shripatrao Patwordhan *v.* State of Bombay, I, 256, 260
Vivendra Singh *v.* State of Uttar Pradesh, I, 253, 259, 261
West Bengal, State of, *v.* Brindaban Chandra, Pramanik, I, 493
West Bengal, State of, *v.* Sirajuddin Batley, I, 406

Ireland

Alex Hull & Co. *v.* M'Kenna, I, 165
Ex parte Duggan, I, 127

Israel

A.B. *v.* M.B., I, 498
Abu Ras *v.* Minister of the Interior, I, 170
Ahmed Shauki El Karbutli *v.* Minister of Defence, I, 131
Albohar *v.* A.G., I, 185
Albrans *v.* Schmetterling, I, 169
Arar *v.* Governor of Tel Mond Prison, I, 132, 171
A.G. for Israel *v.* Sylvester, I, 153
A.G. for Israel *v.* Levitan, I, 191, 225
Benjamin *v.* Commissioner for Migration, II, 157
Bergtal *v.* Schwartzmann, I, 185
Bloch *v.* Selinger, I, 169
Farkas *v.* A.G., I, 191
Feingold *v.* Administrator-General, I, 190
Forer *v.* Guterman, I, 132, 153
Heirs of Mohamed Selim *v.* The Government of Palestine, I, 277
Hussein *v.* Governor of Acre Prison, I, 498
Katz-Cohen *v.* A.G., I, 132, 170
Khayat *v.* A.G., I, 132, 200, 225
Kuk *v.* Minister of Defence, I, 131
L. *v.* Inspector of Income Tax, I, 191
Leon *v.* Gubernik, I, 131
Naqara *v.* Minister of the Interior, I, 499
Oseri *v.* Oseri, I, 498
Pales Ltd *v.* Ministry of Transport, I, 337
Richuk *v.* State of Israel, I, 472
Rosenbaum *v.* Rosenbaum, I, 169
Shehadeh *et al.* *v.* Commissioner of Prisons, II, 159

Shimshon Palestine Portland Cement Factory Ltd *v.* A.G., I, 338
Shiphris, Re Goods of, I, 498
Sifri *v.* A.G., I, 185, 338
Stampfer *v.* A.G., I, 121, 132
Wahib Saleh Kalil *v.* A.G., I, 132
Yosipof *v.* A.G., I, 131

Italy

Affaire de la Ville de Crémone, I, 263
Bessi *v.* Kediro, I, 153
Brossalian, In re, I, 170
Commune of Magenta *v.* Director General of the Treasury, I, 356
Cortegiano Tercuz *v.* Tercuz, I, 158
Costa *v.* Ministero Della Guerra, II, 492
Czario *v.* Valentinis, I, 251
De Falco *v.* La Barbera, I, 357
Durchi *v.* The Commune of Genoa, II, 492
Farrugia *v.* Nuova Comp. Gen Autolinee, I, 159
Finance Department *v.* Dona Boldu, I, 357; II, 26
Galatioto *v.* Ochoa, I, 112
Gastaldi *v.* Lepage Hemery, II, 29, 375
General Administration of War and Finance *v.* Adami, I, 356
Kubelj *v.* Grom, II, 345
Marzari-Fisola Case, I, 357
Marzola *v.* Società Teavibra, I, 159
Minister of Finance *v.* Commune of Lucca, I, 357
Minister of Finance *v.* Siro Corbella, I, 356
Ministers of the Interior and Finance *v.* Commune of Capri, I, 356
Minister of the Treasury *v.* Danante, I, 357
Minister of War *v.* Commune of Pavia, I, 357
Minister of War *v.* Orcesi, I, 357
Olivo *v.* Mordini, II, 345
Orobia *v.* Ministero delle Finanze, I, 153
Orti-Manara *v.* Italian Government & Austrian Government, I, 356
Panagos *v.* Drossopulous, I, 158
Pisati *v.* Pellizari, I, 153
Rainoldo *v.* Ministero dello Guerra, I, 492
Saadoun *v.* Ditta Vaccarino, II, 142
Simi, In re, I, 170
Società Zanini *v.* Busato, I, 158
Sorkis *v.* Amed, I, 159
Tancredi, Re, I, 508
Verlengo *v.* Finance Department, I, 356
Walter *v.* Minister of War, I, 356

Jordan

Ottoman Bank *v.* Jabaji, I, 148

Kenya

Hilton *v.* Hilton, I, 128

Lebanon

Syrian State Succession (Haifa Leases) Case, I, 145, 264

Lithuania

Alsys, In re, I, 142, 144

Malagasy Republic

Affaire Ranaiveson, I, 142, 153
Brouette *v.* Andalini, II, 136

Malawi

Hannuth, In re, I, 124
R. *v.* Amihiya, I, 119, 123, 124

Malaya

Hoogstraten *v.* Low Lum Seng, II, 149

Morocco

Veuve Wanègue *v.* S.A.R.L. 'Air Outremer', I, 133

Netherlands

Bergverksaktiebolaget Kosmai *v.* Militär-Liquidierungsamt, I, 4
Czechoslovakian Co-operative Society *v.* Otten, II, 180, 221, 348
Foundation for Claiming Military Income of Prisoners of War *v.* State of the Netherlands, I, 481
Froeling *v.* The State, I, 481
Hausmann *v.* Koninklike Rotterdamse Lloyd, I, 130
Hehanussa, In re, I, 532

Killian v. Hageman, I, 193
Netherlands Beheers-Instituut v. Nimwegen and Manner, I, 508
Pamanoekan & Tjiasemlanden & Anglo-Dutch Plantations of Java Ltd v. Netherlands, I, 438
Poldermans v. State of the Netherlands, I, 481
Ten Amsterdam Oil Companies, In re, I, 508
Ter K. v. State of the Netherlands, Surinam & Indonesia, I, 142
Van der Have v. State of the Netherlands, I, 428
Van Heynsbergen v. Nederlandsche Handelsmaatschappij, I, 130
Van Maren v. Eerste Nederlandse Verzekering Maatschaapij, I, 193
Veeneendaal v. Pommeranz, I, 508
X, In re, I, 130
X v. Jurrissen, I, 144

New Zealand
Godwin v. Walker, I, 121

Nigeria
Ex parte Enahoro, I, 123

Pakistan
Barlas Brothers (Karachi) & Co. v. Yangtze (London) Ltd, I, 57; II, 354
E. M. Bhaba v. The Crown, I, 123
Mohammad v. The Crown, I, 171
Federation of Pakistan v. Dalmia Cement Co. Ltd Karachi and the Union of India, I, 406
Zafar-ul-Ahsan v. Pakistan, I, 183

Philippines
Brownell v. Sun Life Assurance Co. of Canada, I, 129

Poland
Co-operative Farmers in Tarnów v. Polish Treasury, I, 104, 200
Dzierzbicki v. District Electric Assoc. of Czestochowa, I, 158
Feldmann & Feldmann v. Polish State Treasury, II, 181, 221

Fischer v. Einhorn, I, 153, 158
Knoll v. Sobel, I, 155
Kot v. (Polish) Minister of Public Works, I, 181
L. & J.J. v. Polish State Railways, I, 107, 111
Ludwig v. Polish Minister of Finance, I, 469
Matys v. Nipanicz, I, 246
Niedzielskie v. (Polish) Treasury, I, 362
Niemiec and Niemiec v. Bialobrodziec and (Polish) State Treasury, I, 493
Olpinski v. Polish Treasury (Railway Division), I, 493
(Polish) State Treasury v. Kurzrock, I, 153
(Polish) State Treasury v. Osten, I, 362
Polish State Treasury v. Von Bismarck, I, 273
(Polish) Treasury v. Heirs of Dietl, I, 199, 202
Procurator-General for Poland v. S., I, 246
Struzek v. District Appeal Committee for War Cripples in Łódź, I, 103

Privy Council
Abeyesekera v. Jayatilake, I, 36
Amodo Tijani v. Secretary, Southern Nigeria, I, 277
Asrar Ahmed v. Durgah Committee, I, 253, 255, 258
A.G. for Canada v. A.G. for Ontario, II, 65
A.G. of New South Wales v. Trethowan, I, 38
Bonython v. Commonwealth of Australia, I, 371, 425
British Coal Corporation v. The King, I, 165
Dattatraya Krishna Rao Kane v. Secretary of State for India, I, 253
Duff Development Co. v. Government of Kelantan, II, 148
Falkland Islands Co. v. R., I, 37
Gout v. Cimitian, I, 514
Hoani Te Heuheu Tukino v. Aotea District Maori Land Board, I, 255

Table of Cases

Lord Bishop of Natal, Re, I, 37
Nabob of Arcot v. The East India Co., II, 76
Nabob of the Carnatic v. The East India Co., I, 253
Naden v. The King, I, 164
Penhas v. Tan Soo Eng, I, 37
Sammut v. Strickland, I, 36
Secretary of State for India v. Bai Rajbai, I, 255
Secretary of State for India v. Kamachee Boye Sahaba, I, 253; II, 76
Secretary of State for India v. Sardar Rustam Khan, I, 253
Sirdar Bagwan Singh v. Secretary of State for India, I, 253
Sobhuza II v. Miller, I, 37; II, 9
Sultan of Johore v. Abubakar Tunku Aris Bendahar, II, 149
Vajesingji Joravarsingji v. Secretary of State for India, I, 252, 255
Venkata Rao v. Secretary of State for India, I, 178
Wassaw Exploring Syndicate Ltd v. African Rubber Co. Ltd, I, 282

Roumania

Kulin, Emeric v. Roumanian State, I, 266
Mordcovici v. General Administration of Posts and Telegraphs, I, 395
Sechter v. Ministry of the Interior, I, 395

Saar

Saar Territory (Prussian Officials) Case, I, 179

Senegal

Cie Air France v. Consorts Diop, II, 328

Singapore

Westerling Case, II, 137, 138, 379

Somalia

Mohammed Saleh Mijertain Mahamoud Mohammed Omar v. The State, I, 113

South Africa

Halder v. Minister of Defence, I, 517
Lehmkuhl v. Kock, I, 505

Loewenstein v. Custodian of Enemy Property, I, 517
Marburger v. Minister of Finance, I, 517
Pienarr, Re, I, 505
Rabie v. Jansen, I, 505
Radloff, Re, I, 505
R. v. De Jager, I, 169
R. v. Geyer, I, 505
R. v. Jizwa, I, 505
S. v. Eliasov, II, 178
Shingler v. Union Government (Minister of Mines), I, 252
Treasury v. Wolff, I, 507
Van Deventer v. Hancke & Mossop, I, 505
Vereeniging Municipality v. Vereeniging Estates Ltd, I, 252
Verein für Schutzgebietsanleihen E.V. v. Conradie, I, 423
Wessels v. Olivier, I, 505

Switzerland

Bertschinger v. Bertschinger, II, 60, 343, 372
J.Z., In re, II, 180, 221, 348
Lucerne v. Aargau, II, 20, 21
M. and O., In re, II, 181, 221
Stempfel et Cie v. Haertwig, II, 348
Thurgau v. St Gallen, II, 20, 21
Wasservogel v. Federal Department of Justice and Police, I, 508

Syria

Rizcallah Gazalé Case, I, 112

Tanganyika

Partington v. Partington, I, 128

Tunisia

Consorts Ben Bougassas v. Mohamed Ben El Hadj Rahal, I, 516
Pietro Memmi v. Resident General of France et Procureur de la Republique, I, 516

Transvaal

Habib Motan v. The Transvaal Government, I, 169
Postmaster-General v. Taute, I, 252, 318

Uganda

A.G. for Uganda *v.* Katondwaki, I, 169
Kazaairne *v.* The Lukiko, I, 119

United Kingdom
England and Scotland

Bank Voor Handel en Scheepvaart *v.* Administrator of Hungarian Property, I, 289
Bicknell *v.* Brosnan, I, 503
Blankard *v.* Galdy, I, 108
Calvin's Case, I, 108
Campbell *v.* Hall, I, 36, 108, 116, 501
Catterall *v.* Catterall, I, 37
Chamberlain's Settlement, In re, I, 501
Civilian War Claimants Association Ltd, *v.* The King, I, 254
Cook *v.* Sprigg, I, 319
Doe d. Auchmuty *v.* Mulcaster, I, 502, 531
Doe d. Thomas *v.* Acklam, I, 502, 531
Donegani *v.* Donegani, I, 501
Doss *v.* Secretary of State for India, I, 253, 376
Dudfield *v.* Ministry of Works, I, 178
Dundas *v.* Dundas, I, 502
Dunn *v.* The Queen, I, 178
East India Co. *v.* Syed Ally, II, 76
Elphinstone *v.* Bedreechund, I, 253
Emperor of Austria *v.* Day, I, 209
Ex parte Nalder, I, 127
Ex Rajah of Coorg *v.* The East India Company, I, 253
Fibrosa Spolka Akcyjna *v.* Fairbairn, Lawson, Ltd, I, 303
Gibson *v.* East India Co., II, 76
Government of India & Mubarak Ali Ahmed, Re, I, 116, 123
Haile Selassie *v.* Cables Wireless Ltd, I, 209
Henderson, Re, I, 123
King of the Two Sicilies *v.* The Peninsular & Oriental Steam Packet Co., I, 209
Luthor *v.* Sagor & Co., I, 209
Mangolds' Patent, In the matter of, I, 508
Mayor of Lyons *v.* The East India Co., I, 501

Mighell *v.* Sultan of Johore, II, 148
Mostyn *v.* Fabrigas, I, 501
Murray *v.* Parkes, I, 502, 505, 531; II, 123
Oyekan *v.* Adele, I, 280
Performing Right Society *v.* Bray Urban District Council, I, 125
Philippson *v.* Imperial Airways, II, 361
Picton's Case, I, 108
Rederiaktiebolaget Amphitrite *v.* R., I, 305, 371
Republic of Peru *v.* Dreyfus Bros., I, 209
Republic of Peru *v.* Peruvian Guano Co., I, 209
Riorden *v.* The War Office, I, 178
Rustomjee *v.* R., I, 253, 254
The King *v.* The Home Secretary, ex parte L., I, 508
R. *v.* International Trustee for the Protection of Bondholders A.G., I, 371
R. *v.* Ketter, II, 9
R. *v.* Metropolitan Police Commissioner, ex parte Hammond, I, 127
Sayce *v.* Ameer Ruler Sadiq Mohammad Abbasi Bahawalpur State, I, 528
Stoeck *v.* Public Trustee, I, 501
Sutton *v.* Sutton, II, 300
U.S. *v.* McRae, I, 209
West Rand Central Goldmining Co. *v.* The King, I, 244, 253, 257, 321, 378, 463
Zacharia *v.* Republic of Cyprus, I, 123

United States

Alexander *v.* Roulet, I, 110, 177, 203
Alvarez y Sanchez *v.* U.S., I, 110, 180, 247
Amaya *v.* Stanolind Oil and Gas Co., I, 241, 244, 250
American Insurance Company *v.* Canter, I, 109, 502
Artukovic *v.* Boyle, II, 378
Balzac *v.* People of Puerto Rico, I, 109
Bolshanin *v.* Zlobin, I, 241, 248
Boyd *v.* Nebraska, ex rel. Thayer, I, 503, 532
Bricknell *v.* Trammel, I, 110
Brown *v.* U.S., I, 510
Cariño *v.* Insular Government of the Philippine Islands, I, 248
Cessna *v.* U.S., I, 241, 249

Table of Cases

Chicago Rock Island and Pacific Railway Co. *v.* McGlinn, I, 109, 265
Chinese Exclusion Case, I, 61
Clements *v.* Texas Company, I, 249
Coffee *v.* Groover, I, 240
Davis *v.* Police Jury of Concordia, I, 110, 177, 203
De Lassus *v.* U.S., I, 241
De Lima *v.* Bidwell, I, 111
De Montault *v.* U.S., I, 109, 110
Dent *v.* Emmeger, I, 241, 248, 249
Discontogesellschaft *v.* Umbreit, II, 58
Doe *v.* Eslava, I, 241
Dorr *v.* U.S., I, 110
Downes *v.* Bidwell, I, 109, 111
Ehrlich *v.* Weber, II, 59
Ely's Administrator *v.* U.S., I, 177, 240
Ex parte Thomas, II, 59
Flensburger Dampfercompagnie *v.* U.S., II, 58
14 Diamond Rings *v.* U.S., I, 111
Goetze *v.* U.S., I, 503
Gonzales *v.* Williams, I, 504
Harcourt *v.* Gaillard, I, 109, 249
Harrison *v.* Cross, I, 110
Hawaii *v.* Mankichi, I, 109
Henderson *v.* Poindexter's Lessee, I, 110
Holmes *v.* Jennison, II, 61
Iponmatsu Ukichi *v.* U.S., I, 111
Irish Free State *v.* Guarantee Safe Deposit Co., I, 208
Ivancevic *v.* Artukovic, I, 7
Jackson *v.* Porter, I, 110
Jones *v.* McMasters, I, 241
Karnuth *v.* U.S., II, 122, 300
Keene *v.* McDonough, I, 110, 249
Keith *v.* Clark, I, 119
Kennedy *v.* State, I, 110
Kolovrat *v.* Oregon, I, 7
Langdeau *v.* Hanes, I, 241
Leitensdorfer *v.* Webb, I, 109
Les Bois *v.* Bramell, I, 110
Lukich *v.* Department of Labor and Industry, I, 7
Mahoney *v.* U.S., II, 28
Miller *v.* Letzerich, I, 241
Mitchel *v.* U.S., I, 241
More *v.* Steinbach, I, 109, 177, 203
Mumford *v.* Wardwell, I, 110, 177

Municipality of Ponce *v.* Roman Catholic Apostolic Church in Porto Rico, I, 240
Mutual Assurance Society *v.* Watts, I, 241
McCallen *v.* Hodge, I, 241
McCandless *v.* U.S., II, 122, 300
McHenry County *v.* Brady, II, 62
Naamloze Vennootschap Suikerfabriek 'Wono-Aseh' *v.* Chase National Bank of N.Y., I, 130
New Orleans *v.* U.S., I, 109, 110
North German Lloyd *v.* Hedden, II, 58
O'Hara *v.* U.S., I, 249
Olijan *v.* Lublin, I, 7
Opel *v.* Shoup, I, 59
O'Reilly de Camara *v.* Brooke, I, 110, 247
Ortega *v.* Lara, II, 109
People *v.* Fulsom, I, 110
Pfleiger, In re, I, 504
The Philippine Sugar Estates Development Co. *v.* U.S., I, 109
Playa de Flor Land and Improvement Co. *v.* U.S., I, 241
Pollard's Lessee *v.* Hagan, I, 109, 110
Porto Rico Railway, Light & Power Co. *v.* Amador, I, 102, 103
Ramos *v.* U.S., I, 110
Rassmussen *v.* U.S., I, 110
Respublica *v.* Chapman, I, 118
Robinson *v.* Minor, I, 110
Roque Espiritu de la Ysla *v.* U.S., I, 504
Sanches *v.* U.S., I, 109
Shanks *v.* Dupont, I, 502
Shapleigh *et al.* *v.* Mier, I, 109
Smith *v.* U.S., I, 248
Society for the Propagation of the Gospel in Foreign parts *v.* Town of New Haven, I, 240; II, 300
The Sophie Rickmers, II, 58
Soto *v.* U.S., I, 110
Soulard *v.* U.S., I, 240, 248
Spelar *v.* U.S., II, 260
Stearns *v.* U.S., I, 110, 177, 203
Strobel's Estate, Re, II, 59
Strother *v.* Lucas, I, 240, 244
Terlinden *v.* Ames, II, 59
Texas *v.* White, I, 119
Tobin *v.* Walkinshaw, I, 517
Townsend *v.* Greeley, I, 241
Toyota *v.* U.S., I, 504

U.S. v. Arjona, II, 61
U.S. v. Arredondo, I, 241
U.S. v. Auguisola, I, 248
U.S. v. British Schooners, I, 111
U.S. v. Chaves, I, 248
U.S. v. Clarke's Heirs, I, 241
U.S. v. D'Auterive, I, 109, 110
U.S. v. Fullard -Leo, I, 241, 250
U.S. v. Garrow, II, 122, 300
U.S. v. Hanson, I, 110, 248
U.S. v. Heirs of Rillieux, I, 109,
U.S. v. Kingsley, I, 249
U.S. v. Larkin, I, 249
U.S. v. Miranda, I, 249
U.S. v. Pearson Reading, I, 249
U.S. v. Percheman, I, 240
U.S. v. Pico, I, 110, 177, 203
U.S. v. Power's Heir's, I, 109
U.S. v. Prioleau, I, 209
U.S. v. De Repentigny, I, 502, 532
U.S. v. Reynes, I, 110, 203, 250
U.S. v. Rose, I, 250
U.S. v. Roselius et al., I, 241
U.S. v. Sutter, I, 249
U.S. v. Vaca, I, 109, 249
U.S. v. Vallejo, I, 109, 110
U.S. v. Wiggins, I, 249
U.S. v. Yorba, I, 177, 203
U.S. ex rel D'Esquiva v. Uhl, I, 510
U.S. ex rel. Goodwin v. Karnuth, II, 122, 300
U.S. ex rel. Reichel v. Carusi, I, 510
U.S. ex rel. Rodiek, I, 517
U.S. ex rel. Schwartzkopf v. Uhl. I, 509, 510
U.S. ex rel. Umecker v. McCoy, I, 510
U.S. ex rel. Zeller v. Watkins, I, 510
Urbus v. State Compensation Commissioner, I, 7
Vermilya Brown v. Connell, II, 259
Vilas v. City of Manila, I, 109, 452
Virginia v. West Virginia, I, 455
State of Washington v. Rainier National Park Co., I, 109
Wieland v. Renner, II, 59
William P. Frye, The, II, 58

TABLE OF UNITED KINGDOM STATUTES

1773 An Act for Establishing Certain Regulations for the Better Management of the Affairs of the East India Company, I, 49
1833 An Act for Effecting an Arrangement with the East India Company, I, 49
1833 Judicial Committee Act, I, 164
1849 Admiralty Offences (Colonial) Act, I, 121, 132
1851 Petty Sessions (Ireland) Act, I, 127
1858 An Act for the Better Government of India, I, 49; II, 76
1861 The Indian Councils Act, I, 49
1865 Colonial Laws Validity Act, I, 37, 38, 48
1867 British North America Act, I, 48, 386
1873 Slave Trade (East African Courts) Act, II, 337
1873 Slave Trade Consolidation Act, II, 337
1876 Appellate Jurisdiction Committee Act, I, 122, 123, 164
1876 Slave Trade Act, II, 337
1877 Colonial Stock Act, I, 56, 424, 425, 426
1879 Slave Trade (East African Courts) Act, II, 337
1881 Fugitive Offenders Act, I, 56, 116, 119, 120, 121, 122, 123
1887 Appellate Jurisdiction Act, I, 164
1887 British Settlements Act, I, 37
1889 Acts Interpretation Act, I, 37, 120, 122
1890 Foreign Jurisdiction Act, I, 37, 54, 167
1891 Mail Ships Act, II, 337
1894 Merchant Shipping Act, I, 121, 122,
1895 Judicial Committee Amendment Act, I, 164
1900 Commonwealth of Australia Constitution Act, I, 386
1900 Colonial Stock Act, I, 56, 424, 425, 426
1909 Indian Councils Act, I, 49
1909 South Africa Act, I, 386; II, 122
1911 Copyright Act, I, 124, 125; II, 70, 206, 336
1911 Maritime Conventions Act, II, 337
1912 Seal Fisheries (North Pacific) Act, II, 337
1913 Appellate Jurisdiction Act, I, 164
1914 British Nationality Act, I, 519
1919 Government of India Act, I, 49, 50
1920 Maintenance Orders (Facilities for Enforcement) Act, I, 127
1920 Air Navigation Act, II, 157
1925 Merchant Shipping (International Labour Conventions) Act, II, 337
1926 Indian and Colonial (Divorce Jurisdiction) Act, I, 52, 127
1928 Administration of Justice Act, I, 164
1930 Arbitral Awards Act, II, 353
1931 Statute of Westminster, I, 38, 48, 49, 51, 55, 164; II, 90, 132
1932 Carriage by Air Act, II, 336, 337
1932 Merchant Shipping (Safety and Load-lines Conventions) Act, II, 337
1933 Visiting Forces (British Commonwealth) Act, I, 54
1935 Government of India Act, I, 49, 50, 183, 363; II, 353

1935	Government of Burma Act, I, 52, 223, 428
1935	Counterfeiting Currency (Convention) Act, II, 336
1939	National Loan Act, I, 426
1945	Bretton Woods Agreement Act, II, 336
1946	United Nations Act, II, 337
1947	Indian Independence Act, I, 52, 55, 116, 125, 128, 147, 182, 471, 474; II, 75, 76, 77, 184, 352, 355
1947	Burma Independence Act, I, 52, 53, 128, 130, 145, 520, 531, 535; II, 339
1947	Ceylon Independence Act, I, 55, 129
1948	British Nationality Act, I, 121, 122, 424, 503, 519; II, 323
1948	National Service Act, I, 503
1948	Colonial Development Corporation Act, I, 427
1948	Palestine Act, I, 129, 131
1948	Finance Act, I, 432
1948	Merchant Shipping Act, II, 337
1949	British North America Act, I, 112, 146, 225, 427
1949	Ireland Act, I, 127
1949	India (Consequential Provisions) Act, I, 55, 56, 122, 123, 128, 354; II, 354
1949	Export Guarantees Act, I, 426
1949	Patents Act, II, 336, 339
1949	Colonial Loans Act, I, 446
1949	Civil Aviation Act, II, 336, 337
1949	Merchant Shipping (Safety Convention) Act, II, 337
1950	Colonial and Other Territories (Divorce Jurisdiction) Act, I, 52, 127
1950	Arbitration Act, II, 336, 353
1950	International Organisations (Immunities and Privileges) Act, II, 337
1952	Visiting Forces Act, I, 54
1953	Royal Style and Titles Act, I, 49
1953	Federation of Rhodesia and Nyasaland Act, I, 50
1955	International Finance Corporation Act, II, 336
1956	Copyright Act, II, 70, 206, 336
1957	Pakistan (Consequential Provisions) Act, I, 122
1957	Federation of Malaya Independence Act, I, 53, 119, 122, 128, 163
1957	Ghana Independence Act, I, 55, 122, 128
1957	Geneva Conventions Act, II, 337
1957	Export Guarantees Act, I, 426
1958	British Nationality Act, I, 521
1959	Colonial Development and Welfare Act, 426
1959	Overseas Resources Development Act, I, 427
1960	Nigeria Independence Act, I, 128, 521
1960	Cyprus Act, I, 53, 119, 122, 128, 165, 426, 521
1960	Ghana (Consequential Provisions) Act, I, 56, 122, 128
1960	British North America Act, I, 48
1960	International Development Association Act, II, 337
1961	Republic of South Africa (Temporary Provisions) Act, I, 128, 522
1961	Tanganyika Independence Act, I, 128, 521
1961	Sierra Leone Independence Act, I, 55, 128, 521
1962	Tanganyika Republic Act, I, 55, 56, 128
1962	South Africa Act, I, 56, 127, 128, 522; II, 122

Table of United Kingdom Statutes

1962 West Indies Act, 1, 164
1962 Uganda Independence Act, 1, 55, 128, 167, 521
1962 Jamaica Independence Act, 1, 55, 128, 521
1962 Trinidad and Tobago Independence Act, 1, 55, 128, 521
1962 Tanganyika Republic Act, 1, 28, 165
1963 Nigeria Republic Act, 1, 56, 122
1963 Malaysia Act, 1, 54, 113, 119, 163, 186
1963 Zanzibar Act, 1, 54, 119, 521
1963 Tanganyika Republic Act, 1, 28, 165
1963 Kenya Independence Act, 1, 55, 128, 149, 166, 521
1964 Uganda Act, 1, 56, 119, 122, 128, 166
1964 Zambia Independence Act, 1, 54, 119, 149, 521
1964 Malta Independence Act, 1, 55, 521
1964 The Gambia Independence Act, 1, 55, 128, 521
1964 Malawi Independence Act, 1, 55, 128, 521
1964 Kenya Act, 1, 55, 56
1964 British Nationality Act, 1, 521
1964 British Nationality (No. 2) Act, 1, 521, 522

TABLE OF UNITED KINGDOM STATUTORY INSTRUMENTS

1922 Palestine Order, I, 131
1923 The Southern Rhodesia Constitution Letters Patent, I, 50
1924 The Zanzibar Order, I, 114, 119
1930 The Arbitration Convention (Application to the Belgian Congo) Order, II, 356
1931 The Arbitration (Foreign Awards) No. 2 Order, II, 356
1934 The British Protected Persons Order, II, 9
1937 The Carriage by Air (Parties to Convention) (No. 2) Order, II, 157
1946 The Straits Settlement (Repeal) Order, I, 68
1946 The Double Taxation Relief (Estate Duty) (Canada) Order, II, 118
1946 The Ceylon (Constitution) Order, I, 184, 427, 471
1948 The Federation of Malaya Order, I, 522; II, 68
1948 The Termination of Jurisdiction in Palestine (Transitional Provisions) Order, I, 184, 224, 418, 432
1951 The Eastern African (Appeal to Privy Council) Order, I, 167
1953 The Federation of Rhodesia and Nyasaland Order, II, 67
1954 The Gold Coast (Constitution) Order, I, 477
1957 The Ghana (Constitution) Order, I, 119; II, 75
1957 The Federation of Malaya (Constitution) Order, I, 119, 149, 165, 522; II, 149
1957 The Ghana (Appeal to Privy Council) Order, I, 165
1957 The West Indies (Federation) Order, I, 167; II, 261
1957 The Copyright (International Conventions) Order, II, 206, 336
1958 The Federation of Malaya (Appeals to Privy Council) Order, I, 165, 166
1958 The Nigeria (Retirement Benefit) Order, I, 477
1960 The Somaliland Order, I, 54, 119, 149, 165, 366, 477
1960 The Nigeria (Constitution) Order, I, 119, 149, 165
1960 The Ghana (Consequential Provisions) (Colonial Stock Acts) Order, I, 56
1960 The Sierra Leone (Constitution) (Amendment) (No. 3) Order, I, 477
1961 The Southern Rhodesia (Constitution) Order, I, 115
1961 The Sierra Leone (Constitution) Order, I, 119, 149, 165, 279, 521
1961 The Tanganyika (Constitution) Order, I, 119, 166, 521, 522
1961 The Eastern Africa Court of Appeal Order, I, 163
1961 The Sierra Leone (Procedure in Appeals to Privy Council) Order, I, 165
1961 The Eastern African (Appeal to Privy Council) (Amendment) Order, I, 166
1961 The Carriage by Air (Parties to Convention) Order, II, 338
1961 The Tanganyika (Compensation and Retiring Benefits) Order, I, 477
1961 The East African Common Services Organisation (Compensation and Retiring Benefits) Order, I, 477
1962 The West Indies (Dissolution and Interim Commissioner) Order, I, 114, 229; II, 261
1962 The Trinidad and Tobago (Constitution) Order, I, 119, 149, 164, 165, 521
1962 The Jamaica (Constitution) Order, I, 119, 149, 164, 165, 521
1962 The Aden (Constitution) Order, I, 119, 149

Table of United Kingdom Statutory Instruments xxxvii

1962 The Uganda (Independence) Order, 1, 119, 149, 164, 167, 522
1962 The Zanzibar Order, 1, 54, 149, 165, 166
1962 The Eastern Africa Court of Appeal (Revocation) Order, 1, 163
1962 The British Caribbean Court of Appeal Order, 1, 164, 166
1962 The British Caribbean Court of Appeal (Amendment) (No. 2) Order, 1, 164
1962 The British Caribbean (Appeal to Privy Council) Order, 1, 164
1962 The Trinidad and Tobago (Procedure in Appeals to Privy Council) Order, 1, 165, 166
1962 The Jamaica (Procedure in Appeals to Privy Council) Order, 1, 165
1962 The Kenya (Constitution) (Amendment) Order, 1, 166, 167
1962 The Kenya (Procedure in Appeals to Privy Council) Order, 1, 166
1962 The Uganda (Compensation and Retiring Benefits) Order, 1, 477
1962 The West Indies (Retirement and Compensation) Order, 1, 477
1962 The West Indies (Retirement and Compensation) (Amendment) Order, 1, 477
1963 The Federation of Rhodesia and Nyasaland Order, 1, 114
1963 The Federation of Rhodesia and Nyasaland (Dissolution) Order, 1, 115, 167, 185, 196, 230, 366, 392, 474
1963 The Kenya Order, 1, 119, 149, 163, 166, 167, 230, 279, 366, 392, 521
1963 The Kenya Independence Order, 1, 119, 149, 163, 164, 165, 166, 167
1963 The Zanzibar (Abolition of Appeals to the Privy Council) Order, 1, 166
1963 The Fugitive Offenders (South Africa) Order, 1, 56, 123
1963 The Federation of South Arabia (Procedure in Appeals to Privy Council) Order, 1, 165
1963 The Tanganyika (Pending Appeals to Privy Council) Order, 1, 165
1963 The Malaysia (Appeals to Privy Council) Order, 1, 166
1963 The Court of Appeal for Eastern Africa (Appeal to Privy Council) (Amendment) (No. 2) Order, 1, 166
1963 The Kenya (Procedure in Appeals to Privy Council) (Amendment) Order, 1, 166
1963 The Kenya (Compensation and Retiring Benefits) Order, 1, 477
1963 The West Indies (Retirement and Compensation) (Amendment) Order, 1, 477
1963 The West Indies (Retirement and Compensation) (Amendment) (No. 2) Order, 1, 477
1963 The North Borneo (Compensation and Retiring Benefits) Order, 1, 186, 477
1963 The Bahama Islands (Constitution) Order, 1, 477
1963 The Sarawak (Compensation and Retiring Benefits) Order, 1, 186, 477
1963 The Sabah (Compensation and Retiring Benefits) Order, 1, 477
1964 The Zambia Independence Order, 1, 54, 119, 149, 165, 166, 210, 344, 367, 522
1964 The Malawi Independence Order, 1, 119, 165, 522
1964 The Malta Independence Order, 1, 119, 165
1964 The Malawi (Compensation and Retiring Benefits) Order, 1, 477
1964 The Zambia (Compensation and Retiring Benefits) Order, 1, 477
1965 The Gambia Independence Order, 1, 119, 149
1965 The Gambia (Compensation and Retiring Benefits) Order, 1, 477

TABLE OF COMMONWEALTH AND OTHER STATUTES AND STATUTORY INSTRUMENTS

Australia
1912–58 Commonwealth Navigation Act, I, 122

Federation of Rhodesia and Nyasaland
Customs and Excise Act, 1955, II, 176

Ghana
1957 Nationality and Citizenship Act, I, 521
1960 State Property and Contracts Act, I, 284
1960 Courts Act, I, 149
1961 Federation of Nigeria Act, I, 57
1961 Republic of Cyprus Act, I, 57
1961 Republic of South Africa Act, I, 57
1961 Sierra Leone Act, I, 57
1962 Concessions Act, I, 283
1962 Administration of Lands Act, I, 284
1962 Minerals Act, I, 284

India
1914 Copyright Act, I, 124, 125
1934 Carriage by Air Act, II, 326
1947 The Indian Independence (Rights, Property and Liabilities) Order, I, 22, 147, 221, 363, 364, 365, 404, 405, 450, 470, 493
1947 The Indian Independence (Partition Councils) Order, I, 363
1947 The Indian Independence (International Arrangements) Order, I, 116, 185, 353, 358; II, 128, 353, 354, 355, 358
1947 The Indian Independence (Income Tax Proceedings) Order, I, 191
1947 The Indian Independence (Legal Proceedings) Order, I, 147, 155, 156, 168, 171
1947 High Court (Punjab) Order, I, 147
1947 High Court (Bengal) Order, I, 147
1948 Displaced Persons (Institution of Suits) Act, I, 155
1949 States Merger (Governor's Provinces) Order, I, 148
1950 Preventative Detention Act, I, 358
1955 Citizenship Act, I, 520

Israel
1948 Law and Administration Ordinance, I, 131, 132, 224, 225, 288
1948 Palestine Government Employees Ordinance, I, 184
1949 Tariff Act, II, 157
1950 Law on State Property, I, 224

Jamaica

1961 Jamaica (Constitution) (Retirement of Entitled Officers) Regulations, I, 477
1962 The Judicature (Appellate Jurisdiction) Law, I, 164
1962 Government Securities Act, I, 426

Kenya

1962 The East Africa Common Services Organization Ordinance, I, 163
1962 The Appellate Jurisdiction Ordinance, I, 163, 164
1963 The Kenya (Jurisdiction of Courts and Pending Proceedings) Regulations, I, 119
1964 The Constitution of Kenya (Amendment) Act, I, 120, 149, 210, 296, 367

Malawi

1963 Cessation of Application of Federal Laws Order, I, 115
1963 Double Tax Ordinance, II, 177
1964 Malawi Enactments (Adaptation and Modification) Order, I, 115, 123
1964 Supreme Court of Appeal Ordinance, I, 167
1964 Privy Council Appeals Ordinance, I, 167
1964 Relief from Double Taxation (U.K.) Order, II, 177
1964 Nationality Act, I, 522

Malaysia

1958 Federation of Malaya (Agreement) (Amendment No. 4) Ordinance, I, 477, 478
1960 Sarawak Merchant Shipping Ordinance, II, 69
1965 Malaysia Law No. 53, I, 118, 163, 232; II, 178

New Zealand

1947 Statute of Westminster Adoption Act, II, 90
1950 Republic of India Act, I, 57
1952 Republic of Ireland Act, I, 57
1952 Shipping and Seamen Act, I, 122
1957 Republic of Pakistan Act, I, 57
1960 Republic of Ghana Act, I, 57, 522
1961 Republic of Cyprus Act, I, 57, 522
1962 British Nationality and New Zealand Citizenship Amendment Act, I, 522
1963 Republic of Nigeria Act, I, 57, 522
1963 Republic of Tanganyika Act, I, 57, 522
1964 Uganda Act, I, 57, 522
1965 Republic of Kenya Act, I, 57
1965 Republic of Zambia Act, I, 57

Nigeria

1961 Pensions (Special Provisions) Act, I, 479
1962 Niger Dams Act, I, 281
1963 Constitution of the Federal Republic of Nigeria Act, I, 120, 149, 165, 367

Pakistan

1947 Pakistan (Monetary System and Reserve Bank) Order, I, 221, 222, 404

Sierra Leone
1961 Compulsory Acquisition of Property (Constitutional Safeguards) Act, I, 281
1961 Government Securities Act, I, 426

Singapore
1956 Retirement from the Public Service (Compensation) Ordinance, I, 477, 478

South Africa
1962 The Commonwealth Relations Act, I, 56, 522

Southern Rhodesia
1962 Republic of South Africa (Construction of Laws) Act, I, 522
1963 Federal Laws (Cesser) Order, I, 115
1964 High Court Act, I, 167

Tanzania
1961 The Tanganyika Judicature and Application of Laws Ordinance, I, 119
1961 Citizenship Act, I, 521
1962 The Republic of Tanganyika (Consequential, Transitional and Temporary Provisions) Act, I, 120, 129, 149, 210, 367
1962 The Constitution of Tanganyika Act, I, 164
1962 The Appellate Jurisdiction Act, I, 164, 165, 166
1962 The Retirement (Special Provisions) Act, I, 478
1964 The Union of Tanganyika and Zanzibar Act, I, 113
1964 The Transitional Provisions Decree, I, 150
1964 High Court Decree, I, 150

Trinidad and Tobago
1960 Trinidad and Tobago (Constitution) (Retirement of Entitled Officers) Regulations, I, 477
1962 Trinidad and Tobago (Voluntary Retirement and Compensation) Regulations, I, 477

Uganda
1934 Buganda Tax Law, I, 119
1962 The Judicature Ordinance, I, 119, 149
1962 The Uganda (Appellate Jurisdiction) Act, I, 164, 165, 166, 167
1962 The Court of Appeal Order, I, 164
1962 The Uganda Government Securities Ordinance, I, 426
1964 The Constitution of Uganda (First Amendment) Act, I, 120, 149, 210, 367; II, 117
1964 Extradition Act, I, 123

Zambia
1963 The Federal Laws (Discontinuance) Order, I, 115
1964 Court of Appeal for Northern Rhodesia Ordinance, I, 167
1964 Citizenship of Zambia Ordinance, I, 522
1964 Income Tax Act, II, 177
1965 The Federal Laws (Repeal) Act, I, 115, 123

Zanzibar

- 1963 Courts Decree, I, 150, 163, 164
- 1964 Confiscation of Immovable Property Decree, I, 296
- 1964 Constitution Decree, I, 477
- 1964 Abrogation of Constitution Decree, I, 113, 150
- 1964 Existing Laws Decree, I, 114, 119
- 1964 High Court Decree, I, 150
- 1964 Income Tax Act, II, 177

TABLE OF TREATIES

A. MULTILATERAL TREATIES

1648 Peace of Westphalia (Congresses at Münster and Osnabrück), I, 418; II, 342
1807 Treaty of Tilsit, I, 396
1814 Treaty of Paris, I, 108, 448; II, 96, 263, 264
1815 Act of The Congress of Vienna, I, 169; II, 167, 232, 239, 240, 263, 270
1815 Treaty of Paris, II, 239, 241, 255, 341
1818 Congress of Aix-la-Chapelle (Aachen Protocol), II, 188
1831 Treaty concerning the Netherlands and Belgium, I, 388; II, 264
1839 Treaty of London, concerning the Netherlands and Belgium, I, 269, 388, 448
1855 Treaty guaranteeing the territorial integrity of Sweden and Norway, II, 168
1856 General Treaty for the Reestablishment of Peace, II, 17, 212
1856 Declaration of Paris respecting Maritime Law, II, 222
1856 Treaty respecting the Danube, II, 191
1857 Treaty with Denmark for the Abolition of the Sound dues to Merchandise in Transit, II, 265, 266
1857 Treaty regarding Lake Constance, II, 87
1857 Treaty concerning the Status of New Nationals, II, 87
1864 Geneva Convention for the Amelioration of the condition of wounded in Armies in the field, II, 191
1865 Convention concerning the Cape Spartel Lighthouse, II, 253
1865 Act Governing the Navigation of the Danube, II, 191
1867 Treaty concerning the Shipping on Lake Constance between Riparian States of Lake Constance, II, 87
1868 Shipping Treaty Concerning Lake Constance, between the Riparian States of Lake Constance, II, 85, 86
1868 St Petersburg Declaration regarding Explosive Projectiles, II, 222
1868 Convention for the Navigation of the Rhine (Mannheim Convention), II, 191, 270, 271
1870 Railway Treaty between Switzerland, Baden, Austria-Hungary, II, 87
1870 Revision of the Acts Governing the Navigation of the Danube, II, 191
1875 International Metric Convention, II, 222
1875 Revision of the Acts Governing the Navigation of the Danube, II, 192
1875 International Telegraphic Convention, II, 222
1878 Act of the Congress of Berlin for the Settlement of Affairs of the East, I, 307, 398; II, 45, 103, 104
1880 Treaty regarding Lake Constance, II, 87
1881 Treaty concerning the Turko-Greek Frontier, I, 269
1881 Revision of the Acts Governing the Navigation of the Danube, II, 192
1883 Convention for the Protection of Industrial Property, I, 46; II, 144, 206, 222
1884 Convention for the Protection of Submarine Cables, I, 40; II, 221, 222, 223
1885 General Act of Berlin, II, 17, 307, 308, 309, 310
1886 Berne Convention for the Protection of Literary and Artistic Works, II, 222, 374

Table of Treaties

1888   Convention respecting Free Navigation of the Suez Canal, II, 222, 271, 361
1890   Berne Convention on International Transport of Goods, II, 181, 379
1890   Berne Convention for the Protection of Literary and Artistic Property, II, 204, 205, 221
1891   Madrid Arrangements for international registration of marks of manufacture or of commerce, II, 206
1891   Madrid arrangement concerning the repression of false indications of origin, II, 206
1893   Treaty regarding Lake Constance, II, 87
1894   Sanitary Convention, II, 130
1895   Protocol of Application concerning the Rhine, II, 191
1896   Convention on Civil Procedure, II, 347
1897   Sanitary Convention, II, 222
1899   Hague Convention for the Pacific Settlement of International Disputes, II, 127, 148, 220, 222
1900   Additional Act to the Industrial Property Convention, 1883, I, 46
1902   Hague Conventions on Private International Law, II, 139
1904   Convention for the Suppression of White Slave Traffic, II, 142, 149, 153, 155, 222, 223, 224, 225, 226
1905   Convention on Civil Procedure, I, 181; II, 180, 181, 347, 348
1906   General Act of the International Conference of Algeciras, relating to Morocco, II, 50, 51, 52, 313
1906   Geneva Convention concerning the Red Cross, II, 191, 222
1907   Hague Conventions concerning the Laws and Customs of War on Land, I, 206; II, 148, 222
1907   Hague Convention for the Pacific Settlement of International Disputes, II, 148, 222
1907   Hague Convention Relative to the Status of Enemy Merchant Ships, II, 148, 222, 223
1908   Joint Declaration concerning the Baltic, II, 268
1908   Convention on Literary and Artistic Copyright, II, 130, 157, 205
1910   Convention on Collisions at Sea, II, 130, 227
1910   Obscene Publications Convention, II, 149, 153, 154, 223, 224, 225, 226
1910   Convention Concerning White Slave Traffic, II, 142, 144, 149, 153, 155, 223, 224, 225, 226
1911   Fur Seals Convention, II, 337
1912   Opium Convention, I, 153, 154; II, 149, 153, 154, 224, 225
1914   Additional Protocol to the Berne Convention, II, 144, 205
1919   Treaty of Peace with Bulgaria, I, 402
1919   Peace Treaty between Allied and Associated Powers and Czechoslovakia, II, 138, 179
1919   Treaty of Peace Between Allied and Associated Powers and the Kingdom of the Serbs, Croats and Slovenes, I, 199, 205, 233, 401, 420; II, 178, 179
1919   Poland and The Allied and Associated Powers, II, 181
1919   Treaty of Peace between Allied and Associated Powers and Germany, I, 153, 400–1, 421; II, 17, 80, 181, 187, 191, 224, 238, 241, 270, 313, 348
1919   Minorities Treaty, I, 264
1919   Treaty of Trianon, I, 199, 401, 420; II, 17, 138, 178, 179, 221
1919   Paris Convention on Airspace, II, 212

1919	Convention concerning the Congo and the Niger Rivers signed at St Germain, II, 308	
1920	Treaty of Peace, between Allied and Associated Powers and Hungary, II, 17	
1920	Treaty of Peace between the Allied and Associated Powers and Turkey, I, 350; II, 297	
1921	Convention for the Suppression of Traffic in Women and children, II, 129, 149, 153, 155, 159, 223, 224, 225, 226	
1921	Waterways Treaty concerning the Danube, the Rhine and the Elbe, II, 192	
1921	Convention on Freedom of Transit, II, 148	
1921	Convention concerning the Aaland Islands, II, 269	
1922	Tonnage measurement of merchant ships, II, 131	
1923	Protocol on Arbitration Clauses, II, 310, 336, 353, 355	
1923	Convention for the Suppression of Obscene Publications, II, 129, 142, 153, 154, 224, 225, 226	
1923	Convention on Maritime Ports, II, 227	
1923	Convention on Navigable Waterways, II, 227	
1923	Convention on Railways, II, 227	
1923	Treaty of Peace with Turkey, I, 269, 324, 350, 351, 401–2; II, 239	
1923	White Slave Traffic Convention, II, 155	
1924	Brussels Convention concerning Bills of Lading, II, 120	
1924	Convention terminating Capitulations in the Ottoman Empire, II, 298	
1924	Brussels Agreement respecting Facilities to be Accorded Merchant Seamen for the Treatment of Veneral Disease, II, 210	
1925	Workmen's Compensation for Accidents Convention, II, 70	
1925	Hague Agreement for the International Registration of Industrial Designs and Models, II, 144, 206	
1925	Convention for the Suppression of the Manufacture of Opium, I, 153, 154; II, 142, 144, 153, 154, 225	
1925	Prohibition of the use of Asphyxiating Gas in Warfare, II, 227	
1925	Protocol Amending the Opium Convention, 1912, II, 224, 225	
1926	Agreement concerning the Creation of an International Office for Information regarding Locusts and Organic Statute, II, 158	
1926	International Sanitary Convention, II, 142, 144	
1926	Convention to Suppress the Slave Trade and Slavery, II, 153, 159, 224, 225, 226	
1927	Convention on Execution of Foreign Arbitral Awards, II, 336, 353, 355	
1928	General Act for the Pacific Settlement of International Disputes, II, 212, 304, 305, 370	
1928	Economic Statistics Convention, II, 149, 224, 225, 226	
1929	Convention on Air Carriage, II, 142, 157, 215, 325, 326, 327, 328, 336, 337, 338, 361	
1929	Convention on Safety of Life at Sea, II, 337	
1930	Load Line Convention, II, 69, 148, 161, 227, 337	
1931	Commonwealth Merchant Shipping Agreement, I, 122	
1931	Convention providing for a Uniform Law for Cheques, II, 225	
1931	Convention on the Stamp Laws in connection with Cheques, II, 225	
1931	Narcotic Drugs Convention, I, 154; II, 142, 144, 154, 224, 225, 226	
1931	Convention for the Settlement of Certain Conflicts of Laws in connection with Cheques, II, 225	
1931	Protocol Amending the Opium Convention, 1912, II, 224	

Table of Treaties

1933 White Slave Convention, II, 159, 223, 224, 225, 226
1938 Agreement for the Cession to Germany of Sudeten Territory, I, 212
1944 Convention on Civil Aviation (Chicago Convention), II, 129, 325, 329, 336, 337
1944 International Sanitary Convention for Aerial Navigation, II, 211
1945 Charter of the United Nations, II, 337
1945 Articles of Agreement of the International Bank for Reconstruction and Development, II, 189, 190
1945 International Monetary Fund Agreement, II, 189, 190
1946 Convention on the Privileges and Immunities of the United Nations, II, 140, 142, 144, 150, 223
1946 Final Act of Reparations, II, 384, 385, 386
1946 Protocol Amending the Narcotic Drugs Conventions, 1912–36, II, 154, 225
1947 Agreement Establishing the South Pacific Commission, II, 188
1947 Treaty of Peace with Italy, I, 215-7, 233, 334, 404; II, 313
1947 Treaty of Peace between the Allied and Associated Powers and Finland, I, 335
1947 Protocol Amending the White Slave Traffic Conventions of 1921 and 1933, II, 154, 224
1947 Protocol Amending the Convention for the Suppression of Obscene Publications of 1923, II, 129, 153, 223, 224, 226
1947 General Agreement on Tariffs and Trade, II, 156, 208
1948 Convention on Safety of Life at Sea, II, 337
1948 Protocol Amending the Convention Relating to Economic Statistics, 1928, II, 223, 226
1948 Narcotic Drugs Protocol Dealing with Drugs outside the Scope of 1931 Convention, and 1946 Protocol, II, 224
1949 Convention for the Amelioration of the condition of the wounded, sick and shipwrecked members of armed forces at sea, II, 114, 161, 220, 227, 337
1949 Convention for the Amelioration of the condition of the wounded and sick in armed forces in the field, II, 114, 161, 220, 227, 337
1949 Convention Relative to the protection of Civilian persons in time of War, II, 114, 161, 220, 227, 337
1949 Convention Relative to the treatment of Prisoners of War, II, 114, 161, 220, 227, 337
1949 Protocol Amending the White Slave Traffic Conventions of 1904 and 1910, II, 223, 224
1949 Protocol amending the White Slave Traffic Conventions of 1921 and 1933, II, 153, 223
1949 Protocol Amending the Obscene Publications Convention of 1910, II, 153, 223, 224, 226
1949 Road Traffic Convention, I, 178; II, 69, 120, 142, 150, 178
1949 Temporary Importation of Private Road Vehicles Convention, II, 150
1949 Customs Facilities for Touring Convention, II, 150
1949 Agreement for Provisional Application of the Draft International Customs Convention on Touring, Commercial Road Vehicles, etc., II, 150
1949 Protocol Concerning Road Signs and Signals, II, 225
1950 Convention of Pau concerning Navigation of the Mekong River, II, 252
1950 Agreement on the Importation of Educational, Scientific and Cultural Materials Agreement, II, 224

xlvi   *Table of Treaties*

1951 Treaty of Peace with Japan, II, 382
1951 Refugees Convention, II, 217
1952 Importation of Commercial Samples and Advertising Material Agreement, II, 224
1953 Convention on the Political Rights of Women, II, 227
1953 Protocol Amending Slavery Convention of 1926, II, 153, 159, 224, 226
1953 Agreement on the German External Debt, I, 436; II, 385
1954 Quadripartite Convention between France, Cambodia, Laos and Vietnam, II, 148
1954 First International Tin Agreement, II, 219
1954 Agreement on the Importation of Educational, Scientific and Cultural Materials, II, 149
1954 Geneva Agreement on Indochina, II, 148
1955 Amendment to the Slavery Convention, 1926, II, 226
1955 Austrian State Treaty, I, 436
1956 Final Declaration of the International Conference Terminating the States of Tangier, 1956, I, 293
1957 Treaty of the European Economic Community, II, 309, 310, 311
1958 Protocol terminating the Convention of 1865 and transferring Control of the Cape Spartel Lighthouse to Morocco, II, 253
1958 Articles of Agreement of International Development Association, II, 336
1961 Second International Tin Agreement, II, 219
1962 Protection of Industrial Property Union Convention, II, 206
1962 International Coffee Agreement, II, 219
1962 Sanitary Convention, II, 211
1963 Agreement of Association of the European Economic Community, II, 312
1963 Consular Convention, II, 118
1963 Niger Basin Treaty, II, 310

B. BILATERAL TREATIES

Country	Date	Treaty	
Aargau-Baden	1867	Judicial Assistance Agreement	II, 59
Aargau-Baden-Switzerland	1867	State Treaty Concerning Execution of Judgments	II, 87
Afghanistan-Great Britain	1893	Boundary Treaty	II, 275
Afghanistan-Great Britain	1919	Peace Treaty (Rawalpindi)	II, 275
Afghanistan-Great Britain	1921	Treaty of Friendship and Commerce	II, 275
Algeria-France	1962	Protocol on Financial Control	I, 445
Algeria-France	1962	Evian Agreement	I, 229
Algeria-France	1962	Judicial Protocol	I, 162
Algeria-France	1962	Declaration of Principles concerning Economic and Financial Co-operation	I, 196, 229
Algiers-Portugal	1785	Treaty of Friendship	II, 101
Argentina-France	1948	Air Services Agreement	II, 330
Argentina-Great Britain	1825	Treaty of Amity, Commerce and Navigation	II, 125

Table of Treaties

Country	Date	Treaty	
Argentina-Great Britain	1889	Extradition Convention	II, 125
Argentina-Spain	1859	Treaty of Recognition, Peace and Unity	I, 419
Argentina-Spain	1863	Commercial Treaty	II, 313
Australia-Federation of Rhodesia and Nyasaland	1956	Commercial Agreement	II, 115
Australia-Switzerland	1959	Exchange of Notes concerning the Death Duties Agreement 1872	II, 126
Austria-Hungary-Bavaria	1820	Water Treaty	II, 80
Austria-Hungary-Bavaria	1851	Water Treaty	II, 80
Austria-Hungary-Bavaria	1858	Water Treaty	II, 80
Austria-Hungary-Bavaria	1862	Water Treaty	II, 80
Austria-Hungary-Brazil	1910	Arbitration Convention	II, 179
Austria-Hungary-Denmark-Prussia	1864	Treaty of Peace	I, 269, 307, 355, 398
Austria-Hungary-France	1713	Treaty of Peace (Utrecht)	I, 418; II, 17, 18, 101
Austria-Hungary-France	1797	Treaty of Campo Formio	I, 207, 355, 418
Austria-Hungary-France	1801	Treaty of Lunéville	I, 418, 448
Austria-Hungary-France	1809	Treaty of Peace	I, 418
Austria-Hungary-France	1814	Treaty of Peace	I, 269
Austria-Hungary-France	1859	Treaty of Peace	I, 200, 269, 307, 396, 449
Austria-Hungary-France	1866	Extradition Treaty	II, 179
Austria-Hungary-Germany	1880	Treaty concerning Attestations	II, 87
Austria-Hungary-Germany	1891	Treaty of Commerce	II, 179, 345
Austria-Hungary-Germany	1891	Protocol to Commercial Treaty	II, 179, 345
Austria-Great Britain	1924	Commercial Agreement	II, 319
Austria-Great Britain	1929	Commercial Agreement	II, 319
Austria-Hungary-Holy See	1855	Concordat	II, 30, 179
Austria-Hungary-Italy	1866	Treaty of Peace	I, 306, 356, 418, 469, 530
Austria-Hungary-Netherlands	1814	Treaty concerning the Sovereignty of Belgium	II, 96
Austria-Hungary-Portugal	1816	Treaty of Marriage between Don Pedro I and the Archduchess Leopoldina of Habsburg	II, 102
Austria-Hungary-Prussia	1742	Treaty concerning Silesia (Berlin)	I, 418
Austria-Hungary-Prussia-Denmark	1864	Treaty of Peace	I, 269
Austria-Hungary-Prussia	1866	Treaty of Peace	II, 267
Austria-Hungary-Russia-Germany	1918	Treaty of Peace	II, 268
Austria-Hungary-Saxony	1854	Bankruptcy Treaty	II, 58
Austria-Switzerland	1954	Financial Agreement	I, 437

Table of Treaties

Country	Date	Treaty	
Austria-Hungary-Turkey	1699	Commercial Convention	II, 110
Austria-Hungary-Turkey	1718	Commercial Convention	II, 110
Austria-Hungary-Turkey	1739	Commercial Convention	II, 110
Austria-United States	1928	Treaty of Commerce, Friendship and Consular Rights	II, 38
Austria-United States	1930	Extradition Treaty	II, 39
Baden-Aargau	1867	Judicial Assistance Agreement	II, 59
Baden-Aargau-Switzerland	1867	State Treaty concerning Execution of Judgments	II, 87
Baden-France	1864	Treaty concerning the Execution of Judgments	II, 376
Baden-Holy See	1932	Concordat and Final Protocol	II, 83
Baden-Norway	1847	Exchange of Notes regarding Mutual Reporting of Death Certificates	II, 80
Baden-Norway	1855	Declaration concerning Mutual Abrogation of jus detractus	II, 80
Baden-Switzerland	1841	Water Treaty	II, 85
Baden-Switzerland	1856	Establishment Treaty	II, 59, 60, 81, 343, 350
Baden-Switzerland	1879	Navigation Treaty	II, 81
Baden-Switzerland	1897	Fishery Agreement	II, 86
Baden-Switzerland	1897	Hunting Agreement	II, 86
Baden-Thurgau	1831	Frontier Treaty concerning the City of Constance	II, 87
Baden-United States	1857	Extradition Treaty	II, 59
Baden-United States	1868	Bancroft Treaty	II, 59
Bavaria-Austria-Hungary	1820	Water Treaty	II, 80
Bavaria-Austria-Hungary	1851	Water Treaty	II, 80
Bavaria-Austria-Hungary	1858	Water Treaty	II, 80
Bavaria-Austria-Hungary	1862	Water Treaty	II, 80
Bavaria-France	1865	Treaty concerning Copyright	II, 376
Bavaria-Holy See	1924	Concordat	II, 83
Bavaria-Norway	1847	Exchange of Notes concerning Mutual Reporting of Death Certificates	II, 80
Bavaria-Turkey	1870	Consular Convention	I, 110
Bavaria-United States	1845	Treaty abolishing Taxes on Immigration	I, 59
Bavaria-United States	1853	Extradition Treaty	II, 59
Bavaria-United States	1863	Bancroft Treaty	II, 59
Belgium-Congo	1907	Treaty of Cession of the Independent State of the Congo	I, 89, 380, 439; II, 36
Belgium-Congo	1908	Additional Act to the Treaty of Cession	I, 89; II, 307, 308
Belgium-France	1899	Convention concerning the Reciprocal Enforcement of Judgments	II, 379

Table of Treaties

Country	Date	Treaty	
Belgium-France	1915	Treaty terminating Capitulations in Morocco	II, 50
Belgium-France	1931	Agreement modifying the Treaty of Courtrai	II, 274
Belgium-France	1940	Agreement modifying the Treaty of Courtrai	II, 274
Belgium-Germany	1939	Payments Agreement	I, 383
Belgium-Great Britain-Independent State of the Congo	1894	Treaty concerning the Lease of Land to Great Britain	II, 255
Belgium-Great Britain	1901	Extradition Convention	II, 35, 124, 365
Belgium-Great Britain	1906	Agreement concerning the Waters of the Nile	II, 244
Belgium-Great Britain	1921	Agreement concerning the Ports Dar-es-Salaam and Kigoma	II, 242
Belgium-Great Britain	1929	Agreement concerning identity documents for Aircraft	II, 66
Belgium-United Kingdom	1951	Commercial Agreement relating to interests in East Africa	II, 242
Belgium-United Kingdom	1951	Air Agreement	II, 66
Belgium-Liberia	1895	Extradition Treaty	II, 140
Belgium-Netherlands	1839	Treaty of Separation from Holland	II, 265
Belgium-Orange Free State	1894	Extradition Treaty	II, 35
Belgium-Prussia	1851	Treaty concerning Marriage Certificates	II, 87
Belgium-Saar	1955	Treaty concerning Extradition and Judicial Assistance	II, 41
Belgium-Sardinia	1838	Treaty abolishing the *droit d'aubaine*	II, 96
Belgium-South African Republic	1876	Extradition Treaty	II, 35
Belgium-United States	1948	Double Taxation Convention	II, 161, 182, 367
Berbice-Surinam	1799–1800	Boundary Treaty	II, 275
Protectorate of Bohemia and Moravia-Germany	1940	Agreement concerning Social Service Payments	I, 213
Protectorate of Bohemia and Moravia-Germany	1941	Agreement concerning the Financial consequences of the Transfer of the Sudetenland	I, 233
Bolivia-Great Britain	1911	Commercial Treaty	II, 317, 319
Brazil-Austria-Hungary	1910	Arbitration Convention	II, 179
Brazil-Canada	1931	Commercial Agreement	II, 324
Brazil-Great Britain	1826	Treaty concerning the Abolition of the Slave Trade	II, 102
Brazil-Great Britain	1827	Commercial Convention	II, 102
Brazil-Great Britain	1926	Boundary Treaty	II, 274

Table of Treaties

Country	Date	Treaty	
Brazil-Great Britain	1931	Commercial Agreement	II, 319, 324
Brazil-Great Britain	1936	Trade Agreement	II, 324
Brazil-India	1932	Commercial Agreement	II, 324
Brazil-Portugal	1825	Treaty relating to the Independence of Brazil	I, 396; II, 100
Bremen-France	1847	Extradition Treaty	I, 376
Bremen-Norway	1841	Convention on Trade and Navigation	II, 80
Bremen-Norway	1845	Declaration concerning mutual abrogation of 'jus detractus'	II, 80
Brunswick-Norway	1781	Declaration concerning mutual abrogation of 'jus detractus'	II, 80
Brunswick & Luneberg-United States	1854	Property Convention	II, 59
Bulgaria-Great Britain	1924	Commercial Agreement	II, 319
Bulgaria-Roumania	1940	Agreement of Craiova	I, 214, 233
Bulgaria-Turkey	1913	Treaty of Peace	I, 269, 323
Burma-China	1961	Boundary Treaty	II, 282
Burma-United Kingdom	1947	Financial Agreement	I, 223
Burma (Provisional Govt. of)-United Kingdom	1948	Treaty regarding the recognition of Burmese Independence and related Matters	I, 428; II, 130
Burma-Hong Kong	1959	Commercial Agreement	II, 133
Burma-India	1957	Financial Agreement	I, 428
Burma-Japan	1954	Peace Treaty with Japan	II, 131, 382
Burundi-Rwanda	1962	Agreement on Economic Union	I, 391
Cambodia-France	1867	Treaty of Protection	II, 146
Cambodia-France	1950	Economic Agreement	II, 144
Cambodia-France	1953	Judicial Conventions	I, 143, 158, 174, 226, 234
Cambodia-France	1955	Agreement relative to the transfer of Monetary Institutions	I, 227
Cameroon-France	1958	Judicial Agreement	I, 162
Cameroon-France	1960	Co-operation Agreements	I, 211
Canada-Brazil	1931	Commercial Agreement	II, 324
Canada-United Kingdom	1946	Double Taxation Convention	I, 176; II, 118, 134
Canada-United States	1949	Air Transport Agreement	II, 66
Canada-United States	1952	Exchange of Notes concerning the Air Base at Newfoundland	II, 262
Canada-Venezuela	1941	Exchange of Notes constituting a commercial 'Modus Vivendi'	II, 125
Central African Republic-France	1960	Co-operation Agreements	I, 211
Central African Republic-France	1960	Transitional Agreement concerning Justice	I, 161

Table of Treaties

Country	Date	Treaty	
Central African Republic-France	1960	Economic and Technical Co-operation Agreement	I, 150
Ceylon-United Kingdom	1947	Devolution Agreement	II, 359
Ceylon-Japan	1940	Exchange of Notes concerning Reciprocal Judicial Assistance	II, 131
Chad-France	1960	Co-operation Agreements	I, 67, 88, 211
Chad-France	1960	Transitional Agreement concerning Justice	I, 150, 161
Chile-Great Britain	1937	Trade Agreement	II, 324
Chile-Great Britain	1938	Trade Agreement	II, 324
Chile-United Kingdom	1947	Trade Agreement	II, 324
Chile-Peru	1883	Agreement ceding the Provinces of Tarapaca to Chile	I, 409
Chile-Spain	1844	Treaty of Peace and Friendship and Recognition	I, 419
Chile-United States	1832	Treaty of Commerce and Navigation	II, 92
Chile-Zollverein	1863	Treaty of Commerce and Navigation	II, 59
China-Burma	1961	Boundary Treaty	II, 282
China-Great Britain	1894	Convention concerning the Namwan Assigned Tract	II, 281
China-Great Britain	1897	Boundary Convention	II, 281
China-Great Britain-Tibet	1906	Treaty concerning British Privileges in Tibet	II, 279
China-United Kingdom	1947	Air Transport Agreement	II, 66
China-Japan	1895	Treaty of Peace including the Cession of Formosa	II, 503, 530, 533
China (People's Republic of)-Pakistan	1963	Boundary Treaty	II, 280
China-Zollverein	1861	Treaty of Commerce and Navigation	II, 59
Colombia-France	1850	Extradition Treaty	II, 98
Colombia-France	1892	Commercial Treaty	II, 98
Colombia-Great Britain	1825	Treaty respecting exemption from Navigation Laws	I, 126; II, 165, 166, 167
Colombia-Great Britain	1866	Commercial Treaty	II, 317
Colombia-Great Britain	1912	Protocol to Commercial Agreement	I, 43
Colombia-Peru	1829	Boundary Treaty	II, 94
Colombia-United States	1824	Treaty of Peace, Friendship and Navigation	II, 167
Colombia-United States	1850	Consular Convention	II, 97, 98
Colombia-United States	1857	Treaty concerning Debt	II, 94
Colombia-United States	1888	Extradition Treaty	II, 98
Colombia-United States	1904	Extradition Treaty	II, 98
Congo-Belgium	1907	Treaty of Cession of the Independent State of the Congo	I, 89, 380, 439; II, 36

Table of Treaties

Country	Date	Treaty	
Congo–Belgium	1908	Additional Act to the Treaty of Cession	I, 89; II, 307 308
Congo (B)–France	1960	Economic and Technical Co-operation Agreement	I, 71, 85
Congo (International Association of the)–Germany	1884	Commercial Treaty	II, 256
Congo (International Association of the)–Great Britain	1884	Treaty of Commerce	II, 36
Congo (Independent State of)–Great Britain	1894	Treaty relating to Spheres in the Congo and in East and Central Africa	II, 256
Congo–Holy See	1906	Concordat	II, 36
Congo (B)–Northern Rhodesia	1949	Pedicle Road Agreement	II, 173
Congo–United States	1891	Treaty of Commerce and Navigation	II, 36
Costa Rica–France	1916	Treaty concerning Capitulations in Morocco	II, 50
Costa Rica–Great Britain	1849	Commercial Treaty	II, 317
Costa Rica–Great Britain	1913	Protocol to Commercial Agreement	I, 43
Costa Rica–Spain	1850	Treaty of Recognition, Peace and Friendship	I, 419
Costa Rica–United States	1851	Treaty of Commerce and Navigation	II, 92
Cuba–United States	1902	Treaty of Commerce and Navigation	II, 92
Cuba–United States	1903	Lease of Land for Coaling and Naval Stations	II, 23
Cyprus–United Kingdom	1960	Devolution Agreement	II, 359
Czechoslovakia–Germany	1938	Munich Agreement concerning the Sudetenland	I, 212
Czechoslovakia–Germany	1940	Treaty of Secession of Slovakia to the Reich	I, 212
Czechoslovakia–Great Britain	1923	Commercial Agreement	II, 118, 319
Czechoslovakia–Russia	1945	Treaty concerning the transfer of Carpathia	I, 213
Czechoslovakia–United States	1925	Extradition Treaty	II, 179
Czechoslovakia–Yugoslavia	1928	Treaty of Commerce and Navigation	II, 39
Dahomey–France	1961	Judicial Convention	I, 85, 143
Dahomey–France	1961	Co-operation Agreements	I, 85, 211
Denmark–Austria-Hungary–Prussia	1864	Treaty of Peace	I, 269, 397, 355, 398
Denmark–France	1742	Commercial Treaty	II, 112
Denmark–France	1859	Navigation Treaty	II, 112

Table of Treaties

Country	Date	Treaty	
Denmark-France	1877	Extradition Treaty	II, 112
Denmark-France	1886	Seamen's Convention	II, 112
Denmark-France	1892	Declaration concerning Fees for Certificates of Origin	II, 112
Denmark-France	1904	Exchange of Notes for the Protection of Industrial Designs	II, 112
Denmark-France	1912	Exchange of Notes for the Reciprocal Recognition of Judgment Orders	II, 112
Denmark-Great Britain	1661	Treaty of Peace and Commerce	II, 127
Denmark-Great Britain	1670	Commercial Treaty	II, 169
Denmark-Great Britain	1905	Arbitration Convention	II, 111
Denmark-Great Britain	1912	Protocol to Commercial Agreement	I, 43
Denmark-Great Britain	1933	Trade Agreement	II, 324
Denmark-United Kingdom	1950	Trade Agreement	II, 324
Denmark-United Kingdom	1952	Air Services Agreement	II, 332
Denmark-Prussia	1864	Peace Treaty	I, 398; II, 265
Denmark-Spain	1916	Treaty terminating Capitulations in Morocco	II, 50
Denmark-Sweden	1720	Treaty of Peace	I, 418
Denmark-Sweden	1814	Cession of Norway to Sweden, Treaty of Peace and Friendship	I, 396, 448
Denmark-Turkey	1757	Commercial Convention	II, 110
Denmark-United States	1902	Extradition Treaty Supplemented, 1905	II, 111
Denmark-United States	1914	Treaty for Advancement for the Cause of General Peace	II, 112
Denmark-United States	1916	Treaty ceding territory in the West Indies	I, 146, 172
Dominican Republic-United States	1867	Treaty of Commerce and Navigation	II, 92
Ecuador-Great Britain	1851	Treaty of Amity, Commerce and Navigation	II, 167
Ecuador-Spain	1840	Treaty of Peace, Friendship and Recognition	I, 419
Ecuador-United States	1862	Treaty concerning Debt	II, 94
Egypt-Great Britain	1929	Nile Waters Agreement	II, 245, 246, 247
Egypt-Great Britain	1929	Loan Guarantee Agreement	II, 104
Egypt-Great Britain	1930	Commercial Agreement	II, 118
Egypt-United Kingdom	1954	Agreement concerning the construction of the Owen Falls Dam	II, 247
Egypt-Greece	1884	Commercial Convention	II, 105
Egypt-Greece	1895	Commercial Convention	II, 105, 110

Country	Date	Treaty	
Egypt-Sudan	1959	Agreement concerning technical and Financial Co-operation	II, 241
Egypt-United States	1929	Conciliation Agreement	II, 72
Egypt-United States	1929	Arbitration Agreement	II, 72
Egypt-United States	1930	Narcotics Agreement	II, 72
Egypt-United States	1930	Commercial Agreement	II, 72
Egypt-United States	1932	Consular Agreement	II, 72
Egypt-United States	1946	Air Traffic Agreement	II, 72
Egypt-United States	1946	Air Transport Agreement	II, 72
Egypt-United States	1952	Technical Co-operation Amending Agreement	II, 72
Egypt-United States	1952	Technical Co-operation Agreement	II, 72
Egypt-United States	1952	Mutual Defence Agreement	II, 72
Egypt-United States	1954	Development Assistance Agreement	II, 72
Egypt-United States	1954	Technical Co-operation Agreement	II, 72
Egypt-United States	1946	Commercial Understanding	II, 72
Egypt-United States	1954	Relief Supplies Agreement	II, 72
Egypt-United States	1955	Agreement Relating to an Informational Media Guarantee Programme	II, 72
Egypt-United States	1959	Commodities Agreement for the Northern Region	II, 170
Egypt-United States	1960	Economic and Technical Co-operation Agreement	II, 170
Eire-United Kingdom	1921	Treaty of Independence	I, 404; II, 123
Estonia-Great Britain	1926	Commercial Agreement	II, 319
Estonia-Russia	1920	Treaty of Peace	I, 404
Ethiopia-France	1908	Treaty of Commerce	II, 38
Ethiopia-France	1959	Djibouti-Addis Ababa Treaty	I, 333
Ethiopia-Great Britain	1897	Boundary Treaty	II, 283, 302, 303
Ethiopia-Great Britain	1902	Treaty concerning the Waters of the Nile	II, 244
Ethiopia-United Kingdom	1952	Exchange of Notes concerning the Transfer of Eritrea	I, 195
Ethiopia-United Kingdom	1954	Treaty concerning Grazing Rights	II, 283, 303
Ethiopia-Italy	1896	Peace Treaty	II, 283
Ethiopia-Italy	1908	Boundary Treaty	II, 283
Federation of Rhodesia and Nyasaland-Australia	1956	Commercial Agreement	II, 115, 175
Federation of Rhodesia and Nyasaland-Great Britain	1956	Double Taxation Agreement	II, 176
Federation of Rhodesia and Nyasaland-Japan	1958	Commercial Agreement	II, 175

Table of Treaties

Country	Date	Treaty	
Federation of Rhodesia and Nyasaland-Kenya	1958	Double Taxation Agreement	II, 176
Federation of Rhodesia and Nyasaland-South Africa	1959	Double Taxation Agreement	II, 176
Federation of Rhodesia and Nyasaland-South Africa	1960	Commercial Agreement	II, 115, 175
Federation of Rhodesia and Nyasaland-South Africa	1960	Extradition Treaty	II, 177
Federation of Rhodesia and Nyasaland-Tanganyika	1958	Double Taxation Agreement	II, 176
Federation of Rhodesia and Nyasaland-Uganda	1958	Double Taxation Agreement	II, 176
Fiji Islands-Great Britain	1874	Treaty of Cession	I, 271
Finland-Great Britain	1923	Commercial Convention	II, 319
Finland-Great Britain	1924	Extradition Convention	II, 99
Finland-Great Britain	1933	Commercial Treaty	II, 324
Finland-Norway	1920	Exchange of Notes regulating Fishing	II, 251
Finland-Norway	1922	Treaty controlling Reindeer	II, 251
Finland-Norway	1925	Treaty concerning Rafting of Timber near Petsamo	II, 250
Finland-Norway	1938	Fishery Convention concerning the River Tama	II, 251
Finland-Russia	1920	Treaty of Peace	I, 404
Finland-Sweden	1919	Exchange of notes for the continuance in force of treaties	II, 99
Finland-Sweden	1920	Exchange of notes concerning Timber Rafting	II, 250
Finland-Sweden	1925	Treaty respecting transit rights of Lapps and their herds	II, 251
Finland-Sweden	1925	Salmon Fishing Treaty	II, 250
Finland-United States	1929	Extradition Treaty	II, 99
France-Algeria	1962	Protocol on Financial Control	I, 445
France-Algeria	1962	Evian Agreement	I, 229
France-Algeria	1962	Judicial Protocol	I, 162
France-Algeria	1962	Declaration of Principles concerning Economic and Financial Co-operation	I, 196, 229
France-Argentina	1948	Air Services Agreement	II, 330
France-Austria-Hungary	1713	Treaty of Utrecht	I, 418; II, 17, 18, 101
France-Austria-Hungary	1797	Treaty of Campo Formio	I, 207, 355, 418
France-Austria-Hungary	1801	Treaty of Lunéville	I, 418, 448
France-Austria-Hungary	1809	Treaty of Peace	I, 418
France-Austria-Hungary	1814	Treaty of Peace	I, 269
France-Austria-Hungary	1859	Treaty of Peace	I, 269, 307, 396, 449

Table of Treaties

Country	Date	Treaty	
France-Austria-Hungary	1866	Extradition Treaty	II, 179
France-Baden	1864	Treaty concerning the Execution of Judgments	II, 376
France-Bavaria	1865	Treaty concerning Copyright	II, 376
France-Belgium	1899	Convention concerning the Reciprocal Enforcement of Judgments	II, 379
France-Belgium	1915	Treaty terminating Capitulations in Morocco	II, 50
France-Belgium	1931	Agreement modifying Treaty of Courtrai	II, 274
France-Belgium	1940	Agreement modifying Treaty of Courtrai	II, 274
France-Bolivia	1915	Treaty terminating capitulations in Morocco	II, 50
France-Bremen	1847	Extradition Treaty	I, 376
France-Cambodia	1867	Treaty of Protection	II, 146
France-Cambodia	1950	Economic Agreement	II, 144
France-Cambodia	1953	Judicial Conventions	I, 143, 158, 174, 226, 234
France-Cambodia	1955	Agreement relative to the transfer of monetary institutions	I, 227
France-Cameroon	1958	Judicial Agreement	I, 162
France-Cameroon	1960	Co-operation Agreements	I, 88, 211
France-Central African Republic	1960	Co-operation Agreements	I, 87, 211
France-Central African Republic	1960	Transitional Agreement concerning Justice	I, 161
France-Central African Republic	1960	Economic and Technical Co-operation Agreement	I, 150
France-Chad	1960	Co-operation Agreements	I, 67, 88, 211
France-Chad	1960	Transitional Agreement concerning Justice	I, 150, 161
France-Colombia	1850	Extradition Treaty	II, 98
France-Colombia	1892	Commercial Treaty	II, 98
France-Congo (B)	1960	Economic and Technical Co-operation Agreement	I, 71, 85
France-Costa Rica	1916	Treaty terminating Capitulations in Morocco	II, 50
France-Dahomey	1961	Judicial Convention	I, 85, 143
France-Dahomey	1961	Co-operation Agreements	I, 85, 211
France-Denmark	1742	Commercial Treaty	II, 112
France-Denmark	1859	Navigation Treaty	II, 112
France-Denmark	1877	Extradition Treaty	II, 112
France-Denmark	1886	Seamen's Convention	II, 112

Table of Treaties

Country	Date	Treaty	
France-Denmark	1892	Declaration concerning fees for Certificates of Origin	II, 112
France-Denmark	1904	Exchange of Notes for the Protection of Industrial Designs	II, 112
France-Denmark	1912	Exchange of Notes for the Reciprocal Recognition of Judgment Orders	II, 112
France-Ethiopia	1908	Treaty of Commerce	II, 38
France-Ethiopia	1959	Djibouti-Addis Ababa Treaty	I, 333
France-Gabon	1960	Transitional Agreement concerning Justice	I, 150, 161
France-Gabon	1960	Economic and Technical Co-operation Agreement	I, 88
France-Gabon	1960	Special Agreement concerning Gabon's participation in the Community	I, 88, 150, 211
France-Germany	1871	Treaty of Peace	II, 313, 367
France-Germany	1871	Additional Convention to the Peace Treaty of Frankfurt	I, 152, 167, 207, 269, 307, 357, 398
France-Germany	1896	Treaty renouncing German Capitulations in Tunis	II, 47
France-Germany	1926	Treaty concerning the Saar (Baden-Baden Agreement)	I, 179
France-Germany	1957	Treaty ceding the Saar to Germany	II, 41
France-Great Britain	1713	Treaty of Utrecht	II, 126
France-Great Britain	1763	Treaty of Peace	II, 234
France-Great Britain	1810	Articles of Capitulation concerning Mauritius	II, 27
France-Great Britain	1826	Commercial Convention	II, 316, 361
France-Great Britain-Norway	1855	Treaty Guaranteeing Territorial Integrity	II, 169
France-Great Britain-Russia	1856	Convention on the Demilitarisation of the Aaland Islands	II, 267, 268, 269
France-Great Britain	1862	Treaty guaranteeing the independence of the Sultans of Muscat and Zanzibar	II, 45
France-Great Britain	1890	Convention recognising French Protection over Madagascar	II, 32, 33, 45
France-Great Britain	1891	Mail Ship Convention	II, 337
France-Great Britain	1893	Boundary Treaty Relative to the Gold Coast	II, 17
France-Great Britain	1897	Treaty renouncing Privileges in Tunis	II, 46
France-Great Britain-Italy	1906	Agreement concerning Abyssinia	II, 244

Table of Treaties

Country	Date	Treaty	
France-Great Britain	1912	Protocol to commercial Convention	I, 43
France-Great Britain	1920	Treaty Establishing a Boundary Commission concerning the River Jordan	II, 248
France-Great Britain	1923	Convention relating to Air Fields and Dock Facilities	II, 114
France-Great Britain	1923	Agreement of Good Neighbouring between Palestine and Syria and the Lebanon	II, 249
France-Great Britain-Iraq	1932	Agreements concerning the San Remo Oil Concessions	II, 154
France-Great Britain	1936	Extradition Treaty	II, 127
France-United Kingdom	1946	Air Agreement	II, 66
France-Greece	1914	Treaty terminating Capitulations in Morocco	II, 50
France-Holland	1697	Treaty of Peace	I, 418
France-Holland	1699	Treaty to Execute the Treaty of Peace, 1697	I, 418
France-Holland	1810	Financial Treaty	I, 419
France-Holy See	1438	Pragmatic Sanction	II, 380
France-Holy See	1516	Concordat	II, 380
France-Holy See	1801	Concordat	II, 380
France-Holy See	1802	Concordat	II, 340, 341
France-India	1920	Convention concerning the French Lodge at Balasore	II, 127
France-India	1954	Devolution Agreement relating to Chandernagore	II, 362
France-India	1954	Establishment Treaty	I, 151, 155, 222
France-Italy	1864	Treaty assuming part of the Debt of the Papal States	I, 398
France-Italy	1896	Treaty concerning Italian Nationals in Tunis	II, 47
France-Ivory Coast	1961	Judicial Convention	I, 85
France-Ivory Coast	1961	Co-operation Agreements	I, 85, 211
France-Japan	1915	Treaty terminating Capitulations in Morocco	II, 50
France-Laos	1949	Treaty recognising Laos as an Independent State	II, 251, 327
France-Laos	1950	Economic Convention	II, 144
France-Laos	1953	Devolution Agreement	II, 251, 363
France-Laos	1953	Judicial Convention	I, 143, 158, 174, 226
France-Laos	1955	Agreement relative to the transfer of monetary institutions	I, 227
France-Laos	1953	Judicial Convention	I, 226
France-Lebanon	1937	Treaty of Friendship	II, 158

Table of Treaties

Country	Date	Treaty	
France-Lebanon	1948	Agreement concerning Finance	I, 338
France-Madagascar	1890	Treaty establishing a French Protectorate over Madagascar	II, 32
France-Madagascar	1896	Declaration of Surrender	II, 32
France-Malagasy Republic	1960	Convention on Establishment	I, 84
France-Malagasy Republic	1960	Economic and Technical Co-operation Agreement	I, 84
France-Malagasy Republic	1960	Judicial Convention	I, 84 133, 161
France-Malagasy Republic	1960	Transitional Agreement concerning Justice	I, 84, 133, 161
France-Malagasy Republic	1960	Co-operation Agreements	I, 84, 211
France-Mali	1960	Economic and Technical Co-operation Agreement	I, 83, 170; II, 136
France-Federation of Mali	1960	Co-operation Agreements	I, 83, 212
France-Mauritania	1961	Judicial Convention	I, 84, 143
France-Mauritania	1961	Co-operation Agreements	I, 84, 211
France-Morocco	1845	Boundary Treaty	II, 258, 289, 291
France-Morocco	1901–2	Agreement interpreting the 1845 Boundary Treaty	II, 290
France-Morocco	1912	Treaty for the Establishment of a Regular Regime and the Introduction of Necessary Reforms	II, 50, 51
France-Morocco	1956	Declaration terminating the Treaty of Fez	II, 258
France-Morocco	1956	Devolution Agreement	II, 257, 363
France-Morocco	1957	Convention for Administrative and Technical Assistance	I, 187
France-Morocco	1960	Judicial Convention	I, 143
France-Morocco	1961	Agreement for the withdrawal of French Forces from Morocco	II, 258
France-Netherlands	1820	Treaty of Courtrai	II, 274
France-Netherlands	1886	Declaration regarding Boundaries	II, 274
France-Netherlands	1931	Agreement concerning Boundaries	II, 274
France-Netherlands	1940	Agreement concerning Boundaries	II, 274
France-New Zealand	1949	Air Services Agreement	II, 163
France-Niger	1961	Judicial Convention	I, 86, 143
France-Niger	1961	Co-operation Agreements	I, 86, 211
France-Norway	1869	Extradition Treaty	II, 169
France-Norway	1881	Navigation Treaty	II, 169
France-Norway	1881	Commercial Treaty	II, 169
France-Norway	1886	Distressed Seamen's Convention	II, 169
France-Norway	1900	Tax Relief Exchange of Notes	II, 169
France-Norway	1902	Exchange of Notes concerning Certificates of Origin	II, 169

Country	Date	Treaty	
France-Norway	1904	Arbitration Convention	II, 169
France-Portugal	1713	Treaty of Utrecht	II, 101
France-Prussia	1845	Extradition Treaty	II, 376
France-Russia	1896	Declaration concerning Russian nationals in Tunis	II, 47
France-Saar	1926	Protocol concerning the frontier	II, 81
France-Saar	1953	Treaty concerning treaty application to the Saar	II, 41
France-Saar	1957	Exchange of Notes	II, 41
France-Sardinia	1760	Frontier Treaty	II, 29
France-Sardinia	1760	Treaty for the Mutual Execution of Judgments	II, 375
France-Sardinia	1856	Treaty of Cession and Delimitation	II, 29
France-Sardinia	1857	Sanitary Treaty	II, 29
France-Sardinia	1860	Frontier Treaty	II, 29
France-Sardinia	1860	Treaty of Turin restoring Savoy and Nice to France	I, 269, 307, 355, 397, 530
France-Sardinia	1861	Treaty of Cession and Delimitation	II, 29
France-Savoy	1860	Treaty of Cession	I, 246
France-Senegal	1960	Exchange of Notes respecting Co-operation Agreements	I, 66, 83, 211; II, 171
France-Senegal	1960	Co-operation Agreements	I, 83
France-Siam	1867	Boundary Treaty	II, 251
France-Siam	1893	Treaties relating to Navigation of the Mekong River	II, 251
France-Siam	1904	Treaty concerning Navigation of the Mekong River	II, 147, 251, 306
France-Siam	1926	Treaty concerning the Navigation of the Mekong River	II, 251, 305
France-Siam	1937	Treaty of Friendship	II, 304, 305, 306
France-Siam	1946	Settlement Protocol	II, 305
France-Spain	1659	Treaty of Peace (Treaty of the Pyrenees)	II, 313
France-Spain	1800	Louisiana Cession Treaty	II, 234
France-Spain	1914	Treaty terminating Capitulations in Morocco	II, 50
France-Sweden and Norway	1869	Extradition Treaty	II, 169
France-Sweden and Norway	1877	Treaty ceding St Bartholomew to France	I, 499
France-Sweden and Norway	1881	Commercial Treaty	II, 169
France-Sweden and Norway	1881	Navigation Treaty	II, 169

Table of Treaties

Country	Date	Treaty	
France-Sweden and Norway	1886	Distressed Seamen's Convention	II, 169
France-Sweden and Norway	1900	Tax Relief Exchange of Notes	II, 169
France-Sweden and Norway	1902	Exchange of Notes concerning Certificates of Origin	II, 169
France-Sweden and Norway	1904	Arbitration Convention	II, 169
France-Syria	1926	Treaty incorporating the Sandjak of Alexandretta in Syria	I, 403
France-Syria	1936	Treaty of Friendship	II, 158
France-Texas	1839	Commercial Agreement	II, 62
France-Tunis	1881	Treaty assuming Protection over Tunis	I, 377; II, 46, 48, 143
France-Tunisia	1888	Postal Convention	II, 143
France-Tunisia	1953	Meteorological Convention	II, 143
France-Tunisia	1953	Television Convention	II, 143
France-Tunisia	1953	Broadcasting Convention	II, 143
France-Tunisia	1955	Convention concerning Judicial Arrangements	II, 143, 144
France-Tunisia	1955	War damage claims treaty	II, 143, 144
France-Tunisia	1955	Convention for Administrative and Technical Assistance	I, 187; II, 143, 144
France-Tunisia	1956	Protocol Recognising the Independence of Tunisia	II, 143
France-Turkey	1673	Capitulations	II, 110
France-Turkey	1740	Capitulations	II, 110
France-Turkey	1802	Commercial Convention	II, 109, 110, 111
France-Turkey	1838	Commercial Convention	II, 109, 110, 111
France-Turkey	1861	Commercial Agreement	II, 109, 111
France-Turkey	1921	Treaty granting autonomy within the State of Aleppo to the Sandjak of Alexandretta	I, 403; II, 243
France-Turkey	1926	Further Agreement concerning rights of Transit	II, 243
France-Turkey	1937	Note abrogating the Convention of 1926	II, 244
France-Turkey	1939	Treaty ceding the Sandjak of Alexandretta to Turkey	I, 403; II, 244
France-United States	1783	Treaty of Peace	II, 235
France-United States	1801	Louisiana Cession Treaty	I, 204, 504, 506; II, 234
France-United States	1909	Extradition Treaty	II, 114

Table of Treaties

Country	Date	Treaty	
France-United States	1924	Treaty concerning U.S. rights in Syria	II, 158
France-United States	1937	Exchange of Notes Concerning Customs privileges	II, 158
France-United States	1950	Bases Agreement in Morocco	II, 257, 258, 363
France-Upper Volta	1961	Judicial Convention	I, 143
France-Upper Volta	1961	Co-operation Agreements	I, 211
France-Vietnam	1950	Economic Agreement	II, 144
France-Vietnam	1954	Treaty of Independence	II, 327
France-Vietnam	1955	Convention on Nationality	I, 524
France-Vietnam	1953	Judicial Convention	I, 226–7
France-Vietnam	1954	Judicial Convention	I, 143, 158, 174
France-Vietnam	1955	Agreement relative to the transfer of monetary institutions	I, 227
Gabon-France	1960	Transitional Agreement concerning Justice	I, 88, 150, 161
Gabon-France	1960	Economic and Technical Co-operation Agreement	I, 88
Gabon-France	1960	Special Agreement concerning Gabon's participation in the Community	I, 150, 211
Germany-Austria-Hungary	1880	Treaty concerning Official Attestations	II, 87
Germany-Austria-Hungary	1891	Treaty of Commerce	II, 179, 345
Germany-Austria-Hungary	1891	Protocol to Commercial Treaty	II, 179, 345
Germany-Belgium	1939	Payments Agreement	I, 383
Germany-Protectorate of Bohemia and Moravia	1940	Agreement concerning Social Service Payments	I, 213
Germany-Protectorate of Bohemia and Moravia	1941	Agreement concerning the Financial Consequences of the transfer of the Sudetenland	I, 233
Germany-International Association of the Congo	1884	Commercial Treaty	II, 256
Germany-Czechoslovakia	1938	Munich Agreement concerning the Sudetenland	I, 212
Germany-Czechoslovakia	1940	Treaty of Secession of Slovakia to the Reich	I, 212
Germany-France	1871	Treaty of Peace	II, 313, 376
Germany-France	1871	Additional Treaty to the Peace Treaty of Frankfurt	I, 152, 167, 207, 269, 307, 357, 398
Germany-France	1896	Treaty renouncing German capitulations in Tunis	II, 47

Table of Treaties

Country	Date	Treaty	
Germany-France	1926	Treaty concerning the Saar (Baden-Baden Agreement)	I, 179
Germany-France	1957	Treaty ceding the Saar to Germany	II, 41
Germany-Great Britain-Spain	1885	Protocol Respecting the Sovereignty of Spain over the Sulu Archipelago	II, 286, 288
Germany-Great Britain	1890	Treaty transferring Helgoland and Zanzibar	I, 519, 530
Germany-Great Britain	1924	Treaty of Commerce and Navigation	II, 319
Germany-United Kingdom	1938	Exchange of Notes extending German Treaties to Austria	II, 379
Germany-Holy See	1933	Concordat	II, 83, 84
Germany-Hungary	1940	Treaty of Cession	I, 212
Germany-Hungary	1940	Financial Agreement	I, 212
Germany-Hungary	1942	Extention of Double Taxation Treaty to the Protectorate of Bohemia	II, 380
Germany-Israe	1952	Reparations Agreement	I, 390
Germany-Italy	1872	Extension of 1868 Consular Treaty to the Reich	II, 87
Germany-Netherlands	1938	Payment Agreement	I, 383
Germany-Poland	1919	Convention concerning Polish Upper Silesia	I, 178, 180, 269
Germany-Poland	1920	Convention of Poznan for the Regulation of Judicial Proceedings	I, 146, 168, 169
Germany-Poland	1925	Convention of Oppeln concerning the passing of Property to Poland	I, 204
Germany-Russia-Austria-Hungary	1918	Treaty of Peace	II, 268
Germany-Saar	1935	Agreement concerning civil servants in the Saar Area	I, 179
Germany-Slovakia-Hungary	1940	Convention concerning the Kaschau-Oderberger Railway	I, 213
Germany-Slovakia	1940	Agreement concerning Local Debt	I, 389
Germany-Spain	1885	Treaty concerning the Caroline Islands	II, 256
Germany-Spain	1889	Cession of the Caroline Islands to Germany	II, 256
Germany-Sweden	1938	Payment Agreement	I, 383
Germany-Switzerland	1852	Customs Treaty	II, 87
Germany-Switzerland	1852	Railway Treaty	II, 87
Germany-Switzerland	1854	Boundary Treaty	II, 87
Germany-Switzerland	1858	Railway Treaty	II, 87

Table of Treaties

Country	Date	Treaty	
Germany-Switzerland	1859	Customs Treaty	II, 87
Germany-Switzerland	1863	Customs Treaty	II, 87
Germany-Switzerland	1867	Navigation Treaty	II, 81, 87
Germany-Switzerland	1869	Customs Treaty	II, 87
Germany-Switzerland	1870	Railway Treaty	II, 87
Germany-Switzerland	1875	Railway Treaty	II, 87
Germany-Switzerland	1878	Boundary Treaty	II, 87
Germany-Switzerland	1879	Navigation Treaty	II, 87
Germany-Switzerland	1893	Navigation Treaty	II, 87
Germany-Switzerland	1896	Navigation Treaty	II, 87
Germany-Switzerland	1897	Fishing and Hunting Treaty	II, 87
Germany-Switzerland	1898	Railway Treaty	II, 87
Germany-Switzerland	1906	Treaty respecting the Boundary at Baden	II, 87
Germany-Switzerland	1910	Customs Treaty	II, 87
Germany-Switzerland	1942	Agreement extending the Double Taxation Agreement to the Protectorate of Bohemia	II, 380
Germany-Switzerland	1959	Railway Treaty of Bohemia	II, 380
Germany-United States	1871	Consular Convention	II, 59
Germany-United States	1923	Commercial Treaty	II, 379
Germany-Yugoslavia	1939	Treaty of Commerce	II, 39
Ghana-United Kingdom	1957	Devolution Agreement	II, 359
Great Britain-Afghanistan	1893	Boundary Treaty	II, 275
Great Britain-Afghanistan	1919	Peace Treaty (Rawalpindi)	II, 275
Great Britain-Afghanistan	1921	Treaty of Friendship and Commerce	II, 275
Great Britain-Argentina	1825	Treaty of Amity, Commerce and Navigation	II, 125
Great Britain-Argentina	1889	Extradition Convention	II, 125
Great Britain-Austria	1924	Commercial Agreement	II, 319
Great Britain-Austria	1929	Commercial Agreement	II, 319
Great Britain-Belgium, Independent State of the Congo	1894	Treaty concerning the lease of land to Great Britain	II, 255
Great Britain-Belgium	1901	Extradition Convention	II, 35, 124, 365
Great Britain-Belgium	1906	Agreement concerning the Waters of the Nile	II, 244
Great Britain-Belgium	1921	Agreement concerning the Ports of Dar-es-Salaam and Kigoma	II, 242
Great Britain-Belgium	1929	Agreement concerning Identity Documents for Aircraft	II, 66
United Kingdom-Belgium	1951	Commercial Agreement relating to Interests in East Africa	II, 242
United Kingdom-Belgium	1951	Air Agreement	II, 66
Great Britain-Bolivia	1911	Commercial Treaty	II, 317, 319

Table of Treaties

Country	Date	Treaty	
Great Britain-Brazil	1826	Treaty concerning the Abolition of the Slave Trade	II, 102
Great Britain-Brazil	1827	Commercial Convention	II, 102
Great Britain-Brazil	1926	Boundary Treaty	II, 274
Great Britain-Brazil	1931	Commercial Agreement	II, 319, 324
Great Britain-Brazil	1936	Trade Agreement	II, 324
Great Britain-Bulgaria	1924	Commercial Agreement	II, 319
United Kingdom-Burma	1947	Financial Agreement	I, 223
United Kingdom-Provisional Government of Burma	1948	Treaty regarding the recognition of Burmese Independence and Related Matters	I, 428; II, 130
United Kingdom-Canada	1946	Double Taxation Convention	I, 176; II, 118, 134
United Kingdom-Ceylon	1947	Devolution Agreement	II, 359
Great Britain-Chile	1937	Trade Agreement	II, 324
Great Britain-Chile	1938	Trade Agreement	II, 324
United Kingdom-Chile	1947	Trade Agreement	II, 324
Great Britain-China	1894	Convention concerning the Namwan Assigned Tract	II, 281, 282
Great Britain-China	1897	Boundary Convention	II, 281
Great Britain-China-Tibet	1906	Treaty concerning British Privileges in Tibet	II, 279
United Kingdom-China	1947	Air Transport Agreement	II, 66
Great Britain-Colombia	1825	Treaty respecting exemption from Navigation Laws	I, 126; II, 165, 166, 167
Great Britain-Colombia	1866	Commercial Treaty	II, 317
Great Britain-Colombia	1912	Protocol to Commercial Agreement	I, 43
Great Britain-International Association of the Congo	1884	Treaty of Commerce	II, 36
Great Britain-Independent State of the Congo	1894	Treaty relating to Spheres of Influence in the Congo and in East and Central Africa	II, 256
Great Britain-Costa Rica	1849	Commercial Treaty	II, 317
Great Britain-Costa Rica	1913	Protocol to Commercial Agreement	I, 43
United Kingdom-Cyprus	1960	Devolution Agreement	II, 359
Great Britain-Czechoslovakia	1923	Commercial Agreement	II, 118, 319
Great Britain-Denmark	1662	Commercial Treaty	II, 127
Great Britain-Denmark	1670	Commercial Treaty	II, 169
Great Britain-Denmark	1905	Arbitration Convention	II, 111
Great Britain-Denmark	1912	Protocol to Commercial Agreement	I, 43
Great Britain-Denmark	1933	Trade Agreement	II, 324
United Kingdom-Denmark	1950	Trade Agreement	II, 324

Table of Treaties

Country	Date	Treaty	
United Kingdom-Denmark	1952	Air Services Agreement	II, 332
Great Britain-Ecuador	1851	Treaty of Amity, Commerce and Navigation	II, 167
Great Britain-Egypt	1929	Nile Waters Agreement	II, 245, 246, 247
Great Britain-Egypt	1929	Loan guarantee	II, 104
Great Britain-Egypt	1930	Commercial Agreement	I, 118; II, 118
United Kingdom-Egypt	1954	Agreement concerning the Construction of the Owen Falls Dam	II, 247
Great Britain-Eire	1921	Treaty of Independence	I, 404; II, 123
Great Britain-Estonia	1926	Commercial Agreement	II, 319
Great Britain-Ethiopia	1897	Boundary Treaty	II, 283, 302, 303
Great Britain-Ethiopia	1902	Treaty concerning the Nile	II, 244
United Kingdom-Ethiopia	1952	Exchange of Notes concerning the Transfer of Eritrea	I, 195
United Kingdom-Ethiopia	1954	Treaty concerning Grazing Rights	II, 283, 303
Great Britain-Federation of Rhodesia and Nyasaland	1956	Double Taxation Agreement	II, 176
Great Britain-Fiji Islands	1874	Treaty of Cession	I, 271
Great Britain-Finland	1923	Commercial Agreement	II, 319
Great Britain-Finland	1924	Extradition Convention	II, 99
Great Britain-Finland	1933	Commercial Treaty	II, 324
Great Britain-France	1713	Treaty of Peace and Friendship (Utrecht)	II, 126
Great Britain-France	1763	Treaty of Peace	II, 234
Great Britain-France	1819	Articles of Capitulation concerning Mauritius	II, 27
Great Britain France	1826	Commercial Convention	II, 361
Great Britain-France-United Kingdom of Norway and Sweden	1855	Treaty guaranteeing Territorial Integrity	II, 169
Great Britain-France	1856	Convention on the Demilitarisation of the Aaland Islands	II, 267, 268, 269
Great Britain-France	1862	Treaty guaranteeing the independence of the Sultans of Muscat and Zanzibar	II, 45
Great Britain-France	1890	Convention recognising French Protection of Madagascar	II, 32, 33, 45
Great Britain-France	1891	Mail Ship Convention	II, 337
Great Britain-France	1893	Boundary Treaty relative to the Gold Coast	II, 17
Great Britain-France	1897	Treaty renouncing privileges in Tunis	II, 46
Great Britain-France-Italy	1906	Agreement concerning Abyssinia	II, 244

Table of Treaties

Country	Date	Treaty	
United Kingdom-France	1912	Protocol to Commercial Agreement	I, 43
Great Britain-France	1920	Treaty establishing a Boundary commission respecting the River Jordan	II, 248
Great Britain-France	1923	Convention relating to Air-Fields and Dock Facilities	II, 114
Great Britain-France	1923	Agreement of Good Neighbouring between Palestine, Syria and the Lebanon	II, 249
Great Britain-France-Iraq	1932	Agreement concerning the San Remo Oil concessions	II, 154
United Kingdom-France	1936	Extradition Treaty	II, 127
United Kingdom-France	1946	Air Agreement	II, 66
Great Britain-Germany-Spain	1885	Protocol respecting the Sovereignty of Spain over the Sulu Archipelago	II, 286, 288
Great Britain-Germany	1890	Treaty transferring Helgoland and Zanzibar	I, 519, 530
Great Britain-Germany	1924	Commercial Agreement	II, 319
United Kingdom-Germany	1938	Exchange of Notes extending German Treaties to Austria	II, 379
United Kingdom-Ghana	1957	Devolution Agreement	II, 359
Great Britain-Greece	1864	Treaty ceding the Ionian Islands	I, 356, 419
Great Britain-Greece	1886	Commercial Agreement	II, 41
Great Britain-Greece	1904	Protocol to Commercial Agreement 1886	II, 41
Great Britain-Greece	1910	Extradition Treaty	II, 377
Great Britain-Guatemala	1928	Commercial Agreement	II, 319
Great Britain-Honduras	1887	Commercial Treaty	I, 41, 43
Great Britain-Honduras	1900	Protocol to Commercial Agreement 1887	I, 41
United Kingdom-Hungary	1926	Commercial Agreement	II, 118
Great Britain-Iceland	1953	Arbitration Convention	II, 111
Great Britain-Iceland	1933	Trade Agreement	II, 324
United Kingdom-India-Thailand	1946	Agreement Terminating the State of War	II, 7, 9
United Kingdom-India	1947	Financial Agreement	I, 404
United Kingdom-India	1948	Financial Agreement	I, 404
Great Britain-Iraq	1922	Treaty of Alliance	II, 153, 295, 299, 359
Great Britain-Iraq	1927	Treaty of Alliance	II, 295, 359
Great Britain-Iraq	1930	Agreement concerning devolution of obligations	II, 153
United Kingdom-Israel	1950	Financial Agreement	I, 193, 195, 200, 223, 224, 234; II, 386

lxviii   *Table of Treaties*

Country	Date	Treaty	
United Kingdom-Italy	1883	Treaty of Commerce and Navigation	II, 125
Great Britain-Italy	1891	Protocol concerning Spheres of Influence in Eastern Africa	II, 244
Great Britain-Italy	1894	Treaty recognising Italian Somaliland	II, 283
Great Britain-Italy	1924	Treaty regulating Boundaries of their respective Territories in East Africa	II, 284
Great Britain-Italy	1925	Treaty transferring Jubaland to Italian Somaliland	II, 284
Great Britain-Italy	1925	Agreement concerning the Waters of the Blue Nile	II, 244
Great Britain-Italy	1938	Declaration concerning Lake Tsana	I, 332
United Kingdom-Italy	1951	Exchange of Notes concerning the Disposal of Italian Property in Cyrenaica and Tripolitania	I, 218
United Kingdom-Jamaica	1962	Devolution Agreement	II, 262, 359
Great Britain-Japan	1984	Treaty of Commerce	I, 42; II, 64, 321
Great Britain-Japan	1922	Agreement relating to Tonnage Measurement of Merchant Ships	II, 131
United Kingdom-Jordan	1946	Devolution Agreement	II, 154
Great Britain-Latvia	1923	Commercial Agreement	II, 319
Great Britain-Liberia	1849	Commercial Treaty	II, 316
Great Britain-Liberia	1908	Protocol to Commercial Agreement	I, 43
United Kingdom-Libya	1951	Financial Agreement	I, 218
Great Britain-Lithuania	1922	Commercial Treaty	II, 317, 319
Great Britain-Lithuania	1934	Trade Agreement	II, 324
Great Britain-Madagascar	1865	Treaty of Commerce	II, 31, 32, 33, 49
United Kingdom-Malaya	1957	Devolution Agreement	II, 359, 362
United Kingdom-Malaya	1957	Agreement on External Defence and Mutual Assistance	II, 380
United Kingdom-Malaysia	1963	Agreement Relating to Malaysia	I, 186; II, 380
Great Britain-Mexico	1888	Commercial Agreement	I, 41, 43
Great Britain-Mexico	1926	Convention setting up the Anglo-Mexican Claims Commission	I, 537
Great Britain-Morocco	1783	Treaty of Commerce	II, 43, 52
Great Britain-Morocco	1856	Commercial Treaty	II, 48, 141, 317
Great Britain-Muscat	1891	Treaty of Friendship, Commerce and Navigation	I, 41
Great Britain-Netherlands	1814	Treaty ceding Dutch Colonies	II, 274

Table of Treaties

Country	Date	Treaty	
Great Britain-Netherlands	1856	Consular Convention	II, 65
Great Britain-Netherlands	1898	Extradition Treaty	II, 137, 138
United Kingdom-Netherlands	1948	Exchange of Notes concerning the Regulation of Trade between Singapore and Malaya and the Netherlands Indies	II, 139
United Kingdom-New Zealand	1932	Ottawa Trade Agreement	II, 134
United Kingdom-New Zealand	1959	Trade Agreement	II, 134
United Kingdom-New Zealand	1961	Air Services Agreement	II, 162
United Kingdom-Federation of Nigeria	1960	Devolution Agreement	II, 359
United Kingdom-Federation of Nigeria	1961	Exchange of Letters agreeing to the inclusion of the Northern Cameroons in the Federation	II, 359
United Kingdom-Norway	1907	Supplementary Agreement extending the Extradition Treaty, 1873	II, 169
Great Britain-Norway	1909	Extension of the 1904 Arbitration Convention	II, 169
Great Britain-Norway	1913	Protocol to Commercial Agreement	I, 43; II, 169
United Kingdom-Norway	1950	Trade Agreement	II, 324
United Kingdom-Norway	1952	Air Services Agreement	II, 332
Great Britain-Orange River Colony	1854	Convention for the Recognition of the Orange River Colony	I, 269
Great Britain-Panama	1906	Extradition Treaty	II, 98
Great Britain-Panama	1928	Commercial Agreement	I, 98; II, 319
United Kingdom-Paraguay	1884	Commercial Agreement	I, 41, 43
Great Britain-Persia	1857	Commercial Agreement	II, 107, 317
Great Britain-Persia	1903	Commercial Treaty	II, 109, 148
Great Britain-Peru	1850	Commercial Agreement	II, 317
Great Britain-Poland	1923	Commercial Agreement	II, 118
Great Britain-Portugal	1810	Treaty of Commerce	II, 101, 102
Great Britain-Portugal	1815	Treaty concerning the Slave Trade	II, 102
Great Britain-Portugal	1817	Treaty concerning the Slave Trade	II, 102
Great Britain-Portugal	1901	Treaty concerning Railway Traffic and the Recruitment of Native Labour	II, 35
Great Britain-Portugal	1914	Commercial Treaty	II, 317
Great Britain-Portugal	1920	Treaty renouncing Capitulatory Rights in Egypt	II, 293
United Kingdom-Portugal	1950	Air Agreement	II, 331

lxx   *Table of Treaties*

Country	Date	Treaty	
United Kingdom-Portugal	1954	Visa Abolition Agreement	II, 177
Great Britain-Prussia	1864	Treaty concerning Salvage of Life at Sea	II, 58
Great Britain-Roumania	1930	Commercial Agreement	II, 118, 319
Great Britain-Russia	1825	Treaty concerning Commerce, Navigation and Fisheries	II, 40, 235 236, 237, 274, 302
Great Britain-Russia	1859	Commercial Agreement	II, 235
Great Britain-Russia	1880	Declaration concerning the estates of deceased seamen	II, 99
Great Britain-Russia	1882	Declaration concerning tonnage measurement	II, 99
Great Britain-Russia	1886	Extradition Treaty	II, 99
Great Britain-Russia	1896	Agreement concerning Commercial relations with Zanzibar	II, 99
Great Britain-Russia	1904	Agreement concerning joint stock Companies	II, 99
Great Britain-Russia	1904	Agreement concerning the Exchange of Money Orders	II, 99
Great Britain-Russia	1906	Exchange of notes concerning trademarks in China	II, 99, 100
Great Britain-Russia	1908	Exchange of Notes on Trade Marks and Patents in Morocco	II, 99, 100
Great Britain-Russia	1915	Waiver of Consular Fees on Certificates of Origin	II, 99
Great Britain-Russia	1934	Commercial Agreement	II, 118, 324
United Kingdom-Russia	1956	Exchange of Notes Concerning South Vietnam	II, 148
Great Britain-Salvador	1862	Treaty of Commerce and Navigation	I, 43
Great Britain-Salvador	1886	Protocol to Commercial Agreement	I, 43
United Kingdom-Salvador	1945	Trade Agreement	II, 324
Great Britain-Sardinia	1863	Treaty of Commerce and Navigation	II, 29
Great Britain-Serbia	1880	Commercial Treaty	I, 41
Great Britain-Kingdom of the Two Sicilies	1863	Treaty of Commerce and Navigation	II, 29
United Kingdom-Sierra Leone	1961	Devolution Agreement	II, 359
Great Britain-Spain	1713	Treaty of Peace and Friendship (Utrecht)	I, 418
Great Britain-Spain	1790	Convention concerning Fishery rights in the South Seas	II, 91
Great Britain-Spain-Germany	1855	Protocol concerning various claims in the Sulu Archipelago	II, 286
Great Britain-Spain	1894	Commercial Modus Vivendi	I, 42
Great Britain-Spain	1922	Commercial Agreement	II, 319

Table of Treaties

lxxi

Country	Date	Treaty	
Great Britain-Sweden	1654	Treaty of Uppsala	II, 126, 316, 320
Great Britain-Sweden	1661	Commercial Treaty	II, 91, 316, 320
Great Britain-Sweden and Norway	1826	Commercial Treaty	II, 169, 316
Great Britain-Sweden and Norway-France	1855	Treaty guaranteeing Territorial Integrity	II, 168
Great Britain-Sweden and Norway	1873	Extradition Treaty	II, 156, 169
Great Britain-Sweden and Norway	1881	Distressed Seamen's Convention	II, 169
Great Britain-Sweden	1911	Protocol to Commercial Agreement	I, 43; II, 169
Great Britain-Sweden	1920	Declaration renouncing Capitulatory Rights in Egypt	II, 293
Great Britain-Sweden	1933	Trade Agreement	II, 324
United Kingdom-Sweden	1946	Air Services Agreement	II, 332
Great Britain-Switzerland	1855	Commercial Treaty	II, 317
Great Britain-Switzerland	1872	Treaty concerning Estate Duties	II, 126
Great Britain-Switzerland	1914	Protocol to Commercial Agreement	I, 43
Great Britain-Switzerland	1937	Civil Procedure Agreement	II, 118
Great Britain-Switzerland	1880	Extradition Convention	II, 118, 124
Great Britain-Texas	1840	Commercial Agreement	II, 62
Great Britain-Texas	1840	Treaty concerning Texan contribution to the Public Debt of Mexico	II, 63
Great Britain-Texas	1840	Treaty for the Suppression of the African Slave Trade	II, 63
Great Britain-Thailand (Siam)	1937	Trade Agreement	II, 6, 125, 315, 318, 319, 320, 323, 324, 370
Great Britain-Tibet	1914	Trade Regulations	II, 358
Great Britain-Tibet-China	1913	Simla Agreement	II, 278, 280
Great Britain-Tonga	1900	Treaty assuming Protection	II, 50
British Government in India-Tonk	1869	Extradition Treaty	II, 77
United Kingdom-Trans-Jordan	1946	Treaty of Alliance	I, 334; II, 359
Great Britain-Transvaal	1881	Pretoria Convention	I, 269, 376
United Kingdom-Trinidad and Tobago	1962	Devolution Agreement	II, 262, 360
Great Britain-Tunis	1875	Treaty of Friendship	II, 46, 47, 48
Great Britain-Turkey	1675	Capitulations	II, 104

lxxii Table of Treaties

Country	Date	Treaty	
Great Britain-Turkey	1861	Commercial Agreement	II, 104, 111
Great Britain-Turkey-France	1885	Financial Agreement	II, 104
Great Britain-Tuscany	1847	Treaty of Commerce and Navigation	II, 29
United Kingdom-United Nations Special Fund	1960	Agreement respecting projects in Singapore	II, 70
Great Britain-United States	1783	Treaty of Peace	II, 234
Great Britain-United States	1794	Treaty of Amity, Commerce and Navigation (Jay Treaty)	II, 122, 300
Great Britain-United States	1815	Treaty of Commerce and Navigation	II, 378
Great Britain-United States	1818	Treaty concerning Fishing off Newfoundland	II, 19
Great Britain-United States	1826	Treaty concerning Trading Rights in the Straits Settlements	II, 375
Great Britain-United States	1842	Convention concerning Boundaries, Suppression of the Slave Trade and Extradition (Webster Ashburton Treaty)	II, 90, 122, 124
Great Britain-United States	1871	Treaty of Washington	II, 17, 236, 237
Great Britain-United States	1889	Extradition Convention	II, 124
Great Britain-United States	1899	Treaty concerning Real Property	II, 123
Great Britain-United States	1903	Treaty concerning Light and Harbour Dues in Zanzibar and Pemba	II, 103
Great Britain-United States	1914	Arbitration Agreement	II, 127
Great Britain-United States	1924	Customs Treaty (Liquor Traffic)	I, 44
Great Britain-United States	1930	Boundary Agreement concerning North Borneo and the Philippines	II, 253, 287
Great Britain-United States	1931	Extradition Treaty	II, 75, 90, 115, 118, 131, 156, 367
Great Britain-United States	1937	Agreement concerning Reciprocal Reduction of Passport Visa Fees	II, 75
United Kingdom-United States	1941	Air Bases Agreement	II, 259, 260, 261
United Kingdom-United States	1946	Agreement respecting Air Services	II, 72, 75, 330, 333, 368, 369
United Kingdom-United States	1948	Economy and Technical Co-operation Agreement	II, 369, 75

Table of Treaties

Country	Date	Treaty	
United Kingdom-United States	1950	Mutual Defence Assistance Agreement	II, 369
United Kingdom-United States	1951	Technical Co-operation Agreement	II, 369
United Kingdom-United States	1951	Consular Convention	II, 75
Great Britain-Uruguay	1889	Protocol to Commercial Agreement	I, 43
Great Britain-Uruguay	1819	Arbitration Treaty	I, 46
Great Britain-Vaud	1872	Death Duties Agreement	II, 126
Great Britain-Venezuela	1825	Treaty of Amity, Commerce and Navigation	I, 165; II, 125, 167
Great Britain-Yugoslavia	1937	Commercial Agreement	II, 319
Greece-Egypt	1884	Commercial Convention	II, 105
Greece-Egypt	1895	Commercial Convention	II, 105, 110
Greece-France	1914	Treaty terminating capitulations in Morocco	II, 50
Greece-Great Britain	1864	Treating ceding the Ionian Island	I, 356, 419
Greece-Great Britain	1886	Commercial Agreement	I, 41
Greece-Great Britain	1904	Protocol to Commercial Agreement 1886	I, 41
Greece-Great Britain	1910	Extradition Treaty	II, 377
Greece-Turkey	1913	Treaty of Peace and Friendship	I, 269
Greece-Turkey	1920	Declaration renouncing Capitulatory Rights	II, 293
Guatemala-Great Britain	1928	Commercial Agreement	II, 319
Guatemala-Spain	1863	Treaty of Friendship, Recognition and Independence	I, 419
Guatemala-United States	1849	Treaty of Commerce and Navigation	II, 92
Hamburg-Norway	1844	Convention of Trade and Navigation	II, 80
Hamburg-Norway	1845	Declaration concerning Mutual abrogation of 'Jus Detractus'	II, 80
Hanover-United States	1846	Treaty of Commerce and Navigation	II, 30
Hansa Cities-United States	1826	Treaty of Friendship	II, 58
Hesse-Cassel-Norway	1819	Declaration concerning Mutual abrogation of 'jus detractus'	II, 80
Hesse-Darmstadt-Norway	1819	Declaration concerning Mutual abrogation of 'jus detractus'	II, 80
Hesse-Darmstadt-United States	1868	Bancroft Treaty	II, 59
Holland-France	1697	Treaty of Peace	II, 418
Holland-France	1699	Treaty to Execute the Treaty of Peace 1697	I, 418
Holland-France	1801	Financial Treaty	I, 419
Holland-Prussia	1816	Treaty of Limits	I, 307

Table of Treaties

Country	Date	Treaty	
Honduras-Great Britain	1887	Commercial Treaty	I, 41, 43
Honduras-Great Britain	1900	Protocol to Commercial Agreement 1887	I, 41
Holy See-Austria-Hungary	1855	Concordat	II, 179
Holy See-Baden	1932	Concordat and Final Protocol	II, 83
Holy See-Bavaria	1925	Concordat	II, 83
Holy See-Congo	1906	Concordat	II, 36
Holy See-France	1438	Pragmatic Sanction	II, 380
Holy See-France	1516	Concordat	II, 380
Holy See-France	1801	Concordat	II, 27, 380
Holy See-France	1802	Concordat	II, 340, 341, 350
Holy See-Germany	1933	Concordat	II, 83, 84
Holy See-Netherlands	1927	Concordat	II, 97
Hong Kong-Burma	1959	Commercial Agreement	II, 133
Hungary-Germany	1940	Treaty and Cession	I, 212
Hungary-Germany	1940	Treaty concerning Administrative assistance in fiscal matters	I, 212
Hungary-Germany	1942	Extension of Double Taxation Treaty to the Protectorate of Bohemia	II, 380
Hungary-Great Britain	1926	Commercial Agreement	II, 118
Iceland-Great Britain	1935	Arbitration Convention	II, 111
Iceland-Great Britain	1933	Trade Agreement	II, 324
Iceland-United States	1902	Extradition Treaty	II, 111
Iceland-United States	1950	Consular Convention	II, 123
Iceland-United States	1950	Treaty of Friendship	II, 123
India-Brazil	1932	Commercial Agreement	II, 324
India-Burma	1957	Financial Agreement	I, 428
India-France	1920	Convention concerning French Lodge of Balasore	II, 127
India-France	1954	Revolution Agreement relating to Chandernagore	II, 362
India-France	1954	Establishment Treaty	II, 151, 155, 222
India-United Kingdom-Thailand	1946	Treaty for the Termination of a State of War	II, 79
India-United Kingdom	1947	Financial Agreement	I, 404
India-United Kingdom	1948	Financial Agreement	I, 404
India-Japan	1952	Peace Treaty with Japan	II, 382
India-Pakistan	1947	Financial Agreement	I, 406
India-Thailand	1948	Exchange of Notes	II, 7
India-Tibet	1954	Exchange of Notes Concerning Extra territorial Rights	II, 279, 280
Indonesia-Japan	1958	Peace Treaty with Japan	II, 382
Indonesia-Netherlands	1949	Round Table Agreement	II, 137, 364
Indonesia-Netherlands	1959	Agreement concerning Claims of Netherlands Nationals	I, 286

Table of Treaties

Country	Date	Treaty	
Indonesia-Netherlands	1962	Treaty transferring West New Guinea to Indonesia	II, 41
Iraq-Great Britain	1922	Treaty of Alliance	II, 153, 295, 299, 359
Iraq-Great Britain	1927	Treaty of Alliance	II, 295, 359
Iraq-Great Britain	1930	Agreement concerning Revolution of Obligations	II, 153
Israel-Germany	1952	Reparations Agreement	I, 288
Israel-United Kingdom	1950	Financial Agreement	I, 193, 195, 200, 223, 224, 234; II, 386
Italy-Austria-Hungary	1866	Treaty of Peace	I, 306, 356, 418, 469, 530
Italy-Ethiopia	1896	Treaty of Peace	II, 283
Italy-Ethiopia	1908	Treaty to Delimit the Frontier	II, 283
Italy-France	1864	Convention under which Italy assumed part of debt of Papal States	I, 398
Italy-France	1896	Treaty concerning Italian Nationals in Tunis	II, 47
Italy-Germany	1872	Extension of 1868 Consular Treaty to the Reich	II, 87
Italy-Great Britain	1883	Treaty of Commerce and Navigation	II, 125
Italy-Great Britain	1891	Protocol concerning Spheres of Influence in Eastern Africa	II, 244
Italy-Great Britain	1894	Treaty recognising Italian Somaliland	II, 283
Italy-United Kingdom	1924	Treaty concerning the Boundaries of their respective territories in East Africa	II, 284
Italy-Great Britain	1925	Treaty transferring Tubaland to Italian Somaliland	II, 284
Italy-Great Britain	1925	Agreement concerning the Waters of the Blue Nile	II, 244
Italy-Great Britain	1938	Declaration concerning Lake Tsana	I, 332
Italy-Great Britain	1951	Exchange of Notes Concerning the disposal of Italian property in Cyrenaica and Tripolitania	I, 218
Italy-North German Confederation	1868	Consular Treaty	II, 87
Italy-Saar	1951	Social Security Treaty	II, 41
Italy-Somalia	1960	Devolution Agreement	II, 163, 364
Italy-Switzerland	1862	Extension of Swiss Sardinian Treaties to Italy	II, 29

Table of Treaties

Country	Date	Treaty	
Italy-Switzerland	1864	Treaty extending Swiss Sardinian Telegraph Treaties	II, 29
Italy-Tunis	1865	Treaty conferring customs privileges	II, 47
Italy-Turkey	1912	Treaty of Peace	I, 399
Italy-Turkey	1923	Exchange of Notes concerning the Protocol relating to certain concessions granted in the Ottoman Empire	I, 323
Italy-United States	1871	Treaty of Commerce	II, 30
Italy-United States	1954	Technical Co-operation Agreement Concerning Somalia	II, 74
Italy-United States	1961	Treaty transferring 1954 Agreement to the Republic of Somalia	II, 74
Italy-Yugoslavia	1920	Trade Agreement	I, 323
Ivory Coast-France	1961	Judicial Convention	I, 85
Ivory Coast-France	1961	Co-operation Agreement	I, 85, 211
Jamaica-United Kingdom	1962	Devolution Agreement	II, 262, 359
Japan-Burma	1954	Peace Treaty with Japan	II, 131
Japan-Ceylon	1940	Exchange of Notes concerning reciprocal judicial assistance	II, 131
Japan-China	1895	Treaty of Peace including the Cession of Formosa	II, 503, 530, 533
Japan-Fed. Rhodesia and Nyasaland	1958	Commercial Agreement	II, 175
Japan-France	1915	Treaty terminating capitulations in Morocco	II, 50
Japan-Great Britain	1894	Treaty of Commerce	I, 42; II, 64
Japan-Great Britain	1922	Agreement relating to tonnage measurement of Merchant Ships	II, 131
Japan-India	1952	Peace Treaty with Japan	II, 382
Japan-Indonesia	1958	Peace Treaty with Japan	II, 382
Japan-Korea	1905	Treaty of Protection	II, 37, 49
Japan-Korea	1910	Annexation of Korea	II, 36, 37
Japan-Queensland	1897	Commercial Agreement	I, 41
Japan-Russia	1905	Treaty of Peace	I, 269, 514, 530, 533
Jordan-United Kingdom	1946	Revolution Agreement	II, 154
Kenya-Fed. Rhodesia and Nyasaland	1958	Double Taxation Convention	II, 176
Kenya-Switzerland	1965	Exchange of Notes confirming Treaties	II, 118
Korea-Japan	1905	Treaty of Protection	II, 37, 49
Korea-Japan	1910	Annexation of Korea	II, 36, 37
Korea-United States	1882	Treaty of Peace, Amity, Commerce and Navigation	II, 37
Laos-France	1949	Treaty recognising Laos as an Independent State	II, 251, 327

Table of Treaties lxxvii

Country	Date	Treaty	
Laos-France	1950	Economic Convention	II, 144
Laos-France	1953	Devolution Agreement	II, 251, 363
Laos-France	1953	Judicial Convention	II, 143, 148, 174, 226
Laos-France	1955	Agreement relative to the transfer of monetary institutions	II, 227
Laos-France	1953	Judicial Convention	II, 226
Latvia-Great Britain	1923	Commercial Agreement	II, 319
Latvia-Russia	1920	Treaty of Peace	I, 404
Lebanon-France	1937	Treaty of Friendship	II, 158
Lebanon-France	1948	Financial Agreement	I, 338
Liberia-Belgium	1895	Extradition Treaty	II, 140
Liberia-Great Britain	1849	Commmercial Treaty	II, 316
Liberia-Great Britain	1908	Protocol to Commercial Agreement	I, 43
Libya-United Kingdom	1951	Financial Agreement	I, 218
Lithuania-Great Britain	1922	Commercial Treaty	II, 317, 319
Lithuania-Great Britain	1934	Trade Agreement	II, 324
Lithuania-Russia	1920	Treaty of Peace	I, 404
Lubeck-Norway	1852	Convention on Trade and Navigation	II, 80
Lubeck-Norway	1855	Declaration of Mutual Abrogation of 'jus detractus'	II, 80
Lubeck-Norway	1856	Exchange of Notes regarding coastal navigation	II, 80
Luxembourg-Prussia	1849	Treaty concerning Border Forests	II, 80
Luxembourg (Knight of)-Speyer	1281	Hunting Treaty	II, 22
Madagascar-France	1890	Treaty establishing a French Protectorate over Madagascar	II, 32
Madagascar-France	1896	Declaration of Surrender	II, 32
Madagascar-United States	1881	Treaty of Commerce and Friendship	II, 34
Malagasy Republic-France	1960	Convention on Establishment	I, 84
Malagasy Republic-France	1960	Economic and Technical co-operation Agreement	I, 84
Malagasy Republic-France	1960	Judicial Convention	I, 84, 133, 161
Malagasy Republic-France	1960	Transitional Agreement concerning Justice	I, 84, 133, 161
Malagasy Republic-France	1960	Co-operation Agreements	I, 84, 211
Malawi-Rhodesia	1964	Trade Agreement	II, 174
Mali-France	1960	Economic and Technical Co-operation Agreement	I, 83, 170, II, 136
Mali, (Federation of)-France	1960	Co-operation Agreements	I, 83, 212

Table of Treaties

Country	Date	Treaty	
Malaya-United Kingdom	1957	Devolution Agreement	II, 359, 362
Malaya-United Kingdom	1957	Agreement on External Defence and Mutual Assistance	II, 380
Malaysia-United Kingdom	1963	Agreement Relating to Malaysia	I, 186; II, 380
Malaya-New Zealand	1961	Trade Agreement	II, 134
Maratha-Portugal	1779	Treaty of Punnam	II, 129, 130
Mauritania-France	1961	Judicial Convention	I, 84, 143
Mauritania-France	1961	Co-operation Agreements	I, 84, 211
Mecklenburg-Schwerin-Germany	1819	Declaratory Notes concerning mutual abrogation of 'jus detractus'	II, 80
Mecklenburg-Schwerin-Norway	1846	Trade and Navigation Agreement	II, 80
Mecklenburg-Schwerin-Norway	1847	Exchange of Notes concerning mutual reporting of death certificates	II, 80
Mecklenburg-Schwerin-Norway	1855	Declarations regarding mutual rights to coastal navigation	II, 80
Mecklenburg-Strelitz-Norway	1819	Declaratory notes concerning mutual abrogation of 'jus detractus'	II, 80
Mecklenburg-Strelitz-Norway	1847	Exchange of Notes concerning mutual reporting of death certificates	II, 80
Mecklenburg-Schwerin-Sweden	1830	Treaty granting the revenues of the City of Wismar to Mecklenburg-Schwerin	II, 254, 255
Mecklenburg-Schwerin-Sweden	1903	Treaty ceding the City of Wismar to Mecklenburg-Schwerin	II, 254
Mexico-Great Britain	1888	Commercial Agreement	I, 41, 43
Mexico-Great Britain	1926	Convention setting up the Anglo-Mexican Claims Commission	I, 537
Mexico-Spain	1836	Treaty of Peace and Friendship	I, 419
Mexico-United States	1828	Treaty of Limits	II, 92, 273, 301
Mexico-United States	1831	Treaty of Commerce and Navigation	II, 92, 97
Mexico-United States	1848	Treaty of Peace, Friendship Limits and Settlement	I, 269
Morocco-France	1845	Boundary Treaty	II, 258, 289, 291
Morocco-France	1901–2	Agreement interpreting the 1845 Boundary Treaty	II, 290
Morocco-France	1912	Treaty for the Establishment of a Regular Regime and the Introduction of Necessary Reforms	II, 50, 51

Table of Treaties

Country	Date	Treaty	
Morocco-France	1956	Declarations terminating the Treaty of Fez	II, 258
Morocco-France	1956	Devolution Agreement	II, 257, 363
Morocco-France	1957	Convention for Administrative and Technical Assistance	I, 187
Morocco-France	1960	Judicial Convention	I, 143
Morocco-France	1961	Agreement for the Withdrawal of French Forces from Morocco	II, 258
Morocco-Great Britain	1783	Treaty of Commerce	II, 43
Morocco-Great Britain	1856	Treaty of Commerce	II, 48, 141, 317
Morocco-Norway	1767	Treaty of Amity and Commerce	II, 53
Morocco-Norway	1880	Status of Aliens Convention	II, 53
Morocco-Norway	1896	Exchange of Notes concerning Duties on Tobacco	II, 53
Morocco-Sardinia	1857	Exchange of Notes concerning contraband	II, 29
Morocco-United States	1856	Treaty of Peace	II, 53
Morocco-United States	1936	Treaty of Trade and Commerce	II, 52
Muscat-Great Britain	1891	Treaty of Friendship, Commerce and Navigation	I, 41
Muscat-United States	1833	Treaty of Commerce and Navigation	II, 45, 102, 103
Naples-Turkey	1740	Commercial Convention	II, 110
Netherlands-Austria-Hungary	1814	Treaty concerning the Sovereignty of Belgium	II, 96
Netherlands-Belgium	1839	Treaty of Separation from Holland	II, 97, 265
Netherlands-France	1820	Treaty of Courtrai	II, 274
Netherlands-France	1940	Agreement concerning Boundaries	II, 274
Netherlands-France	1931	Agreement concerning Boundaries	II, 274
Netherlands-Germany	1938	Payment Agreement	I, 383
Netherlands-Germany	1939	Treaty and General Relations	II, 80
Netherlands-Great Britain	1814	Treaty ceding Dutch Colonies	II, 274
Netherlands-Great Britain	1856	Consular Convention	II, 65
Netherlands-Great Britain	1898	Extradition Treaty	II, 137, 138
Netherlands-United Kingdom	1948	Exchange of Notes concerning the Regulation of Trade between Singapore and Malaya and the Netherlands Indies	II, 139
Netherland-Holy See	1927	Concordat	II, 97
Netherlands-Indonesia	1959	Agreement concerning the transfer by Indonesia to the Netherlands of Claims against Netherlands Nationals	I, 286

Table of Treaties

Country	Date	Treaty	
Netherlands-Indonesia	1962	Treaty transferring West New Guinea to Indonesia	II, 41
Netherlands-Prussia	1816	Boundary Treaty	II, 12, 80
Netherlands-Texas	1840	Commercial Agreement	II, 62
New Granada-United States	1846	Treaty of Friendship, Commerce and Navigation	II, 167, 253
New Zealand-France	1949	Exchange of Notes concerning Air Traffic	II, 163
New Zealand-United Kingdom	1932	Ottowa Trade Agreement	II, 134
New Zealand-United Kingdom	1959	Trade Agreement	II, 139
New Zealand-United Kingdom	1961	Air Services Agreement	II, 162
New Zealand-Malaya	1961	Trade Agreement	II, 134
New Zealand-Switzerland	1959	Exchange of Notes concerning the Death Duties Agreement of 1872	II, 126
New Zealand-United States	1940	Arbitration Agreement	II, 127
New Zealand-Western Samoa	1962	Devolution Agreement	II, 360
Nicaragua-Spain	1850	Treaty of Independence	I, 419
Nicaragua-United States	1867	Treaty of Commerce and Navigation	II, 92
Niger-France	1961	Judicial Convention	I, 86, 143
Niger-France	1961	Co-operation Agreements	I, 86, 211
Federation of Nigeria-United Kingdom	1960	Agreement concerning the Inheritance of International Obligations	II, 359
Federation of Nigeria-United Kingdom	1961	Exchange of Letters agreeing to the Inclusion of the Northern Cameroons in the Federation	II, 359
North Germany Confederation-Italy	1868	Consular Treaty	II, 87
North German Confederation-United States	1852	Extradition Treaty	II, 59
North German Confederation-United States	1868	Bancroft Treaty	II, 59, 376, 377
Northern Rhodesia-Congo (B)	1949	Pedicle Road Agreement	I, 173
Norway-Baden	1847	Exchange of Notes regarding Mutual reporting of Death Certificates	II, 80
Norway-Baden	1855	Declaration concerning Mutual Abrogation of 'jus detractus'	II, 80
Norway-Bavaria	1847	Exchange of Notes concerning Mutual Reporting of Death Certificates	II, 80

Table of Treaties

Country	Date	Treaty	
Norway-Bremen	1841	Convention on Trade and Navigation	II, 80
Norway-Bremen	1845	Declaration concerning Mutual Abrogation of 'jus detractus'	II, 80
Norway-Brunswick	1781	Declaration concerning mutual abrogation of 'jus detractus'	II, 80
Norway-Finland	1920	Exchange of Notes regulating Fishing	II, 251
Norway-Finland	1922	Treaty controlling Reindeer	II, 251
Norway-Finland	1925	Treaty concerning rafting of Timber near Petsamo	II, 250
Norway-Finland	1939	Fishery Convention concerning the River Tana	II, 251
Norway-France	1869	Extradition Treaty	II, 169
Norway-France	1881	Navigation Treaty	II, 169
Norway-France	1881	Commercial Treaty	II, 169
Norway-France	1886	Distressed Seamen's Convention	II, 169
Norway-France	1900	Tax Relief Exchange of Notes	II, 169
Norway-France	1902	Exchange of Notes concerning Certificates of Origin	II, 169
Norway-France	1904	Arbitration Convention	II, 169
Norway-Great Britain	1909	Extension of the 1904 Arbitration Convention	II, 169
Norway-Great Britain	1913	Protocol to Commercial Agreement	I, 43; II, 169
Norway-United Kingdom	1950	Trade Agreement	II, 324
Norway-United Kingdom	1952	Air Services Agreement	II, 332
Norway-Hamburg	1844	Convention on Trade and Navigation	II, 80
Norway-Hamburg	1845	Declaration concerning Mutual abrogation of 'jus detractus'	II, 80
Norway-Hesse-Cassel	1918	Declaration concerning Mutual abrogation of 'jus detractus'	II, 80
Norway-Hesse-Darmstadt	1819	Declaration concerning Mutual abrogation of 'jus detractus'	II, 80
Norway-Lubeck	1852	Convention of Trade and Navigation	II, 80
Norway-Lubeck	1855	Declaration on Mutual Abrogation of 'jus detractus'	II, 80
Norway-Lubeck	1856	Exchange of Notes regarding Coastal Navigation	II, 80
Norway-Mecklenburg-Schwerin	1919	Declaratory Notes concerning mutual abrogation of 'jus detractus'	II, 80
Norway-Mecklenburg-Schwerin	1846	Trade and Navigation Agreement	II, 80
Norway-Mecklenberg-Schwerin	1847	Exchange of Notes concerning mutual reporting of death certificates	II, 80

Country	Date	Treaty	
Norway-Mecklenburg-Schwerin	1855	Declarations regarding mutual rights to coastal navigation	II, 80
Norway-Mecklenburg-Strelitz	1847	Exchange of Notes concerning mutual reporting of death certificates	II, 80
Norway-Mecklenburg-Strelitz	1819	Declaratory Notes concerning mutual abrogation of the 'jus detractus'	II, 80
Norway-Morocco	1767	Treaty of Amity and Commerce	II, 53
Norway-Morocco	1880	Status of Aliens Convention	II, 53
Norway-Morocco	1896	Exchange of Notes concerning Duties on Tobacco	II, 53
Norway-Oldenburg	1776	Agreement on mutual abrogation of 'jus detractus'	II, 80
Norway-Oldenburg	1843	Declarations on Trade and Navigation	II, 80
Norway-Oldenburg	1847	Exchange of notes concerning mutual reporting of death certificates	II, 80
Norway-Oldenburg	1859	Declarations concerning mutual right to coastal navigation	II, 80
Norway-Prussia	1815	Treaty to settle questions arising out of the Treaty of Kiel	I, 396
Norway-Prussia	1826	Declaratory Notes concerning mutual abrogation of 'jus detractus'	II, 80
Norway-Prussia	1827	Agreement on Trade and Navigation	II, 80
Norway-Prussia	1847	Exchange of Notes concerning mutual reporting of death certificates	II, 80
Norway-Prussia	1858	Declarations concerning mutual rights to coastal navigation	II, 80
Norway-Prussia	1859	Declarations concerning expansion of mutual rights to coastal navigation	II, 80 II, 80
Norway-Prussia	1861	Agreement concluded with the former Kingdom of Hanover concerning Redemption of Customs	II, 80
Norway-Prussia	1847	Agreement on mutual abrogation of 'jus detractus'	II, 80
Norway-Prussia	1847	Exchange of Notes concerning mutual reporting of death certificates	II, 80
Norway and Sweden-Russia	1826	Treaty of St Petersburg	II, 251

… Table of Treaties … lxxxiii

Country	Date	Treaty	
Norway-Saxe-Altenburg	1847	Exchange of Notes concerning mutual reporting of death certificates	II, 80
Norway-Saxe-Coburg-Gotha	1847	Exchange of notes concerning mutual reporting of death certificates	II, 80
Norway-Saxe-Coburg-Gotha	1862	Declaration concerning mutual abrogation of 'jus detractus'	II, 80
Norway-Saxe-Weimar	1792	Agreement on mutual abrogation of 'jus detractus'	II, 80
Norway-Saxe-Weimar	1847	Exchange of notes concerning mutual reporting of death certificates	II, 80
Norway-United States	1827	Treaty of Commerce and Navigation	II, 169
Norway-United States	1869	Naturalization Convention and Protocol	II, 169
Norway-United States	1887	Money Order Convention	II, 169
Norway-United States	1893	Extradition Treaty	II, 169
Norway-Württemberg	1847	Exchange of Notes concerning mutual reporting of death certificates	II, 80
Norway-Württemberg	1829	Declaration concerning mutual abrogation of 'jus detractus'	II, 80
Oldenburg-Norway	1776	Agreement on mutual abrogation of 'jus detractus'	II, 80
Oldenburg-Norway	1843	Declaration on Trade and Navigation	II, 80
Oldenburg-Norway	1847	Exchange of notes concerning mutual reporting of death certificates	II, 80
Oldenburg-Norway	1859	Declarations concerning mutual right to coastal navigation	II, 80
Orange Free State-Belgium	1894	Extradition Treaty	II, 35
Pakistan-China (People's Republic)	1963	Boundary Treaty	II, 280
Pakistan-India	1947	Financial Agreement	I, 406
Pakistan-Thailand	1958	Commercial Treaty	II, 7
Panama-Great Britain	1906	Extradition Treaty	II, 98
Panama-Great Britain	1928	Commercial Agreement	II, 98
Panama-United States	1904	Extradition Treaty	II, 98
Paraguay-Great Britain	1884	Commercial Agreement	I, 41, 43
Persia-Great Britain	1857	Commercial Agreement	II, 107, 317
Persia-Great Britain	1903	Commercial Treaty	II, 109, 148
Persia-Iraq	1937	Boundary Treaty	II, 248
Persia-Turkey	1823	Commercial Treaty	II, 106
Persia-Turkey	1847	Treaty of Erzerum	II, 106, 247, 248

f-2

Table of Treaties

Country	Date	Treaty	
Persia-Turkey	1913	Boundary Treaty	II, 248
Peru-Chile	1883	Agreement ceding province of Tarapaca to Chile	I, 409
Peru-Chile	1829	Boundary Treaty	II, 94
Peru-Great Britain	1850	Commercial Agreement	II, 317
Peru-United States	1851	Treaty of Commerce and Navigation	II, 92
Philippines-United States	1946	Treaty of Independence and General Relations	I, 146, 366, 433; II, 225
Poland-Germany	1919	Convention concerning Polish Upper Silesia	I, 178, 180, 269
Poland-Germany	1920	Convention of Poznan for the regulation of Judicial Proceedings	I, 146, 168, 169
Poland-Germany	1925	Convention of Oppeln concerning the passing of Property to Poland	I, 205;
Poland-Great Britain	1923	Commercial Agreement	II, 118
Poland-Russia-Ukraine	1921	Peace Treaty	I, 404
Portugal-Algiers	1785	Treaty of Friendship and Commerce	II, 101
Portugal-Austria	1816	Treaty of Marriage of Don Pedro I and the Archduchess Leopoldina of Habsburg	II, 102
Portugal-Brazil	1825	Treaty of Independence	I, 396; II, 100
Portugal-France	1713	Treaty of Utrecht	II, 101
Portugal-Great Britain	1810	Treaty of Commerce	II, 101
Portugal-Great Britain	1815	Treaty concerning the Slave Trade	II, 102
Portugal-Great Britain	1817	Treaty concerning the Slave Trade	II, 102
Portugal-Great Britain	1901	Treaty concerning Railway Traffic and the Recruitment of Native Labour	II, 35
Portugal-Great Britain	1914	Commercial Treaty	II, 317
Portugal-Great Britain	1920	Treaty renouncing Capitulatory rights in Egypt	II, 293
Portugal-United Kingdom	1950	Air Agreement	II, 331
Portugal-United Kingdom	1954	Visa Abolition Agreement	II, 177
Portugal-Maratha	1779	Treaty of Punnam	II, 128, 130
Portugal-Spain	1777	Treaty of Limits	II, 102
Prussia-Austria-Hungary	1742	Treaty concerning Silesia (Berlin)	II, 418
Prussia-Austria-Hungary-Denmark	1864	Treaty of Peace	I, 269
Prussia-Austria-Hungary	1866	Treaty of Peace	II, 267
Prussia-Belgium	1851	Treaty concerning Marriage Certificates	II, 87
Prussia-Denmark	1864	Peace Treaty	I, 398

Table of Treaties

Country	Date	Treaty	
Prussia-France	1845	Extradition Treaty	II, 376
Prussia-Great Britain	1864	Salvage of Life at Sea	II, 58
Prussia-Holland	1816	Treaty of Limits	I, 307
Prussia-Holy See	1929	Concordat	II, 83
Prussia-Luxembourg	1849	Treaty concerning Border Forests	II, 80
Prussia-Netherlands	1816	Boundary Treaties	II, 12, 80
Prussia-Norway and Sweden	1815	Treaty to settle questions arising out of the Treaty of Kiel	I, 396
Prussia-Norway and Sweden	1826	Declaratory Notes concerning mutual abrogation of 'jus detractus'	II, 80
Prussia-Norway and Sweden	1827	Agreement on Trade and Navigation	II, 80
Prussia-Norway and Sweden	1847	Exchange of notes concerning mutual reporting of death certificates	II, 80
Prussia-Norway and Sweden	1858	Declarations concerning mutual rights to coastal navigation	II, 80
Prussia-Norway and Sweden	1859	Declarations concerning expansion of mutual rights to coastal navigation	II, 80
Prussia-Norway and Sweden	1861	Agreement concluded with the former kingdom of Hanover concerning redemption of customs	II, 80
Prussia-Norway and Sweden	1847	Agreement on mutual abrogation of 'jus detractus'	II, 80
Prussia-Norway and Sweden	1847	Exchange of notes concerning mutual reporting of death certificates	II, 80
Prussia-Turkey	1761	Capitulations	II, 110
Prussia-United States	1785	Commercial Treaty	II, 58
Prussia-United States	1799	Commercial Treaty	II, 58
Prussia-United States	1828	Treaty of Commerce and Navigation	II, 58
Prussia-Westphalia	1811	Convention relating to debt of Rhenish Confederation	I, 396
Queensland-Japan	1897	Commercial Agreement	I, 41
Rhodesia-Malawi	1964	Trade Agreement	II, 174
Rhodesia and Nyasaland, Federation of, *see under* Federation			
Roumania-Bulgaria	1940	Agreement of Craiova	I, 214
Roumania-Great Britain	1930	Commercial Agreement	II, 118
Russia-Czechoslovakia	1945	Treaty concerning the transfer of Carpathia	I, 213
Russia-Estonia	1920	Treaty of Peace	II, 404
Russia-Finland	1920	Treaty of Peace	II, 404
Russia-France	1896	Declaration concerning Russian Nationals in Tunis	II, 47

Table of Treaties

Country	Date	Treaty	
Russia-Germany-Austria-Hungary	1918	Treaty of Peace	II, 268
Russia-Great Britain	1825	Treaty of Commerce, Navigation and Fisheries	II, 40, 235, 236, 237, 274, 302
Russia-Great Britain	1859	Commercial Agreement	II, 235
Russia-Great Britain	1880	Declaration concerning the estates of deceased seamen	II, 99
Russia-Great Britain	1882	Declaration concerning tonnage measurement	II, 99
Russia-Great Britain	1886	Extradition Treaty	II, 99
Russia-Great Britain	1896	Agreement concerning commercial relations with Zanzibar	II, 99
Russia-Great Britain	1904	Agreement concerning joint stock Companies	II, 99
Russia-Great Britain	1904	Agreement concerning the Exchange of Money Orders	II, 99
Russia-Great Britain	1906	Exchange of notes concerning trademarks in China	II, 99, 100
Russia-Great Britain	1908	Exchange of Notes on Trade Marks and Patents in Morocco	II, 99, 100
Russia-Great Britain	1915	Waiver of Consular Fees on Certificates of Origin	II, 99
Russia-Great Britain	1934	Commercial Agreement	II, 118, 324
Russia-United Kingdom	1956	Exchange of Notes concerning South Vietnam	II, 148
Russia-Japan	1905	Treaty of Peace	I, 269, 514, 530, 533
Russia-Latvia	1920	Treaty of Peace	II, 404
Russia-Lithuania	1920	Treaty of Peace	II, 404
Russia-Norway and Sweden	1826	Treaty of St Petersburg	II, 251, 304
Russia-Spain	1915	Treaty terminating capitulations in Morocco	II, 50
Russia-Sweden	1720	Peace Treaty of Stockholm	I, 418; II, 254
Russia-Sweden	1917	Joint Declaration concerning Rafting of Timber	II, 250
Russia-Turkey	1739	Commercial Convention	II, 110
Russia-Turkey	1774	Commercial Convention	II, 110
Russia-Turkey	1783	Commercial Convention	II, 110
Russia-Turkey	1878	Treaty of Peace	II, 20
Russia-Ukraine-Poland	1921	Treaty of Peace	I, 404
Russia-United States	1867	Treaty ceding Alaska to the United States	I, 204, 269; II, 40, 235, 236, 237
Rwandi-Burundi	1962	Agreement on Economic Union	I, 391

Table of Treaties

Country	Date	Treaty	
Saar–Belgium	1955	Treaty concerning Extradition and Judicial Assistance	II, 41
Saar–France	1926	Protocol concerning the Frontier	II, 81
Saar–France	1953	Treaty concerning Treaty Application to the Saar	II, 41
Saar–France	1957	Exchange of Notes	II, 41
Saar–Germany	1935	Agreement concerning Civil Servants in the Saar District	I, 179
Saar–Italy	1951	Social Security Treaty	II, 41
Salvador–Great Britain	1862	Treaty of Commerce and Navigation	I, 43
Salvador–Great Britain	1886	Protocol to Commercial Agreement	I, 43
Salvador–United Kingdom	1945	Trade Agreement	II, 324
Salvador–Sardinia	1860	Treaty of Amity	II, 29
Salvador–Spain	1865	Treaty of Independence	I, 419
Sardinia–Belgium	1838	Treaty abolishing the droit d'aubaine	II, 96
Sardinia–France	1760	Frontier Treaty	II, 29
Sardinia–France	1760	Treaty concerning Mutual Execution of Judgments	II, 375
Sardinia–France	1856	Treaty of Cession and Delimitation	II, 29
Sardinia–France	1857	Sanitary Treaty	II, 29
Sardinia–France	1860	Frontier Treaty	II, 29
Sardinia–France	1860	Treaty of Cession and Delimitation	II, 29
Sardinia–Great Britain	1863	Treaty of Commerce and Navigation	II, 29
Sardinia–Morocco	1857	Exchange of Notes concerning contraband	II, 29
Sardinia–Salvador	1860	Treaty of Amity	II, 29
Sardinia–Spain	1851	Judicial Assistance Treaty	II, 29
Sardinia–Switzerland	1843	Extradition Treaty	II, 29
Sardinia–Switzerland	1851	Treaty of Commerce	II, 29
Sardinia–Turkey	1823	Commercial Convention	II, 110
Sardinia–United States	1838	Treaty of Commerce	II, 30
Savoy–France	1860	Treaty of Cession	I, 246
Savoy–Turkey	1839	Treaty of Commerce	II, 29
Saxe–Norway	1847	Exchange of notes concerning mutual reporting of death certificates	II, 80
Saxe–Norway–Coburg-Gotha	1847	Exchange of notes concerning mutual reporting of death certificates	II, 80
Saxe–Norway–Coburg-Gotha	1862	Declaration concerning mutual abrogation of 'jus detractus'	II, 80

Country	Date	Treaty	
Saxe-Norway-Weimar	1792	Agreement on mutual abrogation of 'jus detractus'	II, 80
Saxe-Norway-Weimar	1847	Exchange of notes concerning mutual reporting of death certificates	II, 80
Saxony-Austria	1854	Bankruptcy Treaty	II, 58
Senegal-France	1960	Exchange of Notes respecting Co-operation Agreements	I, 66, 83, 211; II, 171
Senegal-France	1960	Co-operation Agreement	II, 83
Serbia-Great Britain	1880	Commercial Treaty	I, 41
Serbia-United States	1902	Extradition Treaty	II, 379
Siam, see Thailand			
Kingdom of the Two Sicilies-Great Britain	1863	Treaty of Commerce and Navigation	II, 29
Sierra Leone-United Kingdom	1961	Devolution Agreement	II, 359
Slovakia-Germany	1940	Convention concerning the Kaschau-Oderberger Railway	I, 213
Slovakia-Germany	1940	Agreement concerning Local Debt	I, 389
Somalia-Italy	1960	Devolution Agreement	II, 163, 364
South Africa-Fed. Rhodesia and Nyasaland	1959	Double Taxation Agreement	II, 176
South Africa-Fed. Rhodesia and Nyasaland	1960	Commercial Agreement	II, 115, 175
South African Republic-Belgium	1876	Extradition Treaty	II, 35
Spain-Argentina	1859	Treaty of Recognition, Peace and Unity	I, 419
Spain-Argentina	1863	Commercial Treaty	II, 313
Spain-Chile	1844	Treaty of Peace and Friendship and Recognition	I, 419
Spain-Costa Rica	1850	Treaty of Recognition, Peace and Friendship	I, 419
Spain-Ecuador	1840	Treaty of Peace, Friendship and Recognition	I, 419
Spain-France	1659	Treaty of Peace (Treaty of the 'Pyrenees')	II, 313
Spain-France	1800	Louisiana Cession Treaty	II, 234
Spain-France	1914	Treaty terminating Capitulations in Morocco	II, 50
Spain-Germany	1885	Treaty concerning the Caroline Islands	II, 256
Spain-Germany	1889	Cession of the Caroline Islands to Germany	II, 256
Spain-Great Britain	1713	Treaty of Peace and Friendship (Utrecht)	I, 418

Table of Treaties

Country	Date	Treaty	
Spain-Great Britain	1790	Convention concerning Fishery rights in the South Seas	II, 91
Spain-Great Britain-Germany	1855	Protocol concerning various claims in the Sulu Archipelago	II, 286
Spain-Great Britain	1894	Commercial Modus Vivendi	I, 42
Spain-Great Britain	1922	Commercial Agreement	II, 319
Spain-Guatemala	1863	Treaty of Friendship, Recognition and Independence	I, 419
Spain-Mexico	1836	Treaty of Peace and Friendship	I, 419
Spain-Nicaragua	1850	Treaty of Independence	I, 419
Spain-Portugal	1777	Treaty of Limits	II, 102
Spain-Salvador	1865	Treaty of Independence	I, 419
Spain-Sardinia	1851	Judicial Assistance Treaty	II, 29
Spain-Sultan of Sulu	1850	Capitulations	II, 285
Spain-Sultan of Sulu	1851	Capitulations	II, 285
Spain-Sultan of Sulu	1878	Capitulations of Peace	II, 285
Spain-Turkey	1782	Commercial Convention	II, 110
Spain-United States	1789	Treaty of Amity, Boundaries and Navigation	II, 92
Spain-United States	1795	Treaty of Friendship, Boundaries, Commerce and Navigation	I, 92, 93, 94, 95, 234, 302
Spain-United States	1819	Treaty of Friendship, Cession of the Floridas and Boundaries	I, 244, 269; II, 92, 95, 301, 302
Spain-United States	1898	Treaty of Peace	I, 146, 152, 169, 244, 269, 366; II, 225, 252, 299
Spain-United States	1900	Cession of Islands in the Philippines Archipelago	II, 225
Spain-Uruguay	1841	Treaty of Peace, Friendship, Commerce, Navigation and Recognition	I, 419
Spain-Venezuela	1845	Treaty of Peace, Friendship and Recognition	I, 419
Speyer-(Knight of) Luxembourg	1281	Hunting Treaty	II, 22
Sudan-Egypt	1959	Agreement concerning Technical and financial co-operation	I, 241
Sulu (Sultan of)-Spain	1850	Capitulations	II, 285
Sulu (Sultan of)-Spain	1851	Capitulations	II, 285
Sulu (Sultan of)-Spain	1878	Capitulations of Peace	II, 285
Sulu (Sultan of)-United States	1899	Bates Treaty	II, 286
Surinam-Berbice	1799–1800	Boundary Treaty	II, 275

Table of Treaties

Country	Date	Treaty	
Sweden-Denmark	1720	Treaty of Peace	II, 418
Sweden-Denmark	1814	Cession of Norway to Sweden, Treaty of Peace and Friendship	I, 396, 448
Sweden-Finland	1919	Exchange of Notes respecting the continuance in Force of Treaties	II, 99
Sweden-Finland	1920	Treaty respecting the Rafting of Timber	II, 250
Sweden-Finland	1925	Treaty respecting Transit Rights of Lapps and their Herds	II, 251
Sweden-Finland	1927	Salmon Fishing Treaty	II, 250
Sweden and Norway-France	1877	Treaty ceding St Bartholomew to France	I, 449
Sweden and Norway-France	1869	Extradition Treaty	II, 169
Sweden and Norway-France	1881	Commercial Treaty	II, 169
Sweden and Norway-France	1881	Navigation Treaty	II, 169
Sweden and Norway-France	1886	Distressed Seamen's Convention	II, 169
Sweden and Norway-France	1900	Tax Relief Exchange	II, 169
Sweden and Norway-France	1902	Exchange of notes concerning Certificates of Origin	II, 169
Sweden and Norway-France	1904	Arbitration Convention	II, 169
Sweden-Germany	1938	Payments Agreement	I, 383
Sweden-Great Britain	1661	Commercial Treaty	II, 91, 316, 320
Sweden-Great Britain	1654	Treaty of Uppsala	II, 126, 316, 320
Sweden and Norway-Great Britain	1826	Commercial Treaty	II, 169, 316
Sweden and Norway-Great Britain	1873	Extradition Treaty	I, 156, 169
Sweden and Norway-Great Britain	1881	Distressed Seamen's Convention	II, 169
Sweden-Great Britain	1911	Protocol to Commercial Agreement	I, 43; II, 169
Sweden-Great Britain	1921	Declaration renouncing capitulatory Rights in Egypt	II, 293
Sweden-Great Britain	1913	Trade Agreement	II, 324
Sweden-United Kingdom	1946	Air Services	II, 332
Sweden-Mecklenburg-Schwerin	1803	Treaty concerning Administrative Contracts	I, 355
Sweden-Mecklenburg-Schwerin	1830	Treaty of Malmo	II, 254, 255

Table of Treaties

Country	Date	Treaty	
Sweden-Mecklenburg-Schwerin	1903	Treaty ceding the City of Wismar to Mecklenburg-Schwerin	II, 254
Sweden-Russia	1720	Peace Treaty of Stockholm	I, 418; II, 254
Sweden-Russia	1917	Joint declaration concerning the Rafting of Timber	II, 250
Sweden-United States-Norway	1827	Commerce and Navigation	II, 169
Sweden and Norway-United States	1869	Naturalization Convention	II, 169
Sweden and Norway-United States	1887	Money Order Convention	II, 169
Sweden and Norway-United States	1893	Extradition Treaty	II, 169
Switzerland-Australia	1959	Exchange of Notes concerning the Death Duties Agreement 1872	II, 126
Switzerland-Austria	1954	Financial Agreement	I, 437
Switzerland-Baden	1841	Water Treaty	II, 85
Switzerland-Baden	1856	Establishment Treaty	II, 59, 60, 81, 343, 350
Switzerland-Baden-Aargau	1867	State Treaty concerning Execution of Judgments	II, 87
Switzerland-Baden	1879	Navigation Treaty	I, 81
Switzerland-Baden	1897	Fishery Agreement	I, 86
Switzerland-Germany	1852	Railway Treaty	II, 87
Switzerland-Germany	1852	Customs Treaty	II, 87
Switzerland-Germany	1854	Boundary Treaty	II, 87
Switzerland-Germany	1858	Railway Treaty	II, 87
Switzerland-Germany	1859	Customs Treaty	II, 87
Switzerland-Germany	1863	Customs Treaty	II, 87
Switzerland-Germany	1867	Navigation Treaty	II, 81, 87
Switzerland-Germany	1869	Customs Treaty	II, 87
Switzerland-Germany	1870	Railway Treaty	II, 87
Switzerland-Germany	1875	Railway Treaty	II, 87
Switzerland-Germany	1878	Boundary Treaty	II, 87
Switzerland-Germany	1879	Navigation Treaty	II, 87
Switzerland-Germany	1893	Navigation Treaty	II, 87
Switzerland-Germany	1897	Fishing and Hunting Treaty	II, 87
Switzerland-Germany	1898	Railway Treaty	II, 87
Switzerland-Germany	1906	Treaty respecting the Boundary at Baden	II, 87
Switzerland-Germany	1910	Customs Treaty	II, 87
Switzerland-Germany	1942	Agreement extending the Double Taxation Agreement to the Protectorate of Bohemia	II, 380
Switzerland-Germany	1959	Railway Treaty	II, 87
Switzerland-Great Britain	1855	Commercial Agreement	II, 317

Table of Treaties

Country	Date	Treaty	
Switzerland-Great Britain	1872	Treaty concerning Estate Duties	II, 126
Switzerland-Great Britain	1914	Protocol to Commercial Agreement	I, 43
Switzerland-Great Britain	1937	Civil Procedure Agreement	II, 118
Switzerland-Italy	1862	Extension of Swiss-Sardinian Treaties to Italy	II, 29
Switzerland-Italy	1864	Treaty extending Swiss Sardinian telegraph Treaties	II, 29
Switzerland-Sardinia	1816	Treaty fixing Political Frontier	II, 29, 237
Switzerland-Sardinia	1843	Extradition Treaty	II, 29
Switzerland-Sardinia	1851	Treaty of Commerce	II, 29
Switzerland-Württemberg	1826	Bankruptcy Treaty	II, 59
Syria-France	1926	Treaty incorporating the Sandjak of Alexandretta in Syria	I, 403
Syria-France	1936	Treaty of Friendship	II, 158
Syria-Lebanon	1921	Provisional Agreement for the Extradition of Offenders	II, 159
Syria-United States	1924	General Relations Convention	II, 72
Syria-United States	1937	Customs Agreement	II, 72
Syria-United States	1944	General Relations Convention	II, 72, 294
Tanganyika-Fed. of Rhodesia and Naysaland	1958	Double Taxation Agreement	II, 176
Tanzania-United States	1966	Exchange of Notes concerning Continuity of Treaties	II, 414
Texas-France	1839	Commercial Treaty	II, 62
Texas-Great Britain	1840	Commercial Agreement	II, 62
Texas-Great Britain	1840	Treaty concerning Texan contribution to the Public Debt of Mexico	II, 63
Texas-Great Britain	1840	Treaty for Suppression of the African Slave Trade	II, 63
Texas-Netherlands	1840	Commercial Agreement	II, 62
Thailand (Siam)-France	1867	Boundary Treaty	II, 251
Thailand (Siam)-France	1893	Treaties relating to Navigation of the Mekong River	II, 251
Thailand (Siam)-France	1904	Treaty concerning Navigation of the Mekong River	II, 147, 251, 306
Thailand (Siam)-France	1926	Treaty concerning the Navigation of the Mekong River	II, 251, 305
Thailand (Siam)-France	1937	Treaty of Friendship	II, 304, 305, 306
Thailand (Siam)-France	1946	Settlement Protocol	II, 305
Thailand (Siam)-Great Britain	1937	Trade Agreement	II, 6, 125, 315, 318, 319, 320, 323, 324, 370
Thailand-Pakistan	1958	Commercial Treaty	II, 7

Table of Treaties xciii

Country	Date	Treaty	
Tibet-Great Britain-China	1913	Simla Agreement	II, 278, 280
Tibet-Great Britain	1914	Trade Regulations	II, 358
Tibet-India	1954	Exchange of Notes concerning Extra-territorial Rights	II, 279, 280
Thurgau-Baden	1831	Frontier Treaty concerning the City of Constance	II, 87
Tonga-Great Britain	1900	Treaty assuming Protection	II, 50
Tonga-United States	1886	Commerce and Navigation Treaty	II, 50
Tonk-British Government in India	1900	Extradition Treaty	II, 77
Transjordan-United Kingdom	1946	Treaty of Alliance	I, 334
Transvaal-Great Britain	1881	Pretoria Convention	I, 269, 376
Tunis-France	1881	Treaty assuming Protection over Tunis	I, 377; II, 46 48, 143
Tunisia-France	1888	Postal Convention	II, 143
Tunisia-France	1953	Meteorological Convention	II, 143
Tunisia-France	1953	Television Convention	II, 143
Tunisia-France	1953	Broadcasting Convention	II, 143
Tunisia-France	1955	Convention concerning judicial Arrangements	II, 143, 144
Tunisia-France	1955	War Damage Claims Treaty	II, 143, 144
Tunisia-France	1955	Convention for Administrative and Technical Assistance	I, 187; II, 143, 144
Tunisia-France	1956	Protocol Recognising the independence of Tunisia	II, 143
Tunis-Great Britain	1875	General Convention of Commerce	II, 46, 47, 48
Tunis-Italy	1865	Treaty conferring Customs privileges	II, 47
Tunis-United States	1797	Treaty of Capitulation	II, 47
Tunis-United States	1824	Treaty of Capitulation	II, 47
Turkey-Austria-Hungary	1699	Commercial Convention	I, 110
Turkey-Austria-Hungary	1718	Commercial Convention	I, 110
Turkey-Austria-Hungary	1739	Commercial Convention	I, 110
Turkey-Bavaria	1870	Consular Convention	I, 110
Turkey-Bulgaria	1913	Treaty of Peace	I, 269, 323
Turkey-Denmark	1757	Commercial Convention	I, 110
Turkey-France	1673	Capitulations	II, 110
Turkey-France	1740	Capitulations	II, 110
Turkey-France	1802	Commercial Convention	II, 109, 110, 111
Turkey-France	1838	Commercial Convention	II, 109, 110, 111
Turkey-France	1861	Commercial Agreement	II, 109, 111
Turkey-France	1921	Treaty granting autonomy within the State of Aleppo to the Sandjak of Alexandretta	I, 403; II, 243

Country	Date	Treaty	
Turkey-France	1926	Further Agreement concerning rights of Transit	II, 243
Turkey-France	1937	Note abrogating the Convention of 1926	II, 244
Turkey-France	1939	Treaty ceding the Sandjak of Alexandretta to Turkey	I, 403; II, 243
Turkey-Genoa	1535	Capitulations	II, 110
Turkey-Genoa	1606	Capitulations	II, 110
Turkey-Great Britain	1675	Capitulations	II, 104
Turkey-Great Britain	1861	Commercial Convention	II, 104, 111
Turkey-Great Britain-France	1885	Financial Agreement	II, 104
Turkey-Greece	1913	Treaty of Peace and Friendship	I, 269
Turkey-Greece	1920	Declaration terminating Capitulatory Rights	II, 293
Turkey-Italy	1861	Treaty of Commerce and Navigation	II, 29
Turkey-Italy	1912	Treaty of Peace	I, 399
Turkey-Italy	1923	Exchange of Notes concerning Concessions in the Ottoman Empire	I, 323
Turkey-Naples	1740	Commercial Convention	II, 110
Turkey-Persia	1823	Commercial Treaty	II, 106
Turkey-Persia	1847	Treaty of Erzerum	II, 106, 247, 248
Turkey-Persia	1913	Boundary Treaty	II, 248
Turkey-Prussia	1761	Capitulations	II, 110
Turkey-Russia	1739	Commercial Convention	II, 110
Turkey-Russia	1774	Commercial Convention	II, 110
Turkey-Russia	1783	Commercial Convention	II, 110
Turkey-Russia	1878	Treaty of San Stephano	II, 20
Turkey-Sardinia	1823	Commercial Convention	II, 110
Turkey-Savoy	1839	Treaty of Commerce	II, 29
Turkey-Spain	1782	Commercial Convention	II, 110
Turkey-Tuscany	1833	Commercial Convention	II, 110, 111
Turkey-United States	1830	Commercial Convention	II, 104
Turkey-Venice	1454	Capitulations	II, 110
Turkey-Venice	1718	Commercial Convention	II, 110
Tuscany-Great Britain	1847	Treaty of Commerce and Navigation	II, 29
Tuscany-Turkey	1833	Commercial Convention	II, 110, 111
Uganda-Fed. of Rhodesia and Nyasaland	1958	Double Taxation convention	II, 176
Uganda-Switzerland	1965	Exchange of Notes continuing Treaties	II, 118
United Kingdom, see Great Britain			
United Nations Special Fund-United Kingdom	1960	Agreement respecting Projects in Singapore	II, 70

Table of Treaties

Country	Date	Treaty	
United States-Austria	1928	Treaty of Commerce, Friendship and consular rights	II, 38
United States-Austria	1930	Extradition Treaty	II, 39
United States-Baden	1857	Extradition Treaty	II, 59
United States-Baden	1868	Bancroft Treaty	II, 59
United States-Bavaria	1845	Treaty abolishing Taxes	II, 59
United States-Bavaria	1853	Extradition Treaty	II, 59
United States-Bavaria	1868	Bancroft Treaty	II, 59
United States-Belgium	1948	Double Taxation Conventions	II, 161, 182, 367
United States-Brunswick and Luneburg	1854	Property Convention	I, 59
United States-Canada	1949	Air Transport Agreement	II, 66
United States-Canada	1952	Exchange of Notes concerning the Air Base at Newfoundland	II, 262
United States-Chile	1832	Treaty of Commerce and Navigation	I, 92
United States-Colombia	1824	Treaty of Peace, Friendship and Navigation	II, 167
United States-Colombia	1850	Consular Convention	II, 97
United States-Colombia	1857	Treaty concerning Debt	II, 94
United States-Colombia	1888	Extradition Treaty	II, 98
United States-Colombia	1904	Extradition Treaty	II, 98
United States-International Association of the Congo	1884	Treaty of Commerce	II, 36
United States-Costa Rica	1851	Treaty of Commerce and Navigation	II, 92
United States-Cuba	1902	Treaty of Commerce and Navigation	II, 92
United States-Cuba	1903	Lease of Land for coaling and Naval Stations	II, 23
United States-Czechoslovakia	1925	Extradition Treaty	II, 179
United States-Denmark	1902	Extradition Treaty, Supplemented 1905	II, 111
United States-Denmark	1914	Treaty for Advancement for the cause of General Peace	II, 112
United States-Denmark	1916	Treaty ceding Territory in the West Indies	I, 146, 172
United States-Dominician Republic	1867	Treaty of Commerce and Navigation	II, 92
United States-Ecuador	1862	Treaty concerning Debt	II, 94
United States-Egypt	1929	Conciliation Agreement	II, 72
United States-Egypt	1929	Arbitration Agreement	II, 72
United States-Egypt	1930	Narcotics Agreement	II, 72
United States-Egypt	1930	Commercial Agreement	II, 72
United States-Egypt	1932	Consular Agreement	II, 72
United States-Egypt	1946	Air Traffic Agreement	II, 72

Table of Treaties

Country	Date	Treaty	
United States-Egypt	1946	Air Transport Agreement	II, 72
United States-Egypt	1952	Technical Co-operation Amending Agreement	II, 72
United States-Egypt	1952	Technical Co-operation Agreement	II, 72
United States-Egypt	1952	Mutual Defence Agreement	II, 72
United States-Egypt	1954	Development Assistance Agreement	II, 72
United States-Egypt	1954	Technical Co-operation Agreement	II, 72
United States-Egypt	1946	Commercial Understanding	II, 72
United States-Egypt	1954	Relief Supplies Agreement	II, 72
United States-Egypt	1955	Agreement Relating to an (programme) Informational Media Guarantee	II, 72
United States-Egypt	1959	Commodities Agreement for the Northern Region	II, 170
United States-Egypt	1960	Economic and Technical Co-operation Agreement	II, 170
United States-Finland	1929	Extradition Treaty	II, 99
United States-France	1783	Treaty of Peace	II, 235
United States-France	1803	Treaty for Cession of Louisiana	I, 204, 540, 506; II, 234
United States-France	1909	Extradition Treaty	II, 114
United States-France	1924	Treaty concerning US Rights in Syria	II, 158
United States-France	1937	Exchange of Notes concerning customs privileges	II, 158
United States-France	1950	Base Agreement in Morocco	II, 257, 258, 363
United States-Germany	1871	Consular Convention	II, 59
United States-Germany	1923	Commercial Agreement	II, 379
United States-Great Britain	1783	Treaty of Peace	II, 234, 235
United States-Great Britain	1794	Treaty of Amity, Commerce and Navigation (Jay Treaty)	II, 122, 300
United States-Great Britain	1815	General Treaty of Commerce and Navigation	II, 378
United States-Great Britain	1818	Convention concerning Commerce, Slavery and Fishing off Newfoundland	II, 19
United States-Great Britain	1826	Treaty concerning Trading Rights in the Straits Settlements	II, 375
United States-Great Britain	1842	Convention concerning Boundaries, Suppression of the Slave Trade and Extradition (Webster-Ashburton Treaty)	II, 90, 122, 124
United States-Great Britain	1871	Treaty of Washington	II, 17, 236, 237

Table of Treaties

Country	Date	Treaty	
United States-Great Britain	1889	Extradition Convention	I, 124
United States-Great Britain	1899	Treaty concerning Real Property	II, 123
United States-Great Britain	1903	Treaty concerning Light and Harbour Dues in Zanzibar and Pemba	II, 103
United States-Great Britain	1914	Arbitration Agreement	II, 127
United States-Great Britain	1924	Customs Treaty (Liquor Traffic)	I, 44
United States-United Kingdom	1930	Boundary Agreement concerning North Borneo and the Philippines	II, 253, 287
United States-Great Britain	1931	Extradition Treaty	II, 75, 90, 115, 118, 131, 156, 367
United States-United Kingdom	1937	Agreement concerning Reciprocal Reduction of Passport Visa Fees	II, 75
United States-United Kingdom	1941	Air Bases Agreement	II, 259, 260, 261
United States-United Kingdom	1946	Agreement respecting Air Services	II, 72, 75, 330, 333, 368, 369
United States-United Kingdom	1948	Economic and Technical Co-operation Agreement	II, 75, 369
United States-United Kingdom	1950	Mutual Defence Assistance Agreement	II, 369
United States-United Kingdom	1951	Technical Co-operation Agreement	II, 369
United States-United Kingdom	1951	Consular Convention	II, 75
United States-Hanover	1846	Treaty of Commerce and Navigation	II, 30
United States-Hansa Cities	1827	Treaty of Friendship	II, 58
United States-Hesse-Darmstadt	1868	Bancroft Treaty	II, 59
United States-Iceland	1902	Extradition Treaty	II, 111
United States-Iceland	1950	Consular Convention	II, 123
United States-Iceland	1950	Treaty of Friendship, Commerce and Navigation	II, 123
United States-Italy	1871	Treaty of Commerce	II, 30
United States-Italy	1954	Technical Co-operation Agreement concerning Somalia	II, 74
United States-Italy	1961	Treaty transferring the 1954 Agreement to the Republic of Somali	II, 74
United States-Kenya	1965	Exchange of Notes confirming Treaties	II, 110
United States-Korea	1882	Treaty of Peace, Amity, Commerce and Navigation	II, 37
United States-Madagascar	1881	Treaty of Commerce and Friendship	II, 34

xcviii   *Table of Treaties*

Country	Date	Treaty	
United States-Mecklenburg-Schwerin	1847	Treaty of Commerce and Navigation	II, 58
United States-Mexico	1828	Treaty of Limits	II, 92, 273, 301
United States-Mexico	1831	Treaty of Commerce and Navigation	II, 92, 97
United States-Mexico	1848	Treaty of Peace, Friendship, Limits and Settlement	I, 269
United States-Morocco	1836	Treaty of Peace	II, 53
United States-Morocco	1936	Treaty of Trade and Commerce	II, 52
United States-Muscat	1833	Treaty of Commerce and Navigation	II, 45, 102, 103
United States-New Granada	1846	Treaty of Friendship, Commerce and Navigation	II, 167, 253
United States-New Zealand	1840	Arbitration Agreement	II, 127
United States-Nicaragua	1867	Treaty of Commerce and Navigation	II, 92
United States-North German Confederation	1852	Extradition Treaty	II, 59
United States-North German Confederation	1868	Bancroft Treaty	II, 59, 376
United States-Norway	1827	Treaty of Commerce and Navigation	II, 169
United States-Norway	1869	Naturalization Convention and Protocol	II, 169
United States-Norway	1887	Money Order Convention	II, 169
United States-Norway	1893	Extradition Treaty	II, 169
United States-Panama	1904	Extradition Treaty	II, 98
United States-Philippines	1946	Treaty of Independence and General Relations	I, 146, 366, 433; II, 225
United States-Prussia	1785	Commercial Treaty	II, 58
United States-Prussia	1799	Commercial Treaty	II, 58
United States-Prussia	1828	Treaty of Commerce and Navigation	II, 58
United States-Russia	1867	Treaty for the cession of Alaska	I, 204, 269; II, 40, 235, 236, 237
United States-Sardinia	1838	Treaty of Commerce	II, 30
United States-Serbia	1902	Extradition Treaty	II, 379
United States-Somalia	1961	Technical Co-operation Agreement	II, 74
United States-Spain	1789	Treaty of Amity Boundaries and Navigation	II, 92
United States-Spain	1795	Treaty of Friendship, Boundaries, Commerce and Navigation	II, 92, 93, 94, 95, 234, 302
United States-Spain	1819	Treaty of Friendship, Cession of the Floridas and Boundaries	I, 244, 269; II, 92, 95, 301, 302

Table of Treaties

Country	Date	Treaty	
United States-Spain	1898	Treaty of Peace	I, 146, 152, 169, 244, 269, 366; II, 225, 252, 299
United States-Spain	1900	Cession of Islands in the Philippine Archipelago	II, 225
United States-Sultan of Sulu	1899	Bates Treaty	II, 286
United States-Sweden and Norway	1826	Commerce and Navigation	II, 169
United States-Sweden and Norway	1869	Naturalization Convention	II, 169
United States-Sweden and Norway	1887	Money Order Convention	II, 169
United States-Sweden and Norway	1893	Extradition Treaty	II, 169
United States-Syria	1924	General Relations Convention	II, 72
United States-Syria	1937	Customs Agreement	II, 72
United States-Syria	1944	General Relations Convention	II, 72, 294
United States-Tanzania	1966	Exchange of Notes concerning continuity of Treaties	II, 114, II, 114
United States-Tonga	1886	Commerce and Navigation Treaty	II, 50
United States-Tunis	1797	Treaty of Capitulation	II, 47
United States-Tunis	1824	Treaty of Capitulations	II, 47
United States-Turkey	1830	Commercial Convention	II, 104
United States-United Arab Republic	1955	Money Order Arrangements	II, 73
United States-United Arab Republic	1958	Money Order Arrangements	II, 73
United States-Venezuela	1836	Treaty of Commerce and Navigation	II, 92
United States-West Indies Federation	1961	Defence Areas Agreement	II, 261
United States-Württemberg	1868	Bancroft Treaty	II, 59
United States-Zanzibar	1886	Treaty of Commerce and relating to Consuls	II, 102, 103
Upper Volta-France	1961	Judicial Convention	I, 143
Upper Volta-France	1961	Co-operation Agreements	I, 211
Uruguay-Great Britain	1889	Protocol to Commercial Agreement	I, 43
Uruguay-Great Britain	1918	Arbitration Treaty	I, 46
Uruguay-Spain	1841	Treaty of Peace, Friendship, Commerce and Navigation	I, 419
Vaud-Great Britain	1872	Death Duties Agreement	II, 126
Venezuela-Canada	1941	Exchange of Notes constituting a commercial 'Modus Vivendi'	II, 125
Venezuela-Great Britain	1825	Treaty of Amity, Commerce and Navigation	I, 165; II, 125, 167

c   Table of Treaties

Country	Date	Treaty	
Venezuela-Spain	1845	Treaty of Peace, Friendship and Recognition	I, 419
Venice-Turkey	1454	Capitulations	II, 110
Venice-Turkey	1718	Commercial Convention	II, 110
Vietnam-France	1950	Economic Agreement	II, 144
Vietnam-France	1954	Treaty of Independence	II, 327
Vietnam-France	1955	Convention on Nationality	I, 524
Vietnam-France	1953	Judicial Convention	I, 226, 227
Vietnam-France	1954	Judicial Convention	I, 143, 158, 174
Vietnam-France	1955	Agreement relative to the transfer of monetary institutions	I, 227
West Indies Federation-United States	1961	Defence Areas Agreement	II, 261
Western Samoa-New Zealand	1962	Devolution Agreement	II, 360
Westphalia-Prussia	1811	Convention relating to Debt of the Rhenish Confederation	I, 396
Württemberg-Norway	1829	Declaration concerning mutual abrogation of 'jus detractus'	II, 80
Württemberg-Norway	1847	Exchange of Notes concerning mutual reporting of death certificates	II, 80
Württemberg-Switzerland	1826	Bankruptcy Treaty	II, 59
Württemberg-United States	1868	Bancroft Treaty	II, 59
Yugoslavia-Czechoslovakia	1928	Treaty of Commerce and Navigation	II, 39
Yugoslavia-Germany	1939	Treaty of Commerce	II, 39
Yugoslavia-Great Britain	1937	Commercial Agreement	II, 319
Yugoslavia-Italy	1920	Trade Agreement	I, 323
Zanzibar-United States	1886	Treaty of Commerce and relating to Consuls	II, 102, 103
Zollverein-China	1861	Treaty of Commerce and Navigation	II, 59
Zollverein-Netherlands	1851	Treaty of Commerce and Navigation	II, 59
Zollverein-Siam	1862	Treaty of Commerce and Navigation	II, 59

TABLE OF UNITED NATIONS DOCUMENTS RELATING TO STATE SUCCESSION

A/CN. 4/149 and Add. 1. The succession of states in relation to membership in the UN. Memorandum prepared by the Secretariat.

A/CN. 4/150 and Corr. 1. Succession of states in relation to general multilateral treaties of which the Secretary-General is the depositary. Memorandum prepared by the Secretariat.

A/CN. 4/151. Digest of the decisions of international tribunals relating to state succession. Study prepared by the Secretariat.

A/CN. 4/157. Digest of decisions of national courts relating to succession of states and governments. Study prepared by the Secretariat.

A/CN. 4/160. Report by Mr Manfred Lachs, Chairman of the Sub-Committee on succession of states and governments.

ST/LEG/1. Handbook of final clauses.

ST/LEG/3 and Revisions. Status of multilateral conventions of which the Secretary-General acts as depositary.

ST/LEG/6. Handbook of final clauses.

ST/LEG/7. Précis de la pratique du Secrétaire Général dépositaire d'accords multilateraux.

ABBREVIATIONS

A.C.	Appeal Cases (United Kingdom).
A.I.R.	All India Reporter (India).
A.J.	*American Journal of International Law.*
A. J. Comp. L.	*American Journal of Comparative Law.*
Agrawala	'Law of Nations as Interpreted and Applied by Indian Courts and Legislature' in *India Journal of International Law*, vol. II (1962), p. 431.
Al.	Alabama Reports (United States).
All E.R.	All England Law Reports (England).
Ann. Dig.	*Annual Digest of Public international Law Cases.*
Annuaire de l'Institut	*Annuaire de l'Institut de Droit International.*
Annuaire français	*Annuaire français de droit international.*
Anzilotti	*Corso di diritto internazionale* (1912).
Appleton	*Des effets des annexions de territoire sur les dettes de l'État démembré ou annexé* (1895).
B. & C.	Barnewall and Cresswell, King's Bench Reports, 1822–30 (United Kingdom).
B.F.S.P.	*British & Foreign State Papers.*
BGE	*Entscheidungen des schweizerischen Bundesgerichtes* (*Arrêts du Tribunal féderal suisse*) (Switzerland).
B.T.S.	*British Treaty Series.*
B.Y.	*British Year Book of International Law.*
Bad. Ges. VOBl.	*Gesetz-und Verordnungs-Blatt für Baden.*
Bad. Reg. Bl.	*Regierungsblatt für das Grossherzogtum Baden.*
Bad.-Württ. Ges. Bl.	*Gesetzblatt für Baden-Württemberg.*
Bartoš	'Les nouveaux Etats et les traités internationaux', in *Jugoslovenska Revija za Medunarodno Pravo*, vol. II (1962).
Basdevant	*Traités et conventions en vigueur entre la France et les Puissances étrangères.* 4 vols. (1918–1922).
Bayer. Ges. u. VOBl.	*Gesetz-und Verordnungs-Blatt für Bayern.*
Beavan	Beavan's Reports, Rolls Series, 1838–66 (United Kingdom).
Beisswingert	*Die Einwirkung bundes-staatlicher Kompetenzverschiebungen auf völkerrechtliche Verträge unter besonderer Berücksichtigung der deutschen Entwicklung* (1960).
Ber. Slg.	*Schweizerische bereinigte Sammlung der Bundesgesetze und Verordnungen.*
Berber	*Lehrbuch des Völkerrechts.* 3 vols. (1960–2).
Bing. N.C.	Bingham New Cases, Common Pleas Series, 1834–40 (United Kingdom).
Black.	Blackstone, H., Common Pleas Reports, 1788–96 (United Kingdom).
	Blackstone, W., King's Bench Reports. 1746–80. (United Kingdom).
Blatchf.	Blatchford's United States Circuit Court Reports, 1845–81.

Abbreviations

Bluntschli	*Das moderne Völkerrecht der civilisirten Staten als Rechtsbuch dargestellt* (1867).
Bomb.	Bombay Series, Indian Law Reports.
Bro. C.C.	Brown's Chancery Cases, 1778–94 (United Kingdom).
Bulmerincq	*Völkerrecht oder internationales Recht* (1887).
Bustamante	*Derecho internacional público* (1936).
C.	Papers presented to Parliament by Command of His (Her) Majesty.
	–1–4222 1836–1869
	C. 1–9550 1870–1899
	Cd. 1–9239 1900–1918
	Cmd. 1–9889 1919–1956
	Cmnd. 1– 1956
C.L.R.	Common Law Reports.
C.L.R.	Commonwealth Law Reports.
C.W.N.	Calcutta Weekly Notes.
Cabouat	*Des annexions de territoire et de leurs principales conséquences* (1881).
Cal.	Calcutta Series, Indian Law Reports.
Cal. L.J.	*Calcutta Law Journal.*
Calvo	*Droit international théorique et pratique,* 5th ed. (1896).
Cansacchi	'*Sullo* "Stato di appartenenza" dei comandi giuridici nei transferimenti territoriali' in *Rivista di diritto internazionale,* vol. XXXVII (1954).
Castren	'La Succession d'États' in Hague *Recueil,* vol. LXXVIII (1951), pp. 385 *et seq.*
Cavaglieri	*La dottrina della successione di stato a stato e il suo valore giuridico* (1910).
Cavaré	*Le droit international public positif* (1951).
Cd.	See C.
cert. den	certiorari denied (U.S.).
Ch. D.	Chancery Division (England).
Clunet	*Journal du droit international,* fondé par E. Clunet. 1874. (France).
Clute	*The International Legal Status of Austria, 1938–1955* (1962).
Cmd.	See C.
Cmnd.	See C.
Co. Rep.	Coke's Reports, 1572–1616 (United Kingdom).
Coccejus	*Introductio ad Henrici 1.6 de Cocceji, Grotivm illustratvm.*
Coleman Phillipson	*Termination of War and Treaties of Peace* (1916).
Costa	*Manuel de derecho international público* (2nd ed. 1947).
Cowp.	Cowper's King's Bench Reports, 1774–8 (United Kingdom).
Cranch	Cranch's U.S. Supreme Court Reports, 1801–15 (United States).
Crandall	*Treaties, their Making and Enforcement* (2nd ed. 1947).
Crusen	In Hague *Recueil,* vol. XXII (1928).
Ct. Cl.	Court of Claims (United States).
D.	Dalloz, *Jurisprudence général* (France):
	D.P. 1845–1924 Recueil périodique et critique.

Abbreviations

	D.P. 1924–1941 Dalloz périodique.
	D.H. 1924–1941 Dalloz Hebdomadaire.
	D.A. 1941–1945 Dalloz (Recueil) analytique.
	D.C. 1941–1945 Dalloz (Recueil) critique.
	D. 1946–1955 Recueil Dalloz.
	D.S. 1955–1956 Recueil Dalloz et Sirey.
	D. 1956–
D.L.R.	Dominion Law Reports, 1912– (Canada).
Dahm	*Völkerrecht* (1958).
Delbez	*Manuel de droit international public, droit general et droit particulier des Nations Unies* (2nd ed. 1951).
de Louter	*Le droit international public positif.* 2 vols. (1920).
De Muralt	*The Problem of State Succession with Regard to Treaties* (1954).
Despagnet	*Cours de droit international public* (4th ed. 1910).
de Visscher	'Problem de la succession d'états en visage dans l'histoire diplomatique du Congo', in *Communicazioni e Studi*, vol. XI (1960).
Duparc	*Traités et accords en vigueur. Liste des engagements bilatéraux souscrits par la France en vigeur au 1 er Janvier 1958* (1962).
E.A.S.	Executive Acts Series (United States).
E.R.	English Reports Reprint. 1220–1865 (United Kingdom).
Ehrlich	*Prawo miedzynarodowe* (1958).
Eq	Equity Reports (United Kingdom).
Ex. D.	Exchequer Division Reports (United Kingdom).
F 2d.	Federal Reporter 2nd Series (United States).
F.C.R.	Federal Court Reports.
F.O.	Foreign Office (United Kingdom).
F.R. & N.	Federation of Rhodesia and Nyasaland.
F. Supp.	Federal Supplement (United States).
Fauchille	*Traité de droit international public* (1922).
Fed. Cas.	Federal Cases (United States).
Feilchenfeld	*Public Debts and State Succession* (1931).
Fenwick	*International Law* (4th ed. 1965).
Feuille Fédérale	*Feuille Fédérale de la Confédération Suisse; Bundesblatt der Schweizerischen Eidgenossenschaft.*
Fiore, *Int. Law Code*	*International Law Codified, and its Legal Sanction, or the Legal Organization of the Society of States*, trans. with Introduction by Borchard (1918).
Fiore, *Nouv. droit int.*	*Nouveau droit international public* (1868).
Fontes Juris Gent.	*Fontes Juris Gentium*, edited by Victor Bruns: Ser. A, sect. 1, vol. 1, Digest of the Decisions of the Permanent Court of International Justice 1922–30 (1931); vol. II, Digest of the Decisions of the Permanent Court of Arbitration 1902–28 (1931); Ser. A, sect. 2, vol. 1, Decisions of the German Supreme Court relating to International Law 1879–1929 (1931); Ser. B, sect. 1, vol. 1, pt. 1, Digest of the Diplomatic Correspondence of the European States 1856–71 (1932); pt. 2, *ibid.* (1933); pt. 3, *ibid.* (1938); vol. II, pt. 1, *ibid.* (1937); pt. 2 (1937).

Abbreviations

For. Rel.	Foreign Relations of the United States (United States).
Foro It.	Foro Italiano (Italy).
Friedrich	Grundzüge des Völkerrechts (1915).
Fusinato	'Annessione', in Enciclopedia giuridica, vol. 1, pt. 2.
G.A. Off. Rec.	General Assembly of the United Nations, Official Record.
Gabba	'Successione di Stato a Stato' in Quistioni di diritto civile (2nd ed. 1885).
Gareis	Institutionen des Völkerrechts (1887).
Genovskij	Osnovi na meždunarodnoto prava (1956).
Ghosh	Treaties and Federal Constitutions (1961).
Gidel	Des effets de l'annexion sur les concessions (1904).
Giur. It.	Giurisprudenza Italiana (Italy).
Gooch and Temperley	British Documents on the Origins of the War (1898–1914). 2 vols. (1926–7).
Gould	An Introduction to International Law (1957).
Grotius	De jure belli ac pacis libri tres (1625).
Guggenheim	Beiträge zur völkerrechtlichen Lehre vom Staatenwechsel (Staatensukzession) (1925).
Guggenheim, Traité	Traité de droit international public (1953–4).
H.C. Deb.	See Parl. Deb.
H.L. Deb.	See Parl. Deb.
H.M.S.O.	His (Her) Majesty's Stationery Office.
Hackworth	Digest of International Law, 8 vols. (1940–4).
Hague Recueil	Académie de droit international, Recueil des cours. 1923– .
Hall	International Law, 8th ed.; revised by A. Pearce Higgins (1926).
Halleck	Elements of International Law (2nd ed. 1885).
Handelsverträge	Die Handelsverträge des Deutschen Reiches, hrsg. Reichsamt des Inneren, Berlin, 1906 (Ergänzungsband 1915).
Hatschek	Völkerrecht als System rechtlich bedeutsamer Staatsakte (1923).
Hecker	Staatensukzession und Ungemeindung (1932).
Henrich	Theorie des Staatsgebiets (1922).
Herbst	Staatensukzession und Staatsservituten (1962).
Hershey	Essentials of International Public Law (2nd ed. 1929).
Hertslet	Hertslet's Commercial Treaties, A Collection of Treaties and Conventions between Great Britain and Foreign Powers.
Heydte, von der	Völkerrecht (1958).
Hoijer	Les traités internationaux (1928).
Hold-Ferneck	Lehrbuch des Völkerrechts (1930).
Holzendorff	Handbuch der Völkerrechts (1885–9).
How.	Howard's United States Supreme Court Reports, 1843–60.
How. Pr. Repts.	Howard's Practice Reports (United States).
Huber	Die Staatensuccession (1898).
L'Huillier	Eléménts de droit international public (1950).
Hyde	International Law; chiefly as interpreted and applied by the United States (2nd ed. 1951).
I.A.	Indian Appeal Cases, Law Reports (England).
I.C.J. Rep.	International Court of Justice, Reports of Judgments, Advisory Opinions and Orders.

I.C.L.Q.	International & Comparative Law Quarterly.
I.L.A. Handbook	The Effect of Independence on Treaties; A Handbook Published under the Auspices of the International Law Association (1965).
I.L.C.	International Law Commission.
I.L.Q.	International Law Quarterly.
I.L.R.	International Law Reports.
I.R.	Irish Reports, 1894– .
J.C.P.	La Semaine Juridique Juris Classeur Périodique, 1927– (France).
Jellinek	Allgemeine Staatslehre (1900).
Jèze	Le partage des dettes publiques au cas de démembrement du territoire (1921).
Jones, Mervyn	'State Succession in the Matter of Treaties' in B.Y. vol. XXIV (1947), p. 360.
Journal Officiel	Journal Officiel de la République Française (France).
K.B.	King's Bench Reports 1906– (England).
Keith	The Theory of State Succession with special reference to English and Colonial Law (1907).
Kiatibian	Conséquences juridiques des transformations territoriales des États sur les traités (1892).
Knapp	Knapp's Appeal Cases (Privy Council Cases), 1829–36 (United Kingdom).
Konkordatsprozess, Der	Der Konkordatsprozess—Veröffentlichungen des Instituts für Staatslehre und Politik e.V. Mainz— (München 1956–8).
Kunz	Die völkerrechtliche Option (1925).
L.J. Ch.	Law Journal Chancery Reports (England).
L.J. Eq.	Law Journal Equity Reports (England).
L.N. Off. J.	League of Nations Official Journal (1920–46).
L.N.P.M.C.	League of Nations Permanent Mandates Commission.
L.N.T.S.	League of Nations Treaty Series.
L.Q.R.	Law Quarterly Review, 1885– (United Kingdom).
L.R.	Law Reports.
Laband	Das Staatsrecht des Deutschen Reiches (5th ed. 1911).
Lah.	Lahore Series, Indian Law Reports.
Lapradelle and Politis	Recueil des arbitrages internationaux.
Larivière	Des conséquences des transformations territoriales des États sur les traités antérieurs (1892).
Lawrence	A Handbook of Public International Law (10th ed. 1925).
Lester	'State Succession to Treaties in the Commonwealth' in I.C.L.Q. vol. XII (1963), p. 175.
Liszt	Le droit international (9th ed. 1913).
M.L.R.	Modern Law Review.
M.N.R.G.	Nouveau recueil général de traités, etc., edited by a number of editors in continuation of the work of M. de Martens.
M.R.	Recueil de traités, etc., edited by Geo. Fréd. de Martens. 7 vols. (1801–26).
McNair	The Law of Treaties (1962).
Magoon	Reports on the Law of Civil Government under Military Occupation (1902).

Abbreviations cvii

Malloy	*Treaties, Conventions, International Acts, Protocols and Agreements between the United States of America and Other Powers, 1776–1909*, 2 vols. Compiled by William M. Malloy, under Resolution of the Senate, 18 January 1909, 1909 Senate Documents No. 357, Sixty-first Congress, Second Session, 2 vols. (1910).
Marek	*Identity and Continuity of States in Public International Law* (1954).
Marinoni	In *Rivista di diritto internazionale*, vol. VII (1912).
Martens	*Traité de droit international* (1883–7).
Mercier	*Les servitudes internationales* (1939).
Mérignhac	*Traité de droit international public* (1907).
Meyer-Lindenberg	*Völkerrecht* (1957).
Minn. L.R.	*Minnesota Law Review*, 1917– (United States).
Mod.	Modern Reports, King's Bench Series, 1669–1732 (United Kingdom).
Monaco	*Manuale di diritto internazionale púbblico e privato* (1959).
Moo. I.A.	Moore's Indian Appeals, Privy Council Series, 1836–72 (United Kingdom).
Moo. P.C.C.	Moore's Privy Council Cases, 1836–62 (United Kingdom).
Moore, Dig.	*A Digest of International Law*, 8 vols. (1906).
Moore, I.A.	*History and Digest of the International Arbitrations to which the United States has been a Party*, 5 vols. (1898).
Mosler	*Wirtschaftskonzessionen bei Änderungen der Staatshoheit* (1948).
Münch	*Ist an dem Begriff der völkerrechtlichen Servitut festzuhalten?* (1931).
N. Dak	North Dakota Reports (United States).
N.E.	Northeastern Reporter (United States).
N.S.	New Series.
N.W.	Northwestern Reporter (United States).
N.Z.L.R.	New Zealand Law Reports, 1883– .
Ned. Tijd.	*Nederlands Tijdschrift voor International Recht*, 1953– (Netherlands).
Nielsen	*American and British Claims Arbitration. Under special Agreement between United States of America and Great Britain, 18 August 1920. Report of F. K. Nielsen* (1926).
Niemeyer	*Völkerrecht* (1923).
Nys	*Le droit international* (2nd ed. 1904).
O.R.C. Reps	Orange River Colony Reports.
O'Connell	*The Law of State Succession* (1956).
Op. A.G.	Opinions of the Attorneys-General of the United States.
Oppenheim	*International Law* (8th ed., by H. Lauterpacht, vol. I, 1958).
Outrata	*Mezinárodní právo veřejoe* (1960).
P.C.I.J.	Permanent Court of International Justice Reports.
P.L.D.	Pakistan Legal Decisions.
P.M.C.	Permanent Mandates Commission.
P. Wms.	Peere Williams Reports, Chancery Series, 1695–1735 (United Kingdom).

Paenson,	*Les conséquences financières de la succession des États (1932–1953)*, (1954).
Pal. L.R.	Palestine Law Reports.
Panhuys	'La succession de L'Indonésie aux accords internationaux conclus par les Pays-Bas avant l'indépendance de l'Indonésie' in *Ned. Tijd.* vol. II (1955), p. 55.
Parl. Deb.	Parliamentary Debates (Hansard). House of Commons Official Report; Parliamentary Debates (Hansard). House of Lords Official Report.
Paul	*Studie z mezinárodního práva.*
Pet.	Peter's U.S. Supreme Court Reports, 1828–42 (United States).
Phil. S.C.	Philippines Supreme Court.
Phillimore	*Commentaries on International Law* (1st ed. 1854; 2nd ed. 1871 used).
Phillipson	*Termination of War and Treaties of Peace* (1916).
Piédelièvre	*Précis de droit international public ou droit des gens* (1894).
Podesta Costa	*Manual de derecho internacional publico* (2nd ed. 1947).
Pradier-Fodéré	*Traité de droit international public européen et américain* (1885–94).
Preuss, GBl.	*Gesetzblatt für die Königlich Preussischen Staaten.*
Preuss Ges. Sammlung	*Gesetz-Sammlung für die Königlich Preussischen Staaten.*
Pufendorf	*De jure naturae et gentium.*
Q.B.	Queen's Bench Reports 1906– (England).
Q.B.D.	Queen's Bench Division, 1875–1905 (England).
RGBl.	*Reichsgesetzblatt* (Germany).
RGSt.	*Entscheidungen des Reichsgerichts in Strafsachen*, 1880–1944 (Germany).
RGZ.	*Entscheidungen des Reichsgerichts in Zivilsachen*, 1880–1945 (Germany).
R.I.I.A.	Royal Institute of International Affairs, *Documents on International Affairs*, published under the auspices of the Royal Institute of International Affairs, and edited by: John W. Wheeler-Bennett, 1928 (1929); 1929 (1930); John W. Wheeler-Bennett and Stephen A. Heald, 1930 (1931); 1931 (1932); 1932 (1933); 1934 (1938); Stephen A. Heald, 1935, vol. I (1936); vol. II (1937); 1936 (1937); 1937 (1939); Monica Curtis, 1938, vol. I (1942); vol. II (1943).
R.O.	Recueil officiel des lois fédérales (Switzerland).
Rauchaupt	*Völkerrecht* (1936).
Rauschning	*Das Schicksal völkerrechtlichen Verträge bei Änderung des Status ihrer Partner* (1963).
Redmond	Third vol. of Malloy. See Malloy.
Reid	*International Servitudes in Law and Practice* (1932).
Reuter	*Droit international public* (1958).
Rev. crit. de droit int. privé	*Revue critique de droit international privé* (1933–).
Rev. de droit int.	*Revue de droit international.*

Abbreviations

Rev. de droit int. et de lég. comp.	Revue de droit international et de legislation comparée (1899–).
Rev. gén. de droit int. pub.	Revue générale de droit international public (1894–).
Rev. jur. et pol.	Revue juridique et politique: indépendence et coopération. Vols. I–XII published as Revue juridique et politique de l'Union français; XIII–XVII as Revue juridique et politique d'outremer.
Riv. D.I.	Rivista di diritto internazionale (1906–).
Rivier	Principes du droit des gens (1896).
Rob. Eccl.	Robertson's Ecclesiastical Reports, 1844–53 (United Kingdom).
Rogister	Zur Lehre von der Staatennachfolge (1902).
Rosenne	In B.Y. vol. XXVII (1950).
Ross	Textbook of International Law (1947).
Rousseau	Droit international public (1953).
S.	Sirey, Recueil général des lois et des arrêts fondé par J.-B. Sirey (1801–).
S.A.L.R.	South African Law Reports, 1948– (South Africa).
S.C. Off. Rec.	Security Council of the United Nations, Official Record.
S.C.R.	Supreme Court Reports, 1876–1922 (Canada).
S.C.R. (N.S.W.)	Supreme Court Reports, New South Wales, 1862–79 (Australia).
S. Ct. R.	Supreme Court Reports (India).
S.E.	South Eastern Reporter (United States).
S.I.	Statutory Instrument (United Kingdom).
S.R. & O.	Statutory Rules and Orders (United Kingdom).
S.W.	South Western Reporter (United States).
Sack	Les effets des transformations des États sur leurs dettes publiques et autres obligations financières (1927).
Salk	Salkeld's King's Bench Reports, 1689–1712 (United Kingdom).
Sauer	System des Völkerrechts (1952).
Scelle	Précis de droit des gens, principes et systématique (1932–4).
Schnitzer	Staat und Gebietshoheit (1935).
Schönborn	Einige Probleme der Staatennachfolge (1913).
Schrodt	Systema juris gentium (2nd ed. 1780).
Schuschnigg	International Law (1959).
Schwarzenberger	Manual of International Law (4th ed. 1960).
Selosse	Traité de l'annexion au territoire français et de son démembrement (1880).
Sen	In Indian Law Review, vol. 1 (1947).
Sereni	Diritto internazionale (1956–60).
Sibert	Traité de droit international public: le droit de la paix (1951).
So.	Southern Reporter (United States).
Spiropoulos	Théorie générale du droit international (1930).
St. Tr.	Howell's State Trials, 1163–1820 (United Kingdom).
Stael-Holstein	'La doctrine des servitudes internationales en Scandinavie' in Rev. de droit int. et de lég. comp., 3rd ser., vol. III (1922), p. 424.

Abbreviations

Strupp	Eléménts du droit international, européen et américain (1930).
Strupp-Schlochauer	Wörterbuch des Völkerrechts by Karl Strupp, 1911, 2nd ed., by H.-J. Schlochauer (1960).
Sup. Ct. C.G.H. Rep.	Supreme Court Reports of the Cape of Good Hope (South Africa).
Svarlien	(An) Introduction to the Law of Nations (1955).
T.I.A.S.	Treaties and Other International Acts Series (United States).
T.P.D.	Transvaal Province Division (S.A.L.R.).
T.S.C.R.	Transvaal Supreme Court Reports.
Temperley	(ed.) A History of the Peace Conference of Paris, 6 vols. (1920–2).
Term.	Term Reports, King's Bench Series, 1785–1800 (United Kingdom).
Tervooren	Statenopvolging en de financiële verplichtingen van Indonesië (1957).
Tex.	Texas Reports (United States).
Trans. Grot. Soc.	Transactions of the Grotius Society.
Trans. L.R.	Transvaal Law Reports.
U.N. Doc.	United Nations Documents.
U.N. Rep.	Reports of International Arbitral Awards, United Nations publication.
U.N.T.S.	United Nations Treaty Series.
U.S.	United States Reports.
U.S.T.S.	United States Treaty Series.
Udina	'L'estinzione dell'imperio Austro-Ungarico nel diritto internazionale' in Hague Recueil, vol. XLIV (1933).
Ullmann	Völkerrecht (1898).
V.L.R.	Victorian Law Reports, 1875– (Australia).
Váli	Servitudes of international law; a study of rights in foreign territory (2nd ed. 1958).
Vallat	'Some Aspects of the Law of State Succession' in Transactions of the Grotius Society, vol. 41 (1956), p. 123.
Vanselow	Völkerrecht, Einführung in die Praxis der Staaten (1931).
Vattel	Le Droit des Gens.
Vážný	Collection of the Decisions of the Czechoslovak Supreme Court of Justice (Sbírka rozhodnutí nejvyššího soudu). Edited by Vážný (Czechoslovakia).
Verdross	In Hague Recueil, vol. XXX (1929), p. 437.
Verdross–Zemanek	Völkerrecht (1959).
Vesey	Vesey Junior's Chancery Reports, 1789–1816 (United Kingdom).
W.L.R.	Weekly Law Reports.
W. Va.	West Virginia Reports (United States).
Wagnon	Concordats et droit international (1935).
Waldkirch	Das Völkerrecht in seinen Grundzügen dargestellt (1926).
Wall.	Wallace's U.S. Court Reports, 1865–76 (United States).
Wash.	Washington Reports (Va.) (United States).
Westlake	International Law (1904).

Wharton	*A Digest of International Law of the United States, taken from Documents issued by Presidents and Secretaries of State and from Decisions of Federal Courts and Opinions of Attorneys-General*, 3 vols. (1887).
Wheat	Wheaton's United States Supreme Court Reports, 1816–27.
Wheaton	*Elements of International Law* (1866).
Whiteman	*Digest of International Law* (1963).
Wilkinson	*The American Doctrine of State Succession* (1934).
Württ. Reg. Bl.	*Regierungsblatt für Württemberg.*
Z.f.a.ö.R.u.V.	*Zeitschrift für ausländisches öffentliches Recht und Völkerrecht*, begr. von Bruns, 1929–44, 1950–1 (Germany).
Zemanek	*Gegenwärtige Fragen der Staatensukzession* (1964).
Zorn	*Grundzüge des Völkerrechts* (2nd ed. 1903).

PART I
THE THEORY AND PROCESS OF STATE SUCCESSION

Chapter 1

THE NATURE AND THEORY OF STATE SUCCESSION

1. THE NATURE OF STATE SUCCESSION

The transfer of territory from one national community to another gives rise to legal problems of a difficult and complex character. Such transfers have been frequent in modern history, and often drastic in their extent and consequences. They have been effected in a variety of ways: by violent annexation, by peaceful cession, by revolution or emancipation of subject regions, and by extensive territorial resettlements. Despite their formal differences these changes possess one common feature: one State ceases to rule in a territory, while another takes its place.[1] This is a fact which has legal consequences. A sudden and often serious influence is exerted upon the international relations of the territory concerned, and upon its economic, social and legal structure. The body of law which has been built up for the solution of the problems arising from transfer of territory has for its object the minimizing of the effects of this change.

This body of law is known as the 'law of State succession'. The term 'State succession' has been objected to as begging the question which any investigation of the consequences of change of sovereignty seeks to resolve. It seems to suggest that the State which extends its sovereignty over a specific territory thereby becomes invested with all the juridical consequences of its predecessor's acts, that it is, in law as well as in fact, the latter's 'successor'.[2] The significance of the term is to be limited, however, to the factual situation which arises when one State is substituted for another in sovereignty over a given territory, and in this sense it enjoys the authority of an extensive literature. It does not necessarily presuppose a juridical substitution of the acquiring State in the complex of rights and duties possessed by the previous sovereign.

As Hall, in a much quoted passage,[3] expressed it, personality has been regarded as the key to the problem of State succession. The consequences of change of sovereignty vary according to the extent to which such

---

[1] Feilchenfeld, p. v; *Encyclopedia of the Social Sciences*, vol. XIV (1934), p. 345.
[2] Mervyn Jones in *B.Y.* vol. XXIV (1947), p. 360; Sen in *Indian Law Review*, vol. I (1947), p. 200; Caflisch in *Ned. Tijd.* vol. X (1963), p. 351.
[3] Hall, p. 114.

personality is affected. If the legal identity of a community is completely destroyed there is said to be a 'total succession' of States. If territory is lost while personality and legal responsibility remain unimpaired, the process is described as 'partial succession'.[1] This does not imply a total or partial succession respectively to the legal relations of the previous sovereign, but is merely an abbreviated way of defining the extent of the change. There is a variety of ways in which States can combine with or separate from one another. The older forms were those of annexation and cession, and the early literature of State succession was directed specifically to the consequences of these two methods of transferring territory. International personality may also be affected by less complete amalgamations, as in the case of unions or federations of States.[2] At the present time the most characteristic form of State succession is the secession of colonial areas or the emergence of subject territories to full sovereignty.[3]

2. THE RELATIONSHIP BETWEEN STATE SUCCESSION AND CONTINUITY OF STATES

It is at times difficult to determine whether the dismemberment of a State constitutes a total or partial succession. It is, for example, controversial whether the break-up of the Austro-Hungarian Empire in 1919 involved the extinction of the personalities of the States of Austria and Hungary, or merely the dissolution of the union that had existed between them, and the secession from them of several national groups to form new States.[4] Such a question, difficult to resolve as it may be, is of considerable

1 Oppenheim, vol. I, p. 156; Hershey in *A.J.* vol. V (1911), p. 185; Mervyn Jones, *loc. cit.* pp. 363 *et seq.* For a criticism of the traditional distinction see Scelle, vol. II, p. 152.
2 Feilchenfeld, p. 613.
3 The independence of Finland in 1918 was described in the *Aaland Islands* dispute as 'a new political phenomenon and not as a mere continuation of a previously existing political entity': *L.N. Off. J.* October 1920, Special Supplement no. 3 at p. 9. The succession of Henri IV to the throne of France raised the question of continuity of States for the first time. France regarded Navarre as absorbed in a unitary realm. The States of Béarn claimed that Navarre remained a separate legal person, joined to France by personal union of the crowns. When Louis XIII enforced French ecclesiastical law in Béarn in 1621 the Hugenot revolt occurred. French lawyers of the time debated the question hotly. See Hanotaux and La Force, *L'Histoire du cardinal de Richelieu*, vol. 2 (1895), pp. 418 *et seq.*
4 See *Bergverksaktiebolaget Kosmai* v. *Militär-Liquidierungsamt*, Ann. Dig. vol. I, Case no. 86; *Military Decoration Pension Case*, Ann. Dig. vol. III, Case no. 58; Lenz, *Untersuchung zur Frage der Identität der Republik Österrreich mit der Monarchie der Habsburger* (1939); Udina, *L'estinzione dell'imperio Austro-Ungarico nel diritto internazionale* (1933); Antonucci, *Réparation et règlement de la dette publique autrichienne et*

The Nature and Theory of State Succession 5

importance in the law of State succession. If the personality of the divided State survives there is only a partial and not a total succession. One portion of the State retains the rights and duties, while the others commence their lives as new legal beings. On the other hand, if such personality is completely lost in the dissolution no portion of the territory can be said to remain invested with rights and duties, and the problem is to what extent the successor States are entitled to such rights and obliged by such duties.

Evidently, then, a conceptual distinction must be made between succession of States and continuity of States. This work is concerned only with the legal problems that arise from a succession of States, and not with the question of when a succession, or discontinuity in legal personality, occurs.[1] However, these problems will differ from the problems raised by political changes not affecting the continuity of States only to the extent to which the legal régime governing the consequences of a change of sovereignty differs from that governing the consequences of a change of governments. Until the middle of the nineteenth century both types of change were assimilated, and the problems they raised were uniformly solved.[2] With the abstraction of the concept of sovereignty, however, a

---

hongroise d'avant guerre (1932); Decoudu, *Le partage des dettes publiques autrichiennes et hongroises* (1926); Herz, *Die Identität des Staates* (1931); Schilling, *Ist das Königreich Jugoslawien mit dem früheren Königreich Serbien völkerrechtlichen identisch?* (1939). See Baty in *Trans. Grot. Soc.* vol. IX (1923), p. 120; Feilchenfeld, p. 435; Udina in Hague *Recueil*, vol. XLIV (1933), p. 686; Hyde, vol. I, p. 362; Crisafulli in *Rivista di diritto internazionale*, vol. 47 (1964), p. 365. See also Letter of Allied and Associated Powers transmitting to the Austrian Delegation the Treaty of Peace with Austria; *A History of the Peace Conference of Paris* (1921), edited by H. W. V. Temperley, vol. IV, p. 400. A similar controversy exists with respect to the dismemberment of the Ottoman Empire. The award in the Ottoman Debt Arbitration considered Turkey as 'continuing the personality of the Ottoman Empire': *Répartition des annuités de la dette publique ottomane, Sentence Arbitrale* (1925), pp. 61–2. Italy regarded itself as a mere expansion of Sardinia: *Costa v. Military Service Commission of Genoa, Foro Italiano*, 62 (1937), vol. I, p. 1167. Whether or not the dissolution of the United Netherlands in 1830 constituted the extinction of the personality of the Netherlands or the secession of Belgium is disputed. See Pradier-Fodéré, vol. I, p. 251; Fauchille, vol. I, pt. I, p. 380; Sen, *loc. cit.* p. 197.

1 See Marek, *Identity and Continuity of States in Public International Law* (1954), pp. 10 *et seq*. Rausching, p. 42.

2 Grotius, II, xiv, 11; Pufendorf, VIII, x, 8 (he persists in the assimilation in a converse fashion, arguing that colonies founded by emigration, but apparently not independent, are free of the parent's debts: VIII, xii, 5); Vattel, II, xii, 191; G. F. de Martens, *Précis du droit des gens modernes de l'Europe* (1788), II, ii, 60; Klüber, *Europäisches Völkerrecht* (1821), p. 422; Wheaton, *Elements of International Law* (1836, 1st pub.), (8th ed. by Dana 1866 used) in *Carnegie Classics of International Law*, pt. I, s. 29; Manning, *Commentaries on the Law of Nations* (1839), (1875 ed. by Sheldon Amos used), p. 91; Wildman, *Institutes of International Law* (1849), vol. I, p. 68; Kent, *Commentaries on American Law* (1826), (1860 ed. used), vol. I, p. 28; Phillimore, vol. I,

conceptual chasm was opened between change of sovereignty and change of government; in the one instance a problem of substitution in the possession of rights and obligations was raised; in the other, continuity of these rights and obligations was presumed in virtue of continuity in the personality of the possessor.[1]

At the present time the boundary between change of sovereignty and change of government often wears thin to the point of disappearance, and the question has now arisen whether or not there is any utility in maintaining a rigid distinction between the legal consequences of the one and the other situation. The grant of independence to a colonial territory theoretically involves a change of sovereignty, and the problems raised by it are accordingly subsumed under the category of State succession. In fact, however, this type of change exhibits more affinity, at least with respect to most of the legal institutions affected by it, with the traditional case of succession of governments than with the classical instances of transfers of territory from one State to another. The formation of composite political entities by union or federation raises the same issue. A United States Court of Appeals, holding that the Serbian–United States Extradition Treaty of 1901 was in force *vis-à-vis* Yugoslavia, said that the latter country

was formed by a movement of the Slav people to govern themselves in one sovereign nation, with Serbia as the central or nucleus nation. Great changes in the going government were in the planning, and were brought about, but the combination was not an entirely new sovereignty without parentage. But even if it is appropriate to designate the combination as a new country, the fact that it started to function under the Serbian constitution as the home government and under Serbian legations and consular service in foreign countries, and has con-

p. 168 (he continues to assimilate change of government and change of sovereignty); Zachariä, *Deutsches Staats- und Bundesstaatsrecht* (1841), p. 58; Twiss, *The Law of Nations* (1861), (2nd ed. 1884 used), p. 28; F. de Martens, *Traité de droit international* (1883), p. 369. The early practice of the United States also assimilated them, arguing that the Latin American States and the Netherlands had succeeded respectively to Spanish and French commitments: Wharton, vol. II, p. 19; Moore, *Dig.* vol. v, p. 345. On 10 August 1818 Secretary of State Adams wrote to the United States Ambassador to Chile, arguing with respect to Chile's duty to discharge the liabilities of Spain that 'no principle of international law can be more clearly established than this, that the *rights* and the *obligations* of a nation in regard to other States are independent of its internal revolutions of government. It extends even to the case of conquest. The conqueror who reduces a nation to his subjection receives it subject to all its engagements and duties towards others, the fulfilment of which then becomes its own duty': Wharton, vol. I, p. 19.

[1] Bluntschli, Bk. II, s. 48; Bulmerincq, p. 195; von Liszt, p. 274; Pradier-Fodéré, ss. 158–60; Heffter, *Das Europäische Völkerrecht der Gegenwart auf den bisherigen Grundlagen* (1884), s. 61; Calvo, vol. II, pp. 248, 262; vol. IV, p. 404; von Holtzendorff, vol. II, pp. 33 *et seq.*

The Nature and Theory of State Succession

tinued to act under Serbian treaties ... is conclusive proof that if the combination constituted a new country it was the successor of Serbia in its international rights and obligations.[1]

This instance demonstrates that the solution of the problem raised by political change cannot be left to the hazard of characterizing the event as a succession of States or a succession of governments. There is evident at the present time a developing pressure in the direction of assimilating these two categories of events, and as the nineteenth-century theory of the State, with its concomitant metaphysics of political personality, loses its cogency, legal theory will tend more and more to return to its eighteenth-century position.

This issue of personality became of great importance in the partition of British India in 1947. This country had, since the Treaty of Versailles, gradually attained international personality.[2] When India and Pakistan were formed out of it the question arose whether that personality had continued to exist in one or other of the new Dominions, or had been extinguished altogether. Pakistan claimed automatic membership of the United Nations. If the personality of British India had been sustained in the new India, Pakistan would have been in the position of a seceding State, and India alone, on the conclusions which will later be reached, would have retained membership of international organizations. On the other hand, if British India had been dismembered so that neither Dominion continued its juristic personality, then, it would seem, neither should have inherited its membership. India alleged that the former was the case,[3] and this view was supported by a legal opinion given on the question by the Secretariat of the United Nations.[4] This opinion, which will be quoted in full in a subsequent chapter, considered that there was 'no change in the international status of India; it continues as a State with all treaty rights and obligations, and consequently with all rights and obligations of membership in the United Nations'. Pakistan was regarded as a new State. In international law, it was argued, the situation was analogous to the separation of the Irish Free State from Great Britain, and of Belgium from the Netherlands.

This opinion did not pass unchallenged. When Pakistan applied in the

1 *Ivancevic* v. *Artukovic*, 211 F. 2d. 565 at p. 573 (1954); cert. den. 348 U.S. 818; rehearing denied, 348 U.S. 889. For other evidence of continuity of Serbian treaties see Whiteman, vol. II, p. 944 *et seq.*; *Kolovrat* v. *Oregon*, 366 U.S. 187 (1961); *Lukich* v. *Department of Labor and Industry*, 176 Wash. 221, 22 P. 2d. 388 (1934); *Urbus* v. *State Compensation Commissioner*, 113 W. Va. 563; 169 S.E. 164 (1933); *Olijan* v. *Lublin*, 50 N.E. 2d. 264 (1943); Exchanges of Notes of 1946, T.I.A.S. 1572; 1948, T.I.A.S. 1803. 2 Sen, p. 192; Mervyn Jones, p. 370.
3 *The Statesman*, 17 July 1947; Sen, p. 193. 4 See *infra*, vol. II, p. 184.

ordinary way for membership in the United Nations, objection was raised in both the Security Council and the First Committee of the General Assembly to the assumption that India was still the same person as British India.[1] In the Security Council France adopted Pakistan's original argument, and maintained that the latter had inherited, along with India, the original membership of British India, and that therefore no application for membership was necessary.[2] In the First Committee Argentina voiced the opinions of a number of delegations in contending that the division had effected the extinction of British India, and that therefore neither of the new Dominions should be considered a successor in membership.[3] As a result, the legal committee was requested to advise on the course to be followed in similar circumstances. Its opinion was that a State does not cease to be a member merely because its frontier and constitution have been subjected to changes. This effect, it held, can only be brought about by proof that the international personality of the State has been extinguished. It was also of opinion that when a new State is formed it cannot claim to be automatically a member of the United Nations and must make application for membership.[4]

The opinion of the Secretariat has been criticized as drawing an improper analogy from the cases of the Irish Free State and Belgium.[5] In those cases the old sovereigns actively participated in the act which created the new States. The creation of Pakistan, on the other hand, was not the act of India, nor did India directly participate in it. It was a division enacted by a constitutional superior, and in no sense of the word could it be considered that there was any secession on the part of Pakistan. Both the Dominions were in the position of new States. Whatever the merits of this view, the example illustrates the extreme difficulty experienced at times in forcing changes of sovereignty within the confines of one category.

3. THE THEORY OF STATE SUCCESSION

The State acquiring territory from another is usually described as the 'successor State'. The losing State may conveniently be referred to as the 'predecessor State'. The nature of the substitution of the one for the other, however, and even the question whether such a substitution is possible are subjects of controversy. It is often thought that the problem raised by change of sovereignty over territory, or by political reconstructions, is

1 See Schachter in *B.Y.* vol. XXV (1948), p. 103.
2 U.N. Doc. S/496, 18 August 1947.
3 U.N. Doc. A/C 6/156, 2 October 1947.
4 U.N. Doc. A/C 1/212, 11 October 1947.
5 Sen, pp. 196 *et seq.* See *infra*, vol. II, p. 185.

soluble only by reference to international law. In fact, however, and except with respect to the question of treaties, international law plays only a minor role in the matter, and the majority of theories on State succession have dealt with the question as one partly of legal philosophy and partly of constitutional law, and have found it unnecessary to resort to international law. These theories group themselves, in virtue of their conclusions, into two categories: the first category of theories achieves a total, or at least a large degree of, legal continuity throughout the process of change of sovereignty; the second category negatives this continuity and leaves the territory subjected to the change in a condition more or less of legal vacuum. Within each of the two categories theories may be isolated which are mutually incompatible, and each of these theories will be found to be an emanation from the theories of State and the law prevalent when they were formulated. This makes it evident that the doctrine on State succession is far less pragmatic than philosophical; that the historical precedents must be evaluated in the context of changing political theory; and that the opinions of the authors on State succession are no more persuasive than the conceptions of the State, of the law, and of the international society which prompt them.

I. Theories of Continuity

(a) *The theory of universal succession*

The earliest doctrine of State succession resolved the problem of political change by importing the Roman law conception of the continuity of legal personality in the estate which falls by inheritance. Rights and duties, as incidents of this personality, and as elements of the estate, pass *ipso jure* to the successor. They retain their identity, despite accidental changes in the identity of those who are from time to time their bearers, because they derive from absolute natural rights and hence are constant.[1] Change of rulers, then, whether effected by cession of territory, by revolution or by death, cannot involve the replacement of one right or duty by another, but only a replacement of their subjects. If a ruler acts in a private capacity his contracts expire with his death or expulsion; but if he acts in his princely office his commitments relate not to himself but to the people through whom, in virtue of the social contract, he ultimately derives his authority.[2]

---

[1] Grotius, II, ix, 9, 10, 12. The best treatment of Grotius is in Feilchenfeld, *Public Debts and State Succession* (1931), ch. II, but is restricted to Grotius' discussion of financial obligations. He finds Grotius' views doubtful, p. 27.

[2] Grotius, II, xiv, 1, 2. The distinction between debts contracted by a prince in his private interest (which his successor need not honour) and those contracted by him in his public interest had a history in French constitutional law, and this probably

Property, although antecedent to the creation of society, is affected by whatever legal arrangements are made for it by the ruler;[1] and since territory is only a form of property,[2] it follows that debts contracted by the ruler in exercise of his public functions continue to affect it after he has lost his authority.[3]

This theory, which persisted up to the middle of the nineteenth century, and even beyond,[4] achieves succession in virtue of a legal principle ante-

influenced Grotius. See von Albertini, *Das politische Denken in Frankreich zur Zeit Richelieus* (1951), p. 184. The successor was also not obliged by acts of his predecessor 'au préjudice de Couronne qui est inalienable', Jacques de Cassan, *La recherche des droicts de Roy et la Couronne de France* (1632), p. 85.

1 Grotius, II, xiv, 10.

2 *Ibid.* II, viii, 4. That Grotius intended his principle to encompass succession by transfer of territory as well as by internal change seems to be clear from II, xiv, 11. See Cocceijus' criticism, 'negamus, in successionibus regnorum successoris personam pro eadem censeri cum persona defuncti'; the text is published in Huber, p. 191, n. 42. Keith copied from it, p. 3.

3 Pufendorf, *De jure naturae et gentium libri octo* (1698), VIII, x, 8. He is the first writer to regard public assets as permanently burdened with debts: VIII, xii, 2, 3. However, he thought colonies founded by emigration to be free of the parent's debts: VIII, xii, 5.

4 Rutherforth, *Institutes of International Law* (2nd ed., 1779), p. 673; Vattel, *Le droit des gens*, II, xii, 191. Schrodt believed in a universal succession in cases of conquest: *Systema juris gentium*, (2nd ed., 1780), pt. iii, iv, xxxviii–xl; G. F. de Martens, *Précis du droit des gens modernes de l'Europe* (1788), II, ii, 60; citing Neyron, *de Vi federum inter gentes* (1778); Klüber, *Europäisches Völkerrecht* (1821), p. 422. After 1815 a controversy arose over the liabilities of the puppet State of Westphalia; most writers considered King Jerome to be a belligerent occupant: Kamptz, *Beiträge zum Staats- und Völkerrecht* (1816), I, p. 183; von Bülow, *Abhandlungen über einzelne Materien des bürgerlichen Rechts* (1819), p. 9; Pfeiffer, *Das Recht der Kriegseroberung in Bezug auf Staatscapitalien* (1823), p. 23; Zachariä, *Über die Verpflichtung zur Aufrechthaltung der Handlungen der Regierung des Königreichs Westphalen* (1817), p. 17. Pfeiffer thought a conqueror did not succeed to debts, Kamptz thought he did. The question was also discussed by Haas, *Über das Repartitions-Princip der Staatschulden bei Länderzerstückelungen* (1831). Pfeiffer and Haas are mentioned by Huber, p. 189, n. 8, and this reference is taken by Gidel, p. 22. There is no evidence that any writer before Feilchenfeld actually examined these works, and he admitted he could not find a copy of Haas. Attempts by the present author to have this work photocopied have also failed. Wheaton, *Elements of International Law* (1836, 1st pub.), (8th ed. by Dana 1866 used) in *Carnegie Classics of International Law*, pt. I, s. 29; Manning, *Commentaries on the Law of Nations* (1839), (1875 ed. by Sheldon Amos used), p. 91; Wildman, *Institutes of International Law* (1849), vol. I, p. 68; Kent, *Commentaries on American Law* (1826) (1860 ed. used), vol. I, p. 28; Phillimore, *Commentaries on International Law* (1st ed. 1854), (2nd ed. 1871 used), vol. I, p. 168 (he continues to assimilate change of government and change of sovereignty); Twiss, *The Law of Nations* (1861) (2nd ed. 1884 used), p. 20; F. de Martens, *Traité de droit international* (1883), p. 369; Rivier, vol. I, pp. 65 *et seq.*; Despagnet, p. 117; Nys, vol. II, p. 31; Fiore, *Nuovo diritto internazionale europeo* (1865), republished under the title *Trattato di diritto internazionale pubblico* (4th ed. 1904 used), vol. I, pp. 217–30; *Nouveau droit international public suivant les besoins de la civilisation moderne*, Fr. trans. by Pradier-Fodéré (1868), vol. I, p. 311; Mérignhac, *Traité de droit international public* (1907), vol. II, p. 14.

cedent to the enacted law of any society, and hence antecedent to the positive law of nations. Succession occurs, not in virtue of an external legal prescription, but in virtue of a legal quality which reposes in the object of succession.[1]

(b) *The theory of popular continuity*

Once the concept of sovereignty had been isolated and endowed with metaphysical quality by the philosophers of the eighteenth century, it became difficult to resist the importation of a distinction between change of sovereignty and change of government. However, it did not immediately follow that these two events were subjected, so far as concerned their consequences, to differing rules of law. The sense of nationalism which underlay the Risorgimento in Italy prompted the view that, while a formal distinction had to be recognized between change of sovereignty and change of government, in substance neither change can affect the legal condition of peoples.[2] Change of sovereignty involves no more than a change in the fictitious element in political organization, the real element surviving intact.[3] Obligations of a political character, such as treaties, attach to the element of sovereignty and lapse with it;[4] obligations of a patrimonial character, including most economic and judicial matters, attach to society and remain attached. The distinction adumbrated by the universal succession theorists between obligations of the prince in his princely capacity and his obligations in his personal capacity, which in Vattel became a distinction between 'real' and 'personal' obligations,[5] is now transformed into a distinction between social and political commitments. While the emphasis in this theory is upon legal continuity, therefore, the degree of continuity actually achieved is, in virtue of this transformation, considerably less than that achieved in the theory of universal succession.[6]

[1] Schönborn expresses it thus, p. 7: 'Es soll nicht ein neues Recht an Stelle des früheren treten, sondern das Recht des neuen Subjekts als identisch mit dem des alten Subjekts gelten.'
[2] In his famous inaugural lecture in 1851 Mancini, *Prelezioni* (1873), applied Mazzini's theory of nationalism to the State.
[3] Fiore, *op. cit.*, and Pradier-Fodéré anticipated this view. Mancini's thesis was taken up by Gabba, who wrote the first essay on State succession: 'Successione di Stato a Stato', in *Questioni di diritto civile* (2nd ed. 1885), pp. 356–92. Also see Mantellini, *Lo Stato ed il codice civile* (1882), vol. II, pp. 364, 682.
[4] Gabba, *op. cit.*
[5] *Le droit des gens*, II, xii, 191. He consolidated the theory that financial obligations attach permanently to assets, basing himself on the Silesian debt problem in 1742, II, xiii, 203.
[6] Gabba's theory influenced Fiore, 'Revue de la jurisprudence italienne', in Clunet (1883), p. 78, and Chrétian, 'Revue de la jurisprudence italienne', *ibid.* (1886),

(c) *The theory of organic substitution*

The nationalist sentiment which underlay the theory just discussed affected in varying ways the views of French as well as Italian authors on the question of the effects of State succession, and led, indeed, to the isolation of the problem of 'State succession' as one calling for specific legal treatment.[1] But it was in the organic theory of the State in Germany at the end of the nineteenth century that it had its principal influence. The publication of von Gierke's famous work[2] on the theory of corporate association had an instantaneous and important impact on the theory of State succession through its adoption by Huber. In the course of his examination of the juridical aspects of association, Gierke was led to investigate the problem of the disposition of the assets and related rights and duties of a social body after its formal dissolution. Since, in his doctrine, the State is no more than the ultimate moral organism, the solution of the problem in the event of State succession is no different from what it would be in the event of the disappearance of any other social grouping. A social organism, unlike a natural organism, rarely disappears in death. What normally happens is that its identity is lost with the destruction of the hard core of its life, but the organic forces which previously governed it remain unaffected. A succession in the place of the dissolved social personality is an immediate and primary consequence of the change. 'The property of the former composite person[3] passes to its new owner as a single entity, with all the rights and obligations attaching to it.'[4]

The emphasis in this theory, as developed by Huber, is rather less on the legal effects of political change than on the nature of the change itself.[5] When States appear and disappear the factual elements of people and territory are integrated in a new organic being; there is a change in the juridical element of organization, which does not occur in cases of change of government; and the problem is to distinguish the legal institutions which attach to the factual elements, and hence survive the change, from

p. 747; *Principes de droit international public* (1893), p. 144. Two other followers projected the dual personality into the distinction between *beni disponibile* and *beni indisponibile*: Fusinato, *Enciclopedia giuridica*, vol. I, pt. 2, pp. 2055–140, 'Annessione'; Corso, 'Transmissione di obblighi patrimoniali degli stati in caso di mutazione territoriale, in *Studi di diritto internazionale privato* (1896) (concerning the Chilean debt controversy). The factor of social solidarity also figures in the first systematic treatise on State succession by Selosse in 1880. There is an echo of Gabba's thesis in Romano as late as 1925, in *Rivista di diritto internazionale*, vol. XX (1925).

1 E.g. Selosse, Cabouat, Kiatibian, Appleton, Larivière and Rivier.
2 *Die Genossenschaftstheorie und die deutsche Rechtsprechung* (1887) (photographic reproduction of this edition issued in 1963), pp. 809–905.
3 'Verbandperson'.   4 P. 876.   5 P. 27.

The Nature and Theory of State Succession

those which attach to the organizational element and do not survive it. To argue, as one French author[1] had, that the organizational element is integrated in the new political structure, or to argue as the theorists of the Risorgimento had, that legal personality is fictitious, and hence irrelevant, confuses this question, in Huber's opinion.[2] For, to Huber, a political organism is a real thing, and is isolated from other organisms, not only in virtue of the grouping of people and territory, but also in virtue of the gravitational factor of the political life centre.[3]

In actual fact, the organic theory does not, in its conclusions with respect to the rights and duties affected by change of sovereignty, radically differ from the preceding ones. Rather, it offers a new explanation by denying that there is either succession of bearers in an identical legal relationship, or a juridical continuity in the bearers themselves, and arguing instead for a substitution in respect of both bearers and their rights and duties. The successor State takes over nothing; rather it absorbs the factual situation brought about by the predecessor's legal commitments, and in the very act of substituting itself as the new life centre substitutes itself in the juridical incubus deriving from the previous life centre, and embodied in the organic structure of the integrated society. In practical terms, this means that the successor State takes over all the rights and duties of its predecessor, save those which are essentially political; if it substitutes itself factually in the property of its predecessor it must also substitute itself in the encumbrances upon that property; there is, therefore, a perpetuation of the *passif* as well as of the *actif*.[4]

1 Appleton, p. 38, arguing from the analogy of *adrogatio*.
2 Huber's criticism, p. 13.   3 P. 28.
4 P. 24. Westlake was the only author of importance to adopt Huber's doctrine, *International Law* (1904), p. 69; also in *Law Quarterly Review*, vol. XVII (1901), p. 392, and vol. XXI (1905), p. 335. A similar position was reached by Olivart, *Tratado de derecho público* (1903), vol. I, p. 174; *De los principios que regien la succesión territorial en los cambios de soberanía* (1906). Oppenheim's doctrine seems also to reflect Huber's views: *International Law* (1907), s. 80. Von Bar advanced a similar doctrine, 'Die kubanische Staatsschuld', in *Die Nation*, vol. XVI (1899), p. 425. His argument was adopted by Kohler, *Grundlagen des Völkerrechts* (1918), p. 99. Meile adopted Huber's thesis in an opinion on the Netherlands South African Railway Co. concession: *Die Rechtsstellung der Niederländisch-Südafrikanischen Eisenbahngesellschaft in Amsterdam, sowie ihrer Aktionäre und Obligationäre gegenüber Grossbritannien als Rechtsnachfolger der südafrikanischen Republik* (1903). See also Kaufmann, *Zur Transvaalbahnfrage* (1901), which was based on respect for private rights.

(d) The theory of self-abnegation

Jellinek's great work[1] on the State, which appeared five years after Huber's book, was the most important single influence in State succession writings in the next twenty-five years, because it stated categorically for the first time the obstacles which an imperative theory of law opposes to the burdening of successor States with the commitments of their predecessors. But Jellinek did not derive from this a negative thesis respecting continuity of the predecessor's legal relationships. The solution to the problem of continuity he considered to lie in his general theory of international law, according to which the State, in exercise of its own will, or in virtue of an act of 'auto-limitation', agrees to observe the rules of international law, and perform the obligations towards other States created under them.[2] Successor States may become subject to the commitments of their predecessors through this process of self-abnegation. While the State is formally at liberty to take over or reject whatever suits it in the previous legal order, it is in fact materially required in the interest of realizing its own aims to permit only the least disturbance thereof.[3] Therefore, in practice, it integrates within its own legal order all existing law which is compatible therewith and which is not expressly repealed.

Jellinek thus thrusts the emphasis on continuity rather than disruption, and constructs the legal bonds of continuity on the basis of tacit consent of all the parties concerned. So, pragmatic policy decisions are transformed by silence and presumption into new legal bonds. Since rights and duties mutually arise from a coincidence of wills of equally placed partners, it follows that the successor State is not the only free policy-making agent. Other States may insist on performance of existing obligations, and may even make their recognition of a new State explicitly or tacitly dependent upon the maintenance by the latter of existing legal relationships. Since in Jellinek's system recognition is constitutive and may be conditional, the new State may therefore be burdened with antecedent obligations in the very act of legal birth.[4]

II. Negative Theories

The lack of correspondence between the universal succession theory and the facts of international practice contributed, during the latter half of the nineteenth century and the early part of this century, to a new doctrine which denied all the premises of the earlier. It was contended that the

---

[1] *Allgemeine Staatslehre* (1900) (revised in 1905, and more considerably revised in 1914) (1960 reprint of the 5th ed., 1928 used).
[2] Pp. 367–75.   [3] P. 279.
[4] P. 273. Van Panhuys advances a similar argument in *Ned. Tijd.* vol. II (1955), p. 55.

sovereignty of the predecessor State over the absorbed territory is abandoned. A hiatus is thus created between the expulsion of the one sovereignty and the extension of the other. The successor State does not exercise its jurisdiction over the territory in virtue of a transfer of power from its predecessor, but solely because it has acquired the possibility of expanding its own sovereignty in the manner dictated by its own will. None of the incidences of sovereignty passes to the successor State. The latter seizes what it can and repudiates what it will. From the notion of the 'absolute independence of all sovereign power' it is argued that 'there is no general rule of law which obliges the annexing State to take upon itself the juridical consequences of acts of the extinguished State'.[1] There is no legal tie between the two, and therefore the extinguished State's rights and obligations 'no longer have a subject, its creditors have lost their debtor'.[2] Within this general thesis specific theories may be identified which vary from the crude to the highly sophisticated.

(a) Imperative theories of law

Once the unifications of Italy and Germany had been achieved, political theory tended to concentrate less on the identity of national peoples and more on the State as the vehicle of national expression. This added a dynamic element to the theory that law is the expression of the sovereign will, and reinforced the abstraction of the concept of political sovereignty. If law is an expression of the sovereign will, it is dependent for its survival upon the continuity thereof.[3] Change of sovereignty, involving lapse of the will, implies the total collapse of the legal order.[4] If continuity is in

[1] Cavaglieri in Hague *Recueil*, vol. XXVI (1929), p. 378.   [2] *Ibid.*
[3] Among the earliest exponents of this view were Gareis, *Institutionen des Völkerrechts* (1887), p. 61; and Zorn, *Grundzüge des Völkerrechts* (2nd ed. 1903 used), p. 150.
[4] Cavaglieri, pp. 17, 191. He criticizes Huber on the ground that it is impossible to transform the material fact of supersession of territorial authority into a juridical title, p. 54. See Feilchenfeld, p. 617; Sereni, pp. 397 *et seq.*; Balladore-Pallieri, *Diritto internazionale pubblico* (6th ed. 1952), pp. 180 *et seq.*; Ross, pp. 127 *et seq.*; Berber, vol. II, pp. 249 *et seq.* The imperative system dominated German literature before the War: Waldkirch, *Das Völkerrecht* (1926), pp. 116–20; Vanselow, *Völkerrecht* (1931), p. 142 (although he allowed for obligations to continue to attach to assets); Wolgast, *Völkerrecht* (1934), p. 827; von Rauchhaupt, *Völkerrecht* (1936), p. 63; Schwartz in Niemeyer's *Zeitschrift für internationales Recht*, vol. XLVIII (1934), p. 166; Hecker's dissertation has not been available: *Staatensukzession und Umgemeindung* (1932). On the special problem of localized treaties contributions were made by von Moos, *Zur Lehre von den Staatsservituten* (1933), pp. 83–6; Münch, *Ist an dem Begriff der völkerrechtlichen Servitut festzuhalten?* (1931), pp. 39, 56–9, 75–81; Rosenne, p. 267. Cf. his views with those of Cansacchi in *Scritti di diritto internazionale in onore di Tomaso Perassi* (1957), vol. I, p. 251; and in *Rivista di diritto internazionale*, vol. XXXVII (1954), p. 19. Rosenne's negative views on treaties are contained in Clunet, vol. LXXVII (1950), p. 1140; Mosler, p. 23. Von Holtzendorff was probably the first to propagate this view, vol. II, pp. 33 *et seq.*

fact achieved, this can only be in virtue of an act of will of the successor State.[1] Also, once sovereignty is envisaged as a mere competence to legislate, its rigid isolation from the concept of public ownership is inevitable. Hence, territory ceased to be regarded as something that could be transferred, and came to be regarded as an object of sovereign functions,[2] and later as no more than the area within which these functions are exercised.[3] Since sovereignty is the formal aspect of power, and power is a fact, sovereignty is not transferable;[4] and since neither sovereignty nor territory can be an object of assignment, the notion of State succession is fallacious, and the expression itself a metaphor.

So far as State-to-State relations are concerned, there can be no succession because these are entered into *intuitu personae*, that is to say, in intimate connexion with the circumstances, including the quality of the contracting partners.[5] Even 'real' rights and obligations fall because, as a category, they are no less fallacious than the theory that territory is property on which they depend.[6] The same doctrine applies to the non-international relationships of the predecessor State. These derive from the latter's municipal law and vanish with it. If they are maintained by the

1 Cavaglieri, pp. 75, 86, 91, 103; Focherini, *La successione degli Stati* (1910); Marinoni in *Rivista di diritto internazionale*, vol. VII (1912), p. 312; Anzilotti, *Corso di diritto internazionale* (1912), p. 297; Hall, p. 114; Schönborn, p. 11; Strupp, *Grundzüge des positiven Völkerrechts* (1921), p. 49; and in Hague *Recueil*, vol. XLVII (1934); Schätzel, *Gebietserwerb* in Strupp's *Wörterbuch des Völkerrechts*, vol. II, pp. 366, 578; Henrich, *Theorie des Staatsgebiets* (1922), p. 115; Zucchelli, *Il Debito pubblico nelle conseguenze giuridiche patrimoniali delli annexioni* (1919); Olivi, *Considerazioni giuridiche interne al problema della successione di Stato a Stato* (1927); Guggenheim, *Traité*, p. 459. In the *Robert E. Brown Claim* Great Britain argued that 'conquest and annexation is merely an act of appropriation by force; the title of the conqueror is founded on might; his title to the property of the former Government upon the fact of the physical control and his expressed intention to maintain it': Answer of His Britannic Majesty's Government in the *Robert E. Brown Claim*, p. 17.

2 See *infra*, p. 22.   3 See *infra*, p. 23.

4 Appleton was the first to make this point clearly, pp. 46, 109. See Cavaglieri, pp. 17, 191; von Rogister, p. 13; Gidel, p. 62; Feilchenfeld, p. 611; Sereni, pp. 397 *et seq.*; Ross, pp. 127 *et seq.*; Berber, vol. II, pp. 249 *et seq.*; Castren in Hague *Recueil*, vol. LXXVIII (1958), p. 379; Mosler, pp. 16, 22, 93, 160. This view is ably contested by Udina, pp. 693–8.   5 Cavaglieri, p. 75.

6 Cavaglieri, pp. 79, 96, 126; Schönborn, p. 73; Herbst, *passim*; Lester, p. 475. An earlier work by Freund had argued for the intimate attachment of debts (*Anleihen*) to State property (*Vermögen*). There is no succession in the debt relationship, but each asset remains burdened by its debt: *Die Rechtsverhältnisse der öffentlichen Anleihen* (1907), pp. 172 *et seq.* Another work by Schmidt, published in the same year as Schönborn's, argued for succession in the debt relationship: *Der Übergang der Staatsschulden bei Gebietsabtretung* (1913). Neither work was known to Guggenheim. He was, however, familiar with Koch, *Die territorialen Veränderungen der Staaten und ihr Einfluss auf die Schuldenhaftung* (1913). The argument that there is an intimate connexion between debts and revenues was made by Andreadès in *Rev. gén. de droit int. pub.* vol. XV (1908), p. 585.

successor State, as it is conceded they usually are, this is in response to moral considerations which are extraneous to legal analysis.[1]

(b) *Theories of a sceptical character*

Most of the imperative theorists, recognizing that chaos would result if successor States failed to endorse the legal acts of their predecessors, argued either that positive international law directed the successor to fulfil the predecessor's obligations or that successor States should voluntarily undertake these. They have examined State practice, either to establish the rules of international law, or to demonstrate the utility of a voluntary substitution. However, from time to time authors of a sceptical turn of mind have refuted the evidence and have resisted even the hortatory suggestion that successor States should exercise their discretion in favour of their predecessors' creditors. Keith is the outstanding example of this attitude. His work, constituting an academic apologia of the British policy with respect to the debts of the Boer Republics, merits Feilchenfeld's comment that it is more of an advocate's brief than an entirely detached opinion.[2] It is probably the most thoroughgoing essay in legal positivism that had up to the date of its publication been attempted, and it must be conceded that in its empirical fashion it demolished, in the most devastating fashion, the constructions of all Keith's predecessors, even if, in the process, it did violence to considerations both of justice and of social stability.

III. Theories Importing International Law

The universal succession theory and the theory of continuity of the people and territory both solve the legal problem raised by State succession without needing to import international law. Some imperative theorists, conceding that the process of change of sovereignty is one of the substitution of one competence to rule by another, and nothing more, nonetheless argue that international law, based on the positive practice of States, directs the successor State to discharge certain of its predecessor's obligations, and vests in it certain of its predecessor's rights.[3] This approach is useful with respect to the effect of change of sovereignty on relationships governed by international law, such as treaties; and, indeed, it may be the only feasible approach with respect to these. But it is quite irrelevant to the solution of problems raised by change of sovereignty with respect to relationships governed exclusively by municipal law, and even of the problem of the survival of that law itself.

1 Cavaglieri, pp. 108-14; Schönborn, pp. 58, 83.   2 P. 404.
3 Hall, p. 114; Halleck, *Elements of International Law* (2nd ed. 1885), p. 97.

Resort to positive international law characterizes the earlier French writings on State succession.[1] French authors approached the problem without too sharp a distinction in mind between law and justice, and hence they tended to thrust the emphasis onto continuity in virtue of the moral urge to achieve an equitable result. The German theorists, whose Kantian position dictated an unbridgeable gulf between rules of law and concepts of justice, found themselves inhibited in this respect, and as a result their emphasis is more negative. As Strupp expresses it, 'it is juridically impossible to imagine a transmission of credits of the extinguished State to the other unless this is authorized by a special international norm'.[2] But when he and his colleagues seek this norm they generally fail to discover it.[3] A constant and uniform solution adopted in treaties of cession is considered to be capable of inducing a positive rule of law which can be availed of when no such treaty is entered into, but there is a marked tendency to stop short of enunciating such a rule, and to acknowledge merely a 'developing rule'.[4]

The theory of 'auto-limitation' lacks sufficient intellectual dynamism to promote conviction that consent has produced law. The alternative view that international law derives from sources superior to the will of States is not so inhibited, because it envisages rules of State succession as incumbent on any State entering the international community.[5] If positive international law contains a criterion for distinguishing between continuity and discontinuity of States, it must also contain rules for bridging the gap which discontinuity creates. This approach can even result in the reintroduction of the concept of succession, for if succession is a general principle of law, and the general principles of law are part of international law, then a legal succession can be achieved in virtue of the supervening authority of international law.[6]

1 The first to use the pragmatic method effectively was Larivière. Appleton also resorted to a supranational legal conception, although it is doubtful if it could be called international law. Sack's views are similar. Reference to an international law solution is made by Le Fur, in *Rev. gén. de droit int. pub.* vol. VI (1899), p. 620; Gidel, *passim*.
2 Hague *Recueil*, vol. XLVII (1934), p. 474.
3 Cavaglieri, p. 199; Schönborn, pp. 59, 61.
4 Schönborn, pp. 59, 61; von Rogister, pp. 13 *et seq.*; Cahn in *A.J.* vol. XLIV (1950), p. 478.
5 Udina, p. 694; Guggenheim, pp. 11, 17, 18, 26; Feilchenfeld, p. 621; Rousseau, p. 283; also in *Annales de droit et de sciences politiques*, vol. XII (1962), p. 3; Reuter, pp. 120 *et seq.*; Dahm, vol. I, pp. 102 *et seq.*; Gould, pp. 412 *et seq.*; Castren, *loc. cit.*; Paenson, *passim*; Tervooren, *passim*; van Panhuys; Vallat; Mosler, pp. 33, 376; De Muralt, *passim*.
6 Guggenheim, p. 43; Bello, *Principios de derecho internacional* (1946), p. 149; Bustamante y Sirven, *Derecho internacional público* (1936), vol. III, p. 321; Quadri, *Diritto internazionale pubblico* (1960), pp. 436 *et seq.*

The Nature and Theory of State Succession

IV. Communist Theory of State Succession

One would expect that Communist theory would proceed logically from the dismantling of the superstructure of capitalist exploitation to the conclusion that a successor State is unencumbered by the economic and political commitments of the predecessor,[1] and indeed, until recently, this is the sentiment to be found in the standard Soviet works[2] on international law. In the introduction by Barsegow to the Russian version of a treatise on State succession,[3] however, an air of revision is apparent. Barsegow, adverting to the Soviet acquisitions after the Second World War, is clearly in doubt whether the negative thesis is the line to be maintained, and accordingly he takes a deliberately ambiguous position. In East Germany, Communist doctrine has returned to the thesis of universal succession, this expression, indeed, actually being employed.[4]

In a dissertation[5] published in 1962 under the auspices of the *Akademie für Staats- und Rechtswissenschaft 'Walter Ulbricht'*, Kirsten distinguishes dialectically four periods of State succession doctrine: first, the pre-monopolistic period of capitalism, that is, the period down to the Franco-Prussian War, and corresponding with the period of universal succession doctrine; secondly, the period of monopolistic capitalism, that is, the period prior to the October Revolution, and corresponding with the period of negative succession doctrine; thirdly, the period of the international

[1] Bartoš in *Jugoslovenska Revija za Medunarodno Pravo*, vol. IX (1962), p. 185.
[2] Korovin, pp. 211 et seq., says that some treaties may remain in force, but only with the consent of the successor State. Localized (dispositive) treaties, however, are succeeded to. This view was followed in *Mĕždunarodroe pravo Učebnik* (1957), pp. 120 et seq., in the Soviet Union, and corresponds with the prevailing views in Eastern Europe, e.g. Bartoš, vol. I, pp. 324 et seq.; Ehrlich, p. 549; *Zarys prawa międzynarodowego publicznego* (1955), vol. I, pp. 150 et seq.; Paul, pp. 56 et seq., who does, however, find the question of multilateral conventions 'embarrassing'; Outrata, pp. 114 et seq.; Genovskij, vol. I, pp. 111 et seq.
[3] *Pravopreemstvo Gosudarstv* (1957), unauthorized translation of O'Connell, *The Law of State Succession* (1956). Zacharova in *Sovĕtskij Ježegodnik mĕždunarodnogo prava* (1960), pp. 157 et seq. is cautious—there is succession to some treaties and none to others; Avakov, *Pravopreenstvo Sovĕtskogo Gosudarstva* (1961), pp. 22 et seq., dealing with the succession of the Soviet to Tsarist Russia, says that the principle of *successio juris* applies not only in the relations between individuals, but also between States. The Soviet, as a new State, succeeded to economic treaties that were not contrary to the socialist economy, and multilateral treaties regulating economic, technical and cultural questions. Koževnikov takes a qualified position, but affirms succession in respect of technical matters, peaceful settlement, transport facilities, including the Constantinople Convention, and localized treaties, for example, loan agreements, but in cases of independence the consent of the new sovereign will be needed.
[4] Wünsche and Pahl in *Wissenschaftliche Zeitschrift der Deutschen Akademie für Staats- und Rechtswissenschaft 'Walter Ulbricht'*, Sondernummer zum 40 Jahrestag der Grossen Sozialistischen Oktoberrevolution, p. 126.
[5] *Einige Probleme der Staatennachfolge* (1962).

class struggle initiated by the Revolution, and corresponding with the attempt by the capitalist Powers to dictate a solution to the problem of State succession in Central Europe that would suit their imperialist aims; and fourthly, the present period of transition from capitalism to socialism, when a universal succession doctrine is dictated by the principles of peaceful coexistence. In capitalist countries territorial changes are reflexions of the law of unequal economic and political development of States, and therefore an important means of distributing profits.[1] As the Communist Manifesto pointed out, the *bourgeoisie*, through the exploitation of world markets, created a cosmopolitan system of exploitation. All States were more or less interested in maintaining this system during the first of the four periods, and the doctrine of universal succession was a response to the need for disrupting the distribution of profits as little as possible in consequence of political change.[2] In the second period, however, the German *haute bourgeoisie* became aggressive and predatory, and the new doctrine aimed at preserving to the economic victor the spoils of conquest. The English capitalists responded in kind, and the 'predatory'[3] thesis found its ultimate expression in Keith's negative view.[4]

Kirsten's analysis of the third period is almost entirely confined to establishing two propositions necessary to his conclusion, first, that the Soviet is a successor State and, secondly, that it undertook all the rights and obligations of its Tsarist predecessor. With respect to the first proposition, he contends that the socialist revolution so fundamentally destroyed the basis of the capitalist State as to terminate its identity.[5] With respect to the second proposition, that the Soviet took over Tsarist rights and obligations not connected with exploitation, Kirsten relies on a statement of Lenin to this effect.[6] This is the relevant precedent for all peace-loving States in the

1 P. 12.   2 P. 13.
3 'Räuberischen'.   4 P. 31.
5 The following Soviet writers say the same thing: Avakov, *op. cit.*; Zacharova, *loc. cit.*; and by implication Koževnikov, Genovskij, Korovin. However, the pre-Soviet Russian debt remains in total default: *Report of the Council of the Corporation of Foreign Bondholders* (1964), p. 314. Since, however, the People's Republic of China has claimed the United Nations seat as China, not as a new State, despite the fact that the social change there is more complete than it was in Russia, the thesis of Soviet succession is exposed to a dialectical challenge which Kirsten does not attempt to disguise, pp. 59 *et seq.* What is worthy of more criticism is Kirsten's evasion of the evidence that Czechoslovakia and Poland took a negative attitude towards legal succession to the Central Powers and Tsarist Russia. In 1949 the Chinese People's Government stated that it would study the treaties of the Kuomingtang to decide which of them it would acknowledge as binding. Korovin, p. 211, thinks this was a correct approach.
6 'Wir lehnen alle Punkte über Raub und Vergewaltigung ab, aber alle Punkte, in denen gutnachbarliche Beziehungen und wirtschaftliche Abkommen vereinbart sind, nehmen wir freudig an, diese Punkte können wir nicht ablehnen', p. 52.

era of peaceful coexistence, one of the principles of which is the 'peaceful working together of States'.[1] This principle must not be negatived by change of sovereignty.[2] The result is universal succession, but in a sense different from that of the pre-monopolistic capitalist period. In that period universal succession implied a complete succession; now it implies a complete succession only with respect to those rights and obligations which do not aim to produce a new World War, enslave or plunder other peoples, or harm the socialist camp, which alone aims at the preservation and strengthening of peace.[3] Therefore, 'today universal succession is a legal institution of common democratic international law, which raises in its fundamental principles a barrier that may not be breached'.[4] The distinction between 'political' and 'non-political', or 'personal' and 'non-personal', rights and obligations is merely a reflexion of *bourgeois* legal doctrine, and is rejected[5] as incompatible with peaceful coexistence. The way to this conclusion had been prepared by Barsegow,[6] when he pointed out that the distinction emanated from the theory that territory is property, and was thus rooted in the capitalist property conception of the means of production.[7]

Russian scholars have adopted a reserved attitude with respect to the East German thesis. They recognize that it is important to East Germany's claim to be a successor to the *Reich* in participation in international arrangements, but they are privately critical of the thesis of universal succession. Although Soviet doctrine remains unclear and uncertain it appears to be tending towards the separation of the categories of 'succession' and decolonization, the one admitting of a more complete succession than the latter. The case of East Germany is treated as one of succession.[8]

1 'Friedliche Zusammenarbeit'.
2 Pp. 83, 89: 'Es entspricht dem völkerrechtlichen Prinzip der friedlichen Zusammenarbeit der Staaten, dass der erreichte Stand der internationalen Zusammenarbeit durch Staatenwechselfälle nicht eingeschränkt wird. Das erwähnte Prinzip verlangt gleichfalls, dass die friedliche Zusammenarbeit der Staaten durch Staatenwechselfälle so wenig wie möglich gestört wird.'
3 P. 89.
4 P. 91. 'Heute ist die Universalsukzession ein Rechtsinstitut des allgemeindemokratischen Völkerrechts, das mit seinen Grundprinzipien eine Barriere errichtet, die nicht überschritten werden darf.'
5 P. 92.
6 *Loc. cit.*
7 Wünsche and Pahl, when they argued that bilateral treaties are not succeeded to, but multilateral treaties are, fell, in Kirsten's opinion, into error because they failed to recognize this connexion, p. 93.
8 The distinction crystallized in comments of the Soviet delegation at the Helsinki Conference of the International Law Association in 1966.

V. Implications for State Succession of Theories of Territory

There are two ways of regarding a change of sovereignty over territory: as a transfer of sovereignty, or as a displacement of sovereignty.[1] The one approach tends to admit the feasibility of a legal succession, that is, an implied assignment of rights and obligations along with the conveyance of the land, the other to deny it. The theoretical issue thus posed is between entry of the successor State into the legal relationships of its predecessor and a mere assertion on the former's part of its sovereign power in the vacuum left by the latter's withdrawal, and this issue is, in part at least, a reflexion of a complex conceptual disagreement on the relationship between territory and sovereignty.

The primitive theory of territory was conditioned by feudal conceptions of the relationship between the sovereign and the soil, and it has been called the 'theory of property' (*Eigentumstheorie*). It envisages the State as exercising 'primordial' power over territory. The theory tends to govern Anglo-American thinking, which is still dominated by the feudal conception of eminent domain, and which resists the disengagement of *imperium* and *dominium*. It tends also to be reflected in French doctrine, owing to the French conception of public property, and the *droit patrimonial*. Although Italian jurisprudence accepts the distinction between *imperium* and *dominium* to the extent of recognizing that a State may have sovereignty over territory without enjoying proprietary rights therein, there are Italian writers who perpetuate the property conception of territory for the same reason as the French, distinguishing *dominium* as the power over territory, and *imperium* as the power over people.[2]

The Hegelian theory of the State, as it permeated German jurisprudence in the nineteenth century, led to the absorption of the concept of territory, and the concomitant concept of people, in the concept of the State itself. The resulting explanation of the relationship between territory and sovereignty (the *Eigenschaftstheorie*) is that territory is an element of the State, the physical aspect, indeed the very 'body'[3] of the State, and not a fortuitous accessory thereof.[4] A mutation of territory is, consistently with

---

[1] Generally on territory see Bastid, *Le territoire dans le droit international contemporain* (1954); Schönborn in Hague *Recueil*, vol. XXX (1929), p. 85. Two brief recent discussions are in Dahm, vol. I, p. 538, and Berber, *op. cit.* vol. I, p. 296. See also Thalmann, *Grundprinzipien des modernen Zwischenstaatlichen Nachbarrechts* (1951), p. 19.

[2] Donati, *Stato e territorio* (1924), p. 117. A German writer of the same view is Hamel, *Das Wesen des Staatsgebiets* (1938).

[3] 'Körper'.

[4] Fricker, *Vom Staatsbegiet und Gebietshoheit* (1867), pp. 66–75. His theory is an anticipation of the *Raumstheorie*, i.e. territory is the physical domain within which the State manifests itself; von Holtzendorff, pp. 225–8; Jellinek, *op. cit.* p. 402.

the organic theory of the State, not a mutation in possession, but a modification of the State's personality formulated in its power to command. This theory was the *Raumstheorie*,[1] according to which territory is not an object of State domination, but its spatial extent. Early in the century the next step was taken of disengaging altogether the two concepts of territory and State authority.[2] Territory was stated to be merely the physical sphere (*Bereich*) within which the competence of the State is exercised. The new thesis, known as the *Kompetenztheorie*, became a focal point of the 'pure theory' of law as it evolved in Austrian jurisprudence.[3] Competence is to be examined not only from the point of view of isolating the authority within the State who is empowered to command, but also from the point of view of identifying to whom, and in respect of where, the command may be addressed. Competence is thus divisible into 'personal' and 'local' competence, and competence in its widest sense is the sum of the powers of the State to deal with people and with things. The emphasis is thus thrust on 'territorial sovereignty', and not on territory, which becomes a secondary concept, the 'reflex', as Radnitzky put it, of the juridical quality of the State.

The *Kompetenztheorie* differs from the *Eigentumstheorie* in that it denies that territory can be regarded as landed property subjected to the *jus utendi et abutendi*, without recognition of the peculiar relationship of sovereign and subject that exists in respect of the inhabitants. It differs also from the *Eigenschaftstheorie* and the *Raumstheorie* in refusing to identify the power to command with the territorial sovereignty, and in regarding mere territorial sovereignty as an empty concept in the absence of specific competence over individuals. Since valid competence exists extraterritorially, the theory of sovereignty must be independent of territorial conceptions; territorial boundaries are merely a regulatory limitation. The validity of acts intra- and extraterritorially performed cannot be made to depend upon a territorial nexus, but upon a higher norm which specifies permissible acts by reference either to territory or to extraterritorial factors.[4]

The cession of territory from one State to another is treated differently in these respective theories. To the *Eigentumstheorie*, it is a mere transfer

1 So called by Henrich in *Zeitschrift für Völkerrecht*, vol. XIII (1926), p. 28.
2 Radnitzky in *Archiv des öffentlichen Rechts*, vol. XX (1906), p. 313.
3 Henrich, *op. cit.*; Kelsen, *General Theory of Law and State* (1949), p. 208; *Allgemeine Staatslehre* (1925), p. 137; Verdross in Niemeyer's *Zeitschrift für internationales Recht*, vol. XXXVII (1927), p. 293. Generally see Verosta in *Österreichische Zeitschrift für öffentliches Recht*, vol. IX (1954), p. 241; Caflisch in *Ned. Tijd.* vol. X (1963), pp. 353 et seq.
4 Schnitzer, *Staat und Gebietshoheit* (1935), p. 128; Costes, *Des cessions de territoires* (1914), p. 45.

of real estate from one owner to another; to the *Eigenschaftstheorie* and the *Raumstheorie* it constitutes a modification of the identity of the State, and a substitution of two new entities for two old ones; to the *Kompetenztheorie* it is merely a displacement of one set of specific faculties by another. The interconnexion of the respective theories of territory and succession now becomes obvious: the universal succession theory presupposes a transfer of territory with all the legal qualities attaching to it; the organic theory, whether in Gabba's or Huber's form, presumes the destruction of an element of the State, of something personal to it, and the consequent inconceivability of its transfer; the one leads to a doctrine of inherited, the other to a doctrine of substituted, authority. The *Kompetenztheorie* refutes the possibility both of transfer and of survival of the organic element of the population to which rights and duties attach, and denies that a substitution in such rights and duties can occur merely in virtue of a substitution of authority.

VI. Criticisms of these Theories

The doctrine of universal succession in its various manifestations has merited severe and extensive criticism,[1] and is now largely rejected by theorists. In so far as it was based on analogy with Roman law it would seem to have commenced from untenable premises. The rights and duties of individuals and those of States are not comparable. The former are personal to a real being, the latter to a fictitious one. Personality, as a juridical term signifying the homogeneous and autonomous character of a community, is not transmissible. The Roman law analogy is justifiable only as a metaphor, and the validity of the metaphor is not substantiated by an examination of the body of diplomatic and judicial practice. Internal as much as external politics have militated against the acceptance by States of an absolute inheritance of obligations. On the other hand, theories of succession which base themselves on the continued identity of the absorbed territory itself are defective in ascribing to the territory after the change of sovereignty the capacity to retain rights and duties. Although such a concept found an early response in State practice in the

---

[1] Specifically by Pradier-Fodéré, ss. 158–60; Heffter, *Das europäisches Völkerrecht der Gegenwart auf den bisherigen Grundlagen* (1884), s. 61; *Le droit international de l'Europe* (1873), p. 50; Calvo, vol. II, pp. 248, 262; vol. IV, p. 404; von Holtzendorff, p. 33; Hall, p. 114; Gareis, p. 61; Zorn, p. 150; Fischer, *Das Problem der Identität und der Neuheit* (1892); Huber, pp. 9, 18, 20, 24; Gidel, pp. 36 *et seq.*, 51 *et seq.*; Keith, p. 3; Cavaglieri, pp. 17 *et seq.*; and in Hague *Recueil*, vol. XXVI (1929), p. 378; Schönborn, pp. 7 *et seq.*; Guggenheim, pp. 30 *et seq.*; Jones, p. 360; Feilchenfeld, pp. 616, 620; Ripert in Hague *Recueil*, vol. XLIV (1933), p. 640; Kelsen in *ibid.* vol. XLII (1932), p. 314; Mosler, pp. 20 *et seq.*

growth of the notion of a *dette hypothéquée sur le sol*, referred to as such in many treaties of the Napoleonic period, it has been found to be one impossible to apply in its entirety. Relationships of municipal law may continue to bind a territory which remains fiscally autonomous, but such territory cannot be bound by jural relationships of international law which were properly personal to the extinguished or expelled sovereignty.

The difficulty with all theories that base themselves on the continuity of the social substratum to which rights and duties are alleged to attach is that, once the distinction between change of sovereignty and change of government is conceded, it is the fact of a substitution in sovereignty which is alone relevant.[1] There may be excellent reasons for attributing rights and duties to the successor State in virtue of the stability of the social structure, but a legal rule to this effect does not derive merely from the fact of social continuity.[2] In any event, a thesis of factual continuity fails to provide a criterion for the division of debts when a State is dismembered.

The rejection of the theories of continuity does not, however, necessarily involve the conclusion that there can be no legal continuity throughout the process of change of sovereignty. Indeed Jellinek, the principal architect of the imperative theory, contrived this continuity, though his reasoning is not beyond challenge on his own premises. His critics[3] have commented that in arguing from the need for stability in human relationships he is striving to reconcile morality and law, which logically are irreconcilable if one isolates the category of law in terms exclusively of command. The categorical imperative in the Kantian system can yield only a subjective direction, that is, a direction to the will of the moral actor; it cannot, because of the formal separation of the 'is' and the 'ought', assist in the subjection of the actor to an external authority. But in Jellinek this is precisely what occurs, for he says that when a new State is created it 'recognizes' itself to be bound by international law in virtue of the needs of international intercourse. The moral act of self-abnegation is thus transformed into a juridical bond, from which no withdrawal, save with the consent of all, is permitted.[4]

1 Huber, while admitting (p. 12) that the consequences of his own doctrine approximated those of Gabba, contested the notion that legal personality is a mere fiction, and the social personality the only effective legal consideration. Respecting Appleton's doctrine, he pointed out that the question whether acquired territory is permitted to survive as an administrative entity is a matter of the successor's will, and that the doctrine is inapplicable in the case of fully centralized States, p. 16. Huber is criticized, along with Gabba, by Gidel, pp. 65 *et seq.*; Keith, p. 4.
2 Criticism made by Cavaglieri, p. 54.
3 Triepel, *Völkerrecht und Landesrecht* (1899; reprinted 1958), p. 77; Guggenheim, p. 13 and (referring to Schönborn) p. 40. Cf. Udina, p. 697.
4 Cavaglieri, p. 112. But he follows his theory of auto-limitation, p. 214; also Schönborn, pp. 7 *et seq.*

Jellinek's primary contribution to the debate on State succession, however, is not his argument for continuity but his clarification of the notion of change of sovereignty. His followers derived from this a negative view of State succession, but this is not really necessary. Even if territorial changes are merely replacements of sovereignty it does not follow that positive international law may not attach to them legal consequences, even the consequences of a juridical succession.[1] Sovereignty connotes nothing more than the supreme legal competence within a defined region, a competence which is relative only. 'Change of sovereignty' implies nothing more than the substitution of one such competence for another. The successor State in no sense 'continues' the sovereignty of its predecessor; neither is it necessarily irresponsible for the juridical consequences of its predecessor's acts. The territory, the people, the complex of legal relations existing between them, all remain unaffected by the change. The imposition upon the successor State by international law of duties with respect to such territory is not incompatible with the extension of its sovereign jurisdiction.

The imperative theory may thus be circumvented if one tolerates the supervening authority of international law, but only with respect to matters governed by international law. The weak point in the theory is its solution of the problem of succession to public property. The sophisticated Continentals recognized that, to be consistent with their theory that change of sovereignty involves the expulsion of the competence to rule, and does not involve a transfer of territory, they would have to admit that the successor State does not 'succeed' to the property and rights of its predecessor. They accordingly argued that these, like the territory itself, become *bona vacantia* at the instant of the change, and are appropriated by the successor State in manifestation of its own will.[2] The less sophisticated Keith glosses over this refinement by saying that the successor State 'succeeds' to the property of its predecessor.[3] The curious thing is that Keith is almost alone in saying that the successor State cannot claim its predecessor's property located in third States,[4] which one would have thought to be a necessary corollary of the theory that the successor State gains title only in virtue of its actual power over the *res*, but which is a corollary studiously avoided by almost all exponents of the theory.

It would be misleading to conclude that the theory of State succession is dictated by that of territory, for it is still possible to argue that international law directs a successor State with respect to the rights and duties

---

[1] Kelsen, in Hague *Recueil*, vol. XLII (1932), pp. 121 *et seq.*
[2] For authorities see *infra*, pp. 199, 200.
[3] P. 49. [4] P. 52. Also Sereni, pp. 397–400.

of its successor, and this direction might be sufficiently explicit to make the distinction between 'succession', 'substitution' and 'continuity' irrelevant. It is equally misleading to imagine that either the *Eigentumstheorie* or the *Kompetenztheorie* is logically imposed upon the analysis of concrete instances of State succession, for it is not international law but municipal law which determines the intrinsic relationship between territory and the authority of the State. The concepts of territory and of sovereignty are merely intellectual artifacts, not metaphysical entities, and their delineation is only possible in the light of the actual systems which utilize them. The Anglo-American system is fundamentally based upon a property concept. The *Kompetenztheorie* may be a perfectly valid emanation from the Austrian constitutional system. It does not follow that either theory will dictate a universal solution.

In fact, scarcely any author has confined himself to any one of the theories in all its purity. The struggle for originality, the pressure towards adopting a median position, the reluctance to press conclusions to too logical an end have all prompted modifications, amalgamations, and mutations of the various theories. It follows that the supposed deductions with respect to State succession lack the authority that theory pretends to confer on them. Schönborn,[1] for example, who was the first to recognize a relationship between theories of territory and theories of sovereignty, thought that both the *Eigentumstheorie* and the *Eigenschaftstheorie* would lead, in differing degrees, to the negation of succession. If, he said, territory is an object of State authority, territorial sovereignty is a property right of public law (*staatsrechtliches Sachenrecht*), the content of which is always a matter of internal law. Therefore, it is impossible for identical rights to persist when a change of sovereignty may involve a change in the legal status of the object. Even if one were to assume that all modern States have the same conception of territorial sovereignty, so that change of sovereignty would not involve a change in the relationship of the State to the territory, this would only be true in a negative sense, for inevitably the positive details of the relationship will vary according to different legal conceptions. If, on the other hand, one adopts the *Raumstheorie*, another, but even more fundamental, objection to the possibility of succession arises, and that is that all that can pass from one State to another is the right to exercise sovereignty and have this exercise recognized by other States. The particular rights which flow from the exercise are clearly dependent upon the identity of the sovereign, and cannot possess an identity of their own independently thereof.

Territory, to Guggenheim, is an object of sovereignty, not an element

[1] P. 10.

of it.[1] He criticizes Jellinek for speaking in the same sentence of a 'transmission' of sovereignty and of the successor State 'extending' its sovereignty over the territory and the predecessor State 'withdrawing' its own sovereignty. This, Guggenheim objects, is a flagrant contradiction: sovereignty is either transferred or expelled. The object theory of territory, he points out, derives largely from doctrine on State succession, for only if territory is conceived in terms of possession can the notion of a transfer of international competence be supported.[2] Succession, to Guggenheim, then, is a consequence of the 'passing' of the competence of a State over its territory to another State. But since it is 'competence' which passes, and not ownership, it follows that only the public domain and not the private domain of the predecessor State falls to the successor, and it does so in virtue of a positive rule of international law.[3]

Verdross, a leading exponent of the *Kompetenztheorie* in his treatment of territory, departs radically from it in his discussion of succession, for he subdivides competence into specific faculties, each of which separately, or all of which jointly, may be assigned.[4] Indeed, it is difficult to understand why international law, as a superior system, may not effect a transfer of power or an assignment of rights and duties along with a conveyance of territory, and clearly the impediment arises only from subscription to the imperative theory of law in all its dogmatic intractability.

Each of the above doctrines has its own method of approaching the problems of State succession. The universal succession theory commences from an *a priori* analogy between international law and private law, and seeks to force State practice within the confines of a single rubric. The negative theory looks to State practice alone and refuses to admit any general principle. It divides the problems of State succession into arbitrary categories and seeks for a positive rule relating to each. It demonstrates that large-scale economic considerations tend to override legal reasoning, that States have been compelled to resort to treaties and agreements to solve the problems which change of sovereignty habitually raises, and that the various solutions are dictated more by policy than by principle. Upon conflicting treaty provisions, it is argued, no harmonious body of doctrine can be constructed. The attempt to decide whether one particular treaty substantiates a principle or creates an exception to another principle leads only to a vicious circle.

Despite these objections, however, it must be admitted that an ex-

[1] P. 46.   [2] P. 48.   [3] Pp. 63–83, 98.
[4] *Die Verfassung der Völkerrechtsgemeinschaft* (1926), pp. 182–4; and in Hague *Recueil*, vol. xxx (1929), p. 374.

The Nature and Theory of State Succession 29

tensive examination of treaty provisions is not entirely uninstructive. It is possible to discover and formulate the principles and fundamental considerations which lie behind them. In this respect it is perhaps more valuable to ascertain on what points agreement has in the past been reached than to analyse the points of controversy. It is significant that, in the history of State succession, controversy has developed not so much around the question whether such and such a principle exists as over application of such a principle. States which, for political or economic reasons, have found it expedient to acknowledge a principle detrimental to their supposed vital interests have sought to establish exceptions to it. Such was the case when France refused to acknowledge the obligations of Madagascar, the United States those of Spain in Cuba and the Philippines, Italy those of Ethiopia, and Germany those of Austria. To deny from a consideration of these cases the existence of a general principle is to adopt an unnecessarily restricted interpretation. In other cases States have sought to emancipate themselves from the operation of a general principle by refusing to admit that they were successors to other States.

Contemporary literature on State succession tends to lack the philosophical depth and academic cosmopolitanism which are so evident in the writers of the specialist monographs in the earlier part of this century and the last years of the nineteenth century. These writers—except for Keith—clearly had read everything that had been written on the subject, and appear to have been at home with the literature of four languages. They erected doctrinal edifices of a pleasing symmetry on theories of the State that were philosophically integrated. Admittedly these constructions were easily demolished, or rendered evanescent, if one disputed the relevant philosophy, but at least the critic had an instant point of departure for the purpose of evaluation. The modern pragmatic approach, while in given instances it may yield results far more consonant with moral and social needs, tends towards superficiality. Authors nibble piecemeal at the problems of succession, picking and choosing attitudes without, apparently, recognizing that these may be exposed to serious philosophical objection. In the result, strands of Hegel and of Thomas Aquinas become inextricably interwoven in a patchwork of rubrics, and the critic is hard put to it to say just what theory of the State, or what philosophy of law, underlies the formulation.

Unless one identifies the relevant strands, and is aware of their philosophical origins, the doctrine of State succession will appear to be an unpalatable mélange of incoherent and contradictory ideas, and there will be a tendency to despair of ever formulating an acceptable concept. An awareness of the need for theoretical criticism is thus a precondition of sound speculation and accurate analysis. The critic who examines the writings on State succession carefully cannot fail to be struck by the startling persistence of the view that the successor State should, as a matter of 'equity' or 'justice', take over its predecessor's obligations,[1] and by the constant admission that in practice it almost always does so; and he must come to the arresting conclusion that only some profound gulf between law and ethics inhibits the translation of this moral attitude into rules of law. When it is realized that the gulf is contrived by Kant's categories, which have dominated the European legal mind, the problem of expressing social, economic and moral needs in terms of law may not appear so intractable. The jurist's function is to channel the normative pressures in society and organize them in rubric form. A positive approach from the position of fact is essential for verification of the pressures, but a positive approach alone cannot make the facts congruous, or raise the analysis beyond the anecdotal. To list together the authors *pro* and *contra* a proposition, without enquiring why they take the view they do, is really only to argue *ad hominem*. Inevitably the negative scales are depressed by this quantitative method, for the observer, confronted with a catalogue of opposed authorities, will in despair take a non-committal position, and this will be translated into State practice by those who have to make decisions. Incoherency of practice is thus both occasioned and compounded by incoherence in theory.

4. CONCLUSIONS

Since law is a spontaneous generation from the needs and aspirations of man in community, it follows that there is no unbridgeable gap between international law and municipal law. Both systems are founded on the 'general principles of law', and they differ only in respect of the areas of human activity which they seek to regulate. A contradiction between international law and municipal law must not be supposed, and when the

---

[1] Selosse, pp. 116, 185; Le Fur in *Rev. gén. de droit int. pub.* vol. VI (1899), p. 620; von Bar in *Die Nation*, vol. XVI (1899), p. 425; Kohler, *Grundlagen des Völkerrechts* (1918), p. 99; Gidel, pp. 14 *et seq.*; Cavaglieri, p. 103; Schönborn, p. 58 (Guggenheim said Schönborn was quieting scruples, p. 40); Jèze in *Revue de science et législation financière*, vol. XIX (1921), p. 59; vol. XXI (1923), p. 81; Mosler, p. 37. The equitable doctrine has gained greatest currency in the 'burdens with the benefits' theory in the United States. As Hyde states it, 'it would be unjust to permit the transferee to gain the benefits accruing to the territory acquired from the use of borrowed funds unless the obligation to make repayment were undertaken': vol. I, p. 402. It is not clear whether the upholders of the burden-and-benefit theory regard the obligation as one of law or equity. Wilkinson, for example, after expounding the connexion of burdens attaching to benefits, concludes that there is 'no legal obligation on the part of a successor State to assume the public financial obligations of its predecessor': p. 95.

two systems are accidentally antithetical it is the function of juristic logic to effect a reconciliation between them. It follows that international law is always available to a municipal law judge, unless he is directed to the contrary, as a relevant corpus of doctrine for the solution of litigious problems. Modern constitutions, in the endeavour to guarantee this mandate, incorporate international law into municipal law. Two conclusions relevant to the doctrine of State succession follow from this view of law, and from this statement of the relationship between international law and municipal law: the first is that change of sovereignty does not occasion the total and automatic collapse of the internal legal order, and the second is that international law is not incapable of regulating in municipal law the consequences of the change.

The alternative view of law is that it is a creation of the sovereign will, and sustained only so long as the sovereign will remains effective.[1] While in some respects, and in some countries in more respects than in others, law formally derives from the legislative will, its content constitutes an essential part of the pattern of human activity. Every human actor every day makes many decisions which presuppose rules of law. No one can contemplate with equanimity the anarchy that would result from an instantaneous legal vacuum, or even from the instantaneous displacement of one legal system by another. The concept of legal certainty and the presumption of legal knowledge would lose their cogency, and injustice would result. Such consequences cannot be presupposed in any legal philosophy which seeks to effect a correspondence between justice and the positive law. This does not mean that a successor State is restricted in its competence to replace the previous legal system with its own, for this may in fact be judiciously achieved; but it does mean that juristic speculation is not permitted to presume that the legal system, five minutes after change of sovereignty, and before the successor State has had time to formulate its views, no longer exists. Needless to say, no author has drawn so fatuous a conclusion. The theorists who commence with the conception of law as a manifestation of sovereign will avoid it by presuming that the successor State has impliedly willed to continue the legal system, which now derives its validity from a new source.[2] But it must be

[1] For authors see *infra*, p. 101. The most able contemporary exposition of this view is by Rosenne, pp. 266 *et seq.*
[2] As Rosenne has demonstrated, this view has results which differ markedly from the view of legal continuity. See Huber, p. 16; Westlake, p. 75; von Rogister, p. 13; Gidel, p. 64; Keith, *passim*; Jellinek, *op. cit.* p. 82; Cavaglieri, p. 103; Marinoni, *loc. cit.* p. 312; Schönborn, p. 83; Udina, p. 697; Guggenheim, *Traité*, p. 459; Feilchenfeld, p. 611; Caflisch in *Ned. Tijd.* vol. x (1963), pp. 353 *et seq.* who discusses the difficulties involved in protecting nationals of the successor State.

observed that the bridge so constructed across the hiatus in sovereignty is a fiction, and theories are suspect which accept that their own logical consequences must be fictitiously avoided.

If the internal legal system, save in its constitutional aspects, is unaffected by change of sovereignty, the most fundamental difficulties of State succession disappear, for all those institutions created by the law survive. Hence, private property rights, and rights deriving from judicial decisions, subsist unchanged. This does not mean that the successor State is legally inhibited from affecting them, but it does mean that it must act specifically to do so. Up to this point international law as such has not entered into the problem, for the survival of the legal order is not an achievement of international law, but a consequence of the nature of law itself, a conclusion of philosophy, not of positive direction. International law plays no more than its ordinary role of setting the standard of alien treatment. It follows that the extent to which rights created under the predecessor's law may be terminated by the successor State is determined by the international rules of State responsibility.[1] The rights of those who before the change of sovereignty were nationals of the successor State, or become its nationals after that event, do not, in the present state of international law, enjoy this protection, and unless guaranteed by the successor's own constitution (as is the case in the United States) are perilously situated. But in this respect the case after succession is no different from what it was before, and the successor State is no more and no less privileged than the predecessor State. When the courts of the successor State, say, therefore, as they have regularly done, that international law maintains private rights, this is true only with respect to alien rights, and then only in the complex sense outlined. It would be more accurate if they said that law of itself is unaffected by anything other than formal repeal by the sovereign of the moment, and then the statement would be true equally of alien and of national rights.

The real problem raised by change of sovereignty, then, is restricted by this view of the nature of law to the problem which arises respecting the rights and duties of the predecessor State itself. One may subscribe to the view that change of sovereignty is not a transfer of sovereignty, that it is a total displacement of one set of powers by another and not an assignment of these powers, and still reach the conclusion that the successor State is entitled to exercise the predecessor's rights and is obliged to discharge the predecessor's duties, because international law so directs. Perhaps, if international law is capable of this achievement, it does not

[1] Mosler subsumes the whole problem under the category of State responsibility, pp. 40, 41.

matter very much whether the process is regarded as one of devolution, assignment or inheritance (that is, succession) or novation or substitution, for the result is the same. And it is possible for international law to occasion a succession in respect of certain institutions, for example, the public domain of the predecessor State, and a substitution in respect of others where succession may be inappropriate, for example, governmental contracts. The real point is whether or not international law is competent to regulate the question at all. The main objection to presuming such competence is that it concedes superior normative power to international law in the direction of municipal law. A dualist solution of the problem would be that international law may direct the successor State as such to undertake its predecessor's commitments, but it cannot direct this with internal effect in the successor's courts; hence, in practice only alien interests can be affected by the supposed international law rule, and then only through the processes of diplomatic protection. It is, however, unnecessary to postulate the solution on the outcome of the monist-dualist debate if one accepts the fundamental integrity of international law and municipal law, and admits the effectiveness of the former in municipal courts. Then it becomes possible for a judge to say that he finds that international law in cases of State succession effects an assignment of, or substitution in, the rights and duties of the predecessor State; that this is a relevant norm when municipal law does not direct to the contrary; and that it is equally available to aliens and nationals.

The ultimate question, therefore, is whether international law contains rules for regulating the disposition of public rights and duties as a consequence of a succession of States, and how these rules are to be established. Although most writers on State succession have conceded the possibility of proving international law rules by recording the practice of States, they have been inhibited in their evaluation of this practice by the presupposition that the successor State's will is a pre-eminent source of law, and that moral and sociological pressures are irrelevant. Once the view is accepted that law is rooted in the metaphysics of community existence the inhibition disappears, for then the moral and sociological pressures, which all the authors have recognized, become juristically normative: 'equity' or 'justice' is more easily transformed into rules of positive law, *lex ferenda* into *lex lata*.[1] The appreciation of the law of State succession is, then, ultimately one of emphasis. A rational approach will thrust the emphasis on positive manifestation of the need for order and stability to be discovered in regular solutions devised by States in their day-to-day practice; an imperative approach will thrust it on the formal divergencies

[1] Cf. Dahm, vol. I, pp. 102 *et seq.*

and discrepancies in this practice. The two approaches tend respectively towards affirmation and denial.

The process of evaluation is one of juristic logic, not one of mere description, for description cannot make practice coherent which, in nearly every respect, is factually incoherent. The jurist has tools of reason at his disposal; and a theory which commences with the necessity, rationality and moral good of law will find no obstacle to their utilization. The ultimate principles of legal reasoning are formulated in rubrics known as the 'general principles of law'. They are available, not because in one form or another they are part of all developed legal systems, but because they are conceptually cogent in any scheme of legal reasoning. The concept of unjust enrichment is such a principle, and its mediating role between the categories of justice and of law endows it with special significance in the solution of problems of State succession when one party to a legal relationship has disappeared, just as it is important in the solution of the analogous problem of frustration of contract in private law. State practice, of course, is never avowedly based on general principles of law; it consists either of positive conduct or of asseverations of a much more concrete character. But the jurists will add meaning to the practice, and give form to its unstable patterns, by confining it within the structure of speculation which the general principles promote. Only when empirical techniques are informed by juristic logic are satisfactory results likely to be achieved.

Such an approach gains in flexibility what it loses in dogma. It avoids the search for a blanket formula to cover all contingencies, and tends to leave the solution to analysis of concrete instances; in other words, to avoid prejudgment. This is not to submerge the problem in intolerable relativism. Rather, it is to recognize the relativity of problems and the intractability of facts. All legal systems which are uncodified raise problems of judicial application to concrete circumstances of principles of very general character, and juristic logic has proved adequate to their solution. The law must remain consonant with the affirmative pressures which the patterns of human conduct generate, and sensitive to the products of experience. It must not be constricted by theories of the State whose momentum is largely expended, or by theories of justice which fail to reconcile human differences that take on juristic form. The law of State succession in the mid-twentieth century has reached a position of crisis, because evident moral and sociological pressures emphasize the need for continuity and the avoidance of disruption, while theory remains enmeshed in the nineteenth-century conception of sovereign will. The problem is to give expression in normative form to a reconciliation of two competitive pressures, that of stability in the international and internal orders, and that of adjustment of legal relationships to the social and economic effects of change. The solution lies in a presumption of continuity which concrete analysis may rebut, and it can only be perceived chapter by chapter in relation to specific issues. It does not lie in a universal touchstone of succession or non-succession.

Chapter 2

EVOLUTION OF THE BRITISH EMPIRE AND COMMONWEALTH

1. INTRODUCTION

The settlement of the constitutional crisis of the seventeenth century in England resulted in a sharper division between executive and legislative functions, and therefore between the powers of the royal prerogative and the powers of Parliament, than had been traditional in English law. The Crown lost its power of proclaiming new laws, or of suspending laws or dispensing from them, so that henceforth Parliament alone could engage the subject in new or modified legal liability, or invest in him novel legal rights. But in the process the Crown came to be exclusive in the fields reserved to it. For example, treaties, so long as they did not affect the rights and duties of the subject—which meant, in effect, so long as they did not touch his pocket—were a matter of indifference to Parliament, and remain so today, except in those instances where the executive seeks parliamentary approval for ratification of a treaty of controversial character, or where legislation is necessary to secure performance of the treaty in municipal law.

A like area of power was reserved to the Crown in the matter of its overseas territories. In the eighteenth century a distinction came to be drawn between ceded and settled colonies. When a colony was acquired by conquest or cession from another State, the Crown had the power to establish executive, judicial and legislative instrumentalities of government by Order in Council, Letters Patent or Proclamation. However, it might not contravene any Act of Parliament extending to the colony; and once a representative legislature had been granted by prerogative act, the right of government by Order in Council lapsed for the duration of the grant unless expressly reserved therein. When the conquered or ceded colony was already occupied by a system of law, English law (except the prerogatives of the Crown) did not extend thereto, unless by prerogative or parliamentary action.[1]

A settled colony is one in which British subjects were the first settlers with a developed system of laws. In the case of such a colony the settlers carried with them the common law, and such statute law as was

---

[1] *Campbell* v. *Hall* (1774) 20 State Tr. 329 at p. 323; *Abeyesekera* v. *Jayatilake* [1932] A.C. 260; *Sammut* v. *Strickland* [1938] A.C. 678.

applicable.[1] Statutes enacted subsequently to the date of settlement do not apply unless expressly extended to the colony.[2] Two difficulties arise from this proposition: The first is the question of the date of settlement, which has usually been fixed at a later stage by a section in the Acts Interpretation Act of the colonial legislature. The second is the question of applicability: it has been taken that statutes of Westminster unsuited to the condition of the colony at the date of settlement do not apply,[3] but there has been a tendency to ascertain suitability at the date when the issue is raised rather than retrospectively at the date of the reception of English law, so that the whole question remains controversial.[4]

In a settled colony, the Crown had prerogative power to create legislative, executive and judicial bodies, but once representative government was granted it lost the power of legislating by Order in Council.[5] In 1887 the British Settlements Act[6] authorized the Queen in Council in respect of settled colonies without a legislature to make laws for the peace, order and good government of the settlement, and since this is a continuous grant of power the Crown's prerogative to legislate generally by Order in Council was preserved. In the cases of Protectorates and Trust Territories, the Crown's power derives from the Foreign Jurisdiction Act, 1890,[7] and is as plenary as in the case of conquered or ceded colonies.[8] Orders in Council are made under the Act, and are invalid only if repugnant to Acts of Parliament extending to the territory.

Once the colonies were granted representative government the question arose whether they were entitled to alter the common law only, or even at all; and as a result of a constitutional crisis in this matter in South Australia, the Colonial Laws Validity Act, 1865 was enacted.[9] This provided that in the case of any Crown possession in which a legislature might exist, no colonial law should be deemed void on the ground of repugnancy to the law of England, unless it should be repugnant to the provisions of some Act of Parliament, order or regulation extending to the colony, or having in the colony the force and effect of law. The colonial legislatures might,

---

1 *Penhas* v. *Tan Soo Eng* [1953] A.C. 304.
2 *Memorandum* (1722), 2 P. Wms. 74; *Catterall* v. *Catterall* (1847), 1 Rob. Eccl. 580; *Falkland Islands Co.* v. *R.* (1864), 2 Moo. P.C.C. (N.S.) 266.
3 *Quan Yuk* v. *Hinds* (1905), 2 C.L.R. 345.
4 Castles in *Public Law* (1962), p. 182, and in *Adelaide Law Review*, vol. II (1963), p. 1.
5 *Re Lord Bishop of Natal* (1865), 3 Moo. P.C.C. (N.S.) 115.
6 50 & 51 Vict., c. 54.
7 54 & 55 Vict., c. 37, as amended in 1913 by 3 & 4 Geo.V, c. 16. See generally Jenkyns, *British Rule and Jurisdiction beyond the Seas* (1902).
8 *Sobhuza II* v. *Miller* [1926] A.C. 518, at p. 524.
9 28 & 29 Vict., c. 63. Castles in *Public Law* (1962), p. 183, and generally Todd, *Parliamentary Government in the British Colonies* (1894).

however, amend their constitutions, provided they did so in the manner and form required by imperial or colonial legislation, which meant that a colonial parliament might prescribe a mandatory manner and form of voting which would be a precondition of validity of colonial legislation.[1]

The Colonial Laws Validity Act has been regarded as the Magna Charta of the colonies, but in fact it constituted, in its system of legislative repugnancy, the keystone of colonial dependence upon the United Kingdom. It was reinforced by other doctrines: the first of which was that no colonial legislature was competent to legislate for things, persons and events beyond its territorial jurisdiction (which meant its territorial sea)[2] unless authorized by Imperial Act of Parliament.[3] The second of these was the legislative requirement of reservation of certain colonial bills for the personal assent of the Sovereign, involving the theoretical possibility of disallowance upon the advice of the Cabinet at Westminster. As it happened, disallowance ceased to be an issue by the end of the nineteenth century, although legislation continued to be held invalid by the courts on the ground of repugnancy or extraterritoriality.

In the last years of the century an awareness of the maturity of certain of the older colonies led to an accretion of their competence in the matter of the royal prerogative of treaty-making, and the evolution of this competence must be analysed before a study can be made of the termination of the legislative and doctrinal inhibitions upon colonial legal activity.

2. TREATY-MAKING POWER AND AUTONOMY OF THE OLDER DOMINIONS

The Imperial Conferences of 1923[4] and 1926[5] recognized the autonomy of the self-governing Dominions, and the Statute of Westminster, 1931,[6] endowed their legislatures with plenary competence and immunity from the jurisdiction of the Imperial Parliament. The position of the Crown was not, however, precisely defined, and as long as the conception prevailed that it was 'one and indivisible' throughout the Empire it was difficult to concede like autonomy to the Dominions in the initiation of foreign policy. Since treaty-making is an executive and not a legislative act in the British Constitution, this posed the problem of the extent to which a United Kingdom signature upon a treaty should commit the Dominions. Coupled with this was the question of the extent to which the Dominions

---

1 *A. G. of New South Wales* v. *Trethowan* [1932] A.C. 526.
2 O'Connell in *B.Y.* vol. XXXIV (1958), p. 199.
3 O'Connell in *L.Q.R.* vol. LXXV (1959), p. 318.
4 Cmd. 1987.   5 Cmd. 2768.   6 22 Geo. V, c. 4.

had, by evolutionary processes, attained the faculty in international law of independent treaty-making. Before dealing with the solutions arrived at in the 1920s it is important to trace these processes, for it has been alleged that they constitute the juridical basis for distinguishing, in respect of succession to Imperial treaties, the older Dominions from the newly independent countries, which in the main have attained international personality quickly, and in some cases without passing through the intermediate stages of autonomy which are sometimes conceded to create a status of 'semi-sovereignty'.[1]

I. The Situation prior to Dominion Status

In 1912 Keith committed himself to the proposition that the Imperial Crown had an absolute power of concluding treaties, and that in doing so it was advised by the Imperial Cabinet.[2] He failed to make the qualification that the more advanced colonies had already, for nearly half a century, claimed an ever extended faculty of concluding intergovernmental agreements of international character. At this early stage the clear distinction that subsequently emerged between Head-of-State and intergovernmental treaties was not fully appreciated, and the Crown was in both instances the active governmental instrumentality in the issuance of powers to sign and in the ratification of agreements. It was taken for granted in the early stages of independent contracting by the colonies that the Governor should in each instance receive a specific delegation from the Crown in Whitehall. Perhaps more important in assessing the autonomy of the colonies was the increasing recognition that colonial governments possessed the initiative in both the denunciation and application of Imperial treaties of a commercial and technical character. The reservation of initiative to Whitehall in the case only of 'political' treaties seems to be of great significance in appreciating the devolution of British treaties upon the Dominions, and in analysing the treaty lists which purport to record this devolution.

Australian colonies began to conclude agreements in their own names as early as 1874 in respect of postal matters. At this date postal agreements were not regarded as treaties in the strict sense of the word, and were concluded by postal administrations, but the procedure of making agreements was still laid down by a direction from Whitehall to the colonial postmasters-general, who recorded that they were authorized 'by their respective governments' to sign. Although ratification was not always

[1] Lester, pp. 480 et seq.
[2] *Responsible Government in the Dominions* (1912), vol. III, p. 1101.

reserved it seems that the Governor normally played a role in the approval of the negotiations, and on occasions either signed or ratified. Inevitably after this experience the colonies grew bold in demanding from Whitehall the right to enter into direct negotiations with foreign powers in commercial matters, and the subject was debated at the Colonial Conference of 1887[1] on the basis of the experience of Canada,[2] which had shortly before negotiated a differential tariff agreement with the United States and, with the consent of Whitehall and through the British Ambassador in Paris, a similar agreement with France in 1878. In 1884 Canada had also signed the International Cable Convention,[3] and at the time of the Colonial Conference was negotiating a tariff agreement with Spain. That already Canada was regarded as enjoying a special international status is evident from the veto imposed by Whitehall shortly before on the negotiations initiated by the West Indies for a provisional tariff agreement with the United States. The West Indies planters in retaliation urged annexation by the United States.[4] This offered Sir Francis Dillon Bell of New Zealand the opportunity at the 1887 Conference of urging the extension to all the colonies of the Canadian privilege.[5]

The immediate occasion of his paper was the present opportunity and strong desire of the New Zealand Government to negotiate a favourable tariff arrangement with France in respect of frozen meat. Permission was being currently sought of the British Government to enter into supervised negotiations with the French authorities, but it was thought appropriate that the whole subject should be thrown open for debate at this Conference. While it was true that, in the case of Canada at least, permission to negotiate with foreign countries in matters of trade had never been withheld where this did not interfere with the provisions of treaties or with the general fiscal structure of the Empire,[6] it was desirable that the privilege should be extended to all the colonies alike.[7]

No doubt because of the marked division of opinion on the subject of independent colonial negotiation in trade matters, the subject was not taken to a vote. It was only recorded as one of the suggestions made at the Conference. By a resolution carried at the 1894 Colonial Conference,

1 C. 5091.   2 *Ibid.* p. xii. Also *Report of Proceedings*, pp. 464, 476.
3 *B.F.S.P.* vol. LXXV, p. 356; Malloy, vol. II, p. 1949.
4 *Report of Proceedings* per J. H. Hofmeyer, p. 464.
5 *Ibid.* 'Negotiations with Foreign Powers in Matters of Trade', Appendix no. 43, p. 135, discussed pp. 476–84.   6 *Ibid.* p. 477.
7 There was some dissent from this proposal. Mr Hofmeyer favoured, instead, an Imperial Customs Tariff to meet the situation (*ibid.* p. 463 *et seq.*); this view was supported by, *inter alios*, Sir John Downer (p. 470) and Sir Thomas Uppington (pp. 479–80), on the ground that an eventual treaty-making freedom of colonies would destroy the Empire.

however, the privileges already granted to Canada were extended to Australia and New Zealand.

(a) *Reserved application of commercial treaties*

This discussion, in advance of its time, took no account of a significant development which had occurred shortly before the Conference of 1887, and which necessarily involved the undertaking of an obligation of consultation between the Imperial Government and the more advanced colonies in the application of commercial treaties. This was the practice of ceasing to make application of such treaties automatic to the colonies, but to include a clause providing for voluntary adherence by those colonies (usually named) that wished to do so. Normally a time limit ranging from six months to two years was specified as the time within which colonies could exercise their free right of adherence.[1]

While these clauses provided for separate adherence on the part of colonies, no provision was made for the corresponding right of separate withdrawal. This privilege came later, and marks the second stage of colonial commercial 'emancipation'. Meanwhile, apart from the voluntary adherence system, two other devices were used during the first stage: (1) A special protocol was sometimes executed providing for the accession of named colonies to a commercial treaty, from which they were previously excepted as above, subject to special concessions.[2] (2) In 1905, for the first time, a device was used which later became almost standard form in British commercial treaties of the 1902s and 1930s. The treaty with Bulgaria[3] did not apply to British colonies, but the products of colonies

[1] The first such treaty was that with Italy of 15 June 1883, Hertslet, vol. xv, p. 776; B.F.S.P. vol. LXXIV, p. 63. South Australia, alone among the Australian colonies, did not accede to this treaty. The treaty is no longer in force in respect to the other States, not having been revived by the Peace Treaty of 1947. The last instance in which colonies were included in a commercial treaty without their consent was in 1880 with Serbia: Hertslet, vol. xv, p. 342; B.F.S.P. vol. LXXII, p. 144. This form was followed in the treaties with: Greece, 1886, Hertslet, vol. XVII, p. 757, art. XVII; B.F.S.P. vol. LXXVII, p. 100; N.S.W. did not accede. Honduras, 1887, Hertslet, vol. XXI, p. 660, art XIV; Mexico, 1888, *ibid.* vol. XVIII, p. 855, art. XIV; B.F.S.P. vol. LXXIX, p. 25; N.S.W. did not accede. Egypt, 1889, Hertslet, vol. XVIII, p. 379, art. XV; B.F.S.P. vol. LXXXI, p. 1274; India was not excepted by this clause; Queensland and Tasmania acceded. Muscat, 1891, Hertslet, vol. XIX, p. 745, art. XXI; B.F.S.P. vol. LXXXIII, p. 11; India was not excepted; of Australian colonies only Queensland acceded. Bulgaria, 1894, Hertslet, vol. XX, p. 201, art. V; B.F.S.P. vol. LXXXIX, p. 5; all States acceded.

[2] Victoria, Queensland and Tasmania acceded with reservations to the treaty with Paraguay, 1884, Hertslet, vol. XVII, p. 851; *idem*, vol. XVIII, p. 944; B.F.S.P. vol. LXXXII, p. 1039. See also Japan–Queensland, Hertslet, vol. XXIV, p. 694; B.F.S.P. vol. LXXXIX, p. 1129.

[3] Cd. 3592, Hertslet, vol. XXV, p. 53, art. XX; B.F.S.P. vol. XCVIII, pp. 864, 1179.

enjoyed most-favoured-nation treatment on the basis of reciprocity. In this way, the colonies undertook no obligations under the treaty, but inherited the important privilege of most-favoured-nation treatment, which they could bring to an end, if desired, simply by ceasing to grant the same privilege to the other party. There are nineteen such treaties still in force whereby Australia claims most-favoured-nation treatment. This practice has ceased since the Second World War.

A confidential Board of Trade circular distributed at the 1907 Colonial Conference confirmed that no commercial treaty would be made applicable to the self-governing colonies without their consent; and that provision for their separate adherence and denunciation would be inserted instead.[1]

(b) Power of separate denunciation

When the practice of separate adherence was established, it seemed a necessary corollary that colonies which acceded separately could withdraw without affecting the application of the treaty to other parts of the Empire. The earliest example of a provision permitting colonial withdrawal would seem to be a 'voluntary adherence' clause in reverse which appeared in the Anglo-Spanish Commercial Modus Vivendi of 1894.[2] This exchange of notes applied to all colonies, but it was provided that 'it shall be open to any British Colony to withdraw from the present agreement, on notice to that effect being given... within six months after the date of its signature'.

It is noteworthy that when Queensland desired voluntarily to adhere to the Anglo-Japanese Commercial Treaty of 1894, pursuant to article XIX,[3] the British Government and Japan signed a protocol in 1897 reciting that Queensland had acceded, that certain provisions of the treaty would not apply to Queensland in given circumstances, and that 'the said Treaty shall cease to be binding, as between Japan and the said Colony of Queensland, at the expiration of twelve months after notice shall have been given on either side of a desire to terminate the same'.[4]

It became increasingly desirable, especially after 1897, that any obstacles in the way of granting commercial concessions to Great Britain by the colonies be got rid of.[5] While the recently concluded commercial treaties provided for separate accession, the older treaties did not offer any avenue for withdrawal by the colonies without affecting their

1 Not published; discussed in Conference Proceedings 1907, *Parliamentary Papers*, vol. LV, p. 483.   2 Hertslet, vol. XIX, p. 843.
3 *Ibid.* vol. XIX, p. 691; B.F.S.P. vol. LXXXVI, p. 39.
4 Hertslet, vol. XXIV, p. 694; B.F.S.P. vol. LXXXIX, p. 1129.
5 See e.g. the cases of Belgium and Germany, 1897, *Parliamentary Papers*, vol. LIX, pp. 640–1, 644–5.

Evolution of the British Empire and Commonwealth 43

operation elsewhere in the Empire. It was urged upon the Imperial Government by Sir Wilfrid Laurier in 1911 that the older treaties be brought into line with the more recent ones, so that colonial freedom of action would be complete.[1]

Australia withdrew from the treaties of commerce with Mexico in 1912, Paraguay in 1911, Egypt in 1910, Belgium in 1919 and Muscat in 1923. In these five cases an extensive search has failed to reveal any protocol or declaration granting the right of separate withdrawal. The explanation is probably that it was informally agreed between the parties, at the time when Australia sought to withdraw, that the separate accession clauses by virtue of which Australia had become a party implied a separate right of withdrawal.

(c) Colonial participation in the negotiation of a treaty

After 1923 the Dominions either requested that reciprocal most-favoured-nation treatment be made applicable to them, or negotiated a trade agreement direct with the foreign country concerned without the mediation of the British Government. Since 1902 it had been felt that the obtaining of the consent of a colony before a commercial treaty was made applicable to it was insufficient to guarantee that local economic interests would be consulted during diplomatic negotiations. Unless the views of colonies were made known effectively at the time of negotiating the treaty, the right of voluntary adherence would in many cases be of very limited value. A resolution was passed at the Colonial Conference of 1902 'that so far as may be consistent with the confidential negotiation of treaties with foreign powers, the views of the Colonies affected should be obtained in order that they may be in a better position to give adhesion to such treaties'.[2] Apparently nothing had been done in this direction by 1907 when Mr Deakin (Australia) pressed the matter again.[3] The confidential Board of Trade circular distributed at that Conference, but not published, apparently provided avenues of prior consultation which satisfied delegates.

[1] Imperial Conference 1911, Rep. of Proceedings, *Parliamentary Papers*, vol. LIV, p. 64. Australia wanted the right of separate denunciation so that it could get rid of treaties standing in the way of the Navigation Bills which were designed to give preference to British shipping over the heavily subsidised foreign shipping lines: ibid. pp. 135–40. Protocols permitting separate withdrawal were concluded with El Salvador, 1886, Hertslet, vol. XVII, p. 929; Uruguay, 1889, *ibid.* vol. XXI, p. 1120; B.F.S.P. vol. XCI, p. 122; Honduras, 1900, *B.F.S.P.* vol. LXXIX, p. 1121; Greece, 1904, *ibid.* vol. XCVIII, p. 53; Liberia, 1908, *ibid.* vol. CI, p. 194; Sweden, 1911, *ibid.* vol. CIV, p. 202; Colombia, 1912, *ibid.* vol. CV, p. 266; Denmark, 1912, *ibid.* p. 267; France, 1912, *ibid.* p. 271; Costa Rica, 1913, *ibid.* vol. CVI, p. 754; Norway, 1913, *ibid.* p. 809; Switzerland, 1914, *ibid.* vol. CVII, p. 564.

[2] Cd. 1299.   [3] Cd. 3523.

(d) Non-commercial agreements

It has already been noted that the colonies could not participate in or conduct their own negotiations with foreign countries in respect to 'political treaties'. After the Imperial Conferences of 1923 and 1926 this became possible, subject of course to the usual practice of Commonwealth-wide consultation in the event of possible effects which such a treaty might have on other members. Following the Conferences, a number of 'political' treaties were made applicable to Australia; the Australian Treaty List notes in each of these cases that 'the Australian Government concurred in the conclusion of this Treaty'.[1]

(e) The international law implications of colonial competence

The significance of these events for purposes of the law of succession seems to be considerable. The more advanced colonies gradually gained the initiative in negotiation of commercial agreements until, by the time their status as Dominions came to be recognized in the years preceding 1914, their separate membership of treaties, though generally contrived through Imperial agencies, was recognized to the extent that they could separately enter and withdraw. This was done by means of United Kingdom protocol whenever they were territorially affected by implication (i.e. in the older treaties as a rule), and by direct recourse to the withdrawal clause when affected by separate adherence. At this point in time they must have been recognized to have international treaty-making faculties of a sort, and to this extent to be 'successor States' in fact. It is of importance to recognize that no doubt of their being successors in law arose; whenever they wished to contract out they had to negotiate to this end and did not dream of pleading the lapse of the treaty. At the same time it was recognized that they were bound by Imperial 'political' treaties out of which they could not contract, so that their succession *de facto* was incomplete. But when it became complete they omitted these treaties from their treaty lists, which prompts the suggestion that the rationale of the devolution of Imperial treaties was their territorial application, which was specific (by implication or by declaration) only in the case of those categories of treaties which are found in the treaty lists, and which were the sorts of treaties in respect of which the colonial authorities possessed initiative.

There is nothing theoretically contradictory in the notion of subordinate territories having the right to enter into treaties on their own initiative, even though the other parties may be entitled to look for

[1] E.g. the note accompanying the Liquor Traffic Convention with U.S.A. in 1924.

Evolution of the British Empire and Commonwealth 45

performance to the suzerain or constitutional superior. This is exactly the case with Protectorates, and, probably, Mandated and Trust Territories: the treaties are legally those of the territories, though the instrumentality of contracting and implementation is the protecting Power. Why the same should not be the case with colonies which gain status in treaty-making is not clear, and the British Government was obviously perplexed by the question, as the change in emphasis in its legal advice illustrated.

On 7 January 1882, for example, Hertslet prepared a memorandum[1] on the *Right of the British Colonies to Enter into Separate Arrangements with Foreign Countries*, in which he said that he was of opinion that no colony had a right to conclude any separate arrangement of an international character with any foreign country, without the express sanction of the British Government. Although many colonies had concluded postal conventions with the United States, in no case had they done so without the express sanction of the Secretary of State for the Colonies. He said that the usual course had been for the government of the colony to submit to the Secretary of State a memorandum containing the outline of the postal arrangement proposed to be entered into between the colony and the United States; for the Colonial Office then to put itself in communication with the Post Office upon the subject; for the Treasury and Foreign Office to be eventually consulted; and, should there be no objection thereto, for the Secretary of State for the Colonies then to convey his sanction to the colony to enter into the arrangement thus approved by the Imperial Government. He thought that, should it be the desire of Her Majesty's Government to allow Canada or any of the Australian colonies to enter into commercial arrangements direct with France or any other Power, it would be necessary to obtain an Act of Parliament for that purpose. He added:

But although power could be thus conveyed to any Colony to enter into direct commercial agreements with foreign Powers, I think it would be far more satisfactory that the Imperial Government should conduct those negotiations, aided by a Representative of the Colony, and that when those negotiations should be concluded, the Treaty should be signed in the name of Her Majesty and in that of the Ruler of that foreign State; and that it should eventually be duly ratified by Her Majesty.

By 1905 the situation had so altered that the Law Officers (Finlay and Carson) were able to advise that the colonies could, like Egypt, remain separately bound by treaties which the United Kingdom had modified. The Legal Assistant in the Colonial Office had advised that the

[1] F.O. Confidential Paper no. 4578.

International Institute at Berne was correct in regarding New Zealand and Queensland, which were territorially affected by the Industrial Property Convention, 1883,[1] as having been automatically affected by the British signature of the Additional Act of 1900.[2] This view was contested by the British delegate who signed the Additional Act, and the Law Officers advised that 'the Colonies in question are still bound by the Convention of 1883 unmodified by the Additional Act of 1900'.[3]

II. Dominion Status and Treaties

If a date must be assigned for complete succession of the older Dominions in fact, it is clearly that of the Versailles Peace Conference. Not only did the Dominion delegations sign with the United Kingdom, but, coincidentally, it was acknowledged that even 'political' treaties were not to affect the Dominions without their consent. For example, in 1918 Australia 'concurred' in the conclusion of an arbitration treaty with Uruguay.[4] After the Imperial Conference of 1923[5] it was taken for granted that the Dominions must 'concur', and the only 'political' treaties to be found in the Australian and New Zealand lists are those in which this concurrence was expressed. The Imperial Conference of 1926[6] took into account the problem of reconciling the prerogative of treaty-making in a system of imperial relations, the essence of which was the unity and indivisibility of the Crown, with the equality in status of the Dominions with the United Kingdom. The Report to the Conference of the Inter-Imperial Relations Committee recommended that the practice of signing treaties for the Empire and enumerating the Dominions and India, if these wished to be included, should terminate as inconsistent with the view that these countries were on a footing of equality with Great Britain. Instead, all treaties to include the Empire should be in Head-of-State form and made in the name of the Crown as the symbol of the Imperial relationship.

The making of the treaty in the name of the King as the symbol of the special relationship between the different parts of the Empire will render superfluous the inclusion of any provision that its terms must not be regarded as regulating *inter se* the rights and obligations of the various territories on behalf of which it has been signed in the name of the King.[7]

[1] B.F.S.P. vol. LXXIV, p. 44.
[2] Ibid. vol. CI, p. 165.
[3] 26 January 1905. Unnumbered. General. New Zealand still regards the Additional Act as applying to it in virtue of the British signature.
[4] B.F.S.P. vol. CXII, p. 779.
[5] Cmd. 1987.
[6] Cmd. 2768.
[7] Cmd. 2763, p. 27.

Evolution of the British Empire and Commonwealth 47

Although some authorities took this as implying the juridical identity of the Dominions and Great Britain, with the consequence that the latter would alone be internationally responsible for breach of treaty by the former, in fact this theory was quickly demonstrated to be untenable when the normal method of treaty-making came to be intergovernmental contracting, with the Dominions signing in their own right, and when the treaty in Head-of-State form fell rapidly into disuse.

This history of the evolution of the older Dominions to plenary competence in treaty-making seems to establish that the attainment of Dominion status was (before the theoretical reconstruction of the Commonwealth that occurred in 1949 and the obsolescence of the 'Dominion' notion) an instance of State succession. There has been a tendency to reject this view and regard the *inter se* doctrine of Commonwealth treaty relations as creating a screen around the whole Commonwealth, so that devolution occurred in circumstances of insulation from the operation of ordinary rules of international law, and exclusively for reasons of constitutional law; that in consequence what occurred was not succession in the international law sense.[1] Apart from the fact that the *inter se* doctrine[2] proved ephemeral, and was breached by treaty-application devices and legislative implementation almost as soon as it was devised, it was never more than a doctrine of treaty construction to the effect that, unless otherwise stated, a multilateral treaty was not to operate *inter se* the members of the Commonwealth, just as bilateral agreements *inter se* were to be construed as governed by municipal law and not international law (if, in fact, governed by law at all). It raised no implications for the multipartite *vincula juris* forged by a single Imperial act between a foreign power and several British territories whose autonomy was ever on the increase.

III. The Statute of Westminster, 1931

The Balfour Declaration of 1926[3] undoubtedly stated the constitutional and international position of the Dominions, but the exceptional position occupied by the legislative process in the British Constitution prompted

---

1 Lester, *loc. cit.*
2 See generally Keith, *Constitutional Law of the British Dominions* (1933), p. 82; *Speeches and Documents on the British Dominions, 1918–1931*, pp. 410–17; Latham, *The Law and the Commonwealth* (1937); Noel-Baker, *The Present Juridical Status of the Dominions in International Law* (1929); Stewart, *Treaty Relations of the British Commonwealth* (1939), p. 351; Wade and Phillips, *Constitutional Law* (4th ed., 1950), p. 191; Jennings in *B.Y.* vol. xxx (1953), p. 320; Mervyn Jones in *B.Y.* vol. xxv (1948), p. 160; Imperial Conference, 1926, Cmd. 2768; Imperial Conference, 1930, Cmd. 3717, pp. 22–4. Fawcett, *The British Commonwealth in International Law* (1963), ch. 15.
3 Cmd. 2768, p. 14.

doubts whether the courts would be competent to give effect to the statement without legislative direction. Hence, after a further Imperial Conference in 1930, the Statute of Westminster[1] was enacted. This affected Canada, South Africa and Eire immediately, but the vital sections were withheld from effect in relation to Australia, New Zealand or Newfoundland until those sections should be adopted by the Parliaments of those Dominions. Australia adopted the Act in 1942[2] and New Zealand in 1947.[3] Newfoundland had not adopted it when transferred to Canada in 1949. The legislative technique of guaranteeing complete internal independence to the Dominions was to recite in the preamble the Balfour Declaration that the Crown was the symbol of free association; that no alteration in the Succession to the Throne or the Royal Style and Titles should occur without the assent of all the Dominion Parliaments; that no law of the Parliament of the United Kingdom should henceforth extend to the Dominions without their request and consent; and then to repeal the Colonial Laws Validity Act[4] in its relation to the legislature of any Dominion (the Australian States remained unaffected), and state positively that the Dominion Parliaments might legislate repugnantly to legislation of the United Kingdom.[5] The other doctrines of imperial constitutional law were cancelled expressly or by implication in their relationship to the Dominions. Thus, the latter were empowered to legislate extraterritorially[6] and, in virtue of the grant of power to legislate repugnantly, they ceased to be affected by the constitutional requirement of reservation of bills.[7]

The removal of legislative constraints upon the Dominions in virtue of the Statute of Westminster was not accompanied by the removal of prerogative restraints, and hence independence in the external order did not match independence in the internal order. The Crown, in legal theory, remained one and indivisible, and, since contradictory advice offered it by several governments in the matter of foreign affairs seemed logically impossible, the conclusion continued to be drawn by many constitutional authorities that United Kingdom Ministers occupied a paramount position in the matter of committing the Dominions in international relations. Dominion status was thus not equivalent to complete independ-

[1] 22 Geo. V, c. 4.   [2] No. 56 of 1942.   [3] No. 38 of 1947.
[4] See *supra*, p. 37.   [5] S. 2.
[6] S. 3. But not the constituent elements of the federations.
[7] Except the Australian States. Sometimes constitutional amendments must be made by U.K. Act. For example, in 1960, s. 99 of the British North America Act, 1867 was amended by The British North America Act, 1960, 9 & 10 Eliz. II, c. 2, because the Statute of Westminster did not confer power on the Canadian Parliament to amend its Constitution.

ence. Once, however, the structure of legislative unity was demolished, an accretion of competence in the matter of foreign affairs was inevitable, and even before the Statute of Westminster the mysterious process whereby the Crown ceased to be unitary and became divisible had set in. The process was completed at the outbreak of war in 1939,[1] and was formally recognized with respect to the Royal Style and Titles[2] upon the accession of Queen Elizabeth II. In the outcome, the relationship between the monarchies of the Commonwealth is that of personal union, achieved not by the coalescence of two Crowns but by the fragmentation of a corporation sole, and it is indistinguishable from the union between Great Britain and Hanover in 1714. This has reduced the Commonwealth to a voluntary association, of virtually no constitutional status, and much less organic than the French system of co-operation, which remains enmeshed in political and economic bonds contrived by treaty.

3. THE EVOLUTION OF THE OTHER COMMONWEALTH COUNTRIES

I. Pre-independence Autonomy

The existence of a local legislature, while not a precondition for the evolution of a local legal order, separate from that of the United Kingdom, was nonetheless its inevitable accompaniment. In India the Charter Act of 1833[3] created a central legislature by withdrawing power to legislate by regulation from the Presidencies and enlarging the Governor-General's Council. At this stage the executive and the legislature were fused; and although the creation of a Legislative Council in 1858[4] achieved some separation of functions, the fusion was continued by the empowering in 1861[5] of the Governor-General to legislate by ordinance, which would have the same authority as Acts of the Legislature. In 1909[6] the Central Legislature was enlarged, and in 1919[7] transformed into a bicameral organ. The final step to complete Parliamentary Government was the Government of India Act, 1935[8] which federated the country, and obliged the Viceroy to consult his Ministers, though not necessarily to accept their advice.

The Regulating Act of 1773[9] provided that the Presidencies might not make any treaty with any of the Indian Princes or Powers without the

1 O'Connell in *I.C.L.Q.* vol. VI (1957), p. 103.   2 1 & 2 Eliz. II, c. 9.
3 3 & 4 W. IV, c. 85.   4 21 & 22 Vict., c. 106.
5 24 & 25 Vict., c. 67.   6 9 Edw. VII, c. 4.
7 9 & 10 Geo. V, c. 101.   8 25 & 26 Geo. V, c. 42.
9 13 Geo. III, c. 63, s. 9. Ghosh, *Treaties and Federal Constitutions* (1961), p. 56.

consent of the Governor-General in Council, except in cases of imminent necessity. This provision remained on the statute book during the nineteenth century, though not acted upon. The implication favoured a treaty-making capacity in the Central Government; but since treaty-making remained a Crown prerogative, specific delegation would in each instance have been required from Whitehall. The Schedule to the Devolution Rules under Section 45 A of the Government of India Act, 1919[1] separated external relations from relations with States in India, but made the Governor-General in Council responsible to the Secretary of State for India with respect to both. There was no general delegation of the prerogative of treaty making to the Governor-General, but only a specific delegation from time to time. Conventions signed 'for India' usually included a territorial application provision whereby application would be withheld from the Indian States until these had agreed to enforce them in their territories. In 1927 an understanding was reached with the International Labour Organization whereby I.L.O. conventions ratified by India would apply only to British India. In the Government of India Act, 1935, the power to legislate with respect to external affairs and the implementation of treaties was made exclusive to the federation,[2] but ratification continued to remain a prerogative function.

The development of India's separate status in treaty-making is roughly coincidental with that of the Dominions. As early as 1883[3] India gained the right of separate accession to and withdrawal from commercial treaties, although the officers who participated in their negotiation remained responsible to the British Cabinet through the Governor-General, unlike the representatives of the Dominions who were responsible to their own legislatures.[4] This situation prevailed until 1947.

The process whereby the Federation of Rhodesia and Nyasaland evolved in international status (before its dissolution in 1963) is reminiscent more of that of the older Dominions than of that of India. In 1945[5] a Central African Council was established linking the colony of Southern Rhodesia, which had enjoyed responsible government since 1923,[6] and the Protectorates of Northern Rhodesia and Nyasaland; and eventually in 1953[7] a federation was established by United Kingdom legislation. Complete internal independence was achieved except in respect of bills to

1 9 & 10 Geo. V, c. 101, sch. I, pt. II, nos. 2, 3.
2 S. 100 (1).
3 The British-Italian Commercial Treaty, Hertslet, vol. XV, p. 776; also the 1900 treaty with Honduras, Cd. 254.
4 Ghosh, *op. cit.* p. 17.
5 Franck, *Race and Nationalism* (1960), p. 36.
6 S.R. & O. 1078.   7 1 & 2 Eliz. II, c. 30.

Evolution of the British Empire and Commonwealth

amend the Constitution, some of which had to be reserved, and some of which were restricted altogether. The ultimate power to dissolve the federation remained in the United Kingdom; and in the United Nations the view has been taken that the Federation remained a dependent territory affected by the Charter provisions relating to self-determination. So far as external affairs are concerned, no grant of competence was included in the Federal Constitution, but delegations of the prerogative of treaty-making were made.[1]

That the Statute of Westminster was declaratory of the legal situation reached by the self-governing parts of the Empire has been recognized by implication by the United Kingdom in relation to Southern Rhodesia. The United Kingdom stated in a White Paper of June 1961:

> The constitution of 1923 conferred responsible government on Southern Rhodesia. Since then it has become an established convention for Parliament at Westminster not to legislate for Southern Rhodesia on matters within the competence of the Legislative Assembly of Southern Rhodesia, except with the agreement of the Southern Rhodesia Government.[2]

Therefore, although Southern Rhodesia was not specifically covered by legislation equivalent to the Statute of Westminster, legislative independence, it has been argued,[3] had been achieved by the grant of responsible government. The implication for treaty-making is that no United Kingdom treaty could be applied to Southern Rhodesia which required legislative implementation, without Southern Rhodesia's participation.

Apart from Ceylon and Burma, and the West Indian territories, evolution to independence has occurred elsewhere in the Commonwealth in a somewhat similar fashion, though the process through representative to responsible government and then to independence has been more rapid. Legislative Councils had existed in West Africa since the middle of the nineteenth century, but it was not until after the Second World War that an unofficial African majority was introduced, and not until after 1950 that the responsibility of the Cabinet to the legislature was fully achieved. In East Africa, Legislative Councils were set up after the Second World War, but completely representative assemblies were not created until the 1950s. In Somaliland the Governor and the Executive Council ruled. In none of these instances was there any delegation of the prerogative of foreign affairs.

[1] See *infra*, vol. II, p.172. For dissolution of the Federation, see *infra*, vol. II, pp. 172–8.
[2] Cmnd. 1399.
[3] Correspondence between Her Majesty's Government and the Government of Southern Rhodesia: Cmnd. 2000.

II. The Technique of Granting Independence

The older Dominions achieved independence by evolution and not by specific grant. The first deliberate action to grant independence was with respect to Burma, followed closely by India and Ceylon. A distinction, however, was drawn between the first of these countries and the other two, which has dominated the draftsmanship on subsequent occasions. Burma did not wish to remain in the Commonwealth, and hence it was legislatively severed from the British Constitution.[1] India and Pakistan, however, were deliberately placed in the same legal position as the older Dominions, and in the official parlance of the period were described as having attained Dominion status.[2] The distinction first drawn in 1947 has crystallized between independence with retention of the royal prerogative and independence with republican status. At one time it was considered that the latter form of independence implied automatic exclusion from the Commonwealth, even though in 1949 it had been decided that a monarchy within the Commonwealth might opt to become a republic and yet remain within the Commonwealth. So, Burma automatically ceased to be part of the Commonwealth upon withdrawal of the royal prerogative. Views have, however, altered. When Cyprus and Zambia wished to retain the Commonwealth connexion and yet become republics, this was conceded.

(a) Grant of independence as a republic (or foreign monarchy)

The Burmese Independence Act[3] is described as an Act to provide for the independence of Burma as a country not within His Majesty's dominions and not entitled to His Majesty's protection, and for consequential and connected matters. The first operative section implements this formula. Section 2 deals with the persons who ceased to be British subjects. Section 3 provides for the retention of certain customs privileges under United Kingdom customs enactments. Section 4 abates appeals to the Privy Council and suits under the Government of Burma Act not pending, but preserves the jurisdiction of United Kingdom courts in respect of the Indian and Colonial Divorce Jurisdiction Acts. Section 5 repeals references to Burma in fifty-four statutes, with the proviso that if, by the law of Burma, any of these enactments, which included the Admiralty Jurisdiction, Colonial Courts, Interpretation, Merchant Shipping and

---

1 Burma Independence Act, 1947, 11 & 12 Geo. VI, c. 3.
2 Indian Independence Act, 1947, 10 & 11 Geo. VI, c. 30. For discussion on techniques of independence of Dominions see Fischer in *Annuaire français* (1962), p. 805.
3 11 & 12 Geo. VI, c. 3.

Extradition Acts, continue to be part of the law of Burma they should be recognized as such in the United Kingdom. Further, all references to Burma in all instruments and other enactments should not in future include references to the independent country of Burma, provided that any power to make a new order under such enactments in relation to independent Burma should not be affected.

Article 226 of the Burmese Constitution provides that, subject to the Constitution and to the extent to which they are not inconsistent therewith, the existing laws should continue to be in force until the same or any of them shall have been repealed or amended by a competent legislature or other competent authority, but the expression 'existing laws' was defined in the interpretation section to mean only laws made by legislatures 'within the Union of Burma'. Therefore, presumably, no United Kingdom statutory law survived in Burma, irrespective of the repeal provisions of the Burmese Independence Act.[1]

The Cyprus Act, 1960[2] is entitled an Act to make provision for, and in connexion with, the establishment of an independent republic in Cyprus. It provides for the Crown by Order in Council to declare the constitution of Cyprus to be in effect, and establishes on that day the Republic of Cyprus. It then states that 'Her Majesty shall have no sovereignty or jurisdiction over the Republic of Cyprus'. Section 3 provides that 'only existing law which operates as law of, or of any part of, the United Kingdom being a law applying in relation to Cyprus' shall, subject to subsequent repeal, continue to apply in like manner in relation to the Republic of Cyprus. 'Existing law' is defined to mean Act of Parliament, enactment or instrument, and any rule of law which was in force on the date of independence. Article 188 of the Cyprus Constitution continues in force all laws not contradictory to the Constitution. The Schedule to the Cyprus Act makes certain consequential amendments to several United Kingdom Acts, mainly by adding the expression 'Republic of Cyprus'. Whereas, therefore, Burma continued no United Kingdom statutory law, Cyprus, despite its becoming a Republic, did so, with the consequence that, although a Republic, Cyprus has remained one of 'Her Majesty's dominions or possessions' within the meaning of statutory enactments.

The Federation of Malaya Act, 1957[3] adopted a different formula altogether. Owing to the fact that the Federation was protected, it was only necessary for Parliament to approve the conclusion by Her Majesty

1 Cf. Maung Maung, *Burma's Constitution* (1959), p. 211.
2 8 & 9 Eliz. II, c. 52.
3 5 & 6 Eliz. II, c. 60.

of an agreement with the Rulers of the Malay States for the establishment of the Federation as an independent sovereign country 'within the Commonwealth'. No legislative withdrawal of the Crown's jurisdiction was required. The peculiar effect of this provision was to achieve Malaya's membership in the Commonwealth by Act of Parliament of one only of the Commonwealth members, although Malaya, while not becoming a republic, ceased to be under Her Majesty's sovereignty. Section 2 contained a formula for survival of existing law which was the model for that adopted in the case of Cyprus. The consequential provisions schedule is more extensive than in the case of Cyprus. Certain sections of the Army Act and the Air Force Act were repealed in relation to Malaya, but Malayan forces were included in the Visiting Forces (British Commonwealth) Act, 1933, with consequential change in the Visiting Forces Act, 1952. The Merchant Shipping Acts, with two consequential changes, are specified to continue to apply in relation to the Federation as they apply in relation to the other Commonwealth members, but the copyright legislation ceased in relation to the Federation.

Since the fusion of Sabah, Sarawak and Singapore with Malaya to form Malaysia involved the withdrawal of Her Majesty's sovereignty and jurisdiction therefrom, it was necessary for United Kingdom legislation to achieve this.[1] Reference had also to be made to operation of existing law and to appeals from the State Courts to the Supreme Court of Malaya.

The British Protectorate of Somaliland became independent on 26 June 1960 by Proclamation of Her Majesty, and provision for the government of the territory was made by the Somaliland Independence Order in Council.[2] Zanzibar became independent on 3 December 1963,[3] and provision was made for continuity of existing law.[4] The Constitution of Zambia, as a Republic, was enacted by Order in Council[5] pursuant to the Foreign Jurisdiction Act, 1890[6], and the Zambia Independence Act, 1964.[7] Apart from saving existing laws,[8] it provided for the succession of the Republic to the Crown's rights and obligations.[9]

[1] Malaysia Act 1963, c. 35.
[2] S.I. 1960, no. 1060.
[3] The Zanzibar Act, 1963, c. 55, provided for continuity of certain Acts referring to Zanzibar.
[4] The Zanzibar Independence Order in Council, S.I. 1962, no. 2784.
[5] The Zambia Independence Order in Council, S.I. 1964, no. 1652.
[6] 53 & 54 Vict., c. 37.
[7] C. 65, s. 65.
[8] S. 4. See *infra*, p. 119.
[9] Ss. 19, 20.

Evolution of the British Empire and Commonwealth

(b) Grant of independence as a monarchy

The Indian Independence Act[1] specifically referred to 'two independent Dominions'. Section 7 provided that His Majesty's Government in the United Kingdom should have no responsibility as respects the government of any of the territories of British India, and that his suzerainty over the Indian States lapsed with all treaties or agreements relating to the tribal areas. Section 8 made provision for transitional government of each Dominion by a Constituent Assembly, and section 9 for the issuing of Orders to bring the Act into effect. Section 18 provided for continuity of existing laws, and their application to each Dominion.[2] At that stage the only consequential legislative amendments which were necessary were those respecting the Armed Forces.

The Ceylon Independence Act[3] did not refer to 'Dominion' but to 'fully responsible status', and the legislative device by which this status was achieved was the extension of the fundamental provisions of the Statue of Westminster to Ceylon, placing it thereby in precisely the same legal situation as Australia, New Zealand or Canada. Certain consequential provisions were incorporated, mainly substituting the expression 'Dominion' for 'Colony' in relevant legislation, and terminating the applicability of legislation referring to 'Colonies'.

The presumption that retention of the monarchical link involves only minimal consequential changes upon independence has dominated the draftsmanship in all subsequent cases. The Ghana Independence Act, 1957[4] followed closely the pattern of the Ceylon Independence Act, and has been followed in turn by the Acts relating to Sierra Leone,[5] Jamaica,[6] Trinidad and Tobago,[7] Kenya,[8] Malta[9] and the Gambia[10] and, subject to their transformation into Her Majesty's Dominions, Tanganyika,[11] Uganda,[12] and Malawi.[13]

When India became a Republic in 1949 it was recognized that further changes in law would result, which would require additional legislation. Accordingly, the Indian Independence (Consequential Provisions) Act[14] was enacted, which has become standard in the case of all independent Commonwealth countries becoming republics after a period of retention

1 10 & 11 Geo. VI, c. 30.
2 See *infra*, p. 116.
3 11 & 12 Geo VI, c. 7.
4 5 & 6 Eliz. II, c. 6.
5 1961, 9 & 10 Eliz. II, c. 16.
6 1962, 10 & 11 Eliz. II, c. 40.
7 1962, 10 & 11 Eliz. II, c. 54.
8 1963, c. 54.
9 1964, c. 86.
10 1964, c. 93.
11 1961, 10 & 11 Eliz. II, c. 1.
12 1962, 10 & 11 Eliz. II, c. 57.
13 1964, c. 46; Malawi Independence Order in Council, S.I. 1964, no. 916.
14 India (Consequential Provisions) Act, 1949, 12, 13 & 14 Geo. VI, c. 92.

of the monarchy. Similar Acts were passed in relation to Ghana,[1] Tanganyika,[2] Nigeria,[3] Uganda[4] and Kenya.[5] The formula adopted in these Acts is to recite the intention of the countries concerned to become republics 'while remaining' members of the Commonwealth, and then to provide that the fact of their becoming republics is to have no effect on the operation of existing law, except that by Order in Council legislation may be modified. In the case of Ghana, the only modification thus effected was with respect to the Colonial Stock Acts.[6]

The effect of these Consequential Provisions Acts has been to achieve the continuity *mutatis mutandis* of United Kingdom legislation in respect to the countries concerned, but only within the legal systems of the United Kingdom, colonies, protectorates, and Southern Rhodesia. In virtue of the Independence Acts, these later enactments have had no effect upon the internal laws of the countries concerned, which, if they do not enact in like fashion, achieve survival of the legislation only by drastically extended interpretation. In the case of India, for example, the question whether India can any longer be described as one of 'Her Majesty's dominions' or a 'British possession' within the meaning of legislation has been controverted,[7] though, in virtue of the Indian (Consequential Provisions) Act, an English court is obliged to hold that India falls within this definition.[8]

There is, therefore, a remarkable difference in the situation which resulted in the change to a republican form of government, in the case of those countries which remained within the Commonwealth, from that achieved *tout d'un coup* in the case of Burma. Commonwealth membership has thus proved a catalytic factor in the legal results of a grant of independence. This is more clearly evidenced in the case of South Africa, which became a republic and withdrew from the Commonwealth in 1962. The United Kingdom enacted[9] to implement a standstill arrangement, and modify certain legislation, such as the Fugitive Offenders Act,[10] which had been enacted for the Empire but had been incorporated piecemeal into the Commonwealth system. South Africa enacted[11] to bring

1 1960, 8 & 9 Eliz. II, c. 41. 2 1962, 11 & 12 Eliz. II, c. 1.
3 1963, c. 57. 4 1964, c. 20.
5 1965, c. 5
6 The Ghana (Consequential Provisions) Colonial Stock Acts) Order in Council, S.I. 1960, no. 969.
7 See *infra*, p. 122.
8 See *infra*, p. 123.
9 The South Africa Act, 1962, 10 & 11 Eliz. II, c. 23.
10 *Ibid.* 4th sch. The Act was repealed in relation to South Africa by the Fugitive Offenders (South Africa) Order in Council, S.I. 1963, no 613.
11 The Commonwealth Relations Act, no. 69 of 1962.

about consequential changes respecting diplomatic privileges,[1] companies,[2] merchant shipping,[3] and colonial stock.[4] The Commonwealth Merchant Shipping Agreement, 1931[5] was considered to have lapsed in the case of South Africa, but not the Ottawa Trade Agreement of that year, which still secures commercial advantages for South African goods. South Africa retained Imperial legislation which had been applied to it, but provided for its adaptation to the new situation.[6]

One further point must be noticed: in the case of those territories which had not been Crown colonies, such as Tanganyika which had been a Trust Territory, and Uganda and Malawi which had been Protectorates, and which wished for a period to retain the monarchical connexion with the United Kingdom, an additional formula was introduced into the opening sections of the Independence Acts providing for the territories to be Her Majesty's Dominions. The effect of this has been to achieve, in the very act by which independence was granted, the application to the countries concerned of Acts of the United Kingdom Parliament affecting the Crown's Dominions but not other dependent territories.

The curious feature of this process is that the draftsmanship of the Independence Acts has allegedly determined the extent to which the new States continue British statutory law, and even the extent to which they become affected by it in the instant of independence. If the constitutions of the new States reflect these provisions precisely, there can be no question of the effects in the legal systems of both the United Kingdom and the new State; but in the event of their failing to do so, it is just arguable, as the Supreme Court of Pakistan has decided,[7] that the effect of the legislation is restricted to United Kingdom law.[8]

1 S. 61.
2 Ss. 3, 4.
3 Ss. 31–60.
4 S. 11.
5 Cmd. 3994; *B.F.S.P.* vol. CXXXIV, p. 318; *L.N.T.S.* vol. 129, p. 177.
6 The Republic of South Africa Constitution Act, no. 32 of 1961. S. 3.
7 *Barlas Brothers (Karachi) and Co.* v. *Yangtze (London) Ltd*, Pakistan Legal Decisions, vol. XI (1961), p. 573.
8 Consequential provisions legislation has also been enacted by Ghana: Federation of Nigeria Act, 1961, Act no. 35; Republic of Cyprus Act, 1961, no. 72; Republic of South Africa Act, 1961, no. 61; Sierra Leone Act, 1961, no. 74; and by New Zealand: Republic of India Act, 1950, no. 14; Republic of Ireland Act, 1950, no. 13; Republic of Pakistan Act, 1956, no. 10; Republic of Ghana Act, 1960, no. 6; Republic of Cyprus Act, 1961, no. 14; Republic of Nigeria Act, 1963, no. 58; Republic of Tanganyika Act, 1963, no. 1; Uganda Act, 1964, no. 21; Republic of Kenya Act, 1965, no. 51; Republic of Zambia Act, 1965, no. 50.

Chapter 3

EVOLUTION OF THE FRENCH COMMUNITY AND FRANCOPHONE STATES

I. THE PRE-INDEPENDENCE SITUATION

There is a temptation to compare the evolution of the French Community with that of the Commonwealth, but, while the comparison is in certain respects apt, there are significant differences between the processes by which independence has been granted to British territories, and those by which it has been attained by French territories. The French Community, as conceived, exhibited the ordinary characteristics of an international entity, with a conventional foundation, a secretariat-general, and a complex of rights and duties akin to those which arise in the case of economic and political organizations of a more traditional character. The evolution of the Community has also been somewhat different, with formal institutional changes occurring at recognizable intervals. The relevant dates are 1946, 1956, 1958 and 1960.[1]

I. The French Union of 1946

The Constitution of the Fourth Republic created in Title VIII the French Union, comprising metropolitan France and the Overseas Departments and Territories on the one hand, and on the other the Associated Territories and States, each of which defined its relationship with France in a particular manner. The organs of the Union were: the Presidency, occupied *ex officio* by the President of the French Republic; the High Council, presided over by the President and composed of delegates from France and each Associated State, whose function was to assist the government in the general conduct of the affairs of the Union; and an Assembly composed half of representatives of metropolitan France and half of members representing the Overseas Departments and Territories and the Associated States, these being elected by the respective Assemblies.

The Overseas Territories were to be given a special status which took

---

[1] Pierson-Mathy in *Évolution politique de l'Afrique, Chronique de politique étrangère*, vol. XIV (1961), pp. 1–236; Gonidec in *Public Law* (1960), p. 177; de Lacharrière in *Annuaire français* (1960), p. 9; Borella, in *ibid.* (1960), p. 925; Feuer, in *ibid.* (1961), p. 762; Gandolfi in *Rev. jur. et pol.* vol. XVII (1963), p. 202; Gharsallah, in *ibid.* p. 235; Fischer in *Annuaire français* (1962), p. 827. The most complete summary of the system of co-operation as it affects the Malagasy Republic is by Conac and Feuer in *Annales Malgaches*, vol. I (1964), p. 111.

into account their particular interests within the framework of the general interests of the Union. Those interests were to be determined by the Assembly of the Union. In each Overseas Territory an elective Assembly was to be instituted, whose powers were to be determined by French legislation. The Overseas Territories also sent representatives to the National Assembly and the Council of the Republic. All nationals of the Overseas Territories were stated to have French nationality and citizenship in the same capacity as French nationals of metropolitan France. But the exercise of their rights as citizens would be determined by special laws. At the same time, all citizens and nationals of territories within the French Union would have the status of citizens of the French Union, which ensured them the enjoyment of the rights and liberties guaranteed by the Constitution.

Under the Constitution of the Fourth Republic the following had the status of Overseas Territories: Senegal, Mauritania, Soudan, Guinea, Ivory Coast, Volta, Dahomey, Niger, all constituting French West Africa; Gabon, Congo, Ubangi-Shari, and Chad, all constituting French Equatorial Africa; and Madagascar, French Somaliland, St Pierre and Miquelon, the Comoro Archipelago, and the Pacific Islands.

II. The Loi-cadre of 23 June 1956

In 1956 a *loi-cadre* of the French Parliament, pursuant to the Constitutional provisions just discussed, gave the Overseas Territories internal autonomy and permitted their local Assemblies to elect to the Executive Councils ministers responsible to the Assemblies. The situation thus arrived at was comparable with that reached in the British cases of Canada, New Zealand and the Australian colonies in the middle of the nineteenth century. In July 1958 the chairmanship of the government councils was transferred to elected prime ministers.

In the actual operation of the French Union between 1946 and 1960 the tendency was for France to devise various forms of differentiation between citizens of metropolitan France and French nationals of the Overseas Territories, particularly in the electoral mechanism and in the proportion of representation in the French legislature. Confronted with a developing self-consciousness in Africa, French politics sought a federal solution to the problems that increasingly manifested themselves. The grant of local autonomy failed to satisfy local aspirations, and at the same time it induced anxiety among the European residents and administrators with respect to interests such as public order, the treasury, personal rights and social legislation. Federalism appeared to be an attractive technique for reconciling these differences, but since it implied a division of power with a reservation to the metropolitan authorities of the most important matters, including foreign policy, defence and utilization of common resources, it was fundamentally unacceptable to nationalist opinion, and inevitably was a short-lived experiment. Hence developments under the Constitution of 1958 occurred in two stages at short intervals, and culminated in full independence.

III. The Community of 4 October 1958

The word 'Community' was devised as a substitute for the word 'Union' in the Constitution of the Fifth Republic, and Title XII was devoted to its fundamental characteristics.[1] Generally speaking, the new scheme represented no radical departure from the old.[2] The Preamble recited the principle of free determination of peoples, but the remainder of the Constitution is inspired with the hope that the inevitable consequences of the recognition of this principle could be avoided. Article I states that the Republic and the peoples of the Overseas Territories, by adopting the present Constitution by an act of free determination, form a Community. This was interpreted as implying that a negative vote would be one for secession. The only State which voted negatively was Guinea, and it was immediately stated by the French Government that in virtue of this fact Guinea was separated from the other territories of French West Africa, which had approved the Constitution, and the Constitution would not, therefore, be promulgated in Guinea. On 2 October the Territorial Assembly of Guinea voted for independence without any objection being raised on the part of the French Government, although the latter temporarily adjourned recognition *de jure*.[3] Independence was available for the other member States of the Community in virtue of article 86, which reads as follows:

A change in the status of a member State of the Community may be requested either by the Republic or by a resolution of the legislative assembly of the State concerned, confirmed by a local referendum organized and supervised by the institutions of the Community. The actual change is effected by an agreement approved by the Parliament of the Republic and the legislative assembly concerned.

A member State of the Community may become independent by the same means. It then ceases to belong to the Community.

1 *Journal Officiel*, 5 October 1958, p. 9151. The *ordonnances* of 19 December 1958 containing the *lois organiques de la Communauté* were put into effect in *Journal Officiel*, 20 December 1958, p. 11455.
2 Borella in *Annuaire français* (1958), p. 659; Kirsch in *Rev. jur. et pol.* vol. XIV (1960), p. 334; Ordonneau, in *ibid.* vol. XVI (1962), p. 541.
3 Fischer in *Annuaire français* (1958), p. 711; Erhard, *Communauté ou Sécession* (1959).

The effect of action under this article would be that a member State becoming independent would cease to belong to the Community.

Article 76 reads as follows:

The overseas territories may keep their status within the Republic. If they express the wish, by formal deliberation in their territorial assembly within the time limit prescribed in the first paragraph of article 91, they become either overseas departments of the Republic or, separately or grouped together, member States of the Community.

This gave the member States the faculty of choosing to enter the status of Department, Territory or Member of the Community. The only regions which opted for the quality of a Department overseas were Guadeloupe, Martinique, Réunion and Cayenne. The States which maintained the *status quo* were Somaliland, Comores, New Caledonia, French Polynesia, St Pierre and Miquelon. These remained within the Republic with the rights resulting from the Decree of Autonomy conferred by the law of 23 June 1956 and the decrees made in execution thereof.

Article 78 states that by special agreements the jurisdiction of the Community might be transferred from the Community to one of its members. The implication of this article is that, should the matters referred to as being within the Community's jurisdiction, namely, foreign policy, defence, currency, common economic and financial policy, and policy concerning strategic raw materials, be conveyed to the members, these would have achieved virtual independence through being invested with all the incidents of sovereignty.

In the belief that unity of direction by a sort of presidential federation could be achieved, and the dissolution of the French overseas system thus avoided, the Constitution provided for organs of centripetal operation. The Community would contribute to the election of the French President through the participation of the Assemblies of the Overseas Territories, and, by agreement of the member States, in the workings of the electoral college. Article 80 provides that the President of the Community is the President of the French Republic. The primary characteristics of the system as designed were (*a*) international unity and (*b*) centralization of power in respect of common matters.

(*a*) *International unity*

According to article 77 there is only one citizenship of the Community, although this did not exclude the possibility of each of the member States having its own citizenship. Common citizenship is part and parcel of common foreign policy, and it was not long before the implications of this connexion became evident with the demand for transfer from the Community to the States of foreign policy jurisdiction under article 78. Initially the Community did not take on the aspects of a separate international person because, although the French Republic formed part of the Community, it occupied such a peculiar place that the expression 'member State' was in practice used only to designate the other States. By Presidential Decisions of 9 February[1] and 14 April 1959,[2] the unity of foreign policy was affirmed, and the subordination of the States of the Community to treaties already concluded by the French Republic was achieved. On the other hand, by Presidential decision of 12 June 1959,[3] it was envisaged that nationals of the States of the Community could be proposed by their governments for the diplomatic and consular service of the French Republic and for inclusion in French delegations in international conferences. About twenty diplomatic agents were in fact designated under this provision.

(b) Centralization

Article 78 includes among the competences of the Community, defence, currency, economic and financial policy, strategic matters, control of justice, higher education, the organization of common transport and telecommunications. But these were not exclusive powers in the traditional federal sense; for, on the one hand, the possibility of a partial or a total transfer of competence to the States was envisaged; and, on the other hand, the fact that a matter remained within the competence of the Community did not necessarily imply that it would be subject to a single authority exercising a totality of power. The competences of the Community could be extended to, as well as concurrently exercised by, each of the member States, according to different rules of co-operation or different procedures for harmonizing decisions. There were thus, at the same time, tendencies towards centralization of competence and towards greater autonomy in the exercise of Community competence on the part of the States. On 9 February 1959[4] the army was unified, and on 14 April 1959[5] the power to proclaim a state of emergency and to withdraw from member States the responsibility for public order was vested in the President of the Community. In the economic domain, on 12 June 1959[6] a decision was taken with respect to the unity of the franc zone, and consequential authority was vested in the minister charged with currency

1 *Journal Officiel de la Communauté*, 15 February 1959, p. 9.
2 *Ibid.* 15 April 1959, p. 24.
3 *Ibid.* 15 June 1959, p. 42.
4 Presidential Decision, *ibid.* 15 February 1959, p. 9.
5 Presidential Decision, *ibid.* 15 April 1959, p. 25.
6 Presidential Decision, *ibid.* 15 June 1959, p. 43.

and common economic and financial policy with respect to the regulation of exchange and its control. A decision of the same date maintained in the Community customs-free circulation of products originating in the member States. With respect to the control of justice, provision was made for a reference to the *Cour de Cassation*, and the prerogative of mercy was vested in the President. Regulations were also issued concerning higher education, transport and telecommunications.

The Community developed partly by means of organic laws and partly by Presidential decisions. The President acquired, in virtue of articles 91 and 92 (those relating to the implementation of the Community provisions of the Constitution), a significance greater than the text of Title XII would appear to confer on him. The functioning of the Executive Council and to some extent of the Senate and the Court of Arbitration was subject to Presidential power in the following respects:

Article 82 placed the Executive Council under the presidency of the President; it was composed of the Prime Minister of the French Republic, the heads of government of each of the member States and ministers in charge of Community affairs, and its function was to organize the co-operation of members of the Community at the governmental and administrative levels. As its chairman, the President had great power in the manipulation of the Council. By Ordinance of 19 December 1958 a mechanism was devised whereby the President could, of his own decision, vary the composition of the Council, convoke it, settle its agenda, appoint the ministers in charge of Community affairs, and be the authority for the implementation of the organic laws of the Community, its agreements and treaties, and decisions of the Court of Arbitration. The Ordinance of the same date respecting the Senate likewise extended the powers of the President in relation to the fixing of the agenda and to the deciding of its priorities. As to the Arbitration Court, the Constitution mentioned its existence only in article 84 dealing with litigation between members of the Community and with its jurisdiction. The Ordinance of the same date provided that its members would be nominated by the President, that he would draft its rules of procedure, and that he could ask for advisory opinions which would not be published, and which would be reserved for his own use.

The power which the President exercised in the Community unavoidably corresponded with that which he exercised in the Republic, and the result was something in the nature of a 'personal union', represented by the common chief of State, between two legal orders which in other respects remained distinct. The international unity of the Community could have led to the absorption of the external relationships of the Republic in the Community, but if this had occurred, the Republic would have risked losing its international personality.

2. THE CONVENTIONAL COMMUNITY OF 1960

The Constitutional Community had scarcely come into being when the pressure towards independence became irresistible. The logic pursued in the case of Guinea of excluding States from the Community in the event of independence ceased to be attractive because, when faced with the issue of membership of the Community or independence, the member States would clearly elect for a complete rupture. The only solution was a revision of the Community to permit continued participation after independence. Within the constitutional framework, independence could be achieved by article 86, resulting from the vote of the Assembly of a member State confirmed by a referendum controlled by the institutions of the Community, and effected by an agreement approved by legislation of both the French Republic and the legislative Assembly concerned. The effect of action under this article, however, was exclusion from the Community. A possible alternative technique was offered by article 78 (3) which provided for the transfer of Community competences to the member States. Action under this article would not involve expulsion from the Community, but the Constitutional Consultative Committee had gone on record to the effect that certain matters could not be transferred under this article, including foreign policy. Although the French Government and some of the States tended towards an interpretation in favour of action under article 78 (3) it was by no means certain that the United Nations, on application for membership, would regard the transfer of competences under the Constitution as qualifying for real independence and sovereignty.

The problem was posed by Mali's demand for independence at the end of 1959. The procedure of article 86 was rejected because of the risk of an adverse vote on the referendum which that article required. Accordingly, the Executive Council of the Community, at its sixth session in Senegal in December 1959, approved the utilization of the procedure in article 78, and the following day, General de Gaulle, as President of the Community, announced to the Federal Assembly of Mali that it could take steps to become independent, although he preferred to call them steps to international sovereignty.[1] This procedure, it was understood, did not require a constitutional revision.

However, the transfer of all the competences of a member State, if

[1] *Le Monde*, 15 December 1959.

Evolution of the Francophone States

permitted by article 78, raised implications with respect to other provisions of Title XII, for example article 77 (2) which refers to the common citizenship of the Community. Furthermore, the institutions of the Community, in their operation, depend upon the presumption that there are common competences. Therefore, to admit accession to independence in virtue of article 78 would seem to prevent a revision by means of agreement of the whole of the matters dealt with in the other provisions of Title XII. Negotiations with respect to the revision of these provisions in the case of Mali began in Paris in January 1960, when the French delegation asserted the need for a constitutional amendment. At the same time, Madagascar demanded the opening of similar negotiations, which began in Paris in February. Three sets of negotiations led to the seventh session of the Executive Council of the Community in March. Although its final communiqué simply declared that the Council had taken into consideration the progress of negotiations with Mali and Madagascar, it acknowledged the need for a constitutional amendment which would be as simple as possible, providing for compatibility between independence and membership of the Community, and permitting the fixing, by means of bilateral conventions, of the conditions of participation in the Community. The conventions with the Malagasy Republic were signed on 2 April 1960, and those with the Federation of Mali on 4 April, although the text of the constitutional amendment was not adopted by the French Government until 4 June 1960.[1] The procedure of article 85 was then used to revise the dispositions of Title XII, concerning the function of the common institutions. Having refused, in virtue of article 44 (3), any amendment to its bill, other than one of form, the French Government submitted a constitutional amendment to the National Assembly and the Senate, where it survived motions of rejection on the ground of unconstitutionality. In virtue of this legislation, a second clause was added to article 85:

Les dispositions du présent titre peuvent être également révisées par accords conclus entre tous les États de la Communauté; les dispositions nouvelles sont mises en vigueur dans les conditions requises par la Constitution de chaque État.

And a third, fourth and fifth to article 86:

AI. 3: Un État membre de la Communauté peut également, par voie d'accords, devenir indépendant sans cesser de ce fait d'appartenir à la Communauté.

AI. 4: Un État indépendant non membre de la Communauté peut, par voie d'accords, adhérer à la Communauté, sans cesser d'être indépendant.

[1] Loi constitutionnelle, no. 60/525, Journal Officiel, 8 June 1960, p. 5183.

AI. 5: La situation de ces États au sein de la Communauté est déterminée par les accords conclus à cet effet, notamment les accords visés aux alinéas précédents ainsi que, le cas échéant, les accords prévus au deuxième alinéa de l'article 85.

These paragraphs contained two sets of rules. The first permits accession of a State to independence within the Community. The second envisages that the Constitution of such a State and, as a result, the institutions of the Community depend only upon the signature of agreements. There are thus two techniques of independence, with the agreement of France or without it, and to these correspond two different procedures. Independence-association (with the agreement of France) is obtained by means of agreements of transfer of competences, while independence-secession (against the will of France) is obtained by means of a resolution of the Legislative Assembly of the State, confirmed by a local referendum organized and controlled by the Community. In both cases, the continuance of the new State in the Community depends upon subsequent agreement, and this means that adhesion to the Community is reopened to the States formerly under protection and trusteeship, as well as to Guinea.

The various States of the Community rapidly utilized the possibilities offered by this constitutional reform, none preferring autonomy to independence. The situation was complicated by Mali, the Federation of which dissolved on 20 August 1960, when Senegal decided to withdraw and proclaim its independence. The Soudanese Republic at first refused to accept this dissolution but, eventually recognizing the *fait accompli*, changed its name to the Republic of Mali on 22 September 1960, proclaimed its independence, and withdrew from the Community. France recognized the Republic of Senegal on 11 September and that of Mali on 26 September, and both States were admitted to the United Nations on 29 September.[1] There followed an exchange of notes between Senegal and France[2] in which the former recognized that, according to the principles of international law, it was totally subrogated in the agreements made between France and the Federation of Mali. By this means, Senegal continued its position in the Community.

The second group of States which acceded to independence and adhered to the Community is composed of the former territories of French Equatorial Africa, that is, Chad, Central African Republic, Congo and Gabon, the first three of which formed a Union of the Republics of Central Africa on 17 May 1960. This was described in the communiqué of the Executive Council of the Community as a Union of a confederal type,

---

[1] Gandolfi in *Annuaire français* (1960), p. 881.
[2] Decree no. 61-536, *Journal Officiel*, 2 June 1961, p. 4971; *Rev. gén. de droit int. pub.* vol. LXV (1961), p. 695.

suitable at some opportune time for being invested with attributes of international sovereignty,[1] so that it was clearly envisaged that a single international person might be substituted for the three constituent States. Gabon agreed only to maintain a customs and currency union with them, in addition to accepting a common system of defence and a harmonization of foreign policy. The agreements of transfer were signed by France and the three States of the Union on 12 July 1960 and with Gabon on 15 July 1960. The agreements involving adhesion to the Community were signed a month later.

The new Community comprises only seven former members, France, Senegal, Malagasy Republic, Gabon, Chad, Central Africa and Congo. Five States did not adhere to the Community: the Ivory Coast, Dahomey, Upper Volta, Niger and Mauritania. The first four demanded a transfer of all competences in virtue of article 78, but refused to sign any agreement of participation or co-operation until after their admission to the United Nations. Hence only agreements for the transfer of competences were signed. The technique of independence utilized by them, however, was that which, under the French Constitution, and hence in the eyes of French law, preserved various of the incidences of Community membership, such as the Community citizenship. The publication of the decree of the French law giving effect to the agreements of transfer on 29 July 1960 expressly states that the new States have become independent without ceasing, in virtue of this fact, to belong to the Community.[2]

The decision of Mauritania was peculiar. It was envisaged that upon independence Mauritania would sign agreements of co-operation, but independence occurred in face of the hostility of Morocco, which claimed Mauritanian territory. As there was no opposition in the United Nations to the admission of Mauritania, the latter decided to postpone signature of agreements with France until after its admission. The agreements of transfer were signed on 19 October 1960.

Subsequently all five States, and also Cameroon, signed agreements of co-operation with France. These cover most of the matters contained in the corresponding agreements made with the Community members. In addition, the Ivory Coast, Dahomey and Niger signed a defence agreement with France and Cameroon, and a judicial convention with France. While the technical result achieved by these agreements is to bring the countries into the closest possible economic, financial and judicial links with France, and thus into the essentials of the Community system, all six

1 *Le Monde*, 23 March 1960.
2 Decree no. 60-758, *Journal Officiel*, 30 July 1960, p. 7049.

States continue to remain formally outside the Community. It follows that the institutions of co-operation are bilateral, and are not necessarily those of the Community.

The slight changes effected in the Constitution in 1960 left the institutions of the Community unaffected, but since, apart from the Presidency, these were loosely defined and were to be given their character and accorded their actual functions by organic laws ranking as legislation and not as constitutional provisions, they were readily adaptable to the new situation. The President of the French Republic remained the President of the Community, but the Executive Council was transformed into a periodical Conference of the Heads of State and of Governments. Since it had no real power of decision, and each State was left to carry out its resolutions, it remained a forum of debate, subject to the rules of unanimity on the lines of the North Atlantic Council; should a member State resile from its affirmative vote this would involve no juridical consequences.[1] The interparliamentary Senate as it was envisaged was a modest affair. The comparison between it and the Assemblies of the European Communities seems at first sight apt, but in actuality the two bodies were radically dissimilar; the European Assemblies look towards an accession of competence with the developing centripetal pressure of European integration, whereas the Senate of the French Community represented the effort to preserve unity in dissolution.[2] In fact the Senate was still-born.

3. THE SYSTEM OF CO-OPERATION

The situation produced by the transfer of competences was ambiguous: those States which adhered to the Community in fact enjoy a relationship with France no different from that enjoyed by the other States which, while not adhering to the Community, signed agreements of co-operation; and, since not all the States have signed identical agreements, the actual links between them and France are not uniform, whether they adhered to the Community or not. Although the provisions of the French Constitution concerning the Community remain unchanged, they are effective only with respect to the territories under French sovereignty. Accordingly, the concept of the Community has been quietly abandoned, and replaced by that of co-operation. The system of co-operation is, in fact, no more than an aggregation of bilateral treaties between France on the one hand and each of the African States on the other, supplemented

---

1 De Lacharrière in *Annuaire français* (1960), p. 28.
2 Piquemal in *Rev. jur. et pol.* vol. XV (1961), p. 394. The Senate was instituted by *Ordonnance* no. 58–1255, *Journal Officiel*, 20 December 1958, p. 11455.

Evolution of the Francophone States 69

in some respects by agreements between the African States.[1] But in appreciating the process whereby these States have become successor States the system is of relevance inasmuch as it contrives the maximum legal continuity consistent with grants of independence. The co-operation agreements may be catalogued as follows:

1. Special Agreements on Participation in the Community
2. Co-operation Agreement in the Field of Foreign Affairs
3. Defence and Technical Military Assistance Agreements
4. Co-operation Agreements in Respect of Strategic Raw Materials
5. Co-operation Agreements in Monetary, Economic and Financial Matters
6. Co-operation Agreements in Matters of Higher Education
7. Co-operation Agreements in Matters of Civil Aviation
8. Co-operation Agreements in Matters of Merchant Navy
9. Co-operation Agreements in Matters of Justice
10. Convention on Establishment
11. Co-operation Agreement in Postal and Telecommunications Matters
12. Agreement on Cultural Co-operation
13. Multilateral Agreement on the Fundamental Rights of the Nationals of the States of the Community
14. Convention on Conciliation and the Arbitration Court

I. Agreements on Participation in the Community and the *Union Africaine et Malgache*

These emphasize the voluntary nature of the association. They specify that the States are members of the Community, and recognize the President of the French Republic to be *de jure* President of the Community, thereby disposing of any argument that his functions in relation to them stem from the French Constitution. Participation of both France and the Member States in Conference of Heads of State and of Government assembled under the chairmanship of the President is provided for, and the States are said to be entitled to send delegations to the Senate. The original Franco-Gabonese agreement merely confirmed membership of Gabon in the Community and referred to the co-operation agreements as specifying the conditions of participation, but subsequently an additional

[1] Plantey in *Rev. jur. et pol.* vol. XVIII (1964), p. 6; Ligot in *ibid.* vol. XVI (1962), p. 3; Gandolfi in *ibid.* vol. XVII (1963), p. 202; Conac and Feuer in *Annuaire français* (1960), p. 859, and in *Annales Malgaches*, vol. I (1964), p. 116. 'Panorama de la législation sur les conventions conclues par les pays africains d'expression française et par Madagascar, (Penant, 1964), pp. 271 *et seq.*; pp. 402 *et seq.*

special agreement was signed which contained provisions identical with those in the other agreements.[1]

The Community thus contrived is the result of bilateral agreements to which France is the only common party. All rights and duties are reciprocal, and it is left to the member States to create identical legal relationships *inter se*. In fact, the development of these relationships has virtually aborted the Community, and when the President of Senegal in 1963 proposed the assembling of the Conference envisaged in the agreements, but including also the non-Community Francophone States, the suggestion was coldly received. The linking of all the successor States with France in a multilateral system has therefore not been achieved. However, a multilateral system was brought about among the successor States by the creation of the *Union Africaine et Malgache* in 1961. This provided a structural framework of co-operation and consultation for twelve of the ex-French States, the actual links being constituted by a series of co-operation agreements,[2] namely:

1 L'Organisation Africaine et Malgache de Coopération Économique
2 L'Organisation du Pacte de Défense
3 L'Union Africaine et Malgache des Postes et Télécommunications
4 The General Convention Relative to Diplomatic Representation
5 The General Convention of Co-operation in the Matter of Justice
6 The General Convention Relative to the Situation of Persons and the Conditions of Establishment

The Union was transformed into an economic organization on the creation of the Organization of African Unity, but even as such it has retained the organic character of a francophone system.

To this extent, the deliberate continuity achieved by the system of co-operation has minimized the consequences of State succession. Other regional contrivances have reinforced this continuity. For example, the Customs Union of West Africa has been maintained throughout the process of independence (except for the withdrawal of Guinea in 1958) and has been supplemented by the Monetary Union of West Africa and Togo created in 1962; a similar Customs Union for Equatorial Africa has also been continued, and supplemented by the Monetary Union of Equatorial Africa and Cameroon; and the Ivory Coast, Dahomey, Upper Volta and Niger constitute the Council of the Entente, created before independence.

1 Decree no. 60–1231, *Journal Officiel*, 24 November 1960, p. 10480.
2 Lampué in *Rev. jur. et pol.* vol. XVIII (1964), p. 21; Ligot and Devernois in *ibid.* vol. XVI (1962), p. 339; Peureux in *ibid.* vol. XV (1961), p. 541.

II. The Co-operation Agreements

(a) *The diplomatic, economic and defence agreements*

The Agreements in the field of Foreign Affairs, apart from creating diplomatic and consular relations *inter se*, specify that the French Republic shall ensure that the interests of the States and their nationals shall be represented in countries where the States have no representation of their own, and provide for the seconding of diplomats from the States to offices of the French Republic and of the Community to watch over matters affecting the States. France and the States shall keep each other mutually informed and shall consult on matters of foreign policy.[1]

The Economic Co-operation Agreements maintain the principle of a reciprocal preferential operation between France and each State. They make reference to free circulation of merchandise as a possible eventuality. They also envisage co-ordination of commercial policy towards third States, and tariff policy towards foreign States is unified by means of a Mixed Commission according to policies laid down by the Conference of the Heads of State.

Agreements also achieve unity of policy with respect to strategic materials. They envisage the exchange of information, consultation and uniform policy; and, if the interests of defence require it, the exportation of strategic materials to other countries will be limited or forbidden. In the military sphere, the agreements provide for military aid, and, to guarantee homogeneity in the forces of the Community, each State agrees to resort only to France for purposes of training and supply of equipment. The French Army is permitted to recruit nationals of the Community States which permit the stationing and movement of French forces on their territory, air space and territorial sea.

The Defence Agreements envisage considerable technical assistance in the military domain and facilities for the French Army in the territories of other States.[2] They mention co-operation and mutual aid for the defence of the contracting parties and of the whole Community (with a common plan of defence and co-operation in the agreement with the Central African Republic, the Congo and Chad and an engagement to consult on any permanent matter in the agreements with the Malagasy Republic and Gabon) but contain no formal clause of guarantee. They seem to permit the participants to remain neutral in the event of a conflict involving one or other party.

1 Gandolfi in *Rev. jur. et pol.* vol. XVII (1963), p. 202.
2 Ligot in *ibid.* p. 517.

(b) The arbitration convention

By the Convention of 22 June 1960 on Conciliation and the Court of Arbitration signed by France, the Malagasy Republic and the Federation of Mali, and open to accession by other Community States, a Conciliation Commission was set up, formed by two delegates of each party, which is required to formulate initial recommendations within a period of six months. If these recommendations addressed to the parties do not lead to settlement, arbitration results from a *compromis* or a unilateral application to the Court. In default of agreement of the parties, jurisdiction is constituted by arbitrators nominated in advance, two by each State, and an umpire who has to be chosen, in the event of disagreement, according to the rules laid down, which confer on the President a significant role.

(c) The franc zone

The Economic and Technical Co-operation Agreements provided first of all for the continuation of the franc zone.[1] The logic of independence implies that each State is at liberty with respect to its own financial and foreign policy, and this is in fact recited in article I of the agreements. If there were not a national currency, it would be impossible for each State to balance its budget freely and decide its own loan policy. However, the agreements aim at unity of money among the Francophone States and recognize that this cannot be achieved if each State is submitted to independent fluctuations in the market of its external exchange. Under the Constitutional Community, the unitary franc zone implied a rigorous centralization of power in favour of the French Government, which alone could decide monetary policy. Under the system of co-operation, monetary policy is decided multilaterally. Agreements were entered into with the Federation of Mali on 22 June 1960, the Malagasy Republic on 27 June 1960, and with Chad, the Central African Republic, Congo and Gabon on 11, 13, 15 and 17 August 1960 respectively, with the object of maintaining a fixed relation between local moneys and the French franc, any modification of parity between them being subordinated to the agreement between the two States. Further, any modification of the relationship between the franc and foreign moneys could only occur after consultation with the States of the Community, and this involves the obligation upon France to take appropriate measures to safeguard the legitimate interests of the States. In the interests of maintaining the unity of the monetary block and the strength of the national currencies, credit is subject to complex rules.

[1] Piquemal in *ibid.* vol. XVI (1962), p. 437.

Evolution of the Francophone States

For example, the Malagasy Agreement entrusts the issuing of money to a public establishment, called the Malagasy Institute of Issue, which shall take over this function, during a transitionary period, from the Bank of Madagascar and the Comores. France guarantees the Malagasy issue, and maintains freedom of transfers between the two Republics. The Central African Republic, Congo, Chad and Gabon reserve currency issue to the Central Bank of the States of Equatorial Africa and the Comores. On 12 May 1962 a Co-operation Agreement was negotiated between France and the member Republics of the West African Monetary Union instituted on that day between Ivory Coast, Dahomey, Upper Volta, Mali, Mauritania, Niger and Senegal.[1] This provided for the Central Bank of West Africa to be governed by annexed statutes, and for the cession to it by France of a capital establishment fund of 500 million francs, to be shared equally by the Members, and contributed to equally by them. France undertook to ensure the free convertibility into French francs of the franc of the African Financial Community, which would be operated by the Bank. The definition and parity of the latter with the former would be those in force at the date of signature. This might not be varied except by agreement of all the parties. In July 1962 Mali unilaterally replaced the African Financial Community franc with a Mali franc.[2] In short, the operation of the franc zone depends upon discussion and reciprocal concessions and the satisfactory operation of the Monetary Department, the Committee of Foreign Investment, the Commission of Commercial Agreements, the Committees for Economic and Financial Affairs of the Community, and the Higher Council of Credit.

(d) Co-operation in the matter of justice

Upon independence certain of the French States entered into Transitional Agreements in Matters of Justice with France.[3] In virtue of the processes of ratification and promulgation these became internal law in the States concerned. They provided that pending the setting up of local appellate jurisdictions, appeals to set aside decisions given by the local administrative and judicial jurisdictions should be brought before the Community Division of the *Conseil d'État*, and the Community Chamber of the *Cour de Cassation*. In the event of the decision being set aside the case would be sent back to the jurisdiction of the trial courts, and if this jurisdiction should have been annulled after independence, it would be

1 Decree no. 63-488, *Journal Officiel*, 18 May 1963, p. 4541; decree no. 63-1078, *ibid.* 13 October 1963, p. 9709. Muracciole in *Rev. jur. et pol.* vol. XVI (1962), p. 375; Conac and Feuer in *Annales Malgaches*, vol. I (1964), p. 120.
2 *The Times*, 2 October 1962, p. 40.
3 Mangin in *Rev. jur. et pol.* vol. XVI (1962), p. 339.

differently constituted. The trial court is bound to comply with the decision of the *Cour de Cassation* on the point of law which the latter has decided.

So far as trial is concerned, jurisdictions sitting on the territory of the French Republic or on that of the State becoming independent should continue, for a transitional period, to be enforced in the territory of the other State under the procedures provided by the Constitution of 1958. At the end of the transitional period the *Conseil d'État* and the *Cour de Cassation* would remain seized of the cases which had been the subject matter of appeal prior to that date.

Agreements to this effect were signed by the Malagasy Republic, the Republic of Central Africa, Congo, Chad and Gabon. At a later stage, Co-operation Agreements in the Matter of Justice were signed, which provided that the supreme national appellate jurisdictions would have exclusive authority. France, however, undertook to provide judicial assistance with respect to personnel and facilities. Regular exchange of judicial information was provided for, and nationals sentenced to imprisonment for more than one year in the courts of another State would be handed over to the national State on request. The courts of each State would have exclusive jurisdiction to decide whether an individual has the nationality of that State. Elaborate provisions were inserted concerning the transmission and service of judicial and extra-judicial acts, the collection of evidence, and the exchange of police records. The decisions of the courts of one State would be *res judicata* in those of the other subject to the rules of the conflict of laws. Agreement was also reached respecting extradition, and the conditions for extradition.

(e) Agreement on fundamental rights and establishment

An agreement was entered into between France, the Federation of Mali and the Malagasy Republic at the same time as the Co-operation Agreements, in which uniform public liberties were to be enjoyed on the territories of both States. Every national of a State of the Community might freely enter the territory of any other State of the Community and set up his residence there, provided that each State might determine by its own laws the conditions for the free exercise of civic and political rights by the nationals of the other States of the Community. Equality with nationals was guaranteed with respect to judicial process, investment, and the acquisition and enjoyment of property rights of all kinds.

This agreement was open to accession by any State of the Community. It was complemented by Conventions on Establishment signed with the Federation of Mali on 22 June 1960, the Malagasy Republic on 27 June

1960, Chad on 11 August 1960, the Central African Republic on 13 August 1960, Congo on 15 August 1960, and Gabon on 17 August 1960.

4. THE IMPLICATIONS OF COMMUNITY EVOLUTION IN THE LAW OF STATE SUCCESSION

I. The Legal Orders of the Overseas Territories

The geographical isolation of the Overseas Territories from France prompted, as it did in the similar instance of the British Empire, local legal orders more or less distinguishable from the legal order of the metropolitan territory. However, the local orders, together with that of the metropolitan territory, were, as French texts put it, 'englobes'[1] in the wider and more fundamental legal order which constituted the internal aspect of the international personality of France. From the international point of view, indeed, the autonomous legal orders of the Territories were identical with the systems respecting local and decentralized collectivities within France herself. While this remained theoretically true, however, in practice the Territories came increasingly to be distinguished from the metropolitan territory in respect of the consequences of France's international activity. Various international organizations accepted representation less of France, in the political sense, than of the local technical administrations, thereby taking into account the implications in the international sphere of autonomous local legal orders. In discussing the survival of the legal system after the independence of the Territories, therefore, one must recognize the completeness and the separateness of that system before independence. And so far as the international acts binding the Empire, Union or Community in its successive stages are concerned, through promulgation these gradually became part of the local legal orders, so that they survived the transfer of sovereignty in virtue of the survival of the legal system. The emphasis is upon continuity through 'localization' rather more than upon collapse and disappearance through rupture.

II. The Evolutionary Character of the Community and the Survival of the Legal Order

It is evident that the process of becoming independent through which the French Overseas Territories have passed is quite distinct from secession in the ordinary sense of the word, certainly distinct from any political liberation, save in the instance of the Commonwealth, that had hitherto

[1] Lampué in *Annuaire français* (1960), p. 907.

occurred. The essential change was wrought entirely within the context of the French Constitution, so that the rupture with the existing legal situation was as slight as it could be, consistent with accession to international sovereignty. The French legal order, embracing the more particular legal orders of the Territories, survived in its essential aspects, and was transformed into national legal orders of the new States in virtue of the operation of the French Constitution upon which that order depended. A devolution of the ensemble of rights and obligations created under the French legal order is thus only to be expected, and this expectation is reinforced by the character of the co-operation agreements signed with France, which minimize the implications of accession to sovereignty, and by the evolutionary rather than revolutionary process by which that accession took place. Even before the final steps to independence were taken, the member States asserted themselves to be independent, and yet did not deny that they remained affected by the international acts of the former French administrations. In January 1960, for example, the Economic Commission of the United Nations for Africa disputed the right of the Vice-President of the Council of Chad to speak on behalf of France as delegate of the Community. The Vice-President replied:

Nos rapports avec la France résultent du consentement mutuel. Nous sommes une Communauté librement structurée et acceptée par chacun des États. La France, dont le nom est inscrit sur la table où je siège, n'est qu'un État de cette Communauté. Il n'est pas possible d'accepter que la Commission considère que nous parlons au nom de la France seule, je ne veux pas non plus que par un biais de procédure, on en vienne à conclure que nous souhaitons rester dans le régime colonial. L'exercice de notre souveraineté se fait en commun. Un africain peut donc représenter cette Communauté, comme un Ministre français peut parler au nom de cette même Communauté.[1]

Implicit in this argument is the shifting of the legal order from France to the Community, a shift of a constitutional character clearly not involving any alteration either of international commitments or of the legal consequences of internal governmental activity, and being decidedly more akin to change of government, as traditionally understood in international law, than to change of sovereignty. It is not surprising that Senegal,[2] Congo (Brazzaville) and the Malagasy Republic have recognized themselves to be bound in principle by French treaties.

1 *Le Monde*, 29 January 1960.
2 See *infra*, vol. II, p. 171. There is some controversy about the method whereby Community competence was transferred to the Federation of Mali. One view is that the transfer was made to Senegal and Soudan, who 'retransferred' it to the Federation. This view was expressed by the Secretary of State for Community Affairs on 9 June 1960, *Journal Officiel, Assemblée Nationale*, 11 June 1960, p. 1218. The Federation was

At no point in time, in this evolutionary process, could it be said that a decisive break in the chain of legal continuity had occurred. The Overseas Territories had, under the Constitution of the Fourth Republic, advanced to full internal autonomy; at this stage the change was a change of governments only, and the ensemble of French rights and duties settled on the territorial administrations. Then in two stages internal autonomy crystallized into external autonomy, involving the plenitude of international personality. There was, then, save in the case of Guinea, only a formal breach with French institutions, the substance of the former relationship being preserved by agreement. Despite the dubious usage of the expression 'confederal', the following view of the French Prime Minister provides the proper emphasis:

Certes, celle-ci comporte à l'égard de ces États des changements importants par rapport aux règles fixées en 1958; mais dans cette Communauté nouvelle, où la vocation confédérale est plus accentuée que dans la communauté telle qu'elle a été créée en 1958, il est entendu que des institutions demeurent en même temps qu'une volonté de politique coordonnée affirmant, non seulement entre la France et les nouveaux États, mais entre tous les États de la Communauté, une solidarité qui est la caractéristique de cette Communauté.[1]

The Secretary of State for Community Relations added:

C'est parce que ces accords ne traduisent pas seulement une union d'intérêts que nous avons réussi, sous une forme nouvelle, à maintenir la Communauté. Celle-ci subsiste sous la forme d'une union d'États indépendants. Les juristes s'attacheront à la qualifier au regard des catégories du droit international. Je voudrais en démontrer la réalité, cette réalité qui apparaît aujourd'hui dans les conventions conclues et qui se manifestera demain dans son organisation. . . .[2]

III. Application of French Treaties to the Overseas Territories

As early as 1777, in a Ministerial Letter addressed to the Council of San Domingo, it was stated that French treaties 'ne sont pas applicables aux colonies'.[3] This has remained the consistent attitude of French

formed on 10 June 1959 (*L'Année politique*, 1959, p. 271), and until June 1960 it was an autonomous member of the Community. The transfers of competence were signed on 4 April 1960 by the President of Senegal, who was also Vice-President of the Federation, and by the President of Soudan, who was also President of the Federation. The expression used was ambiguous: 'Les compétences . . . sont . . . transférées à la République du Sénégal et à la République Soudanaise, groupées au sein de la fédération du Mali.' From this the alternative conclusion is drawn that the transfer was made to the existing member of the Community, the Federation, and when this entity disappeared the agreements made with it lapsed also.

1 *Journal Officiel, Assemblée Nationale*, 10 June 1960, p. 1219.
2 *Ibid.* 7 July 1960, p. 1724.   3 Lampué, *loc. cit.* p. 920.

governments, and in 1928 it was stated in the debates on a tariff law that no commercial treaty was applicable to a colony, save in virtue of a territorial application clause, and that such a clause was ordinarily inserted only upon the advice of authorized representatives of each territory.[1] The law itself provided that 'les dispositions des conventions de commerce ne sont applicables aux colonies que si elles le stipulent expressément'. This provision was amended in 1954 to read: 'Le Chéf de Territoire rend provisoirement exécutoires les accords douaniers internationaux applicables avant ratification législative, lorsque ces accords prévoient expressément leur extension dans ces territoires.'

The Law of 20 September 1947 creating an organic status for the Department of Algeria recognized that in virtue of the Constitution French treaties were of full effect in the Department. In the case of the Overseas Territories, the practice persisted of extending treaties to them in virtue of territorial application clauses, and the Territories were in fact separately listed in the United Nations Treaty Series.

From the period of the Restoration French overseas authorities often participated in the drafting of treaties, and this practice was endorsed in Ordinances of 1825, 1827 and 1828 concerning the organization of the territories. The governor was empowered, when authorized by his instructions, to negotiate 'toutes conventions et autres', though he could not conclude them without the ratification of the Head of State.[2] Right up to the independence of the Overseas Territories in 1960 the French Government remained the sole authority with a discretion to enter into international engagements. The decrees of 4 April 1957 and 23 June 1956 implementing the *loi-cadre* of 23 June 1956 in French West and Equatorial Africa and Madagascar make this abundantly clear.

French practice distinguishes treaties which contain territorial application provisions from those which do not. Such provisions might be restrictive, as in the case of the Hague Conventions on Private International Law of 1902 which were limited to European territories, or they might be permissive, in the sense that a contracting party may extend the treaty's application to its overseas territories, but until it does so the treaty affects the metropolitan territory only. The Convention of Paris for the Protection of Industrial Property, 1883, is one of the earliest of such treaties. In a negative form, some treaties, such as the Warsaw Conven-

1 Lampué, *loc. cit.* p. 920
2 This is still the rule in St Pierre and Miquelon (since 1844) and New Caledonia (since 1885), in the decree organizing the *Établissements de l'Océanie*. In the decree of 23 August 1898 with respect to Algeria this local competence was denied, and the governor-general was forbidden to engage in any political or diplomatic activity without the authorization of Paris.

tion, 1929, permit States to exclude particular territories from the operation of the treaty. So far as treaties which omit a territorial reference are concerned, the question is whether they are inherently applicable to overseas territories. Gradually French doctrine has progressed in the direction of presuming that treaties not containing territorial provisions do not affect the Overseas Territories, partly because territorial clauses are so regularly inserted that their omission can only imply the irrelevance of the treaty to other than the metropolitan territory, but principally because in the French constitutional system a treaty gains the force of law internally, and must be transformed into two distinct legal orders, the metropolitan and the colonial. While there is nothing in the Constitution directly inhibiting the multi-legislative functions of the central authority, these functions, except in respect of fundamental constitutional matters, are, and for a long time have been, left to the local legislatures. A treaty concerning labour conditions, for example, would modify local labour law, a matter in which ordinarily the French legislature would not interfere. The argument has been widely accepted that a treaty as legislation should not achieve what ordinary legislation would not be designed to achieve, and it was specifically adopted by the *Comité juridique de l'Union française* in an opinion of 19 April 1950 'concernant l'application des traités internationaux aux différents éléments de l'Union française'.[1] At the same time, the *Comité* recognized that there are treaties which are analogous to fundamental constitutional law, such as peace treaties, and which would inherently affect all of the national territory in virtue of the central legislative act. The category into which any particular treaty, other than a peace treaty, falls has been controversial, and the application of extradition treaties in particular has been questioned, and the matter is uncertain.

The whole problem in French law is complicated by the tendency of authors and of courts to assume that there are universal principles governing the applicability of treaties to colonial territories, and that the internal constitutional norm is merely the obverse of these.[2]

[1] *Rev. jur. et pol.* vol. VII (1953), p. 124.
[2] Hence, it has been taken for granted that the applicability of Franco-British treaties to British colonies would be the index of applicability to the French, and vice versa. So the *Cour d'Appel* of Paris in 1879, *Boch* v. *Tinchant*: Clunet, 1879, p. 548, held that a Franco-Spanish treaty respecting protection of trademarks did not apply to Cuba, and the *Cour de Cassation* in 1913 decided that a Franco-Chinese treaty of 1886 did not apply to an Annamese, even though it created a most-favoured-nation treatment for Chinese living in Indochina, because it had not been locally promulgated: *Affaire de Du-Ngoc-Truong*, Dareste, 1913, 3.175. Clearly, the latter decision reflects an internal legislative notion which may or may not exist in other legal systems. The most important French decision on the point of treaty applicability is

IV. Treaties in the French Internal Legal Order after 1946

Under the Constitution of the French Union, treaties which were applicable in the legal relations subsisting between private parties, or which affected the powers and functions of the administration, were transformed into internal law in virtue of the process of ratification and publication. Article 26 (3) of the Constitution of 1946 stipulated that

properly ratified and published diplomatic treaties have the authority of law even in the case where they are contrary to French laws, without any other legislative provisions being necessary to ensure their application than those which were necessary for their ratification.

Article 28 stated that such treaties, 'having superior authority to that of municipal laws, their provisions can only be repealed, modified or suspended after regular denunciation, notified through diplomatic channels'. The Constitution of 1958 effected some alteration. Article 55 reads: 'Once published, properly ratified or approved treaties or agreements have priority over municipal law, provided that the other contracting parties fully apply them.' The change was to include 'treaties' and 'agreements', so as to make it clear that executive agreements have the same legislative status as treaties; and to place 'ratified' and 'approved' in the alternative so as to permit this status to be attained by agreements signed by officers of State other than the President, provided, according to the practice developed during the Fourth Republic, the latter 'approves' of them by presidential decree. The President is specified by article 52 to be the ratifying authority. Hence, whether the instrument is a treaty or an executive agreement, it is the action of the President which transforms it into internal law, provided publication has occurred in the *Journal Officiel*.[1]

that of the *Cour de Cassation* of 12 November 1957, concerning whether a Franco-Swiss treaty of 1869, not specifically applied to Somaliland, was in fact in force there. It was held that it was not in force in virtue of a '*principe de la spécialité législative*': *Société générale de surveillance de Genève* v. *Banque de l'Indochine*, *Bull. civ.* I, no. 427. This principle was not recognized as governing the applicability of a judicial convention in the Belgian colonies: *Cour d'Appel* at Aix, 22 July 1937, *Nouvelle revue de droit international privé*, p. 769. The Belgian Congo, in virtue of its separate personality, was held by the *Tribunal de la Seine* not to be affected by the Franco-Belgian judicial Convention of 1899: *Gazette du Tribunal*, 30 January 1935; or by an extradition treaty in British India, 1937: *Davidson's* Case, *Ann. Dig.* vol. VIII, Case no. 24; although both decisions have been criticized for failure to recognize the autonomous character of the territories concerned. For other authorities see Kiss, *Répertoire de la pratique française en matière de droit international public*, vol. I, ss. 795–803.

1 Pursuant to decree no. 53-192 of 14 March 1953 concerning Ratification and Publication of International Obligations Subscribed by France: *Journal Officiel*, 15 March 1953, p. 2436.

The legislature has the exceptional role of ratification or approval, under article 53, in the case of peace treaties, commercial treaties, treaties or agreements relating to international organization, and treaties or agreements involving State finances, legislative changes, personal status, or the cession, exchange or acquisition of territory.

Since the Constitution of 1946 created a unitary legal order for France and the Overseas Territories,[1] one view was that treaties extended automatically to all French territories, *en plein droit*, save where there was incorporated a territorial application clause.[2] The contrary view was that the Constitution of 1946 was in this respect no different from that of 1848, and that the traditional rule remained unaffected that treaties, with limited exceptions, must be specifically extended, whether there was a territorial clause or not.[3] In an Opinion of 22 April 1953[4] the *Comité juridique de l'Union française* took the view that engagements undertaken with respect to specialized international organizations were deemed to apply to the Overseas Territories only when these had participated by means of delegations in the drafting, had been consulted, or had participated in regional conferences and committees on the subject. For example, the Council of Europe Statute failed to mention Overseas Territories, but the law of 23 July 1949 approving it provided for representation of the Territories in the Consultative Assembly, thus implying the extension of the Treaty to the whole Union.

It may be considered that the application of a treaty to the Overseas Territories, pursuant to a territorial application or otherwise, had the effect of implementing the treaty or agreement internally in those Territories, in virtue solely of the constitutional ratification or approval of the President or, as the case may be, of the French legislature. That the survival of the legal order would imply the survival of the relevant treaties or agreements in the internal legal system of the countries becoming independent would appear, theoretically, to be beyond question. In actual practice serious difficulties might arise in the implementation of such treaties should their clauses not prove adaptable to the changed circumstances. For example, it is clearly impermissible to argue that the Statute of the Council of Europe still affects the former French States, or even the Overseas Territories.

Also, the survival of a treaty as internal law does not imply that it has survived as an international contract. Hence other parties may choose not

1 Title VIII, s. 1.
2 Luchaire, in *Études en l'honneur de Georges Scelle* (1950), p. 851; Rousseau, p. 45.
3 Lampué, *loc. cit.* p. 921.
4 *Annuaire français* (1960), p. 922.

to recognize the continuity effected in internal law, and might prefer to rely upon international rules of succession. It is noteworthy that, although G.A.T.T. was expressly extended to the French Overseas Territories, the Organization felt impelled to devise a *de facto* system of continuity at the international level.[1] Similarly, the Bureaux for the Protection of Industrial and Literary Property have assumed that a declaration of continuity on the part of the new States is necessary before they may be regarded administratively as parties to the treaties concerned.[2] It does not follow that a private litigant might not successfully invoke the relevant Convention as part of the surviving internal legal order in the courts of the French successor States to protect his legal interests.

Table 1. *Principal agreements of multilateral co-operation between France and the Francophone States*

	I	II	III	IV	V	VI	VII
France	★	★	★	★	★	★	★
Central African Republic	★	★	★	—	★	★	★
Congo	★	★	★	—	★	★	★
Chad	★	★	★	—	★	★	★
Gabon	(★)	(★)	—	—	★	★	★
Ivory Coast	—	—	—	★	—	—	★
Dahomey	—	—	—	★	—	—	★
Niger	—	—	—	★	—	—	★
Senegal	—	—	—	—	★3	★3	★
Mali	—	—	—	—	—	—	—
Cameroon	—	—	—	—	—	—	★
Togo	—	—	—	—	—	—	—
Upper Volta	—	—	—	—	—	—	★
Mauritania	—	—	—	—	—	—	★
Malagasy Republic	—	—	—	—	★	★	★
Guinea	—	—	—	—	—	—	—

   I Quadripartite agreement on defence, decree no. 60–1230 (France), *Journal Officiel*, 24 November 1960, p. 10459.
  II Quadripartite agreement on higher education, *ibid*. Gabon has participated in these two agreements.
 III Quadripartite agreement on monetary, economic and financial matters, *ibid*.
 IV Quadripartite agreement on defence, decree no. 62-136 (France), *Journal Officiel*, 6 February 1962, p. 1261.
  V Convention on conciliation and the court of arbitration, decree no. 60–694 (France), *Journal Officiel*, 20 July 1960, p. 6642.
 VI Multilateral convention on the fundamental rights of nationals of States of the Community, *ibid*.
VII Convention of co-operation in the control of insurance businesses and operations, decree no. 63–981 (France), 24 October 1963, p. 9499.

1 See *infra*, vol II, p. 209.   2 See *infra*, vol II, pp. 206–8.
3 Senegal has succeeded to these agreements concluded by the Federation of Mali.

Table 2. *Bilateral co-operation agreements of the Francophone States*

Nature, date and place of signature	Reference
FEDERATION OF MALI	
1. Transfer of competence, 4 April 1960, Paris	loi no. 60–569, *Journal Officiel*, 18 June 1960, p. 5471 decree no. 60–628, *Journal Officiel*, 2 July 1960, p. 5969
2. Co-operation agreements, 22 June 1960, Paris (*a*) participation in Community (*b*) co-operation in foreign affairs (*c*) co-operation in defence (*d*) co-operation in primary materials and strategic products (*e*) co-operation in economic monetary and financial matters (*f*) co-operation in higher education (*g*) co-operation in merchant navy (*h*) co-operation in civil aviation (*i*) convention of establishment	loi no. 60–682, *Journal Officiel*, 19 July 1960, p. 6575 decree no. 60–693, *Journal Officiel*, 20 July 1960, p. 6629
SENEGAL	
1. Exchange of notes on succession to agreements of the Federation of Mali, 16/19 September 1960, Dakar/Paris	decree no. 61–536, *Journal Officiel*, 2 June 1961, p. 4971
2. Further co-operation agreements (*a*) co-operation in higher education (not yet in force) (*b*) co-operation in matters of justice, 14 June 1962, Paris	*Journal Officiel du Sénégal*, 3 February 1962, p. 180
REPUBLIC OF MALI	
1. Denunciation of agreements of Federation of Mali	
2. Later co-operation agreements (*a*) general technical co-operation, 2 February 1962, Paris (*b*) cultural co-operation, 2 February 1962, Paris (*c*) co-operation in matters of justice, 9 March 1962, Bamako (*d*) co-operation in economic monetary and financial matters, 9 March 1962, Bamako (*e*) consular convention, 9 March 1962, Bamako	loi no. 63–812, *Journal Officiel*, 8 August 1963, p. 7354

Table 2. (cont.)

Nature, date and place of signature	Reference
MALAGASY REPUBLIC	
1. Transfer of competence, 2 April 1960, Paris	loi no. 60–568, *Journal Officiel*, 18 June 1960, p. 5471 decree no. 60–627, *Journal Officiel*, 2 July 1960, p. 5968
2. Co-operation agreements, 27 June 1960, Tananarive (a) participation in Community (b) co-operation in foreign affairs (c) defence agreement (d) co-operation in primary materials and strategic products (e) co-operation in monetary, economic and financial matters (f) co-operation in matters of justice (g) co-operation in higher education (h) co-operation in civil aviation (i) co-operation in merchant navy (j) co-operation in posts and telecommunications (k) establishment convention (l) agreement on the state of persons originally of Île Sainte-Marie.	loi no. 60–681, *Journal Officiel*, 19 July 1960, p. 6575 decree no. 60–692, *Journal Officiel*, 20 July 1960, p. 6607
MAURITANIA	
1. Transfer of competence, 19 October 1960, Paris	loi no. 60–1199, *Journal Officiel*, 17 November 1960, p. 10252 decree no. 60–1229, *Journal Officiel*, 24 November 1960, p. 10459
2. Co-operation agreements, 19 June 1961, Paris (a) treaty of co-operation (b) defence agreement (c) military and technical assistance (d) co-operation in economic, monetary and financial matters (e) agreement in matters of justice (f) cultural co-operation (g) co-operation in posts and telecommunications (h) co-operation in civil aviation (i) co-operation in merchant navy (j) general agreement of technical co-operation in matters of personnel	loi no. 61–848, *Journal Officiel*, 4 August 1961, p. 7243 decree no. 62–137, *Journal Officiel*, 6 February 1962, p. 1324

Table 2. (cont.)

Nature, date and place of signature — Reference

IVORY COAST

1. Transfer of competence, 11 July 1960, Paris — loi no. 60–735, *Journal Officiel*, 29 July 1960, p. 6992
   decree no. 60–758, *Journal Officiel*, 30 July 1960, p. 7049

2. Co-operation agreements, 24 April 1961, Paris — loi no. 61–768, *Journal Officiel*, 27 July 1961, p. 6908
   decree no. 62–136, *Journal Officiel*, 6 February 1962, p. 1261
   (a) treaty of co-operation
   (b) co-operation in economic, monetary and financial matters
   (c) technical and military assistance
   (d) co-operation in matters of justice
   (e) co-operation in higher education
   (f) cultural co-operation
   (g) co-operation in posts and telecommunications
   (h) co-operation in civil aviation
   (i) co-operation in merchant navy
   (j) general agreement of technical co-operation in matters of personnel

DAHOMEY

1. Transfer of competence, 11 July 1960, Paris — loi no. 60–735, *Journal Officiel*, 29 July 1960, p. 6992
   decree no. 60–758, *Journal Officiel*, 30 July 1960, p. 7049

2. Co-operation agreements, 24 April 1961, Paris — loi no. 61–771, *Journal Officiel*, 27 July 1961, p. 6909
   decree no. 62–136, *Journal Officiel*, 6 February 1962, p. 1261
   (a) treaty of co-operation
   (b) co-operation in economic, monetary and financial matters
   (c) military and technical assistance
   (d) co-operation in matters of justice
   (e) co-operation in higher education
   (f) cultural co-operation
   (g) co-operation in posts and telecommunications
   (h) co-operation in civil aviation
   (i) co-operation in merchant navy
   (j) general agreement of technical co-operation in matters of personnel

Table 2. (cont.)

Nature, date and place of signature	Reference
UPPER VOLTA	
1. Transfer of competence, 11 July 1960, Paris	loi no. 60–735, *Journal Officiel*, 29 July 1960, p. 6992 decree no. 60–758, *Journal Officiel*, 30 July 1960, p. 7049
2. Co-operation agreements, 24 April 1961, Paris (a) treaty of co-operation (b) co-operation in economic, monetary and financial matters (c) military and technical assistance (d) co-operation in matters of justice (e) co-operation in higher education (f) cultural co-operation (g) co-operation in posts and telecommunications (h) co-operation in civil aviation (i) co-operation in merchant navy (j) general agreement of technical co-operation in matters of personnel	loi no. 61–767, *Journal Officiel*, 27 July 1961, p. 6907 decree no. 62–136, *Journal Officiel*, 6 February 1962, p. 1261
NIGER	
1. Transfer of competence, 11 July 1960	loi no. 60–735, *Journal Officiel*, 29 July 1960, p. 6992 decree no. 60–758, *Journal Officiel*, 30 July 1960, p. 7049
2. Co-operation agreements, 24 April 1961, Paris (a) treaty of co-operation (b) co-operation in economic, monetary and financial matters (c) military and technical assistance (d) co-operation in higher education (e) cultural co-operation (f) co-operation in matters of justice (g) general agreement on technical co-operation in matters of personnel (h) co-operation in posts and telecommunications (i) co-operation in civil aviation (j) co-operation in merchant navy	loi no. 61–770, *Journal Officiel*, 27 July 1961, p. 6908 decree no. 62–136, *Journal Officiel*, 6 February 1962, p. 1261

Evolution of the Francophone States

Table 2. (cont.)

Nature, date and place of signature	Reference

CHAD

1. Transfer of competence, 12 July 1960, Paris

    loi no. 60–733, *Journal Officiel*, 29 July 1960, p. 6992
    decree no. 60–756, *Journal Officiel*, 30 July 1960, p. 7041

2. Co-operation agreements, 11 August 1960, Fort Lamy
    (a) conditions of participation in the Community
    (b) co-operation in foreign affairs
    (c) military and technical assistance
    (d) aid agreement
    (e) domain agreement
    (f) cultural co-operation
    (g) establishment convention

    loi no. 60–1255, *Journal Officiel*, 23 November 1960, p. 10427
    decree no. 60–1230, *Journal Officiel*, 24 November 1960, p. 10459

CENTRAL AFRICAN REPUBLIC

1. Transfer of competence, 12 July 1960, Paris

    loi no. 60–733, *Journal Officiel*, 29 July 1960, p. 6992
    decree no. 60–756, *Journal Officiel*, 30 July 1960, p. 7041

2. Co-operation agreements, 13 August 1960, Bangui
    (a) conditions of participation in Community
    (b) co-operation in foreign affairs
    (c) military and technical assistance
    (d) aid agreement
    (e) domain agreement
    (f) cultural co-operation
    (g) establishment convention

    loi no. 60–1225, *Journal Officiel*, 29 November 1960, p. 10427
    decree no. 60–1230, *Journal Officiel*, 24 November 1960, p. 10459

CONGO

1. Transfer of competence, 12 July 1960, Paris

    loi no. 60–733, *Journal Officiel*, 29 July 1960, p. 6992
    decree no. 60–756, *Journal Officiel*, 30 July 1960, p. 7041

2. Co-operation agreements, 15 August 1960, Brazzaville
    (a) conditions of participation in Community
    (b) co-operation in foreign affairs
    (c) military and technical assistance
    (d) aid agreement
    (e) domain agreement
    (f) cultural co-operation
    (g) establishment convention
    (h) agreement on the centre of higher education at Brazzaville

    loi no. 60–1225, *Journal Officiel*, 23 November 1960, p. 10427
    decree no. 60–1230, *Journal Officiel*, 24 November 1960, p. 10459

Table 2. (cont.)

Nature, date and place of signature — *Reference*

GABON

1. Transfer of competence, 15 July 1960, Paris

   loi no. 60–734, *Journal Officiel*, 29 July 1960, p. 6992
   decree no. 60–757, *Journal Officiel*, 30 July 1960, p. 7047

2. Co-operation agreements, 17 August 1960, Libreville
   - (a) participation in the Community
   - (b) co-operation in foreign affairs
   - (c) defence agreement
   - (d) co-operation in economic, monetary and financial matters
   - (e) co-operation in merchant navy
   - (f) co-operation in civil aviation
   - (g) co-operation in higher education
   - (h) establishment convention

   loi no. 60–1226, *Journal Officiel*, 23 November 1960, p. 10428
   decree no. 60–1231, *Journal Officiel*, 24 November 1960, p. 10480

CAMEROON

Co-operation agreements, 13 November 1960, Yaoundé
- (a) treaty of co-operation
- (b) co-operation in economic, monetary and financial matters
- (c) organization of relations between the Cameroon and French treasuries
- (d) cultural convention
- (e) general agreement on technical co-operation in matters of personnel
- (f) co-operation in civil aviation
- (g) military and technical assistance to Cameroon armed forces
- (h) role and status of French military mission in Cameroon
- (i) consular convention
- (j) judicial convention

loi no. 60–1435, *Journal Officiel*, 28 December 1960, p. 11908
decree no. 61–877, *Journal Officiel*, 9 August 1961, p. 7429

TOGO

Co-operation agreements, 10 July 1963, Paris
- (a) diplomatic convention
- (b) defence agreement
- (c) judicial convention
- (d) establishment convention
- (e) cultural co-operation
- (f) technical co-operation
- (g) co-operation in economic monetary, and financial matters
- (h) relations between the Togo and French treasuries

loi no. 63–1253, *Journal Officiel*, 22 December 1963, p. 11455
decree no. 64–523, *Journal Officiel*, 10 June 1964, p. 4990

Chapter 4

EVOLUTION OF THE CONGO

1. THE CESSION OF THE CONGO TO BELGIUM, 1907

The Treaty for the Cession of the Independent State of the Congo to Belgium of 28 November 1907 provided for the transfer of the Congo

avec tous les droits et obligations qui y sont attachés. L'État belge déclare accepter cette cession, reprendre et faire siennes les obligations de l'État Indépendant du Congo, telles qu'elles sont détaillées en l'annexe A, et s'engage à respecter les fondations existantes au Congo, ainsi que les droits acquis légalement reconnus à des tiers, indigènes, et non indigènes.

D'autre part, la cession comprend tout le passif et tous les engagements financiers de l'État Indépendant, tels qu'ils sont détaillés dans l'annexe C.[1]

An Additional Act of 5 March 1908 excepted from the cession the *Fondation de la Couronne* as constituted by decrees of 1896, 1901, 1904, 1906 and 1907, and included listed *terres vacantes*, mainly in the east-centre part of the country, and the assets which had constituted the *Fondation* were ceded as *domaine privé de l'État*.[2] By decree of the same date of the Sovereign of the Independent State, the *Fondation de la Couronne* assumed civil personality, and the *terres vacantes* were ceded to the State, with reservation of the usufruct in the case of immovables, and rights of concessionaires.

The legislative process whereby the Congo was absorbed within the domain of Belgian sovereignty is complicated. There were, in fact, three enactments, all dated 18 October 1908: the first was that 'réalisant le transfert à la Belgique de l'Etat Indépendant du Congo', which approved the treaty of cession; the second was another law which similarly approved the additional act to the treaty of cession; and the third was that providing for the future administration of the colony, known popularly as the *Charte Coloniale* and formally as the *Loi sur le Gouvernement du Congo belge*. Article 1 of the last mentioned stated:

Le Congo belge a une personnalité distincte de celle de la métropole. Il est régi par des lois particulières.

L'actif et le passif de la Belgique et de la colonie demeurent séparés. En conséquence, le service de la rente congolaise demeure exclusivement à la charge de la colonie, à moins qu'une loi n'en décide autrement.

[1] B.F.S.P. vol. c, p. 705.   [2] *Ibid.* vol. CI, p. 728.

The *Loi* then proceeded to establish the government of the Congo, and to provide for the separate treasury and related fiscal matters. Article 27 provided thus:

> Le roi fait les traités concernant la colonie. Les dispositions de l'article 68 de la constitution belge relatives aux traités s'appliquent aux traités qui concernent la colonie. Le Ministre des Affaires Étrangères du Royaume a dans ses attributions les relations de la Belgique avec les Puissances étrangères au sujet de la colonie.

The Independent State of the Congo had made fifty-two treaties, agreements and accessions before the cession, and most of these were regarded as still in force before independence in 1960.[1] At the time of the cession no question as to continuity of these treaties was raised. On 1 July 1916 the United States gave notice of abrogation of article 5 of its treaty with the Congo of 1891, and the Belgian Government replied with the statement that the other provisions of the treaty were understood to remain in force.[2] On 24 April 1918, Belgium and France made a declaration modifying the Franco-Congo Telegraphic Convention of 1903.[3] On 23 December 1908 France and Belgium promulgated an arrangement concerning the preferential right of France in respect of the territories of the Independent State, acquired in 1884, which recited that 'considérant qu'à la suite du transfert à la Belgique des possessions de l'État Indépendant du Congo ... le Gouvernement belge se trouve substitué à l'obligation contractée sous ce rapport par le Gouvernement dudit État'.[4] The informal French Treaty List of 1962 continued to list as in force treaties between France and the Congo of 1885, 1887, 1894 (all frontier) and 1899 (extradition).[5] In 1956 the Court of Appeal of Paris applied the treaty of commerce of 31 October 1901 between the Congo and France,[6] which is not included in the French list.

The Belgian Congo had treaties made for it by the King of the Belgians, pursuant to the *Loi* of 1908, but it was subjected to international con-

---

1 De Visscher in *Communicazioni e Studi*, vol. XI (1960), p. 63. Italy, when it recognized the cession in 1908, was sure that Belgium would respect the Act of Berlin 'ainsi que les autres conventions faites au profit des ressortissants Italiens', Jentgen, *La terre belge du Congo* (1937), p. 337. Austria-Hungary made a similar observation, *ibid.* p. 338. At the time of independence of the Belgian Congo a list of treaties was prepared which included all relevant pre-1908 treaties, *Chronique de politique étrangère*, vol. XIII (1960), p. 913. Document no. 86.
2 *Ibid.* vol. CXII, p. 1198.
3 *Ibid.* vol. CXI, p. 655; *Journal Officiel*, 1 June 1918.
4 *B.F.S.P.* vol. CII, p. 358; *Rev. gén. de droit int. pub.* vol. XI (1911), p. 208.
5 Duparc, pp. 11 *et seq.*
6 *Congo Belge*, v. *Montefiore I.L.R.* vol. XXIII, p. 191; reversed on a different ground in Dalloz, *Jurisprudence Générale* (1963), p. 37. *Rev. jur. et pol.*, vol X (1957), p. 356, with a note by S. Bastid. She regards the cession of the Congo in 1907 as comparable with entry into a federation, p. 374. See *infra*, vol II, pp. 255–6.

Evolution of the Congo

ventions by separate accession, and at some international conferences the Belgian delegation separately represented the Congo. With respect to bilateral treaties made by the King of the Belgians, the general opinion was that these would not affect the Congo as a separate juridical person unless territorially applied. The *Tribunal de la Seine* on 27 December 1934 held that in virtue of this opinion a Franco-Belgian judicial convention of 1899 was not applicable to the Congo.[1]

The legislative history of the formula 'distinct personality' as used in the *Loi* of 18 October 1908 is important if this inconstant expression is to be given precise meaning.[2] At the time of the cession both the Belgian Senate and the House of Representatives appointed select Commissions to report on the matter.[3] It was proposed to the House Commission that the colony should be stated to have 'autonomie financière'. This expression was criticized, and efforts were made to insert the text of article 115 of the Belgian constitution into the law. Eventually the expression 'personnalité' was adopted on a compromise motion. The Government was consulted on the point, and proposed the formula that 'toute possession coloniale de la Belgique a une personnalité juridique distincte de celle de l'État'. The Commission then began to entertain doubts, members pointing out that the term 'personnalité juridique' smacked too much of status in the internal civil law, and would result in equating the Belgian Congo with any other corporation of Belgian law, whereas something larger and more fundamental was intended. Accordingly it was decided to omit the qualification 'juridique' and substitute 'distincte', although it was not a term of art. The Commission then reported that the intention behind the expression was to achieve 'the separation of the *actif* and the *passif* of respectively Belgium and the Congo'. This implied that Belgium would not take over any of the existing debts of the Congo,[4] and that all

---

[1] But cf. the decision of the *Cour d'Appel* at Aix, 22 July 1937, *Nouvelle revue de droit international privé*, p. 769, which overlooked the autonomous status of the Congo.

[2] Durieux, *Le problème juridique des dettes du Congo belge et l'État du Congo* (1961); 'La Belgique et le Congo', *Zaïre*, vol. VII, no. 4 (1953), p. 339; *Institutions politiques, administratives et judiciaires du Congo belge et du Ruanda-Urundi* (4th ed. 1957); *Souveraineté et communauté belgo-congolaise* (1959); Halewyck, *La charte coloniale* (1914–19), 3 vols.; Waelbroeck in *Chronique de politique étrangère*, vol. XV (1962), p. 59; Stengers, *Belgique et Congo*; *l'Élaboration de la Charte Coloniale* (1963) gives the history of the question; de Visscher in *Communicazioni e Studi*, vol. XI (1960), p. 53; Marrès and Henri, *L'État belge responsable du désastre congolais* (1961); De Bandt in *Revue belge de droit international* (1965), p. 497; 'Décolonisation et indépendance du Ruanda et du Burundi', *Chronique politique étrangère*, vol. XVI (1953), p. 445; *Congo, Effets de l'indépendance* (Penant, 1964), p. 559.

[3] Reports, *Ch. des Représentants*, Doc. no. 150, meeting of 3 April 1908, *Sénat de Belgique*, Doc. no. 12, meeting of 26 August 1908.

[4] For the final settlement of the Belgian-Congo Debt problem, see *infra*, p. 344.

future financial transactions would be with the Congo alone: that the transfer of the *actif* and *passif* to Belgium in the treaty of cession was a transfer of the ultimate competence to regulate the legal situation, but that the situation would, in virtue of the law of ratification, remain unaltered, so far as the maintenance of budgetary rights and obligations in public and private law were concerned. The report went on: 'En ce qui concerne la dette de l'État, le système est que la colonie pourra faire des emprunts non garantis, comme il pourra y avoir aussi des emprunts dont la Belgique consentira à assumer la garantie.' To ensure that Belgium did not, in virtue of the treaty of cession, fall heir to the existing debt it was unanimously resolved to specify the separation of the *actif* and the *passif* of Belgium and the Congo. When the Government commented that 'l'État belge, reprenant tout l'actif et tous les engagements actuels de l'État Indépendant, se trouve engagé à assurer le service de la dette antérieure à la reprise dans le cas où la colonie serait dans l'impossibilité d'y faire face', the Commission refused to modify its formula.

The Senate Commission approached the question from the more fundamental position that 'les lois qui régissent la Belgique ne sont pas applicables à la colonie; celle-ci sera régie par des lois particulières, par des lois spéciales qui devront être appropriées aux besoins matériels et moraux de la colonie et conformes aux intérêts matériels et moraux de la mère patrie'. The conclusion to be drawn from this was specified to be the 'existence propre' of the colony, and that 'les charges et les ressources de la colonie ne sont pas identifiées avec celles de la métropole'. The implications were then spelled out in detail: there would be a clear distinction between the finances of Belgium and those of the colony, between the engagements of Belgium and the colony, and the latter would have the power to execute its own commitments, 'sous le contrôle et la sauvegarde' of the former; and it would have to discover the means of doing so from its own resources, without resort to the assistance, guarantee or subsidy of Belgium except in exceptional circumstances which would be regarded as such only when the question might arise. There would thus be a maximal institutional continuity between the independent State and the colony. 'La Belgique n'assume donc pas les dettes du Congo. Les créanciers de la colonie sont prévenus qu'ils n'auront pas d'action directe contre la Belgique pour les emprunts futures, à moins d'une garantie expressément stipulée par une loi.' As to past debts,

la question est plus délicate parce qu'elle se complique de celle de savoir à qui passent, lors du transfert, l'actif et le passif de l'État Indépendant.

En principe, l'État qui succède à une autre État reprend l'actif et le passif de l'État qui disparaît.

Evolution of the Congo 93

Or, objectera-t-on, la Belgique succède à l'État Indépendant. C'est exact pour ce qui concerne la souveraineté, mais l'actif et le passif de l'État Indépendant seront échus au Congo belge et non à la Belgique.

Il en résulte que la Belgique ne doit pas même répondre pour les dettes antérieures du Congo, ni pour le capital des dettes, ni pour le service de la rente congolaise.

The Commission discovered nothing inequitable in this conclusion, for the creditors of the Congo had no ground of complaint. 'Leur gage n'est pas diminué par l'annexion; ils profitent, au contraire, des décisions prises au sujet de la Fondation de la Couronne.' To make the conclusion explicit, the Commission resolved that the fourth line be added to the text of article 1 of the *Loi*.

These principles, as acted upon in interpretation of this article, became the basic constitutional law of the Belgian Congo, and were recognized in Belgian courts, which always distinguished between the colony and the metropolis, and discharged the latter from all suits in which the former was answerable.[1]

The constitutional device whereby effect was given to the Reports of the Commissions was to pass the law ratifying the treaty before the law known as the Colonial Charter was passed, so that, both laws ranking equal, the second prevailed in the event of contradiction between the terms of the cession and the terms of the basic law. This was made clear in the House of Representatives by the Minister of Justice when he summarized the procedure as being that

la Belgique reprend le Congo et puis elle l'organise comme elle le veut. Elle peut donc lui attribuer comme patrimoine propre à la Colonie, les mêmes biens qui appartenaient à l'État Indépendant du Congo comme État. Réserve sera faite des immeubles, situés en Belgique, qui rentreront dans le patrimoine de l'État belge.[2]

2. THE INDEPENDENCE OF THE CONGO, 1960

The Belgian Congo gained independence after a Round Table Conference of January 1960 which did not, however, lead to the signature of a formal agreement between Belgium and the Congo; and by means of Belgian legislation,[3] which was intended to give the Congo institutions necessary

---

[1] *Cour d'Appel* of Brussels, 2 October 1930, *Pasicrisie Belge* (1930), vol. II, p. 170; *Cour de premiere instance* of Brussels, 13 July 1927, *Revue de doctrine et de jurisprudence coloniales* (1929), p. 19; *idem*, of 18 March 1953, Brussels, *Journal des Tribunaux* (1953), *Jurispr.* no. 264.

[2] Ch. des Reprs. *Annales parlementaires*, sess. extraord., 3 July 1908, p. 199, col. 2.

[3] The history is set out in *Les Dossiers du Centre de Recherche et d'Information Socio-Politiques* (Congo, 1959; Congo, 1960 in two vols; Congo, 1961). There is also a volume on Ruanda-Urundi. Also see Ganshof van der Meersch, *Fin de la Souveraineté belge au Congo* (1963), esp. pp. 161–80; de Visscher, *loc. cit.*

to enable it to function provisionally as a new State, pending the adoption of a definitive Constitution. This legislation of 19 May 1966 is known as the *loi fondamentale relative aux structures du Congo*.[1] Article 2 assures the continuity of laws in providing for the continuing in force as at 30 June 1960 (the date of independence) of all laws and decrees. Article 259 states: 'Sont abrogées au 30 juin 1960: la loi du 18 octobre 1908, telle que modifiée à ce jour, sur le gouvernement du Congo belge en tant qu'elle s'applique au Congo belge.' The effect of this annulment is highly controversial. The Auditor-General's department gave an opinion to the *Conseil d'État* on 21 October 1960[2] that it involved the automatic suppression of the *patrimoines* which the abrogated law had intended to create. To the contrary, it has been pointed out that the Colonial Charter was repealed on the day when the Congo acceded to independence, and the repealing legislation thus purported to regulate a situation already beyond Belgian legislative control; that this accession had the effect of dismemberment of a unitary State composed of the metropolis and the Congo and organized on the basis of *la séparation des patrimoines*. Therefore, neither in law nor in fact, was the Colonial Charter in force at the date. The effect of article 259 was declaratory of this situation only so far as the Congo was concerned, and this was acknowledged in the *projet de loi* presented to the House of Representatives on 31 March 1960,[3] where it was stated that 'toutefois, ce n'est qu'en tant qu'elle s'applique au Congo belge que la loi du 18 octobre 1908 est abrogée. Jusqu'à ce qu'une législation distincte intervienne pour le Ruanda-Urundi, ce territoire demeure en effet régi par cette législation.' If the legislature had wished to negative the separation of the *patrimoines* it would have had to put article 259 into force at the latest on 29 June 1960; because on the next day it would be incapable of affecting matters concerning the Congo.

The point of the debate is whether, in virtue of the abrogation of the *Loi* of 1908, Belgium had, by suppressing the separation of the *patrimoines*, revived the provisions of the law ratifying the treaty of cession (the first of the three enactments mentioned above), and thereby fallen heir to the debts and liabilities of the colony *dans le cadre de son autonomie financière légale*; or whether it had merely disengaged the Congo from the legislative device whereby its competence was defined in Belgian law, without affecting the separation of *patrimoines*, so that the *patrimoine du Congo belge*

---

1 *Moniteur belge*, 27–28 May 1960; erratum *ibid.* 2 June 1960; Muracciolo in *Rev. iur. et pol.* vol. XVI (1962), p. 279.

2 *Meert Case, Avis no.* 8166, *Journal des Tribunaux* (1960), p. 738, esp. at p. 741. De Visscher says it is strange to see a court applying after the independence of the Congo, a treaty providing for the annexation of the Congo, in *loc. cit.* p. 81.

3 *Ch. des Représ.* Doc. no. 489 (1959–60), no. 1, sess. 1959–60, *Exposé des motifs*, p. 68.

would remain that of *l'État du Congo*, with the implication that the debts of the one would become the debts of the other. But in the case of obligations contracted under municipal law, whether the law of Belgium, or of the Congo, or of another State, the personality of the contracting party is the important thing, and under the scheme of international protection of private law relationships of governments, it would be difficult to see how Belgium could be engaged in direct international liability.

On 30 December 1961 the *Cour d'Appel* of Ruanda-Urundi held[1] that the law approving cession had given birth to the Colony, and the *Charte Coloniale* had merely organized it administratively. The conclusion was drawn that the Colony had not become an entity distinct from Belgium in the sense of possessing its own sovereignty, but was merely the location of a *patrimoine distinct*. While the Colony was a legal order separate from that of the metropolis, the legislative competence respecting it remained 'd'abord et en toute souveraineté' with the Belgian Parliament. The *Loi* of 19 May 1960 had abrogated the *Charte Coloniale*, but not the *loi de transfert*, which was thus still in force in Belgian territory a year after the independence of the Congo, although it had 'nécessairement cessé de produire effet à cette date' in the latter's territory. This merely means that effects produced in Belgian law concerning the Congo before independence had not been nullified in the act of independence, and that the separation of the Belgian and Colonial *patrimoines* had been terminated by article 259. From the relevant date there was only one entity in whom the rights and obligations ultimately dependent on the Belgian State could vest, and that was the *patrimoine* of the metropolis.

Four days previous to this judgment a similar decision had been given by the *Tribunal Civil* of Brussels,[2] after an extensive survey of the literature on State succession to the public debt. But on 14 January 1963[3] another chamber of this Court gave a decision rejecting the fusion of the *éléments actifs et passifs du patrimoine colonial non repris par la République du Congo avec le patrimoine de la Métropole*, and on the basis thereof non-suited a plaintiff whose action against Belgium had been brought after the date of Congolese independence, but was founded on a claim against the Colonial administration. A similar decision was given by the *Tribunal Civil* of Ghent on 9 December 1963,[4] but with the additional reason that debts

1 *The Northern Assurance Co. Ltd* v. *Gouvernement du Congo belge*, *Journal des Tribunaux* (1962), p. 318.
2 *Dumont* v. *État belge*, *ibid*. p. 22. On appeal the *Charte Coloniale* was held to be irrelevant on the ground that judicial officials had rights against Belgium; *ibid*. decision of 4 December 1963, p. 727.
3 *Ibid*. 1963, p. 64.
4 *Meert Case*, Avis no. 8166, *Journal des Tribunaux* (1960), p. 738, esp. at p. 741.

contracted in the exclusive interest of the Congo had passed to the successor State, even in the absence of a treaty to this effect;[1] and also on appeal disposed of by the *Cour d'Appel* of Brussels on 4 December 1963,[2] in an action on bailment brought against the Belgian State in lieu of the colonial authorities. The thesis was adopted that the achievement of independence by the Congo terminated the *Charte Coloniale*, and that article 259 was included in the Law relating to the Structures of the Congo only *ex abundanti cautela*. Since legislation is not retroactive in character, the article could not have had the effect of creating a legal bond between the appellant and the Belgian State which did not exist when the cause of action arose.

The Belgian courts have not been content to hold that the Belgian State, save in respect of judicial officers,[3] is not responsible for the obligations of the Belgian Congo. They have gone further and stated, after examination of the textbooks, that these obligations, being local in character, have passed to the independent Republic of the Congo.[4]

[1] *De Keer v. État belge*, ibid. (1964), p. 61; *Demol v. État belge, Ministre des Finances*, ibid. p. 600; *Pittacos v. État belge*, ibid. (1965), p. 7.
[2] *Baugnet-Hock v. État belge*, ibid. (1963), p. 732.
[3] *État belge v. Dumont*, decision of 4 December 1963, ibid. (1963), p. 727.
[4] *Dumont v. État belge*, ibid. (1962), p. 22; *Creplet v. État belge et Société des forces hydro-électriques de la colonie*, decision of 30 January 1962, ibid. p. 242. But cf. *Meert Case*, ibid. (1960), p. 738.

Chapter 5

EVOLUTION OF THE NETHERLANDS INDIES

Until 1854 the Crown of the Netherlands, through the Governor-General, had direct and plenary authority in the Indies, but in that year the Council of the Indies, which had previously enjoyed only consultative status, was endowed with legislative and executive functions. The effect of this was to inhibit the Netherlands Council of State from exercising too direct a jurisdiction over the Indies, and thus indirectly to promote their juridical separation from the Netherlands.[1] In 1864 it was enacted that the Indies should have a separate treasury and system of accounts.[2] Thereafter various government departments were set up in the Indies under the Governor-General, who remained responsible to the Crown and not to the Netherlands Government. In 1912 a further law of the Netherlands[3] was enacted to provide that the Netherlands Indies should constitute a separate juristic person, with property and liabilities separate from those of the Netherlands. The official representative of this separate person was the Governor-General, or the Minister of the Colonies, according to the functions exercised. The finances of the Indies should be administered and accounted for in accordance with the system of accountability laid down in the Act.

In fact the Act of 1912 was merely confirmatory of an opinion long held by Netherlands lawyers that the Indies constituted a particular legal order; and the conclusion was generally drawn that the enactment of itself did not create the financial autonomy of the Indies, which would depend as much upon administrative procedure and financial practice as upon legislation. Attention, accordingly, must be directed to the method of raising loans for the Indies. Until 1875 there was no public debt of the Indies as such, and some Indies revenues flowed into the Netherlands Treasury. Later the Indies incurred a debt to the Netherlands by reason of funds received from loans issued in 1883 and 1898 in the name of, and chargeable to, the Netherlands, the greater part of which were made available to the Indies. This debt took the form of a charge on the Indies accounts for the payment of interest and amortization in proportion to the part of the loans received. The loan of 1898 was completely

1 De Kat Angelino, *Le problème colonial* (1932), vol. II, pp. 55–82.
2 *Staatsblad*, no. 106.
3 *Indische Comptabiliteitswet*, 1912.

discharged in 1935, and the last payment was made on that of 1883 by Indonesia in 1952.[1]

The principal effect of the Act of 1912 was to provide a basis for a separate credit system of the Indies. Creditors no longer doubted the legal capacity of the Indies to raise moneys directly, and no longer expected the Netherlands Treasury to discharge them. A series of loans issued by the Indies in its own name, and charged on its own accounts, began in 1915, and from 1931 onwards were converted by a conversion loan guaranteed by the Netherlands. In 1934 the Minister for the Colonies was authorized by Netherlands legislation[2] to issue conversion loans in the name of, and chargeable to, the Netherlands Indies, and to issue a guarantee of the Kingdom as to performance of the obligations attaching thereto. Eventually all Indies loans became subject to guarantee.[3]

The administration of the Indies, as constituted under the Governor-General, was juridically separate from that of the Netherlands, and the rights of civil servants and soldiers in the Indies derived from regulations specifying the Indies Government as the employing authority.[4]

Independence was achieved by Indonesia at a Round Table Conference in 1949, and the details of the settlement reached concerning Indonesia's succession to the Indies will be dealt with in the proper context.[5]

1 Tervooren, pp. 39–73.
2 *Staatsblad*, no. 274.
3 Tervooren, pp. 91–3.
4 De Kat Angelino, *op. cit.* pp. 114–52.
5 See *infra*, pp. 437–8.

PART II

THE EFFECT OF CHANGE OF SOVEREIGNTY ON THE LEGAL AND ADMINISTRATIVE STRUCTURE OF THE AFFECTED TERRITORY

Chapter 6

THE EFFECT OF CHANGE OF SOVEREIGNTY ON THE LEGAL SYSTEM IN THE AFFECTED TERRITORY

The laws and ordinances of a State fall, generally speaking, into two categories. Those which are promulgated by the Government for the effective administration of the country constitute in their totality its administrative or public law. Such law is political in character, concerns the relations of the people to the State, and pertains to the prerogatives of the sovereign authority. Its object is either the realization of public policy or the regulation and disposition of the public domain. On the other hand, those customs which grow out of the social structure of the community and have reference to the private relations of citizens one to another fall within the category of private law. Such customs, whether written, codified, modified by statute, or located only in the habits of the people, are concerned with the property of individuals and the settlement of their differences. They do not concern the administration of the State.

I. THE BASIS OF LEGAL CONTINUITY

As a matter of historical fact, change of sovereignty has not disturbed, except incidentally, the legal relations *inter se* of the inhabitants of territory affected, or even, in some cases, their relations with the administrative authorities. The explanation of this survival of law goes to the heart of legal philosophy; the theory that law is a concomitant of man's social nature presumes survival of the legal system;[1] the theory that law is a manifestation of the sovereign will—the imperative theory—predicates this survival on the tacit or explicit consent of the successor State.[2]

---

1 Piédelièvre says: 'the laws of a people are the living expression of its character and customs', vol. I, p. 128. See Sibert, vol. I, p. 214.
2 Accioly, *Traité de droit international public*, vol. I (Fr. trans. 1940), p. 200; Berber, vol. I, p. 260; Briggs, *Law of Nations Cases and Documents* (1952), p. 237; Bustamante, vol. III, p. 275; Cansacchi, 'La sopravivenza dell' ordinamento giuridico antecedente in territorio annesso', in *Studi Perassi* (1957), vol. I, p. 251; Cavaglieri in Hague *Recueil*, vol. XXVI (1929), p. 378; Feilchenfeld, p. 617; Gould, p. 419; Guggenheim, p. 136; *Traité*, p. 459; Jellinek, p. 272; Lapradelle states that 'the effect of this act of will, express or tacit, of the new sovereign, is necessarily to confer on legislation a national character. The law of the old state ceases, and after the annexation is maintained in the territory by a different title', p. 395. Mosler, p. 23; von

Neither theory contrives continuity of all legislation, but the former presumes survival of a wider spectrum of laws than does the latter. In recent times it has become usual for successor States to specify that the law to be applied in the new context is the previous law. The imperative theory considers that the previous law has now been transformed into the successor's law by a sovereign act,[1] and that no other explanation of its survival is needed. However, a situation such as occurred with the partition of India does not accommodate itself so readily to this thesis. The legislative provision for the continuity of English law in both India and Pakistan is the Indian Independence Act, an enactment of the predecessor sovereign.[2] Only if one presumes continuity of the previous law is one entitled to treat this provision, as the Indian courts have done, as a statutory direction to apply the previous law. Likewise, only a philosophical explanation is available with respect to continuity of law in countries where this continuity has not been legislatively regulated at all.

Some subscribers to the imperative theory of law[3] have been content with the bare proposition that under international law the legal system survives a change of sovereignty,[4] apparently unaware of the need for some explanation of the phenomenon of survival, and in particular of the function that international law may have in directing this survival. Critical minds within the imperative school have pointed out[5] that, unless one concedes a role to international law in directing the solution in municipal courts of the internal problem of municipal law survival, the question of this survival or otherwise is entirely one of municipal law.[6]

Rauchhaupt, p. 63; Rosenne in *B.Y.* vol. XXVII (1950), pp. 273, 277, 279–82; Schönborn, p. 50; Sereni, vol. II, p. 386; Spiropoulos, p. 63; Strupp, *Éléments*, p. 95; Vanselow, p. 142.

[1] Rosenne, *loc. cit.* pp. 279–81; Cansacchi, *loc. cit.*; Sereni, *op. cit.* p. 386, says that the formal validity of the law derives from the successor State, but its content from the predecessor State.

[2] See *infra*, p. 116.

[3] Particularly Keith, pp. 27 *et seq.*

[4] Kaeckenbeeck in *B.Y.* vol. XVII (1936), p. 8.

[5] E.g. Rosenne, *loc. cit.* p. 277. See *Porto Rico Railway, Light and Power Co. v. Amador, Ann. Dig.* vol. I, Case no. 49, a case involving the grant of licences to operate as common carriers. In this case it was held that the use of public places in Porto Rico was to be decided according to the principles of the freer common law prevailing in the United States, although private rights and civil law were retained 'by will of the American Government'. See also a Belgian case which assumed that Czechoslovakia had substituted its own financial law for that of Austria in the district of Marienbad: *Lipschutz v. Böhmische Esconto Bank and Credit Anstalt, Ann. Dig.* vol. VII, Case no. 41.

[6] Kelsen in Hague *Recueil*, vol. XLII (1932), p. 317. His normative system recognizes the problem but does little to resolve it beyond requiring the promulgation in municipal law of a direction whose authority resides elsewhere. 'Neither generally binding principles nor any single rule of international law can be found which oblige a State

But since a dualism of international law and municipal law prescinds from an imperative theory of law, this concession is insupportable. The alternative theory that juridical institutions are spontaneously generated, and that law is a crystallization of a people's pattern of life into norms of conduct, yields the conclusion that legal survival is independent of an intervention of sovereignty; and it also, without denying the intrinsically harmonious connexion of international law and municipal law,[1] does not need to rely on international law to achieve this survival. It considers continuity of law throughout the process of change of sovereignty to result from the nature of law itself, and not from positive direction of either the sovereign or of international law.

Sometimes the problem is complicated by importing the question of recognition of foreign laws.[2] Are the rules of law in newly acquired territory to be regarded as foreign in the eyes of courts of other territory of the successor sovereign, so as to be proved as facts and not as laws? It has sometimes been assumed that because the answer is in the negative, this constitutes proof that the surviving law is now part of the municipal law of the successor State, as a result of a sovereign intervention. No such implication arises or is dictated by any of the possible explanations of the survival of law. The law of the predecessor State certainly becomes the law of the successor State,[3] but it does not necessarily derive from the latter's sovereignty.

It has also been argued that without the transformation of the municipal law of the old into the municipal law of the new sovereign, acquired rights created under the former would become frozen.[4] The conclusion is by no means necessary to the premises, for acquired rights are as much at the legislative discretion of the new sovereign as they were at that of the old; the only question is whether five minutes after a change of sovereignty they exist at all, not whether they may be legitimately expropriated or modified by the successor State. Unless a legislative will to maintain the

which takes a territory under its sovereignty to take over at the same time laws which until then had been in force there. Such an obligation would, therefore, have to result in each case from special agreements concluded between the States in question. Such agreements, as forming special and exceptional law, must be interpreted most restrictively': *Struzek v. District Appeal Committee for War Cripples in Łódź, Ann. Dig.* vol. VI, Case no. 42.

1 See O'Connell, *International Law* (1965), pp. 44 *et seq.*
2 Rosenne, *loc. cit.* p. 277; *Porto Rico Railway, Light and Power Co. v. Amador, Ann. Dig.* vol. I, Case no. 49; *Occupation of Crete Case, ibid.* vol. III, Case no. 69.
3 The Belgian Minister of Justice said on 23 January 1964 in a written answer to a parliamentary question: 'L'octroi de la souveraineté a eu pour effet d'enlever à la législation coloniale en vigueur au 30 juin 1960 son caractère de législation belge particulière et de lui donner celui d'une législation étrangère.'
4 Rosenne, *loc. cit.* p. 281.

law in being is presumed to exist five minutes after change of sovereignty (which is a fiction), it is necessary to presume a retroactivity of the legislative will when manifested. But if this will is never manifested, except by implication, conviction of legislative endorsement of the legal system can grow but slowly. In actual fact, all legal transactions concluded in this twilight period of uncertainty will be founded on the presumption of legal continuity, and the human necessity for regulation and certainty is clearly a more viable intellectual factor than the supposition of a collective will.

The claims of one man against another, whether founded on contract, quasi-contract or tort, or on enforceable judgments of competent courts, constitute acquired rights which the successor State must respect.[1] They are 'property' no less than rights to the ownership of land, and their abrogation by the successor State is only legitimate when accompanied by a payment of reasonable compensation. The cancellation of claims possessed by foreign nationals, or the failure to provide machinery for their settlement, is not an unjust enrichment on the part of the successor State, it is true, but it does constitute a denial of justice for which redress may be demanded through the appropriate diplomatic channels. The doctrine of acquired rights applies *a fortiori* to interests which are governed entirely by private law.[2]

2. THE DISTINCTION BETWEEN PUBLIC LAW AND PRIVATE LAW

Since obviously not all the laws of the predecessor State survive change of sovereignty, it is important to ascertain the test for determining which of them have lapsed.

The traditional doctrine of State succession is that the private law survives a change of sovereignty but the public law does not.[3] The suggested distinction was made by French authors in the nineteenth century, and no doubt to the French lawyer it is a clear and workable distinction, though he makes it on somewhat different premises from the German or the Dutch lawyer. To the English or American lawyer,

---

1 Feilchenfeld, pp. 617 *et seq.*
2 *Co-operative Farmers in Tarnów* v. *Polish Treasury*, Ann. Dig. vol. II, Case no. 32.
3 Fauchille, vol. I, pt. I, p. 371; Piédelièvre, vol. I, p. 125; Phillipson, p. 305; Hershey in *A.J.* vol. v (1911), p. 285; *Essentials of International Public Law* (2nd ed., 1927), p. 224; Hoijer, p. 484; Kaeckenbeeck, *The International Experiment of Upper Silesia* (1942), p. 31; Selosse, pp. 164 *et seq.*; Dahm, vol. I, p. 110; Delbez, p. 181; Schwarzenberger, *Manual*, p. 81; Schönborn recognized that a new State is under a pressing need to leave the public law in force, p. 78.

however, it is a purely verbal distinction, for the common law recognizes only rudimentarily a division between public and private functions, and the statute law is based on premises which do not import it. In the case of succession in sovereignty of territories subject to English law, therefore, the suggestion is misleading that the distinction between public law and private law is the touchstone for determining which legal institutions survive; and the extent to which they do survive can only be measured by the extent to which political and administrative continuity is achieved throughout the change. In the case of independence of British territories when maximum continuity is maintained, doctrines of a public law character remain as applicable after the event as before it.

The doctrine of Act of State is an example. This denies an English court competence to entertain suits against the Crown arising out of the acquisition of territory by the Crown. The doctrine has its public aspects, inasmuch as it is concerned with a transfer of political power, and it rightly figures among those disparate legal institutions assembled in the textbooks under the heading of constitutional law. But as a common law doctrine it no doubt passes with the whole corpus of English law, and it has been applied in Indian courts to bar claims arising out of the merger of the Indian States in the Union.[1] Similarly, the whole doctrine of the royal prerogative is inherited by the successor State so long as the successor State remains a monarchy; and, so long as that State maintains a parliamentary form of government, all the law relating to parliamentary privilege, and institutions of review of executive action, such as certiorari, mandamus or prohibition, are likewise inherited.

Even in the case of territories subject to French law, the distinction between public law and private law manifests itself differently according to different forms of change of sovereignty. Independence within the context of the French Community was achieved by tranfers of specific competence under the Constitution, and as a result the maximum legal continuity was guaranteed. The whole body of French administrative and constitutional law was thus inherited, save for those institutions, including judicial institutions, by which the dependency of the territories upon France was achieved. Even in the case of cession of French territory it is incorrect to postulate a complete lapse of public law, for a great deal of the *droit administratif*, including the French ecclesiastical law,[2] continued in force in Alsace-Lorraine during the period of its transference to Germany. In 1955 the criminal court at Strasbourg held that German legislation of 1906 making billposting an offence was still in force in Alsace-Lorraine.[3]

[1] See *infra*, pp. 258 *et seq*. [2] See *infra*, vol. II, p. 340.
[3] *Annuaire français* (1956), p. 759.

A year later the *Tribunal de la Seine* held that the paternity provisions of the German civil code also prevailed there.[1] This makes it clear that, even in French law, the touchstone of the dichotomy between public law and private law is elusive.

French legal opinion differs on the question whether French law extends to newly acquired territory, and therefore, by implication, differs on the question whether the laws in force in the territory at the date of cession lapse. One view is that French law automatically applies to absorbed territory, and expels the contradictory laws in force there; the other view is that each French law must be specifically promulgated in the territory, and until this promulgation occurs all relevant legislation operating therein survives. Between these extreme opinions are more discriminating views: it is thought that, if there is no principle of the unity of legislation in the law of the annexing State, there is nothing to prevent the laws of the absorbed State prevailing; alternatively, it is suggested that a distinction should be drawn between laws which would be immediately applicable and those which would require promulgation; and, finally, there is a view that the only laws which apply to annexed territory are constitutional laws.[2] By a law of 9 June 1871 the Emperor of Germany appointed a date for the introduction of the German imperial administration in Alsace-Lorraine, and this provision was regarded as keeping French administrative law in subsistence in the provinces until the date of the application of the German law.[3] The extension of French constitutional law to Alsace-Lorraine was not proclaimed until 1 June 1924.[4] In French law it is a matter of interpretation in each case to what extent administrative law extends to acquired territory.[5]

1 *Annuaire français* (1957), p. 719.
2 French *ordonnances royales* did not apply to new territory unless promulgated: *Report in the Parlement of Paris*, 1683, Selosse, p. 142. In 1919 France enacted that all the law in Alsace-Lorraine should remain in force until French law should be legislatively introduced, *Journal Officiel*, 18 October 1919, p. 522. Generally see Lapradelle in *Rev. gén. de droit int. pub.* vol. XXXII (1925), pp. 388 *et seq.* Piédelièvre says that it is necessary to promulgate the successor's public laws *en bloc* in the absorbed territory: vol. I, p. 129. He makes an exception in the case of constitutional law, however, and says that it applies as from the moment of the change of sovereignty. Other writers agree with him: Strupp, *Éléments*, vol. I, p. 95; Fauchille, vol. I, pt. I, p. 366. For the opposite view see Fiore, *Int. Law Code*, p. 139; *Nouv. Droit int.* vol. I, p. 311.
3 Despagnet, p. 121.
4 See the decision of the *Tribunal des Conflits* of 27 February 1933 in the case of *Cie d'Assurances Rhin et Moselle*, *Rev. gén. de droit int. pub.* vol. XLII (1935), p. 220. See Fauchille, vol. I, pt. I, p. 372.
5 *Clunet*, vol. XCI (1964), p. 131, for decisions.

3. INCONSISTENCY BETWEEN LAWS OF THE PREDECESSOR AND SUCCESSOR STATES

If the distinction between public law and private law proves too rigid to provide a touchstone for determining which laws survive in territory subjected to change of sovereignty, a new test must be sought. The appropriate test seems to be inconsistency between the laws of the predecessor and successor States. Unless this inconsistency occurs, the laws in force in the territory are unaffected by the change; and the extent to which it occurs will depend upon the extent of the change. (1) In cases of annexation or cession a direct contradiction between the public laws of predecessor and successor States will occur, depending upon whether the territory is totally absorbed in a central administrative system or is left legally autonomous. (2) In cases of partition or dismemberment, the fragmented parts of a State will take with them all laws which are compatible with the new state of affairs, including all relevant public laws; but sometimes difficulties will arise in the transformation of federal law into the law of the dismembered portion. (3) In cases of secession and grants of independence, the only contradiction that can occur will be in respect of those legal institutions by which the previous dependence of the territory on the metropolitan government was secured; all other laws remain laws of the new State.

Tests of inconsistency in constitutional law have not, however, proved easy to manipulate. It is permissible to limit inconsistency to those occasions when it is impossible for the subject of the law to obey both laws; but it is equally permissible to extend it to those occasions when, though obedience to both laws is feasible, the superior law was intended, on construction, to cover the field of the legislative subject-matter. It is not permissible, in the rudimentary state of authority on State succession, to argue that one or other of these solutions is dictated, either by international law or by juristic logic; and the choice must be left to the law of the successor State, which is thus at liberty to determine the extent to which it supersedes that of the predecessor State.

The principle of continuity of law is only a presumption, which is displaced by positive legislative enactment, and if the new sovereign evinces the intention to introduce uniform law in the acquired territories this intention will prevail.[1] When political sentiment is acute, the intention

---

[1] *L. and J.J.* v. *Polish State Railways*, I.L.R. vol. XXIV, p. 77. Hyde, following Beale's view of the permanence of a legal norm (*Treatise on the Conflict of Laws* (1916), s. 131) argues that only laws at variance with those of the new sovereign cease to operate, but this cessation is not to be ascribed to the bare change of

of the new sovereign to substitute its law for that of the old is more easily established than when the change of sovereignty is perfunctory.

At times treaties of cession have stipulated for the continuance in force of the constitutional or administrative law of the ceding State in the territory transferred,[1] or have fixed a date upon which the successor's law would apply. Such a provision is ineffective until it becomes part of the municipal law of the successor State, and even then does not fetter the latter's constitutional competence to abrogate or alter the whole or part of the adopted law.

4. CONTINUITY OF LAW IN CEDED OR ANNEXED TERRITORY

(i) *British cessions and annexations*

The English common law was held to take effect in territories ceded to Great Britain only when promulgated,[2] and 'the laws of a conquered country continue until they are altered by the conqueror'.[3] In many of the territories acquired by the Crown the private law which operated under the old sovereign has been permitted to continue to regulate the relations of the inhabitants. Thus, Roman Dutch law remained the law of South Africa and of Ceylon, French that of Quebec and Mauritius,[4] and native law in many other regions. Included in this private law is the competence of public corporations established under charter or act of a supreme legislature to continue their operations. Local authorities are thus entitled to continue to levy rates and prosecute under by-laws, and trust corporations, public utility undertakings, and all bodies constituted for other than political purposes maintain their function. English constitutional law, and particularly the royal prerogative concerning government of ceded and conquered territory, extends thereto; and in so far as it extends, the previous law which is inconsistent with it lapses. However, the test of inconsistency has never been before a British court, and English law has therefore no experience to offer. Much depends upon whether newly

sovereignty but to conditions which are themselves consequences of that change: vol. I, p. 397. Fauchille, vol. I, pt. I, p. 390; Hershey in *A.J.* vol. V (1911), pp. 219, 224.

1 E.g. Convention between France and Sardinia of 1860 to regulate questions arising out of the cession of Savoy and Nice to France, *M.N.R.G.* vol. XVII, pt. II, p. 22.

2 *Calvin's Case* (1608), 7 Co. Rep. 1*a*; 77 E.R. 377; *Blankard* v. *Galdy* (1693), 2 Salk, 411; 4 Mod. 215 91 E.R. 356.

3 *Campbell* v. *Hall*, 98 E.R. 1045; 1 Cowp. 204 per Lord Mansfield at p. 208; *Picton's* Case, 30 St. Tr. 226, per Lord Ellenborough at p. 944.

4 The Articles of Capitulation, 1810, confirmed by the Treaty of Paris, 1814, provided for the inhabitants to preserve their religion, law and customs. See *infra*, vol. II, p. 207.

acquired territory becomes part of the Crown's dominions, or is administered by the Crown as foreign territory; and in the latter case, much depends upon the extent to which the foreign territory is administratively assimilated to the Crown's dominions.

In India the law concerning private rights of a State merged with other States in the Union was held to have continued in force,[1] and the same rule was applied to the case of retrocession of British Indian territory to Gwalior State on the date of partition.[2]

(ii) *United States cessions*

The United States Supreme Court stated with respect to the inhabitants of territory ceded to the United States:

Their relations with their former sovereign are dissolved, and new relations are created between them and the government which has acquired their territory. The same act which transfers their country, transfers the allegiance of those who remain in it; and the law, which may be denominated political, is necessarily changed, although that which regulated the intercourse, and general conduct of individuals, remains in force, until altered by the newly-created power of the State.[3]

United States practice has been consistently founded on the principle that only those laws which upheld the former sovereign lapse upon its disappearance. But application of the principle has not proved easy:[4]

1 *Mihan Singh* v. *The Subdivisional Canal Officer*, I.L.R. vol. XXI, p. 64; *State of Bihar* v. *Santo Kumar Mitra*, A.I.R. (1952), Pat. 148; *Anand Balkrishna Behare* v. *Police Leshkar* [1949], Madhya Bharat Law Reports 160.
2 *State of Madhya Bharat* v. *Mohanlal Motilal*, A.I.R. (1957), M.B. 58.
3 *American Insurance Co.* v. *Canter*, 1 Pet. 511 at p. 536. See also *U.S.* v. *Power's Heirs*, 11 How. 570; *U.S.* v. *Heirs of Rillieux*, 14 How. 189; *Leitensdorfer* v. *Webb*, 20 How. 176; *Shapleigh et al.* v. *Mier*, 83 F. 2d. 673 at p. 676; *The Philippine Sugar Estates Development Co.* v. *U.S.*, 39 C. Cl. (1904), 225 at pp. 244–7; *Ortega* v. *Lara*, 202 U.S. 339 at p. 342; *Vilas* v. *City of Manila*, 220 U.S. 345 at p. 357; *Chicago Rock Island and Pacific Railway Co.* v. *McGlinn*, 114 U.S. 542; *State of Washington* v. *Rainier National Park Co.* 192 Wash. 592. See also the Opinions of the Attorney-General of 9 September 1899; 22 Op. A.G. pp. 574–7; 21 November 1899, *ibid.* pp. 627–31.
4 *Downes* v. *Bidwell*, 182 U.S. 244. The Constitution and laws of the United States apply to acquired territory: *Pollard's Lessee* v. *Hagan*, 3 How. 212 at p. 225; *U.S.* v. *D'Auterive*, 10 How. 609; *De Montault* v. *U.S.*, 12 How. 47; *U.S.* v. *Power's Heirs*, 11 How, 570; *Sanches* v. *U.S.*, 42 Ct. Cl. 458; *U.S.* v. *Heirs of Rillieux*, 14 How. 189; *Hawaii* v. *Mankichi*, 190 U.S. 197; *New Orleans* v. *U.S.*, 10 Pet. 662; *Balzac* v. *People of Puerto Rico*, 258 U.S. 298. Hence, previous laws at variance with them lapse: *More* v. *Steinbach*, 127 U.S. 70 at p. 81; *U.S.* v. *Vaca*, 18 How. 556. Hence, too, the United States does not succeed to the prerogatives of the previous sovereign: *Pollard's Lessee* v. *Hagan*, 3 How. 212 at p. 225; Magoon, p. 372. But only political laws are at variance with United States law: *U.S.* v. *Vallejo*, 1 Black 541; *Harcourt* v. *Gaillard*, 12 Wheat. 523; Magoon, pp. 11, 19, 86, 490; 22 Op. A.G., pp. 566, 574, 627.

Immigration laws have been held to be political in nature,[1] as well as laws creating vested interest in political office.[2] Likewise, the laws granting authority to the previous sovereign to alienate the public domain have been held to lapse as political laws.[3] But when Hawaii was annexed in 1900, Congress designated[4] the laws which it considered to have been abrogated as contrary to United States public policy, and these included not only laws governing the flag, naturalization and consular agents, but also laws concerning flour, development of resources, savings banks, juries, *habeas corpus*, vagrancy, and master and servant.

At first, the opinion in the United States was that American law, including not only revenue laws,[5] but commercial law,[6] and shipping law,[7] extended *ex proprio vigore* with United States sovereignty, but later this was modified to require either an express extension of legislation by Congress to newly acquired territory or an implication in the acts by which that territory is incorporated in the United States.[8] The prevailing American opinion is that laws embodying grants of power to governmental agencies to govern acquired territory extend thereto *ex proprio vigore*, but laws embodying limitations on the power of Congress or these agencies do not.[9] When Andrew Jackson arrested a Spanish military officer after the transfer of power in Florida, the officer's release was ordered by the United States territorial court on a *habeas corpus* application. Jackson appealed to the President and cabinet, who upheld him on the ground that the constitutional guarantees had not been extended.[10] The Supreme Court held in 1922 that Congress had manifested the

1 *People* v. *Fulsom*, 5 Cal. 373.
2 *Alvarez* v. *U.S.*, 216 U.S. 167; *O'Reilly de Camara* v. *Brooke*, 209 U.S. 45.
3 *Henderson* v. *Poindexter's Lessee*, 12 Wheat, 530; *U.S.* v. *Reynes*, 9 How. 127; *Alexander* v. *Roulet*, 12 Wall. 423; *De Montault* v. *U.S.*, 12 How. 47; *U.S.* v. *D'Auterive*, 10 How. 280, 289; *New Orleans* v. *U.S.*, 10 Pet. 662; *Pollard's Lessee* v. *Hagan*, 3 How. 212, 225; *U.S.* v. *Vallejo*, 1 Black, 541; *Davis* v. *Concordia*, 9 How. 280 at p. 289; *Mumford* v. *Wardwell*, 6 Wall. 423; *Les Bois* v. *Bramell*, 4 How. 449; *Kennedy* v. *State*, 231 S.W. 683, 258 U.S. 617; *Jackson* v. *Porter*, Fed. Cas. No. 7143; *Stearns* v. *U.S.*, 6 Wall. 589; *Keene* v. *McDonough*, 8 Pet. 308; *Robinson* v. *Minor*, 10 How. 627; *U.S.* v. *Hanson*, 16 Pet. 196; *U.S.* v. *Pico*, 23 How. 321; also Wharton s. 51; 1 Op. A.G., 108; 11 *ibid*. 191; 22 *ibid*. 627; Magoon, p. 467.
4 31 Stat. L. 141, ch. 339. Wilkinson, p. 63.
5 *Bricknell* v. *Trammel*, 82 So. 221.
6 22 Op. A.G., 578. It was held that Acts of Congress regulating foreign commerce took effect *ipso facto* in incorporated territory: *Harrison* v. *Cross*, 16 How. 164 at p. 202.
7 *Ramos* v. *U.S.* 12 F. 2d. 761.
8 *Rassmussen* v. *U.S.*, 197 U.S. 516; *Dorr* v. *U.S.*, 195 U.S. 138; *Soto* v. *U.S.*, 273 F. 2d. 628 at pp. 632–5.
9 Wilkinson, p. 31.
10 Magoon, p. 137 *et seq.*, Annals of Congress, 17th Cong. 1st sess. II, 1374–7, 2300, 2413.

The Effect on the Legal System

intention to extend to Hawaii all laws which were not inherently inapplicable.[1] After the cession of Alaska it was held that Congress had intended to extend customs and navigation laws thereto.[2] But United States copyright laws were considered not to benefit Hawaiians.[3] Puerto Rico was held not to have come within the operation of United States tariff laws, even though the territory was not foreign territory within their intendment.[4] The United States as a result has, as one authority has described it, 'fashioned a uniquely complicated doctrine'.[5]

(iii) *The Anschluss of Austria to the Reich, 1938*

The Law of Reunion of Austria to the *Reich* of 13 March 1938 proclaimed in article 2 that 'the law now prevailing in Austria remains in force until further notice. The introduction of *Reich* law into Austria will be effected by the Leader and *Reich* Chancellor, or by the *Reich* Minister empowered by him to do so.'[6] In a case concerning the liability of a servant of the *Reich* who was involved in a collision during the occurrence of the *Anschluss*, the *Reichsgericht* held that the Austrian law had continued in effect after the annexation, and that article 131 of the Weimar Constitution, which the defendant had pleaded, had not been extended to Austria and did not apply to it automatically.[7]

(iv) *The acquisition of German territory by Poland, 1945*

On 13 November 1945 Polish legislation provided that the body of law in force in the judicial district of Poznan should take effect in the territories removed from German administration. The legislation failed, however, to regulate the question of the law in force there between 2 August 1945, when this event occurred, and its promulgation. A special bench of the Polish Supreme Court in 1948 was constituted to decide the question. It held that Polish law immediately superseded German law in the territories on the twin grounds that the German population was dispersed and had lacked social cohesion, and that the group consciousness of the Polish nation objected to applying German law to Poles.[8]

1 *Iponmatsu Ukichi* v. *U.S.*, 281 F. 525.
2 *U.S.* v. *British Schooners*, 5 Al. 11.
3 22 Op. A.G., 268.
4 *De Lima* v. *Bidwell*, 182 U.S. 1; *Downes* v. *Bidwell*, 182 U.S. 244; *14 Diamond Rings* v. *U.S.*, 183 U.S. 176.
5 Magoon, p. 50.
6 R.I.I.A., Docs. on Int. Aff. 1938 (1943), vol. II, p. 74.
7 *R. and G.* v. *H. Hochbahn A.G., Ann. Dig.* vol. X, Case no. 24.
8 *L. and J.J.* v. *Polish State Railway, I.L.R.* vol. XXIV, p. 77.

(v) *Other cases*

The Syrian Court of Appeal held that the law of the Ottoman Empire relating to the rights of Christians had continued in force in Syria.[1] The *Reichsgericht* decided in 1882 that French law did not lose its validity in Alsace-Lorraine through the transfer of those provinces to Germany.[2] An Italian court held that the enactments of the Italian Social Republic, as a *de facto* government, retained their validity even after the legitimate government had recovered the territory administered by the Republic, unless such exactments were of a purely political character.[3]

(vi) *The cession of Newfoundland to Canada, 1949*

By virtue of the British North America Act, 1949,[4] laws operating in Newfoundland were to continue so to operate until repealed or altered by the Parliament of Canada or that of the new province, and Canadian statutes were only to come into force in the province when extended by Act of the Canadian Parliament, or by Proclamation of the Governor-General in Council.

5. CONTINUITY OF LAW UPON THE FORMATION AND DISSOLUTION OF COMPOSITE STATES, AND DISMEMBERMENT OF STATES

(i) *The formation of the United Arab Republic, 1958*

Article 68 of the Provisional Constitution of the United Arab Republic maintained in force all laws, decrees and regulations of Egypt and Syria within the respective regions.

(ii) *The formation of the Somali Republic, 1960*

Article 42 of the Somaliland Constitution provided that the law administered by the courts would be in conformity with the substance of the common law, the doctrines of equity, and the statutes of general application in force in England on 16 March 1900. Following the fusion of the Republic of Somalia and Somaliland in 1960, the Government of the United Republic created a Permanent Consultative Commission for Integration.[5] Article 3 of the Act of Union, which was retrospective to

1 *Rizéallah Gazaló* Case, *Ann. Dig.* vol. IV, Case no. 65.
2 *Fontes Juris Gent.*, ser. A, sec. 2, vol. I, p. 117.
3 *Galatioto v. Ochoa*, *Foro Italiano* (1946), vol. I, p. 217.
4 12, 13 & 14 Geo. VI, c. 22.
5 Cotran in *I.C.L.Q.* (1963), p. 1017.

1 July 1960, provided that the laws in force in both territories at the establishment of the Union should remain in force, and the courts as then constituted should continue to exercise the jurisdiction conferred on them. Following review by the Consultative Commission, the judicial systems were unified by the Organization of the Judiciary Decree of June 1962, with district courts, regional courts, courts of appeal for each region, and a Supreme Court of the Republic, as provided for in the Constitution. The decree provides for the administration by the courts of the Shariat law of customary law in civil matters, where the cause of action has arisen under that law, and for the statutory law in other matters. Since the statutory law is English in two of the Regions and Italian in the remainder, it follows that unification has not been completely achieved. The Commission is proceeding towards it by codifying statutes in various fields. The Supreme Court has held that the survival of laws with differing statutory penalties from the days before independence cannot be challenged on the ground of unconstitutionality for offence against the equality provisions in the Constitution.[1] The procedure is broadly that which prevailed in each of the two territories before independence.

(iii) *The formation of Malaysia, 1963*

The Constitution of Malaysia[2] preserves all law in force on Malaysia Day, *mutatis mutandis*. All federal law already enacted would extend to any part of Malaysia to which it was expressed to extend, but would not otherwise extend to a Borneo State or Singapore except by special legislation. Present laws of the latter would be treated as federal laws if falling within federal areas of power. Continuity of law was also achieved by the Constitutions of the States,[3] and in the law of the United Kingdom by the Malaysia Act, 1963.[4]

(iv) *The formation of Tanzania, 1964*

When Tanganyika and Zanzibar united, the Articles of Union preserved the existing laws of the territories, save as they should be construed with necessary modification to bring them into conformity with the Union.[5] Since Zanzibar had abrogated the Constitution at the time of the overthrow of the Sultan,[6] it was necessary for the Revolutionary

1 *Mohammed Saleh Mijertain Mahamoud Mohammed Omar* v. *The State*, Criminal Appeal no. 19 of 1961. *Ibid.*
2 Cmnd. 2094, s. 73.
3 *Ibid.* Sabah, s. 48; Sarawak, s. 46; Singapore, s. 105.   4 Ch. 35, s. 3.
5 Union of Tanganyika and Zanzibar Act, no. 22 of 1964, s. 8. Govt. Notice no. 243 of 1 May 1964. 'Existing law' was defined in s. 2.
6 Zanzibar General Notice no. 73 of 12 January 1964.

Government to legislate to preserve existing laws.[1] An exception with respect to this saving provision was made in the case of the Zanzibar Order in Council, 1924,[2] but a further saving was made with respect to the sections which had specified the law in force in Zanzibar, including the statutes of general application in force in England on 7 July 1897.[3]

(v) *The dismemberment of Ruanda-Urundi, 1962*

By agreement signed at Brussels on 21 December 1961, Belgium undertook to transfer the powers of internal autonomy to Rwanda and Burundi. This was achieved by issuing some thirty-six legislative orders concerning decentralization, and Belgium stated that it went without saying that all the measures of application taken on the basis of these laws and regulations were within the jurisdiction of the two countries. As a consequence of these measures, complete continuity of law was achieved throughout the process of separation of Rwanda and Burundi. In particular, by Legislative Order no. 23, decentralization was achieved of the decree governing contracts and obligations. In order to work out how the Brussels Protocols were to be applied, a mission was despatched from Brussels to Rwanda and Burundi in January 1962 and provisional constitutions proposed by the countries themselves were then promulgated to provide a legal framework for the powers which were vested in the local governments by the Legislative Orders.[4]

(vi) *The dissolution of the Federation of the West Indies, 1962*

The Order in Council dissolving the Federation of the West Indies[5] provided that all federal laws should remain in force in the Territories. The Commissioner for the Territories, who would be responsible for the process of dissolution, would, however, have power to adapt or modify any such laws.[6]

(vii) *The dissolution of the Federation of Rhodesia and Nyasaland, 1963*

The Federation of Rhodesia and Nyasaland Order in Council, 1963,[7] provided that the power of the federal legislature to make laws should cease, but it preserved the continuity of the scheduled list of laws. The

1 Existing Laws Decree no. 1 of 1964.
2 S.R. & O. no. 1401 of 1924.
3 S. 24.
4 U.N. Doc. A/5126/Add. 1, Annex XXIV.
5 The West Indies (Dissolution and Interim Commissioner) Order in Council, S.I. 1962, no. 1084, s. 15.
6 S. 14.
7 S.I. 1963, no. 1635, ss. 1 and 3.

The Effect on the Legal System

subsequent Order in Council[1] dissolving the Federation provided that all law in force in a Territory immediately before dissolution, including all federal legislation, should continue in force, but the Governor might, by Order made before dissolution, declare that any law of the federal legislature should cease to have effect, or should be modified. Southern Rhodesia declared[2] that 148 Federal Acts should cease to apply, including Acts relating to federal loans and guarantees. In addition, modifications were effected in respect of seventy-nine other Acts, including those affecting copyright and exchange control. However, the Southern Rhodesian Constitution[3] had excluded federal legislation from the operation of the Declaration of Rights provisions in the Constitution, and neither the Dissolution Order nor the Southern Rhodesian interpretation enactment covered this omission. The fact that, after dissolution, federal law, though now part of Southern Rhodesian law, would continue to escape the constitutional guarantees was pointed out before the Order dissolving the Federation was drafted,[4] but any attempt on the part of the United Kingdom to rectify the situation would have complicated the negotiation of the dissolution agreements. In 1964 the I.L.O. criticized Southern Rhodesia for maintaining federal legislation in force relating to prisons which was alleged to contradict the convention relating to forced labour. The relevant Southern Rhodesian legislation excluded forced labour. This raised the question whether the inconsistency provisions of the Federal Constitution were still applicable, or whether the two Acts now ranked *pari passu*, and if so whether the federal Act, being subsequent in time, should now be interpreted as having repealed the Territorial law.

Northern Rhodesia provided for the lapse of only thirteen federal enactments,[5] but subsequently Zambia repealed thirty-five federal Acts, mostly relating to federal pensions and finance.[6] It modified sixty-six enactments. Nyasaland provided for the cessation of forty enactments,[7] and, after independence, for a number of consequential modifications.[8]

1 S.I. 1963, no. 2085, s. 2.
2 Federal Laws (Cesser) Order, 1963, Southern Rhodesia Govt. Notice no. 786.
3 The Southern Rhodesia (Constitution) Order, S.I. 1961, no. 2314, s. 70 (3).
4 Southern Rhodesia Legislative Assembly Debates, 1963, col. 1809.
5 Federal Laws (Discontinuance) Order, 1963, Govt. Notice no. 447 of 1963.
6 The Federal Laws (Repeal) Act, 1965.
7 Cessation of Application of Federal Laws Order, 1963, Govt. Notice no. 16 of 1964, *Nyasaland Gazette* of 6 January 1964, p. 39.
8 Malawi Enactments (Adaptation and Modification) Order, 1964, Govt. Notice no. 219, *Malawi Gazette* of 3 July 1964, p. 631.

(viii) *The partition of India, 1947*

Section 18 of the Indian Independence Act provided that, apart from construction of the relevant legislation to refer to both India and Pakistan, according to the circumstances, the law of British India, including all Orders in Council made under section 311 of the Government of India Act for adapting and modifying Acts of Parliament, would, so far as applicable and with the necessary adaptations, continue as the law of each of the new Dominions until altered by legislation thereof. Instruments of Instruction to the Governor-General and the Governors, would, however, lapse. Continuity of law was also achieved in article 372 (1) of the Indian Constitution.

Indian courts have rejected contentions that these provisions were ineffective to secure a continuity of United Kingdom statute law in India,[1] at least where no reconstruction of its provisions would be necessary.[2]

Lord Goddard, in a case under the Fugitive Offenders Act, referring to section 18, said: 'It seems to me clear that that Act, which was passed in direct contemplation of India becoming a Republic within some five weeks of its passing, preserves in force all the laws of this country relating to India which were in force at the date of the Republic coming into existence.'[3]

The Supreme Court of Pakistan, however, held that the Order in Council by which a devolution of British Indian treaties in Pakistan had occurred was ineffective to apply to Pakistan the legislation giving internal effect to the Convention on Arbitral Awards. This decision has been criticized.[4]

The partition of India gave rise to certain technical problems stemming from the continuity of law, and these may be briefly mentioned:

(A) Taxation. The Indian Income Tax Act was kept in force, but the High Court of Calcutta refused to presume that a tax assessment on land revenue made before partition still subsisted after the land passed to Pakistan, without proof of the law of Pakistan.[5]

---

1 See *infra*, p. 124. In *Babu s/o Kalu* v. *Parsam s/o Salam* (1951), *Criminal Law Journal* (1954), p. 795, the High Court of Madhya Bharat held that on the authority of *Campbell* v. *Hall* the continuity of law in India was consistent with the principles of international law.

2 See *infra*, p. 125.

3 *Re Government of India and Mukarak Ali Ahmed* [1952] 1 All E.R. 1060 at p. 1062.

4 See *supra*, p. 57.

5 *Kumar Jagadish Chandra Sinha* v. *Commissioner of Income Tax*, I.L.R. vol. XXIII, p. 112.

The Effect on the Legal System

On 10 December 1947 an agreement between India and Pakistan for the avoidance of double taxation was notified under section 49 AA of the Act.[1] Firms which had done business in both countries when they were part of British India had made profits in one part and incurred losses in the other, and the question arose whether under section 23 (5) (a) of the Act the net income of these firms should be apportioned. In one instance where the firm constituted a partnership, the Indian income tax authority split up the loss and added it to the income of one of the partners who had other business in Pakistan which operated profitably. This was held by the Punjab High Court to involve an alteration of the incidence of tax and not to be a mere avoidance of double taxation.[2] The continued obligation of the subject of assessment was upheld by the Supreme Court of Madras in 1958.[3]

(B) *Companies.* An effect of the partition of India was that companies resident in Pakistan became domiciled there for purposes of the conflict of laws, whereas they had previously been domiciled in India. It was held by the Punjab High Court that it followed that the *situs* of the shareholding of Indian shareholders in such companies would be Pakistan.[4]

(C) *Private contracts.* Three categories of contracts between private parties were affected by the partition: where the parties were both resident in Pakistan and after partition migrated into India or vice versa; where they were both in India and the contract was to be performed in Pakistan; and where one party was residing in Pakistan and the other in India and one left Pakistan or India, as the case might be. The question of frustration of the contract in these situations was raised.[5] The Indian Supreme Court held that the only doctrine of frustration is that of supervening impossibility or illegality as laid down in section 56 of the Indian Contract Act.[6] It was held in two Punjab cases that an arbitration clause in a contract by which disputes should be referred to arbitration of two 'European merchants' in Karachi was subjected to supervening impossibility because of the hazards of a journey from India to Pakistan by non-Moslems. Also, the parties were to be taken to have contracted to be governed by the laws of India to be administered by the courts of India.[7]

1 *U.N.T.S.* vol. LI, p. 173, Notification no. 28.
2 *In the matter of Seth Satya Pal Virmani,* Civil Reference no. 15 of 1952.
3 *Sree Rajendra Mills Ltd, Gandhinagar, Salem* v. *The Income Tax Officer* A.I.R. (1958), Mad. 220.
4 *Batala Civil Engineering Co.,* Civil Original, no. 4 of 1949.
5 Kapur in *Indian Law Review,* vol. IX (1957), p. 13.
6 *Satyabrata Chose* v. *Mugneeram Bangur & Co.* (1954), S.C.A. 187.
7 *Rama Nand Vijay Parkash* v. *Gokal Chand,* A.I.R. (1951), Simla 189; *Messrs Parmeshri Das Mehra & Sons* v. *Ram Chand Om Prakesh* (1951), 53 Punjab L.R. 432.

(ix) *The separation of Singapore from Malaysia, 1965*
The legislation concerning Singapore's separation from Malaysia contained a continuity of laws provision.[1]

6. CONTINUITY OF LAW IN NEW STATES

In most instances of independence of dependent territories, legislative provision has been made for the continuity of the previous legal system. The provisions in question fall into two categories: (*a*) those in which no condition is expressly imported that the laws shall be consistent with the transfer of sovereignty and (*b*) those in which this condition is imported.

(i) *Independence of British territories*
Until the modern grants of independence there had been no historical example of the successful secession of British territory from the Crown since the independence of the United States. On that occasion the colonial charters, and all English law and relevant statutes, continued to apply in the colonies, and have been given effect to on many occasions. However, at the time of secession it was not clear whether the law relating to the allegiance to the Crown lapsed in virtue of a total evacuation of English law, or whether it lapsed only in virtue of its public character. The Supreme Court of Pennsylvania interpreted the Act of 28 January 1779 of that State 'for the revival of the laws' as 'virtually declaring that they were suspended from 14th May, 1776 till the 11th February, 1777'. The constitution agreed upon on 29 July 1786 'was incontrovertibly a dissolution of the government, as far as related to the powers of Great Britain, but not in relation to the powers which had been before exercised by councils and committees'. The Chief Justice thought that the Act of 1779 was intended merely to declare that the laws originally enacted under the authority of the Crown ceased any longer to derive their virtue and validity from that source, but that the draftsman thought that the separation from Great Britain 'worked a dissolution of all government, and that the force, not only of the acts of Assembly but of the common law and statute law of England, was actually extinguished by that event'. In view of these doubts arising from the construction of the Act, it would be safer not to convict for treason occurring during the twilight period.[2]

[1] *State of Singapore Govt. Gazette*, 9 August 1965, no. 1824; *Malaysia Law* no. 53 of 1965, s. 7; *International Legal Materials*, vol. IV (1965), p. 939.
[2] *Respublica* v. *Chapman*, 1 Law Ed., U.S. 33, at p. 53 (1781). After the American Civil War it was sufficient to hold that the law of the States had remained in force in virtue of the claim of the States to have seceded, and to hold that the United States

The Effect on the Legal System 119

On the grant of self-government, and later of independence, to British territories it has become customary to incorporate a provision for the preservation of existing laws.[1] And even though this provision is itself an enactment of the predecessor State, no argument has yet been addressed to a court of a newly independent State that it in itself has lapsed, and with it necessarily has lapsed the formula for the survival of existing law. Most new States have their own legislation specifying that the common law and doctrines of equity form part of the existing law together with English statutes of general application as at a specific date, but in some instances these enactments were made before independence.[2]

Constitution continued to determine the validity of State laws in virtue of the failure of the secession: e.g. *Keith* v. *Clark*, 97 U.S. 455; *Texas* v. *White*, 7 Wall. 700.

1 The Ghana (Constitution) Order, S.I. 1957, no. 277, ss. 3 (4), 79, 80; The Federation of Malaya Independence Act, 1957, 5 & 6 Eliz. II, c. 60, s. 2; Federation of Malaya (Constitution) Order, S.I. 1957, no. 1533, s. 162; Malaysia Act, 1963, c. 35, s. 3; The Cyprus Act, 1960, 8 & 9 Eliz. II, c. 52, s. 3; Somaliland (Constitution) Order, S.I. 1960, no. 1060, s. 54; The Sierra Leone (Constitution) Order, S.I. 1961, no. 741, s. 4; The Tanganyika (Constitution) Order, S.I. 1961, no. 2274, s. 4; The Trinidad and Tobago (Constitution) Order, S.I. 1962, no. 1875, s. 4; The Jamaica (Constitution) Order, S.I. 1962, no. 1550, s. 4; The Aden (Constitution) Order, S.I. 1962, no. 2177, s. 5; The Kenya Order in Council, S.I. 1963, no 791, s. 4; The Kenya Independence Order, S.I. 1963, no. 1968, s. 4; The Uganda Independence Order, S.I. 1962, no. 2175, s. 4; The Uganda Act, 1964, c. 20, s. 1; The Zambia Independence Order, S.I. 1964, no. 1652, s. 4; The Zambia Independence Act, 1964, c. 65, s. 2; The Malawi Independence Order, S.I. 1964, no. 916, s. 4; The Malta Independence Order, S.I. 1964, no. 1398, s. 4; The Zanzibar Act, 1963, c. 55, s. 1; The Gambia Independence Order, S.I. 1965, no. 135, s. 4. In *Kazaairne* v. *The Lukiko* [1963] *The East African Law Reports*, 472, it was held that s. 26 (3) of the Uganda Independence Order in Council had no effect on art. 41 of the Constitution of Buganda, and the Buganda Tax law 1934 was an existing law to which s. 4 (1) of the Uganda Independence Order applied, and s. 74 (1) of the Constitution of Uganda had no effect on it. The definition of 'existing laws' was held by the High Court of Malawi to include the Fugitive Offenders Act, 1881, *R.* v. *Amihiya*, Criminal Appeal no. 301 of 1964, *The Times*, 22 October 1964, p. 10.

2 Tanganyika Judicature and Application of Laws Ordinance, no. 57 of 1961. The Schedule to this Act substitutes Tanganyika where relevant for the expressions British Colony or Possession and the Fugitive Offenders Act is preserved. The date of application of Statutes is 22 July 1920. For Uganda see Judicature Ordinance no. 62 of 1962, s. 2 (date of application 11 August 1902). For Kenya see The Kenya (Jurisdiction of Courts and Pending Proceedings) Regulations 1963, s. 3 (date of application 12 August 1897), made under s. 11 of the Kenya Order in Council, 1963. In Zanzibar the application of English law and statutes, as provided in the Zanzibar Order in Council, S.R. & O. no. 1401 of 1924, s. 25 (date of application, 2 March 1925), is preserved by the Zanzibar Existing Laws Decree, no. 1 of 1964, s. 3. The Nigerian (Constitution) Order in Council, 1960, provided for the law to be administered in federal courts in the Western Region to be the common law and equity administered concurrently as they are administered in the High Court of Justice in England; and in Lagos and the Eastern and Northern Regions, the common law, equity, and statutes of general application in force in England on 1 January 1900, as varied by United Kingdom legislation expressly extending to Nigeria, and Nigerian Ordinances. (The Northern Cameroons adopted the legal system of the Northern Region of Nigeria.)

When a newly independent country abolishes the British Crown it is desirable for further saving of existing law to be made, because otherwise much legislation which includes references to the Crown's functions might lapse.[1] In countries where this legislation has been enacted it is possible that, for example, the Fugitive Offenders Act, the operation of which is predicated on two territories being 'British possessions', has survived as part of existing law. But even if it has survived as part of existing law in two Republics within the Commonwealth, it does not follow that it operates between them. For example, the statute is probably in force in both Tanzania and Kenya. But a Tanzanian court would have to hold that in Tanzanian law both Tanzania and Kenya are still affected by it; and it is not clear to what extent the Tanzanian court is obliged to recognize that the Act is in force in Kenya, in order to determine that in Tanzanian law it is in force in both countries.[2]

Some of the problems raised by specific statutes will be discussed.

(A) *The definition of 'British possession'*. Certain Acts of the United Kingdom Parliament predicate legal consequences upon action by, or in respect of, 'British possessions'. The question arises whether independent States still qualify as British possessions for the relevant purpose.

The Acts Interpretation Act, 1889[3] defined a British possession as part of 'Her Majesty's dominions'. The latter expression has not been statutorily defined, but it is taken for granted that those Commonwealth countries which remain connected with the royal prerogative continue to be Her Majesty's dominions, while certain territories which, because they were not colonial territories, and hence were not part of the Crown's dominions, became, in the independence enactments, part of Her Majesty's dominions by statute. These countries were Tanganyika, Uganda[4] and Malawi. Also, the Consequential Provisions Acts of the United Kingdom, passed to regulate the effects of Commonwealth countries becoming republics, have continued, for purposes of statutory operation in the United Kingdom, to define the countries concerned as Her Majesty's dominions, and hence as British possessions.[5]

---

1 Such provision has been made in the Constitution of the Federal Republic of Nigeria Act, no. 20 of 1963, s. 156; the Republic of Tanganyika (Consequential, Transitional and Temporary Provisions) Act, no. 2 of 1962, s. 5, which requires that the existing law shall be construed with the republican constitution. Similar provision is made in The Constitution of Kenya (Amendment) Act, no. 28 of 1964, s. 14, and The Constitution of Uganda (First Amendment) Act, no. 61 of 1963, s. 39 (1) (this defines 'existing law' in s. 2).

2 See *infra*, p. 123.

3 52 & 53 Vict., c. 63.

4 See *supra*, p. 57.   5 See *supra*, p. 55.

The Effect on the Legal System

It cannot automatically be presumed that when a country separates from the United Kingdom, and especially from the Crown, it ceases to be affected by legislation which had referred to 'British possessions' or 'Her Majesty's dominions', for, as the Supreme Court of New Zealand pointed out, the question of interpretation that is involved is less one of the political status of a territory than one of geographical reference. Callan J. said: 'I have no doubt from this definition of "British Possession" (in the Fugitive Offenders Act) that this expression is used in the statute as descriptive of a geographical area—and not as a political description.'[1] The Supreme Court of Israel, pursuing this reasoning, held that Israeli courts have Admiralty Jurisdiction under the Admiralty Offences (Colonial) Act, 1849, even though Israel could not be regarded as a 'colony'. The important factor, it apprehended, was continuity of the law, not commitment to a political condition.[2]

(B) *The definition of 'British ship'*. A frequent requirement for the exercise of Admiralty jurisdiction is either that the ship is a British ship, or that the person sought to be charged with an offence is a British subject. What, then, is a British ship? Ownership by a British subject has always been the test applied; if ownership cannot be proved, the fact that the ship is British may be inferred from the circumstances, for example, that the ship flies the British flag and sails from a British port.[3] The Merchant Shipping Act, 1894 enacts that a ship shall not be deemed to be a British ship unless it is owned wholly by British subjects or by a body corporate established under and subject to the laws of some part of Her Majesty's dominions and having its principal place of business in those dominions.[4] Furthermore, a British ship is required by the Merchant Shipping Act to be registered thereunder,[5] and a ship which is not so registered shall not be recognized as a British ship for the purposes of the Act.[6] An unregistered British ship would no doubt be subject to the Admiralty jurisdiction generally for criminal purposes.

A British subject is a citizen of any Commonwealth country and the expression 'Her Majesty's dominions' embraces the monarchies of the Commonwealth, and also, by statute, the republics.[7] The place of registra-

---

1 *Godwin* v. *Walker* [1938] N.Z.L.R. 712 at p. 753.
2 *Stampfer* v. *A.G.* I.L.R. vol. xxiii, p. 284.
3 *Bell* v. *Mansfield* (1893) 19 V.L.R. 165; *R.* v. *Ross* (1854) 1 S.C.R. (N.S.W.) 857.
4 57 & 58 Vict., c. 60, s. 1. The British Nationality Act, 1948, Sched. IV, amended the definition to mean ship owned by a British subject, however he acquired this status.   5 S. 2.   6 S. 2 (2).
7 India, 12, 13 & 14 Geo. VI, c. 92, s. 1; Pakistan, 4 & 5 Eliz. II, c. 31, s. 1; Malaya, 5 & 6 Eliz. II, c. 60, s. 2; Ghana, 8 & 9 Eliz. II, c. 41, s. 1; Cyprus, 8 & 9 Eliz. II, c. 52, s. 3; Uganda, 1964, c. 20, s. 1; Nigeria, 1963, c. 57, s. 1.

tion of the ship must be the United Kingdom or a port approved by the governor in any 'British possession', which term is statutorily defined to mean 'Her Majesty's dominions',[1] and has been held to include India. The question then arises whether a ship registered in a Commonwealth country is a British ship. The British Nationality Act, section 3, preserves offences under the Merchant Shipping legislation, and equates non-United Kingdom citizens who are British subjects with aliens only in respect of acts done or omitted in another Commonwealth country, and not upon the high seas. United Kingdom courts may thus have criminal jurisdiction, at least in respect of Commonwealth citizens, over events on board ships registered in other Commonwealth countries. But have those other Commonwealth countries a like jurisdiction?

Should the Admiralty Offences (Colonial) legislation be treated by the courts as applying to ships defined as British ships in the British Merchant Shipping Act, it is clear that the courts of one part of the Commonwealth have jurisdiction over the ships of another part in circumstances that international law would not permit in the case of totally foreign ships. In fact, however, the link between the Admiralty Offences (Colonial) legislation and the British Merchant Shipping Act is not explicit but notional. It arises from the decision in R. v. Keyn[2] that the Admiralty jurisdiction does not affect foreign ships, and it assumes that foreign ships and non-British ships are coincidental categories. It is arguable that international law should now be resorted to in order to qualify this coincidence, so that, although a ship for purposes of the British Merchant Shipping Act is a British ship, it may for purposes of the Admiralty jurisdiction be a foreign ship. The notion of 'British ship' may thus no longer be totally comprehensive.[3]

(C) *The Fugitive Offenders Act, 1881.* The Fugitive Offenders Act,[4] as extended to Protectorates,[5] provided for rendition of criminals from one 'British possession' to another, under procedures involving the signature of the Governor of the Colony. The Act could be applied to any territory by Order in Council. In 1952 the High Court in England held that the

1 Acts Interpretation Act 1889, 52 & 53 Vict., c. 63, s. 18 (2).
2 (1876) 2 Ex. D. 63.
3 Cf. definition of 'Commonwealth ship' in New Zealand Shipping and Seamen Act, 1952, s. 1, and of 'British ship' in Australian Commonwealth Navigation Act, 1912–1958, s. 6. See the British Commonwealth Merchant Shipping Agreement, 1931, *L.N.T.S.* vol. 129, p. 177, Cmd. 3994; *B.F.S.P.* vol. 134, p. 138, which promises 'national' treatment by 'Each Part' of the Commonwealth to ships of other 'Parts'. Does this bind the new Commonwealth Members?
4 44 & 45 Vict., c. 69.
5 5 & 6 Geo. V, c. 39.

effect of the Indian (Consequential Provisions) Act, 1949 was to preserve in force all United Kingdom laws relating to India, and that the Fugitive Offenders Act continued to govern the rendition to India of an offender at India's request.[1] In 1957, however, the Supreme Court of India held that India could no longer be described as a 'British possession', and hence rendition to other Commonwealth countries under the Act was no longer possible.[2] In contrast with this decision, and also with India's own policy of seeking rendition under the Act, both previously and subsequently thereto,[3] the Federal Court of Pakistan held the Act to apply in Pakistan while that country was a monarchy.[4] Nigeria[5] and Ghana[6] have both utilized the Act, although at the time the one was a monarchy and the other a republic. The Act has also been utilized by Cyprus,[7] a republic, and between Australia and Ceylon,[8] both of which are monarchies.

A Commonwealth country which abolishes the monarchy certainly ceases to be one of the Crown's dominions, and hence, pursuant to the definition in the Acts Interpretation Act, 1889, a British possession. However, the provision made for the continuity of existing law by those countries which have become republics has the effect of retaining the Fugitive Offenders Act in force in those countries. Hence, a fugitive can be delivered from any one of those countries to one of the Crown's dominions. But can he be delivered to another republic? Or can another republic, or another of the Crown's dominions, reciprocally deliver? The High Court of Malawi has dealt twice with the question. In the first case a fugitive was not delivered by the hearing magistrate to Ghana on the ground, subsequently overruled by the Hight Court, that the Act was not in force in Malawi.[9] In the second case Kenya sought rendition of a

1 Re *Government of India and Mubarak Ali Ahmed* [1952] 1 All E.R. 1060.
2 *State of Madras* v. *C. G. Menon*, A I.R. (1954), S.C. 517. Clute in *A.J. Comp. L.* vol. VIII (1959), p. 25. When South Africa withdrew from the Commonwealth the application thereto of the Fugitive Offenders Act was withdrawn: Fugitive Offenders (South Africa) Order, S.I. 1963, no. 613. The Federation of Rhodesia and Nyasaland had its own Extradition Act, permitting extradition to South Africa. This was repealed by Northern Rhodesia and Nyasaland (see *supra*, p. 115), and Southern Rhodesia enacted new legislation. The Fugitive Offenders Act was saved in Uganda by the Extradition Act, no. 16 of 1964, s. 3 (1).
3 *Re Henderson* [1950] 1 All E.R. p. 283; *Re Government of India and Mubarak Ali Ahmed* [1952] 1 All E.R. 1060.   4 *E. M. Bhaba* v. *The Crown* (1954) 2 Tindh. 101.
5 *Ex parte Enahoro*, The Times, 16 January 1963.
6 *Ex parte Otchere*, The Times, 12 October 1962. Also *R.* v. *Amihiya*, The Times, 22 October 1964, p. 10.
7 *Zacharia* v. *Republic of Cyprus* [1962] 2 All E.R. 438. The Act was saved in respect of Cyprus by The Cyprus Act, 1960, 8 & 9 Eliz. II, c. 52, s. 3.
8 *In re Bradley*, unreported.
9 *R.* v. *Amihiya*, Criminal Appeal no. 301 or 1964. Reported in *The Times*, 22 October 1964, p. 10.

fugitive, but an order for his delivery made by the magistrate had not been executed when Kenya became a republic. The order was reversed on appeal to the High Court, on the ground that Kenya had ceased to be a British possession, and the retention of the Act in the legislation of Kenya amounted to 'one way traffic only'. It might authorize a fugitive to be sent from Kenya to Malawi (because the latter remains a British possession), but it could not make lawful the return of a prisoner from Malawi to Kenya.[1] In other words, the retention of the Act in force between Kenya and Malawi was a matter of Malawi law, and the Kenyan law on the matter was irrelevant. The edifice of rendition in the Commonwealth is seriously undermined by these considerations.

(D) *The Copyright Acts.* The Copyright Act, 1911[2] does not directly implement any of the Conventions of the Berne Union to which the United Kingdom is a party, but certain of its provisions are based upon them, and are to be construed accordingly. Except in the case of the self-governing Dominions, the Act extended to all the Crown's dominions, and might be extended by Order in Council to all protectorates and to Cyprus. The effect is to bring the Act into internal effect in all British dependencies, the legislatures of which might modify it,[3] but not enact repugnantly to it. Accordingly, copyright protection was achieved within the territories respecting works originating outside them, as well as to works first published within them, irrespective of the nationality of the author. After independence, the Act continues in force as internal law. There is no reciprocal provision respecting foreign territories, and hence the fact that a work originates in a foreign dependent territory which has become independent is irrelevant.

In 1958 the continuing effect in India of the Copyright Act was discussed in a Madras decision in the case of *Blackwood & Sons Ltd* v. *Parasuraman*,[4] in which an injunction was sought. The defendants pleaded that the Copyright Act, 1911, upon which the plaintiffs relied, ceased to be operative in India when that country became independent, or *a fortiori* when it became a republic, on the ground that the Act referred to copyright subsisting 'throughout the parts of His Majesty's dominions'. The plaintiffs pleaded the Indian Copyright Act of 1914, to which the defendants replied that, in making this enactment, the Indian legislature was exercising a power and jurisdiction conferred upon it by section 77 of the Imperial Act. The Court held that the effect of section 18 (2) of the Indian Independence Act[5] was to confer power on the Indian legislature

1 *In re Hannath*, Misc. Criminal Case no. 1 of 1965.
2 1 & 2 Geo. V, c. 46. 3 S. 27.
4 A.I.R. (1959), Mad. 410. 5 See *supra*, p. 116.

The Effect on the Legal System

to amend the Imperial Act, and that pursuant to section 18 (1) all existing Imperial laws would remain in force until so amended. Article 372 of the Indian Constitution also achieved continuity of Imperial legislation. It was pointed out that powers derived through the Act of 1914 from the Act of 1911 had in fact been exercised on several occasions by Indian authorities since 1950, on the presumption of continuity of the covering enactments.

The defendants also argued that, even if Imperial legislation remained in force in India, the Copyright Act did not, for its provisions were expressly inapplicable to self-governing Dominions, and hence ceased to apply upon construction with the enactment of the Indian Independence Act. The Court found itself bound on the authority of the Privy Council[1] to reject this contention, and expressly adverting to the logical connexion between the Copyright Act and the Copyright Union, referred to India's membership of the latter as establishing an absence of repugnance between Indian independence and the provisions of the Act. As to the argument that the Act could not apply after India ceased to be a British possession, the Court was careful to distinguish private rights from public ones. Copyright was clearly 'part of the private law of this country and governed the rights and obligations between its inhabitants in regard to one type of property'. The objection upheld in the Supreme Court of India[2] that for extradition purposes 'the grouping of India with other British Possessions could no longer be valid after India ceased to be a British Possession' concerned principles of public law which 'have no application for the determination of private rights and it would be subversive of all principles of international law to hold that the *inter se* rights of individuals concerning their property were affected by political changes'. Hence the Act of 1911 was still in force, and the implication is that the indirect implementation of the International Copyright Conventions which it achieves is unaffected by independence.

On 4 May 1950 there occurred an exchange of notes between Israel and the United States respecting reciprocal copyright protection. Previous to 14 May 1948 copyright relations existed between Palestine and the United States by virtue of a Palestine Order in Council and a Proclamation of the President in 1933 under Title 17, section 9, of the United States Code. This provides for protection 'when the foreign state or nation of which such author or proprietor is a citizen or subject grants, either by treaty, convention, agreement or law, to citizens of the United States the

---

[1] *Performing Right Society* v. *Bray Urban District Council* [1930] A.C. p. 377.
[2] *State of Madras* v. *C. G. Menon*, A.I.R. (1954), S.C. 517. See *supra*, p. 123.

benefit of copyright on substantially the same basis as to its own citizens'. The President determines when the reciprocal conditions exist. The Proclamation relating to Palestine was not made pursuant to a treaty, but in virtue of the reciprocity achieved by the Order in Council.

The Israeli note drew the attention of the United States to the fact that section 29 of the Israel Copyright Law was similar to the American law on the subject, and that it was the desire of the Israeli Government to conclude a reciprocal copyright arrangement with the United States. Israel would be prepared to regard the present note and a concurring reply as constituting an agreement between the two Governments. The United States replied that 'with a view to giving effect to the commitment proposed in the note under acknowledgment, the President of the United States of America has issued today a proclamation' implementing the Code provisions. Accordingly, it considered the exchange of notes as constituting an agreement.[1]

The proclamations of 1 July 1891 and 9 April 1910 made by the President of the United States applied to 'Great Britain and the British Possessions', but those of 1 January 1915 and 10 April 1920 specifically excepted the five Dominions. The proclamations of 10 March 1944 and 26 May 1950 enumerate the British territories to which they apply, excluding the areas specifically excepted in the proclamations of 1915 and 1920. The continued effect of these proclamations in respect of countries which have attained independence within or from the Commonwealth has proved a matter of some perplexity. The proclamations of 1891, 1915, 1920 and 1944 covered Burma, Ceylon, India and Pakistan. No announcement has been made as to their continued application to Burma, Ceylon and Pakistan, and the question seems to be open. In 1954, however, following an exchange of notes between the two countries,[2] a new proclamation was issued with respect to India which affirmed the existence of copyright relations with India continuously before and after independence. In the case of Ireland, a proclamation was issued in 1929, and the Department of State in 1949 took the view that the creation of the Republic of Ireland Act had had no effect upon this proclamation. The proclamations of 1944 and 1960 regarding Great Britain also specifically referred to 'Palestine', excluding Transjordan, and Israel continued to be listed in the 1952 edition of the Code as the beneficiary of these proclamations.

France was the beneficiary of proclamations of 1891, 1910, 1918, 1947, and 1950, and in 1952 became a co-contracting party with the United States in the Universal Copyright Convention. The fate of copyright relations in the French countries which have attained independence since 1952 depends

[1] *U.N.T.S.* vol. CXXXII, p. 189.   [2] *Ibid.* vol. CXXXIV, p. 119.

The Effect on the Legal System

upon the devolution or otherwise of the convention. Laos and Cambodia are also parties to the convention. Vietnam, however, is not, and a note in *Treaties in Force* says that the Department of State has made no announcement as to the proclamations of 1891–1947 in relation to Vietnam.

No reference is made to any Commonwealth country other than India in the United States lists of proclamations.

(E) *English warrants in Ireland.* In *Ex parte Nalder*,[1] which was decided before the Ireland Act, 1949,[2] it was held that the Petty Sessions (Ireland) Act, 1851[3] was still in force to give effect to an Irish warrant in the United Kingdom. After the Ireland Act came into force the Irish Supreme Court in *Ex parte Duggan*[4] gave effect to a United Kingdom warrant. In 1952, one Davidson, who was sentenced in the United Kingdom for illegally importing a car from Ireland, was returned under an Irish warrant to Ireland and sentenced for illegally exporting it.[5]

(F) *The Enforcement of Maintenance Orders Acts.* The United Kingdom Maintenance Orders (Facilities for Enforcement) Act, 1920[6] provides for enforcement in England of maintenance orders made in any part of Her Majesty's dominions, and for reciprocal enforcement against residents of such dominions of orders made in England. Where the legislature of any part of Her Majesty's dominions provides for reciprocal enforcement, the Act may be extended to orders of such dominions by Order in Council. Provision was also made for extension to any British protectorate. No judicial decision has been given on the continued application of the Act in respect of independent countries, especially the republics. Whereas in the United Kingdom the expression 'Ireland' was altered in 1923[7] to read 'Northern Ireland', this change was not effected in the corresponding legislation of certain other Commonwealth jurisdictions, which thus may continue to apply the Act to the Republic of Ireland as if it were part of Her Majesty's dominions.

(G) *The Colonial Divorce Acts.* The Indian and Colonial (Divorce Jurisdiction) Act, 1926[8] applied to any part of Her Majesty's dominions other than self-governing dominions, and empowered the courts in these

---

1 [1948] 1 K.B. 251.   2 12 & 13 Geo. VI, c. 41.
3 14 & 15 Vict., c. 93.
4 [1952] I.R. 62; 85 I.L.T.R. 22.
5 See also *R. v. Metropolitan Police Commissioner. Ex parte Hammond* [1964] 2 W.L.R. 777.   6 10 & 11 Geo. VI, c. 33.
7 S.R. & O. 1923, no. 405. The Act has been saved in relation to South Africa by the South Africa Act, 1962, 10 & 11 Eliz. II, c. 23, 2nd sch.
8 16 & 17 Geo. V, c. 40. Extended to protectorates and trust territories by the Colonial and Other Territories (Divorce Jurisdiction) Act, 1950, 14 Geo. VI, c. 20.

territories to grant English divorces. The Indian Independence Act[1] preserved only pending proceedings under the Act, and terminated the jurisdiction of Indian courts thereunder. When Tanganyika became independent an amendment was scheduled, the effect of which was to take away the power of applying the Act to Tanganyika by Order in Council after the amendment.[2] The High Court of Tanganyika held that this did not revoke the grant of jurisdiction to the Tanganyikan courts under the existing Order in Council, which had become 'part of the law of Tanganyika'. It said: 'It is a well-recognized principle of constitutional law that all legislation applicable to a Territory remains applicable unless the instrument setting up the new constitution provides otherwise in clear terms.'[3] When Tanganyika became a Republic the High Court held that the Act remained in force as part of the law of Tanganyika in virtue of Tanganyikan saving legislation.[4]

The Kenya Independence Act[5] reverted to the Indian precedent. Before the High Court of Kenya it was argued that this did not have the effect of revoking the Order in Council by which the Act had been constituted part of the 'existing law' of Kenya preserved in the Independence Act. The High Court held that the Order was preserved as part of the existing law, but the jurisdiction of the Court thereunder had been revoked.[6]

(H) *The effect of legislative repeal in United Kingdom Acts.* In various of the Independence Acts[7] or Consequential Provisions Acts certain scheduled statutes are repealed in respect of the country becoming independent or a

---

1 10 & 11 Geo. VI, c. 30.
2 Tanganyika Independence Act, 1961, 10 & 11 Eliz. II, c. 1, second schedule, item 15.
3 *Partington* v. *Partington* [1962] The Eastern Africa Law Reports 579.
4 *Partington* v. *Partington* [1963] The Eastern Africa Law Reports 77.
5 S. 7.
6 *Hilton* v. *Hilton* [1964] The Eastern Africa Law Reports 359.
7 Burma Independence Act, 1947, 11 & 12 Geo. VI, c. 3; Indian Independence Act, 1947, 10 & 11 Geo. VI, c. 30; India (Consequential Provisions) Act, 1949, 12, 13 & 14 Geo. VI, c. 92; Ghana Independence Act, 1957, 5 & 6 Eliz. II, c. 6; Ghana (Consequential Provisions) Act, 1960, 8 & 9 Eliz. II, c. 41; Federation of Malaya Act, 1957, 5 & 6 Eliz. II, c. 60; Cyprus Act, 1960, 8 & 9 Eliz. II, c. 52; Nigeria Independence Act, 1960, 8 & 9 Eliz. II, c. 55; Sierra Leone Independence Act, 1961, 9 & 10 Eliz. II, c. 16; Tanganyika Independence Act, 1961, 10 & 11 Eliz. II, c. 1; Tanganyika Republic Act, 11 Eliz. II, c. 1; Republic of South Africa (Temporary Provisions) Act, 1961, 9 & 10 Eliz. II, c. 23; South Africa Act, 1962, 10 & 11 Eliz. II, c. 23; Jamaica Independence Act, 1962, 10 & 11 Eliz. II, c. 46; Trinidad & Tobago Independence Act, 1962, 10 & 11 Eliz. II, c. 54; Uganda Independence Act, 1962, 10 & 11 Eliz. II, c. 57; Kenya Independence Act, 1963, c. 54; Uganda Act, 1964, c. 20; Malawi Independence Act, 1964, c. 46; Malta Independence Act, 1964, c. 86; The Gambia Independence Act, 1964, c. 93.

republic. In one of these Acts, the Palestine Act,[1] a reservation was expressly incorporated to the effect that this repeal would not affect the question of the continuity of the statutes concerned as part of the internal law of Palestine. The Explanatory Memorandum to the Palestine Bill stated that the Act 'repeals Acts of Parliament having application to Palestine, but leaves them to continue in force as part of the domestic law of Palestine'. In the debate on the second reading of the Bill, the Attorney-General said:

So far as the law in Palestine is concerned, the position will be that the existing law will continue in operation. How far it continues in operation will depend upon what, if any, authority takes over the effective government of Palestine when we leave.... It is a well-established rule of international law ... that the laws of a country which has been ceded, or abandoned, continue, in the presumption of international law, to be those which existed at the time of the cession or abandonment.[2]

And in the House of Lords it was stated that the new Palestine authorities would 'inherit as a working basis an existing body of laws which, in its validity in Palestine, is in no way affected by this Bill'.[3]

It has been taken for granted[4] that, even in the absence of a provision with respect to the law in the territory concerned, this sort of repeal, or, as in the case of the Ceylon Independence Act,[5] the express continuity, is for purposes of the internal law of the United Kingdom only.

(ii) *The independence of the Philippines, 1946*

The Philippines Independence Act of the United States Congress enacted that the laws in force in the Philippine Islands were to continue in force in the Commonwealth of the Philippines until repealed.[6] In 1954 the Philippines Supreme Court considered an appeal involving the question whether a United States Act, the Philippine Property Act of 1946, was still operative in the Philippines. In holding affirmatively the Court found that executive action and legislation of Congress had assumed the continuity of the Act, and therefore the Philippines had consented to it. Without this consent, the Court added, the Act would not have applied.[7]

1 11 & 12 Geo. VI, c. 27.   2 448. H.C. Deb. 5 s., cols. 1322–3.
3 *Ibid.* vol. 154, col. 1207.   4 Rosenne in *B.Y.* vol. XXVII (1950), p. 269.
5 11 Geo. VI, c. 7.
6 U.S. Statutes at Large, 73rd Cong., 1933–4, vol. XLVIII, pt. I, Public Laws, no. 127.
7 *Brownell* v. *Sun Life Assurance Co. of Canada* (1954) Phil. S.C. vol. X (1954), 608, affirmed in *Brownell* v. *Bautista, ibid.* p. 846.

(iii) *The independence of Indonesia, 1949*

The Transitional Regulations agreed upon between the Netherlands and Indonesia at the Round Table Conference in 1949 were subsequently incorporated into Indonesian law.[1] This provided that Netherlands law would remain applicable in Indonesia only to the extent to which it would be inconsistent or incompatible with the transfer of sovereignty to Indonesia. The effect of this qualification was examined in 1953 by a United States District Court which held that a law promulgated by the Netherlands Government in 1940, permitting Netherlands companies to transfer their head offices from part of the Netherlands to another, and which was an emergency war measure, was inconsistent with the sovereignty of Indonesia, and hence was no longer in force there. Hence a company incorporated in the Netherlands Indies was not entitled to transfer its head office to Surinam under this law after the transfer of sovereignty to Indonesia; and hence action by the company in United States courts to recover securities deposited under Netherlands law with the Escomptobank which held them on behalf of Indonesia was met with the defence that the Foreign Exchange Institute of Indonesia had refused their release.[2] Other laws were held by other courts not to have been affected by the proviso. For example, Netherlands courts held that Netherlands legislation on the conflict of laws continued in force in Indonesia,[3] and that a Netherlands bankruptcy decree preserved its non-foreign character in respect of breaches occurring in the Netherlands Indies under Indies law, notwithstanding the change of sovereignty.[4]

(iv) *The independence of Burma, 1947*

Article 226 of the Constitution of Burma states that, subject to the Constitution, and to the extent to which they are not inconsistent therewith, the existing laws should continue in force until repealed, but that the President might by Order adapt and modify them as expedient or necessary, with due regard to the provisions of the Constitution. The Burma Independence Act repealed certain statutes in so far as they related to Burma.[5]

[1] See *supra*, p. 98.
[2] *Naamloze Vennootschap Suikerfabrik 'Wono-Aseh'* v. *Chase National Bank of New York*, I.L.R. vol. XX, p. 82.
[3] *In re X*, ibid. vol. XIX, p. 138; *Hausmann* v. *Koninklijke Rotterdamse Lloyd*, ibid. p. 139.
[4] *Van Heynsbergen* v. *Nederlandsche Handelsmaatschappij*, ibid. vol. XXIV, p. 76.
[5] 11 & 12 Geo. VI, c. 3, second schedule.

(v) *The independence of Israel, 1948*

The Palestine Act, 1948[1] provided for the repeal of scheduled enactments referring to Palestine, and for the cessation of application to Palestine of any enactment, but added that nothing in the section should be construed as preventing the continuance in force of any such enactment as part of the law of Palestine. Concurrently with its formation the Provisional Government of Israel promulgated the Law and Administration Ordinance,[2] section 11 of which provided that the law which existed in Palestine on 14 May 1948 should remain in force, in so far as there was nothing therein repugnant to the Ordinance or to other laws to be enacted, and subject to such modifications as might result from the establishment of the State and its authorities. Section 13 repealed certain sections of the Immigration Ordinance, 1941, and the Defence (Emergency) Regulations, 1945. The Land Transfers Regulations, 1940 were repealed with retroactive force to 18 May 1939, the date of their enactment. All these repeals concerned matters affecting the Jewish settlement in Palestine. Section 12 nullified any privileges or special powers granted to British officials by any law, and section 14 provided for the devolution of all powers vested in the Crown, the Secretaries of State or the High Commission to the Government of Israel.

On 20 July 1949 the Knesset enacted legislation prescribing that the law which existed in Palestine on 14 May 1948 would remain in force, except only as modified by the establishment of the State and the termination of the Mandate.[3]

These provisions were held by the Israeli Supreme Court to have continued in force the internal effects of the Mandate,[4] and the Court could examine legislation of the British High Commission to determine its consistency with the Mandate.[5] Only when found to be consistent therewith would the previous law be regarded as *intra vires* to affect continuing interests after the formation of Israel.[6] For example, the courts examined whether polygamy was consistent with the freedom of conscience provisions of the Mandate.[7] Save as repealed, the Defence (Emergency Regulations) Order 1945 was held to have been kept alive.[8] The

[1] 11 & 12 Geo. VI, c. 27.
[2] *Official Gazette*, no. 2, 21 May 1948.
[3] Law and Administration Ordinance, no. 1 of 5708.
[4] Which had been transformed into the municipal law of Palestine by Palestine Order in Council, 1922–47, art. 46.
[5] *Leon v. Gubernik, Ann. Dig.* vol. XV, p. 42.
[6] *Ahmed Shauki el Karbutli v. Minister of Defence*, ibid. vol. XVI, Case no. 19.
[7] *Yosipof v. A.G., I.L.R.* vol. XVIII, Case no. 58.
[8] *Kuk v. Minister of Defence, Ann. Dig.* vol. XV, Case no. 15.

provisions were also held to govern the question of *res judicata* in the Privy Council,[1] title to public property,[2] and continuity of criminal jurisdiction.[3]

In 1956 the Supreme Court considered whether the Admiralty Offences (Colonial) Act, 1849,[4] which gave colonial courts admiralty jurisdiction, and had been applied to Palestine by Order in Council in 1922, gave jurisdiction to the courts of Israel with respect to crimes committed on the high seas in Israeli ships. The objection had been made that since the Act referred to 'colonies' it could not have survived the termination of the Mandate. The Supreme Court rejected the contention, holding that Palestine shipping had been brought under the Admiralty jurisdiction, and that this jurisdiction had been kept alive in Israel by the Law and Administration Ordinance.[5]

Article 46 of the Palestine Order in Council of 1922 invested the courts of the Mandated Territory with jurisdiction in conformity with the Ottoman law in force in Palestine on 1 November 1914, and also British Orders in Council, the substance of the common law, and the doctrines of equity in force in England. The law thus applied in Israeli courts is primarily Ottoman law, with English law utilized when Ottoman law is inadequate to the solution of a problem. One feature is that no part of English statute law, not even that which alters common law rules, constituted part of Palestine law, though Palestine legislation in most respects rectified this situation. While Israeli statutes have radically altered many branches of the law, they have in some respects failed to adjust the common law to changes subsequently effected in England by statute.[6]

(vi) *The continuity of law in the French Community*

Under the Constitution of the Fifth Republic, the Member States of the Community continued to be affected by all laws and regulations in force on the date of its promulgation, except when contrary to the provisions of the Constitution, and until abrogated or modified by the competent authorities.[7] Most of these States, in the legislation reconstructing their

1 *Forer* v. *Guterman, ibid.* Case no. 21. See *infra*, p. 153.
2 *Khayat* v. *A.G., I.L.R.* vol. XXII, p. 123. See *infra*, pp. 200, 225.
3 *Katz-Cohen* v. *A.G., Ann. Dig.* vol. XVI, Case no. 26; *Wahib Saleh Kalil* v. *A.G., ibid.* p. 70; *Arar* v. *Governor of Tel Mond Prison, I.L.R.* vol. XIX, Case no. 30. See *infra*, p. 171.   4 12 & 13 Vict., c. 96.
5 *Stampfer* v. *A.G., I.L.R.* vol. XVIII, p. 284.   6 Yadin in *I.C.L.Q.* (1962), p. 70.
7 With only two exceptions continuity of law was ensured in the Francophone States by constitutional provision. That of Chad is typical: 'La législation et la réglementation actuellement en vigueur au Tchad restent applicables, sauf intervention de textes nouveaux, en ce qu'elles n'ont pas de contraire à la présente Constitution'

judicial systems after independence, provided for legal continuity.[1] Their laws became, *vis-à-vis* France, foreign laws.[2]

(vii) *The independence of the Congo (Léopoldville), 1960*

On 19 May 1960 the Belgian Parliament enacted the *Loi fondamentale relative aux structures du Congo*.[3] This was intended as a transitional measure to permit the Congo and its institutions to function independently of Belgium during the process of independence. Article 2 contained a provision for continuity legislation, but article 3 stated that the *Loi* would remain in force only until the Congo had adopted its own alternative institutions.[4] It created the offices of State, a bicameral legislature and a judicial system. The Belgian Constitution was not applicable to the Congo, in virtue of the latter's separate juridical personality, but the Law of 18 October 1908 on the Government of the Belgian Congo had the characteristics of a local constitution. Because Belgium's direct rule in the Congo was designed to remedy a notorious social and racial injustice, the fundamental rights embodied in the Law were extraordinarily liberal. In view of the repeal of this Law it was necessary in the *Loi fondamentale* to restore these rights, and accordingly reference was made to human rights and their universal application. The references in the Law of 1908 to the freedom of the press and association were not reproduced, but they had already been guaranteed to the inhabitants of the Congo by decree of 17 August 1959, which would remain in force after independence.

(Constitution of 11 November 1960, article 77, *Journal Officiel du Tchad*, 15 December 1960, special number). Thus by law of 27 May 1959 Upper Volta repealed the French Law on the Press of 29 July 1881; and in 1964 a fugitive O.A.S. leader condemned in France was arrested at Dakar airport in flight between Italy and Brazil, under French legislation still in force in Senegal. The two exceptions were the Malagasy Republic and Guinea. On the difficulties of continuity of Law in Senegal see Inez in *Southern California Law Review*, vol. XXXVII (1964), p. 21. For Guinea and Ivory Coast see Whiteman, vol. II, p. 878. The Co-operation Agreement in Matters of Justice between France and the Malagasy Republic provided that 'à défaut de textes malgaches, les dispositions législatives et réglementaires du droit français en vigueur à Madagascar à la date à laquelle prend effet le présent accord continuent à être appliquées par les juridictions malgaches'. On 26 January 1965 Morocco unified its judicial and legal systems and moroccanized them. Clause 3 contained a continuity of laws provision: *loi* no. 3-64, *Bulletin Officiel* (1965), p. 103. This came into force on 1 October 1965, *Le Petit Marocain*, 28 September 1965, p. 1.

1 See *infra*, p. 150.
2 *Cozzolino v. Cozzolino, Gazette du Palais* (1963), 2,320; *Clunet*, vol. XCI (1964), p. 594. See also *ibid.* p. 319. Also with respect to Indochina: *Pornot v. French State, Annuaire français* (1963), p. 985; *Veuve Wanègue v. S.A.R.L. 'Air Outre-mer'*, *ibid.* (1963), p. 985.
3 See *supra*, p. 94.
4 De Visscher in *Communicazioni e Studi*, vol. XI (1960), p. 11.

On 4 August 1961 the Congolese legislature enacted that Congolese courts should apply existing law. This was held by a Belgian court to have no internal effect in Belgian law, so that Belgian courts were not deprived of any jurisdiction by the continued competence of Congolese courts to administer the law of the Belgian Congo.[1]

By a Law of 17 June 1960 the *Caisse d'assurance du Congo belge et du Ruanda-Urundi*, which had been incorporated under colonial law, was transformed into an organ of Belgian law. Similar action was taken with respect to the social security funds of the Congo civil service, which were transferred to Belgium and placed under the guarantee of Belgian law.

So far as the Law of 1908 was concerned, the *Conseil d'État* in Brussels held that the Belgian State was obliged by administrative actions performed under its sovereignty, notwithstanding the subsequent repeal of the Law and the accession of the Congo to independence, and notwithstanding the circumstance that the Belgian Congo was a separate juridical person. It was pointed out that neither the *Loi fondamentale relative aux structures du Congo* nor any other law had determined the responsibility which the Congo should assume with respect to acts performed by the authorities which administered territory under Belgian sovereignty, and no international agreement had been entered into to settle the question.[2]

(viii) *The problem of continuity of law in Poland after 1919*

In 1917 Germany and Austria formally proclaimed a Polish kingdom in their respective sectors of the then occupied Russian provinces of Warsaw and Lublin, and inaugurated a Regency Council as the nominal representative, or trustee, of this kingdom.[3] The Regency Council by two acts of a legislative character[4] set up a provisional government and vested the legislative powers of the kingdom in a State Council. In the meantime the monarchy in Russia was deposed and the revolutionary government concluded with Germany and Austria a peace treaty in which it surrendered to Germany and Austria the territories in which the Polish Kingdom had been proclaimed.[5] The Regency Council was denied participation in

1 S.A. *Caisse patronale* v. *Cox, Journal des Tribunaux* (1964), p. 509.
2 *Meert* Case, *Journal des Tribunaux* (1960), p. 738. See *supra*, p. 95.
3 A. Burda, R. Klimowiecki, *Prawo Państwowe* [The State Law] (Warsaw, 1959), p. 44.
4 The decree of 3 January 1918: *Dekret Rady Regencyjnej o tymczasowej organizacji władz naczelnych w Królestwie Polskim* [A decree relating to the provisional organization of the supreme authorities in the Polish Kingdom], *Dziennik Praw Królestwa Polskiego (Journal of Laws of the Polish Kingdom)*, no. 1 of 1918, item 1; the Act of 1 February 1918: *Ustawa o Radzie Stanu Królestwa Polskiego* [An Act relating to the State Council of the Polish Kingdom], *ibid.* no. 2 of 1918, item 2.
5 The Treaty of Brest-Litovsk of 3 March 1918; Dybowski in *The Cambridge History of Poland (1697–1935)*, ch. XX, p. 488.

the making of this treaty.[1] In November 1918 the Regency Council transferred its powers to Józef Piłsudski,[2] who became Head of State and announced its dissolution. Piłsudski in turn proclaimed the creation of the Polish Republic,[3] declared himself its provisional chief, and appointed a government. A legislative assembly was later to be convoked to give the new Republic a proper constitution.[4] The Republic[5] was represented at the Peace Conference in Paris in 1919, and became a party to the Versailles Treaty of 28 June 1919,[6] which purported to establish the boundaries of the Republic, although it was not until 1923 that they were finally fixed[7] by a series of treaties—the result of either peaceful negotiations,[8] or international plebiscites,[9] or hostilities.[10]

The difficulties arising out of the existence of different administrative systems introduced by the partitioning Powers were overcome by the retention in principle, and for a transitional period, of the three foreign administrative organizations of the territories.[11] Various enactments were made to integrate administrative services; for example: with respect to the administration of the former province of Galicia;[12] the taking over by the Treasury of the fiscal administration in the Polish territories formerly annexed by Austria;[13] the provisional organization of the administration

1 *Ibid.* pp. 473, 487.
2 Declaration of 14 November 1918, *Dz.P.P.P.*[*Journal of Laws of the Polish State*], no. 17 of 1918, item 39.
3 Decree of 14 November 1918, *ibid.* item 41.
4 Burda, Klimowiecki, *op. cit.* p. 47.
5 The Fourteen Points of President Wilson's message to Congress on 8 January 1918 included as point 13 the reconstruction of an independent Poland; this point was confirmed as one of the aims of the War by a Joint Resolution of the Prime Ministers of Great Britain, France and Italy on 3 June 1918: see Dybowski, *loc. cit.* p. 477.
6 Halecki, *A History of Poland* (1961), p. 280.   7 *Ibid.* p. 275.
8 The treaty with Rumania signed in March 1921: see Penson in *The Cambridge History of Poland (1697–1935)*, ch. XXIV, p. 573.
9 The frontiers with Germany in Upper Silesia and East Prussia, and the frontier with Czechoslovakia in Zips and Orava: see Kutrzeba in *The Cambridge History of Poland, supra,* ch. XXII, pp. 512–20.
10 Reddaway, in *The Cambridge History of Poland, supra,* ch. XXI, p. 511; Kutrzeba, *op. cit.* pp. 521–34; 'Traktat pokoju między Polską a Rosją i Ukrainą' [The Peace Treaty between Poland and Russia and the Ukraine], *Dz.U.R.P.* [*The Journal of Statutes of the Polish Republic*], no. 49 of 1921, item 299.
11 Later superseded by a uniform organization provided by the Order relating to the organization and competence of the administrative authorities.
12 'Rozporządzenie Rady Ministrów w przedmiocie administracji państwowej w Galicji', *Dz.U.P.P.* no 24 of 1919, item 240.
13 'Ustawa w przedmiocie objęcia przez Ministerstwo Skarbu administracji skarbowej na ziemiach polskich b. zaboru austriackiego', *Dz.U.P.P.* no 31 of 1919, item 261.

of the provinces formerly annexed by Prussia;[1] the taking over by the Minister for Labour and Social Welfare of all matters remaining within his departmental competence and arising in the provinces formerly annexed by Austria;[2] the extension of the provisions of the decree of 4 February 1919, regulating the municipal self-government, to municipalities in the provinces formerly annexed by Russia;[3] normalization of the legal and political order in the territories incorporated by the Republic;[4] the extension of decrees, acts and statutory rules to, and the future reconciliation of legislation in, the provinces formerly annexed by Prussia;[5] and the introduction of the Act relative to the publication of the Journal of Statutes of the Polish Republic in the provinces formerly annexed by Prussia.[6]

The difficulties arising out of the partitions of the Polish territories in the domain of judicial organization were overcome by the provisional retention,[7] with certain modifications, of the existing various judicial systems originated by the partitioning Powers. Modifications were introduced respecting the location of courts of justice,[8] the constitution of the supreme court,[9] the judicial system in the provinces formerly annexed by Austria,[10] and the provisional constitution of courts martial.[11]

The various criminal laws made by the partitioning Powers for the territories were provisionally retained with certain necessary modifications.[12]

1 'Ustawa o tymczasowej organizacji zarządu b. dzielnicy pruskiej', Dz.P.P.P. no. 64 of 1919, item 385.
2 'Rozporządzenie Rady Ministrów w przedmiocie przejęcia w b. dzielnicy austriackiej przez Ministra Pracy i Opieki Społecznej spraw wchodzących w zakres działania tego Ministerstwa', Dz.U.R.P. no. 3 of 1920, item 16.
3 'Ustawa w przedmiocie rozciągnięcia na miasta b. zaboru rosyjskiego dekretu z 4 lutego 1919 o samorządzie miejskim', Dz.U.R.P. no. 19 of 1920, item 91.
4 'Ustawa o unormowaniu stanu prawno-politycznego na ziemiach przyłączonych do obszaru Rzeczypospolitej', Dz.U.R.P. no. 16 of 1921, item 93.
5 'Ustawa o wprowadzeniu dekretów, ustaw sejmowych i rozporządzeń rządu, oraz o dalszym uzgadnianiu ustawodawstwa na obszarze b. dzielnicy pruskiej', Dz.U.R.P. no. 75 of 1921, item 511.
6 'Rozporządzenie Rady Ministrów o wprowadzeniu w życie na obszarze b. dzielnicy pruskiej ustawy w sprawie wydawania Dziennika Ustaw R.P.', Dz.U.R.P. no. 47 of 1921, item 288.
7 Ludwiczak, Międzynarodowe Prawo Prywatne [Private International Law] (1958), p. 13.
8 'Dekret w przedmiocie dyzlokacji sądów', Dz.P.P.P. no. 14 of 1919, item 170.
9 'Dekret w przedmiocie ustroju Sądu Najwyższego', Dz.P.P.P. no. 15 of 1919, item 190.
10 'Dekret w przedmiocie zmian w urządzeniach wymiaru sprawiedliwości w b. zaborze austriackim', supra, item 200.
11 'Ustawa o tymczasowym sądownictwie wojskowym', Dz.P.P.P. no. 65 of 1919, item 393.
12 Zdzisław Keck, Skorowidz Przepisów Prawnych—Przepisy ogłoszone w Dzienniku Ustaw Rzeczypospolitej Polskiej w latach 1918–1949 [Index to laws published in the

The Effect on the Legal System 137

In the sphere of civil law there existed in the territories several foreign systems and their various traditions, namely: (a) the Prussian General Code of 1794; (b) the German Civil Code of 1896; (c) the Austrian Civil Code of 1811; (d) the Hungarian customary law and a Code of 1825; (e) the II and III book of the French Code of 1852; (f) the old Russian Civil Law, the 'Zvod Zakanov'; (g) the Canon Law, in so far as it was relied upon, or referred to, by Civil Law in matrimonial matters and benefices (*beneficia*); (h) various other codes, statutes and regulations. The first Polish legislature accorded recognition to all these foreign laws and transformed them into Polish law for those territorial parts of the Polish Republic in which the laws had already been in operation.[1]

A system of conflicts of law by which full faith and credit was extended to the various territorial laws was effected by a code of interlocal law[2] in 1926.[3]

After the legal *modus vivendi* had been established, a codifying commission was set up by the Act of 3 June 1919[4] to work out a body of uniform codes of law for the whole of the Polish Republic.[5] The work of the commission resulted in uniform parliamentary legislation respecting different subject-matters, and after 1926 was implemented by way of presidential decrees.[6] Up to 1939 the commission drafted the following bills which went through the parliamentary machinery and became uniform laws: (a) the law relating to the organization and structure of civil and criminal courts of justice;[7] (b) a series of statutes relating to the administrative law and procedure;[8] (c) the Code of Criminal Procedure;[9] (d) the Code of Civil Procedure;[10] (e) the Penal Code and the Law relating

---

Journal of Statutes of the Polish Republic in the years 1918–1949], 2nd ed. (Warszawa, 1949), p. 61 at (152), *Karne Prawo* [Criminal Law].

1 Gwiazdomorski, *Prawo Spadkowe* [The Law of Inheritance] (1959), p. 16.
2 Wolff, *Private International Law* (1945), p. 43.
3 'Ustawa o prawie właściwym dla stosunków prywatnych wewnętrznych', *Dz.U.R.P.* no. 101 of 1926, item 580.
4 'Ustawa o utworzeniu Komisji Kodyfikacyjnej', *Dz. P.P.P.* no. 44 of 1919, item 315.
5 Jakób Litauer, *Kodeks postępowania niespornego* [Code of Procedure in non-litigious matters], vol. I, pp. 4–6; vol. II, pp. 4–5.
6 'Ustawa z dnia 2 sierpnia 1926 r. o upoważnieniu Prezydenta Rzeczypospolitej do wydawania rozporządzeń z mocą ustawy', *Dz.U.R.P.* no. 78 of 1926, item 443.
7 'Prawo o ustroju sądów powszechnych', *Dz.U.R.P.* no. 16 of 1928, item 93.
8 'Prawo o postępowaniu administracyjnym', *Dz.U.R.P.* no. 36 of 1928, item 341; 'Prawo o postępowaniu przymusowym w administracji', *ibid.* item 342; 'Prawo o postępowaniu karno-administracyjnym', *ibid.* no. 38 of 1928, item 365.
9 'Kodeks Postępowania Karnego z dnia 19 marca 1928 r.', *Dz.U.R.P.* no. 33 of 1928, item 243.
10 'Kodeks Postępowania Cywilnego', *Dz.U.R.P.* no. 83 of 1930, item 651.

to non-indictable offences;[1] (*f*) the Code of the Law of Obligations;[2] (*g*) the Code of Mercantile Law.[3] These laws superseded the foreign legal systems initially retained. Each codification of a branch of law was accompanied by appropriate provisions which introduced the uniform law thus codified and set out in detail the various laws repealed by it, for example the Presidential Decree of 29 November 1930 which made Regulations introducing the Code of Civil Procedure.[4] Other unifying public Acts related to citizenship,[5] resting in principle on the *jus sanguinis*,[6] the right of option to acquire or renounce Polish citizenship by subjects and former subjects of Austria, Germany and Russia,[7] and the repeal of legal disabilities imposed by the former partitioning Powers on the Established Church.[8]

The normal functioning of courts of justice and the civil and criminal proceedings before these courts were disrupted by the wartime situation, and there was no need of systematic legislation for an orderly transition of pending matters. As a rule, orders made by the old courts could not be executed, and only an evidentiary significance could be attached to all judgments. Convictions for indictable common offences remained with certain exceptions unaffected by the changes, but no special machinery was provided for their enforcement.[9]

Doubtful legal situations were clarified by legislation, for instance, validating contracts entered into by the occupying authorities,[10] mitigating

1 'Kodeks Karny z dnia 15 lipca 1932', *Dz.U.R.P.* no. 60 of 1932, item 571; 'Prawo o Wykroczeniach z dnia 15 lipca 1932', *ibid.* item 572.
2 'Kodeks Zobowiązań', *Dz.U.R.P.* no. 82 of 1933, item 598.
3 'Kodeks Handlowy', *Dz.U.R.P.* no. 57 of 1934, item 502.
4 'Przepisy wprowadzające Kodeks Postępowania Cywilnego, Rozporządzenie Prezydenta Rzeczypospolitej z dnia 29 listopada 1930', *Dz.U.R.P.* no. 83 of 1930, item 652. Section 1 of the regulations, for instance, repealed the former Russian Act of 20 November 1864 relating to civil procedure *ex* the *Zvod Zakonov*, vol. XVI, pt. 1; the former Austrian Juridical Rule and Civil Procedure introduced by the Act of 1 August 1895 *Reichsgesetzblatt* (Austria–Hungary), 1895, p. 329, nos. 110–13; and the former German Act relating to civil procedure introduced by the Act of 30 January 1877, *RGBl.*, 1877, p. 83,
5 'Ustawa o obywatelstwie Państwa Polskiego', *Dz.U.R.P.* no. 7 of 1920, item 44.   6 Dolski, *Kształtowanie Elementów Państwa* (1943), p. 65.
7 'Rozporządzenie Prezydenta Rzeczypospolitej o nabyciu i utracie obywatelstwa polskiego w myśl traktatu wersalskiego', *Dz.U.R.P.* no. 57 of 1920, item 358; 'Ustawa o uregulowaniu prawa wyboru obywatelstwa polskiego przez obywateli b. cesarstwa austriackiego lub b. królestwa węgierskiego i prawa wyboru obywatelstwa polskiego przez b. obywateli tych państw, posiadających obywatelstwo polskie', *Dz.U.R.P.* no. 88 of 1922, item 791.
8 'Rozporządzenie Prezydenta Rzeczypospolitej o uchyleniu przepisów zaborczych w sprawach Kościoła Rzymsko-Katolickiego', *Dz.U.R.P.* no. 51 of 1931, item 424.
9 Keck, *op. cit.* pp. 151–63.
10 'Dekret w przedmiocie umów zawartych przez byłe władze okupacyjne', *Dz.P.P.P.* no. 5 of 1919, item 99.

The Effect on the Legal System 139

convictions in criminal courts set up by the occupants,[1] or restoring property confiscated by the former partitioning Powers[2] and civil rights to persons deprived of these rights following convictions for political or military offences in the latter's courts.[3] Legislation also regulated the taking over by the new State of the railways,[4] the taking over by the Polish Treasury of the liability for debts incurred by the former partitioning Powers with persons who later became Polish subjects,[5] the registration of debentures issued by the treasuries of the former partitioning Powers,[6] and the transfer to the Polish Treasury of fiscal rights formerly vested in the treasuries of the German States and members of the German ruling royal families.[7] Rules were also made for the registration of claims against the former non-Polish superannuation funds,[8] the making of by-laws for certain statutory finance companies,[9] the reorganization of the insurance industry,[10] the liability of the new State to former shareholders of the nationalized railways[11] and the centralization of archives.[12] The initial monetary order established in 1919 and 1920[13] and the currency reform of

1 'Dekret w przedmiocie złagodzenia kar orzeczonych przez sądy okupacyjne', Dz.P.P.P. no. 21 of 1918, item 73.
2 'Ustawa o dobrach skonfiskowanych przez byłe rządy zaborcze uczestnikom walk o niepodległość', Dz.U.R.P. no. 91 of 1932, item 771.
3 'Ustawa o przywróceniu praw utraconych wskutek przestępstw politycznych i wojskowych z wyroków sądów b. państw zaborczych' Dz.U.R.P. no 39. of 1920, item 230.
4 'Dekret o przejściu kolei', Dz.P.P.P. no. 14 of 1919, item 155.
5 'Ustawa w przedmiocie wypłaty zastępczej pewnych kategorii wierzytelności należnych obywatelom Państwa Polskiego od niemieckich, austro-węgierskich i austriackich b. rządów zaborczych względnie okupacyjnych', Dz. U.R.P. no. 70 of 1920, item 465.
6 E.g. 'Ustawa o rejestracji i stemplowaniu tytułów długu przedwojennego Austro-Węgier', Dz.U.R.P. no. 45 of 1921, item 269.
7 'Ustawa o przelaniu praw skarbowych państw niemieckich oraz praw członków niemieckich domów panujących na Skarb Państwa Polskiego,' Dz.U.R.P. no. 62 of 1920, item 400.
8 E.g. 'Rozporządzenie Prezydenta Rzeczypospolitej o rejestracji pretensji z tytułu emerytur i złożonych składek emerytalnych b. pracowników byłych rosyjskich kolei rządowych', Dz.U.R.P. no. 21 of 1929, item 217.
9 E.g. 'Rozporządzenie Prezydenta Rzeczypospolitej o statutach towarzystw kredytowych ziemskich i miejskich oraz zmianach statutów instytucji kredytowych, zatwierdzonych w drodze ustawodawczej przez b. władze zaborcze', Dz.U.R.P. no. 35 of 1928, item 326.   10 Keck, op. cit. pp. 183–7.
11 E.g. 'Rozporządzenie Prezydenta Rzeczypospolitej o uregulowaniu zobowiązań Państwa z tytułu przejęcia państwowych i prywatnych kolei w b. zaborze austriackim', Dz.U.R.P. no. 115 of 1924, item 1027.
12 'Dekret w przedmiocie organizacji archiwów państwowych i opieki nad archiwaliami', Dz.P.P.P. no. 14 of 1919, item 182; also Zdzisław Keck, op. cit. p. 5.
13 'Dekret w przedmiocie jednostki monetarnej waluty polskiej', Dz.P.P.P. no.14 of 1919, item 174; 'Ustawa w sprawie nazwy monety polskiej', Dz. U.P.P. no. 20 of 1919, item 230; 'Ustawa w przedmiocie ustanowienia marki polskiej prawnym środkiem płatniczym na całym obszarze Rzeczypospolitej', Dz.U.R.P. no. 5 of 1920, item 26.

1923[1] required further legislation for the conversion of the former national debts[2] and private debts[3] into the new legal tender introduced by the new State.

In the public and private domain outside the absorbed territories an orderly winding-up of rights and obligations vested in the former sovereigns and their non-Polish subjects was secured by the registration of non-Polish property,[4] the setting up of a Central Liquidation Authority[5] and some liquidation committees.[6] The Treaty of Versailles provided some directives for the liquidation of German property not affected by the change.[7] Clause 304 of the treaty established a mixed arbitration tribunal for this purpose.[8] The treaties which fixed the boundaries of the new republic also dealt with the winding-up of foreign property rights.[9] Some bilateral agreements, for instance those concluded with Austria, dealt with such matters as the former unsecured Austro-Hungarian national debt,[10] debts incurred before 1918,[11] the payment of superannuation pensions granted by the former Austrian government,[12] and moneys deposited with the Austrian Post Office Savings Bank.[13]

In 1938 the Czech part of the Olza District was ceded to the Polish

1 'Ustawa o reformie walutowej', *Dz.U.R.P.* no. 4 of 1924, item 28.
2 E.g. 'Rozporządzenie Prezydenta Rzeczypospolitej o przerachowaniu zobowiązań Skarbu Państwa Austriackiego i Węgierskiego oraz zobowiązań funduszu krajowego galicyjskiego, które ciążą na Skarbie Państwa Polskiego', *Dz.U.R.P.* no. 115 of 1924, item 1028.
3 'Rozporządzenie Prezydenta Rzeczypospolitej o przerachowaniu zobowiązań prywatno-prawnych', *Dz.U.R.P.* no. 30 of 1925, item 213.
4 E.g. 'Ustawa o rejestracji i zabezpieczeniu majątków niemieckich', *Dz.U.R.P.* no. 25 of 1920, item 153.
5 'Dekret o utworzeniu Głównego Urzędu Likwidacyjnego', *Dz.P.P.P.* no. 12 of 1919, item 132.
6 E.g. 'Rozporządzenie w przedmiocie Regulaminu Komitetu Likwidacyjnego do spraw b. rosyjskich osób prawnych', *Dz.U.R.P.* no. 95 of 1928, item 839.
7 Kierski, *Likwidacja majątków niemieckich według traktatu pokoju* [The liquidation of German property according to the Peace Treaty] (Poznań, 1921), pp. 3–4.
8 Namitkiewicz, *Mieszany Trybunał Rozjemczy polsko-niemiecki* [The Mixed Polish-German Arbitration Tribunal] (Warszawa, 1922), pp. 50–69.
9 Raczyński, *Traktaty pokojowe wobec praw majątkowych* [Peace treaties and property rights] (Kraków–Warszawa, 1920), pp. viii and 102.
10 'Układ dotyczący długów publicznych niezabezpieczonych austriacko-węgierskich', concluded in Paris on 11 February 1931, *Dz.U.R.P.* no. 64 of 1931, item 492 and 493.
11 'Układ dotyczący długów austro-węgierskich sprzed 1918 roku', *Dz.U.R.P.* no. 32 of 1931, item 229.
12 'Konwencja dotycząca emerytur przyznanych przez b. Rząd Austriacki', concluded in Rome on 6 April 1922, *Dz.U.R.P.* nos. 3, 71 of 1929, items 26, 533 and 534.
13 'Konwencja w sprawie przejęcia wierzytelności i depozytów spod zarządu Pocztowej Kasy Oszczędności w Wiedniu', concluded in Rome on 6 April 1922, *Dz.U.R.P.* nos. 5, 69 and 81 of 1929, items 48, 528, 529 and 610.

The Effect on the Legal System 141

Republic. The cession, preceded by a Polish claim to this territory,[1] was the result of a bilateral agreement between the two States concerned.[2] It was followed by the incorporation of some square miles of Czech territory into the Polish Republic. While the basis for the transfer was provided by the Polish-Czechoslovak Agreement,[3] the actual changes were effected by legislation of the Polish Republic. Presidential Decrees were issued relating to the union of the recovered territories with the Republic;[4] the introduction into these territories of certain Polish legislation;[5] the introduction of the Polish citizenship law of 20 January 1920 and certain amendments thereto;[6] the introduction of certain civil law and mercantile law provisions;[7] the conversion of debts payable in Czechoslovak currency;[8] and the currency regulations.[9]

[1] Harrison Thompson, *Czechoslovakia in European History* (1944), p. 349.
[2] Boratyński, *Obrona suwerenności małych państw* [The Protection of Sovereignty of Small States] (Warszawa, 1949], pp. 195–6.
[3] 'Miesięczny Przegląd Polityczny' in *Polityka Narodów*, no. 5 of 1938, pp. 341–5.
[4] 'Dekret Prezydenta Rzeczypospolitej o zjednoczeniu Odzyskanych Ziem Śląska Cieszyńskiego z Rzecząpospolitą Polską, *Dz.U.R.P.* no. 78 of 1938, item 533.
[5] 'Dekret Prezydenta Rzeczypospolitej o rozciągnięciu mocy obowiązującej niektórych aktów ustawodawczych na odzyskane ziemie Śląska Cieszynskiego', *Dz.U.R.P.* no. 81 of 1938, item 549.
[6] 'Dekret Prezydenta Rzeczypospolitej o rozciągnięciu mocy obowiązującej ustawy z dnia 20 stycznia 1920 roku o obywatelstwie Państwa Polskiego na odzyskane ziemie Śląska Cieszyńskiego oraz o zmianie niektórych jej prezepisów', *Dz.U.R.P.* no. 81 of 1938, item 548.
[7] 'Dekret Prezydenta Rzeczypospolitej o rozciągnięciu mocy obowiązującej niektórych przepisów prawa cywilnego i handlowego na odzyskanych ziemiach Śląska Cieszyńskiego', *Dz.U.R.P.* no. 89, item 604.
[8] 'Dekret Prezydenta Rzeczypospolitej o przerachowaniu zobowiązań opierających się o walutę czesko-słowacką', *Dz.U.R.P.* no. 79, item 535.
[9] Treasury Orders, *Dz.U.R.P.* no. 92 of 1938, item 633, and *Dz.U.R.P.* no. 95 of 1938, item 640.

Chapter 7

THE EFFECT OF STATE SUCCESSION ON THE JUDICIAL SYSTEM

1. THE JUDICIAL ORGANIZATION

The jurisdiction accorded to courts of justice is a matter of public law, and the judicial system is part of the structure of government. When a State loses sovereignty over a territory, the courts established under its public law suffer the fate of the law itself. They lose their competence. Accordingly a Lithuanian court held[1] that Lithuania was an independent State which did not derive its sovereignty from Russia; its courts were not successors of the Russian courts; and an action begun in the Russian courts could not be continued in those of Lithuania. Conversely, courts of the predecessor State lose their competence with respect to actions against the administration of the successor State. The District Court of the Hague held that it had lost jurisdiction over actions in tort against the Netherlands Indies, on the ground that Indonesia had acquired sovereign status and was no longer subject to the court's jurisdiction.[2]

However, in the case of dependent territories which were autonomous legal orders, independence has no effect upon the continued jurisdiction of the local courts, though there might be some impact upon the process of appeal, as there has been in the case of the ex-French territories. A certain continuity of judicial relationships between the metropolis and the former French territories was achieved by the judicial co-operation conventions, although the jurisdiction exercised by the courts of the newly independent countries ceased to be French and became foreign.[3] In the case of Indo-

---

[1] *In re Alsys*, Ann. Dig. vol. V, Case no. 42; Phillipson, p. 311; Keith, p. 34; Selosse, p. 226; Paone in *Riv. D.I.* vol. XXXVII (1954), p. 584.

[2] *Ter K. v. State of the Netherlands, Surinam & Indonesia*, I.L.R. vol. XVIII, Case no. 53.

[3] *Guyen v. Frein*, Gazette du Palais (1963), II, 431. *Crédit du Nord v. Wilkin*, 7 May 1963, Cour de Bordeaux (unreported), *Annuaire français* (1964), p. 867; *C. v. Dame C.*, D. (1964), 28; *Dubois v. Dame Dubois*, Gazette du Palais (1964), I, 374. Also on the conflict of laws rules in French courts respecting attribution of jurisdiction of French colonial courts; for authorities see Clunet, vol. LXXXIX (1962), p. 1020; vol. XCI (1964), pp. 112, 319, 594; *Société comptoir commercial franco-africain v. Carabiber*, Revue critique de droit international privé, vol. LIII (1964), p. 530; *Lévy v. Cie d'assurances L'Equité et Cie d'assurances La Paternelle africaine*, Rev. gén. de droit int. pub. vol. LXVIII (1964), p. 753; *Affaire Ranaiveson*, 1 July 1963, Cour criminelle de Tananarive (unreported).

china the agreements[1] provided for the transfer to Vietnam, Cambodia and Laos of all judicial jurisdiction, but for the provision of French magistrates as expert advisers, and for special privileges for French citizens. Court records and judicial deposits would be handed over. On 9 March 1957 the French Minister of Foreign Affairs stated that the transfer of judicial competence to the States of Indochina had left certain French magistrates competent to function, but 'à un titre nouveau'.[2] The agreements with Morocco,[3] and the Francophone States,[4] provide for the employment of French judicial officers, harmonization of law, the status of French litigants, reciprocal judicial assistance and extradition.

A convention of 3 June 1955 between France and Tunisia[5] provided for special judicial guarantees for French citizens. The protocol of 20 March 1956 by which Tunisia's independence was recognized[6] stated that those provisions of the convention of 1955 which would be contradictory to Tunisia's new status as an independent country would be modified or abrogated. In a statement in the French National Assembly on 2 October 1956, the Secretary of State for Tunisian Affairs stated that this would necessarily modify the status of French citizens, and on 9 March 1957 the Foreign Minister stated that the maintenance of a special régime of justice for French citizens in Tunisia was no longer conceivable and that the existence of French courts in Tunisia had become incompatible with the new international status of the country. Accordingly, a new judicial relations agreement between the countries had become necessary, which would contain appropriate guarantees for French citizens, including the regulation in Tunisia of their personal status by French law. Also, in civil and commercial matters French law already in force in Tunisia would continue to be applied by Tunisian courts in the absence of any Tunisian legislation.[7]

1 Conventions of 29 August 1953 and 9 September 1953 with Cambodia; 22 October 1953 with Laos; 15 September 1954 with Vietnam. Decree no. 59–593, *Journal Officiel*, 3 May 1959, p. 4758.
2 *Annuaire français* (1957), p. 823.
3 Decree no. 60–11, *Journal Officiel*, 14 January 1960, p. 421.
4 Malagasy Republic, decree no. 60–692, *ibid.* 20 July 1960, p. 6616; Dahomey, decree no. 62–136, *ibid.* 6 February 1962, p. 1281; Niger, *ibid.* p. 1299; Upper Volta, *ibid.* p. 1311; Ivory Coast, *ibid.* p. 1265; Mauritania, decree no. 62–137, *ibid.* p. 1330; Republic of Mali, decree no. 64–694, *ibid.* 10 July 1964, p. 6128.
5 Decree no. 55–1179, *ibid.* 6 September 1955, p. 8909.
6 *Revue égyptienne de droit international*, vol. XIII, 1957, p. 222.
7 *Annuaire français* (1957), p. 807.

2. THE JUDICIAL JURISDICTION

I. Civil Proceedings

Unless the question is regulated by treaty or legislation, or both, complex issues are raised by a change of sovereignty after the institution of civil proceedings, and with respect to pending appeals and execution of judgments already issued.

(a) *Pending claims*

(A) *Solution in the absence of legislation.* Change of sovereignty may influence a pending claim in several ways. One or both of the parties may change nationality. The court before which the action is to be tried, or in which documents have been filed,[1] may or may not be located in the lost territory. The *situs* of property subject to proceedings, or the *locus* of the cause of action, may or may not be removed outside the jurisdiction.

Although the court before which the claim is pending may, because it is situated in absorbed territory, lose its jurisdiction,[2] the claim itself, if it is constituted under the private law of the predecessor State, remains an acquired right. The District Court of Maastricht held that, even though the transfer of German territory to the Netherlands changed the *locus delicti* for the purposes of the conflict of laws, acts previously performed there were to be characterized as tortious by German law, because civil rights already acquired could not be affected by political changes.[3] If the claim of a foreign national falls, according to the rules of private international law, within the jurisdiction of its courts, the successor State is obliged to permit the recommencement of the proceedings. On the other hand, the court may be situated in territory which remains subject to the old sovereign, while loss of a province affects either the status of the parties or the *situs* of property or the *locus* of the cause of action. In this case the continuing competence of the court to entertain the claim is dependent on its jurisdiction over the defendant, the movable or immovable property subject to the action, or the place where the cause of action arose. Should the pending action concern immovable property the *situs* of which ceases to be within the jurisdiction of the court, it must be recommenced in the appropriate tribunal. A Syrian court held that,

---

1 Delbez, p. 182; Piédelièvre, vol. I, p. 156; Selosse, pp. 250–4; Sibert, vol. I, p. 215.
2 *In re Alsys, Ann. Dig.* vol. V, Case no. 42. Fauchille is of opinion that proceedings need not be recommenced: vol. I, pt. I, p. 367. Strupp agrees with him: *Éléments*, vol. I, p. 95.
3 *X.* v. *Jurrissen, I.L.R.* vol. XVII, p. 82.

consequent upon the transfer of Palestine from Turkey to Great Britain, and the separation of Palestine from Syria, it could no longer exercise jurisdiction in a case which concerned immovable property in Palestine.[1] This is a question to be determined by the rules of private international law. The successor State is obliged to permit the recommencement of the proceedings in its courts only if the latter are, by such rules, the only tribunals competent to adjudicate on the matter.[2] On the other hand, litigation pending against the successor State in respect of liabilities which the successor assumes must be recommenced in the latter's courts.[3]

The successor State is bound to respect the rights of the parties as they existed at the moment of the change of sovereignty. Hence, procedural steps taken by either party must be recognized in subsequent litigation, and disclosures in the pleadings or on discovery or interrogatories are effective if admissible in the law of evidence of the successor State.[4] The substantive law under which the rights and claims in dispute are alleged to have arisen will require to be proved as foreign law only if the successor's private law has superseded that of the predecessor. The former's law of evidence and procedure, however, will govern the conduct of the case, and may affect the rules of prescription and limitation to which the claim was previously subject.

(B) *Solution provided by treaties and legislation*
(i) *State practice generally*

Various methods have been chosen from time to time to regulate the problem of pending proceedings: the Convention of Frankfurt, 1871, provided that, where actions were pending before French courts in Alsace-Lorraine at the date of the cession of those provinces to Germany, they were to be continued in the courts of the territory where the defendant had his domicile immediately after the change of sovereignty. Similar rules were to be applied to processes decided in courts of first or second instance which had not yet the force of a *res judicata* but against which appeals had not been lodged.[5] In the Treaty of Paris, 1898, the

[1] *Syrian State Succession (Haifa Leases) Case, Ann. Dig.* vol. III, Case no. 70.
[2] See Fauchille, vol. I, pt. I, p. 367; Piédelièvre, vol. I, pp. 155–6; Fiore, *Int. Law Cod.* p. 163. The Austrian Supreme Court held in the *Paternity Suit (Austria) Case* that a paternity suit commenced in the Vienna *Landesgericht* could be continued under the Transitional Law of 20 July 1945 by the District Court of the City of Vienna, *I.L.R.* vol. XX, p. 93.
[3] Actions brought against the Secretary of State in respect to the liability of Burma were, by the provisions of the Burma Independence Act, 1947, expressed to abate on the transfer of sovereignty to that country, 11 & 12 Geo. VI, c. 3, s. 4 (2).
[4] Fauchille, vol. I, pt. I, p. 367; Piédelièvre, vol. I, p. 155.
[5] *M.N.R.G.* vol. XX, p. 847, art. 3.

United States and Spain agreed that civil suits would be prosecuted to a conclusion in the courts before which they were pending at the date of the change of sovereignty, or in courts substituted therefor.[1] A similar provision was incorporated in the Convention of Poznan signed by Germany and Poland in 1920 for the regulation of judicial proceedings in territory ceded to the latter. Actions pending were to be continued in the court in which they were commenced, or, if the court was no longer in existence, in the German or Polish court of the same standing in the same district.[2] The British North America Act, 1949 provided for the continuance in force of jurisdiction of Newfoundland courts.[3] When the Philippine Islands attained independence, it was agreed between the new Republic and the United States that cases pending before the United States Supreme Court in respect of claims arising in the seceding territory were to continue to be subject to review until disposed of, despite the change of sovereignty.[4] On the other hand, when Denmark ceded territory in the West Indies to the United States in 1916, the treaty of cession enacted that pending actions were to be continued in the Danish courts, and executed by the 'competent authorities'.[5] The Constitution of Malaysia provided for the continuity of the existing jurisdictions of subordinate courts, and for the continued validity of all judicial actions.[6]

(ii) *The partition of India, 1947*

The separation of India and Pakistan, especially since it was accompanied by extensive population movement, raised such complex problems respecting judicial jurisdiction that a solution based upon customary law and juristic logic would obviously be hazardous.[7] In particular, although each of the Dominions would become a foreign country in the eyes of the other's, conflict of laws rules, the implications of this had to be legislatively minimized. As the Calcutta High Court said:

> The circumstances were abnormal and unprecedented and it must not be forgotten that the division of India and the creation of the two Dominions of India and Pakistan gave rise to new problems which could not be solved under the existing principles of law—private and international. These problems were sought to be

1 *M.N.R.G.* ser. 2, vol. XXXII, p. 74, art. 12 (2), p. 77.
2 *L.N.T.S.* (1927), vol. IX, p. 103.
3 12, 13 & 14 Geo. VI, c. 22, s. 18 (4).
4 *U.N.T.S.* vol. VII (1947), no. 1, art. 5.
5 *M.N.R.G.* 3rd ser. vol. X, p. 357, art. 8, at p. 365.
6 Cmnd. 2694, s. 88.
7 Agrawala in *Indian Journal of International Law*, vol. II (1962), p. 448; Kapur in *Indian Law Journal*, vol. IX (1957), pp. 11 *et seq.*

The Effect on the Judicial System

solved and the attending difficulties were sought to be resolved by the transitional enactments.[1]

Since the provinces of Punjab, Bengal and Assam were partitioned, it was necessary to partition the judicial system of which the High Courts at Lahore and Calcutta were the regional apexes. This was done by sections 13 of the High Court (Punjab) and of the High Court (Bengal) Orders, 1947. The Lahore High Court continued to have jurisdiction in West Punjab, which became part of Pakistan, and the Calcutta High Court in West Bengal, which remained part of India. It was necessary to make provision concerning the continuance of proceedings pending in the other territory in each instance, and for appeals and reviews. Section 4 of the Indian Independence (Legal Proceedings) Order, 1947 provided that all proceedings pending immediately after the date of partition in any civil or criminal court other than a High Court in the three provinces should be continued in the court in which commenced, and that that court would retain all jurisdiction and powers which it had immediately previous thereto.

The Calcutta High Court interpreted the expression 'proceedings pending' to cover execution proceedings, and even decrees which were filed before partition but respecting which execution proceedings had not be filed.[2]

With respect to actions against the administration the following solution was devised: It was enacted that actions and rights of action against the Secretary of State were to cease; in England they were to be brought against the High Commissioner and in India against such other person as the Governor-General should designate.[3] Where the Governor-General in Council was a party to any legal proceedings in British India with respect to the rights, property and liabilities apportioned between India and Pakistan, the Dominion succeeding to them was deemed to be substituted for him, and the proceedings were to continue accordingly.[4] A like arrangement was made in respect of the provinces. Proceedings which immediately before the partition were pending against the Secretary of State in respect of a liability of the Governor-General in Council or a province were to continue against the Dominion or province which

---

[1] *Ahidbar Ghose* v. *Jagabandhu Roy*, A.I.R. (1952), Cal. 846.
[2] *Bonbehari Roy* v. *Dhirendra Nath Roy*, A.I.R. (1956), Cal. 132. Hence, the non-satisfaction certificate and the application for execution with the certificate in another court constitute the same proceedings: *Ayub Ali* v. *Harinarayan Kanu*, A.I.R. (1957), Assam 155.
[3] Indian Independence Act, 1947, 10 & 11 Geo. VI, c. 30, s. 15.
[4] Indian Independence (Rights, Property and Liabilities) Order, 1947, s. 12 (1).

succeeded to the liability.[1] Where the Governor-General in Council was a party to proceedings in respect of 'actionable wrongs' the liability was to become that of the Dominion within whose territory the cause of action arose.[2]

The Supreme Court of India interpreted these provisions in a case in which the cause of action arose in Dacca in 1945, and the suit was pending in the Court of the First Subordinate Judge in Dacca at the date of partition. The Subordinate Judge of Alipore framed a preliminary question of jurisdiction when the Province of East Bengal was substituted for the Province of Bengal. The Supreme Court held this was a substitution under the legislation, and that the Alipore court had jurisdiction.[3] The High Court of the Punjab held that a claim based upon the wrongful confiscation of goods by the Government of the Punjab could only be adjudicated upon by the courts within that part of Punjab where the confiscation occurred, and since this was in Pakistan, the Indian courts had no jurisdiction.[4]

A similar arrangement regarding pending proceedings was made with respect to the merged States in the States Merger (Governor's Provinces) Order, 1949. This was held to have transferred to the High Court of Allahabad proceedings commenced in the State of Rampur which merged with the United Provinces, as if the proceedings had been instituted or commenced in that court.[5]

(iii) *The dismemberment of Palestine, 1947*

In 1949 the General Military Governor of the Western Side of Jordan issued a proclamation which had the force of law in accordance with article 6 of the Law Amending the General Administrative Law in Palestine. In virtue of this the Supreme Court of Cassation in Jordan held that the Jerusalem Court of First Instance had jurisdiction to hear cases which were originally included in the jurisdiction of the Jaffa District Court, and hence was competent to examine the legal relationship between a customer and the Jaffa branch of the Ottoman Bank.[6]

1 Indian Independence (Rights, Property and Liabilities) Order, 1947, s. 12 (3).
2 *Ibid.* s. 10 (1).
3 *State of Tripura* v. *Province of East Bengal* A.I.R.[1951] S.C., 23 See also *Midnapore Zemindary* v. *Province of Bengal* [1948] F.C.R. 309. Generally on the effect of s. 4 of the Order see *The Associated Hotels of India Ltd* v. *R. B. Jodha Mal Kothalia*, A.I.R. (1957), Pun. 201; *Ganguli Engineering Ltd* v. *Shrimati Sushila Bala Dasi*, A.I.R. (1957), Cal. 103.
4 *Lakhmi Chand* v. *Punjab State*, I.L.R. vol. xx, p. 91.
5 *Nazakat Ali Khan* v. *Bankey*, A.I.R. (1958), All. 106.
6 *Ottoman Bank* v. *Jabaji*, I.L.R. vol. xxi, p. 457.

The Effect on the Judicial System

(iv) *The independence of British territories*

It is the practice when granting independence to British territories to enact their independence Constitutions, which include the judicial system. Generally provision is made for cases pending before the courts established under the previous Constitutions to be continued before those established under the new ones.[1] Since the courts are royal courts, provision for continuity has also been made when the monarchy has been abolished.[2] The grant of jurisdiction to the new courts is sometimes explicit,[3] but in the case of Uganda is unclear. It was there provided that the High Court should have the jurisdiction to be conferred upon it by the Constitution or any other law.[4] In fact, no jurisdiction has been explicitly conferred upon it, the Uganda legislation merely stating that the High Court should exercise its jurisdiction in conformity with existing law.[5]

(v) *The union of Tanganyika and Zanzibar, 1964*

When Tanganyika and Zanzibar united, provision was made for pending proceedings to be continued before the court having jurisdiction

---

1 Federation of Malaya (Constitution) Order, S.I. 1957, no. 1533, ss. 168, 172; Somaliland (Constitution) Order, S.I. 1960, no. 1060, s. 56; The Nigeria (Constitution) Order, S.I. 1960, no. 1652, s. 5; The Sierra Leone (Constitution) Order, S.I. 1961, no. 741, s. 9; The Trinidad and Tobago (Constitution) Order, S.I. 1962, no. 1875, ss. 8, 9 (appeals only); The Aden (constitution) Order, S.I. 1962, no. 2177, s. 7 (High Court proceedings only); The Jamaica (Constitution) Order, S.I. 1962, no. 1550, s. 14 (appeals only); The Kenya Independence Order, S.I. 1963, no. 1968, s. 16; The Uganda Independence Order, S.I. 1962, no. 2175, s. 17; The Zambia Independence Order, S.I. 1964, no. 1652, s. 17; The Gambia Independence Order, S.I. 1965, no. 135, s. 12; Zanzibar Independence Order, S.I. 1962, no. 2784, s. 3. The Zambia Independence Act, 1964, c. 65, s. 7, continues to vest jurisdiction in the courts to make a decree for the dissolution of a marriage with respect to those proceedings which were instituted before 24 October 1964. A similar provision is contained in the Kenya Independence Act, 1963, c. 55, s. 7. The Nigerian judicial system was reconstructed as at the date of independence by the Nigerian (Constitution) Order in Council, 1960, S.I. 1960, no. 1652. The Supreme Court of Ghana was set up in 1853, Ordinance no. 4 of 1853, and reconstituted in 1935, Ordinance no. 7 of 1935, 1957 and 1958. The judicial system was reconstructed when Ghana became a Republic on 1 July 1960, Courts Act, 1960, no. 9.

2 The Constitution of the Federal Republic of Nigeria Act, no. 20 of 1963, chap. VIII, established the courts, and saving was made in ss. 155 and 156; The Republic of Tanganyika (Consequential, Transitional and Temporary Provisions) Act, no. 2 of 1962, ss. 9 and 10; The Constitution of Uganda (First Amendment) Act, no. 61 of 1963, s. 39 (1); The Constitution of Kenya (Amendment) Act, no. 28 of 1964, ss. 17, 18.

3 E.g. Zambia, The Zambia Independence Order, S.I. 1964, no. 1652, s. 98.

4 The Uganda Independence Order, S.I. 1962, no. 2175, s. 90 (1).

5 The Uganda Judicature Ordinance, no. 62 of 1962, s. 2.

in the matter.[1] Since the Revolutionary Council in Zanzibar had abrogated the Constitution,[2] it was necessary to legislate for the reconstitution of the High Court, and for the continuing of pending proceedings.[3]

(vi) *The independence of the Francophone States*

The judicial conventions entered into between France and the three States of Indochina transferred all judicial jurisdiction to the latter, but provided for pending proceedings to be determined according to the law hitherto applying to them.[4] In the case of Vietnam proceedings pending before the mixed *Cour de Cassation* would be remitted to the Vietnamese Ministry of Justice. Criminal proceedings already commenced before the Mixed Courts would be continued before the Vietnamese Courts, and be subject to Vietnamese criminal law, unless its provisions would be more severe than French law, when the latter would continue to govern the matter. Administrative proceedings would be transferred as they stood to the Vietnam authorities if concerning the public services of Vietnam, and to the French if concerning the French State.

The creation of separate judicial systems in the Malagasy Republic[5] and the African States[6] was achieved by legislation of the new States themselves, which contained no specific provision for continuity of pending cases. The transitional agreements in the matter of justice entered into between France and the Malagasy Republic,[7] the Central African Republic,[8] Gabon,[9] Congo and Chad,[10] however, provided for the continuity of all jurisdictions and for temporary continuity of appeals to the *Cour de Cassation* and the *Conseil d'État*. Until Malagasy rules of procedure were promulgated, French rules governed the jurisdiction of Malagasy courts.[11]

1 Transitional Provisions Decree, Govt. Notice no. 245 of 1 May 1964, s. 8.
2 Zanzibar Govt. Notice no. 73.
3 High Court Decree no. 2 of 1964, s. 5. In anticipation of independence the Sultan in 1963 had reconstituted the High Court, and similar provision had been made for pending proceedings, Courts Decree, no. 22 of 1963, s. 30.
4 See *supra*, p. 143.
5 Art. 18 of the Malagasy Constitution provided for a High Court of Justice, whose organization was fixed by a Law of 2 June 1959, *Journal Officiel de la République malgache*, 6 June 1959, p. 1300. An administrative court was created by a Law of 7 December 1959, *ibid*. 12 Dec. 1959, p. 2446.
6 See *infra*, p. 176.
7 Decree no. 60–627, *Journal Officiel*, 2 July 1960, p. 5968.
8 Decree no. 60–756, *ibid*. 30 July 1960, p. 7041.
9 Decree no. 60–757, *ibid*. 30 July 1960, p. 7047.
10 Decree no. 60–756, *ibid*. 30 July 1960, p. 7041. See *Cie des transports régionaux de l'Est et du Centre*, *Gazette du Palais* (1962), 1, 251.
11 *Annuaire français* (1961), p. 967.

(vii) *The independence of Algeria, 1962*

On the independence of Algeria a judicial protocol of 28 August 1962[1] provided that civil suits pending before Algerian courts in which both parties were of French nationality and were domiciled in France would, at the request of either of them, be remitted to French courts, unless the suit affected Algerian immovables. The same provision operated vice versa in favour of Algerians and also affected suits which involved the French State and its public organs, and in which the principal object was to establish that some person had French nationality.

(viii) *The cession of the French Establishments in India, 1954*

The agreement between France and India of 21 October 1954[2] relative to the cession of the French Establishments provided that court processes pending at the date of the transfer would be completed and decisions given in accordance with the laws and regulations in force in the Establishments. The local jurisdiction would continue to function, and would be administered by 'magistrates legally qualified, well known and domiciled in the Establishments', who would be chosen by the Indian Consul-General before the transfer and appointed to office temporarily, according to French law. However, if the parties agreed, pending suits could be transferred to the jurisdiction of Indian courts, and suits in respect of which the pleadings had been issued but no appearance had been made would no longer appear on the lists of French courts.

(ix) *The independence of the Congo (Léopoldville), 1960*

The *Loi fondamentale*,[3] by which the Belgian Congo was given an interim constitution as an independent State, contained provisions for the continuity of the existing judicial system. However, political events occasioned a breakdown in the operation of the system. Many Belgian magistrates and judges left the country without giving judgment in cases before them, and for some time they were not replaced.[4] In order that actions could be recommenced in Belgian courts the Belgian Parliament legislated on 7 August 1961 to grant jurisdiction to Belgian courts, which, in virtue of *dispositions conventionnelles*, would have had to be

---

[1] Decree no. 62–1020, *Journal Officiel*, 30 August 1962, p. 8506. Interpreted by the *Conseil d'État* in the *Union régionale Algérienne de la C.F.T.C.* Case, Clunet, vol. XC (1963), p. 603.
[2] *Annuaire français* (1955), p. 703, art. 10; B.F.S.P., vol. CLXI, p. 533.
[3] The Congo reorganized its legal system on 4 August 1961. See *supra*, p. 133.
[4] Parliamentary Answer of the Minister of Justice, 21 January 1964, *Journal des Tribunaux* (1964), p. 138.

brought before Congolese courts.[1] This was held to mean that, unless a judicial convention existed between Belgium and the Congo, Belgian courts could administer justice in any matter governed by Belgian law.[2] And, since there was no treaty between Belgium and the Congo creating *exception de litispendance*, the fact that the same matter might remain within the jurisdiction of the Congolese courts was irrelevant to the jurisdiction of Belgian courts.[3]

(x) *The dismemberment of Ruanda-Urundi, 1962*

By Legislative Order of 8 January 1962, Belgium amended a Decree of 16 June 1960 which constituted the Code of Judicial Organization and Competence of Ruanda-Urundi so as to add to the Court of First Instance and the Court of Appeal, as previously constituted, two Burundi assisting judges having a deliberative voice for criminal matters and an advisory voice in civil matters. Since the Burundi Government felt that this reform measure failed to implement its right to self-government, it did not put the measure into effect and it demanded complete self-government for the judicial system without supervision of any kind. It was noted that all Belgian judges would be withdrawn from 1 July 1962 and that Burundi would find itself without any judiciary. Hence the government wished to affirm its desire to organize the courts in accordance with the will of the nation.

(b) *Judgments*

(i) *State practice generally*

A judgment in the courts of the predecessor State is an acquired right, and effect must be given to it in the courts of the successor State if the judgment creditor is a foreign national.[4] Execution, however, may not, it

1 Recueil des lois et arrêtés royaux de Belgique (1961), p. 2886.
2 S.A. *Caisse patronale* v. *Cox*, *Journal des Tribunaux* (1964), p. 509.
3 Parliamentary Answer of the Minister of Justice, 21 January 1964, *Journal des Tribunaux* (1964), p. 138.
4 Delbez, p. 182; Fauchille, vol. I, p. 368; Guggenheim, *Traité*, p. 475; Phillipson, p. 311; Piédelièvre, vol. I, p. 149; Selosse, p. 238; Sibert, vol. I, p. 215; Verdross-Zemanek, p. 201; Wilkinson, p. 36. It was acknowledged in the Convention Additional to the Convention of Frankfurt, 1871, that every judgment given by French courts in Alsace-Lorraine, and having the force of a *res judicata* should be considered as definite and binding in the ceded territory: *M.N.R.G.* vol. XX, p. 847, art. 3. The Treaty of Paris, 1898, provided that judgments rendered in civil suits between private persons before the exchange of ratifications, and in respect of which there was no right of revision under Spanish law, would be deemed final, and would be executed in due form by competent authorities in the territory within which such judgments should be carried out: *M.N.R.G.* (ser. 2), vol. XXXII, p. 74, art. 12 (1). In *Clements* v. *Texas Company* the Texan Court of Civil Appeals held that 'a valid judgment upon title to land rendered in a province of Mexico by a court of competent jurisdiction under the Mexican Government was not affected as a valid

would seem, be issued directly upon the judgment. The latter is a foreign judgment, and must be proved as such.[1] Proceedings upon it for confirmation in the courts of the successor State will be subject to the formalities of the new legal system; but, as the rights of the judgment creditor are acquired, their enforcement is not dependent upon the existence of a treaty for mutual enforcement of judgments between his national State and the successor State.[2]

The question of judgments of the predecessor's courts was discussed at length in a case before an Italian court in Addis Ababa after the annexation of Ethiopia. Action was being taken upon a judgment of an Ethiopian court, and it was held that, as there was no formal legal continuity between the old and the new judicial systems, the judgments given by courts of the previous sovereign could not be enforced automatically in the annexed territories, and had to be rendered executive by a new judgment in the Italian courts. However, the earlier judgments, it was stated, could be adduced as proof of the existence of rights duly acquired.[3]

It is controversial whether or not the successor State is obliged to execute against persons resident in the ceded territory the judgments of courts of the predecessor State located outside this territory. The Law Officers in 1865 were of opinion that the successor State must treat such a judgment in the same way as it must treat any other foreign judgment. The issue in this instance arose after the cession of the Ionian Islands to

---

obligation by a revolution and the subsequent setting up of the new Republic of Texas in the Mexican province where it was rendered', 273 S.W. 993. In a case in 1903 before a British court in the Transvaal, an injunction granted by a court of the South African Republic was repeated, on the ground that it was a final order, although it was said that the court would not have made such an order *ab initio*: Keith, p. 36. Judgments given by the courts set up in the Italian Social Republic in 1943 were considered as binding on Italian courts after the recovery of the territory subject to the Republic's jurisdiction: *Pisati* v. *Pellizari*, Foro Italiano, 70 (1947), vol. I, p. 336; *Orobia* v. *Ministero delle Finanze*, Foro Italiano, 70 (1947), vol. I, p. 277. In *Forer* v. *Guterman* the district court of Tel Aviv held that an Order of the Privy Council made before the termination of the mandate for Palestine was binding on the parties afterwards: *Ann. Dig.* vol. XV, Case no. 21. See *A.-G. for Israel* v. *Sylvester*, ibid., Case no. 190.

[1] Fauchille, vol. I, pt. I, p. 348; Piédelièvre, vol. I, pp. 148 *et seq.*; Rousseau, p. 281; Selosse, p. 249. The Treaty of Versailles enacted that judgments delivered by German courts in Alsace-Lorraine were to be capable of execution only after the issue of an exequatur by the corresponding French tribunal: B.T.S. (1919), no. 4, Cmd. 153, art. 78, p. 45. The *Cour criminelle* of Tananarive held that a *condamnation* of the accused by a French court in Réunion had become a foreign judgment after the independence of Madagascar, and could not be taken into account in determining recidivist penalties, *Affaire Ranaiveson*, 1 July 1963 (unreported).

[2] See (*Polish*) *State Treasury* v. *Kurzrock*, *Ann. Dig.* vol. I, Case no. 52; *Fischer* v. *Einhorn*, *Ann. Dig.* vol. III, Case no. 71.

[3] *Bessi* v. *Kediro*, *Ann. Dig.* vol. IX, Case no. 39.

Greece. Two Italian nationals had obtained in the British consular court at Constantinople a judgment against a resident of the islands. After the cession, the judgment creditors sought execution of the judgment. The Greek Government adopted the view that the judgment had become a 'Greek judgment by the cession of the Islands' and was subject to review in the Greek courts. The Italian Government, on behalf of its nationals, requested the good offices of the British Ambassador at Athens to induce the Greek Government to recognize the validity of rights previously acquired. The Law Officers were asked to give an opinion on the matter. They pointed out that this was a case of a judgment pronounced within the extraterritorial Turkish jurisdiction of Great Britain. The Court which pronounced the judgment remained

> just what it was before; and the only change is, that the person of a Greek defendant is no longer amenable to the authority of that Court, and that we have lost the power to *compel* his obedience to a sentence by which he was and is bound.
> ... the analogy most in point is that of a foreign Judgment; and ..., under the peculiar circumstances of these cases, Her Majesty's Government has a right to expect from the Greek Government that they shall be treated as valid English judgments, not open to appeal or cassation before any Greek Court.[1]

The same matter was again reported upon in the following year. The effect of the transfer, the Law Officers advised,

> (according to sound principles of international law) was only that the successful plaintiffs, if they desired afterwards to obtain the benefit of those judgments before the new tribunals to which the defendants had now become amenable, might be obliged to do so upon the same terms, and with the same advantages or disadvantages, as in other cases, in which the benefit of foreign judgments may have to be sought before the Courts of a country different from that in which they have been pronounced.[2]

A like conclusion was reached by a Polish court which was asked to enforce a judgment of the Supreme Court of the Austro-Hungarian Empire at Vienna, respecting property located in territory incorporated into Poland in 1919. The judgment was one of a district court of Vienna in the first instance, of the Court of Appeal at Vienna in the second instance, and only in the third instance of the Supreme Court, which alone had jurisdiction over the whole Empire, and consequently over Poland. It was held that the judgment in question was a foreign judgment, and could not be enforced by a Polish court because of the absence of any agreement between Poland and Austria for the mutual enforcement of

---

1 Opinion of 28 March 1865, F.O. 83/2287; O'Connell, Appendix, no. 24.
2 Opinion of 6 July 1866, F.O. 83/2287; O'Connell, Appendix, no. 27a.

judgments, and an entire want of reciprocity.[1] This case would appear to have been correctly decided. It would seem logical to limit the obligation of the successor State to enforce the judgments of the courts of its predecessor to those cases in which the jurisdiction of such courts in the first instance embraced the absorbed territory. It is not clear that the jurisdiction of the consular court in Constantinople did embrace the Ionian Islands, and the opinion of the Law Officers would seem to be defective in not taking this criterion into consideration.

(ii) *The partition of India, 1947*

The effect of the partition of India upon judgments of the British Indian courts, and of the merger in India of the States and of the French Establishments,[2] has been controversial. One theory is that a judgment of a British Indian Court in territory which fell to Pakistan could never be a foreign judgment *vis-à-vis* India,[3] for a foreign judgment means a judgment of any country which is 'not Indian'.[4] Before the partition, it is argued, India and Pakistan were one country and judgments given in territory which fell to Pakistan were judgments of Indian courts. It follows that they could not lose their Indian nationality simply because the place where they were given became foreign territory.[5] Hence no difficulties of interpretation could arise respecting the provision in the Indian Independence (Legal Proceedings) Order, 1947[6] which provided that effect would be given within the territories of either of the two Dominions to any judgment, decree, order or sentence of any court, other than a High Court, in Bengal, Punjab and Assam, as if it had been passed by a court of competent jurisdiction within that Dominion; and which was construed to include execution against property in either Dominion.[7]

However, the alternative theory, that the judgments of courts in territory which fell to Pakistan, were foreign, tended to dominate for a time the interpretation of Indian legislation[8] providing for execution of

1 *Knoll* v. *Sobel, Ann. Dig.* vol. III, Case no. 72.
2 India undertook to execute judgments and orders which were given by French courts before the transfer of the French Establishments in India and which were either final or would become final after the time for appeal would have lapsed, *Annuaire français* (1955), p. 709, art. 10. Actions valid under French law treating private rights before the transfer would remain valid.
3 Kapur in *Indian Law Journal*, vol. IX (1957), pp. 9 *et seq.*
4 Paraphrasing Dicey's rule incorporated in the Indian Civil Procedure Code.
5 *Kishori Lal* v. *Shrimati Shanti Devi*, A.I.R. (1953), S.C. 441, per Bose, J. at p. 442.
6 S. 4 (3).
7 *Ahidhar Ghose* v. *Jagabandhu Roy*, A.I.R. (1952), Cal. 846.
8 Displaced Persons (Institution of Suits) Act, 1948, no. 47 of 1948, amended by no. 25 of 1949.

decrees made before partition in favour of persons who had been displaced from Pakistan to India. The High Courts of Calcutta[1] and Punjab[2] held these decrees to be foreign, but the Supreme Court stated in respect of their decisions that

if those decisions are not based on matters which are special to them and which do not apply here and if the learned Judges intended to enunciate a general principle which would affect the rights of parties before us, then, with the greatest respect, we consider that they are, to that extent, wrong.[3]

The Legal Proceedings Order was ambiguous respecting whether the judgments to be enforced were to be given before the date of partition, or whether judgments subsequently given in respect of litigation pending at that date were also included. Several High Courts tended to the view that only the former judgments were covered by the Order,[4] and an attempt was made on the basis of them to argue before the Punjab High Court that the Order could have covered only proceedings over which the court had lost jurisdiction through partition, and not proceedings in courts whose jurisdiction had not been affected, and whose judgments, in consequence, would remain foreign judgments. The Court held that the expression 'proceedings pending' in the Order included also judgments pending, and went on to decide that the Order could not have intended to leave unenforceable a large residue of cases which had been heard and decided in the court in which action was brought but in respect of which execution could only be effected in the other Dominion.[5]

The more liberal interpretation of the Order seems to be required by the English rule of the conflict of laws that a decree pronounced in the absence of the defendant by a foreign court, to the jurisdiction of which he has not in any way submitted himself, is an 'absolute nullity'.[6] If it were to be argued that, consequent upon partition, the defendant had

1 *Naresh Chander Bose* v. *Sachinder Nath*, 53 C.W.N. 700; *Dominion of India* v. *Hira Lal*, 53 C.W.N. 817.
2 *Said ul-Hamid* v. *Federal Indian Assurance Co. Ltd*, A.I.R. (1951), Simla. 255.
3 *Kishori Lal* v. *Shrimati Shanti Devi*, A.I.R. (1953), S.C. 441, per Bose, J. at p. 442.
4 *Dominion of India* v. *Hiralal Bothra*, A.I.R. (1950), Cal. 12; *Surendra Nath Kolay* v. *Milan Mia Laskar*, A.I.R. (1955), Assam 12; *Ayub Ali* v. *Harinarayan kanu*, A.I.R. (1957), Assam 155; *Said ul-Hamid* v. *Federal Indian Assurance Co.*, A.I.R. (1951), Pun. 255; *Hiranand Dobey* v. *Jyoti Ram Goel*, A.I.R. (1952), J. & K. 30; The Calcutta High Court contradicted this decision in *Protap Kumar Sen* v. *Nagendra Nath Mazumdar*, A.I.R. (1951), Cal. 511.
5 *The Associated Hotels of India Ltd* v. *R. B. Jodha Mal Kothalia*, A.I.R. (1957), Pun. 201. But if the court of action, refuses a warrant of execution, the judgment creditor cannot on the basis of a fresh non-satisfaction certificate from the court in Pakistan proceed to execution in India, because the proceedings in this case could not be described as pending: *Surendra Nath* v. *Milan Mia Laskar*, A.I.R. (1955), Assam 12; Agrawala, *loc. cit.* p. 51.
6 *Sirdar Gurdoyal Singh* v. *Rajah of Faridkote* (1894), A.C. 670

The Effect on the Judicial System

ceased to submit himself to a foreign court, then the judgment of that court, in the absence of legislation rectifying the matter, would be unenforceable. The whole question remains controversial, both as to the nature and extent of the conflict rule, and as to its application in the context of partition and merger.

The Full Bench of the High Court of Bombay in 1951 considered the effect upon judgments of the merger of the State of Akalkot in the Union of Bombay. The Bombay Code of Civil Procedure laid down the principle of no jurisdiction over non-resident aliens, and when a judgment creditor sought to enforce a judgment given in 1947 by the court of Sholapur against a debtor at that time resident in Akalkot, this was utilized by the defence to resist execution. It was held that the effect of the Code rules was not to render the decree of the Sholapur court a legal nullity, but merely to create a procedural impediment, which was removed when the defendant fell within the jurisdiction in virtue of the merger of Akalkot. (The Court distinguished *Gurdyal Singh* v. *Rajah of Faridkote* on the ground that the expression there used was 'mere nullity', and was not intended to mean an 'absolute nullity'.)[1]

Some Indian courts have held that the validity of a judgment or decree is to be determined by reference to the law in force on the date when the court was called upon to execute the decree, which would, in the context, be a date after partition or merger.[2] Other courts have held that the relevant date is the date of the judgment.[3] The better view appears to be that, since a foreign judgment is not a nullity, but is simply inexecutable, no fresh right needs to be vested in the decree holder, but merely a removal of procedural impediments to rights already vested. This was achieved by the Indian Civil Procedure Code.[4]

(iii) *The independence of the Francophone States*

A Presidential Decision of 12 June 1959[5] on the judicial jurisdiction within the French Community provided that decisions of any courts within the Community would be executory within all States of the

---

1 *Bhagwan Shankar* v. *Rajarum Bapu Vithal*, I.L.R. vol. XVIII, Case no. 30.
2 *Braj mohan Bose Benimadhav* v. *Kishorilal Kishanlal*, A.I.R. (1955), M.B. 1; *Lunaji Narayan* v. *Purshottam Charan*, A.I.R. (1953), M.B. 225; *Bhagwan Shankar* v. *Rajaram Bapu Vithal*, A.I.R. (1951), Bom. 125; *Meherunnissa Begum* v. *Venkat Muril Manohar Rao*, A.1.R. (1955), Hyd. 184; *Radheyshiam* v. *Firm Sawai Modi Basdeo Prasad*, A.I.R. (1953), Raj. 204.
3 *H. M. Subbaraya Setty & Sons* v. *S. K. Palani Chetty & Sons*, A.I.R. (1952), Mys. 69; *Shah Kantilal* v. *Dominion of India*, A.I.R. (1954), Cal. 67; *Shah Premchand* v. *Shah Danmel*, A.I.R. (1954), Raj. 4; *Chintamoni Padhan* v. *Paika Samal*, A.I.R. (1956), Orissa, 136; *Maloji Rao* v. *Sankar Saran*, A.I.R. (1955), All. 490.
4 Agrawala, *loc. cit.* p. 452.   5 *Journal Officiel*, 27 June 1959, p. 6405.

Community according to machinery which would be fixed by convention. No conventions, however, were promulgated before the transfer of Community competence in 1960, and the *Tribunal de Grande Instance* of St Nazaire held on 21 November 1961 that a decision of a court of Niger, even given before the transfer of Community competence in 1960, was a foreign judgment, and was not executory within France.[1]

In an exchange of notes[2] accompanying the protocol by which France transferred to Cambodia its judicial jurisdiction, it was agreed that judgments delivered by French courts before the transfer of jurisdiction would be executed in countries falling under the authority of the French Government, and that records would be made available for this purpose. Similar provision was made with respect to Laos and Vietnam. The judicial co-operation agreements between France and the other Francophone States provide for reciprocal execution of judgments.[3]

(c) Appeals

Action upon a judgment of the predecessor's court can be taken only if the judgment is final, and this is a matter to be solved by reference to the law under which it was delivered.[4] If a right of appeal against the judgment has vested in one of the parties it is part of the acquired right which the successor State must respect,[5] even though the court to which the appeal lies loses all jurisdiction.[6] Whether the appeal must be taken anew in the courts of the predecessor or successor State is a matter for private international law to determine in accordance with the principles suggested above in the case of pending proceedings. If the case on appeal must be tried in the courts of the successor State it is governed by the latter's law of procedure and evidence.[7]

---

1 *Consorts Marteau v. Receveur des finances de Saint-Nazaire*, Annuaire français (1962), p. 933.

2 Conventions of 29 August 1953 and 9 September 1953 with Cambodia; 22 October 1953 with Laos; 15 September 1954 with Vietnam, decree no. 59–593, *Journal Officiel*, 3 May 1959, p. 4758.   3 See *supra*, p. 143.

4 Fauchille, vol. I, pt. I, p. 369; Sibert, vol. I, p. 216; *Dzierzbicki v. District Electric Assoc. of Czestochowa*, Ann. Dig. vol. VII, Case no. 38.

5 *Fischer v. Einhorn*, Ann. Dig. vol. III, Case no. 71.

6 Fauchille is of opinion that the court retains its jurisdiction, but this is difficult to admit: vol. I, pt. I, p. 369. In *Panagos v. Drossopulous* the Italian Court of Cassation held that it had lost jurisdiction to entertain an appeal from Rhodes: *Foro Italiano*, 71 (1948), vol. I, p. 1033; also *Cortegiano Tercuz v. Tercuz*, ibid. 73; *Società Zanini v. Busato*, ibid. 817.

7 When a case is heard on appeal by the courts of the successor State it must be governed by the substantive law in force at the time of the judgment appealed from. In the *Salonica Appeals* Case the Greek Areopagus held that it was substituted for the Ottoman court at Salonica, but had to be guided by Turkish law in force at the time when judgment was given: Ann. Dig. vol. II, Case no. 45.

(i) *Appeals to the Italian Court of Cassation and Council of State*

If the court from which the appeal lies is situated in the successor State, and the court to which it lies is that of the predecessor State, there is a severance in the chain of jurisdiction. The Italian Court of Cassation held that it had lost jurisdiction to entertain appeals from Eritrea[1] and Tripoli, though in the latter case it was decided that, so long as Tripoli remained, in virtue of article 23 of the Peace Treaty, under Italian administration, this jurisdiction was temporarily preserved as an aspect of such administration.[2] The Italian Court of Cassation also held that judgments of the courts in Trieste given during the Anglo-American occupation, and prior to the conclusion of the Peace Treaty of 1947, had been made within the organic Italian judicial system, and appeals lay to the higher Italian courts after the cession of the territory.[3]

The Italian rules of procedure which were in force in Somalia under Trusteeship provided for appeal to the Italian Council of State against final administrative acts of the Government of Italian East Africa. In 1956 an Ordinance created a Court of Justice for Somalia with jurisdiction over appeals on the grounds of incompetence, *ultra vires* or excess of jurisdiction on the part of administrative authorities. The Italian Council of State held that its jurisdiction lapsed with the creation of this new jurisdiction, except in respect of cases pending in which the Council of State had already adjudicated. The decision was arrived at on the basis that the rules of procedure had been revived with the creation of the Trust Territory, and this measure was provisional pending the growth of autonomous institutions in the territory.[4]

(ii) *Appeals to the French Cour de Cassation and Conseil d'État*

Following the Presidential Decision of 12 June 1959 on the control of justice within the Community,[5] recourse to the *Conseil d'État* and the *Cour de Cassation* was to be maintained, but, in the case of decisions of African or Madagascan courts, the two tribunals would be constituted so as to include judges nominated by the President of the Community on the advice of the Governments of the States. It was recognized that the organization and administration of the judicial jurisdiction was appropriate to each State. By *Ordonnance* of 6 October 1958 the *Conseil*

---

1 *Sorkis v. Amed*, I.L.R. vol. XVII, Case no. 24.
2 *Farrugia v. Nuova Comp. Gen. Autolinee*, I.L.R. vol. XVIII, Case no. 32.
3 *Marzola v. Società Teavibra*, Ann. Dig. vol. XVI, Case no. 24.
4 Cotron in *I.C.L.Q.* vol. XII (1963), p. 1010.
5 See *supra*, p. 62.

d'État would lose its competence when the new States legislated to this effect.[1]

The *Conseil d'État* was seized of constitutional jurisdiction in respect of Morocco and Tunisia in virtue of Moroccan and Tunisian pre-independence legislation making it an organ of their respective administrative systems, and also in virtue of French legislation granting it competence as such. This produced a 'parallelism' of legal sources which, after the independence of the two countries, raised the question of the appropriate law to be applied. It was held that the *Conseil d'État*, although it might be a Tunisian or Moroccan jurisdictional organ, was still a French organ, and, when the parallel enactments did not give sufficient directions for the solution of a litigious problem, reference should be made to the 'general principles of law'. French procedure was always applied.[2]

After the publication of the Franco-Tunisian Judicial Assistance Agreement of 9 March 1957,[3] the question arose whether this implied the suppression of the competence granted the *Conseil d'État* by decree of the Bey of Tunis of 3 January 1927. The *Conseil d'État* referred the matter to the French Foreign Office, and upon receipt of its opinion ruled that its jurisdiction in respect of Tunisian administrative decisions had lapsed.

Respecting civil jurisdiction, all processes pending before French courts in Tunisia on 1 July 1957 were remitted to Tunisian courts. This included appeals before the *Cour de Cassation*. However, if both parties were French citizens one of them could, before that date, secure remission of the suit to French courts, or to the *Cour de Cassation*, which, losing the right to reverse decisions of the Tunisian Court of Appeals on the relevant date, might substitute therefor a Court of Appeal of French jurisdiction, such as that of Constantine.[4]

In an exchange of notes in 1957 between France and Morocco[5] it was agreed that appeals to the *Cour de Cassation* should not be continued, but that pending appeals might be heard. Other appeals would be remitted to the Moroccan Supreme Court. Motions to quash decisions of the courts instituted by the *dahir* of 1913 would not be entertained after the date when the Supreme Court of Morocco was established.

Provision for the temporary jurisdiction of the *Cour de Cassation* and the *Conseil d'État* was made in respect of certain of the French African

1 Ordonnance no. 58–513, *Journal Officiel*, 7 October 1958, p. 9182.
2 *Annuaire français* (1958), p. 751.
3 Decree no. 58–86, *Journal Officiel*, 1 February 1958, p. 1266.
4 *Annuaire français* (1959), p. 858. Re Hedi Ben Zakour, I.L.R. vol. xxv, p. 99. This provision was correctly utilized in a motion *d'assistance judiciaire à fin de pouvoir*, Anna Gueisse v. Nauche, Bull. Civ. (1962), I, p. 31.
5 Decree no. 60–11, *Journal Officiel*, 14 January 1960, p. 421.

The Effect on the Judicial System

States in the Transitional Agreements in the Matter of Justice which they signed with France.[1] Upon the expiry of the stated time, the jurisdiction would lapse. The question of continued jurisdiction in the case of those States which did not enter into such agreements was raised in 1961 before both tribunals in respect of a decision of the *Tribunal Supérieur d'Appel* of Niger delivered before independence. An exchange of notes followed between the Presidents of France and of Niger, in which it was agreed that both tribunals had ceased to be competent with respect to Niger on the date of transfer to that country of Community competence. It was further agreed that the Supreme Court of Niger had become competent to entertain an appeal from the decision in question.[2] The *Conseil d'État* also held that it had lost its jurisdiction with respect to administrative action in Cameroon and Chad when these became independent.[3]

In 1961 certain of the Francophone African States addressed uniform letters to France in which they pointed out that one effect of the transfer of Community competence to them was to bring about the lapse of competence of the *Cour de Cassation* and the *Conseil d'État* with respect to their judicial systems. France was requested to concede this interpretation. In each case the French Prime Minister replied affirmatively, and informed the other party that he had given instructions for the dossiers relative to matters before these tribunals to be remitted to the minister of justice of the new State.[4]

An ordinance of 30 December 1958 transferred the administration of justice to Cameroon as an aspect of the autonomy granted it within the Community.[5] Under article 6 of the Franco-Cameroon Judicial Agreement of 31 December 1958,[6] an appeal was maintained from the highest courts of Cameroon to the French *Cour de Cassation* in civil matters, and

---

1 Malagasy Republic, decree no. 60-627, *Journal Officiel*, 2 July 1960, p. 5968; Central African Republic, decree no. 60-756, *ibid.* 30 July 1960, p. 7041; Congo, *ibid.*; Chad, *ibid.*; Gabon, decree no. 60-757, *ibid.* p. 7047. See *Cie des transports régionaux de l'Est et du Centre, Gazette du Palais*, (1962), I, 251. However, this was limited to *juridiction de l'ordre administratif*, and did not extend to *juridiction relevant du contentieux local, Fédération des Syndicats des Travailleurs de la Fonction publique de Madagascar, R.D.P.* (1962), p. 777. Duvernoy Case, *Rev. jur. et pol.* vol. XVI (1962), p. 601, interpreting the Congo Agreement. See the Report of the *Avocat-général* therein. Also, respecting the Malagasy Agreement, *Suprema* Case, *ibid.* p. 544, and the Central African Agreement, *ibid.* p. 543.   2 *Annuaire français* (1962), p. 1029.
3 *Affaire union des populations du Cameroun, R.D.P.* (1962), p. 778; *Société frigarifique des produits des éleveurs tchadiens, ibid.* p. 777. Mayi-Matip Case, *Rev. jur. et pol.*, vol. XVI (1962), p. 581.
4 Ivory Coast, decree no. 62-136, *Journal Officiel*, 6 February 1962, pp. 1261, 1962; Dahomey, *ibid.* p. 1285; Niger, *ibid.* p. 1306; Upper Volta, *ibid.* p. 1315; Mauritania, decree no. 62-137, *ibid.* pp. 1324, 1335.
5 *Journal Officiel du Cameroun*, 1 January 1959, p. 1.
6 *Journal Officiel du Cameroun*, 1 January 1959, p. 9.

to the *Conseil d'État* in administrative matters. By decree of 4 June 1959 Cameroon reorganized its internal administrative judicial system, transforming the *Conseil du Contentieux Administratif* into the *Tribunal d'État*.[1] In a judicial protocol of 28 August 1962[2] it was agreed between France and Algeria that the files of appeals pending before the *Conseil d'État* and the *Cour de Cassation* were to be immediately transmitted to the Algerian authorities if the suit affected Algeria or Algerian companies. Decisions of these two organs given between 1 July 1962 and 28 August 1962 would be executed at the discretion of Algeria. Decisions of the *Cour de Cassation* in matters of private law would have the authority of *res judicatae* in Algeria. The *Cour de Cassation* and the *Conseil d'État* would retain their competence in respect of cases concerning the French State and French companies, and which involved principally questions of French nationality.

In an Agreed Franco-Indian Minute of 16 March 1963 it was resolved that cases pending before the *Cour de Cassation*, the *Conseil d'État* and the *Cour supérieur d'Arbitrage* on 16 August 1962 would be referred to the appropriate Indian court. All judgments and orders made would be enforced by the Indian authorities except in cases within the previous thirty months in which the defendant had not had the opportunity to appear.

(iii) *Appeals to the Belgian Cour de Cassation and Conseil d'État*

The *Loi fondamentale*[3] provided for the provisional continuity of the existing judicial system, including the competence of the Belgian *Cour de Cassation* and *Conseil d'État*.[4] However, with the breaking off of diplomatic relations between Belgium and the Congo in 1960 these provisions were regarded as having lapsed, and the Belgian tribunals lost their jurisdiction.[5] On 18 July 1965 the Congo enacted legislation modifying

1 Decree no. 59–31, *ibid.* 1 July 1959, p. 832. Following the independence of Cameroon pursuant to U.N. resolution the *Conseil d'État* found it had lost jurisdiction in respect of an administrative act performed there in 1955; *Mbounya* Case, *Rev. gén. de droit int. pub.* vol. LXVI (1963) with a note by Rousseau. Since Guinea was regarded as a seceding State, the French Cour de Cassation held that the French West African administrative courts lost jurisdiction on the date of its independence, *Affaire Dame Milo*, R.D.P. (1963), p. 794; *Annuaire français* (1964), p. 870.

2 Decree no. 62–1020, *Journal Officiel*, 30 August 1962, p. 8506.

3 See *supra*, p. 94, arts. 189, 263.

4 The Conseil d'État held in January 1963 that it was competent only with respect to cases pending on 1 November 1954, pursuant to the Treaty of Cession of 1954, (*Annuaire français*, 1955, p. 703, arts. 14, 16), *Affaire Coumarassamy Vanier, Recueil des décisions* (1963), p. 45; *Affaire Mohammed*, R.D.P. (1963), p. 794.

5 *Mahamba* Case, 24 March 1961, *Journal des Tribunaux* (1962), p. 8. De Visscher in *Communiazioni e Studi*, vol. XI (1960), p. 78. De Bandt in *Revue belge du droit international* (1965), p. 500.

the *Loi fondamentale*, in which all reference to the Belgian *Cour de Cassation* and *Conseil d'État* was terminated.[1] It was held by the *Conseil d'État* that this had the effect of depriving it of all competence.[2]

(iv) *The formation of Malaysia, 1963, and the separation of Singapore, 1965*

The Malaysia Act[3] provided for appeals to proceed from the Borneo States and Singapore to the Supreme Court of the Federation, but arrangements might be made under section 3 of the Malaya Independence Act 1957 with respect to appeals pending before the Privy Council, whose jurisdiction otherwise would lapse.[4]

When Singapore separated from Malaysia it was enacted that the Singapore courts would retain their jurisdiction, and that pending legislative change appeals would continue to be to the Federal Court of Appeals of Malaysia, and thence to the Privy Council.[5]

(v) *Appeals to the Court of Appeal of Eastern Africa*

When Tanganyika, Uganda, Kenya and Zanzibar became independent it was necessary to provide for the continued appellate jurisdiction of the Court of Appeal of Eastern Africa, which was constituted in 1961,[6] and reconstituted[7] as an organ of the East Africa Common Services Organization.[8] The Act of reconstitution, and also the relevant legislation of the four member States conceding appellate jurisdiction to the Court,[9]

---

1 Moniteur congolais, 15 September 1963.
2 Tshombe v. République du Congo, *Journal des Tribunaux* (1965), p. 121.
3 1963, c. 35, s. 5.
4 5 & 6 Eliz. II, c. 60.
5 *State of Singapore Govt. Gazette*, 9 August 1965, no. 1824; Malaysia Law no. 53 of 1965, s. 8; *International Legal Materials*, vol. IV (1965), p. 939.
6 The Eastern Africa Court of Appeal Order, S.I. 1961, no. 2323, revoked by The Eastern Africa Court of Appeal (Revocation) Order, S.I. 1962, no. 2598.
7 Court of Appeal of Eastern Africa Act of the Common Services Organization, no. 130 of 1962.
8 The Organization was set up with a scheduled list of functions by agreement of Tanganyika, Kenya and Uganda, the latter two being entrusted by the United Kingdom with power to contract it. Acts of the Organization have legislative force, s. 4. The instrument will be found in The East Africa Common Services Organization Ordinance, Laws of Kenya, cap. 4, rev. 1962; The *Tanganyika Gazette* of 10 December 1961, Govt. Notice no. 437 of 1961.
9 The Kenya Order, S.I. 1963, no. 791, s. 166, provided that the Court should be the Court of Appeal constituted under the Constitution, should the Central Legislature so provide. This was repeated in The Kenya Independence Order, S.I. 1963, no. 1968, s. 176. Kenya enacted accordingly in The Appellate Jurisdiction Ordinance, no. 3 of 1962, s. 3. The Constitution of Tanganyika Act, no. 1 of 1962, Supplement no. 1A to the *Tanganyika Gazette*, vol. XLIII, no. 65 of 7 December 1962, s. 51, authorized Parliament to provide for appeals to the Court. Parliament enacted the Appellate Jurisdiction Act, no. 9 of 1962, s. 3. Under The Uganda (Independence)

provide for appeals pending before the old court to be continued before the new one;[1] and also for the decisions of the Court to be enforced through the States' judicial systems.

(vi) *Appeals to the British Caribbean Court of Appeal*

When the Federation of the West Indies was dissolved,[2] Jamaica[3] and Trinidad and Tobago[4] substituted their own Courts of Appeal for the British Caribbean Court of Appeal, and provision was made for pending appeals to be continued before the new courts.[5] The British Caribbean Court of Appeal was then reconstituted as the Court of Appeal of the other West Indian territories.[6]

(vii) *Appeals to the Privy Council*

The jurisdiction of the Privy Council, originally derived from the royal prerogative, is now defined by legislation of 1833.[7] Before the Statute of Westminster no portion of the Crown's dominions could revoke appeals to the Privy Council,[8] but the Dominions to which the Statute was applied acquired this competence.[9] With the obsolescence of Dominion status the question arose whether continued appeals were

Order, S.I. 1962, no. 2175, s. 18, the Court was deemed to have been established under s. 96 (2) (*a*) of the Constitution. Jurisdiction was conferred by the Uganda (Appellate Jurisdiction) Act, no. 1 of 1962, brought into effect by the Court of Appeal Order, 1962, Supplement to the *Uganda Gazette* of 7 December 1962, p. 1066. Zanzibar Courts Decree, no. 22 of 1963, s. 25.

1 The Kenya Appellate Jurisdiction Ordinance, no. 3 of 1963, s. 11; The Tanganyika Appellate Jurisdiction Act, no. 9 of 1962, s. 4; The Uganda (Appellate Jurisdiction) Act, no. 1 of 1962, s. 4. The Court of Appeal of Eastern Africa interpreted s. 16 (1) of the Kenya Independence Order relating to appeals before the Court in *Sunderdass Hariram* v. *Bhupendra Shamjibhai* [1964] The Eastern Africa Law Reports 241.

2 The West Indies Act, 1962, 10 & 11 Eliz. II, c. 19.

3 The Jamaica (Constitution) Order, S.I. 1962, no. 1550, schedule, s. 103; The Judicature (Appellate Jurisdiction) Law, no. 15 of 1962.

4 The Trinidad and Tobago (Constitution) Order, S.I. 1962, no. 1875, schedule, s. 78; The British Caribbean Court of Appeal (Amendment) (no. 2) Order, S.I. 1962, no. 1870.

5 The Jamaica (Constitution) Order, S.I. 1962, no. 1550, s. 14; The Trinidad and Tobago (Constitution) Order, S.I. 1962, no. 1875, s. 9.

6 The British Caribbean Court of Appeal Order, S.I. 1962, no. 1086; The British Caribbean (Appeal to Privy Council) Order, S.I. 1962, no. 1087.

7 Judicial Committee Act, 3 & 4 Will. IV, c. 41. As extended by the Appellate Jurisdiction Committee Act, 1876, 39 & 40 Vict. c. 59; the Appellate Jurisdiction Act, 1887, 50 & 51 Vict. c. 70; the Judicial Committee Amendment Act, 1895, 58 & 59 Vict. c. 44; the Appellate Jurisdiction Act, 1913, 3 & 4 Geo. V, c. 21; the Administration of Justice Act, 1928, 18 & 19 Geo. V, c. 26.

8 *Naden* v. *The King* [1926] A.C. 482.

9 *British Coal Corporation* v. *The King* [1935] A.C. 500.

consistent with independence. In October 1963 the Chief Justice of Ceylon ruled that the Order in Council, by which the Crown gives effect to a decision of the Privy Council, since it was a manifestation of the prerogative, was ineffective in Ceylon. It was unthinkable, he said, that the Queen would claim that Ceylon was yet a colony in respect of which she enjoyed the judicial prerogative; it was equally unthinkable that she would do anything that would in the slightest degree impair the independence of Ceylon.[1] On appeal from this ruling, the Privy Council held that it was a mistake to regard the Orders in Council by which the decisions of the Privy Council are made effective as legislative and not judicial acts. The legislative framework for these Orders was part of Ceylon's law. Furthermore, the Privy Council was not an institution of the United Kingdom, but part of the judicial structure of all countries still permitting appeals to it.[2]

Since the independence of Ceylon it has become the practice to provide for appeals to the Privy Council, or to abolish them, either in the constitutions of the new States or in their own legislation.[3] Where appeals have been abolished, it has been usual to provide for the disposal of those pending.[4] A special problem arises when a new State, some time after independence, becomes a republic, or ceases to be part of the Crown's dominions. Since orders of the Privy Council are communicated to the

1 Unpublished. *The Times*, 15 October 1963, p. 10.
2 *Alex Hull & Co.* v. *M'Kenna* [1926] I.R. 402.
3 The Federation of Malaya (Appeal to Privy Council) Order, S.I. 1958, no. 426, s. 3. The Federation of Malaya (Constitution) Order, S.I. 1957, no. 1533, s. 131. Ghana (Appeal to Privy Council) Order, S.I. 1957, no. 1361. The Nigeria (Constitution) Order, S.I. 1960, no. 1652, schedule, s. 114. The Sierra Leone (Constitution) Order, S.I. 1961, no. 741, s. 84; The Sierra Leone (Procedure in Appeals to Privy Council) Order, S.I. 1961, no. 742. The Zambia Independence Order, S.I. 1964, no. 1652, leaves it to the President to declare that the Judicial Committee is a court of appeal, schedule, s. 102. The Trinidad and Tobago (Constitution) Order in Council, S.I. 1962, no. 1875, schedule, s. 82. The Trinidad and Tobago (Procedure in Appeals to Privy Council) Order, S.I. 1962, no. 1876. The Jamaica (Constitution) Order, S.I. 1962, no. 1550, ss. 18, 110; The Jamaica (Procedure in Appeals to Privy Council) Order, S.I. 1962, no. 1650. The Federation of South Arabia (Procedure in Appeals to Privy Council) Order, S.I. 1963, no. 83. The Malawi Independence Order, S.I. 1964, no. 916, s. 14; The Malta Independence Order, S.I. 1964, no. 1398, s. 103; The Gambia Independence Order, S.I. 1965, no. 135, s.13.
4 The Tanganyika (Pending Appeals to Privy Council) Order in Council, S.I. 1963, no. 789, made under the Tanganyika Republic Act, 1962, 11 & 12 Eliz. II, c. 1; The Tanganyika Appellate Jurisdiction Act, no. 9 of 1962, s. 12; The Uganda Appellate Jurisdiction (Amendment) Act, no. 1 of 1964, s. 2. The Zanzibar Independence Order, S.I. 1962, no. 2784, schedule, s. 133. Kenya Independence Order, S.I. 1963, no. 791, s. 17. Nigeria Republic Act, 1963, chapter 57, s. 1 (3). Except in the case of Somaliland, where any pending appeals to the Privy Council or the Eastern Africa Court of Appeal were deemed to have abated, S.I. 1960, no. 1060, s. 3 (2) (c), and Cyprus, 8 & 9 Eliz. II, c. 52, s. 5.

appropriate judicial authorities through prerogative channels, it may be that the competence of the Crown to make such orders has lapsed, even in the event of both the United Kingdom and the new State legislating for enforcement thereof.[1] The question has been discussed in the case of Uganda, which legislated to abolish appeals in all but constitutional matters, and in delphic terms purported to regulate the appellate jurisdiction in cases where there was an appeal under the Constitution to both the Court of Appeal and the Privy Council.[2] The United Kingdom, according to the usual practice,[3] legislated for the Privy Council to retain jurisdiction only with respect to pending cases, and for future jurisdiction only pursuant to the 'law of Uganda'.[4] Presumably the law of Uganda includes the Constitution, so that appeals might still lie in respect of constitutional matters. However, the manner in which the Privy Council could communicate its decision on appeal was left unclear. Where, under the Constitution of the new State, a Judicial Committee is established as a final court of appeal, its decision is not a prerogative matter, and this difficulty would not arise.[5] The Privy Council in such cases advises the Head of State (in the case of Malaya it reports to the Agong).

When the Court of Appeal for Eastern Africa was reconstituted by an Act of the East African Common Services Organization,[6] an Order in

[1] The Malaya (Appeals to Privy Council) Order, S.I. 1958, no. 426; The Malaysia (Appeals to Privy Council) Order, S.I. 1963, no. 2086. The Trinidad and Tobago (Procedure in Appeals to Privy Council) Order, S.I. 1962, no 1876, s. 20. The Tanganyika Appellate Jurisdiction Act, no. 9 of 1962, s. 14. The Zambia Independence Order, S.I. 1964, no. 1652, s. 102. The Uganda Appellate Jurisdiction Act, no. 1 of 1962, s. 8 (2), with detailed rules in schedule 7 (2). The Court of Appeal for Eastern Africa (Appeals to Privy Council) Order, S.I. 1961, no. 2601, s. 21. The Zanzibar Independence Order, S.I. 1962, no. 2784, schedule, s. 133.

[2] The Appellate Jurisdiction (Amendment) Act, 1964, nos. 1, s. 1.

[3] The Trinidad and Tobago (Procedure in Appeals to Privy Council) Order, S.I. 1962, no. 1876, s. 21, dealing with pending proceedings from the British Caribbean Court of Appeal under the British Caribbean Court of Appeal Order, S.I. 1962, no. 1086; The Court of Appeal for Eastern Africa (Appeal to Privy Council) (Amendment) (No. 2) Order, S.I. 1963, no. 1920.

[4] The Uganda Act, 1964, c. 20, s. 3.

[5] As, e.g., in Kenya and Zambia.

[6] See *supra*, p. 163. The East African States were in a special position, inasmuch as appeals lay directly only in some constitutional matters, and in other matters from the Eastern Africa Court of Appeal. The Tanganyika (Constitution) Order, S.I. 1961, no. 2274, schedule, s. 62. The Kenya (Constitution) (Amendment) Order, S.I. 1962, no. 2599; The Kenya (Procedure in Appeals to Privy Council) Order, S.I. 1962, no. 2600, as amended by S.I. 1963, no. 612; The Kenya Order, S.I. 1963, no. 791, ss. 170 (constitutional) and 171 (others); The Kenya Independence Order, S.I. 1963, no. 1968, ss. 180 and 181 (re-enacting) under the Kenya Independence Act, 1963, no. 54 of 1963, s. 6. Uganda before independence was subject to appellate jurisdiction under the Foreign Jurisdiction Act, 1890, 53 & 54 Vict. c. 37. The East African (Appeals to Privy Council) Order, S.I. 1951, no. 609. The jurisdiction was preserved when Uganda was transformed into one of Her Majesty's dominions, The Uganda

Council was made providing for appeals therefrom to Her Majesty in Council from Kenya.[1] Appeals to the Privy Council were abolished by a further Order in Council upon the independence of Kenya,[2] whose Constitution, however, substituted therefor an appeal to the Judicial Committee of the Privy Council.[3] A right of appeal from the decisions of the Court of Appeal to the Judicial Committee was preserved by the combined effect of the Constitution, the Kenya Independence Order in Council[4] and the Kenya Order in Council, 1963.[5]

(viii) *The dissolution of the Federation of Rhodesia and Nyasaland, 1963*

The Order in Council[6] dissolving the Federation provided that, where necessary, the Territories would be substituted for the Federation in pending cases, and appeals might be taken to the existing Supreme Court, which, along with other Federal tribunals, would continue to hear the pending proceedings. All the Territories enacted legislation creating Courts of Appeal to replace the Supreme Court.[7] Appeals pending from the Federal Supreme Court to the Privy Council continued, but the Order omitted to provide for their decisions to be executed by the Territorial courts.[8]

(ix) *Treaty provisions for pending appeals*

Various conventional solutions to the problem of pending appeals have been devised. The Treaty of Frankfurt provided that appeals were to be decided by the courts before which they had been taken, unless, by reason of the annexation of Alsace-Lorraine, both parties found themselves in personal matters subject to the courts of the other State.[9] The Treaty of St Germain gave jurisdiction to the courts of the successor State to entertain

Independence Act, 1962, 10 & 11 Eliz. II, c. 57. Appeals would lie as of right in constitutional matters, and in cases of human rights from the Court of Appeal of Eastern Africa, The Uganda Independence Order, S.I. 1962, no. 2175. Uganda enacted that appeals should also lie as of right in certain cases and at discretion in others from the Court of Appeal of Eastern Africa, The Appellate Jurisdiction Act, no. 1 of 1962, s. 5.

1 The Kenya (Constitution) (Amendment) Order in Council, 1962, S.I. 1962, no. 2599.
2 The Kenya Independence Order in Council, S.I. 1963, no. 1968, ss. 180, 181.
3 *Ibid.* schedule 2, s. 181.   4 *Loc. cit.*
5 S.I. 1963, no. 791, ss. 170, 171. *Sunderdass Hariram* v. *Bhupendra Shamjibhai* [1964] The Eastern Africa Law Reports 240.
6 S.I. 1963, no. 2085, ss. 8, 9.
7 Southern Rhodesia, High Court Act, no. 22 of 1964; Court of Appeal for Northern Rhodesia Ordinance, no. 52 of 1964; Nyasaland, Supreme Court of Appeal Ordinance no. 17 of 1964.
8 This was covered in Nyasaland by Ordinance no. 17 of 1964.
9 Protocol, *M.N.R.G.* vol. XX, p. 847, art. 6.

appeals from courts situated in the ceded territory.[1] In the Convention of Poznan, Germany and Poland agreed that appeals were to be heard in the court in whose district the court appealed from was situated at the time of the coming into force of the Convention.[2] A Prussian court of appeal held that its jurisdiction had not been lost by reason of the fact that both the land to which the appeal referred and the seat of the court of first instance had passed to Poland.[3]

(x) *The partition of India, 1947*

In the Indian Independence (Legal Proceedings) Order[4] it was enacted that appeals from proceedings in the courts of British India were to be subject to the jurisdiction of the court in which such appeals would ordinarily lie if proceedings had been commenced in the proper court. Before the Supreme Court of India it was argued that this was ineffective to confer jurisdiction upon the High Court of Calcutta with respect to an appeal in a suit involving immovable property in territory which fell to Pakistan. The Supreme Court held that the High Court of Calcutta was the court which had appellate jurisdiction in respect of the proceedings which were pending at the date of partition, and it was, therefore, the 'proper court' and there was no basis for adding a gloss to the Order.[5]

(d) Judicial precedent

The judgments of the courts of the predecessor State are not binding as precedents upon the courts of the successor State, even where a doctrine of judicial precedent prevails in the law of both countries. They are, at the most, of persuasive value. In a case before a British court in the Transvaal after the annexation of the Boer Republics in 1900, it was stated that the decisions of the High Court of the South African Republic were not binding upon the courts of the conquering Power. The Chief Justice said:

This Court is not, in the full sense of the term, the successor of the High Court, and the decisions of the latter upon legal matters, though we regard them with the highest respect, and would differ from them only with the greatest reluctance, do not stand, as far as we are concerned, on the same footing as our own. They are decisions of a different court, and though the same system of law is common

---

1 *B.T.S.* (1919), no. 11, Cmd. 400, art. 45 at p. 15.
2 Art. 1 (7) (1).
3 *Baron A.* v. *Prussian Treasury, Fontes Juris Gent.*, ser. A, sect. 2, vol. 1, p. 126.
4 *Gazette of India Extraordinary*, 14 August 1947.
5 *Ashalata Debi* v. *Sri Jadu nath Roy*, A.I.R. (1954), S.C. 409. See also *Tirlok Nath* v. *Moti Ram*, A.I.R. (1950), E. Punj. 149.

to both tribunals, we are bound by the rule of the Privy Council in the past as well as in the future, whereas the High Court was not.[1]

After the independence of Uganda the High Court dealt with the argument that it was no longer bound by precedent in the following words: 'The constitutional position of Uganda is now that of independence within the Commonwealth, we are, nevertheless, in our opinion, entitled to rely upon previous judicial decisions to guide us in our findings.'[2]

II. Criminal Proceedings

Very few definite principles can be said to exist in the case of criminal proceedings pending, or in the process of determination before the courts of the predecessor State. The proceedings are terminated only by loss of jurisdiction over the accused. Since criminal prosecution is a matter of discretion there can, in this case, be no obligation on the part of the successor State to undertake the prosecution.[3] On the other hand, the limits of the jurisdiction of the successor State to prosecute crimes committed under the sovereignty of its predecessor must be severely circumscribed. It seems that the successor State is competent to prosecute only if it acquires jurisdiction over the place where the crime was committed. 'Objective territorial jurisdiction' is the criterion for determining the right of a State to undertake prosecution, and there is no reason why an exception to this rule should be made in the case of a successor State.[4]

---

1 *Habib Motan* v. *The Transvaal Government*, Transvaal Supreme Court Rep. (1904), 404. In *Bloch* v. *Selinger* the District Court of Tel Aviv held that it was not rigidly bound by English precedents. In *Albrans* v. *Schmetterling*, the district court of Jerusalem held that, while continuity and stability in the law led the court generally to follow a precedent which had been acted upon for eleven years, the Supreme Court of Israel was free to review any decision of the former Supreme Court; also *Rosenbaum* v. *Rosenbaum*. See note in *Ann. Dig.* vol. xv, p. 43.

2 *A.G. for Uganda* v. *Katondwaki* [1963], The Eastern Africa Law Reports 323 at p. 330.

3 In the Convention of Poznan, Poland agreed that criminal cases pending before a court in territory which became Polish should be continued in the same court: Cmd. 400. art. 2 (1). The Treaty of Paris, 1898 provided that criminal actions pending against citizens of territory which ceased to be Spanish were to be continued under the jurisdiction of the Supreme Court of Spain until final judgment, but when such judgment had been rendered, the execution of it should be committed to the competent authority of the place in which the case arose: *M.N.R.G.* (2nd ser.), XXXII, p. 74, s. 12 (3).

4 Delbez, p. 183; Piédelièvre, vol. I, p. 157; Selosse, pp. 261–8; Sibert, vol. I, p. 216. In the case of *R.* v. *de Jager*, the accused was committed for trial before a special criminal court at Pretoria for a crime committed in territory which was within its jurisdiction after the offence. The court decided it was competent by virtue of its jurisdiction over the place where the crime was committed and the accused was apprehended: (1903), T.S.C.R. 36.

This issue was raised in an Italian court set up in Ethiopia after the annexation of that country. In the case of *In re Simi* the jurisdiction of the courts of the successor State over crimes committed before the annexation was challenged. The court admitted that 'rules of International Criminal Law in matters of state succession are non-existent' but considered that, as the Italian State was the successor of Ethiopia, 'crimes committee prior to the annexation must be regarded as having taken place in Italian territory'. The competence to prosecute for such crimes, it was stated, 'must be regarded as a logical corollary of sovereignty'.[1] *Simi's* Case was followed by another before the same tribunal in which the accused was prosecuted for a crime committed prior to the annexation. The court found that it had jurisdiction, but as the time allowed by Abyssinian law for undertaking the prosecution had expired the accused was discharged.[2] An interesting case on the same issue came before the Supreme Court of Israel after the emergence of that country to full sovereignty. In *Katz-Cohen v. Attorney-General*[3] it was pleaded by an accused indicted for murder committed before the termination of the Mandate that the criminal law of the Palestine administration, being an attribute of sovereignty, had not been continued in force by the Israeli law and Administration Ordinance which provided for the operation in Israel of the law of Palestine.[4] In rejecting this plea the court pointed out that the root of the appellant's argument was the fundamental distinction between civil and criminal procedures. It failed to see, however, that this distinction was vital to the question of jurisdiction. Why should not the same community (it inquired) 'against whom the offence was committed, demand its punishment merely because the Government of Israel has now replaced the Mandatory Government?' The court then proceeded to expand the theory of the 'continuity of law despite change of sovereignty'. The law of the Palestine administration was not 're-enacted as new law of the State of Israel... but remained in force, and this gives us continuity from the legal point of view'.[5]

This rule was extended to cover jurisdiction over an offence which had been committed prior to the ending of the Mandate in territory which came under Israeli jurisdiction as a result of the Armistice Agreements, 1949.[6] Although the court found that there was no ground for deportation as a result thereof, it held that preventive measures taken for political reasons by the Mandate authorities had continuing validity.[7]

1 *Ann. Dig.* vol. VIII, Case no. 46.   2 *In re Brossalian*, ibid. Case no. 47.
3 *Ann. Dig.* vol. XVI, Case no. 26.   4 *Official Gazette*, no. 2, 21 May 1948.
5 *Ann. Dig.* vol. XVI, p. 70.
6 *Wahib Saleh Kalil v. A.-G.* ibid. p. 70.
7 *Abu Ras v. Minister of the Interior*, Piskei Din, 6 (1952), p. 480.

The Effect on the Judicial System

In 1952 the Court Rules (Adaptation of Criminal Proceedings) Order was promulgated. Regulation 2 provided that a judgment given in a criminal case by a Court in Palestine after 14 May 1948 which had not yet been executed would be executed as if rendered by a Court which functioned in Israel. A 'Court in Palestine' was defined as a Court which functioned in the territory under the Mandate for Palestine outside the area over which the law of Israel applies. This Regulation was applied to validate a prison sentence upon conviction by the Palestine authorities.[1]

Rosenne distinguishes between the Italian and Israeli cases.[2] The Italian court, he argues, admitted that rules of international criminal law in matters of State succession are non-existent, and based the right of prosecution squarely upon the doctrine of sovereignty; whereas the Israeli court in the *Katz-Cohen* case, in his opinion wrongly, based its right upon the continuity of law. The question at issue is not whether the criminal law survives, but whether jurisdiction is given to the court of the successor State. Jurisdiction is an attribute of sovereignty, and the continuity of law is relevant only in so far as it is necessary to determine whether there is or is not a law in existence under which the prosecution on behalf of the successor State may be conducted. Both the Italian and Israeli cases are deficient, the former in not considering the existence of Ethiopian law after the annexation, the latter in not considering the question of jurisdiction after independence. They are, however, complementary to each other.

The Indian Independence (Legal Proceedings) Order covered criminal as well as civil proceedings in its reference to continuity of pending proceedings. In the case of Pakistan the applicability of the Order was unsuccessfully contested on the ground that since detention had been ordered at Kamal, in India, its continuance in Pakistan, to which the accused had been transported, was illegal.[3]

The promulgation of the Constitution of India, with its definition of 'Indian citizen', may have altered the situation of offenders whose acts had been committed before partition in territory which fell to Pakistan. The criminal jurisdiction of Indian courts derived after partition from the Criminal Procedure Code of British India. Section 177 of the Code prescribed the place of trial, and section 186 provided for issue of process for offences committed beyond the local jurisdiction in respect of offences committed within or without British India. The latter section clearly

1 *Arar* v. *Governor of Tel Mond Prison, I.L.R.* vol. XIX, p. 141.
2 *B.Y.* vol. XXVII (1950), p. 284.
3 *Mohammed* v. *The Crown, Ann. Dig.* vol. XV, p. 72. See also *Babu s./o. Kalu* v. *Parsam s./o. Salam* [1954] Crim. L.J. 795, in which the jurisdiction to convict was deduced from the continuity of law.

conferred on Indian courts jurisdiction over offences committed within either British India before partition or India after partition;[1] but the Punjab High Court held that there was no jurisdiction over a person who remained in Pakistan after partition, subsequently committed an offence there, and then fled to India, because the offence was committed extraterritorially and the offender was not at the time an Indian citizen.[2] It has been argued that the coming into force of the Constitution had the effect of treating the subjects of British India as aliens, and on the authority of this case the conclusion has been drawn that even pre-partition offences committed in Pakistan were not subject to the jurisdiction.[3]

The protocols[4] for the transfer of the French judicial jurisdiction to the Indochinese States provided that detained persons finally convicted and serving sentences at the date of the transfer should, if French citizens, be evacuated to French penal establishments, and otherwise become the responsibility of the French authorities. The prerogative of mercy should continue to be exercised by the French President in the case of French citizens, who would also preserve any right of appeal to French courts. All other appeals would go to local courts.

Jurisdiction of the successor State is limited to those actions which are crimes within the law of the predecessor State. Whether or not such an action is a crime in that of the successor State is immaterial.[5] If a prosecution is undertaken by the successor State it is governed by the latter's law of procedure and evidence. The fact that sentence has been passed in the courts of the predecessor State imposes no obligation on the successor State. Punishment is a matter of administrative discretion.[6] On the other

1 On the authority of *Kishori Lal* v. *Shrimati Shanti Devi*, A.I.R. (1953), S.C. 441.
2 *Ram Narain* v. *Central Bank of India Ltd*, A.I.R. (1952), Pun. 178.
3 Kapur in *Indian Law Journal*, vol. IX (1957), p. 35.
4 Protocol with Cambodia of 29 August 1953, Laos of 22 October 1953, and Vietnam of 15 August 1954, decree no. 59–593, *Journal Officiel*, 3 May 1959, p. 4758.
5 On the other hand, there is a body of opinion to the effect that an offence should not be prosecuted by the successor State if not a crime within its law: Fauchille, vol. I, pt. I, p. 370; Hatschek, p. 128; Phillipson, p. 313; Selosse, p. 269.
6 Fauchille is of opinion, however, that if sentence has been pronounced in the courts of the predecessor State it should be executed by the successor State unless the penalty is not one admitted under the latter's law: vol. I, pt. I, p. 378. Piédelièvre agrees with him: vol. I, p. 159. Strupp says that the crime is punishable 'after the laws of the successor' but that the judgment must nevertheless be executed: *Éléments*, vol. I, p. 96. In the Treaty between Denmark and the United States in 1916 respecting the cession of territory in the West Indies, it was provided that where the penalty prescribed in the judgment of the court of the predecessor State was not recognized in the law of the United States, a corresponding one should be applied, 39 Stat. 1706; U.S.T.S. no. 629. It is difficult to justify, in the absence of such agreement, any limitation of this character on the sovereign discretion of the successor State: *M.N.R.G.* 3rd ser. vol. X, p. 357. Before the independence of Rwanda and Burundi five persons

The Effect on the Judicial System

hand, the successor State should not prosecute a second time for the same offence unless a second trial is sanctioned under the law of the predecessor. Nor, it would seem, is the successor State competent to prosecute crimes which are essentially political in character, such as treason to the previous sovereign, or sedition. The criminality of these actions is dependent upon political purposes which cannot survive a change of sovereignty. The political law under which criminality arose lapses, and with it jurisdiction over the offence.

There is no reason why the predecessor State should not remain competent to prosecute its own nationals for criminal acts committed by them in territory lost to the prosecuting State after commission of the offence. The French *Cour de Cassation* has held that article 692 of the Code of Penal Procedure (which exempts an accused from trial in France if he has been tried abroad) does not apply to French nationals in respect of crimes committed in Algeria before the independence of that country.[1]

Table of legislation of the Francophone States effecting changes in their judicial systems after independence

Federation of Mali, Constitution title IX: concerning judicial authority; title X: of the High Court of Justice, *Journal Officiel de la Fédération du Mali*, 25 June 1960, p. 405.

Senegal, Constitution, title IX: concerning judicial authority; title X: of the High Court of Justice, *Journal Officiel du Sénégal*, 31 April 1960.
    Ordonnance n°. 60–17, *loi organique* of the Supreme Court, *ibid*. 12 September 1960, p. 926.
    Decree n°. 60–390 fixing the composition and the competence of courts of appeal, of tribunals of first instance and of justices of the peace, *ibid*. 19 November 1960, p. 1246.
    Loi organique n°. 61–65 on the organization of the High Court of Justice and the procedure followed before it, *ibid*. 6 January 1962.

Mali, Constitution, title VII: concerning judicial power; title VIII: of the Cour d'État; title IX: of the High Court of Justice, *Journal Officiel de la République du Mali*, 29 September 1960.
    Loi n°. 61–55 concerning judicial organization, *ibid*. 24 June 1961, p. 1.
    Loi n°. 61–56 concerning organization of the Cour d'État and determining the procedure before it, *ibid*.
    Loi n°. 61–55 concerning judicial organization in the Republic of Mali, *ibid*. 24 June 1961, p. 11.

---

were prosecuted by the Belgians for complicity in the murder of Crown Prince Louis Rwagasore, and sentenced to imprisonment. The day after independence, Burundi reopened the case and the death sentence was imposed and carried out: *The Times*, 16 January 1963.

1 Cour de Cassation, Ch. crim. 26 June 1963, Vilella, *Bull. Crim.* (1963), p. 485.

Mauritania, Constitution, title VI: concerning justice, *Journal Officiel de la Mauritanie*, 3 June 1961.
Loi n°. 61–123 fixing the judicial organization of the Islamic Republic of Mauritania, *ibid.* 4 July 1961.
Decree n°. 61–142 installing the Supreme Court within its constitutional provision, *ibid.* 16 August 1961, p. 337.

Guinea, Ordonnance n°. 4 creating a court of appeal at Conakry, unpublished.
Constitution, title IX: concerning judicial authority, *Journal Officiel de la Guinée*, 12 November 1958.
Ordonnance n°. 18 creating a superior tribunal of cassation to sit at Conakry, *ibid.* 1 March 1959, p. 125.
Ordonnance n°. 29 creating a High Court of Justice, *ibid.* 1 May 1959, p. 282.
Ordonnance n°. 38 reorganizing the superior tribunal of cassation, *ibid.* 1 August 1959, p. 473.

Ivory Coast, Constitution, title VI: of the Supreme Court; title VII: concerning judicial authority; title VIII: of the High Court of Justice, *Journal Officiel de la Côte d'Ivoire*, 4 November 1960.
Loi n°. 61–155 concerning judicial organization, *ibid.* 1 June 1961, p. 780.
Loi n°. 61–201 determining the composition, organization, attributions and functioning of the Supreme Court, *ibid.* 13 June 1961, p. 843.
Decree n°. 62–30 regulating internally the Supreme Court, *ibid.* 1 March 1962, p. 236.

Upper Volta, Constitution, title VI: of the Supreme Court; title VII: concerning judicial authority; title VIII: of the High Court of Justice, *Journal Officiel de la Haute-Volta*, 12 November 1960.
Loi n°. 5–62 creating an administrative tribunal and determining the procedure applicable before it, *ibid.* 27 January 1962, p. 98.
Loi n°. 33–60 creating a superior tribunal of appeal, *ibid.* 28 May 1960, p. 427.
Loi n°. 13–61 completing the above, *ibid.* 17 June 1961, p. 541, promulgated by decree n°. 188, *ibid.* 27 May 1961, p. 489.
Decree n°. 250 promulgating loi n°. 9–63 concerning judicial organization, *ibid.* 25 May 1963, p. 330.
Decree n°. 251 promulgating loi n°. 10–63 relative to the Supreme Court, *ibid.* p. 332.

Dahomey, Constitution title VI: of the Supreme Court; title VII: concerning judicial authority; title VIII: of the High Court of Justice, *Journal Officiel de Dahomey*, 26 November 1960.
Loi n°. 61–41 creating an administrative tribunal, *ibid.* 1 November 1961, p. 829.
Loi n°. 61–42 organizing the Supreme Court, *ibid.* p. 830.

Niger, Constitution, title VI: of the Supreme Court; title VII: concerning judicial authority; title VIII: of the High Court of Justice, *Journal Officiel du Niger*, 8 November 1960.
Loi n°. 61–28 determining the composition, organization, attributions and the functioning of the Supreme Court, *ibid.* 31 August 1961, p. 71.
Loi n°. 62–11 fixing the organizations and competence of jurisdictions in Niger, *ibid.* 1 April 1962, p. 116; and annexe, *ibid.* 25 August 1962, p. 81.

Togo, Constitution, title IV: concerning judicial power; title V: the High Court of Justice, *Journal Officiel du Togo*, 17 April 1961, p. 293.
Loi n°. 61–17 relative to judicial organization, *ibid.* 15 June 1961, p. 393.

The Effect on the Judicial System

Loi n°. 61–26 instituting the Supreme Court, *ibid.* 1 September 1961, p. 536; rectification, *ibid.* 1 November 1961, p. 665.
Loi n°. 62–9 relative to the procedure followed before the Supreme Court, *ibid.* 1 April 1962, p. 280.

Congo, decree n°. 60–625 relative to the composition of the Court of Appeal, *Journal Officiel du Congo*, 1 October 1960, p. 696.
Loi n°. 6–61 fixing the judicial organization, *ibid.* 1 February 1961, p. 85.
Constitution, title VI: of the Supreme Court; title VII: concerning judicial authority; title VIII: of the High Court of Justice, *ibid.* 4 March 1961, p. 9.
Loi n°. 6–62 relative to the competence of the Court of Appeal and superior tribunals and to the procedure followed before these jurisdictions in administrative matters, *ibid.* 1 February 1962, p. 97.
Loi n°. 4–62 creating the Supreme Court, *ibid.* 15 February 1962, p. 149; applied by decree n°. 62–165, *ibid.* 1 July 1962, p. 543.
Ordonnance n°. 63–10 fixing the judicial organization and the competence of jurisdictions, *ibid.* 15 November 1963, p. 929.

Gabon, decree n°. 11 organizing jurisdictions, *Journal Officiel du Gabon*, 15 January 1961, p. 49.
Constitution, title VI: concerning judicial power; title VII: of the Supreme Court; title VIII: of the High Court of Justice, *ibid.* 25 February 1961, p. 147.
Loi n°. 24–62 creating the Supreme Court, *ibid.* 15 December 1962, p. 829.
Loi n°. 27–62 determining the organization and functioning of the High Court of Justice and the procedure applicable before it, *ibid.* 15 December 1962, p. 833.

Central African Republic, Decree n°. 60–219 on the provisional functioning of the appellate jurisdiction, *Journal Officiel de la République Centrafricaine*, 15 November 1960, p. 596.
Constitution, title IV: article 32 of the Constitutional Council; title V: concerning judicial authority, *ibid.* 15 December 1960.
Loi n°. 60–182 organizing justice, *ibid.* 1 February 1961, p. 31.
Loi n°. 60–183 fixing the organization of tribunals, *ibid.* 15 February 1961, p. 64.
Loi n°. 61–249 concerning the organization and functioning of the Supreme Court, *ibid.* 1 December 1961; completed and modified by loi n°. 63–418, *ibid.* 15 December 1963, p. 612.
Loi n°. 61–250 concerning judicial organization, *ibid.*; and decree n°. 62–099 concerning judicial organization, *ibid.* 1 May 1962, p. 290.

Chad, Constitution, title VII: concerning judicial authority; title VIII: of the Supreme Court; title XI: of the High Court of Justice, *Journal Officiel du Tchad*, 15 December 1960, p. 571.
Ordonnance n°. 1 reforming the Criminal Court, *ibid.* 1 April 1961, p. 181.
Decree n°. 170 instituting a supreme court at Fort-Lamy, *ibid.* 15 September 1962, p. 691.
Decree n°. 120 creating a court of appeal at Fort-Lamy, *ibid.* 15 July 1963, p. 424.

Cameroon, decree n°. 60–33 fixing the internal regulation and functioning of the Supreme Court, *Journal Officiel du Cameroun*, 24 February 1960, p. 285.
Constitution, title VII: concerning judicial authority; title VIII: of the High Court of Justice, *ibid.* 4 March 1960, p. 315.
Ordonnance n°. 60–56, *loi organique* of the High Court of Justice, *ibid.* 12 May 1960, p. 683.
Loi n°. 61–12 relative to administrative law, *ibid.* 13 July 1961, p. 805.

Decree n°. 61–96 relative to the functioning and procedure of the Supreme Court in administrative matters, *ibid.* 12 August 1961, p. 908.

Ordonnance n°. 61–4 relative to judicial organization, *Journal Officiel de la République Fédérale du Cameroun*, 1 October to 6 November 1961.

Ordonnance n°. 61–6 fixing the composition and procedure of the Federal Court of Justice, *ibid.* p. 10; completed by Ordonnance n°. 62–1, *ibid.* 15 January 1962, p. 40.

Ordonnance n°. 61–9 creating a supreme court in the Federated State of West Cameroon . . . , *ibid.* 1 October to 6 November 1961, p. 17.

Ordonnance n°. 61–18 organizing the Federal High Court of Justice, *ibid.* 15 January 1962, p. 36.

Decree n°. 62–188 fixing the composition of the Supreme Court of East Cameroon, *ibid.* 15 June 1962, p. 575.

Decree n°. 64–218 relative to the functioning of the Federal Court of Justice in administrative matters, *ibid.* 1 September 1964, p. 128.

Madagascar, loi organique n°. 2 organizing the High Court of Justice, *Journal Officiel de la République Malgache*, 6 June 1959, p. 1300.

Decree n°. 60–032 reorganizing jurisdictions in Madagascar, *ibid.* 20 February 1960, p. 387.

Ordonnance n°. 60–107 reforming the judicial organization, *ibid.* 1 October 1960, p. 1952.

Loi n°. 60–013 creating the Supreme Court, *ibid.* 29 July 1961, p. 1266; correction, *ibid.* 12 August 1961, p. 1411.

Chapter 8

THE EFFECT OF CHANGE OF SOVEREIGNTY ON THE ADMINISTRATION OF ABSORBED TERRITORY

I. THE CIVIL SERVICE

A State which acquires territory from another has a complete discretion as to the manner in which it will be administered. The governmental agencies of the predecessor State lose their competence at the moment of the change of sovereignty,[1] and any official function performed by them after that date is valid only in so far as it is sanctioned by the new government. The civil servants of the old administration, if retained in their offices, derive their authority for the future from the new sovereign, and exercise it in accordance with the latter's administrative law, if such has been extended to the territory.[2]

It is controversial to what extent the successor State is obliged by international law to continue the employment of the officials of its predecessor. The analysis of this question depends on the status of the contract of employment, and with respect to this there are two theories. The first, largely adhered to in Germany until 1920, regards the appointment of a civil servant as creating a contractual relationship of private law between him and the State which can be terminated only by reference to the provisions of the contract, or to the law under which it was constituted.[3] According to this theory, the relationship in question confers upon a civil servant an acquired right to his office which a successor State should respect.[4] The second theory considers the relationship of an official to the

---

[1] The United States Government was advised on 14 June 1899 that, when Spanish sovereignty ceased in Porto Rico, the officers of Spain ceased to have authority to exercise the royal prerogative there: Moore, *Dig.* vol. I, p. 307. Similar advice was given with respect to Hawaii on 21 November 1899: 22 Op. A.-G. p. 627. A number of United States cases illustrate the working of this principle: *U.S.* v. *Yorba*, 1 Wall. 412; *Stearns* v. *U.S.* 6 Wall. 589; *U.S.* v. *Pico*, 23 How. 321; *More* v. *Steinbach*, 127 U.S. 70; *Alexander* v. *Roulet*, 13 Wall. 386; *Mumford* v. *Wardwell*, 6 Wall 423. See Piédelièvre, vol. I, p. 166.

[2] *U.S.* v. *Reynes*, 9 How. 127; *Davis* v. *Concordia Policy Jury*, 9 How. 280; *Ely's Administrator* v. *U.S.* 171 U.S. 220.

[3] Kaeckenbeeck, *The International Experiment of Upper Silesia* (1942), p. 72.

[4] Selosse, pp. 183–95; Piédelièvre, vol. I, p. 143; Keith, p. 34; Phillipson, p. 310; Guggenheim, p. 130; Huber, pp. 115–24; Schönborn, p. 54; Rousseau, p. 281; Schnitzer, p. 141.

State as one exclusively of public law. His status is constituted by public appointment, and is a matter of discretion on the part of the State. It follows that a successor State incurs in the act of change of sovereignty no obligation whatever towards him.[1]

The latter theory is the more widely held and the more easily defensible. An official exercises a public function, and his right so to exercise it cannot in any sense be regarded as absolute. In the last analysis it is dependent upon the public policy of the State, and upon the official's satisfactory performance of his duties. In English law civil servants hold office at the pleasure of the Crown,[2] and it is not to be assumed that those of them employed in territory which is lost to British sovereignty would enjoy any greater measure of security after the succession than before it. The Colonial Regulations[3] specifically state that appointment to public offices does not constitute a contract between the Crown and its servants, and is made by the Crown's authority and maintained during the Crown's pleasure. In the case of the former colonies, officials of alien race, customs and ideas have necessarily had to be replaced, to some extent at least, by administrators more sympathetic to the aspirations of the new régimes.

A choice between the two theories was imposed, after the cession of German territory to Poland in 1919, upon the Upper Silesian Arbitral Tribunal in a number of cases decided by it. The issue in these cases was whether or not the relations between the State and former German officials who were absorbed into the Polish Civil Service were governed by Polish law, or by German law as it existed at the time of the transfer of sovereignty. It was contended on behalf of the officials concerned that their status was contractual, and invested them with acquired rights, the protection of which was guaranteed by article 4 of the Geneva Convention of 1922.[4] The position of these officials, it was argued, could not be altered by Polish legislation or administrative action, save with the payment of full compensation. The tribunal, however, adopted the public appointment theory, and held that in international law change of sovereignty did not of itself imply the subrogation of the successor State in the relations which had existed between the officials and the German and Polish Governments. It was further held that the rights of the officials were

1 After 1920 the *Reichsgericht* tended to favour the public appointment theory: Kaeckenbeeck, *op. cit.* p. 72. In French law, if an official is kept on he has the same pension and service rights as French officials: Selosse, p. 187; Bull, 11 Ser., no. 7722, Decree of 11 June 1860, art. 5.
2 Keith, *Constitutional Law* (7th ed. 1939), p. 196; *Dunn* v. *R.* [1896] Q.B. 116; *Riorden* v. *War Office* [1961] 1 W.L.R. 210; *Venkata Rao* v. *Secretary of State for Ind*ia [1937] A.C. 248; *Dudfield* v. *Ministry of Works*, The Times, 24 January 1964, p 15.
3 Part I, Public Officers, 1956.
4 *L.N.T.S.* vol. IX, p. 465; *B.F.S.P.* vol. CXVIII, p. 365.

not acquired rights since they were not 'rights which had an economic value'.[1] The tribunal decided that the office of a teacher in a State school in territory transferred to Poland was constituted under public law, and, since it gave rise to no right of a private character, was not subject to protection under article 4 of the convention. 'In matters of State succession', it was said, 'this opinion is in accordance with the attitude of general international law according to which on a change of sovereignty relations of public law are not automatically taken over by the successor State.'[2]

Even a contract of employment expressed to be for a definite period and absolute in its terms is founded upon public law. The Supreme Court of the Saar was called upon after the detachment of that territory from Germany in 1919 to consider the obligations of the Governing Commission with respect to a contract of employment made between an official and the previous German administration, and expressed to be for life. It was held that the Commission could not be 'restricted in its choice of officials by appointments made by the former Government'. There was in international law, it was stated, no general obligation upon the successor State to take over the officials of the former State, or to compensate them for loss of employment. A successor State has an unrestricted right to deprive a private individual of the office previously held by him.[3] When the Saar was reoccupied by Germany in 1935, an agreement was entered into between the *Reich* and the Government Commission concerning civil servants in the area.[4] Those of German nationality who fell within the scope of the Baden-Baden Agreement of 1926[5] returned to their respective administrations.

A further important case on the question of the status of civil servants was decided by the *Conseil d'État* in France in 1936.[6] The plaintiff had been a judge in Strasbourg upon appointment for life made by the German administration. In 1919 he was requested to resign, and was given another appointment as compensation. He claimed he was entitled to a pension on a proportional basis in respect of service up to 1919. The Government Commissioner, during the hearing, insisted that 'the successor State is not

1 Kaeckenbeeck, *op. cit.* pp. 71–4.
2 *Hausen* v. *Polish State*, *Ann. Dig.* vol. VII, Case no. 40. Lauterpacht criticizes these cases as failing to consider the doctrine of acquired rights as 'a basis for decision'. While admitting the right of the successor State to dispense with the service of officials, he appears to argue that the doctrine of acquired rights guarantees them compensation: *The Function of Law in the International Community* (1933), p. 92.
3 *Saar Territory (Prussian Officials) Case*, *Ann. Dig.* vol. III, Case no. 68.
4 *L.N.Off.J.* (1935), pt. 1, p. 484.
5 *L.N.T.S.* vol. LV, p. 350.
6 *In re Kremer*, *Ann. Dig.* vol. VIII, Case no. 43.

bound to maintain in its service the officials of the partitioned State'.[1] The court, in adopting and expounding this view, stated that 'all juridical connexion ceases to exist between the State and its officials. The successor State must reinvest in their office agents whom it intends to keep in its service, but it also has an absolute, discretionary, sovereign power to refuse to grant such investiture.'[2]

A successor State is therefore, it is believed, under no obligation to retain the services of officials in the absorbed territory. In addition, since the officials have no rights of an enforceable and permanent character, it cannot be obliged to grant compensation to those of them whom it chooses not to employ.

After the annexation of Burma in 1886 Great Britain rejected claims for indemnity for loss of State employment. Great Britain was 'under no legal obligation either to continue to employ servants of the late Government, or to compensate them for the loss of their appointment'.[3]

A convention of 1920 between Germany and Poland reserved to the latter the right 'to dispense with the services of individual German officials'.[4] A Czech court held that the Czechoslovak State was not a continuation of the former Hungarian State and was not obliged to take over the pecuniary obligations resulting from the appointment of officials of the former Hungarian State.[5] In another case the Upper Silesian Arbitral Tribunal stated that 'there is no rule of international law to the effect that a State which acquires territory is *ipso facto* bound to take over officials employed by its predecessor'. Such taking over of officials can take place only by virtue of treaties or special agreements.[6] The United States Supreme Court decided[7] in 1910 that compensation need not be paid for the abolition of a quasi-public office in territory ceded to the United States by Spain. Such compensation has often been paid, more especially in the case of those countries which have attained independence within the Commonwealth, but this is no more than a gratuitous undertaking, and is without significance in the law of State succession. Should civil servants whose employment is terminated by the change of sover-

[1] *Rev. gén. de droit int. pub.* vol. XLV (1938), p. 479.
[2] *Ibid.* p. 482.
[3] Letter of the Secretary for Upper Burma to the Secretary to the Government of India, Burma: For. Dept., no. X, Annex 6, to the *Answer of His Britannic Majesty's Government in the Robert E. Brown Claim*, p. 99.
[4] L.N.T.S. vol. IX, no. 245, arts. 3, 7.
[5] *Hungarian Officials (Succession)* Case, *Ann. Dig.* vol. III, Case no. 67.
[6] *Frystatzki v. Polish State, ibid.* vol. IV, Case no. 62. See also the decision of the Austrian Constitutional Court in *Post Office Official (Austrian) Succession* Case, *ibid.* vol. I, Case no. 47.
[7] *Alvarez y Sanchez v. U.S.* 216 U.S. 167.

eignty not receive compensation, however, the successor State is obliged to respect their pension and superannuation rights accrued up to the date of the change of sovereignty.[1]

A specific administrative act is necessary to create a relationship of employment between an official and the new sovereign. A plaintiff who had been a servant of the Austrian Government claimed before a Czech court that he had continued to exercise his functions in territory which had been incorporated into Czechoslovakia, and alleged that wages were due to him during the period in which he had so acted. This plea was rejected by the court, which stated that Czechoslovakia had not automatically entered as legal successor into the public service relations of the old Austrian State.[2]

Officials in absorbed territory do not necessarily lose their rank in the service of the predecessor State. This is a matter which is dependent entirely upon that State's public law, but as a general rule such officials remain the servants of the employing State unless they were employed by a totally destroyed local administrative agency, or have lost the nationality which they previously enjoyed.

2. THE ARMED FORCES

The relation between officers and other ranks of the armed forces and the State is no different from that of other servants. In the early literature of the law of State succession some space was devoted to the position of conscripts and mercenaries, who were generally treated as specific instances of public property. Much of this discussion relates to outmoded types of military service, and was not based on sound principle. The relationship of a soldier to the State is an administrative one, and ceases, like other administrative functions, when the soldier loses the nationality of the predecessor State through the transfer of sovereignty. The successor

---

[1] Kaeckenbeeck in Hague *Recueil*, vol. LIX (1937), p. 346. In the *Kremer* Case it was admitted by the court that 'by the general principle of international law, the measures which deprived Kremer of his post in 1919 rendered the French Government liable to grant some reparation for the damage caused to him'. Such reparation, however, did not necessarily consist in the grant of a pension: see *infra*, p. 465.

[2] *Austrian Officials (Succession)* Case, *Ann. Dig.* vol. I, Case no. 46. That such a formal act is necessary was insisted on also in the Polish courts. In *Kot* v. *(Polish) Minister of Public Works* it was held that 'Polish authorities had the right to use their free discretion in accepting or not accepting for Polish service employees of the States responsible for the partitioning of Poland, who were serving in the territories which came to Poland... The admission of such an employee to the Polish service would require a distinct act on the part of the competent authority': *ibid.* vol. IV, Case no. 63. See also *Hungarian Officials (Succession)* Case, no. 11, *ibid.* vol. V, Case no. 44.

State has a complete discretion whether or not it will absorb such a person in its own armed forces.[1] If it fails to accord equivalent rank, it is obliged, however, to respect pension and superannuation rights.

Similarly, there can be no restraint upon the competence of the successor State to conscript persons who become its nationals upon absorption of territory, and this is irrespective of whether the persons in question have performed military duty for the predecessor State. If members of the armed forces are absorbed into those of the successor State their enlistment is only effective in municipal law if properly performed. For example, in England such persons would require to be gazetted. Jurisdiction over them ceases, however, if they exercise a right of option to retain the nationality of the predecessor State.

3. PRACTICE IN THE MATTER OF CIVIL SERVICE CONTINUITY

(i) *The partition of India, 1947*

It was announced by the Viceroy that the 'Government of India agrees that compensation should be payable to those who are not invited to continue to serve under the Government in India after the transfer of power'. A scale of compensation was evolved.[2] That this was a matter of grace only would appear from the statement of the Prime Minister in the House of Commons that promises of compensation in the event of termination of service had been made to encourage recruiting after the war.[3] Many officials, however, were taken over by the Governments of India and Pakistan, and the Indian Independence Act, 1947 included a provision that every person appointed to the Indian Civil Service or judiciary who continued to serve in office after the establishment of the Dominions should be entitled to receive from the successor State the same conditions of service in respect of remuneration, leave and pensions, and the same rights in respect of disciplinary matters and tenure of office, as he was entitled to previously.[4]

On 18 June 1947 a circular letter was issued by the Government of India to the Chief Secretaries of Provincial Governments, in which it was stated that the transfer of power from Britain to India had brought about an automatic termination of the Indian Civil Service, and that it was open to any servant concerned either to decline to continue in the service of the new Government or to offer his services, and it was open to the Government to accept the offer or not.

[1] Keith, p. 34; Piédelièvre accepts the opposite view, vol. 1, p. 143.
[2] Cmd. 7116, p. 17.   [3] *Ibid.*
[4] 10 & 11 Geo. VI, c. 30, s. 10.

In 1959 the Indian Supreme Court heard an appeal by a former official of the Province of Madras, who was recruited to the Indian Civil Service in 1936. His employment was governed by section 240 of the Government of India Act, 1935, according to which it was to be at the pleasure of the Crown, and under the control of the Secretary of State. In 1947 the appellant was asked by the Indian Government whether he was prepared to continue in government service after the transfer of power, and he replied affirmatively. Before independence, however, he was informed by the Madras Government that his services would be terminated on the date of independence. He filed suit against the State of Madras. The Supreme Court held that upon withdrawal of British rule from India all services of the Indian Civil Service were automatically terminated, and would be continued only subject to the decision of the new Government of India. This was stated to be in accordance with international law. It was further held[1] that continuity of service could only be achieved by the Government accepting an offer of a former servant to work for that Government, and discontinuance of service was at the option of either party. Even if the argument of the appellant was conceded that after independence the civil service was still in the employ of the Crown, section 240 would not give the protection claimed for it. But as a matter of law, the Crown in right of India was symbolic, and the severance of India from the ultimate authority and responsibility of the British Government had effected a basic alteration in the contractual-cum-statutory tenure of service.

In the case of claims of officials of the States which merged in the Union of India, the question was resolved by reference to the Act of State doctrine.[2]

A Pakistan court adopted a similar reasoning to that of the Indian courts. A petitioner who joined the Indian Civil Service in 1936, his conditions of service being laid down in a covenant with the Secretary of State for India, was transferred on partition to the Pakistan Administrative Service, and was prematurely retired therefrom when the Constitution was suspended in 1956. He sought a writ of mandamus to quash the order under which the retirement was authorized, on the ground that it was a violation of the covenant and of the law of State succession. The court held, however, that international law could not be invoked by a subject to deny constitutional validity to a legislative enactment.[3]

1 *State of Madras* v. *Rajagopalan*, A.I.R. (1955) S.C. 817.
2 See *supra*, p. 258.
3 *Zafar-ul-Ahsan* v. *Pakistan*, P.L.D. (1959) Lah. 879.

(ii) *The independence of Burma and Ceylon, 1947*

In the case of Burma, it was announced that few opportunities for continued service would be offered to European officers, but that those whose service was discontinued would be compensated. The Prime Minister stated in the House of Commons that the source of the moneys from which the compensation would be derived had not been agreed upon.[1] The Governor of Burma notified officials there that 'the Government of Burma take the view that all Secretary of States' officers, Burman and British alike, should have their present service terminated on the transfer of power under the conditions laid down in the rules governing ordinary or premature retirement as may be appropriate'. He added: 'Those who wish to continue in service under the Government of Burma and are acceptable to that Government will enter on new relations settled between the Government of Burma and the officers themselves.'[2] With respect to Ceylon, it was laid down that officials 'may retire from the public service, and on retirement be granted a pension or gratuity'.[3]

(iii) *The independence of Israel, 1948*

When British jurisdiction ceased in Palestine, it was arranged that any person holding office in the service of the Government of Palestine immediately before the appointed day should be deemed to continue in his office until either he should be appointed to the service of the Crown elsewhere, or, if he were not so appointed, he should retire or should be removed from office.[4] Shortly after its formation Israel legislated to require every person who on 14 May 1948 was in the service of the Government of Palestine, and whose ordinary place of residence was on that date within the territory of Israel, to continue to serve temporarily in accordance with the instructions of the Government, unless, before publication of the ordinance on 3 June 1948, he would be otherwise notified. The Government was given a discretion to terminate employment or to post to other appointments within six months of that date.[5] The Israel Supreme Court held that, apart from this legislation, no official of the Palestine administration had any right to continue to serve, and it was a prerequisite to reinstatement under the legislation that the official

1 Cmd. 7189, p. 43.   2 *Ibid.*
3 Ceylon Constitution Order in Council, 1946, S.R. & O. 1946, Appendix of Prerogative Orders, no. 2, s. 63.
4 Termination of Jurisdiction in Palestine (Transitional Arrangements) Order in Council, 1948, S.R. & O. 1948, no. 1603, s. 7. In effect most of the officials were given alternative employment in Malaya and elsewhere: 459 H.C. Deb. 5 s., Written Answers, col. 206.
5 Palestine Government Employees Ordinance, Laws of Israel, 1 (5708–1948), p. 19.

reported for duty within the stated time,[1] and had not been discharged before the relevant date.[2]

(iv) *Independence within the Commonwealth*

Each British dependency constitutes a separate legal organization, and all government officials are employed by this organization, and not by the United Kingdom. All appointments are charged on the territorial accounts, and are advertised and competed for by officials within the territory, in other territories, and sometimes from outside the Colonial Service altogether. It follows from this decentralization of the service, as well as from the terms of employment, which negative any suggestion of a contract with the Crown,[3] that, upon separation of the territory from the United Kingdom, officers thereof have no claims upon the United Kingdom for future employment in the event of their redundancy. Nor, since their tenure was not of a vested right character, could the territories, after independence, be called upon to maintain employment.

The situation thus produced by independence placed in hazard the pension rights of officials whose tenure of service had not expired, and it was rectified by the Public Officers Agreements.[4]

(v) *The dissolution of the Federation of Rhodesia and Nyasaland, 1963*

The Order in Council dissolving the Federation[5] provided for the creation of a Staff Commission[6] to exercise jurisdiction over Federal officers on secondment to the Territories,[7] whose status was preserved.[8] All officials were invited to continue in office until May 1964, and those declared redundant would be compensated by the addition of one third to their pensions. About 3,000 out of 35,000 civil servants were declared redundant.[9] It was announced that after the independence of Northern Rhodesia about 1,800 officers would be designated redundant with the Africanization of the service, and that the United Kingdom would bear half the cost of their compensation.

1 *Sifri* v. *Attorney-General*, I.L.R. vol. XVII, Case no. 22; *Albohar* v. *Attorney-General*, ibid. p. 94.
2 *Bergtal* v. *Schwartzmann*, ibid. p. 93.
3 See *supra*, p. 178.
4 See *infra*, p. 474. For the financial disabilities of redundant colonial officers see *The Times*, 5 September 1963, p. 13.
5 S.I. 1963, no. 2085.
6 S. 21.
7 S. 22.   8 S. 20.
9 *The Times*, 19 November 1963, p. 11. This was questioned and a figure of 800 suggested in the Rhodesia and Nyasaland Parliament. *Parliamentary Debates* (1963), col. 1528.

(vi) *The formation of Malaysia, 1963*

At the time of the creation of the Federation of Malaysia steps were taken to protect government officials of the Borneo States and of Singapore who were to continue in the service of either the State or Federal governments or to be retired.[1] The Malaysia Bill annexed to the Malaysia Agreement provides for preservation of pensions as under the Constitution of the Federation of Malaya;[2] it also allows special protection for pensions of serving members of the State service in the Borneo States,[3] and appeals by those officials against decisions affecting pensions or compensation.[4] The Constitutions of Sabah and Sarawak provide for the transfer of existing officers[5] and secondment of members of the State services to the Federal service.[6] There are also clauses allowing compulsory retirement of government officials to facilitate appointment of local candidates.[7] These officials are affected by the terms of the British North Borneo and Sarawak (Compensation and Retirement Benefits) Orders in Council of 1963[8] and the Public Officers Agreements between the United Kingdom and Malaysia respecting the North Borneo States.[9] These instruments lay down minimum standards for conditions of service and retirement, together with the granting, preservation and payment of pensions. The Singapore Constitution contains sections relating to protection of pension rights,[10] pension rights on transfer,[11] continuance in office of public officers[12] and terms of office of those continuing,[13] as well as secondment to the Federal service.[14] The Singapore Public Officers Agreement contains protective provisions similar to those of the agreements relating to the Borneo States.[15]

(vii) *The Francophone States*

In the Fifth Republic the French civil service was unified and centralized, so that all officials, whether on home or overseas postings, belonged to a single system and were subject to its rules and conditions. Each French civil servant has a defined rating, financially calculated by reference to a basic index figure, and this is his sole entitlement. On overseas postings he might receive a location allowance which would double his salary, but

---

1 The relevant documents were published in London in July 1963: Cmnd. 2094.
2 S. 81. 3 S. 82. 4 S. 83.
5 Sabah: s. 55; Sarawak: s. 54. 6 Ss. 56 and 55 respectively.
7 Ss. 57 and 56 respectively.
8 Cmnd. 2094, p. 201; the two Orders are identical in terms.
9 Cmnd. 2094, p. 220; the two agreements are also identical.
10 Ss. 76, 77. 11 S. 79. 12 S. 100.
13 S. 101. 14 S. 102. 15 Cmnd. 2094, p. 224.

this would not be a matter of entitlement save during the period of the posting. The problem raised by the independence of the French overseas territories has not, then, been a problem of continuity by the successor States of the contracts of employment of previous civil servants, but of continuity of rights under the predecessor's law. French officials on postings in countries which became independent have been posted home or to other dependent territories, without loss of their *cadre* status.

The States of the Community and other ex-French States have not entered into any agreements concerning officials comparable with those entered into with the United Kingdom. However, the policy of providing French administrative and technical assistance has to some extent bridged the gap. Although it is conceded that the States upon independence were not committed to maintaining French officials in their service,[1] they have signed agreements with France in which the fate of existing officials has, by implication, been absorbed in general regulation of recruitment, conditions of service and guarantees of emolument. The prototypes of these agreements were those signed with Cambodia on 8 November 1949 (no longer in force), Laos on 19 July 1949 and 13 April 1957, and Vietnam on 30 December 1949 (also no longer in force),[2] which were followed by the Convention for Administrative and Technical Assistance made with Morocco on 6 February 1957,[3] and with Tunisia on 3 June 1955[4] (also no longer in force).

These agreements were imitated in the case of the African States which became independent in 1960,[5] and with Algeria in 1962.[6] The common feature in all the arrangements is that France places its personnel at the disposal of the new State, and this personnel is generally composed of the former servants. For example, in 1950 in Indochina 5,966 French officials remained, and the figures for Morocco and Tunisia were 30,000 and 6,500 respectively, including judges and schoolteachers. Since the agreements substantially altered the terms and conditions of employment, and often provided for this to be temporary, France itself took the necessary measures to reclassify its officials, and used persuasion to ensure that the necessary proportion of them would agree to secondment under the governmental arrangements.

1 Fischer in *Annuaire français* (1957), p. 93; *Le statut des salariés français expatriés outre-mer*, publn. of the *Commission des Investisseurs* (1963).
2 Decree no. 53-191, *Journal Officiel*, 14 March 1953, p. 2403.
3 Decree no. 60-93, *Journal Officiel*, 2 February 1960, p. 1100. *Bulletin Officiel Marocain*, 21 June 1957, no. 2266.
4 Decree no. 55-1179, *Journal Officiel*, 6 September 1955, p. 8909.
5 See *supra*, p. 83.
6 Decree no. 62-1020, *Journal Officiel*, 30 August 1962, p. 8506.

Morocco offered French officials a private law contract concerning their terms of employment. Generally these terms are fixed in the intergovernmental agreements, and in some instances special terms are created for fixed categories. For example, the agreements with Morocco and Tunisia provided for French magistrates to be governed by their own statute, which would assure them the same privileges, immunities, honours and prerogatives to which they would be accustomed in France, including a guarantee of their judicial independence.

In addition to members of the French civil service on postings to the overseas territories, the administrations of the latter also included locally recruited personnel, mainly of indigenous character. Since there was no break in legal continuity throughout the processes of independence, employment of these persons was unaffected. On 12 December 1959 an Ordinance on the *Statut général des fonctionnaires* was promulgated by the State of Cameroon, designed to introduce flexibility into the law of 22 July 1958, which regulated the civil services of the Trust Territory, and, being designed for French officials, was rigid. The ordinance defined the rights of public servants, excluded from entry into the public service all but Cameroon citizens (except magistrates and members of the armed forces), and guaranteed the legal and political rights already in existence, including the right of forming *organisations syndicales*.[1] The effect of this was to maintain the status of all indigenous personnel. Similar action was taken in Upper Volta.[2]

The agreement between France and India of 21 October 1954 relative to the cession of the French Establishments in India provided for India to take charge of all officers and agents of the Establishments.[3]

(viii) *The independence of the Congo (Léopoldville), 1960*

The *Loi fondamentale relative aux structures du Congo* of 19 May 1960,[4] contained reference in article 250 to the public service of the Belgian Congo, which was placed at the disposal of the Congo. This service was organized separately from that of Belgium, and its legal basis was the Law of 18 October 1908 on the government of the Congo, which would cease to apply on independence. Accordingly an alternative basis had to be created, and this was provided by an *Arrêté royal* of 28 June 1960 *portant statut des agents de l'Administration d'Afrique*, including teachers, magistrates and police.[5] This created the same legal status for Belgian

1 Ordonnance no. 59–170, *Journal Officiel du Cameroun*, 12 December 1959, p. 1703.
2 *Journal Officiel de la Haute-Volta*, 30 November 1959 (special number).
3 *Annuaire français* (1955), p. 703, art. 5.   4 See *supra*, p. 94.
5 *Moniteur belge* of 27 July 1960. Modified, *ibid.* 17 September 1960, 14 November 1960.

officials in the Congo as was created by article 66(2) of the Belgian Constitution.

On 14 March 1960 a law was promulgated modifying the *Loi générale* of 21 July 1844 concerning pensions, which had hitherto been payable by the Treasury of the Belgian Congo, the effect of which was a guarantee of payment of all pensions and annuities, and all other benefits, payable by the Belgian Congo and by Ruanda-Urundi.[1] On 21 March 1960 a law was also promulgated integrating the personnel of the *Administration d'Afrique*, the *Force publique* and the magistracy in the public service of Belgium, thereby guaranteeing employment to those officers who would be prevented from pursuing their careers in Africa 'pour des raisons indépendantes de leur volonté'.[2] It regulated the status and conditions under which such officers would be admitted into the relevant metropolitan departments, and provided for compensation and pensions for those who did not request service in Belgium. Similar provision was made with respect to lay teachers by a Law of 24 June 1960, and with respect to *agents des parastataux* on 27 June 1960.[3]

This legislation did not envisage the mass exodus of Belgian officials from the Congo which was forced by political events, and the result was to strain the structure of the Belgian civil service by an influx of personnel, and to impose severe budgetary pressures on the Government. Numerous departmental regulations had to be issued to deal with the unexpected situation. Furthermore, some officers were not included in the guaranteeing legislation, and one of these, the *procureur-général* of Léopoldville, succeeded in an action for indemnity against Belgium. The *Cour d'Appel* of Brussels held that, despite the juridical separation of the metropolis and the Colony, judicial officers exercised Crown functions.[4]

4. CONTINUITY OF GOVERNMENT DEPARTMENTS

In the case of annexation or cession, where one administration supersedes another, governmental departments are substituted. In the case of federation or union this substitution occurs only in respect of departments administering matters within the federal or union exclusive competence. The transfer of Newfoundland to Canada illustrates this situation. In the case of independence, when the legal system continues substantially unaffected by the change, government departments retain their competence.

1 *Ibid.* 4 April 1960.
2 *Ibid.* 13 April 1960. Modified, *ibid.* 21 July 1960, *Arrêts d'exécution* of 18 June 1960 and 8 July 1960, *ibid.* 30 July 1960, 15 and 16 July 1960.
3 *Ibid.* 21 July 1960.
4 *État belge* v. *Dumont*, decision of 4 December 1963, *Journal des Tribunaux* (1963), p. 727.

However, this continuity may not occur with respect to institutions which, though authorized by a continuing law, are in fact elements of the previous sovereignty. The Israel Supreme Court reviewed proceedings in the winding up of an estate which had been instituted by the Mandate authorities and heard by an Israel court. The court held that the Administrator-General of Israel was not the substitute or successor of the Administrator-General of Palestine, and that the argument that the Administrator-General, as a corporation sole, remained in existence in virtue of the Law and Administration Ordinance was met with the point that the Mandate office was 'under the shield of the Crown', and was not analogous to a corporation of private law. The Supreme Court pointed out that it had no evidence whether the officials of the Administrator-General were those of the Government, and what happened to his funds on termination of the Mandate.[1]

It is also possible that institutions of the predecessor State retain competence in respect of matters affecting the successor State's territory or subjects. Everything depends upon the concrete situation. It was held in a New York court that a power of attorney granted to the Consul-General of the Netherlands in respect of letters of administration had not been *ipso facto* revoked in virtue of the subsequent independence of the Netherlands Indies, of which the grantor was a denizen. This decision was based on the interpretation of the power, which was not contingent upon duration or continuity of citizenship.[2]

5. THE RIGHT TO TAX

The successor State acquires at the moment of change of sovereignty the competence to tax the inhabitants of the absorbed area and levy rates on their property.[3] It is not obliged by the taxation laws or exemptions of its predecessor, and if it collects unpaid taxes due to the latter it does so in the exercise of its own sovereign discretion, and not by virtue of any right which it had inherited.

There is little merit in the view at one time proposed by several French writers[4] that unpaid taxes must be apportioned between the old and the new States. The obligation to pay the taxes in question is one owed to the old State, and the debt relationship, being constituted under public law,

1 *Feingold* v. *Administrator-General, I.L.R.* vol. XVIII, p. 72.
2 *In re Ameyund, ibid.*, vol. XIX, Case no. 25.
3 See the authors listed in connexion with public property claims, *infra*, p. 200.
4 Piédelièvre bases his argument on 'equity': vol. I, p. 142; Despagnet holds that an apportionment of taxes should date from the change of sovereignty: p. 126; Selosse, p. 197.

expires with the change of nationality of the debtor and the loss of sovereign authority over him. If the tax is demanded by the successor State a new legal relationship is established, based on the latter's sovereign authority, and the predecessor State has no interest in the money paid.[1]

According to the Indian Independence Income Tax Proceedings Order, 1947,[2] each of the Dominions preserved the sums created by way of taxation after the date of partition. Pakistan proposed that these sums be deposited in a common pool up to the end of March 1948 and then be distributed, but India refused.[3]

It was held by the Israeli courts[4] that the collection by Israeli authorities of all taxes and dues struck before termination of the Mandate was authorized by the Law and Administration Ordinance.[5] The question of Algeria's rights to recover French-levied taxes is discussed in connexion with the problem of public property.[6]

6. THE CURRENCY

(A) A successor State has a discretion as to whether it will retain in circulation the currency of its predecessor. If it fails to do so, however, it must respect rights duly acquired in the old currency. Paper money is a debt covered by the bank which has issued it. The relationship of the bearer to the bank is one of credit, and is constituted under private law. If the notes are issued by the State treasury or reserve bank the debt is one between the bearer and the State, but is no less of a private character. The successor State is thus obliged by international law either to permit the continued circulation of the old currency or to establish parity between it and the new and establish the machinery for its exchange.[7]

[1] The Treaty of St Germain provided that 'the Italian Government will collect for its own account the taxes, dues and charges of every kind leviable in the territories transferred to Italy, and not collected on 3 November 1918': art. 39. In the *Czechoslovakia Succession in Taxes* Case, the Government of Czechoslovakia claimed a tax due to the former German Empire, and paid to it in 1918. It was held that Czechoslovakia had, as the successor State of Germany, the right to tax, and the defendant had to pay the tax when demanded in the manner consistent with the change of sovereignty: *Ann. Dig.* vol. IV, Case no. 53.
[2] *Gazette of India Extraordinary*, 14 August 1947.
[3] Paenson, p. 73.
[4] *Attorney-General* v. *Levitan*, I.L.R. vol. XVIII, Case no. 28, respecting suit over bond to the Attorney-General of Palestine; *L.* v. *Inspector of Income Tax, Pesakim Elyonium*, vol. VII (1953), p. 233, respecting unpaid tax; *Farkas* v. *Attorney-General, Ann. Dig.* vol. XVI, p. 71.
[5] See *supra*, p. 131.   [6] See *infra*, p. 229.
[7] Nolde in Hague *Recueil*, vol. XXVII (1929), pp. 285 *et seq.*; Selosse, p. 132, Huber, p. 104. After the attainment of independence by Poland, a new currency was issued, but the circulation of the old was not prohibited.

If the State is divided, such currency goes to the successor State as is proportionate to the amount of treasury acquired. The debt to the bearer is similarly divided, and the easiest way to resolve the question of its apportionment is to withdraw the old currency from circulation, issue notes of equivalent value, and adjust the balance between the interested States.[1] Notes of the Austro-Hungarian Empire continued to circulate after 1919 in the successor States until stamped, and the inter-state balances were adjusted from time to time on the basis of the value of the notes stamped.[2]

German money became legal tender in Austria on 17 March 1938 at the same rate of exchange as the previous Austrian schilling.[3]

The Reserve Bank of India transferred to Pakistan a sum equivalent to the volume of bank notes in circulation in Pakistan at the time of partition. Indian rupees continued to circulate locally in Pakistan until replaced by Pakistan bank notes at the same rate of exchange as from 1 April 1948, until 30 September 1948. The Reserve Bank of India continued to possess the exclusive privilege of issuing Pakistan bank notes.

While effective cancellation by the successor State of the rights of holders of the predecessor's currency at the time of succession would be confiscation, and engage international responsibility, it does not follow that the successor State is any less competent in international law than any other State to devalue its currency subsequently to change of sovereignty. Apart from treaty commitments and the obligations under the Articles of Agreement of the International Monetary Fund,[4] currency valuation is a domestic matter. As to commitments made before devaluation, and expressed in the currency of the devaluing country, international law is unclear. In some circumstances there could be a contractual commitment to a standard of valuation different from that embodied in the actual currency of payment,[5] but generally it must be conceded that the currency of payment is to be calculated in reference to its actual value at the date of payment.

(B) The problem becomes different and more difficult when the devaluation occurs after a duty to compensate has arisen, and it is obviously more complex when that duty affected the predecessor State and has been inherited by the successor State. Is the currency of payment to be valued at par with the currency of account? It might be argued that, since

1 Sack, *Partage des dettes de l'État* (1923), pp. 90 et seq.
2 Sulkowski in Hague *Recueil*, vol. XXIX (1929), p. 62.
3 *RGBl.* I, 17 March 1938.
4 A devaluation without the Fund's consent is nonetheless effective. See O'Connell, *International Law* (1965), vol. II, p. 1096.
5 *Serbian and Brazilian Loans* Case, P.C.I.J. Ser. A, nos. 20-1.

compensation is designed as a restitutionary measure, and is of its nature a purchase price for assets taken, the duty to pay it arises at the moment of taking. If that duty is unfulfilled at the date of devaluation the conclusion should be that payment must be made in the currency of account, because it is a payment wrongfully postponed. If the duty to pay has not been discharged by the predecessor State this may be an argument against transferring the burden to the successor State (an argument to be resolved by reference to whether the latter has benefited from the taking), but it can scarcely be an argument against payment at the rate prevailing on the date of the taking.

The question of devaluation by a successor State has arisen acutely in three instances, those of Indonesia, the Congo (Léopoldville), and Israel. In the case of Indonesia the question was whether payments expressed to be made in Netherlands Indies guilders were to be made at par with Netherlands guilders or at par with the devalued Indonesian rupiahs. Netherlands courts have decided the question both ways.[1] Belgian courts have held that the Congolese franc is not an object of merchandise subject to valuation, but a mode of payment. Hence, if a transaction is regulated by Congolese law a payment in Congolese francs validly discharges the obligation of the purchaser, even though the rate of conversion to Belgian francs may have altered.[2] However, if a judgment expressed in Congolese francs was given before depreciation of the currency it can be enforced at par in Belgian courts, because under Belgian law the debtor must repair the damage caused by delayed payment.[3]

The case of Israel is classic. In 1926 the Palestine Currency Board was created, composed of representatives of the United Kingdom and the Bank of England, and represented in Palestine by an Accountant-General. The Board was authorized to issue Palestine currency at par with the pound sterling. At the termination of the Mandate all the reserves of the Palestine Currency Board which had been invested in loans of the United Kingdom had to be transferred into a Currency Reserve Fund. According to article 2 (*d*) of the agreement of 30 March 1950,[4] Israel renounced its claim on this Fund to the amount of £2,000,000. Ordinance no. 18 of 1948, the Bank Notes Ordinance, which came into force on 17 August,

[1] *Van Maren* v. *Eerste Nederlandse Verzekering Maatschaapij*, I.L.R. vol. XXI, p. 63; *Killian* v. *Hageman*, ibid. vol. XXIV, p. 73.
[2] *Sidaf* v. *Cimenki*, *Journal des Tribunaux* (1964), p. 616; *Entreprises Fernand Gillion en Afrique 'Sogiaf'* v. *Banque centrale du Congo belge et du Ruanda-Urundi*, ibid. p. 639; *Deleers* v. *De Rosen de Borgharen*, ibid. (1965), p. 153; *Windey* v. *Fonds des invalides des employés du Congo et du Ruanda-Urundi*, ibid. p. 352, holding that the Belgian Congolese franc was distinct from the Belgian franc. See Lejeune and Dierickx, ibid. (1962), p. 217.   [3] *Dupret* v. *Van den Hove*, ibid. (1965), p. 89.
[4] *U.N.T.S.* vol. LXXXVI, p. 232.

embodied an agreement between Israel and the Anglo-Palestine Bank granting the latter the exclusive privilege of issuing bank notes for the nominal value of 500 mils (equals 10s.). The Bank was required to exchange up to 15 September 1948 all the bank notes of the Palestine Currency Board at the fixed rate of exchange. The notes of the Palestine Bank were then credited by the United Kingdom to Account no. 2 of the Government of Israel.[1]

A year later the Israeli pound was devalued along with sterling in relation to the dollar. Between February 1952 and April 1953 three official rates of exchange existed against the dollar, namely 2.80, 1.40 and 1. On 1 May 1953 Israel fixed an exchange rate of $0.566 to the Israeli pound for travel and certain export transactions. Germany, in the *Templar Mediation*,[2] argued that the rate of exchange on the day of taking is the criterion of compensation for expropriation,[3] whereas Israel argued that the rate was that prevailing on the date when the final proposals of the mediator would be delivered. This conversion rate, it was contended, was a reflexion of a rule that the obligation to pay is an obligation to pay in local currency alone. The agreement with Germany, and the special agreement to mediate, distinguished, according to Israel, between the money of account and the money of payment. In the special agreement the property would be assessed in local currency.

Israel relied upon the award in the *Diverted Cargoes* Case,[4] where the f.o.b. cost had been expressed in dollars, and the question was whether the credit due to the Greek Government was to be converted into sterling at the exchange rate on the day of payment, as Greece contended, or at the rates prevailing at the date of requisition. The arbitrator in that case had ascertained what currency was to be considered as the money of contract, and found it to be sterling. He then asked whether the obligation should be calculated by reference to the dollar regarded as the unit of value and as the money of account, and held that the dollar was selected as the standard of value; that is, the currency by reference to which the amount in sterling was due from the United Kingdom to Greece. As to the rate of exchange, it was necessary to go into the substance of the obligation. The majority of States had enacted rules according to which the rate of conversion from the money of account to the money of payment is that prevailing at the time of the payment of the debt. The arbitrator adopted the 'judgment day' rule and not the 'breach day' rule, and Israel argued that this was also the appropriate solution in expropriation matters.[5]

1 Paenson, p. 80.
2 See *infra*, p. 281.
3 Memorial, p. 172.
4 *I.L.R.* vol. XXII, p. 820.
5 Counter-memorial, pp. 100–6.

The Effect on Administration

Germany stated that it could not accept the view that, not only the fixing of the amount of compensation, but also the payment of the sum, should be effected in the currency of the expropriating country. The compensation should be sufficient to enable the dispossessed, who had waited long enough for their money, to purchase assets of equivalent value to those taken. The *Diverted Cargoes* Case was irrelevant because there genuine contractual rights were involved, and it was not possible to apply rules pertaining to such a case to a claim for compensation.[1]

(C) Sometimes the effect of a separation of territory which had been part of a unitary monetary system is to create a volume of currency which, owing to exchange control regulations of the predecessor State, ceases to be readily convertible. When this situation occurs agreement on exchange of bank notes is sometimes reached between the predecessor and successor States. For example, in an exchange of notes of 27 September 1952[2] between the United Kingdom and Ethiopia respecting the financial settlement reached on the transfer of Eritrea from the United Kingdom administration to Ethiopia as a federated State, it was agreed that Ethiopia would exchange in Eritrea Ethiopian dollars for the East African currency in circulation there, and that the East African Currency Board, which administered exchange control, would give full sterling value or credit to Ethiopia for all East African currency withdrawn from circulation and returned to Nairobi. In the Financial Agreement of 30 March 1950 between Israel and the United Kingdom it was agreed that, where payments were provided for, the necessary exchange would be made available. This was particularly applicable to pensions.[3]

When the Saar was restored to Germany agreement was reached that Germany would exchange French currency in circulation in the Saar at the existing rate of exchange, and would withdraw such currency in circulation to an amount of 40 milliards of francs to neutralize the volume of accumulated currency. Since the circulation in the Saar was estimated to be 50 milliards of francs Germany was, in effect, permitting one fifth of the circulating currency to remain in circulation and to constitute a debt of France to Germany. Had France refused repatriation of the 40 milliards, the effect would have been, not to make the Saar resistant to an inflow of German bank notes, but to create an excess of French bank notes in Germany and a depreciation of French currency on the free market.

The question of the franc zone has been discussed.[4] Algeria agreed to

---

1 Reply, p. 80.   2 *U.N.T.S.* vol. CXLIX, p. 64, s. (3).
3 *Ibid.* vol. LXXXVI, p. 250.
4 See *supra*, p. 72. For official French views see *Annuaire français* (1963), p. 1046.

belong to it, but transactions relating to conversion of Algerian currency into French currency, and vice versa, could be made on the basis of official parities recognized by the International Monetary Fund. Agreement would be reached on the terms and conditions of transferring the privilege of issue, and the conditions of Algeria's participation in the currency pool.[1]

The Order in Council dissolving the Federation of Rhodesia and Nyasaland[2] contained provisions for the stabilization of the currency. Federal currency would be legal tender until 1 January 1965, and parity during this period would be maintained with sterling. The capital stock of the Bank of Rhodesia and Nyasaland would be transferred to the Liquidating Agency, and a Committee of Ministers of the Territories would exercise former Federal functions in respect of currency issue and exchange control. The Bank would be dissolved as at 31 December 1965, and its backing and assets distributed among the Territories in proportion to the amount of Federal currency which before the date of demonetization would have been redeemed by the Bank to the Central Banks of the Territories. On 16 November 1964 the Central Banks of the Territories began issuing currency, and the banking offices began handing over whatever Federal currency they received. On 1 June 1965 the Bank of Rhodesia and Nyasaland ceased to function. It had been calculated that the Federal currency was related to the respective goods and services of the three Territories in the ratio of 30:22:10. Theoretically, on 1 June 1965 the volume of Federal currency exchanged for Territorial currency in each of the former Territories should have corresponded with this ratio. In actual fact, there was a margin in Malawi's favour as against Rhodesia, although Zambia was as predicted. The imbalance may have been due in part to the remittance of currency by expatriate Nyasas in Rhodesia, thereby adding to the volume of currency representing the goods and services of Malawi. Sound banking practice would suggest that the key to repartition should have been the productivity backing of the currency, not its accidental location at the date of repartition; but the haste with which the Federation was dismantled prevented agreement being reached on the productivity base. It has been estimated that the hazards of the procedure adopted in this instance could have involved a margin of error of 5 per cent, with considerable influence on the economy of Malawi in particular. For example, while Federal currency was exchanged at par, Territorial currency was discounted 2½ per cent. This encouraged the export

[1] Declaration of Principles Concerning Economic and Financial Co-operation, 19 March 1962, *A.J.* vol. LVII (1963), p. 717, *Journal Officiel*, 20 March 1962, p. 3024, arts. 8, 9.
[2] S.I. 1963, no. 2085.

of Federal currency in exchange transactions. Also, there was some speculation that Zambian exchange controls would be more flexible than Rhodesian, leading to the export of Federal currency to Zambia during the period when no exchange control operated between the former Territories. This was roughly offset by export of currency by expatriates in Zambia, but the result was fortuitous and unforeseen when the repartition key was devised.

Had sterling been devalued at any time before 1 June 1965, Federal currency, in virtue of the Order in Council, would have been automatically devalued. However, legal opinion in one of the former Territories was that the Territories were free to maintain the existing exchange rate. The effect of this would have been that less Territorial currency would be issued in exchange for Federal currency. Had the converse situation occurred, and a former Territory devalued its currency, the question would have arisen whether more of the latter would have had to be exchanged for Federal currency. If it had, the effect would not have been to disturb the economic basis of the repartition, so long as the new currency was universally convertible at the new rate; and, provided the devaluation had been consistent with the Articles of Agreement of the International Monetary Fund, no violation of international law would have occurred.

The East African Currency Board was created in 1919 under Colonial Regulations, with its headquarters in London. Its purpose was to issue and manage a local currency in East Africa to replace the Indian rupee which was widely in circulation.

In 1960 a change was made to African personnel representing the constituent Territories, and the headquarters were moved to East Africa. No alteration was made in the competence of the Board, which was limited to issue of East African currency backed by sterling, with a restricted power to make fiduciary issues.

After the independence of the member States, in accordance with the movement towards federation in East Africa, negotiations were commenced with a view to instituting a central bank common to Tanzania, Kenya and Uganda. This would replace the Board as issuing authority, and would in addition have all the competences of the central bank of a sovereign State. In June 1965, however, it was announced that each State would create its own central bank and currency.

Each of the new central banks would be a successor to the Board. It would present East African currency to the Board to be redeemed in sterling, and would take over its own fiduciary issues, that is, it would present notes to redeem its own securities. The proportion in which the currency would be deemed to be distributed was not decided. The fiduciary issue presented no problem since it was composed entirely of crop finance advances to private banks, which were territorially located. The Board would continue to operate for an indefinite time while notes and currency still in circulation remain unredeemed.

Aden, the other member of the East African Currency Board, was in a different position from Uganda, Kenya and Tanzania. In April 1965 a new Southern Arabian currency authority, to which Aden was attached, commenced operations. Under the legislation creating the new authority the latter took over all the East African Currency Board's operations in the territories under its jurisdiction.[1] It agreed to take over the paper money of Aden from the Board; but Aden would remain indefinitely a member of the Board to protect its outstanding interest in profits and currency still in circulation.[2]

[1] Federation of South Arabia, law no. 10 of 1960, ss. 3 (3), 3 (4), 32.
[2] See generally Loynes, *The Currency of South Arabia* (1962), report prepared for the Government of Aden; East African Currency Board, report for 1964.

Chapter 9

THE EFFECT OF CHANGE OF SOVEREIGNTY ON THE PUBLIC PROPERTY OF THE STATE

I. THE PUBLIC AND PRIVATE DOMAINS

1. The Distinction between the Public Domain and Private Domain, and the Factor of Territorial Identity

The State in its character of a legal person owns movable and immovable property employed both in administration and in commercial enterprises. A distinction is drawn between public property of the State and its private property. Some authors consider that only the former 'passes to' the successor State, the latter remaining with the predecessor State.[1] However, the distinction is as elusive as the distinction, of which it is a projection, between public law and private law;[2] and the most that can be said[3] is that only such property as pertains to sovereignty, and only such

[1] Castren, pp. 452 et seq.; Cavaglieri, pp. 130 et seq.; Dahm, vol. I, p. 112 (he admits that modern treaties tend to eliminate the distinction); Delbez, p. 180; Gould, p. 413; Guggenheim, pp. 84 et seq.; Traité, pp. 466 et seq.; Huber, pp. 75 et seq.; Meyer-Lindenberg, p. 85; Schnitzer, p. 143; Schönborn, pp. 57, 81, 99; Selosse, pp. 141, 178; Sereni, vol. II, p. 397; Sibert, vol. I, p. 213; Vanselow, p. 142; Verdross-Zemanek, p. 194; Monaco, p. 218. The distinction played an important role in the Protocol to the Frankfurt Conference, 1871, no. 1 of 7 July 1871, M.N.R.G., 1st ser., vol. XX, p. 807.

[2] See supra, p. 104.

[3] Piédelièvre, vol. I, p, 135; Phillipson, p. 314; Keith, pp. 6, 49 et seq.; Westlake, pt. I, p. 75; Lawrence, p. 90; Szászy in Rev. de droit int. vol. V (1931), p. 588; Kelsen in Hague Recueil, vol XLII (1932), p. 328; Martens, vol. I, p. 369; Gidel, p. 82; Despagnet, p. 120; Wilkinson, pp. 23 et seq.; Fauchille, vol. I, pt. I, p. 380; Hall, p. 115; Rousseau, p. 272; Bluntschli, Bk. II, s. 54; Hershey, p. 220; Gould, p. 413; von Holtzendorff, p. 38; Heffter, p. 50; von der Heydte, p. 304. See the Treaty of St Germain, art. 208; Treaty of Trianon, art. 191. The Allies informed Germany in 1919 that 'in conformity with the rules of International Law and Equity' they were 'applying to the German Colonies the general principle in accordance with which the transfer of sovereignty involves the transfer under the same conditions to the State to which the surrender is made of the immovable and movable property of the ceding State': Reply of the Allied and Associated Powers to the Observations of the German Delegation on the Conditions of Peace, 1919, Cmd. 258, p. 20. In the case of (Polish) Treasury v. Heirs of Dietl a Polish court explained the relationship of such property to sovereignty. 'The Polish State', it quoted from a previous case, 'the moment its independence had been restored, had by virtue of its sovereignty become possessed of all public law and private law property of the partitioning State which was situated in the territories occupied by it': Ann. Dig. vol. IV, Case no. 51. See also

part of it as is identified with ceded or annexed or seceding territory can be claimed by a successor State *ipso jure*.[1]

The way in which property 'passes to' a successor State is also controversial. Theories on this subject are interwoven with theories of the relationship of territory and sovereignty,[2] and influence the criterion by which private property and public property are distinguished. The universal succession theorists had no difficulty in assuming that the successor State 'succeeds to' the property of its predecessor in the same way that the heir at private law succeeds to the estate of the deceased, because they conceived of territory in proprietary terms. But the theory current early in this century that territory is merely the physical sphere within which competence is exercised prompted the thesis that, when the predecessor State vacates territory, those of its assets located there which appertained to its sovereign functions become *bona vacantia*, and are then appropriated by the successor State as an act of its own will. The Anglo-Americans have not adverted to these theoretical disagreements, which the expression 'passing to' conceals, because their conception of the public domain is rooted in feudal law. This explains why the English and American authors have not recognized any distinction between the public and private domains of the State. Such a distinction is fundamental in Continental legal systems: the public domain is attributed to the State in virtue of sovereignty; and, since State succession constitutes a substitution of sovereigns, it follows that the public domain is appropriated by the successor State. The private domain, however, is 'owned' by the predecessor State, and, if the latter continues to exist, the private domain is unaffected by change of sovereignty. If the predecessor State is totally destroyed, then ownership lapses and the private domain, like the public domain, becomes *bona vacantia*.[3]

The distinction between the public and the private domains of the State emanates logically from the new conception of State property which the French Revolution introduced,[4] and which the Code Civil consecrated,[5]

Co-operative Farmers in Tarnów v. *Polish Treasury*, where it was held that Poland took over the property of the former Austrian Treasury by actually assuming supreme power in the territory: *Ann. Dig.* vol. II, Case no. 32.

[1] The expression was used in the Israel–U.K. Agreement, *infra*, p. 223 and *Khayat* v. *Attorney-General*, I.L.R. vol. XX, p. 123, and the Netherlands–Indonesian Agreement, *infra*, p. 226. It was held that all movable property *garnissant* public buildings in the territories ceded by Savoy to France in 1859 followed the fate of the buildings: D. 1860, 4, 158. On devolution to public service see Guggenheim, *Traité*, p. 466.

[2] See *supra*, p. 22.

[3] Von Rogister, p. 13; Huber, p. 20; Gidel, p. 64; Gareis, p. 60; Cavaré, vol. I, p. 376; Sereni, vol. II, p. 397; Hold-Ferneck, vol. I, p. 114.

[4] *Loi domaniale* of 22 November–2 December 1790.

[5] Arts. 537 (2), 538–41, 1128, 1558, 2226.

when it defined as *domaine public* those assets which are not susceptible of private ownership.[1] In a work by Proudhon, published in 1833, the conclusion is drawn that the public domain is that which is dedicated to the functions of government, while the private domain is that which the State owns in the same manner as a private individual owns property.[2] This criterion of dedication was eventually to be transformed in Duguit's constitutional theory into one of inalienability.[3] At the same time French law evolved the theory that administrative districts, communes and other bodies, inasmuch as their property is dedicated to public services distinct from those of the State, possess it in the right of private persons.

Not surprisingly, the French authors on State succession, beginning with Pradier-Fodéré,[4] assumed that, at least in cases of partial succession, neither the private domain of the State nor the property of local bodies would fall to the successor State.[5] Since Italian law followed the French distinction the Italian authors made the same assumption. Cavaglieri, for example, distinguished the *patrimonio indisponibile*, which consists of assets inalienably connected with the public service, and hence commercially beyond valuation, from the *patrimonio disponibile*, which consists of merchantable property. The former belongs to (*spettare*) the actual sovereign, and does not pass by succession but is appropriated; therefore, any attempt to link the *actif* and the *passif* is, in his opinion, fallacious.[6] So far as the *actif* is concerned, it continues to remain the property of the owner, even if located in the ceded territory, and hence in what has now become, *vis-à-vis* the owner, foreign soil.[7] The difficulty with this theory is that it affords no ground for the successor State to claim the public property of the predecessor (and also its private property in cases of total extinction) located abroad, for if this becomes *bona vacantia* the logical party to acquire it would be the State on whose territory it is located. The successor State can claim it only by succession. None of the exponents of the doctrine push it to this absurd extreme, save Keith,[8] and, it seems, Sereni[9].

Recently the Continental and English concepts have collided in practice. The English negotiators in the settlement with Israel in 1950 found, when dealing with Continentally trained lawyers, that the distinction

1 Art. 538. See Guggenheim, p. 67.
2 Quoted by Barckhausen in *Revue de droit public*, 1902, as cited by Guggenheim, p. 67.
3 *Traité de droit constitutionnel*, vol. III (1923), p. 360.
4 Vol. I, p. 277. See, e.g., Fauchille, vol. I, pt. I, p. 360.
5 Fiore, vol. I, p. 229; Bluntschli, p. 84; Huber, p. 45; Schönborn, p. 64; Guggenheim, pp. 63–83; Schnitzer, pp. 128, 143.
6 P. 130.   7 P. 131.   8 P. 52.   9 Pp. 397–400.

between the public and private domains assumed an unexpected relevance. Also, in the drafting of the Italian Peace Treaty, this dictinction was given an importance which the British administration in Libya does not appear fully to have appreciated. As the Franco-Italian Conciliation Commission[1] and the United Nations Tribunal for Libya[2] both discovered, even in those systems of law which recognize a distinction between property owned by the State *de jure imperii* and property used by it *de jure gestionis*, it is by no means easy to determine that all institutions maintained at public expense appertain to sovereignty. Whether or not property is identified with territory is a matter of internal law which may, or may not, predicate the identification on the property being devoted to public purposes; and the criterion of public character and the criterion of territorial identification may thus contradict each other. For example, Israel succeeded to all the property in the accounts of the Palestine administration, irrespective of whether the property could be described as public or private, and did not succeed to any property, public or private, including military property, in the accounts of the United Kingdom.[3]

Poland in 1919, according to a decision of the Polish courts,[4] succeeded, in virtue of its sovereignty, to all 'public law and private law property' of the three predecessor States; but the United Nations Tribunal for Libya held that it was a rule of customary international law that private property of the predecessor State does not pass to the successor State, and, indeed, continues to be owned by the former though still located in the territory of the latter.[5] On 5 Deember 1866 the Law Officers gave an opinion on the effect of the Prussian annexation of Hanover upon the reversionary interest of the Queen of England in the Crown property of that State. They advised that 'the King of Prussia has a right to at least all property movable and immovable which appertained to the Crown and Kingdom and which the sovereign could not sever from the Crown'. The Queen's interest was limited to such property as was personal to the King of Hanover, and the British Government was justified in claiming compensation from Prussia only in respect of such property as was seized by that country.[6] The distinction here between public and private property is rudimentary and easily comprehended, but applied to sophisticated modern State enterprises it is fraught with hazard.

Clearly the law of the predecessor State in the first instance determines what constitutes public property.[7] But the determination is not, for

1 See *infra*, p. 216.   2 See *infra*, p. 218.   3 See *infra*, p. 224.
4 (Polish) *Treasury* v. *Heirs of Dietl*, Ann. Dig. vol. IV, Case no. 51.
5 See *infra*, p. 218.
6 Opinion of 5 December 1866, F.O. 83/2289; O'Connell, Appendix, no. 30.
7 United Nations Tribunal for Libya, *infra*, p. 218.

purposes of State succession, decisive. On the one hand, a country acquiring territory from another cannot treat as public property religious or charitable institutions owned by private persons, merely because in its law such institutions are designated as public. The Law Officers' opinion on this issue in the case of the Madagascar concessions will later be considered.[1] Such institutions may be expropriated by a subsequent act, but only subject to the rules relating to acquired rights. A State can only inherit what was the public property of its predecessor, and hence cannot succeed automatically, for example, to the ownership of a private railway, but only to such rights of regulation and control as its predecessor enjoyed. On the other hand, a successor State acquires property which was owned by its predecessor even if such property is designated as 'private' in that State's law, provided it is employed in a governmental capacity. Hungarian law, for example, made no distinction between public and private property, and treated as heritable all assets owned by the State or by territorial corporations of public law. The Permanent Court of International Justice, however, in dealing with the status of property of the Austro-Hungarian monarchy in territory transferred in 1919 to Czechoslovakia, observed that the provisions of the Treaty of Trianon relative to the passing of Hungarian State property 'applies the principle of the generally accepted law of State succession'.[2]

The predecessor State is competent up to the moment of change of sovereignty to alienate the public domain or any portion of it, and the property so alienated cannot be appropriated *ipso jure* by its successor. The Polish Government in the *German Settlers* Case denied that Germany, after the signature of the Treaty of Versailles and before the transfer of the ceded territories to Poland, could impress a private character on State property. This contention was rejected by the Permanent Court, which held that Germany 'retained, until the actual transfer of sovereignty, the right to dispose of her property'.[3]

When the change of sovereignty affects only part of the territory of a State the problem of a division of tangible State property is not easy. It

1 See *supra*, p. 310.
2 *Peter Pázmány University* Case, P.C.I.J. ser. A/B, no. 61, p. 237.
3 P.C.I.J. ser. A, no. 7. The same principle has been recognized in the courts of the United States: *Davis* v. *The Police Jury of Concordia*, 9 How. 280; *U.S.* v. *Reynes*, 9 How. 127; *More* v. *Steinbach*, 127 U.S. 70; *Alexander* v. *Roulet*, 13 Wall. 386; *Stearns* v. *U.S.* 6 Wall. 589; *U.S.* v. *Pico*, 23 How. 321; *U.S.* v. *Yorba*, 1 Wall. 412. The capacity to transfer property situated in the ceded territory ceases, however, at the moment of the change of sovereignty. The British Government announced that it would regard as invalid all transfers of property made by the Republic of South Africa and the Orange Free State after 19 March 1900: Cd. 53, p. 747; Cd. 128, p. 751.

is a general principle that only such property as is destined specifically for local use is acquired by the successor State. The application of this principle to State railways, telegraph and telephone systems, public lands and buildings, and immovable property generally, admits of little dispute. The identification of movable property with the ceded or annexed area, however, is rarely so obvious. The rolling stock of a State railway, public transport vehicles, military supplies and equipment not in fixed installations usually belong to the State as a whole, and may be located only accidentally in the absorbed territory.[1]

The opinion of publicists is that all movable property 'situated'[2] in the territory and partaking of the character of 'fixtures' passes to the successor State.[3] When, for example, Spain sought to remove every category of military equipment from San Juan after the transfer of sovereignty over Porto Rico to the United States in 1898, the latter objected, and argued that 'under the law movable things become immovable property when constructed or destined for the permanent use or service of immovable property'. The United States insisted on taking over all ordnance and fixed batteries, military and naval repair shops and their equipment, and all machinery in public buildings.[4] Movables not so identified with immovables in ceded territory as to be regarded as 'fixtures' would seem to remain the property of the predecessor State.

II. The National Exchequer

All public funds of a totally absorbed State become the property of the successor. The division of such funds in the case of partial succession, however, admits of some dispute. Within the last half century the financial operations of States have increased immeasurably in complexity. Schemes of social security, national health, compulsory personal insurance, savings bank deposits, mortgage advances and fire insurance investments have created specialized funds contributed to by the bulk of the population. It is

[1] Treaties of cession have at times specified the property that was to pass with the ceded territory. For example, the treaty for the cession of Louisiana to the United States, designated such property as 'all public lots and squares, vacant lands and all public buildings, fortifications, barracks and other edifices': *M.R. (Suppl.)*, vol. III, p. 465, art. 2 at p. 467. The treaty for the cession of Alaska to the United States by Russia in 1867 provided similarly: *B.S.F.P.* vol. LVII, p. 452.

[2] The words 'situated in' were employed in the Convention of Oppeln to designate the public property of Germany which passed to Poland: *L.N.T.S.* 1925, vol. XXXIV, no. 875, art. 1 (1).

[3] Despagnet, p. 128. Piédelièvre denies that the private property of the State passes to the successor in the case of partial succession. The distinction between public and private property of the State, however, seems artificial: vol. I, p. 135.

[4] *For. Rel.*, 1898, pp. 910–13.

perhaps just that a successor State should acquire such proportion of these funds as is represented by the contributions of the absorbed territory, and that the benefit of the contributions be applied to its population. No rule of international law to this effect can, however, be said to exist. The funds in question do not constitute a trust so as to attach to a specified locality.

The successor State therefore acquires *ipso jure* only local treasury balances and reserves, and funds specially allocated to the absorbed territory.[1] The Treaty of Versailles, for example, enacted that the German Government was to transfer to those Powers which undertook the administration of the German colonies, or to which German provinces were ceded, only such portions of the reserves accumulated by Germany as were attributable to the carrying on of social or State insurance in the areas concerned.[2] The successor State also acquires all funds applied to the liquidation of local debts, including savings bank deposits and pension and superannuation funds payable to persons in the acquired territory.[3]

Whatever funds are taken over by the successor State, however, remain subject to the equities attached to them. Thus, it can claim only the balance of money outstanding after all properly drawn cheques have been met, and after deduction of disbursements.[4]

III. Incorporeal Rights

The same principles apply to incorporeal as to corporeal property.[5] A successor State acquires all the liquidated rights of its predecessor in the absorbed territory, and hence can collect rents on leased public lands, repayment of mortgage moneys and the interest thereon, industrial loans, local body advances and ordinary contract debts. This is not because of any transmission of the legal relationship from the old to the new State, but merely because the capital of a public investment constitutes 'property' which pertains to the sovereign authority and can be recovered by it. Even when only in military occupation of territory, a conquering State

---

1 Despagnet, p. 128.
2 Arts. 77 and 312. See also the Treaty of St Germain, art. 275.
3 See specially India, *infra*, p. 404.
4 Phillipson, p. 320. Great Britain, when it annexed the Transvaal, took over the balances of the National Bank as they stood after the payment of cheques previously drawn and routine administration expenses: *ibid*.
5 However, this is not universally held. Some authors consider that public claims lapse and the successor State pursues them as a manifestation of its own sovereignty. This view is connected with the *Kompetenztheorie* of territory: Guggenheim, p. 84; Huber, p. 75.

has the right to liquidate realizable securities,[1] and when sovereignty is transferred its rights can be no less absolute. It can enforce all claims of its predecessor which relate to public assets in the absorbed territory, or to money advanced from local treasury funds.

Some authors have experienced difficulty in treating unliquidated claims of a State as 'public' property which is capable of being appropriated by its successor. Such claims, it is thought, are personal to the State in which they are invested, and are dependent upon the continuance of a legal relationship which does not survive the change of sovereignty; hence, although there is no known authority on the point, it has been considered difficult to justify in principle the competence of the successor State to recover damages for a tort against its predecessor, except when the succession process is such that legal continuity is scarcely, if at all, disrupted.[2] But if the arguments later to be addressed[3] to the question of tortious claims against the predecessor State are valid, they are equally valid with respect to similar claims of the State. It must be admitted, however, that if the predecessor State's private contractors cannot insist on all the stipulations of their contracts against the successor State, the latter is equally inhibited, for the contractual relationship between the parties, in so far as it relates to the absorbed territory, must be considered to be terminated. Liquidated claims arising out of the performance of the contract can be enforced by the successor State as falling within the category of 'public property', or as constituting acquired rights, but in the absence of a novation of the contract, tacit or express, the ensemble of rights and obligations created in the instrument of contract expires with the instrument itself. Hence, the successor State, if it is not administratively identical with the predecessor, can incur no rights, it is suggested, in a purely executory contract of the latter.

To the rule of succession to incorporeal rights an exception may exist in the case of rights inseparably connected with the previous Government's policy, and not arising out of perfunctory administration. The Austrian Constitutional Court in 1958 considered the extent to which the claims of a predecessor State devolve under international law upon the successor. The claim in this instance was one arising out of a decree of the German Ministry of the Interior requiring the City of Vienna to pay outstanding fees for inspection of foodstuffs, and it was made by the Austrian Government on the contention that all rights formerly vested in

[1] Hague Conventions concerning the Laws and Customs of War on Land, no. IV (1907), art. 53.
[2] For example, France paid the U.A.R. the sum of £20m. for damage done in Egypt in 1956.
[3] See *infra*, p. 482.

the *Reich* now vest in Austria. The court rejected the claim on the ground that international law does not effect a transfer to the successor State of the rights created under the public law of the predecessor State and indissolubly linked with the exercise of governmental power over the territory.[1]

2. THE PUBLIC AND PRIVATE DOMAIN SITUATED OUTSIDE THE AFFECTED TERRITORY

The discussion of the principles relating to the effect of change of sovereignty on the public property of a State has so far been limited to assets situated in the territory absorbed. There is little authority on the question of the competence of the successor State to claim assets located outside its territory. It would seem that in the case of partial succession, property of the predecessor State not actually located in the territory does not change its ownership. It has not come within the sovereign jurisdiction of the successor State, and the latter can claim only so much of it as it can seize or as is ceded to it.[2] In the case of total succession, however, the predecessor loses its competence to own property. Such of its assets, therefore, as are situated in foreign countries must either become property of the successor State or cease to have any owner. There is no reason to adopt the latter alternative. A successor State in the case of total succession acquires all the rights of its predecessor that appertain to sovereign jurisdiction. Such jurisdiction embraces the capacity to possess assets located in foreign countries. It is reasonable to conclude, therefore, that the claims of the successor State to be the owner of the assets of its predecessor located in other States must be recognized by the States concerned.

The problem was first discussed at length in the case of *United States* v. *McRae*, decided by the Court of Equity[3] in England in 1869. In this case the United States claimed from an agent of the Confederate Government in England moneys deposited with him during the Civil War on behalf of that Government, and the defendant sought to set off claims which he had against the Confederate Government. It is not clear if the court regarded the question as one relating to change of government or to

[1] *Republic of Austria* v. *City of Vienna*, I.L.R. vol. XXVI, p. 77.
[2] The German Government agreed in 1871 to repurchase French rights in a railway company in Alsace-Lorraine in property located in Switzerland: Keith, p. 52. Hall maintains that in the case of land situated outside the territory, there is at the most a right to its value: p. 115. Meyer-Lindenberg, p. 85; Dahm, vol. I, p. 113; Verdross-Zemanek, p. 194; Guggenheim, *Traité*, p. 468 admit succession abroad in cases of total succession. The Palazzo Venezia was acknowledged to have passed to Austria with the Treaty of Campo Formio, 1797: Sereni, vol. II, p. 398.
[3] (1869), L.R. 8 Eq. 69.

succession of States. Upon the suppression of a rebellion, it stated, the restored legitimate government is entitled, as of right, to its property seized by the usurping government, and can recover it by title paramount. On the other hand, property acquired by the insurrectionary government in the exercise of its authority can be claimed by the legitimate government as successor only. This being the case it could have no greater rights than its predecessor, and the set-off would have to be admitted. The court apprehended it

> to be the clear public universal law that any government which *de facto* succeeds to any other government, whether by revolution or restoration, conquest or reconquest, succeeds to all the public property, to everything in the nature of public property, and to all rights in respect of the public property of the displaced power. . . . But this right . . . can only be enforced in the same way and to the same extent, and subject to the same correlative obligations and rights, as if that authority had not been suppressed and displaced, and was itself seeking to enforce it.

The succession of the United States to the Confederate States would seem to have been more a succession of States than a succession of governments. The Confederate States constituted more than a rebel government. They were a number of semi-sovereign States which claimed the right to secede from one federation and form another. They exercised an effective and independent administration for a lengthy period of time over the territories which they comprised. The court in *McRae's* Case, in speaking of a succession by 'revolution or restoration, conquest or reconquest', would seem to have intended more than a succession of governments, and if this view is correct the decision is authority for the proposition that the public property of a totally absorbed state located in a foreign country can be claimed by the successor State. The court of first instance and counsel for the defendants appear so to have considered it in the *Haile Selassie* Case.[1]

A similar problem was considered by the Supreme Court of New York in *Irish Free State* v. *Guaranty Safe Deposit Co.*[2] In this case the Irish Free State took action to recover funds collected and deposited in that country by an agent of the revolutionary government of the so-called Republic of Ireland, set up before the transfer of sovereignty from Great Britain to the Irish Free State had been effected. The plaintiff rested its claim on the ground that the Irish Free State was the successor to the revolutionary government. The court held, however, that the Irish Free State, having been established by Act of the Imperial Parliament of Great Britain, had

---

1 [1939] Ch. 182 at pp. 184 and 189.
2 *Ann. Dig.* vol. III, Case no. 77.

succeeded, not to the revolutionary organization, but to the *de jure* government of Great Britain, and that therefore no derivative title could be claimed to the funds in question. Great Britain alone would have been competent to recover these funds. The case is not a direct authority in the law of State succession,[1] but it is interesting in that no objection was raised to the proposition that the Irish Free State would have been entitled to these funds if they had already been claimed by Great Britain.[2]

The country in which public property of the predecessor is situated is not, however, obliged to acknowledge the pretensions of the successor unless it has recognized the latter as the *de jure* sovereign. A decision to this effect was delivered by the Court of Appeal in England in 1939 in the case of *Haile Selassie* v. *Cable and Wireless Limited*.

The Emperor of Ethiopia, after the annexation of his country by Italy, sought to recover money owing to Ethiopia by the defendant company. The latter pleaded in defence that the claim pertained, not to the Emperor personally, but to the Emperor as sovereign of Ethiopia, and that, in consequence of the recognition by Great Britain of the King of Italy as the *de facto* sovereign of that country, the claim was either suspended or transferred to the Government of Italy. In its argument the defendant relied on the dictum in *United States* v. *McRae* to the effect that a government which *de facto* succeeds to any other government succeeds to all the public property of the displaced Power. The Court of Chancery, before which the action was first tried,[3] drew a distinction, however, between the case of *United States* v. *McRae*, where there had been only one *de jure* claimant, and the present case, where there were in effect two claimants, one recognized *de jure* and the other *de facto*. It denied that the *de facto* recognition operated to vest in the *de facto* government a title to property of the *de jure* sovereign situated in England. The case was taken on appeal[4] and before trial it was announced that Great Britain had recognized Italy as the *de jure* sovereign of Ethiopia. The court thereupon held that 'the right to sue in respect of public property must be treated in the Courts of this country as having become vested in His Majesty the King of Italy as from the date, at the latest, in December 1936... Now, that being so, the

---

[1] The extent of the analogy between the cases of succession of government and succession of States is not clear. Most of the authorities on the problem relate to the former: *U.S.* v. *Prioleau* (1866), 35 L.J. Ch. (N.S.) 7; *Republic of Peru* v. *Dreyfus Brothers* (1888), 38 Ch. D. 348; *Republic of Peru* v. *Peruvian Guano Co.* (1887), 36 Ch. D. 489; *King of the Two Sicilies* v. *The Peninsular & Oriental Steam Packet Company* (1850), 19 L.J. Eq. (N.S.) 202; *Emperor of Austria* v. *Day* (1861), 30 L.J. 690; *Luther* v. *Sagor and Company* [1921] 3 K.B. 532.

[2] See Dickinson in *A.J.* vol. XXI (1927), p. 747; Uren in *Michigan Law Review*, vol. XXVIII (1929), p. 149.

[3] [1939] Ch. 182. [4] *Ibid.* p. 194.

title of the plaintiff to sue is necessarily displaced.'[1] At no time during the hearing of the case was it asserted that a successor State recognized *de jure* could not claim the public property of its predecessor situated outside the absorbed territory.

3. PRACTICE IN THE MATTER OF THE PUBLIC AND PRIVATE DOMAINS

(i) *The abolition of the Crown in Commonwealth countries*

When a dependent British territory becomes independent and retains the monarchy there is no necessity to make provision for the assignment to it of public property, because this remains Crown property. Property of the United Kingdom Government in the territory is unaffected by the change; property of the territorial government is henceforth held by the Crown in right of the newly independent country. When the latter abolishes the connexion with the Crown it is sometimes provided for Crown property to vest, either in the President,[2] who is invested with the Crown's prerogatives, or in the Government,[3] or in the Republic.[4]

(ii) *The independence of the Francophone States*

The property of the State in the former French territories fell into four categories: the public domain of France, the private domain of France, the public domain of the territories, and the private domain of the territories. Following the *loi-cadre* of 1956,[5] the unappropriated public lands were transferred to the territories, and following independence in 1960 it was assumed that the first category of property had automatically vested in the new States.[6] As for the French private domain, in theory this would remain French; but certain of its elements were too important economically to the new States for the theory to be followed.

The problem of succession to the public and private domain was approached in three different ways. The co-operation agreements with

---

[1] *Ibid.* p. 197.
[2] Zambia Independence Order, S.I. 1964, no. 1652, s. 19. (Zambia became a republic in the act of independence.)
[3] The Constitution of Kenya (Amendment) Act, no. 28 of 1964, s. 25. Certain provision was also made with respect to Regional property, s. 17; The Constitution of Uganda (First Amendment) Act, no. 61 of 1963, s. 42.
[4] Republic of Tanganyika (Consequential, Transitional and Temporary Provisions) Act, 1962, no. 2 of 1962, s. 12.
[5] See *supra*, p. 59.
[6] On 10 November 1961 the *Cour d'Appel* of Dakar upheld this assumption, and denied the right of a French governmental agency to act as plaintiff in an action concerning aerial navigation installations at Dakar: *Annuaire français* (1962), p. 842.

certain of the Francophone States, while they contained no provision for the transfer of governmental property, did provide for mixed commissions to draft further agreements should there be difficulty in the distribution thereof.[1] Only in one case, that of Senegal in September 1962 as successor to the Federation of Mali, was a subsequent agreement made involving a detailed settlement. The second technique was to conclude a special agreement on property at the same time as the other co-operation agreements. This was done in three cases,[2] and provided for the creation of mixed commissions with the exclusive function of drafting detailed protocols. The commissioners were directed to list the immovable property charged on the French budget, which would be retained by France, and to determine where, and in what amount, compensation would be payable on the transfer of French property. Supplementary protocols were ratified by France in the cases of the Central African Republic and Chad in March 1963, but no further settlement with the Congo appears to have been made.

The third approach was also employed in three cases. In the economic co-operation agreements with Gabon, the Malagasy Republic and Mauritania there was special reference to the transfer of public property,[3] and mixed commissions were created with directions to determine the needs of continuing French services in these countries, to recommend exchanges of buildings where desirable, and to list the French public bodies which were administratively autonomous for the purpose of classifying their property as private.

The second and third approaches resulted in six follow-up agreements,[4] those with Senegal and the Malagasy Republic providing for the general transfer of all public property with subsequent specific exceptions contained in unpublished annexes, the others listing comprehensively the property which was to be transferred, and that which was to be reserved to France. Generally, France retained property for the accommodation of diplomatic representation, military and sometimes technical personnel

1 Cameroon, decree no. 61–877, *Journal Officiel*, 9 August 1961, p. 7429, arts. 5, 42; Ivory Coast, decree no. 62–136, *ibid.* 6 February, 1942, p. 1262, arts. 5, 38; Dahomey, *ibid.* p. 1277, arts. 5, 38; Upper Volta, *ibid.* p. 1307, arts. 5, 38; Niger, *ibid.* p. 1292, arts. 5, 38.

2 Central African Republic, decree no. 60–1230, *ibid.* 24 November 1960, p. 10466; Congo, *ibid.* p. 10472; Chad, *ibid.* p. 10478.

3 Gabon, decree no. 60–1231, *ibid.* 24 November 1960, p. 10484; Malagasy Republic, decree no. 60–692, *ibid.* 20 July 1960, p. 6612; Mauritania, decree no. 62–137, *ibid.* 6 February 1962, p. 1328.

4 Senegal, decree no. 63–270, *ibid.* 21 March 1963, p. 2720; Central African Republic, decree no. 63–267, *ibid.* p. 2718; Chad, decree no. 63–271, *ibid.* p. 2721; Gabon, decree no. 63–268, *ibid.* p. 2718; Malagasy Republic, decree no. 63–269, *ibid.* p. 2719; Mauritania, decree no. 63–1077, *ibid.* 31 October 1963, p. 9707.

stationed in the Francophone States under the defence and technical assistance agreements. The property of independent French public bodies was listed. In all cases the *palais de justice* and *palais du haut commissariat* were transferred to the new States. In the agreement with the Federation of Mali the test for the apportionment of property was its budgetary source, whether French or territorial.[1] The commission in this case drafted an agreement which provided for the transfer to Senegal, as successor to the Federation, of the *dépendances domaniales* registered in the name of France, save those listed in an unpublished annex.[2] In the cases of Togo, Guinea and Morocco there has been no formal agreement on the question of transfer of public property. In the last named instances, however, there has been no serious controversy. France retained the property which it considered necessary for the administration of its services in the country, and as these services have been terminated the property has been gradually transferred. As in the case of the other countries, however, France has retained the official palace as its embassy.

(iii) *The dismemberment of Czechoslovakia, 1938–9*

The Munich Agreement of 27 November 1938, which dealt with the Sudeten question, contained no provisions concerning the succession of Germany to the rights of Czechoslovakia. However, an agreement between the puppet Protectorate of Bohemia and Moravia and the *Reich* on 4 October 1941 dealt with the financial consequences of the transfer of the Sudeten areas to Germany.[3] All the public property of Czechoslovakia situated in the Sudeten territories, and all those assets which on 15 March 1939 were located outside the frontiers of Czechoslovakia, were transferred to the *Reich*, and were released from all mortgages. The Protectorates of Bohemia, Moravia and Silesia continued the rights and obligations of Czechoslovakia so far as these were not transferred to the *Reich*, to Hungary, or to Slovakia. The secession of Slovakia was dealt with by a treaty with the *Reich* of 13 April 1940.[4] All the property of Czechoslovakia, factories and public funds situated in the territory of Slovakia became *ipso jure*, and without compensation, the latter's property, and Czechoslovakia had no claims on any of the property of Czechoslovakia situated outside Slovakia territory. The agreement of 21 May 1940[5] provided for the *ipso jure* succession of Hungary to all the private and public

1 Decree no. 60–693, *ibid.* 20 July 1960, p. 6634, art. 36. For Senegal see Gautron in *Annuaire français* (1962), p. 342; in *ibid.* 1964, p. 839. Generally see Fouilloux in *ibid.* (1965), p. 885; Tixier in *ibid.* p. 916.
2 Decree no. 632–70, *Journal Officiel*, 21 March 1963, p. 2720.
3 *RGBl.* 2, 24 April 1942.   4 *Ibid.* 20 August 1941.
5 *Ibid.* 6 June 1941.

The Effect on the Public Property of the State

property of Czechoslovakia located in the ceded areas. The treaty between Czechoslovakia and the Soviet of 29 June 1945, relating to the transfer of Carpathia, provided in a protocol for the transfer without compensation of all state property in the territory.[1]

The agreements between the *Reich* and the Protectorate of Bohemia and Moravia of 4 October 1941 and Slovakia of 13 April 1940 and Hungary of 21 May 1940 dealt with debts owing to the State on the same basis as other property. Each of the States succeeded to credits affecting the territories of Czechoslovakia to which it had succeeded. Mortgages passed to the State on whose territory the mortgaged property was situated.

In the agreement between the *Reich* and the Protectorate it was stipulated that the *Reich* acquired all the claims of Czechoslovakia in respect of enterprises carrying on business outside Czechoslovakia within its new frontiers, even if their head office was located in the territory of the Protectorate. Enterprises which carried on business within the new frontiers and partly outside the *Reich* would have the right to demand a repartition. The *Reich* also succeeded to the rights of Czechoslovakia in respect of mortgages of immovable property in the Sudeten lands, and to claims against individuals or companies resident there, as at the date of the transfer of the Sudeten lands. The same principle was applied with respect to mortgages and claims relating to property transferred on 15 March 1939. A similar principle was applied with respect to Slovakia.[2]

By convention of 15 November 1940 between the *Reich*, Slovakia and Hungary,[3] the assets of the Kashau-Oderberger Railway were divided between the three signatories on a territorial basis. The *Reich* received 25 per cent, Slovakia 69.625 per cent and Hungary 5.375 per cent.

With respect to securities in favour of the State, the principle adopted was that, if the rights attached to them could no longer be exercised, then they were returnable to the depositary; and if they could continue to be exercised they were to be transferred to the State which would be competent to do so. Securities deposited in the courts were dealt with differently by the conventions with Hungary and Czechoslovakia. In the former they were to pass to the State which exercised jurisdiction in the account, and in the latter the question was reserved for specific decision.[4]

The conventions concerning Czechoslovakia provided that the rights of local bodies which were not divided in virtue of the territorial cessions would remain intact, and when they were divided then there would be an equitable repartition.

[1] *B.F.S.P.* vol. CXLV, p. 1096; Paenson, p. 104. [2] *Ibid.* p. 109.
[3] *RGBl.* 2, 20 August 1941. [4] Paenson, p. 111.

(iv) *The 'Anschluss' of Austria to the 'Reich', 1938*

Austria attained the same internal status as the other *Länder* in Germany, which after the constitutional reorganization of 1934 became administrative districts. Although it continued thereby to enjoy a certain degree of financial autonomy, under the new *Reich* constitution all the public and private assets of Austria passed to Germany. The Federal Railway system became part of the *Deutsche Reichsbahn*,[1] and all the rights and liabilities attached to the railways became *Reich* public property (*Sondervermögen des Reichs*). The Austrian National Bank was absorbed by the *Reichsbank*.[2]

(v) *The absorption of the Baltic States in the Soviet Union, 1939*

The public and private property of the Baltic States did not pass to the Soviet Union but remained the property of the three Baltic Soviets.

(vi) *The cession of Roumanian territory, 1940*

In the Agreement of Craiova of 7 November 1940, Roumania ceded to Bulgaria part of Dobroudja. This cession was accompanied by a financial agreement in which Bulgaria undertook to pay Roumania a milliard lei, intended to settle all the financial consequences of the transfer, in particular the claims expressly enumerated in Annex D. Roumania ceded all the public property of the State, its provinces and communes, the national bank and various other installations. All other claims were waived. Roumania relinquished all claims in respect of arrears of payments due from persons resident in the ceded territories, as well as from those persons who opted from Bulgarian nationality.[3]

(vii) *The dismemberment of Yugoslavia, 1942*

In 1942 Yugoslavia was partitioned, Croatia and Montenegro becoming vassal States of Italy, the *Reich* annexing part of Croatia, and Italy, Hungary and Bulgaria annexing other parts of Yugoslavia. Serbia retained its personality, but under German occupation. The public property of Yugoslavia was divided between the conquering States. In the event of immovable property being severed by the altered frontiers, the assets were to be divided according to the principles of equity.[4] Arrears of taxes and customs were to be claimable by the State in whose territory the competent office was located, even if the jurisdictional area of the office had been dismembered. Secured credits passed with the territory on which the assets were located.[5]

1 *RGBl.* 1, 17 March 1938.   2 Paenson, p. 143.
3 *Ibid.* p. 109.   4 *Ibid.* p. 154.   5 *Ibid.* p. 153.

(viii) *The Italian Peace Treaty, 1947*

The Peace Treaty with Italy, 1947, referred to public property in very general terms. 'All objects having juridically the character of public property' removed since 4 November 1918 from the territory of Trieste, and those connected with the territory which Italy had received under the Peace Treaties of 1919 and 1920, were to be returned to Yugoslavia.[1] In Annex VI of the Treaty it was provided that the Free Territory of Trieste should receive, without payment, Italian state and para-state property within the Free Territory. These included movable and immovable property of the Italian State, local authorities and public institutions or publicly owned companies and associations, and submarine cables within the territory.[2]

Ethiopia was treated on the same basis.[3] However, the case of Eritrea was reserved for United Nations action, and on 2 September 1950 the General Assembly adopted a Resolution[4] federating Eritrea and Ethiopia. On 19 January 1951 it further resolved[5] to approve the economic and financial provisions in respect of Eritrea arising out of paragraph 19 of Annex XIV of the Peace Treaty, and to adopt a recommendation that Eritrea would receive, without payment, all movable and immovable property located in Eritrea and owned by Italy or by the Italian administration there. This property should comprise the public property of the State (*demanio pubblico*); the inalienable property of the State (*patrimonio indisponibile*); the property of the Italian Fascist party; the alienable property of the State (*patrimonio disponibile*); property belonging to the autonomous agencies of the State, i.e. *Ferrovie dell'Eritrea, Azienda speciale Approvigionamenti, Azienda miniere Africa Orientale (A.M.A.O.), Azienda autonoma strade statali (A.A.S.S.)*; the rights of the Italian State in the form of shares, and similar rights in the capital of institutions, companies and associations of a public character which had a *siège social* in Eritrea. Where the operations of such companies should extend to countries other than Eritrea, then Eritrea should receive only those rights of the Italian State which appertained to operations in Eritrea. The properties mentioned were to be transferred to Eritrea as they stood at the date of transfer, and Eritrea should take over all commitments and liabilities outstanding at that date in connexion with those concerns.[6]

Annex XIV of the Peace Treaty with Italy provided that the Italian

---

1 B.T.S. 1948, no. 50, Cmd. 7481, art. 12 (2).   2 Art. 1.
3 Art. 34.   4 Res. 490 a (V).
5 Gen. Ass. Off. Rec., 6th Sess., 366th meet., p. 413 (U.N. Docs. A/2077, A/2801).
6 U.N. Doc. A/2077.

successor States would receive, without payment, Italian State and parastate property within territory ceded in the Treaty, including movable and immovable property of the Italian State, local authorities, public institutions, and publicly owned companies and associations, as well as property of the Fascist party.[1] It was further agreed that Italy and the successor States would conclude agreements for a just and equitable apportionment of the property of any existing local authority whose area was divided by a frontier settlement.[2] In the areas of Savoy transferred to France part of the common property of some Italian communes passed under French sovereignty, while the inhabitants remained under Italian sovereignty, and vice versa. Since Italy and France were unable to agree on a division of this property, the matter was referred to the Franco-Italian Conciliation Commission.

Italy's position was that the treaty provisions could not be literally applied since this would involve the suppression of the local authorities. Communes in the ceded territory would pass to France while retaining their property, and it was not the intention that this property should fall into the ownership of the French State. The treaty should not be construed as effecting eminent domain, and the apportionment provisions made this evident. France argued that it was clear from the omission of any reservations in the case of the communes that the intention was to transfer the communal property to French national ownership. France could then, in exercise of her sovereignty, reallocate this among the frontier communes.

The Commission upheld the Italian contention,[3] commencing with the assumption[4] that, unless modified by treaty, territorial changes should leave untouched property rights regularly acquired before the change. It held that this assumption operated in favour of communes and other local authorities. The treaty explicitly distinguished between *biens communaux* situated in ceded territory, and those situated anywhere, provided that the commune to which they belonged was divided by the frontier settlement. The former would be transferred to France, while the latter would fall under the principle of apportionment. In so far as *biens communaux* governed by the apportionment paragraph were situated in ceded territory they came within the wider category of *biens communaux* transferred to France. The apportionment rule brought about a derogation in respect of certain *biens communaux*, which would otherwise be regulated by the transfer provision. The *biens communaux* of divided communes were not

1 Art. 1. 2 Art. 18.
3 I.L.R. vol. XX, p. 63. Expressing a view long previously expounded by Selosse, p. 185.
4 At p. 68.

to be subjected to a double treatment, namely transfer to French national ownership, followed by apportionment by agreement, for this would involve a retrocession of the property. The conclusion followed that property reallocated to Italian communes ought to belong to them as private property, even if located in France, for the alternative would not only offend the presumption of non-interference with acquired rights, but transform these into State servitudes, which would not ordinarily be a result of apportionment.

(ix) *The independence of Libya, 1951*

The Italian Peace Treaty made no provision respecting the disposition of the property of Libya, and left this to be dealt with jointly by the United Kingdom, the United States, France and the Soviet at the time of their determination of the future of the country.

The General Assembly resolved[1] to set up a tribunal to determine the economic and financial provisions of the transfer of power from the Italian to the Libyan administration. The resolution provided for Libya to receive, without payment, the movable and immovable property located in Libya and owned by the Italian State, either in its own name or in the name of the Italian administration of Libya. The public property of the State (*demanio pubblico*) and the inalienable property of the State (*patrimonio indisponibile*) in Libya,[2] as well as the relevant archives and documents of an administrative character or technical value concerning either Libya or the property in question, would be immediately transferred, along with the property in Libya of the Fascist party. In addition, Italy and Libya would agree on the conditions of transfer of the alienable property of the State in Libya (*patrimonio disponibile*) and the property in Libya belonging to the autonomous agencies (*aziende autonome*) of the State, as well as the rights of the State in the capital and property of institutions, companies and associations of a public character located in Libya, and, in the case of companies etc. operating outside as well as inside Libya, appertaining to operations in Libya.

The *Ad Hoc* Political Committee annexed an Explanation of Certain Points in the Draft Resolution submitted to the General Assembly,[3] in which it was stated that the rights in question included shareholding and similar rights owned by the Italian State, either in its own name, or in that of the Italian administration in Libya. It also added that the tribunal, 'whose decisions should be based on law', should apply the rules of law

[1] Res. 388 (V) Gen. Ass. Off. Rec., 5th Sess., Supp., no. 20. U.N. Doc. A/1775.
[2] See Italian Civil Code, 1942, arts. 822, 826, 828.
[3] U.N. Doc. A/1726.

and not decide *ex aequo et bono*, and it would 'thus apply the General Assembly resolution in the light of the principles of international law and of the rules for the interpretation of international texts'.

On 28 June 1951, Italy and the United Kingdom entered into an accord concerning the disposition of Italian property in Libya, pursuant to the General Assembly Resolution.[1] Article 5 provided that the United Kingdom would release the property of some twenty-five named 'institutions, companies and associations', including the Bank of Naples, the Bank of Sicily, the National Assurance Institute, the Royal Automobile Club of Italy, and the Institute for the Colonization of Libya, and stated that the property of three of these would be released to liquidators and would be liquidated in accordance with the law in force in Libya, while the property of the remainder would be handed over to 'duly appointed representatives'. The final arrangements for dealing with the property of the Institute for the Colonization of Libya would be made in due course in accordance with the terms of article IX of the General Assembly Resolution. On 7 November 1951[2] the two Governments further agreed that the management of all property in Cyrenaica, other than the property referred to in article 5 (5), and (9), would be undertaken by an officer nominated by the Italian Government, until the property could be released to the owners.

The assumption underlying this agreement was that the property which was not to be liquidated was privately owned property, and this assumption was contested by Libya, which sought a ruling from the Tribunal set up by the General Assembly Resolution. Italy argued that, in order to decide whether the Italian State possessed a *droit patrimonial* in the concerns mentioned in the article, it was necessary to ascertain first whether their operation was confined to Libya. The public nature of the concerns was a matter to be determined by Italian law alone. Libya's case was that in the Peace Treaty Italy had renounced all rights and titles belonging to her in Libya, and the resolution, being based on the treaty, had the effect only of realizing a right which had already come into existence as a result of the general renunciation, which included not only rights attaching to the State in the exercise of its sovereignty but also rights belonging to it in its capacity of a juridical person of private law. Therefore, Libya argued, she was entitled to public institutions belonging to the Italian State in its entirety, the part owned by Italy of public utility undertakings which were not public institutions, and the shares and *droit patrimonial* of any kind owned by the Italian State in private institutions.

[1] *U.N.T.S.* vol. CXVIII, p. 115.
[2] *Ibid.* p. 133.

The Effect on the Public Property of the State

The Tribunal held[1] that it should resort to the treaty only when the resolution was insufficiently clear. From a survey of the *travaux préparatoires* of the resolution it concluded that the draftsman intended the expression *ente pubblico* to have a meaning wider than that in Italian law, and that hence Italian law would not be decisive. In any event, Italian law did not support the Libyan contention that the property of all public institutions belonged to the State. So far as shares and *droit patrimonial* were concerned, the resolution, as explained by the *Ad Hoc* Committee, excluded the notion that concerns of a private nature were affected. The fact that such concerns were not mentioned could only be explained by the fact that such rights belonging to the Italian State were not to be transferred to Libya.

The Italian Government also contended that the resolution did not apply to concerns having their *siège social* in Italy, but the Tribunal held that the expression 'located' in Libya related to the 'rights of the State' and not to the 'institutions, companies and associations' mentioned. On the other hand, the Tribunal upheld the Italian contention that the only rights transferable to Libya were those possessed by the Italian State in its own name, or in the name of the Italian administration in Libya. In the case of the Bank of Naples, it was found that the Italian Government had no capital in the institution, nor any rights with respect to profits, and the fact that the Bank was subject to close governmental control and participated in Government enterprises was insufficient to constitute it a public concern. The test of ultimate vesting of the assets on liquidation led to the conclusion that the property of certain of the institutions was transferable to Italy, but not that of others.

So far as the private property, or *patrimonio disponibile*, of Italy was concerned, the United Nations Tribunal for Libya held that the Peace Treaty provisions must be interpreted in favour of the customary rule of international law that private State property, that is, property which the State possesses in the same manner as a private person in order to derive income from it, does not pass to the successor State.[2] Accordingly, title to the Italian *patrimonio disponibile* in Libya had not been lost. Libya, pursuant to the resolution of the General Assembly, was entitled to hold the property, but was required to abstain from disposing of it without Italy's consent, and was obliged to maintain the existing administrative agency entrusted with its custodianship.

1 *Italy v. Libya*, I.L.R. vol. XXII, p. 103.
2 *Italy v. Great Britain and Libya*, ibid. vol. XXV, p. 2.

(x) The partition of India, 1948

All the lands vested in the Viceroy were transferred three days before independence to the Governor-General so that they became the public property of the Dominion of India and passed to it without compensation. The official description of these lands was 'land vested in His Majesty for the purpose of the Governor-General in Council'. Land situated outside British India became joint property of the two Dominions. If the land was situated in an Indian State which in the course of one month from independence acceded to one or other Dominion, then the land would become the property of that Dominion. If the land was situated outside the subcontinent it would become the property of India.[1] All the land belonging to the governments of the provinces of Bengal, Punjab and Assam was divided between the two parts of each province according to their locality. The same principle was applied with respect to the lands of the Central Government.

On 18 June 1947 an Expert Committee (no. II) was appointed to examine the problem of apportionment of the assets and liabilities of British India. The presumption guiding its deliberations was that India would remain a constant international person, and Pakistan would constitute a successor State. The assets to be distributed consisted of capitalized assets of a non-productive character, capital assets acquired out of revenue and borne on charge either with value, such as buildings, stores, factories, or without value, such as stores in ordnance depots; assets acquired out of revenue and not borne on charge, such as shop tools and consumable stores drawn for current use; assets not paid for by the Government of India, but received as gifts; buildings and stores belonging to the British Government and in the custody of the Government of India; and assets taken over from the American army.

An agreement was concluded between India and Pakistan on 1 December 1947[2] which confirmed the principle of automatic succession of each of the Dominions to the public lands within its territory, including railways, post offices and other public buildings. The equipment and stores of the Post and Telegraph Department and the Railways were, however, divided according to a complicated formula which took into account the distances involved and the density of the traffic. All arms factories and munitions were attributed to the Dominion of India according to their book valuation, and India undertook to pay Pakistan a sum of 6 crores of rupees for the construction of new munitions factories in

[1] In fact, this was mainly diplomatic real estate.
[2] *Reserve Bank of India Bulletin* (1948), no. 2, p. 72.

Pakistan. Pakistan was to take over one third of military equipment and material.[1] All the military installations and material and equipment of the United Kingdom located in India were transferred on 1 April 1947 to the Government of India.[2] In virtue of the Financial Agreement of 9 July 1948[3] they were divided between the Dominion of India and the United Kingdom acting on behalf of Pakistan, against compensation of £100,000,000. Movable property and cash of the Government of British India and/or the Governments of the Provinces of Bengal and Punjab were divided between the Dominions and/or the provinces respectively, on the same basis as real property.[4] All other assets were to be transferred jointly. India succeeded to the funds of the Reserve Bank estimated at £1,160,000,000.[5] This sum was divided into two more or less equal accounts, known as no. 1 and no. 2 accounts. One of these was in freed currency and the other in blocked currency. India also undertook to transfer balances to an account to be opened in the Bank of England under the name of Pakistan. Funds of the Central Government and the partitioned provinces were to be divided. It was arranged that the Government of India would pay to that of Pakistan that portion of the Government's bank profits in respect of the period commencing 1 July 1947 and ending 30 September 1948 which bore to the total of such profits in respect of this period the same proportion as the total value of the Pakistan notes to the total value of all notes in circulation in that Dominion on 30 September 1948.[6] As soon after that date as practicable, there were to be transferred from the issue department of the bank to the Government of Pakistan assets which had together a value equal to the total liability in respect of Pakistan notes in circulation on that date.[7] Reserve funds of the bank were apportioned on the basis of the uncovered debt.[8] It was also laid down that where either of the Dominions or any Province became entitled to any property or obtained any other benefit, and it was 'just and equitable' that that property or those benefits should be transferred to or shared with the other Dominion, or with any other Province, then they were to be allocated in such manner as, in default of agreement, might be determined by the Arbitral Tribunal.[9]

1 For Pakistan's difficulty in getting control of these assets see Rushbrook Williams, *The State of Pakistan* (1962), p. 33.
2 Financial Agreement of 14 August 1947, Cmd. 7195.
3 Cmd. 7472.
4 Indian Independence (Rights, Property and Liabilities) Order, 1947, s. 6.
5 Financial Agreement of 14 August 1947, Cmd. 7195.
6 Pakistan (Monetary System and Reserve Bank) Order, 1947, pt. IV, s. 1 (2).
7 S. 4 (1).   8 S. 4 (6).
9 Indian Independence (Rights, Property and Liabilities) Order, 1947.

The agreement between India and Pakistan of 1 December 1947[1] and the Pakistan Monetary System and Reserve Bank Order, 1947, fixed the division of the cash and bullion of the Reserve Bank of India amounting to 400 crores of rupees, of which Pakistan received 75 crores. Pakistan also received from the Reserve Bank part of its assets calculated on a percentage of paper money circulating in Pakistan, adjusted by reference to certain obligations of Pakistan towards the Bank, and under this heading Pakistan received 75 per cent.

(xi) *The cession of the Indian Establishments, 1954*

The agreement of 21 October 1954[2] between France and India respecting the cession of the French Establishments in India provided that the latter would be substituted for the former in all credits, debts and deficits relating to the local administration.[3] All food stocks accumulated in the territory for the local population, whether charged to the metropolitan or local budgets, would be repurchased by the Indian Government.[4] Immovable property situated in the territory would be ceded to the Government of India, with the exception of property reserved to French political and cultural missions in the territory.[5]

(xii) *The independence of the Philippines, 1946*

According to the Act of 1934,[6] all the public and private domain acquired by the United States in 1898 was transferred to the Commonwealth of the Philippines with the exception of lands reserved for military bases of the United States or already disposed of.

(xiii) *The independence of Syria and the Lebanon, 1946*

The public domain of these two mandated territories was attributed to them as legal entities.[7] French military installations and material were transferred with possession at a fixed valuation of 20,000,000 Lebanese pounds and 23,200,000 Syrian pounds by treaties of 24 January 1948[8] with the Lebanon and of 7 February 1949 with Syria. Both countries succeeded jointly to the assets of the *intérêts communs*, which consisted of 5,660,000 Syrian pounds in cash and other items representing the interest of the State in various concessions. Both countries also succeeded to the funds of the Bank of Syria and Lebanon, amounting to 10,203,864,576 French francs, respecting Syria. The amount for Lebanon is not indicated. The

1 *Reserve Bank of India Bulletin* (1948), no. 2.
2 *Annuaire français* (1955), p. 703.
3 Art. 20.   4 Art. 21.   5 Art. 22.
6 Tydings-McDuffie Act, sect. II, art. 5, 48 Stat. 127.
7 Paenson, p. 65.   8 *Journal Officiel*, 15 March 1949, p. 2651.

total sum was in blocked currency which was to be liberated progressively up to 1958. During this period the contracting parties mutually agreed upon the stability of the rate of exchange, basing it on parity between the French franc and the pound sterling, as fixed by the International Monetary Fund. There were certain provisions relating to the use to which the released currency was to be put.

The agreement between France and Turkey of 23 June 1939[1] concerning the cession of the Sandjak of Alexandretta provided for the cession to Turkey of all the property rights and interests of all French companies and of the immovable property of every French national against global compensation of 35,000,000 French francs. This sum was intended also to compensate the French State for the military installations which were transferred.

(xiv) *The independence of Burma, 1948*

Burma succeeded to all the property of the Government of Burma as constituted in the Government of Burma Act, 1935.[2] The United Kingdom gave important financial aid in the Financial Agreement of 30 April 1947[3] and the Defence Agreement of 29 August 1947.[4] In virtue of its Independence Agreement,[5] Burma succeeded without compensation to all the military installations, equipment, etc., of the United Kingdom in Burma, but undertook to transfer to the United Kingdom the proceeds of the sale of provisions and material of the civil and military administrations.

(xv) *The independence of Israel, 1948*

The opinion of the Permanent Mandates Commission, confirmed by a memorandum of the Legal Section of the League of Nations of 20 May 1924, was that the public and private domain of a State situated within the territories constituted territorial assets, and that the mandatories had only *pouvoirs de gestion*. This point of view was accepted in principle by the mandatories.[6]

The operative principle underlying the agreement between Israel and the United Kingdom of 30 March 1950[7] was that Israel had succeeded to the property of the Palestine High Commission, whereas property of the

1 *Ibid.* 14 July 1939; *B.F.S.P.* vol. CXLIII, p. 477.
2 26 Geo. V & Edw. VIII, c. 2.
3 *Hansard*, 22 May 1947, 437 *H. C. Deb.* 5 s., col. 276.
4 Annexed to the Treaty of Independence, Cmd. 7360, p. 9.
5 *B.T.S.* 1948, no. 16; Cmd. 7360.
6 *L.N. Off. J.* vol. V (1924), p. 333, 4th meeting.
7 *B.T.S.* 1950, no. 26; Cmd. 7941; *U.N.T.S.* vol. LXXVI, p. 231.

United Kingdom in Israel was to be purchased by Israel if neither withdrawn by the United Kingdom nor transferred by it to the Israeli Government. Israel, then, succeeded to the public domain of the High Commission in Palestine *ipso jure*, and without compensation, and this was recognized municipally by retroactive legislation in 1951.[1] The domain was defined as all immovable property, and mines, minerals, all movable property, and all rights, whether vested or contingent, which on 14 May 1948 were held by the Government of Palestine or any of its departments or services, or by the High Commissioner, whether as trustee for the Government of Palestine or otherwise, or by some other functionary of the Government of Palestine. The United Kingdom owned the lands and installations of the War Office and the R.A.F. In article 7 of the agreement of 30 March 1950[2] Israel acquired these on limited compensation of £1,700,000 of the £5,882,000 which it had to pay the United Kingdom.

With respect to financial matters, provisional arrangements were made as follows: Government funds were to be transferred to trustees;[3] sinking fund accumulations held by trustees nominated by the Treasury under the Palestine Loan Ordinance of 1942 were to continue to be held by the trustees in trust for the repayment of the principal moneys;[4] sinking funds held by the Crown agents in trust for the Government of Palestine under any ordinance providing for the issue of bearer bonds should vest in the Crown agents, and be held by them until the Secretary of State should direct the transfer of the funds to some authority or authorities succeeding to the Government of Palestine.[5]

All the local funds of the administration other than enemy property were transferred to the Government of the United Kingdom by the agreement of 30 March 1950.[6] The balance was £381,000 and the final accounting between Israel and the United Kingdom was to be settled in thirty biennial remittances. Israel and the United Kingdom agreed to renounce sums due to the Mandatory Administration by way of income tax and company profits tax, but, by the Law and Administration Ordinance of 21 May 1948,[7] the Government of Israel required payment to it of all sums due to the Government of Palestine not liquidated on 14 May 1948. Israel succeeded to the credits of the Mandatory Administration in respect of loans granted to local bodies,[8] but renounced any claim to property of

---

1 Law on State Property, Laws of the State of Israel, 5 (5711–1950/51), p. 45.
2 *U.N.T.S.* vol. LXXXVI, p. 231.
3 Termination of Jurisdiction in Palestine (Transitional Provisions) Order in Council, 1948, S.R. & O. 1946, no. 1603, s. 3.
4 *Ibid.* s. 4.   5 *Ibid.* s. 5.   6 Art. 2 (*a*) (2).
7 Law and Administration Ordinance, Official Gazette no. 2, 21 May 1948.
8 Art. 4 of the agreement of 30 March 1950.

The Effect on the Public Property of the State

the Mandatory Administration not situated in Israel, and also, in article 2 (*d*), to the surplus of £2,000,000 of the Palestine Currency Board. Israel did not succeed to the credit of the United Kingdom in respect of certain deliveries made to the Mandatory Administration and amounting to £669,000.

In 1954 the District Court of Haifa considered the provision in the agreement of 30 March 1950 in which the United Kingdom transferred to Israel its rights and interests in assets, including land, in Israel, held by or on behalf of the War Office. The Israel Defence Ministry claimed that it was entitled to land requisitioned by the British army in Palestine in 1941, on which the British army had erected buildings. In an action brought by the titleholder of the land it was held that the Government of Israel was not the successor to the British administration, and that the British army remained the legal owner of the requisitioned property. Since the British army had agreed with the plaintiff after the termination of the mandate to restore the land and buildings to the plaintiff in consideration of the waiver by the latter of all claims arising from the requisition, an agreement of a private character had been made which was enforceable in the courts. The agreement of 1950 could affect only property at that date in the ownership of the British army, and could not affect property already the subject of an agreement for restitution.[1]

The Israel Supreme Court held that Israel could sue on a bond previously given in favour of the Attorney-General of Palestine. This was based on Section 21 of the Law and Administration Ordinance, 1948, by which taxes and payments of every kind which had not been paid to the Government of Palestine were payable to Israel, and by the State Property Law of 1951, which asserted the right of Israel to all vested and contingent, movable and immovable property of the Government of Palestine.[2]

(xvi) *The transfer of Newfoundland to Canada, 1949*

The British North America Act, 1949, provided[3] that Canada would take over certain services, and the property connected with them. This included the real and personal property of the Newfoundland Railway, the airport at Gander, the Newfoundland Hotel, harbours, wharves, navigation aids, bait depots, certain ships, military and naval property, stores and equipment, the public telecommunication and broadcasting services, and all public works and property used primarily for services taken over by Canada. Where buildings were used partly for services

---

[1] *Khayat* v. *Attorney-General, I.L.R.* vol. XXII, p. 123.
[2] *Attorney-General* v. *Levitan*, ibid. vol. XVIII, p. 64.
[3] 12 & 13 Geo. V, c. 22, ss. 33 and 34.

taken over by Canada, and partly for services retained by Newfoundland, a scheme of division was agreed upon.

The case of Newfoundland was one of integration in a federal society of territory which had been an autonomous administrative entity, so that it involved really an extension of federal jurisdiction only in accordance with the distribution of legislative powers. The retention by Newfoundland of property dedicated to functions within the provincial powers was a logical solution.

(xvii) *The independence of Indonesia, 1949*

In the Agreement on Transitional Measures, 2 November 1949,[1] article 4, Indonesia succeeded to all the public and private property of the Netherlands Indies, and was recognized by the Netherlands also to have acquired title to certain military and naval installations and material of the Netherlands transferred by agreement. It was conceded that the rights and duties of the Indies were proper to them as a separate juridical entity.[2] However, an unexpected use was made by Indonesia of this recognition. Numerous Netherlands citizens were billed by Indonesia for payment of obligations alleged to have been due to the Indies.[3] Considerable political feeling was aroused in the Netherlands on the subject, and in the Financial and Economic Agreement of 1954[4] between the Netherlands and Indonesia, the latter was 'bought off' by the former for a sum of 20 million guilders, a global payment in satisfaction of all outstanding private obligations.

(xviii) *The independence of Indochina, 1953*

The public domain in Indochina consisted of (1) French public property known as the *domaine colonial*; (2) the property of a former federation of Indochina administered by the former Governor-General and known as the *domaine général*; (3) the property of each colony or protectorate known as the *domaines locals*; (4) the property of the provinces and communes.[5]

The protocol of 29 August 1953[6] transferring French judicial jurisdiction to Cambodia provided for the acquisition by Cambodia of all movable and immovable property of the French judicial services, as well as of all immovable property used by them for administrative purposes. The same provision was included in the Franco-Laotian Judicial Convention of 22 October 1953[7] and the similar Convention with Vietnam of

1 *U.N.T.S.* vol. LXIX, p. 3.   2 See *supra*, p. 97.
3 Tervooren, pp. 189, 234.   4 *U.N.T.S.* vol. CCXLI, p. 129.
5 Paenson, p. 67.
6 Decree no. 59–593, *Journal Officiel*, 3 May 1959, p. 4758.
7 *Ibid.*

15 September 1954.[1] In 1956, in reply to a question in the French Assembly, the French Foreign Minister stated that the transfer to the Government of Vietnam of competence arising from the French *réquisition du logement* had been effected by an exchange of letters of 16 September 1954. He stated that it was for the Vietnamese authorities *à se prononcer ultérieurement* on the renewal of requisitions.[2]

The test employed for partitioning the assets and credits of the Governor-Generalate of Indochina was that of territorial, or 'geographical', connexion. Credits and debits were to be identified territorially, and the elements of the *actif* and *passif* were to be balanced by compensating accounts between Vietnam, Cambodia and Laos, all of which guaranteed equality of exchange during the period. The national issuing bodies were subrogated in the rights and duties of the Union of Indochina, and operations of the Trésor Indochinois were taken in charge by the French Treasury, and covered by a loan of 318 million piastres. The balance was to be imputed as a debit on account of the Trésor Indochinois to the French Treasury, which would service the loans issued by the Governor-Generalate. The *actif* and *passif* were to be divided geographically, and where this was not possible the national State, or the State of domicile of the creditor, was to be responsible. The public domain would become the property of the State where it was located; the balance of the private domain, after liquidation of the treasury accounts, would be distributed in the proportion 19.75 per cent to Cambodia, 6 per cent to Laos, and 74.25 per cent to Vietnam. Where possible the distribution was to be effected by allocating property situated in the territories of the States, and otherwise by a cash adjustment. A technical commission was set up to implement the plan.[3]

(xix) *The formation of Somalia, 1960*

Section 57 of the Constitution of Somaliland, which was annexed to the Somaliland Order in Council, 1960, by which British Somaliland attained independence, provided for the vesting in the Government of Somaliland of all property, including any rights arising from contract or otherwise, which immediately before the commencement of the Constitution vested in the Crown. There was no such provision respecting the trust territory, but when the Somali Republic and Somaliland fused, provision was made in the Act of Union (which was retrospective to 1 July 1960) for the transfer to the Somali Republic of all rights vested in

1 *Ibid.* 2 *Annuaire français* (1955), p. 778.
3 'Accord relatif au transfer des institutions monétaires aux États du Cambodge, du Laos, et du Vietnam', Protocols 1 and 2, Decree no. 73–NG, 17 March 1955, *Cong Báo Vietnam*, 1955, p. 670.

the independent Governments of Somaliland and Somalia. As there was never an independent Somalia, it has been argued that the effect of article 4 was to make the Somali Republic the successor of the Government of Somaliland only.[1]

(xx) *The dismemberment of the Mali Federation, 1960*

In 1961 a conference was held between Mali and Senegal in which the assets of the Mali Federation were divided in proportions of 62 per cent for Senegal and 38 per cent for Mali.[2] Against these figures was offset the service of debts which the Federation had assumed, arising out of the liquidation of the property of the French West African group of territories. With respect to postal orders and similar charges, each State undertook to reimburse holders resident in its territory. The same principle of localization governed the division of the credits of the federal post office, railways, and the port of Dakar.

(xxi) *The independence of the Congo (Léopoldville), 1960*

The political crisis in the Congo that occurred immediately after independence presented a formal transfer of property to the new State. Assets of the colony located in the territory were assumed to have passed with the grant of independence. But the colony had owned a portfolio of shares in Belgian companies, valued in 1959 at $750 million. (This had declined by 1965 to $300 million on the New York Stock Exchange.[3]) A *Comité spécial du Katanga* was set up in Brussels to manage the assets which were in issue pending a political settlement. Such a settlement was negotiated early in 1964,[4] but had to be renegotiated in February 1965. The *Compagnie du Katanga* recognized the transmission to the Congo of all assets managed by the *Comité spécial*, and all profits deriving therefrom, and conceded to the Republic the right to collect its share of royalties from the companies holding concessions from the *Compagnie du Katanga* (see *infra*, p. 444). It ceded to the Congo 12,500 shares of common stock in *Union Minière du Haut-Katanga*. In return the Republic recognized the transmission to the Company of assets and profits managed in Belgium by the *Comité spécial*, and retroceded to it the 1,800 preferred shares and the 143,962 shares of common stock still registered in the name of the Belgian Congo.[5]

1 Cotran in *I.C.L.Q.* (1963), p. 1011.
2 *Annuaire français* (1961), p. 1024; Gautron in *ibid.* (1962), p. 861.
3 *New York Times*, 6 February 1965, p. 1.
4 *The Times*, 21 March 1964, p. 7.
5 Press Release, 11 February 1965 of the Belgo-American Development Corporation: *International Legal Materials*, vol. IV (1965), p. 239.

The Republic of the Congo agreed to assume the liabilities of the *Comité spécial* in the Congo, while the *Compagnie du Katanga* agreed to assume its liabilities in Belgium. The Republic also agreed to compensate Belgian private interests for the acquisition of Congo mining rights (see *infra*, p. 343), amounting to $25 million, including $20 million to the Company in respect of *Union Minière* shareholding. A debt-discharging institution would be set up to replace $250 million in Congolese bonds with a forty-year issue, and accumulated interest on bonds would be paid.[1]

The financial settlement reached between Belgium and the Congo (Léopoldville) in March 1964 involved the transfer to the latter of incorporeal assets and claims calculated in the schedule of interests in the budget of the Belgian Congo in 1960.[2]

(xxii) *The independence of Algeria, 1962*

The Evian Agreement of 19 March 1962[3] dealt with Algeria's succession to French assets in the most general terms. Algeria would enjoy the rights contracted in its name, and in the name of Algerian public establishments by French authorities; public real estate would be transferred to it, together with patrimonial funds allotted for the administration of the public services. The French Government has taken the view that Algeria thereby became entitled to arrears of tax, and the problem of recovery of these in France was made the subject of investigation. The relations between the French and Algerian Treasuries resulting from an agreement of 31 December 1962 would not seem to make recovery possible under French law.[4]

(xxiii) *The dissolution of the Federation of the West Indies, 1962*

The process of dismantling the Federation's structure[5] was committed to a Commissioner for the Territories, with extensive powers.[6] All the property, rights, liabilities and contracts of the Federation would vest in him,[7] and he would be responsible for determining their allocation. To date the accounts have not been completed.

1 *New York Times*, 6 February 1965, p. 1.
2 See *supra*, p. 444. Renegotiated in January 1965, see *ibid*.
3 Declaration of Principles Concerning Economic and Financial Co-operation, *A.J.* vol. LVII (1963), arts. 18, 19; *Journal Officiel* (March 1962), p. 3019.
4 *Annuaire français* (1963), p. 1017.
5 The West Indies (Dissolution and Interim Commission) Order in Council, S.I. 1962, no. 1084.
6 S. 4.   7 S. 8.

(xxiv) *The dissolution of the Federation of Rhodesia and Nyasaland, 1963*

The Order in Council[1] dissolving the Federation created a body corporate called the Liquidating Agency whose functions were the disposal of the assets and liabilities of the Federation by way of apportionment and distribution. It would also exercise until 31 March 1963 the functions of the Federal Commissioner of Taxes. Its statutory powers were considerable.[2] It was provided that freehold property of the Federation situate in a Territory would vest in the Crown in right of the Territory, and property not so situate would vest in the Liquidating Agency. Movable property of the Federation would entirely vest in the Agency, and be subject to antecedent liabilities.[3] Claims by and against the Federal Government would vest in and against the Agency.[4] Assets and liabilities of the Post Office Savings Bank were also vested in the Agency,[5] but would be apportioned among the Territories according to the location of the depositors. Certain Federal bodies concerned with marketing, broadcasting and airways[6] were wound up and their property vested in the Agency.[7] Separate joint bodies were created by agreement between Northern Rhodesia and Southern Rhodesia, and given statutory authority in the Order. These related to electricity,[8] railways[9] and air.[10] A modified customs union was also created.[11]

The Liquidating Agency consisted of the Treasurers of the three Territories, whose resolutions were deemed to indicate the agreement of their respective governments. The framework within which decisions were taken was the Order in Council read in conjunction with the Reports of a Committee (known as Committee A), which had been set up under the presidency of the United Kingdom before the Order was drafted.[12] Report No. 6 of this Committee dealt with the distribution of uncollected taxes and the Federal revenue surplus. The key to the distribution of taxes would be as follows: during the period of federation the Federal Government had retained 62 per cent of taxes, and distributed the balance to the

1 Federation of Rhodesia and Nyasaland (Dissolution) Order in Council, S.I. 1963, no. 2085.
2 Ss. 5–9. 3 S. 10. 4 S. 11.
5 S. 14.   6 S. 56. 7 S. 17.
8 Central African Power Corporation, Southern Rhodesia Govt. Notice no. 657A of 1963.
9 Rhodesia Railways, *ibid.* no. 750B of 1962.
10 Central African Airways Corporation, *ibid.* no. 750A of 1963.
11 *Ibid.*; no. 25A of 1964.
12 These Reports have not been made public and are classified documents. They have been examined by courtesy of the Liquidating Agency. For background to Committee A's work see Rhodesia and Nyasaland Parliamentary Debates, 1963, col. 1565.

The Effect on the Public Property of the State

Territories in the ratio of 14 per cent to Southern Rhodesia, 18 per cent to Northern Rhodesia, and 6 per cent to Nyasaland. This account would be closed as at 31 December, and the taxation revenue for the remaining six months of the fiscal year would be totally distributed to the Territories, which now, in addition to their ordinary percentages, would participate in the 62 per cent representing the Federal Government's income in the ratio respectively of 14/38 : 18/38 : 6/38.

Nyasaland repudiated the Federation and withdrew from it *de facto*, although not *de jure*, on 31 July 1963. During the five months between its withdrawal from the Federation and the latter's final dissolution Nyasaland gradually took over various services. Up to the date of taking them over it paid the Federal Government for the cost of maintaining them, and after that date it collected the revenues attaching to them. The net result of this taking over, plus the distribution of federal taxes, was to accord Nyasaland a financial gain. For this reason it was resolved that Nyasaland would not participate in the distribution of the revenue account surplus (excluding taxes), which would be distributed to Southern and Northern Rhodesia in the ratios respectively of 44/65 and 21/65.[1] Included in this surplus were items, such as Federal Government diplomatic property abroad, which were not covered by either the Order in Council or the Reports of Committee A. The Liquidating Agency resolved that these would be distributed according to the same formula. After all items which could properly be related to services taken over by the Territories had been accounted for, there remained, as at November 1964, a sum denominated 'unallocatable revenue' of £401,470 available for distribution, offset against which was a sum denominated 'unallocatable expenditure' of £178,597.[2]

Many Federal assets were divided by agreement. For example, departmental libraries and furnishings were allocated after a process of bargaining. Southern Rhodesia was given Rhodesia House in London and Zambia the Rhodesian High Commissioner's house.

The Order in Council provided for the Liquidating Agency to satisfy claims existing before the date of dissolution. This was interpreted by the Liquidating Agency to mean rights of action accruing before 31 December 1963, but not thereafter. A particular problem arose with respect to property leased by the Federal Government. The Liquidating Agency resolved that all leases had expired on the date of dissolution, and only

---

1 The basis of this key is explained, *infra*, p. 393.
2 The accounts of the Federation up to 31 December 1963, and those of the Liquidating Agency have not been published and are classified documents. They have been examined by courtesy of the Liquidating Agency.

rights of action under the lease already accrued could be pursued. For example, if the lease contained a clause that the lessee should restore the premises to the condition they were in at the commencement of the leasehold, this was considered to create an obligation already in existence at the date of termination of the lease, and all claims arising under such clauses were honoured.

(xxv) *The formation of Malaysia, 1963, and the separation of Singapore, 1965*

The Constitution of Malaysia provided for the succession of the Federal Government of Malaysia to any land vested in a Borneo State or Singapore and used by the United Kingdom or a State for purposes which on Malaysia Day would become federal purposes.[1] Other property used for government services would be apportioned between the Federal Government and the State with regard to the respective needs of the Federal and State Governments, the balance of apportionment to be preserved by adjustment of the burden, as between the Federation and the State, of the latter's financial liabilities.[2] All rights, liabilities and obligations relating to any matter which was the responsibility of a Borneo State or of Singapore, but which on that date would become the responsibility of the Federal Government, would devolve upon the Federation. The Attorney-General would certify whether the right, liability or obligation was that of the State or the Federation.[3] The Constitutions of the States provided for the vesting therein of 'all property and assets', and all 'rights, liabilities and obligations' which were vested in the British Crown.[4]

When Singapore separated, it was enacted that property which before Malaysia day had been that of Singapore, and on that day or after became that of Malaysia, should devolve again on Singapore.[5]

4. ARCHIVES

Documents which relate to absorbed territory fall within the category of public property.[6] If the territory is a separate administrative division, the ownership of archives maintained by the local administration is transferred with the territory. Difficulties arise, however, in the case of those documents which relate to the predecessor State as a whole, and only incidentally constitute a record of its transactions in the absorbed territory.

1 Cmd. 2094. 2 S. 75. 3 S. 76.
4 *State of Singapore Govt. Gazette*, 9 August 1965, no. 1824; Malaysia Law no. 53 of 1965, s. 9; *International Legal Materials*, vol. IV (1965), p. 939.
5 Sabah, ss. 49, 50; Sarawak, ss. 47, 48; Singapore, ss. 103, 104.
6 Schönborn, p. 82; Huber, p. 68.

The Effect on the Public Property of the State

Such documents remain the property of the predecessor State, but it is generally agreed that copies of them must be furnished to the successor State on demand. Although there is no substantial authority for the proposition, it would seem in principle that taxation records become the property of the State having the right to collect taxes in a territory, staff files of officials go to the State which retains their services, and public trust documents and land registration instruments pass to the State taking over the rights and responsibilities relating to these matters.

The Treaty of Versailles provided that the German Government would hand over without delay to France all archives, registers, plans, titles and documents of every kind concerning the civil, military and financial, judicial or other administrative institutions of the territories restored to French sovereignty.[1] Under the Peace Treaty with Italy of 1947, the several successor States of Italy received all relevant archives and documents of an administrative character and historical value relating to the transferred territory. In addition, Italy was obliged to restore all archives relating to territory taken from France in 1940, and at other times from Yugoslavia and Ethiopia. With respect to Trieste, all archives held by both Italy and Yugoslavia were to be delivered to the Free Territory.[2] The Franco-Italian Conciliation Commission held that the provisions of the Italian Peace Treaty referring to the apportionment of property of communes whose area was divided by the cession of Italian territory to France were not applicable to archives, which, even if they belonged to a commune whose area was divided, would pass to the successor State if they concerned the territory or related to the property transferred; otherwise they remained with Italy.[3]

The treaty between the Protectorate of Bohemia and Moravia and Germany of 4 October 1941[4] provided that all the assets of Czechoslovakia not expressly transferred to the *Reich* would remain the property of the Protectorate. Archives concerning the assets transferred to the *Reich*, Hungary or Slovakia passed to these countries. The Treaty of Craiova[5] provided that the local archives of municipalities, communes, departments, etc., in the ceded territory would be passed to Bulgaria, together with certified copies of documents located in Bucharest.

The agreement of 21 October 1954[6] between France and India respecting the French Establishments in India provided that France would

1 Art. 52. See also Treaty of St Germain, art. 93.
2 *U.N.T.S.* vol. XLIX, p. 126, Annex XIV (18) (1).
3 *Frontier (Local Authorities) Award*, I.L.R. vol. XX, p. 69.
4 *RGBl.* II, 24 November 1942.
5 *B.F.S.P.* vol. CXLIV, p. 247.
6 *Annuaire français* (1955), p. 703.

keep archives of historical interest, and deliver to India those which would be necessary for the administration of the territory,[1] including judicial records.[2] The protocol of 29 August 1953[3] transferring French judicial jurisdiction to Cambodia provided for the transfer to Cambodia of all judicial records, with the exception of documents relating to French civil status, which should be deposited with the French High Commissioner.

According to the agreement of 30 March 1950[4] with the United Kingdom, Israel retained the archives of the Mandatory Administration, but undertook to grant free access to the United Kingdom, India and Pakistan. Land registration records concerning former German-owned property in Palestine had been removed to Australia during the war. These were not returned, but Israel was given access to them. Australia held the documents for Germany pending settlement of the *Templar Case*.[5] The archives transferred to India or Pakistan were the subject of agreement of 1 December 1947 between the two Dominions. Archives relating to one of the Dominions exclusively went to it. The others were copied and distributed.

1 Art. 33.   2 Art. 10.
3 Clunet, vol. LXXXVII, p. 251. For Laos see *ibid*. p. 255, art. 3.
4 *U.N.T.S.* vol. LXXXVI, p. 231.   5 See *infra*, p. 287.

PART III

THE DOCTRINE OF ACQUIRED RIGHTS IN THE LAW OF STATE SUCCESSION

The municipal law obligations of the predecessor State which are to be considered in this Part are many and diverse. The most obviously important obligation is the national debt, which is owed either to an international organization, to other States, or to private creditors. This national debt may, for the purposes of study, be conveniently subdivided into the general public debt and local administrative debts. The obligation which the predecessor State has in both cases is to repay the principal and interest in the stipulated manner. Partaking to some extent of the character of administrative debts, but possessing different legal constituents, are administrative contracts. The rights acquired against the State by a private person under such a contract are purely incorporeal. In this sense an administrative contract may be distinguished from a concessionary contract. A concessionaire ordinarily acquires under his contract not only rights *in personam* against the State, but also an interest *in re* in real property. His rights are at once corporeal and incorporeal. In the subsequent chapters an inquiry will be made as to the extent to which international law requires the successor State to respect the rights and obligations constituted by these various legal relationships.

Chapter 10

STATE SUCCESSION AND THE DOCTRINE OF ACQUIRED RIGHTS

1. THE NATURE OF THE MUNICIPAL LAW OBLIGATIONS OF THE STATE

The rights of private persons may consist in their ownership and possession of assets, their claims against other private persons, or their claims against the State. In the terminology of international law, all three categories of rights are referred to as 'acquired rights'. Only if one presumes that the legal system under which rights have been created has evaporated in the instant of change of sovereignty is it necessary to question the survival of private rights in movable and immovable property, or the claims of private persons *inter se*. If the legal system survives the vicissitude of State succession, then these rights are as effective after the event as before it. The problem that then arises is whether the successor State may act to alter them, and the answer to the question depends upon whether the rights are vested in nationals of the successor State or in nationals of other States. If vested in the former, they are protected only to the extent to which the successor State's constitution guarantees private rights: this is the purport of the decisions of United States courts to be considered later. If vested in the latter, they are protected to the extent to which international law protects any alien property.

In respect of claims against the predecessor State the situation is somewhat different. Such claims may only be pursued against the successor State if the liability has devolved upon it; and it may devolve in virtue of the successor State's own law, or in virtue of international law, or, perhaps, in virtue of both. International law, since it is the only legal system available to regulate the consequences of the international event of State succession, is competent to achieve such a devolution; but even if a devolution occurs, the successor State is only inhibited from adversely affecting the rights of its own national creditors by its own unilateral act in the event of these being protected by its own constitution; in the case of alien creditors, it is inhibited by the ordinary rules of international law concerning contractual responsibility. There are, therefore, three questions to be clarified. First, does the legal system survive change of sovereignty? An affirmative answer to this has already been given. Secondly, does positive international law impose any liability on the successor State in respect of private rights subsisting against its predecessor? To this an affirmative answer will be given. And thirdly, may the successor State cancel these rights after the change of sovereignty? To this the answer will be given that it may only do so to the extent to which international law permits any State to abrogate rights.

To the problem of a devolution on the successor State of the predecessor State's obligations to private persons, two approaches have been made. In the first place, it has been argued that the successor State inherits, according to some principle or other of law, the ensemble of rights and obligations which the predecessor State possessed, and henceforth is bound in exactly the same way, and under exactly the same terms, as the latter. The second approach is the converse of the first. It has been denied that there is any such inheritance, and it has been claimed that there is at the moment of succession a complete severance between the state of affairs existing under the old sovereignty and that arising under the new,[1] so that the new sovereign is irresponsible for the juridical consequences of its predecessor's acts. Neither method, however, always gives strictly accurate results. On the one hand, the existence in international law of the notion of absolute inheritance has not been acknowledged by modern scientific research. On the other hand, to argue that rights and duties do not pass *ipso jure* from the predecessor to the successor State is not to deny that the latter may incur some obligation in international law towards the former's creditors and co-contractors. The legal relationship which existed between the predecessor State and the person to whom it owed a duty is something more than a mere *vinculum juris*: it also gives rise to a certain state of facts. Should the predecessor State have borrowed money, for example, two things are created. There is, first, the juridical link between the parties, which exists until either the money is repaid or the State itself has disappeared. There is, secondly, the factual situation which consists in the actual detention by the State of money in which the lender has an equitable interest. When the debtor State is superseded the legal duty to repay this money is not always inherited *ipso jure* by its successor. What is always 'inherited' is the state of facts which the now extinguished legal relationship has brought about; and the equitable interest which the lender has in this factual situation is as much an 'acquired right', 'property right' or 'vested right'[2] as the interest of a titleholder in tangible property. The obligation of the successor State is to respect this interest. It is not an obligation derived from the predecessor, but one imposed *ab exteriore* by

[1] Udina in Hague *Recueil*, vol. XLIV (1933), p. 754; Baty in *Yale Law Journal*, vol. XXXV (1926), p. 434.
[2] Descamps in *Rev. gén. de droit into pub.* vol. XV (1908), p. 394.

State Succession and Acquired Rights 239

international law. It arises when the successor, through its own action in extending its sovereignty, becomes competent to destroy the titleholder's interest. The general principle in which this obligation is embodied, and which underlies the whole problem of State succession, is the principle that acquired rights must be respected.[1]

While subrogation of the successor State in the rights and obligations of the predecessor State is generally indefensible, no implications arise with respect to instances of State continuity as distinct from those of State succession; and a particular transformation of sovereignty may be at once an instance of continuity and of succession, so that each concrete *vinculum juris* calls for specific appraisal according to the preponderance of elements of legal continuity and of legal disruption. Such is the situation which arises when a colony attains independence. Previous to this event it was an autonomous legal and fiscal order, strictly distinguished from that of the metropolis; and the local government departments, usually without even a change of name, and with no more than a change in the upper official echelons, continue their operations under existing statutes and regulations without interruption. Hence, except in the few respects in which the colony was absorbed within an imperial legal order, the change is one of governments rather than one of sovereignty, and the *vincula juris* persist.

2. THE HISTORY OF THE DOCTRINE OF ACQUIRED RIGHTS

The doctrine of acquired rights, although not adequately defined either in literature or in judicial or diplomatic practice, has long been accepted in international law, and has been sanctioned by a considerable body of

---

[1] That acquired rights subsist after change of sovereignty is acknowledged by: Calvo, vol. III, p. 399; Cansacchi in *Scritti in onere di T. Perassi* (1957), vol. I, pp. 253 et seq.; Dahm, vol. I, p. 110; Despagnet, p. 122; Fiore, *Nouv. Droit. int.* vol. I, p. 312; *Int. Law Cod.* p. 142; Fusinato, p. 2094; Gidel, pp. 84–91; Gould, p. 423; Guggenheim, pp. 124–35, *Traité*, p. 474; Huber, pp. 57–9, 135–49; Hershey, p. 224; Hoijer, p. 484; von der Heydte, p. 309; Kaeckenbeeck in *B.Y.* vol. XVII (1936), p. 8; Hague *Recueil*, vol. LIX (1937), p. 340; Mosler, pp. 13, 14, 25–36; Nys, vol. II, p. 33; Coleman Phillipson, p. 50; Reuter, p. 130; Rousseau, p. 274; Schönborn, p. 53; Schuschnigg, p. 157; Sibert, vol. I, p. 215; Svarlien, p. 115; Trotabas, *Le droit public dans l'annexion et le respect des droits acquis* (1921); Ullmann, p. 131; Verdross–Zemanek, p. 199; de Visscher, p. 191.

Cavaglieri, pp. 122 *et seq.*, criticizes the doctrine as unnecessary to explain the fact that private titles survive, and as unable to engage the successor State in obligation with respect to them. Strupp in Hague *Recueil*, vol. XLVII (1934), p. 478, denies any international law protection for private rights on a thesis of sovereign jurisdiction. Schnitzer argues that the principle of continuity must find its basis in the successor's public law, p. 142. Berber also contests the doctrine of acquired rights, although he is hesitant: vol. I, p. 261. Sereni points out that the problem is not one of succession but of protection of alien property, vol. II, pp. 390, 402.

decisions of international and municipal tribunals. With the passing of the patrimonial State in the seventeenth century, and the consequent possibility of drawing a distinction between *imperium* and *dominium*, it was recognized that only sovereignty and its incidents expired with the personality of a State. The relationships of the inhabitants one to another and their right of property were recognized to remain undisturbed.[1] This distinction was reinforced during the nineteenth century in England by the *laissez-faire* philosophy of ownership, and in America by the provisions of the Constitution referring to the rights of property. In the latter country the doctrine of acquired rights evolved rapidly with the incorporation into the Union of a number of territories previously belonging to France, Spain and Mexico. The doctrine was stated in complete terms by Marshall, C. J. In the classic case of *U.S.* v. *Percheman* he said:

> It is very unusual, even in cases of conquest, for the conqueror to do more than to displace the sovereign and assume dominion over the country. The modern usage of nations, which has become law, would be violated; that sense of justice and of right which is acknowledged and felt by the whole civilized world would be outraged, if private property should be generally confiscated, and private rights annulled. The people change their allegiance; their relation to their ancient sovereign is dissolved; but their relations to each other, and their rights of property, remain undisturbed.[2]

As all the cases[3] which followed *U.S.* v. *Percheman* dealt with the question of the United States' duty to respect the ownership of land in the absorbed territories, it was inevitable that the doctrine of acquired rights should have become in America a doctrine of respect for land tenure. The sanctity of such tenure was upheld in a long series of cases[4] in which often

---

[1] In *U.S.* v. *Percheman* it was said that 'the cession of territory . . . would be necessarily understood to pass the sovereignty only, and not to interfere with private property': 7 Pet. 51 at p. 87.   [2] 7 Pet. 51 at pp. 86–7.
[3] *Strother* v. *Lucas*, 12 Pet. 410 at pp. 435–6: 'This government put itself in place of the former sovereigns, and became invested with all their rights, subject to their concomitant obligations to the inhabitants'; *Ely's Administrators* v. *U.S.*, 171 U.S. 220 at p. 223: 'In harmony with the rules of international law, as well as with the terms of the treaties of cession, the change of sovereignty should work no change in respect of rights and titles; that which was good before should be good after; that which the law would enforce before should be enforceable after the cession'; *Coffee* v. *Groover*, 123 U.S. 1 at p. 9: 'It is no doubt the received doctrine, that in cases of ceded or conquered territory, the rights of private property in lands are respected. Grants made by the former government, being rightful when made, are not usually disturbed.' Such sanctity of property does not depend upon treaties, but the United States, 'as a just nation, regard this stipulation as the avowal of a principle which could have been held equally sacred, though it had not been inserted in the contract': *Soulard* v. *U.S.*, 4 Pet. 511 per Marshall, C. J., at p. 512.
[4] *Municipality of Ponce* v. *Roman Catholic Apostolic Church in Porto Rico*, 210 U.S. 296 at p. 324; *Society for the Propagation of the Gospel in Foreign Parts* v. *Town of New*

State Succession and Acquired Rights

exaggerated language was employed, and in which the term 'law of nations' was more often a reference to the natural law basis of the Constitution than to international law. The absolute duty of a successor State to respect the rights of landowners was enunciated in no less vigorous terms in United States diplomatic practice. In 1886 the Secretary of State wrote to the American Ambassador in Chile asserting that the landed interests of American citizens in territory acquired by Chile from Peru were

> consecrated by the law of nations. . . . The Government of the United States is therefore prepared to insist on the continued validity of such titles, as held by citizens of the United States, when attacked by foreign Governments succeeding that by which they (were) granted. Title to land and landed improvements, is, by the law of nations, a continuous right, not subject to be divested by any retroactive legislation of new Governments taking the place of that by which such title was lawfully granted.[1]

The problem of survival of rights created under the previous legal system is inseparably connected with the explanation of the survival of law.[2] If the legal order of the predecessor State totally collapses, all acquired rights lapse, and they can only be revived if the successor State, by an act of will, permits this.[3] It follows that, if the successor treats the law as abrogated, it cannot be engaged in international responsibility should the acquired rights of aliens not be honoured. The English doctrine of Act of State was explained by Keith[4] as emanating from this thesis.

The practice of the courts, both international and municipal,

---

Haven, 8 Wheat. 464 at p. 493; *Mitchel v. U.S.*, 9 Pet. 711 at p. 734; *Delassus v. U.S.*, 9 Pet. 117 at p. 133; *Mutual Assurance Society v. Watts*, 1 Wheat. 279 at p. 279; *U.S. v. Arredondo*, 6 Pet. 691 at p. 712; *U.S. v. Roselius et al.*, 15 How. 31; *McCallen v. Hodge*, 5 Tex. 34, 279 at p. 282; *U.S. v. Clarke's Heirs*, 16 Pet. 228 at p. 232; *Townsend v. Greeley*, 5 Wall. 326 at p. 335; *Dent v. Emmeger*, 14 Wall. 308 at p. 312; *Langdeau v. Hanes*, 21 Wall. 521 at p. 527; *Cessna v. U.S.*, 169 U.S. 165 at p. 186; *Doe v. Eslava*, 9 How. 421 at p. 443; *Jones v. McMasters*, 20 How. 17 at p. 21; *Playa de Flor Land and Improvement Co. v. U.S.*, 70 F. Supp. 281; *U.S. v. Fullard-Leo*, 156 F. 2d. 756; *Amaya v. Stanolind Oil and Gas Co.* 158 F. 2d. 554; *Miller v. Letzerich*, 49 S.W. 2d. 404; *Bolshanin v. Zlobin*, 76 F. Supp. 281; *Terrett v. Taylor*, 9 Cranch 43 at p. 50.

1 Wharton, vol. I, p. 17.

2 Berber, vol. I, p. 260; Cansacchi in *Scritti in onore de T. Perassi* (1957), vol. I, p. 253; Cavaglieri, pp. 117 *et seq.*; Gould, p. 419; Guggenheim, *Traité*, p. 459; von Holtzendorff, p. 34; Huber, p. 22; Jellinek, p. 279; Sereni, p. 386; Schnitzer, p. 142; Rosenne in *B.Y.* vol. XXVII (1950), p. 267. See *supra*, p. 101.

3 Mosler concedes that the law of the predecessor State lapses, pp. 16, 22, 23, 93, 160, but overcomes the implications of this by postulating that rights are 'acquired' in virtue of international law and not municipal law, and therefore do not participate in this lapse: p. 33.

4 Pp. 13 *et seq.*

contradicts this explanation, and, except in England, the negative attitude respecting acquired rights. In a series of decisions concerning the effect of the treaty of cession of Nice and Savoy to France, the French courts held that the doctrine of non-retroactivity required an interpretation in favour of maintenance of rights already acquired (*droits privés antérieurement acquis*), and consequently limited the competence of the French jurisdiction to deciding whether they conformed or not with the law under which they purported to have been created.[1] Although the doctrine of acquired rights had been adumbrated by Savigny,[2] it seems to have its genesis in these cases,[3] and only later was it employed to rationalize the survival of property rights in the territories acquired by the United States.[4] Grivaz,[5] considering the legal effect on church institutions of the cession of Savoy, utilized the expression *théorie des droits acquis*, and for the first time comprehended therein not only what Vareilles-Sommières[6] had referred to as 'inherent rights' (*droits innés*), that is, rights of property, in the primitive sense, but also contractual rights (*droits concédés*) deriving from the State. These *droits concédés* were divided into two categories, corresponding with the distinction between public law and private law: that is, rights granted by the law, to which the principle of non-retroactivity was absolutely inapplicable, and rights resulting from the exercise of natural freedom. The latter were further subdivided into mere concessions of legal 'aptitudes', which were also immune to the same principle, and vested interests of a truly private character, which were governed by it. There was, therefore, some speculative background to Gidel's distinction between the terms of a contract made by the predecessor State, which would not necessarily oblige the successor State, and the *droits réels* resulting from such a contract, which survive (*survivent*) the change.[7] Upon this doctrine Gidel erected his thesis of the effects of annexation upon concessions.

Although the concept of 'acquired rights' had not been propounded as such, the authors throughout the nineteenth century had taken it for granted that private property rights were unaffected by change of sovereignty. Wheaton had mentioned that the successor State must pay

1 D. 1862. 1. 355, 7 July 1862; D. 1883. 1. 147, 22 January 1883.
2 *System des heutigen römischen Rechts*, vol. VIII, p. 370; *Traité de droit romain* (1851), vol. VIII, p. 368, sec. CCCLXXXIV; Guggenheim, p. 126.
3 The earliest doctrinal analysis appears to be by Vareilles-Sommières in *Revue critique de législation et de jurisprudence* (1893), p. 444. It was taken up by Merlin on the subject of non-retroactivity of legislation in *Répertoire, Effet rétroactif*, s. 3, no. 3, para. 1; Descamps in *Rev. gén. de droit int. pub.* vol. XV (1908), p. 385; Goupy, *Des droits civils maintenus en cas d'annexion* (1907).
4 Gidel, pp. 147 et seq.   5 In *Rev. gén de droit int. pub.* vol. IV (1897), p. 645.
6 Loc. cit.   7 P. 96.

compensation if, subsequent to the change, it confiscates private property.[1] Selosse regarded judicial judgments as rights of this nature.[2] Perhaps the first important exposition was that of Fiore,[3] who was followed by Despagnet,[4] but the discussion which attracted most attention was in an article by Descamps in 1908.[5]

Descamps' article was dealt with for the first time critically by Cavaglieri, who described as 'unhappy' Descamps' argument that to permit the successor State unilaterally to cancel titles would be offensive to the doctrine of non-retroactivity of law.[6] He thought the doctrine of acquired rights insufficiently established on the basis of disparate judicial decisions of various States. Since the burden of Descamps' theory was that the successor State was committed to performance or recognition absolutely and for the term of the right,[7] it places a successor State, Cavaglieri said, in a less favourable position *vis-à-vis* the titleholders than its predecessor, and to this extent it is clearly unsound. But it does not follow, he conceded, that acquired rights are of no legal value after succession. They survive change of sovereignty in so far as they are not creations of sovereignty, but they survive only for the purposes of the conflict of laws, and hence only so long as the successor State maintains title to which foreign recognition may be given.[8] No *vinculum juris* can exist between the successor State and the titleholder except at the former's instance.

The view, shared by Descamps and Gidel, that acquired rights are sacrosanct to the extent that they may not be touched by the successor State is clearly not admissible today. Also, the successor State, should it expropriate without compensation, can only be liable with respect to alien titleholders, for only towards them can it be internationally responsible.[9] Various authors who have considered that contractual relations with the predecessor State have lapsed have attempted to gain compensation for the parties who have lost financially by utilizing the doctrine of unjust enrichment. This solution makes its appearance quite early in the literature, and has proved persistent.[10] It has been controverted by at least as many authors as have propounded it, mainly on the ground that it is impossible technically to prove (*a*) that the successor State has been enriched, (*b*) that the enrichment is connected with the detriment to the

1 S. 31.   2 P. 238.
3 *Trattado di diritto internazionale pubblico*, 3rd ed., 1887–91, p. 221.
4 P. 108.
5 In *Rev. gén. de droit int. pub.* vol. XV (1908), p. 385.
6 P. 122.
7 On this ground he also criticized Fiore, p. 221.
8 P. 125.   9 A point first made by Selosse, p. 165.
10 Dahm, vol. I, p. 117; Descamps in *Rev. gén. de droit int. pub.* vol. XV (1908), p. 400; Despagnet, p. 121; Gidel, pp. 134 *et seq.*; Jèze, p. 12; Reuter, p. 128.

creditor, or (c) that the enrichment is unjustified.[1] Cavaglieri, who was clearly uneasy at the implications of his doctrine that international law does not provide for succession, thought it an effective remedy in the municipal courts of the successor State whose law embodied it.[2] Guggenheim, who prefers to reject outright the utilization of the unjust enrichment concept in the solution of problems of State succession,[3] criticizes Cavaglieri as failing to draw the logical conclusion from his thesis of non-subrogation in legal liability.[4]

3 THE ELEMENTS OF THE DOCTRINE OF ACQUIRED RIGHTS

The tendency of the American cases[5] to imply that the doctrine of respect for acquired rights relates only to ownership of land was substantiated by the words 'rights of property',[6] or the even vaguer term 'private right', which they employed. Feilchenfeld, for example, seeks to demonstrate that incorporeal rights, among which he specifically includes concessions, are to be 'distinguished from' acquired rights to tangible property.[7] In addition, the judgment in the *West Rand Gold Mining Company* v. *The King* asserted that the 'obligations of conquering States with regard to private property of private individuals, particularly land as to which the title had already been perfected before the conquest or annexation, are altogether different from the obligations which arise in respect of personal rights by contract'.[8] It cannot, however, be admitted that the doctrine of respect for acquired rights is restricted in its operation to corporeal interests.[9] It includes 'all things and rights considered as

---

1 Appleton, p. 49; Caflisch in *Ned. Tijd.* vol. x (1963), p. 352; Feilchenfeld, p. 820; Schönborn, pp. 100 *et seq.*
2 P. 136. 3 P. 91.
4 P. 92; Castren, p. 462. 5 See *supra*, p. 240.
6 Sayre adopts this interpretation in *A.J.* vol. XII (1918), p. 478. See Kaeckenbeeck in Hague *Recueil*, vol. LIX (1937), p. 341. In *Strother* v. *Lucas* the doctrine was specifically restricted to landholding. 'This court has defined property to be any right, legal or equitable, inceptive, inchoate, or perfect, which before the treaty with France in 1803, or with Spain in 1819, had so attached to any piece or tract of land, great or small, as to affect the conscience of the former sovereign "with a trust"'; 12 Pet. 410 at p. 436; *Amaya* v. *Stanolind Oil Co.* 158 F. 2d. 554.
7 P. 626. 8 [1905] 2 K.B. 391 at p. 411.
9 Gidel cites a number of French decisions in support of the extension of the doctrine of *droits acquis* to include judgment debts and marital and family relationships: p. 87. 'Property of all kinds', as protected by the Treaty of Paris, 1898, was held by the Solicitor to the War Department of the United States to include trade marks: Magoon, *Reports on the Law of Civil Government under Military Occupation* (1902), p. 305. Planiol considers that 'no one has ever been able to give a definition of acquired right': *Traité élémentaire de droit civil*, 2nd ed., vol. I, p. 96, quoted by Nys, vol. II, p. 33.

State Succession and Acquired Rights 245

having a money value . . . such as trade marks and copyright, patents and rights *in personam* capable of transfer or transmission as debts',[1] and in the *Forests of Central Rhodope* Case emphasis was thrust on the element of acquired rights in a concession which did not necessarily involve an interest in the land.[2] In English legal language the words 'acquired rights' have not yet assumed the significance of a term of art. They do not immediately suggest all the elements of the concept to which they refer. A similar deficiency exists in French, Italian and Spanish. In this respect the German term *Vermögensrecht* is a more adequate one than its foreign equivalents since it clearly signifies any right, whether *in rem* or *in personam*, of an assessable monetary value.[3] Such possibility of assessing the value of the interest is an important attribute of the concept of acquired right.

Acquired rights, therefore, as understood in international law, are any rights, corporeal or incorporeal, properly vested in a natural or juristic person, and of an assessable monetary value. Within the scope of such *Vermögensrechte* fall rights which have their basis in contract no less than those relating to the ownership of real property, providing they concern an undertaking or investment of a more or less permanent character. Some attempt to assess the elements of an acquired right was made by the Upper Silesian Arbitral Tribunal in a case brought before it by an advocate who claimed that his practice, located in territory transferred to Poland in 1919, had been destroyed by an official boycott imposed because he was a Jew. The interest possessed by him in his practice, he alleged, was an 'acquired right' within the scope of article 4 of the Geneva Convention of 1922.[4] His claim was rejected by the tribunal. The mere freedom to use one's working capacity and to exercise a profitable activity did not, it considered, constitute a subjective acquired right. For such a right to exist there must be a title of acquisition and the recognition by the law of some concrete power, as in the case of an established business involving a definite undertaking protected by the law on the same basis as the ownership of land. Such a business exhibits the characteristics of an economic concession, in which rights of exploitation are embodied in an undertaking, plant or definite object. The tribunal pointed out that the *Reichsgericht* in Germany had only admitted the existence in the medical profession of an 'acquired right' when the right concerned the operation of a private clinic. In the absence of such an undertaking the exercise of the medical profession was, having regard to its scientific and ethical aspects, outside the conception of a business. So also, the tribunal argued, the

---

[1] Byrne, *A Dictionary of English Law* (1923), p. 709.
[2] U.N. Rep. vol. III, p. 1426. See *infra*, p. 331.
[3] Mosler, pp. 140–2.   [4] B.F.S.P. vol. CXVIII, p. 365.

notary's practice, since it constitutes a public function, could not fall within the category of an acquired right. Something more permanent is demanded than an undertaking which consists only in the exercise of a personal activity.[1] Attempts have been made to argue that the privilege of French advocates practising at the bar in former French countries is an acquired right, violation of which could justify French diplomatic protest.[2] France, however, has preferred to negotiate the continuity of this privilege in the Judicial Co-operation Agreements which have been signed with most of these countries.[3]

Commercial privileges which do not embody interests capable of financial valuation are not acquired rights. In the *Oscar Chinn* Case[4] the Permanent Court of International Justice held that the reduction of transport rates on the Congo River by the Belgian Government in the interests of correcting an economic disequilibrium was not offensive to the freedom of trade guaranteed to British subjects in the Act of Berlin, 1885, as modified by the Convention of St Germain, 1919, even though the economic effect of the measure was to create a *de facto* monopoly in a Belgian concern. As Judge Cecil Hurst admitted in his dissenting opinion,[5] 'Chinn possessed no right, either under the Treaty of St Germain or under general international law, which entitled him to find customers in the Congo'.

In 1948 the French *Conseil d'État* held that the extension of French law governing public hospitals in France to the territories of Nice and Savoy, which France acquired in 1860 from Sardinia, cancelled licences held from the King of Sardinia granting the right to dispense drugs to the public.[6] The closing of public dispensaries under French law violated no right protected by the Treaty of Cession[7] because this was an administrative act terminating a privilege which did not amount to a property interest.

It is impossible to lay down exact rules as to the interests which are protected as acquired rights. Many private investments possess at the same time a public character, and are conditional, more or less, on the continued sovereignty of the predecessor State.[8] Very real difficulties are

---

1 *Jablonsky* v. *German Reich*, Ann. Dig. vol. VIII, Case no. 42. In *Kügele* v. *Polish State* the same tribunal held that the degree of remunerativeness of property or business does not constitute an acquired right: *ibid*. vol. VI, Case no. 34. See also *Niederstrasser* v. *Polish State*, *ibid*. Case no. 33.
2 *Annuaire français* (1959), p. 891.   3 See *supra*, p. 143.
4 P.C.I.J. ser. A/B, no. 63, p. 65, at pp. 84, 85.   5 At p. 121.
6 *In re Hospices Civil de Chambéry*, Ann. Dig. vol. XV, Case no. 20.
7 M.N.R.G. vol. XVII, pt. II, p. 22.
8 A Polish court held that a condition restricting the alienation of land was a political condition and fell with the change of sovereignty: *Matys* v. *Nipanicz*, Ann. Dig. vol. I, Case no. 48. See also *Procurator-General of Poland* v. *S.*, *ibid*. vol. III, Case no. 366.

experienced by judicial organs which are required to deal with rights of a mixed public and private character in determining whether it is the private or the public character of the right that is to prevail.[1] Mosler says:

> The more a legal relationship between persons or between persons and things belongs to the private sphere, the easier it is to answer this problem positively. It can be answered negatively when there is a connexion with the political order of sovereignty. Difficulties arise in those cases which do not belong exclusively to the private sphere, but in which the state participates in its public interest.[2]

On the one side the principle of acquired rights demands that the interest of a private investor be not abrogated; on the other side the public interest of the acquiring State has to be considered. The tension between the public and private aspects of the interest prevents the laying down of hard and fast rules. It is, however, clearly established that rights to public offices, whether purchased or inherited, and whether or not the grant is by implication for the duration of political power of the sovereignty under which the rights were created, are political in essence and not protected by international law.[3] Neither are monopolies for the sale of offices within the category of acquired rights.[4]

To receive the protection of international law an interest must have been properly vested, *bona fide* acquired and duly evidenced. Strict evidence of title, however, has not been insisted upon in practice. In many of the territories incorporated from time to time in the United States, grants of land had been made by the officials of the predecessor State which were either conditional or not substantiated by written documents. Commencing from the assumption that acquired rights are not abrogated by change of sovereignty, the courts of the United States endeavoured to restrict as far as possible the conditions necessary to constitute an acquired right.[5] Although it is international law which defines which rights are to

---

1 Kaeckenbeeck in *B.Y.* vol. XVII (1936), p. 12. For a distinction between private rights which were to be respected and rights of a mixed public and private character see the Treaty of Washington, 1867, Malloy, vol. II, p. 1522. Szászy is of opinion that rights must be respected even if contrary to the public order of the successor State, *Rev. de droit int.* vol. V (1930), p. 591.

2 P. 35. In *Alvarez y Sanchez* v. *U.S.* an American court held that the provisions relating to private rights in the Treaty of Paris, 1898 had no reference to 'public or quasi-public stations, the functions and duties of which it is the province of the government to regulate'; 216 U.S. 167 at p. 175.

3 Piédelièvre, vol. I, p. 140; *The Application of the Countess of Buena Vista*, Magoon, *op. cit.* p. 209.

4 *O'Reilly de Camara* v. *Brooke*, 209 U.S. 45; *Alvarez y Sanchez* v. *U.S.*, 216 U.S. 167; Moore, *Dig.* vol. I, pp. 428–9; Bordwell in *A.J.* vol. III (1909), p. 119; *ibid.* vol. IV (1910), p. 463.

5 Sayre in *A.J.* vol. XII (1918), pp. 483 *et seq.*

be protected, it is, it was held, the law of the predecessor State under which the rights are alleged to have arisen which is to determine whether or not they have been properly acquired. In applying the above principles the courts of the United States went behind the circumstances of absence of title-deeds, or of defective title-deeds, and sought to ascertain the intention of the predecessor State. If this intention was reasonably beyond doubt the courts did not insist upon every legal formality being completed.[1]

In *Delassus* v. *U.S.*, in which case the claimant to land in territory transferred to the United States by Spain had no title which could be produced, it was said that the circumstances were such as to induce a presumption that he had an acquired right. These circumstances were that the land had been regularly surveyed, the claimant was in possession, and according to Spanish law he could have demanded a title as of right at any time.[2] Other cases went further than this. In *U.S.* v. *Chaves* it was said that long and uninterrupted possession of real property, in the absence of rebutting circumstances, creates a presumption that formal instruments and records of title have once existed, even though they cannot be found.[3]

Out of these cases has developed a doctrine of inchoate title.[4] Once it is proved that the claimant had a judicially enforceable right *ad rem*, whether it be legal or equitable, this is sufficient to establish his interest as an acquired right in international law. The test is the claimant's right, under the law of the predecessor State, to an indefeasible title, either in perpetuity or for a term. Contingent rights, and certainly future expectancies, do not fulfil this test.[5] The criterion was adopted also by the French courts in Algeria in 1854, where the inhabitants held land without written titles.[6] It was confirmed by the decision of the *German Settlers* Case, where rights to land under contract were held by the Permanent Court of

---

[1] In *U.S.* v. *Hanson* it was held that the Spanish authorities had power to make grants of the public domain of Florida, and the United States courts could only consider whether the grant was made in point of fact, and what was its legal effect, and not whether it was made in accordance with the ideas of the United States courts on the merits of the claim: 16 Pet. 196. When Chile applied its own municipal law to test the validity of titles existing in territory incorporated within it the United States protested on behalf of its nationals who were adversely affected that this was contrary to international law: Wharton, vol. I, p. 16; *U.S.* v. *Auguisola*, 1 Wall. 352. The court will take judicial notice of the law under which the right arose: *U.S.* v. *Chaves*, 159 U.S. 452. For a lengthy review of the negotiations between the United States and Spain respecting rights of Spanish subjects in Florida see Gidel, pp. 151 *et seq.*

[2] 9 Pet. 117. See also *Dent* v. *Emmeger*, 14 Wall. 308; *Cariña* v. *Insular Government of the Philippine Islands*, 212 U.S. 449.

[3] 159 U.S. 452 at p. 464. But see *Bolshanin* v. *Zlobin*, 76 F. Supp. 281.

[4] See also *Soulard* v. *U.S.* 4 Pet. 511; *Smith* v. *U.S.* 10 Pet. 326; *Bolshanin* v. *Zlobin*, 76 F. Supp. 281.

[5] Descamps, *loc. cit.* p. 388.   [6] Gidel, p. 112.

International Justice to be rights *ad rem* protected by international law.[1]

It has also been held that a decision as to title given by the courts of the predecessor State must be accepted, even though the evidence upon which it is based is insufficient in the law of the successor State.[2] A right which is conditional, however, is not an acquired right until fulfilment of the condition. If the condition has not been fulfilled before the change of sovereignty, it would seem that there is no duty of respect imposed on the successor State. On 15 July 1849 the Queen's Advocate gave an opinion on the obligation of the United States to compensate a British company for the confiscation in 1836 by the Texan legislature of lands originally granted to it by Mexico. He pointed out that the conditions upon which the lands in question had been granted had not been complied with, and this was in itself sufficient to render the grant invalid and establish a bar to the claim for compensation.[3] On the other hand, there is some authority for suggesting that, if performance of the condition has been rendered impossible by the action of the successor State itself, the latter is responsible to the titleholder, and must respect whatever interest he has acquired. The same Queen's Advocate some years earlier had advised upon the claim of British subjects to lands in Texas. These persons had alleged that they had been prevented by the disturbed state of affairs in Texas from fulfilling the conditions attached to grants of land made to them by Mexico. He reported that the failure to fulfil the conditions in question was not due to any fault of the claimants, and that the confiscation of their lands upon an alleged failure so to fulfil them would render the British Government competent to intervene on their behalf.[4]

A grant of land is not an acquired right if it is indefinite, though the test of its indefiniteness lies in the fact that the land has not been located rather than that it has not been surveyed.[5] The grant must not have been

[1] P.C.I.J. ser. B, no. 6. In the *Robert E. Brown* Case it was held that, though licences had never been issued, Brown had substantial rights of a character entitling him to an interest in real property: U.N. Rep. vol. VI, p. 120.

[2] *Clements* v. *Texas Company*, Ann. Dig. vol. III, Case no. 73. See also *Keene* v. *McDonough*, 8 Pet. 308. The American agent stated in his brief in the *Robert E. Brown* Case that 'just as it is clearly established that under international law private rights should be respected by an absorbing state, so it is well established that appropriate judicial acts of an extinguishing state, defining such rights, should not be disregarded by the absorbing state': Nielsen, p. 180.

[3] Opinion of 25 July 1849, F.O. 83/2208; O'Connell, Appendix no. 17.

[4] Opinion of 23 July 1839, F.O. 83/2382; O'Connell, Appendix no. 14. See also *Cessna* v. *U.S.*, 169 U.S. 165 at p. 186; *U.S.* v. *Kingsley*, 12 Pet. 476; *U.S.* v. *Wiggins*, 14 Pet. 334; *U.S.* v. *Vaca*, 18 How. 556; *U.S.* v. *Larkin*, 18 How. 557.

[5] *O'Hara* v. *U.S.*, 15 Pet. 275; *U.S.* v. *Miranda*, 16 Pet. 153; *U.S.* v. *Sutter*, 21 How. 170; *U.S.* v. *Pearson Reading*, 18 How. 1; *Dent* v. *Emmeger*, 14 Wall. 308; *Harcourt* v *Gaillard*, 12 Wheat. 523.

voidable at the option of the predecessor State, and must have been within its competence.[1] Nor are grants obtained by fraud to be considered as acquired rights, though fraud in this context should be defined by the predecessor's law rather than by that of the successor.[2]

However, in the eyes of United States courts, an occupant of land is entitled to the benefit of every presumption, and to have all doubts resolved in his favour.[3] This does not mean that the occupant is immune from the operation of American law, even if enacted subsequently, concerning foreclosure, sale upon execution, trespass, or adverse possession.[4]

4. THE DOCTRINE OF ACQUIRED RIGHTS AND THE DOCTRINE OF ACT OF STATE

Some authors limit the operation of the doctrine of acquired rights to the interests of nationals of States other than the successor State, basing their argument on the now largely discredited theory that the individual cannot be a subject of international law, and on the consequent assumption that a duty in international law is a duty owed only to a sovereign State; nationals of the successor State, and those of the predecessor State who become nationals of the former by virtue of the change of sovereignty, do not enjoy any international law protection of their interests.[5] This statement of the position is only partially true. Speaking generally, the machinery for protection of acquired rights exists only in the case of nationals of foreign States. In some European legal systems there is no provision for claims arising out of the change of sovereignty to be brought against the successor State in its own courts. And, as a State's own nationals, in the absence of any such empowering agreement as the Geneva Convention, 1922, cannot have their claims presented on their behalf by another sovereign State, they are without a remedy.

This is not to prove, however, that such persons are not the subjects of rights given them by international law. The fact that a right cannot be enforced does not mean that it does not exist. Where the machinery for enforcement is provided in the municipal law of the successor State, there can be no doubt that the subjects of the latter can invoke the doctrine of acquired rights no less than the subjects of foreign States. The long

[1] *U.S.* v. *Reynes*, 9 How. 127; *U.S.* v. *Rose*, 23 How. 262.
[2] Gidel, p. 146. In *Schwerdtfeger* v. *Danish Government* a Danish court held that the rule of acquired rights could not apply to a case where an investment in land was made with an eye to the impending cession: *Ann. Dig.* vol. II, Case no. 40.
[3] *U.S.* v. *Fullard-Leo*, 156 F. 2d. 756.
[4] *Amaya* v. *Stanolind Oil and Gas Co.* 158 F. 2d. 554.
[5] Mosler, pp. 41 *et seq.*, 80, 92.

State Succession and Acquired Rights

tradition of the United States decisions is adequate testimony on this point, while the *German Settlers* Case is explicitly in favour of the protection of the acquired rights of persons who became Polish nationals with the transfer of German territory.[1] It must be recognized, also, that the prevailing tendency to give persons other than sovereign States the right of appearance before international tribunals is breaking down the old assumption that States only are the subjects of international law. It is not inconceivable that in the future international law will provide the machinery for enforcement of rights vested in the subjects of a successor State no less than those of nationals of other States. Where domestic machinery is available, subjects of the successor State have successfully invoked the doctrine of acquired rights to establish claims against the new sovereign. The Italian Court of Cassation in 1927 took the view that a contract of lease made between the Austrian administration and a private party in respect of property situated in the territory which fell to Italy in 1919, bound the latter as successor in sovereignty. The lease was regarded as only a species of the category of acquired rights, and its continued validity was to be assumed in virtue of the general replacement of Austria by Italy in the former's juridical relations of private law.[2]

(i) *The doctrine of act of State in English law*

In the present state of affairs, domestic courts of most States are not given jurisdiction over claims arising out of the assumption of sovereignty. In England the doctrine in which this limitation is expressed is known as act of State.[3] It has been summarized in the following words:

When a territory is acquired by a sovereign state for the first time, that is an act of state. It matters not how the acquisition has been brought about. It may be by conquest, it may be by cession following on treaty, it may be by occupation of territory hitherto unoccupied by a recognized ruler. In all cases the result is the same. Any inhabitant of the territory can make good in the municipal Courts established by the new sovereign only such rights as that sovereign has, through

[1] See *infra*, pp. 273. The Upper Silesian Arbitral Tribunal adhered to the older doctrine, stating that there is no rule of international law on which a claim for compensation for the abrogation of the acquired right by officials of the State can be based, and this because international law is a law between States only: *Niederstrasser* v. *Polish State*, Ann. Dig. vol. VI, Case no. 33.
[2] *Czario* v. *Valentinis*, Ann. Dig. vol. IV, Case no. 52.
[3] McNair states that English authority can fairly be summarized by saying that cession does not *per se* affect private property, immovable and movable, within the ceded territory, and that the State acquiring the territory ought not to act to the detriment of the owners of the property; but if the Crown upon acquiring territory were so to act no municipal tribunal would be competent to deal with the matter: *Legal Effects of War* (3rd ed. 1948), p. 386. See Harrison Moore, *Act of State in English Law* (1906), pp. 157 *et seq.*; Bentwich in *B.Y.* vol. XXIII (1946), p. 330.

his officers, recognized. Such rights as he had under the rule of predecessors avail him nothing. Nay more, even if in a treaty of cession it is stipulated that certain inhabitants should enjoy certain rights, that does not give a title to those inhabitants to enforce these stipulations in the municipal courts. The right to enforce remains only with the high contracting parties.[1]

The doctrine of act of State has been misinterpreted in both literature and judicial pronouncement. From a statement of the doctrine the conclusion has not infrequently been drawn that legal rights acquired under the predecessor State, in so far as they are vested in persons who become subjects of the successor State, no longer exist at all after the change of sovereignty.[2] The case that was originally responsible for this interpretation was *Cook* v. *Sprigg*, which was decided in connexion with the annexation by Great Britain of certain territory in South Africa. It was held that a treaty of cession, or annexation, made by the Crown, and its results, are not within the cognizance of municipal courts.

It is a well-established principle of law that the transactions of independent States between each other are governed by other laws than those which municipal courts administer. It is no answer to say that by the ordinary principles of international law private property is respected by the sovereign which accepts the cession and assumes the duties and legal obligations of the former sovereign with respect to such private property within the ceded territory. All that can be properly meant by such a proposition is that according to the well-understood rules of international law, a change of sovereignty by cession ought not to affect private property, but no municipal tribunal has authority to enforce such an obligation.[3]

The case of *Secretary of State for India* v. *Bai Rajbai* which was decided in 1915, relying on this enunciation of the law, specifically implied that

1 *Vajesingji Joravarsingji* v. *Secretary of State for India* (1923), L.R. 51 I.A. 357 at p. 360.
2 See the interpretation of the Transvaal Concessions Commission, Cd. 623, p. 7.
3 [1899] A.C. 572 at p. 578. This case was followed in the Transvaal Supreme Court in *Postmaster-General* v. *Taute*, in which it was held that it is impossible for British courts 'to declare that, as a result of annexation, any contractual obligations have been transferred from the one Government to the other': [1905] Trans. L.R. (S.C.) 582. See also *Vereeniging Municipality* v. *Vereeniging Estates Limited*, where the defendant claimed the right to erect electric cables across streets vested in the plaintiff, relying on a contract entered into between its predecessors in title and the Government of the South African Republic. It was held that in the absence of express recognition of his rights by the Government the courts could not entertain the action. 'It has already been decided by our courts ... that, where a person had a personal right against the Government of the South African Republic, he could not vindicate that personal right in the courts of the Transvaal Colony after annexation. He could not set up a right that he had as against the extinct Government': [1919] S.A.L.R. T.P.D. 159. See also *Shingler* v. *Union Government* (*Minister of Mines*) [1925] S.A.L.R. (S.C.) 556.

State Succession and Acquired Rights

the private rights of persons who became British nationals by virtue of the transfer of territory to British India had not survived the change.

The relation in which they stood to their native sovereigns before this cession, and the legal rights they enjoyed under them, are, save in one respect, entirely irrelevant matters. They could not carry on under the new régime the legal rights, if any, which they might have enjoyed under the old. The only enforceable rights they could have as against their new sovereign were those and only those, which that new sovereign, by agreement express or implied, or by legislation, chose to confer upon them.[1]

Any such interpretation would seem to be unfounded and to be beyond the limits established in a long series of cases.[2] The doctrine of act of State is one of English municipal law. It merely denies an English court jurisdiction to inquire into the consequences of acts of the British Government which are inseparable from the extension of its sovereignty. The court is not entitled to ask if such acts are 'just or unjust, politic or impolitic',[3] or what legal rights and duties have been carried over in the change of sovereignty. The doctrine is not intended, however, to deny a rule of international law.[4] In fact an English municipal court, in considering the effect of acts of sovereign power on the rights of individuals, may be forced to uphold a breach of international law[5]. Nor is the doctrine to be interpreted as denying that persons who become British subjects by virtue of cession or annexation *ipso facto* lose their rights. On the contrary, as was said by Stirling, J., in *Salaman* v. *Secretary of State of India*,[6] a case

---

1 (1915) L.R. 42 I.A. 229 at p. 237.
2 *Elphinstone* v. *Bedreechund* (1830), 1 Knapp P. C. 316; *Secretary of State in Council of India* v. *Kamachee Boye Sahaba* (1859), 7 Moo. Ind. App. 476; *Ex Rajah of Coorg* v. *The East India Company* (1860), 29 Bevan 300; *Nabob of the Carnatic* v. *The East India Company*, 1 Vesey Jun. 371; 2 Vesey Jun. 56; *Sirdar Bhagwan Singh* v. *Secretary of State for India* (1874), L.R. 2 I.A. 38; *Rustomjee* v. *R.* (1876), 1 Q.B.D. 487; *Doss* v. *Secretary of State for India*, L.R. 19 Eq. 509 at p. 534; *West Rand Gold Mining Company* v. *The King* [1905] 2 K.B. 391 at p. 409; *Dattatraya Krishna Rao Kane* v. *Secretary of State for India* (1930), L.R. 57 I.A. 318. *Asrar Ahmed* v. *Durgah Committee, Ajmer, Ann. Dig.* vol. XIII, Case no. 17; *Farid Ahmad* v. *Government of the United Provinces*, ibid. vol. XVI, Case no. 22; *Mithan Singh* v. *The Sub-Divisional Canal Officer, I.L.R.* vol. XXI, p. 64; *Dalmia Dadri Cement Co. Ltd* v. *Commissioner of Income Tax*, ibid. vol. XXV, p. 79; *Raja Rajinder Chand* v. *Mst. Sukhi*, ibid. vol. XXIV, p. 74; *Vivendra Singh* v. *State of Uttar Pradesh*, ibid. vol. XXII, p. 131; *Gajjan Singh* v. *Union of India*, ibid. vol. XXIII, p. 101; *Maharaj Umeg Singh* v. *State of Bombay*, ibid. vol. XXII, p. 138; *Idumati* v. *State of Saurashtra*, ibid. vol. XXIII, p. 109; *Bapu and Bapu* v. *Central Provinces*, ibid. p. 110.
3 *Secretary of State for India* v. *Sardar Rustam Khan* [1941] A.C. 356 at p. 372.
4 Westlake, pt. I, p. 81; Kaeckenbeeck in Hague *Recueil*, vol. LIX (1937), p. 349; Wade in *B.Y.* vol. XV (1934), p. 101.
5 *Loc. cit.* p. 105.
6 [1906] 1 K.B. 613.

respecting private interests in lands acquired by the East India Company, 'obligations unquestionably exist which bind the East India Company and the British Government as their successor and which ought most scrupulously to be observed, none the less that they cannot be enforced by an action'.[1]

In the same decision Fletcher-Moulton, L.J., went even further and suggested that the intention and effect of an act of State may be to create rights as between the Government and individuals who are, or who are about to become, subjects of the British Government. If, he argued, the successor State can enforce rights of its predecessor in its own courts, there is no reason why in such a case 'a claim of a converse character might not equally be entertained by municipal Courts, and a subject recover from the existing Government by the processes of law applicable to such a case any debts due from the former ruler'. 'Claims', he went on later, 'are not necessarily beyond the cognizance of municipal Courts merely because their origin is connected more or less directly with an act of State.'[2]

This view has raised the question of the exact scope of the doctrine of act of State. It suggests that if a municipal court is clearly of the opinion that a treaty of cession is intended to confirm the rights of subjects of the successor State, then these rights may be enforced irrespective of their connexion with an act of State. The cases which argue that such a treaty confers no rights of itself on British subjects[3] were cases in which this intention was excluded in evidence. Such a view derives some support from the judgment of the Privy Council delivered by Lord Haldane in *Amodu Tijani* v. *Secretary, Southern Nigeria*.[4] Lord Haldane did not require that the intention of a treaty to confer rights on British subjects should be explicit. The cession of territory in Africa to Great Britain appeared, he said, 'to have been made on the footing that the rights of property of the inhabitants were to be fully respected. This principle is a usual one under British policy and law when such occupations take place'.[5]

If this interpretation is correct it affords a serious limitation to the doctrine of act of State. The conclusion, according to Lord Haldane, is 'that a mere change of sovereignty is not to be presumed as meant to disturb rights of private owners; and the general terms of a cession are *prima facie* to be construed accordingly'.[6] An undertaking to respect rights of inhabitants need not, it would seem from this opinion, be express. It

---

[1] At p. 638. [2] At pp. 640–1.
[3] *Rustomjee* v. *The Queen* (1876), 1 Q.B.D. 487; *Civilian War Claimants' Association, Ltd* v. *The King* [1932] A.C. 14.
[4] [1921] 2 A.C. 399.
[5] At p. 407. It was held that compensation was payable for land expropriated.
[6] *Ibid.*

may be deduced from the circumstances of the cession.[1] However, the development of this theory of the implied intention of a treaty has, for the moment, been halted by the cases of *Secretary of State for India* v. *Sardar Rustam Khan*[2] and *Hoani Te Heuheu Tukino* v. *Aotea District Maori Land Board*,[3] both of which are merely a restatement of *Cook* v. *Sprigg*. In the latter case the Privy Council examined the provisions respecting native lands in the treaty by which the Maori chiefs ceded sovereignty over New Zealand to Great Britain. It was clearly of opinion that 'any rights purporting to be conferred by such a treaty of cession cannot be enforced in the courts, except in so far as they have been incorporated in the municipal law'.[4] Neither case denies the clearly enunciated opinion in the *Salaman* and *Amodu Tijani* judgments that persons who become British subjects by the annexation or cession of territory do not lose their duly acquired rights. The only point of conflict between the former and the latter is on the question of the extent to which machinery for enforcement of these rights exists in English municipal law.

However, a more significant check upon the operation of Lord Haldane's thesis was imposed by the Privy Council in *Oyekan* v. *Adele*[5] in 1957 when it was held that the courts will not construe a treaty of cession to determine whether it maintains rights, but will look exclusively to the conduct of the Crown, for 'the effect of the Act of State is to give to the British Crown sovereign power to make laws and to enforce them, and, therefore, the power to recognize existing rights or extinguish them, or create new ones'.[6]

(ii) *Recognition of rights by the successor sovereign in English law*

If the doctrine of act of State is a substantive one, then it would require legislation on the part of the successor State whose law is English law before claims antecedent to a transfer of sovereignty could be pursued against it. On the other hand, if it is merely a procedural bar, it might be executively waived, and this waiver could occur either as a matter of intention in the act of State itself, as Fletcher Moulton, C. J., and Lord Haldane have recognized,[7] or it might, as the Privy Council has stated on several occasions, occur subsequently by acknowledgment or by agreement express or implied.[8] The question what amounts to subsequent

---

1 See also Holdsworth in *Columbia Law Review*, vol. XLI (1941), pt. 2, p. 1328.
2 [1941] A.C. 356. 3 [1941] A.C. 308.
4 At p. 324. 5 [1957] 2 All E.R. 785.
6 At p. 788. 7 See *supra*, p. 254.
8 *Secretary of State for India* v. *Bai Rajbai* [1915] L.R. 42 I.A. 229; *Vajesingji Joravarsingji* v. *Secretary of State for India* [1923] L.R. 51 I.A. 357; *Asrar Ahmed* v. *Durgah Committee, Ajmer*, Ann. Dig. vol. XIII, Case no. 17.

acknowledgment or agreement was dealt with only incidentally by English courts previous to the opinion of the Privy Council in *Asrar Ahmed* v. *Dungah Committee, Ajmer*.[1] This case concerned a claim to the hereditary custodianship of a shrine which derived from a grant in 1813 by the State of Ajmer, which five years later was ceded to the Crown. Lord Simonds thought that a claim to an office to which material benefits appertained was one to which the principle of subsequent recognition was peculiarly applicable, and his opinion was founded on the inability of the appellant to point to any instrument, conduct or mode of dealing which could constitute recognition.

The Indian courts since independence have explored the question of recognition of rights by the successor State. They have held from a survey of governmental reports, and action or inaction on the part of British officials, that the British Government did not wish to dispossess the Fakirs who held land in territory conquered in 1803; and that the doctrine of act of State does not apply when the claimants were left after change of sovereignty in possession of their rights.[2] In a claim against the Patiala and East Punjab States Union, based on a grant of irrigation rights without liability to water-rating made by the Ruler of Nabha State, it was held that the fact that the Union did not move to demand water rates for nearly four years after the merger was an indication that the new sovereign accepted the position.[3] When the State of Bombay took possession of the properties of a limited liability company in which the merged State of Idar had purchased shareholding, and proceeded to exercise the rights attached to the shares, it had 'by implication accepted the liability of the merged State to pay the unpaid call money on shares'.[4] This was stated to be an exception to the rule laid down by the Divisional Bench of the Bombay Court that Bombay was not liable in respect of any contract entered into by the Idar State.[5] It was said that 'the Court cannot permit a party to allow itself to take only the benefits arising out of a contract or a bargain and dispute the liabilities arising therefrom'.[6]

1 *Ann. Dig.*, vol. XIII, Case no. 17.
2 *Farid Ahmad* v. *Government of the United Provinces*, ibid. vol. XVI, Case no. 22.
3 *Mihan Singh* v. *The Sub-Divisional Canal Officer*, I.L.R. vol. XXI, p. 64.
4 *The Collector of Sabarkantha* v. *Shankarlal Kalidas Patel*, A.I.R. (1960), Bomb. 516.
5 *Ganapatrao Shankarrao* v. *State of Bombay*, A.I.R. (1959), Bomb. 263.
6 At p. 518. *Promod Chandra Deb.* v *The State of Orissa*, A.I.R.|(1962), S.C. 1288. But there must be proof of an acceptance of benefits: *Vinayak Shripatrao Patwardhan* v. *State of Bombay*, A.I.R. (1961), Bomb. 11; *Raj Kumar Narasingh Pratap Singh Deo* v. *State of Orissa*, A.I.R. (1962), Orissa 60.

(iii) *The date of an act of State*

There has been a general assumption running through the English cases on act of State that the defence can be set up only in respect of a refusal on the part of the Crown to acknowledge rights acquired from the previous sovereign; and that even though the dispute on the point might arise some time after the change of sovereignty the refusal must be at least notionally continuous from the date of the change. The assumption would exclude the possibility of the defence of act of State being raised in respect of a dispossession by the successor sovereign of the titleholder after that date. In *Dalmia Dadri Cement Co.* v. *Commissioner of Income Tax* the Indian Supreme Court[1] stated that 'in law, the process of acquisition is one continuous "Act of State"—terminating on the assumption of sovereign powers *de jure* over them by the new sovereign and it is only thereafter that rights accrue to the residents of those territories as subjects of that sovereign'.[2]

The meaning of this passage was considered by the Supreme Court in two cases in 1962. In *Jagannath Agarwala* v. *State of Orissa*[3] the Mayurbhanj State had merged with the province of Orissa in 1949. Subsequent to that, the appellant filed a suit in respect of monetary transactions against the former ruler of Mayurbhanj State. The Supreme Court held that it could not entertain the appellant's claim unless Orissa had either expressly or impliedly admitted it. The Court accepted the principle that, even after the act of succession is completed, the successor State can validly press the plea of act of State as against the claims of the subjects of the State acquired.[4] But in *The State of Saurashtra* v. *Abdulla*,[5] the Supreme Court held that the act of State terminates when succession takes place.

(iv) *The distinction between property and contractual claims*

The presumption that the Crown intends to maintain existing titles is apparently restricted to claims to tangible property, or at least is minimized in the case of rights arising against the predecessor State out of contract. The distinction between property and contractual rights was adverted to by Lord Alverstone, C. J., in *West Rand Central Gold Mining Co.* v. *The King*,[6] where he described the obligations of conquering States with regard to the private property of private individuals, particularly

[1] I.L.R. vol. XXV, p. 79.
[2] Per Aujar, J., at p. 823.
[3] Supreme Court Appeals, 1962, no. 10.
[4] *Raj Kumar Narasingh Pratap Singh Deo* v. *State of Orissa*, A.I.R. (1962), Orissa, 60; *The State of Orissa* v. *Harichandan Babu*, A.I.R. (1964), Orissa, 73.
[5] Supreme Court Appeals, 1962, no. 20.　　[6] [1905] 2 K.B. 391 at p. 411.

land as to which a title had already been perfected before the conquest, as 'altogether different' from the obligations which arise in respect of personal rights by contracts.

If a particular piece of property has been conveyed to a private owner or has been pledged, or a lien has been created upon it, considerations arise which are different from those which have to be considered when the question is whether the contractual obligation of the conquered State towards individuals is to be undertaken by the conquering State.[1]

In his separate judgment in *Dalmia Dadri Cement Co. Ltd* v. *Commissioner of Income Tax*,[2] Bose, J., distinguished the instant case, which arose out of the failure of the successor to maintain a taxation privilege granted before merger by the previous Ruler, from previous decisions that the doctrine of act of State could not apply to bar an action arising out of land grants. He said: 'In the present case, in so far as the right is claimed on the basis of contract, it would fall to the ground on any view.' This was because the doctrine that private rights are unaffected by change of sovereignty 'does not extend to personal rights such as those based on contract'. He then concluded: 'I therefore want to make it clear that this decision must not be used as a precedent in a case in which rights to immovable property are concerned.'[3]

(v) *The act of State doctrine in the law of India*

The Indian courts have regarded the act of State doctrine as forming part of the corpus of the common law which constitutes part of the law of India, and they have proceeded to solve the problems of claims antecedent to State succession by reference to it. They have been confronted with four distinct instances of succession, the extension of British sovereignty over the Indian States during the nineteenth century, the independence of India, the merger in the Federal States of India of the princely States, and the cession of Chandernagore from France.[4] It was logical that the doctrine of act of State as applied to the first situation by the Privy Council should continue to be applied by the Indian courts. These, accordingly, held that the defence of act of State could be maintained against a plaintiff who claimed ownership of a plot of land belonging to his family before the conquest of Muttra in 1803,[5] and against a plaintiff who claimed an hereditary custodianship of a shrine.[6] It was also

[1] Ibid.   [2] I.L.R. vol. XXV, p. 79.
[3] At p. 87.
[4] *Union of India* v. *Manmull Jain*, A.I.R. 1954, Cal. 615.
[5] *Farid Ahmad* v. *Government of the United Provinces*, Ann. Dig. vol. XVI, Case no. 22.
[6] *Asrar Ahmed* v. *Durgah Committee, Ajmer*, ibid. vol. XIII, Case no. 17.

resorted to in a claim to pine trees on the lands of the defendants which was based on an alleged grant by the Rajah of Kangra, whose principality was in 1827 annexed by Rajah Ranjit Singh, the Sikh conqueror. When the latter's territory was taken over by the British Crown the relevant sanad did not have the effect of reviving the lost rights.[1]

Indian courts have not recognized that the act of State doctrine would apply to oust the jurisdiction of the courts respecting claims against the Government of India arising before independence. They have treated the relevant Independence Orders in Council as achieving legislative continuity of all claims.[2] However, despite the Indian Independence Act provisions regarding continuity of conditions of service of officials[3] who continued to serve in office after independence, the act of State doctrine prevailed in an action by an official of the Government of Madras who had been declared redundant.[4]

Indian courts have assimilated the process of merger of the Princely States in the States of the Union to the process of annexation and cession as it occurred in the nineteenth century. In an action based on a claim that a grant of irrigation water in perpetuity to the appellant's father by Nabha State, which in 1948 was merged with the Patiala and East Punjab States Union, the latter pleaded that the rights of a subject of a former Covenanting State could not be enforced by the subject in the courts of the new sovereign without recognition of those rights by the new sovereign. The court found that there had been such recognition, and that the act of State doctrine would not apply.[5] On the other hand, the doctrine was applied in an action seeking reinstatement in office brought by an official of the State of Bikaner, which was merged in Rajasthan, the court deliberately assimilating accession, conquest, merger and integration.[6]

In 1954 the Supreme Court held that, with respect to grants of land made by the State of Vindhya Pradesh before its merger in Uttar Pradesh, the doctrine of act of State was no bar to enforcement, even if the grants were *mala fide*; and the grants, being valid, fell under the property guarantees of the Indian Constitution (art. 32) and could only be withdrawn upon due legal process.[7] The judgment, delivered by Bose, J.,

[1] *Raja Rajinder Chand* v. *Mst. Sukhi*, I.L.R. vol. XXIV, p. 74.
[2] See *supra*, p. 116.   [3] S. 10.
[4] *State of Madras* v. *Rajagopalan*, A.I.R. (1955), S.C. 817. See *supra*, p. 182. The case was treated on the same basis as a case arising out of the merger of several States: *Rajvi Amar Singh* v. *State of Rajasthan*, A.I.R. (1958), S.C. 228.
[5] *Mihan Singh* v. *The Sub-divisional Canal Officer*, I.L.R. vol. XXI, p. 64.
[6] *Rajvi Amar Singh* v. *State of Rajasthan*, A.I.R. (1958), S.C. 228.
[7] *Vivendra Singh* v. *State of Uttar Pradesh*, I.L.R. vol. XXII, p. 131. Followed by *Gajjan Singh* v. *Union of India*, ibid. vol. XXIII, p. 101.

distinguished the process of merger which occurred in India from the analogous events in the nineteenth century, on the ground that the titleholders were at all times Indian citizens protected by the Constitution, and it is impossible for a sovereign to exercise an act of State against its own subjects.

It is impossible to think of those who sat down together in the Constituent Assembly and of those who sent representatives there, as conqueror and conquered, as those who ceded and as those who absorbed, as sovereigns or their plenipotentiaries contracting alliances and entering into treaties as high contracting parties to an Act of State.

However, the issue of act of State came before the Supreme Court again in 1958 on a different set of facts, and it was this time held to bar a claim based on a contract with the previous sovereign.[1] The appellant was the holder of a concession granted by the ruler of Jind in 1938, which entitled him to a monopoly in the manufacture of cement for a period of twenty-five years. The concession agreement provided that the concessionaire would be assessed for income tax in accordance with the State procedure, but that the rate of tax could always be 4 per cent up to a limit of an income of 5 lakhs, and 5 per cent on any income in excess. Jind acceded to the Dominion of India on 15 August 1947, and on 5 May 1948 joined the Patiala and East Punjab States Union. The Covenant of Merger provided that:

all rights, authority and jurisdiction belonging to the ruler which appertain or are incidental to the Government of the Covenanting States shall vest in the Union and shall therefore be exercisable only as provided by this Covenant or by the constitution to be framed thereunder; all duties and obligations of the ruler pertaining or incidental to the Government of the Covenanting State shall devolve on the Union and shall be discharged by it.

On 20 August 1948 the Rajapramukh issued an Ordinance which provided that all laws in Patiala should apply *mutatis mutandis* to the territories of the Union, and all laws in force in any Covenanting State taken over by the Union would be repealed. On 24 November 1949 the Rajapramukh accepted the Indian Constitution, and in 1950 the Patiala Union accepted the Federal Financial Integration Scheme, thereby becoming taxable by the Union of India. The cement company sought to maintain its privileged taxable position by reliance upon the terms of the Covenant of

1 *Dalmia Dadri Cement Co.* v. *Commissioner of Income Tax*, ibid. vol. xxv, p. 79. Followed in *The State of Saurashtra* v. *Jamadar Mohammed Abdulla*, A.I.R. (1962), S.C. 445; *Promod Chandra Deb* v. *The State of Orissa*, A.I.R. (1962), S.C. 1288; *Buland Sugar Co. Ltd* v. *Union of India*, A.I.R. (1962), All. 425; *Vinayak Shripatrao Patwordhan* v. *State of Bombay*, A.I.R. (1961), Bomb. 11.

Merger, and was met with the defence of act of State. The plaintiff sought to exclude the defence by contending that, since the Ruler of Jind had been an absolute monarch, the concession was a law, and that the Ordinance should be interpreted by reference to the rule of construction that general laws do not interfere with rights under special laws; and that if the intention was so to interfere, the Act was constitutionally invalid as offending property guarantees. Furthermore, the Ruler had, in the Covenant of Merger, assigned the concession to the new State, which was bound by agreement. The defence was upheld by the majority, the Supreme Court saying: 'It is also well established that in the new situation these residents do not carry with them the rights which they possessed as subjects of the ex-sovereign, and that, as subjects of the new sovereign, they have only such rights as are granted or recognized by him.'[1]

Various legal strands are interwoven in the decision. The plaintiff's claim was based upon a contract with the previous government, not upon legislation, which was repealed by the ordinance of the new government. The issue, therefore, was not one of legislative cancellation of rights, but continuity of the concession. The Covenant was pleaded, not to bridge the abyss between two sovereignties, but rather as reinforcement of the continuity which was alleged to exist in virtue of succession. The Supreme Court's references to the automatic abrogation of rights are not to be taken as statements on the substantive law of succession, but as conclusions from the bar imposed with respect to claims based on continuity by the act of State doctrine. On the appositeness of the latter in the case of merger Bose, J., delivered a significant separate judgment. He pointed out that opinion increasingly favoured the survival of personal rights upon State succession, and that to rely uncritically on English decisions withdrawn from their context would be to disregard modern conceptions about immovable property. The instant decision must be taken to be no more than a ruling that the Covenant of Merger, as a public agreement, was unenforceable in the courts, whereupon the act of State doctrine would appear as an aspect of the constitutional principle that no executive agreement, unsupported by legislation, can modify the legal position of the subject. So far as the extension of the doctrine to exclude the claim based upon succession was concerned, it must be understood, Bose, J., concluded, as restricted to contractual relations with the government, and no implication was to be raised respecting rights in immovable property.[2]

In this decision the Supreme Court ignored the principles it had itself laid down in 1954[3] in holding that the only point was whether an existing

1 I.L.R. vol. xxv, p. 82. 2 At p. 87.
3 *Vivendra Singh* v. *State of Uttar Pradesh*, I.L.R. vol. xxii, p. 131.

State had acquired the territory of another State; the nationality of the claimants and the form of the amalgamation were both treated as irrelevant factors. The majority also seem to have treated as irrelevant the distinction made by Bose, J., which he had also made in the 1954 decision, between claims to property and claims under governmental contracts. Both were assimilated in the one ruling that in the new situation these residents do not carry with them the rights which they possessed as subjects of the ex-sovereign, and that, as subjects of the new sovereign, they have only such rights as are granted or recognized by him.[1] As for the point made in the 1954 decision[2] that the claimants were at all times Indian citizens protected by the Constitution, the Court now held that the right of citizenship commences when the Act of State terminates, and the two cannot therefore coexist.[3] And as for the international law rule on the subject, it was held to be no answer to say that private property must be respected by the sovereign who accepts the cession, because this is something that cannot be domestically enforced.

Whatever be the situation with respect to act of State, it is clear that the competence of a unitary State to legislate to cancel title granted in merged territory can only be controlled by the Constitution. Even if the Constitution contains property guarantees,[4] it might also forbid the courts to exercise jurisdiction in any dispute arising out of agreements between the merged and the absorbing States.[5]

(vi) *The act of State doctrine in civil law systems*

While civil law systems do not possess a doctrine of act of State as such, certain of them do have a rule concerning the relationship of the executive and the judiciary in the matter of treaty interpretation, which in some circumstances achieves the same result.[6] This rule is that a court is required to seek an executive ruling on the interpretation of a treaty which is ambiguous, and, if the treaty contains provisions for the transfer of obligations and the executive chooses to direct the court that the plaintiff's rights are excluded, the latter's suit is arrested. In Italy this rule was laid down by the Court of Cassation in 1885 as follows:

> It does not belong to the judicial authority to pass an opinion on the existence of obligations which it is asserted resulted from a diplomatic treaty and bind a State

---

1 *Promod Chandra Deb* v. *The State of Orissa*, A.I.R. (1962), S.C. 1288
2 At p. 1289.   3 At p. 1301.
4 *Idumati* v. *State of Saurashtra*, I.L.R. vol. XXIII, p. 109.
5 *Maharaj Umeg Singh* v. *State of Bombay*, ibid. vol. XXII, p. 138.
6 Gidel, p. 217; Guggenheim, p. 93. *Association des porteurs de parts de scripts lombards* v. *Italian State and Comité des obligataires de la Compagnie des chemins de fer Danube-Save-Adriatique*, Clunet, vol. XC (1963), p. 781.

in relation to individuals, no more than to decide that such obligations, supposing they exist, have passed from one State to another as a result of the cession of provinces.[1]

If the treaty containing transmission clauses is clear, French courts may apply it, but if it requires to be interpreted then they must refer it to the executive. In 1874 a court at Montpellier stated:

L'État qui absorbe l'autre est censé de l'annexer avec ses obligations et ses droits, ses charges et ses avantages résultant des traités, à moins qu'il ne manifeste une intention contraire dans la forme et dans les limites du droit international.[2]

Where there is no treaty with a transmission clause, then antecedent obligations of the predecessor State cannot be established against France by administrative law procedure. This was laid down by the *Conseil d'État* in 1906 in respect of claims arising after the French conquest of Dahomey. It was held that:

A la vérité, les requérants soutiennent que, par suite de la prise de possession du Dahomey par la France, le Gouvernement français est tenu des dettes qui auraient pu incomber à l'ancien gouvernement du Dahomey; mais que cette prétention soulève un débat relatif à l'exercice des droits de souveraineté résultant pour la France de l'annexion du Dahomey, et que ce n'est pas au Conseil d'État qu'il appartient de se prononcer sur un litige de cette nature.[3]

5. EXPROPRIATION OF ACQUIRED RIGHTS AND THE PRINCIPLE OF COMPENSATION

There is little doubt that the respect for acquired rights is a principle well established in international law.[4] Just how far this protection extends and what exactly is its nature are matters of considerable controversy. Is the successor State bound to maintain acquired rights in existence in perpetuity, or may it abrogate these rights by an exercise of its own sovereign power? If it may so abrogate them, what then is its obligation towards the titleholders? This question the Permanent Court of International Justice in the *German Settlers* Case was not called on to determine

1 *L'Affaire de la Ville de Crémone*, Clunet (1886), p. 746.
2 *Iconomidis* v. *Couve, Dugrip R. et Cie*, ibid. (1874), p. 184.
3 *Mante et Borelli de Régis* v. *État Français*, ibid. (1906), p. 785. See also D. 91, 3. 41; *Affaire Dame Ravero, Recueil des arrêts du Conseil d'État* (1904), p. 662.
4 Kaeckenbeeck in Hague *Recueil*, vol. LIX (1937), p. 354; *B.Y.* vol. XVII (1936), p. 12; Gidel, p. 84. Freeman suggests that the real cause of much of the confusion surrounding the doctrine of acquired rights is due to the attempt to lay down a broad principle of immunity from expropriating legislation: *The International Responsibility of States for Denial of Justice* (1938), p. 515. See Fitzmaurice in Hague *Recueil*, vol. LXXIII (1948), p. 286.

because Poland was bound by treaty not to legislate to terminate acquired rights, and the court was only concerned to establish which rights were acquired. 'The general question', it said, 'whether and under what circumstances a State may modify and cancel private rights by its sovereign legislative power, requires no consideration here.'[1]

It cannot be admitted that an acquired right always persists under the new sovereign on exactly the same terms as it existed under the old. To admit this would be to admit that the legal relationship which existed between the old sovereign and the titleholder has been inherited by the successor State. This is not necessarily the case. What the new sovereign does inherit is the fact of the existence of the titleholder's interest. In placing itself into a relationship with this factual situation it incurs a new legal duty to the titleholder, which duty is not necessarily coterminous with that which was previously owed by the old State. An acquired right becomes in the act of the change of sovereignty subject to the law of the successor State.[2] The latter may assimilate it into its own legal order. It may make it subject to its own legal formalities,[3] to its own taxation laws,[4] to its own rules governing user and alienation; and its own law will be recognized by third States as governing testamentary capacity to dispose of the right[5] and jurisdiction of its courts to entertain actions with respect to it.[6] On 16 November 1861 the Queen's Advocate reported on the mining rights of a British subject in San Domingo, which that year was annexed by Spain. He could see no reason for the British Government's insisting that the rights in question should be preserved in all respects as they were enjoyed before the annexation. Spain, he considered, was entitled to make them subject to its own mining laws.[7]

---

[1] P.C.I.J., Ser. B, no. 6 at p. 36. Article 15 of the Minorities Treaty: 'The right of the optants to retain immovable property in Poland shall not be affected in any way by laws, ordinances or other measures which are not applicable to Polish nationals': *B.T.S.* 1919, no. 20, Cmd. 479.

[2] Brierly in Hague *Recueil*, vol. LVIII (1936), p. 65.

[3] The Attorney-General of the United States was of the opinion that 'if any substantial act remains to be done, resting on the grace, favour or discretion of the government to secure to an applicant or alleged concessionary a franchise or right in public property thus ceded by one nation to another, such additional actions must be obtained in accordance with the laws of the present and not former owner': 22 Op. A.-G. p. 546; see Mosler, p. 35.

[4] *In re Potters Works of Ziegler Brothers*, *A.J.* vol. I (1907), p. 237. See also *Kügele v. Polish State*, *Ann. Dig.* vol. VI, Case no. 34.

[5] Although in the case of *Re Wayda's Estate* it was held by a United States court that the estate of a Galician who died resident in the United States must pass by Austrian law of succession because the right to it had vested under that law: *Ann. Dig.* vol. II, Case no. 44.

[6] *Syrian State Succession (Haifa Leases)* Case, *Ann. Dig.* vol. III, Case no. 70.

[7] Opinion of 16 November 1861, F.O. 83/2262; O'Connell, Appendix no. 21.

During the past century the prevailing concept of the sanctity of private property led to an assumption that a successor State could not interfere with such property in absorbed territories. This assumption was supported by the long line of American decisions which established that private property in the regions incorporated into the United States had not been abrogated by the act of incorporation, and were after the act protected by the provisions of the Constitution relating to property rights. More recently, however, the tendency towards nationalization of certain basic industries in some countries, and of all forms of property in others, has compelled the abandonment of any such assumption. It is now recognized that a sovereign State has the competence in international law to expropriate rights possessed by foreigners in its territory.[1] There is no reason why a successor State should be in any less strong a position in this respect than any other State, or why acquired rights should be invested after a change of sovereignty with a 'sanctity and permanence'[2] greater than they had before. Change of sovereignty often involves corresponding changes in the social and economic structure of the community, and a successor State must focus the principle of respect for acquired rights against the demands made by these changes. 'Expropriation for reasons of public utility, judicial liquidation and similar measures' was recognized by the Permanent Court of International Justice in the *Upper Silesia* Case to be beyond the measures which generally accepted international law does not sanction in respect of foreign nationals.[3] Until a successor State legislates to terminate acquired rights, however, these remain in existence as facts. Legislation to abrogate them must therefore be specific and express, and a judge must interpret it strictly so as to maintain in being acquired rights which are not unequivocally destroyed.[4]

1 O'Connell, *International Law* (1965), vol. II, ch. 25.
2 Kaeckenbeeck in Hague *Recueil*, vol. LIX (1937), p. 355.
3 P.C.I.J. ser. A, no. 7, p. 22. In *Niederstrasser* v. *Polish State*, the Upper Silesian Arbitral Tribunal held that 'the successor State may, like the ceding State, take away and modify these rights by legislative action': *Ann. Dig.* vol. VI, Case no. 33. In his brief in the *Brown* Case the British agent said: 'When you come to deal with private rights, I agree that, speaking generally, there has been more or less a general consensus as to the way in which it should be treated, that, as between themselves and the annexed State, let the private rights that have accrued to other individuals be maintained and do not interfere with them; certainly not at the time of annexation, or only interfere with them after a Government has been set up': Nielsen, p. 185.
4 Kaeckenbeeck describes this as the principle of 'non-retroactivity', which binds the judge of the successor State as a rule of interpretation: *B.Y.* vol. XVII (1936), p. 13; Hague *Recueil*, vol. LIX (1937), p. 355. In *Chicago Railway Company* v. *McGlinn*, it was said that 'after annexation the new sovereign may apply its law to alter rights, but not arbitrarily and only in accordance with its own law': 114 U.S. 542 at p. 546. See Verdross in Hague *Recueil*, vol. XXXVII (1931), p. 358. It is, however, not sufficient

The principle of respect for acquired rights in international law is no more than a principle that change of sovereignty should not touch the interests of individuals more than is necessary. This does not mean that these interests may not be interfered with at all. The doctrine merely indemnifies the titleholders from complete and arbitrary destruction of their interests, and secures for them an impartiality on the part of the successor State in the exercise of its discretion.[1] There can be no general immunity from expropriating legislation. Such expropriation, however, is only justified when accompanied by a recognition of the equities involved. If the doctrine of acquired rights does not protect the titleholders from expropriation, it at least guarantees them restitution. The successor State, once it extends its sovereignty over the absorbed area, has a choice as to the course it will adopt. On the one hand it may permit acquired rights to continue in existence; on the other hand, it may legislate to alter or entirely cancel them. If it adopts the latter course it must then comply with the minimum standards set by international law, and either pay compensation or grant new titles of some equivalent value.[2] A successor State thus stands in the same position with respect to acquired rights as any other State, and the fact that the rights have come into existence under its predecessor is immaterial. In the case of *Kulin, Emeric* v. *Roumanian State* the Roumanian–Hungarian Mixed Arbitral Tribunal entertained the claim of certain persons whose landed estates situated in territory transferred from Hungary to Roumania had been expropriated without compensation. It was alleged that this was a violation of article 250 of the Treaty of Trianon. The Tribunal, without deciding upon the application of this article, held that 'a measure as a result of which the property of an ex-enemy is taken away in its entirety from the owner constitutes *prima facie* a violation of the general principle of respect of acquired rights and oversteps the limits of common international law'.[3]

The juridical justification for the obligation to pay compensation is to be found in the concept of unjustified enrichment, which lies at the basis of the doctrine of acquired rights, and constitutes, as Gidel says, 'a positive obligation which exists in the relations between individuals and which has been sanctioned in every legislation and has a fixed place in international

---

to hold that the doctrine of acquired rights merely ensures equality of treatment for aliens and nationals. This is to deny any minimum standard of international law applicable to them both: see Freeman, *op. cit.* p. 504.

1 Freeman, *op. cit.* p. 502.
2 Dupuis, in Hague *Recueil*, vol. XXXII (1930), p. 163. The American-Great Britian Claims Arbitration Tribunal appeared to regard expropriation as a legitimate act which created an obligation to compensate: *Robert E. Brown* Case, U.N. Rep. vol. VI, p. 128.   3 *Ann. Dig.* vol. IV, Case no. 59.

law'.[1] If a successor State legislates to abrogate the interest of a private person the latter has suffered a detriment, and the former is enriched at his expense. The enrichment consists in the value of the interest which is appropriated. The duty which international law imposes on the successor State is a duty to satisfy the equities involved in the factual situation with which it has come into relationship.[2] 'Individual confiscation of property without indemity', writes Kaeckenbeeck, 'undoubtedly falls short of the international standard of civilized society, because it violates the sense of equity of the civilized world, on which its deepest legal convictions rest, which is at the root of all legislation on expropriation, and which has been ratified by a long international custom.'[3]

It is upon the basis of unjustified enrichment that the principles of compensation can best be rationalized.[4] The titleholder is not indemnified because the State has committed some tortious act, nor because it has broken a legal relationship existing between him and itself. On the contrary, compensation is paid, as Kaeckenbeeck points out, 'simply as an equitable alleviation of the economic sacrifice demanded on behalf of the community'.[5] For this reason, the compensation which must be paid need not be the maximum. The injustice is relieved by a payment which is reasonable and approximates to the lowest market value of the interest. This is a standard established in diplomatic practice, and it is as yet only rudimentary.[6]

The doctrine of acquired rights is perhaps one of the few principles firmly established in the law of State succession, and the one which admits of least dispute. But there is, as the memorandum submitted by the Secretary-General of the United Nations to the International Law Commission in 1949 suggests, 'no adequate measure of certainty with regard to its application to the various categories of private rights such as those grounded in the public debt, in concessionary contracts, in relations of public service and the like'.[7] Despite this uncertainty, the assimilation

1 Gidel, p. 134.
2 Mosler, p. 37. 'The idea of equity', he says, 'is the motive; the obligation is found in international custom.'
3 *B.Y.* vol. XVII (1936), p. 16.
4 'The fact of refusing compensation', says Kaeckenbeeck, would 'constitute a notorious injustice': Hague *Recueil*, vol. LIX (1937), p. 360. Mosler locates the basis of obligation in equity (*Billigkeit*), p. 37.
5 *B.Y.* vol. XVII (1936), p. 16; Hague *Recueil*, vol. LIX (1937), p. 359. The author's views on the subject of expropriation and compensation, with supporting citations, will be found in *International Law* (1965), vol. II, ch. 25.
6 Kaeckenbeeck, *loc. cit.* p. 361.
7 Survey of International Law in Relation to the work of Codification of the International Law Commission. Preparatory Work. Memorandum submitted by the Secretary-General: A/CN. 4/1/Rev. 1.

of these categories of rights to the concept of acquired rights is probably the basis upon which the treatment of most of the problems of State succession may profitably be attempted.[1] In the following chapters such an attempt will be made.

[1] That unjust enrichment is a juridical concept fundamental to Western European legal systems is now well acknowledged. It is found in Roman law, it was formulated in modern legal systems on a natural law basis, and it is found today in the principal of them. The author's views on the subject will be found, with citations, in *American Journal of Comparative Law*, vol. v (1956), p. 2. For the doctrine in international law see Cheng, *General Principles of Law, as Applied by International Courts and Tribunals* (1953) and in *Current Legal Problems*, vol. VIII (1955), p. 185.

Chapter 11

DIPLOMATIC AND JUDICIAL PRACTICE IN THE MATTER OF ACQUIRED RIGHTS

I. Practice in Cases of Cession and Annexation

Most of the treaties of cession of the nineteenth century, whether relating to European, American or undeveloped countries, contained provisions for the protection of acquired rights.[1] As a result of the regularity of such practice diplomatic correspondence on the subject is not extensive, and judicial authority, as McNair points out,[2] is scanty. In this chapter consideration will be given to State practice in the matter of private interests in tangible property.

[1] The most important of such treaties were: Treaty of Peace between France and Austria, 1814, *M.R. Suppl.* vol. VI, p. 1, art. 27 at p. 11; Act of the Congress of Vienna, 1815, *ibid.* p. 379, art. 103 at p. 426; Treaty of Cession of Florida, 1819, *M.R. Suppl.* vol. IX, p. 328, art. 8 at p. 334; Treaty of London, 1839, *M.R. Suppl.* vol. XX, p. 773, art. 23 at p. 787; Treaty of Guadalupe Hidalgo, 1848, *M.N.R.G.* vol. XIV, p. 7, art. 8 at p. 19; Bloemfontein Convention, 1854, *B.F.S.P.* vol. LVI (1854), p. 331, art. 4 at p. 332; Treaty between France and Austria, 1859, *M.N.R.G.* vol. XVI, pt. II, p. 516, art. 21 at p. 564; Convention between France and Sardinia, 1860, to settle questions arising out of the cession of Savoy and Nice, *M.N.R.G.* vol. XVII, pt. II, p. 22, art. 8 at p. 24; Treaty of Vienna, 1864, *M.N.R.G.* vol. XVII, pt. II, p. 474, art. 17 at p. 482; Treaty of Washington, 1867, Malloy, vol. II, p. 1521, art. 3 at p. 1523; Additional Convention to the Treaty of Frankfurt, 1871, *M.N.R.G.* vol. XX, p. 847, arts. 3 and 10 at pp. 849, 855; Convention of 1881 relative to the settlement of questions arising from the rectification of the Turko-Greek boundary, *M.N.R.G.* 2nd ser., vol. VI, p. 753, arts. 3 and 4 at p. 755; Pretoria Convention, 1881, *B.F.S.P.* vol. LXXII (1881), p. 900, art. 2 at p. 907; Treaty of Paris, 1898, Malloy, vol. II, p. 1690, arts. 8, 9, 12 and 13 at pp. 1692 *et seq.*; Treaty of Portsmouth, 1905, *B.F.S.P.* vol. XCVIII (1905), p. 735, art. V at p. 737; Treaty of Constantinople, 1913, *B.F.S.P.* vol. CVII (1914), pt. I, p. 706, art. IX at p. 711; Treaty of Athens, 1913, *B.F.S.P.* vol. CVII (1914), pt. I, p. 892, art. VI at p. 895; Treaty of Lausanne, 1923, *L.N.T.S.* (1924), vol. XXVIII, p. 11, art. 65 at p. 55. This provision followed a declaration that the property of *ressortissants* would be treated in accordance with 'ordinary international law': art. 2, p. 11; Geneva Convention, 1922, *B.F.S.P.* vol. CXVIII, p. 365, art. 4 at p. 367. In the Patents of Annexation of Hesse, Nassau, Hanover and Frankfurt in 1866, Prussia proclaimed that acquired rights would not be interfered with: *B.F.S.P.* vol. LVI (1866), pp. 1034, 1078, 1087, 1094. The most recent treaties do not mention acquired rights, which suggests that practice in this regard is now so well formulated that no treaty provision is regarded as necessary.

[2] *Legal Effects of War* (3rd ed. 1948), p. 386.

(i) *The cession of Java by Great Britain to the Netherlands, 1830*

After the transfer of Java to Holland in 1830 certain British subjects complained that the Dutch administration was violating the conditions of tenure of land granted to the complainants by the British Government in 1813. The latter instructed the British Ambassador at the Hague that the

> obligation on the British Government, arising from the Contract, could not be discharged by the transfer of the Island to a third party, and the original purchasers of the Estates, or those to whom they might have assigned them, were entitled to expect that their interests would be secured in any arrangements which might be made for effecting such transfer.... His Majesty's Government, therefore, consider that the Netherland Government when they succeeded to the rights which the British Government possessed in Java, became subject and liable to all the obligations and engagements into which the latter had entered or had contracted with the proprietors of these Estates.[1]

Negotiations with the Dutch Government respecting the claims of the British landholders persisted for some four years without result. In 1834 the Foreign Office requested the advice of the King's Advocate as to the further steps to be taken. It was pointed out in the reference that the Dutch administration had altered the conditions of tenure, and also imposed taxation on the estates. They had, in addition, requisitioned certain of the equipment of the estates. The King's Advocate admitted the right of the administration to levy taxation. So far as the other actions were concerned, they constituted 'a direct violation of the terms of the Contract, to which they [the Dutch] as deriving their Title from the British Government, the original Vendors, were bound to conform'.[2] This Opinion, in asserting a transmission of the contract of sale from the old sovereign to the new, indicates an acceptance of the universal succession theory.

1 Instructions of 20 April 1830, F.O. 238/46, no. 11.
2 Opinion of 29 September 1934, F.O. 83/2291 O'Connell, Appendix no. 12. In 1885 the Law Officers gave an Opinion on the question of the recognition by Greece of Turkish land titles in territory ceded by Turkey in 1878. Greece insisted on proof of title. Turkey argued that production of any document purporting to have conveyed land was sufficient. The Foreign Office upheld the Turkish view. The Law Officers did not advise on the merits; Opinion of 6 February 1885, F.O. Confidential Papers (5246), no. 159, O'Connell, Appendix no. 45. A similar Opinion was given by the Law Officers on 3 February 1876 respecting the rights of a British subject in the Sulu Islands which were ceded in that year by their sultan to Spain: F.O. Confidential Papers (4328), no. 69, O'Connell, Appendix no. 36.

(ii) *The cession of Fiji to Great Britain, 1874*

The annexation of the Fiji Islands by Great Britain in 1874 gave rise to disputes with the United States and Germany concerning the titles to land held in the islands by citizens of these countries.[1] There was complete agreement upon the general principle that title to land was not affected by the change of sovereignty, and the dispute turned on the practical application of that principle rather than on the principle itself. The Treaty of Cession of 19 October 1874[2] recognized that 'the absolute proprietorship of all lands not shown to be alienated so as to become *bona fide* the property of Europeans or other foreigners' had become vested in the Queen. Claims to alienated land were in due course to be investigated and equitably adjusted. For this purpose a Commission was subsequently appointed. It rejected the claims of certain nationals of the United States and Germany.[3] The Governments of these two countries objected to the procedure adopted by the Commission, and in particular to the throwing of the onus of proof on the landholders that the claims had been acquired *bona fide*. The German Ambassador in London, in a memorandum submitted to the Foreign Office in 1883, rejected the test of *bona fides*:

> Both according to the wording of this document [the Treaty of Cession] and according to the common principles of international law the right to lands which German subjects had acquired there previous to the English annexation could only be unrecognized in cases of proved *mala fides*, and according to the opinion of the German Government, in all cases where the legal acquisition is duly proved by documentary evidence in forms recognized as valid under the earlier sovereignty, or where in default of such documentary evidence the proofs have not been brought against the *bona fide* acquisition, the property of the respective subjects of the German Empire should be recognized and confirmed.[4]

The German claims were settled in 1884 by payment of compensation,[5] but the controversy with the United States continued. While Great Britain made no attempt to deny that by international law property rights are unaffected by annexation, it nevertheless adhered to the decisions of the Commission respecting the claims of United States nationals. Eventually, as late as 1922, the United States brought the principal of these claims—that of one Burt—before the British American Claims Tribunal.[6] In 1865 Burt had bought land in Fiji from a native chief. Subsequently he had been

---

1 In the instructions to the Governor of Fiji in 1875 the British Government clearly indicated its intention to respect rights of property: C. 1114.
2 C. 3584.
3 For the Report of the Commission see *B.F.S.P.* vol. LXXIII, p. 1184.
4 C. 3815, p. 2.   5 *B.F.S.P.* vol. LXXVI, p. 887.
6 *George Rodney Burt* Case, U.N. Rep. vol. VI, p. 93.

expelled by the natives. He had filed a claim to the land after the annexation of the islands, and in due course his alleged rights had been examined by the Commission. The latter had rejected his claim as insufficiently evidenced. In its argument before the tribunal the British Government contended that Burt had not acquired a valid title as the chief had no power to dispose of the land without the concurrence of a certain class of persons known as 'occupiers of the soil'. The tribunal found that evidence of native law to this effect was vague, that Britain had itself acted on the assumption that the chiefs had power to dispose of the land, and, therefore, that Burt had suffered a denial of a validly acquired right.[1] In delivering its award the tribunal considered the obligation of a successor State with respect to the acquired rights of private persons. It stated:

> If Burt had at the time a valid title to the lands it is plain that under all the circumstances the Government was bound to recognize and respect it.... The Crown authorities by refusing to recognize his title, failed to carry out the obligation which Great Britain, as the succeeding Power in the islands, must be held to have assumed.[2]

(iii) *The establishment of British protectorate over the Gilbert Islands, 1892*

In 1892 when the British Government established a protectorate over the Gilbert Islands the American Government took the view that

> it has a right to expect that the rights and interests of American citizens established in the Gilbert Islands will be as fully respected and confirmed under Her Majesty's Protectorate as they could have been had the United States accepted the offer of protection not long since solicited by the rulers of those islands.[3]

The British Government replied assuring the United States that 'the rights and interests of United States citizens established in the Gilbert Islands will be fully recognized and respected'.[4]

(iv) *The cession of German territory to Poland, 1919*

The doctrine of acquired rights was emphatically held to be part of international law in two important cases which related to private land

---

[1] *Ibid.* p. 99. In another claim brought by the United States before the same tribunal in respect of land in New Zealand, it was held that the claimant had acquired no more than a native customary title, the content and scope of which were very uncertain, and which could not be held to extend to full property or *dominium*: *William Webster* Claim, ibid. p. 166 at p. 168; see also the claims of *Benson Robert Henry*, ibid. p. 100; *Heirs of John B. W. Williams*, ibid. p. 104; *Isaac M. Brower*, ibid. p. 109.
[2] *Ibid.* p. 98.   [3] *For. Rel.* 1892, p. 241.
[4] *Ibid.* p. 246.

tenure in territories incorporated in Poland under the Treaty of Versailles. The first of these cases, known as the *German Settlers* Case, was concerned with the interpretation of titles to lands held by German settlers in Poland. In 1886 the Prussian Government had enacted a law which created a Settlement Commission for the purpose of compulsorily acquiring land in a Polish province of Prussia, and for the settling thereon of Germans. A rather unusual system of landholding was devised, based on two kinds of contract.[1] Under the first, known as *Rentengutsvertrag*, lands were made over to the settlers in perpetuity under a contract of sale, pursuant to which a transfer might be obtained on payment of the balance of a fixed redeemable rent. Under the second type of contract, known as *Pachtvertrag*, the lands were leased to the settlers for a term of years with considerable security of tenure.

In 1920 Poland evicted all the settlers who had not taken the transfer of title before the date of the Armistice, and a complaint was made on behalf of the interested parties to the League of Nations. The Council of the League, after some hesitation, exercised the powers granted to it under article 12 of the Minorities Treaty of 28 June 1919, and requested an advisory opinion on the matter from the Permanent Court. In its pleadings before the court Poland argued that Germany was incapacitated from executing a transfer of land after the date of the Armistice, and that the transfers granted to the settlers after that date were consequently invalid. It was also alleged that the contracts were intended to secure the German colonization of Poland and that they could be disregarded under article 92 of the Treaty of Versailles, which excluded from the share of financial liabilities of Germany and Prussia to be borne by Poland that part of the debt which 'arises from measures adopted by the German and Prussian Governments with a view to the German colonization of Poland'.[2] The court rejected each of the Polish allegations. It decided that the granting of a transfer after the date of the Armistice was giving effect to rights

---

1 *Settlers of German Origin in Territory ceded by Germany to Poland*, P.C.I.J. ser. B, no. 6, p. 15. See Barclay, Kaufmann, Struycken and Kipp, *Études concernant la doctrine de la succession d'État; quatre consultations* (1924).

2 The Polish courts expressed the official point of view in their decisions regarding the rights of Germans in the incorporated territories. In one case, in which a claim was made before a Polish court alleging that Poland had contravened international law in expropriating land, title to which had been given in 1919 pursuant to a contract of sale made in 1912, the court held that there was no provision in the Treaty of Versailles compelling Poland to take over the obligations of the German Empire. 'No generally recognized international custom prescribes that a State which is the successor to another State accepts solely by reason of State succession the obligations of private law of the State which was its predecessor.' It was further argued that since the dismemberment of Poland had not been acquiesced in, these lands had never ceased to be Polish: *Polish State Treasury* v. *von Bismarck*, *Ann. Dig.* vol. II, Case no. 39.

already created.[1] 'The German Government as well as the Prussian State', it found, 'is to be considered as having continued to be competent to undertake transactions falling within the normal administration of the country during that period.'[2] The contracts themselves were not, as Poland claimed, only inchoate or imperfect rights unenforceable in law until the grant of a transfer,[3] but were proper legal rights. The State had no arbitrary power to refuse a transfer if the conditions had been fulfilled.[4] The purchasers had rights to the lands even before the transfer, and this was an interest recognized and protected by the law. Even while holding under contract they had acquired something in the nature of a *jus ad rem* analogous to the right possessed by the usufructuary in Roman law. After the transfer they acquired a *jus in re*.[5] The interests in question were held to be protected by article 7 of the Minorities Treaty of 1919, which made all Polish nationals equal before the law, and secured for them the enjoyment of 'the same civil and political rights without distinction as to race, language or religion'. The expression 'civil rights', it was decided, included 'rights acquired under a contract for the possession or use of property'.[6]

The court, however, went beyond the treaty provisions and rested its decision also on the international law doctrine of respect for acquired rights. It was of opinion that

private rights acquired under existing law do not cease on a change of sovereignty.... It can hardly be maintained that, although the law survives, private rights acquired under it have perished. Such a contention is based on no principle and would be contrary to an almost universal opinion and practice.... Even those who contest the existence in international law of a general principle of State succession do not go so far as to maintain that private rights including those acquired from the State as the owner of the property are invalid as against a successor in sovereignty.[7]

To Poland's contention that it took all the property of the German Empire unburdened because the Treaty of Versailles did not state otherwise, the court answered that 'no treaty is required for the preservation of the rights and obligations now in question'. In its opinion 'no conclusion can be drawn from the silence of the Treaty of Peace'. On the contrary, the treaty appeared to sanction the principle of survival of acquired rights; the court stated:

It is true that the Treaty of Peace does not in terms formally announce the principle that, in the case of a change of sovereignty, private rights are to be respected, but

---

1 P.C.I.J. ser. B, no. 6, p. 40.   2 Ibid. p. 28.   3 Ibid. p. 30.
4 Ibid. p. 32.   5 Ibid. p. 33.   6 Ibid. p. 23.   7 Ibid. p. 36.

this principle is clearly recognized by the Treaty. Under Article 75, contracts between the inhabitants of Alsace-Lorraine and the former German authorities are as a rule maintained, and if terminated by France in the general interest, equitable compensation must be accorded under certain conditions.

If this rule prevailed in Alsace-Lorraine, which was returned to France, 'it is hardly conceivable that it was intended by the Treaty to give discretionary powers as regards similar rights in territories the sovereignty of which was acquired only by cession'. It was pointed out that the treaty provided for the maintenance of a wide category of contracts between former enemies, and the conclusion was drawn that 'if as between enemies such contracts are maintained, it seems impossible that the Treaty should have countenanced the annulment of contracts between a State and its newly acquired nationals'.[1]

With respect to the *Pachtverträge*, the court was of opinion that 'a certain security of tenure is assured.... The holder becomes personally attached to the land, with a reasonable expectancy of permanent occupancy.'[2] Such rights also survived the change of sovereignty.[3]

The importance of this case lies not only in its explicit pronouncement in favour of the existence in international law of the doctrine of acquired rights,[4] but also because it defined as acquired rights certain interests which were of a mixed public and private character.[5] The original political motive behind them, the court considered, did not deprive the contracts of their legal character.

The fact that there was a political purpose behind the colonization scheme cannot affect the private rights acquired under the law.... The political motive originally connected with the *Rentengutsverträge* does not in any way deprive them of their character as contracts under civil law, and the few clauses which they contain of a distinctively political character become inoperative without interfering in the least with the normal execution of their essential clauses.[6]

The second case considered by the court related to the Geneva Convention of 1922.[7] This convention contained three headings: the first was intended to secure for a certain time the maintenance of German law in force in Polish Upper Silesia; the second contained a guarantee of acquired rights; the third gave Poland power to 'expropriate in Polish

1 *Ibid.* pp. 37–9. 2 *Ibid.* p. 41. 3 *Ibid.* p. 42.
4 Salvioli in Hague *Recueil*, vol. XII (1926), p. 105; Kaeckenbeeck in Hague *Recueil*, vol. LIX (1937), p. 343; to the contrary conclusion see Udina in Hague *Recueil*, vol. XLIV (1933), p. 741.
5 See Lauterpacht, *The Development of International Law by the Permanent Court of International Justice* (1958), p. 320.
6 P.C.I.J. ser. B, no. 6, p. 39.
7 *Certain German Interests in Polish Upper Silesia*, P.C.I.J. ser. A, no. 7.

Upper Silesia . . . undertakings belonging to the category of major industries'. Other property of German nationals was not to be liquidated. Purporting to act under the third head of the convention, Poland in June 1922 extended by decree to Upper Silesia the operation of a Polish law declaring void certain rights acquired by persons under deeds executed by the German Government after the date of the Armistice. One of the interests so expropriated was the Chorzów factory, owned by a German corporation. In 1915 a contract had been concluded between the *Reich* and a company which undertook to erect this factory at Chorzów. The *Reich* continued to own the land and could terminate the contract upon certain conditions. In 1919 a new company was formed which bought the factory outright from the *Reich*. The question of the expropriation of this factory was referred to the court by Germany. Poland argued that the alienation and creation of real rights after the date of the Armistice and before the transfer of sovereignty was invalid.

This argument the court rejected. It was of opinion that 'Germany undoubtedly retained until the actual transfer of sovereignty the right to dispose of her property, and only a misuse of this right could endow an act of alienation with the character of a breach of the Treaty'.[1] Although not expressly and positively enunciated, the principle of respect for acquired rights was, the court found, recognized by the Treaty of Versailles.[2] Those provisions of the treaty which related to the transfer of public property to the successor States as a result of cession of territory, 'must, in accordance with the principles governing State succession— principles maintained in the Treaty of Versailles and based on considerations of stability of legal rights—be construed in the light of the law in force at the time when the transfer of sovereignty took place'.[3] At that time, it was held, the ownership of the factory did not belong to the *Reich*. The *rights* possessed by the company were acquired, and the principle of respect for acquired rights is 'a principle which, as the Court has already had occasion to observe, forms part of generally accepted international law, which, as regards this point, amongst others, constitutes the basis of the Geneva Convention'.[4]

The expropriation allowed under Head III of the Convention, therefore, it was decided,

is a derogation from the rules generally applied in regard to the treatment of foreigners and the principle of respect for vested rights. As this derogation itself is strictly in the nature of an exception, it is permissible to conclude that no further derogation is allowed. Any measure affecting the property, rights and interests of

1 *Ibid.* p. 30.   2 *Ibid.* p. 31.
3 *Ibid.* p. 41.   4 *Ibid.* p. 42.

German subjects covered by Head III of the Convention, which is not justified ... and which oversteps the limits set by the generally accepted principles of international law, is therefore incompatible with the régime established under the Convention. . . . It follows from these same principles that the only measures prohibited are those which generally accepted international law does not sanction in respect of foreigners; expropriation for reasons of public utility, judicial liquidation and similar measures are not affected by the Convention.[1]

(v) *General judicial practice*

The *Reichsgericht* decided in 1924 that 'the circumstances that under article 51 of the Versailles Treaty Alsace-Lorraine, from a constitutional point of view, passed to France as from 11 November 1918, can exercise no effect on private legal relations established before the coming in force of the Treaty'.[2] The Italian Court of Cassation held that Italy was not entitled to question grants of land of the Austrian Government in territories ceded to it by Austria in the Treaty of St Germain.[3] The Judicial Committee of the Privy Council upheld native titles to land existing in territory ceded to the Crown by certain African chiefs. 'A mere change of sovereignty', it stated, 'is not to be presumed as meant to disturb rights of private owners; and the general terms of a cession are *prima facie* to be construed accordingly.'[4] A Palestine court considered in 1937 the effect of the separation of the mandated territories from the Ottoman Empire upon property rights previously acquired. The claimants alleged that the lands occupied by them were private property in Turkish law, even though registered in the name of the Sultan. The British Government contended that because the lands were so registered in the sovereign's name they were public property which passed to the successor State. The court, in the course of deciding the issue, observed that

the mere change of state, however, is not an act of confiscation of such property. This theory supports the generally accepted view that the substitution of a new State for an old can make no difference to existing private rights in property, unless such rights are specifically extinguished by the treaty itself, or by the subsequent acts of the conqueror.[5]

1 *Ibid.* p. 22.
2 *Fontes Jur. Gent.* ser. A, sect. II, vol. I, p. 118; see also p. 116.
3 Mosler, p. 30.
4 *Amodo Tijani* v. *Secretary, Southern Nigeria* [1921] 2 A.C. 399 per Lord Haldane, at p. 407.
5 *Heirs of Mohammed Selim* v. *The Government of Palestine*, *Ann. Dig.* vol. VIII, Case no. 39. The International Law Association at its meeting in Vienna in 1926 adopted a resolution that the Peace Treaties had given effect to international law, and that 'liquidation of acquired rights was not in conformity with international law': *Report of the 34th Conference of the International Law Association* (1927), p. 248.

(vi) *The termination of the federal status of Eritrea, 1962*

Eritrea, which had been an Italian colony, was federated with Ethiopia under United Nations auspices in 1952.[1] In 1952 Ethiopia unilaterally terminated the Federal status of Eritrea and applied to the territory the system of Unitary Administration of the Empire. The Imperial Order states:

> All rights, including the right to own and dispose of real property, exemptions, concessions and privileges of whatsoever nature heretofore granted, conferred or acquired within Eritrea, whether by law, order, contract or otherwise, and whether granted or conferred upon or acquired by Ethiopian or foreign persons, whether natural or legal, shall remain in full force and effect.[2]

The Order provides for the transfer to the Imperial Government of all rights, powers, duties and obligations of the Administration of Ethiopia.

(vii) *The cession of West New Guinea (West Irian) to Indonesia, 1962*

In virtue of the agreement of 15 August 1962 between Indonesia and the Netherlands[3] by which the latter transferred West New Guinea to the former, the United Nations would exercise a temporary authority in the territory pending introduction of the Indonesian administration. It was provided that the United Nations Temporary Executive Authority would take over existing Netherlands commitments in respect of concessions and property rights, and that after Indonesia had taken over the administration it would honour those commitments which were 'not inconsistent with the interests and economic development of the people of the territory'. A joint Indonesian-Netherlands commission would be set up to study the problem.[4]

(viii) *The cession of the French Establishments in India, 1954*

On 21 October 1954 France and India signed an agreement concerning the cession of the French Establishments to India.[5] The autonomous character of these Establishments was to be maintained by India's agreement to keep in force the special administrative statute which had previously governed them and to modify this only after consultation with the people. Similarly the law governing the Assembly of the municipality would continue to function. Article 3 provided that the Government of India would succeed to the rights and obligations resulting from all acts of

---

1 U.N. Res. 390 A (V); *U.N. Yearbook* 1952, p. 262.
2 No. 27 of 1962. 3 S. 4.
4 U.N. Doc. A/5170, art. XXII. 5 *Annuaire français* (1956), p. 703.

French administration and engaging the territory. All French citizens and citizens of the French Union who originated in the Establishments, who were domiciled there at the date of the transfer and actually carried on a profession there would be entitled to continue their activities without having to acquire new diplomas or licences or fulfil other requirements. Special provision was inserted respecting religious and cultural assets and the administration of the religious missions.

(ix) *The formation of the United Arab Republic, 1958*

Article 5 of the Provisional Constitution of the United Arab Republic stated: 'Private property is inviolable. The law organizes its social function. Property may not be expropriated except for purposes of public utility and in consideration of just compensation in accordance with the law.' The Land Reform Law of Egypt was extended to Syria, but in both instances compensation was paid.[1]

On 13 July 1958 an agreement was signed between the U.A.R. and the *Société Financière de Suez*, under which the U.A.R., as successor to the Government of Egypt, agreed to pay a fixed sum as compensation for the nationalization of the Suez Canal. Moreover, the U.A.R. agreed to release French and British property sequestrated in 1956 by Egypt, and to pay compensation for nationalized property. The U.A.R. also agreed to resume payment of pensions to British nationals.[2]

II. Practice in Cases of Independence

On 14 December 1962 the General Assembly of the United Nations adopted a resolution on Permanent Sovereignty over Natural Resources, in which it was proclaimed that nationalization, expropriation or requisitioning should be based on grounds of public utility, security or national interest, and be accompanied by appropriate compensation. This formula was stated not in any way to prejudice the position of any member State on any aspect of the question of the rights and obligations of successor States and Governments in respect of property acquired before the accession to complete sovereignty of countries formerly under colonial rule. The Assembly noted that the subject of succession was being examined as a matter of priority by the International Law Commission.[3]

Guarantees respecting property have been incorporated in the constitutions of several of the emerging African nations,[4] and these ensure for the

---

[1] Cotran in *I.C.L.Q.* vol. VIII (1959), p. 365. [2] Cmnd. 639.
[3] U.N. Res. 1803 (XVII), U.N.G.A. 17th Sess., Off. Rec., Supp. no. 17 (U.N. Doc. A/5217), p. 15.
[4] E.g. Constitution of Sierra Leone, S.I. 1961, no. 741, s. 17 (1). The Constitution of Kenya, S.I. 1963, no. 791, schedule 2, s. 1 (c), provides that all persons in

benefit of persons whose titles antedate the grant of independence. In some cases, however, the exact nature of these titles is unclear. Provision has also been made in the legislation of some successor States guaranteeing overseas investment, although in no instance does it directly affect investments made before independence.[1]

(i) *Land tenure in West Africa*

Although the Crown made land grants in the English form in West Africa, it does not follow that the grantees gained a title superior to that of any of the inhabitants whose land tenure had been unaffected by the extension of British rule. The expression 'his heirs, executors, administrators and assigns forever' has been held to be meaningless and inapplicable in its African setting.[2] The effect of such a grant is only to ascertain the chief or headman who has charge of the land for the time being, and it leaves the interest of the family or occupiers to be determined by the native customary law. Subject to this comment, all titles continued to be governed by the local law and legislation, one example of which is section 3 of the Crown Grants (Township of Lagos) Ordinance which states that

> all grants of land situate within the township of Lagos . . . shall be deemed to have been validly made; and each of such grants shall be deemed to have vested in the grantee an estate free from competing interests and restrictions, save only such interests and restrictions, recognized by native law and custom, as at the date of the grant affected such estate.

The survival of the local law and legislation of this character after independence, which the constitutions of the African States provide for,[3] makes it clear that the doctrine of act of State is inapplicable in the circumstances, as it proved to be inapplicable in India.[4] Recognition by the new

Kenya are entitled to 'protection . . . from deprivation of property without compensation'. Mention is not made of property owned by persons not resident in Kenya. There is provision for the taking of property in the public interest, but prompt payment of full compensation must be made, s. 6 (1).

1 Dahomey, 21 December 1961, *Journal Officiel de la République du Dahomey*, 15 January 1962, p. 17, *loi* no. 61–53; Ghana, Capital Investments Act, 1963, no. 172 of 1963 (for criticism of the working of this see *The Times*, 16 December 1963, p. 9); Guinea, 5 April 1962, *Journal Officiel*, 4th yr., no. 6, 7 April 1962, *loi* no. 50 AN/62; Ivory Coast, *Journal Officiel de la République de la Côte d'Ivoire*, no. 58, 10 September 1959, p. 823, *loi* no. 59–134; Mauritania, *Journal Officiel de la République Islamique de Mauritanie*, 16 August 1961, p. 309, *loi* no. 61–122; Senegal, *Journal Officiel de la République de Sénégal*, no. 3520, 31 April 1962, p. 587, *loi* no. 61–33, U.N. Doc. E/3840.
2 *Oyekan* v. *Adele* [1957] 2 All E.R. 785.
3 E.g. Ghana, s. 40. See *supra*, pp.149, 150
4 See *supra*, p. 258.

States of pre-existing rights is evidenced in the statutory provisions enacted after independence and providing for compensation to be payable in the event of expropriation. For example, the Niger Dams Act, 1962 of Nigeria[1] provides in section 5 for the Land and Native Rights Act to have effect in the event of the Niger Dams Authority compulsorily acquiring land for the purpose of the exercise of its electricity generation, navigation, pisciculture and irrigation functions, and prescribes the duty of the authority to secure that as little damage as is reasonably possible is done in the exercise of the power of acquisition. Any person who suffers loss in the exercise of this power is to be compensated adequately, and the High Court was invested with jurisdiction as to the subject-matter of the loss, and the amount of compensation payable.

Four months after independence Sierra Leone enacted the Compulsory Acquisition of Property (Constitutional Safeguards) Act, 1961.[2] This states that where any law, then in operation or thereafter to be made, provides for compulsory acquisition of property and effective provision is made for the prompt payment of adequate compensation, and for the securing to any person having an interest in the property a right of access to a court of other authority for the determination of the interest and the amount of compensation, then an application to the courts may be filed according to procedure laid down. The courts are empowered on their own motion to call and hear evidence and assess compensation, which is then to be payable according to the procedure laid down in the Act.

(ii) *The Ghana land concessions*

Section 13 (1) of the Constitution of 29 June 1960 embodies a declaration of fundamental principles made by President Nkrumah, one of which is that 'no person should be deprived of his property save where the public interest so requires and the law so provides'. The proviso is important in considering the legislative action taken with respect to the land concessions.

In order to protect the native inhabitants, the Colony of the Gold Coast in 1900, and Ashanti in 1903, promulgated a Concessions Ordinance, which required the issuing of a certificate of validity before any grant of land to a non-native could be effective. A concession was defined as 'any writing whereby any right interest or property in or over land with respect to minerals precious stones timber rubber or other products of the soil' purported to be granted by a native. This was held not to extend to a demise of the surface of the land, nor to a sale or lease of the

1 No. 23 of 1962.
2 No. 42 of 1961.

land itself.[1] Subsequently the definition of a concession was widened, and the final Ordinance issued in 1939, and revised in 1950,[2] included within it the conveyance of any right title or interest in or to land, other than an assignment or sub-demise of rights granted by any concession, or a sale, mortgage, lease or agreement to lease land within a town or village, and from which rights to minerals were excepted. Any agreement dealing with any interest in the land or its products made between a native and a non-native was required to be in writing, and the court should have jurisdiction to enquire into and certify as valid or invalid any such agreement, and no effect might be given to any concession unless it had been so certified. Notice of the concession was required to be given the court within two months of its execution. The court was given power to enquire into certain questions, such as the adequacy of the consideration, the terms of the grant, and the preservation of traditional rights. A registry of concessions was established, and all certificates of validity were entered therein.

Sections 25 and 26 dealt with cancellation of concessions. Should it appear to the Attorney-General that there was any contravention of the true intent and purpose of the provisions of the Ordinance relating to the areas of land, the aggregation of concessions, or financial intimacy of separate concession-holders, he might apply to the court for a rule *nisi* calling on the concession-holder to show cause why the concession should not be cancelled; and the court was empowered to make the rule absolute.

This was the land law affecting non-native interests at the date of independence, and the acquired rights of alien holders were defined by it. After independence the Government of Ghana set up a Commission of Enquiry into Concessions which reported on 31 December 1958.[3] It was found that four hundred and sixty concessions had been validated in respect of the Gold Coast, and sixty-seven in respect of Ashanti. No indication was given as to the national character of the companies possessing grants, but it is clear that they included Ghanaian, United Kingdom, South African and Netherland companies. There was a general and unqualified finding that: the grantors had been illiterate and did not understand what they were conceding; the method of granting timber and mining rights was obsolescent; it was a practice to obtain excessive areas of granted land and to leave them unexploited; the agreements were drawn up by the grantees to their advantage; the consideration was inadequate; royalties

[1] *Wassaw Exploring Syndicate Ltd* v. *African Rubber Co. Ltd* [1914] A.C. 626 at p. 631.
[2] *Revised Edition of the Laws* (1956), c. 136.
[3] Report of the Commission of Enquiry into Concessions, 1961, Government Printer, Accra.

were rarely payable; the grantees were making excessive profits. It was recommended that a Special Court be established to review all concession agreements, and that some body be empowered to terminate all unexploited concessions. Another recommendation was that the expression 'native', used to designate the grantor, was outmoded and should be replaced by the expression 'citizen of Ghana'.

In 1961 the Government of Ghana issued a White Paper[1] on the Report in which it agreed with these findings. It preferred that the ordinary courts continue to deal with concessions, but in fact in 1962 the recommended Special Courts were set up. The Government thought it would be equitable to compute royalties on a basis relating to sale prices. The policy of Ghana to welcome overseas capital, and provide attractive conditions for investment, was mentioned. One of these conditions was said to be the policy of honouring agreements, and this would be borne in mind in the revisions of the existing concession agreements. However, where rents and royalties were too low, the remedy should be by fiscal measures which would yield extra revenue for the community as a whole, rather than a remedy which would increase the revenue of the grantors.

In 1962 a Concessions Act[2] was passed which repealed relevant sections of the Ordinance, and confirmed existing concessions.[3] A Tribunal was set up consisting of five members appointed by the President, and the Minister may apply to it to terminate any concession if he is satisfied that there has been a breach of its terms, that two or more holders are in a relationship of financial intimacy as defined under the law in force, that a holder unreasonably withholds consent to a variation of terms that the Minister thinks have become oppressive by reason of a change in economic conditions, that a holder has lost the financial ability to develop the concession, or that the land has not been developed or the prescribed limits have been exceeded. Alternatively, the Minister might apply to the Tribunal for a modification of the terms of the concession.

These provisions do not directly and adversely modify the acquired rights of the holders as they existed under the law in force at the date of independence, though undoubtedly they distort them. What is new and potentially subversive of these rights is section 5, which confers power on the President to cancel any concession held by an individual who is not a citizen of Ghana or by a company which is not incorporated in Ghana or whose 'effective control' is in the hands of such an individual, 'if he considers that it is or may prove prejudicial to public safety or interests. Such cancellation shall have effect notwithstanding anything to the contrary in any law.' No court has any power of review, but the Tribunal

[1] No. 4 of 1961.   [2] No. 124 of 1962.   [3] S. 2.

is empowered to settle outstanding rights between the parties resulting from such cancellation.

At the same time an Administration of Lands Act, 1962[1] was passed which empowered the President to declare any Stool land to be vested in him in trust, if it appeared to him to be in the public interest so to do, and it is made lawful for him to execute any deed or do any act as a trustee in respect of the land specified. Stool land includes land controlled by any person for the benefit of the members of a Stool, clan, company or community. Further, a Minerals Act[2] was passed which vests in the President the entire property in and control of all minerals in, under or upon, the land, rivers and territorial waters of Ghana. He was empowered to grant mining licences, and to exercise the right of preemption of all minerals raised in Ghana by any existing holder or by any holder of a licence granted by this Act, and of products derived from the refining or treatment of such minerals,[3] at the publicly quoted market rate ruling for such minerals, or at the price decided upon by the High Court.[4]

In 1960 Ghana enacted a State Property and Contracts Act[5] which provided that all references to the 'Crown' in Acts relating to the acquisition of property should be read as references to the 'President'. The Act deals with the procedure of acquisition, the acquisition of industrial land, and the settlement of questions of title and compensation by the High Court. The formula of compensation is the market value of the property acquired, which is the amount which it might have been expected to realize if sold on the open market by a willing seller. The compensation provisions of this Act, governing acquisition by the State, do not affect the cancellation of concessions.

(iii) *The expropriation of Netherlands property in Indonesia, 1957–9*

In 1957 events began in Indonesia which resulted in the termination of the private rights of Netherlands citizens which had been guaranteed in the Round Table Agreement.[6] The initial action consisted in the occupation by Indonesian trade unions of Netherlands-owned enterprises and the prevention of such enterprises from freely carrying on business. In a note of 11 December 1957 the Netherlands protested that these 'measures' were incompatible with international law and the obligations entered into by Indonesia, and with the guarantees in the Indonesian Constitution. This was followed on 28 December 1957 with a note in which it was observed that further measures had been taken, and that the Netherlands

1 No. 123 of 1962. 2 No. 126 of 1962. 3 S. 5.
4 S. 6. 5 No. 6 of 1960. 6 *U.N.T.S.* vol. LXIX, p. 3.

refused to recognize the appearance of legality in the application of existing statutory provisions in a manner at variance with their enacted object. Furthermore, they were acts arbitrary and discriminatory in character, and hence devoid of any reasonable basis. On 14 May 1958 the Netherlands further protested at the default of Indonesia in meeting its obligations under the loan agreement of 1 April 1950 to an amount of 280 million florins, and on 23 January 1958 at the Indonesian cessation of payment of all pensions, relief payments and retaining pay of former civil servants of Indonesia of Netherlands nationality. On 16 September 1958 a further protest was addressed at various administrative measures taken in Indonesia to interfere with Netherlands enterprises, characterizing these as disguised confiscation without indemnification and without legal grounds. The threefold legal objections mentioned in the first note were reiterated.

Indonesia replied on 8 October 1958, stating that from 1950 to 1956 it had been at great pains to fulfil its financial and economic agreements with the Netherlands, although these constituted a heavy burden. A connexion was acknowledged between the measures taken and the failure of the Netherlands to respond in accordance with Indonesia's interpretation of the Round Table Agreement provisions relative to West New Guinea, though no mention was made of reprisals, and a legal justification was offered by basing the action on the provisions of the Central Authorization Ordinance[1] and the Enterprises Co-operation Decree,[2] which were Netherlands enactments still in force. The Netherlands responded on 2 February 1959, refusing to acknowledge the diplomatic interconnexion of the Indonesian measures and the West New Guinea question, and reiterating Indonesia's 'obligation under international law to reinstate the injured parties and to compensate them for the losses suffered.'

Meanwhile, on 31 December 1958, the Indonesian Government had promulgated an Act for the nationalization of Netherlands enterprises, and the Netherlands note proceeded to challenge the international law validity of this on the ground of discrimination, of admission in the preamble that the Act was a means for exerting political pressures, and of failure to compensate.

On the strength of this the Netherlands Government takes the view that the nationalization announced can neither annul nor transfer the property and other rights of Netherlands nationals owning property in Indonesia, either natural or legal persons. This also applies to the produce of this property. The Netherlands Government will therefore continue to regard this property and this produce as still fully belonging to the lawful owners.

[1] *Staatsblad* (1939), no. 557.
[2] *Ibid.* (1945), no. 136.

Postponement of compensation until settlement of the political dispute would not merely occasion a deviation from actual practice, it would constitute an actual violation of international law. 'It characterizes the measure announced, if it should be at all legally valid, which is not the case, all the more as an act invalid and unlawful under international law.'

On 8 April 1959 the Netherlands received a note from Indonesia in which the latter claimed that the question whether a law is legal or not is to be determined by the legislation of the country concerned, and not by the judgment of a foreign country, and that the Nationalization Act was based on the sovereign right of a State. As regards compensation, despite the fact that the obligation to compensate is not unanimously recognized as a clear principle of international law, the Nationalization Law clearly recognized it, and laid down that compensation should be granted, the amount to be fixed by a special commission in accordance with article 27 of the Provisional Constitution. A decree of 2 April 1959 had already regulated the procedure for obtaining compensation.

The correspondence terminated on 18 December 1959 with a Netherlands note in which protest was directed at ordinances of 23 February 1959[1] and 2 April 1959[2] concerning the principles of the Nationalization Act, the setting up of the Board for the Nationalization of Dutch-owned enterprises, and the terms of reference of the Committee for the Fixation of Compensations, and the way in which applications for compensation were to be submitted. It was reiterated that the measures were 'unlawful and invalid' because the preamble to the Act showed that they were not 'based on the general interest in connexion with the use to be made of the property to be nationalized, but have been taken for the purpose of exerting pressure in a political dispute', and that they were discriminatory and also confiscatory because there was no question of any prompt payment of an adequate and effective compensation.[3] Negotiations on compensation began towards the end of 1964 between the Netherlands and Indonesia.

(iv) *The nationalization of Indian property in Burma, 1948–1955*

A fundamental policy of the Burmese Government after independence was the resumption and redistribution of land from the bigger landowners, absentee landlords, the South Indian Chettyars and moneylenders.[4] The Burmese Constitution provides that the State is the ultimate

1 Nos. 2 and 3.   2 No. 9.
3 For three academic opinions on the legality of the Indonesian action, in which the Round Table provisions are mentioned, see McNair, Rolin and Verdross in *Ned. Tijd.* (July 1959).
4 Maung Maung, *The Constitution of Burma*, pp. 107–8.

owner of all lands, and has the right to regulate, alter or abolish land tenures, and to fix a maximum size to private land, provided, however, that compensation should be paid in accordance with law.[1] This constitutional guarantee is of limited importance, since it leaves the quantum of compensation to the Burmese legislature. In 1948 a Land Nationalization Act was passed which fixed the maximum landholding of a joint family at fifty acres, and provided for compensation of twelve times the land tax. The South Indian Chettyars, who owned about one quarter of the paddy, were dissatisfied with the amount of compensation, and made representations to the Burmese Government.[2] When the Bill was enacted without modification the Indians took the matter up with the Government of India. The national status of the complainants was not clear: those who had been born in British India or Burma and had opted for Burmese nationality had become Burmese; while those who had been citizens of the Indian States had become citizens of India. Since the claimants sought representation as a group, the status of the Indian Government in the matter was uncertain. Nonetheless the latter took the matter up with the Burmese Government in 1949 and made representations, as the Deputy Minister for External Affairs stated in the Constituent Assembly, 'to safeguard the legitimate interests of Indians in Burma'.[3]

However, the breakdown of law and order in Burma interrupted the process of land resumption and put an end to the Indian representations. In 1953 Burma began to implement the legislation, and calculated that about two and one-third millions of acres, or one third of the total to be distributed, belonged to Indian Chettyars. The total compensation at the rate of twelve times the annual land revenue would amount to kyats 13.7 crores, of which the Chettyars would receive K. 4·6 crores. In 1957 the Government invited claims for compensation for land taken over between 1953 and 1955, for which the total compensation due was K. 155 lakhs. Of the claims received, K. 82 worth were passed for payment, and each claimant received up to R. 2,500 in cash and the balance, if any, in Government bonds which were negotiable for certain specified investments.[4] The Indian Government took no further action.

(v) *German property in Israel: the Templar mediation*

In 1939 the British Administration in Palestine promulgated a Trading with the Enemy Ordinance, which created the Office of Custodian of Enemy Property, and provided for the vesting therein of property of

1 Ch. III, s. 30.   2 Kondapi, *Indians Overseas 1888–1949*. (1951), p. 297.
3 India, Constitutive Assembly Debates, Legislative, vol. I, no. 12 (1949), p. 766.
4 Maung Maung, *op. cit.* p. 108.

enemy aliens.[1] Further legislation with respect to vesting took the form of an Order of the High Commissioner of 1 November 1939. Pursuant to this the property of certain German nationals in Palestine was vested by successive Orders in the Custodian, and since most of this, consisting of urban and agricultural realty, belonged to the members of a Unitarian religio-economic society known as the Templar Society, the German assets in Palestine are usually referred to as the Templar Assets. The property remained vested in the Custodian until April 1948 when various of the vesting Orders were revoked. The revoking Orders were not published before termination of the Mandate owing to the destruction by sabotage of the Government printing press in Jerusalem, but they were printed in a collection of Legislation Enacted and Notices Issued which were later gazetted in London by instruction of the Palestine Attorney-General.

The United Kingdom withdrew from Palestine on 14 May 1948, and Israel was founded by its own act.[2] The Israeli Provisional Council of State issued the Law and Administration Ordinance retrospective to that date, which maintained in force the law in Palestine and all orders made.[3] An amendment to this Ordinance excluded from continuity all laws and orders which had not been published in the Palestine Gazette, so that in Israeli internal law the revocation of the vesting orders was ineffective, and the German property remained in the hands of the Custodian. In 1950 Israel enacted a German Property Law,[4] which created a Custodian of German property, and vested in him all German property vested in the Custodian of Enemy Property, as security against settlement by Germany of claims of Israeli citizens against that country.

In 1952 Germany and Israel began negotiations for a settlement of financial issues, and on 10 September 1952 concluded an agreement[5] on German property in Israel as part of the general restitutionary settlement affecting Jews who had suffered at the hands of Germany. Israel agreed to pay compensation for the vested German property in an amount corresponding to such value of the property as would be assessed in the course of the negotiations, and provisions for mediation was included in the event of a breakdown in negotiations. The negotiations in fact broke down after some years, and the matter was referred to mediation in Geneva in May 1962. Owing to the procedure of mediation, no reasoned award of the mediator was possible, and the dispute terminated after agreement with the mediator's proposals, under which Israel paid the

1 No. 36 of 1939.   2 See *supra*, p. 128.
3 Law and Administration Ordinance of 15 May 1948.
4 12th Av, 5710.   5 *U.N.T.S.* vol. CLXII, p. 205.

sum of 54,000,000 DM, or about half of the total value claimed. The legal arguments of Germany and Israel, though inconclusive, shed a great deal of light on the problems of State succession.

Germany's case was that the United Kingdom did not expropriate German property, so that this remained private property at the date of Israel's foundation. In fact, all that the United Kingdom had done was vest about one third of the total German property during the war, and the remaining two thirds in November 1947, solely as a means of liquidating the property of Germans who wished permanently to migrate and could not individually dispose of their real estate in face of Jewish hostility. It had been the intention of the British administration to hand the proceeds of this property to the German emigrants, but this was only partially accomplished by the date of withdrawal from the Mandate, owing to the stopping of a cheque of £1,500,000 by the Jewish employees of the Bank of Palestine. The balance of vested property was divested when it became clear that liquidation would not be carried out, and was a measure taken to preserve private rights. Even if the divesting was ineffective, the most that had occurred was a transfer of ownership to the Custodian, with a *spes restitutionis* in the titleholders,[1] and that, when the Ordinance 'flew off'[2] with the collapse of public law on the change of sovereignty,[3] the property automatically revested in the titleholders. Therefore, no matter how one looked at it, at the date of the change the property was private property, and the taking of it was an Israeli act.

Germany did not dispute the legality of this taking, on the ground that the purpose of the law was to utilize the property as security for the satisfaction of claims against Germany of persons residing in Israel. (This seems to have been a gratuitous concession for obvious political reasons.) Nonetheless, the formula for compensation in the *Chorzów Factory* Case[4] was applicable, and the recognition of the principle of compensation in the agreement of 1952 was a recognition that full compensation was payable. This interpretation flowed not only from general international law, but also from the relationship between the provisions for compensation to German titleholders and those relating to the indemnification of Jewish refugees.[5] Once the quantum of this indemnification had been agreed upon, the need to retain German property as security had lapsed, and the monetary equivalent of a *restitutio in integrum* was payable. Apart from this, no interconnexion between the two sets of provisions existed.

1 *Bank voor Handel en Scheepvaart* v. *Administrator of Hungarian Property* [1959] A.C. 584.
2 Per Lord Keith at p. 640.
3 See *supra*, p. 104.
4 P.C.I.J. ser. A, no. 17 (1928).
5 Memorial, p. 26.

In any event, the German argument concluded, even if Israel did not itself take over the property and incur the obligation to compensate, it inherited the obligations of restitution of the Palestine administration.[1]

The Israeli argument commenced with the proposition that outside the agreement of 1952 no compensation was payable, and that consequently the parties could not be held bound to an objective standard of payment. The contention was supported with the submission that on the date of Israel's foundation the German property was vested in the Palestine administration, and the owners had been finally deprived of it: that the property was Palestine public property and had fallen to the sovereignty of Israel.[2] Since Israel was not the successor of the Palestine administration no obligation to compensate, assuming it to have pre-existed, could have been inherited from the Mandatory. Israel merely determined the legal régime under which the property was to be administered, and did not take it. Israel, further, was entitled to retain the property because Palestine had been involved in the war against Germany, and Germany had occasioned losses to European Jewry which involved the duty to compensate.[3] The holding of the property could be regarded as a measure of reprisals or reparations. This factor established an interrelationship between the provisions for payment of indemnity by Germany to Israel and the provisions for payment of compensation by Israel to the German property holders, an interrelationship evident from the circumstance that the indemnification provisions were a condition precedent to the validity of the compensation provisions.[4] Furthermore, the agreement was a *pactum de contrahendo*, so that no liability would arise until the mediator's proposals had been accepted.[5] Since Israel was receiving only a small proportion of the total value of Jewish loss under the idemnification provisions, it was not required to pay more than a similar proportion of the value of German property by way of compensation, the balance of the property being held to the account of the unindemnified amount of Jewish loss.

The arguments of Israel concerning its succession to a state of war with Germany, and its consequent entitlement to reparations, and also its argument on the rate of exchange, are discussed elsewhere,[6] and it is sufficient to consider the issue on the quantum of compensation. Israel argued that the expression in the agreement 'such value of the said property as shall be assessed' meant that it was not the value but the property which was to be assessed, and that the word 'assessment' means a fixing, not an ascertainment.[7] Even if Israel were held liable to an

[1] Ibid. p. 86.
[2] Counter-memorial, p. 31.
[3] Ibid. p. 32.
[4] Ibid. p. 47.
[5] Ibid. p. 50.
[6] See *supra*, p. 193.
[7] Counter-memorial, p. 58.

objective quantum of compensation, this could not, in the light of Germany's admission of the legality of the taking, mean a full compensation, since all the international judicial authorities which required full compensation to be paid were with respect to unlawful takings.[1] Even in respect of these, international lawyers no longer contend for more than 'adequate' compensation, which does not mean full compensation.

It followed that market value was not the appropriate test, and in any event, this standard is only to be used when there is a free and competitive market based on non-speculative prices.[2] In 1948, owing to the disturbed condition of Palestine, there was no such market. The alternative standard of the 'use' value would yield a very low figure since, owing to the existence of rent restriction legislation, the use to which the property could be put was limited. Furthermore, the agreement envisaged global payment and not payment related to specific assets. Israel contested the existence in international law of a conception of unjust enrichment.[3]

Germany countered these contentions with the argument that a taking is never unlawful provided it is followed by adequate, effective and prompt compensation.[4] The provisions for indemnification were in recognition of a moral and not a legal obligation, and no interrelation between them and the provisions for compensation for German property could exist, because the former would be a payment from German revenue, and could not be total, whereas the latter would not be a payment out of revenue but out of the value of the assets. The right to expropriate could not derive from the claims of individual Israeli citizens, who, in addition to the benefits deriving from the global payment by Germany to Israel, preserved rights against Germany under German legislation respecting *Wiedergutmachung* of Jewish losses.

(vi) *Acquired rights in North Vietnam*

In an exchange of letters of 21 July 1954 between France and North Vietnam officials, it was provided that the property of French citizens and companies would be safeguarded and respected. In 1956 the French Minister for Foreign Affairs reported that the Democratic Republic of Vietnam was bound by this engagement but had failed to keep it. Nonetheless, negotiations were continuing and the French Government had threatened to refuse to carry out a certain number of its engagements if North Vietnam failed in its obligations. It was by these means that the principle of payment of pensions had been recognized.[5] However, the French Government would not interfere with the control in North

---

1 *Ibid.* p. 68.   2 *Ibid.* p. 73.   3 *Ibid.* p. 79.
4 Reply, p. 7.   5 *Annuaire français* (1956), p. 838.

Vietnam of the installations of the Yunnan Railway Company, whose assets had reverted to public ownership.[1]

(vii) *Acquired rights in the Philippines*

Article VI of the Treaty of General Relations between the United States and the Philippines of 1946 stipulated that the property rights of citizens and corporations of each party would be respected.[2]

(viii) *Acquired rights of French citizens in Morocco and Tunisia*

Upon the release of Morocco from French protection, the question arose whether Morocco could alter the existing legislation respecting compensation payments made to French citizens who were the victims of industrial accidents in Morocco and were subsequently resident in France. A question was asked the Minister of Foreign Affairs in the Assembly of 16 January 1960 to which he replied that the payments allocated to accident victims in Morocco were affected by Moroccan legislation whatever the nationality of the recipients or their place of residence might be. Wherever a French citizen objected to the standard of payment, the French Ambassador would intervene with the Government of Morocco to re-establish his rights. French law in the matter of industrial accidents could not apply to the victims of accidents in Morocco because these were only entitled to payment in respect of accidents occurring on French territory.[3]

In 1958 Morocco issued a *dahir* which modified the existing taxation laws relating to deductions from public and private incomes, indemnities, emoluments, salaries, pensions and life annuities, and provided that the new *régime* would apply to persons domiciled in France, Algeria, Tunisia, French West Africa and Togo who had been previously exempted from impositions of this sort. On 27 November 1957 the French Foreign Minister had stated that the abrogation of the Protectorate *régimes* in Tunisia and Morocco did not entitle these countries to affect a juridical and political situation which had existed for many years. He asked Morocco if the *dahir* were not contrary to the spirit or the terms of the Franco-Moroccan Administration and Technical Convention of 1957 that the two countries had negotiated.

To a question asked in the French Parliament in 1960 the Minister of Foreign Affairs stated that the *dahir* was not in fact contrary to the terms of the convention of 1957 and that, pending the conclusion of a double taxation convention, the French Ambassador had proposed to Morocco

[1] *Ibid.* (1955), p. 614.   [2] T.I.A.S. 1568.
[3] *Annuaire français* (1960), p. 1073.

that a provisional exemption be created, achieving the same situation for French beneficiaries as they had previously enjoyed. The Minister stated that no agreement had yet been reached on this question with the Moroccan authorities.

Article 15 of the Moroccan Constitution contains a guarantee of property rights. Nonetheless, the property rights of French agricultural settlers, which had been unaffected by independence, have been gradually encroached upon. Dahirs of 9 May 1959[1] and 30 June 1959[2] provided for the compulsory acquisition of certain lots of collective land. The French Ambassador drew the attention of the Moroccan Government to the serious repercussions which this would have on the French agricultural community in Morocco. The French Government demanded that compensation be paid to French farmers affected, and that this should be paid before any dispossession of them should occur. It also insisted on representation for French subjects before the Consultative Commission established by the *dahirs*. These overtures were unsuccessful, and the total expropriation of *lots de colonisation* was envisaged as part of a Moroccan triennial plan of agricultural reform.[3] This was effected by *dahirs* of 20 September 1963.[4] All French agricultural land (other than melk land) was taken by the State without compensation. French protest that this action violated the Constitution has been met with the reply that the Constitution contemplates only privately owned property in the strict sense, and not colonized land held on government lease; and the further demand that compensation be paid to satisfy the requirements of international law has not been acceded to.[5]

When Tangier was returned to Morocco in 1956, a Protocol was annexed to the Final Declaration of the International Conference providing that persons carrying on a liberal profession would be entitled to continue therein.[6]

With respect to the withdrawal of privileges of French transportation companies in Tunis and Morocco, the French Ambassadors to both

1 *Bulletin Officiel* (Morocco), 10 July 1959, p. 1120.
2 *Ibid*. 12 August 1960, p. 1537.
3 Le Plan triennial, 1965–7, Cabinet Royal, p. 123.
4 *Dahir* no. 63–289, *fixant les conditions de la reprise par l'État des lots de colonisation;* Dahir no. 1–63–288, *relatif au contrôle des opérations immobilières à réaliser par certaines personnes et portant sur des propriétés agricoles rurales, Bulletin Officiel* (1963), p. 1527.
5 *Dahir* no. 1–63–288 contemplates permission to continue holding agricultural land on the perimeters of urban areas. In fact this permission has very rarely been given. Altogether about 400,000 hectares of land have been affected: Cassaigne, *La situation des Français au Maroc depuis l'indépendance*, pub. of the *Fondation nationale des sciences politiques*, p. 27.
6 B.T.S. (1957), no. 9; Cmnd. 60; *U.N.T.S.* vol. CCLXIII, p. 165 at p. 177.

countries protested and insisted that Morocco and Tunis should be internationally responsible for the payment of compensation. It appeared that only French carriers in Tunis whose licences had been withdrawn for October 1956 had in fact been compensated.

The Tunisian Electricity and Transport Company was a Tunisian incorporated body of which 80 per cent of the capital was held by French shareholders. It had made the declaration required by article 35(b) of the Economic and Financial Convention between France and Tunisia of 1955, but in 1958 Tunisia resumed control of both transportation and electricity. The Company demanded compensation in virtue of the contracts of concession, one of the terms of which had anticipated resumption. For two years it had received no reply from the Tunisian Government, and on 3 September 1960 the French Minister for Foreign Affairs stated in the Assembly that the French Ambassador had not awaited the execution of the Tunisian Decree before protesting and insisting that the Company be compensated in accordance with the terms of this contract. Since then it had been reported that the French Government had maintained a constant interest in the question and was in contact with the Company.[1]

(ix) *Rights of lawyers in Guinea*

In 1959 only barristers of Guinean nationality were permitted to practise at the Bar in Guinea. In reply to a question in the Assembly, the French Foreign Minister stated that, as an independent State, Guinea was incontestably entitled to restrict various functions and that in any event the new law did not necessarily exclude the possibility of alien barristers obtaining special permission to plead in certain cases.

The French Government hoped to negotiate a judicial co-operation convention which would offer the maximum guarantee to the nationals of each State resident in the territory of the other.[2]

(x) *Acquired rights of French citizens in Algeria*

The Evian Agreement of 18 March 1962,[3] which terminated the negotiations leading to Algerian independence, contained provisions for the protection of acquired rights of French nationals in Algeria. These were, however, of very general character, and it is arguable that they were con-

[1] *Annuaire français* (1960), p. 1074.
[2] *Ibid.* (1959), p. 891.
[3] Declaration of Principles Concerning Economic and Financial Co-operation, *A.J.* vol. LVII (1963), p. 729, arts. 1, 12; General Declaration, art. 2; Declaration of Guarantees, art. 5; *Journal Officiel*, 20 March 1962, p. 3019. A summary will be found in U.N. Doc. E/3840. See Segovia, *Los acuerdos de Evian, Foro Internacional*, vol. III (1962/63), p. 368.

tractually dependent on French technical assistance. A distinction was drawn, respecting French acquired rights in the exploitation of mineral resources, between the Saharan and non-Saharan departments. Respecting the latter, joint technical organs were to be established. There were provisions concerning guarantees for French nationals of equal and non-discriminatory treatment, and against taking without compensation. France would grant aid for the repurchase of property rights of French nationals for purposes of land reform, and in pursuance of a repurchase plan to be drawn up by Algerian authorities. There were provisions for arbitration of disputes.

The agreement did not function smoothly. In January 1963 Algeria signed agreements in Paris for French economic aid to the value of 1,700 millions of francs, and conceded that French property taken over by Algerians would be regarded as legally in the possession of absent French owners.[1] On 15 April 1963 the Algerian Prime Minister stated that his Government took its stand on the Evian Agreement and had opened negotiations with France for indemnification of the property taken over. In the meanwhile, Algeria would refund the outlay for the current year's crops. France, he said, had not replied.[2] On 16 September 1963 he stated that Algeria had been duped, and intended to take over all French settlers' land.[3] The following day France protested to Algeria at the nationalization of three French-owned newspapers.[4] On 20 September 1963 two French-owned hotels in Algiers were nationalized.[5]

The general looseness of the Evian Agreement has not assisted in clarifying the issues. While French property is guaranteed, it is provided that no dispossession measures shall be taken without fair compensation previously agreed upon. This envisages expropriation. At the same time, there is an implication that agrarian properties can only be taken by a process of repurchase with French financial aid, pursuant to a repurchase plan agreed upon by the two countries.[6] At first France appeared to accept the Algerian claim to be able to recover usufruct of lands declared vacant because their proprietors had migrated to France. When, however, Algeria took the next step of expropriating certain of the larger vacant properties, France stated that this constituted a violation of the Evian

1 *The Times*, 23 January 1963, p. 9. This expropriation seems to be unsupported by formal legislation. Requests made to the Governments of France, Algeria and Morocco for copies of the relevant texts have been refused.
2 *The Times*, 17 April 1963, p. 9.
3 *Ibid.* 17 September 1963, p. 11.
4 *Ibid.* 19 September 1963, p. 10.
5 *Ibid.* 21 September 1963, p. 7.
6 Declaration of Principles Concerning Economic and Financial Co-operation, *A.J.* vol. LVII (1963), art. 13.

Agreement, and withheld a fifth of its aid subvention under the agreement to deal with 'certain consequences of these measures'. Subsequent French protests at the extension of the Algerian programme of expropriation met with no response.[1]

(xi) *Acquired rights of French citizens in the Francophone States*

In the establishment agreements concluded between France and certain of its former African dependencies and Madagascar, as part of the system of co-operation, provision was made respecting the acquired rights of natural and juridical persons of each party in the territories of the other.[2] These rights were specified to include the free exercise of a profession, and generally for national treatment and reciprocal recognition of incorporation of each other's companies. In certain of the agreements concerning the transfer of French property, provision was made for the new States to confirm concessions already granted.[3]

(xii) *Acquired rights in Zanzibar*

On 22 March 1964 it was announced that the President of the People's Republic of Zanzibar had powers enabling him to confiscate, without compensation, any immovable property, without right of appeal, and subject to payment of compensation only if the Government deemed that 'undue hardship' might befall the property owner.[4] All land in the Republic was stated to be subject to nationalization. No reservation of alien rights was made.

(xiii) *Acquired rights in Kenya*

When Kenya became a republic it legislated to confirm all real estate interests which had subsisted at the date of Kenyan independence.[5]

1 *Annuaire français* (1963), pp. 1023–5. Charpentier in *ibid.* pp. 903 *et seq.*
2 Central African Republic, decree no. 60–1230, *Journal Officiel*, 24 November 1960, p. 10468, arts. 3, 11, 12; Congo, *ibid.* p. 10473, arts. 3, 11, 12; Chad, *ibid.* p. 10479, arts. 3, 11, 12; Gabon, *ibid.* arts. 3, 11, 12; Malagasy Republic, decree no. 60–692, *Journal Officiel*, 20 July 1960, p. 6628, arts. 3, 11, 12.
3 Central African Republic, decree no. 60–1230, *Journal Officiel*, 24 November 1960, p. 10466, art. 5; Congo, *ibid.* p. 10472, art. 5; Chad, *ibid.* p. 10478, art. 5.
4 *The Times*, 23 March 1964, p. 9; Confiscation of Immovable Property, Decree no. 4 of 1964.
5 The Constitution of Kenya (Amendment) Act, no. 28 of 1964, s. 20. For the Constitution see *supra*, p. 279.

(xiv) *Acquired rights in the Congo (Léopoldville)*

On 17 June 1960 the Congo enacted legislation concerning public liberties, section 14 of which embodied a guarantee of acquired rights.[1] Confirmation of these was made by the Congolese Minister of Lands in a declaration of October 1961.[2] Belgian and other alien concessions were covered by the legislation and the declaration. On 19 November 1964 the Congolese Government cancelled the right of the *Compagnie du Katanga* to grant mining concessions, a right which had been enjoyed in virtue of an agreement of 1900 with the Congo Free State. In an explanatory memorandum it was argued that the Company was not engaged in ordinary business, but was a substitute in sovereignty, inasmuch as it had the power to appropriate land by police action, exploit it, and colonize it at the expense of the native population. The rights of the Company were not, therefore, 'acquired rights'; and rights 'arising from the public power and the royal authority disappear, *ipso facto*, with the liquidation of the previous legal order'.[3]

Action by the Congolese Government with respect to concessions is discussed later.[4] This action was legislatively consolidated on 7 June 1966, when it was decreed that the State had full sovereignty over its natural resources.[5]

1 De Visscher in *Communicazioni e Studi*, vol. XI (1963), p. 78.
2 *Bulletin de la Féderation des Associations Provinciales des Entreprises du Congo*, no. 28 of 15 October 1961, p. 132; de Visscher, *loc. cit.*
3 *International Legal Materials*, vol. IV (1965), p. 232. But for the subsequent nationalization of certain mining concessions see *infra*, p. 344.
4 See *infra*, p. 342.
5 Ordonnance–loi no. 66–343 assurant à la République Démocratique du Congo la plénitude de ses droits de propriété sur son domaine et la pleine souveraineté dans la concession des droits fonciers, forestiers et miniers sur toute l'étendue de son territoire, *Moniteur Congolais*, 15 August 1966.

Chapter 12

THE THEORY OF STATE SUCCESSION RESPECTING GOVERNMENTAL CONTRACTS

The negative theorists denied that there could be any transmission of rights and obligations under governmental contracts upon a change of sovereignty.[1] The universal succession theorists contended that there was such a transmission.[2] When the practice is examined it discloses that a subrogation of successor States in contractual relationships is not universally admitted, though it has occurred, but also that a complete repudiation of all liability under the contract on the part of successor States is rare, and to be explained on grounds of exception. The middle-way solution seems to have been to admit that upon a change of sovereignty one of the parties to the contract has disappeared from the place of performance, and that the contract as such lapses from 'frustration', but to argue that the benefit to the private contractor under the contract, in so far as it has been performed, must be satisfied under the doctrine of unjust enrichment.[3] This is a solution suggested by the comparable problem under both English law and the civil law. The result is that the government is released under the contract, but must pay the contractor whatever is due to him at the date of change of sovereignty if the benefits of his work accrue to the territory affected.[4] If the contract is totally executory the matter is at an end altogether.[5]

The middle-way solution is appropriate only in those cases where the change of sovereignty involves a destruction of the legal competence of the governmental instrumentality with whom the contract has been made. In cases of independence of colonial territories, and even in some cases of territorial cession, this competence has not been disturbed.[6] Government departments such as Boards of Works continue to function without interruption, not even, in many instances, changing their staffs. It would be artificial to contend that the contracts of such departments lapse merely because the ultimate political authority has altered. Nor, as a matter of practice, are such contracts discontinued.

The important factor in the attitude of States towards the question of

1 See the authors mentioned *supra*, p. 15.
2 See *supra*, chapters 1 and 2.
3 See *supra*, pp. 243, 266
4 See *infra*, p. 353.
5 See *infra*, p. 354.
6 See *supra*, p. 119.

the survival of governmental contracts has been a reluctance to be saddled with contracts that could be described as survivals of imperialist exploitation, and consequently as abhorrent to the policies of the new government. The practice of the United States with respect to concessionary contracts of Spain in Cuba and the Philippines was motivated by this consideration,[1] and in turn has motivated subsequent practice. It must be conceded that there is justice in the argument that a successor State should have the right to scrutinize contracts to decide which of them conforms with its own economic, social and political policies. But it must also be remembered that the right was asserted at a time when it was generally thought that international law protected contracts to the date of their full performance, so that if the successor State became a party to the contract it would have to see it through to the bitter end or incur responsibility for wrongful repudiation.

Clearly, the central point for investigation is the extent to which international law protects contractual performance. If it does not guarantee specific performance, then the question of inheritance of the contract becomes, from a practical point of view, irrelevant; for the successor State may utilize ordinary legal techniques for disengaging itself from inconvenient commitments. In actual fact, the problem of contractual performance in international law is immensely complex, and the solution depends mainly upon the subtleties of municipal law. Briefly, the position, without throwing the picture into too high relief, may be stated as follows:[2] International law protects only rights acquired under the proper law of the contract. If specific performance is not a feature of the proper law, then international law does not enjoin it; if it is, then it does enjoin it. If municipal law is altered by the contracting State so as to modify the rights of the contract-holder, this will engage the interest of international law only if this modification fundamentally alters the acquired right to the holder's disadvantage. The problem is very much more complex if the governing law is international law or the general principles of law,[3] but such a situation is rare. In essence, then, what international law protects is the resort to local remedies to sue for breach of contract. If the damages likely to be awarded against a State in its own courts for breach of contract are scarcely greater than the compensation which would be payable in any event by the successor State pursuant to the middle-way solution, the effort to argue a case for non-succession seems scarcely worthwhile, and only raises legal conundrums in the majority of cases where the contracts are continued. The chances of a

---

[1] See *infra*, p. 311. [2] O'Connell, *International Law* (1965), p. 1057.
[3] *Ibid.*

successor State being permanently affected by an inconvenient contract are very slight indeed when it is reflected that, even in cases where no change of sovereignty was involved, governmental repudiation of a contract has not been followed by an award of specific performance or *restitutio in integrum* by tribunals empowered to deal with the case, but by an award of *damnum emergens* and *lucrum cessans*. This means that, at the most, a repudiating State may have to pay a forfeiting contract-holder his loss of expected profits. The question is whether it is better to accept this possibility with good grace in one case in a thousand and preserve an orderly continuity in the remaining nine hundred and ninety-nine contracts, or seek to escape altogether from the payment of more than the capital investment in the one inconvenient case and thereby place in legal jeopardy the nine hundred and ninety-nine cases.

It is unrealistic to assume that in every case it is the private contract-holder who is seeking to enforce rights against the successor State, and the latter whose right to repudiate is in issue. There must be at least as many instances where the State would want to sue the private contractor for breach of contract. Yet if there is to be no subrogation in the contract, this must hold for both sides of it. What attitude will a court of the successor State take towards a private contractor who pleads by way of defence the frustration of the contract upon change of sovereignty, and argues that the only damages which the State can claim are those accrued before the date of the change? One might hazard the guess that the defence would not succeed, and if exhaustive research were made into actual cases support for this opinion might be forthcoming.

As a matter of practice, there has been no important recorded instance since the Boer War[1] of successor States claiming the right forthwith upon the change of sovereignty to repudiate contracts. Rather, the repudiation has come at a later date and has all the characteristics of an ordinary expropriation or nationalization. Indeed, the most obvious instance, that of Indonesian expropriation of Dutch property, was in face of a treaty guaranteeing the performance of the contracts.[2] Indonesia was, legally, in a far more dubious position as affected by the treaty than if she had accepted as a matter of customary law her automatic succession to contracts; for then her liabilities under international law would have depended upon what remedies existed under Dutch law for breach of contract, and these were certainly less than those arising under the treaty.

Once the fear is allayed that, by accepting succession to contracts as the norm, States are disabled from expropriation, the practical obstacle is removed to the argument in favour of succession, at least where the

1 See *infra*, p. 360.   2 See *supra*, p. 284.

contract is that of an autonomous local administration. The American cases of the nineteenth century misled most writers into believing that once succession was acknowledged the private rights persisted in perpetuity.[1] This occurred in the United States only because the rights, once vested, fell under the protective provisions of the Constitution. No implication as to the international law rule need or should be drawn. Similarly, the famous enunciations in favour of the doctrine of acquired rights by the International Court[2] in the 1920s are not to be taken as inhibiting the successor State's competence to expropriate, because that competence was in the actual cases affected by treaty. In short, a doctrine of succession to contracts would place the successor State in a different legal position from the predecessor State with respect to performance in only a residue of cases, and in most instances national interest can be preserved by resort to the ordinary law of expropriation, even if this means an increase in the measure of damages.

It must also be borne in mind that the problem of State succession is not only a problem of continuing legal relationship between governmental authorities and alien vested interests but also one of the survival of rights of local inhabitants who become nationals of the successor State. If contracts expire, this means contracts of nationals as well as of aliens. It is only because the question of succession has been confused with the question of how to get rid of inconvenient alien control of natural resources or public utilities that such a legal upheaval comes into contemplation at all. The confusion has been worse confounded by the English doctrine of act of State,[3] which has prevented English property- and contract-holders from pursuing the question of the survival of their interests in English courts following the acquisition of territory by the Crown. This, in its results, has assimilated the problem of the national with that of the alien, and has given the impression, erroneous but widespread, that upon change of sovereignty all claims lapse.

The question whether change of sovereignty puts an end to a contract made with the predecessor State is one which can only be answered in the concrete context. The assimilation of annexation, cession, union, dismemberment and independence as categories of succession has prompted the excessively rigid conclusion that every instance of change of sovereignty involves a termination of the legal personality of one contracting party. But, as the Permanent Court of Arbitration in the *Lighthouses Arbitration*[4] pointed out, 'it is impossible to formulate a general, identical solution for every imaginable hypothesis of territorial succession, and any

[1] See *supra*, p. 240.   [2] See *supra*, p. 273.
[3] See *supra*, p. 250.   [4] *I.L.R.* vol. XXIII, p. 81.

attempt to formulate such a solution must necessarily fail in view of the extreme diversity of cases of this kind'.[1] A tribunal, it held, must reckon with the formal mode by which the change is effected, whether it is a case of complete dismemberment of a pre-existing State, secession of a colony or of a part of a State, or a matter of the merger of two previously independent States; and it must take into account the relationship between the incorporating State and the incorporated State, the voluntary or involuntary nature of their union, the pre-existing constitutional status of the predecessor State, and the concrete circumstances of the performance or breach of the contract.

In the *Lighthouses* Arbitration one of the claims concerned the breach of an Ottoman concession contract on the part of the autonomous Cretan State. This breach consisted in granting a Greek shipping company exemption from the payment of lighthouse dues, and it was known to the Greek Government and persisted in by it after Crete became part of Greece. The concrete facts, the Tribunal found, were the violation of a term of the contract by the legislature of an autonomous State, the population of which had aspired for decades to be united, by force of arms if necessary, with Greece. The violation had been recognized by the State of Crete as constituting a breach of contract, and Greece had endorsed it as effected in favour of one of its nationals.[2]

In these circumstances, the Tribunal can only come to the conclusion that Greece, having adopted the illegal conduct of Crete in its recent past as an autonomous State, is bound, as successor State, to take upon its charge the financial consequences of the breach of the concession contract. Otherwise, the avowed violation of a contract committed by one of the two States, linked by a common past and a common destiny,

would have the effect of a 'thoroughly unjust' cancelling of financial responsibility.[3] The so-called general principle of non-transmission was not acknowledged to be a general and absolute principle, and the Tribunal would not utilize it to sacrifice undoubted rights of a private nature.

Perhaps the most scientifically correct scheme of rules to solve the problem of the effect of change of sovereignty on contracts is the following: The proper law of the contract, which will ordinarily be the law of the predecessor State, should be looked to in order to ascertain if the contract has expired from frustration; in most legal systems the disappearance of the contracting State from the place of performance will have this effect, but if the law of the successor State provides for complete

---

[1] At p. 91.   [2] At p. 92.   [3] *Ibid.*

succession the effect will be negatived. International law looks to the proper law to determine what it should protect. In the event of frustration of the contract in virtue of the proper law, and as a consequence of State succession, what remains to be protected is the equitable interest that survives the frustration. In civil law systems this interest is governed by the doctrine of unjust enrichment;[1] in the common law it is governed by rules which prescind from the theory of unjust enrichment.[2] Therefore, the successor State will incur, in virtue of international law, the obligation of satisfying the equities created by the proper law, should the contract be frustrated, and the obligation of performance should it not be frustrated. The obligation is owed to nationals of the successor State as well as aliens, in virtue of the capacity of international law to regulate the consequences of the international event of State succession; but only in the case of aliens is there machinery for enforcing the obligation; nationals have no resort beyond local remedies. And this scheme of rules derives from the theory that the legal system of the predecessor State survives change of sovereignty; a proposition which is one of legal philosophy, not one of positive international law.

[1] Cavaglieri perceived this point, p. 138
[2] *Fibrosa Spolka Akcyjna* v. *Fairbairn Lawson Ltd* [1943] A.C. 32, per Lord Wright.

Chapter 13

THE DOCTRINE OF ACQUIRED RIGHTS AND ECONOMIC CONCESSIONS

1. THE NATURE OF A CONCESSIONARY CONTRACT

An economic concession is usually a licence granted by the State to a private individual or corporation to undertake works of a public character extending over a considerable period of time, and involving the investment of more or less large sums of capital. It may also consist in the grant of mining or mineral or other rights over State property. To this type of concession there are usually annexed rights of marketing and export, as well as provisions concerning royalties. Thirdly, a concession may be merely a grant of occupation of public land for the carrying on of some public purpose, such a concession taking the form of a contract between the State and the concessionaire. Of this type were the concessions granted by the Queen of Madagascar to English mission societies for the erection of hospitals.

According to the definition which Gidel adopted from Auroc,[1] a concession is 'a contract by which one or several persons are engaged to execute a work on the consideration of being remunerated for their efforts and expenses, not by a sum of money paid directly to them by the administration after the completion of the work, but by a receipt of a return levied for a more or less lengthy period of time on the individuals who profit from the work'.[2] It is, as Mosler describes it, 'the grant to an individual of rights under municipal law which touch public interest'.[3] Beyond this, he points out, the term 'concession' has no fixed legal meaning.[4]

1 *Conférence sur les droits administratives*, vol. II, p. 269, no. 615.
2 Gidel, p. 123. The concessions maintained in the Treaty of Zürich, 1859 included railways built at the private expense of the concessionaire, reimbursement being effected out of income derived therefrom.
3 Mosler, p. 66.
4 *Ibid.* p. 79. Carlston in *Northwestern University Law Review*, vol. LII (1957), p. 618, and in *A.J.* vol. LII (1958), p. 260; Hyde in *ibid.* vol. L (1956), p. 854, at p. 862; Huang in *ibid.* vol. LI (1957), p. 277 at pp. 289 *et seq.*; Develle, *La Concession en droit international public* (1936); Guldberg in *Acta Scandinavica Juris Gentium*, vol. XXV (1955), p. 18; Mallarmé in *Rev. gén. de droit int. pub.* vol. X (1903), p. 282. The continuity of concessions after change of sovereignty is examined by: Cabouat, *passim*; Gidel, *passim*; Guggenheim, p. 132, *Traité*, p. 477; Huber, p. 43; von der Heydte, p. 309; Rousseau, p. 274; Reuter, p. 130; Schönborn, p. 53; Svarlien, p. 116; Sereni, p. 404; Sibert, vol. I, p. 213.

Acquired Rights and Economic Concessions 305

An economic concession thus embodies the following characteristics: it is a contract between a public authority and the concessionaire; it involves the investment of capital by the latter in an undertaking for the erection of public works or the exploitation of the public domain; the reward which the concessionaire expects to derive is usually in the form of profits which the public authority, under the terms of the contract, permits him to make; it may also consist in subsidies paid by the public authority itself. In the case of a concession for the exploitation of public lands there is usually provision for the payment to the public authority of royalties on the profits. Whatever be its form, a concession always involves a more or less complicated system of reciprocal rights and duties between the concessionaire on the one hand and the State on the other.[1]

The exact legal régime constituting the relationship between the concessionaire and the conceding State is a matter of choice by the parties. In some exceptional instances international law itself, or the general principles of law, may be selected, and the result may be a protection of the bargain for its full maturity.[2] Generally, however, the proper law of the contract is that of the conceding State, and it is this law which will characterize the concessionaire's legal interest.[3] In English law this interest is analogous to a leasehold, and, indeed, usually is in the form of a Crown lease. It will be affected by the relevant minerals legislation, which will be imported explicitly or implicitly into the bargain. The contractual provisions concerning royalties, exemptions and subventions are usually embodied in a document ancillary to the deed of lease, which will be in the usual technical form. From the aspect of international law, what is protected is the value of the lease, which is assessable in the usual land and improvement valuation manner, and the ancillary contract which is subject to the usual rules of English law concerning contracts made with the Crown. In the absence of statutory cover there is some doubt whether contracts of the Crown, other than purely commercial contracts,[4] are ever enforceable against the Crown, since the bargain is a concession of governmental interest, and is inherently revocable.[5] Although English law lacks a coherent distinction between public law and private law, this structure of contractual performance is a reflexion of something akin to it,

1 Mosler, p. 74.
2 Further discussion in O'Connell, *International Law* (1965), pp. 1057 *et seq.*
3 *Petroleum Development Ltd* v. *Sheikh of Abu Dhabi*, I.L.R. vol. XVIII, Case no. 37.
4 *N.S.W.* v. *Bardolph* (1934), 52 C.L.R. 455, esp. per Evatt, J., at p. 474.
5 *Rederiaktiebolaget Amphitrite* v. *R.* [1921] 3 K.B. 500. The authority was criticized by Denning, J., in *Robertson* v. *Minister of Pensions* [1949] 1 K.B. 227 at p. 231; this was not sustained in the House of Lords in *Howell* v. *Falmouth Boat Construction Co. Ltd* [1951] A.C. 837 at p. 845.

namely, a distinction between the Crown's commercial activity and concessions of the Crown's sovereignty.

In civil law systems a concession is regarded as governed by elements of both public law and private law, the admixture varying according to the nature of the functions conceded.[1] The relationship comes into being, as the arbitrator appointed to interpret article 160 of the Treaty of Versailles pointed out, through the grant 'by the State, or by an authority dependent on the State, by special act, in virtue of a power which in principle was of a discretionary character'.[2] The contract is thus constituted in the first instance under public law, but it gives rise to rights of a private nature. Although it is at times difficult to decide whether it is the public or the private aspects of a concessionary contract which are predominant, there is little doubt that the interest which the concessionaire acquires is one governed and protected by private law.

A concession of this kind may thus readily be distinguished from an outright conveyance of land,[3] and from a licence to practice a profession,[4] both of which grants are sometimes referred to as concessions. For this reason a concession in this context is described as an economic concession. It differs from an ordinary grant of land in two principal respects: in the first instance, the State, which is one party to the contract of concession, is subject to a positive contractual duty; secondly, the concessionaire has the right to extend the operations of the concession beyond the limits of the land subject to exploitation, as, for example, in the marketing of products.[5] Since an economic concession involves, on the one hand, the occupation of land and, on the other, a system of contractual relationships with the State, it is an interest at once corporeal and incorporeal,[6] and stands midway between the category of a debt owed by the State and the category of the private ownership of land.[7]

1 Develle, *op. cit.* p. 26; Mosler, pp. 72 *et seq.* In the *Lighthouses* Case Greece argued that 'la concession d'un service public—et tel est le case en l'espèce—n'est pas un contrat du droit privé. C'est un véritable act de puissance publique, auquel s'ajoute seulement un élément contractuel. Il puise ses droits de son pouvoir souverain': P.C.I.J. ser. C, no. 74.

2 *Germany* v. *Reparations Commission*, U.N. Rep., vol. I, p. 429 at p. 479. The article in question provided for the transfer to the Reparations Commission of German concessions in certain successor States. The arbitrator was concerned with the application of this article to Germany's allies.

3 Mosler, p. 77; Gidel, p. 105.
4 Mosler, p. 76.
5 Gidel, p. 116.
6 *Ibid.* p. 128. See Fiore, *Nouv. Droit. int.* vol. I, p. 312.

7 Mosler points out that a concessionary obligation is merely an administrative debt: 'These claims, seen from the conceding department's point of view, and after the disappearance of the department from that of the acquiring state, are administrative liabilities. Therefore, the protection of acquired rights is closely connected with

Acquired Rights and Economic Concessions

The judicial and diplomatic practice of States in the matter of concessions can conveniently be considered in two sections. In the first place it is necessary to inquire to what extent such practice establishes the duty of the successor State to respect the interest of a concessionaire as an acquired right.[1] Secondly, it is necessary to examine the juridical character of any such duty.

2. JUDICIAL AND DIPLOMATIC PRACTICE IN THE MATTER OF CONCESSIONS

(i) *The cession of the Ionian Islands to Greece, 1864*

When negotiations were pending in 1863 for the transfer of the Ionian Islands from British protectorate to Greek sovereignty, the Austrian Foreign Minister informed the British Ambassador at Vienna that he was disturbed at the fate of concessions which had been granted in the Islands to the Austrian Lloyd Company. He contended that such concessions ought not to be interfered with. It could not be admitted that 'an obligation contracted by either side should cease because the territory passed into other hands', and he insisted that the stipulations of the contract of concession should continue to be binding on the administration of the Islands after the cession.[2] Upon receipt of this correspondence the Foreign Office requested the Law Officers to advise 'on the general question of the validity in the event of the cession of the Ionian Islands to Greece, of contracts made by the Government of those Islands, when under the

the liability of the acquiring state for the administrative debts of the losing state', p. 143. Huber, p. 43. Schönborn, p. 53, considers concessionary rights to be entirely governed by public law. Cf. Sereni, vol. I, p. 404.

1 Concessions were specifically mentioned as obligating the successor States in the following treaties: Treaty between Prussia and Holland, 1816, *B.F.S.P.* vol. III (1816), p. 720, art. 31 at p. 731; Treaty of Zürich, 1859, *M.N.R.G.* vol. XVI, pt. II, p. 516, art. 11 at p. 521; Convention between France and Sardinia to settle questions arising out of the union of Savoy and Nice to France, *ibid.* vol. XVII, pt. II, p. 22, art. 6 at p. 24; Treaty of Vienna, 1866, *ibid.* vol. XVIII, p. 405, art. 7 at p. 407. The Additional Convention to the Treaty of Frankfurt of 11 December 1871 transferred to Germany all concessions in mines in Alsace-Lorraine, *ibid.* vol. XX, p. 847, art. 13 at p. 855. Germany refused to acknowledge concessions respecting the Alsace-Lorraine railways, but only because the concessions had not been ratified by the French Government: Mosler, p. 130. The Act of the Congress of Berlin, 1878, substituted Bulgaria for the Ottoman Empire in its obligations towards the Rustchuk–Varna Railway: *M.N.R.G.* 2nd ser., vol. III, p. 447, art. 10 at p. 454. Similar provision was made with respect to Serbia and Roumania. These stipulations were accepted by the delegates 'without discussion': Protocol 7 to the Act of Congress, C. 2083. In 1866 the *Cour de Cassation* held that a water concession in Savoy was unaffected by the fact that the waters had ceased to belong to Sardinia: S. 1866, I, 261.

2 C. 3347, no. 5, p. 5.

protectorate of Great Britain'. The Law Officers, one of whom was Sir Robert Phillimore, stated that they entertained 'no doubt upon the general question of the continued obligation of all lawful contracts, existing at the time of the cession of these Islands to the Kingdom of Greece. . . . Both according to the principles of International Law', they advised, 'and the practice of all civilized States, ceded territories pass, *cum onere*, to the new Sovereign.'[1]

(ii) *The cession of Peruvian territory to Chile, 1883*

In 1883 Peru ceded the province of Tarapacá to Chile. Shortly afterwards the latter cancelled the concession of the Nitrate Railway Company, a British corporation, and invited tenders for the construction of competing railway lines. Attempts made by the Company to have its claims adjudicated in the Chilean courts were frustrated by actions of the government of that country, and the Company eventually appealed to the British Government, and requested it to protest against the violation of the terms of the concession. Before taking such action the Foreign Office sought from the Law Officers an opinion as to the grounds upon which a diplomatic note might be based. The latter advised that 'Her Majesty's Government would be justified in protesting against the proposed infraction of the exclusive privilege granted by the Concession'. There had been no breach of the terms of the concession on the part of the Company, and if the Chilean Government alleged that there had, the Company was entitled to have 'the question of the legality of the forfeiture of the Concession determined in due course by the Chilean Tribunals'.[2]

(iii) *The annexation of Madagascar by France, 1896*

The question of the maintenance of concessions by a successor State became a diplomatic issue on a larger scale upon the annexation of Madagascar by France on 6 August 1896. A projected treaty of cession, which was annexed, before the decree of annexation, to the instructions given to the French Resident-General, specified that 'the Government of the French Republic does not assume any responsibility by reason of . . . concessions which the Government of Her Majesty the Queen of Madagascar had contracted before the signature of the present treaty'.[3] Acting upon his instructions, the Resident-General required the holders of concessions to prove the validity of their instruments of title, and to conform to certain French ordinances which were promulgated for their

---

1 Opinion of 15 August 1863, F.O. 83/2287; O'Connell, Appendix, no. 22.
2 F.O. Confidential Papers (6113), no. 5. Opinion of 10 February 1890; O'Connell, Appendix, no. 53.   3 *Rev. gén. de droit int. pub.* vol. IV (1897), p. 231, n. (2), art. 6.

'regularization'. Those who did not comply with these requirements were to be considered as having renounced their concessions.[1]

The United States took the view that this requirement was not binding upon American concessionaires, whose rights were considered inviolable, and instructions to this effect were contained in a dispatch of the Secretary of State to the American Ambassador at Paris on 29 May 1897. To the overtures of the Ambassador the French Minister of Foreign Affairs replied that the only purpose of the requirement was 'to establish the validity of the said concessions, and would not therefore affect property acquired in a regular manner'.[2] After a consideration of this reply the Secretary of State informed the *Chargé d'Affaires* at Paris that 'this Government can not admit the right of the French Government, in the event of the noncompliance of any American citizen with the order in question, to treat his concession as forfeited or subject to disposition by that Government'.[3]

Great Britain took a corresponding attitude and addressed protests to France on behalf of a British firm, Messrs Harrison Smith and Company. That firm, which possessed mining concessions in Madagascar, was informed by the Resident-General that 'although the French Government attached no value to the ancient contracts, they had decided to recognize, as far as was permitted by the new Law, the rights of priority acquired by persons already established'. The firm was accordingly invited to 'regularize' its concession, but in the meantime the sale of its products without authorization was prohibited. The application of the Company for the 'regularization' of its concession resulted in a disagreement between it and the French Government, and the latter registered the claims of other persons to lands in districts covered by the concession.[4] The Company thereupon invoked the assistance of the British Government, and its claims were referred to the Law Officers for opinion. In its reference to them the Foreign Office stated that it was disposed to think that a 'formal protest' should be made to the French Government against the application of the Law 'to destroy rights and privileges regularly granted to British subjects by the proper authority, previous to the annexation of Madagascar by the French'. The attention of the Law Officers was drawn to the previously quoted correspondence between the United States and France, and the Foreign Office considered that concessions granted to British subjects should be treated on the same footing. The Law Officers advised on 3 March 1899:

[1] Moore, *Dig.* vol. 1 (1906), p. 387.   [2] *Ibid.* p. 388.
[3] Letter of 12 August 1897, *ibid.* p. 388.
[4] Opinion of 3 March 1899, F.O. Confidential Papers (7356), no. 24, Appendix, no. 61.

These Concessions were private property, and there is no pretence for saying that they can be forfeited on the conquest of the island by the French. . . . The French Government, pending negotiations as to the recognition of these Concessions, have allotted to others the ground covered by them. We are unable to see on what ground of international law, and of ordinary justice, the course pursued by the French Government in this matter can be defended.[1]

Reference was also made to the Law Officers on the question of concessions granted by the Queen of Madagascar to British missionaries to erect and maintain hospitals on public land. Attempts had been made by the Queen during the period of the French protectorate over the island to eject certain of these missionaries, and, after the annexation, the French authorities, relying on the proceedings of the Queen, requisitioned one of the hospitals. The missionaries objected on the ground that the compensation offered was quite inadequate, and appealed to the British Government. The Law Officers, to whom the question was referred, felt no doubt

that on the true construction of the instrument the use of the land on which the hospital is built was granted by the Queen to the missionaries so long as it should be used for hospital purposes.

We cannot see any justification for the resumption, nominally by the Queen, of the land and buildings. It appears to us to be a mere act of spoliation.

Accordingly, they recommended that the matter be taken up diplomatically with the French Government, and that the claim should be based on the terms of the grant.[2]

The French Government, however, took the view that under French law all religious buildings were the property of the State, and on this ground sought to justify the expropriation of mission concessions. No satisfaction being obtained, the Foreign Office referred the question to the Law Officers, and suggested that 'the fact that the original Agreement was made at a time when Malagasy, and not French law, governed the matter was of importance'. The Law Officers advised on 2 February 1898, that

1 *Ibid.* The company had arranged with the previous Resident-General to export gold from their mines free of duty according to the terms of their concessions. The Law Officers were of opinion that 'the ore was extracted by them on the faith of the assurance given by M. Laroche that it might be exported. . . . We think that the French Government may be fairly asked to give effect to the arrangement made by M. Laroche pending the regularization of the concession.' This opinion does not state any rule of law, but it appears to be based on the assumption that the decree of the French Resident-General was ineffective to deprive the Company of its concessionary rights: Opinion of 29 March 1897, F.O. Confidential Papers (7058), no. 14, O'Connell, Appendix, no. 57.

2 F.O. Confidential Papers (7058), no. 13, Opinion of 22 March 1897, O'Connell, Appendix, no. 66.

the grants made by the Malagasy Queen for hospital purposes—while reserving to the Queen the title to the land—amount in substance to a contract that so long as it was used for the purpose mentioned in the grant, the holders would not be disturbed....

It appears to us that the French Government inherit this obligation, and that it would be a breach of contract if the holders of land under such grants were evicted, unless the land were wanted for public purposes and adequate compensation was paid.[1]

(iv) *The cession of Cuba and the Philippines by Spain, 1898*

The question of the maintenance of concessions was presented in a critical form in the case of transfers of territory that followed the Spanish-American War of 1898. Among the British companies which had concessions in the ceded territories of Cuba and the Philippines were the Eastern Extension, Australasia and China Telegraph Company Ltd, the Cuba Submarine Telegraph Company and the Manila Railway Company. From time to time the Law Officers rendered opinions to the Foreign Office with respect to the obligations which the United States had incurred towards these companies.

During the negotiations that preceded the treaty of peace between Spain and America the Spanish Commissioners listed the contracts which they suggested should be confirmed by treaty. The American Commissioners replied that 'the United States does not propose to repudiate any contract found upon investigation to be binding under international law ... and would deal justly and equitably in respect of contracts that were binding under the principles of international law'.[2] At a further stage in the negotiations the Commissioners repeated this assurance, and the Treaty of Paris confirmed all concessions properly granted.[3] There was therefore never any question that the United States felt itself obliged, as a general principle, to respect concessions. It was the interpretation of this obligation that brought the United States into collision with Great Britain.

In order that it be valid and binding on the successor State, the United States alleged that a concession must not only be related or attached to the

---

[1] Opinion of 2 February 1898, F.O. Confidential Papers (7199), no. 16, O'Connell, Appendix, no. 58. According to Gidel, it is not certain that France refused to recognize concessions as binding. He suggests that she relied on the terms of the concessions themselves to avoid fulfilling them: p. 248. Mosler is of the opinion that the French Government drew a distinction between concessions granted in civilized countries, and those granted in undeveloped countries. He suggests that while the former were recognized as binding the latter were not: p. 183. This was a distinction later to be drawn to her own advantage by Italy after the annexation of Ethiopia.

[2] Moore, *Dig.* vol. I, p. 389.   [3] *Ibid.* p. 390.

territory ceded, but also granted for its exclusive benefit.[1] The Attorney-General of the United States advised his Government that the concession granted to the Manila Railway Company to build a railway in the Philippines had been inspired by Spanish imperialistic motives. Hence, he argued, it was not in the exclusive interest of the ceded territories, and the United States was not obliged to respect it. The most that could be said was that there was an obligation of equity[2] imposed on the United States to compensate the concessionaire for the advantages which would accrue to the new administration from the laying of the railway.

The Law Officers were requested by the Foreign Office to advise on the merits of this Opinion of the Attorney-General, and they reported on 30 November 1900. They pointed out

that there is no warrant for the contention raised by the Attorney-General of the United States that the obligations undertaken by Spain in relation to the Companies in question are divisible into those for the general benefit of Spain and those exclusively for local benefit. To admit such a contention would leave it open, in all cases of conquest and cession, to the succeeding Government to repudiate the obligations of their predecessors on alleged grounds of motives, which, even if they could be proved to have existed, cannot affect the rights of property secured to individuals or Companies as a consideration for executing works of local improvement.

Such a contention is, in our opinion, contrary to the recognized principles of international law.[3]

Reports were also rendered by the same Law Officers on the general question of the liability of the United States with respect to the concessions of the Eastern Extension and Cuba Telegraph Companies. In the case of the concession of the first named company, the Spanish Government had been under a contractual obligation to pay annual subsidies to the concessionaire, and in consideration of this undertaking had the right to transmit messages at a reduced tariff. After the cession of the Philippines

1 These conditions were deemed by the War Department to be fulfilled in the case of a concession to construct a canal in Cuba, and by the Attorney-General in the case of a concession to construct tramways in Cuba. The latter also held that a concession to lay cables in Cuba had sufficient local identification and benefit to prevent the United States from granting similar privileges to other companies: Sayre in *A.J.* vol. XII (1918), p. 712.

2 Moore, *Dig.* vol. I, pp. 399–404. 'The Provinces of the Philippines have undoubtedly received, and they retain and will retain, the chief benefit from the railroad; the revenues out of which that part of the benefit was to be paid for are now in the hands of their new government; the creditor was induced very properly to look to those revenues for that purpose': *ibid.* p. 404. 'To regard the concession as exclusively for local benefit', he said, 'would be to ignore obvious facts': *ibid.* p. 402.

3 Opinion of 30 November 1900, F.O. Confidential Papers (7516), no. 44, O'Connell, Appendix, no. 71.

Acquired Rights and Economic Concessions 313

the United States used the facilities of the Company, and paid for messages at the same rate as had the Spanish administration. It nevertheless refused to continue the subsidy. The Foreign Office advised the Law Officers that it was important for the Company that the United States take over this obligation to pay subsidies, and requested an Opinion on the point. The Law Officers gave this Opinion on 4 January 1899, as follows:

> The United States are bound, on taking possession of the Philippine Islands, or assuming effective control over them, whether under the form of a Protectorate or otherwise, to respect the Concessions granted by Spain to the Eastern Extension Company both as to exclusive rights and as to subsidy. The obligation is one of a local nature, although contracted by the Government of Spain. On the faith of it, the Company has expended a large sum of money on works for the benefit of the Philippines, and the obligations in respect of the Concessions seem to us to belong clearly to that class of local obligations which have always been held to pass with the territory.[1]

With respect to the Cuba Telegraph Company's concession, the United States took the view that it was only in military occupation of Cuba and was not obliged to permit the Company to exercise rights granted by the defeated sovereign. The Law Officers were consulted on the validity of this argument. They considered that the occupation of Cuba by the United States was a direct exercise of sovereignty, and was not

> in the slightest degree analogous to a mere military occupation. It may or may not be temporary, but so long as it lasts it carries with it the obligation to respect such local obligations as the Concessions of the Telegraph Company.
>
> It need not be contended that the United States assumed absolute responsibility for the permanent observation of these Concessions in Cuba, but they are bound to respect them during the occupation, and to 'advise' any succeeding Government to do the like.[2]

Acting on these various opinions, the Foreign Office instructed the British Ambassador at Washington on a number of occasions to present 'official' and 'unofficial' claims, chiefly for the payment of interest and subsidies under the concessions of the Eastern Extension and Manila Railway Companies. The substance of the British claims was that the burden of all concessions which relate to the ceded territory must be accepted by the cessionary State, and not merely those granted exclusively

---

[1] Opinion of 4 January 1899, F.O. Confidential Papers (7356), no. 52, O'Connell, Appendix, no. 60.
[2] Opinion of 2 May 1899, F.O. Confidential Papers (7356), no. 54, O'Connell, Appendix, no. 63.

for local benefit. In a memorandum addressed to the United States Secretary of State, the Ambassador said:

> The obligations contracted by Spain under those concessions are of a local nature and it will not be contested, as Her Majesty's Government believe, that they become binding on the United States Government on their taking possession of the islands.... On the faith of those concessions the company has expended vast sums for the benefit of the islands, and the obligations in question clearly belong to that class of local obligations which have always been held to be transferred with the sovereignty and to pass with the territory.
>
> The question is really governed by general principles of international law as to the effect of conquest, and therefore Her Majesty's Government do not contend that the use by the United States Government of the company's cable, without availing themselves of the Government rights reserved by the concessions (such as those of free telegrams, etc.) would of itself render the concessions binding on them. But the use of the cable by the United States Government may fairly be mentioned as illustrating the local nature of obligations and as strengthening the claim put forward by the company, and which Her Majesty's Government consider to be well founded.[1]

The United States Government, however, held to its view that the concessions in question were not binding as contracts and were, at the most, 'equitable' claims on the ceded provinces.[2] The Foreign Office requested the view of the Law Officers on this distinction, and on 12 December 1900, they reported that they were unable to agree with the reasoning of the United States. They argued that the full claims of the respective companies should be recognized.[3]

There the matter from a diplomatic point of view rested. Subsequently, however, action was taken by the Eastern Extension Company before the United States Court for Claims for payment of subsidies contracted for under the concessions. This action was dismissed for want of jurisdiction, and the Company then brought an action on implied contract, which went on appeal to the Supreme Court.[4] As any claim based on State succession was barred for procedural reasons, the case proceeded on the assumption that an obligation to pay the subsidy could arise only by a contract, express or implied, made by the United States, or through unjust enrichment at the expense of the claimant. It was held that no contract 'was made by any officer of the United States',[5] and the sending of telegrams at a special premium was alone insufficient to establish unjust

1 Moore, *Dig.* vol. I, pp. 406–7.
2 Sayre, *loc. cit.* p. 713.
3 Opinion of 12 December 1900, F.O. Confidential Papers (7516), no. 45, O'Connell, Appendix, no. 72.
4 251 U.S. 355. 5 At p. 366.

Acquired Rights and Economic Concessions

enrichment.[1] Since the court was unable to take cognizance of the effect of the change of sovereignty the case is unimportant in the law of State succession.

The Cuban Republic, which was established on 20 May 1902, was approached by the Cuba Telegraph Company for payment of subsidies which the Spanish Government had agreed to pay under the terms of the concession. The attitude of Cuba was that an engagement contracted with Spain remained the engagement of that country, and did not pass to the successor. This conclusion is justified on the doctrine propounded by the United States that concessions not exclusively for local benefit were not binding. The concession to the Company was considered by the Cuban Government to have been granted as a 'measure of war' against the Cuban people. The Company thereupon took action in the Supreme Court of Cuba, and judgment was given on 11 October 1906, upholding the view of the Government. When the British Government was asked to further the claims of the Company diplomatically, it agreed that the concession had *prima facie* passed to Cuba, but it reserved its opinion on the question of the concession being an 'act of war'.

In 1907 the matter was again drawn to the attention of the Law Officers when it was pointed out that by a Spanish Decree of 1895 a subsidy was to be paid to the Company by the Treasury of Cuba until 1910. When the payments were refused by the United States, the British Government, it was reported, had taken the matter up with the new Cuban Republic after its formation in 1902, being met with a refusal on the ground that the subsidy was an engagement of Spain.

Sir Edward Grey recognized that, while it might be held that the obligations originally attaching to Spain in Cuba had devolved upon her successors, it would appear to him on a full examination of the peculiar circumstances in which the concession was granted that the liability of Spain could not properly be held to have devolved upon them. The reason for the grant of the concession was the necessity for uninterrupted telegraphic communication between points of strategic importance in the island, and to overcome the impediment to military operations through the interception by the insurgents of land communications. The Law Officers were requested to report whether they considered that this was a case where the Spanish Government should be looked to. They reported affirmatively but with some doubts:

The claim should be based on the grounds that the obligation was contracted by the Spanish Government personally in the name of the King, and not by the

[1] At p. 363.

colonial Cuban authorities, and that it was undertaken as a military measure in the interests of the Spanish Government, who have had the benefit of the performance of the contract by the claimants.

It cannot be said, however, that the question is free from doubt. The contract related to a local undertaking, and payment was to be made out of the local Exchequer.

Although we think that the latter stipulation was merely a direction as to payment for the convenience of the parties, it is perhaps open to the contention that it was intended as a condition attaching to payment.

In pressing the claim, His Majesty's Government will be in some degree prejudiced by reason of the delay, and the fact that they have on previous occasions made the claim against the successors in Cuba of the Spanish Government.[1]

(v) *The annexation of the Boer Republics, 1900*

The attitude which Great Britain took towards concessions granted by the Boer Republics prior to their annexation in 1900 has been the occasion of considerable controversy. It has given substance to the 'negativist' doctrine, and as such is one of the most important precedents in the law of State succession. Criticism of the British treatment of these concessions has been intensified in more recent times,[2] and the question must be reconsidered in the light of the Law Officers' Opinions which have subsequently become available.

The Orange Free State was annexed by Proclamation on 24 May 1900, and the South African Republic on 1 September 1900. The British High Commissioner announced by notice that the British Government would consider all concessions on their merits.[3] The Colonial Office, before taking definite steps with respect to these concessions, considered an opinion submitted by the legal adviser to the High Commissioner. This opinion was to the effect that the British Government was 'justified in holding that all concessions granted by the annexed States had expired, and that the concessionaires had no legal claim which they could enforce against Her Majesty's Government'. A complete refusal to be bound by the obligations of the annexed States 'was the stronger and more correct position to assume'. Expressing itself as not entirely convinced of the validity of this argument, the Colonial Office requested the advice of the Law Officers on the following questions: Whether the British Government was justified in holding that all concessions had lapsed and that the concessionaires had no legal claim which they could enforce against the

1 Unnumbered, unclassified F.O. Documents.
2 Mosler, p. 113; Drost in *Rev. de droit int. et de lég. comp.*, ser. 3, vol. xx (1939), p. 701.
3 Cd. 623, p. 5.

Acquired Rights and Economic Concessions

Government; and whether the Government was free to determine what obligations they would take upon themselves.

The Law Officers reported:

A Government annexing territory after conquest so annexes it subject, speaking generally, to such legal obligations as have been incurred by the previously existing Government before the outbreak of war, and not from their nature conditional on the continued existence of the territory as an independent State.

They did not agree with the legal adviser to the High Commissioner that 'it would be open to Her Majesty's Government, acting upon any recognized principles of international law, to repudiate responsibility for all the obligations incurred by the Governments of the South African Republic and the Orange Free State'. Within the term 'obligation' they specifically included concessionary contracts. They were careful to explain, however, that 'the duty to observe such contracts cannot be forced by a Municipal Court: it rests merely on the recognition of international law of what is equitable upon the acquisition of the property of the conquered State'. They were also of opinion that contracts incurred during the war, or in contemplation of the war, need not be recognized, making, to this extent, some concession to the American doctrine of 'odious' concessions.[1]

This opinion which was adhered to consistently by the Law Officers, despite the policy subsequently adopted by the Government, robs the Report of the Transvaal Concessions Commission of some of its authority. This Commission, which was set up in August 1900, was required to examine the merits of the concessions granted by the Boer Governments, and to advise the Colonial Office whether or not they should be maintained. Its Report, which was published on 19 April 1901,[2] made recommendations in respect of twenty-five concessions, and these recommendations were prefaced by some general observations on the law of State succession.

An annexing State, it was argued, is not legally bound by contracts made with the annexed State, and no court of law has authority to enforce them.

After annexation, it has been said, the people change their allegiance, but their relations to each other and their rights of property remain undisturbed; and property includes those rights which lie in contract. . . . Concessions of the nature of those which were the subject of enquiry presented examples of mixed public

[1] Opinion of 30 November 1900, F.O. Confidential Papers (7516), no. 22A, O'Connell, Appendix, no. 70.
[2] Cd. 623.

and private rights:[1] they probably continue to exist after annexation until abrogated by the annexing State, and, as matter of practice in modern times, where treaties have been made on the cession of territory, have been often maintained by agreement.

Nevertheless, the Report went on to deny that international law places any responsibility on the successor State with respect to such rights:

> We doubt whether the duties of an annexing State towards those claiming under concessions or contracts granted or made by the annexed State have been defined with such precision in authoritative statement, or acted upon with such uniformity in civilized practice, as to warrant their being termed rules of international law.

Despite this denial, however, the Report concluded that 'we are convinced that the best modern opinion favours the view that, as a general rule, the obligations of the annexed State towards private persons should be respected'. This general rule the Report considered to be a rule of 'ethics rather than of law'.[2] In making this distinction between law and ethics the Report betrayed too great an adherence to the Austinian definition.[3] It was a distinction unsupported by arguments of law or discussions of precedents, and it ignored not only the practice of Great Britain and other States during the previous century, but even the contemporary practice of the former with respect to the Madagascar and Spanish concessions. Its view of sovereignty led the Commission to assume that a successor State takes the rights but not the liabilities of a contract. This was the thesis subsequently to be propounded by Keith, and it was the dictum of the Transvaal Supreme Court at about the same time, when it was said that 'the conqueror becomes, by right of conquest, the successor to all the property corporeal and incorporeal of the vanquished', and hence to its rights under contract.[4]

To the general equitable principle that concessions should be respected the Commission annexed certain conditions. The contract must have been valid under the laws of the annexed State and not *ultra vires* of the authorities who granted it; it must also have been duly and *bona fide* acquired. On this ground the Report recommended the cancellation of a concession

---

1 If the Commission intended by this reference to mixed public and private rights to allege that such rights fail precisely because of their public character its argument is repudiated by the decision of the Permanent Court in the *German Settlers* Case, where rights of a distinctly public and imperialistic character were upheld: see *supra*, p. 274.
2 *Loc. cit.* p. 7.
3 Westlake in *Law Quarterly Review*, vol. XVII (1901), p. 395; Kaeckenbeeck in Hague *Recueil*, vol. LIX (1937), p. 350.
4 *Postmaster General* v. *Taute* [1905] Trans. L.R. (S.C.), 582.

Acquired Rights and Economic Concessions 319

which had been obtained by bribery.[1] The contract must not have been in breach of a treaty with the annexing State; it must not be injurious to the latter, and it must not have been revocable. On this last ground the Report advised against recognition of concessions which had depended on the discretion of the South African Government.[2]

The procedure adopted by the Commission was no less objectionable than its law. It followed the precedent of the French Government in the case of the Madagascar concessions, and that of the Fiji Land Commission, in shifting the *onus probandi* on to the concession-holders, who were required to establish that the above conditions were fulfilled in their cases.[3]

Most of the concessions which the Report analysed were upheld. The most significant case in which a recommendation was made that the concession be cancelled was that of the Netherlands South African Railway Company. This Company had made its facilities available to the Boer Governments during the war, and in this manner had undoubtedly made its contribution to the prolongation of hostilities. Because the Company had thus identified itself with the enemy it was considered inappropriate that its concession be continued, and this decision was justified by the importation of the doctrine of 'unneutral service'. 'We have seen', it was said, 'that the operations of the company during the war were acts of aggression, redress for which, as it cannot be sought against the person, may justly be exacted against the property of the aggressor.' This application, to the case of a railway, of laws which had hitherto been restricted to ships of neutral nations was a novelty which has found sanction in no other instance.[4]

Shareholders of the Company were not compensated because it was argued that they were the proprietors, they elected the directors, and they attended meetings.[5] 'Nothing, however, disentitles the bond-holders from

---

1 In doing so it would appear to have acted illogically. It should first have considered if bribery was a sufficient ground in the law under which the contract was made to warrant its cancellation. Instead it adopted its own canons of law.

2 Cd. 623, p. 8. In this it followed *Cook* v. *Sprigg* [1899] A.C. 572, which arose out of the refusal of the British Government to recognize a concession granted by a Swaziland chief prior to the annexation of his territory, not because the concession was never valid, but because even a valid concession could have been revoked at any time by the chief, who was not subject to any law, and was a mere despot.

3 'In each case we held that the onus of proof was upon the concessionaire to establish the validity of his concession': Cd. 623, p. 8.

4 Gidel regards the distinction drawn between 'normal' and 'abnormal' operations as fictitious. He asks if any railway which transports troops or munitions is guilty of an act of war, and maintains that the principle is the thin end of the wedge to destroy respect for acquired rights: p. 196. It is impossible, he says, to invoke the idea of neutrality when the railway could be requisitioned: p. 199. See also Mosler, who rejects the Commission's arguments as untenable: p. 170.

5 Cd. 623, p. 36.

full recognition,' it was decided, because these had lent money *bona fide* to the Company and had no control over its activities.[1] The decision in this instance was also bolstered up by the contention that the Company was a monopoly against the public interest. Other concessions were cancelled on similar grounds, notably that of the Johannesburg and Zuibekom Water Supply Concession whose monopoly gave it a complete discretion in the matter of supplying water to Johannesburg.[2] There is, however, no authority elsewhere for the contention that a concession may be cancelled without compensation merely on the ground that it is a monopoly.[3] There is little doubt that the question of monopolies figures largely in the considerations of the Commission, since English lawyers tend to view with distaste the idea of a private monopoly of public utilities.

If the Report was opposed to the opinions of the Law Officers it was similarly opposed to the opinions of other States who were interested in the matter. Even before the Report had been filed, the German and Austrian Embassies in London had made representations on behalf of national shareholders of the Netherlands South African Railway Company, and during the subsequent three years repeated diplomatic steps were taken. Germany in particular was insistent that a legal obligation to respect the Company's concession had been incurred by Great Britain.[4] The Company itself took legal opinion, which contended that Great Britain had succeeded to all contractual obligations of the late Republics, and asserted that private property rights, including concessions, were protected by international law.[5] Fortified with this opinion the Company, which was incorporated in Holland, invoked the assistance of the Dutch Government. The latter embarked on a long and fruitless correspondence with Great Britain, and eventually suggested arbitration.[6] This Great Britain refused, but after protracted negotiations she settled most of the outstanding claims with *ex gratia* compensation, though still with a denial of legal liability.[7]

1 *Ibid.* p. 37.   2 *Ibid.* p. 34.
3 The United States Attorney-General was of opinion that 'the mere fact that the Western Union Telegraph Company is enjoying under a grant of exclusive right what amounts to a monopoly is no reason of itself why it should be deprived of its concession. It is easy to say that monopolies are odious, but there are concessions which amount to monopolies which are lawful and cannot be disturbed except by a violation of public faith. Concessions of this kind, which carry with them exclusive rights for a period of years, constitute property of which the concessionary can no more be deprived arbitrarily and without lawful reason than it can be deprived of its personal tangible assets': 22 *Op. A.-G.* pp. 516, 518. See on the question Fuller in *Columbia Law Review*, vol. III (1903), p. 245.
4 Mosler, p. 133; Gidel, p. 195.   5 *Ibid.* p. 9.
6 Feilchenfeld, p. 383.
7 Pitt Cobbett, *Cases on International Law* (4th ed. 1924), vol. II, p. 353.

Acquired Rights and Economic Concessions 321

In the meantime, some appearance of authority for the views of the Commission had been given in the dictum in the case of the *West Rand Gold Mining Company* v. *The King*,[1] in which it was said that a conqueror is at liberty to fix the financial conditions on which it desires to acquire the conquered country. As was the case with the Report itself, this conclusion was arrived at without adequate analysis of precedents or discussion of theory, and in consequence is of little value.

The British Government would appear to have been fully aware that its policy towards the Transvaal concessions was inconsistent with that which it adopted at the same time towards the Spanish concessions in Cuba and the Philippines. On 23 October 1900 the Foreign Office asked the Law Officers

whether it is necessary or desirable, in view of the attitude which has been taken up by Her Majesty's Government in regard to the Concessions granted by the South African Republic, that Her Majesty's Ambassador at Washington should be instructed to advance any further arguments in reply to the opinion of the United States' Attorney-General.

To this inquiry the Law Officers replied that they did not think that this attitude formed 'any obstacle to pressing the claim' on the United States Government.[2]

The Foreign Office, however, still experienced qualms of conscience, and observed a month later that

it is thought that the attitude already adopted . . . in somewhat analogous circumstances towards holders of Concessions in South Africa may afford an important indication of the limits within which the claims of British concessionaires in Cuba or Manila may consistently and properly be pressed on the attention of the United States' Government.

This doubt would appear to have made little impression on the Law Officers, who merely referred to their previous opinion.[3] Neither Great Britain nor the United States established in the two controversies any

---

1 [1905] 2 K.B. 391 at p. 402.
2 Opinion of 3 November 1900, F.O. Confidential Papers (7615), no. 44, O'Connell, Appendix, no. 71.
3 Opinion of 12 December 1900, Confidential Papers, no. 45, O'Connell, Appendix, no. 72. It is interesting to observe that the same Law Officers, R. B. Finlay and E. Carson, as counsel in the *West Rand* Case argued there that 'there is no principle of international law by which a conquering State becomes *ipso facto* liable to discharge all the contractual obligations of the conquered State': [1905] 2 K.B. at p. 394. The subsequent opinion of the Law Officers was that the Commission did not put forward legal principles, but only suggestions as to the manner in which the discretion of the Government should be exercised.

conclusive authority for a denial of rules of international law. Subsequent practice tends to uphold such rules.[1]

(vi) *The annexation of Korea by Japan, 1910*

When Japan annexed Korea in 1910 it was announced that foreigners resident in Korea would, so far as conditions permitted, enjoy the same rights and immunities as in Japan proper, and the protection of their legally acquired rights. The British Foreign Secretary was disturbed as to the effect of this pronouncement upon British mining concessions and property rights in general, because the privileges enjoyed by British subjects in Korea were materially greater than those accorded them in Japan. 'It would seem fair', he wrote to the Japanese Ambassador, 'that the former should not be placed in a less favourable position in consequence of the annexation.'[2] The British Ambassador in Tokyo, acting on instructions from the Foreign Secretary, took up the matter with the Japanese Foreign Minister, and on 21 July 1910 reported that the latter had informed him that 'all commercial, industrial and property rights, mining and land ownership, foreign settlements and perpetual leases would not immediately be disturbed by annexation, but would form subject for later discussion with powers'.[3]

In a subsequent conference with the Foreign Minister, the Ambassador pointed out that 'it is very important that British subjects in Corea should know what would be the fate of the commercial, industrial and property rights which they had acquired in Corea in the matter of mines, missions and land ownership in general'. The Japanese Minister assured him that 'no change would be made at the time of annexation, but the Japanese Government would wish that all these points should be subsequently discussed with the foreign Governments concerned'.[4] Shortly afterwards the Japanese Government delivered a note to Great Britain in which it was stated that they fully recognized British land and mining interests in Korea, and that all the terms of the concessions were confirmed and all rights and privileges thereby granted would be duly maintained and respected.[5]

It must be admitted that there is little in this correspondence to substantiate the recognition of a rule of law. In fact, the Foreign Secretary's

---

1 A Swiss court in 1905 upheld a concession concerning water rights in territory transferred from one canton to another: *In re Potters Works of Ziegler Brothers*, reported in *A.J.* vol. 1 (1907), p. 237.
2 Cd. 5717.
3 F.O. 371/877. 26451/988/10/12, Gooch and Temperley, vol. VIII (1932), p. 493.
4 F.O. 371/878. 28688/988/10/12, Gooch and Temperley, *ibid.* p. 494.
5 Cd. 5717.

reference to it seeming 'fair' would appear to be an echo of the 'ethics rather than law' doctrine of the Transvaal Concessions Commission. The instance is valuable, however, as evidence of the tendency in modern practice to confirm concessionary and other private rights in absorbed territory.

(vii) *General practice, 1911–20*

The committee of experts which sat in Paris in 1913 to draft the terms of settlement of the First Balkan War adopted a formula that 'cessionary States are subrogated in all the rights and charges of the Imperial Ottoman Government in what concerns concessions having their exploitation on the territories ceded by the present treaty; they equally engage to respect and execute contracts in these territories validly entered into by the Imperial Government or competent authorities'.[1] Under the Treaty of Constantinople Bulgaria assumed the rights and obligations of Turkey in respect to concessions of the Oriental Railway Company in the territories ceded to her.[2]

Notes were exchanged between Italy and Turkey in 1923 in which the former agreed to maintain concessions in territories ceded to it in 1912. It was nevertheless accorded the power to bring such concessions 'into conformity with the new economic conditions'.[3] In the Treaty of Rapallo in 1920 Yugoslavia declared its recognition of the concessions in Dalmatia of an economic character granted to Italian citizens by the Austrian administration.[4]

(viii) *The dissolution of the Ottoman Empire, 1923: the Mavrommatis and Lighthouses Cases*

Some difficulty was experienced in regulating the numerous concessions which had been granted by the Ottoman Government in territories which at the end of the First World War were ceded to the Allied and Associated Powers as mandates or otherwise. There would seem to have been no question that the concessions were, as a general principle, to be maintained, but problems arose with their adaptation to quite different economic circumstances.

[1] F.O. 4328/1/13/44, Gooch and Temperley, vol. IX (1933), pt. II, p. 455. Austria proposed an amendment specifically to include railway concessions: F.O. 4786/1/13/44, Gooch and Temperley, *ibid.* p. 455. The British view was that the matter should be settled in a manner 'equitable to Turkey': F.O. 8858/5729/13/44, Gooch and Temperley, *ibid.* p. 517.
[2] B.F.S.P. vol. CVII, pt. I, p. 706.
[3] L.N.T.S. vol. XXXVI, no. 921.
[4] *Ibid.* vol. XVIII (1923), p. 396, art. 7 at p. 403.

As early as 17 March 1920, the Acting Secretary of State of the United States wrote to the American Chargé d'Affaires in London explaining the policy of the United States with respect to American concessions in these territories. The State Department, he said,

> had examined Standard Oil Company permits and concessions in Palestine, and finds (1) that in respect of all its claims it has certain vested rights under Turkish law; (2) that Great Britain in its temporary occupation of Palestine may legally enjoin the acquisition of further vested rights but must by virtue of its position as quasi-trustee recognize and protect the vested rights of the Standard Oil Company already existing; and (3) Great Britain as trustee cannot legally allow discrimination in favour of her own and other nationals.[1]

On 3 April 1922 he wrote to the Ambassador in London with regard to other American concessions in Palestine. 'It is also to be understood, of course,' he stated, 'that the existing legal rights of American citizens or companies in Palestine are to be fully respected and safeguarded.'[2]

Protocol XII annexed to the Treaty of Lausanne dealt with the question of these concessions.[3] All those entered into before 29 October 1914 between the Ottoman Government or any local authority and nationals of the contracting parties were to be maintained.[4] In addition, the successor States were to be fully 'subrogated' as regards the rights and obligations of Turkey towards the nationals of other States.[5] Provision was made for the 'readaptation of concessions' to the new economic circumstances.[6] Concessions which were still executory might be dissolved 'at the request of the concessionaire' subject to indemnification for expenses incurred.[7]

This protocol gave rise to the *Mavrommatis* Case,[8] a claim instituted by the Greek Government before the Permanent Court of International Justice on behalf of a national, who alleged that the British Government, as Mandatory of Palestine, was obliged to respect his concession. Mavrommatis had been the holder of two concessions to undertake public works, known respectively as the Jerusalem and Jaffa Concessions. With respect to the latter the court decided that for technical reasons it had no jurisdiction, but in arriving at this conclusion it observed that

> if Protocol XII leaves intact the general principle of subrogation ... the Administration of Palestine would be bound to recognize the Jaffa concessions, not in conse-

---

1 *For. Rel.* 1920, vol. II, p. 650. See also *ibid.* 1923, vol. II, p. 1033.
2 *Ibid.* 1922, vol. II, p. 273.
3 B.T.S. 1923, no. 16; Cmd. 1929.
4 Art. 1.   5 Art. 9.
6 Art. 5.   7 Art. 6.
8 *Mavrommatis Concessions* Case, P.C.I.J. ser. A, no. 5.

Acquired Rights and Economic Concessions 325

quence of an obligation undertaken by the Mandatory, but in virtue of a general principle of international law to the application of which the obligations entered into by the Mandatory created no exception.[1]

The claim in respect of the Jerusalem concessions was the only one considered on its merits. The Greek Government alleged that the concession had begun to be put into operation and that therefore the Mandatory was bound to maintain it and to agree to its 'adaptation to the new economic conditions of the country, or to redeem it by paying to the claimant reasonable compensation'. It was alleged that a concession had been granted to a third party which rendered impossible the fulfilment of the obligations owed to Mavrommatis, and that therefore compensation must be paid.[2] The court refused to entertain the claimant's plea that the provisions of Protocol XII should be supplemented by 'principles taken from general international law' because the protocol was complete in itself.[3]

It was held that the grant of the competitive concession had not rendered the fulfilment of that of Mavrommatis impossible.[4] As the case was decided entirely on the provisions of the protocol it is no authority for general international law, and the only dictum which makes reference to general international law is that quoted in respect of the Jaffa concession. The Greek Government's pleading, however, clearly indicates a reliance, not only on the protocol, but also on the 'general principles of international law'. In its memorial it stated that

it is indeed established in International Law that all rights validly acquired by individuals in a given territory preserve their force and value despite any change of sovereignty which has come over this territory. The new sovereign is, on the same ground as the previous ones, bound to respect them, or, if need be, to have them respected.[5]

In 1952 the Greek Council of State considered the fate of a concession granted in 1908 by the Ottoman Government to exploit a sulphur mine on the island of Nisyros which had been transferred from Turkey to Italy in 1924, and was again transferred from Italy to Greece in 1947. The appellants applied for renewal of the concession under Greek mining law, which was extended to the island by Royal Decree in 1949. The Administrative Tribunal rejected the application on the ground that the concession had been terminated by the Italian authorities acting under a

1 *Ibid.* no. 2, p. 28. 2 *Ibid.* p. 8.
3 *Ibid.* no. 5, p. 27.
4 *Ibid.* p. 45.
5 P.C.I.J., ser. A, no. 5, p. 105. See also *Lighthouses* Case, P.C.I.J. ser. A/B, no. 62.

law of 1933 which provided that all Ottoman concessions which had not been regularly exploited during the previous five years were to be considered as null and void, even though the reason for non-exploitation was *force majeure* or Act of God. The Council of State held that, even if the concession had in fact not been exploited, the law of 1933 was in violation of international usage concerning acquired rights, and any doubt upon the correct interpretation of a legal provision should be resolved by a construction in favour of the general principles of international law. In the instant case the law of 1933 violated Protocol XII which had been ratified by both Italy and Greece.[1] (It was also held that it violated the Hague Conventions, the Council maintaining the fiction that between 1924 and 1947 Italy was merely in belligerent occupation.)

A French company, Collas and Michel, had a concession from the Ottoman Government to erect and operate lighthouses throughout the Ottoman Empire. The territories upon which the lighthouses were erected suffered various vicissitudes, but some of them were incorporated in Greece as a result of the Treaty of London, 1913, the confirmation of the Great Powers in 1914, and the Treaties of Neuilly, Sèvres and Lausanne. The territories affected were parts of Macedonia, Epirus and Thrace, the autonomous State of Samos and the autonomous State of Crete. When in April 1913 the concession contract was renewed by the Ottoman Government, some of these territories were under belligerent occupation, and were never returned to Turkish control. Furthermore, the renewal was not ratified until the Turkish Parliament met after the outbreak of the First World War. Various claims of the concessionaire had arisen against the Ottoman Government before the cessions of these territories. Greece disclaimed responsibility with respect to both the concession and the claims, and in 1931 France and Greece signed a special arbitration agreement which requested the Permanent Court of International Justice to decide whether the renewal was regularly concluded, and accordingly operative as regards the Greek Government in so far as concerned lighthouses situated in the territories assigned to it after the Balkan wars or at a later date. Upon the delivery of the Court's decision, a settlement would be negotiated with the company, and failing agreement the issues would be submitted to arbitration.

The Permanent Court held[2] that the matter was governed by Protocol XII of the Treaty of Lausanne, which had provided that the successor States should be subrogated as regards concession contracts entered into with the Ottoman authorities prior to 29 October 1914, in so far as concerned

[1] *Nisyros Mines* Case, *I.L.R.* vol. XIX, Case no. 27.
[2] P.C.I.J. ser. A/B, no. 62 (1934).

territories detached from Turkey after the Balkan wars. According to Ottoman law, the concession renewal dated from April 1913, that is, before the cessions following the Balkan wars, and since the matter was regulated by treaty it was unnecessary for the Court to express any opinion on the effect of the grant of concessionary rights in territory under belligerent occupation. The Court accordingly ruled that the contract 'was duly entered into and is accordingly operative as regards the Greek Government in so far as concerns lighthouses situated in the territories assigned to it after the Balkan wars or subsequently'.[1]

Greece contested the applicability of this ruling to Samos and Crete, which were autonomous States under Ottoman sovereignty, on the ground that the contract was not validly concluded for them, and the Court was requested to indicate whether its judgment applied as regards the lighthouses situated in these territories. The Court held[2] that, since the States would only be regarded as ceasing to be part of the Ottoman Empire and under the sovereignty of the Sultan if there had been an entire disappearance of a political link, its ruling also extended to them.

The decision that the concession was in force in virtue of subrogation between Greece and the company then raised the question whether the various claims of the company arising out of the terms of the contract before the dates of cession also affected Greece. This question, together with various Greek counterclaims, was then submitted to the Permanent Court of Arbitration after the interruption of the Second World War. Most of the issues which the Court now had to deal with were technical issues concerning the dates of the cessions of territory, the applicability to this issue of the decision in the *Ottoman Public Debt* Case,[3] the currency of payment and interest. Several claims, however, were of general interest to the customary law of State succession.

The Permanent Court of Arbitration seems to have taken as its ultimate criterion of Greece's succession in respect of the financial consequences of breach of the concession contract the question whether the events involved Greece's discredit.[4] Claim no. 11[5] was based on the following facts: In 1903 the Government of the autonomous State of Crete asked the firm of Collas and Michel to construct two new lighthouses on Crete. Since 1899 the firm had not been bound under its concession with Turkey to build new lighthouses at its own expense, and accordingly it referred the request to the Ottoman Government, seeking credit for the work. The

---

[1] At p. 29. [2] P.C.I.J. ser. A/B, no. 71 (1937).
[3] U.N. Rep., vol. I, p. 329.
[4] *Lighthouses Arbitration between France and Greece*, I.L.R. vol. XXIII, p. 93.
[5] *Ibid*. p. 81.

latter granted credit at the expense, not of the Cretan but of the Ottoman budget, and to set it off regarded itself as being entitled to that part of the dues received by the firm's Cretan agencies, which belonged to the State granting the concession. The Cretan Government, however, insisted on payment of the receipts from the Cretan lighthouses into its own treasury. On that obstacle the proposal foundered, and the company claimed for payment of initial expenses. The Court rejected the claim on the coincidence of the following factors: neither the Ottoman Empire nor Crete had recognized the claim; it had not been determined by a tribunal; it was not liquidated, nor easily liquidable on the facts giving rise to it; the firm had undertaken the preparatory work rashly without assuring themselves of the eventual financial consequences; the Cretan Government was partly responsible since its final refusal was in contradiction with its original request; the Ottoman Government was partly responsible for failing to assure construction of facilities necessary for navigation and insisted upon by the Great Powers.

In view of this division between the three parties concerned of the responsibility for the events of 1903 to 1908, the Tribunal sees no real reason to saddle, after the event, Greece, who had absolutely nothing to do with the dealings between those parties, with this responsibility, in whole or in part.[1]

The decision is a reminder that in the law of international claims other than purely formal factors are involved. The fundamental factor was that it was unclear in Turkish law whether there was any contract or breach of contract for which the State could be liable; assessment of damages in the event of breach was problematical; Greece had not been enriched by the work; responsibility for the loss was distributed. In short, all the factors operated to leave the loss where it fell.

In Claim no. 4,[2] however, the release of a Greek shipping company from payment of dues to the lighthouses concessionaire constituted a breach of the concession contract, from which a Greek national had benefited, and in which Greece was implicated.

When the rights and duties under the contract were clear, and the amount liquidated, the Court had no difficulty in awarding payment. Hence, in Counterclaims nos. 3–6[3] it found that Greece was entitled to recover from the concessionaire the costs of maintaining and operating lighthouses from which it had expelled the concessionaire for a period of more than thirteen years, because the concessionaire had continued to collect the shipping dues and had incurred no charges to offset against them. It did not follow, however, that Greece was entitled to recover what

1 At p. 89.   2 At p. 90.   3 At p. 99.

it had actually expended, and the entitlement would have to be professionally appraised.

At various times during the administration of the Mandate of Palestine, Great Britain had to decide whether or not to maintain concessions held by its own subjects, and therefore not within the scope of Protocol XII. One such concession, claimed by a Captain Bennett, was rejected, and the Report of the Transvaal Concessions Commission was invoked to justify the conclusion that 'international law is not sufficiently settled on the point'. A claim by a Mr Edwards and a Major Henry to salt concessions on the Dead Sea was likewise rejected on the ground that 'a succeeding Government, in the absence of express stipulations, has it in its discretion whether to recognize or not to recognize concessionary contracts entered into by the preceding Government'. Concessions not protected by treaty provisions, the British Government considered, were not maintained by principles of international law. Hence, the right was asserted to abrogate concessions granted by Germany to Tanganyika, where the only concessions actually recognized were those on which a considerable amount of work had been done. These decisions of the British Government, being based on the dicta of the Transvaal Concessions Commission, and hence on what has been alleged here to be a mistaken view of the law, do not, it is submitted, carry great weight as precedents. They were clearly prompted by the distinction that concessions are contracts pure and simple, and subject to different rules from land tenure. This distinction led the Government to the conclusion that a concession granted by Turkey to the Baghdad Railway Company was not binding as a contract on the British Government, but was a 'property right' within the definition of article 65 of the Treaty of Lausanne. The right to run trains on the line was regarded, not as a contractual right, but as a justified user of realty.

(ix) *The Sopron–Köszeg Local Railway Company Arbitration, 1929*

Rules of international law were recognized by the arbitrators appointed to give a decision on the readaptation of the concession of the Sopron–Köszeg Local Railway Company in Austria and Hungary. Article 330 of the Treaty of St Germain and article 304 of the Treaty of Trianon had enacted that the administrative and technical reorganization of railway lines which were situated in the territories of several successor States would be effected by agreement between the companies and the States concerned. In the absence of such agreement, the matter was to be referred to arbitration. In the case of the Sopron–Köszeg Railway, which ran partly through Austria and partly through Hungary, negotiations with the Austrian Government led to a controversy, and arbitrators were appointed under the terms of the treaty to determine the basis of agreement. They prefaced their decision on the details of the reorganization of the railway by some general remarks on the position of a concession in ceded territory. Assuming that Austria was a new sovereign person, they stated:

> In principle the rights which a private company derives from a deed of concession cannot be nullified or affected by the mere fact of a change in the nationality of the territory on which the public service conceded is operated. Most authorities and international judgments which conform most nearly to modern views of international law take this view. . . . The contract clauses under which the Sopron Köszeg Local Railway Company was working before the war can be pronounced neither wholly invalidated by the change of sovereignty affecting the territories on which its undertaking is situated, nor indeed wholly valid and enforceable according to their drafting and tenor up to the expiration of the concession; that the arbitrators appointed by the Council of the League of Nations are called upon ... to make such changes in the position under the contracts as are rendered necessary by the events of the last fifteen years, which could not be anticipated in the joint intentions of the Parties when the concession was granted; that the arbitrators should, with that end in view, take account both of the legitimate interests involved in the public-utility undertaking concerned and of the purpose set before them by the Treaties of Peace, which is to restore the regular operation of the railways of the former Austro-Hungarian Monarchy, in the higher interests of the facility and freedom of international communication.[1]

The case is important for its clear exposition of the issue which is presented to a successor State. It recognized that a successor State must take account of the 'legitimate interests involved' in the undertaking. It also recognized that such a State cannot be obliged by every term of the concession and must have the competence to 'make such changes in the position under the contracts' as are rendered necessary by the change.

In a further arbitration in 1933 concerning the effect of the division of the Zeltsweg–Wolfsberg and Unterdrauberg–Woellen Railway by the reconstructed frontier of Austria and Yugoslavia, article 320 was stated to be a reflexion of the principles of international law concerning the technical reorganization of concessions consequent upon State succession. It was said that

> l'article 320 se borne à confirmer, ainsi que l'a reconnu la jurisprudence antérieure, ce principe du droit public international que les droits tenus par une compagnie privée, d'un acte de concession, ne sauraient être mis à néant ou lésés du seul fait que le territoire sur lequel est assis le service public concédé a changé de nationalité.[2]

[1] *Ann. Dig.* vol. v, Case no. 34, p. 59. See also *Barcs–Pakrac Railway* v. *Yugoslavia, ibid.* vol. vii, Case no. 190.
[2] U.N. Rep., vol. iii, p. 1803.

(x) *The Forests of Central Rhodope Case, 1934*

The Treaty of Neuilly of 1919 provided that private rights guaranteed in the treaties by which territory was ceded at the end of the Balkan Wars of 1913–14 were not to be affected by the further cessions of such territory following the First World War. The owners of a forestry company which had been granted a concession by the Ottoman Government became Greek nationals in virtue of these cessions, although the forests subject to the concession remained in Bulgaria, which had acquired them by cession in 1913. Bulgaria refused to recognize the concession and granted a new concession to a Bulgarian company. Greece referred the matter to the Council of the League of Nations, which appointed an arbitrator under article 181 of the Treaty of Neuilly. Bulgaria disputed the application of the article to the facts of the case, arguing that the concessionary rights were merely personal rights to the cutting of timber, and involved no element of interest in land so as to fall within the conception of acquired rights. This contention was rejected by the arbitrator, who held that 'un principe général du droit commun international, celui du respect, sur un territoire annexé, des droits privés régulièrement acquis sous le régime antérieur, se trouve expressément sanctionné par le Traité de Neuilly, suivant l'example des traités de paix de 1913–1914'.[1] It followed that article 181 was 'une consécration expresse du principe bien connu du respect des droits acquis dans des territoires cédés, c'est-à-dire le renouvellement, à la charge de l'État cessionnaire, d'une obligation incombant à l'État cédant'.[2]

The Treaty of Neuilly referred to 'private rights' and the Treaty of Constantinople of 1913 to 'acquired rights' as well as to 'rights of real property', and the arbitrator considered that it was logical that the narrower expression in the later treaty be interpreted as equivalent to the wider expression in the earlier, which certainly included financial claims. Therefore, whether the rights of the concessionaire were rights affecting land, or rights under contract for which an indemnity could be claimed, was not in point. Even if, under Ottoman law, the right, deriving from the concession, to enter upon the land and cut the timber was so precarious that the alienation of the title to the land would involve an exclusion therefrom of the concessionaire, the latter would still possess his rights under contract. In actual fact, the exclusion of the concessionaire had occurred, not as a result of the alienation of the title, but as a result of the prohibition upon exploitation which the Bulgarian Government had interposed upon the ground that under existing Bulgarian forestry

1 *Ibid.* p. 1396.   2 *Ibid.* p. 1401.

legislation the forests were State property. 'Le Gouvernement bulgare a donc pris une mesure directement dirigée contre les droits du coupe aussi et basée sur la thèse—non légitime—que la cession de ce genre de droits aurait été inadmissible parce que les forêts étaient propriété d'État.'[1] However, even though Bulgaria was in violation of its obligations under the treaty, *restitutio in integrum* had become impossible, and damages alone could be awarded. The assessment of these presented difficulty, inasmuch as the valuation of speculative activity such as forestry was hazardous, especially when the forests were situated in a politically unstable frontier area.[2] Subject to this, and 'conformément aux principes généraux du droit international',[3] damages were based on the value of the forests subject to contracts of exploitation at the date of actual dispossession, together with interest from that date.

(xi) *The annexation of Ethiopia by Italy, 1935*

On 20 December 1925, notes were exchanged between Great Britain and Italy relating to a British concession to build a dam on Lake Tsana in Ethiopia. On 3 April 1936, after the annexation of that country, Italy guaranteed the continuation of the British rights, and this guarantee was repeated in the Anglo-Italian Agreement of April 1938.[4] Nevertheless, the Italian Government did not consider itself under any legal obligation to recognize concessions in Ethiopia, because, it was argued, principles of international law could not apply to the conquest of an undeveloped country.[5] The effect of this attitude upon the concession of the Djibouti–Addis Ababa Railway Company, a French corporation, was considered in the French National Assembly. M. Laval stated that the French Government was not interested in Italy's actions so long as it respected acquired rights. An agreement was entered into between the two countries confirming this concession in most particulars.[6]

The Djibouti–Addis Ababa Railway Company was incorporated in Paris in 1908, with its *siège social* there, of French nationality, and governed by French law. It received two concessions for the construction of a railway, one in 1908 from the Emperor Menelik II of Ethiopia for the portion

---

[1] *Ibid*. p. 1426.   [2] *Ibid*. p. 1434.
[3] *Ibid*. p. 1435.
[4] L.N.T.S. vol. CXCV, p. 86; B.F.S.P. CXLII, p. 152.
[5] Mosler, p. 107. In this instance Italy appears to have followed the French view with respect to the Madagascar concessions. In a Decreto-Legge of 9 May 1935, there was no mention of Ethiopia as a country, but only of 'the tribes'. Those in Italy who were opposed to the theory of State succession argued that monopolies had been granted by Ethiopia because she was unable to exploit her own resources: *ibid*. p. 185.
[6] *Rev. de droit int. et de lég. comp.* vol. XVII (1936), p. 588; Mosler, pp. 107, 186.

of the line on Ethiopian territory and one from the French State in 1909 with respect to that portion of the line situated in French Somaliland. The concessions were unaffected by the Italian conquest of Ethiopia, and again by the independence of Ethiopia after the Italian expulsion. However, political and economic developments made it desirable that they should be reconstructed, and since the process of reconstruction is in some ways a model it is useful to refer to it. However, at no stage during the negotiations was the continued validity of the concessions in dispute.

The Federation of Eritrea with Ethiopia in 1950 made it possible for the latter to construct alternative routes to the coast. The Addis Ababa–Assab route was modernized and important port installations were constructed at Assab. The port of Djibouti, and consequently the railway, thereby lost the economic monopoly which had been enjoyed from 1909. In 1954 the railway was compelled to reduce its freight rates, thereby incurring an accumulated deficit between 1954 and 1956 of 865,000,000 francs, and since the French Treasury was guarantor of the company's debts to the extent of 4 milliards of francs, the French Government was interested in negotiating a new arrangement with Ethiopia. By 1958 the return in traffic in the port of Djibouti had declined, and the construction of a road from Assab to Diredawa aggravated the situation further by interfering with the economic monopoly which the railways still enjoyed in respect of the products of Pharar.

It was recognized further that any negotiations with Ethiopia for restoration of the economic situation of the railway must be governed by acknowledgement that political factors warranted a greater participation of Ethiopia in the administration of the railway. Accordingly, the negotiations which began in 1958 between France and Ethiopia and culminated in a treaty of 12 November 1959[1] were based, as the *avant-propos* of the treaty mentioned, on complete equality between the two countries.

The company was reconstituted as an Ethiopian incorporated company with its head office in Addis Ababa and governed by the treaty, that is to say, as the *avant-propos* admits, by international rules. Where, however, the treaty is silent, the relevant code of reference was to be the Ethiopian Commercial Code, the text of which was annexed to the treaty. The capital of the company was now divided equally between France and Ethiopia, and guarantees of the maintenance of this parity were incorporated in the treaty. The equality of direction, choice of the president and vice-president, and composition of the administrative council were also

[1] Djibouti–Addis Ababa Railway Treaty, *Documentation français: Notes et études documentaires*, no. 2658 (1959).

agreed upon. The French Government guaranteed to Ethiopia freedom to utilize the port of Djibouti in time of peace and in time of war, as well as the grant to Ethiopia, without conceding extraterritorial rights, of the facilities normally available in a free port, that is, national treatment of the usage of installations, customs and treatment of officials.

In order to maintain the fundamental concessionary character of the railway's rights to the date of expiration, both governments unilaterally confirmed their validity, subject to the modifications effected by the treaty. Under a new statute, three-quarters of the capital would henceforth belong to the two governments, and an extraordinary general meeting would be called for this purpose. The transfer of the headquarters to Ethiopia and the change in the nationality of the company were stated not to put an end to its legal personality, and to have no effect on the fiscal situation of either country. The company was not to be subjected to any tax other than that existing at the date of entry into force of the treaty. Provisions for double taxation in respect of salaries, dividends and interest paid by the company were included. The Ethiopian Government would arrange the necessary exchange facilities. The two governments undertook equal and conjoint responsibility with respect to the eventual deficits of the company, but while Ethiopia did not contest that it should in the future support half the eventual debt, it did not regard itself as obliged to undertake any proportion of the existing debt, which would remain a charge on the French Treasury.

(xii) *The independence of Transjordan, 1946*

In the Treaty of Recognition of Transjordan it was agreed that commercial concessions granted in respect of Transjordan territory prior to the signature of the treaty should be valid for the periods specified in their texts.[1]

(xiii) *The Peace Treaty with Italy, 1947*

The Peace Treaty with Italy of 1947 provided that Albania and Ethiopia might cancel within one year concessions or special rights granted to Italian nationals.[2] This seems to be a derogation from a general principle, and it would seem to imply that concessions not cancelled within the year, and concessions to others than Italians, were to be maintained.

1 *U.N.T.S.* vol. VI, p. 143; *B.T.S.* 1946, no. 32 (Cmd. 6916), art. 10.
2 *U.N.T.S.* vol. XLIX, p. 126; *B.T.S.* 1948, no. 50 (Cmd. 7481), arts. 30 and 36.

Acquired Rights and Economic Concessions   335

(xiv) *The Petsamo Nickel Concession Issue, 1947*

The Treaty of Peace of 10 February 1947 with Finland[1] provided for the retrocession of Petsamo to the Soviet Union, which recognized the validity of any obligation contracted by Finland. This included the concessions for the exploitation of nickel at Petsamo granted to a Finnish company in association with the Mond Nickel Company and the International Nickel Company of Canada. The Canadian Government sought to protect the interests of these companies and, together with the British Government, negotiated with the Soviet. The outcome was an agreement according to which the Soviet undertook to pay the Canadian Government the sum of $20,000,000 over a period of six years. This company was a subsidiary of a British company, which in turn was a subsidiary of a Canadian company. The compensation was paid to the latter.[2]

(xv) *Concessions in Indonesia*

At the Round Table Conference held at the Hague, provisions were incorporated in the agreement arrived at between the Netherlands and Indonesia on 2 November 1949, respecting outstanding rights and liabilities. The latter undertook to 'adhere to the basic principle of recognizing' concessions, and would restore the titleholders to the actual exercise of their rights.[3]

However, Indonesia reserved the right to conduct an investigation in respect of important rights, concessions and licences granted after the Japanese occupation of the territory, which might influence the economic policy of the Republic. Account was to be taken of the occupation by the populace with the approval of the Japanese authorities of certain estates. Infringement of the rights mentioned would be permitted only in the public interest, and through amicable settlement with the claimants, or, in the absence of settlement, by expropriation exclusively for the public benefit against previously enjoyed or guaranteed indemnity to be fixed by judicial decision at the real value.[4]

(xvi) *Concessions in Mandated Territories*

It would appear that general principles of succession bound Mandatories to respect vested rights of third States and their nationals in the Mandated Territory.[5] There are, however, several factors which support the

1 *U.N.T.S.* vol. XLVIII, p. 228; *B.T.S.* 1948, no. 53 (Cmd. 7484).
2 Mosler, p. 135.
3 *U.N.T.S.* vol. LXIX, pp. 3, 200.
4 The fate of Netherlands concessions in Indonesia is discussed *supra*, p. 284.
5 See Wright, *Mandates under the League of Nations* (1930), p. 480.

proposition that Mandatories were not obliged to honour obligations previously incurred in the territory which were in any way burdensome upon it. In the first place there are, in the terms of the Mandates, certain provisions dealing with protection of foreign interests. Under A class Mandates the Mandatory was required to provide judicial protection of the rights of natives and foreigners.[1] In B class Mandates the provision was more specialized in that the Mandatory was bound to 'secure to all nationals of states members of the League of Nations the same rights as are enjoyed in the territory by his own nationals in respect of . . . the protection afforded to their person and property'.[2] In C class Mandates no specific mention was made of protecting interests of other nationals. Thus on the basis that Mandatory States were required to act only within the terms of the Mandates, and applying the principle *expressio unius est exclusio alterius*, it seems justifiable to assume that burdensome concessions could have been dishonoured. In addition the United States' treaties with the Mandatory States, which put the United States on an equal footing with League members in Mandated Territories, included an express provision promising security for United States interests which, had there been any definite general devolution, would appear superfluous.[3] Finally, a jurisdictional point lends additional weight to this argument. Under the Mandate clauses the Permanent Court did not have compulsory jurisdiction over controversies involving alien interests except in so far as they were expressly recognized by the Mandates, an indication that no general obligation was succeeded to by the Mandatory.[4]

(xvii) *Concessions in Israel*

The maintenance of concessions in Israel was originally provided for in a declaration contained in the resolution of the General Assembly of the United Nations of 29 November 1947.[5] As, however, this agreement was never implemented, the question of economic concessions was left to be determined, if at all, by international law. In the negotiations which took place at Tel Aviv in July 1949, the British representatives were insistent

[1] British Mandate for Palestine, art. 9, *L.N. Off. J.* vol. III, p. 1008; article 8 excluded continuance of extraterritorial privileges by capitulations. French Mandate for Syria, art. 6, *ibid.* p. 1014.

[2] *L.N. Off. J.* vol. III, p. 867; the other B Mandates contain similar clauses.

[3] E.g. U.S.-Japanese treaty, 1922, concerning Yap Island: *L.N.T.S.* vol. XII, p. 202, art. 2 (2).

[4] E.g. British Mandate for Nauru, art. 7, para. 2; there is corresponding provision in each of the thirteen other Mandates: see Fachiri, *Permanent Court of International Justice* (2nd ed. 1932), p. 87, n. 4.

[5] U.N. Doc. A/516, resolving to adopt the report of the *ad hoc* committee contained in A/AC 14/34.

that 'according to the principles of international law private property must be respected by the successor Government, and concessions must be maintained'. These concessions were, however, in a rather unusual situation since, consequent upon the decision in the *Mavrommatis* Case,[1] and in exercise of the powers granted by the protocol to the Treaty of Lausanne, Great Britain, as Mandatory of Palestine, had regulated their exercise by municipal ordinance. Such acts of legislation were continued in force after the setting up of the State of Israel by Act of the Knesset maintaining the law of Palestine as it existed on 14 May 1948.[2] These concessions were 'readapted to the new economic circumstances' in accordance with the powers contained in the Palestine ordinances.

At the date of Israel's foundation there were several concessions in force in Israeli territory: the Mavrommatis concessions, the Iraq Petroleum Company concession of 1939, the Anglo-Iranian Oil Company concession of 1933, the Trans-Arabian Pipeline Company concession of 1946, and the Palestine Potash Ltd concession. Israel continued to respect existing concessionary rights, but opened negotiations with the concessionaires for their adaptation. In 1950 an agreement was reached extending the duration of the concession of the Palestine Potash Ltd, under which Israel lent the Company $2,500,000 to assist it to reconstruct its factory which had been damaged by war. Negotiations with the Anglo-Iranian Oil Company broke down, and the Company withdrew from Israel. The Government of Israel has been approached regarding concessionary rights allegedly granted by the Ottoman authorities before 1917, but, in the absence of any recognition of these by the Mandatory Administration, has declined to deal with them.

In 1955 the Israel Supreme Court reviewed the liability of Israel respecting concessions granted by the British High Commission, and rejected the thesis of subrogation.[3] The case concerned a contract made in 1938 between the appellants and the Palestine Railways by which a concession was granted for newspaper kiosks and bookstalls on the Haifa Central Railway Station. The contract was terminable on three months' notice in writing. It was maintained in force until March 1948, when the railway administration informed the concessionaire that the contract could not be regarded as binding any substitute for the Palestine Railways after the end of the Mandate, though there was no intention to give notice of termination. The Israel Ministry of Transport refused to recognize the contract, whereupon the appellants brought action. It was agreed between the parties, on the basis of previous decisions of the courts

1 P.C.I.J. ser. A, no. 5.   2 See *supra*, p. 128.
3 *Pales Ltd* v. *Ministry of Transport, I.L.R.* vol. XXII, p. 113.

of Israel,[1] that Israel was not the successor of Palestine,[2] and the appeal was argued on the basis of an enquiry into the rights of the appellants to sell under a contract which provided a method of cancellation. The contract was alleged to have been recognized by the Law and Administration Ordinance of 1948,[3] which had kept concessions in force until varied by legislation.

The Supreme Court held that Israel was not bound by the contract, which did not fall within the scope of the Ordinance because a distinction had to be drawn between acts performed by the previous Government in its capacity as the Government and transactions concluded by it in its capacity as owner of property. The new State would be interested in recognizing activities of the first category because it would be unwilling to snap the chain of continuity in the legal régimes of the citizen; but perfunctory transactions such as leasing of houses, sale of land and conclusion of commercial contracts in which the government appears as the other party in relation to a citizen are not required by logic to be recognized by the successor State. Since Israel was not the successor in the Mandate it did not automatically step into the shoes of the Government of Palestine, and the draftsman of the Ordinance clearly had this distinction in mind when he associated concessions with authorizations, licences, patents, trademarks, etc., which were activities performed by the authorities of the Mandate as the Government of the country. Applying the *ejusdem generis* rule of construction the court concluded that the expression 'concession' must be restricted to grants by the Mandatory authorities in their governmental capacity, and not to contracts of a landlord-and-tenant character. As examples of concessions validated by the ordinance the court instanced the Palestine Electric Corporation and the Dead Sea Concession.

(xviii) *Concessions in the Lebanon*

In 1948 France and the Lebanon concluded an agreement[4] modifying that of 1944, and containing provisions for the settling of financial problems resulting from the Mandate period. In a letter annexed (no. 12) to the agreement, the Lebanese Government stated that

in view of the termination of the mandate and the proclamation of Lebanese independence, it may be desirable to make certain modifications in the acts and annexes governing the concessions of French companies or companies financed by French capital operating in Lebanon.

1 *Sifri* v. *Attorney-General*, I.L.R. vol. XVII, Case no. 22; *Shimshon Palestine Portland Cement Factory Ltd* v. *Attorney-General*, ibid. Case no. 19.
2 For the Israeli position see *supra*, p. 287.
3 *Official Gazette*, no. 2, 21 May 1948.
4 *U.N.T.S.* vol. CLXXIII, p. 99.

Acquired Rights and Economic Concessions 339

Conversations would be initiated with each of the companies concerned to arrive at a solution in a contractual manner and within the framework of existing law. One of the companies with which conversations were initiated was the *Sociéte d'Électricité de Beyrouth*, a French company with its *siège social* in Paris, incorporated in 1923 for a period of ninety-nine years, and the holder of five concessions in the Lebanon. Before the conversations resulted in agreement, the Lebanon put the concession under provisional State control by decree in 1953. This action resulted from a campaign begun in 1951 with the object of securing a reduction of the charges for electricity, which went as far as a collective refusal of consumers to pay the rates corresponding to their consumption of electricity. The Government also refused to permit the Company to raise certain reduced charges, an action which was permitted by the General Conditions governing the operation of the concession issued in 1955. The company proposed to allow the dispute to be settled by the legal means provided for in the General Conditions, but its offer was unanswered. Eventually, France alleged, the public campaign against the electricity rates developed into an invitation to the public to refuse to pay for electricity. The Government refused either to support the Company's tariff or to permit it to cut off its electricity supply. Four Dutch experts were called in by the Lebanese Government to undertake an enquiry. They upheld the charges, and made certain recommendations, which, however, the Government did not implement. Instead it issued decrees reducing the tariffs, and the Company claimed that this measure upset the financial equilibrium of the concession. Negotiations continued fruitlessly, and the Company's request for arbitration, to which it was entitled under the General Conditions, was ignored. The Government appointed receivers in March and April 1953, who took possession of the offices and archives of the Company.

France delivered notes to Lebanon making representations on behalf of the Company, but when these brought no satisfaction proceedings were instituted in August 1953 in the International Court of Justice under the judicial settlement provisions of the agreement of 1948. France alleged that violations of international law had occurred in the breach of the concessionary contract and the Government's refusal to accept arbitration; and asked that the rules of international law applicable to its nationals be respected, and that adequate reparation be made for the failure to observe them.

Cette obligation concernait, non seulement les rapports du Gouvernement libanais avec la société, mais aussi et surtout les relations avec le Gouvernement de la République française; il s'agit d'une obligation d'État à État, contractée dans un traité destiné à régler l'ensemble des problèmes financiers résultant de la liquidation du passé et à fixer pour l'avenir les relations monétaires et financières entre les deux pays. Toute violation de cette obligation constitue donc *ipso facto* un acte illicite en droit international.[1]

On 26 March 1954 an agreement was reached between the company and the Lebanese Government, and this was ratified by the Lebanese Parliament on 30 June 1954. The case was then removed from the court's list.

A similar issue arose with respect to the concession granted in 1887 by the Ottoman Government 'aux droits duquel se trouve actuellement substitué l'État libanais'[2] to the *Compagnie du Port, des Quais et des Entrepôts de Beyrouth*, which was converted into a French company on 7 February 1926 in accordance with the provisions of Protocol XII of the Treaty of Lausanne. The concession is due to expire in 1990. The concessionary contract of 1887 was readapted by agreement with France in 1925, and again in 1934 when the harbour was extended. It fell also under the provisions of the letter annexed to the agreement of 1948 between France and the Lebanon.

Article 8 of the contract provided that the materials and plant used in the construction of the harbour installations should be exempt from customs duties, and throughout the whole period of the concession, the land, harbour beds, quays and outbuildings should be exempt from any tax. In 1956 the Lebanese Government promulgated a law stipulating that all companies enjoying exemption from taxes under agreements satisfied by special laws should, as from 1 January 1952, be subject to income tax and to all other fiscal and municipal taxes and dues. In virtue of this the *Compagnie du Port* found itself levied with income tax, land tax, municipal tax on rental value, and customs duties.

The Company pursued negotiations, which had been in train since 1948, with a view to settling the tax question in a single document dealing also with the modification of the concession in relation to the extension of the harbour desired by Lebanon. In August 1957 an agreement was reached which dealt with the extensions and also modified the application to the company of the taxation decree of 1956. This was to be approved by a general meeting of shareholders and to be ratified by the Lebanese Parliament. Although the shareholders ratified promptly, the Parliament did not, but coercion was nevertheless applied with respect to the taxation. The Company on 22 December 1958 proposed arbitration, to

---

[1] *Electricité de Beyrouth Co.* Case, I.C.J., 1954, Pleadings, p. 55, quoting the *Chorzów Factory* Case.
[2] *Case Concerning the Compagnie du Port, des Quais et des Entrepôts de Beyrouth and the Société Radio-Orient*, I.C.J. Pleadings, 1960.

Acquired Rights and Economic Concessions 341

which it was entitled under the agreement of 1925. No reply was received from the Lebanese Government, and in February 1959 France made an application to the International Court of Justice under the agreement of 1948.

At the same time France also made application with respect to Radio-Orient, a French company with its *siège social* in Paris, which in 1922 became the successor to the *Compagnie Générale de Telegraphie sans Fil*, which in 1921 had been granted by the French High Commission in the Lebanon the right to construct and exploit the radio-electric centre of Beirut. Pursuant to the protocol of 7 June 1944 between the French and Lebanese Governments concerning the transfer of the postal and telegraphic service, the Lebanese Administration took over the rights and obligations of the agreement of 1921, which fell under the provisions of the agreement of 1948. One of the clauses of the concession exempted the Company from payment of customs duties on equipment imported for installation. The Company was subjected to taxation in virtue of the law of 1956, and was levied with duty in respect of equipment imported for the purpose of carrying out supplementary work of installation.

France claimed that, leaving aside the obligations stipulated in the agreement of 1948, application to the two companies of the law of 1956 would have

given them a right to compensation in respect of the modifications thus introduced into the financial clauses of their original agreements and into the subsequent concessionary instruments. Failing this, the contractual equilibrium would be upset and the Lebanese Republic, which is the cause of this injury to foreign nationals, would *ipso facto* incur responsibility towards the State to which those nationals belong.[1]

France alleged that the case was one of formal denial of justice, because the Company had not been permitted to have its rights validated by the processes to which it was contractually entitled.

Ce déni de justice constitue à un double titre un acte illicite international, puisque se trouvent violées non seulement l'obligation incombant à l'État libanais de mettre tout étranger en mesure de faire valoir effectivement ses droits, mais encore les dispositions de la Convention de 1925 et celles de l'accord de 1948.[2]

Owing to the legislative character of the breaches of contract neither Company had local remedies to exhaust.[3]

On 13 April 1960 an agreement was reached between Lebanon and the *Compagnie du Port*, and in the case of *Radio-Orient* the Lebanese Council

---

1 At p. 8.   2 At p. 39.
3 See *supra*, p. 299.

of Ministers ruled on 11 May 1960 that the law of 1956 would not be applied to it. The case was removed from the court's list on 31 August 1960.

(xix) *Concessions in the Congo (Léopoldville)*

No binding provisions were made at the time of independence of the Belgian Congo for the safeguarding of concessionary interests. However, the question arose at the Round Table Conference in January 1960, when the Congo representative took the view that the State instrumentalities with which concessionary interests were connected, particularly respecting mining, could not be continued after independence. The Belgian representatives considered that it was impossible to make the concessionaires accept the dissolution of bodies with which they were contractually bound, without having previously fixed compensation which would be satisfactory to them. At this point the objection was raised that it was useless to prescribe compensation in advance for the ensemble of rights which had not been exercised, and respecting assets which had never been valued. The Congo delegation continued to insist on the principle of dissolution of concessionary powers, and argued that, since the conference was purely consultative, no undertaking could be made concerning the principle or the amount of indemnity payable.[1]

The conference decided to work through two Commissions, the first to examine financial assistance, and the second the problem of investments. Since the conference was consultative, the results of the work of the commissions was not binding, and did not attain legal definition. However, certain interesting resolutions were adopted by them. It was recognized that in 1960 the ordinary Congo Budget would be about 1,050 millions of francs, and that this would have to be subsidized by Belgium. In order to maintain local administration and service the public debt, as well as to balance the budget without further resort to borrowing, continued Belgian financial assistance would be required. It was recommended that public and private investment be organized on a planned basis through a central programming office; that existing private enterprises abstain from interference in public affairs and adapt themselves to incorporate more Congo management and improve labour conditions; and that in return the Congo authorities would avoid any discrimination against private enterprises on grounds of nationality or otherwise. It would be desirable if the Congo gave guarantees respecting private rights, in particular the guarantees required by international law of judicial

[1] *Les dossiers du Centre de Recherche et d'Information Socio-Politiques* (Congo, 1960), vol. I, p. 92.

Acquired Rights and Economic Concessions 343

protection of these rights against administrative interference.[1] Expropriation would only be permitted for reasons of public interest; and in case of partial or total expropriation, compensation in accordance with the principles of the fundamental law and public liberties should be payable. If the expropriated concerns should be alien, the compensation should be freely convertible.

In the case of concessions it was recommended that contracts should be respected, without, however, negativing the right of public authorities to withdraw concessions if the conditions of their grant were not respected. However, in the cases of mining and forestry concessions, no compensation need be paid except reimbursement of justified expenses, should the grants not be exploited according to the terms of the contracts or of a programme agreed upon with the authorities.

Finally, the conference expressed the hope that, until a double taxation convention should be signed, Belgium would maintain the fiscal provisions in force which currently regulated Congo companies.

On 21 July 1960 the Congo Senate adopted an *Avant-projet de programme gouvernemental*, in which internal financial policy was reviewed. It rejected nationalization as a general principle, and declared that it would encourage private investment in agriculture and mining. It added:

Pour le passé, les droits acquis des propriétaires terrains seront consacrés s'ils ont satisfait au programme de mise en valeur et s'ils n'ont pas excédé les limites des terrains accordés. Pour l'avenir, les propriétaires coutumiers recevront une juste rémunération pour la cession de leurs terres, s'ils le désirent.[2]

On 3 December 1964 the Congolese Government decreed the 'reappropriation' of all mining concessions throughout the Congo. Four mainly Belgian-owned and interlocked companies, which had received mineral, forestry and land concessions from Belgium, were principally affected. These companies had all been taken over by *Union Minière du Haut-Katanga*. However, it was stated that the 'reappropriation' did not constitute 'nationalization', but implied that in future mining companies would buy the rights to exploit the land from the government. The preamble to the decree states that alien property rights would be safeguarded. In substance, therefore, the concessions were adapted to the new financial situation, and payments to the government would be increased.[3] The settlement of this question was included in the general financial agreement between the Congo and Belgium of January 1965.[4]

1 *Ibid.* p. 95.
2 *Ibid.* vol. II, p. 577.
3 *The Times*, 3 December 1964, p. 8. For further details see *supra*, p. 297.
4 See *infra*, p. 444; *New York Times*, 8 February 1965, p. 1.

(xx) *Concessions in the United Arab Republic*

The formation of the United Arab Republic did not affect the concessions granted by Egypt and Syria, and in the case of the Anglo-Egyptian Oilfields Ltd a concession was renewed.[1]

(xxi) *Concessions in Algeria, Malagasy Republic and Mali*

The Evian Agreement between France and the Algerian National Liberation Front[2] on 19 March 1962 contained a guarantee to French companies that their activities would not be affected, and that Algeria would assume the obligations and enjoy the rights contracted by the competent French authorities. With respect to the Sahara, it was also provided that Algeria would inherit the concessions granted by France. Similar guarantees were incorporated in the Co-operation Agreements with the Malagasy Republic[3] and Mali Federation.[4]

(xxii) *Mining Concessions in Zambia*

In the early 1890s the British South Africa Company obtained concessions from the Rhodesian chiefs. According to counsel's opinion taken by the government of Zambia these did not cover mineral rights in the Northern Rhodesian Copperbelt, although such rights accrued from the Devonshire Agreement of 1923, when the Crown took over the administration of the territory, and an agreement of 1950 made between the Company, the Crown, and the Government of Northern Rhodesia.[5] The United Kingdom proposed to entrench property rights in the Constitution of Zambia, which was to be promulgated in the Order in Council by which independence was granted the territory in 1964.[6] The Government of Northern Rhodesia wished to except the Company's mineral rights from this entrenchment, partly on the grounds of the disputed character of the rights themselves, and partly on the grounds of the alleged exploitationary history of the Company.[7] It threatened that, should the Constitution be promulgated without a settlement of the question of the Company's rights it would immediately after independence seek by referendum a constitu-

1 Cotran in *I.C.L.Q.* vol. VIII (1959), p. 367.
2 See *supra*, p. 294.
3 Decree no. 60–692 of 20 July 1960, *Journal Officiel* (1960), pp. 6612, 6615.
4 *Ibid.* pp. 6634, 6637.
5 The British South Africa Company's Claims to Mineral Royalties in Northern Rhodesia, White Paper published by the Government Printer, Lusaka, 21 September 1964.
6 S.I. 1964, no. 1652.
7 White Paper; *The Times*, 21 September 1964, p. 13.

Acquired Rights and Economic Concessions 345

tional change to permit expropriation.[1] The Company challenged this suggestion as a threat of 'seizure without proper compensation'.[2] The United Kingdom, while regarding the question as one between the Company and the Government of Northern Rhodesia, urged the latter to test the validity of the Company's rights in court, but this the Government declined to do. It argued that 'the draft constitution which the British Government is asking us to accept enshrines—and strengthens— the B.S.A. Company's claims to ownership of our minerals in a way which is contrary to our understanding of what was agreed at the May constitutional conference'.[3] The position of the Northern Rhodesian Government was that the British South Africa Company was not necessarily engaged in mining itself, but was entitled to royalties from all companies which were. It was, therefore, substituted for the people of Zambia as the ultimate owners of the country's natural resources. The Government was anxious to obtain a settlement before independence, because thereafter the problem would be complicated in virtue of the operation of international law rules of protection of foreign investment.

On the eve of independence a settlement was reached in tripartite negotiations between the Company and the United Kingdom and Northern Rhodesian Governments, in which the Company was compensated[4] in the sum of £4 million, contributed to equally by each Government.

3. EXPROPRIATION OF CONCESSIONS AND THE PRINCIPLES OF COMPENSATION

The generally consistent practice which has just been analysed is clearly based on the principle that the acquired rights of a concessionaire must be respected by a successor State.[5] The only instances when such a duty was categorically denied were the policies adopted by Great Britain with respect to the Transvaal and Ottoman concessions. An attempt has been

---

1 *The Times*, 30 September 1964, p. 12.   2 *Ibid*. 18 September 1964, p. 13.
3 *Ibid*. 23 September 1964, p. 10; 1 October 1964, p. 16; 2 October 1964, p. 10; 9 October 1964, p. 9.
4 The Company received £2 million each from Zambia and the United Kingdom, *Commonwealth Survey*, vol. X (1964), p. 1131.
5 In the view of Kaeckenbeeck 'il n'y a aucun doute que l'opinion juridique moderne pèse entièrement en faveur de l'obligation de respecter les concessions': Hague *Recueil*, vol. LIX (1937), p. 348. Mosler maintains that 'respect for concessionary rights has its root in the respect for acquired rights': p. 92. Elsewhere he says that concessions are protected because they belong to the category of private rights and are subject to the principle that change of sovereignty shall affect the rights of individuals as little as possible: *ibid*. p. 132. See Cabouat, p. 171; Salem in Clunet, vol. XLI (1914), pp. 38–59.

made to demonstrate that the attitude adopted on these occasions was not only based on a mistaken view of the law and the problems involved, but was inconsistent with that of Great Britain on other occasions. The United States, France and Italy did not deny the existence of the general principle, but sought only to establish, in the particular cases in which they were concerned, exceptions to it.

It is not immediately clear, however, in what exactly the duty of the successor State consists. In some cases the emphasis is thrust upon legal continuity, as in an orderly grant of independence, or a cession of territory without disruption of local administrative autonomy (the instance of Crete in the *Lighthouses* Case[1] being an example), or a subrogation of the successor State by treaty or contract. The successor State in these cases remains, or becomes, a party to the contract of concession, and the problem that then arises is whether the concession may, in the eyes of international law, be revoked. Where, on the other hand, the emphasis is upon legal disruption, as in the case of annexation, the subrogation of the successor State in the contract could only occur in virtue of a general devolution of rights and obligations pursuant to a thesis of universal succession.[2] If this thesis is rejected, then the successor State may not be regarded as a party to the contract, which terminates with the change of sovereignty. In such a case no question of continuing the contract for the term of its performance can arise.[3] This conclusion was arrived at by the Attorney-General of the United States in his opinion relating to the Manila Railway Company's concession. 'All the promises of every contract', he advised, 'entered into by the former government of a province wrested from it by victory in war do not transfer themselves to the new Government in defiance of the natural proposition that a man cannot be bound by a stranger's promise.'[4] The heart of the matter, then, is whether

1 P.C.I.J. ser. A/B, no. 71.

2 Earlier writers upheld subrogation with some unanimity: Fiore, *Nouv. droit int.* (2nd ed. 1885), vol. I, p. 315; Martens, vol. I, p. 368; Westlake, vol. I, p. 75.

3 The Opinion of the Law Officers relating to the Nitrate Railway Company concession of 10 February 1890 was based on the argument that the Company's monopoly could not be infringed. That of 30 November 1900 respecting the Transvaal concessions seems to be in favour of the universal subrogation of the successor State in the 'legal obligations' of its predecessor. That the Law Officers were not in favour of universal subrogation is clear from the exception they made in the case of concessions granted during the war. The formula adopted at the Conference of Paris prior to the Treaty of Constantinople employed the term 'subrogation'. The judgment in the *Mavrommatis* Case speaks of the 'general principle of subrogation' as one of international law 'to the application of which the obligations entered into by the Mandatory created no exception'. See *supra*, p. 324.

4 21 *Op. A.-G.* p. 180. Elsewhere he said: 'Concessions here in question were executory contracts, not concerning the public domain owned by Spain, but containing many personal obligations of Spain and of other parties. Spain is regarded

in cases of continuity and subrogation the successor State is in a less advantageous legal position with respect to cancellation of a concession than it is in cases of non-continuity and non-subrogation. If a State is always entitled to revoke concessions and terminate contracts in virtue of its general competence to expropriate against compensation, then the argument as to subrogation or non-subrogation may not be worth making.

The rules of international law governing State responsibility with respect to contracts are unclear, but analysis has yielded the following systems:[1] If the contract provides for non-cancellation, and if this provision can be interpreted as a divesting of its power to expropriate on the part of the contracting State,[2] then the contract must be specifically performed. If, on the other hand, the contract remains subject to an exercise of sovereign discretion, and specific performance is not an essential feature of the proper law, damages are the only remedy for unilateral termination.[3] If the quantum of damages in such a case is the same as the quantum of compensation would be in the case of failure to perform a contract in which the successor State is not subrogated, then, save in the exceptional instances where the concession is non-revocable, a successor State is in no different position from its predecessor. But if, as seems likely, the quantum of damages payable by the predecessor State would be calculated on a basis of *lucrum cessans* as well as *damnum emergens* (that is, on a loss of expected benefits to accrue during the term of the contract),[4] whereas the quantum of compensation payable by the successor State would be the capital value of the undertaking without reference to the loss of expected benefits, then the successor State is in a different position from the predecessor State.

The arguments in favour of the inherent revocability of concession agreements tend to be *a fortiori* in the case of successor States, which cannot

by the law of nations as having a personality of her own distinct from that of the power which has succeeded her in control of the ceded territory, and I am not aware of any authority for saying that such personal obligations, either on the part of the Government of Spain or the other contracting parties, become binding as contractual obligations upon a government which made no such promises': Moore, *Dig.* vol. I, p. 401. See also Keith, p. 6. From a legal point of view, Mosler points out, the contract does not continue to exist, but there is a new relationship which is based on the obligation which the acquiring state has under international law with respect to the national State of the concessionaire: p. 92. It is preferable, however, to base the relationship on the obligation owed, not to the national State, but to the individual directly. Hyde appears to believe that the contract continues until cancelled, but this can only mean the interest which the concessionaire has in the factual situation which the contract has brought into being: Hyde, vol. I, p. 428.

1 O'Connell, *International Law*, vol. II (1965), p. 1072.
2 E.g. *Saudi Arabia* v. *Arabian American Oil Co. (Aramco), I.L.R.* vol. XXVII, p. 117.
3 *Delagoa Bay Railway Co.* Case, Moore, *I. A.*, vol. II, p. 1865.
4 O'Connell, *International Law*, vol. II (1965), pp. 1069, 1077, 1205.

be compelled to carry on with arrangements made by their predecessors which are either contrary to their public interests or obstructive of the realization of their own ideas of social development.[1] Change of sovereignty often involves changes in the economic structure of the country which demand that modifications be effected in the exercise of concessionary rights. Italy, for example, was acknowledged to have the right to bring concessions granted by Turkey in Libya 'into conformity with the new economic conditions'. Protocol XII of the Treaty of Lausanne, despite the fact that it speaks of 'subrogation', recognized the necessity for the 're-adaptation of concessions'. The Sopron Köszeg Railway arbitration accepted the general principle that rights to which the concession gave rise could not be nullified, but qualified it by stating that the terms of the concession, 'according to their drafting and tenor', could not be considered as wholly 'valid and enforceable'. While the 'legitimate interests involved' demanded recognition, it was considered that they were subject to 'such changes' as were 'rendered necessary by the new circumstances'. In the agreement between the Netherlands and Indonesia by which the problems resulting from the independence of the latter were resolved, it was specifically agreed that the successor State had a complete discretion with respect to 'fiscal measures and social and other measures customary in a modern country'. Had Great Britain been subrogated in the duties of the Transvaal concessions, it would have had to maintain the Johannesburg Water Supply Concession, a monopoly which left that city in the power of a group of private individuals. It cannot be pretended that any State would ever consent to this situation, and even Westlake, who was uncompromisingly opposed to the principles of the Transvaal Report, would have agreed that Great Britain was justified in claiming the right to decline to recognize or modify concessions which might prejudicially affect the interests of the public.[2]

The expropriation of a concession, however, is only justified when accompanied by a recognition of the equities involved. The situation in which the concessionaire is interested may be more or less complex. He may have undertaken work, expended capital, bound himself by subcontracts to third parties, and committed himself to extensive operations upon the assumption of deriving therefrom at a later date adequate remuneration. For the successor State to ignore this expenditure of capital and labour, and to appropriate to itself the benefits accruing therefrom, is

1 Mosler, pp. 94, 163–6; Gidel, p. 208; Hershey, p. 226; Sereni, p. 405; Sibert, vol. I, p. 203. In *Niederstrasser* v. *Polish State*, the Upper Silesian Arbitral Tribunal stated that 'the successor State, like the ceding State, may take away these rights by legislative action': *Ann. Dig.* vol. VI, Case no. 33.
2 Westlake in *Law Quarterly Review*, vol. XVII (1901), p. 397.

unjustifiably to enrich itself. The concessionaire's equitable interest is an acquired right constituted by his activity, and international law imposes on the successor State a correlative duty to make restitution to the extent of its enrichment. So long as it satisfies the equities, it is immaterial whether the successor State modifies the concession, grants alternative facilities, or expropriates outright. Its obligation may be satisfied if it subrogates itself in the rights and duties of the original contract, and permits the concessionaire to continue with his operations. Such subrogation is effected by a new agreement, or a novation of the contract, whether it be tacit or express. On the other hand, the minimum which international law demands is the payment of reasonable compensation, and wherever concessions have been cancelled there has always been such reimbursement.[1] Even the Transvaal Concessions Commission, although denying any legal obligation in the matter, admitted that

> the question of compensation arises, inasmuch as it would be inequitable that a concessionaire should lose without compensation a right duly acquired, and whose conditions he had duly fulfilled, because the new Government differed from the old in its view as to what was, or was not, injurious to public interest even though the opinion of the new Government were obviously the true one.[2]

The question of the Ottoman concessions in the Mandated Territories was first disposed of in the Treaty of Sèvres, which was never ratified and was replaced by the Treaty of Lausanne. In this treaty the principles suggested above find clear expression. The successor State, 'if it considers that the maintenance of any of these concessions would be contrary to the public interests, shall be entitled, within a period of six months from the date on which the territory was to be placed under its

---

[1] 'The minimum is that compensation must be paid', says Mosler, pp. 37, 165. For his sociological basis see pp. 122, 124. See also p. 165; Szászy in *Rev. de droit int.* vol. v (1930), p. 492. Mosler's view leads him here to a conclusion which is perhaps open to question. He admits that the successor State has a discretion as to whether it will subrogate itself in the contract, but he holds the view that if it does so subrogate itself the consent of the concessionaire to the novation is not required. 'The legal relationship between it [the successor State] and the concessionaire is created once again with the same contents it had under the losing State', and this by a unilateral act of the acquiring State: p. 91. However, it may be doubted if a new legal relationship can be created without the consent of the concessionaire. If it is admitted that the contract of concession has expired with the change of sovereignty, then it would seem that the agreement of both the concessionaire and the new party is necessary to the novation. This agreement may be tacit, but Mosler appears to be of the opinion that the successor State can bring about this novation because it has sovereign power to bind the concessionaire irrespective of his will. Schönborn considers that if a concession is contrary to the public law of the successor State it lapses without compensation: p. 54. Sereni, vol. II, p. 405, thinks compensation payable.

[2] Cd. 623, p. 8.

authority or tutelage, to buy out such concessions and in such event shall be bound to pay to the concessionaire equitable compensation'.[1] This right to cancel the concession was not incorporated in the Treaty of Lausanne, but was recognized in an exchange of notes between the British and French delegations. The British Government agreed not to avail itself as regards the French Government of the provisions of Protocol XII.

In consequence, and within a period of one year from the coming into force of the Treaty of Peace of today's date, the French Government will have the power, in the territories detached from Turkey in which it exercises authority as mandatory, to proceed to the repurchase of concessions for public services of which British nationals may be the beneficiaries. In this event, the concessionaire will receive equitable compensation.[2]

In its pleadings in the *Mavrommatis* Case, the Greek Government was in favour of the view that the successor State had the right to expropriate the concession, but only subject to payment of compensation.[3] The agreement between the Netherlands and Indonesia not only admits the principle of compensation, but limits its operation in a way that may well serve as a model for similar arrangements in the future. 'Expropriation, nationalization, liquidation, compulsory cession, and transfer of properties or rights' might take place exclusively for the public benefit 'against previously enjoyed or guaranteed indemnity to be fixed by judicial decision at the real value of the object involved'.[4]

It is also to be noted that the claims of British concessionaires in Madagascar which were considered by the Law Officers arose out of disputes, not so much concerning the competence of France to expropriate the concessions, but rather the amount of compensation offered. The Opinion of 2 February 1898 is an example of the inexactitude of much of the legal argument to be found in diplomatic correspondence relative to problems of State succession. It commenced by asserting that the grant 'amounted in substance to a contract'; it would be a 'breach of contract if the holders of such land were evicted'. This argument seems on the face of it to be in favour of subrogation. It concludes, however, by admitting the competence of the French Government to reclaim the lands if they were 'wanted for public purposes and adequate compensation was paid'.[5]

1 B.F.S.P. vol. CXIII, p. 652.
2 B.T.S. 1923, no. 17, Cmd. 1946.
3 'Whereas', it was stated in the judgment, 'the British Government is of opinion that the fact that the successor States are placed under an obligation to maintain the concessions..., whilst no mention is made of a right to expropriate them, is indicative of an intention to exclude such a right, the Greek Government, on the other hand, considers that the existence of such a right of expropriation is to be assumed': P.C.I.J. ser. A, no. 5, p. 38.   4 U.N.T.S. vol. LXIX, art. 3, p. 234.
5 F.O. Confidential Paper (7199), no. 16; O'Connell, Appendix, no. 58.

If compensation is the only obligation which international law imposes on the successor State, the qualifications introduced into the Transvaal Report become more consistent. The successor State can be under no obligation to put the concessionaire in a better equitable position than he was in before the change of sovereignty. Hence, as the Report emphasizes, if the predecessor State was insolvent, its worthless obligations could not be converted into valuable ones upon its extinction. Furthermore, as the Report went on,

in determining the amount of compensation in respect of losses sustained by the owner of a concession cancelled or modified as injurious to the public interest, regard may justly be paid to the question whether the owner, at the time when he received, or acquired the concession, knew, or ought reasonably to have known, that it was precarious. A concession may be precarious for many reasons, but it certainly is so, if the subject matter of it is closely related to large and changing public interests.[1]

In order that the rule of international law with respect to compensation shall be operative, certain conditions clearly must be fulfilled. The concession must have been regularly and *bona fide* obtained, with a proper observance of legal forms, and it must not be conditional either on the continued survival of the predecessor State, or upon any other factor which cannot be fulfilled. The law of the predecessor State is the criterion for determining these matters.[2] As there is no question of an obligation to continue the terms of the concession, it is immaterial that the concession is contrary to the public interest of the successor State, or in violation of its treaty obligations.

The doctrine which the United States tended to develop after the Spanish American War concerning the 'odious' character of certain concessions has not been sanctioned by subsequent practice, and remains as vague as when it was enunciated.[3] The principle of restitution is applicable to 'odious' concessions as much as to any others because the works undertaken are useful to the successor State and do in fact enrich it. The origin of the concession is thus immaterial.[4] The only acknowledgment of the doctrine of 'odious' concessions made by the Law Officers was with respect to grants made during a war with the annexing State. It is possible that a qualification to the general principle is here admitted in State

1 Cd. 623, p. 8. See also Mosler, p. 158.
2 Kaeckenbeeck in Hague *Recueil*, vol. LIX (1937), p. 351.
3 See Mosler, p. 168.
4 *Ibid.* p. 169. It is to be noted that Protocol XII to the Treaty of Lausanne excludes from protection concessions granted after the outbreak of war. Concessions of this type are frequently assimilated to 'war debts'.

practice, but it requires more evidence to establish itself as recognized in international law. Similar reasoning disposes of the argument that concessions in undeveloped lands need not be respected. Such concessions, it is true, may have been granted precisely because the undeveloped country was incapable of exploiting its own natural resources. However, as the successor State is enriched by the work done it owes a duty of compensation.[1]

[1] Mosler, p. 178.

Chapter 14

THE DOCTRINE OF ACQUIRED RIGHTS AND ADMINISTRATIVE CONTRACTS

The ambiguity in the term 'property' as used by English and American publicists has made it difficult to extend the category of acquired rights to pure *res incorporales*. In German writings there has never been this difficulty, and contractual obligations have always been included within the scope of *Vermögensrechte*. A careful analysis of international practice within recent times discloses that private law interests arising out of contractual relations with the State are regarded by international law as acquired rights no different in their essential character from tangible interests.[1] Once this is admitted, the principles set out in the foregoing chapters with respect to

[1] In the arbitration between Norway and the United States in 1921 relative to the requisitioning by the latter of ships of the former, and the consequent damage through interference with contracts of carriage, the United States Government tried to argue that contractual claims are not property rights. The tribunal rejected this argument and held that the cancellation of contractual rights is equivalent to the taking of private property as defined by the 5th Amendment to the Constitution, and 'just compensation is due to the claimants under the municipal law of the United States, as well as under international law, based upon the respect for private property': *Norwegian Shipowners' Claims*, U.N. Rep. vol. I, p. 307.
Judge Nielsen in a dissenting judgment in *U.S.A. (International Fisheries Co.) v. United Mexican States* arbitration said: 'In the ultimate determination of responsibility under international law, I think an international tribunal in a case grounded on a complaint of breach of contract can properly give effect to principles of law with respect to compensation. . . . If a government agrees to pay money for commodities and fails to make payment, it seems to me that an international tribunal may properly say that the purchase price of the commodities has been confiscated, or that the commodities have been confiscated, or that property rights in a contract have been destroyed or confiscated': U.N. Rep. vol. IV, p. 691.
In the *Venezuelan Bond* Cases heard before the United States–Venezuelan Claims Commission it was in the award stated that 'a claim is none the less a claim because it originates in contract. . . . The refusal to pay an honest claim is no less a wrong because it happens to arise from an obligation to pay money instead of originating in violence offered to persons or property', Moore, *I.A.*, vol. IV, p. 3649. See also the *Delagoa Bay Railway Co.* Arbitration, *ibid.* vol. II, pp. 1865 *et seq.* and the *Sicilian Sulphur Monopoly* Case, B.F.S.P. vol. XXVIII (1839), pp. 1163 *et seq.*; vol. XXIX (1840), pp. 175 *et seq.*; vol. XXX (1841), pp. 111 *et seq.* See *For. Rel.* 1902, pp. 838 *et seq.*; *A.J.* vol. XXI (1927), pp. 160 *et seq.* See the following writers: Brierly in Hague *Recueil*, vol. LVIII (1936), p. 169; Verdross in Hague *Recueil*, vol. XXXVII (1932), p. 364, pp. 372 *et seq.*; Kelsen in Hague *Recueil*, vol. XLII (1932), p. 257; Eagleton, *Responsibility of States in International Law* (1928), pp. 165 *et seq.*; Feller, *The Mexican Claims Commissions* (1935), p. 173; Herz in *A.J.* vol. XXXV (1941), p. 245.

expropriation and restitution become applicable to the problem which administrative contracts present. Contracts of this kind differ from concessionary contracts in lacking any interest in realty. They are by nature more ephemeral, and since they ordinarily involve no monopoly of public functions their private element predominates.[1] Within the scope of administrative contracts are included all those arrangements made by the State or its functionaries with private individuals for the supply of goods and the carrying out of public works. They are matters of ordinary governmental routine. There is no exploitation on the part of the private contractor, only a right to a fair remuneration.

Whether or not a contract expires at the moment of the change of sovereignty mainly depends upon the survival or otherwise of the governmental instrumentality with which the contract was made. Should it not survive, and should the contract at this moment be executory on both sides, there can be no liability to perform it on the part of either the private contractor or the successor State.[2] On 30 November 1900 the Law Officers gave an opinion on the question of the effect of the annexation of the Transvaal upon an executory contract made by the Government of that country with Messrs Spicer and Sons for the delivery of goods. They said that 'it seems to belong to the class of contracts which, in their very nature, are conditional upon the continued existence of the Transvaal Government, and being executory only not capable in strictness of being regarded as binding on the conqueror'.[3] On the other hand, should the contract be only partly executed, the private contractor has an acquired right to the extent of his investment, and the successor State has a correlative duty imposed on it by international law to make restitution to the extent to which it has been enriched by delivery of goods or performance of work. The standard of competition will, in most cases, be the contract price, but it may be a lower market value.

Since the contractual relationship expires with change of sovereignty those clauses of an administrative contract relating to indemnity or guarantees cannot oblige the successor State. The private contractor cannot be said to have an equitable interest in such a provision, and there is no enrichment on the part of the successor State which might create it. In 1924 the Franco-German Mixed Arbitral Tribunal considered the claim of a contractor who had lost goods on the Alsatian railways before the cession of Alsace-Lorraine. The question was whether he should sue

[1] Mosler, p. 163.
[2] *Leo Foe Siong* v. *Netherlands New Guinea*, Ned. Tijd. vol. XII (1965), p. 317.
[3] Opinion of 30 November 1900, F.O. Confidential Papers (7516), no. 22 A; O'Connell, Appendix, no. 70.

Acquired Rights and Administrative Contracts

France or Germany for indemnity under the contract of carriage. The tribunal decided that there was no proof that France took over obligations of this character in respect of the Alsatian railways.[1] The case is complicated by the provisions of the Treaty of Versailles exempting France from participation in the national debt of Germany, but it is also consistent with the doctrine of unjustified enrichment. On the other hand, the doctrine of unjustified enrichment affords ground for a claim against the successor State of a quasi-contractual character. In 1925 a plaintiff brought a claim before a Czechoslovak court for the recovery of fees paid in error to the Hungarian Treasury before the formation of Czechoslovakia. It was held that a repayment of the fee could not be refused by the successor State on the ground that the money had been deposited in the predecessor's Treasury. The change of sovereignty had brought about no change in the existing legal order.[2]

Authority for the above propositions is not extensive because administrative contracts have usually been assimilated in practice to administrative debts, from which, indeed, they are often indistinguishable except in origin. Such practice as exists is the outcome of an attempt to create a contractual relationship between the private contractor and the successor State, and it is therefore of a controversial character. The most that can be extracted from a consideration of such practice is the obligation of the successor State to respect the acquired rights of the contractor. There is no justification for assuming a transmission of the contract itself.

I. PRACTICE OF STATES

(i) *General practice, 1797–1866*

A treaty between Sweden and Mecklenburg-Schwerin in 1803 maintained all contracts which had been made with the royal authority in respect of the ceded areas.[3] The Treaty of Campo Formio confirmed all obligations contracted by the Government of Venice for the maintenance of Napoleon's armies.[4] Contracts of an administrative character were specifically mentioned in the convention between France and Sardinia of 1860 to settle questions arising out of the cession to the former of Savoy and Nice,[5] and also in the Treaty of Vienna of 1864.[6] The Treaty of London of the same year transferred to Greece all the engagements of

---

1 *Lévy v. German State*, Ann. Dig. vol. II, Case no. 27.
2 *Succession in Obligations (Fees paid in Error)* Case, Ann. Dig. vol. III, Case no. 50.
3 M.R. (Suppl.), vol. III, p. 488, art. 19 at p. 508.
4 M.R. (Suppl.), vol. VII, p. 208, art. 12 at p. 212.
5 M.N.R.G. vol. XVII, pt. II, p. 22, art. 5 at p. 24.
6 *Ibid.* p. 474, art. 17 at p. 482.

contracts lawfully concluded by the former administration of the Ionian Islands.[1] By the Treaty of Vienna of 1866 the Government of Italy was to succeed to the 'rights and obligations resulting from contracts regularly stipulated by the Austrian administration for objects of public interest specially concerning the ceded territories'.[2]

(ii) *Judicial practice in Italian courts, 1877–86*

The latter treaty was followed by a number of decisions of Italian courts which held that acts of confiscation and requisition done by Austria within the ceded areas were to be regarded as contractual obligations as defined by the treaty. These Italian cases are virtually the only judicial decisions before 1919 on the question of the obligations of a successor State with respect to the ordinary contractual relations of its predecessor. At first the Italian courts were cautious, and hesitated to apply any principle of succession. In the case of *Orti-Manara* v. *Italian Government and Austrian Government* it was said that 'the very fact that the two Governments made special agreements on the subject with a view to precisely regulating along financial lines the succession of one to the other is against the hypothesis of a general and absolute succession of the second to the first'.[3] In another case the doctrine that was subsequently to find expression in the Report of the Transvaal Concessions Commission was propounded as follows: 'The principle that a Government which succeeds another is bound to satisfy the obligations of the preceding Government constitutes only a moral obligation.'[4]

A change in the trend of the Italian decisions came with a judgment of the Court of Cassation at Florence in 1878, when it was held that 'by public law the state which succeeds in a part of the territory of another state is bound, independently of special conventions, by the obligations legally contracted by the latter in relation to the territory to which it succeeds'.[5] Thereafter the Italian courts leaned definitely towards a theory of universal succession.[6] It was decided in one case that Italy was

[1] *B.F.S.P.* vol. LIV (1864), p. 11, art. 7 at p. 15.
[2] *M.N.R.G.* vol. XVIII, p. 405, art. 8 at p. 406.
[3] *Giurisprudenza italiana* (1877), vol. XXX, pt. I, sec. 2, col. 1.
[4] *Walter* v. *Minister of War* (1871), *Monitore dei Tribunali* (1872), p. 133. See also *Ministers of the Interior and Finance* v. *Commune of Capri*, quoted in the Answer of His Britannic Majesty's Government in the *Robert E. Brown* Claim, p. 14; *Minister of Finance* v. *Siro Corbella, Giurisprudenza italiana* (1877), vol. XXIX, pt. I, sec. 1, col. 996; *General Administration of War and Finance* v. *Adami*, ibid. col. 999; *Commune of Magenta* v. *Director General of the Treasury*, ibid. (1877), vol. XXX, pt. I, sec. 2, col. 118.
[5] *Verlengo* v. *Finance Department*, ibid. col. 1206. The court held, however, that debts contracted in the general interests of the ceding State need not be assumed by the acquiring State, thus anticipating the American 'odious' doctrine.
[6] See Hurst in *B.Y.* vol. V (1925), pp. 174 *et seq.*

Acquired Rights and Administrative Contracts 357

bound to pay compensation for the bailment of the claimant's horses to the late Government of Parma. 'All obligations', it was said, 'contracted during the legitimate rule of the old State with respect to the preservation and defence of its dominion', and consequently those having reference to requisitions of forage and horses made upon private individuals, pass to the State which may have succeeded the State having contracted the said claims before the latter had been paid.... The principle of succession from State to State in *universum jus* does not alter the rights of single individuals as against the new State, for which reason it is applied without limitation, whether the acquisition has been effected pacifically or in a bellicose manner, or, more or less, in accordance with the political ideas and aspiration of the people.[1]

In another case it was stated that upon annexation 'the new State succeeds the preceding one by uninterrupted continuity and takes over in *activis et passivis* the patrimonial *universum jus*'.[2] The remaining cases which dealt with the same question followed more or less the pattern set by the Court of Cassation in 1878.[3]

(iii) *Decision of the French Conseil d'État, 1876*

The Additional Convention to the Treaty of Frankfurt, 1871, recognized all contracts for the letting and working of public property in Alsace-Lorraine.[4] This provision was considered by the *Conseil d'État* in an *arrêt* of 28 April 1876, in which the rights of a private contractor arising out of a contract of public works made with the French Government were assimilated to administrative debts. Considering whether or not the rights in question were to be pursued against the French or the German Government the court said:

Une loi n'aurait pas été nécessaire pour rendre obligatoire à l'égard des créanciers ayant des droits acquis contre l'État français, la substitution de l'État allemand comme débiteur de leurs créances. Cette substitution est le résultat d'un fait plus puissant que la loi, d'un fait de force majeure, c'est-à-dire de l'annexion même à un autre pays du territoire sur lequel les travaux ont été exécutés. Un principe généralement admis par le droit des gens, c'est que, du jour où s'effectue la séparation d'un

1 *Minister of War* v. *Orcesi*, translated in the Answer of His Britannic Majesty's Government in the *Robert E. Brown* Claim, p. 182.
2 *Marzari-Fisola* Case, *Giurisprudenza italiana*, vol. XLVIII (1896), pt. I, sec. 2, col. 662.
3 *Minister of War* v. *Commune of Pavia*, *Giurisprudenza italiana*, vol. XXXII (1880), pt. I, sec. I, col. 1314; *Finance Department* v. *Dona Boldu*, ibid. col. 293; *Minister of the Treasury* v. *Danante*, ibid. col. 760; *De Falco* v. *La Barbera*, ibid, col. 1068; *Minister of Finance* v. *Commune of Lucca*, ibid. sec. 2, col. 868. All these Italian cases are translated *in extenso* in the brief of the American agent in the *Hawaiian Claims* Arbitration, Nielsen, pp. 115 *et seq.*, and in the Answer of His Britannic Majesty's Government in the *Robert E. Brown* Claim, Annexes 8 *et seq.*
4 M.N.R.G. vol. XX, p. 847, art. 17 at p. 859.

territoire, l'État cessionnaire prend les lieu et place du cédant vis-à-vis de tous ceux qui ont passé des contrats avec ce dernier: il en recueille les avantages et en supporte les charges.

This decision the court justified on the doctrine of universal succession. 'The Government, in favour of which the cession has taken place, it asserted, is in respect of the ceding Government, a true heir, a successor to its personality.'[1]

(iv) *The annexation of Burma by Great Britain, 1886*

Burma was annexed by Great Britain in 1886. The attitude which the British Government adopted towards administrative contracts which the Burmese Government had made before the annexation is disclosed in interdepartmental correspondence. 'Such obligation as there may be on the British Government is a mere moral obligation,' wrote the Secretary to the Government of India.

In dealing with the claimants, it will, we consider, be the safest course to act on the defensive and insist on the position that they have no legal remedy, while, measuring the extent of our moral obligations, we decline to entertain any claims for the recognition of which authority or precedent cannot be clearly established. As a matter of principle no claim should be admitted unless based on service actually performed by the State, or unless on account of goods supplied or money advanced for State purposes. We would leave it to the claimants to show, if they can, that any wider interpretation than this has in practice been placed on the general doctrine that a Government taking by conquest inherits the liabilities of its predecessors.[2]

The Secretary for Upper Burma reported that 'claims based on service actually performed for the State, and on goods supplied for Government purposes, have been investigated. The British Government having taken the place of the Burmese Government may perhaps hold itself responsible for payments due on account of services rendered or goods supplied to the State.'[3] As it happened, however, claims by Europeans alone were admitted, and those of Burmese were rejected outright, chiefly on the ground that it was impossible to discover the actual terms on which any work was done or goods supplied by them.[4] Likewise, all claims in respect of contracts made with the King in his personal capacity were rejected

1 D. 1876, 3. 84, quoted by Gidel, pp. 33–4.
2 Letter from the Secretary to the Government of India to the Secretary of State for India, no. 177 of 1886, dated 4 October 1886.
3 Letter from the Secretary for Upper Burma to the Secretary to the Government of India, Burma: For. Dept. no. X, dated 30 May 1886.
4 Letter from the Secretary for Upper Burma to the Secretary to the Government of India: For. Dept. no. Y, dated 8 June 1886.

because of the absolute character of the monarchy, and the risks ordinarily incidental to a contract with a person irresponsible in law.[1]

It seems clear, however, that the British Government, in denying any legal liability with respect to these contracts, did not intend to deny any general rule of international law. Its policy was undoubtedly based on the distinction that Burma was not a civilized community, and that it had been subject to a Government that was notorious for its corruption and mismanagement. The admission of any general principle would have been to open the door to claims which it would have been impolitic to admit. Such is the general tenor of the correspondence. Legal opinion was given by the solicitor to the Government of India almost as soon as the conquest was completed. 'A new Government', he advised, 'succeeds to fiscal rights and is bound to fulfil the fiscal obligations of the former Government, and it is also responsible for debts previously contracted.' The Chief Commissioner for Burma was quite prepared to admit that this was the general rule of law. He wrote:

I find that international law authorities say pretty broadly and clearly: A power which succeeds another power in sovereignty over a State should fulfil the fiscal obligations and discharge the public debts of the State contracted previously. Under public debts would be includable such as have been contracted in the name of the State by its authorized agents and for public purposes, not private debts of the sovereign.[2]

The reasons for his policy with respect to Burmese contracts are given in a subsequent letter in which the Secretary for Upper Burma reported that

in cases in which it appears that the claims are *bona fide* and that they are based on work really done, or for goods supplied to the State ... the Chief Commission [sic] would not admit any legal liability to pay these claims. It seems to him that when a civilized Government succeeds a Government like that of the Kingdom of Upper Burma, it is under no obligation to accept and to discharge, subject to the conditions imposed by civilization and good Government, the obligations incurred by its predecessor under entirely unlike conditions.[3]

1 Letter from the Secretary for Upper Burma to the Secretary to the Government of India, Burma: For. Dept. no. X, dated 30 May 1886.
2 Letter from the Chief Commissioner for Burma to the Government of India, no. 20, dated 5 January 1886, enclosure 4.
3 Letter from the Secretary for Upper Burma to the Secretary to the Government of India, Burma: For. Dept. no. Y, dated 8 June 1886. The documents relating to the Burmese contracts are published in Annex 6 and Annex 6A to the Answer of His Britannic Majesty's Government in the *Robert E. Brown* Claim. A complete list of claims and the minutes made in connexion with them is contained in enclosures to the letter of 14 October 1886, and in a letter from the Government of India to the Secretary of State for India dated 28 February 1886. A number of letters from the French and Italian Governments are enclosed but are not significant.

That the Colonial Office did not attach great importance to this policy as affording a precedent is clear from a reference made by it to the Law Officers in 1900. The department admitted that Upper Burma was 'an uncivilized country, and it was possible that in dealing with such a State rules more favourable to the succeeding Government could be applied than to the case where two civilized States have been incorporated with Her Majesty's Dominions'. The Law Officers did not comment on this distinction, but reported that a successor State takes over such legal liabilities as have been incurred by the previously existing Government.[1]

(v) *The annexation of the Boer Republics, 1900*

When the Boer Republics were annexed in 1900, existing contracts were in some cases replaced by new ones. Generally speaking, where goods had been delivered under contract to the predecessor Governments they were paid for, but the same limitation on legal liability was assumed as in the case of concessions.

James Spicer and Son, a London firm, received before the Boer War an order from the South African Republic to supply certain postage stamp paper. Delivery could not be made because of the outbreak of war, and after the annexation of the Republic the company sought payment from the Colonial Office. The latter replied that it was under no legal obligation to purchase the paper but in fact it did purchase such part of it as was of use to the Office. No compensation was paid for the loss incurred owing to the company's inability to dispose of portion of the paper which was of special character.[2]

Messrs Siemens and Company, also of London, presented the Colonial Office with a claim for telegraphic and telephone material some of which had been seized in transit by the British Government in South Africa, and some of which was still in Siemens' hands. The Colonial Office accepted liability with respect to the first two categories but not with respect to the third, stating that there was no principle of law which made the conqueror liable to take delivery of goods ordered by the conquered government. However, some of the goods were in fact purchased. The Transvaal Government agreed to complete the purchase of a zoological textbook which had been ordered by the Republic on the ground that it would be of use, but copies had to be supplied in English instead of Dutch. Claims for payment of natural history specimens supplied before the war for museum cabinets and other items were paid. The Colonial Office refused

1 Opinion of 30 November 1900, F.O. Confidential Papers (7516), no. 22A; O'Connell, Appendix, no. 70.
2 F.O. Confidential Paper, no. 8144, April 1904, p. 1.

to proceed with the contract for the supply of furniture on the ground that it had got the required furniture elsewhere. It also refused to pay for the preparation of certain mining plans which were ready to be despatched before the war, on the ground that the plans were now useless owing to the issuing of new instructions to mine surveyors. Payment of a picture commissioned in Berlin of the Boer Executive, for a Paris exhibition, was also refused.[1]

Although the Colonial Office in principle accepted liability for payment of goods actually delivered to the Republic, it refused to do so when the goods were of a military character. These included hospital beds supplied to the Republic Ambulance Corps, hats and rice. There was also a refusal to pay for repairs done to a munitions factory. All these claims were made by Dutch and French firms. The Italian Government took up a claim on behalf of the Austro-Italian Trading Company for goods supplied to the Republic in 1900. The reply delivered to Italy was that the Transvaal Government recognized no obligation as regards debts of the Republic and the question whether any specific debt would be settled as a matter of course depended on the circumstances. Italy does not appear to have taken the matter further.[2]

The practice of the Transvaal Government in dealing with claims by individuals was summarized by the Treasurer in September 1901.[3] He stated that the general principle followed was that where a particular asset had been taken over it was considered as remaining subject to any liability attaching to it. For instance, credit balances of government accounts in the National Bank were taken over to the credit of the Civil Government account. A claim was subsequently put in by the National Bank amounting to £4,000 in respect of cheques which had been drawn on these accounts at branches of the Bank and had been paid but had not been returned to the head office in time to allow of their being debited against the Government balances before these were taken over. Where money was entrusted to private persons for specific purposes, these were permitted to charge against the rebatable balances properly attested disbursements.

Where goods had been supplied to the Republican Government and had been used for public purposes, claims for payment were made; also, where an unfinished contract had been taken over and continued by the new administration, any claims for sums due to the contractor were met as part of the contract.

On the other hand, claims on account of salaries due from, but left unpaid by, the Republican Government were rejected, as also claims on

1 *Ibid.* pp. 2, 3.   2 *Ibid.* pp. 3, 4.   3 F.O. Docket No. 37505 of 1901.

account of goods supplied or services rendered where these had not been used by the new administration.

In the case of the Pretoria–Pietersburg Railway Company a further report was made by the Law Officers on 24 February 1903,[1] stating that they did not have the contract between the company and its contractor before them, but so far as they could gather from the reports of an arbitration under the contract, the claim of the contractor against the company rested on breach of contract and an allegation of collusion between officials of the company and officials of the Transvaal Government in delaying the progress of the works. It appeared that the arbitrators decided against the company on the ground of collusion or incompetence of the representatives of the company, and if there was actual collusion then it appeared to be obvious that the company could not have recovered against the government of the Republic and could not now recover against its successors in title.

The breach of contract on which they would have to rest their case would be one to which, according to the evidence before the Arbitrators, the Company were themselves parties, and no action can be maintained by one who has been himself a party to the matters complained of.

(vi) *Judicial practice in Polish courts, 1919*

The few cases that followed the resettlement of Europe in 1919 are not very conclusive. The Polish courts generally adopted the view that State property had passed to Poland under article 256 of the Treaty of Versailles, and not on any theory of succession, and that therefore no obligations existed with respect to contracts or debts relating to it. In a case brought on a contract for work and labour done on buildings formerly owned by the Austrian Government, it was held by a Polish court that,

in contradistinction to the older doctrine of International Law, the modern law of nations no longer recognizes the private law principles of succession as applicable to the transfer of territory from one State to another. The successor State takes over the debts of its predecessor only in so far as it has expressly accepted them.[2]

---

1 F.O. Confidential Paper, no. 8144. Memorandum on the Practice of His Majesty's Government and the Governments of the Transvaal and Orange River Colony with respect to accepting Liability for Obligations of the Late Republics, April 1904, Appendix no. 4.

2 *Niedzielskie* v. *(Polish) Treasury, Ann. Dig.* vol. III, Case no. 53. See also *(Polish) State Treasury* v. *Osten, Ann. Dig.* vol. I, Case no. 37. In this case it was held that 'there is no general international custom ordering a State which acquires property under an international treaty to respect contracts of lease concluded by the predecessor State'.

Acquired Rights and Administrative Contracts 363

(vii) *The partition of India, 1947*

The division of contracts between India and Pakistan was provided for in an Order under the Indian Independence Act. Contracts of British India which were for purposes exclusively relating to territory incorporated in Pakistan should be deemed to have been made on behalf of that Dominion.[1] Pakistan was to be invested with all rights and liabilities which had accrued or should accrue in the future under any such contract,[2] and there was to be included in such liabilities the obligation to satisfy an award or order made by any court or other tribunal in proceedings in connexion with the contract, and expenses incurred in connexion therewith.[3] All other contracts should be deemed to have been made on behalf of India.[4] Similar arrangements were made with respect to contracts of the partitioned provinces of Bengal and Punjab.[5] Detailed assignments were to be effected by the Partition Council.

The Partition Council[6] set up an Expert Committee No. IV to propose a method of allocating outstanding contracts between India and Pakistan.[7] The Committee decided that it was concerned only with contracts of the nature covered by section 175 of the Government of India Act, 1935, which excluded reference to post office cash certificates, and post office insurance policies, which were regarded as falling more under the heading of financial obligations than contractual obligations. The contracts falling within the terms of reference were, therefore, contracts pertaining to immovable property, contracts pertaining to supplies to be made and services to be performed by the public or rendered to the public, contracts pertaining to the personal services of Government Services, and contracts pertaining to the sale of surplus, waste or obsolete stores.

With regard to contracts affecting immovable property the Committee recommended[8] that they should be deemed to have been made by the Dominion in which the property was situated. Contracts relating to supplies and services to be made by or rendered to the public exclusively for the purpose of either Dominion should be deemed to have been

---

[1] Indian Independence (Rights, Property and Liabilities) Order, 1947, *Gazette of India Extraordinary*, 14 August 1947, s. 8 (1) (*a*).
[2] Indian Independence (Rights, Property and Liabilities) Order, 1947, *Gazette of India Extraordinary*, 14 August 1947, s. 8 (1).
[3] *Ibid.* s. 8 (5) (*a*) and (*b*).
[4] *Ibid.* s. 8 (1) (*b*).
[5] *Ibid.* s. 8 (2) and 3).
[6] Constituted by the Indian Independence (Partition Councils) Order, 1947, *Gazette of India Extraordinary*, 12 August 1947.
[7] *Partition Proceedings*, vol. III, p. 35.
[8] *Ibid.*

entered into by that Dominion, and this would cover all contracts placed for stores which were of local interest. Contracts concerning government servants would be considered as the obligations of the respective Dominion under which they would serve after 1947. Contracts such as that for the catering of the railway system as a whole would be divided as contracts made separately with the two Dominions. Contracts for purchase of stores intended for the purposes of both Dominions should be deemed to have been made with the Dominion in whose territory the consignee under the contract was located, and if there were several consignees, some located within the territory of the other, the contract should be deemed to have been entered into with each Dominion in respect of the stores to be delivered to the consignees within its respective jurisdiction. If the consignee's name was not mentioned, then the contract should be regarded as that of the Dominion within whose territory the place of performance of the contract was situated.[1] Contracts entered into abroad would be the obligation of the Dominion of India unless destined for the requirements of Pakistan. With respect to Defence Agency Contracts, which were partly Indian and partly Pakistani, the recommendation was that they should be transferred to India with effect from the date of independence, that India could administer the contracts as a whole, leaving Pakistan to effect a financial adjustment in the final accounting between the Dominions. Where division would be impossible, the recommendation was that each Dominion should be put in a position to operate independently the maximum number of contracts or parts of contracts in which it was interested.[2]

The final recommendation was that in the case of more complicated contracts, such as railway contracts, departmental committees should be appointed to make proposals for the division, based upon ascertainment of the consignees and the share of the Dominions in the goods forthcoming against the various contracts.

The Partition Council approved[3] the recommendations of the Steering Committee on the report of the Export Committee, and accepted the draft sections of the Order in Council, which formed part of the Indian Independence (Rights, Property and Liabilities) Order, 1947.

The interpretation of the Order might be expected, in view of the attempt made to devise an overall formula for solution of highly variant contractual situations, to provide material for litigation, and this expectation has been realized. It has been held that where construction work under a contract with the Defence Department was carried on in territory which

[1] *Partition Proceedings*, vol. III, p. 36.   [2] *Ibid.* p. 37.
[3] *Ibid.* p. 54.

became part of Pakistan, it was no longer the liability of India.[1] But not every situation was so simple. Where residents of Baroda sued on a contract made with the Government of India for the purchase of cloth lying at the Ordnance Parachute Factory in Lahore, and had paid in full the cost and stamp duty but had not received the goods owing to riots following partition, the court held that the responsibility was that of Pakistan, because the test to be applied in interpreting the Order was which of the two Dominions would have been entitled to exercise rights of ownership with regard to the undelivered goods; clearly this depended upon the locality in which the goods were at the date of partition.[2] Contracts not exclusively for the purposes of East Bengal and made with the Provincial Government of Assam fell to Pakistan,[3] and a contract for the supply of fodder to the Lahore Cantonment was held to be the responsibility of Pakistan.[4] The test formulated by Chagla J., was

whether if the contract had been entered into on 15 August, 1947, it would have been a contract for the purposes of the Dominion of Pakistan or if the Dominion of Pakistan had been in existence when the contract was entered into, whether it would have been a contract for the purpose of Pakistan.[5]

In the case of contracts made with the Governments of the merged States, the solution was based on the act of State doctrine.[6] Contracts broken before the date of partition were held to be affected by the legislation.[7]

The question of the liability of the Indian Railways for non-delivery of goods consigned from railway depots in what subsequently became Pakistan arose in several cases. Interpreting the Indian Independence (Rights, Property and Liabilities) Order, an Assam court held that in such instances India was liable because the contract was not exclusively for the benefit of Pakistan territory.[8] A Calcutta court followed this decision in a case in which both the place of despatch and the place of destination were in Pakistan, but the goods had to cross Indian territory *in transitu*.[9] It has

1 *Elahi Bux* v. *Union of India*, A.I.R. (1952), Cal. 471; *Pannalal Mukherjee* v. *Union of India*, A.I.R. (1957), Cal. 156.
2 *Union of India* v. *Chinubhai Jeshingbhai*, A.I.R. (1953), Bomb. 13.
3 *Chunilal Patua* v. *The State of Assam*, A.I.R. (1953), Assam 113.
4 *Union of India* v. *Chaman Lal Loona & Co.*, A.I.R. (1957), S.C. 652; *Union of India* v. *Balwant Singh Jaswant Singh*, A.I.R. (1957), Pun. 27; *Hari Trading Co.* v. *Dominion of India*, 99 Cal. L.J. 62.
5 Ibid., adopting *Union of India* v. *Chinubhai Jeshingbhai*, A.I.R. (1953), Bomb. 13.
6 See *supra*, p. 258.
7 *Krishna Ranjan Basu Ray* v. *Union of India*, A.I.R. (1954), Cal. 623. Agrawala in *Indian Journal of International Law*, vol. II (1962), p. 441.
8 *Assam Suppliers Ltd* v. *Union of India*, A.I.R. (1952), Assam 88.
9 *Union of India* v. *Loke Nath Saha*, A.I.R. (1952), Cal. 140. The decision was distinguished in *Chaman Lal Loona & Co.* v. *Dominion of India*, A.I.R. (1954), Punj. 129.

been argued that when proof was forthcoming that the goods had never left the Pakistan station this rule would not apply.[1]

(viii) *The independence of the Philippines, 1946*

The Republic of the Philippines agreed to assume all liabilities of the islands and their local bodies, and all continuing obligations which the United States had assumed under the Treaty of Paris, 1898.[2]

(ix) *The independence of Libya, 1950*

Two public corporations of the Italian State in Libya—*Ente per la Colonizzazione della Libia*, and *Istituto della Providenza Sociale*—made many contracts and concessions with Italian colonists. All the rights arising from these contracts were fully maintained, while the lands belonging to the corporations were transferred to Libya, and the corporations themselves were liquidated.[3]

(x) *The independence of Somalia, 1960*

Section 58 of the Constitution of Somaliland,[4] which was annexed to the Somaliland Order in Council, 1960, by which British Somaliland attained independence, provided for the vesting in the Government of Somaliland of any liability or obligation, whether arising from contract or otherwise incurred by the Crown for the purposes of the Government of the Protectorate of Somaliland. There was no such provision respecting the Trust Territory, but when the Somali Republic and Somaliland fused, provision was made in the Act of Union (which was retrospective to 1 July 1960), for the transfer to the Somali Republic of all obligations lawfully incurred by the independent Governments of Somaliland and Somalia. As there was never an independent Somalia, it has been argued that the effect of this provision was to make the Somali Republic the successor of the Government of Somaliland only.[5]

(xi) *The dissolution of the Federation of Rhodesia and Nyasaland, 1963*

The Order in Council[6] dissolving the Federation provided for Federal assets and liabilities to vest in the Liquidating Agency. The latter was directed by a Report of a Committee (known as Committee A) under the chairmanship of the United Kingdom, which formed the basis of the Order. The legal sub-committee of Committee A advised that all claims

1 Kapur in *Indian Law Review*, vol. IX (1957), p. 26.
2 *U.N.T.S.* vol. VII (1947), p. 4, art. 7.
3 U.N. Res. 388 (v), art. 6. 4 S.I. 1960, no. 1060.
5 *I.C.L.Q.* vol. XII (1963), p. 1011. 6 S.I. 1963, no. 2085.

would be settled as at the date of dissolution, and the Liquidating Agency hence treated all contracts as subsisting only to that date. Leaseholds in which the Federation was lessee accordingly expired on that date, although leaseholds abroad were treated as assets and assigned for a consideration after that date. The legal sub-committee also advised that the contracts of Federal public corporations would expire with the entities created under Federal law. Hence, the contract of the Rhodesian Broadcasting Company with the Federal Broadcasting Corporation was regarded as having lapsed when the Corporation went out of existence.

(xii) *Abolition of the Crown in Commonwealth countries*

When a dependency of the United Kingdom is granted independence it is unnecessary to provide for succession to rights, liabilities and obligations of the previous administration, provided that the new State retains the monarchy, for in theory it is the Crown in which these are vested. However, when a new State, either in the act of independence,[1] or subsequently,[2] abolishes the monarchy, it is the practice to provide for this succession to the President or the Government provided for under the constitutional change.

2. CONCLUSION

A review of these cases discloses how difficult it is to apply the doctrine of acquired rights in practice. The more locally identified is the contract the greater is the presumption that it has benefited the absorbed territory. It is impossible to set down *a priori* cases in which this presumption will arise. It is a matter which judicial analysis alone can determine. Nevertheless, the general principle of respect for acquired rights, and its corollary principle of restitution, are, it is submitted, clearly accepted in international law as applying to administrative contracts. A decision of the Austrian Supreme Court in 1948 in the case of *Kleihs* v. *Republic of Austria* illustrates the operation of the principle. An engineering firm in Vienna sued for payment for work executed for the Austrian State Railways. The work had been commissioned by the German State Railways while Austria was incorporated in the *Reich*. The Republic contended that it was doubtful if the Austrian State Railways would derive any lasting benefit

[1] Zambia Independence Order, S.I. 1964, no. 1625, s. 20.
[2] Republic of Tanganyika (Consequential, Transitional and Temporary Provisions) Act, 1962, no. 2 of 1962, s. 13; The Constitution of Kenya (Amendment) Act, 1964, no. 28 of 1964, s. 26; The Constitution of Uganda (First Amendment) Act, 1963, no. 61 of 1963, s. 43; The Constitution of the Federal Republic of Nigeria Act, 1963, no. 20 of 1963 contained in s. 155 a general saving.

from the work. It is interesting to note that both parties as well as the court assumed the existence of some doctrine of 'benefit' or enrichment. The latter held that, although the German State Railways had not intended to commission the work for the present respondent, and the appellant had not intended to benefit it, in actual fact the work did benefit, or must be presumed to have benefited, the Republic, which must pay for it.[1]

[1] *Ann. Dig.* vol. xv, Case no. 18. Unreported in Austria.

Chapter 15

THE DOCTRINE OF ACQUIRED RIGHTS AND THE NATIONAL DEBT

1. INTRODUCTION

The history of the effect of change of sovereignty on the public debt is confused and complicated.[1] Undue reliance cannot be placed on treaty provisions because these have usually been the outcome of compromise dictated by the successor State's capacity to pay. Economic considerations, it must be admitted, have obtruded to such an extent on the topic as to obscure whatever fundamental principles exist.

The general public, or national, debt is that contracted by the central government in the interests of the entire State. The creditor of the debt may be another State, an international organization, a public corporation or a private creditor. The debt may be owed under international law, the municipal law of the creditor, or that of the debtor.[2] It may be secured or unsecured, bonded or unbonded. A secured debt is one for which liquidation is provided from predetermined assets or revenues. It is said to be charged or pledged on such assets and revenues, and the creditor may be given the right to pursue the debt against them. An unsecured debt is merely a right to receive payment of money at a fixed date, a right which can be pursued against the debtor only, and not by a transfer of the debtor's assets.[3]

If the debtor is totally extinguished, its international capacity for rights and obligations, though not necessarily its fiscal capacity, is extinguished with it. The successor State which takes over the entire territory of the debtor assumes a position in which it can prevent the servicing of the debt. Henceforth the juridical competence of the absorbed territory to incur

---

[1] Hackworth is of opinion that no definite conclusions can be arrived at 'except that no universal rule of international law on the subject can be said to exist', *Dig.* vol. I, p. 539. See also Feilchenfeld, p. vi; Dahm, vol. I, pp. 115–8; Ross, p. 129. Jèze suggests that the uncertainty is due to the fact that Anglo-American practice is dictated by the circumstance that England and America were annexing States, *Le Partage des dettes publiques au cas de démembrement de territoire* (1921), p. 6. The topic has been considered ever since international law became a discipline: Gentili, III, v, 22; Grotius, II, IX, viii; Pufendorf, VIII, xii, ii; Vattel, II, XIII, 203; Bynkershoek, *Quaestionum juris publici*, II, xxv.
[2] Feilchenfeld, pp. 648 et seq.
[3] *Ibid.* pp. 655 et seq.

and discharge obligations, and to raise the means of doing so, can only exist as a particular manifestation of the municipal law of the successor State. Discharge of the debt is completely subject to the latter's control. The problem that confronts the successor State is this: must it provide itself for the servicing of the debt, or may it leave the absorbed territory to do so, or may it ignore the debt altogether?[1] Should the debtor be dismembered, the problem is only slightly different. In this case the territory and assets necessary to liquidate the debt come under two or more sovereigns. The international identity and the fiscal capacity of the debtor are both destroyed. There can be no question of leaving the absorbed territory to discharge the debt because it no longer exists as an integral unit. The question in such a case is this: are the successor States jointly and severally liable to service the debt and, if so, what proportion of it?

When only part of the debtor's territory is lost, both international personality and fiscal capacity remain, though the actual ability to liquidate the debt may be severely circumscribed by a substantial loss of revenue and assets. The successor State in this case does not become competent to interfere with the formal debt relationship, and the rights of creditors against the debtor remain, in law, completely undisturbed, though they may, in fact, be rendered considerably precarious.[2] The question is whether the debt must be allocated between the debtor State and its successor or successors. The fundamental distinction is thus between total and partial succession. The rules of international law, being intended to secure the rights of creditors, will vary in the two instances.

Such rules must be assumed to exist, if only to preserve the relative distribution of wealth amongst States from arbitrary changes. The doctrine of acquired rights, it is believed, not only achieves this purpose, but renders intelligible the mass of historical precedents.[3]

[1] Feilchenfeld, pp. 664 *et seq.*
[2] *Ibid.* p. 667. See de Louter, vol. I, p. 230.
[3] Jèze contends that 'absolute respect for the rights of creditors is the rule', *op. cit.* p. 8. Sack argues that 'the principle of succession to the debts of a State rests on that of the safeguard of acquired rights of private persons. Persons possessing movable or immovable goods having rights *in rem* or rights of credit preserve these rights notwithstanding the eventual change of sovereignty over the territory in question. The new government, though it be sovereign and independent, must recognize and respect the rights which they have acquired', *Dettes publiques*, pp. 59–60; see also pp. 61 and 74. See Feilchenfeld, who analyses the weaknesses of debts as species of private property, p. 655; Castren, pp. 462 *et seq.*; Schnitzer, p. 135.

2. THE RELATIONSHIP BETWEEN CREDITOR AND SOVEREIGN DEBTOR

If a State borrows from the World Bank,[1] its obligations are probably governed by international law.[2] Most other loans, however, are contracted according to a municipal law system,[3] which characterizes the rights of the creditors to be protected by international law. Should the proper law of the contract not permit suit against the debtor government (which, in the absence of covering legislation[4] is the case with English law[5]) then it is doubtful if any international protection whatever is available to the creditors. This is especially true of loans which are raised by local and not international subscription, for States are less disposed to protect their nationals who come into possession of bearer certificates respecting domesticated borrowings than they are in the case of raisings on the international loan market.

International practice respecting defaulted bondholdings is neither sufficiently extensive nor sufficiently coherent to permit of a definitive statement of the rules of law governing alien claims.[6] The reluctance on the part of Foreign Offices to pursue defaulting States has resulted partly from an unwillingness of governments to become international debt collectors, and partly from a recognition of the fact that pursuit of a financially embarrassed State is not only likely to be unsuccessful but will certainly generate political tension. Accordingly, mere non-payment of the loan on the due date is not regarded as an occasion for an international claim, and it is only on the rare occasion when the loan is directly repudiated, or when the non-payment has been so continuous and unwarranted by economic circumstances as to amount to repudiation, that claims are in fact made. Of course, if the proper law permits access to the courts on defaulted bonds, and this access is refused, or the courts are directed by the executive to reject the suit, then a denial of justice has occurred for which a claim, extraneous to the claim respecting default, might be made.

Change of sovereignty may affect the legal rights of creditors in varying ways, but may not, depending on the circumstances, greatly modify their actual financial position. If the debtor State is so dismembered that

---

[1] Broches in Hague *Recueil*, vol. XCVIII (1959), p. 300.
[2] Mann in *B.Y.* vol. XXXV (1959), p. 38.
[3] *Serbian and Brazilian Loans* Case, P.C.I.J. ser. A, no. 20–21 (1929); *R. v. International Trustee for the Protection of Bondholders*, A.G. [1937] A.C. 500; *Bonython v. Commonwealth of Australia* [1951] A.C. 201.
[4] *Bonython v. Commonwealth of Australia* [1951] A.C. 201.
[5] *Rederiaktiebolaget Amphitrite v. R.* [1921] 3 K.B. 500. See *supra*, p. 305.
[6] O'Connell, *International Law* (1965), vol. II, p. 1080.

amortization becomes impossible, then creditors will look to the successor State for payment. If the nominal debtor survives as an entity competent to service the debt, the creditor's rights are unaffected. In either event, however, a diplomatic claim is unlikely to be made on behalf of alien bondholders if the debtor is financially embarrassed by the change. A creditor whose rights are preserved against the predecessor State, therefore, is ordinarily in no stronger position than a creditor whose only recourse is against a successor State, for mere non-payment in either case is unlikely to give rise to a formal dispute, while repudiation can, at the most, justify a claim for payment, without interest, and perhaps spread over a long time. In monetary terms, it does not matter whether the claimant State seeks payment from the predecessor State, or argues for a subrogation on the part of the successor State in the formal debtor–creditor relationship, or is content to claim equitable compensation from the successor State.

The question of survival of the *vinculum juris* between debtor and creditor appears, then, to be practically important only in the case where, under the proper law, the debtor State can be sued in its own courts, or in the courts of other countries. But such a case is likely to be rare. Although the tendency is to relax the rule concerning resistance to suit by sovereigns, this relaxation, neither in the laws of borrowing countries, nor in those of other countries, has, generally speaking, extended to borrowings for public purposes. This explains why there are virtually no judicial authorities of municipal courts on the effect of State succession on the national debt, though there are decisions on its effect upon credits and debits of administrative contracts.

Perhaps the most important effect of a subrogation of the successor State in the debt of its predecessor is with respect to the currency and mode of payment. In the *Lighthouses* Case[1] the Permanent Court of Arbitration treated credits and debits arising from contracts of loan as aspects of private vested rights, which, according to the 'general principles of public international common law', are unaffected by territorial changes. Protocol XII of the Treaty of Lausanne, which 'fully subrogated' Greece as regards the rights and obligations of Turkey towards the beneficiaries of concessionary contracts, was inspired by this principle, and hence it covered debits and credits arising from operations associated with concessionary contracts. This had led M. Borel, the Arbitrator in the *Ottoman Debt* Arbitration,[2] to comment that, in omitting to include in the Treaty of Lausanne any provision respecting the currency in which loans were

[1] I.L.R. vol. XXIII, p. 659.
[2] U.N. Rep., vol. I, p. 529 (1925); see *infra*, p. 402.

to be repaid, the High Contracting Parties had intended to leave completely intact the respective rights of the bondholders of the Ottoman Debt and of the debtor States. The Permanent Court of Arbitration concluded from this that contracts of advance made with Turkey ought to be regarded as having been in no way affected by the Treaty of Lausanne.

The contracts continue to be governed by their own law and there is no good reason to except from that principle the special clauses protecting the legitimate rights of the lenders, such as that by which they are given an essential guarantee of the repayment of their capital and interest in the form of an assignment of the part belonging to the borrower State, in its capacity of grantor State, in the lighthouse dues to be collected by a third party, the concessionaire firm.[1]

3. TOTAL SUCCESSION

I. Annexation

(A) Should the debtor State be extinguished, the legal relationship between it and the creditor disappears. What is left is the creditor's equitable interest in the money advanced. Should the debt be pledged, he has, in addition, an interest also in State property, an interest *ad rem*. It cannot be asserted with confidence that he can still pursue his remedy against public assets, and it cannot be denied that the successor State has the right to expropriate his interest in them. But should the successor State so act it incurs a duty in international law to effect compensation. When it is said, therefore, that a territory passes to a successor State *cum onere*, '*grevé*', or 'burdened', this is the most that can be meant. Many writers, on the contrary, have tried to assert that there is impressed on a State's territory a real and transitory obligation.[2] This, however, is not substantiated by State practice, and is another facet of the universal succession theory.[3]

[1] *I.L.R.* vol. XXIII, p. 97.

[2] Cavaglieri suggests that the successor State takes over debts of which the predecessor was '*grevé au profit de ses créanciers étrangers*', in *Annuaire de l'Institut de Droit International*, Session de Paris, 1934, vol. XXXIV, p. 479. Calvo maintains that debts inhere in the soil and are not personal to the sovereign under whose reign they were contracted: vol. IV, p. 404. See Rivier, vol. I, p. 70. On the other hand, see Hall, p. 114, and Jèze, *op. cit.* p. 17, who regard the debt of State as a personal obligation.

[3] There is a large body of opinion which considers that a successor State must 'take over' the debts of the extinguished one: Despagnet, p. 120; Fauchille, who says that payment is 'absolutely incumbent' on the successor State: vol. I, pt. I, p. 380; Fiore, *Int. Law Cod.* p. 142 and *Nouv. droit int.* vol. I, p. 316; Martens, vol. I,; p. 369; Rivier, vol. I, p. 70; Spiropoulos, p. 75; Piédelièvre, vol. I, pp. 169–70;

The difficulties attending the proof of such a real obligation were avoided by Sack, who argued that the relationship between a debtor State and its creditor is a matter neither of international law, nor of municipal law, but of something in between, which he called international financial law.[1] To such a law he ascribed the capacity of binding the territory of a State, and of impressing on it a burden of an absolute and permanent, and therefore transmissible, character.[2] The necessary corollary of this theory is the assertion that creditors have the right to pursue the debt against the accidental sovereign of the territory.[3]

Sack's theory would seem to fail in two respects. First, it was rendered necessary by his adherence to the view that international law is a law between States only. It follows, he contended, that a successor State can neither acquire nor inherit any duty in international law to a creditor. This thesis has already been rejected. Secondly, to substantiate the conclusion that a creditor has an enduring right against the accidental owner of public assets, it would be necessary to prove that he has a right to demand payment out of such assets. This could only be proved where there exists over the assets a pledge or lien recognized by the successor State. No examples of State practice can be found where this right to payment has been acknowledged, or in which a State's budgetary provisions have been regarded as other than matters of internal regulation.

Strupp, *Éléments*, p. 109; Kiatibian, p. 23; Bustamante, vol. III, p. 339; Kelsen in Hague *Recueil*, vol. LXII (1932), p. 332; Udina in Hague *Recueil*, vol. LXIV (1933), p. 755; Szaszy in *Rev. de droit int.* vol. V (1930), p. 588; Sauser-Hall in *Schweizerische Juristenzeitung*, 35th year (1938), pp. 161–5; *Law Times*, vol. CLXX (1931), pp. 379–81; Sedillot in *L'Europe nouvelle*, 18 April 1939, 22e année, pp. 287–8; Cavaglieri in Hague *Recueil*, vol. XXVI (1929), p. 380. The negative view is taken by Drost in *Rev. de droit int.* ser. 3, vol. XX (1939), pp. 702 *et seq.*; Sereni, vol. I, p. 406; Schönborn, p. 106; Hoijer, *Les traités internationaux* (1928), p. 484; Meyer-Lindenberg, p. 86; von Schuschnigg, p. 158; Wheaton, s. 20; Gould, p. 415; Dahm, who thinks the argument for succession is strongest in cases of total succession, vol. I, p. 116; Verdross-Zemanek, p. 195; Delbez, p. 180; de Visscher, p. 191; while Brierly has expressed doubt: Hague *Recueil*, vol. LVIII (1936), p. 68. Rousseau objects to the negative theory as an emanation from a voluntarist theory of law, p. 275.

1 *Dettes publiques*, p. 87.

2 *Ibid.* pp. 54 and 88. See also in Hague *Recueil*, vol. XXIII (1928), pp. 228, 237. 'The legal responsibility of the state for its public debts extends to all the resources of the commonwealth': *ibid.* p. 231. 'The juridical basis of public wealth resides precisely in the fact that debts bind the territory of the debtor': *Dettes publiques*, p. 54. The debt which binds the territory of the State obliges governments, old and new, extending jurisdiction over this territory on the principle *res transit cum suo onere*: *ibid.* p. 58. 'Only debts contracted while such and such a territory forms part of the old state burden its territory; only such debts must be assumed by the states in which the territories in question are incorporated': *ibid.* p. 301. See also in *New York University Law Quarterly Review*, vol. 10 (1932).

3 'Creditors have a juridical guarantee in the fact that their credits bind the territory of the debtor state': Hague *Recueil*, vol. XXIII (1928), p. 276.

(B) In the act of change of sovereignty the successor State acquires the capacity to destroy the interest of the creditor in the secured or unsecured debt. The principle of respect for acquired rights, however, obliges it to respect this interest.[1] So long as the creditor is reimbursed to the extent of his investment it is immaterial to him in which way this respect is effected. The successor State may, in the first place, permit the absorbed State to preserve a fiscal and economic autonomy.[2] In such a case it is the fiscal unit which is enriched by the invested capital, and it is out of the revenues of the unit that restitution, in the municipal law of the successor, must be made. Should the unit fail to provide for the servicing of the debt the successor State does not necessarily incur an international responsibility. The most it must do is provide the means in its own municipal law for the creditor to enforce his rights. Should it fail to do so, or should the unit fail to give effect to the municipal law, then, and only then, does the successor State itself become directly responsible to the creditor's own State, and it does so under the doctrine of denial of justice.[3]

On the other hand, should the successor State either directly absorb the predecessor within its own fiscal system, or otherwise destroy its fiscal competence, then it is the State as a whole which is enriched, and it is the State itself which must respect the creditor's acquired right.[4] This respect it may effect in various ways: First, it may continue to repay the debt and interest on the terms stipulated, thereby making an express or tacit novation of the debt relationship. Secondly, it may repay the capital and interest up to the date of absorption. If it is not to incur the presumption of a novation, it must effect such repayment within reasonable time. If the debt was secured, it may either permit the creditor's interest in the security to persist, or it may expropriate the security in the same way as it may expropriate other types of acquired rights. If it adopts the latter course, it owes a duty to pay compensation.[5] The standard of compensation

---

1 Fitzmaurice in Hague *Recueil*, vol. LXXIII (1948), p. 288.

2 Sack admits that the absorbed territory can preserve its character as an autonomous region, *Dettes publiques*, p. 155. Appleton argues that though the State may be dead in international law it is not dead in administrative law: it exists under the form of a department or province: p. 36. Gidel replies that this is interesting only as a matter of machinery of repartition. The absorbed State cannot remain a debtor since its international personality has been destroyed: p. 70. See Jèze, *op. cit.* p. 19; Garner in *A.J.* vol. XXXII (1938), p. 430.

3 See Feilchenfeld, p. 665; Jèze, *op. cit.* p. 19; Castren, pp. 470 *et seq.*

4 Jèze accepts the doctrine of unjust enrichment in this context, pointing out that the debt has been used to construct things of benefit to the inhabitants, and concluding that 'one must not be enriched at another's expense', *op. cit.* p. 12.

5 There is no inheritance of the debt relationship. For example, when Great Britain annexed the Transvaal in 1877 it was suggested that the debenture-holders might be forced to pay for increased security by a lowering of the interest rate. Had

in such cases must be the value of the creditor's investment at the moment of change of sovereignty. The doctrine of unjust enrichment in this context is usually rejected because it is argued that proof that the debt has benefited the absorbed territory is impossible.[1] Such proof is not needed. Apart from the fact that there is a presumption of benefit, there is a detriment to the creditor, and detriment, allied with a presumption of benefit, is sufficient to constitute unjust enrichment. State practice generally bears out the contention that the successor State need not liquidate the debt of its predecessor, provided it leaves the absorbed State as a fiscal unit. Such practice will now be considered:

(i) *British annexations, 1874–7*

When Fiji was annexed the Colonial Secretary requested from the consul there full particulars of the financial obligations of Fiji 'which would have to be assumed'. But he observed that the British Government could not consent to make the revenues of Great Britain liable in any way for this debt.[2] Subsequently the Colonial Office adopted the attitude that if Fiji's debts were discharged out of such revenues this would be an 'act of grace'. During the negotiations preliminary to the annexation of the Transvaal in 1877 the President of that country was assured that Transvaal's debt would 'be guaranteed'.[3] The Proclamation of Annexation asserted that 'payment of debts of the State must be provided for'.[4]

there been any contractual relationship this alteration would have been legally unjustifiable, *B.F.S.P.* vol. LXVIII (1877), p. 140. The only principle which Feilchenfeld admits is that 'maintenance of financial obligations must not be impaired', p. 222. Feilchenfeld's maintenance theory is correct, but it does not go far enough. An isolated rule that debts must be maintained must have some juridical basis against which the whole problem can be focused. It is necessary to go behind the rule itself to the principle which it formulates.

1 Sack objects that it is impossible to estimate the benefit to the territory, and points out that if a benefit theory were accepted debts would have to be divided in proportion to the benefit, and not in proportion to the paying capacity of the territory, *Dettes publiques*, pp. 76–7.

2 Letter from the Colonial Secretary to the Governor of Fiji, 4 March 1875, C. 1337, p. 237.

3 Answer of His Britannic Majesty's Government in the *Robert E. Brown* Claim, p. 9.

4 *B.F.S.P.* vol. LXVIII (1877), p. 140. The Treaty of Pretoria in 1881 made the Transvaal liable not only for debts of the old South African Republic, but also for expenses incurred in the administration of the State between 1877 and 1881: C. 3098, p. 601. The case of *Doss* v. *Secretary of State for India* contained a dictum which was referred to on several occasions by the Foreign Office in its references to the Law Officers. This dictum was to the effect that 'every State which takes possession of the territories of another . . . is liable for the debts and loans which exist on its revenues': (1875), 19 Eq. 509, at p. 530.

(ii) *The annexation of Hawaii by the United States, 1898*

The joint Resolution of Congress providing for the annexation of Hawaii in 1898 declared that 'the public debt of the Republic of Hawaii, lawfully existing at the date of the passage of this joint resolution . . ., is hereby assumed'. The liabilities of the Federal Government, however, were not to exceed 4 million dollars because Hawaii was to remain a fiscal unit with its own budget, and to provide for the amortization of its own debt.[1] In a subsequent opinion on this Joint Resolution the Attorney-General of the United States said that 'the general doctrine of international law, founded upon obvious principles of justice, is that, in the case of annexation of a state or cession of territory, the substituted sovereignty assumes the debts and obligations of the absorbed state or territory—it takes the burdens with the benefits. . . . There is nothing in the Hawaiian resolution of annexation which gives the negative to this theory.'[2]

(iii) *French annexations, 1881–96*

When France annexed Tahiti the latter ceased to have any fiscal autonomy, and France provided for the servicing of its debt.[3] On the other hand, when a French protectorate was declared over Tunis the latter did preserve such autonomy,[4] and the view was taken that France incurred no financial liability.[5] The Treaty of Cession projected with Madagascar provided that the island was to remain charged with its own debts, and liquidation of them was to be effected out of its own revenues. No responsibility was to rest on France.[6] Subsequently, the French Minister for Foreign Affairs declared that rules of international law relating to the obligations of conquered territories would be strictly followed. He was careful, however, to avoid any implication that France was obliged by such rules to guarantee or take over the Madagascan debt.[7]

---

1 Moore, *Dig.* vol. I, p. 351.
2 22 *Op. A.-G.* p. 583.
3 *M.N.R.G.* 2nd ser., vol. IX, p. 223.
4 *B.F.S.P.*, vol. LXXII, p. 247.
5 Hertslet, *The Map of Africa by Treaty* (3rd ed. 1909), vol. III, p. 1185, vol. II, p. 720.
6 *Rev. gén. de droit int. pub.* vol. IV (1897), p. 231, n. 2, art. 6. See Garner in *A.J.* vol. XXXII (1938), p. 771.
7 *Rev. gén. de droit int. pub.* vol. IV (1897), p. 250. Fauchille repudiates all suggestion that France was not bound by the Madagascan debt: vol. I, pt. 1, p. 379. The reason for the French refusal, as explained by the Minister of the Colonies in the *Conseil d'État*, was the impossibility of determining the authoritative character or otherwise of the debts alleged to have been contracted by Madagascar: *Conseil d'État, Recueil des arrêts*, vol. LXXIV, 3rd ser. 1904, 5 August 1904, 4361, quoted by Sack, *Dettes publiques*, p. 65, no. 1.

(iv) *The British annexations of Burma, 1886, and the Boer Republics, 1900*

Great Britain refused to recognize any legal duty to discharge the financial obligations of Burma because the latter had no regular national debt.[1] The entire national debt of the South African Republic, however, including a deficit of £1,500,000, was taken over by Great Britain in 1900.[2] Before such action was taken the Colonial Office referred the matter to the Law Officers. The latter were asked to advise whether or not the British Government was bound to take over the public debts of the extinct Republics. If they were so bound the Colonial Office would require to know if they must 'carry out to the letter all the obligations of the late Republic, or whether they might modify these obligations and decline to be bound by every term of the contracts entered into by the late Republic'. They suggested that in view of the increased security given for the payment of these loans by the substitution of the British Government as a debtor for the extinct government it would not be 'inequitable to reduce the rate of interest'. The Colonial Office also desired to know if the loans might be converted before the due date and if it would be justifiable to 'carry out such conversion on terms based on its own credit'.

The Law Officers were clearly of the opinion that there was no obligation on the part of Great Britain to do more than leave the annexed States competent to discharge their own debts. They advised that

Her Majesty's Government, as successor to the Governments of the South African Republic and the Orange Free State, are bound to take over the public debts of these States as a charge thereon, but not, of course, as debts payable otherwise than from revenue derived from the conquered States respectively.

(*a*) The conditions attaching to such debts will still continue, but it will be open to Her Majesty's Government to alter such conditions in any respect that may be more equitable, having regard to the altered condition of affairs.

(*b*) Her Majesty's Government are bound to pay any instalments of principal and interest which may be due in so far as they have revenue from the conquered territory available for that purpose.[3]

In the negotiations for peace in South Africa, the British Government in general repudiated liability for debts contracted during the war. The

1 C. 4887, p. 590.
2 C. 1552, p. 125. De Louter contends that Great Britain was without doubt bound to assume the South Africa debt: *op. cit.* vol. I, p. 229. See to the contrary the *West Rand Gold Mining Company* v. *The King* [1905] 2 K.B. 391 at p. 402, where it was said that there is no principle of international law by which after annexation of conquered territory the conquering State becomes liable to discharge liabilities of the conquered State.
3 Opinion of 30 November 1900, F.O. Confidential Papers (7516), no. 22A; O'Connell, Appendix, no. 70.

Boer and British negotiators agreed[1] that a Judicial Commission would be appointed to which Government notes issued under a law of 1900 of the South African Republic might be presented within six months. All notes for which valuable consideration had been given would be paid without interest. All receipts given by officers in the field, if found to have been given *bona fide* for goods used by the forces in the field, would be paid out to the persons to whom they were originally given. The total liability was not to exceed more than £3,000,000 and if the total amount of proved claims would be more than this sum there would be a *pro rata* diminution.

In a memorandum of the Colonial Office of 27 November 1903 it was observed that the position taken by the Law Officers in the British and Colonial Governments differed widely from Continental writings, and that the proposal of the Law Officers that it has never been laid down that a conquering State takes over liability for wrongs 'seems hardly to have been confirmed in point of fact'. Reference was made to Huber's work and especially to section 7, in which he refers to all administrative acts which were then completed having to be recognized by the new sovereign so far as new parties have acquired rights. It was commented that the tendency generally of foreign writers on international law was to insist on the need for protecting the neutral.[2]

The debt of the Orange River Colony consisted mainly of a loan for railway purposes from the Cape Government. Interest on this was paid regularly from the date of annexation. The instalments of capital were paid but with the proviso that neither the government of the Colony nor the British Government was to be taken as in any way admitting any liability as to the payment of interest in the future or as to repayment of capital. The only considerable direct debt of either of the Republics was the Rothschild loan, payment of interest on which was not resumed until 18 August 1901, and then only on conditions involving an agreement, part of which was that bondholders should surrender coupons due before 1 July 1901. They were also required to agree to being paid off at par on three months' notice. Bondholders who failed to surrender their bonds on the date named would be held to have forfeited all claims on the British Government and would be dependent for payment of both principal and interest on the revenues of the Transvaal only. Advances made by the British Government for the settlement of this debt and for other purposes would be a prior charge on these revenues.[3]

1 Cd. 1096, p. 7. See Meile, *Die niederländisch-südafrikanische Eisenbahngesellschaft* (1902), p. 23, where the opinion of the Transvaal Concessions Commission on debts of the Boer Republics is controverted. Also Gidel, p. 8.
2 F.O. Confidential Paper no. 8144, p. 16.
3 *Ibid.*

(v) *The annexations of the Congo, 1907, and Korea, 1910*

The Treaty of Brussels, 1907 charged the debts of the Congo exclusively on the territory itself.[1] The debt of Korea, on the other hand, was assumed in 1910 by the Japanese Imperial Treasury.[2]

(vi) *The annexation of Austria, 1938*

When Germany annexed Austria in 1938 it took over a country that was heavily in debt. Apart from loans granted by the United States, and secured by first charge on the assets and revenues of the State, Austria was indebted to the League of Nations for large loans floated under its auspices. These sums were guaranteed in specific portions by various members of the League,[3] who, with the exception of Italy, met in London in June 1938 to consider the effect of the German annexation on their obligations. They had before them a letter from the German Foreign Office, stating that Germany did not feel under any 'legal obligation to take over the external debts of the former Austrian Federal Government'. The guarantor States resolved to address a united protest to the German Government.[4]

On 6 April 1938 the United States informed the *Reich* that it would look to it 'for discharge of the relief indebtedness of the Government of Austria', and it would expect that the other obligations of Austria and its local governments would continue to be freely recognized and that their service would be continued by the German authorities who had succeeded in control of the means and machinery of payment.[5] No satisfactory reply being received, the United States on 9 June delivered a note which stated that

1 M.N.R.G. 3rd ser., vol. II, p. 101, art. 3 at p. 102. For a discussion see *supra*, p. 91.
2 Hackworth, *Dig.* vol. I, p. 543.
3 Garner in *A.J.* vol. XXXII (1938), pp. 424 *et seq.*; Guggenheim, *Traité*, p. 471; Clute, *The International Legal Status of Austria*, (1962), pp. 82 *et seq*. The Austrian debt also included the pre-1914 debts. In respect of these agreement was reached between Germany and the *Caisse commune des porteurs des dettes publiques autrichiennes* in 1952. The Rome Agreement of 1952 signed at the International Conference on Austrian External Debts dealt with the question of global interest on these loans. For details see *Report of the Council of the Corporation of Foreign Bondholders* (1964), p. 79.
4 337 H.C. Deb. 5s., c. 34. The Austrian debts which affected Great Britain were the Austrian Guaranteed International Loan, 1933–53, of which the amount guaranteed and outstanding in 1938 was £3,824,500; the Austrian Conversion Loan, 1934–59, of which the amount issued in London and outstanding was £10,082,200; and a direct loan of £2,473,000, 332 H.C. Deb. 5s., col. 10. On 1 May 1938 the Prime Minister stated that the British Government's guarantee was unaffected by the annexation: 335 H.C. Deb. 5s., col. 494. The Swiss Federal Court held in 1940 that the obligations of the Austrian fiscus had continued: *Blätter für zürcherische Rechtsprechung* (1940), p. 318.
5 Hackworth, *Dig.* vol. I, p. 543.

it is believed that the weight of authority clearly supports the general doctrine of international law founded upon obvious principles of justice that in case of absorption of a state, the substituted sovereignty assumes the debts and obligations of the absorbed state, and takes the burdens with the benefits. A few exceptions to this general proposition have sometimes been asserted, but these exceptions appear to find no application to the circumstances of the instant case.[1]

On the 16th of the same month the *Reichsminister* of Economic Affairs stated in reply that 'neither by international law nor in the interest of economic policy, nor morally, is there any obligation on the part of the *Reich* to acknowledge the legal responsibility for Austria's Federal debts'. He did not attempt to deny that principles of international law on the question do exist, but rather sought to exclude Austria's debts from the operation of such principles by asserting, first, that the law of State succession does not apply in the case of the self-extinction of a debtor State; secondly, that the political character of the Austrian debts removed them from the category of legal obligations to which the law of State succession applies; and thirdly, that there were historical instances in which other States, notably Great Britain, France and the United States, had declined to assume responsibility for the payment of debts.[2] On 17 November 1938 the German Foreign Office communicated with the United States Government, declaring that, after careful study of the pertinent procedures and principles based upon international law, it 'was not of the opinion that it was under any legal obligation to assume the foreign debts of the former Austrian Federal Government', and that, supported by historical precedents, it took a negative stand with regard to the debts of the Austrian Government. It repeated this on 3 January 1939, whereupon the United States, on 20 January, replied that it could not accept the legal interpretation of Germany.[3]

At the time of the German annexation of Austria the latter was burdened with six categories of debt. These were, first, the debts of Austria–Hungary, which had been assumed by the Federal Republic of Austria and were administered out of a common fund established by the Protocol of Innsbruck in 1923; secondly, certain urgent loan raisings immediately after the First World War, which were subject to general security on the assets and revenues of Austria: these ranked after the payment of reparations, and took first priority after the suspension of reparations payment with the moratorium of 1931; thirdly, the Seventh International Loan of

[1] *Ibid.* p. 545.
[2] *The Times*, 17 June 1938, p. 16; see Garner in *A.J.* vol. XXXII (1938), pp. 766–75.
[3] Hyde, vol. I, p. 419; see Garner in *A.J.* vol. XXXII (1938), pp. 421 and 766 *et seq.*; R.I.I.A. *Docs. on Int. Aff. 1938*, vol. II, pp. 100–1.

1930–57 which had been invested in the Railways and Post and Telegraph Department: as a condition of this raising, Austria had to obtain the consent of the creditors of the same category to the hypothecation with first priority of the assets and revenues on customs and the State tobacco monopoly: the loan was administered through the Bank of International Settlements; fourthly, the International Loan of 1933–53 which had been guaranteed in respect of specific parts by six States: this loan was hypothecated on the customs and tobacco reveunes and took second priority: it was regulated according to a Protocol signed at Geneva on 15 July 1932; fifthly, the International Conversion Loan, 1934–59 which had converted a loan of 1923–43 and which was guaranteed in different proportions by eight States; sixthly, debts in respect of Austria's assumption of liability in respect of the Österreichische Kreditanstalt which had gone into liquidation in 1931.[1] Germany ceased payment of Austrian debts on 1 June 1938.[2]

On 16 May 1938 the Under-Secretary for Foreign Affairs stated in the House of Commons that

> on 23rd March His Majesty's Embassy in Berlin were informed that the German Government desired to revise the Anglo-German Payments Agreements of 1st November, 1934, in order to meet the commercial questions arising from the inclusion of Austria in the *Reich*. On 12th April the German Government were informed in reply that His Majesty's Government were prepared to enter into discussions which would cover both the trade and financial interests of the United Kingdom. It was stated that His Majesty's Government assumed that the German Government accepted full responsibility for all financial liabilities of the former Austrian Government in respect of its external indebtedness. The German Government have now informed His Majesty's Embassy that they are willing to make the problem of Austrian foreign indebtedness one of the subjects of the negotiations which are due to begin on the 24th May. His Majesty's Government, for their part, are prepared to take the opportunity afforded by the negotiations to discuss this matter with the German Government, but I ought to make it clear that they consider that the German Government should negotiate arrangements on an international basis providing for payment of all issues of Austrian Government loans.[3]

The Chancellor of the Exchequer informed the House on 1 July 1938 that the British and German delegations had arrived at a settlement. 'Without prejudice to the question of legal liability', the German Government would reimburse the United Kingdom Government any sums paid in respect of their guarantees of the Austrian Guaranteed Loans and assume the full service of bonds of these loans owned by British holders on 1 July 1938.[4]

1 Paenson, p. 144.   2 *Ibid.* p. 145.
3 336 H.C. Deb. 5s., col. 6.   4 337 H.C. Deb. 5s., col. 2362.

Under the agreement with the United Kingdom,[1] Germany, without assuming any legal obligation, undertook responsibility with respect to that part of the Austrian debt which was guaranteed by the United Kingdom. Germany agreed to pay off entirely those bonds belonging to persons resident in the United Kingdom or ordinarily carrying on business there, to British subjects, independently of their place of residence, to companies incorporated under English law, or to British protected persons provided the bonds were denominated in pounds sterling; and also to redeem bonds denominated in other currencies if the holders were resident in the United Kingdom or were companies incorporated under English law. Germany also undertook responsibility in respect of British titles to the 7 per cent 1930–57 loan and the obligations of the *Österreichische Kreditanstalt*, but the rate of interest was reduced to 5 per cent. This settlement with the United Kingdom was tied up with a general settlement of outstanding financial questions.

The agreement with the United Kingdom was followed by agreements with France on 2 August 1938, the Netherlands on 13 September 1938, Sweden on 28 October 1938, and Belgium on 31 January 1939.[2] In addition to these agreements, Germany offered all the bondholders the right to exchange their Austrian bonds for German bonds *ex gratia*, the German bonds carrying interest at the rate of 4½ per cent. In respect of the Austro-Hungarian Treasury bonds, the offer was promised only to creditors who had resided in Germany at the date of 14 April 1938 and who resided there at the date of publication of the offer. In respect of the other issues, the offer was addressed to all creditors, whether resident in Germany or not, and irrespective of their nationality. Most of the international raisings of Austria had been expressed in pounds sterling or French francs, and their conversion into German loans made them subject to German denomination. The rate of exchange of the raisings expressed in foreign money varied according to the loan. The pound sterling was fixed at 11.50 marks in the case of the 1933–53 loan but at 12.97 in the case of the 1930–57 loan. The French franc was fixed at 0.07 marks in respect of the loans carrying 5 per cent and at 0.078 marks in respect of those carrying 5½ per cent.[3] Bonds converted into German issues suffered the ordinary fate of other German borrowings in the currency reform of 1948.

An International Conference on Austrian External Debts was held in Rome in 1952 of Austria and the governments which guaranteed the 1933 and 1934 loans, and also creditors. At the same time settlement was

[1] Cmd. 5788.
[2] Brandt in *Z.f.a.ö.R.u.V.* vol. IX, p. 128.
[3] Paenson, p. 149.

reached with Germany respecting its liability for Austrian debts during the period of the *Anschluss*. Austria resumed servicing its debt in 1954.[1]

(vii) *The annexation of Danzig by Poland, 1945*

When Poland assumed responsibility for Danzig in 1946 the British and Polish Governments agreed that the question of the indebtedness of the Free City of Danzig would be settled at a later date in the light of the relevant provisions of a future German peace treaty.[2] The League Loans Committee protested to the British Treasury that, in view of the remote prospects of such a treaty and of the fact that Poland was *de facto* in possession of the City, 'the Polish Government should be urged to recognize the normal obligations of a successor State and assume Danzig's liabilities'. The Polish Government has declined to discuss the question since that date.[3]

II. Federation

The case of federation of a State, or the formation of a real or personal union, is only a particular application of the rules above suggested. Everything depends on the extent to which the fiscal autonomy of the federating State is preserved. Should the constitution of the federation deprive the State of its competence to incur financial obligations or raise revenues for their discharge the federation becomes directly responsible for reimbursing the creditor. On the other hand, should the constitution recognize such competence, the federation is in the same position as an annexing State which leaves its incorporated territory a fiscal unit.

(i) *The incorporation of Texas into the United States, 1845*

The issue arose with the incorporation of Texas in the United States in 1945. In the first instance Texas ceded all its territory by treaty to the United States, and the latter agreed to assume its debts, which were to be paid in full if they did not exceed $10,000,000, and if they did were to be reduced *pro rata*.[4] The Texas debt consisted chiefly of an issue of treasury bills, a number of which were owned by British nationals. The treaty was not ratified by the United States, and Texas was annexed by Act of Congress. An agreement was subsequently entered into by which Texas modified its boundary and relinquished claims upon the United States for

---

1 Clute, *op. cit.*, pp. 90 *et seq*. Austrian State Treaty, *U.N.T.S.*, vol. 217, p. 233, art. 28 at p. 281. For details see the *Report of the Council of the Corporation of Foreign Bondholders* (1964), p. 79.
2 Trade Agreement of 9 June 1947.
3 *Report of the Council of the Corporation of Foreign Bondholders* (1964), p. 302.
4 Moore, *Dig.* vol. I, p. 343.

Acquired Rights and the National Debt

liability for debts, and the United States undertook to pay Texas the $10,000,000 in stock. Half of this stock was to be held until creditors possessing Texan bonds or stock certificates in respect of which duties on imports had been specifically pledged, had filed a release of all claims against the United States.[1] In 1851 the second half of the stock was issued, and in the following year Texas legislated for payment of only part of its debt.[2] Great Britain took up the matter on behalf of its nationals who held Texan stock certificates, and in 1854 brought a claim before a mixed commission which had been set up under the Claims Convention of 1853.

The argument turned on the issue whether or not Texas retained its fiscal autonomy. The Finance Committee of the Senate had already reported that in its view the United States had become liable for the Texan debts,[3] but the Attorney-General was of opinion that 'it by no means follows that the United States have assumed any liability thereby, or impliedly recognized the existence of any liability on their part'. To what extent, and when, the United States would in justice or equity be liable, if ever, to the creditors of the Republic of Texas 'because of a lien held by them upon the revenue of that Republic to arise from duties on imports, and the transfer, by the act of annexation, to the United States of the sole and exclusive power to levy money by duties and customs, imports and tonnage' was not a question which the Executive of the United States could decide. That question belonged properly to the Congress of the United States.[4]

The British Commissioner argued that the capacity of Texas to discharge the debt had been impaired by the transfer to the United States of the competence to levy duties.[5] He said:

> The obligation of Texas to pay her debts is not in dispute, nor has it been argued that the mere act of her annexation to the United States has transferred her liabilities to the Federal Government, though certainly, as regards foreign governments, the United States is now bound to see that the obligations of Texas are fulfilled. It is the transfer of the integral revenues of Texas to the Federal Government that is relied on as creating the new liability.[6]

The United States Commissioner, on the other hand, rejected the view that the competence of Texas had been impaired.

> Whether the United States should be liable for this indebtedness I do not feel called on to decide. It is clear Texas is not exonerated from the debt.[7] ... Texas is

---

1 *Ibid.* p. 344.   2 Feilchenfeld, p. 274.
3 *Ibid.* p. 281. The liability of the United States was alleged to arise, not from the merger, but from the transfer of imposts to federal hands, see Wilkinson, p. 78.
4 6 *Op. A.-G.* p. 130; Moore, *Dig.* vol. I, p. 345.
5 *Ibid.* p. 346.   6 Wharton, vol. I, p. 23.   7 *Ibid.* p. 21.

still a sovereign State, with all the rights and capacities of government except that her international relations are controlled by the United States, and she has transferred to the United States her right of duties on imports.[1]

The Commissioners having disagreed, the matter was referred to the umpire, who gave a decision on purely technical grounds. The arbitration was thus inconclusive in the law of State succession, but it is important for the emphasis placed on the fiscal autonomy of an incorporated area, and for a discussion on the nature of revenue pledges.[2]

(ii) *The federation of British colonies*

In the cases of the federation of colonies into the unions of Canada, Australia and South Africa, all the constituent units remained charged with their own debts.[3]

(iii) *The creation of the United Arab Republic, 1958*

Under the Provisional Constitution of the United Arab Republic[4] only the National Assembly had the power to contract loans. The implication is that neither of the regions representing Syria and Egypt had this power. During a transitional period the two regions maintained separate budgets, but a single budget had already been projected pursuant to article 70 of the Provisional Constitution when Syria withdrew from the Republic. The U.A.R. would seem to have been the only entity competent to service the debts of the two regions, and the International Monetary Fund recognized this to the extent of regarding the U.A.R. as the debtor, though, pending the creation of a central banking system, Fund operations were based on the separate identities of the regions for borrowing and quota purposes.[5]

(iv) *The incorporation of the Baltic States in the Soviet Union, 1940*

When the Soviet incorporated Latvia, Lithuania and Estonia and transferred Vilna from Poland to Lithuania the debts of all four entities went

[1] *Ibid.* p. 23.
[2] Moore, *I.A.* vol. IV, p. 3593. Subsequently Congress enacted that the Treasury should pay to the creditors the sum of $7,750,000 to be apportioned among the holders *pro rata*: Moore, *Dig.* vol. I, p. 347. The issue in the case was restated subsequently by the American Commissioners during the negotiations preliminary to the Treaty of Paris, 1898. In a memorandum rebutting certain Spanish arguments, they said: 'Texas was an independent state which yielded up its independence to the United States and became a part of the American Republic. In view of this extinction of the national sovereignty the United States discharged the Texan debt': *ibid.* p. 372.
[3] British North America Act, 1867, 30 Vict., c. 3, s. 111; Commonwealth of Australia Constitution Act, 1900, 63 & 64 Vict., c. 17, s. 105; South Africa Act, 1909, 9 Edw. VII, c. 9, s. 124.
[4] Art. 29.
[5] See *infra*, vol. II, p. 194; Cotran, in *I.C.L.Q.* vol. VIII (1959), p. 346.

into default. In 1959 discussions were held in Moscow between the British Government and the Soviet, but the latter refused to discuss claims which arose before 1939. Lists of registered British claims have been presented to the Soviet, but examination of them has taken longer than expected. A proposal has been made to transfer to creditors the assets of the debts which have been blocked in the United Kingdom since 1963.[1]

III. Dismemberment

When the entire territory of a State is divided up among several successors, whether the latter be a group of annexing States, or States formed out of the extinguished State itself, the fiscal composition of the area is likewise divided. There is no question of the successor States preserving the fiscal competence of the debtor. It follows, therefore, that the several successor States, in the act of destroying this competence, render themselves responsible for their predecessor's financial engagements and must effect restitution.[2] This can be only a very general principle, and its application is always attended with the gravest difficulties. There is little agreement among writers[3] on the key of distribution, and as any assessment of the degree of benefit to each successor State is virtually impossible, the doctrine of unjust enrichment does not give much assistance.

Where the debt is secured and the security passes intact to one of the successor States, it would seem that this State alone should become responsible for the debt, on the ground that there must be a presumption that the area benefited by the loan is the area upon which the loan is secured.[4] This again can be no more than a very general principle, and there is no evidence that it has been acknowledged in practice.[5] On the other hand, where the security is dismembered along with the State,

---

[1] *Report of the Council of the Corporation of Foreign Bondholders* (1964), p. 314.
[2] Feilchenfeld, p. 679; Sack, *Dettes publiques*, pp. 205–7; Huber, p. 91; Meyer-Lindenberg, p. 86; Phillimore, vol. I, p. 211; Dahm, vol. I, p. 116. Cf. Sauer, p. 150; Verdross–Zemanek, p. 196; and Ross, p. 130, who require an agreement of repartition. Schönborn, though generally negative, concedes that a repartition is usual, p. 118.
[3] Halleck says that the obligations accruing before the division are ratably binding upon the different parts: vol. I, p. 91. Phillipson finds that as the debt has been incurred for the whole country the successors ought to assume a fair proportion but it is not clear if he intends this to be a rule of law, or of equity: p. 322. Feilchenfeld's maintenance theory, having no theoretical basis, does not assist the problem of dismemberment. There is no State or fiscal unit which can maintain debts, and some juridical concept of repartition must be discovered.
[4] Sack, *Dettes publiques*, p. 205.
[5] Sack demonstrates the practical impossibility that may be found in carrying out the obligations of the security: p. 211. If it is impossible to maintain the security he suggests that the debt should be divided in proportion to the respective contributions of the areas: *ibid.* p. 217.

similar reasoning suggests that the proportion of the debt to be borne by each successor should be in relation to the value of the security acquired by it.

(i) *The dissolution of the United Netherlands, 1830*

The establishment of Belgium in 1830 as an independent State has usually been regarded as a dismemberment of the personality of the United Netherlands.[1] The London Conference passed a resolution to the effect that questions of debt had already given rise to decisions in the past the principles of which, far from being new, it was said, had at all times governed the reciprocal relations of States, and been consecrated by special conventions.[2] The debt was to have been divided between Belgium and the Netherlands in proportion to their respective revenues,[3] but after objection had been raised to this test it was enacted that Belgium contribute half of the 'new debts', that is, those contracted since the union, and be exclusively charged with the 'old debts' of the Austrian Netherlands.[4]

(ii) *The dissolution of the Union of Colombia, 1829*

When the Union of Colombia was divided into its constituent States, New Granada, Ecuador and Venezuela, the King's Advocate advised the Foreign Office that

all the three States will continue responsible for any Debt due from Colombia, contracted during their Union. If it should be proposed to apportion this debt between the several States, and that each should be responsible only for a part, the consent of His Majesty's Government, if it has any demands upon the Government of Colombia, must be obtained to such an alteration of its Security.[5]

This assertion of joint responsibility was not pursued, however, when in December 1834 the debt of Colombia was divided in the proportion of New Granada 50 per cent, Ecuador 21½ per cent and Venezuela 28½ per cent, and in a letter of 7 May 1835 the British Ambassador asked Ecuador to pay only its 'share'.[6]

1 Pradier-Fodéré, vol. I, p. 251; Fauchille, vol. I, p. 380.
2 M.R. (Suppl.), vol. XIV, p. 164, Protocol 12; B.F.S.P. vol. XXVII, p. 990.
3 Act of the Draft Treaty, M.R. (Suppl.), vol. XV, p. 269.
4 Treaty of 1831, M.R. (Suppl.), vol. XVI, p. 398, art. 13. This was confirmed in the Treaty of London, 1839, M.R. (Suppl.), vol. XX, pt. 2, p. 773, art. 13 at p. 782. See Sack, *Dettes publiques*, pp. 279 *et seq.*; Bustamante, vol. III, pp. 336-7.
5 Opinion of 3 June 1834, F.O. 83/2254; O'Connell, Appendix, no. 9.
6 Moore, *I.A.* vol. IV, p. 3636. There was considerable correspondence between Great Britain on the one hand, and the three States on the other, in which each was separately asked to satisfy the creditors of Colombia, B.F.S.P. vol. XXVIII (1938), pp. 958 *et seq.*, especially p. 997. Colombia had raised a 10 per cent loan in

Ecuador subsequently fixed a time limit for the presentation of claims, and the validity of this action was discussed by the Queen's Advocate, Sir Robert Phillimore, in 1863. He advised that 'the obligation of this State to pay its *quota* of the debt contracted by the original Republic of Colombia, in which it was incorporated at the time when the debt was contracted, appears not to be directly controverted'. That this conclusion was reached not only upon consideration of the fact that the debt had been divided but also upon 'right and justice' would appear from the quotations approved from Grotius, Kent and Story. Phillimore's conclusion was that 'apart from the consideration of Municipal Act', the obligation of Ecuador was binding 'according to the general principles of Public International Law', and the only question to be considered was whether or not Ecuador could 'put a bar to the satisfaction of a just debt by fixing a period of time within which it must be demanded'. He said: 'I am not aware of any principle of reason or justice, or any dictum of authority which enables the debtor State to cancel its obligation to a Foreign Creditor by importing an *ex post facto* condition, without the consent of the Foreign Creditor, into the original obligation. I am of opinion that this cannot lawfully be done.'[1]

(iii) *The dismemberment of Czechoslovakia, 1939*

Following the dismemberment of Czechoslovakia in 1939, a partition of the Czech debt was devised by agreement between the successor States. Slovakia and Hungary did not participate in the repartition of debts relating to military expenditure because these were considered odious. In the agreement of 4 October 1941,[2] the *Reich* assumed the obligation of discharging 10 milliards of crowns, being a proportion of the debt of Czechoslovakia, including the consolidated internal debt, the floating debt, and the debts of government departments respecting social security, public utilities and pensions. Respecting the debts of the constituent provinces of Czechoslovakia, the *Reich* assumed responsibility for debts

1820 and 6 per cent loan at 88½ in 1824, but both were in default at the time of the dissolution. New Granada became responsible for £4,903,205, Ecuador for £2,108,377 and Venezuela for £2,794,826. Histories of these debts will be found in the *Report of the Council of the Corporation of Foreign Bondholders* (1939), pp. 195, 226 and 509 *et seq.*

[1] Opinion of 4 November 1863, F.O. 83/2263; O'Connell, Appendix, no. 23. The debts of each of the three States, as distinct from the debt of the Union itself, would appear to have been regarded as local debts which continued to bind them. The Queen's Advocate in an Opinion of 23 March 1867, concerning the value of bonds issued by the Government of New Granada before the formation of the Union in 1824, was clearly of the view that neither the formation nor the subsequent dissolution of the Union affected Colombia's obligation: F.O. 83/2257; O'Connell, Appendix, no. 32.   [2] *RGBl.* II, 24 April 1942.

secured by mortgage on property transferred to it, and debts due to all persons resident outside the frontiers of the Protectorate of Bohemia, and also the debts of all the former Czech armed forces dating before 15 March 1939, independently of the place of residence of the creditors. An exchange of bond certificates was effected between the Protectorate and the *Reich*, and German Treasury bonds at 3½ per cent were issued, inscribed at their nominal value in the *Reichsschuldbuch*. The Protectorate succeeded to the remainder of the Czech debts amounting to 52 milliards of crowns, of which about 8½ milliards represented the external debt of 10 milliards—those debts classified as odious. Slovakia took over 1,850 millions of crowns in respect of bonds located in Slovakia, and also a proportion of the consolidated debt and judgment debts against the State, as well as outstanding lottery coupons. The settlement was complicated by transactions with Germany respecting military aid. Hungary took over a sum of 1,678,959,959.60 crowns which was reduced on conversion and reassessment of the interest rate to a final sum of 1,580,246,874.50. All certificates circulating on Hungarian territory were transferred to the Protectorate, and Hungary assumed an obligation to pay 5.07 per cent of its calculated part of the total debt. The final amortization of the debt was to be a complicated procedure extending until 1987.[1]

In the agreement of 4 October 1941 the Reich agreed to contribute to unliquidated debts of Czechoslovakia only when the claimants were German subjects.

(iv) *The dismemberment of Yugoslavia, 1941*

All the debts of Yugoslavia after its dismemberment in 1941 were converted into a single debt, and distributed in the proportions of Croatia 42 per cent, Serbia 29 per cent, Italy, Hungary and Bulgaria 8 per cent, and Germany 5 per cent. The basis of repartition was the population and the economic potential of the territories. All mortgages on public immovable property acquired by the conquering States were released. The debts of Yugoslavia respecting the nationalization of the railway and agrarian reform were to be assumed by the acquiring States on whose territory the assets appropriated were located. Each acquiring State would honour the guarantees of Yugoslavia affecting its territory. If a guarantee was in the form of a guarantee of mortgage, the responsible State would be the State on whose territory the mortgaged property was located. In other situations, the location of the creditor was the test, and if the creditor was a company whose assets were located in the territory of several of the acquiring States, then an equitable repartition was to occur.[2]

[1] Paenson, pp. 112 *et seq.*   [2] *Ibid.* p. 153.

(v) *The dismemberment of Ruanda-Urundi, 1962*

The budget estimate for 1962 for Ruanda-Urundi showed a deficit of nearly 800 million francs or almost 70 per cent of the total estimated revenue. This was on the assumption that services would be jointly maintained on independence. In the event of their not being maintained and services being decentralized, the deficit would be increased and the collection of duties and taxes would be adversely affected as the cost of administration increased.[1] The issued currency at the end of December 1961 amounted to 1,773 million francs of which 900 million represented the total of sums deposited with the Bank of Issue and private banks. In view of this limited monetary base, the setting up of two distinct monetary systems and two banking organizations would present endless difficulties.[2] The population density of Ruanda-Urundi was considerably greater than that of its neighbouring States, but the annual *per capita* income, estimated at 2,500 francs, was far lower.[3] At a conference of the Governments of Rwanda and Burundi called at Addis Ababa in April 1962 by the United Nations Commission for Ruanda-Urundi, an agreement on economic union between the two new countries after independence was signed.[4] It was agreed that a monetary union be maintained, and that this be administered by a common central banking institution, namely the existing Bank of Issue of Rwanda and Burundi situated at Usumbura. This would continue to perform its functions in accordance with its existing Statute and Regulations, which could only be amended by agreement between the two governments. The bank would have the exclusive right to issue and administer the common currency of the Union, and it would both serve as Treasury for each of the governments and organize their exchange services and foreign exchange control and their licensing systems. It would also act as adviser on financial and monetary matters to both governments as well as make short-term advances to them. It was also agreed that there should be a customs union with a joint customs office and a common tariff. Eighty per cent of the customs revenue would be equally divided between the two governments and the balance paid into a blocked account.

A common taxation service was to be set up and taxes would be levied at the same rates and in accordance with the same regulations in both countries. The revenue would be divided after deduction of the

1 U.N. Doc. A/5126/Add. 1, 30 May 1962, Annex VII, p. 3.
2 *Ibid.* p. 5.
3 *Ibid.* p. 6. Further information is available in the extract from the Report of the U.N. Commission in Annex VII.   4 Annex XVI.

cost of collection according to a formula to be determined on the basis of a technical study to be undertaken. In the meantime, it was agreed that the balance of revenue would be divided in the proportion of 35 per cent for Rwanda and 35 per cent for Burundi, the balance of 30 per cent being paid into a blocked account.

A joint Civil Service Commission would also be appointed in which both Governments would be equally represented to study the administration and budgetary problems involved in operating these and other common services. Finally, there would be a Council of the Union composed of four ministers from each government, which would assist the two governments in co-ordinating the main principles of their economic, financial and commercial policy and would apply the joint decisions of the two governments concerning common services and supervise the execution of those decisions.

No particular reference was made in the agreement to the public debt of Ruanda-Urundi because the Economic Committee organized by the United Nations Commission, whose report formed the basis of the agreement between the two governments, found that a study of the public debt problem could only be undertaken in consultation with Belgium, and that further economic and financial discussions should be undertaken.

(vi) *The dissolution of the Federation of Rhodesia and Nyasaland, 1963*

The Order in Council dissolving the Federation[1] provided for the distribution of the Federal Public Debt. The following categories of debt were nominated: categories A and B consisted of local registered stock; category C of sundry loans; category D of registered stock; category E of external bonds; category F of one International Bank Loan; category G of a second International Bank Loan, the United Kingdom credit of 1962 and the foreign railways loan. The apportionments between the three Territories varied according to the category of debt. The liability of the Federation in respect of categories A, B and C was transferred to the respective Territory, which was authorized to convert the loans. Interest would be paid and bonds be redeemable at the place stated in the titles, and in the currency of the Territory of issue, and on the dates and at the percentage rate applicable, but all rights and trusts would be preserved. Territorial sinking funds would be established in lieu of those of the Federation.[2] With respect to the outstanding external debt, categories D, E, F and G, variable apportionments were also effected. Bonds or stock issued under Federal legislation would be valid and the holders would

[1] S.I. 1963, no. 2085.   [2] S. 12.

continue to enjoy identical rights, but the Territories would assume several liability.[1] The effect of this would be to split the bonds into three. Rights under the Colonial Stock Acts were preserved.[2]

The Federal debt amounted to £264m. This included loans for hydro-electric projects amounting to £26m., liability for which would be shared equally between Northern Rhodesia and Southern Rhodesia. Liability respecting the railway debt would also be shared between the two Territories. Territorial loans taken over by the Federation and amounting to £90m. would revert, and the balance of general funded debt was £118m. The apportionments averaged a distribution of 52 per cent to Southern Rhodesia (£161,781,000 out of £269,428,000), 37 per cent to Northern Rhodesia (£88,250,000), and 11 per cent to Nyasaland (£19,397,000), calculated on the respective share of the federal assets allocated to each territory. Moving the approval of the Order in the House of Commons on 17 December 1963, Mr Sandys said that a division on the basis of allocation of assets seemed the only possibility.[3]

This mode of repartition was controverted by the Territorial Governments, members of the United Kingdom Parliament and associations of bondholders. During the negotiations preceding the decision to dissolve the Federation, the Federal Government argued that the United Kingdom should, in the interests of the Territories and the creditors, assume responsibility for the Federal debt, and look to the Territories for reimbursement on a scale related to the Territories' assets and revenues.[4] In the House of Lords on 8 December 1963 Lord Dilhorne stated that the British Government would not give a guarantee in relation to the public debt of the Federation.[5] The Northern Rhodesian Government stated on 16 December 1963 that it had at no time agreed to the allocation laid down in the Order, and had only reluctantly acquiesced in the settlement. It objected that the debt calculation did not take into account 'the very large net contribution by a territory to the other territories of the Federation since 1953', amounting to £73m., or the 'very large' contribution by Northern Rhodesia from current revenue to the federal capital account.[6]

At the dissolution of the Federal Parliament on 10 December 1963, the Minister of Finance stated that the Order had never been communicated for criticism to the Federal Government. The Governments of

1 S. 16.   2 Ibid.
3 The Times, 18 December 1963, p. 7.
4 680 H.C. Deb. 5s., 11 July 1963, col. 1430.
5 The Times, 16 December 1963, p. 8.
6 Ibid. 17 December 1963, p. 8. Zambia persisted in this claim, but agreed to waive it in virtue of the aid granted by the U.K. Government. See 709 H.C. Deb. 5s., 23 March 1965, p. 76.

Northern and Southern Rhodesia, and the Federal Government, had criticized the proposed apportionment, and minority reports had been made to the British Government, which the latter had rejected. The Federal Government had been concerned at the diminution of the security of federal stockholders, who had virtually unanimously rejected the treatment proposed for them.[1] In a letter written by the Federal Treasury to all holders of federal stock in November 1963 it was disclosed that the British Government would not join in any action designed to preserve the value of investment in that stock. The Territorial Governments had rejected joint and several liability, and the British Government would not act as guarantor. It was believed that the security for the stock would be prejudiced,[2] especially since creditors would have to look to three Territorial Governments, one of which, Nyasaland, would be faced with an initial budgetary deficit of £5m. a year.[3] At the Central Africa Conference in July 1963 the Federal Government had submitted a paper pointing out that its financial obligations rested on the resources and reflected the credit-worthiness of the federal economy. Dissolution of the Federation as an economic unit would involve a loss of economic strength, and the separate Territorial economies should not be expected between them to meet the obligations which had been incurred on a scale appropriate to the Federation as a whole. Since the dissolution was an exercise of Britain's sovereign power, Britain should assume responsibility.[4] Southern Rhodesia had pointed out that, since some federal assets would depreciate on reversion to the Territories, an apportionment calculated on them would be unfair.[5]

The Colonial Secretary, referring to the charge that the Order radically altered the nature of the backing for the loans, justified the action of the British Government in not guaranteeing them by drawing attention to the facts precipitating the dissolution, and refuting the thesis that the dissolution was effected by the United Kingdom. The principle of joint and several responsibility was incompatible with the principle of dissolution.

4. PARTIAL SUCCESSION

I. The Unsecured Debt

Where only part of the debtor State is absorbed, both its international personality and its fiscal competence remain undisturbed, although its paying capacity may be diminished. The debtor State is still the debtor,

[1] *The Times*, 11 December 1963, p. 10.
[2] Ibid. 26 November 1963, p. 9.
[3] Ibid. 27 September 1963, p. 9.
[4] Cmnd. 2093, p. 7.   [5] Ibid. p. 8.

and if the debt is unsecured the legal relationship between it and the creditor is intact.[1] There is no interference by the successor State with the acquired rights of the creditor, and although the former is enriched by the loan, it is not enriched to the direct and immediate detriment of the latter. There can, therefore, be no obligation imposed on the successor State with respect to the creditor.

Since the doctrine of acquired rights and its corollary doctrine of unjust enrichment do not operate between the successor State and its predecessor, they do not assist in the determination of the question that arises in the case of partial succession: must the successor State assume a proportional part of its predecessor's public debt? Such an obligation must be one imposed by international law as a specific rule since it is not demanded by any general principle. The precedents on the topic, however, are confused and contradictory. The justice of a repartition has been universally admitted,[2] but the impossible task of assessing a stable basis for repartition has frustrated the growth of a consistent practice, and prompted a wide divergency of view among publicists.[3]

---

[1] See Martens, vol. I, p. 370; Piédelièvre, vol. I, p. 122; Hall, p. 116, n. 1; Fitzmaurice in Hague *Recueil*, vol. LXXIII (1948), p. 289; Huber, p. 81.

[2] The obligation of repartition has been asserted by a considerable bulk of writers: Despagnet, p. 132; Fiore, *Int. Law Cod.* p. 141; *Nouv. droit. int.* vol. I, p. 360; Rivier, vol. I, p. 70; Hatschek, p. 129; Calvo, vol. I, p. 249; Szászy in *Rev. de droit int.* vol. V (1930), p. 587; Hershey, p. 222; Reuter, p. 127; Wheaton, s. 20; Gould, p. 415; Selosse, pp. 166, 169; Verdross–Zemanek, p. 195; Delbez, p. 180; Sibert, vol. I, p. 211; de Louter, who holds the rule to be without the slighest doubt, p. 228; Podesta Costa, p. 82; Strupp, who holds that the greater number of authors, and of examples of State practice, are almost unanimous: *Éléments*, vol. I, p. 108; Cavaglieri, in *Annuaire de l'Institut de Droit International, session de Paris* (1934), vol. XXXIV, p. 214; Huber, whose view is that creditors lend to a territorial whole with economic resources, and that the owner of these resources is liable for a proportional part of the debt relating to the territory in which they are located: p. 88; Taylor, *A Treatise on International Public Law* (1901), p. 201. Appleton's view is that the debtor itself is divided, and the ceded area remains 'charged' with a proportional part of the debt. The ceded area, which was a debtor before the cession, has merely changed its status, and he supports this theory by analogy with the *capitis diminutio* theory of Roman law: p. 150. Piédelièvre expresses himself doubtful: pp. 130 *et seq.*; Phillipson thinks that the successors must assume a 'fair proportion'; but it is not certain if he means this as a rule of law, p. 322. See to the contrary: Pradier-Fodéré, who bases his denial on the precedent of Alsace-Lorraine in 1871, vol. I, p. 274; Hall, p. 116, n. 1; Halleck, vol. I, p. 91; Oppenheim, vol. I, p. 161; Keith, p. 60. Guggenheim, pp. 95–113 says equity dictates a taking over of part of the debt, and this has stimulated a practice. Also, Zorn, pp. 31, 77; Sereni, vol. I, p. 406, Hold-Ferneck, vol. I, p. 115; Schönborn, pp. 56–8, 100–6; Gareis, p. 67; Sauer, 151; Waldkirch, p. 119; Dahm, vol. I. p. 115. Rousseau, p. 280; de Visscher, p. 191; Cavaré, vol. I, p. 376; Udina in Hague *Recueil*, vol. LXIV (1933), pp. 755–6; Hackworth, *Dig.* vol, I, p. 538.

[3] In *Sechter v. Ministry of the Interior* a Roumanian court held that international law sanctions the principle of universal succession to rights and obligations only in the case of total succession: *Ann. Dig.* vol. V, Case no. 37. See also *Mordcovici v. General*

The liability of a successor State to assume a proportional part of the unsecured debt of its predecessor, when the latter's personality continues, cannot be said with any certainty to be as yet part of international law. The general principle governing the Peace Treaties is at the most one which is, in the words of Hyde, 'indicative of the requirements of international law', and will 'exercise a profound influence in the future'.[1] He continues:

It is not without significance, that the principle of apportionment was applied to the general as well as the local indebtedness of Germany, a result doubtless attributable to the opinion of the principal Allied and Associated Governments that both forms of obligation were to be deemed as closely and beneficially related to the territory transferred as to that regained by the former sovereign.[2]

The tendency towards repartition clearly evidenced in the most recent practice leads to the conviction, it is submitted, that a positive rule of international law is in the process of crystallization.

(i) *General practice, 1783–1825*

The United States did not take over any portion of the public debt of Great Britain in 1783.[3] Proportional distribution of debts, however, was effected in the formation of the Rhenish Confederation,[4] in the Treaty of Tilsit,[5] and in a convention between Prussia and Westphalia in 1811.[6] The national debt was first treated as such in the Treaty of Kiel, when Norway was ceded by Denmark to Sweden in 1814. It was considered, on analogy with secured debts, as 'resting on the whole Monarchy'.[7] The distribution in this case was followed in the Prussian treaties of 1815.[8] Brazil took over a portion of the debt of Portugal in 1825 as part of a general adjustment of financial arrangements.[9]

Administration of Posts and Telegraph, ibid. Case no. 38. In 1850 the Court of Appeal at Jena delivered a judgment based on two opinions rendered by the law faculties of Halle and Berlin relating to the obligations of Saxe-Weimar to liquidate a debt of the Prussian treasury in ceded territory. The Berlin opinion held that 'if a part of the territory is ceded, it cannot be said that the personal obligations of the ceding Power pass wholly or partly to the acquiring state unless this has been expressly stipulated. The Power originally obligated remains the real debtor, although its means have been diminished': Feilchenfeld, pp. 219 *et seq.*

1 Vol. I, p. 409.
2 *Ibid.* p. 407.
3 Feilchenfeld, p. 53; Wilkinson, p. 72.
4 *M.R.* (*Suppl.*), vol. IV, p. 313, art. 30.
5 *Ibid.* p. 444, art. 24.
6 *Idem*, vol. V, p. 363, art. 16.
7 *Ibid.* p. 666, art. 5.
8 *Idem*, vol. VI, p. 349; *idem*, vol. VIII, p. 150.
9 Treaty of Rio de Janeiro, 1825, *M.R.* (*Suppl.*), vol. X, pt. II, p. 796, arts. 1 and 2.

(ii) *The secession of Texas from Mexico, 1840*

When Texas became independent in 1840 British creditors of Mexico felt their security threatened, and some correspondence took place between Great Britain and Texas. The Texas point of view was presented on 5 November 1840 to Lord Palmerston as follows: 'I must enter a *protest tanto* against the inference that Texas is bound in any degree, for any portion of the said Debt, on any principle of international Law, or by any one obligation of private justice.' Mexico had violated its agreement with the colonists and had assigned Texan bonds as security after Texas had declared her independence. But as a consideration for a peace treaty, Texas, in a convention with Great Britain, agreed to take upon itself a portion of the debt contracted by Mexico before 1835 amounting to £1,000,000 sterling. The manner and transfer of the debt were to be settled by agreement between Texas and Mexico under mediation of Her Majesty. It was, however, a voluntary consideration, since it was assumed that Texas was 'no more bound to assume that portion of the Public Debt of Mexico, than the thirteen American Colonies, after they achieved their independence were bound to assume a Share of the National Debt of Great Britain'.[1]

(iii) *General practice, 1859–71*

In the Treaty of Zürich, 1859, Sardinia assumed a proportion of the national loan of Austria in 1854.[2] This was regarded by the Austrian Government as 'the recognition of a general principle' which had regulated the repartition of debts up to that time.[3] Metternich's view was that the treaty was an admission of a 'principle generally admitted, in virtue of which each ceded province must continue to support a portion of the charges of the state of which it forms a part'.[4]

The Treaty of Turin, 1860 made provision for a mixed commission to ascertain the 'constitutive part' of Savoy and Nice in the public debt of Sardinia, and implied that the ceded provinces should remain charged with the contributions which they had been accustomed to make to the national debt.[5] This constitutive part was fixed in the convention of the same year.[6]

The preliminary Peace Treaty between Denmark and Prussia of 1864

1 F.O. 75/1. Smith, *Great Britain and the Law of Nations* (1932), vol. I, p. 383.
2 M.N.R.G. vol. XVI, pt. II, p. 539, art. 4.
3 *Idem*, vol. XVII, pt. II, p. 22, art. 2. Convention between France and Sardinia to regulate questions arising out of the reunion of Savoy and Nice to France.
4 *Idem*, vol. XVI, pt. II, p. 516, art. 4.
5 *Fontes Juris Gent.* ser. B, sect. I, vol. I, pt. I, p. 594.
6 *Ibid.* p. 596.

arranged for a general distribution of the debt between Denmark and Schleswig-Holstein in proportion to their populations.[1] The Peace Treaty of Vienna made Denmark the sole debtor, and the ceded territories were to make contributions.[2] In 1864 Italy and France signed a convention by which the former declared its willingness to assume a proportion of the debt of the Papal States.[3] The Treaty of Frankfurt of 1871 was concerned more with the question of an indemnity to Germany than with the question of the distribution of the French national debt or the local debt of Alsace-Lorraine, and no mention of such debts was made.[4]

(iv) *The Act of the Congress of Berlin, 1878*

At the Congress of Berlin, Turkey proposed the allocation to Bulgaria of a portion of the Ottoman public debt.[5] It was asserted that 'participation in the debt is merely the consequence of recognition, or rather of simple admission, of a right of creditors'.[6] It was agreed by all the delegates that Bulgaria should assume some portion of the Ottoman debt.[7] Lord Salisbury regarded the Roumanian and Serbian tributes as part of the security of the Ottoman creditors, 'a pledge which should not be taken away from them'.[8] On the other hand, when Turkey proposed that Russia take over part of the Ottoman debt, along with the territories acquired in Asia, the Russian plenipotentiary contended that this was incompatible with the rights of a conqueror, and the proposal was not pressed.[9] In the final Act of the Congress, Russia did not assume any debts, and there was no mention of Cyprus, Bosnia, or Herzegovina, which were to be administered by Great Britain and Austria. Distribution was made, however, to Bulgaria, Montenegro and Serbia of those portions of the Ottoman public debt which these States 'should support on an equitable basis'.[10]

(v) *General practice, 1903–13*

When Panama became independent in 1903 it did not admit any liability to take over part of the Colombian debt, and all claims of Colombia in this respect were abandoned as part of a general settlement.[11] In the Treaty of Lausanne, 1912, between Italy and Turkey, however, the

1 *M.N.R.G.* vol. XVII, pt. II, p. 470, art. 3. 2 *Ibid.* p. 474, art. 9.
3 *Idem*, vol. XVIII, p. 24, art. 4.
4 *Idem*, vol. XIX, p. 678; see Sack, *Dettes publiques*, p. 81.
5 *B.F.S.P.* vol. LXIX (1878), p. 918. 6 *Ibid.* p. 939.
7 *Ibid.* p. 940. 8 *Ibid.* p. 1066.
9 See C. 2083, at p. 645.
10 *Ibid.* arts. 35 (2) and 42 (2), pp. 685 and 687.
11 Feilchenfeld, pp. 346 *et seq.*

former undertook to pay the latter an annuity towards the amortization of the Ottoman public debt corresponding to the average for the three years preceding the beginning of the war of those revenues from Tripoli which had been used for payment of that debt.[1] The agreement appears to have been solely the result of bargaining.[2]

The committee of experts who sat in Paris in 1913 to resolve on the terms of the armistice to end the First Balkan War evolved the following formula: 'Each of the signatory States of the present Treaty who receives accession of portion of territories hitherto belonging to the Ottoman Empire will support a part of the whole debt of the Ottoman Empire proportionate to the revenue of the ceded territories.' The portion to be assumed was to be calculated on the average contribution made by the territories during the previous three financial years.[3] When the Armistice Conference was convened France proposed an even stronger formula:

> Every cession of territory stipulated for in the present treaty implies [*comportera*] for the cessionary State the obligation to respect the rights which the Imperial Government or other competent Ottoman authorities have constituted for the benefit of third parties. The State shall assume a part of the whole of the general debt of the Ottoman Empire proportional to the revenues of the ceded territory.[4]

The Austrian Ambassador to London was of opinion that 'the belligerent States shall have [*devront*] to assume numerous charges at the conclusion of the peace, resulting from the public debt, and concessions accorded to private companies which will pass into their hands'.[5]

(vi) *The Peace Treaties, 1919–23*

The Peace Treaties of 1919 and 1923 could not be expected to adhere strictly to any general principle because to do so would be to destroy the economic structure of Europe and prejudice the large numbers of Allied private creditors. In addition, the entire problem of public debt was inextricably involved with the question of reparations. 'By all the rules of international law', writes Temperley in the official history of the Versailles Conference, 'broadly speaking, a successor State is liable for the debts contracted by its predecessor. How far was this responsibility to be affected by the new status of debtors as allies in conference and other considerations?' Italy maintained that the territories ceded to it were in the same position as Alsace-Lorraine. Roumania argued similarly. Czechoslovakia

1 *M.N.R.G.* 3rd ser., vol. VII, p. 3, art. 10.
2 F.O. 44674/4/12/44 (no. 873); Gooch and Temperley, vol. IX, pt. I, p. 431.
3 F.O. 4328/1/13/44 (no. 20); Gooch and Temperley, vol. IX, pt. II, p. 448.
4 F.O. 3575/1/13/44; Gooch and Temperley, vol. IX, pt. II, p. 435.
5 F.O. 23705/9564/13/44; Gooch and Temperley, vol. IX, pt. II, p. 803.

insisted that its representative had long ago given notice of their intention to secede, that their participation in the war had been forced on them, and that therefore the full doctrine of succession could not apply. So great were the difficulties, Temperley concludes, 'that the Conference discarded all attempts to proceed on any distinct doctrinal basis, and to settle the principle of the law of succession. They put all theories on one side and came down to facts and figures.'[1]

The Treaty of Versailles[2] distinguished three categories of successor States. There were, first, those who were to assume portion of the German debt, such as Czechoslovakia; secondly, there were designated certain privileged successors, such as Poland; and thirdly, some successors were exempted from all financial responsibility.[3] The Saar Administration was so exempted because the territory was regarded as compensation for the destruction of French coalmines, and part payment towards the total reparation.[4] France recovered Alsace-Lorraine free from debt because Germany had not assumed any part of the French debt in 1871.[5] Germany protested that this was contrary to international law, whereupon the Allies replied that

> the treaty has no other object than to restore persons and things to the legal position in which they were in 1871. It is easy to justify the exception made in favour of France to the general principle admitted in the Treaty according to which the State receiving territory takes over part of the public debt of the ceding State and pays for the property of the said State in the ceded territory. In 1871, Germany... refused to take over any part of the French debt. France... should take over no part of the German debt nor pay for any State property. This solution is just.[6]

In other cases the Allies admitted a general principle that the successor States of Germany should 'undertake to pay a portion of the debt of the German Empire as it stood on 1 August 1914', and a portion of the debt as it stood on this date of 'the German State to which the territory belonged'. The basis of repartition was to be the ratios between the average for the three financial years 1911, 1912 and 1913 of the revenues of the

---

1 *A History of the Peace Conference of Paris* (1921), edited by Temperley, vol. v, pp. 13 *et seq.*; see *A.J.* vol. XIII (Suppl. 1919), pp. 151–386; *A.J.* vol. XIV (Suppl. 1920), pp. 344–55.
2 *B.T.S.* 1919, no. 4, Cmd. 153.
3 Art. 254.   4 Art. 45.   5 Arts. 55 and 56.
6 Reply of the Allied and Associated Powers to the Observations of the German Delegation on the Conditions of Peace, Cmd. 258, p. 11. 'If', says Feilchenfeld, 'the treaties had recognized legal rights of creditors to demand distribution of debts in case of cession, it would have been impossible to justify a violation of rights of neutral creditors of Germany on the ground that Germany had violated rights of neutral creditors of France': p. 440.

ceded territories and the total revenue of the German Empire and States 'as in the judgment of the Reparations Commission are best calculated to represent the relative ability of the respective territories to make payment'.[1]

The Peace Conferences of Trianon and St Germain adhered, says Temperley, 'to the principle, long recognized in international law, that when a State is divided, each portion so divided shall assume its proportionate share of all debts duly and properly contracted by the whole community before the date of separation'. There was no doubt felt about debts contracted before the outbreak of the war, both secured and unsecured. 'They were the legal obligations of the whole Empire, and had to be divided proportionately between the new constituent States.'[2]

The successor States of the Austro-Hungarian Empire assumed responsibility for such portions of the pre-war bonded debt as were determined by the Reparations Commission.[3] Those of Turkey took over a share of the Ottoman public debt charges on a basis determined by the proportion of total revenues contracted by each during the financial years 1910–12.[4] In fixing this basis the Ottoman Debt Council excluded revenues from territories which had since 1912 ceased to be part of the Ottoman Empire. Iraq, Palestine and Transjordan protested, contending

1 Art. 254, p. 124.
2 *Op. cit.* vol. v, p. 22.
3 Treaty of St Germain, *B.T.S.* 1919, no. 11; Cmd. 400, art. 203; Treaty of Trianon, *B.T.S.* 1920, no. 10; Cmd. 896, art. 186. Decoudu, *Le partage des dettes publiques autrichiennes et hongroises* (1926). The settlement is complex. At the instance of the Sub-Committee of Repartition, authorized by the Reparations Commission, a conference was held at Innsbruck in 1923 which produced a Protocol, ratified by Austria and Hungary and the successor States, and implemented by the Prague Agreement of 1925 and the Paris Annex of 1926. *Report of the Council of the Corporation of Foreign Bondholders* (1925), pp. 87 *et seq.*; (1925), pp. 84 *et seq.*; (1926), pp. 82 *et seq.* In 1929 the Reparations Commission determined the capital amounts incumbent upon each of the successor States. Payments were suspended during the Second World War, and with some exceptions were not renewed until agreement in 1950 between Czechoslovakia and the *Caisse commune des porteurs des dettes publiques autrichiennes*. For Austria see *supra*, p. 383. Agreement was reached between the *Caisse commune* and Hungary in 1956 and Yugoslavia in 1961, the latter being a final settlement of Yugoslavia's liability in respect of the pre-1918 loans. The full history is set out in the *Report of the Council of the Corporation of Foreign Bondholders* (1964), pp. 64 *et seq.* The situation in that year was: Austrian pre-1918 debt: 4 per cent gold rentes, Poland 66,617,779, Roumania 7,342,488, Czechoslovakia, 9,841,933, Yugoslavia 8,897,141, all gold florins; 4½ per cent Treasury notes, Poland 21,958,069, Roumania 3,763,153, Czechoslovakia 3,037,042, Yugoslavia 4,701,189, all Swiss francs. Hungarian pre-1918 debt: 4 per cent gold rentes, Roumania 136,569,293, Yugoslavia 84,484,579, all gold florins; 4½ per cent rentes 1913, Roumania 33,090,246, Yugoslavia 19,335,708, all Swiss francs; 4½ per cent loan, 1914, Roumania 107,625,039, Yugoslavia 70,344,846, all Swiss francs; 4 per cent consolidated State rentes, 1910, 63,128,835, 38,959,767 all Swiss francs. There were also railway bonds, and the Iron Gates Loan, 1895, outstanding.
4 Treaty of Lausanne, *B.T.S.* 1923, no. 16, Cmd. 1929, art. 51 at p. 41.

that the Turkish Republic was burdened with such part of the debt as remained after the contributions laid down in the treaty had been paid, and that, apart from the Treaty of Lausanne, there was no principle of international law according to which a State acquiring part of the territory of another ought to be charged with a corresponding portion of the public debt of the ceding State.

The matter was referred to arbitration, and before the tribunal Turkey argued that the Treaty of Lausanne merely applied a rule of international law to the effect that cessionary States must take over a part of their predecessors' debt.[1] The arbitrator held, however, that it was impossible to say that the State which acquires territory by cession is in strict law bound to take over a corresponding part of the public debt of the ceding State. The distribution in the treaty was a favour since the debtor remained, in law, solely responsible. Only those revenues, he decided, which had been public revenues of the Ottoman Empire were to be included in the distribution, and he excluded revenues which proceeded from commercial operations of the Ottoman public debt.[2]

(vii) *The Mandate over Syria and the Lebanon*

The Mandate over Syria and Lebanon imposed on France the duty to advise, aid and guide the territories in their administration in conformity with article 22 (4) of the Covenant of the League. A constitution was to be granted which would involve the transfer of local affairs to local authorities. There was, therefore, a greater administrative autonomy achieved in Syria and Lebanon than in Palestine, although France governed scarcely less directly. Syria and Lebanon were divided into five parts, which were administratively distinct.[3] The *administration des intérêts communs* directed customs, tobacco monopoly, public services, special military forces of the Levant, and the Ottoman public debt. The *quote-part* of

---

1 *Répartition des annuités de la dette publique ottomane, sentence arbitrale rendue par Eugène Borel* (1925), p. 62, U.N. Rep., vol. I, p. 541. The arbitrator said: 'On ne peut considérer comme acquis en droit international positif le principe qu'un État acquérant partie du territoire d'un autre doit en même temps se charger d'une fraction correspondante de la dette publique de ce dernier. Pareille obligation ne peut découler que du traité où l'assume l'État en cause et elle n'existe que dans les conditions et limites où elle s'y trouve stipulée', at p. 571.

2 *Sentence*, pp. 66–7, U.N. Rep., vol. I, p. 560. See also Treaty of Neuilly, *B.T.S.* 1920, no. 5; Cmd. 522, art. 134. Italy's liability was discharged in 1926, Palestine's in 1928, Iraq's in 1934, Syria and Lebanon's in 1933, Jordan's in 1945 and Yugoslavia's in 1960. Albania, Bulgaria (except for French bondholders), Greece, Saudi Arabia and Yemen remain in default: *Report of the Council of the Corporation of Foreign Bondholders* (1964), p. 280. The total outstanding is £21,712,417 out of a total of £162,547,878.

3 Paenson, p. 35.

Syria, Lebanon, Latakieh and Djebel Druze was determined by article 51 (2) of the Treaty of Lausanne as follows: debts contracted before 17 October 1912, 81.7 per cent; and before 1 November 1914, 10.05 per cent. Distribution of this between the four States was not made until 1926.[1] Up to 1 May 1926 the administration of the Ottoman debt continued to recover the sums destined for the service of this debt. After this date the different States proceeded independently to recover them.[2] An agreement was reached with the Council of the Ottoman Public Debt by Syria and Lebanon on 19 January 1929, and ratified by the French Government, which provided that Syria and Lebanon should pay their part in the form of annuities spread over a number of years. The Council ceded to the two States its immovable property in their territory as well as the sum standing to its credit in the Bank of Syria and Lebanon. In fact, Syria and Lebanon reimbursed their *quote-part* in advance and terminated reimbursement almost entirely in 1933. In 1930 the *Conférence des intérêts communs* was created by the High Commissioner, composed of delegates of the different States.

The customs tariff was applied according to the principle of the open door under the terms of the Mandate.

In 1919 the Bank of Syria took over the functions of the Ottoman Bank. In 1920 a Syrian pound was introduced, based on the French franc and backed by the *bons de la défense nationale déposés à Paris*. The privilege of issuing money was accorded to the Bank of Syria. In 1937 and 1938 the two countries established their own national currencies by agreement with the Bank.

A treaty was signed between France and Turkey on 20 October 1921,[3] by which autonomy was granted within the State of Aleppo to the Sandjak of Alexandretta, which would have its separate budget. When the treaty of 1926 was signed which involved the incorporation of the Sandjak in Syria,[4] Turkey protested to the League of Nations, and in January 1937 the Council of the League decided upon a special status for the territory guaranteed by France and Turkey.[5] The Sandjak would have a large degree of internal autonomy, but would be linked with Syria by fiscal union. Syria would also control its international relations. No treaty could be applied to Alexandretta without the approval of a delegate of the Council of the League, who was to be of French nationality. On 23 June 1939 France, without consulting Syria, ceded the Sandjak to Turkey.[6]

[1] Permanent Mandates Commission Report, *L.N. Off. J.* (1926), p. 182.
[2] Paenson, p. 38.   [3] *L.N.T.S.* vol. LVI, p. 177.
[4] *L.N.T.S.* vol. CXXV, p. 651.
[5] *L.N. Off. J.* 18th Year, no. 1, January 1937, Seventh Meeting.
[6] *L.N.T.S.* vol. CXLIII, p. 477; Paenson, p. 39.

(viii) *General practice, 1920–46*

In the treaties of 1920 between Soviet Russia and its successor States it was stipulated that none of the latter was to contribute to the debts of Imperial Russia.[1] The Soviet had already repudiated such debts. Poland, however, agreed with the Allies to assume such portion of the Russian public debt as might be assigned to it under a special convention to be drafted by a commission.[2] Eire also took over part of the public debt of the United Kingdom 'in such proportion as may be fair and equitable having regard to any just claims on the part of Ireland by way of set off or counterclaim'.[3] The Peace Treaty with Italy, 1947, exempted the Free Territory of Trieste and the other successors from any contribution towards the Italian public debt.[4]

(ix) *The partition of British India, 1947*

Whether the partition of British India constituted a dismemberment of the old international person, or merely a secession of Pakistan, is a question which is probably insoluble. As the latter, however, is the interpretation usually accepted, the precedent in this instance is included under the heading of partial succession. There was no direct repartition of the debt between the two Dominions. All financial obligations, including loans and guarantees, of the Central Government of British India remained the responsibility of India.[5] Those of the partitioned provinces of Bengal and the Punjab, however, became the liabilities of those halves of the provinces which were incorporated in Pakistan.[6] The obligations of the other provinces remained with them.[7] While India continued to be the sole debtor of the central debt, Pakistan's share of this debt, proportionate to the assets it received, became a debt to India.[8] In this manner the difficulties attending the substitution of debtors over arbitrary portions of the public debt were avoided.[9]

1 *M.N.R.G.* 3rd ser., vol. XII, art. 26, p. 45; vol. XI, p. 872; *ibid.* p. 899.
2 *B.F.S.P.* vol. CXII, p. 225, art. 21; cf. Treaty of Riga, *L.N.T.S.* vol. VI, p. 121, art. 19 at p. 153.
3 *L.N.T.S.* vol. XXVI, p. 9, art. 5. See 186 H.C. Deb. 5 s., col. 2656.
4 *B.T.S.* 1948, no. 50; Cmd. 7481, Annex X, art. 5, and Annex XIV, art. 6.
5 Indian Independence (Rights, Property and Liabilities) Order, 1947, *Gazette of India Extraordinary*, 14 August 1947, s. 9 (*a*).
6 Ss. 9 (*b*) and (*c*). 7 S. 9 (*d*).
8 The Hon. Shri R. K. Shanmukham Chetty stated in Congress that the entire outstanding public debt of the late Central Government, amounting to Rs. 18,03,97 lakhs, had been assumed by the Indian Government, while Pakistan's 'share' would be included in its debt to India, Constituent Assembly of India (Legislative) Debates, 19 March 1948, vol. IV, no. 1, Official Report.
9 *Indian Finance*, Special Partition Supplement, 28 June 1947, vol. XXXIX, no. 28.

The Expert Committee set up[1] to recommend the apportionment of the assets and liabilities of British India listed the major financial liabilities outstanding at the time of partition as falling into two categories, the public debt and the unfunded debt. The first category consisted of permanent loans, treasury bills and special loans, and the second category consisted of post office savings banks deposits, national and defence certificates, provident funds, pensions in payment and miscellaneous items.[2]

India was regarded as remaining the contracting debtor against which primary resort might be had. The Governor-General explained the necessity for this interpretation of the events as follows: 'The fear was that a country might borrow money much in excess of her needs, then go through a formal partition and claim that neither part of the divided country was responsible for the debts incurred prior to that partition.'[3] Pakistan, as the successor State, would have to undertake a proportion of the liabilities of India. The Pakistan members of the Expert Committee proposed that

the responsibility for the whole of the debt may be assumed by one Government, the other Government becoming its debtor to the extent of its share of the debt. In such a case the liability of the debtor Government to the creditor Government will be discharged on a mutually agreed basis such as the payment of annuities.[4]

With respect to the uncovered debt, they argued that the allocation of liability should be 'in proportion to the contributions made by the areas which will be included in the Dominions of India and Pakistan to the revenues of the present Central Government'. The Indian members, however, considered that the allocation should be based on population in conjunction with the respective contribution of the two States. The final solution adopted by the Steering Committee, to which the Expert Committee reported, was embodied in section 9 of the Indian Independence (Rights, Property and Liabilities) Order. The Indian members submitted a note stating: 'All the discussion in the Expert Committee and the final settlement with Pakistan will now take the form of an inter-State debt by that Dominion to India. It is now necessary to decide the lines on which this debt should be repaid.'[5] The Partition Council was requested to decide the rate of interest that should be adopted, the date of first instalment, and the number of annual instalments.[6] The capital sum should be calculated by including the value of physical assets taken over in Pakistan territory or allocated to Pakistan, and cash balances allocated to

1 *Partition Proceedings*, vol. II, p. 1.
2 *Ibid.* p. 5.
3 *Idem*, vol. IV, p. 429.
4 *Idem*, vol. II, pp. 6–11.
5 *Idem*, vol. IV, p. 559.
6 *Ibid.* p. 560.

Pakistan. Pakistan's share of the net excess of liabilities, including pension liabilities, over assets, less the value of liabilities under postal cash certificates, postal savings bank deposits, and provident fund balances.

An agreement of 1 December 1947 between the Dominions fixed the contribution of Pakistan to the debts of India. This was to be equal to the accountable value of all the property to which Pakistan had succeeded, plus 17.5 per cent of the surplus of the obligations of India over its assets. In calculating this surplus, it was necessary to deduct the obligations directly assumed by Pakistan from the total obligations of India. Pakistan was to undertake to pay its portion in fifty equal annuities, beginning on 15 August 1952.

India's calculation was that the liabilities of the undivided government would exceed its assets by 4,000 crores of rupees, but eventually it claimed 300 crores from Pakistan.[1] This sum has not been paid because Pakistan counterclaims that a sum of Rs. 180 crores is due to her from India.[2]

The Indian courts have interpreted the expression 'other financial obligations' in the Order which continued the vesting of financial responsibility of the Central Government in India as being *ejusdem generis* with 'loans and guarantees'.[3] The effect of this construction has been to exclude from the operation of the Order administrative and contractual debts which were unconnected with revenue, State finance, or the financial assistance of the Union to any State.

In 1962 the Supreme Court of Pakistan held that a statutory obligation of British India to pay compensation was not a 'financial obligation' which in virtue of the Order of 1947 would devolve on Pakistan. It went further and propounded the thesis that in international law a sovereign, when granting independence, has powers to impose on the new State what terms and conditions it pleases in regard to his own obligations. It stated that there is no established practice that locally connected rights and duties continue after change of sovereignty.[4]

(x) *The independence of Libya, 1950*

The General Assembly of the United Nations by resolution[5] of 15 December 1950 regulated the question of the succession to rights and obligations of Italy during a transitional period. The British and French

1 Constituent Assembly of India (Legislative) Debates, vol. 1, p. 174.
2 Foreign Affairs Records, vol. v (1959), pp. 130, 189, 192.
3 *Province of Bengal* v. *Midnapore Zamindary Co.* A.I.R. (1950), Cal. 159; *State of West Bengal* v. *Sirajuddin Batley*, A.I.R. (1950), S.C. 193; *Iswar Madan Gopal* v. *Province of West Bengal*, A.I.R. (1950), Cal. 463.
4 *Federation of Pakistan* v. *Dalmia Cement Co. Ltd, Karachi and the Union of India*, 14 All Pakistan Legal Decisions (S.C.) 260 (1962).   5 U.N.G.A. Res. 388v.

administrations were to continue, and Libya signed financial agreements with the United Kingdom[1] and France[2] whereby the United Kingdom agreed to subsidize the federal budget for the first year of independence, and France the deficit in the provincial budget of the Fezzan. Both States also agreed to underwrite the organization created to develop the Libyan economy. The United Kingdom would nominate, with the agreement of the Libyan Government, an Inspector-General of Finances, and France a financial counsel for the Fezzan. In March 1952 a mandatory reform was carried out by which Libyan money was attached to the pound sterling, and Libya entered the sterling zone.

II. The Secured Debt

The public debt of a State, or some portion of it, is often secured on public revenues and assets. The security may take one of two forms. In the first place, there may be a real mortgage, pledge or lien of tangible State property. In the second place, there may be security only in the sense that certain revenues or certain funds are allocated to the amortization of specified loans. These two types of debt securities are not often distinguished either in State practice or by publicists.

The question of succession to secured debts is interwoven with the general theory of territory.[3] The universal succession theory is a reflexion of the thesis that territory is an object of national *dominium*, and, as such, something that can be indefeasibly encumbered with mortgages or pledges. Even Appleton and Sack, who maintain the continuity of land and people as the basis of a succession to debt relationships, have not succeeded in disengaging the problem from property concepts of private law, although they have striven to do so. The alternative theory that territory is merely the spatial extent of jurisdictional competence prompts the view that a change of sovereignty affects, not only the competence to raise income, but also security annexed to national assets.[4] It is argued that the relationship of a creditor to a thing is fundamentally personal, and is a matter which only municipal law can regulate. Since international law is merely a law of 'co-ordination'[5] between States, it cannot govern such a relationship, but at the most can concede competence to a State with

1 U.N.T.S. vol. CXXIII, p. 167.
2 U.N.T.S. vol. LXXXII, p. 172.
3 Schnitzer, pp. 135–8.
4 Huber says debts can never be 'real', because the *Reallast* is only *vis-à-vis* the predecessor State, and not *vis-à-vis* the creditor, pp. 88, 100. Pledges of revenue lapse, p. 101, though a general succession to personal liability occurs. Schönborn says a real pledging of territory is antiquated, p. 61.
5 Schnitzer, p. 138; Ross, p. 130; Sereni, vol. I, p. 408.

respect to it. The conclusion is drawn that no State is competent to burden a territory with obligations that restrict its successor's competence. The internal law of the successor State must be free to determine the rights of individuals *in rebus*.

Both approaches to the problem misapprehend it. There is no reason why the interest which a creditor acquires in State property should be any less an acquired right than that which he acquires in privately owned property; and there is a valid conceptual foundation in the doctrine of acquired rights for the view that the security for a loan, as well as the interest in the loan itself, survives a transfer of sovereignty. However, it is always for the law of the predecessor State to determine what interest a creditor has in a security. Continental writers have distinguished between *dettes hypothéquées*, that is, debts actually secured by mortgage of assets, and *dettes hypothéquaires*, that is, debts generally related to sources of income.[1] The tendency is to regard only the former type of security as surviving transfer of the territory.

(a) Pledged assets

The true character of a debt pledge has never been adequately explored. It is not certain if a creditor acquires over State assets a true equitable right of property, or if the assets retain their pledged character after their ownership has passed to a successor State.[2] If the creditor has a real property right in the mortgage then it would seem that the successor State must treat this as a fact giving rise to a legal duty. Possibly in such case the predecessor and the successor States become jointly liable to the creditor, the one on a contractual basis, the other on a basis of restitution. State practice, however, is not sufficiently extensive to give approbation to this proposition.

1 Von Liszt, p. 278; de Louter, p. 228; Sibert, vol. I, p. 210.

2 Wolff demonstrates that a mortgage in the international sense is not the same as a mortgage in the civil sense because there can be no right of sale: Hague *Recueil*, vol. XXXVI (1931), p. 547. Sack does not believe that mortgages are always binding on the successor State because this might prejudice the interests of the latter's creditors: pp. 201 *et seq*. Udina says that 'quant aux dettes dites "hypothécaires", c'est-à-dire dont le paiement est garanti par des immeubles, droits de douane, monopoles ou produits d'impôts, données en gage, on ne peut affirmer qu'il y ait succession dans le cas de diminution territoriale du débiteur que lorsqu'elles sont en même temps des dettes localisées dans le territoire détaché, ou, peut-être, encore, si l'État acquéreur du territoire s'est emparé des biens donnés en gage': Hague *Recueil*, vol. LXIV (1933), p. 756. Jèze believes that the assets retain their mortgaged character after cession: *op. cit.* p. 19, also Guggenheim, *Traité*, p. 472. Vanselow says debts attach to assets, p. 142; also Reuter, p. 128.

(i) *The cession of the province of Tarapacá by Peru to Chile, 1883*

The nature of a pledge was examined to some extent in a controversy with Chile respecting the cession of Peruvian territory to that country in 1883. Peru had pledged guano deposits in the province of Tarapacá, and the proceeds of these deposits, as security for certain national loans. In 1882 Chile, being then in military occupation of the province, decreed the sale of the guano, half of the proceeds to remain with Chile, the other half to be deposited in the Bank of England for distribution among the creditors of Peru, whose rights should be recognized as guaranteed by the guano. When the Treaty of Ancon in the following year transferred the province to Chile this provision was incorporated in it.[1] Various creditors protested against the limitation of their rights to only half the guano proceeds, and Notes were sent by several of the Powers, notably Great Britain, the United States, Italy, France, and Spain. Chile insisted that the rights of the bondholders lay in the Chilean courts, but expressed its willingness to enter into an equitable understanding with them. Moore, commenting on the Secretary of State's instructions to the American Ambassador to Chile, states that: 'Chile, in taking possession, at the close of the war with Peru, of the guano deposits belonging to Peru, took them subject only to such liens as were binding under Peruvian law at the time of cession.'[2]

On 5 November 1884 the Law Officers advised the Foreign Office that they did not consider it necessary to examine critically all the propositions in the Chilean reply because the Chilean Government

declare that they will not refuse to enter into an equitable understanding with the creditors of Peru, who may have rights that merit consideration, and which have originated in acts and contracts legally established. And this declaration is in addition to an admission that if there be creditors who have the rights of mortgagees in respect of the property ceded to Chile, they are still entitled to enforce those rights.[3]

It was further stated, however, that a passage in the Chilean reply which referred to creditors other than pretended mortgagees 'appears to us to be an undertaking on the part of the Government independent of the decision of any Tribunal, or of strict legal right'. The Law Officers were thus, apparently, of the opinion that in general creditors have no rights against a partial successor unless their rights be those of mortgagees of

1 *M.N.R.G.* 2nd ser., vol. x, p. 191, art. 2 at p. 192.
2 Moore, *Dig.* vol. I, p. 336.
3 Opinion of 5 November 1883, F.O. Confidential Papers (5121), no. 66; O'Connell, Appendix, no. 44.

State assets. This distinction is clearly explicit in an Opinion delivered by the same Officers on 22 January 1884. The reference to them stated that the case 'appears to raise a question of international right in regard to the obligations of a State acquiring new territory by conquest or cession to respect the private rights of property therein and to assume the obligation of discharging the public debts charged on such territory'. The Law Officers advised as follows:

Although it would be more equitable that when a part of the territory of one State is acquired by another by conquest, a part of the debt of the conquered country, if any exist, proportionate to the territory so acquired, should be taken over with it; yet there cannot be said to be any absolutely settled rule of international law to that effect. An equitable apportionment of the debt has been frequently, but not invariably, provided for in Treaties of Peace. If, therefore, there were no special circumstances in the present case, it might be doubted whether there was ground for intervention on the part of Her Majesty's Government.

The circumstances which exist in the present case are, however, certainly peculiar. There can be no doubt that the money was lent by the bondholders, in reliance mainly on the security of the valuable guano deposits belonging to the Peruvian Government. And, as some of the most important of these deposits are included in the territory to be ceded, we think there is an equitable claim on the part of the bondholders of a special character, which may justly be strongly urged upon the consideration of the Governments.[1]

On 2 February 1884 opinion was given that nitrate deposit holders were in the same position as the bondholders, and the reference noted that Chile was prepared to deal with the question according to rules of international law.[2] A draft note was drawn up by the Law Officers on 3 August 1886 to the French Government, which observed that the British Government would unite with other governments in taking steps to clear up the controversy 'on a fair and equitable basis'. They were willing to take steps to have an arbitration, which implies that what was 'fair and equitable' was regarded as 'legal'. However, it was pointed out that 'the Chilean Government have not shown themselves unwilling to do justice in the matter, for they have already set apart for the bondholders large sums of money derived from the revenues of Tarapacá, thus admitting in principle the validity of the claim'. In the conclusion of the note the rights of the creditors would appear to have been regarded as enforceable against Chile. 'Her Majesty's Government are ready to support by diplomatic means the reasonable claims of the creditors on the revenues

[1] Opinion of 22 January 1884; F.O. Confidential Papers (5121), no. 65; O'Connell, Appendix, no. 42.
[2] Opinion of 2 February 1884, F.O. Confidential Papers (5121), no. 84; O'Connell, Appendix, no. 43.

of Tarapacá to the fullest extent that is warranted by justice and International Law.'[1]

In due course Chile abandoned its claim to the half of the deposits and its right to sell them, and eventually the dispute developed around the problem of distribution of the proceeds among the creditors. An arbitral tribunal was set up to settle this question. Before the tribunal Chile denied that there was any mortgage of the assets in Peruvian law, and the award, delivered in 1901, was in favour of this contention. It decided that the rights of the creditors depended upon the existence of civil mortgages, but that no such mortgages had been established. Under Peruvian law the creditors had not acquired any security that was transmissible and the relationship between them and Peru was solely one of contract.[2] The controversy does not, therefore, establish with certainty the legal character of a debt pledge.

(ii) *Decision of the Reichsgericht, 1885*

In 1885 the *Reichsgericht* stated that 'all encumbrances of a public character resting on a piece of property in so far as they are not owed to the State itself, continue to subsist in spite of the incorporation of the property in another State'.[3]

(iii) *Secured debts in the Peace Treaties, 1919*

The Treaties of St Germain and Trianon[4] distinguished secured debts as those 'specifically secured' on 'railways, salt mines or other property'. Property so pledged to secure a debt was to remain pledged, and, when divided among several States, that portion of it situated in a particular State was to constitute the security only for that part of the debt which was apportioned to that State, and not for any other part of the debt. The amount of the liability in respect of such secured debts was to be deducted from the amount payable by the successor State to Austria for Austrian property transferred with the cession of territory.

(b) *Pledged revenues*

If a portion of the national debt is charged to a local revenue merely because the latter offers a convenient basis of credit, it would seem that such pledge need not be respected by a successor State. It is difficult to agree that a revenue pledge is a mortgage in the same sense as hypothecated

---
1 Opinion of 3 August 1886, F.O. Confidential Papers (5440), no. 8; O'Connell, Appendix, no. 47.
2 Feilchenfeld, p. 328, nn. 28 and 29.
3 *RGZ* 13, 8, 204; *Fontes Juris Gent.* ser. A, sect. II, vol. I, p. 114.
4 St Germain, *loc. cit.* art. 203; Trianon, *loc. cit.* art. 186.

assets. There can at the most be only a right to repayment out of such revenues, and there is no authority for the proposition that a creditor can foreclose on them or possess equitable property in them. The real nature of a revenue pledge, however, is not sufficiently determined for the subject to be treated with any degree of assurance.[1]

(i) *The incorporation of Texas in the United States, 1845: Texan Bonds Arbitration*

During the contention with respect to the Texan bonds both the British agent[2] and the Attorney-General[3] of the United States were of opinion that revenue pledges are tantamount to mortgages. The American agent, however, rejected this view and argued that Texas could still borrow money on pledged revenues.[4] The American Commissioner observed in addition that the pledging of a revenue could give no rights of control over it to a creditor.[5]

(ii) *The projected transfer of a province by Mexico to the United States, 1866*

On 11 July 1866 the Queen's Advocate advised that,

if part of the Mexican territory, the revenues of which are already pledged or hypothecated to the British bondholders, be sold without their consent, it will still be liable to discharge its due share of the interest or principal of the debt to the bondholders. Care should be taken that the purchaser be duly affected, previously to the purchase, with the knowledge of the lien which the foreign creditor has upon the territory in question.[6]

(iii) *The cession of Cuba by Spain, 1898: Cuban debt controversy*

The only substantial authority on revenue pledges is that afforded by the controversy between the United States and Spain during the negotiations preliminary to the Treaty of Paris, 1898, relative to the loans charged on the Cuban revenues. Spain argued that the debts were contracted by it as sovereign of Cuba, and being charged on the Cuban revenues were locally connected. The principles of repartition, the Spanish Commissioners argued,

1 On 5 July 1825 the King's Advocate gave an opinion on the obligation of Mexico to undertake payments of certain ecclesiastical annuities to the late Cardinal of York. The Spanish Government had pledged these annuities on the Mexican revenues. The King's Advocate was doubtful of the legal character of the pledge, but in any event he was of opinion that a seceding State would not be responsible for such a debt: F.O. 83/2289; O'Connell, Appendix, no. 2.
2 Feilchenfeld, p. 282.
3 6 *Op. A.-G.* p. 146.
4 Feilchenfeld, p. 283.   5 *Ibid.* p. 283.
6 Opinion of 11 July 1866, F.O. 83/2225; O'Connell, Appendix, no. 28.

seem to be observed by all cultured nations that are unwilling to trample upon the eternal principles of justice, including those in which such cessions were made by force of arms, and as a reward for victories through treaties relating to territorial cessions. . . . When creditors have been granted by the very certificate of their contract a direct lien on certain defined property or certain defined income, in order thus to recover the loaned capital and its legitimate interest, the sovereign cannot then, without first reckoning with their consent, cede or freely dispose of such property and incomes as if they were his full and exclusive property. . . . The Spanish Commissioners only wish that the principle, up to this time always admitted, to wit, that a debt being exclusively the debt of a colony and affecting its territory goes with the colony itself, be also recognized in this treaty.[1]

The American Commissioners replied that

as to that part of the Spanish memorandum in which the so-called Cuban bonds are treated as 'mortgage bonds', and the rights of the holders as 'mortgage rights', it is necessary to say only that the legal difference between the pledge of revenues yet to be derived from taxation and a mortgage of property cannot be confused by calling the two things by the same name.[2]

In addition to describing the debts as 'odious' because imposed on the Cuban people without their consent, the United States imported a doctrine of 'the national character' of debts.[3] Spain pointed out that Cuba should remain charged because the Cuban revenues constituted a first pledge, and Spain was a party to the debt only as guarantor.[4] The United States, however, held that Spain was the sole debtor, and that the debt was part of Spain's national debt and protected by two securities, the principal one of the Cuban revenues, and the ancillary one of Spain's guarantee.[5]

(iv) *The cession of Ottoman territory, 1913*

The German Ambassador to London suggested in 1913 that the Conference to be called to draw up the peace terms at the end of the First Balkan War might adopt the principle that

rights belonging to the bearers of the public debt of the Ottoman Empire on revenues which have been charged as special pledges to the service of the different

[1] Moore, *Dig.* vol. I, pp. 353, 362 *et seq.* There was never any question of transferring a proportionate part of the whole Spanish public debt, but only that part of it locally assigned, *ibid.* p. 353. 'From no point of view can the debts above described be considered as local debts of Cuba, or as debts incurred for the benefit of Cuba,' said the United States Commissioners. 'They are debts created by Spain for its own purposes, and through its own agents, in whose creation Cuba has no voice': *ibid.* p. 358.
[2] *Ibid.* p. 383.
[3] *Ibid.* pp. 358, 367, 378, 381, 382.
[4] *Ibid.* p. 379.
[5] *Ibid.* pp. 368 *et seq.*, 379.

departments of state... shall be fully safeguarded in the territories acquired by the Balkan States. The cessionary Balkan States of the Ottoman territory shall have [*auront*] thus to support a part of the said Public Debt of the Ottoman State, whether by means of payment of annual contributive parts to the services of the different Departments, or by means of a reimbursement of capital of the part incumbent upon them of the debt of the Ottoman Empire.[1]

(v) *Pledged revenues in the Peace Treaties, 1919–23*

Germany in 1919 had no secured debt, and except for loans secured on the Egyptian tribute no distinction was made in the other Peace Treaties between loans secured by revenue pledge and unsecured loans.[2] The system applied to Egypt was described in the Ottoman Debt Arbitration as a 'specialization of securities'.[3] Turkey was released from all undertakings and obligations in regard to the Ottoman loans guaranteed on the Egyptian tribute.[4]

(vi) *Pledged revenues in the Lighthouses Case, 1955*

In this arbitration[5] Greece counterclaimed for recovery of its share of the lighthouse dues collected by the concessionaire between 1913 and 1928. The counterclaim failed on the ground that, although Greece was entitled to a share in the lighthouse receipts which had previously gone to Turkey, the receipts in question were subject to an assignment to Turkey's creditors by way of guarantee of State loans raised in 1904, 1907 and 1913. These loans had been maintained, and their amortization partitioned among the successor States of the Ottoman Empire, in the Treaty of Lausanne, and Greece was one of the successor States affected. It was stated by the Arbitrator that the maintenance and repartition of debts effected by the treaty were in accordance with the principles of international law prescribing respect for *droits patrimoniaux acquis*, included in which were contracts of loan between the State and private creditors. In the event of default on the part of the successor State in making repayment according to the treaty provisions, the pre-existing rights and obligations continued *dans leur teneur primitive*.

The case illustrates that, where an intimate connexion exists between certain revenues and the national debt as a whole, the problem often becomes one of succession to a 'local' debt rather than one of a repartition of the general debt, the basis of the repartition becoming not a proportion

1 F.O. 2208/1/13/44, Gooch and Temperley, vol. IX, pt. II, p. 402.
2 Treaty of Lausanne, *B.T.S.* 1919, no. 11; Cmd. 400, art. 18.
3 *Loc. cit.* p. 64.
4 For a thorough analysis of the Egyptian tribute see Sack, pp. 109–28.
5 *I.L.R.* vol. XXIII, pp. 94 *et seq.* See *supra*, p. 327.

Acquired Rights and the National Debt

of the debt, calculated by reference to population, income, etc., but that proportion amortizable out of the pledged revenues derivable from the ceded territory. While it is possible, therefore, that interests in hypothecated assets must be recognized as acquired rights by a successor State, it cannot be asserted with any conclusive authority that a successor State incurs any liability to either the creditor or the predecessor State by virtue of taking over hypothecated revenues.

Chapter 16

THE DOCTRINE OF ACQUIRED RIGHTS AND LOCAL DEBTS

1. DEBTS OF A FISCALLY AUTONOMOUS REGION

A successor State is under no legal obligation to take over a part of the national debt of its predecessor so long as the latter's sovereignty survives and the debt relationship is unaffected. Where, however, the absorbed territory is fiscally autonomous, the situation is different. In this case the contracting authority is a local agent of the central government, or perhaps a provincial government, and the security for the debt rests entirely on the revenues of the territory. The central government, except perhaps indirectly, is not concerned with the amortization of the debt.

Where such territory is ceded to a successor State, or annexed by it, or where it becomes independent, the situation is analogous to that of total succession.[1] Not only would the central government of the predecessor State be unjustly encumbered by a transfer to it of the debts of its lost region, but the creditors of such debts would be so severely prejudiced as to have suffered a detriment and possible deprivation of acquired rights. If the situation in this case, therefore, is to be assimilated to that arising in the case of total succession, it would be reasonable to expect that the successor State incurs in the change of sovereignty an obligation to either the predecessor State or the creditor.[2]

---

[1] Mosler, p. 157. If it is maintained, he says, that there is a general principle of international law according to which the State is obliged to take over local debts, there is no difference in the nature of total and partial succession: p. 157. See Jèze, p. 18; Westlake, vol. I, p. 62. See also the opinion of the Queen's Advocate quoted above with respect to the debt of New Granada: F.O. 83/2257; O'Connell, Appendix, no. 32.

[2] Redslob in *Rev. de droit int.* vol. XIII (1934), p. 482; François in Hague *Recueil*, vol. LXVI (1938), p. 81; Despagnet, pp. 123, 132; Appleton, p. 156; Podesta Costa, p. 81; Piédelièvre, vol. I, p. 132; Udina in Hague *Recueil*, vol. XLVII (1934), p. 490; Cavaglieri in *Annuaire de l'Institut de Droit International, session de Paris* (1934), vol. XXXIV, p. 218. Sack considers that regional debts do not bind the whole territory, but follow the provinces to which they are attached: Hague *Recueil*, vol. XXIII (1928), p. 265. Debts charged by the central government on an area he calls 'provincial debts', and those contracted for the exclusive benefit of the area he calls 'regional' debts: *ibid.* p. 263. See also *Dettes publiques*, pp. 72 *et seq.*, 135 *et seq.*, 185 *et seq.* See Hyde, vol. I, p. 409. Fenwick thinks the category of local debts is vague, p. 154; while Hackworth expresses doubt: *Dig.* vol. I, p. 540. Schönborn refers to a 'developing rule' concerning local debts, p. 61. Also Wengler, vol. II, p. 1010; Monaco, p. 218. See Bustamante y Sirven, *Derecho internacional público* (1936), vol. III, p. 321; Hershey, *Essentials of International Public Law* (2nd ed. 1927), p. 220; Meyer-Lindenberg, p. 86; Reuter, p. 128; Sauer, p. 151; Waldkirch, p. 119; Castren, p. 482; Gould, p. 416;

The maintenance of the debt of a fiscally autonomous region depends upon the retention by the region, after change of sovereignty, of its legal capacity in internal law. The personality of an administrative entity is less defined in English law, and hence more controversial in its incidence, than in civil law systems, where a regional government may enjoy a clearly formulated civil status, which is to some extent independent of the attributes of sovereignty. If such an entity ceases to be competent in internal law to exercise rights and be subject to duties, then a case of succession has occurred; but, if it remains competent with respect to rights and duties, even though subjected to change of sovereignty, no question of succession arises. The problem in every case, then, is whether the creditors may still proceed against the regional government under the original contract; and its solution depends upon the extent to which change of sovereignty raises implications respecting survival of civil identity.

In 1956 the *Cour d'Appel* of Paris dealt with the question whether the debt liability of the Independent State of the Congo had become that of Belgium in 1907.[1] Referring to the terms of the cession and of the Colonial Charter, by which the Congo remained a separate juridical person, the Court held that, even if the creditors had no right of recourse against Belgium, but only against the Belgian Congo, the latter was still part of the sovereignty of Belgium, and could invoke the latter's sovereign immunity when sued domestically.[2]

When the Palestine Mandate terminated it was necessary to enact

---

Selosse, p. 167; Dahm, vol. I, pp. 117 *et seq.*; Verdross–Zemanek, pp. 195 *et seq.*; Ross, p. 130; Schwarzenberger (as a matter of equity), p. 81; de Visscher in *Communicazioni e Studi*, vol. XI (1962), p. 78. Sereni's view is negative, on the ground that the successor's own subjects might be the creditors: vol. II, p. 407.

The Court of Cassation at Florence stated on 15 December 1879: 'La sentenza ben rileva il principio, che nel diritto pubblico lo Stato che succede in una parte di territorie d'un altro Stato, sia tenuto, independentemente da convenzioni speciali alle obbligazioni contratte legalmente da quest'ultimo riguardo al territorio nel quale succede': *Giurisprudenza Italiana* (1880), I, 1, 293 at p. 295. The passing of debts was linked by the same court with the *res transit cum suo onere* notion in a judgment of 25 May 1896: 'il nuovo Stato succede al precedente, per modo non interrotta continuità e raccolga in activis e passivis l'universum jus patrimoniale': *Giurisprudenza Italiana* (1896), I, 1, 662 at p. 668. Also the Hungarian–Roumanian Mixed Arbitral Tribunal in *Koranyi* v. *Roumania*: 'Attendu que dans le cas où la dette a été contractée dans l'intérêt du territoire transféré que l'argent a servi dans le passé ou servira dans l'avenir à procurer quelques améliorations ou enrichissements au dit territoire, il n'est pas juste et équitable d'en rendre comptable l'État successeur qui en assume de ce chef la responsabilité': *Recueil des décisions des Tribunaux Arbitraux Mixtes*, VIII, 980 at p. 982.

1 See *supra*, pp. 22, 90.
2 *État indépendant du Congo Belge* v. *Montefiore*, I.L.R. vol. XXIII, p. 191. Reversed on cassation on a different ground. D. 1963, 37.

legislation in the United Kingdom for service by the British Treasury of certain bonds which would not be taken over by Israel.[1]

A contract of loan, especially in the form of bondholding, is made in reference to a context of constitutional and municipal law, by which the paying authority and the conditions of performance are determined. It is possible that under some constitutional systems, including the English, loans, unless backed by statute, are unaccompanied by any legal recourse against any designated debtor. It is equally possible that loans made by regional or colonial administrations are, under the terms of the proper law, amortizable only out of nominated revenue, or by nominated local authorities, even if these do not constitute, in municipal law, a separate juridical entity. To permit the bondholder, after a change of sovereignty has occurred, to pursue the central government might well be to enlarge the rights of the creditor, and alter the content of the proper law.

The successor State should not be permitted to avoid responsibility for terminating the fiscal capacity of a regional government by shifting this on to the predecessor State, which, but for the change of sovereignty, could never have been the subject of pursuit.

(i) *General practice, 1648–1866*

From the Treaty of Westphalia, 1648, onwards[2] local treasury debts were generally divided, and during the eighteenth century a new category of debts emerged, designated as debts 'hypothecated on the soil',[3] and based on the conception of the territory as something which could be mortgaged in its entirety. The character of *dettes hypothéquées* was never very clear. The category appears to have included both debts for which a local source of revenue was assigned and debts actually charged on the territory.[4] In a treaty between France and Holland in 1810 it was enacted

1 S.I. 1949, no. 138; *B.F.S.P.* vol. CLIII, p. 29.
2 Treaty of Westphalia: *M.N.R.* vol. II, p. 157; Treaties of Ryswick, 1679 and 1699: Dumont, *Corps Universel diplomatique du droit des gens* (1731), vol. VII, pt. II, pp. 381, 470; Treaty of Utrecht, 1713: *B.F.S.P.* vol. I, p. 420; Treaty of Stockholm, 1720: *B.F.S.P.* vol. I, p. 218. These were all cases of succession under feudal law. Succession under a law other than feudal first took place in the Treaty of Berlin, 1742, when Prussia undertook the servicing of Austrian loans secured on Silesian revenues and owed to creditors in England and Holland. Austria, however, remained charged with such loans as were owed to her own nationals in the Austrian Netherlands: Feilchenfeld, pp. 35 *et seq.*
3 Treaty of Copenhagen, 1767, *M.R.* vol. I, p. 426, art. 2.
4 Treaty of Campo Formio, *M.R.* vol. VII, p. 208, art. 4 at p. 210; the Treaty of Lunéville, 1801, specified the debts within the category of *dettes hypothéquées* as those for which the estates had formally contracted for the administration of the ceded areas: *M.R.* vol. VII, p. 538, art. 8 at p. 541; Treaty of Vienna, 1809, *M.R.* (*Suppl.*), vol. V, p. 210, art. 5 at p. 213.

that such debts had to be contracted by the administration of the ceded territory for its special interest,[1] and in a subsequent dispute between these countries it was stated that 'there exists an intimate connexion between charges and revenues of states'.[2]

After 1830 the theory that public debts of territories were mortgages on the soil disappeared,[3] and theories of permanence of burden, referring to territories and population rather than to soil, became dominant. In the discussions preliminary to the Treaty of Vienna, 1866, Austria contended that Italy should take over the whole Lombardo-Venetian debt. It was said:

> The only logical basis of all discussion is that which has been admitted either in the Treaty of Zürich, or in the negotiations which have taken place recently between France and Prussia on the one side, and Austria on the other, that is to say, that the Lombardo-Venetian Kingdom has its own debt distinct and separate from the general debt.[4]

(ii) *The secession of the Spanish–American colonies*

All the treaties by which Spain recognized the independence of its revolted colonies in South America transferred to the new States debts owed by or charged to the Spanish treasuries in those territories, or debts owed by Spain in respect of their administration.[5] Most of these treaties consider the matter as one of 'grace, equity and justice', but the treaty of 1859 with Argentina recognized that such debts had passed *ipso facto* with the change of sovereignty.[6]

(iii) *General practice, 1864–1905*

By the Treaty of London, 1864, Greece assumed all the public debt of the Ionian Islands.[7] In an Opinion of 12 December 1866, the Queen's Advocate advised that the Greek Government was bound to continue to

---

1 M.R. (Suppl.), vol. v, p. 327, art. 7 at p. 329. The Treaty of Paris, 1814, redistributed *dettes hypothéquées* which France had assumed in territories ceded to it: M.R. (Suppl.), vol. vi, p. 1, art. 21 at p. 10.
2 Lapradelle and Politis, *Recueil des arbitrages internationaux* (1932), vol. I, p. 279.
3 Feilchenfeld, pp. 175 *et seq.* Piédelièvre calls all debts of a local nature contracted in the exclusive interest of a territory *dettes hypothéquées*, vol. I, p. 132.
4 *Fontes Juris Gent.* ser. B, vol. I, pt. 1, p. 596.
5 Mexico, B.F.S.P. vol. xxiv (1836), p. 864, art. 7 at p. 868; Chile, *ibid.* vol. xxxiv (1844), p. 1108, art. 4 at p. 1109; Ecuador, *ibid.* vol. xxix (1840), p. 1315, art. 5 at p. 1316; Uruguay, *ibid.* vol. xxx (1841), p. 1366, arts. x and xi at p. 1369; Venezuela, *ibid.* vol. xxxv (1845), p. 301, art. 4 at p. 302; Costa Rica, *ibid.* vol. xxxix (1850), p. 40, art. 5 at p. 1341; Nicaragua, *ibid.* p. 1341, art. 5 at p. 1343; Guatemala, *ibid.* vol. lix (1863), p. 1200, art. 4 at p. 1201; San Salvador, *ibid.* vol. lviii (1865), p. 1250, art. 4 at p. 1251. For a discussion on the point see the Spanish memorials on the Cuba debt: Moore, *Dig.* vol. I, p. 355.
6 B.F.S.P. vol. I (1859), p. 1160, art. 4 at p. 1161.
7 M.N.R.G. vol. xviii, p. 63, art. 7.

pay annuities in the form of tithe commutations which the administration of the Islands had contracted.[1] When Norway and Sweden separated in 1905, each retained its personal debt.[2]

(iv) *The Peace Treaties, 1919–23*

The Ottoman Debt Arbitration award in 1925 exempted Crete from the system of proportional distribution adopted in the Treaty of Lausanne, because it had obtained financial autonomy before 1910, and in 1912 had concluded an agreement with the administration of the Ottoman Public Debt which released it from regular contributions.[3] The Reparations Commission was made responsible for arranging the distribution of bonded and unbonded debts of the local areas of the Austro-Hungarian Empire, including those of autonomous provinces and principalities.[4] Debts of undivided areas were taken to pass to the successor States as a matter of course, while secured debts followed the security.[5] 'As regards the local debt of Alsace and Lorraine, and of public institutions of the Province, which existed before 1 August 1914,' the Allies informed Germany, 'it has always been understood between the Allied and Associated Governments that France should accept liability for them.'[6]

Although Czechoslovakia generally did not regard itself as the successor of Austria,[7] its Supreme Administrative Court in 1922 held that, in virtue of the continuity achieved in internal law by the Czech legislature,[8] the Czech Treasury maintained an identity with the previous Austrian Treasury. Rates, taxes, fees and duties continued to be payable to the Czech Treasury under existing legislation, and it followed that fees and taxes paid in error to the Austrian or Hungarian authorities in Bohemia and Moravia were repayable to the claimants.[9] In 1924 Czechoslovakia legislated to authorize the Government to take over claims against the previous administrations and pay them,[10] but in 1926 further legislation was enacted to the effect that Czechoslovakia was not responsible for

1 F.O. 83/2287; O'Connell, Appendix, no. 31.
2 Fauchille, vol. I, pt. I, p. 232.   3 *Loc. cit.* p. 57, n. 2.
4 Treaty of St Germain, *B.T.S.* 1919, no. 7, Cmd. 400, art. 204 at p. 57; Treaty of Trianon, *B.T.S.* 1920, no. 10, Cmd. 896, art. 186 at p. 53.
5 Feilchenfeld, p. 532.
6 Reply of the Allied and Associated Powers to the Observations of the German delegation on the Conditions of Peace, Cmd. 258. Clemenceau replied, in a note of 20 June 1919, that the maintenance of the Alsace-Lorraine debt had never been in doubt, and that France would assume charge of it: Feilchenfeld, p. 547.
7 See *infra*, vol. II. p. 180.
8 Sbirika Zakonu a Mařizeni, 1918, Zakon, no. 11.
9 *Succession in Obligations (Fees Paid in Error)* Case; *Ann. Dig.* vol. III, Case no. 50, *Succession in Obligations (Advance Payment of Duty)* Case, *ibid.* vol. IV, Case no. 58.
10 *Ibid.* vol. III, p. 72.

obligations arising out of transactions of these administrations, except as provided for in the peace treaties.[1] Until that date, Czech courts universally gave effect to contractual debts arising against the Austro-Hungarian government.[2]

(v) *The debts of the German colonies after 1919*

A unique exception to the universal principle adopted with respect to local debts in the Peace Treaties is that afforded by the case of the German colonies placed under Mandate. The Treaty of Versailles enacted that 'neither the territory nor the Mandatory is to be charged with any portion of the debt of the German Empire or States'.[3] The Reparations Commission found itself in the position of having to decide whether this exclusion was intended to embrace the bonded debts of the German colonies themselves.[4] These debts were owed by the colonies as joint debts to the creditors and each other, and were thus undoubtedly debts of fiscally autonomous regions.[5] The Mandatory Powers refused to recognize a responsibility with respect to such debts because, it was contended, the colonial budgets had shown deficits and the colonies had not benefited from foreign investments.[6] Some controversy on the matter persisted between Great Britain and Germany until 1930 when the latter abandoned its claims.[7]

The question of the unbonded debts of the colonies was no less controversial. In 1922 the *Reichsgericht* held that the German Government was liable for rent payable by the administration of German East Africa in 1916–20, on the ground that, even though by general principles of law Great Britain would have been responsible for the private law liabilities of the ceded territories, the Treaty of Versailles had expressly excluded this principle. Germany was therefore held precluded from arguing that it had ceased to be liable for obligations of its lost colonies.[8]

The Court considered the separation of the *Reich* and the colonies, resulting from the latter's financial independence, as fictitious. The Treaty

1 *Ibid.* vol. IV, Case no. 58.
2 U.N. Doc. A/CN. 4/157, p. 110, s. 401.
3 Treaty of Versailles, *B.T.S.* 1919, Cmd. 153, art. 257.
4 It was considered that art. 257 referred only to the debts of the German Empire and States, and not to the debts of the colonies themselves: Mann in *Journal of Comparative Legislation and International Law*, 3rd ser., vol. XVI (1934), no. 4, pp. 281–8.
5 Feilchenfeld, p. 557.
6 Reply to the Allied and Associated Powers, *loc. cit.* p. 20.
7 Feilchenfeld, p. 562.
8 *Tanganyika Succession* Case, *Ann. Dig.* vol. I, Case no. 34; *S. Th.* v. *German Treasury*, *Ann. Dig.* vol. II, Case no. 29. Mann in *Journal of Comparative Legislation and International Law*, 3rd ser., vol. XVI (1934), no. 4, p. 281.

of Versailles provisions, under which Germany assumed liability for certain colonial obligations, were regarded as confirmation of a general principle whereby Germany was the entity fundamentally liable.[1] In 1926 the question came before a different Chamber of the *Reichsgericht* in connexion with a claim for return of a judicial deposit in the court at Windhuk, and the Chamber held that the territory itself was originally liable for the debt, and that this debt could not have passed to the *Reich* in virtue of the transfer of sovereignty to South Africa.[2] In the case of bonded debts of the colonies, Germany had been liable as guarantor, and the *Reichsgericht* held in 1932 that, the corporate character of the colonies having survived the transfer to the Mandatory Powers, the principal debt had not been extinguished, and the guarantee had consequently not been affected by political change.[3]

The distinction drawn by the *Reichsgericht* in these three cases was between obligations which, though contracted by local authorities, could be attributable to the German Empire, and hence to the *Reich*, and obligations arising out of acts of local administration which were not attributable to the *Reich*. This followed from the implied distinction in the Treaty of Versailles[4] itself between the debts of the German Empire, which were not to be undertaken by any of the Mandatory Powers, and administrative debts which were not referred to in the Treaty. The *Reichsgericht* was impressed by the fact that the Mandatory administrations had pursued administrative debts which were owing to the German colonial administrations, and, without deciding that the Mandatory Powers were liable under the law of State succession, concluded from this that there was a general recognition that Germany was not liable.[5] Such a conclusion also appeared to follow from a statute of 1892 which had provided that only colonial property was attachable for colonial administrative debts.

The question was also discussed in the South African courts in 1936 when a suit was prosecuted by a bondholder against the Administrator of the Mandated Territory of South West Africa for payment of capital and interest on bearer bonds issued by the German Protectorate of South West Africa. Although the Protectorate was fiscally autonomous under the law

1 *Tanganyika Succession* Case, ibid. vol. I, Case no. 34. Followed in *S. Th.* v. *German Treasury*, ibid. vol. II, Case no. 29.
2 *X.* v. *German Reich*, RGZ, 113, 281, confirming appeal from the *Kammergericht* decision reported in *Ann. Dig.* vol. III, Case no. 55. Followed in 1929, *Fontes Juris Gent.* ser. A., vol. II, no. 14; and in 1930, *South West Africa (Succession)* Case, *Ann. Dig.* vol. V, Case no. 35.
3 *Sch.* v. *Germany*, *Ann. Dig.* vol. VI, Case no. 31; RGZ 137, 1 (415). Dahm calls this 'indirect succession', vol. I, p. 102.
4 Art. 257.   5 *X.* v. *German Reich*, RGZ, 113, 281 (1926).

Acquired Rights and Local Debts

of the *Reich*, with its own accounts and a separate juridical status from that of the *Reich*, this factor was irrelevant because the creation of the Mandate, and the provisions of the Treaty of Versailles respecting the liability of Germany for the debts of the former colonies, had terminated the territory's personality. The problem, the court concluded, was one of succession, not one of continuity, and it was soluble in an English court by reference to the doctrine of act of State.[1]

In 1923 the Anglo-German Mixed Arbitral Tribunal was concerned with a claim by an English company for payment of a draft drawn to its order before the outbreak of the Second World War by the administration of the German protectorate of Kamerun on the *Kolonialhauptkasse* in Berlin. The Tribunal rejected the contention that the *Reich* was the debtor, saying:

> La tutelle administrative exercée sur le protectorat, et en vertu de laquelle le budget du protectorat doit être arrêté par l'Empire allemand à Berlin, n'exclut pas l'existence séparée du protectorat en tant que personne juridique de droit privé, notamment en matière commerciale. Cette existence séparée résulte, entre autres, de la loi allemande du 30 mars 1892 dont la cinquième section prévoit que les obligations pécuniaires naissant de l'administration du protectorat n'engagent que les seuls avoirs du protectorat. Ceci exclut toute dette ou responsabilité de l'Empire en ce qui concerne les transactions qui sont l'œuvre des agents du protectorat.[2]

(vi) *The independence of British dependencies*

All borrowings of British colonies, in whatever form, are made by the colonial authorities and are charges on colonial revenues alone. The Colonial Service Regulations, Part II—Public Business, 1951, require the presentation of annual estimates in which revenue and expenditure are shown, and expenditure is only permitted in virtue of an annual colonial Appropriation Law. Any grant or loan from the United Kingdom must be credited in the first instance to a suspense account, and transfers to revenue must take place monthly to balance the actual expenditure. Other loans are authorized only by a colonial law, and if this does not specifically authorize the execution of the particular works contemplated, and the amount to be expended upon each, a further Appropriation Law, and the consent of the Secretary of State, are required. Estimated loan expenditure does not appear in the body of the estimates, but a full statement thereof is appended to the general estimates and must receive the approval of the colonial legislature.

1 *Verein für Schutzgebietsanleihen E. V.* v. *Conradie* [1937] S.A.L.R. (Cape Prov. App. Div.), 113; *Ann. Dig.* vol. VIII, Case no. 40.
2 *The Niger Co. Ltd* v. *Germany, Recueil des décisions des Tribunaux Arbitraux Mixtes* (1923–4), p. 232.

All British dependencies at the date of grant of independence were subject to four categories of loans:
  (*a*) Loans under the Colonial Stock Acts;
  (*b*) Loans from the International Bank for Reconstruction and Development;
  (*c*) Colonial Welfare and Development Loans;
  (*d*) Other raisings on the London or local stock markets.

All these loans have remained charged to the territories after independence, and continue to be effective under the legislation authorizing them. They continue to be shown in the relevant financial statements officially produced by the newly independent governments in the post-independence fiscal year.

(*A*) *Colonial Stock Act, 1877*. This Act[1] provided for the inscription in a register kept in the United Kingdom of any stock forming the whole or part of the public debt of a colony. Transfers of stock were to be recorded in the register, but, if authorized by the colonial government, bearer certificates might be issued to which coupons entitling the bearer to dividends would be attached, and transfers of bearer certificates would not be registered. Section 19 provided that any prospectus inviting subscription for stock, and every certificate and coupon, should state that the revenues of the colony alone would be liable in respect of the stock and dividends thereon, and that the Consolidated Fund of the United Kingdom and the United Kingdom Treasury Commissioners would not directly or indirectly be liable or responsible for the payment of the stock or the dividends thereon, or for any matter relating thereto. However, it would be no defence to any legal proceedings in a court in the United Kingdom in relation to the register of colonial stock that the court had no jurisdiction on the ground that the registrar is the agent of a colonial government. Any person claiming an interest in colonial stock might proceed in the United Kingdom by petition of right, but any judgment, decree, rule or order of the court should be complied with only by the registrar or other agent of the colonial government having possession in England of moneys of such government, and not by the United Kingdom Treasury. For the purpose of the Act a colony means any dominion, colony, island, territory, province or settlement situate within the Crown's dominions, but outside the United Kingdom and India. In 1900 colonial stock was made a trustee investment stock in the United Kingdom.[2] In 1929 the Act was extended to the protectorates.[3]

In 1948 legislation[4] was enacted to provide for the extension by United

[1] 1877, 40 & 41 Vict., c. 59. [2] 63 & 64 Vict., c. 62. [3] 20 & 21 Geo. V, c. 5.
[4] 11 & 12 Geo. VI, c. 56, amended by 12 & 13 Geo. VI, c. 1.

Kingdom Order in Council of the provisions of the Colonial Stock Act to stock issued thereafter by any Government or authority administering services or matters of common interest to the inhabitants of more than one of the colonies or territories to whose stock the Act of 1877 and its amendments could be made applicable.

The effect of this legislation was to import into any contract of loan respecting inscribed stock a clause defining the borrower as the colony itself, and making the revenues of the colony alone liable. Under the proper law of the contract there could be no recourse against the United Kingdom government in the event of colonial default. Independence of a colony clearly has no effect upon the contractual nexus between the colony and the creditor, and the United Kingdom cannot, under the terms of the contract, be made liable. This conclusion is reached, whether the emphasis is placed on the fiscal autonomy of the colony, on the continuity of its internal legal system and its borrowing institutions, or on the association between the loan and the revenues nominated for its amortization.

In each of the independence Acts[1] the Colonial Stock legislation is repealed with respect to each former colony. The effect is to transfer the stock register to the newly independent government, and to repeal the grant of jurisdiction to the United Kingdom courts in respect of the relevant stock. It follows that the only avenue of recourse available to a creditor is in the courts of the former colonies. These generally already had jurisdiction under colonial ordinances to permit suit against the colonial government.[2] But where there was no legislation making the colonial government liable there is some doubt whether action under a contract of loan could be taken at all.[3] Much depends in English law upon whether a contract of loan is characterized as an exercise of governmental functions, or whether it can be regarded as in the nature of a commercial contract. But, in either event, the new State would incur international responsibility towards foreign stockholders, because these had, as part of their right, a domestic remedy in United Kingdom courts; and it is arguable that the borrower must restore at least an equivalent remedy after independence.

In an exchange of notes of 16 August 1960 accompanying the signature of the Cyprus Establishment Treaty,[4] Cyprus confirmed that it would submit to the jurisdiction in respect of any action brought in the United Kingdom courts under the Colonial Stock Act, in respect of any stock registered in the United Kingdom before or after independence. Pursuant

---

[1] See *supra*, p. 52.   [2] *Bonython* v. *The Commonwealth* [1951] A.C. 201.
[3] Mitchell in *Modern Law Review*, vol. XIII (1950), pp. 318, 455.
[4] Cmd. 1252, p. 102.

to this undertaking, the Cyprus Act, 1960[1] provided in the Schedule for Cyprus stock to continue to be governed by the Colonial Stock Acts, though certain consequential amendments were made respecting actions in United Kingdom courts.

In anticipation of independence, the Legislature of Uganda on 9 October 1962 enacted the Uganda Government Securities Ordinance,[2] which provided that, whenever a United Kingdom court adjudged any sum of money payable by the Government of Uganda in respect of any Colonial Stock securities, that sum should, without further appropriation than the Ordinance, be charged on and paid out of the revenues of Uganda, and adequate funds should be made available in the United Kingdom by the Government of Uganda to settle the judgment. Also, no legislation affecting these securities in such a way as to involve a departure from the original contract in regard thereto should become law except after agreement with the United Kingdom Government.

(B) *Colonial Development Loans.* In 1958 a Commonwealth Trade and Economic Conference was held in London, which reported[3] that one of the sharpest limitations on the development of underdeveloped countries was a world-wide shortage of capital. Even if these countries increasingly mobilized their own savings to finance their programmes of capital investment, a large gap would still remain which could only be filled by investment from abroad, and that while private investment would play an important part there was also need of governmental assistance.[4] The United Kingdom announced its intention to make Commonwealth assistance loans from Exchequer funds. In the case of already independent Commonwealth countries these loans would be made under authority of the Export Guarantees Acts 1949[5] and 1957,[6] and so far as colonial territories were concerned they would be made under the Colonial Development and Welfare legislation.[7]

The Colonial Development and Welfare Acts 1940–59 were consolidated in 1959.[8] They authorize the Treasury to make loans to the government of any colony for the purposes of a development programme approved by the Secretary of State and by the legislature of the colony. The terms of the loan would be fixed by the United Kingdom Treasury. The funds for lending might be issued from the Consolidated Fund, or raised pursuant to the National Loan Act, 1939.[9] Section 6 provides that a

1 8 & 9 Eliz. II, c. 52.
2 No. 51 of 1962. Similar legislation has been enacted by Sierra Leone, no. 13 of 1961; Jamaica, no. 3 of 1962, and Trinidad and Tobago, no. 14 of 1962.
3 Cmnd. 539.   4 P. 5.   5 12 & 13 Geo. VI, c. 14.
6 5 & 6 Eliz. II, c. 23.   7 Cmnd. 539, p. 13.   8 7 & 8 Eliz. II, c. 71.
9 2 & 3 Geo. VI, c. 117.

scheme which was made solely for the benefit of any colony shall, if the colony at any time ceases to be a colony, cease to have effect at that time, without prejudice to the making of payments in pursuance of the scheme after that time in respect of any period falling before that time. However, a scheme may be made after independence with respect to a body established for the joint benefit of the former colony and any other colony, and sums paid out of moneys provided by Parliament might be employed for the purposes of such a scheme made before independence, if the government of the former colony undertakes to bear a reasonable share of the cost of the scheme.

The Colonial Development Corporation was established by Act of Parliament in 1948,[1] and the legislation was consolidated in the Overseas Resources Development Act, 1959.[2] The function of the Corporation is to assist the development of dependent territories of the Commonwealth, and it is empowered to undertake projects to this end. When a country in which a project has been approved attains independence, the Corporation is authorized to continue the project, but not to start new projects. The Corporation has a statutory obligation to pay its way, and is operated commercially. It may raise up to £150 million on a long- or medium-term basis for the purpose of financing its projects. As at the end of 1963 the Corporation's outlays were expressed in millions of pounds as follows: Caribbean (17.46), Far East (20.685), East Africa (22.98), West Africa (13.129).[3] In both Malaya and Nigeria the Corporation had established participation in local generalized development agencies before independence, and was enabled to carry on its function of helping to promote new development projects, notably in the field of agriculture.

(vii) *The transfer of Newfoundland to Canada, 1949*

By the British North America Act, 1949, Canada was to assume and provide for the servicing of the stock issued and to be issued on the security of Newfoundland.[4]

(viii) *The independence of Ceylon, 1947*

All interest on the public debt, sinking fund payments and the like of Ceylon were charged on the consolidated Fund of the new Dominion.[5]

1 11 & 12 Geo. VI, c. 15. Now Commonwealth Development Corporation (1963).
2 7 & 8 Eliz. II, c. 23.
3 Report and Accounts, 1963.
4 British North America Act, 1949, 12 & 13 Geo. VI, c. 22, s. 23.
5 S.R. & O. 1946, Appendix of Prerogative Orders, no. 2, s. 66.

(ix) *The independence of Burma, 1947*

The financial arrangements made with Burma represent an attempt on the part of Great Britain to rehabilitate that country. The Government of the United Kingdom agreed[1] to cancel £15 million of the sums advanced towards deficits on the Ordinary and Frontier Areas Budget. The balance of the sums was to be repaid by Burma in twenty equal instalments, beginning not later than 1 April 1952, no interest being chargeable. This was accepted by the Provisional Government as a 'further contribution by the Government of the United Kingdom towards the restoration of Burma's financial position, and as a final liquidation of their claim in respect of the cost of supplies and services furnished to the British Military Administration in Burma'. The Provisional Government agreed to repay in full the sums advanced by the Government of the United Kingdom towards expenditure on various projects such as public utilities, according to the terms of existing agreements. Repayment would continue to be made from current receipts in excess of necessary outgoings and working capital, and from the proceeds of liquidation. The balance of advances then outstanding was to be repaid in twenty equal instalments beginning not later than 1 April 1952, no interest being chargeable.

Burma had its own financial system before it became independent, and Burmese loans had the status of trustee stocks.[2] The Governor was obliged to secure the provision of all requisite funds to meet claims, including pensions, of the United Kingdom.[3] Hence Burma's debt was a local one, and there is little doubt that it would have continued to be binding after the change of sovereignty. The Japanese occupation, however, had left Burma in a bankrupt condition, and the figure mentioned above had been advanced by the United Kingdom as an interest-free loan to enable Burma to discharge its indebtedness and balance the budget. Of this sum £8 million had been advanced during the financial year October 1945–September 1946, and it had been agreed that a further sum of £7½ million would be advanced which would be converted into an outright grant if the facts of further study warranted it. This in fact was done when Burma became independent.[4]

When Burma became fiscally autonomous in 1937, the uncovered debt

1 Treaty between the United Kingdom and the Provisional Government of Burma regarding the Recognition of Burmese Independence and Related Matters, *B.T.S.* 1948, no. 16, Cmd. 7360, art. 6 (2).
2 Government of Burma Act, 1935, 26 Geo. V & Edw. VIII, c. 3, s. 65.
3 *Ibid.* s. 58.
4 Cmd. 7029.

Acquired Rights and Local Debts

was allocated on the basis of the respective contributions to the Central Exchequer. Burma's contribution in the form of receipts from income tax, customs and tributes was found to be $9\frac{1}{4}$ per cent. The percentage actually arrived at on the basis of locally collected taxes was 8 per cent, and this was reduced to $7\frac{1}{2}$ per cent. The principal and interest were calculated taking into account the interest payments, discounts, date of redemption, etc., and the rate of interest was based on the average yield over the preceding two years of loan, with a currency of fifteen years and over. On the basis of this financial allocation there was a capital sum repayable to India which initially amounted to Rs. 70,79,81,000 repayable over a period of forty-five years, and exclusive of pensions. The repayment of the debt, and of Burma's share of the pension, was interrupted by the war and not resumed before independence.[1] In 1952 India calculated that the total which Burma owed her was Rs. 707,500,000, comprising Rs. 650,000,000 on account of debt and Rs. 57,500,000 on account of pensions. No payment at that date had been made for ten years.[2] In 1957 an agreement was negotiated with Burma for a final settlement, according to which India agreed to reduce the capital sum to Rs. 200,000,000 and renounce claim to interest, and Burma agreed to pay India out of the purchase price for Burmese rice in 1954 a sum equal to £13 for every ton bought. India agreed that the balance of the Burmese debt, after allowing for receipts of Rs. 156,000,000, should be settled either by treating it as financial aid to Burma under the Colombo Plan, or by part adjustment against the sale price of any Burmese rice bought by India in 1954, as might be agreed upon. The net sum due to or from Burma from or to India in connexion with the termination of the common currency arrangements between the two countries would be deducted from or added to the balance of the debt.[3]

There was, therefore, no question of Burma's liability to service its pre-independence debt, and India's claims in this respect are significant. At the date of independence, apart from the Indian loan, Burma owed the United Kingdom K356 million, which was discharged by agreement by a down payment of K97 million, and $5,042,501.37 due to the United States under the Lease–Lend Agreement. The latter was repayable in twenty instalments beginning in 1947, of which $3,182,182.14 had been paid by 1957. Burma also owed Pakistan K81.50, being its proportion of Indian debt, negotiations respecting which were still in progress.

1 Maung Maung, *Burma's Constitution*, p. 212.
2 India, Parliamentary Debates (Lok Sabha), vol. I, no. 3, pp. 87–8; Cook, *Burma, Economic Survey* (H.M.S.O., 1957), p. 36.
3 Financial Agreement between India and Burma of 12 March 1957 (copy supplied).

(x) *Loans, advances and investment of private capital in Mandated Territories*

The question of continuance of private interests in Mandated Territories in the event of cessation or transfer of the Mandate arose for discussion in the Permanent Mandates Commission and the Council of the League when Australia asked for Council sanction for a loan to New Guinea in 1924. The loan was intended to be a general charge on the revenues of the territory. The Council refused to sanction it on the grounds that the transaction was the sole responsibility of the Mandatory, but it noted and raised no objection to the loan.[1] This incident occurred while a questionnaire was in circulation to all the Mandatory States asking for opinion on the power of Mandatories to hypothecate revenues for loans, and on whether such obligations would devolve upon successive Mandatories. All the Mandatories except Australia considered Council sanction for loans superfluous, and all, including Australia, expressed the view that any succeeding Mandatory would be bound by such contracts.[2] The answers resulted in the Council's adopting the following resolution on 15 September 1925:

The Council:

(1) Declares that the validity of financial obligations assumed by a mandatory Power on behalf of a mandated territory in conformity with the provisions of the mandate and all rights regularly acquired under the mandatory régime are in no way impaired by the fact that the territory is administered under mandate.

(2) Agrees on the following principles:

(*a*) That the cessation or transfer of a mandate cannot take place unless the council has been assured in advance that the financial obligations regularly acquired under the administration of the former mandatory Power shall be respected; and

(*b*) That when this change has been effected the Council will continue to use all its influence to ensure the fulfilment of these obligations.[3]

In the course of the discussion following the Australian request, a distinction was drawn between hypothecating revenues for loans, and charging them on public works in the Mandated Territory. It was suggested that the latter course, in the event of transfer of the Mandate, would have the same effect as annexation of part of the Mandated Territory by the Mandatory if it were to retain the security after transfer. Hence it was suggested that a floating charge on revenues, which would pass to successive governments but which would not burden the territory

---

1 *L.N. Off. J.* vol. V, pp. 1333, 1596.
2 *Ibid.* pp. 497–501.
3 *Idem*, vol. VI, p. 1511.

as a mortgage, would be more acceptable.[1] It was generally considered that this attitude was excessively protective in view of the Council's supervisory powers, and the distinction was not incorporated into the resolution finally adopted by the Council.

(xi) *The independence of Israel, 1948*

The Palestine budget was autonomous, but grants in aid were received from the United Kingdom amounting between 1922 and 1945 to £14,000,000. In 1944–5 the income was £17,496,000 and the expenditure £18,196,000, of which taxation and licence fees brought in £6,450,000 and customs duties £3,576,000.[2]

As long as Great Britain did not recognize Israel, even *de facto*, it was impossible to commence discussions on the latter's liabilities, and it was not until 4 July 1949 that negotiations were opened in Tel Aviv. That a successor to the Mandatory would normally be obliged to undertake the latter's financial responsibilities was never directly contraverted. In fact article 28 of the Mandate itself indicated that the government which followed the Mandatory Administration should fully honour the obligations incurred during the period of the Mandate. Great Britain insisted that international law imposed on Israel a direct responsibility, and sought to extract from that country an assurance that it accepted State succession in principle. The Resolution of the United Nations of 29 November 1947, it was argued, was merely a recognition of the application of this principle to the case of Israel. Israel continued to maintain, however, that the law of State succession could not apply to the present case, and the legal arguments of the two delegations were so divergent that it was decided to discard them altogether. The negotiations were then removed to London, where an agreement was reached in March 1950, based entirely on compromise.[3]

The Government of Palestine in 1927 had issued a loan of £4,475,000 Palestine at 5 per cent, the payment of the principal and interest of which was guaranteed by the United Kingdom.[4] In 1942 this loan was converted into one of 3 per cent, the accumulated funds for discharge having been utilized to reimburse bearers who did not wish to exchange their bonds.

[1] P.M.C. Minutes, 5th Session, p. 179; draft decision submitted by Sir Fredrick Lugard.
[2] Paenson, p. 35.
[3] B.T.S. 1950, no. 26, Cmd. 7941, art. 4. Israel assumed responsibility for the discharge of liability in respect of all such bonds as were held and registered in Israel, provisionally assessed at £4,340,000. The United Kingdom was to remain responsible for bonds not held and registered in Israel.
[4] Finance Act, 1934.

The total raising was expended on railways, ports, telecommunications and construction of buildings. In article 2(*b*) of the agreement of 30 March 1950 the United Kingdom undertook the responsibility of servicing this debt, but Israel made a contribution of £3,500,000 representing the value of railways and other installations located on the territory of Israel. The Government of Palestine had also issued bearer bonds to the amount of £4,340,000 for which Israel assumed responsibility. This was partly in consideration of recognition of Israel's right to recover the loans made by the Government of Palestine to the local bodies, amounting to £2,914,000. The balance was transferred by the United Kingdom to Israel. In effect, Israel assumed responsibility for the payment of creditors resident in Israel of a sum equal to that recoverable from debtors resident therein. The United Kingdom continued to be responsible for all bearer bonds not registered in Israel.[1] Israel received a part of the funds for liquidation valued at £374,000 as well as part of the interest accumulated on the fund and not expended of £2,664,033. This was valued at £86,000. The United Kingdom was credited with the funds for liquidation, and the accumulated interest of the unused portion of the raising of £2,644,033. The Government of Israel regards this agreement as conclusive in respect of any claims against Palestine based upon the former Ottoman Debt.[2]

In 1948 the United Kingdom Parliament legislated to provide that any Defence Bonds or Palestine Savings Certificates issued by the Government of Palestine under the War Loan Ordinance, 1941, should be treated for purposes of the National Loans Act, 1939, as if the money raised thereby had been raised under that Act through United Kingdom agencies, and as if the bonds and securities had been issued under that Act, and the liability had been expressed in currency of the United Kingdom at par with that of Palestine.[3] With respect to the Palestine Loan of 1942, it was provided by Order in Council[4] that the sinking fund thereof would continue to be held by the trustees, and the provisions of the Ordinance would continue to govern them. The sinking funds[5] and unspent capital[6] held by the Crown Agents in trust for the Government of Palestine under any Ordinance providing for the issue of bearer bonds would vest in the Crown Agents, pending directions of the British Government. Like provisions were made with respect to pension and provident funds, post

1 Art. 4.
2 Information submitted by the Government of Israel to the U.N. on the Question of Succession of States and Governments, 1963, p. 13.
3 Finance Act, 1948, 11 & 12 Geo. VI, c. 49, s. 81.
4 S.R. & O. no. 1003 of 1948.   5 S. 5.
6 S.R. & O. no. 138 of 1949, s. 2.

Acquired Rights and Local Debts

office savings bank credits, police and other funds, and these were to be applied to the discharge of all obligations of the former Government of Palestine.[1]

(xii) *The independence of the Philippines, 1946*

The Tydings–McDuffie Act of 1934, by which the United States created the machinery for independence of the Philippines, was accepted by the Philippines legislature, and provided[2] for the Philippines to undertake responsibility for the debts contracted during the colonial period. Since a period of transition to independence was envisaged, it would be possible to liquidate portion of the debt, and provision was made for the allocation of export taxes to this end. A distinction was made between obligations of the Archipelago and its political subdivisions before 1934, which had been authorized by the United States Congress, and other public debts. Provision was made that the United States would not be liable for any post-1934 debts,[3] and the inference has been drawn[4] that it intended to remain liable in respect of the Congress-authorized pre-1934 debts, despite the fact that they were charged on the revenues of the Archipelago. By a law of 1939, the Government of the Philippines assigned the export revenues to the United States Treasury for the purpose of setting up a special fund for the amortization of the pre-1934 debt which had been authorized by Congress, but provided merely for the service by the Philippines of other debts which were payable out of the ordinary revenues. This suggests that the United States felt some responsibility to the bondholders in respect of Congress-authorized debt, but not in respect of other debts, and the suggestion is supported by a provision in the legislation that, if at the date of independence the special fund should be insufficient for service of the Congress-authorized debt, the Philippines would make a payment to balance the account.

Article 17 of the Constitution stipulated that the Philippines would assume all the debts and obligations of the Commonwealth of the Philippines, its provinces and municipalities existing at the date of independence. In the treaty with the United States the Philippines assumed all the debts and liabilities both general and administrative of the islands.[5]

[1] S. 12.   [2] B.F.S.P. vol. CXXXVII, p. 690.   [3] S. 9.
[4] Fischer, *Un Cas de décolonisation: Les États-Unis et les Philippines* (1960), p. 264.
[5] U.N.T.S. vol. VII (1947), no. 1, p. 4, art. 4. Though it cannot be said that Manchukuo became independent in 1932, the attitude of those who claimed that it did might be instructive. In the declaration of 1 March 1932, it was stated that 'money obligations, incurred within the territory of Manchukuo by treaty stipulation with various countries prior to the establishment of the new State, shall be met according to the usual international conventions': R.I.I.A. *Docs. on Int. Aff.* 1932, p. 278.

(xiii) *The independence of Indochina, 1948–53*

By decree of 23 October 1948[1] an Indochinese Treasury was created which undertook charge of all obligations contracted in the name of the former government of Indochina. The Treasury was required to ensure the guarantee of the budgets of the Associated States of Vietnam, Laos and Cambodia and their public bodies and of the financial services of the French Union. It was authorized to contract loans, issue bonds and receive advances from the National Bank of Indochina, which was an issuing authority. At a Conference in Pau in 1951, it was agreed that the National Treasury should be dissolved into treasuries for each of the three Associated States. An independent bank for the servicing of the debt was created, to be directed by a new issuing authority which would take over the functions of the Bank of Indochina. The new Bank was required to service the debt of the three States, and was authorized to contract loans within the limits necessary to honour the obligations of the former Treasury.

The liquidation of the Central Treasury of Indochina was provided for in Protocol no. 2 of the Quadripartite Convention signed in Paris in December 1954 between France, Cambodia, Laos and Vietnam.[2] The *actif* and the *passif* of the Treasury were dealt with uniformly. France undertook the *actif* of advances by the Treasury to French nationals, the credit of Air France, and the losses due to the revaluation of the piastre in 1945; and also the *passif* of the advances agreed to by France for the financing of equipment, the balance on account of the operations of the Indochinese Treasury with the French Treasury, and the service of loans issued by the former Government-General of Indochina, as well as debts not the object of particular agreement. The budgetary deficits as they would appear in the last balance sheet of the Indochina Treasury would be undertaken by the three successor States on the following basis: debit balances on account for the execution of works in a State, advances made for public and collective enterprises of a State, and any other debts notionally related to a State would be attributed to that State. Annexed tables of accounts included current accounts for public works. The agreement of December 1954 relative to the transfer of monetary institutions to Cambodia, Laos and Vietnam transferred 'les créances et les dettes, les droits et les charges qui, par leur nature ou leur origine, s'identifient territorialement ou "géographiquement" au regard de l'un ou de l'autre des États'.

1 Decree no. 48–1656, *Journal Officiel*, 24 October 1948, p. 10403.
2 *Notes et Études Documentaires*, Doc., 1955, no. 1973, p. 17.

(xiv) *The cession of the French Establishments in India, 1954*

The agreement of 21 October 1954 between France and India[1] respecting the transfer to the latter of the French Establishments provided that on the date of transfer *de facto* the local public accounts would be stopped in the entries of the Treasury of the territories, and the Government of India would be substituted for the French Government in all the credits, debts and deficits of the various accounts concerning the local administration. It would reimburse France the sums advanced from the Treasury, other than those by way of gift.

(xv) *The independence of Libya and Ethiopia*

General Assembly Resolution 388 (V) of the United Nations concerning the independence of Libya provided in article 4 that Libya would be exempted from any part of the Italian public debt. Ethiopia also did not succeed to any part of this debt in virtue of article 14 of the Treaty of Peace. However, all Italy's successor States assumed the obligations of the Italian Government towards creditors resident in the ceded territories in respect of debts contracted prior to 10 July 1940 and attributable to public works and civil administrative services of benefit to the territory.

(xvi) *The restoration of Austria's independence, 1945*

At the Potsdam Conference in 1945 the annexation of Austria was declared to be null and void, and it was stated that Austria would not be asked for reparations. This has been regarded as relieving Austria from any financial obligations of Germany resulting from the Second World War.[2] Owing to its having no foreign exchange, Austria was unable to service the pre-*Anschluss* debt, although in 1946 the Austrian Government expressed its willingness to do so in Austrian schillings at the new rate of exchange. The following year it informed the British Council of the Corporation of Foreign Bondholders that it would discuss the external debt after a peace treaty had been concluded and the financial position was known. In 1949 when a 5 per cent internal reconstruction loan was floated, it was announced that it would be possible to cash in 1938 State Loan Bonds in payment therefor, although no obligations would be assumed by Austria for loans raised by the German occupation forces.

On 5 July 1951 the Committee of Control of the Guarantor States for the Reconstruction of Austria met for the first time since the *Anschluss*. The Guarantor States had been honouring their guarantees by servicing

1 *Annuaire français* (1955), p. 703, arts. 19, 20.
2 Clute, *The International Legal Status of Austria, 1938–1955* (1962), p. 89.

the Austrian Government International Guaranteed Loans of 1933 and the Austrian Government Guaranteed Conversion of 1934. The Austrian Government continued to express its willingness to enter into negotiations concerning its pre-*Anschluss* external debt as soon as financial circumstances permitted. In November 1952 a conference was convened at Rome to discuss the matter further, and an agreement was reached which was submitted to interested governments and bodies. Austria undertook to resume service of its external bonded debt as from 1 January 1954, including the Austrian proportion of the Austro-Hungarian debt. Certain foreign securities would require to be revalidated, either because redeemed certificates had not been cancelled or because they had been lost or looted from German and Austrian vaults during the war. Legislation was enacted in 1953 for this purpose, and revalidation agreements were concluded with foreign countries. Apart from a reduction of interest and extension of maturity dates, servicing by Austria of the pre-*Anschluss* debt commenced in 1954.[1]

With respect to the service of the Austrian external bonded debt during the period of the *Anschluss*, Austria took the position that Germany should pay the interest charges and payments of principal which fell due during the period. On 23 October 1950 the Chairman of the Allied Commission for Germany inquired of the German Government whether it agreed with the Austrian position, and in 1951 Germany undertook payment 'for interest and other charges' during the *Anschluss* period, but with a proviso about the extent of Germany's surviving territory.[2] The Agreement on German External Debts signed in London on 27 February 1953 provided that the German Federal Republic would pay 60 per cent of the arrears of interest and amortization of Austria's external bonded debt which had fallen due during the period of the *Anschluss*.[3] On 13 October 1954 Germany announced that it would commence payments on 1 July 1955 of Austrian bonds which had fallen due during this period, and offered to pay 75 per cent instead of the original 60 per cent of the arrears.[4] These arrangements were confirmed in the Austrian State Treaty in 1955.[5]

Although Austria has contested the thesis of her succession to Germany, her courts have in fact given indirect effect to contractual and financial obligations of the administration during the period of the *Anschluss* by applying the principle of unjust enrichment.[6]

1. Clute, *op. cit.*, pp. 90–1.
2. T.I.A.S. 2274, *B.T.S.* 1951, no. 85; Cmnd. 836; *B.F.S.P.* vol. CLVIII, p. 262.
3. T.I.A.S. 2792, *B.T.S.* 1959, no. 7, Cmnd. 626; *B.F.S.P.* vol. CLX, p. 245.
4. Clute, *op. cit.* p. 92.
5. T.I.A.S. 3298, art. 28; *B.F.S.P.* vol. CLXII, p. 1209.   6 See *supra*, p. 368.

Austria agreed in 1954 to reimburse Switzerland for expenses incurred between 13 March 1938 and 31 December 1941 for work done on the River Rhine of benefit to both States, at a time when Austria had been occupied by Germany. Germany had refused after 1938 to take over Austria's obligations in this respect, but in fact voluntarily carried out some work. While Austria was liable to pay the arrears she was able as a part set-off to claim the benefit of the work voluntarily done by Germany. This was accepted by Switzerland.[1]

(xvii) *The independence of Indonesia, 1949*

The Netherlands East Indies constituted a separate juridical and fiscal personality, the history and incidence of which are discussed earlier.[2] The independence of Indonesia therefore constituted a classical instance of continuity of a fiscal entity.

The Agreement on Transitional Measures reached at the Round Table Conference in the Hague in 1949[3] provided in article 4 (1) that all rights and obligations, under private law as well as under public law, of the Netherlands Indies would be transferred to Indonesia. Indonesia alone would be responsible for the performance of the obligations of the public bodies in the Netherlands Indies which were dissolved into the State of Indonesia or into one of its subdivisions; and Indonesia guaranteed the performance of the obligations binding upon those public bodies which continued to exist after the transfer of sovereignty.

The Economic and Financial Agreement of 2 November 1949 listed the debts to be taken over by Indonesia[4] as follows: the consolidated debt of the Government of the Netherlands Indies and the portion attributed to it in the consolidated debt of the Netherlands, the debts contracted under the Marshall Plan and to the United States in 1947, to Canada in 1945 and to Australia in 1949, and to the Netherlands in the credits granted by the United Kingdom. All the other debts of the Netherlands Indies were contracted directly to the Netherlands. Article 25 transferred to Indonesia 'all internal debts', which under article 26 Indonesia undertook to repay with interest, receiving, in return, all rights of the Indies in the debts to the Netherlands. Under article 27 the balance of debts due from the Indies to the Netherlands was cancelled. This resulted in a reduction of the external debt to the Netherlands to 2,000 million guilders as at 31 December 1949.[5] The waiver of claims and the reduction provided in article 27 meant

1 *Feuille Fédérale*, no. 26, 1015–48 (1954).
2 See *supra*, p. 97.
3 *U.N.T.S.* vol. LXIX, pp. 3, 200, 430, 882.
4 Taylor, *Indonesian Independence and the United Nations* (1960), p. 437.
5 See *Bijlage*, IV in Tervooren, p. 358.

merely that a part of the external debt of the Netherlands Indies to the Netherlands was kept out of the succession arrangement, which resulted in the fact that all '*passiva*' on the 'property balance' (assets and liabilities) of the Netherlands Indies as at 31 December 1949 (the time of transfer) were taken over by Indonesia.[1]

It will be seen that article 25 dealt specifically only with the external debts of Indonesia derived from loans and foreign credits, and, because it was agreed that Indonesia would merely take over part of the existing external debt, it became necessary to enumerate these loans and credits in order to limit the general operation of article 4 of the Agreement on Transitional Measures. This limitation was possible because article 4 contained an exception clause referring to the agreements annexed to the Union Statute, one of which was the Financial Agreement.

The Netherlands subsequently contended that the 'internal debts' of Indonesia mentioned in article 25 (D) included the 'remaining debts' of Indonesia to the Netherlands mentioned in article 27—a contention which then and later Indonesia strongly refuted. Remarkably enough, it does not appear that Indonesia at the time argued the question of debts incurred for the purpose of waging a colonial war against the Indonesian people, which must have involved an enormous accumulation of internal debts.

After the independence of Indonesia, action was brought in the Netherlands respecting a balance outstanding as the result of a banking transaction between the plaintiffs and the Netherlands Ministry for the Colonies in exile in London during 1942. A credit balance had accumulated as a result of dollar payments made by the plaintiffs to the Netherlands Purchasing Commission in New York. After the war the Netherlands refused to remit the balance of $750,000 to the plaintiffs out of the Netherlands Treasury, on the ground that the debt attached to the Netherlands Indies as a separate juridical person, and had been succeeded to by Indonesia. The court upheld this, stating that the Netherlands Indies, as a separate person, was legally represented in financial transactions by either the Governor-General or the Minister for the Colonies, and was the only debtor who could be sued.[2]

The same court, however, departed from this principle the following year with respect to a suit arising out of death following an act of a soldier of the Royal Netherlands Indies Army in the Indies.[3]

[1] Tervooren, pp. 140–1.
[2] *Pamanoekan and Tjiasemlanden and Anglo–Dutch Plantations of Java, Ltd* v. *Netherlands*, I.L.R. vol. XIX, Case no. 21.
[3] *Van der Have* v. *State of the Netherlands*, idem, vol. XX, p. 80.

(xviii) *The independence of the Congo (Léopoldville), 1960*

When the Congo was ceded to Belgium in 1907[1] its integration within the Belgian State and its future administration were regulated by two enactments of the Belgian Parliament of 18 October 1908.[2] The first of these ratified the cession; the second, known as the *Charte Coloniale*, effected a separation of the legal personalities of the metropolis and the Colony. Article 18 of this second law stated that the Colony might not contract financial liabilities without legislative authority.[3] The Parliamentary Commissions which examined the *projet* of this law recognized that, in view of the direct control exercised over the Colony's finances by the Belgian Parliament under both article 115 of the Constitution and the *Charte Coloniale*, this fiscal separation was legally somewhat fictitious.[4] It remained, therefore, theoretically possible for a creditor to argue that when the Minister for the Colonies contracted a loan on behalf of the Belgian Congo or Ruanda-Urundi[5] he was indirectly committing the Belgian State to a residual liability.[6] When the Congo attained independence the question of the Colony's debt was carefully avoided, though, at the closing session on 16 May 1960 of the Round Table Conference, a Belgian Minister expressed the opinion that it would remain with the Congo. The political situation in the new Republic after independence made the service of the public debt impossible, and attempts were made to establish that the Belgian State was liable therefor.

The arguments to this end varied according to whether the debt was pre- or post-1908:

With respect to the pre-1908 debts it was argued that the effect of article 3 of the Treaty of Cession in 1908 was to transfer to Belgium the liability in respect of the listed loans of 1898, 1901, 1902, 1904, 1906 and 1907, so that the creditors had gained a direct right against the metropolis. The separation of the metropolitan and colonial *patrimoines* in the *Charte Coloniale* had not negated this transfer, because two laws enacted on the

---

1 *B.F.S.P.* vol. C, p. 705.
2 See *supra*, p. 89.
3 Halewyck, *La Charte coloniale*, vol. I, p. 42; Paulus, *Droit public du Congo*, no. 16.
4 *Documents parlementaires* (Chambre), 1907–8, no. 130; *Documents parlementaires* (Sénat), 1908–9, no. 12. On 17 March 1908 the Government stated that 'l'État belge, reprenant tout l'actif et tous les engagements actuels de l'État indépendant [se trouvait] engagé à assurer le service de la dette antérieure à la reprise dans le cas où la colonie serait dans l'impossibilité d'y faire face': *ibid.* (Chambre), 1907–8, no. 146, p. 143; Halewyck, *op. cit.* vol. I, n. 12.
5 Which had been subjected to the *Charte Coloniale* by a law of 21 August 1925.
6 But this was rejected by the courts: *État belge* v. *De Smet, Journal des Tribunaux* (1960), p. 575.

same day cannot derogate from each other.[1] Since the Belgian courts had already decided that action could be brought in respect of the pre-1908 debt only against the Colony,[2] the proponents of the view that Belgium was liable after Congolese independence took their stand on the contention that the abrogation of the *Charte Coloniale* in the *Loi relative aux structures* of the Congo, by which that independence was achieved, had had the effect of reviving article 3 of the Treaty of Cession, and of fusing the metropolitan and colonial *patrimoines*.

A judgment of the *Cour d'Appel* of Paris[3] in 1956 anticipated the problem that would arise on independence respecting the pre-1908 debt. The action was brought by a holder of a 1901 Congo bond against the Belgian Congo. Though the action was not against the Belgian State, the latter intervened on a plea of immunity to have it dismissed. The *Avocat-Général* was of opinion that Belgium could not, in enacting the *Charte Coloniale*, disengage itself of the obligations which it had assumed in the treaty. He said:

Je suppose, Messieurs, que dans un avenir plus ou moins éloigné, entraînées par un vent qui souffle déjà en Afrique, les populations congolaises se révoltent et fassent acte de sécession, et que, dans le même temps, le nouvel État du Congo refuse de payer les emprunts émis du temps de Léopold. Les porteurs ne pourraient-ils pas s'adresser à la Belgique et lui dire: 'Par le Traité de cession, vous avez hérité des biens et des dettes du Congo. Et si, aujourd'hui, le Congo refuse de payer, payez vous-même. Nous n'avons à connaître, diraient-ils, que le Traité de cession, et la Charte, arrangement particulier entre notre ancien débiteur et notre nouveau débiteur, ne nous concerne pas.'

In a note to the decision, Mme Bastid took the view that the treaty of cession did not achieve the substitution of Belgium as debtor *vis-à-vis* individual bondholders.[4] While her opinion is a sound reflexion of the rules of international law respecting bond protection, it ignores the peculiar situation respecting the Congo, that the treaty, ratified by the Belgian Parliament, ranked internally as law, and, if of self-executing character, was capable of creating rights and duties cognizable by municipal courts.

The argument that the repeal of the *Charte Coloniale* had resulted in a

---

1 The point is discussed in Durieux, *Le problème juridique des dettes du Congo belge et l'État du Congo* (1961); Waelbroeck in *Chronique de politique étrangère*, vol. xv (1962), p. 59; de Visscher in *Communicazioni e Studi*, vol. xi (1962), pp. 78 *et seq*; De Bandt, in *Revue belge du droit international* (1965), p. 497.
2 *Sarrot* v. *Colonie du Congo belge et État belge*, Pasicrisie Belge (1930), vol. ii, p. 170. On appeal decided on another ground, *idem* (1933), vol. i, p. 208.
3 *Congo Belge* v. *Montefiore*, I.L.R. vol. xxiii, p. 191.
4 *Rev. jur. et pol.* vol. x, (1956), p. 375.

fusion of the metropolitan and colonial *patrimoines* prevailed for a time in the Belgian courts, especially in the *Meert* Case before the *Conseil d'État*,[1] but the trend of judicial authority has been against this view,[2] mainly on the ground that, since the repeal was contained in the very act by which Belgium's link with the Congo was severed, it was *ex abundanti cautela*, and intended merely to declare the legal situation which independence would achieve.

With respect to the post-1908 debt, the argument has been made by the *Syndicat des porteurs de la dette coloniale belge* that colonial bonds bore the title *Royaume de Belgique*, were authorized by laws enacted by the Belgian Parliament, and bore the signature of the Minister for the Colonies; and that if these were insufficient to create a contractual nexus with Belgium, then the latter was liable, at least quasi-delictually, for deceiving lenders by creating a false appearance in order to ensure the success of the loans. But, since, in virtue of the *Charte Coloniale*, creditors were aware that they were contracting with the Belgian Congo alone, it would be surprising if, in respect of post-1908 debts, they had any right of recourse against Belgium, unless the latter was a guarantor.

The argument of the *Syndicat* ignores the terms of the bonds themselves. Under their proper law the only recourse was against the Colony, and there was no recourse against the Belgian Treasury. Such a recourse would not arise merely from the fact that the Colony had become independent, and would require a legislative act. The *Syndicat* concedes the point of this objection, but goes on to protest that if the Republic of the Congo is not the legal successor in liability of the Colony, and Belgium is not to be made liable, the intolerable conclusion is reached that the creditors lack any debtor. Recognizing this, the Belgian Government has argued, at times, for Belgium's liability in virtue of the abrogation of the *Charte Coloniale*,[3] and at other times for the Congo's succession and Belgium's exoneration. After a great deal of political debate on the subject in Belgium the Ministry of Finance stated on 2 September 1961[4] that

[1] Decision of 21 October 1960, *Journal des Tribunaux* (1960), p. 738. The Auditor-General's substitute considered that 'le patrimoine du Congo belge, dans le mesure où il n'a pas été transféré à la République du Congo, se trouve confondu, depuis cette date avec le patrimoine de la Belgique-métropole, tant activement que passivement', at p. 739. Also *Cour d'Appel* of Ruanda-Urundi in decision of 30 December 1961, *The Northern Assurance Co. Ltd* v. *Gouvernement du Congo belge, Journal des Tribunaux* (1962), p. 318; *Tribunal civil* of Brussels, decision of 26 December 1961, *Dumont* v. *État belge*, ibid. (1962), p. 22.

[2] *De Keer* v. *État belge*, decision of 9 December 1963, ibid. (1964), p. 61; *Baugnet-Hock* v. *État belge*, decision of 4 December 1963, ibid. (1963), p. 732. *État belge* v. *Dumont*, *Cour d'Appel* of Brussels, decision of 4 December 1963, ibid. p. 727.

[3] E.g. *Meert* Case, ibid. 1960, p. 738.

[4] *Le Soir*, 2 September 1961, p. 1.

conformément au droit international public, toutes les dettes généralement quelconques qui furent contractées par la Colonie du Congo en vertu de son autonomie financière et en fonction de la séparation des patrimoines belge et colonial, pour ses propres besoins et dans son intérêt exclusif, sont passées de plein droit, à la date du 30 juin 1961, dans le patrimoine de l'État du Congo. Il en est donc ainsi des emprunts, même de ceux qui ont put faire l'objet de garantie par une loi belge. Dès lors, le gouvernement doit veiller à ne pas se substituer à la Républic du Congo, qui est le débiteur.

On the question whether the Republic of the Congo and Rwanda and Burundi automatically and *ipso jure* became subject to the obligations of the Belgian Congo and Ruanda-Urundi the Belgian courts are in disagreement. In the *Meert* Case[1] on 21 October 1960 the substitute for the Auditor-General delivered an opinion to the *Conseil d'État* in which he argued that the Congo would not be liable for the obligations of the Belgian Congo. The opinion reflected the theories current early in this century concerning the expulsion of one sovereignty by another,[2] and the negative conclusions that were drawn from this; and it ignored the element of administrative continuity in cases of colonial independence. Although the action was delictual in character, the problem was assimilated with that of debts, and the confusion was worse confounded by inaccurate citation of judicial and doctrinal authority. Nonetheless, the finding was adopted by the *Tribunal Civil* at Brussels on 26 December 1961,[3] which added to the confusion by stating that obligations towards magistrates were not local in character. However, the same court on 30 January 1962[4] held that a claim against the administration of the Congo and the Trust Territory of Ruanda-Urundi for work done constituted a local debt which would pass to the successor State, and gave judgment in respect thereof against the Republic of the Congo. But it held that a second claim in the same action was to be characterized as quasi-delictual, and would not pass to the successor State. Again the authors cited to support the decision on each of the claims by no means say what the Court believed them to say, and are mutually contradictory. Subsequent decisions affirmed that the Congolese debts were local debts and had passed to new States.[5]

At the time of independence the budgetary position of the Belgian

[1] See *supra*, p. 94.   [2] See *supra*, p. 14.
[3] *Dumont* v. *État belge*, Journal des Tribunaux (1962), p. 22.
[4] *Creplet* v. *État belge et Société des forces hydro-éléctriques de colonie*, ibid. p. 242.
[5] *Demol* v. *État belge, Ministre des finances*, ibid. (1964), p. 600. In this case it was held that the fact that Belgium retained a portfolio of the Congolese *actif* pending settlement of the Congo question did not imply the passing of any obligation to Belgium. Also *Pittacos* v. *État belge*, ibid. (1965), p. 7, quoting Mme Bastid's opinion, *supra*, p. 442.

Congo was such that the new State would require a subvention from Belgium of 2,350 millions of francs. The total revenues from all sources, including this subvention, amounted to 17,103 millions, of which fixed charges respecting the service of the public debt amounted to 3,933 millions, and pensions 532 millions. On 11 May 1960 the Minister for the Colonies indicated that the floating debt represented 9,303 millions, of which 4,525 millions was due to be reimbursed in 1960, in 1961 1,266 millions, in 1962 700 millions, in 1963 706 millions, in 1964 1,139 millions, in 1965 565 millions and for each of the years from 1966 to 1972 50 millions, representing the annual charge on the loans granted to Belgium by the International Bank for Reconstruction and Development, and retroceded to the Congo by the issue of treasury bonds. The consolidated debt was stated to amount to 35,909 millions, making a total 'public debt which the independent Congo would have to service of 45,212 millions of francs. Against this sum was listed the portfolio which the Congo would continue as part of its patrimony, reckoned, on stock exchange quotations as at the end of 1959, at 34,975,707 millions of francs.[1]

In the *Avant-projet de programme gouvernemental* adopted by the Senate of the Congo on 21 July 1960, the difficulties of the financial situation following independence were adverted to. Although no specific reference was made to the public debt it is clear that this item was included in the expenses respecting which the budget had to be balanced.[2] However, the political collapse of the Congo brought to an end the regular servicing of the national debt. On 20 March 1963 Congo and Belgium reached a settlement on the question of the former's responsibility. In return for Belgium's transfer to Congo of shares held by the Belgian State in private industry with interests in the Congo, the latter assumed responsibility for the whole of the public debt and incidental obligations, representing a round sum of 46,000 millions of Belgian francs. The total settlement

[1] *Les dossiers du Centre de Recherche et d'Information Socio-Politiques, Congo* (1960), vol. I, p. 103.

	millions of francs
Banks	856,289
Stock companies	9,491,429
Public utility companies	1,122,276
Transportation	10,335,828
Water and electricity	4,609,663
Mining companies	6,547,333
Agriculture	301,928
Loans of public authorities	1,494,179
Diverse	216,782
	34,975,707

[2] *Idem*, vol. II, p. 578.

involved more than 80,000 millions. After difficulties, this settlement was executed by agreement reached in January 1965.[1]

(xix) *The independence of the French African States*

Since the French African territories constituted separate legal and fiscal orders, and since these orders were preserved in the process of independence, no question arose of their continuing to service their respective debts. On 10 March 1962 the French Minister of Finance stated that 'les États africains d'expression française et la République malgache s'acquittent régulièrement des échéances des emprunts contractés par les territoires d'outre-mer auxquels ils ont succédé'.[2] However, Guinea, which had broken away from the French Community, had practically ceased to undertake the servicing of the debt of the former territory of French Guinea. Also, the repartition of the debt of the former federation of French West African colonies had encountered difficulties, and negotiation for a settlement of these was begun in 1962.[3]

(xx) *The independence of Algeria, 1962*

The Evian Agreement of 19 March 1962 provided for Algerian succession to French obligations in only the most general terms.[4] Algeria would assume those contracted in its name or in that of Algerian public establishments by French authorities. It was stated in the French Parliament on 22 February 1963 that Algeria had undertaken the servicing of a loan issued by the former Government-General, but that the actual modalities of payment of coupons were the subject of negotiation with Algerian authorities.[5] A French mission was also sent to Algeria to

[1] *The Times*, 21 March 1964, p. 7. Belgium agreed to transfer $300 million of securities to the Congo; three seats on the board of Union Minière would be given the Congo; Belgian interests in Congo mining companies would be transferred to the Congo; the Congo would compensate Belgian private interests for the acquisition of Congo mining rights (see *infra*, p. 343) amounting to about $25 million, including $20 million to the Compagnie du Katanga for Union Minière shares it owned. A debt-discharging institution would be set up to replace $250 million in Congo bonds with a forty-year issue and accumulated interest on bonds. The portfolio transferable from Belgium to the Congo was valued in 1959 at $750 million, but had declined to $300 million: *New York Times*, 6 February 1965, p. 1.

[2] *Annuaire français* (1962), p. 1030.

[3] It was agreed between France and the former States of French West Africa that consultations would take place concerning the solution of the debt problem raised by the dissolution of the federation: decree no. 62–136, *Journal Officiel*, 6 February 1962, p. 1261. For Niger, see p. 1294, art. 37; Upper Volta, *ibid.* p. 1309, art. 37; Dahomey, *ibid.* p. 1297, art. 37; Ivory Coast, *ibid.* p. 1263, art. 37.

[4] Declaration of Principles Concerning Economic and Financial Co-operation, art. 18, *A.J.* vol. LVII (1963), p. 728; *Journal Officiel*, 20 March 1962, p. 3019 at p. 3024.

[5] *Journal Officiel (Assemblée Nationale)*, 22 February 1963, p. 2306; *Annuaire français* (1963), p. 1016.

negotiate machinery for the settlement of contractual debts, and it was decided to leave the recovery of these to judicial action by private creditors.[1] Where, however, debts could be described as certain and liquidated it was the view of the French Government that they should be paid by the appropriate Algerian ministry, and in certain cases where payment had been delayed the French Government took certain technical action under the co-operation agreements. The test adopted by the French Government for determining which debts passed to Algeria was whether they constituted part of the Algerian or the metropolitan budget.[2]

To the Evian Agreements was annexed on 18 August 1962 a Provisional Protocol on the Execution of French and Algerian Financial Matters.[3] This provided that the financial operations of the Algerian State and its public bodies would be conducted by the Algerian Treasury, and those of France in Algerian territory by the French Treasury. At the end of 1962 a new convention would come into force, but in the meantime both French and Algerian financial matters would be dealt with by the General Treasury in Algiers and the regional financial offices of Colomb-Béchar and Laghout. The expenses of the French army would be met by the French military treasury in Algiers. The regulation of financial matters would be in accordance with requirements as at 30 June 1962, until adjusted by agreement between the governments, and in accordance with the laws and rules in force in Algeria, including those affecting public services. There follow provisions concerning the status of financial officers, the responsibility of the financial services, and the jurisdiction of the French Court of Accounts.

In a further Protocol on Financial Control[4] it was agreed that the administration of the public expenses of Algeria would continue to be regulated by the law in force in Algeria on 30 June 1962, subject to eventual modifications decided upon by the Algerian authorities.

The succession provisions in the Evian Agreement were the subject of litigation concerning France's liability to pay compensation to a French national whose property in Algeria had been requisitioned by the French authorities under the emergency decrees during the secessionary war. The French Treasury argued that Algeria was now liable to pay the amount, and France had been discharged. The court at Riom, however, held that

1 *Journal Officiel (Assemblée Nationale)*, 4 July 1963, p. 3854; 26 July 1963, p. 4548; *Annuaire français* (1963), p. 1017.
2 *Journal Officiel (Assemblée Nationale)*, 24 August 1963, p. 4739; *Annuaire français* (1963), p. 1021.
3 Decree no. 62–1020, *Journal Officiel*, 30 August 1962, p. 8513.
4 *Ibid.* p. 8514.

the obligation was not a local but a metropolitan one, having been contracted in the interests of the French government in Algeria, and hence Algeria had not succeeded to it.[1]

The obligations of Algeria under the Evian Agreements were not regularly discharged, and France as guarantor of certain of these obligations undertook their discharge. From time to time France reminded Algeria of her liability.[2]

2. WORLD BANK LOANS

Loans granted by the International Bank for Reconstruction and Development to dependent territories are governed by the Bank's Loan Regulations no. 4. These denominate the loan, the currencies in which withdrawals are to be made and principal and premium and interest paid, the purchase and valuation of currencies, the delivery, payment and currency of bonds, and interest upon them, the guarantee and redemption of bonds and their enforceability, and the obligations of the guarantor. Article VIII, section 7 (1) provides that the rights and obligations of the borrower and the guarantor shall be valid and enforceable in accordance with their terms, notwithstanding the law of any State to the contrary, and section 7 (2) adds that the obligations of the guarantor under the guarantee agreement shall not be discharged except by performance and then only to the extent of such performance. Such obligations shall not be subject to any prior notice to, demand upon or action against the borrower, or to any prior notice to or demand upon the guarantor with regard to any default by the borrower.

The practice of the Bank in the case of colonial territories may be illustrated from the Loan Agreement of 27 May 1960 to Kenya for the African Agriculture Project.[3] The borrower is designated as the Colony and Protectorate of Kenya. The Loan Regulations are imported into the Agreement in article I 'with the same force and effect as if they were fully set forth' therein. On the same date the United Kingdom signed the Guarantee Agreement in which it is designated as the guarantor. Again, the Loan Regulations are imported into the agreement in article I. In article III the guarantor gives priority to the guaranteed loan on its own revenues.

In 1949 the Colonial Loans Act[4] authorized the Treasury to guarantee

[1] *Chaurand* v. *Agent judiciaire du Trésor public*, Rev. gén. de droit int. pub. vol. LXVIII (1964), p. 750; *Gazette du Palais* (1964), 1–238.
[2] For texts see Charpentier in *Annuaire français* (1964), pp. 900 *et seq.*
[3] International Bank, Fifteenth Annual Report, 1959–60, p. 21.
[4] 12 & 13 Geo. VI, c. 50.

loans by the Bank to colonial territory, upon the latter providing to the satisfaction of the Treasury for the appropriation of the loan to its purpose, for the establishment of a sinking fund for repayment, and for charging the loan on the revenues and assets of the territory.

It follows from this practice that the World Bank is legally disinterested in the effect of independence on the loan, since if repayments are not regularly made by the borrower they will be recoverable from the guarantor, who is the former sovereign authority. The latter must then look to the borrower for recoupment. This situation arose in respect of the Congo (Léopoldville) when, owing to the internal situation, it was unable to meet its indebtedness. The extent of Belgium's commitment has not been published.

The following World Bank loans had been made before independence:

Congo (Léopoldville). Five loans had been made totalling $120 million. In 1951 $40 million were lent to meet the foreign exchange costs of a ten-year development plan. This plan was linked with another $30 million lent directly to Belgium to meet the impact on the Belgian economy of the loss of foreign exchange resulting from its contribution to the development plan, but, since the Belgian franc equivalent of the $30 million was made available by Belgium to the Congo to help the development plan, the Congo was ultimately a beneficiary of both loans. No settlement of the debt relationship in respect of this $30 million had been made between the Congo and Belgium prior to independence, and the conditions in the country subsequent to independence postponed it until the meeting of the joint commission on outstanding questions scheduled to meet in Brussels in 1963. In 1957 the Bank lent $40 million to the Congo to finance imports of equipment, and two transport loans were made in March 1960 of $28 million and $5 million respectively. Work on these projects was interrupted by events in 1960, and the greater part of the funds allocated remained undisbursed.

Federation of Rhodesia and Nyasaland. Five loans totalling $140 million have been made, all guaranteed by the United Kingdom. Details of their repartition are given elsewhere.[1]

French West Africa. In 1954 the Bank made a loan of $7,091,567 for the benefit of the colonies of French West Africa. This was guaranteed by France. The loan helped finance equipment for parts of a railway system serving the area of eight territories which subsequently became independent, namely, Dahomey, Niger, Guinea, Ivory Coast, Mali, Mauritania, Senegal and Upper Volta.

Mauritania. In March 1960 (eight months before independence) the

[1] See *supra*, p. 392.

Bank made a loan of $66 million to Mauritania in connexion with iron ore exploitation.

Gabon. In 1959 a loan was made of $35 million to the Compagnie Minière de Ogooné (COMILOG), the share capital of which is held by various French interests and the United States Steel Corporation, for the exploitation of manganese. The loan would benefit Gabon mainly, but also to some extent the Congo (Brazzaville). Gabon, Congo and France guaranteed the loan.

East Africa. In 1955 the Bank lent the East African High Commission the sum of $24 million for the benefit of transportation in Uganda, Kenya and Tanganyika. The loan is being serviced by the Common Services Organization, but is guaranteed by the United Kingdom.

Kenya. The agricultural loan of 1960 was for $5.6 million.

Nigeria. In 1958 Nigeria borrowed $28 million.

Ruanda-Urundi. In 1957 the Bank made a loan of $4.8 million to finance two projects which were completed before independence.

Uganda. A loan of $8.4 million was made to Uganda in March 1961.

The Bank's annual reports show the various loans against the names of the relevant new States after their independence.

3. ADMINISTRATIVE DEBTS

There has never been any doubt that a successor State is under an obligation to respect those debts incurred in the ordinary routine of governmental administration in the territory acquired by it.[1] Such debts approximate very closely to the obligations of administrative contracts. Adequate practice is afforded in the cases discussed under that subject-matter.[2]

Administrative debts were first treated as special kinds of *dettes hypothéquées*,[3] but before the Treaty of London, 1839[4] had emerged as a separate category. As most of the cessions of territory which took place during the

---

[1] Cavaglieri was the first to make a clear distinction between public and administrative debts, p. 245, though Huber had adumbrated it, p. 112. Jèze, *op. cit.* p. 18; Guggenheim says administrative debts are not owed by the State but by a particular *statio fisci specialis*, and attach to the territory in which the fiscus is located, p. 121; German law, he points out, distinguishes between *Finanz-* and *Verwaltungsschulden*, p. 86; Koch, *Die territorialen Veränderungen der Staaten und ihr Einfluss auf die Schuldenhaftung*, pp. 11 *et seq.*; Laband, *Das deutsche Reichstaatsrecht*, p. 235. Cf. Gareis, p. 67; Zorn, pp. 31, 77.

[2] See *supra*, p. 353.

[3] Treaty of Lunéville, M.R. vol. VII, p. 538, art. 8. The Treaty of Paris, 1814 distinguished administrative debts: M.R. (*Suppl.*), vol. VI, p. 1, art. 21 at p. 10; Treaty of Kiel, 1814, M.R. (*Suppl.*), vol. V, p. 666, art. 6 at p. 668.

[4] M.R. (*Suppl.*), vol. XX, pt. II, p. 773, art. 15 at p. 783.

nineteenth century apportioned all debts, there was no need specifically to designate administrative debts, and they are mentioned only in the Treaty of Paris, 1877, relating to the cession of St Bartholomew from Sweden to France.[1] The Attorney-General of the United States advised with respect to the Spanish debts in the Philippines in 1898 that 'it seems to be the consensus of opinion among authorities on international law, that, upon the separation of part of a country from the sovereignty over it, debts created for the benefit of the departing portion of the country go with it as charged upon its government'.[2]

In the *Robert E. Brown* Claim the memorial of the United States contended that

inasmuch as Great Britain has acquired the entire and complete territory of the South African Republic by conquest, and has succeeded to and holds the full and entire sovereignty thereof, thereby replacing and substituting itself for the South African Republic, which has by such acts ceased to exist, Great Britain is bound to pay the debts of the defunct Republic, and especially so when such debts are in the nature of judgment debts.[3]

The expansion of State activities in recent times has rendered administrative debts of increasing importance in the law of State succession. Such debts are now unlimited in number and kind. Apart from debts contracted for public works and in the course of public business, there are refunds of land registry, judicial and customs deposits, caution money, cheques, post office savings and money order accounts, judgment debts, rents for the hiring of private property, and refunds of income tax.[4] The doctrine of acquired rights protects all these forms of debt, but there is little record of machinery being provided for their allocation.

[1] Protocol of Paris, 1877, *M.N.R.G.* 2nd ser. vol. IV, p. 366, art. 3. Article 8 of the Treaty of Zurich, 1859 stipulated for the substitution of Sardinia in the obligations of Austria arising from contracts regularly concluded by the administration. After the unification of Italy was completed the Italian courts were required to determine whether this was a comprehensive formula, or whether additional categories of obligations had passed to Sardinia in virtue of other than treaty law. In 1860 the Ministry of the Interior had circulated a memorandum in favour of the latter view (Gidel, p. 32), and the Italian courts adopted it with some dissent (Venice: *Giur. It.* XXIX, 2, 638; 30 March 1877; Turin, *ibid.* I, 997; 22 June 1877; *ibid.* XXXII, 1, 1311; 7 September 1880; *Foro It.* 1881, v. 283, 28 December 1880) followed this view (Turin, *Giur. It.* XXIX, 1, 999, 6 July 1877; Florence, XXX, 1, 1206, 21 July 1878; XXXII, 1, 293, 15 December 1879; Venice, XXXI, 2, 724, 19 June 1879). On Alsace-Lorraine debts see *Cour de Cassation*, D. 1876, III, 84, Gidel, p. 33.

[2] 23 *Op. A.-G.* p. 181.

[3] Memorial of the United States in Support of the *Robert E. Brown* Claim (1924), p. 11.

[4] Feilchenfeld doubts if tax refunds are acquired rights, p. 691, n. 69. On insurance funds see Huber, p. 122.

(i) *Administrative debts of British India, 1947*

Deposits in a post office savings bank situate in the Dominion of Pakistan at the time of partition which had not been subsequently removed, and those which had been transferred from India to Pakistan, were to cease to be the liability of India and to become that of Pakistan.[1] Items of excess profits tax, deposits and interest, civil service bonuses, railway company deposits, deferred pay of military personnel, and postal life insurance policies were to follow the assets to which they related, or the domicil of the persons to whom they were payable, as the case might be.[2] Outstanding money orders were to be the responsibility of Pakistan if the post office which received the original credit was situated in its territory.[3]

(ii) *Administrative debts of the Boer Republics, 1900*

After the annexation of the Boer Republics responsibility for savings bank deposits and funds entrusted to the post office was accepted by the British Government unconditionally. However, the British Government declined to pay money orders or postal orders for which payment was made to the post office for the South African Republic because the existence of a large number of unissued orders at the outbreak of war made it impossible to protect the post office against improper claims. Liabilities arising out of postal and telegraph agreements of the Republics with other Governments were recognized even when in respect of past services in which the new Government could not participate, if the arrangement was one which it was in the interest of the colony to continue. A claim by the Eastern Telegraph Company in respect of telegrams sent by them after the outbreak of war, some for the late Government, and some for private persons, prisoners of war and consuls, was paid, as it was considered that the cables formed part of the system under the International Telegraph Convention by which the company was bound to forward telegrams. The exchange of accounts between the company and the South African Republic was a special arrangement adopted on behalf of the Portuguese Government, which was responsible for the telegraph services between Lourenço Marques and the Transvaal, and the Portuguese could have made a claim.[4]

[1] The Indian Independence (Rights, Property and Liabilities) Order, 1948, s. 3 (3).
[2] *Ibid.* s. 3 (4)–(11).
[3] *Ibid.* s. 3 (9); see Proceedings of the Partition Council, 1948–9, Case no. PC/216/20/47.
[4] F.O. Confidential Paper no. 8144.

(iii) *Administrative debts of Czechoslovakia, 1940*

In the agreement of 14 March 1940 between Germany and the Protectorate of Bohemia and Moravia,[1] the *Reich* undertook the responsibility in respect of social service payments in all territories incorporated directly in Germany. In respect of hospital and sickness benefits, the Fund was divided between the three States in proportion to the number of assured persons in respect of whom each of the three States had respectively undertaken responsibility. The Protectorate paid Germany in respect of its proportion of this Fund a sum of 4.5 milliards of crowns. By agreement of 24 June 1940,[2] Hungary undertook the responsibility for beneficiaries residing in the ceded territories on 1 June 1940 who had migrated to Hungary after 1 October 1938 or who were of Hungarian nationality, or who had been resident in territories ceded to Germany and had migrated thereafter to Hungary. In return, Germany or the Protectorate undertook responsibility with respect to beneficiaries resident in the ceded territories on 1 October 1938 who had left to reside either in Germany or in the Protectorate. With respect to obligations contracted after 1 October 1938, Hungary undertook the responsibility with respect to beneficiaries who were resident in the ceded territories on 1 January 1940, or were resident in Slovakia but were working in the Hungarian frontier zone between 1 October 1938 and 1 January 1940; or who were resident in the ceded territories on 1 October 1938 but migrated to Hungary or were resident abroad but had worked in the ceded territories until 1 October 1938 and were of Hungarian nationality; or who were residing in the ceded territories before 1 January 1940 and had been voluntarily assured. The same method of distribution of the insurance funds was devised as in the case of Germany. Hungary received a portion of the Central Social Insurance Fund in Prague and the General Pension Fund, and the *Zentralbruderlade* of the buildings belonging to these Funds in the ceded terirtories. Credits secured on immovable property in the ceded territories, and all credits from local bodies which were not partitioned and were located in the ceded territories, also passed to Hungary. On 20 March 1941 Germany undertook responsibility for the Protectorate's share of the debt in respect of social security.[3]

The agreement between Slovakia and the *Reich* of 13 April 1940 provided that debts would be assumed by Slovakia if the creditor resided there.[4] An agreement concerning the Kashau–Oderberger Railway

1 *RGBl.* 2, 14 June 1940. 2 *RGBl.* 2, 20 September 1940.
3 *RGBl.* 2, 20 February 1942. 4 Paenson, p. 116.

divided the six loans between the three successor States in defined proportions.[1]

(iv) *Administrative debts of the Federation of Rhodesia and Nyasaland, 1963*

Committee A, set up before the dissolution of the Federation to advise on the division of the latter's assets and liabilities,[2] adopted with respect to local rights and obligations a formula which became known as the 'Walk Out — Walk in' Agreement. According to this, the Federal Government would vacate liabilities in respect of services rendered to government offices and instrumentalities located in the Territories, and the relevant Territorial Government would be automatically substituted. Since, pursuant to Order in Council,[3] the Territories acquired all buildings located therein, this was a logical solution. However, it was found that services had been rendered to head offices, and the attachment of the burden to the physical entity would be somewhat fictitious. Such claims were treated by the Liquidating Agency[4] as unallocatable, and fell into the category of unallocatable expenditure which would be offset against the revenue surplus available for distribution.

4. DEBTS OF LOCAL GOVERNMENT BODIES

Change of sovereignty does not affect the juridical character and existence of local government bodies in ceded or annexed territory, and hence debts contracted by such bodies, and the legal relationship between debtor and creditor, remain intact. The creditor's interest is thus an acquired right which can be enforced against the debtor, and which must be respected by the successor State. The Supreme Court of the United States held that a municipality is at once a governmental agency, and hence a mere delegation of sovereignty, and at the same time a legal entity standing for the community in the administration of local affairs wholly beyond the sphere of the public purposes for which its governmental powers are conferred. In view of the dual character of municipal bodies, it was held, there is no reason for presuming their total dissolution in consequence of cession.[5] Should such bodies be dissolved, however, the successor State must compensate their creditors.

These principles are clearly enunciated in a judgment of the *Reichsgericht*[6]

1 *RGBl.* 2, 20 August 1941.   2 See *supra*, p. 230.
3 See *supra*, p. 231.   4 See *supra*, p. 230.
5 *Vilas v. City of Manila*, 220 U.S. 345.
6 *Polish Mining Corporation v. District of Ratibor*, *Ann. Dig.* vol. VII, Case no. 37. Contrast with *Pensions (Prussia) Case*, *ibid.* vol. II, Case no. 28; *Rural District Council of Guttentag v. P.*, *ibid.* vol. VI, Case no. 40; *State Succession (Windhuk in S.W. Africa) Case*, *ibid.* vol. III, Case no. 55.

holding that the District of Ratibor was not, as a consequence of its being bereft of half its ratable area, a different legal person from that which had contracted an administrative loan. It was said that, as a matter of general principle of law, local debts follow the political fortunes of the territory with which they are connected. 'A debt is regarded as "local" when it arises out of a particular place, or is incurred for its benefit.' In any event, the 'new holder' of the benefited assets would be under an 'international legal duty to take over local debts'.

Chapter 17

THE DOCTRINE OF ACQUIRED RIGHTS AND THE REPARTITION OF DEBTS

I. THE BASIS OF REPARTITION

Allocation of debts is consistently provided for in treaties, not only to secure a satisfactory economic adjustment, but also to constitute the machinery necessary for this purpose. International law does no more than lay down very general principles which are ineffective in the absence of some agreed basis of repartition. No one basis is more mandatory than another, and once it is established that international law compels a repartition, the interested States must thereupon work out between themselves the necessary and most satisfactory means to secure recognition of the acquired rights of the creditors.

Most writers have accepted a taxation ratio as the basis upon which to divide the national and local debt,[1] while others have adopted the tests of extent of territory, population, nationality of creditors, taxable value as distinct from actual revenue contributions, value of assets, contributions of ceded areas to the central administration, and any one or more combinations of these.[2] A similar divergency of tests is to be found in treaties dealing with the subject. In some cases revenue has been the important element,[3] but this is not a universally satisfactory test because the allocation of charges and revenues between the central treasury and the organs of local government differs from territory to territory.[4] Since the contributions of a territory might be disproportionate to the allocations of the budget, the source, nature and locality of the revenue must all be taken into consideration.[5] Moreover, to secure an equitable partition, the average

[1] Wheaton (3rd ed. 1889), p. 52; Despagnet, p. 123; Piédelièvre, vol. I, p. 132; Fiore, *Int. Law Cod.* p. 143; Pradier-Fodéré, vol. I, p. 279; Selosse, p. 170; Huber, p. 91; Dahm, vol. I, p. 118; Sibert, vol. I, p. 210; Castren, p. 472.

[2] Huber, p. 91.

[3] Treaty of Constantinople, 1881, M.N.R.G. 2nd ser., vol. VI, p. 756, art. 10; Treaty of Lausanne, B.T.S. 1923, no. 16, Cmd. 1929, art. 51.

[4] For a criticism of the term 'taxable capacity' see *Economist*, 30 October 1924, p. 775. See also Sack, *Dettes publiques*, p. 566.

[5] Ibid. p. 571. Net revenues were taken as the test in the Treaty between Prussia and Nassau of 1815, M.R. (Suppl.), vol. VI, p. 333, art. VIII at p. 344; and a proportion of populations and revenues in the Treaty of Kiel, M.R. (Suppl.), vol. V, p. 666, art. 6 at p. 669.

over several years must be taken.[1] This was done in the Peace Treaties after the First World War. The Treaties of Versailles,[2] St Germain[3] and Trianon[4] followed the principle of distribution proportional to the future paying capacity of the ceded territories, measured by reference to revenues contributed in 'normal' years before the war. The Treaty of Lausanne[5] adopted a proportional distribution based on past contributions without regard to future paying capacity.

There was some illogicality in the failure in these instances to take into consideration paying capacity in all its aspects, and not merely as evidenced by revenues actually contributed at a time when quite different economic circumstances prevailed. In fact the Austrian and Hungarian Governments complained that the treaties did not consider actual paying capacity at all, and Hungary proposed that area and population be the tests.[6] The selection of revenues as the basis of distribution was left to the Reparations Commission, which adopted various tests, and ordinarily disregarded local benefits and securities.[7]

The extent of territory in itself is not a test, because it bears no relationship to population, wealth or revenues.[8] Population is an important factor but it is not decisive because of a possible differentiation in prosperity between one part of a State and another.[9] The Supreme Court of the United States, in a case concerning the division of the debt of dismembered Virginia, held that the repartition which approached nearest to justice was one based on the capital value of assets apportioned on the separation, and not on that of land or population.[10]

The distribution of the debt of the Federation of Rhodesia and Nyasaland was based on two distinct keys, one utilized for the funded debt, the other for current account debts. This distinction resulted from the fact that the Federation's appropriations were divided into two accounts, the loan account and the revenue account. Respecting the former, the key to distribution was the value of distributed federal assets, to which public raisings were notionally related.[11] Respecting the revenue account, however, a more complex, but at the same time equally logical, formula was adopted. All Federal Government departments had budgeted for

1 Sack, *Dettes publiques*, p. 579.
2 B.T.S. 1919, no. 4, Cmd. 153, art. 254, at p. 124.
3 *Ibid.* 1919, no. 11, Cmd. 400, art. 203 at p. 55.
4 *Ibid.* 1920, no. 10, Cmd. 896, art. 186 at p. 51.
5 *Ibid.* 1923, no. 16, Cmd. 1929, art. 51 at p. 41.
6 Feilchenfeld, p. 460.   7 *Idem.*
8 Sack, *Dettes publiques*, p. 547.
9 *Ibid.* p. 550. Bluntschli adopted this test, p. 86.
10 *Virginia* v. *West Virginia*, 220 U.S. 1.
11 See *supra*, p. 231.

expenditure over a twelve-month period to expire six months after the date of dissolution. When all estimates were added together it was found that expenditure in respect of Southern Rhodesia, Northern Rhodesia and Nyasaland (excluding direct Federal expenditure) would total respectively £44,099, £20,421 and £6,102. Since Nyasaland was excluded from the accounting for reasons elsewhere explained, this yielded a rough ratio of 44/65:21/65, which was utilized for the distribution of both the unallocatable revenue and the unallocatable expenditure.[1]

The only principle that emerges from a consideration of all the possible tests is that the distributive key must be related to what Sack calls 'the contributive force' of each part of dismembered territory,[2] and this contributive force can only be realized by a consideration of all the possible influential factors.[3] An analysis of these factors enables one to arrive at the amount of the revenues which the territory can furnish to the Government for the purpose of servicing its appropriate part of the debt, after deduction of normal administrative expenses.[4] 'The contributive force relative to a territory', says Sack, 'is the contributive force envisaged in relationship to that of the whole of the territories of which the territory in question forms part.'[5] All depends on the concrete facts of each particular case.[6]

2. THE RIGHTS OF CREDITORS

It is a matter of vital importance to the creditors in the case of repartition whether it is the successor State which becomes solely responsible to them, or whether the predecessor State remains jointly responsible. There is no direct authority whatever on this point, and very few writers appear to have considered it relevant. A creditor, or his national State, will naturally wish to know against which of the two States a claim must be brought if the debt is not serviced.

If the successor State has interfered with the acquired rights of creditors it becomes directly responsible to them, not by virtue of the debt relationship, but by virtue of its own action. In the case, therefore, of total succession to the general debt or the debt of an autonomous fiscal unit, or the administrative debts of an absorbed area, there is no doubt that the successor State is the one against which a claim must be brought. But the problem is not so easy if the debtor State is dismembered among several successors, and there is no agreed basis of repartition. Although no writer

1 This decision was taken by Committee A. See *supra*, p. 230.
2 *Dettes publiques*, p. 528.   3 *Ibid.* p. 534.
4 *Ibid.* p. 537.   5 *Ibid.* p. 542.
6 *Ibid.* p. 533. The question is one, says Jèze, which depends essentially on the economic condition of the territory: p. 9.

has asserted a joint responsibility of the several successor States, it is difficult to avoid a conclusion in favour of this solution. If the debt is secured it seems that the creditors' rights are limited to the State possessing the security, but this is dependent on the acceptance of the view that creditors can pursue their remedy against public assets and have a right to the liquidation of the security, a proposition by no means conclusively established.

Even though a repartition of debts in the case of partial succession may be agreed upon, the rights of creditors against the debtor State still persist. Though possibly impaired, they cannot, it would seem, in the absence of agreement to the contrary, be pursued against the successor State.[1] The most that can be said is that the predecessor State possesses what Appleton describes as a 'right of contribution'[2] against the successor State. Any agreement between them, while it can confer rights on the creditors, cannot without their consent liberate the debtor from its obligations. Any treaty providing for such emancipation is, according to Sack, invalid as against creditors who have not consented to the assignment.[3]

After the Treaty of Berlin, 1878, the Lord Chancellor wrote a memorandum in which he considered whether the Porte was still liable for administrative debts owed to the Rustchuk–Varna railway. By article 10 of the treaty Bulgaria had been subrogated for the Porte in its undertakings and obligations towards the railway only as from the date of ratification of the treaty. The question of all previous accounts had been reserved for subsequent agreement between the Porte, the Bulgarian Government and the railway. The Lord Chancellor was of opinion that if such an agreement were not reached the 'strict principle' would prevail. 'The Porte was the debtor of the company before the treaty', he argued, 'and continues that debtor unless the three parties concerned agree that the debt shall be undertaken in whole or in part by someone else.'[4] Referring to similar debts owed by the Porte to the Kustendji Railway, he said that

[1] Sack admits that it is simpler to have the old State remain the debtor, and the new settle accounts with it: *Dettes publiques*, p. 417; but this is not a juridical repartition, which the creditors have the right to demand: *ibid*. p. 421. 'The creditors of the public debt', he says, 'have with respect to the governments of several territories burdened by the old debt a right of credit equal to the amount of that part of the debt incumbent on each of the territories': *ibid*. p. 231.

[2] Pp. 2 and 38. The right of contribution, but not a right of pursuit, was recognized in the Recessum Imperii, 1807, *M.R.* vol. VII, p. 435, art. 38.

[3] 'If an arrangement between the debtor states on the subject of the debt of which their territories are burdened', he says, 'affects in practice the rights and interests of creditors it will, so far as the creditors are concerned, be null and void': *Dettes publiques*, p. 13.

[4] Memorandum of 5 August 1879, F.O. Confidential Papers (4328), no. 86; O'Connell, Appendix, no. 40.

if such a claim or demand existed against the old government, and was in process of litigation, or was actually constituted against them, their [the old government's] liability would continue unless it was handed over in express words, and unless the person having the claim assented there would have to be a 'novation' of the debt, and in the novation all the three parties concerned must concur. . . . There was no assent by the Kustendji Railway to the transfer of the claim, and I think it clear that the 51st section puts Roumania in the place of the Porte merely from the time of transfer.[1]

These two Opinions were given irrespective of the question of the liability of the successor States directly to the Porte, and concerned only the rights of the creditors.

No direct rights against the various successor States were given to creditors in the Treaty of Versailles, and the Reparations Commission was to decide whether these States were to discharge their obligations by payment to the creditors or by payment to the debtor State. It was at length decided that they were to make payments directly to the creditors.[2] A direct change of debtorship was made, however, in the Treaties of St Germain[3] and Trianon.[4] Each successor State was to discharge all bonds existing on its territory, and the amounts paid out on these 'nationalized' bonds were then to be adjusted between the States concerned. In the case of unbonded debts the successor States were to be directly responsible to the creditors.[5] Turkey, likewise, was relieved of all obligation in respect of the shares of the debt transferred to its successor States,[6] and the Council of the Ottoman public debt was to distribute to the creditors the contributions made by these States.[7]

3. ODIOUS DEBTS

To the general principle of apportionment of debts set out in the preceding chapters there are some exceptions in the case of those debts which are personal to the power which contracted them, and are, as Sack describes

1 Memorandum of 12 June 1879, F.O. Confidential Papers (4328), no. 83; O'Connell, Appendix, no. 39. See also Memorandum of 1 April 1879, F.O. Confidential Papers (4328), no. 76; O'Connell, Appendix, no. 37.
2 Feilchenfeld, p. 498.
3 *Loc. cit.* art. 203.
4 *Loc. cit.* art. 186.
5 St Germain, art. 205; Trianon, art. 188, arts. 203 and 186 respectively. Sack criticizes these provisions vigorously: *op. cit.* pp. 503 *et seq.*
6 Treaty of Lausanne, *loc. cit.* art. 46.
7 *Ibid.* art. 55. Jèze argues that creditors have a right to a repartition, and goes on 'the *droit de poursuite* of the creditors remains what it was before the partition; only the contribution of the successor State to the partitioned State is concerned; this is a juridical relationship between State and State': p. 13.

them, *dettes de régime*.[1] An interest which a creditor possesses in a debt must, in order to constitute an acquired right protected by international law, be an interest in funds utilized for the needs and interests of the State. Any debt contracted for other purposes is a debt intrinsically 'hostile to the interests of the territory'.[2]

The doctrine of odious debts is a dangerous one which, as Despagnet says, 'favours most arbitrary and iniquitous solutions'.[3] Unanimous agreement as to what constitutes an odious debt has been inhibited by a diversity of economic and political theories. The concept of odious debts tends to be expanded as States seek a pretext for avoiding obligations which otherwise would be imposed upon them, and for this reason it is essential strictly to limit it. Sack suggests that a successor State, in order to justify the invocation of the doctrine of odious debts, should be required to prove, first, that the debt was contrary to the interests of the population of all or part of the absorbed territory and, secondly, that the creditors were aware of this. Once these two things have been proved, he argues, the onus is upon the creditors to show that the funds have in fact been utilized for the benefit of the territory.[4] Two types of debt have been distinguished as odious, those imposed on a community without its consent and contrary to its true interests, and those intended to finance the preparation or prosecution of war against the successor State, and possibly against other States.

I. Hostile Debts

(i) *The Cuban debt controversy, 1898*

The history of the former category begins with the controversy between the United States and Spain in 1898 relative to the Cuban debt. In addition to arguing that this debt was part of the public debt of Spain, and was not a local debt, and therefore not binding on a successor State, the United States contended that it had been contracted without Cuba's consent, and that the funds had been expended in a manner contrary to Cuba's interest.[5] It was alleged, and not disputed by Spain, that the bulk of the Cuban loans had been incurred in financing attempts to reincorporate San Domingo into the Spanish dominions, the Spanish expedition

---

[1] *Dettes publiques*, p. 157.   [2] Hyde, vol. I, p. 404.
[3] Despagnet, p. 125. See also Fauchille, vol. I, pt. I, p. 380; Cavaglieri in Hague *Recueil*, vol. XXVI (1929), p. 381; Sack, *Dettes publiques*, p. 158. Cahn says that 'odious debts are such debts which for ethical, moral or political reasons are disapproved by the successor', in *A.J.* vol. XLIV (1950), p. 480. One must object to the introduction of the word 'political', as any debt must on this formula be 'odious' which is in the slightest manner inconvenient to the successor State.
[4] *Dettes publiques*, p. 163.   [5] Moore, *Dig.* vol. I, pp. 357 *et seq.*

to Mexico,[1] and the suppression of uprisings in Cuba itself.[2] The exact extent to which the existing debt was a consolidation of the loans contracted for these purposes was uncertain,[3] but it is clear that the United States went beyond the premises of its own argument in treating the entire Cuban debt as unbeneficial to the island.

The Spanish Commissioners pressed the point that the creditors had lent money on an implicit acceptance of the debtor's capacity to pay, that this capacity had been impaired, and the tacit security thereby diminished, and that for this reason treaties of cession always endeavour to respect the rights of creditors by means of a partition of the debt.[4] To this the American Commissioners replied that the creditors must have appreciated the purpose of the loans, which were for 'the continuous effort to put down a people struggling for freedom from the Spanish rule', and must be held to have taken the obvious chances of their investment in so precarious a security.

The doctrine as thus expounded by the United States would seem to have been conditioned by peculiarly American notions of self-determination, and by the desirability of emancipation of the continent from European influence. That the debts were 'created by the Government of Spain, for its own purposes and through its own agents, in whose creation Cuba had no voice',[5] was repugnant to American political philosophy as it prevailed at the time. In reply to the American argument it might be objected that a debt contracted without the consent of the charged territory is not necessarily odious provided it is beneficial. Nor is it always justifiable to argue that money raised for the legitimate maintenance of law and order, and the suppression of revolution, is essentially contrary to the true interests of the territory. On this topic politics assume dominance over legal analysis, and for this reason the only exact test of whether or not a debt is odious is the extent to which it is unbeneficial to the population of the territory it burdens.

(ii) *Odious debts in the Peace Treaties, 1919*

This was the test employed in the drafting of the Treaty of Versailles, which exempted Poland from the apportionment of those debts which 'in the opinion of the Reparation Commission are attributable to the measures taken by the German and Prussian Governments for the German colonization of Poland'.[6] When Germany objected to this clause the Allies replied that it was considered a just reversal of one of the 'greatest wrongs of

---

1 Moore, *Dig.* vol. 1, p. 373. 2 *Ibid.* pp. 357 *et seq.*
3 *Ibid.* p. 381. 4 *Ibid.* p. 362.
5 *Ibid.* p. 358. 6 *Loc. cit.* art. 255, and art. 92.

which history has record'.[1] On the other hand the drafting committee of the Treaty of St Germain rejected the argument of Czechoslovakia that no part of the war or pre-war debt of the Austro-Hungarian Empire was binding upon it because such debts had been contracted for purposes hostile to the Czechoslovak nation and the Allies generally.[2] Czechoslovakia thereupon acknowledged that it would 'charge itself to pay' the coupons of this debt.[3]

II. War Debts

There is considerable authority for treating war debts as 'odious',[4] although there is no intrinsic reason why this should be so. The argument that creditors who lend money for the purpose of carrying on a war, or when a war is 'notoriously imminent', are investing in a doubtful security is reasonable,[5] but it is difficult to describe them, as Westlake does,[6] as voluntary enemies of the victor. Debts contracted in the general interest of military preparedness are not odious,[7] but creditors who lend money for warlike purposes during a war are presumed to have taken the chances of their investment.

(i) *The annexation of the Boer Republics, 1900*

This doctrine Sack describes as the doctrine of 'subjective culpability of creditors'. It was first enunciated in connexion with the annexation of the Boer Republics by Great Britain in 1900. In a reference to the Law Officers on the question of the latter's liability for the former's debts, the Colonial Office inquired whether,

even on the assumption that Her Majesty's Government, as the successors of the South African Republic, inherited generally the obligations as well as the rights of the late Republic, the further question arose whether their liability could be held to extend to any obligation arising between the outbreak of war and annexation. That it was possible to argue that the outbreak of war created a situation between the continuance of which no obligations could, in the nature of things, arise which

---

1 Reply of the Allied and Associated Powers, *Parl. Pap.* 1919 (Cmd. 258), vol. LIII, p. 12.
2 *For. Rel.* 1919, vol. IV, p. 350.   3 *Ibid.*
4 Fiore, *Nouv. Droit int.* p. 357, Jèze, *op. cit.* p. 10; Garner in *A.J.* vol. XXXII (1938), p. 769; Mosler, pp. 166 et seq.; Guggenheim, p. 115; Hershey, *Essentials of International Public Law* (2nd ed. 1927), p. 221; Gould, p. 418; Selosse, p. 166; Dahm, vol. I, p. 119; Ross, p. 131; Guggenheim, *Traité*, p. 471; Rousseau, p. 274; Sibert, vol. I, p. 210; Castren, p. 466.
5 Hyde, vol. I, p. 422; *Report of the Transvaal Concessions Commission*, p. 10. See *supra*, p. 316,
6 Westlake, pt. I, p. 78.
7 Sack, *Dettes publiques*, p. 168.

would legally pass from the enemy Government to Her Majesty's Government at the conclusion of hostilities.[1]

The Law Officers replied:

We think that obligations incurred during the war, or in contemplation of the war, stand upon a different footing, and we do not know of any principle of international law which would oblige Her Majesty's Government to recognize such obligations.[2]

Acting upon this Report, the British Government refused to recognize notes issued as security for loans for war purposes.[3]

(ii) *War debts in the Peace Treaties, 1919*

Although the Peace Treaties after the First World War as a general principle excluded war debts from repartition, and in addition, in some cases, debts contracted during the Artmistice,[4] a strict adherence to this principle in the case of Austria-Hungary was impossible because the latter's war debt had risen to immeasurable proportions, while its territories had been correspondingly diminished. Had either Austria or Hungary[5] been burdened with the whole of this war debt it would have been condemned to immediate bankruptcy.[6] A compromise was therefore reached according to which no responsibility was to rest on Austria for the securities representing the bonded war debt of the former Austro-Hungarian Government contracted prior to 28 October 1918, and existing outside Austria, but within the limits of the Empire.[7]

1 Opinion of 30 November 1900, F.O. Confidential Paper (7516), no. 22A; O'Connell, Appendix, no. 70.
2 Ibid. 3 Parl. Pap. 1900, vol. LVI (Cd. 426), p. 9, p. 763.
4 Treaty of Versailles, *loc. cit.* art. 254. 'The Allied and Associated Powers cannot consider the assigning of a part of Germany's war debt to the liberated territories; such a division would in fact make the Powers receiving these territories support a part of Germany's war debt, which is inadmissible': Reply of the Allied and Associated Powers, *loc. cit.* p. 39.
5 The Hungarian delegation argued that 'jurisprudence in matters of international law has always adopted the rule that with territory detached from a state, the beneficiary state is bound to take over a portion of the debts of the old state corresponding to the territory detached, and nowhere can any trace be discovered of a difference between such and such a category of public debts from the standpoint of the origin or nature of those debts, or of the object for which they were created. International law has never admitted an exception to this general rule': quoted by Feilchenfeld, p. 448, n. 73.
6 Temperley, *op. cit.* p. 22; Sack, *Dettes publiques*, p. 159.
7 Treaty of St Germain, *loc. cit.* art. 205; Treaty of Trianon, *loc. cit.* art. 189. In 1924 the *Reichsgericht* summed up the doctrine in these words: 'According to principles of international law, obligations arising out of the conduct of the war, or in any other manner bound up with the war, cannot be enforced against the acquiring State': *RGZ* 108, s. 298. *Fontes Juris Gent.* ser. A, sec. 2, vol. I, p. 121.

4. DEBTS OF A BANKRUPT STATE

The acquired rights of creditors of a State whose debts exceed the possibility of their liquidation from existing revenues and assets are in some degree or other valueless. In such cases it is usual to accord to the successor States a right of inventory.[1] The most that the doctrine of unjustified enrichment demands of a successor State is compensation to the value of the creditors' interests. It follows, therefore, as Sack says, that

> the acquiring state has the right to suspend in part the payment of the debts burdening the acquired territory in that case where the resources of this territory are insufficient to assure the complete service of these debts, even though the acquiring state should possess resources available from its own territories. There can be no obligation to burden the resources of the acquiring state.[2]

Such a limitation was expressly recognized by the Law Officers in their Opinion on the debts of the Boer Republics of 30 November 1900,[3] and it was rationalized by the British agent in the *Hawaiian Claims* Arbitration, when he said:

> It is obviously ridiculous... that after the end of a successful war the State which is the conquering State is bound to take care of the obligations of the State it conquers, which may be bankrupt, for instance. Persons who might have claims against a bankrupt government when there is no earthly chance of getting them paid, will certainly, when a powerful neighbour invades that State and annexes it, present their bills and expect them to be duly honoured. That seems to be ridiculous.[4]

The British agent, however, in denying any obligation in respect of the debts of a bankrupt State went, it is submitted, too far. There must at least be a duty to make a *pro rata* payment.

---

1 Bustamante upholds such a right: vol. III, p. 324; Martens vigorously denies it: vol. I, p. 368. See Huber, p. 158, and Phillipson, p. 322. If the territory and population, says Westlake, are maintained as a distinct fiscal unit, the annexing State may refrain from imposing on them the full taxation which they could bear. If the territory is merged in the successor State for revenue purposes, the latter's liability is unlimited, but otherwise its liability is limited to the value of the assets received, including such taxation as the territory can reasonably bear without interfering with the political convenience of the successor State: pt. I, p. 77.

2 *Dettes publiques*, p. 250.

3 Opinion of 30 November 1900, F.O. Confidential Papers (7516), no. 22A; O'Connell, Appendix, no. 70.

4 Nielsen, p. 90. In the *West Rand Gold Mining Co.* v. *The King* it was said that 'a country has issued obligations to such an extent as wholly to destroy the national credit, and the war, which ends in annexation of the country by another Power, may have been brought about by the very state of insolvency to which the conquered country has been reduced by its own misconduct. Can any valid reason be suggested why the country which had made war and succeeded should take upon itself the

5. ARREARS OF INTEREST

It is generally assumed that the total amount of the debt outstanding at the date of the repartition is the amount to be assumed by the successor State, including all arrears.[1] Such would not seem to be the case. In denial of the suggested obligation reference may be made to a case decided by the Anglo-Austrian and Anglo-Hungarian Mixed Arbitral Tribunal, in which it was held that the predecessor States of the Austro-Hungarian Empire were responsible for arrears accruing up to the date of the coming into force of the Treaties of St Germain and Trianon.[2] This decision would seem to correspond with the doctrine of unjustified enrichment, which does not demand more than a minimum of restitution to the creditors of the amount they invested. On this theory accrued interest is an accretion to the capital investment, and there is no enrichment to the successor State. If the predecessor State is still in existence its contractual obligation to pay these arrears is unimpaired. If it is not, the creditors, it is believed, have no remedy.

liability to pay out of its own revenues the debts of the insolvent state?': [1905] 2 K.B. 391 at p. 403.

[1] Sack, *Dettes publiques*, p. 250.   [2] Feilchenfeld, p. 456, n. 98.

Chapter 18

THE DOCTRINE OF ACQUIRED RIGHTS AND PENSIONS AND SALARIES

I. SERVICE PENSIONS

I. Pensions accruing before Change of Sovereignty

The question of the obligation of a successor State to pay the pensions of officials of its predecessor is topical at the present time when the colonial administrations are being dismantled; and the importance of the subject is evidenced by the large number of claims to pensions which were brought before the Upper Silesian Arbitral Tribunal by officials of the previous administration of the German provinces ceded to Poland in 1919.[1]

Civil and military pensions as a rule are granted to agents of the State as part of the remuneration due to them in respect of their services. They are not gratuitous payments, but are actually earned by labour, and constitute part of the official's undertaking. They thus partake, to some extent, of the character of administrative debts. The relationship which exists between the State and the official is a contractual one.[2] The interest which an official may have in his pension, however, is an acquired right in the sense earlier defined only if he has an unconditional right to its payment. If a retired civil servant cannot recover arrears of pension by action against the predecessor State, it is not to be supposed that he is put in any stronger position by the cession to a foreign Power of the territory in which the pension is payable. As his rights are not acquired, the successor State can incur no duty in international law to respect them. Whether or not pensions constitute administrative debts which a successor is bound to liquidate thus depends exclusively upon their status in the law under which they became payable. Should a pensioner possess under such law an enforceable right to payment of his pension, his interest is an investment in no way distinguishable from a monetary one. The relationship between him and the State is one of mixed public and private character, but it is the

[1] Kaeckenbeeck, *The International Experiment of Upper Silesia* (1942), p. 82.
[2] Feilchenfeld, p. 691; Despagnet, p. 126; Huber, p. 115; Schönborn, who refers to a 'developing rule', p. 61; Selosse, p. 185; von der Heydte, p. 306; Schnitzer takes a negative view, p. 141; Guggenheim regards pensions as central debts, *Traité*, p. 473.

latter which prevails.[1] State practice in the matter of such enforceable pensions will be discussed in the separate cases of total and partial succession.

(a) Total succession

If the State owing a pension is absorbed by another, the contractual relationship between the pensioner and the government is destroyed, but not the pensioner's interest. The successor State is obliged by international law to respect this interest as an acquired right, and it may do so either by continuing the pension payments or by granting some equivalent compensation.

Evidence of practice in such cases, however, is not extensive. When Burma was annexed by Great Britain in 1886, arrears were paid to foreign officials, but, as there was no regular and enforceable pension right vested in a Burmese officer, no other obligations were assumed.[2] Arrears of pensions were paid by Great Britain upon the annexation of the Transvaal in 1877,[3] but after 1900 they were paid only in exceptional cases, and then with a denial of legal liability.[4] There is no evidence of the status of such pensions in the law of the South African Republic, but in any event the precedent is valueless because the British action was dictated by the principles enunciated by the Tranvaal Concessions Commission, which

[1] The Upper Silesian Arbitral Tribunal decided in the case of *Grzesik* v. *Polish State* that salaries and pensions were to be regarded as the objects, not of a private subjective right, but of a right bearing a public character. As such they were not subject to protection as acquired rights: *Ann. Dig.* vol. VIII, Case no. 41. The tribunal had earlier held, in the case of *Hausen* v. *Polish State*, that the exclusion of public rights from protection as acquired rights within the definition of article 4 of the Geneva Convention of 1922 corresponded to a general principle of international law 'according to which, in the case of a transfer of sovereignty, there is, apart from convention stipulations, no subrogation of the cessionary to the ceding state in the matter of public relationships': *idem*, vol. VII, Case no. 40. The test for determining whether the rights in question are predominantly public or private is to be found, however, in the law under which they arose. It is believed that pension rights are predominantly private if enforceable under that law. A Polish court held that a war pension granted under German law could not be recovered from the Polish Government by a pensioner in Upper Silesia (*Struzek* v. *District Appeal Committee for War Cripples in Łódź, ibid.* vol. VI, Case no. 42).

[2] Keith, p. 73.
[3] C. 2144.
[4] Keith, p. 73. The British Government in 1902 repudiated liability with regard to all pensions of the former Boer Governments, although in some cases they were continued as an act of grace, for example in the case of the ex-Chief Justice De Villiers of the Orange Free State. When the widow of an Army officer who died during the Boer War applied for payment of a pension from a fund created by a Law of 1888, she was informed that the Colonial Government had decided it was a matter of course to assume liability for pensions granted under the old law, but that the fund was insufficient to provide for these, and it was accordingly impossible to admit claims arising out of the War: F.O. Confidential Paper no. 8144, p. 5.

principles have already been sufficiently criticized. Prussia, on the other hand, undertook the payment of all pensions, other than municipal debts and personal obligations of deposed sovereigns, payable by the States annexed in 1866.[1]

(b) Partial succession

It is difficult in the case of partial succession to determine in what circumstances the successor State becomes obliged to pay the pensions of its predecessor. During the first half of the nineteenth century pensions were treated either as local administrative debts or as *dettes hypothéquées*, irrespective of whether they were owned by the central or a local treasury.[2] In only a few cases were they specifically distinguished from other categories of debts.[3] After 1850 the tendency developed to transfer to a cessionary State liability to pay only the pensions of those officials whose nationality changed with the cession of territory. France, for example, undertook in 1860 to pay the pensions of Sardinian pensioners who became French by virtue of the cession of Nice and Savoy.[4] Similar provisions were contained in the treaty of 1861 respecting the cession of Mentone.[5] Italy took over the pensions of officials resident in the Papal States absorbed in 1860.[6] In 1871 Germany agreed to pay all civil and military and ecclesiastical pensions of persons resident in Alsace-Lorraine who opted for German nationality and whose pensions had accrued before 2 March 1871.[7] The Treaties of St Germain and Trianon exempted Austria and Hungary for the future from all liability with respect to civil or military pensions which had been payable to persons who became nationals of the several successor States of the Austro-Hungarian Empire.[8] A similar provision was incorporated in the Treaty of Lausanne.[9]

1 B.F.S.P. vol. LVI, pp. 1034, 1067, 1078, 1094.   2 Feilchenfeld, p. 101.
3 Treaty between France and Nassau, 1806, *M.R.* (*Suppl.*), vol. IV, p. 233, art. 5 at p. 234; treaty between Baden and Württemberg, 1810, *M.R.* (*Suppl.*), vol. V, p. 295, art. 6 at p. 298; treaty between Prussia and Westphalia, 1811, *M.R.* (*Suppl.*), vol. V, p. 364, art. 20 at p. 370. The treaty between Bavaria and Austria of 1815 allocated pensions 'belonging to the administration', *M.R.* (*Suppl.*), vol. VI, p. 451, art. 5 at p. 454.
4 Convention between France and Sardinia, 1860, to settle questions arising out of the cession of Savoy and Nice to France, *M.N.R.G.* vol. XVII, pt. II, p. 22, art. 2 at p. 23.   5 *Ibid.* p. 55, art. 4 at p. 57.
6 *Idem*, vol. XVIII, p. 23, art. 5 at p. 30. In the Treaty of Prague, 1866, pensions granted by Austria in Holstein were to be maintained when Holstein became a Prussian province. This is possibly to be explained by the character of the condominium: *M.N.R.G.* vol. XVIII, p. 344, arts. 9 and 10, p. 346. See also the Protocol of 31 October 1877, between Sweden and France, annexed to the treaty for the cession of St Bartholomew: *M.N.R.G.* 2nd ser., vol. IV, p. 366, art. 6 at p. 368.
7 Additional Convention to the Treaty of Frankfurt, 1871, Protocol, *M.N.R.G.* vol. XX, p. 823.   8 B.T.S. 1919, no. 11, Cmd. 400, art. 216 at p. 62.
9 *Idem*, 1923, no. 16, Cmd. 1929, art. 61 at p. 51.

That change of nationality is the test for determining which State is to discharge pension obligations was asserted in a case decided by a court in Danzig respecting a claim to a pension brought by a former official of the German administration against the Government of the Free Territory of Danzig. The court decided that under the rules of international law the obligation to pay the pension had passed to the defendant. It was stated that the literature of international law generally considers obligations with regard to pensions as administrative debts.

According to rules of customary international law, local administrative debts created by a particular administrative authority as well as general public State debts were governed by the principle that they passed to the successor State. A customary rule of international law has been developed to the effect that claims to pensions passed to the succeeding State if the person who claimed the pension became a national of the succeeding State and made no use of the right to opt for the nationality of his former State.[1]

Apparently adopting the same principle, the South African administration took over liability for pensions granted by the German Government to its employees in German South West Africa, provided such persons had been in permanent employment or on pension at the date of the change of sovereignty and were normally resident in the territory and accepted Union citizenship.[2]

It seems difficult, however, to accept change of nationality as the test. There is no reason why a person who becomes a national of a successor State should not continue to be paid his pension by the predecessor State.[3] If the test of change of nationality were adopted it would constitute an exception to the general principle of repartition of debts, according to which liability of the successor State to amortize the debt of the central treasury of the predecessor State arises only in those cases in which the change of sovereignty has destroyed the competence of the debtor State to discharge its obligations. Pensions should be treated as local administrative debts only when payable by a local treasury in the absorbed territory.

(A) *Where the central government was the employer.* Where an official was employed by the central government his rights to a pension are enforce-

1 *Danzig Pension* Case, *Ann. Dig.* vol. v, Case no. 41.
2 *B.T.S.* 1924, no. 27, Cmd. 2220.
3 The Peace Treaty with Italy of 1947 enacted that Italy was 'to continue to be liable for the payment of civil and military pensions earned as of the coming into force of the present treaty, for service under the Italian State, municipal or other local government authorities, by persons who under the treaty acquire the nationality' of the successor States. The provision included pensions not yet matured: *B.T.S.* 1948, no. 50, Cmd. 7481, Annex XIV, art. 8.

able against that organ alone. The change of sovereignty over the territory in which he either is domiciled or was employed does not affect the contractual relationship between him and the treasury, and there is no reason why the successor State should be the authority obliged to satisfy his interest.[1] (Such is the position of an official of the mother country in a ceded colony or province.) Germany in the Treaty of Versailles, for example, was declared to remain burdened with all civil and military pensions which had been earned under its sovereignty by officials in Alsace-Lorraine, and the maintenance of which was a charge on the budget of the German Empire.[2] In addition, the Polish courts held that Poland was not bound by the pension laws of the Austro-Hungarian Empire.[3]

In 1939 the *Reich* assumed the responsibility of payment of pensions in respect of the Sudentenland.[4] If the beneficiaries acquired German nationality in virtue of cession, were of German racial origin and had been pensioned before 10 October 1938, those civil servants who entered the service of the *Reich* before March 1940 were considered to have retained their rights in respect of their service in Czechoslovakia. On 22 November 1938, Czechoslovakia granted autonomy to Slovakia and on 23 December 1938 issued a decree transferring pension obligations from the Central Government to the Governments of the States. Slovakia had the right to select which civil servants it would take over, but undertook to employ officials of Slovak nationality employed in Bohemia and Moravia–Silesia. Certain officials were retained in full employment. In Czechoslovakia those officials who retained Czech nationality and were retained in office were placed on a temporary list. The Czech civil service regulations were to remain in force in Slovakia for a period of three years.[5]

The financial agreement annexed to the Treaty of Craiova[6] in 1940 included a renunciation by Bulgaria of claims in respect of pensions which Roumania had ceased to pay to former officials of Bulgarian origin who became Roumanian subjects upon the cession of territory in 1913.

(B) *Where a regional government was the employer.* If the pensioner was employed by a totally absorbed local administrative unit, and his pension

1 On the other hand, during the negotiations preliminary to the Treaty of Vienna, 1866, the Austrian Government wrote to the Italian Government asserting that, after the change of sovereignty over the areas to be transferred, officials in the ceded territories could legitimately claim from Italy pensions which they had earned previously: *Fontes Juris Gent.* ser. B, sect. I, vol. I, pt. I, p. 589.
2 *B.T.S.* 1919, no. 4, Cmd. 153, art. 62 at p. 40.
3 *Ludwig* v. *Polish Minister of Finance, Ann. Dig.* vol. II, Case no. 43.
4 *RGBl.* I, 21 October 1939, p. 2059.
5 Paenson, p. 119.
6 *Ibid.* Annex is not published with the Treaty in *B.F.S.P.* vol. CXLIV, p. 247; it will be found in *Drujoven Vestnik*, 12 September 1940.

was payable out of the funds of the unit, the debt is a local administrative debt. If the legal relationship between the creditor and the debtor survives change of sovereignty, no problem arises; if it is destroyed by change of sovereignty, the successor State incurs a duty to respect the rights acquired by the pensioner. The only authority which exists on this point is the practice of Great Britain and its successor States, and as the right of British civil servants to pensions is not absolute, such practice is not conclusive. It is, however, evidence of the general tendency in cases of the cession or secession of autonomous regions, and merits analysis.

(i) *The cession of the Ionian Islands, 1864*

When Great Britain ceded the Ionian Islands to Greece in 1864, it was agreed that pensions granted to British subjects who had served the government of the islands were to be paid by Greece. These pensions were owed by the local government of a fiscally autonomous territory, and were a charge on its revenues. In this case machinery was constituted whereby Greece paid to Great Britain the total sums due from time to time in respect of such pensions, and Great Britain then allocated these sums among the recipients.[1] This provision was reported on by the Law Officers on 24 April 1868 respecting a pension claim of an Ionian subject. It was stated in the report that a claim outside the operation of the treaty could be enforced against Greece only if constituted under legislation of the Ionian Islands.[2]

(ii) *The partition of India, 1947*

In the settlement of matters arising out of the partition of British India in 1947, the solution that was devised initially for debts was applied also to pensions. Those payable by the Central Indian Government to late officials of the Indian Civil Service and retired military, naval and air force personnel remained the responsibility of the Dominion of India, while those which had obliged the Punjab and Bengal were to be the liabilities of those halves of the provinces embodied in Pakistan.[3] Subsequently it was proposed by India that each Dominion should assume liabilities for the pensions paid in its territory, and those payable to officers who opted for its service and were accepted. This proposal was adopted by the Partition Council on 1 December 1947,[4] and was embodied in the Indian Independence (Liabilities) Order, 1947, which transferred to

1 *M.N.R.G.* vol. XVIII, p. 65, art. 8 at p. 68.
2 Opinion of 24 April 1868, F.O. 83/2287; O'Connell, Appendix, no. 34.
3 Indian Independence (Rights, Property and Liabilities) Order, 1947, s. II (2) (*a*).
4 Proceedings of the Partition Council, 1948–9, vol. II, p. 86.

Pakistan those pensions which either before or after the partition had been payable at a government treasury, post office, or other place situated in that Dominion after the partition. The respective sums taken over by India and Pakistan were £147,605,125 and £20,516,341. By agreement with India[1] the United Kingdom assumed the payment of pensions up to the year 2007. A similar agreement was concluded with Pakistan,[2] in the sum of £8,166,848. The sums involved were to be deducted from the blocked accounts of the two Dominions. The former civil servants who preserved their employment under the new régime of one or other Dominion had their pension rights safeguarded in section 10 of the Indian Independence Act.

(iii) *The independence of Burma, 1947*

Burma, it was announced by the Prime Minister in the House of Commons on 12 August 1947,[3] was to 'accept liability for pension or proportionate pension earned by service under the Secretary of State'. In the Treaty of Recognition, the Provisional Government of Burma reaffirmed

their obligation to pay to British subjects domiciled on the date of the coming into force of the present Treaty in any country other than India and Pakistan all pensions, proportionate pensions, gratuities, family pension fund and provident fund payments and contributions, leave salaries and other sums payable to them from the revenues of Burma or other funds under the control of the executive authority of Burma in virtue of all periods of service prior to that date under the rules applicable immediately prior thereto.[4]

The United Kingdom promised the former civil servants that their rights would be safeguarded in the same way as those of the officials of India, in accordance with assurances given them at the time of the separation of Burma from India in 1935.[5]

(iv) *The independence of Ceylon, 1947*

All pensions payable to officials of the Ceylon administration were recognized to be a charge on the Consolidated Fund established in the Dominion for the servicing of the public debt.[6]

[1] Cmd. 7472.
[2] Cmd. 7479.
[3] Cmd. 7189.
[4] B.T.S. 1948, no. 16, Cmd. 7360, art. 5.
[5] Cmd. 7189.
[6] Ceylon (Constitution) Order in Council, 1946, s. 64, S.R. & O., 1946, Appendix of Prerogative Orders, no. 2.

(v) *The independence of Indochina, 1949; cession of the French Establishments, 1954*

It was decided at the Conference of Pau in 1950 that the three Associated States of Indochina would shortly after decide on the future status of the Civil Pensions Fund of Indochina. Meanwhile, pensions would continue to be paid by the Debt Fund.[1] In a Franco-Indian Minute of 16 March 1963 it was confirmed that French nationals who had established their domicile outside India would continue to receive their pensions in respect of service in the French Establishments which had been ceded to India.[2]

(vi) *The termination of the Palestine Mandate, 1948*

In the Financial Agreement with the United Kingdom of 30 March 1950[3] Israel undertook to pay the pensions of former officials of the Mandatory Government resident in Israel, whether they had retired before 14 May 1948 or not, up to an amount not exceeding 200,000 Israeli pounds annually, the capitalized value of which was estimated to be £2,400,000; and to refund to the United Kingdom sums disbursed to such pension holders by it between 15 May 1948 and 31 May 1950. Upon devaluation of the Israeli pound[4] difficulties arose with respect to pensions, but action brought by a pensioner in the courts failed on the ground that the financial agreement had not been transformed into municipal law by legislative process.[5]

In 1951 the British Government made a Financial Agreement with the Government of Jordan[6] by which the latter assumed responsibility for the payment of pensions of former officials of the Mandatory Government who were resident in Jordan on the date of signature of the agreement.

Pensioners resident outside Israel and Jordan continued to be paid by the British Government.

(vii) *The independence of Indonesia, 1949*

Since the Netherlands Indies constituted a separate juridical person from the Netherlands,[7] civil servants of the Indies administration had no right of recourse against the Netherlands Government in respect of pensions and other claims. Nonetheless, the latter assumed responsibility as guarantor[8] respecting the rights of both permanent[9] and temporary

---

1 *Documentation français: Notes et Études Documentaires*, no. 1425, 24 January 1951.
2 Decree no. 63–444, *Journal Officiel*, 5 May 1963, p. 4045.
3 *U.N.T.S.* vol. LXXXVI, p. 231, arts. 2 (*c*), 3.   4 See *supra*, p. 193.
5 *Richuk* v. *State of Israel*, *I.L.R.* vol. XXVIII, p. 442.   6 Cmd. 8355.
7 See *supra*, p. 97.
8 *Staatsblad* 1950, Wet no. K 268.   9 Ch. II (1) (1), s. 2.

employees.[1] Detailed provisions was made concerning the amount of maintenance and its conversion into pension rights.[2] Later the benefits of this enactment were extended to public servants settled in Indonesia, including Netherlands citizens who had become Indonesian nationals, provided they remained settled in Indonesia.[3] They were also extended to teachers and other ancillary officers.[4]

(viii) *The independence of Algeria, 1962*

The Evian Agreement concerning the independence of Algeria provided that the latter country would guarantee 'vested rights' with regard to pensions.[5] However, there have been constant difficulties between France and Algeria concerning the performance of this undertaking. First a distinction was drawn between local officials and officials of the Government General of Algeria. Then the agreement was interpreted by Algeria in favour of paying French pensioners a reduced rate which Algerian pensioners were to receive, and refusing to pay certain entitlements. Certain special pensions have not been paid at all.[6]

II. Pensions accruing after Change of Sovereignty

If an official's service is terminated by the change of sovereignty, his only rights are those accrued up to that date. It follows, therefore, that a successor State is obliged to undertake only the payment of a pension proportionate to the extent of his service. The treaty of 1864 between Great Britain and Greece specified that the latter was to be responsible for those pensions 'granted' by the Government of the Ionian Islands. The use of the word 'granted' suggested that the provision referred only to those who were already in receipt of pensions at the date of the cession, and did not apply to those who had a right to a pension contingent only upon their completion of service after that date. Various memorials were addressed on the question to the British Government, and the latter stated that Greece was to be responsible for proportional pensions to this category of persons.[7]

The obligation to pay a proportional pension arises only in those cases in which the officials are not retained by the successor State. If they are so retained and resign of their free will they forfeit all claims to a pension.

1 Ch. II (II) (1), s. 8. 2 Ch. III.
3 *Staatsblad* 1951, Wet no. 591. 4 *Ibid.* Wet no. 590.
5 Declaration of Principles Concerning Economic and Financial Co-operation, *Journal Officiel*, 20 March 1962, p. 3024; *A.J.* vol. LVII (1963), p. 778, art. 15.
6 *Annuaire français* (1963), pp. 1017–21. For details on Algeria's default see Charpentier in *Annuaire français* (1964), pp. 901 *et seq.*
7 Command Paper 3322.

This circumstance arose in 1948 upon the partition of India. As a general principle officials of British India appointed by the Secretary of State were either granted a proportional pension or retained in service.[1] Certain officials who had not been appointed by the Secretary of State, and who were retained in the service of either India or Pakistan, resigned before the completion of their contracts. After some negotiation with the British Government, India and Pakistan agreed to pay pensions to those of them who retired after 1 November 1948, but not to those of them who retired before this date.[2] Debates on the latter category of persons took place in the House of Lords, but at no stage was the liability of India or Pakistan asserted.[3] It was explained by the Secretary of State for Commonwealth Affairs that there was no compelling necessity for the retirement of such officials, that they had 'walked out' on the Governments of India and Pakistan, and that they 'had no right to a proportionate pension'.[4]

The Order in Council dissolving the Federation of Rhodesia and Nyasaland provided for the establishment of a Central African Pension Fund vested in trustees appointed by the United Kingdom, the Federation and the three Territories,[5] and consisting of balances in the Federal Pension Fund and contributions of the Territories and the United Kingdom.[6] In the event of trustees not being appointed before the dissolution, the Fund would vest in the Liquidating Agency. A Central African Pension Agency was also created to perform the functions of the Pensions Officer of Southern Rhodesia.[7] The respective funds would be invested,[8] and charged with the pensions and gratuities listed in Schedule II, including gratuities for abolition of office.[9]

III. Public Officers' Agreements and Localization of the Civil Service

(1) It has become the practice upon independence of British dependent territories for the new Governments to conclude Public Officers' Agreements with the British Government. These Agreements have been

1 Indian Independence Act, 1947, 10 & 11 Geo. VI, c. 30, s. 10.
2 458 H.C. Deb. 5s., col. 540.
3 163 H.L. Deb. 5s., col. 922. Lord Wavell stated that the Government of India was not accused of responsibility for the injustice which had occurred.
4 *Ibid.* col. 927. Viscount Addison explained that those who resigned 'did so of their own volition, with a full appreciation of the consequences of their resignation': 159 H.L. Deb. 5s., col. 541.
5 S.I. 1963, no. 2085, ss. 24, 26. On dissolution of the Federation of Rhodesia and Nyasaland the Central African Public Officers Agreement was enacted in Nyasaland by Government Notice no. 220, *Malawi Gazette* of 3 July 1964, p. 655.
6 S. 25.   7 S. 27.
8 S. 28.   9 S. 29.

concluded in accordance with an undertaking given in Colonial Paper no. 306 of 1954 entitled 'Reorganization of the Colonial Service'. The British Government, recognizing their special obligation towards Colonial Service officers, embodied in the agreements provisions to safeguard the terms of service and retirement benefits of those officers. The Agreements also provided for continuing payments of pensions already awarded to officers and their dependants.

Public Officers' Agreements have been concluded with all newly independent Commonwealth countries with the exception of the Federal Republic of Nigeria.[1] In the cases of Kenya, Tanganyika and the East African Common Services Organization it has been necessary to conclude supplementary agreements to the effect that expatriate officers who become local citizens of the East African territories would cease to be covered by the Public Officers' Agreement. The earliest Public Officers' Agreement was concluded with the Government of Ceylon in 1947,[2] but the first of the agreements made on the basis of Colonial no. 306 was that with the Government of Ghana made in 1957. This provided that an officer who continued in service after independence should be entitled to conditions of service not less favourable than those to which he had been entitled previously. A distinction was drawn, in the case of Ghana, between tenure of office, promotion and discipline, on the one hand, and salary, pension, leave and passages on the other. As regards tenure of office, promotion and discipline, the officer was entitled to conditions not less favourable than those provided for in the Ghana (Constitution) Order in Council, 1957; while with regard to remuneration, pension, leave and passages he was entitled to conditions not less favourable than those in force immediately before independence. Subsequent agreements have not drawn this distinction; they have provided that the conditions of service applicable to an overseas officer who remains in the service shall be not less favourable than those which were applicable to him immediately before

[1] Ghana, Cmnd. 158; Malaya, Cmnd. 854; Western Nigeria, Cmnd. 2178; Northern Nigeria, Cmnd. 2180; Eastern Nigeria, Cmnd. 2179; Cyprus, Cmnd. 1252; Sierra Leone, Cmnd. 1529; Tanganyika, Cmnd. 1813; Trinidad and Tobago, Colonial no. 348; Jamaica, Colonial no. 351; Uganda, Cmnd. 2001; Kenya, Cmnd. 2285; Zanzibar, unpublished (on the revolution in January 1964 Zanzibar defaulted in its commitments; pensions have been continued by the United Kingdom Government); Zambia, Cmnd. 2543; Malawi, Cmnd. 2341; The Gambia, Cmnd. 2661; East African Common Services Organization, Cmnd. 2244; Bahamas, Cmnd. 2289; Barbados, Colonial no. 356; Central Africa, Cmnd. 2387; Somalia, Cmnd. 1101 (following the severance of diplomatic relations between the United Kingdom Government and the Government of the Somali Republic early in 1963, the latter Government ceased payment of pensions; pensions have been continued by the United Kingdom Government); Sabah, Cmnd. 2469; Sarawak, Cmnd. 2470; Singapore, Cmnd. 2468.
[2] Ceylon Independence Agreement, Cmd. 7360.

independence. Conditions of service comprise the rules and regulations which govern the terms of service of the officer, disciplinary control, salary and allowances, and passages. The more recent agreements do not (as did the Ghana agreement) seek to protect promotion prospects.

All colonial territories which have achieved independence have introduced schemes for the localization of the Civil Service before or at the time of independence, and provision has been made in the constitutional instruments for the retirement of expatriate officers to make room for local officers; and for local officers to be preferred to expatriate officers for promotion purposes.

(2) All the agreements provide that pensions paid elsewhere than in the independent country should, after independence, be paid in sterling and be paid at the rate of exchange prevailing immediately before independence. Every officer retiring after independence is entitled to exercise an option as to whether his pension, and after his death that of his dependants, shall be paid in the independent State or elsewhere, and every officer who at the date of independence was already in receipt of a pension in the independent country has a similar right of option within six months. Members of the British Overseas Civil Service and Judiciary who continue to serve the government of the independent State remain eligible to be considered by the British Government for transfer or promotion to employment in the public service elsewhere, and the Government of the independent State undertakes to release them and to preserve their pension rights when they are transferred or promoted. Ghana annexed to its agreement an exchange of notes in which it was stated that Ghana reserved the right to provide that certain positions should only be held by citizens of Ghana. Western Nigeria annexed a list of posts reserved to Nigerian citizens.

The Public Officers' Agreement protects the pension rights of officers who have retired from the service of the independent territories either before or after independence. The standard definition for 'pension' is 'any pension, gratuity, compensation and interest thereon, retiring allowance, or other like benefit, including any increase in pension' payable to the officer by the independent Government, 'and any contribution repayable and interest payable' to widows or children of the officer.

In some agreements (for example the Kenya agreement) special provision was made to protect the pension rights, but not the conditions of service, of non-designated officers (i.e. officers not covered by the relevant Overseas Services Aid Scheme) although there was no obligation to do this in Colonial no. 306.

Acquired Rights and Pensions and Salaries

In October 1960, the British Government published a White Paper[1] entitled 'Service with Overseas Governments'. In this Paper the position of overseas officers in the service of overseas governments was reviewed in the light of the inevitable changes in their conditions of service as constitutional advance proceeded and as territories developed their local Civil Services. The Paper led to the conclusion of Overseas Service Aid Scheme Agreements with a number of overseas governments,[2] as a result of which the British Government accepted financial responsibility for the expatriation or inducement element in the pay of overseas officers and the consequential share of pensions or gratuities. In addition, the British Government paid specified education allowances and half the cost of leave passages and compensation payable on retirement arising from constitutional change. The Paper referred also to a conference of senior officials in the African territories held in the Colonial Office in March 1960, in order to focus attention on the measures required to build up the locally recruited element in the overseas public services. This conference provided a valuable forum for the exchange of ideas and experience in this field.

Some of the independent States have legislated with respect to public officers either before or after independence. In 1957 Malaya enacted[3] that all pensions, gratuities and allowances which had been or might be granted to persons who had been public officers at any time before 1 July 1957, or their dependants, should be governed by the law under which they were granted, or, if granted after that date, by the law in force on that

[1] Cmnd. 1193.
[2] Ghana, S.I. 1954, no. 551; Nigeria, S.I. 1958, no. 1523; Federation of Malaya, Fed. of Malaya Agreement (Amendment no. 4) Ordinance, 1956; Singapore, Retirement from the Public Service (Compensation)—Singapore Ordinance no. 43 of 1956; Cyprus, Cyprus (Retirement Provisions) Order in Council 1960, and Amendment of 1960; Somalia, The Somaliland (Constitution) Order in Council, 1960; The Overseas Officers Retirement (Compensation) Regulations, 1960 and Amendment of 1960; Sierra Leone, S.I. 1960, no. 2415; Tanganyika, S.I. 1961, no. 2037; East African Common Services Organization, S.I. 1961, no. 2321; Uganda, S.I. 1962, no. 2176; Kenya, S.I. 1963, no. 1966; The West Indies, S.I. 1962, nos. 1085 and 1551, S.I. 1963, nos. 166 and 790; Jamaica, Jamaica (Constitution) (Retirement of Entitled Officers) Regulations 1961, *Jamaica Gazette* supplement no. 88; Trinidad and Tobago, Trinidad and Tobago (Constitution) (Retirement of Entitled Officers) Regulations, 1960 and Trinidad and Tobago (Voluntary Retirements and Compensation) Regulations 1962; Barbados, Barbados (Constitution) (Retirement of Entitled Officers) Regulations 1961; The Gambia, S.I. 1965, no. 136; Sabah, S.I. 1963, no. 1492; Sarawak, Sarawak (Compensation and Retiring Benefits) Order in Council 1963; Zanzibar, Constitution Decree no. 10 of 1963; Bahamas, Regulations made under the Bahama Islands (Constitution) Order in Council 1963—Government Notice 75 of 1964; Malawi, S.I. 1964, no. 917; Zambia, S.I. 1964, no. 1653.
[3] Federation of Malaya Agreement (Amendment no. 4) Ordinance no. 59 1956.

date, or, in either case, by any law made thereafter which is not less favourable. Provisions of similar nature were made for future situations. Where a person was entitled to exercise an option for his case to be governed by one of two or more laws, the law chosen by him would be deemed to be more favourable than the other law or laws. Appropriation was made for charging on the general revenues and assets of the Federation, and for disbursement of all compensation, pensions, gratuities and allowances. The compensation referred to was specified to be payable to any officer entitled to a pension who was prematurely retired, this to be calculated according to the most advantageous method on a loss-of-career computation factor (by multiplying the amount of the officer's annual pensionable emoluments by a factor appropriate to his age and pensionable service, with a ceiling of £11,000). Provision was included for an option of service with the new Government or for retirement. The Schedules modified the pensions payable to retired officers who received compensation, and it was provided that an officer to whom a pension was payable might at his option be paid in lieu thereof a reduced pension, plus a gratuity calculated according to the scheduled table. Also, an officer transferred to other public service would be eligible to receive compensation in the form of a lump sum equal to five times the amount by which his last drawn annual pensionable emolument exceeded his initial annual pensionable emoluments in the office to which he might be transferred. The Federation of Malaya Agreement (Amendment) Ordinance, 1958,[1] provided than an officer covered by the Retirement from the Public Service (Compensation) Ordinance, 1956[2] of Singapore who had in his service worked under the Government of the Federation should be entitled to the like advantages. Provision was made on the formation of Malaysia for continuity of pension rights.[3]

Tanganyika in 1962 enacted the Retirement (Special Provisions) Act,[4] which enabled the Public Service Commission at the instance of the Prime Minister to consider whether there are more Africans qualified for appointment to, or promotion in, any branch of the public service than there are vacancies, and then to compulsorily retire non-Tanganyikan citizens to create such vacancies. Alternatively, an officer superseded by an African in pursuance of the Government's policy of Africanization of the public service might retire at any time on notice with the approval of the Public Service Commission. Any officer affected by these provisions may be granted a pension, or, at his option, a reduced pension and a gratuity in

1 Federation of Malaya Agreement (Amendment no. 4) Ordinance no. 38 of 1958.
2 No. 43 of 1956.   3 See *supra*, p. 475.   4 No. 50 of 1962.

accordance with the Pensions Ordinance calculated according to the scheduled formula. In addition to his pension such an officer is entitled to an annual allowance up to the amount of pension he would have received had he continued to serve until normal retirement.

Nigeria passed the Pensions (Special Provisions) Act, 1961,[1] increasing pensions to which, under the Pensions Ordinances, persons were entitled who, but for retirement as expatriate officers, would have been in receipt of a salary, with reservation concerning officers of Western Nigeria.

Jamaica passed an amendment in 1961 to the Pensions Regulations[2] of a consequential character, substituting for named British authorities identical Jamaican authorities.

2. SUPERANNUATION

The effect of change of sovereignty on an official's superannuation rights demands separate treatment. In this case the official has contributed money of his own to superannuation funds. Even if a right to recover these funds is not afforded by the law of the employing State, their passing into the hands of a successor State is an enrichment which creates a duty of restitution. Whether or not there is an acquired right to a full superannuation emolument, there is at least a right to the reimbursement of the invested capital.

3. NON-SERVICE PENSIONS

The grant of a pension by the Government solely as a matter of discretion confers no rights whatever on the recipient, and consequently a successor State incurs no duty with respect to it. All pensions and annuities other than those earned by service or investment are of this character.[3] Even where a separate fund is established under some scheme of national health and insurance, the passing of this fund into the hands of the successor State creates no obligation to continue old age or invalidity payments. The contributions made towards such funds by individuals are indistinguishable from other forms of taxation, and in no sense amount to a trust.

For similar reasons pensions granted in respect of war injuries do not constitute acquired rights. They are *ex gratia* undertakings on the part of the government. Germany in 1871 refused to assume the obligation to pay

---

[1] No. 15 of 1961.   [2] No. 44 of 1961.
[3] A Hungarian court held in *Kalmár* v. *Hungarian Treasury* that a life annuity obligation in favour of Hungarian citizens living in Hungary, granted by Hungary in respect of damage to property in territory detached from Hungary by the Treaty of Trianon, did not pass to the successor State. 'The objection raised by the defendant that the administrative liabilities of the ceded territories *ipso facto* fall on the Successor States is unfounded': *Ann. Dig.* vol. v, Case no. 36.

French pensions to persons who had carried arms during the Franco-Prussian War and became German subjects. France protested that this was contrary to international law, but did not press the point.[1] On the other hand, ordinary military pensions earned by service are not invalidated as against a successor State merely because the recipient's duty had involved hostile activity against that State.

4. SALARIES

Arrears of salary due at the date of the change of sovereignty are indistinguishable in essence from pensions. If, in the municipal law of the employing State, they constitute recoverable administrative debts they are acquired rights which the successor State must respect. If, as is the case with British civil servants, they are irrecoverable as of right,[2] then no such duty arises.[3]

After the Boer War an officer in the Boer Army and a teacher in the employment of the Transvaal education authority and a judge of the High Court claimed from the British Government unpaid balances of salary due by the Government of the South African Republic. The claims were rejected, although in the case of a claim for survey work done for the Republic by a Mr Crewes, the Law Officers reported in 1901 that there was an equitable claim for repayment, subject to the annexed territory having the funds to meet the demand. On this principle, a London consulting engineer was ultimately paid for services rendered to the Orange Free State, although payment was withheld for some time on the ground that the claim could not be paid so long as the Orange River Colony continued to receive assistance from the Imperial Treasury. On 9 March 1903 a notice was issued by the Transvaal Government in which the fact was recognized that certain former civil servants of the Republic were in indigent circumstances. A Commissioner was constituted to receive and enquire into applications from members of the former civil service, who, owing to the change of government, had been deprived of

[1] Proceedings of the Conference of Frankfurt: *M.N.R.G.* vol. xx, p. 823.
[2] See *supra*, p. 178.
[3] In a Czechoslovakian case the plaintiff claimed salary due to him from the Austro-Hungarian military administration while he was a prisoner of war, and alleged that Czechoslovakia had assumed the pecuniary obligations of the former State. The court did not consider the status of the salary right in Austrian law, but delivered a general opinion to the effect that 'it is by no means self-evident that pecuniary obligations of public law incurred in relations of public service pass *eo ipso* to the so-called succeeding State. Neither does international law recognize a transference of such claims': *Salary Due by the Former Government (Czechoslovakia) Case, Ann. Dig.* vol. I, Case no. 35.

Acquired Rights and Pensions and Salaries

their occupation. It was pointed out that the British Government recognized no liability for the arrears of salary and any assistance given would be in the nature of an act of grace. In fact, some £6,000 was paid to applicants.[1]

In 1955 the Netherlands Supreme Court heard an appeal by a schoolmaster who had been employed by the Government of the Netherlands Indies, and had been interned by the Japanese from 1942 to 1945. During this time, although his appointment was not terminated, he received no salary, and his suit was with respect to this. The appeal was rejected on the ground that, although the notion of sovereignty was a useful criterion for determining rights between public bodies, a contract of employment is not regulated by it but by reference to the personality of the parties. The appellant's contract was with the Government of the Indies, and the Agreement on Transitional Measures between the Netherlands and Indonesia had achieved a transfer of the obligations arising from this contract to Indonesia. On no account could the Netherlands be regarded as liable.[2]

Although the Netherlands Government did not consider itself in any respect liable towards the former employees of the Netherlands Indies, and regarded Indonesia as fully bound, the Netherlands Parliament in 1951 passed legislation known as the Members of the Royal Netherlands Indies Army Guarantee Act,[3] which created a right of recourse against the Netherlands respecting all rights and claims under the regulations in force on 26 December 1949. Various former members of the Royal Netherlands Indies Army claimed under this Act salaries which had not been paid while they were prisoners of war, but the Netherlands Supreme Court interpreted the Act as intended to guarantee only rights and claims which accrued after the transfer of sovereignty, for the period during which a service contract continued to exist.[4]

1 F.O. Confidential Paper no. 8144, p. 5.
2 *Poldermans* v. *State of the Netherlands*, I.L.R. vol. XXIV, p. 69.
3 *Staatsblad*, no. 239.
4 *Foundation for Claiming Military Income of Prisoners of War* v. *State of the Netherlands*, I.L.R. vol. XXIV, p. 72; *Froeling* v. *The State*, ibid. p. 73.

Chapter 19

THE EFFECT OF STATE SUCCESSION UPON STATE RESPONSIBILITY FOR DELICTS

I. THE THEORETICAL PROBLEM OF SUCCESSION

It has been taken for granted that a successor State is not liable for the delicts of its predecessor,[1] but what remains unclear is whether the reference is to international delicts giving rise to State responsibility, or to torts in municipal law. Although a tort in municipal law may constitute an international delict, this is not necessarily the case; conversely, an international delict may not amount to municipal law tort. The failure to characterize the event properly has produced a defective jurisprudence on the part of the few international and municipal tribunals which have pronounced upon the effect of State succession upon international responsibility.

An international delict is an injury for which a State is responsible. It need not be an injury arising out of revolutionary violence involving the destruction of alien property or physical assault on alien persons. It may have its origin in a mere breach of contract, in which case the problem is one of contractual performance. Or it may consist in a misapplication of law or a misdemeanour of the courts. The important thing is that until local remedies are denied the injured party there is no international responsibility; therefore, every international delict consists of a denial of local remedies, or, as it is technically called, a denial of justice.[2]

It is therefore clear that the net is too widely cast if it is proposed that there can be no succession with respect to international delicts.[3] But it is equally clear that, reasonable as it may be that successor States should not have to pay the bills of their predecessors with respect to violence,

[1] Phillipson, p. 331; Wheaton p. 70; Keith, pp. 74–7; Hurst in *B.Y.* vol. v (1924), pp. 163 et seq.; Feilchenfeld, pp. 689 et seq.; Schönborn, p. 95; Meyer-Lindenberg, p. 86; von Schuschnigg, p. 158; Gould, p. 428; von Holtzendorff, p. 38 (qualified by the rule that local obligations pass); Dahm, vol. I, p. 109; Verdross-Zemanek, p. 198; Guggenheim, *Traité*, p. 473; Cheng, *General Principles of Law as applied by International Courts and Tribunals* (1953), pp. 167, 342; Svarlien, p. 119; Cavaré, vol. I, p. 379; Schwarzenberger, p. 81; Sereni, vol. II, p. 399; Rousseau, p. 286.

[2] O'Connell, *International Law* (1965), p. 1024.

[3] Monnier in *Annuaire français* (1962), p. 66. Cavaré refers to 'actes dommageables', vol. I, p. 379.

negligence or misdemeanour, any comprehensive rule to this effect should not be made to depend on the accidental characterization of an act as delictual in municipal law. This was done by a Belgian court[1] with respect to claims arising against the administration of the Belgian Congo, which were held not to pass to the Republic of the Congo.

The difficulty of formulating a comprehensive rule may be appreciated by considering claims which arise in respect of the wrongful deprivation of private property, which are delictual in international law, but perhaps quasi-contractual in municipal law. The wrongful act of appropriation constitutes conversion, but at the same time there is an enrichment on the part of the State to the extent of the value of the property, and this gives rise to a quasi-contractual duty of restitution. The value of the property is determinable, and the claim is a liquidated debt, and an acquired right in international law. On this ground the leading decision on non-succession to torts, the *Robert E. Brown* Claim,[2] is questionable. No adequate consideration was given to the plea of the United States that Brown's rights related to compensation for expropriated property, and not to damage for a wrongful act. Once it was decided that Brown possessed 'substantial rights of a character entitling him to an interest in real property', the tribunal should, it is believed, have investigated whether or not the value of the expropriated property could be ascertained, and whether or not there was the obligation to pay compensation in respect of it. The tribunal, however, preferred to base its decision on the fact that there had been a tortious 'denial of justice', and directed itself exclusively to the question whether the liability in respect of this denial of justice had passed to the successor State.

On the other hand, the Italian courts, after the unification of Italy, characterized as administrative contracts claims which arose out of the seizure or destruction of property by various predecessor governments, and held the successor State liable.[3]

In the *Lighthouses* Case[4] the Permanent Court of International Justice in 1955 challenged the cogency of the thesis that delictual claims may not be presented against successor States, though it conceded that there were types of claims which could not be succeeded to. The case involved several claims of contractual, delictual, quasi-contractual and quasi-delictual character. One claim was for compensation for the removal of a

1 *Meert* Case, *Journal des Tribunaux* (1960), p. 741. See *supra*, p. 94. *Creplet* v. *État belge et Société des forces hydro-électriques de la colonie*, *Journal des Tribunaux* (1962), p. 242.
2 See *infra*, p. 488.   3 See *supra*, p. 356.
4 *I.L.R.* vol. XXIII, p. 81. Verdross–Zemanek explain this case on the ground that Greece had adopted the tort, p. 198.

buoy by the Turkish military authorities in 1911 at Kara-Bournon. The claimants relied on the principle of State succession independently of the formal subrogation of Greece under Protocol XII of the Treaty of Lausanne in the contract of succession.[1] The Court rejected the claim on the ground that the Turkish act was a normal measure of national security, and as such 'perfectly legitimate', although there was a duty on the Ottoman Treasury to compensate. There was no transmission of the obligation to Greece under customary international law, and Greece was not subrogated in the claim under Protocol XII for certain technical reasons of construction.[2]

Another claim concerned an exemption granted by the autonomous State of Crete under Turkish sovereignty to a Greek shipping company in violation of an existing concession agreement. To the contention that Greece had succeeded to Turkey's responsibility in virtue of the cession of Crete, the Greek Government argued that there could be no succession to international delicts. The Court said that, 'even if the debt thus created by the breach of a contractual provision is regarded as a delictual or quasi-delictual obligation because it originated in an illegal act of the State, the conclusions arrived at would not be different'.[3] It pointed out that the thesis that there can never be transmission of delictual obligations was one of theory, not of practice, and 'not well founded'. The solution must depend on the particular circumstances of each case. When the act of the State consisted in a direct violation of the law of nations, such as the invasion of neutral territory or the arbitrary destruction of a vessel exempt from capture, the thesis might be sustained. But an obligation which has its origin in private law or administrative law, and which gives rise to an international claim only in consequence of a denial of justice, is something quite different. The Court added that, quite apart from the formal distinguishing of the categories of international claims, an additional consideration in each case was the process of change of sovereignty involved, whether it was by union or federation on the one hand or annexation on the other, and

the dismemberment of a unitary State into two or more new States presents certain characteristic features which differ from those inherent in the secession of a colony from the mother country as a new independent State. All these differences cannot but exercise a decisive influence on the solution of the problem of State succession even in cases of delictual obligation.[4]

1 See *supra*, p. 324.
2 *I.L.R.* vol. XXIII, p. 92.
3 *Ibid.*
4 At p. 93. Dahm urges an exception to the rule of non-succession to torts in cases where the wrong is continuous, as in seizure of alien property, p. 109.

Effect on State Responsibility for Delicts

The Court went on rhetorically to enquire what justice, or even what juridical logic, there would be in regarding both portions of a State which has split into two as being free from an international obligation to make compensation, which would without any doubt have lain on the predecessor State which had committed the wrong. 'Certain tendencies among writers clearly necessitate reconsideration by reason of the different kinds of possible delictual obligations and the diversity of possible hypotheses of territorial succession.'[1] The analogy drawn from civil law by some German writers in support of the theory of non-transmission of delictual or quasi-delictual obligations that such debts are of a character 'in the highest degree personal' (*höchstpersönlich*) the Court found unconvincing, because in civil law, in fact, delictual obligations of the same highly personal nature normally pass to the heirs.

As the criterion of succession, a distinction has been made between claims of a liquidated character and unliquidated claims. It has been argued that a tort committed by the agents of a State merely gives rise to a right of action for unliquidated damages of a penal or compensatory character.[2] It does not create an interest in assets of a fixed or determinable value. The claimant has no more than the capacity to appear before a court, which thereupon may or may not create in his favour a debt against the offending State. Until such a debt is created, however, the claimant's interest is not an acquired right in the sense defined in the preceding chapters. It follows, therefore, that a claim for unliquidated damages is not protected by international law. Should the offending State be extinguished, or should it lose its sovereignty over the territory in which the delictual obligation arose, its successor incurs no duty to respect the claimant's rights. It is bound neither to satisfy the claim nor to provide the judicial machinery to have it liquidated. Cogent as the distinction theoretically is between liquidated and unliquidated damages, it is a distinction difficult to maintain in the jurisprudence of international claims, as the *Robert E. Brown* Case demonstrates; and attempts to maintain it are apt to torture the problem rather than resolve it. But it cannot be said that the touchstone of liquidated amount is altogether irrelevant, either singly or in association with other factors, in distinguishing claims which devolve upon a successor State from those which do not. In the *Lighthouses* Case[3] the Permanent Court of Arbitration held that one of the

---

1 At p. 93.
2 'The action for unliquidated damages', says Winfield, 'is one pretty sure test of tortious liability': *A Textbook of the Law of Tort* (7th ed.), 1963, p. 9.
3 At pp. 83, 93.

claims must succeed, partly on the ground that the amount was 'easily ascertainable'.

The conclusion must be that there is no universal criterion for distinguishing claims which may be made against the successor State from those which may not. As the Court in the *Lighthouses* Case said, concrete factors, especially the continuing nature of the wrong, and its adoption by the successor State, must be taken into account.

2. PRACTICE IN THE MATTER OF SUCCESSION TO DELICTS

(i) *The union of Belgium and the Netherlands, 1815*

After the reconstruction of the Netherlands which occurred in 1815 upon the dissolution of the connexion with France, and the fusion of the Seven Provinces with Brabant and Flanders, the question arose whether the United States might present a claim against the Government of the Netherlands respecting the seizure of certain American ships in Dutch ports in 1809 and 1810. The Netherlands denied responsibility on the ground that there was no legal continuity between it and the entity that had acted illegally. In 1831 the owners of the ships successfully brought their claims before a Commission set up by agreement between France and the United States, on the ground that France was responsible.[1] Eventually, as late as 1873, the United States accepted the Netherlands contention.[2]

(ii) *The dissolution of the Union of Colombia, 1831*

When the Union of Colombia dissolved, the United States persisted in holding the three successor elements, Colombia, Ecuador and Venezuela, responsible with respect to the same proportion of damages payable for the seizure in 1827 of American ships as was payable in respect of the national debt. In a protocol of 1 May 1852[3] Venezuela agreed to pay its share (later calculated as 28.5 per cent) of the indemnity claimed.[4] Similar treaties respecting the balance of the claim were signed with Colombia in 1857 and Ecuador in 1862.[5]

(iii) *The annexation of Burma, 1886*

The British Government in 1886 adopted a negative attitude towards claims arising out of acts of the Government of Burma previous to the annexation of that country by Great Britain. The solicitor to the Government of India had advised that he was not aware 'of any such proposition

---

1 Moore, *I.A.* p. 4447.   2 Wharton, II, p. 49.
3 Malloy, II, p. 1842.   4 *Ibid.*   5 *Ibid.* I, pp. 319, 432.

of law as renders a new government responsible for losses caused by depredations committed by or under the orders of the former government when in a state of war or otherwise'.[1] Acting upon this advice, the British Government disclaimed all responsibility in respect of claims existing against the Burmese Government in respect of appropriated or destroyed property.[2] Nevertheless, an *ex gratia* payment was made to an Italian naturalist whose specimens had been wrongfully seized by the Burmese Government,[3] and various European property owners and American missionaries received compensation for property wrongfully taken or damaged.[4]

(iv) *The annexation of the Boer Republics, 1900*

In March 1900 the South African Republic called on banks in the Transvaal to provide £255,000 in *specie* and offered raw gold in security. The banks, after consulting Lord Milner and with the knowledge of the Colonial Office, refused to accept the security and the money was taken from them under protest. After the conquest, the banks, claiming that the transaction was really a forced loan, put in a claim to the British Government, which, however, declined any obligation. The refusal was justified, not on the tortious character of the action, but on the general principle of no liability with respect to debts incurred for the purpose of carrying on war. The German Government also put in a claim on behalf of the Dresdener Bank with respect to a quantity of raw gold which was commandeered by the Republic a few days before the outbreak of war in the ordinary course of business coming down to the coast. The German Government was given the same reply.[5]

An English company, the Pretoria–Pietersburg Railway Company, was the holder of a concession from the South African Republic which was recognized by the British Government. The company was subject to a judgment debt of £125,000 for which it could have made the South African Republic liable. The company sought to have the British Government take over the debt, but the latter replied that the company's claim against the Republic appeared to be on account of a tort of which it was guilty and that, therefore, no liability could be admitted. The company

---

[1] *Answer of His Britannic Majesty's Government in the Robert E. Brown Claim*, p. 155. Letter of 30 January 1886 from the Solicitor to the Government of India to the Chief Commissioner.

[2] Letter from the Secretary for Upper Burma to the Secretary to the Government of India, 8 June 1886; Annex VI to the *Answer of His Britannic Majesty's Government in the Robert E. Brown Claim*, p. 140.

[3] Claim of Signor Fea, printed in full in Annex VIA to the *Answer of His Britannic Majesty's Government in the Robert E. Brown Claim*, p. 140.

[4] *Ibid.*   [5] F.O. Confidential Paper, no. 8144, p. 4.

subsequently submitted a legal opinion that the claim was based on breach of contract, but the British Government maintained its position. A similar attitude was taken with respect to a claim of the Italian Engineering Company.[1]

Prior to the war, the British Government had preferred claims on behalf of British subjects who had been ill-treated by the Boer Governments. None of these claims had been admitted by the Government of the Republics, and now the claimants sought reimbursement from the British Government. They were told they had no legal claim to compensation for any sum, but in the circumstances an *ex gratia* payment was made. In one of these cases, submission of the question was made to the Law Officers, who reported on 21 December 1900: 'It has never been laid down that the conquering State takes over liabilities for wrongs which have been committed by the Government of the conquered country and any such contention appears to us to be unsound in principle.'[2]

On 27 November 1901 the Law Officers reported on the Pretoria–Pietersburg Railway Company Claim. They said

> that no Court of Law has jurisdiction to enforce the adoption of a Concession by His Majesty's Government, as successors of the government of the late South African Republic. The assumption of the liabilities of the extinct Government is a matter of international usage, but cannot be enforced in Municipal Courts. In the present case, however, His Majesty's Government has not repudiated the Concession, and we do not see how, in face of the Report of the Commission, of the negotiations for purchase and the taking over of shares, His Majesty's Government can now be advised to take up the position that the Concession lapsed with the fall of the South African Republic.
>
> We think His Majesty's Government ought to recognize any legal obligation arising out of the contract of the late Government on the South African Republic with the Company. We are not in a position to advise whether the claim made by the company to be indemnified, wholly or in part, against the Judgment obtained by the contractor can be substantiated as arising from any breach of the contract with the Company. Malice appears to be charged, and if it was a mere tort of which the South African Republic was guilty, His Majesty's Government would not be liable.
>
> We think that His Majesty's Government are bound to pay all arrears of interest due on debts or shares.[3]

The distinction between liquidated and unliquidated claims was drawn by the British American Claims Arbitral Tribunal when considering the case of *Robert E. Brown*, brought before it in 1923. The claim was in-

---

[1] F.O. Confidential Paper, no. 8144, pp. 6, 7.
[2] *Ibid.* Annex no. 2. [3] *Ibid.* Annex no. 3.

stituted by the United States against England as the successor of the South African Republic, and was based on the wrongful actions of the Government of the annexed State. Brown, who had been an American engineer, had undertaken to 'peg off' a number of mining claims in a territory declared by the President of the South African Republic to be a public goldfield. His application for the required licences had been refused by a local official, contrary, Brown alleged, to the law of the Republic. He sought redress in the High Court of the Transvaal, which tribunal rendered a decision in his favour, and made an order for the issue of the licences. The executive refused to carry out the order, and under political pressure an action for damages which Brown subsequently brought against the Government was rejected by the court.[1]

All efforts taken by Brown to have his rights satisfied were unavailing, and when the Republic was annexed by Great Britain he invoked the assistance of the United States to present a claim against the successor State. Great Britain repudiated liability under international law for wrongs committed by the Republic, and the matter was finally referred to the tribunal for decision. The United States contended for two points: First, it was argued that Brown had acquired valuable mining rights in South Africa of which he had been deprived by the authorities of the South African Government, and that Great Britain was obliged to give effect to a valid judgment of the High Court of the Republic respecting these rights. Secondly, it was asserted that Brown had been invested with an acquired right, and that international law requires that a State which absorbs another through conquest must respect such a right.[2]

Great Britain argued that Brown had been prevented by a wrongful act of the South African Government from ever acquiring a right of property. The burden of proof was upon the United States to 'show not only that there was an obligation on the part of the South African Republic to pay compensation in respect to the injury suffered by Brown, but also a liability for such failure of duty on the part of the Government of a conquered State passed to the conqueror upon annexation of the conquered State'.[3] In discussing the nature of a tortious claim, the British agent pointed out that

[1] U.N. Rep. vol. VI, p. 120; Nielsen, p. 162.
[2] U.N. Rep. vol. VI, p. 130; *Ann. Dig.* vol. II, Case no. 35; Memorial of the U.S., p. 10; Nielsen, pp. 163 *et seq.*
[3] Nielsen, pp. 183 *et seq.* See also *Answer of His Britannic Majesty's Government in the Robert E. Brown Claim*, p. 5. 'His Majesty's Government submit', it was said, 'that there is no rule of international law imposing liability for the wrongful acts of the government of the extinct State upon a State which conquers and annexes the territory of another. Such a theory is supported by no precedents and would be contrary to sound principle and mischievous in effect': *ibid.* p. 19.

under Roman Law the successor was never liable for torts; under our English and American law of torts the successor was never liable, or with very rare exceptions, so rare as to say, I think, never is liable for the torts of the dead person. The liability for torts dies with the person, and it would be an extraordinary thing if it were found that in International Law there was a law which did not exist when you are dealing with local law as applied to individuals.

That there is any juridical basis for a succession to tortious obligations was strenuously refuted.[1]

The United States denied that the issue turned on the question whether or not a successor State is liable for the torts of its predecessor,[2] and in fact admitted that 'there is no general liability for the torts of a defunct State'.[3] It continued to base its claim on the plea that Brown had a right of property which Great Britain must respect. The tribunal agreed that Brown had substantial rights of a character entitling him to an interest in real property, or to damages for the deprivation thereof, but considered that whatever acquired right Brown may have possessed had been terminated by the act of the South African Republic. His only claim thereafter was one based on a denial of justice.[4] The liability which the South African Republic incurred in international law in respect of this denial of justice did not pass to and was not assumed by the British Government. 'Brown had simply a pending claim for damages against certain officials' which 'had never become a liquidated debt of the former State'.[5] The contention of the United States, it was said, 'amounts to an assertion that a succeeding State acquiring territory by conquest without any undertaking to assume such liabilities is bound to take affirmative steps to right the wrongs done by the former State. We cannot indorse this doctrine.'[6]

(v) *The annexation of Hawaii, 1898: the Hawaiian claims*

The same tribunal shortly afterwards considered a similar claim brought this time by Great Britain against the United States on behalf of

1 Nielsen, pp. 185–6.
2 U.N. Rep. vol. VI, p. 130; *Reply of the United States in the Robert E. Brown Claim*, p. 9.
3 *Transcript of the 17th sitting*, 9 November 1923, p. 339. The United States also contended that Great Britain was subject to a special liability by virtue of the fact that the Queen enjoyed rights of suzerainty over the Transvaal. 'Even though the broad rule stated by some authorities relative to the inheritance of an absorbing state of obligations of an extinct state could not be conceded to be an established rule of international law,' it was argued, 'similar obligations should be considered as resting upon the nation asserting rights of suzerainty.' The United States contended that here was presented a case of State succession in which liability should properly be fastened on the successor State: *Answer of the United States in the Hawaiian Claims*, p. 5. This argument was rejected by the tribunal: U.N. Rep. vol. VI, pp. 130–1; Nielsen, p. 201.
4 U.N. Rep. vol. VI, p. 130; Nielsen, p. 198.
5 *Ibid.* pp. 199–200.   6 U.N. Rep. vol. VI, p. 130; Nielsen, p. 201.

Effect on State Responsibility for Delicts

certain British subjects who had suffered wrongful imprisonment and other indignities in the Hawaiian Republic, which the United States had annexed in 1898. In this case Great Britain tried to draw the same distinction between conquest and voluntary merger which had first been propounded by the Queen's Advocate in a report dealing with the effect of the incorporation of Texas into the United States upon Anglo-Texan treaties. 'I suggest', argued the British agent, 'that the United States by acquiring the territory of Hawaii has acquired with it the obligations which Hawaii, on the assumption which we have to make here, is bound to pay. I suggest that in a case of this sort, where there has been a voluntary coalition of two States in the union, all obligations pass whether they arise out of contract or out of tort.' While he admitted that, as a general proposition, delictual obligations do not pass to a successor State, he was of opinion that 'peaceful annexation entails the continuation of the life of the state under new auspices. In a sense the State to which the territory is ceded has taken in a new partner, and in taking in a new partner surely the obligations of the individual person who is taken in would become the obligations of the firm into which he entered into partnership.'[1]

In rejecting this distinction[2] the tribunal delivered some observations on the effect of change of sovereignty on the torts of the predecessor State. The British plea, it considered,

assumes a general principle of succession to liability for delict, to which the case of succession of one state to another through conquest would be an exception. We think there is no such principle. It was denied in the Brown case, and has never been contended for to any such extent. The general statements of writers, with respect to succession to obligations, have reference to changes of form of government, where the identity of the legal unit remains, to liability to observe treaties of the extinct state, to contractual liabilities, or at most to quasi-contractual liabilities. Even here, there is much controversy. The analogy of universal succession in private law, which is much relied on by those who argue for a large measure of succession to liability for obligations of the extinct state..., would make against succession to liability for delicts.[3]

The legal unit which does the wrong, it was decided, no longer exists, 'and legal liability for the wrong has been extinguished with it'.[4]

---

1 U.N. Rep. vol. VI, p. 157; Nielsen, pp. 91 *et seq.* The same distinction was contended for by Great Britain in the *Brown* claim: *Answer of His Britannic Majesty's Government in the Robert E. Brown Claim*, p. 12.
2 'Nor do we see any valid reason', it was said, 'for distinguishing termination of a legal unit of International Law through conquest from termination by any other mode of merging in, or swallowing up, by some other legal unit': Nielsen, p. 161.
3 *Ibid.* p. 160.
4 *Ibid.* p. 161.

(vi) *Judicial practice in general*

In only one case has a successor State been held liable to take over the tortious obligations of its predecessor. In an action brought in a Greek court against the Greek State for damages arising from wrongful acts of Turkish officials in the island of Samos, which became Greek in 1923, it was held that the Greek State was substituted for the previous régime in the island, and must be deemed to be responsible for the injuries done. Apart from the fact that the doctrine of universal succession is acknowledged in Greek jurisprudence, the case is possibly to be distinguished on the ground that Samos had been, under Turkish rule, a privileged autonomous province, and its absorption in Greece did not involve a total abolition of the local administration.[1] The decision corresponds with that of the Permanent Court of Arbitration in the *Lighthouses* Case.[2]

Several cases of doubtful merit were decided by Italian courts in 1947, in the course of which certain observations were made on succession to tortious obligations. In one case the plaintiff claimed damages from Italy in respect of the negligence of a servant of the Italian Social Republic, the German puppet state set up under Mussolini in northern Italy in 1943. The claim failed because it was held that this puppet State was never a sovereign State which had seceded from the Kingdom of Italy. In the course of arriving at this conclusion, however, the court implied that, had there been a real succession of States, this tortious action might have been entertained. 'It is admitted, although this is not universally accepted, that international law recognizes state succession by imposing on the successor State the duty to assume the liabilities of the predecessor State, both towards other States, and private persons of foreign nationality.'[3] In another case it was decided that the Italian Social Republic did constitute a *de facto* government, that there had been a true succession of States, and therefore that the legitimate Italian government was liable for damages caused by the negligence of the Republic's servants.[4]

Apart from the fact that the Italian courts tend to accept the doctrine of universal succession, these cases are perhaps to be explained on the ground that the succession of Italy to the Republic was more a succession of governments than of States. There were at the same time two authorities

---

1 *Samos (Liability in Torts) Case, Ann. Dig.* vol. II, Case no. 36.
2 See *supra*, p. 326.
3 *Rainoldo* v. *Ministero della Guerra, Foro Italiano,* 70 (1947), vol. I, p. 151.
4 *Costa* v. *Ministero della Guerra, Foro Italiano,* 70 (1947), vol. I, p. 256. A similar decision was given on the liability of local governments for torts committed by officials of the Italian Social Republic: *Durchi* v. *The Commune of Genoa, Foro Italiano,* 70 (1947), vol. I, p. 334.

Effect on State Responsibility for Delicts

competing to be the government of Italy, and there was never any real secession of the Republic from the Kingdom.

On the other hand, the generally accepted view was adhered to by the Polish Supreme Court in a case decided by it in 1923. It rejected an action for damages brought against Poland by a person injured in a railway accident which happened on Austrian territory subsequently incorporated in Poland. It was stated that Poland did not become liable for the wrongs of its predecessor.[1]

(vii) *The partition of India, 1947*

The Indian Independence (Rights, Property and Liabilities) Order, 1947[2] provided for partition of the rights and liabilities,[3] including 'liabilities in respect of an actionable wrong'. This expression was interpreted by the Supreme Court to mean claims in respect of which damages, injunction or declaratory relief would be granted, whether the damages were liquidated or unliquidated.[4] It was held that 'since the object of the Order was to provide for an initial distribution of liabilities, a wide and liberal construction should be placed upon it, so as to leave no gap or lacuna'. Pursuant to this interpretation, the Indian courts have held the Order to apply to an injunction to restrain the wrongful service of notices[5] or the collection of income from land whose title was in dispute,[6] as well as liability to pay compensation for conversion of goods[7] or requisition of premises.[8] Also included was liability for a declaration of legal discharge from service.[9]

(viii) *Independence of Commonwealth and Francophone countries*

Legislative continuity of delictual liability has been achieved in these cases.[10]

---

1 *Niemiec and Niemiec* v. *Białobrodziec and (Polish) State Treasury, Ann. Dig.* vol. II, Case no. 33. A similar decision on like facts was given by the same court in *Olpinski* v. *Polish Treasury (Railway Division), Ann. Dig.* vol. I, Case no. 36.
2 *Gazette of India Extraordinary*, 14 August 1947.
3 See *supra*, p. 404.
4 *State of Tripura* v. *Province of East Bengal*, A.I.R. (1951), S.C. 23.
5 *Ibid.*
6 *Khagendra Nath* v. *State of West Bengal*, A.I.R. (1952), Cal. 855.
7 *State of West Bengal* v. *Brindaban Chandra Pramank*, A.I.R. (1957), Cal. 44.
8 *Karnaphuli Jute Mills Ltd* v. *Union of India*, A.I.R. (1956), Cal. 71.
9 *Ramesh Chandra* v. *State of West Bengal*, A.I.R. (1953), Cal. 188. Agrawala in *Indian Journal of International Law*, vol. II (1962), p. 442.
10 See *supra*, pp. 119.

PART IV

THE EFFCT OF CHANGE OF SOVEREIGNTY ON NATIONALITY

Chapter 20

THE EFFECT OF CHANGE OF SOVEREIGNTY ON NATIONALITY OF INHABITANTS OF THE AFFECTED TERRITORY

I. INTRODUCTION

The effect of change of sovereignty upon the nationality of the inhabitants of absorbed territory is one of the most difficult problems in the law of State succession. As the Law Officers stated in a Report of 20 September 1899, 'there is a great absence of authority on the question',[1] and there appears, as the Foreign Office admitted in a subsequent reference, 'to be no fixed and universally recognized rule of international law'.[2]

In the first place, there is considerable disagreement as to the manner in which change of nationality may be brought about. One school of thought asserts that the nationality of inhabitants of absorbed territory is automatically changed at the moment of the substitution of the one State for the other. A second opinion considers that the inhabitants in question acquire the nationality of the successor State only by an express or tacit submission to the new sovereign. The more recent and widely accepted theory regards nationality as a matter solely of domestic jurisdiction, and contends that the successor State has a discretion as to the manner in which it extends its nationality to the inhabitants of territory which it acquires.

In the second place, it is not at all certain which categories of persons are susceptible of having their nationality affected by change of sovereignty. Various tests have been proposed, designed to distinguish persons born in the absorbed territory and resident there at the date of the change persons born there but temporarily or permanently absent, and persons born elsewhere but temporarily or permanently resident in the territory.

In the third place, there is no agreement on the question whether or not the inhabitants of absorbed territory may avoid a change of nationality by removing themselves elsewhere or opting for the nationality of some other State.

---

[1] Opinion of 20 September 1899, F.O. Confidential Papers (7356), no. 72; O'Connell, Appendix, no 64.
[2] Opinion of 13 June 1901, F.O. Confidential Papers (7733), no. 8; O'Connell, Appendix, no. 74.

The expression 'nationality' in international law is only shorthand for the ascription of individuals to specific States for the purpose either of jurisdiction or of diplomatic protection. In the sense that a person falls within the plenary jurisdiction of a State, and may be represented by it, such a person is said to be a national of that State. While the State concerned must first claim jurisdiction over the individual, or to represent him internationally, before he will actually be ascribed to it, it does not follow that such a person is regarded as a national by the State concerned, for, as in the case of Israel between 1948 and 1952, the State may lack a domestic conception of nationality.[1] It would be fallacious to assume that, because international law permissively ascribes certain individuals to successor States in virtue of a change of sovereignty, these automatically become nationals in the eyes of municipal law, for the most international law can do is to approve or disapprove of a claim by successor States to bring individuals within their plenary jurisdiction, or of a claim to represent them in diplomatic matters.

Failure to distinguish the respective roles of international law and municipal law in determining the content of the concept of nationality underlay a controversy in the courts of Israel concerning the effect of the termination of the Palestine Mandate upon the status of the former Palestine citizens who were not British subjects and whose citizenship resulted from Orders in Council. The Tel Aviv District Court, correctly it is believed, held such persons to have lost their citizenship without gaining any other, meaning, thereby, that they were not Israeli citizens entitled to exercise domestic rights predicated upon citizenship.[2] Because this conclusion involved treating Palestine citizens as aliens and, thereby, not only denying Israeli diplomatic representation to them, but also excluding them from Israel's plenary jurisdiction, another judge of the same court disagreed with it, and held such persons to be Israel nationals in domestic law. Such a result, he said, followed from the view that, in the eyes of international law, there were Israeli nationals, even though, at the time, there was no domestic law of nationality, and from the ascription by international law of nationality automatically to the inhabitants of successor States.[3] The Israeli Supreme Court upheld the view that Palestine citizenship had lapsed,[4] and later drew the implication that Palestine citizens had not become Israeli nationals, by holding that a former

---

1 See *infra*, p. 498. On the subject see Jellinek, *Der automatische Erwerb und Verlust der Staatsangehörigkeit durch völkerrechtliche Vergänge, zugleich ein Beitrag zur Lehre von der Staatensukzession* (1951), pp. 35 *et seq*.
2 *Re Goods of Shiphris*, I.L.R. vol. XVII, p. 110. Followed by *Oseri v. Oseri*, ibid. p. 111.
3 *A.B. v. M.B.*, ibid. p. 111.   4 *Hussein v. Governor of Acre Prison*, ibid. p. 112.

Palestine citizen could return to Israel only as an immigrant.[1] The controversy to some extent revolved around the question whether the Palestine Citizenship Orders in Council had been kept alive by the Law and Administration Ordinance,[2] but this was put at rest by the enactment in 1952 of the Israel Nationality Act.

Because the question whether a person is a national for purposes of municipal law is left to municipal law,[3] it does not follow that international law is indifferent to the effect of claiming him as such. There must be a sufficient link between the successor State and the persons it claims as its nationals in virtue of the succession, and the sufficiency of the link might be tested if the successor State attempted to exercise a jurisdiction over those persons in circumstances disapproved of by international law, or attempted to represent them diplomatically; provided, that is, there is some State competent to protest on behalf of the persons concerned.[4] International law thus places restrictions upon the categories of persons whose nationality is claimed by the successor State, though, because of the restrictive character of its operation, it cannot dictate to the predecessor State whether or not it is obliged to retain these persons as its nationals. What these restrictions are is a matter for speculation, but the latitude allowed municipal law in the selection of nationals on a basis of birth, residence and descent suggests that they are minimal. It follows that very limited positive guidance can be drawn from international law as to the tests for deciding which categories of persons are affected by a change of sovereignty.[5]

2. THE MANNER IN WHICH CHANGE OF NATIONALITY IS EFFECTED

The majority of writers have asserted that upon change of sovereignty the inhabitants of the territory concerned lose the nationality of the predecessor State and become *ipso facto* nationals of the successor.[6] There is

[1] *Naqara v. Minister of the Interior*, ibid. vol. xx, p. 49.   [2] See *supra*, p. 128.
[3] *Nationality Decrees in Tunis and Morocco Case*, P.C.I.J. ser. B, no. 4 (1923).
[4] *Nottebohm Case*, I.C.J. Rep. 1955, p. 4.
[5] *The arbitration between Germany and Poland in 1924 concerning the interpretation of the Minorities Treaty*, reported in *Ann. Dig.* vol. II, Case no. 117. See Oppenheim, vol. I, p. 643; Mervyn Jones, pp. 18–19; Graupner in *Trans. Grot. Soc.* vol. XXXII (1946), pp. 87 *et seq.*; Strupp in Hague *Recueil*, vol. XLVII (1934), p. 483. Feilchenfeld suggests that nationals are transferred, not *ipso facto* through succession in international law, but through the acts of the successor State, which claims the nationals of the annexed State as its own subjects: p. 614. Also Verdross–Zemanek, p. 193. See Weis, *Nationality and Statelessness in International Law* (1956), ch. 11. This is controverted by Jellinek, *op. cit.* pp. 50 *et seq.* See also Cavaglieri in *Rivista di diritto internazionale*, vol. XIX (1927), p. 349.
[6] Kunz in Hague *Recueil*, vol. XXXI (1930), p. 117; Oppenheim, vol. I, pp. 551, 571; Keith, pp. 6, 42; Phillipson, p. 36; Lawrence, p. 90; Gettys in *A.J.* vol. XXI

a collective naturalization which takes place the moment ratifications of a treaty of cession are exchanged, or, if there is no treaty, upon the declaration of annexation or independence. It would appear to follow from such a theory that once the change of nationality is effected it cannot be undone, and that removal from the territory, no matter how soon afterwards, cannot have the effect of casting off the new allegiance. A number of Opinions to this conclusion were given by the Law Officers respecting the acquisition of British nationality by the Boers in 1900. On 1 September of that year the High Commissioner, in the Proclamation annexing the Orange Free State, announced that 'all persons residing in the Orange River Colony, heretofore Burghers of the Orange Free State, have ... become the subjects of Her Majesty'.[1] This proclamation was drafted according to the tenor of an Opinion given by the Law Officers in the Colonial Office on 5 February 1900, in which it was advised that

> after conquest, and the Proclamation of the Queen's sovereignty, the burghers or citizens of these two territories, as well as any foreigners resident in them who do not claim to be nationals of some civilized foreign Power, and their children, will become British subjects. This is one of the effects of acquisition of territory by conquest.[2]

On 17 May of the same year a further Opinion was given to the effect that 'the inhabitants of the Orange Free State *will* become British subjects upon annexation'.[3] A similar Report was delivered by the Law Officers on 27 September 1899, respecting the effect upon nationality of the lease to Great Britain of Chinese territory. It was advised:

(1927), p. 267; Fauchille, vol. I, pt. I, p. 856; Mann in *Modern Law Review*, vol. V (1942), p. 222; McNair in *Cambridge Law Journal*, vol. VII (1941), p. 384; Schönborn, pp. 33, 34, 90 (the test, he says, is whether persons fall within the successor's physical sphere of competence, p. 69); Selosse, pp. 139, 283; Costes, *Des cessions de territoires* (1914), p. 93. Pothier was the first to recognize the problem, when he said that all inhabitants became French: *Traité des personnes*, p. 139. Earlier authors on State succession who adverted to it were Bluntschli, p. 213; Stoerk, *Option und Plebiscit bei Eroberungen und Gebietscessionen* (1879). The Treaty of Versailles speaks of acquisition of nationality *ipso facto*: B.T.S. 1919, no. 4; Cmd. 153, arts. 36 (p. 24); 84 (p. 49); 91 (p. 54); 105 (p. 61); 112 (p. 65). See also the Minorities Treaty of 1919: B.T.S. 1919, no. 20; Cmd. 479, art. 4; The Treaty of Lausanne, B.T.S. 1923, no. 16; Cmd. 1929, art. 30 at p. 27. For the position of persons in Cuba and the Philippines after 1898 see *Rev. gén. de droit int. pub.* vol. VI (1899), pp. 625–8. For that of persons in districts annexed to Serbia in the Treaty of Berlin see *idem*, vol. VII (1900), pp. 188–214, with a useful statement of doctrine on p. 194. For a special study of the inhabitants of Alsace-Lorraine after 1870, see Cogordan, *La Nationalité au point de vue des rapports internationaux* (1879), pp. 295–370.

1 Proclamation no. 14 of 1900, Cd. 128, p. 15.
2 Opinion of 5 February 1900, F.O. Confidential Papers (7516), no. 10C: O'Connell, Appendix, no. 67.
3 Opinion of 17 May 1900, F.O. Confidential Papers (7516), no. 18A: O'Connell, Appendix, no. 68.

That the persons inhabiting the new territory who were before the cession Chinese subjects are to be regarded as British subjects for all purposes as from the 16th April last. Cession of territory effects a change in the nationality of the inhabitants. The territory has been ceded; it is British territory, and the fact that the cession is for a term of years only does not affect the conclusion that by the cession the inhabitants become for that term British subjects.[1]

A memorandum on the question was drawn up by the Foreign Office on 12 May 1899 concerning the effect of the annexation of the Limbay District by the Rajah of Sarawak. It quoted with approval the conclusion of Hall[2] that 'in each case the population is subjected to the sovereignty of the State by which the territory is acquired'.[3]

These Opinions were based upon generally accepted English municipal law, and they are no authority whatever in international law. Inhabitants of territory acquired by the Crown have ordinarily been held automatically to have acquired British nationality.[4] It does not follow, however, that international law imposes on Great Britain an obligation to extend its nationality, and in so far as the Law Officers intended to imply a rule to this effect they were generalizing from the practice of English courts, which have, in fact, recognized that the question to what State a person belongs must ultimately be settled by the municipal law of the State to which he claims or is alleged to belong.[5] It is the municipal law of the predecessor State which is to determine which persons have lost their nationality as a result of the change; it is that of the successor State which is to determine which persons have acquired its nationality. The function of international law is at the most to delimit the competence of the

[1] Opinion of 27 September 1899, F.O. Confidential Papers (7356), no. 14A: O'Connell, Appendix, no. 65.
[2] Hall, p. 686.
[3] F.O. Memorandum of 2 May 1899, no. 5704/20/1899–1900: O'Connell, Appendix, no. 62.
[4] This principle was laid down by Lord Mansfield in the classic case of *Campbell* v. *Hall*, where it was stated that 'the conquered inhabitants once received under the ruler's protection become subjects and are to be universally considered in that light, not as enemies or aliens': 1 Cowp. 204 at p. 208. The same principle was upheld in succeeding cases: *Donegani* v. *Donegani* (1835), 3 Knapp 63 at p. 85; *Mostyn* v. *Fabrigas* (1774), 1 Cowp. 161, per Lord Mansfield, at p. 171; *Mayor of Lyons* v. *The East India Company* (1837), 1 Moo, I.A. 175. In the last case it had been argued that upon conquest or cession all the inhabitants of the territory continue aliens after the change of dominion unless and until the conqueror grants them naturalization. The court held, however, that according to English law such inhabitants immediately become British subjects. So far as territory acquired by the Crown after 1948 is concerned, the British Nationality Act, s. 11, provides that the persons who shall thereby become citizens of the United Kingdom are to be specified by Order in Council.
[5] *Stoeck* v. *Public Trustee* [1921] 2 Ch. 67; *In re Chamberlain's Settlement* [1921] 2 Ch. 533.

former to retain certain persons as its nationals, and of the latter to claim them as its own.[1] It cannot prescribe that such persons change their nationality, either automatically or by submission.

The predecessor State would seem to lose its competence in international law to claim the inhabitants of absorbed territory as its nationals when the bond uniting it with them is dissolved. According to English law prior to the Nationality Act, 1948, which predicates nationality on events antecedent to a change of sovereignty,[2] inhabitants of territory ceded by or seceding from the Crown lose their British nationality at the moment of the change of sovereignty, subject to a right of election, and become aliens.[3] This was stated in a memorandum of the Foreign Office of 5 February 1900 to have been the view of English law 'constantly held by Her Majesty's Government'. It was recalled that, at the time of the cession by Great Britain of the Bay Islands to Honduras in 1859, the British Government considered that those inhabitants who did not remove themselves from the territory in accordance with the terms of the treaty had lost their British nationality.[4] The same doctrine was affirmed in the Court of Appeal in the case of *Murray* v. *Parkes* where the applicant, who had been born in Eire before the latter's attainment of Dominion status, and was resident in England, claimed that Eire had seceded from the Crown, and that he had been deprived by Irish legislation of his status as a British subject. Although it was held that there had been no secession, it was stated by Caldecote, C. J., in the course of his judgment, that 'there can be no doubt that, apart from some treaty provision to the contrary, a British subject becomes an alien by the cession of British territory in

---

1 *Nottebohm* Case, I.C.J. Rep. 1955, p. 4. The commentary to the Harvard Draft on Nationality of 1929 asserts that the power of a State to confer its nationality is not unlimited: art. 2 of the Draft Convention on Nationality prepared by the Harvard Law School's Research on International Law, *A.J.* (Special Suppl.), vol. XXIII, 1929.
2 11 & 12 Geo. VI, c. 56.
3 *Doe d. Thomas* v. *Acklam* (1824) 2 B. & C. 779; *Doe d. Auchmuty* v. *Mulcaster* (1826), 5 B. & C. 771; *Dundas* v. *Dundas*, 2 D. 31. A similar rule exists in French law (Cogordan, *op. cit.* pp. 293 *et seq.*), in German (*Fontes Juris Gent.* ser. A, sect. 2, vol. I, p. 120) and in American (*American Insurance Company* v. *Canter*, 26 U.S. (1 Pet.) 511 at p. 542; *U.S.* v. *De Repentigny*, 72 U.S. (5 Wall.) 211 at p. 260; *Shanks* v. *Dupont*, 28 U.S. (3 Pet.) 242. See also Moore, *Dig.* vol. III, p. 314; Graupner in *Law Quarterly Review*, vol. LXI (1945), p. 169. *Re A.*, Clunet, 1954, vol. LXXXI, p. 967. When the Transvaal was released from British sovereignty in 1881, the Lord Chancellor, Selborne, wrote a Memorandum on the effect of this upon persons born in and domiciled in the territory. He stated that he knew of no way in which those who are once British subjects can cease to be so except by cession to another independent State or expatriation. Since the territory remained under the Crown's suzerainty this principle did not apply: McNair, *International Law Opinions* (1956), vol. II, p. 24.
4 F.O. Memorandum of 5 February 1900, 5877/1900, vol. XX: O'Connell, Appendix, no. 66.

Effect of Change of Sovereignty on Nationality

which he is resident at the time of cession'.[1] After the transformation of Eire into the Irish Republic the consequences of State succession were somewhat modified by the British Nationality Act, 1948,[2] section 3 (2) of which provides that any law in force in the United Kingdom should 'continue to have effect in relation to citizens of Eire who are not British subjects in like manner as it has effect in relation to British subjects'. This section was held in *Bicknell* v. *Brosnan*[3] to have the effect of rendering liable to conscription under the British National Service Act, 1948, an Irish citizen who had lived in England from 1949 to 1952.

Although inhabitants of territory ceded by or seceding from the Crown lose their British nationality, it does not follow that they acquire either automatically or by submission that of the successor State.[4] The latter may withhold the granting of its nationality to all or portion of the persons concerned. Courts of third States dealing with the question whether or not a subject of the predecessor State has acquired the nationality of the successor State must consider, first, the competence of the latter to extend its nationality; and, secondly, whether or not in municipal law such nationality has been extended. Undesirable as it may be that any persons become stateless as a result of a change of sovereignty, it cannot be asserted with any measure of confidence that international law, at least in its present stage of development, imposes any duty on the successor State to grant nationality.[5]

It has been held by American courts that United States citizenship is not automatically extended to inhabitants of territory acquired by the Union, and that at the most the United States possesses, as the Attorney-General advised in 1907, 'the right to the allegiance' of the subjects.[6] A collective naturalization 'may be effected in accordance with the intention of Congress'.[7] When the United States acquired Porto Rico in 1898, it was held that pending legislation the inhabitants were not citizens of the United States, although they had ceased to be subjects of Spain.[8] They were not, however, aliens, and the United States could protect them as residents

1 [1942] 2 K.B. 123, per Viscount Caldecote, C. J., at p. 129.
2 11 & 12 Geo. VI, c. 56.
3 [1953] 2 Q.B. 77.
4 Even if a treaty provides that inhabitants of absorbed territory are to become nationals of the successor State the enactment is ineffective until embodied in municipal law: Graupner in *Trans. Grot. Soc.* vol. XXXII, pp. 93-4. In the Treaty of Shimonoseki, 1895, it was recognized that Chinese nationals became Japanese nationals only at the option of Japan: *B.F.S.P.* vol. LXXXVII (1895), p. 799.
5 Graupner, *loc. cit.* p. 92. On the other hand see Kaufmann in Hague *Recueil*, vol. LIV (1935), p. 373.
6 Hackworth, vol. III, p. 117.
7 *Boyd* v. *Nebraska, ex rel. Thayer*, 143 U.S. 135 at p. 170.
8 *Goetze* v. *U.S.* 103 Fed. Rep. 72.

of United States territory.[1] The Treaty of Paris was ratified in 1899, but the Act conferring citizenship upon the inhabitants of the Philippines was not passed until 1902. In the meantime the inhabitants owed allegiance to the United States only as residents of United States territory and not as United States citizens.[2] United States practice has been consistent in this matter. In the Treaty for the Cession of Louisiana in 1803 it was agreed that the inhabitants of the territory would be admitted 'as soon as possible' to United States citizenship. In the Treaty of Guadalupe Hidalgo the discretion of the Congress to admit the inhabitants to citizenship 'at the proper time' was specifically recognized.[3]

When Japan annexed Korea in 1910 the Japanese nationality law was not extended thereto, and consequently the inhabitants of Korea were not considered to have become Japanese citizens. For purposes of international claims and jurisdiction, however, it could not be denied that they were claimed by Japan and hence were, in the contemplation of international law, Japanese nationals.[4]

The treaty of 1810 by which Mauritius capitulated stipulated that the inhabitants would conserve their religion, laws and customs. The *Tribunal de première instance* of Tananarive in 1943 held[5] that the act of annexation had not denationalized the Mauritians: 'Attendu que c'est un principe traditionnel que seul ne peut avoir deux nationalités, qu'en acquirant une nouvelle on perd nécessairement la première.' The implication of this is that, in the opinion of the court, Mauritians had not acquired British nationality, and had retained their French nationality. This conclusion is not administratively accepted by either the United Kingdom or France.

Even though the successor State may not in fact extend its nationality to the inhabitants of acquired territory, there is no doubt that it is entitled to do so with respect to those rendered susceptible by the change of sovereignty, irrespective of their wishes.[6] Its own municipal law, however, may prescribe that such nationality is conferred only by a submission on the part of the persons concerned. The older and more prevalent view of

1 *Gonzales* v. *Williams*, 192 U.S. 1; 23 *Op. A.-G.* p. 370; Moore, *Dig.* vol. II, p. 316.
2 *Roque Espiritu de la Ysla* v. *U.S.* 77 F. 2d. 988; *Toyota* v. *U.S.* 268 U.S. 402.
3 *M.N.R.G.* vol. XIV, p. 7.
4 *Japanese Annual of International Law* (1959), p. 89.
5 *Recueil Pénant* (1943), p. 196.
6 Graupner in *Law Quarterly Review*, vol. LXI (1945), p. 168. A similar principle exists in American law: *In re Pfleiger*, 254 F. 2d. 511. This view is controverted by Jellinek, *op. cit.* p. 49. He thinks the grant of nationality by the successor is declaratory of a change effected by international law, and not constitutive. Cf. Makarov, *Allgemeine Lehren des Staatsangehörigkeitsrechts* (1962), pp. 98 *et seq.*

Effect of Change of Sovereignty on Nationality 505

English law asserts that British nationality extends automatically,[1] but this view has not always been adhered to in courts applying English law. Judges have tended to view with disfavour the conclusion that persons resident in territory acquired by or lost to the Crown are rendered incompetent to retain their previous nationality by removal to a foreign country. At various times they have argued that British nationality can be acquired or lost only by a tacit submission to the new sovereign. Failure to remove within a reasonable time from territory ceded to Great Britain has been considered an acquiescence in the new state of affairs, involving, in consequence, a change of allegiance.[2] This theory was expressed in a number of cases arising out of the annexation of the Boer Republics in 1900, and other African territories. It was stated in one case:

A person might choose to go and live somewhere else. The fact of annexation does not make the people living in the annexed territory subjects of the annexing state unless they, within a reasonable time, show by their conduct or acts that they acquiesce in their position, and choose to become subjects of the conquering power.[3]

Remaining within the sphere of the new dominion, and fulfilling the duties of subjects, the Chief Justice of South Africa held in another case,[4] would amount to a tacit submission. The placing of one's name on the electoral roll was decided in a third judgment[5] to be a sufficient submission.

It is clear that there has been a long history of executive reluctance in Whitehall to insist upon claiming as British subjects persons who had previously been connected with acquired territory, unless they submit to the Crown by retaining the connexion, and a converse reluctance, now embodied in the legislative scheme of United Kingdom citizenship devised in 1948, to admit that British subjects lose this status upon separation of territory from the Crown without having the opportunity to elect to retain it.

On 27 July 1764 the Law Officer gave an opinion that the subjects of

---

1 See *supra*, p. 501. Both German and French nationality extends automatically to inhabitants of absorbed territory: Cogordan, *op. cit.* pp. 319 *et seq.*; Graupner, *loc. cit.* p. 168.
2 See Westlake, p. 70; and his *Collected Papers* (1914), p. 486.
3 *Wessels* v. *Olivier* (1903), O.R.C. Rep. 43 at p. 49.
4 *R.* v. *Jizwa* (1894), Sup. Ct. C.G.H. Rep. 387.
5 *R.* v. *Geyer* (1900), 17 S.C. 501. See also *Lehmkuhl* v. *Kock* (1903), O.R.C. Rep. 20; *Rabie* v. *Jansen* (1902), O.R.C. Rep. 72; *Re Pienaar* (1903), 22 S.C. 300; *Re Radloff* (1905), 22 S.C. 298; *Van Deventer* v. *Hancke & Mossop* [1903], T.S.C.R. 401. In *Murray* v. *Parkes*, Humphreys, J., stated his view that upon the loss of territory to the Crown there is at the same time a relinquishment of 'the right to the allegiance of such of its inhabitants as elect to adhere to the new state': *loc. cit.* at p. 132.

France and Spain who were 'inhabitants' of Canada and the ceded Spanish territories 'and continued there under the stipulations of the definitive treaty, having entitled themselves to the benefits thereof by taking the oaths of allegiance, etc.' were not to be considered as aliens incapable of enjoying or acquiring real property.[1] In 1812 an opinion was given that the 'native inhabitants' of Louisiana, which was ceded by Spain to France in October 1800, and by France to the United States in April 1803, were to be regarded as Americans, although, if they returned to France with the intention to settle there, their national character as Frenchmen would revive.[2]

On 26 January 1844 a Law Officer's opinion was given to the effect that British subjects inhabiting Minorca who remained there after its cession to Spain lost their British nationality.

When the King of England cedes by Treaty any part of his Dominions to another State, the Inhabitants of the Part so called, notwithstanding they may have been born under his Protection, whilst it belonged to the Crown of England, become aliens, unless upon the cession taking place, they shew their adherence to the British Crown by removing from the ceded Territory, and resorting to some remaining portion of the King's Dominions.[3]

The submission theory, whether or not it be proposed as one of English municipal law or one of international law, is unsatisfactory. It fails precisely because the test it employs is arbitrary and subjective. At what stage does the submission effect a change of nationality? What is the status of a person during the interim period between the change of sovereignty and the evidencing of a submission? By what law are his legal relationships arising during this period to be governed? These are difficult questions to which no certain answer can be given.

3. THE CATEGORIES OF PERSONS SUBJECT TO CHANGE OF NATIONALITY

International law does not offer any sure guide as to the categories of persons who, by virtue of a change of sovereignty, become susceptible of receiving the nationality of the successor State. The majority of treaties of cession during the last one hundred and fifty years have spoken of a change of nationality on the part of the 'inhabitants' of the ceded territory. There is little agreement, however, as to the classes of persons designated as 'inhabitants'.[4] International practice and the opinions of writers have

1 McNair, *International Law Opinions* (1956), vol. II, p. 20.
2 *Ibid.* p. 22.   3 *Ibid.* p. 23.
4 Szlechter, *Les options conventionnelles de nationalité* (1948), pp. 99, 107.

Effect of Change of Sovereignty on Nationality 507

alternated between the tests of birth and domicile. The former test was adopted by the Law Officers in an Opinion of 24 March 1888, relating to the nationality of one Chong Kham, who had been born in Burma, was resident in Siam when Burma was annexed by Great Britain, and subsequently became a naturalized Siamese. It was pointed out to the Law Officers that at the time of his naturalization he was unaware of the annexation of Burma. The Law Officers advised that 'it may be properly represented to the Siamese Government that Her Majesty's Government consider Chong Kham is entitled to be regarded as a British subject, and to receive a passport from the British Consul'. The naturalization was to be regarded as ineffective in English law because Chong Kham did not know he had become a British subject.[1]

It is in the case of total succession that the test of birth has most often been employed. In the case of *Treasury* v. *Wolff* a Transvaal court was invited to examine the effect of the annexation of the Orange Free State by Great Britain in 1900 upon a person born in Bavaria in 1851, who became a burgher of the Orange Free State in 1880, and subsequently returned to Bavaria. By this return he lost his burghership. In the meantime Bavaria had been incorporated in the *Reich*, and the court was required to decide whether or not he had acquired German nationality. It was held that he had.[2] No attempt was made by the judge to consider whether by the German constitution, or by the laws of Bavaria or of the *Reich*, the *de cuius* had either lost his Bavarian nationality or acquired German. It was assumed that because he had been born in Bavaria he automatically acquired German nationality, although domiciled at the time elsewhere.

That the law of the successor State is decisive in determining the effect of change of sovereignty on nationality underlies the attitude taken by the British Government with respect to nationals of Austria who were domiciled in England at the time of Austria's annexation by Germany in 1938. Such persons were considered by the Home Office to have become German subjects in accordance with the *Reich* decree of 3 July 1938, conferring German nationality on all Austrian nationals without qualification of either birth or domicile.[3] Upon the outbreak of war in 1939 these persons were treated as enemy aliens.[4] English courts also recognized as

1 Opinion of 24 March 1888, F.O. Confidential Papers (5785), O'Connell, Appendix, no. 51.
2 S.A.L.R. [1919] T.P.D. 25.
3 *RGBl.* 1938, p. 790. A second Decree of 30 July 1939 annulled the Austrian Nationality Law of 1925 and extended the German Nationality Law of 1913 to Austria: *ibid.* 1938, I, p. 1072. Jellinek, *op. cit.* pp. 142 *et seq.*
4 360 H.C. Deb., 5s., col. 1059; 361 H.C. Deb., 5s., col. 420; 362 H.C. Deb. cols.

German nationals former Austrian citizens who departed from Austria at the time of the *Anschluss*, on the ground that German domestic law claimed them as such.[1] The same attitude was adopted by the courts of the Netherlands,[2] Belgium,[3] Italy,[4] and Switzerland,[5] none of which distinguished between Austrians domiciled in Austria, or between those who emigrated at the time of the *Anschluss* and those who remained behind. The German Federal Supreme Court, even after the restoration of Austria, and in face of the latter's claim that Austrian nationality had been continuous throughout the *Anschluss*,[6] held that according to the international rules of State succession annexation automatically effected a change of nationality, and that in the eyes of international law membership of a State was a matter to be decided by the law of that State. Only German law, it concluded, could decide on the acquisition or loss of German nationality. The implication left by the Court was that the *de cuius* possessed both German and Austrian nationality.[7] Subsequently the German Federal Administrative Court reached the conclusion that former Austrians who remained in Germany after 1945 remained German nationals, though it departed from the Supreme Court in holding that only municipal law, and not international law, regulated the effects of State succession upon nationality. It introduced an element of submission into the solution of the problem by requiring repatriation to Austria as a precondition of loss of German nationality.[8] In 1955 this decision was overruled by the Federal Constitutional Court, but on the special ground that Germany acknowledged the total nullification of the *Anschluss*, and the legal changes purporting to flow from it.[9]

The test of deference to the law of the successor State was employed by the Roumanian-German Mixed Arbitral Tribunal in 1923 in the case of

222, 1207; 363 H.C. Deb., 5s., col. 1207; 370 H.C. Deb., 5s., col. 39; 378 H.C. Deb. 5s., col. 782; 383 H.C. Deb., 5s., cols. 1755, 2299. On 16 December 1943 former Austrians were permitted to register as Austrians: 395 H.C. Deb., 5s., col. 1677.

1 *In the matter of Mangold's Patent*, Reports of Patent, Design and Trade Mark Cases, vol. LXVIII, p. 1 (1950); *The King* v. *The Home Secretary, ex parte L.* [1945] 1 K.B. 7. Brownlie in Clunet, vol. LXXXVI, pt. II (1959), p. 1168.

2 *In re Ten Amsterdam Oil Companies*, Ann. Dig. vol. XIII, Case no. 20; *Veeneendaal* v. *Pommeranz*, ibid. vol. XV, p. 214; *Nederlands Beheers-Instituut* v. *Nimwegen and Männer*, I.L.R. vol. XVIII, Case no. 63.

3 *Pulenciks* v. *Augustovskis*, ibid. Case no. 20.

4 *Re Tancredi*, ibid. vol. XVII, Case no. 50.

5 *Wasservogel* v. *Federal Dept. of Justice and Police*, Ann. Dig. vol. XVI, Case no. 52.

6 Clute, ch. IV, and authors there cited.

7 *Neue Juristische Wochenschrift* (1952), v, p. 184.

8 Ibid. (1955), VIII, p. 35. The Supreme Court of Bavaria held that repatriates lost German nationality, ibid. (1952), v, p. 788.

9 Ibid. (1955), VI, 1833. Strebel in Z.f.a.ö.R.u.V. vol. XIX (1959), p. 483.

Wildermann v. *Stinnes*.[1] The *de cuius* was born of parents domiciled in Bessarabia, a territory subsequently ceded by Roumania to Russia. He emigrated from Bessarabia on a Russian passport, and did not return until after the reincorporation of the province in Roumania. He claimed for the purpose of the case that he was a Roumanian national. The tribunal held that this question must be determined by the acts of incorporation, and by Roumanian law, both of which provided for the acquisition of Roumanian nationality by the class of persons to which the *de cuius* belonged. 'Roumanian law recognized expressly', it was decided, 'the quality of Roumanian citizens to be persons who at the date of the Union, though not domiciled in one of the Bessarabian procommunes, were, however, born in one of them of parents domiciled there.'[2] In referring thus to the provisions of municipal law of the successor State, the tribunal, it is believed, proceeded along correct lines. It failed, however, to consider whether international law rendered Roumania competent to claim as its nationals persons born in the ceded territory but not resident there. Such an inquiry was perhaps not considered relevant since Roumania had agreed with certain of the Powers in 1920 to recognize as its nationals persons of the class to which the *de cuius* belonged, and a provision to this effect had been incorporated in the instrument of reunion.[3]

The difficulty with a collective change of nationality of all the citizens of an extinguished State is that it affects persons who possess no identification with the absorbed territory other than the accidental one of birth there or of descent from a father born there. The competence of the successor State to make this change was denied in a number of American decisions relative to the effect of the annexation of Austria in 1938 upon the status of Austrian nationals resident at the time outside Austria. In the case of *United States ex rel. Schwartzkopf* v. *Uhl* the facts were as follows. The *de cuius* was born in 1886 in Austrian territory which in 1919 was incorporated in Czechoslovakia. In 1926 he became a German citizen, and in 1933 an Austrian. In 1936 he took up residence in the United States, and upon the outbreak of war with Germany in 1941 was interned as an alien enemy. He took *habeas corpus* proceedings. The United States Attorney argued that he became a German citizen by virtue of the *Reich*

---

1 *Causes célèbres du droit des gens, Affaire Wildermann* v. *Stinnes*, edited by Lapradelle (1931). The same test was employed by the Egyptian Mixed Court of Appeal in 1925, which held that a person born in Rome and resident in Egypt became by the annexation of Rome in 1870 an Italian national: *Romano* v. *Comma*, Ann. Dig. vol. III, Case no. 195.

2 At p. 442: 'The Tribunal must find if and when Roumanian law could confer on the plaintiff the quality which the Roumanian Government had recognized in him.'

3 *B.T.S.* 1922, no. 15, Cmd. 1747.

decree of 3 July 1938. This contention was rejected by the court, which stated that 'under accepted principles of international law, Germany could impose citizenship by annexation (collective naturalization) only on those who were inhabitants of Austria in 1938'.[1] This decision was followed in a subsequent case,[2] and approved in a third.[3] In another case it was held that a person born in the ceded area of Sudetenland but resident in the United States had become an enemy alien because he had voluntarily applied for German citizenship and had stated that he was willing to bear arms for Germany.[4] It is clear that the American test is less the objective one of determining what limits international law places upon extension of nationality to persons not closely identified with a territory than the subjective one of voluntary submission to the new sovereign, and as formulated it is no more than an aspect of the criterion of enmity across the line of war.

If there is no restraint imposed by international law upon the competence of the successor State to claim as its nationals persons whose only connexion with the acquired territory is in virtue of the operation of the *jus soli* or the *jus sanguinis* rule, then foreign States and foreign or international courts have no basis for refusing recognition to a change of nationality effected in the law of the successor State. But if there is such a restraint, then they are justified in refusing, and perhaps even required to refuse, recognition of a change offensive to the limits laid down. The *Nottebohm*[5] decision clearly favours the existence in international law of restrictions upon individual or collective naturalization when a genuine link does not exist.

Whether a sufficient link exists between an individual and a successor

1 137 F. 2d. 898. Also *U.S. ex rel. Zeller* v. *Watkins*, 167 F. 2d. 279.
2 *U.S. ex rel. D'Esquiva* v. *Uhl*, 137 F. 2d. 903.
3 *U.S. ex rel. Umecker* v. *McCoy*, 54 F. Supp. 679. *Schwartzkopf's* Case rejected as unsound the decision of an American court in *Brown* v. *U.S.*, where it was held that a person born in Hanover but domiciled in the United States at the time when Hanover was annexed by Prussia became a Prussian national. The court had refused to accept 'the idea that the matter of domicil affects the fact of citizenship. . . . When the territory and Government of a Kingdom pass to, and become merged in, the territory of another nation, all of its subjects pass also.' This conclusion presupposed that international law prescribes an automatic change of nationality, and that the test of birth is established in international law. In addition, it failed to consider whether or not the category of persons of which the *de cuius* was one was recognized in Prussian law as having become one of Prussian nationals: 5 U.S. Court of Claims, 571. The same failure to consider the municipal law of the successor State is evident in two judgments of the Egyptian Mixed Court of Appeal in Alexandria in 1925: *Romano* v. *Comma*, *Ann. Dig.* vol. III, Case no. 195; *Pini* v. *Pini*, *ibid.* Case no. 196. Graupner has criticized these three cases in *Trans. Grot. Soc.* vol. XXXII (1946), pp. 101 *et seq.*
4 *U.S. ex rel. Reichel* v. *Carusi*, 157 F. 2d. 732.
5 I.C.J. Rep. 1955, p. 4.

Effect of Change of Sovereignty on Nationality

State will depend very much on the concrete circumstances. The case of the *Anschluss* of Austria by Germany was one of total extinction of the State with which individuals had previously been connected. Austrian citizens whose only connexion with Austria was that of birth or descent were not placed in any different legal condition (though the circumstantial condition might have become very different) by a substitution of German for Austrian nationality. The link of birth or descent was no less significant after the *Anschluss* than it was before it, and its automatic severance would have resulted in statelessness, a condition which the *Nottebohm* rule might sometimes produce, but which is certainly not intended by it. In view of these considerations, and in face of the decisions of the courts of several other countries which admitted German nationality to have extended to all former Austrian nationals, the United States decisions can be justified only upon the political non-recognition of the *Anschluss*.

However, when only part of a State is transferred to another State, the primary connexion with the old sovereign can only be severed in the case of persons linked with the territory. Whether birth or descent is a sufficient link with the territory is obviously more questionable in this case than in the case of total succession, because the alternative is between retention of an old nationality and acquisition of a new, and not between acquisition of nationality and statelessness. This was recognized by the German-Yugoslav Mixed Arbitral Tribunal in the case of *Peinitsch v. German State*. The *de cuius*, who was born in Carinthia but domiciled in Germany at the date of the cession of this province to Yugoslavia under the Treaty of St Germain, pleaded that he had become a Yugoslav national. This plea was rejected. 'It is a rule of international law', it was decided, 'that when a territory passes to a new sovereign, it must, in case of doubt, be assumed that those inhabitants of the territory in question who are not domiciled (*domiciliés*) there do not acquire the new nationality.'[1]

Not always, however, has this principle been restricted to cases of partial succession. In their Opinion of 17 May 1900, the Law Officers advised that British nationality 'ought not to be imposed on inhabitants' of the Transvaal 'who are not within the State, unless they return to it afterwards'.[2] That statelessness would be the fate of those emigrants who could not claim another nationality does not seem to have disturbed the advisers.[3]

[1] *Ann. Dig.* vol. II, Case no. 121.
[2] Opinion of 17 May 1900, F.O. Confidential Papers (7516), no. 18 A: O'Connell, Appendix, no. 68.
[3] In an endeavour to avoid the conclusion that such persons become stateless, the Harvard Draft on Nationality in 1929 proposed the following formula: in the case

It is possible to derive from the *Nottebohm* decision the conclusion that not birth but domicile is the only sufficient link in the case of partial succession to justify an extension of nationality upon change of sovereignty. Domicile in this context is taken to mean 'habitual residence' rather than domicile as understood in any one system of municipal law.[1] In German law, for example, a person may have several domiciles,[2] while in English law he may be habitually resident in a territory without being domiciled there. The criterion of habitual residence was adopted in the Peace Treaties of 1919–23.[3] In addition, the Minorities Treaty of 1919 enacted that Poland was to recognize as its nationals persons born in Poland of parents 'habitually resident' there, regardless of domicile.[4] Subsequently this provision was interpreted by the Permanent Court of International Justice, which held that a person 'habitually resident' in Poland was one who had become 'established in a permanent manner, with the intention of remaining'.[5] The difficulties of the matter were not settled, however, by this interpretation, and a further dispute developed between Germany and Poland on the question whether or not a 'permanent establishment' implied 'an exclusive concentration of personal and economic relations in a single place'. This question was referred to arbitration, and the arbitrator, Dr Kaeckenbeeck, decided that 'the establishment contemplated in the notion of habitual residence does not

of total succession nationals of the predecessor State 'regardless of residence' are to become subjects of the successor State 'unless in accordance with the provisions of its law they decline the nationality of the successor State'; in the case of partial succession habitual residence is to be the sole test: *A.J.* vol. XXIII (1929), Sp. Supp., p. 61. The distinction between total and partial succession is rigidly systematized by Weis, *Nationality and Statelessness in International Law* (1956), ch. 11.

1 *Exchange of Greek and Turkish Populations* Case, P.C.I.J. ser. B, no. 10, p. 19 (1925).

2 Kaeckenbeeck, *The International Experiment of Upper Silesia* (1942), p. 135. On the history of domicile as a criterion see Schätzel, *Internationales Staatsgehörigkeitsrecht in Internationales Recht* (1962), pp. 44 *et seq.*; Szlechter *op. cit.* p. 97; Jellinek, *op. cit.* pp. 71 *et seq.*

3 Treaty of Versailles, arts. 36, 84, 91, 105, 112; Treaty of Lausanne, art. 30. So as to exclude German émigrés and their descendants, it was provided that French nationality was to be acquired by only such inhabitants of Alsace-Lorraine as had lost it in 1871: Treaty of Versailles, Annex to sect. 79, *loc. cit.* In the Treaties of St Germain and Trianon a new principle was introduced, that of *indigénat*. In the territories ceded by Austria and Hungary, individuals, besides being nationals of the State, enjoyed a municipal citizenship in a specific commune, and were designated as *indigénats*. Austria and Hungary were to recognize that any person having this designation would lose his old nationality and acquire that of the State to which the territory was transferred: St Germain, *loc. cit.* art. 70; Trianon, *loc. cit.* art. 56. See Niboyet in *Rev. de droit int. et de lég. comp.* 3rd ser. vol. II (1921), p. 287.

4 *Loc. cit.* art. 4.

5 Advisory Opinion on the Acquisition of Polish Nationality, P.C.I.J. ser. B, no. 7, p. 20 (1923).

Effect of Change of Sovereignty on Nationality 513

imply the exclusive concentration of personal and economic relations in a single place' as Poland had argued. 'The existence of an establishment outside Polish territory does not prevent an establishment in Polish territory from constituting a habitual residence.'[1] Following this decision a convention was entered into between Germany and Poland in which it was agreed that a person was deemed to have his habitual residence in territory acquired by Poland when he had 'settled in the territory in order to carry on there his chosen objects in life', and would be 'residing there habitually and regularly without any intention of leaving'.[2] The term 'habitual residence' as used in the Treaty of Versailles was interpreted by a Belgian court as meaning 'fixed, enduring and permanent residence'. It was held that a person who resided only for several months in 1914 and 1915 in territory ceded by Germany to Belgium in 1919 was not habitually resident there. It was stated:

> No one can be regarded as habitually resident in one place who lives in that place only for short periods of time, and at intervals, while habitually carrying on his ordinary day-to-day avocations elsewhere. On the other hand, a person cannot be deemed to be not habitually resident in one place if he has fixed his abode in that place, if he has there his family and home and the centre of his interests and his affections. It does not matter if he goes away occasionally, without, however, manifesting any intention to abandon that place or to set up house elsewhere.[3]

When Great Britain annexed Cyprus in 1915, it was proclaimed that all Ottoman subjects 'resident' there were to become British subjects.[4] The interpretation of the word 'resident' occasioned difficulty, and it was subsequently enacted by Order in Council of 27 November 1917 that a 'resident' was any Ottoman subject 'ordinarily resident' even though temporarily absent.[5] This enactment was considered by the Egyptian Mixed Court of Appeal in the case of *Agapios* v. *Sanitary and Quarantine Council of Egypt*. The *de cuius* was born in Cyprus and was resident in Egypt at the time of the annexation of the island. He claimed to have become a British national. The court approached the question in what is believed to be the correct manner, and inquired as to the effect of the British enactments. It decided that British nationality was clearly restricted to persons resident in Cyprus during 1914–19 (at least with respect

---

1 *Ann. Dig.* vol. II, Case no. 123
2 *L.N.T.S.* (1925), vol. XXXII, no. 824, art. 4. The Convention also introduced the principle of origin. 'German nationals born in the territory of parents who at the time of the birth were habitually resident in that territory will have acquired Polish nationality *ipso facto*, whether or not they were themselves habitually resident in that territory': art. 7.
3 *In re Stoffels*, *Ann. Dig.* vol. IX, Case no. 107.
4 *B.F.S.P.* vol. CIX (1915), p. 429. 5 *B.F.S.P.* vol. CXI, p. 119.

to Ottomans) and that the *de cuius* remained a Turkish citizen.[1] Habitual residence was the criterion adopted in an exchange of notes which passed in 1937 between Great Britain and Siam relative to the consequences of a boundary adjustment,[2] in the Peace Treaty with Italy of 1947,[3] and in the Italian Royal Decree of 1 June 1936 extending Italian nationality to the inhabitants of Ethiopia.[4]

The test of habitual residence renders only a limited category of persons susceptible of being invested with the nationality of the successor State.[5] Those habitually resident in absorbed territory may have such nationality imposed upon them according to municipal law after the change of sovereignty. In such event they cannot cast off the new allegiance by removing elsewhere.[6] Persons habitually resident outside the territory of a State which is totally extinguished become stateless. A decision to this effect was given by a German court which was called upon to determine the nationality of a person who was born in the district of Teschen, which was at the time Austrian, and was subsequently incorporated in Czechoslovakia. In 1930 he emigrated to Belgium, where he resided until 1940.

1 *Ann. Dig.* vol. I, Case no. 136. Compare *Gout* v. *Cimitian* [1922] 1 A.C. 105.
2 *B.T.S.* 1937, no. 23, Cmd. 5475.
3 *B.T.S.* 1948, no. 50, Cmd. 7481, art. 19 at p. 14.
4 Royal Decree XIV, no. 1019, R.I.I.A. *Docs. Int. Aff.* (1935), vol. II, p. 475. The test was also applied in the following treaties: Paris, 1814, *M.R.* (*Suppl.*), vol. VI, p. 1, art. 17 at p. 9; Vienna, 1815, *ibid.* p. 379, art. 20 at p. 39; Turin, 1860, *M.N.R.G.* vol. XVI pt. II, p. 539, art. 6 at p. 540; Washington, 1867, *ibid.* 2nd ser., vol. I, p. 39; Guadalupe Hidalgo, *ibid.* vol. XIV, p. 7; Constantinople, 1914, *B.F.S.P.* vol. CVII, pt. II, p. 579, art. 2 at p. 580; Portsmouth, 1905, *B.F.S.P.* vol. XCVIII, p. 735, art. 10 at p. 737; Athens, 1914, *ibid.* vol. CVII, pt. I, p. 893, art. 4 at p. 894; Zürich, 1859, *M.N.R.G.* vol. XVI, pt. II, p. 516, art. 12 at p. 520; Vienna, 1864, *ibid.* vol. XVII, pt. II, p. 470, art. 19 at p. 482; Frankfurt, 1871, *ibid.* vol. XX, p. 470, art. 19 at p. 482.
5 Kunz, *loc. cit.* pp. 123 *et seq.*; Mann, *loc. cit.* p. 222; Fauchille, vol. I, pt. I, p. 856. In *Murray* v. *Parkes* Humphreys, J., said that the word 'inhabitants' of absorbed territory must receive its ordinary meaning—namely, the people residing in the territory lost to the Crown: [1942] 2 K.B. 123 at p. 132.
6 On the 'French system' see Jellinek, p. 75. This was apparently the doctrine applied in the celebrated case of Count Platen Hallemund, the Prime Minister of Hanover, who left that country at the time of its annexation by Prussia, and was subsequently cited before a Prussian court for an act of treason alleged to have been committed by him as a Prussian subject after his removal to Austria. The case turned on the question whether or not, Hanoverian nationality having been extinguished, the count was to be considered as stateless or as having become invested with Prussian nationality. The latter appears to have been the view taken. The case has often been criticized on the ground that Prussia was incompetent to treat as a national one who did not remain in the absorbed territory. The full facts of the case, however, have not been made available, and it is not known whether the escape from Hanover was effected immediately before or immediately after the declaration of annexation. If the latter is the case, then the decision is consistent with the principle advanced here. The case was first quoted by Forsyth, *Cases and Opinions on Constitutional Law* (1869), p. 335, and is discussed by Graupner in *Trans. Grot. Soc. loc. cit.* p. 88; Rivier, vol. II, p. 349.

In 1938 Teschen was ceded to Poland, and Polish nationality was extended only to persons resident there or born there of Polish origin. The *de cuius* fulfilled neither qualification, and it was held that he had not acquired Polish nationality. It was further held that as Czechoslovakia had ceased to exist and the *de cuius* was not resident at the time in territory incorporated in its successor States, he had become stateless.[1]

French law has not consistently recognized the domicile test. The *Cour de Cassation* said in 1874: 'Il importe peu qu'au moment de l'incorporation du pays conquis . . . le national qui y est né n'y ait point été domicilié, et qu'il ait fixé son principal établissement à l'étranger. . . . Cette résidence même continue hors de son pays natal ne change rien á la situation, quant à sa nationalité.'[2] But articles 12 and 13 of the Nationality Code of 1945 predicate acquisition or loss of French citizenship, in the absence of treaty stipulation, upon domicile in territories *attachés* to or *cédés* by France. No mention is made of independence. The *Cour de Paris* in 1939 decided that the French nationals domiciled in the territories ceded by France in the Treaty of Paris, 1815, had lost their French nationality, whether they had been born there or not.[3] The *Cour de Pau* held in 1955 that a woman, born a French national, conserved her French nationality after marriage with a Turk in Lebanon in 1922. It was stated that the Treaty of Lausanne had made provision for the fate of Turkish nationals in the detached territories, and that effect had been given to this by legislation in Lebanon in 1924, but that since the husband of the *de cuius* had been resident at this date in France, he had retained his Turkish nationality, and that since Turkish law did not extend this nationality to a wife, no change in her status had resulted from the marriage.[4]

However, as a matter of practice French courts look to the inscription of the *de cuius*' name in the communal register, and assume domicile from this, even though the *de cuius* might in fact be totally resident abroad. Interpreting the expression 'domicile' in the Treaty of Paris of 1947 relating to the change of nationality in the territories ceded to France, the Court at Aix held that this must be understood to mean effective and habitual residence, and this could be proved by inscription in a local register, to which the successor administration had taken no exception.[5] The Cour de Cassation held in 1954 that those persons whose parents had been registered in a commune in Alsace-Lorraine, but who were not

1 *Slouzak Minority in Teschen (Nationality) Case, Ann. Dig.* (Suppl. vol.), vol. XI, Case no. 93.
2 *Ickelheimer v. Richault,* S. 1878, 1. 45.
3 *Affaire Max Alkan,* S. 1954, 2. 106 n.
4 *Re Ghattas, Revue critique de droit international privé* (1955), p. 689.
5 *Berutti v. P. & G.* Aix-en-Provence, J.C.P. (1956), 2, 9173.

themselves registered there and had not been born there, might be registered in such a commune, and gain a right to restoration of French nationality under the Treaty of Versailles.[1]

There is thus a tendency on the part of courts whose system of law identifies inhabitants with particular communes to attribute change of nationality in virtue of the form rather than the substance of this identification. The solution of the problem of change of nationality by the inhabitants of Formosa and Korea in virtue of the Japanese Peace Treaty is an illustration of this. Shortly after entering into occupation of Formosa, China conferred Chinese nationality on all Formosans resident in Formosa, and retroactively upon all Overseas Formosans of Chinese origin. Japan, however, has taken the position that, until the Peace Treaty became effective, all Formosans retained Japanese nationality. Following the signature of the treaty the Japanese Ministry of Justice issued a circular stating that, since Formosa and Korea would cease to be territories of Japan, 'Formosans and Koreans, including those residing in the mainland of Japan, shall lose their Japanese nationality. Japanese nationality might be retained by marriage or adoption, or other relevant legal act, and conversely, persons of Japanese origin would lose their Japanese nationality by marriage to or adoption by a Korean or Formosan'. In emphasizing that grounds for registration in Japan were sufficient grounds for retention of Japanese nationality, the Japanese Ministry of Justice seems to have implied that registration in either Korea or Formosa was the criterion for loss of Japanese nationality. This view, however, has not been universally accepted. It has been argued that, since the treaty intended to 'restore' Formosa, it should be interpreted as a renunciation of Japanese supremacy over the category of persons affected by the taking of Formosa by Japan; this interpretation would exclude Japanese women and children married to, or adopted by, Formosans, and also persons of Japanese origin registered in Formosa. It has also been argued that the intention was renunciation by Japan of claims which she had, not only over former Chinese nationals, but over all persons, including Japanese wives and children, who would have become Chinese nationals by marriage or adoption had the Japanese conquest of Formosa not occurred. Both

---

[1] Iltis v. Procureur de la République, Revue critique de droit international privé (1955), p. 97. (Inscription was also regarded as proof by the Trib. civ. de Tunis, 4 June 1954, Rev. tun. de droit (1955), p. 100); Consorts Ben Bougassas v. Mohamed Ben El Hadj Rahal, ibid. (1956), pp. 91, 353; ibid. (1955), p. 356. It was held that a person born in Tunis of parents and grandparents who were enrolled as aliens, and who had claimed Italian nationality, and had served in the Italian army, was not a Tunisian national. Pietro Memmi v. Résident Général de France et Procureur de la République, ibid. (1935), p. 79, with critical note.

Formosa and Korea had been governed by legal systems separate from that of Japan, and the inhabitants had been subject to separate and local registration.[1]

Persons habitually resident in the absorbed territory who are nationals of foreign States and at the same time not nationals of the predecessor State cannot be invested with the successor's nationality.[2] On the other hand, stateless persons so resident there are in the same position as born nationals of the predecessor State.[3] There is an 'inchoate right' on the part of any State to naturalize stateless persons resident upon its territory.[4] Nor is there any distinction to be drawn between the case of naturalized subjects of the predecessor State and born nationals.[5] On 31 October 1900, the Law Officers gave an Opinion with respect to a German who had been naturalized in the Orange Free State, and who claimed to have become a British national by virtue of the annexation. It was reported that 'no distinction should be drawn between the case of a natural-born and that of a naturalized citizen'.[6] Subsequently the German Embassy requested that consideration be given to the case of such nationals of German origin who did not wish to become British subjects, and it was pointed out that many of them, although naturalized in the Boer Republics, had retained German nationality. On 25 June 1901 the Law Officers reported that such a request was reasonable and in accordance with international usage.[7]

The matter of naturalized burghers of the Transvaal, mainly of German or Russian origin, arose again in 1903 from a despatch of Lord Milner from South Africa which included a legal opinion that such persons had been naturalized only for the period of the Transvaal's existence, and had not become British subjects upon the annexation. The Law Officers were asked their views on this opinion, and they repeated that no distinction should be drawn between natural-born and naturalized Transvaal burghers.[8]

1 *Japanese Annual of International Law* (1958), p. 64.
2 Jellinek, *op. cit.* pp. 78 *et seq.*; *Masson v. Mexico*, Moore, *I.A.* vol. III, p. 2542; *Goldbeck v. Mexico*, *ibid.* p. 2507; *Halder v. Minister of Defence* [1915] S.A.L.R., T.P.D. 622; *Marburger v. Minister of Finance* [1918] S.A.L.R., C.P.D. 183; *Loewenstein v. Custodian of Enemy Property* [1921] S.A.L.R., T.P.D. 606.
3 Kaeckenbeeck, *op. cit.* pp. 180 *et seq.*
4 *Des Bois* Case (1812) 2 Marten 185; Graupner in *Trans Grot. Soc. loc. cit.* p. 99. This view is controverted by Jellinek, *op. cit.* p. 79.
5 Keith, p. 48; *U.S. et al. v. Rodiek*, 117 F. 2d. 588. But see *Tobin v. Walkinshaw*, 1 McAllister 186.
6 Opinion of 31 October 1900, F.O. Confidential Papers (7516), no. 21: O'Connell, Appendix, no. 69.
7 Opinion of 13 June 1901, F.O. Confidential Papers (7733), no. 8: O'Connell, Appendix, no. 74.
8 Unnumbered, unclassified, 28 July 1903.

Although habitual residence is the most satisfactory test for determining the competence of the successor State to impress its nationality on specified persons,[1] it cannot be stated with assurance to be the only test admitted in international law. Upon this subject, perhaps more than upon any other in the law of State succession, codification or international legislation is urgently demanded. It is undesirable that as a result of change of sovereignty persons should be rendered stateless against their wills. It is equally undesirable that persons who have only an accidental relationship with absorbed territory should be invested with a nationality which they do not want. For these reasons it is important that international law recognize the right of persons who wish to avoid acquiring the nationality of the successor State to opt for some alternative nationality open to them, and remove themselves from the territory.

Although the inhabitants of territory affected by a change of administration may retain their previous nationality without acquiring another, the domestic law defining their citizenship may in fact differ from that of the remaining territories of the sovereign. This situation is illustrated by the case of the Ryukyu Islands, which remain under United States administration in virtue of article 3 of the Treaty of Peace with Japan. The assumption is that the inhabitants remain Japanese nationals, and article 3 of the provisions of the government of the Ryukyu Islands, in defining 'a Ryukyuan', appears to defer to this assumption. However, a curious situation results from the provisions of the proclamation of the United States Military Government that 'existing laws' would remain in force, for subsequently Japan enacted new nationality legislation, while, in the view of the Ryukyuan administration, the old continues there.[2]

4. THE EFFECT OF INDEPENDENCE ON NATIONALITY

A grant of independence to a dependent territory may affect nationality in a manner different from that in the case of total annexation, but analogous to that in the case of partial cession. Only persons linked with the territory are susceptible of being regarded by the new State as its nationals. In colonial territories residence is an insufficient practical link, for large numbers of residents would not be of the indigenous population, but would be persons of metropolitan origin, perhaps less closely associated with the destinies of the territory than the indigenous people. At the

[1] *Kaufmann* v. *Augustenborg Town Council*, *Ann. Dig.* vol. II, Case no. 140. See Oppenheim, vol. I, p. 505, n. 3.
[2] *Japanese Annual of International Law* (1959), p. 87.

same time indigenous character is an insufficiently inclusive category, because in most territories there are substantial minority populations of neither metropolitan nor indigenous origin, but with no substantial extraterritorial links. The problems raised have been minimized by the schemes of common status in the Commonwealth and reciprocal treatment in the Community and its associates.

(i) *The Commonwealth*

When the independence of the United States was recognized there was considerable doubt whether the inhabitants of the colonies had ceased to owe allegiance to the Crown, and the question was only resolved on a liberal construction of the peace treaty of 1783.[1] It cannot be doubted, however, that in the nineteenth century the common law settled for a rule that denizens of dominions lost to the Crown ceased to be British subjects unless they affirmed their allegiance by withdrawing from the territory.[2] The statutory scheme of nationality now operative has modified this position.

The British Nationality Act, 1948[3] states that every person who is a citizen of the United Kingdom and Colonies, or a citizen of any of the listed Commonwealth members under legislation enacted by them, shall have the status of a British subject or Commonwealth citizen.[4] Each Commonwealth member was intended to enact similarly, so that a common status is achieved in virtue of the continued membership in the Commonwealth. Owing to the predication of rights and duties upon citizenship in a member State, however, and owing to the occasional lack of consistency in the legislation of the member States defining the categories of persons eligible for citizenship, the common status is of diminishing legal significance.

Inhabitants of dependent territories (other than aliens) fell into three categories: first, that of citizen of the United Kingdom and Colonies, if born within the Crown's Dominions or descended from a British subject under certain territorial conditions;[5] secondly, that of British protected person if a denizen of a British Protectorate or Protected State or Trust Territory; and thirdly, residual British subject by descent in circumstances not qualifying for United Kingdom citizenship. The severance

1 Parry, *Nationality and Citizenship Laws of the Commonwealth* (1957), p. 73.
2 See *supra*, p. 501. The rights of British subjects to opt were recognized at the time of the cession of Heligoland (Anglo–German Agreement Act, 1890, 53 & 54 Vict., c. 32, art. 12 (2)).
3 11 & 12 Geo. VI, c. 56.
4 S. 1.
5 British Nationality Act, 1914, 4 & 5 Geo. V, c. 17, s. 1 (1) (*a*); 1948, s. 4.

of citizenship has been achieved by devices incorporated in the various Independence Acts.

The first device was that respecting Burma.[1] Persons born in Burma, or whose fathers or paternal grandfathers were born in Burma, and their wives ceased to be British subjects unless they, their fathers or grandfathers were born within the Crown's Dominions, Protectorates, Protected States, Trust Territories or Foreign Jurisdiction and were British also by descent or naturalization.[2] An option was available to virtually all such persons if domiciled or ordinarily resident outside Burma.[3] This device avoided the problem of categorizing while permitting the denizens of the metropolis to escape the effects of the change. Because they were attaining the status of Dominions, there was no need for a change in nationality in the cases of India, Pakistan and Ceylon. Accordingly, those persons who were already British subjects retained this status, while those who were British protected persons in virtue of their connexion with the Indian States lost this status with the withdrawal of British suzerainty, but, provided the States were merged in India before the British Nationality Act became law, they acquired the status of British subjects.[4] By the British Nationality Act of the following year, the citizens of these three Dominions were designated as British subjects; and legislation of the Dominions defined the persons who became citizens.[5] Until that event persons were designated by the Act[6] as potentially citizens of those countries if they or their nearest ancestors in the male line acquired nationality by birth within the territories or naturalization there, or annexation of the territories, and as such they could not become United Kingdom citizens.[7]

Persons who were already British subjects, but not United Kingdom citizens, and who remained without that citizenship after the Act, could acquire it if they were not included in the provisions of a citizenship law made by the country of which they were 'potentially' citizens[8] and declared to be such by the Secretary of State.[9]

In virtue of these provisions certain persons no doubt remained British subjects without citizenship, and without acquiring Indian citizenship either under the Indian Constitution or under the Indian Citizenship Act, 1955,[10] which both predicate citizenship on domicile,[11] and on birth and

 1 Burma Independence Act, 1948, 11 & 12 Geo. VI, c. 3, s. 2.
 2 Schedule 1.   3 S. 2 (2).
 4 Parry, *op. cit.* pp. 845, 847.
 5 S. 1 (3).   6 S. 32 (7).
 7 S. 12.   8 S. 12.
 9 S. 32 (8).   10 No. 57 of 1955.
 11 Constitution, s. 5.

Effect of Change of Sovereignty on Nationality 521

descent after 26 January 1950.[1] These could only be deprived of this status by action of the Secretary of State following the Indian enactments.[2]

The device employed in the case of countries which became independent after 1949 has been to add the country's name to the list of countries whose citizenship is the qualification for British nationality, and to remove its name from the list of names of Protectorates and Protected States whose denizens had the status of British protected persons contingently upon their becoming citizens of the new State. All persons who before independence were citizens of the United Kingdom and Colonies cease, under the legislation, to be such if under the law of the new country they become citizens of that country and they, their fathers or paternal grandfathers were born there.[3] To preserve the status of persons of metropolitan origin it is provided[4] that no one shall cease to be a United Kingdom citizen if he, his father, or his paternal grandfather was born in the United Kingdom or a colony or Protectorate or Protected State or Trust Territory or was naturalized or registered there, or became a British subject by annexation. The prototype of this type of legislation was with respect to Ghana in 1958,[5] and the provision is incorporated in the other independence legislation.[6] The drafting of the United Kingdom provision is designed to integrate with that of the citizenship laws of the new States so that, generally speaking, the criterion of a change of citizenship is birth within or without the territory of a parent born there. This device substantially restricts the change to persons of indigenous or semi-indigenous character.[7]

1 No. 57 of 1955, ss. 3, 4.
2 S. 32 (8). For the change of nationality of Indians in Madagascar see Bardonnet in *Annuaire français* (1964), p. 178.
3 Nigeria Independence Act, 1960, 8 & 9 Eliz. II, c. 55, s. 2; Tanganyika Independence Act, 1961, 10 & 11 Eliz. II, c. 1, s. 2; Sierra Leone Independence Act, 1961, 9 & 10 Eliz. II, c. 16, s. 2; Kenya Independence Act, 1963, ch. 54, s. 2; Zanzibar Act, 1963, ch. 55, s. 2; Malawi Independence Act, 1964, ch. 46, s. 2; Zambia Indepence Act, 1964, ch. 65, s. 3; Malta Independence Act, 1964, ch. 86, s. 2.
4 British Nationality Act, 1964, ch. 22, s. 2 (2). Safeguards against statelessness were provided for in British Nationality (no. 2) Act, 1964, ch. 54.
5 British Nationality Act, 1958, 6 & 7 Eliz. II, c. 10, s. 2.
6 Nigeria, 8 & 9 Eliz. II, c. 55, s. 2; Cyprus, S.I. 1960, no. 2215, made under s. 4 of the Cyprus Act, 1960, 8 & 9 Eliz. II, c. 52; Sierra Leone, 9 & 10 Eliz. II, c. 16, s. 2; Tanganyika, 10 Eliz. II, c. 1, s. 2; Jamaica, 10 & 11 Eliz. II, c. 40, s. 2; Trinidad and Tobago, 10 & 11 Eliz. II, c. 54, s. 2; Uganda, 10 & 11 Eliz. II, c. 57, s. 2; Kenya, 11 & 12 Eliz. II, c. 54, s. 3; The Gambia 1964, ch 93, s. 3.
7 The Ghana Nationality and Citizenship Act, no. 1 of 1957; The Tanganyika (Constitution) Order in Council, S.I. 1961, no. 2274, schedule, s. 1; The Citizenship Act, 1961, no. 15 of 1961, as continued by no. 2 of 1962; Tanganyika Govt. Notice no. 415 of 1961; The Sierra Leone (Constitution) Order in Council, S.I. 1961, no. 741, schedule s. 1; The Trinidad and Tobago (Constitution) Order in Council, S.I. 1962, no. 1875, schedule, s. 9; The Jamaica (Constitution) Order in Council, S.I. 1962, no. 1550, schedule, s. 3; The Kenya Order in Council, S.I. 1963, no. 791,

522   *Internal Relations*

With the withdrawal of British protection from the Protectorates and Protected States the denizens of those territories ceased to be British protected persons.[1] The usual provision in the constitutions of the new States for all persons born in the territory who were British protected persons to acquire the new citizenship[2] minimizes the possibility of persons becoming stateless.[3] But in the case of Tanganyika two generations of birth in the territory are required,[4] and the effect of this is to render stateless a large number of Asians who failed to apply for Tanzanian citizenship in the requisite time.

In the case of transfers of territory from the United Kingdom to other Commonwealth members the practice has been to ignore the question of change of citizenship. Hence no legislation was enacted to deprive anyone of United Kingdom citizenship in virtue of the transfer of the Cocos Islands and Christmas Island to Australia, or the incorporation of Penang and Malacca in Malaya, or the creation of the State of Singapore.

When South Africa withdrew from the Commonwealth in 1960 this had no effect upon the status of South African citizens as British subjects under the British Nationality Act, and to resolve any doubts in this and other connexions the United Kingdom enacted legislation[5] preserving the situation. A year later it was enacted that the reference to South Africa in the British Nationality Act should be omitted, and that any person who was a British subject only in virtue of South African citizenship should cease to be such. However, until the end of 1965 South African citizens would not be treated as aliens in the United Kingdom and Colonies, and during this period South African citizens might apply for registration in the United Kingdom under the same terms as Commonwealth citizens.[6]

schedule, s. 1; Uganda Independence Order, S.I. 1962, no. 2175, schedule, s.1; The Malawi Independence Order, S.I. 1964, no. 916, schedule, s. 3; the Malawi Nationality Act, no. 2 of 1964; The Zambia Independence Order, S.I. 1964, no. 1652, schedule, s. 3; The Citizenship of Zambia Ordinance, no. 42 of 1964. The Constitution of Malaya leaves open the possibility of plural citizenship. The Federation of Malaya Order, S.I. 1948, no. 108; The Federation of Malaya Independence Order, S.I. 1957, no. 1533.
 1 British Nationality Act, 1964, ch. 22.
 2 E.g. The Zambia Independence Order, S.I. 1964, no. 1652, schedule, s. 3 (1).
 3 British Nationality (no. 2) Act, 1964, ch. 54, s. 5.
 4 The Tanganyika (Constitution) Order in Council, S.I. 1961, no. 2274, schedule, s. 1.
 5 Republic of South Africa (Temporary Provisions) Act, 1961, 9 & 10 Eliz. II, c. 23.
 6 South Africa Act, 1962, 10 & 11 Eliz. II, c. 23, s. 1, and schedule 1. New Zealand enacted similarly, British Nationality and New Zealand Citizenship Amendment Act, 1962, no. 26 of 1962. South Africa brought citizens of Commonwealth countries into the definition of aliens: South Africa Commonwealth Relations Act, 1962, no. 69 of 1962. Southern Rhodesia achieved an 'Irish solution' for South Africans: Republic of South Africa (Construction of Laws) Act, 1962, no. 21 of 1962. New

(ii) *The Community and Associated States*

The French Nationality Code of 19 October 1945 was expressly applied to the Overseas Territories, so that, subject to certain exceptions, the rules of nationality applied to denizens of both the metropolis and the dependencies.[1] The Constitution of the Fourth Republic[2] also eliminated in fact the distinction between subjects and citizens by providing that all the *ressortissants* of the Overseas Territories were to be French citizens.[3] The Constitution of the Fifth Republic (1958) effected no change in nationality when it envisaged the change in status of the Overseas Territories to Member States of the Community, and a Presidential decision of 9 February 1959 assumed that the latter could not have a separate nationality,[4] because only France remained an international person.[5] This interpretation was contested at the time as involving a misconception of the law of nationality.[6] Since nationality is determined by municipal law, and the member States were admittedly autonomous in this respect, the conclusion was drawn that they might define their own nationality. In fact Togo was authorized on 30 December 1958 to establish its own nationality, and Cameroon legislated to this end on 26 November 1959,[7] six weeks before independence.

The fact that the Constitution of 1958 refers to only one citizenship, *de la Communauté* and not *dans la Communauté*, has suggested that there is no incompatibility between the creation of local nationalities and the retention of a common citizenship, the result being likened to the effects of the 'common clause' in the Commonwealth.[8] This approach was reflected in article 1 of the pre-independence Constitution of the Ivory Coast which stated that 'les citoyens de l'État sont, de plein droit, citoyens de la Communauté'. As to the incidences of this common citizenship, these are defined in article 77 of the French Constitution as being equality of rights,

Zealand legislated with respect to the other Republics within the Commonwealth: Republic of Nigeria Act, no. 58 of 1963; Republic of Tanganyika Act, no. 1 of 1963; Republic of Ghana Act, no. 6 of 1960; Republic of Cyprus Act, no. 14 of 1961; Republic of Uganda Act, no. 21 of 1964.

1 Generally on the territorial scope of French nationality law see Lehmann in Clunet, vol. LXXXII (1955), pp. 324 *et seq.* and Zatzépine, *Le droit de la nationalité des Républiques Francophones d'Afrique et de Madagascar* (1963).

2 Art. 80.

3 Gonidec in *Annuaire français* (1959), pp. 748 *et seq.*; and *Droit d'Outre-Mer*, vol. II (1960), pp. 102 *et seq.*

4 Gonidec in *Annuaire français* (1959), p. 750.

5 Luchaire, *Manuel de droit d'outre-mer*, p. 166.

6 Gonidec, *loc. cit.* p. 751.

7 Ordonnance no. 59–66, *Journal Officiel du Cameroun*, no. 1339, 12 December 1959, p. 1697.   8 Gonidec, *loc. cit.* p. 755.

without distinction of origin, race or religion, and also equality of duties. Until the transfer of powers to the member States in 1960 this was taken to involve liability to conscription, as well as enjoyment of equal rights in France to public office. Since that event the situation has remained unclear, but certainly Community citizens are not equated with aliens in the contemplation of French legislation. This raises the question, raised also in connexion with the Commonwealth,[1] whether there is any restraint imposed by international law, either on France's plenary jurisdiction over citizens of the new independent Republics who remain within the Community, or on her competence to represent them diplomatically.[2]

The French Nationality Code provides for loss of French nationality by persons domiciled in ceded French territory, but is silent on the question of the effect of a transfer of powers under the Constitution to former dependencies. The problem is to some extent regulated by the agreements entered into between France and the new associated States, which agreements override internal law.

The process whereby Vietnam became independent tended to confuse the question of retention or loss of French nationality by the inhabitants; and to resolve the matter a Convention on Nationality was signed by the two countries on 16 August 1955.[3] This provided that only persons born of father and mother of Vietnamese birth, or belonging to an ethnic minority whose habitat is on the territory of Vietnam, should be regarded as of Vietnamese origin, and that a Vietnamese should be a person of Vietnamese origin who does not possess the character of a French citizen, or who renounces such character. French citizens not of Vietnamese origin domiciled in South Vietnam, Hanoi, Haiphong and Tourane were to retain French nationality, even when they would not effectively have established their domicile outside Vietnam, while former French subjects whose place of origin was South Vietnam, Hanoi, Haiphong or Tourane should have Vietnamese nationality, irrespective of their domicile, unless they had acquired French nationality prior to 8 March 1949 by administrative or judicial act, and were more than eighteen years of age, subject to a right to opt for Vietnamese nationality. A similar option would be available for Vietnamese who had acquired French nationality after that date. Persons of Vietnamese origin who were French citizens by birth, aged more than eighteen years, would retain French nationality with a

---

1 O'Connell, *International Law* (1965), p. 734; Wilson and Clute in *A.J.* vol. LVII (1963), p. 566; Parry, *op. cit.* ch. 4.
2 The French Nationality Code of 1945 was held to apply to all persons born before that date in any French territory: *Hong Wang Wang Fat* v. *Procureur de la République*, Trib. Papeete, Bull., p. 172.
3 Decree no. 59–593, *Journal Officiel*, 3 May 1959, pp. 4758, 4767.

right of option. French nationality would also be retained by persons aged more than eighteen, one of whose parents was French. In an exchange of notes it was added that Eurasian and African-Asian infants born and residing in Vietnam whose affiliation was not established should have Vietnamese nationality, and the French Government stated that it regarded this as an application of the classical principle of the *jus soli*. The French Minister of Foreign Affairs stated that the Franco-Vietnamese Convention on Nationality of 16 August 1955 could not have the effect of depriving the subjects of Cochin and the concessions of Hanoi and Haiphong of their French nationality, because article 19 expressly provided for the possibility of Vietnamese people acquiring French nationality, and vice versa.[1]

The Convention on Establishment between France and the Malagasy Republic of June 1960[2] sought to transform the implications of common citizenship in the French Constitution into bilateral agreement, by providing for equality, with some qualifications, of French and Malagasy nationals in the following respects: public office, business establishment, access to the liberal professions, concessions and licences, membership of commercial bodies, labour legislation, trade union activity, civil rights (to be exercised in accordance with the conflict of laws), and taxation. Provision was made for deportation through joint consultation procedures, and for recognition of acquired rights in property, commerce and professional practice. Associations and companies incorporated in, and having their *siège social*, in one or other of the parties were to be assimilated to nationals of that party in respect of the enjoyment of rights in the territory of the other party. All most-favoured-nation implication was excluded by defining the privileged position of the nationals of the parties as resulting from the special relationship of the two countries.

In the same convention special arrangements were made for persons born on Sainte-Marie Island. The Malagasy Republic undertook to continue to apply on its territory to such persons and their descendants the personal status to which they were subject at the date of the agreement. The persons concerned would be permitted to exercise on the territory of the French Republic the rights attaching to the status of French citizen, while preserving Malagasy nationality. This was interpreted by the French

1 *Annuaire français* (1958), p. 825.
2 Decree no. 60-692, *Journal Officiel*, 20 July 1960, pp. 6607, 6627. Similar establishment conventions were also concluded between France and the Central African Republic (decree no. 60-1230, *Journal Officiel*, 24 November 1960, pp. 10459, 10467); Congo-Brazzaville (*ibid.* p. 10473); Chad (*ibid.* p. 10479); Gabon (decree no. 60-1231, *ibid.* pp. 10480, 10488); Federation of Mali (decree no. 60-693, *Journal Officiel*, 20 July 1960, pp. 6629, 6640); Togo (decree no. 64-523, *Journal Officiel*, 10 June 1964, pp. 4990, 4995).

Minister of the Interior as involving for Sainte-Mariens the right to vote while in France, but not while abroad.[1]

On 22 June 1960 France, the Mali Federation and the Malagasy Republic signed a Multilateral Agreement on the Fundamental Rights of the Nationals of the States of the Community,[2] which was open to accession by all Community States, and which provided that every national of a Community State should enjoy the same public liberties on the territory of every other Community State as nationals of that State, including free entry, but reserving the conditions of the exercise of civic and political rights to the legislation of each signatory.

The nationality codes of the former French States can be divided into three groups. The first group[3] attributes nationality on the basis solely of the *jus sanguinis* principle; the second group utilizes both the *jus sanguinis* and *jus soli* principles in conjunction;[4] and the third group, while employing both principles, qualifies them by incorporation of an indigeneity concept.[5] The inhabitants of the former Trust Territories of Cameroon and Togo were never French nationals, unlike the inhabitants of the other French territories, and the codes of these two countries, while falling generally within the third group, presuppose an already latent *camerounais* and *togolais* citizenship.[6]

1 *Annuaire français* (1961), p. 967.
2 Decree no. 60–694, *Journal Officiel*, 20 July 1960, pp. 6642–3.
3 Malagasy Republic, Ordonnance no. 60–064, *Journal Officiel de la République malgache*, 30 July 1960, p. 1306; Congo, loi no. 35–61, *Journal Officiel du Congo*, 1 July 1961, p. 383, but allowing also second generation *jus soli*; Chad, loi no. 31–60, *Journal Officiel du Tchad*, 1 March 1961, p. 115.
4 Ivory Coast, loi no. 61–415, *Journal Officiel de la Côte d'Ivoire*, 20 December 1961, p. 1687; Central African Republic, loi no. 61–212, *Journal Officiel de la République centrafricaine*, 1 June 1961, p. 145; Senegal, loi no. 61–10, *Journal Officiel du Sénégal*, 15 March 1961, p. 351; Niger, loi no. 61–26, *Journal Officiel du Niger*, 31 August 1961, p. 67; Gabon, loi no. 89–61, *Journal Officiel du Gabon*, 14 March 1962, p. 251.
5 Guinea, Ordonnance no. 011 of 1 March 1960, unpublished; the Guinean code contains the interesting provision that in the case of further territories being united with or lost from Guinea and the question of nationality not being dealt with in the instruments effecting the unification or cession, the people domiciled in the joined or lost territories shall acquire or lose Guinean nationality (arts. 6–8); Republic of Mali, loi no. 62–18, *Journal Officiel du Mali*, 1 March 1962, p. 168, original in its combination of the *jus soli* second-generation rule with a requirement of African origin (art. 12); Mauritania, loi no. 61–112, *Journal Officiel de la Mauritanie*, 13 June 1961, p. 242; Upper Volta, loi no. 50–61, *Journal Officiel de la Haute Volta*, 23 December 1961, p. 1109.
6 Cameroon, Ordonnance no. 59–66, *Journal Officiel du Cameroun*, 12 December 1959, p. 1697; Togo, loi no. 61–18, *Journal Officiel du Togo*, 16 August 1961, p. 512.
See generally on African francophone nationality Decettignies and de Biéville, *Les nationalités africaines* (1963); Zatzépine, *Le droit de la nationalité des Républiques francophones d'Afrique et de Madagascar* (1963), pp. 10 *et seq.*; in *Rev. jur. et pol.* vol. XVI (1962), p. 455.

The *Tribunal Civil de la Seine* held before the independence of Cameroon that the only persons who could be regarded as Cameroon nationals were 'natives residing in the former German overseas possessions' within the meaning of article 127 of the Treaty of Versailles.[1]

(iii) *Somalia*

Article 5 of the Act of Union which, with retrospective operation to 1 July 1960, fused the Somali Republic and Somaliland, provides that all persons who on the date of the establishment of the union possessed the citizenship of Somaliland or Somalia should become citizens of the Somali Republic. At the date of union, citizenship was governed by different laws in the Northern and Southern Regions, but on 22 December 1962 a unified citizenship law was enacted, by which Somali citizenship was conferred on any person whose father was a Somali citizen, who is of Somali origin, language or tradition, residing in the Republic or abroad, and declared to be willing to renounce any status as citizen of a foreign country.[2]

(iv) *India and Pakistan*

Expert Committee no. IX in its Report to the Partition Council in 1947 stated that persons residing in either India or Pakistan would remain British subjects, but that this would not imply that residents of the one would have equal rights in the other, for recent practice had been to make civic rights flow from citizenship or domicile, and not from common nationality.[3] The Indian Constitution based citizenship on domicile,[4] and provided[5] that migrants from Pakistan should be deemed to be Indian citizens if they, or either parent, or any grandparents had been born in India as defined in the Government of India Act, 1935, and had either been ordinarily resident in India since 19 July 1948, or had been registered as Indian citizens before the coming into force of the Constitution. It also provided[6] that migrants to Pakistan after 1 March 1947 were not to be deemed citizens of India unless they should return to India under a resettlement permit. Various persons claimed to be Indian citizens on the ground that their sojourn in Pakistan had been temporary, but the Indian courts held that use of a Pakistan passport was conclusive,[7] even where

1 Clunet, vol. LXXXVII (1960), p. 771.
2 Cotran in *I.C.L.Q.* vol. XII (1963), p. 1025.
3 *Partition Proceedings*, vol. VIII, p. 204.
4 S. 5.   5 S. 6.   6 S. 7.
7 *Noor Mohammad v. The State*, A.I.R. (1956), Madhya Bharat, 211; *Ghaurul Hasan v. The State of Rajasthan*, A.I.R. (1958), Raj. 172; *Naziranbai v. The State*, A.I.R. (1957), Madhya Bharat, 1; *Dawood Ali Arif v. Deputy Commissioner of Police*, A.I.R. (1958), Cal. 565.

employed by a wife of an Indian citizen permanently resident in India.[1] To prove domicile in India, more than habitual residence was required, and a lack of intention to reside elsewhere must be proved.[2] Migration of parents involved loss of Indian nationality by children.[3] Permanent migration from Indian-occupied Kashmir to Pakistan was required by an Indian court as a precondition of acquisition of Pakistan nationality by a Kashmiri.[4]

With respect to the withdrawal of British suzerainty from the Indian States, it is clear that the inhabitants ceased to be British protected persons,[5] but with the merger of the States in India (except Hyderabad, Junagadh and Kashmir) they became, it was held by the Bombay High Court, British subjects.[6] The subjects of those States which acceded to Pakistan also became British subjects for the same reason.[7] With the enactment of the Pakistan Citizenship Act, 1951, these persons acquired the status of Pakistan citizens and British subjects.[8]

1 *Naziranbai* v. *The State*, A.I.R. (1957), Madhya Bharat 1.
2 *Nisar Ahmed* v. *Union of India*, A.I.R. (1958), Raj. 65.
3 *State* v. *Abdul Hamid*, A.I.R. (1957), Punj. 86.
4 *Jalla Begum* v. *Ghulam Zohra*, A.I.R. (1959), J. & K. 32.
5 So stated by the Attorney-General, 440 H.C. Deb., 5s., col. 102, 14 July 1947.
6 *In re Antonius Raab*, in L.R. Bom. 1949, 537.
7 *Sayce* v. *Ameer Ruler Sadiq Mohammad Abbasi Bahawalpur State* [1952] 2 Q.B. 390.
8 *Ibid.*

Chapter 21

OPTION FOR AN ALTERNATIVE NATIONALITY

Option for an alternative nationality was defined by the Supreme Administrative Court of Czechoslovakia in 1934 as 'an act by which a person availing himself of a right granted to him by a legal provision assumes a new nationality, giving up at the same time the previous one, solely by his own will and without the co-operation or even against the will of the State to which he hitherto belonged'.[1] It cannot be said with any authority that international law imposes a duty upon the successor State to permit the inhabitants of absorbed territory to repudiate its nationality by removing themselves to a foreign country, or by opting for an alternative nationality.[2] It has been customary, however, at least since 1785, to permit such option,[3] and in very few historical instances of cession has the right to opt been denied.[4] States generally have been loth to

1 *Option (Loss of Nationality) Case*, *Ann. Dig.* vol. VII, Case no. 114.
2 Kunz in Hague *Recueil*, vol. XXXI (1930), p. 127; Strupp in Hague *Recueil*, vol. XLVII (1934), p. 488. See *Romano v. Comma*, *Ann. Dig.* vol. III, Case no. 195; Hall, p. 686; McNair, *Legal Effects of War* (3rd ed. 1948), p. 390; Mervyn Jones, p. 43; Szlechter, *Les options conventionnelles de nationalité* (1948), who catalogues the treaties by reference to the categories of persons to opt, the mechanism of option and the effects; Makarov, *Allgemeine Lehren des Staatsangehörigkeitsrechts* (1962), p. 99.
3 Kunz, *loc. cit.* p. 121. The following writers allege that the right to opt is at least customary, if not obligatory, in international law: Podesta Costa, p. 82; Nys, vol. II, p. 23; Mann in *Modern Law Review*, vol. V (1942), p. 222; Graupner in *Trans. Grot. Soc.* vol. XXXII (1947), p. 114; Mervyn Jones, p. 44; Phillipson, p. 295; Calvo, vol. IV, p. 395; Rivier, vol. II, p. 438; Gettys in *A.J.* vol. XXI (1927), p. 271. Cf. Schönborn, p. 37. In a despatch of 1 June 1867, the French Ambassador to Denmark pointed out that 'the right of option is usual': *Fontes Juris Gent.* ser. B, sect. I, vol. I, pt. I, p. 586. On the question of the nationality of the successor State by plebiscite see Auer in *Trans. Grot. Soc.* vol. VI (1921), pp. 45 *et seq.* The history is given by Szlechter, *op. cit.*; Schätzel, *Internationales Staatsangehörigkeitsrecht in Internationales Recht* (1962), pp. 46 *et seq.*; Jellinek, *Der automatische Erwerb und Verlust der Staatsangehörigkeit durch völkerrechtliche Vorgänge, zugleich ein Beitrag zur Lehre von der Staatensukzession* (1951), pp. 12 *et seq.*; Guyomar in *Rev. gén. de droit int. pub.* vol. LXVII (1963), p. 93.
4 The right of option has been acknowledged in the following treaties: Campo Formio, 1797, *M.R.* vol. VII, p. 208, art. 9 at p. 211; Vienna, 1809, *M.R.* (*Suppl.*), vol. V, p. 210, art. 10 at p. 214; Kiel, 1814, *ibid.* p. 666, art. 20 at p. 614; Paris, 1814, *ibid.* vol. VI, p. 1, art. 17 at p. 9; Prussia and Sweden, 1815, *ibid.* vol. VIII, p. 150, art. 6 at p. 153; London, 1839, *ibid.* vol. XX, p. 773, art. 17 at p. 784; Bloemfontein, 1854, *B.F.S.P.* vol. LVI (1864), p. 331, art. 4 at p. 332; United States and Spain, 1819, for the cession of Florida, *M.R.* (*Suppl.*), vol. IX, p. 328, art. 6 at p. 335; Zürich, 1859, *M.N.R.G.* vol. XVI, pt. II, p. 516, art. 12 at p. 520; Turin, 1860, *ibid.* p. 539,

34　　　　　　　　　　　　　　　　　　　　　　　　　　　　　　　　OSSI

impose an allegiance upon persons who either possess little identification with the absorbed territory or signify resentment at the change of sovereignty. Nationality was long conceived by liberal jurists as a voluntary status, and in England in particular it was widely assumed that the relationship of sovereign and subject could only arise by a submission of the latter to the former. Westlake, for example, argued that a conqueror is incompetent in international law to claim the allegiance of the subjects of its predecessor unless they have given evidence of 'accepting its rule and protection'. This they have a 'free option to do or not'.[1] Such a view of the character of nationality is no longer widely adhered to, and, in determining whether or not a specified category of persons is invested with a right of option, regard must be had to the municipal laws of the States concerned. An option in the proper sense of the word can arise only when the predecessor State acknowledges its subjects in lost territory as competent to reclaim its nationality, and when the successor State at the same time permits them to repudiate its own. Should a right to opt exist in the latter's law, while in the law of the former there is no such right, the most the persons in question can do is elect to become stateless. A similar alternative exists if the nationality of the predecessor State is extinguished.

The right in English law of a British subject habitually resident in territory lost to the Crown to retain his British nationality would seem to

art. 6 at p. 540; Vienna, 1864, *ibid.* vol. XVII, pt. II, p. 470, art. 19 at p. 482; Vienna, 1866, *ibid.* vol. XVIII, p. 405, art. 14 at p. 409; Frankfurt, 1871, *ibid.* vol. XIX, p. 688, art. 2 at p. 689; Additional Convention to same, *ibid.* vol. XX, p. 847, art. 1. See Protocol no. 1 at p. 799; Constantinople, 1879, *ibid.* 2nd ser. vol. III, p. 468, art. 7 at p. 469; Great Britain and Germany, 1890, *B.F.S.P.* vol. LXXXII (1890), p. 35; Shimonoseki, 1895, *ibid.* vol. LXXXVII, p. 799, art. 5 at p. 801; Paris, 1898, *M.N.R.G.* ser. II, vol. XXXII, p. 74, art. 9 at p. 76; Portsmouth, 1905, *B.F.S.P.* vol. XCVIII (1905), p. 735, art. 10 at p. 737; Athens, 1914, *ibid.* vol. CVII, pt. I, p. 893, art. 4 at p. 894; Constantinople, 1914, *ibid.* pt. II, p. 579, art. 4 at p. 580; Proclamation for the Annexation of Cyprus 1915, *ibid.* vol. CIX (1915), p. 429; Versailles, *B.T.S.* 1919, no. 4, Cmd. 153, arts. 37, 85, 91, 106 and 113; Trianon, *ibid.* 1920, no. 10, Cmd. 896, art. 63; St Germain, *ibid.* 1919, no. 7, Cmd. 222, art. 78 at p. 54; Lausanne, *ibid.* 1923, no. 16, Cmd. 1929, art. 32 at p. 27; Minorities Treaties of 1919 *ibid.* 1919, no. 20, Cmd. 479, arts. 3 and 4; Rapallo, 1920, *ibid.* 1921, no. 5, Cmd. 1238, art. 2; Roumania and the Powers concerning the incorporation of Bessarabia, 1922, *ibid.*, 1922, no. 15, Cmd. 1747, art. 5; Finland and Russia, 1920, *M.N.R.G.* 3rd ser. vol. XII, p. 37, art. 9 at p. 42; Lithuania and Russia, 1920, *ibid.* 3rd ser. vol. XI, p. 877, art. 6 at p. 881; Latvia and Russia, *ibid.* p. 888, art. 8 at p. 893; Riga, 1921, *L.N.T.S.* vol. VI, p. 123, art. 4; Peace Treaty with Italy, 1947, *B.T.S.* 1948, no. 50, Cmd. 7481, s. 9 and Annex IV; Great Britain and Burma, 1947, *ibid.* no. 16, Cmd. 7360, art. 3; France and Vietnam, 1955, *Journal Officiel*, 3 May 1959; France and India, *Annuaire français* (1955), p. 703. For details of the option clauses in the treaties between the Reich and Estonia, Latvia, Russia and Roumania of 1939–41 see Schechtmann in *A.J.* vol. XXXVIII (1944), pp. 356 *et seq.*; Ginsburgs, *idem*, vol. LV (1961), p. 919.

[1] In *Law Quarterly Review*, vol. XVII (1901), p. 399.

be generally recognized.[1] The law on the matter was restated by Singleton, J., in *Murray* v. *Parkes*[2] in 1941 when he found himself unable to accept the argument:

> that a British subject can be deprived of his status as such merely by the Act of some Government, State or Dominion elsewhere. He always has the right to elect, and there must be some certainty as to the position, else he cannot be called upon to do that.[3]

The right of a British subject to elect was recognized in the Burma Independence Act.[4] Although British subjects may elect, however, it does not follow that by electing they can avoid the acquisition of the nationality of the successor State. This was recognized by the Law Officers in a Report of 12 November 1866, relative to the position of British subjects, and British naturalized subjects, domiciled in the Ionian Islands at the date of their cession to Greece. The persons in question objected to becoming liable to conscription for the Greek army, and the Foreign Office requested an opinion on the question whether they could avoid this conscription by electing to remain British subjects. The Law Officers were of opinion that

> it would be a reasonable and just concession on the part of the Greek Government to allow British subjects, naturalized during the Protectorate of Great Britain, to have the option now of renouncing their Ionian and resuming their British Nationality, provided this option be exercised without delay, and put on formal record as soon as possible.

They went on to point out, however, that

> inasmuch as no stipulation to this effect was made in the Treaty by which Great Britain renounced the Protectorate, we do not think that Her Majesty's Government can properly demand, as a matter of right, that such an option should be conceded to them by the Government of Greece.[5]

A Report was also delivered by the Law Officers on 17 May 1900 relative to the effect of the annexation of the Boer Republics upon the nationality of the burghers of those countries. It was pointed out that it has been 'usual in recent times to allow those who do not desire to become subjects of the conqueror to leave the conquered territory within a reasonable

---

1 *Doe d. Thomas* v. *Acklam* (1824), 2 B. & C. 779; *Doe d. Auchmuty* v. *Mulcaster* (1826), 2 B. & C. 771.
2 [1942] 2 K.B. 123.
3 [1942] 2 K.B. 123, at p. 136.
4 11 & 12 Geo. VI, c. 3, s. 2.
5 Opinion of 12 November 1866, F.O. 83/2287: O'Connell, Appendix, no. 29.

time'.[1] There is no evidence that the Law Officers intended by this observation to assert a principle of law.

The existence of the right of option in American law would seem to be controversial. Such a right was upheld in *Boyd* v. *Nebraska ex rel. Thayer*,[2] but rejected in the case of *United States* v. *De Repentigny*,[3] where it was emphatically stated that provisions in a treaty of cession 'providing for the emigration of those inhabitants who desire to adhere to their ancient allegiance' were merely derogations from the general principle that a conqueror 'has the right to forbid the departure of his new subjects'. An absolute right of option was impliedly denied by the Harvard Draft,[4] but has been accorded in most treaties of cession in the past one hundred and fifty years.[5] A consideration of the machinery for option evolved in these treaties is not significant in establishing rules of international law, but it is of importance in any discussion of the question.

An Amboinese living in the Netherlands formally renounced Indonesian citizenship under the Netherlands-Indonesian convention of 1949 relating to the status of citizens resulting from the transfer of sovereignty from the Netherlands to Indonesia,[6] and then applied for registration on the list of voters as a Netherlands citizen. Since the *de cuius* belonged to the indigenous population of Indonesia he had no right under the convention to renounce Indonesian citizenship, but he contended that on a transfer of territory the population of the territory concerned had a right of option as to nationality. The Court of Appeal of the Hague, while rejecting[7] this submission, since the right of option had unambiguously been granted in the instrument of cession of sovereignty, stated that this notion of right of option could perhaps successfully be invoked in case of silence on the point, or of obscurity in the terms of the relevant agreement.

It must be conceded that if an option is granted the successor State is entitled to demand the withdrawal of the persons who opt, and the re-

1 Opinion of 17 May 1900, F.O. Confidential Papers (7516), no. 18 A: O'Connell, Appendix, no. 68.
2 143 U.S. 135 at p. 162 (1891).
3 5 Wall. 211 at p. 260 (1866).
4 *Loc. cit.* art. 18.
5 Szlechter, *op. cit.*, discusses 122 treaties providing for options between 1640 and 1947. In most treaties the option has taken the form of an election for the nationality of the predecessor State. In a few there has been no more than a recognition of a right of emigration, as in the Act of the Congress of Vienna, 1815, *M.R.* (*Suppl.*), vol. VI, p. 379, art. 29 at p. 390, while in others it has been agreed that no change of nationality was to be effected except by an option in favour of the successor State, as in the case of the Anglo-French Treaty of 1924, *B.F.S.P.* vol. CXIX (1924), p. 433.
6 This was one of the instruments drawn up by the Round Table Conference, 1949.
7 *In re Hehanussa*, I.L.R. vol. XIX, p. 337.

moval of their property. The Austria–Czechoslovakia Minorities Treaty of 1920 specifically declared that neither of the parties would 'regard it as an unfriendly act if the other brings such pressure as is recognized by international law to bear upon those persons who have exercised the right of option but who do not transfer their residence within the period of time afforded them for this purpose'.[1] In some treaties the persons specified as entitled to opt have been permitted to retain landed property, but their emigration has been insisted upon.[2] Others have provided for both emigration and the disposal of landed property.[3] In a few cases neither has been required of the optants. The period specified within which the right to opt is required to be exercised has varied from two months to six years.[4] Occasionally, it is provided that the husband has the right to opt for the wife and children under the age of eighteen years.[5] If there is no such provision the option of the husband can only include the wife and

1 *L.N.T.S.* vol. III, no. 98, art. 13.

2 Withdrawal was required in the following treaties: Campo Formio, 1797; Vienna, 1809; Paris, 1814; Kiel, 1814; Prussia and Sweden, 1815; London, 1839; Bloemfontein, 1854; Constantinople, 1859; Turin, 1860; Vienna, 1866; Constantinople, 1879; Shimonoseki, 1895; Constantinople, 1914; Portsmouth, 1905; Proclamation of the Annexation of Cyprus, 1915; Treaties between Russia and its successor States, 1919; Peace Treaty with Italy, 1946; Athens, 1914; Versailles, 1919; Trianon, 1919; St Germain, 1919; Lausanne, 1923; Roumania and other Powers relative to the incorporation of Bessarabia, 1921. The time for emigration was fixed at two months after the date of option in the Proclamation of Annexation of Cyprus, and one year in the Peace Treaties of 1919 and the treaties between Russia and its successor States. The references of these treaties are given *supra*, p. 529. Exemption from emigration was specifically granted in the Treaty of Rapallo, 1922. On the subject see Oppenheim, vol. I, p. 552; *A.F. v. Government of the Federal Country (Landesregierung) of Vienna, Ann. Dig.* vol. I, Case no. 152; *Spanish Subjects in Cuba (Equality)* Case, ibid. vol. V, Case no. 249.

3 Disposal of landed property was provided for in the following treaties: Campo Formio, 1797; Vienna, 1809; Kiel, 1814; London, 1839; Prussia and Sweden, 1815; Bloemfontein, 1854; Constantinople, 1879; Sihmonoseki, 1895; Portsmouth, 1905. Most of the Peace Treaties of 1919–23 enacted that optants might retain landed property while removing their domicile.

4 Two months in the Proclamation of Annexation of Cyprus, 1915; one year in the following treaties: Turin, 1860; Vienna, 1866; Paris, 1898; Anglo–French, 1904; St Germain, 1919; Trianon, 1919; Rapallo, 1921; Burma, 1947; Peace Treaty with Italy, 1947, and all the Russian treaties of 1919; eighteen months: Anglo–German, 1890; Shimonoseki, 1895; two years: Zürich, 1859; Versailles, 1919; the Minorities Treaty, 1919; Lausanne, 1923; Roumania, 1922; London, 1839; three years: Bloemfontein, 1854; Constantinople, 1879; Athens, 1914; Constantinople, 1914; six years: Vienna, 1809; Prussia and Sweden, 1815; Paris, 1814; Kiel, 1814.

5 Anglo–French, 1904; Peace Treaties, 1919–23; Peace Treaty with Italy, 1947; see *G.M. v. (Austrian) Federal Minister for the Interior, Ann. Dig.* vol. I, Case, no. 151. The Austrian Supreme Administrative Court held that a married woman cannot opt in the absence of her husband's consent: *Kugler v. (Austrian) Federal Minister for the Interior, ibid.* Case no. 153. A divorced woman, however, has been held to have the right to opt: *A.P. v. Federal Minister of the Interior, ibid.* vol. IV, Case no. 212.

children when such is recognized in the municipal law of the successor State.

There was a departure in the Peace Treaties of 1919 from the traditional practice of naturalization according to territorial designation. An attempt was made to resettle Europe according to the principle of uniting on the same territory, and under the same government, peoples of a common race, language and cultural heritage. Persons possessing rights of citizenship and differing in race and language from the majority of the population of territory incorporated in the successor States of Austria and Hungary were given the right to opt for any other successor State, or for the predecessor State, if the majority of the population of the State selected was of the same race and language as the person exercising the right.[1] In most cases new nationality was acquired by naturalization.

Article 91 of the Treaty of Versailles deviated from the principle adopted in the other peace treaties in failing to render it mandatory upon the optants to emigrate from the successor State. It was merely stated that such persons might emigrate. The question subsequently arose as to the competence of Poland to insist on the emigration of those inhabitants of Upper Silesia who opted for German nationality. This question was referred to the Upper Silesian Arbitral Tribunal, which held that a successor State normally has the right to require the emigration of such persons as have opted against the nationality of the successor State. This principle was found to be 'sanctioned by the practice of States, and was expressly admitted by writers, and underlay the option provisions of the treaties'. The suppression of this right of the successor State would have a character so exceptional that it could not be presumed. It was further held that an option was not invalidated by failure to emigrate within the specified time. A provision in a treaty requiring emigration at the expiration of a period merely suspended the right of the successor State during that period to require such emigration.[2]

It is controversial whether the exercise of a right of option operates retrospectively or constitutes a divesting of a nationality already acquired. It might be presumed that the optant has never acquired the nationality of the successor State, but it might equally well be presumed that he cast off the new allegiance and regained the old. This is the view adopted by Westlake, who argues that, as more people accept the new nationality than opt, there must be a presumption that the new nationality had been

[1] St Germain, art. 80; Trianon, art. 65; Szlechter, *op. cit.* pp. 216–30.
[2] Arbitration between Germany and Poland, *Ann. Dig.* vol. II, Case no. 136. See the discussion of the case in Kaeckenbeeck, *The International Experiment of Upper Silesia* (1942), p. 183.

acquired.[1] The more correct view is believed to be the former. The option, as Kunz argues, is merely a suspensive condition, upon fulfilment of which the change of nationality is effected.[2] The question arose in a direct form before the Czechoslovak-Hungarian Mixed Arbitral Tribunal concerning the effect of the exercise of the right of option granted by the Treaty of Trianon. The *de cuius*, who had been born in territory transferred from Hungary to Czechoslovakia, opted for the nationality of the former. It was necessary to determine whether he had ever lost Hungarian nationality by virtue of the cession, and whether or not he was a Czech national during the period between the coming into force of the treaty and the exercise of the right of option. The tribunal attributed retroactive effect to the option, and held that the *de cuius* had never ceased to be a Hungarian national.[3] In the Burma Independence Act of 1947 it is specifically enacted that, so far as those who might opt were concerned, they were to be deemed as never having become subject to the provisions for change of nationality.[4] A similar clause was incorporated in the Minorities Treaty of 1919[5] with Czechoslovakia, and repeated in the Peace Treaty of 1947[6] with Italy.

The right of the optant to re-establish himself in the absorbed territory is dependent upon the municipal law of the successor State. Should he return he accepts the status of any resident alien. Many optants took up their domicile again in Schleswig-Holstein after its incorporation in Prussia in 1866, and their children born in the territory were regarded by Denmark as Prussians, on the principle of the *jus soli*, and by Prussia as Danes, on the principle of the *jus sanguinis*. A convention was entered into in 1907 in which Prussia agreed to confer Prussian nationality on the persons concerned.[7]

An option must be exercised according to the terms of the treaty granting it or it will be null and void. The Treaty of Lausanne contained provisions by which certain Turkish nationals who were natives of territories detached from Turkey under the Treaty, could in certain

1 Pt. I, p. 73.
2 *Loc. cit.* p. 130. See Keith, p. 45; Isay in Hague *Recueil*, vol. v (1924), p. 439; Szlechter, *op. cit.* p. 335.
3 *Ladislaus Chira Fils* v. *Czechoslovak State, Ann. Dig.* vol. v, Case no. 149. There are, however, decisions to the effect that the acquisition of nationality by option dates only from the exercise of the right of option: *S. Ferdinand* v. *(Austrian) Federal Chancellery, ibid.* vol. I, Case no. 138; *Arbitration between Germany and Poland, ibid.* Case no. 135.
4 Burma Independence Act, 1947, s. 2.
5 B.T.S. 1919, no. 20, Cmd. 474, art. 4.
6 *Idem*, 1948, no. 50, Cmd. 7481, art. 9 and Annex IV. Kunz in *A.J.* vol. XLI (1947), p. 622.
7 Gettys, *loc. cit.* p. 273.

circumstances opt for the nationality of that territory. The Egyptian *Conseil d'État* decided[1] in 1950 that the *de cuius*, originally a subject of the Ottoman Empire, could not opt for Egyptian nationality since the purported option took place before the Treaty of Lausanne entered into force, though after it was signed. However, Egyptian municipal law provided that Ottoman nationals who habitually resided in Egypt were Egyptian nationals. It must be remembered that a provision for option contained in a treaty must become municipal law before it can be effective, and that should the successor fail to implement such provision, as France failed after the Treaty of Vienna in 1815,[2] an option does not become available.[3] In addition, the validity of an option must be determined in the same way as any other act of volition under the municipal law of the successor State.[4]

1 *Messih v. Minister of the Interior*, I.L.R. vol. xxvIII, p. 291.
2 Cogordan, *op. cit.* p. 333.
3 Graupner, *loc. cit.* p. 115.
4 See *Arbitration between Germany and Poland*, Ann. Dig. vol. II, Case no. 135.

Chapter 22

STATE SUCCESSION AND THE NATIONALITY OF CLAIMS

1. THE DOCTRINE OF CONTINUOUS NATIONALITY

States are permitted by international law to espouse only the claims of their own nationals, or of persons assimilated to nationals, but it is sometimes said that a person must be continuously a national of the claimant State from the time when an injury arises until the time when the claim is made. If this is a substantive rule of international law then the question arises whether a change of nationality effected by State succession is an exception to it.

The doctrine of continuous nationality appears to have its origins in the *Santangelo* Case in 1839 when the United States failed in a claim against Mexico respecting an injury done to a person while he was an aspirant to United States citizenship, and succeeded in a second claim respecting one done to him after he acquired this citizenship.[1] The explanation of the rule is that, if it did not exist, persons would seek naturalization in States which were parties to arbitration agreements merely to get a hearing for their claims.[2] If this is its only rationalization, then the rule obviously lacks cogency when the change of nationality is effected by transfer of territory and not by act of the claimant, and the conclusion should be drawn that State succession constitutes an exception to it.

However, there are serious reasons for doubting whether the rule in fact exists as one of substantive international law, and whether it may not be a procedural practice emanating from the construction of arbitration agreements. Clearly, if an agreement specifies that a State may make claims only on behalf of its nationals, in respect of wrongs done to its nationals, a tribunal has jurisdiction only when the claimant is a national at both points in time; and even when an agreement is not specific it might, in fact, yield such a jurisdictional rule upon interpretation. For example, the Convention of 1926 setting up the Anglo-Mexican Claims Commission referred to claims for 'losses or damages suffered by British subjects',[3] and to presentation of matters to the Commissioner by 'British

---

1 Moore, *I.A.* p. 3334, although adumbrated by writers much earlier.
2 Administrative Decision (no. v) of the United States–German Mixed Claims Commission, U.N. Rep. vol. VII, p. 119 per Umpire Parker at p. 141.
3 U.N. Rep. vol. v, p. 8.

claimants'. This was interpreted as importing the rule of continuous nationality into the jurisdiction of the tribunal.[1] Obviously, when the agreement is conclusive on the point of continuous nationality no excepton in favour of change of nationality brought about by change of sovereignty may be cogently urged, whether the rule is to be regarded as substantive or procedural.

If the tribunal's jurisdiction is with respect to a claim arising out of breach of a treaty, it is clear that only the offended signatory State is entitled to take action, and the question that arises is whether it remains entitled so to do if the injured party has lost its nationality through State succession. Unless the rule of continuous nationality is one of substantive law, a distinction might be urged between cases where action is brought by the State in its own right, as a signatory, and cases where it is brought to recover damages on behalf of the injured individual. Since it is unlikely that a State will claim damages on behalf of persons who have lost its nationality, and since the successor State is incompetent to complain of the breach of a treaty to which it was not a party, the principle of continuous nationality operates here to inhibit any claim being made on behalf of the individual, but not on behalf of the signatory.

Also, if the injury was done to a national of the respondent State it is not transformed from a domestic into an international wrong in virtue of a change of nationality achieved by State succession, and hence the question of the successor State taking action on behalf of the individual concerned cannot arise. In the *Forests of Central Rhodope* Case[2] it was held that persons who at the date of the wrong had been Bulgarian nationals, but had become Greek nationals, could not be represented by Greece in respect of claims brought under the Treaty of Neuilly for damages for interference by Bulgaria with acquired rights in territory ceded at the end of the Balkan Wars.

However, if the injury was done to an individual in breach of customary international law, and the arbitration agreement gives no jurisdictional direction to the tribunal, it is doubtful if the rule of continuous nationality is relevant; and even if it is relevant, the rationalization of it prompts the conclusion that a change of nationality effected by change of sovereignty is an exception to it. Any alternative conclusion would mean that large numbers and extensive categories of persons would be deprived of international remedies, and this would not only not be contemplated by

---

[1] *Captain W. H. Gleadell (G.B.)* v. *United Mexican States*, U.N. Rep. vol. v, p. 44 (1929); *Minnie Stevens Eschauzier (G.B.)* v. *United Mexican States*, U.N. Rep. vol. v, p. 207 (1931).
[2] U.N. Rep. vol. III, p. 1405, at p. 1421.

the motives underlying the notion of continuous nationality, but would be offensive to modern conceptions of the role of international law in protecting the individual.[1] The question was raised in the Institute of International Law in 1931 and again in 1932. On the former occasion several members disputed the application of the role of continuous nationality in circumstances of State succession,[2] and on the second occasion several of them, de Lapradelle, Scott, Politis, de Taube, Mandelstam, Alvarez, Séfériadès and Le Fur, moved a resolution to the effect that the only qualification for a claim was that the injured party should be a national of the claimant State when the claim is made.[3]

The question of the effect of State succession upon the nationality of a claim arising from breach of customary international law was an issue before the Permanent Court of International Justice in the *Panevezys–Saldutiskis Railway Co.* Case[4] in 1939. Estonia's claim was based upon the wrongful seizure of a railway company's assets by Lithuania. In a Preliminary Objection Lithuania argued that Estonia could not claim on behalf of the Company, which had been incorporated in Tsarist Russia, and became Estonian after the wrong complained of, in virtue of the secession of Estonia from Russia. Estonia contested the existence and applicability of the rule of continuous nationality. The Court did not deal with the question directly, for it held that local remedies had not been exhausted, and the rule of continuous nationality raised issues of merit. But, in reiterating its view, expressed in the *Mavrommatis* Case,[5] that the law of claims is founded on the right of a State to require international law to be respected in the persons of its nationals, it tended to favour the Lithuanian contention. The link between an individual and a State, it said, is, in the absence of treaty, the only basis of diplomatic protection, and it follows that this protection is restricted in favour of nationals. When an injury is done to a national of a third State, it went on, a claim based upon it does not fall within the domain of diplomatic protection. Every case where a claim had been admitted in face of a change of nationality had been one where the parties had agreed to waive the strict requirements of the rule.

In the present case no grounds exist for holding that the Parties intended to exclude the application of the rule. The Lithuanian Agent is therefore right in maintaining that Estonia must prove that at the time when the injury occurred which is

[1] Monnier in *Annuaire français* (1962), p. 69; Mosler, p. 133.
[2] *Annuaire de l'Institut* (1931), II, p. 210.
[3] *Ibid.* (1932), p. 502. See also Salvioli in Hague *Recueil*, vol. XLVI (1933), p. 126.
[4] P.C.I.J. ser. A/B, no. 76.
[5] P.C.I.J. ser. A, no. 5.

alleged to involve the international responsibility of Lithuania the company suffering the injury possessed Estonian nationality.[1]

This conclusion was contested in the dissenting opinion of Judge van Eysinga. He said:

> The legal life of the new State in all its aspects proceeds in succession to the legal life of the old State. Thus in all matters where the Government of the latter had jurisdiction, its place is now taken by the Government of the new State. This holds good as regards diplomatic protection.[2]

If debts can pass into the hands of the successor State, he argued, it is difficult to see why a claim against a third State arising out of an unlawful act should not also pass from the old to the new State.

> Such a 'succession' is an absolutely characteristic and even essential feature of the law of the State succession. The successor State is continually exercising rights which previously belonged exclusively to the old State, and the same holds good as regard obligations. Accordingly it would be quite normal that in this case the successor State should have protected both diplomatically and before the Court a company the diplomatic protection of which formerly fell to Russia alone.[3]

Judge van Eysinga then went on to add his doubts to those of de Lapradelle as to the existence of the rule of continuous nationality, except as an emanation of the jurisdiction habitually conferred on Mixed Commissions.

Assuming the rule of continuous nationality to exist as one of substantive law, there are two ways of avoiding its operation in cases of State succession. The first way, dependent on the view that the claim is primarily that of the individual and only secondarily that of the State, is to argue that the rationalization of the rule excludes its operation when the change of nationality occurs through change of sovereignty, and that the successor State is competent to claim on his behalf. The second way, dependent on the alternative view that a claim is always that of the State, is that the successor State inherits the claim, so that it is asserting its predecessor's rights by transmission, and not protecting an individual previous susceptible of protection by another State. Judge van Eysinga, in the above passage, adopts the second method. But in denying the existence of the rule of continuous nationality he is in fact subscribing to the philosophy that an injury to an individual is a wrong done primarily to him and only secondarily to his State, and hence is adopting the reasoning behind the first method. That the first method is inseparably con-

---

1 P.C.I.J. ser. A/B, no. 76 at p. 16. Monnier concludes from this that the rule of continuous nationality applies in cases of State succession: *loc. cit.* p. 71.
2 P.C.I.J. ser. A/B, no. 76, at p. 32.
3 *Ibid.*

nected with the individualistic philosophy is clear from the reasoning advanced by de Lapradelle,[1] which Judge van Eysinga adopts, and also clear from the alignment of opinion at the Institute meeting in 1932, which contained avowed natural lawyers such as Scott and Le Fur, and sympathizers with this position such as Politis, Alvarez, and de Lapradelle himself.

2. DIPLOMATIC PROTECTION OF COMPANIES OF ALIEN SHAREHOLDING

The rules concerning diplomatic protection of corporations whose shareholding may be in alien hands are complex and obscure, and the problem may be further complicated when State succession effects the alienation of shareholders whose corporation was previously national. States have not felt inhibited from seeking satisfaction from the successor State in respect of their nationals who owned substantial shareholding in companies incorporated in the territory lost to the predecessor State. The question arose in connexion with the Netherlands–South African Railway Company's concession after the Boer War, when the debenture holders were considered by the Transvaal Concessions Commission to be entitled to better treatment than the shareholders, who were implicated in the non-neutral attituted of the Company during the war. In fact, Netherlands, German and French shareholders were compensated after diplomatic pressures on the part of the respective Governments.[2] A somewhat different circumstance arose in the *Alsop* Case,[3] when the company concerned was incorporated under the law of the successor State, but derived its claim from the predecessor State. The company was Chilean, the shareholding was United States, and the question was Chile's obligation with respect to a debt of Bolivia. The arbitration award given by the King of Great Britain in 1911 referred to the 'American citizens who owned the firm', as distinct from the 'artificial entity of Alsop and Company', as the interested parties. It must be noticed, however, that the arbitration agreement had empowered the King to give an equitable decision. Perhaps of greater significance is the claim for compensation made by Canada against the Soviet Union arising from the latter's cancellation of the concession agreement between Finland and the

---

1 *Loc. cit.* For the question whether jurisdiction under treaty was lost because of the withdrawal of protection from a territory whose nationals were invested with a claim see *National Bank of Egypt* v. *Austro–Hungarian Bank*, Ann. Dig. vol. II, Case no. 10. For a treaty jurisdiction contemplating change of nationality from one Allied Power to another see *Radziwill* v. *Germany, ibid.* vol. III, Case no. 174.
2 Feilchenfeld, p. 382; Mosler, p. 133.
3 U.N. Rep. vol. XI, p. 349.

Finnish subsidiary of the Mond Nickel Company, whose capital was held by the International Nickel Company of Canada, after the cession of Petsamo from Finland to Russia. Canada claimed not only compensation for the actual capital invested but a sum by way of indemnity for the deprivation of the use of the mines. Initially the Soviet took the position that it was not obliged to compensate, but the political situation at the time favoured a settlement, and a sum of $20,000,000 was paid.[1]

[1] See *supra*, p. 335.

BIBLIOGRAPHY

A. STUDIES IN THE LAW OF STATE SUCCESSION

Agrawala, S. K. 'Doctrine of Act of State and the Law of State Succession in India', in *I.C.L.Q.* vol. XII (1963), p. 1399.
Andréadès, G. 'Les obligations financières, envers la dette publique ottomane, des provinces detachées de l'Empire turc dupuis le traité de Berlin', in *Rev. gén. de droit int. pub.* vol. XV (1908), p. 585.
Antonucci, A. *Réparation et règlement de la dette publique autrichienne et hongroise d'avant-guerre* (1932).
Appleton, H. *Des effets des annexions de territoire sur les dettes de l'État démembré ou annexé* (1895).
Audinet, 'Annexion, cession et démembrement de territoires', in *Répertoire de droit international* (Lapradelle-Niboyet) (1929).
Aufricht, H. 'State Succession under the Law and Practice of the International Monetary Fund', in *I.C.L.Q.* vol. XI (1962), p. 154.
Badaoui, M. T. 'L'emprunt public et les transformations politiques et territoriales de l'État', in *Revue égyptienne de droit international*, vol. XIV (1958), p. 22.
Balladore-Pallieri, G. 'Applicabilita ai nuovi stati africani delle convenzioni anteriori', in *Diritto internazionale; rivista trimest rale di dottrina e documentazione*, vol. XVII (1963), p. 269.
Bar, C. L. von. 'Die kubanische Staatsschuld' in *Die Nation*, vol. XVI (1899).
Barclay, Kaufmann, Struycken and Kipp. *Études concernant la doctrine de la succession d'État; quatre consultations* (1923).
Bartoš, M. 'Les nouveaux États et les traités internationaux', in *Jugoslovenska Revija za Medunarodno Pravo*, vol. II (1962), p. 185.
Baty, T. 'Division of States: Its Effects on Obligations', in *Trans. Grot. Soc.* vol. IX (1923), p. 119.
Baty, T. 'The Obligations of Extinct States', in *Yale Law Journal*, vol. XXXV (1926), p. 434.
Bentwich, N. 'State Succession and Act of State in the Palestine Courts', in *B.Y.* vol. XXIII (1946), p. 330.
Binz, R. Staatensukzession und Meistbegünstigung (unpublished dissertation, Munich, 1961).
Bokorné-Szegö, H. 'Succession des nouveaux Etats et les traités internationaux', in *Acta Juridica Academiae Scientiarium Hungaricae*, vol. V (1963), p. 333.
Brandt. 'Die Regelung der österreichischen Bundesschulden', in *Z.F.a.ö.R.u.V.* vol. IX (1939–40), p. 127.
Cabouat, J. *Des annexions de territoire et de leurs principales conséquences* (1881).
Caflisch, L. 'The Law of State Succession, Theoretical Observations', in *Ned. Tijd.* vol. X (1963), p. 337.
Caflisch, L. 'Gründung Italiens in Schweizerische Sicht', in *Schweizerisches Jahrbuch für Internationales Recht*, vol. XIX (1962), p. 103.
Cahn, H. J. 'The Responsibility of the Successor State for War Debts', in *A.J.* vol. XLIV (1950), p. 477.
Cansacchi, G. 'Sullo "Stato di appartenenza" dei comandi giuridici nei transferimenti territoriali', in *Rivista di diritto internazionale*, vol. XXXVII (1954), p. 19.

Cansacchi, G. 'La sopravivenza dell'ordinamento guiridico antecedente in territorio annesso', in *Scritti di diritto internazionale in onore di Tomaso Perassi* (1957).

Castren, E. J. 'La Succession d'États', in Hague *Recueil*, vol. LXXVIII (1951), pp. 385 *et seq*.

Castren, E. J. 'On State succession in Practice and Theory', in *Nordisk Tidsskrift*, vol. XXIV (1954), p. 55.

Cavaglieri, A. *La dottrina della successione di stato a stato e il suo valore giuridico* (1910).

Cavaglieri, A. 'Trapassi di territorio senze trattato', in *Rivista di diritto internazionale*, vol. XIX (1927), p. 317.

Cohen, R. 'Legal Problems arising from the Dissolution of the Mali Federation', in *B.Y.* vol. XXXVI (1960), p. 375.

Corsi, A. '*Transmissione di obblighi patrimoniali degli stati in caso di mutazione territoriale*, vol. I of *Studi di diritto internazionale privato* (1896).

Cotran, E. 'Legal Problems arising out of the formation of the Somali Republic', in *I.C.L.Q.* vol. XII (1963), p. 1010.

Cotran, E. 'Some Legal Aspects of the Formation of the United Arab Republic and the United Arab States', in *I.C.L.Q.* vol. VIII (1959), p. 346.

Coursier, H. 'Accession des nouveaux États Africains aux Conventions de Genève', in *Annuaire français* (1961), p. 760.

De Bandt, J. P. 'La jurisprudence belge: De quelques problèmes de succession d'État à la suite de l'accession à l'independance de la République du Congo (Léopoldville)', in *Revue belge de droit international* (1965), p. 500

Decoudu, J. *Le partage des dettes publiques autrichiennes et hongroises* (1926).

Delson, R. 'Comments on State Succession', in *Proceedings of the American Society of International Law* (1966), p. 111.

De Muralt, R. W. G. *The Problem of State Succession with Regard to Treaties* (1954).

De Visscher, P. 'Problème de la succession d'États envisagé dans l'histoire diplomatique du Congo', in *Communicazioni e Studi*, vol. XI (1960), p. 53.

Drost, P. N. 'Le problème de la succession en matière d'obligations juridiques des États', in *Rév. de droit int. et de lég. comp.*, 3rd ser. vol. XX (1939).

Durieux, A. *Le problème juridique des dettes du Congo belge et l'État du Congo* (1961).

Elias, T. O. 'The Berlin Treaty and the River Niger Commission', in *A.J.* vol. LVII (1963), p. 873.

Feilchenfeld, E. H. *Public Debts and State Succession* (1931).

Fel'dman, D. I. and Farukshin, M. 'Krakh Kolonial'noi sistemy i nekotorye voprosy mezdunarodno-pravovogo priznaniia i pravopreemstva', in *Pravovederiio*, vol. VI (1962), p. 1115.

Ferid, M. *Der Neubürger im internationalen Privatrecht. Fortwirkungen früheren Status bei Wechsel der massgebenden Rechtsordnung* (1949).

Fitzgerald, P. J. 'State Succession and Personal Treaties', in *I.C.L.Q.* vol. XI (1962), p. 843.

Focherini, A. *Le successione degli Stati, loro effetti sulla nazionalità degli abitanti e sulle questioni giuridiche pendenti* (1910).

Fouilloux, G. 'La succession aux biens publics français dans les États nouveaux d'Afrique', in *Annuaire français* (1965), p. 885.

Francis, L. B. 'Jamaica Assumes Treaty Rights and Obligations: Some Aspects of Foreign Policy', in *I.C.L.Q.* vol. XIV (1965), p. 612.

Fuller, P. 'Are Franchises Affected by Change of Sovereignty', in *Columbia Law Review*, vol. 3 (1903), p. 241.

Bibliography

Gabba, C. F. 'Succession di Stato a Stato' in *Quistioni di diritto civile* (2nd ed. 1885).
Garner, J. W. 'State Succession raised by German Annexation of Austria', in *A.J.* vol. XXXII (1938), p. 421.
Gautron, J. C. 'Sur quelques aspects de la succession d'États au Sénégal', in *Annuaire français* (1962), p. 836.
Gettys. L. 'The Effect of Changes of Sovereignty on Nationality', in *A.J.* vol. XXI (1927), p. 268.
Gidel, G. *Des effects de l'annexion sur les concessions* (1904).
Gonzales Campos, J. D. 'Algunas consideraciones sobre las problemas de la sucesión de estados', in *Rivista española de derecho internacional*, vol. XV (1962), p. 465.
Gonzales Campos, J. D. 'Notas sobre la práctica de las organizaciones internacionales respecto a los efectos de la sucesión de estados en el estatuto de miembro de la organización', in *Rivista de derecho española y americano*, vol. III (1963), p. 71.
Goupy, G. *Des droits civils maintenus en cas d'annexion* (1907).
Graupner, R. 'Nationality and State Succession', in *Trans. Grot. Soc.* vol. XXXII (1946), p. 87.
Graupner, R. 'British Nationality and State Succession', in *The Law Quarterly Review*, vol. LXI (1945), p. 161.
Green, L. C. 'Malaya/Singapore/Malaysia: Comments on State Competence, Succession and Continuity', in *The Canadian Yearbook of International Law* (1966), p. 3.
Guggenheim, P. *Beiträge zur völkerrechtlichen Lehre vom Staatenwechsel (Staatensukzession)* (1925).
Guyomar, G. 'Succession d'État et le respect de la volonté des populations', in *Rev. gén. de droit int. pub.* vol. LXVII (1963), p. 92.
Haas, F. J. *Über das Repartitions-Princip der Staatschulden bei Länderzerstückelungen* (1831).
Hecker, H. *Staatensukzession und Ungemeindung* (1932).
Herbst, L. 'Successione fra stati e trattati non localizzati', in *Diritto internazionale*, vol. XVIII (1964), p. 99.
Herbst, L. *Staatensukzession und Staatsservituten* (1962).
Herndl, L. 'Les accords internationaux et la succession d'États', in *Annuaire de l'Association des auditeurs et anciens auditeurs de l'Académie de droit international de la Haye*, vols. XXXII–XXXIII (1962–3).
Hershey, A. S. 'The Succession of States', in *A.J.* vol. V (1911), p. 285.
Herz, J. H. *Die Identität des Staates* (1931).
Hönig. *Zur Liquidation der altösterreichischen Staatsschuld* (1926).
Huber, M. *Die Staatensuccession* (1898).
Hurst, Sir C. 'State Succession in Matters of Tort', in *B.Y.* vol. V (1925), p. 163.
Jellinek, H. *Der automatische Erwerb und Verlust der Staatsangehörigkeit durch Völkerrechtliche Vorgänge, zugleich ein Beitrag zur Lehre von der Staatensukzession* (1951).
Jenks, C. W. 'State Succession in Respect of Law Making Treaties', in *B.Y.* vol. XXIX (1952), p. 105.
Jèze, G. *Le partage des dettes publiques au cas de démembrement du territoire* (1921).
Jones, J. Mervyn. 'State Succession in the Matter of Treaties', in *B.Y.* vol. XXIV (1947), p. 360.
Kamal Hossain. 'International Commercial Arbitration, State Succession and the Commonwealth', in *B.Y.* vol. XXXVI (1960), p. 370.
Kapur, J. L. 'Some Legal Consequences of the Partition of India', in *Indian Law Review*, vol. IX (1957).

Kaufmann, W. *Zur Transvaalbahnfrage* (1901).
Keith, A. B. *The Theory of State Succession with special reference to English and Colonial Law* (1907).
Keith, K. J. 'State Succession to Treaties in the Commonwealth: Two replies', in *I.C.L.Q.* vol. XIII (1964), p. 1441.
Kiatibian, S. *Conséquences juridiques des transformations territoriales des États sur les traités* (1892).
Kirsten, J. *Einige Probleme der Staatennachfolge* (1962).
Kirsten, J. 'Zum völkerrechtlichen Institut der Staatennachfolge', in *Staat und Recht*, vol. IX (1960), p. 975.
Kirsten, J. and others. 'Friedensvertrag und Klassenkampf', in *Staat und Recht*, vol. X (1961), p. 2053.
Koch, T. *Die territorialen Veränderungen der Staaten und ihr Einfluss auf die Schuldenhaftung* (1913).
Krenz, F. E. 'Newly Independent States and the Problem of State Succession', in *Nordisk Tidsskrift*, vol. XXXIII (1963), p. 97.
Kunugi, T. 'State Succession in the Framework of GATT', in *A.J.* vol. LIX (1965), p. 268.
Kunz, J. L. *Die völkerrechtliche Option* (1925).
Kunz, J. L. 'Nationality and Option Clauses in the Italian Peace Treaty of 1947', in *A.J.* vol. XLI (1947), p. 622.
La Forest, G. V. 'Towards a Reformulation of the Law of State Succession', in *Proceedings of the American Society of International Law* (1966), p. 103.
Lapradelle, A. de. 'De l'influence du changement de souveraineté sur la loi territoriale', in *Rév. gén. de droit int. pub.* vol. XXXII (1925), p. 388.
Larivière, L. *Des conséquences des transformations territoriales des États sur les traites antérieurs* (1892).
Le Fur, L. 'Chronique des faits internationaux—Traité de paix du 10 Décembre 1898', in *Rev. gén. de droit int. pub.* vol. VI (1899), p. 572.
Lenz, H. *Untersuchung zur Frage der Identität der Republik Oesterreich mit der Monarchie der Habsburger* (1939).
Leriche, A. 'Aspects formels de la dévolution d'obligations résultant des traités dans le cas d'un nouvel Etat', in *Revue de droit international pour le Moyen Orient* (1953), p. 105.
Lester, A. P. 'State Succession to Treaties in the Commonwealth', in *I.C.L.Q.* vol. XII (1963), p. 175.
Lester, A. P. 'State Succession to Treaties in the Commonwealth. A Rejoinder', in *I.C.L.Q.* vol. XIV (1965), p. 262.
Louis-Lucas, P. 'The Tunisian Republic and the Treaties prior to Independence', in *Clunet*, vol. LXXXVIII (1961), p. 87.
Mallarmé, A. 'Étude sur la condition juridique des chemins de fer privés sud africains depuis l'annexion du Transvaal', in *Rev. gén. de droit int. pub.* vol. X (1903), p. 282.
Mann, F. A. 'The Effects of Changes of Sovereignty upon Nationality', in *The Modern Law Review*, vol. V (1942), p. 218.
Meile, F. *Die Rechtsstellung der Niederländisch–Sudafrikanischen Eisenbahn–gesellschaft im Amsterdam sowie ihrer Aktionäre und Obligationäre gegenüber Grossbritannien als Rechtsnachfolger des südafrikanischen Republic* (1903).
Mertens. *Die Rechtsverbindlichkeit der thüringischen Auseinandersetzungsverträge für das Land Thüringen* (1931).

Bibliography

Meyer. *Die Staatensukzession und ihre Wirkungen bei Abtretung des Memelgebiets* (1934).
Michel. *Die Einverleibung Frankfurts in den preussischen Staat, als Fall einer Staatensukzession* (1910).
Monier, J. P. 'Succession d'État en matière de responsibilité internationale', in *Annuaire français* (1962), p. 65.
Mosler, H. *Wirtschaftskonzessionen bei Änderungen der Staatshoheit* (1948).
Nevanlinna, E. *La Findlande et la dette publique de la Russie* (1925).
O'Connell, D. P. *The Law of State Succession* (1956).
O'Connell, D. P. *Pravopreemstvo Gosudarstv*. (With an introduction by O. P. Barsegow 1957.)
O'Connell, D. P. 'New Zealand and the Law of State Succession', in *The A. G. Davis Essays in Law*, edited by J. F. Northey (1965), p. 180.
O'Connell, D. P. 'State Succession and Problems of Treaty Interpretation', in *A.J.* vol. LVIII (1964), p. 41.
O'Connell, D. P. 'Independence and Succession to Treaties', in *B.Y.* vol. XXXVII (1962), p. 84.
O'Connell, D. P. 'State Succession in the British Commonwealth since the Second World War', in *B.Y.* vol. XXVI (1949), p. 454.
O'Connell, D. P. 'Economic Concessions in the Law of State Succession', in *B.Y.* vol. XXVII (1950), p. 93.
O'Connell, D. P. 'Secured and Unsecured Debts in the Law of State Succession', in *B.Y.* vol. XXVIII (1951), p. 204.
O'Connell, D. P. 'Change of Sovereignty and the Doctrine of Act of State', in *Australian Law Journal*, vol. XXVI (1952-3), p. 201.
O'Connell, D. P. 'State Succession and the Effect upon Treaties of Entry into a Composite Relationship', in *B.Y.* vol. XXXIX (1963), p. 54.
Olivart, R. de D. Y. *De los principios que regien la succession territorial en los cambios de soberanía* (1906).
Olivi, A. *Considerazioni giuridiche intorno al problema della successione di Stato a Stato* (1927).
Ordonneau, P. 'Les problèmes posés par l'indépendance des nouveaux États africaines et malagache sur le plan du contentieux administratif', in *Rev. jur. et pol.* vol. XVI (1962), p. 541.
Paenson, I. *Les consequences financières de la succession des États* (1932-53), (1954).
Panhuys, Jhr. H. F. van. 'La succession de L'Indonésie aux accords internationaux conclus par les Pays-Bas avant l'indépendance de L'Indonésie', in *Ned. Tijd.* vol. II (1955), p. 55.
Paone, P. 'Mutamenti di sovranità ed esercisio della giurisdizione', in *Rivista di diritto internazionale*, vol. XXXVII (1954), p. 584.
Parlavantzas, P. B. 'L'application de la succession à l'établissement, la modification et la dissolution des liens fédératifs', in *Revue hellénique de droit international*, vol. XVI (1963), p. 53.
Pic, P. 'Influence de l'établissement d'un protectorat sur les traités antérieurement conclus avec des puissances tierces par l'État protégé', in *Rev. gén. de droit int. pub.* vol. III (1896), p. 613.
Rauschning, D. *Das Schicksal völkerrechtlichen Verträge bei Änderung des Status ihrer Partner* (1963).
Rogister, L. von. *Zur Lehre von der Staatennachfolge; gibtes stillschweigenden Eintritt in Staatsverträge?* (1902).

Ronga, G. 'The Position in the Berne Union of the Countries which have recently become independent', in *Le droit d'auteur* (1960), p. 320.
Rosenne, S. 'The Effect of Change of Sovereignty upon Municipal Law', in *B.Y.* vol. XXVII (1950), p. 267.
Rosenne, S. 'Israël et les traités internationaux de la Palestine', in Clunet, vol. LXXVII (1950), p. 1140.
Rousseau, C. 'Chronique des faits internationaux: Syrie: Sécession de la Syrie et de la R.U.A.', in *Rev. gén. de droit int. pub.* vol. LXVI (1962), p. 413.
Rousseau, C. 'La pratique récente en matière de succession d'États', in *Annales de droit et de sciences politiques,* vol. XXII (1963).
Sack, A. N. *Les effets des transformations des États sur leurs dettes publiques et autres obligations financières* (1927).
Sack, A. N. *Partage des dettes de l'État* (1923).
Sack, A. N. 'La succession aux dettes publiques d'État', in Hague *Recueil*, vol. XXIII (1928).
Salem, E. R. 'Effets de l'annexion sur la nationalité des sociétés anonymes Ottomanes', in Clunet, vol. XLI (1914), p. 38.
Sayre, F. B. 'Change of Sovereignty and Private Ownership of Land', and 'Change of Sovereignty and Concessions', in *A.J.* vol. XII (1918), pp. 475 and 705.
Schilling, K. *Ist das Königreich Jugoslawien mit dem früheren Königreich Serbien völkerrechtlich identisch?* (1939).
Schmidt, F. F. *Der Übergang der Staatsschulden bei Gebietsabtretung* (1913).
Schönborn, W. *Staatensukzessionen,* 2nd vol. of *Handbuch des Völkerrechts of Stier-Somlo* (1913).
Schönborn, W. Note, in *Juristische Wochenschrift* (1919), pp. 393, 936.
Scott, J. B. *The Treaties of 1785, 1799 and 1878 between United States and Prussia* (1918).
Sedillot. 'Les problèmes financières du démembrement', in *L'Europe nouvelle,* 22 année, no. 1101.
Segovia, R. 'Los acuerdos de Evian', in *Foro internacional,* vol. III (1962/3), p. 368.
Selosse, R. *Traité de l'annexion au territoire français et de son démembrement* (1880).
Sen, Sirdar D. K. 'The Partition of India and Succession in International Law', in *Indian Law Review,* vol. I (1947), p. 190.
Shearer, I. A. 'La succession d'États et les traités non-localisés', in *Rev. gén. de droit int. pub.* vol. LXVIII (1964), p. 5.
Sompong Sucharitkul. 'Succession of States in Regard to Treaties', (in Thai) in *Bot Bandit,* vol. XXI (1963), p. 388.
Stoerk, F. *Option und Plebiscit bei Eroberungen und Gibietscessionen* (1879).
Sukiennicki, W. *La question de la succession par la Pologne des créances hypothécaires et d'autres droits réels grévant, au bénéfice de l'État Prussien* (1931).
Szászy, I. 'La théorie de la succession d'État à État'. An analysis in French of a 700-page book in Hungarian. *Rév. de droit int.* vol. V (1930).
Szlechter, E. *Les options conventionelles de nationalité* (1948).
Tabata, Shigejiro. 'Interim Report by the Committee on State Succession', *The Japanese Annual of International Law,* no. 9 (1965), p. 167.
Tervooren, E. P. M. *Statenopvolging en de financiële verplichtingen van Indonesië* (1957).
Tixier, G. 'La succession à la régie des chemins de fer de l'A.O.F. Problèmes posé par l'apparition de nouveaux États', in *Annuaire français* (1965), p. 916.
Treves, T. 'In tema di applicabilità al Marocco di accordi Italo-Francesi', in *Rivista di diritto internazionale privato e processuale,* vol. I (1965), p. 83.

Udina, M. *L'estinzione dell'imperio Austro-Ungarico nel diritto internazionale* (1933).
Udina, M. 'La succession des États quant aux obligations internationales autres que les dettes publiques', in Hague *Recueil*, vol. XLIV (1933).
Vallat, Sir F. A. 'Some Aspects of the Law of State Succession', in *Trans. Grot. Soc.* vol. XLI (1956), p. 123.
Verbit, G. P. 'State Succession in the New Nations', in *Proceedings of the American Society of International Law* (1966), p. 119.
Waelbroeck, M. 'A propos des emprunts congolais', in *Chronique de politique étrangère*, vol. XV (1962), p. 59.
Wilkinson, H. A. *The American Doctrine of State Succession* (1934).
Wolf, F. 'Conventions internationales du travail et le succession d'États', in *Annuaire français* (1961), p. 742.
Wünsche, H. and Pahl, G. 'Zu einigen Fragen der Staatennachfolge und ihrer Beteutung für die Deutsche Demokratische Republik', in *Deutsche Akademie für Staatsund Rechtswissenschaft 'Walter Ulbricht'. Wissenschaftliche Zeitschrift; Sondernummer zum 40 Jahrestag der Grossen Sozialistischen Oktoberrevolution* (1958).
Zemanek, K. 'State Succession after Decolonisation', in Hague *Recueil*, vol. 116 (1965), p. 187.
Zemanek, K. 'Anmerkung in Das Urteil des Obersten Gerichtshofes von Pakistan in Sachen Yangtze (London) Ltd. *v.* Barlas Bros', in *Z.f.a.ö.R.u.V.* vol. XXII (1962), p. 788.
Zemanek, K. *Gegenwärtige Fragen der Staatensukzession. Sonderdruck. Berichte der Deutschen Gesellschaft für Völkerrecht*, vol. V (1964).
Zucchelli, R. *Il debito púbblico nelle consequenze giuridico patrimoniali dell'annessione* (1919).

B. WORKS CONTAINING MATERIAL RELEVANT TO THE LAW OF STATE SUCCESSION

Abendroth, W. 'Servitut', in Strupp-Schlochauer (R–Z), p. 262.
Accioly, H. *Tratado de derecho internacional público* (1945–6).
Accioly, H. *Traité de droit international public* (1940).
Adam. *L'Angleterre en Egypte* (1927).
Agrawala, S. K. 'Law of Nations as Interpreted and Applied by Indian Courts and Legislature', in *Indian Journal of International Law*, vol. II (1962), p. 431.
Andrassy, J. 'Accord sur les eaux du Nil', in *Jugoslovenska Revija za Medunarodno pravo*, vol. VII (1960), p. 244.
André, J. C. 'L'Évolution du statut des fleuves internationaux d'Afrique noire', in *Rev. jur. et pol.* vol. XIX, p. 285.
Anzilotti, D. *Corso di diritto internazionale* (1912).
Auer, P. de. 'Plebiscites and the League of Nations Covenant', in *Trans. Grot. Soc.* vol. VI (1921), p. 45.
Avakov, M. M. *Pravopreenstvo Sovětskogo Gosudarstva* (1961).
Balas, E. P. 'Zur Lehre von der Staatensukzession: die Frage der Herkunftsbezeichnung "Tokajer Wein"', in *Zeitschrift für Völkerrecht*, vol. XIV (1928), p. 392.
Balladore-Pallieri, G. *Diritto internazionale púbblico* (6th ed. 1952).
Baddour, A el-F. I. el-S. *Sudanese Egyptian Relations* (1960).
Baddour, A. el-F. I. el-S. 'Parallels between Postliminium and State Succession (with special reference to the case of Algeria and Ethiopia)', in *Revue 'Al Quanoun Wal Iqtisad, Droit et economic politique* (Univ. of Cairo), vol. XXXIII (1965), p. 131.

Badr, G. M. 'The Nile Water Question', in *Revue égyptienne de droit international*, vol. XV (1959), p. 94.
Banerjee, A. C. *The Making of the Indian Constitution 1939–1947, Documents* (1948).
Bardonnet, D. 'Les minorités asiatiques à Madagascar', in *Annuaire français* (1964), p. 127.
Bartoš, M. *Medjunarodno janvo pravo* (1954).
Bastid, S. 'La succession du Congo belge aux obligations de l'État independant du Congo devant la Cour de Paris', in *Rev. jur. et pol.* vol. XI (1957), p. 356.
Bastid, S. *Le territoire dans le droit international contemporain* (1954).
Batstone, R. K. 'The Utilisation of the Nile Waters', in *I.C.L.Q.* vol. VIII (1959), p. 523.
Baxter, R. R. *The Law of International Waterways* (1964).
Becker, L. E. 'Zur Rechtsproblematik des Reichskonkordats', in *Neue Juristische Wochenschrift* (1957), p. 1062.
Beisswingert, R. Die Einwirkung bundesstaatlicher Kompetenzverschiebungen auf völkerrechtliche Verträge unter besonderer Berücksichtigung der deutschen Entwicklung (1960) (unpublished doctoral dissertation, Munich).
Bello, A. *Principios de derecho internacional* (2nd ed. 1946).
Berber, F. J. *Lehrbuch des Volkerrechts*, 3 vols. (1960–2).
Bernhardt, R. *Der Abschluss völkerrechtlicher Verträge im Bundesstaat* (1957).
Biscottini, G. 'L'annessione e la frisione di Stati ed i loro reflessi sul fenomeno successorio', in *Rivista di diritto internazionale*, vol. XIX (1940), pp. 133, 321.
Bluntschli, J. K. *Das moderne Völkerrecht der civilisirten Staten als Rechtsbuch dargestellt* (1867).
Boratyński, S. *Obrona suwerenności małych państw* (1949).
Bordwell, P. 'Purchasable Offices in Ceded Territory', in *A.J.* vol. III (1909), p. 119.
Borel, E. *Répartition des annuitées de la Dette publique Ottomane, Sentence Arbitrale* (1925).
Borella, F. 'L'évolution de la Communauté en 1960: de la Communauté institutionelle à la Communauté conventionelle', in *Annuaire français* (1960), p. 925.
Boschan, S. *Europäisches Familienrecht* (1954).
Brandt. 'Die Regelung der österreichischen Bundesschulden', in *Z.f.a.ö.R.u.V.* vol. IX (1939), p. 127.
Braütigam, H. O. 'Abkommen zwischen der Vereinigten Arabischen Republik und der Republik Sudan über die volle Nutzung des Nilwassers vom 8 November 1959', in *Z.f.a.ö.R.u.V.* vol. XXI (1961), p. 81.
Brierly, J. L. 'Règles générales du droit de la paix', in Hague *Recueil*, vol. LVIII (1936), p. 5.
Brierly, J. L. *The Law of Nations* (6th ed. by Sir H. Waldock, 1965).
Briggs, H. W. *Law of Nations Cases and Documents* (1952).
Broches, A. 'International Legal Aspects of the Operation of the World Bank', in Hague *Recueil*, vol. XCVIII (1959), p. 297.
Brown, D. J. L. 'The Ethiopia-Somaliland Frontier Dispute', in *I.C.L.Q.* vol. V (1956), p. 245.
Brown, D. J. L. 'Recent Developments in the Ethiopia-Somaliland Frontier Dispute', in *I.C.L.Q.* vol. X (1961), p. 167.
Brown, E. G. 'British Statutes in the Emergent Nations of Africa: 1844–1962', in *University of Pittsburg Law Review*, vol. XXIV (1963), p. 502.
Brown, P. M. 'The Aaland Islands Question', in *A.J.* vol. XV (1921), p. 268.

Brownlie, I. Notes on British judicial decisions, in *Clunet*, vol. LXXXVI (1959), p. 1166.
Bruce, A. A. 'Compacts and Agreements of States with One Another, and with Foreign Powers', in *Minnesota Law Review*, vol. II (1917–18).
Bulmerincq, A. von. *Völkerrecht oder internationales Recht* (1884).
Bülow, G. P. von. *Abhandlungen über einzelne Materien des bürgerlichen Rechts* (1819).
Burckhardt, W. 'L'Affaire des Zones Franches de la Haute-Savoie et du pays de Gex', in *Rev. de droit int. et de lég. comp.* 3rd ser. vol. XI (1930), p. 90.
Burda, A. and Kimowiecki, R. *Prawo Panśtwowe* (1959).
Burr, C. H. *The Treaty Making Power of the United States and the Methods of its Enforcement as Affecting the Police Powers of the States* (1912).
Bustamante Y. Sirven, A. S. *Derecho internacional público* (1936).
Bynkershoek, C. van. *Quaestionum juris publici*, Libri duo, 1737.
Calvo, C. *Le droit international théorique et pratique précédé d'un exposé historique des progrès de la science du droit des gens*, 5th ed. 6 vols. (1896).
Cansacchi, G. In *Rassegna di diritto púbblico*, vol. IX (1951).
Caponera, D. 'Le bacino internazionale del Nilo', in *La Communità Internazionale*, vol. XIV, p. 60.
Carlston, K. S. 'Concession Agreements and Nationalization', in *A.J.* vol. LII (1958), p. 200.
Carlston, K. S. 'International Role of Concession Agreements', in *Northwestern University Law Review*, vol. LII (1957), p. 618.
Castles, A. C. 'The Reception and Status of English Law in Australia', in *Adelaide Law Review*, vol. II (1963), p. 1.
Castles, A. C. 'Limitations of the Autonomy of the Australian States', in *Public Law*, (1962), p. 175.
Castren, E. 'Obligations of States arising from the Dismemberment of another State', in *Z.f.a.ö.R.u.V.* vol. XIII (1951), p. 753.
Cavaglieri, A. 'Regles générales du droit de la paix', in Hague *Recueil*, vol. XXVI (1929), p. 315.
Cavaglieri, A. In *Annuaire de l'Institut de droit international*. Session de Paris (1934), vol. XXXIV.
Cavaré, L. *Le droit internationale public positif* (1951).
Cavaretta, G. 'Effetti del transferimento della soveranita su un territorio', in *Scritti giuridichi in onore Santi Romano*, vol. III (1940), p. 77.
Chailley, P. *La nature juridique des traités internationaux selon le droit contemporain* (1932).
Charpentier, J. Summary of French practice in international law in *Annuaire français* (1964), p. 900.
Cheng, Bin. *General Principles of Law as Applied by International Courts and Tribunals* (1953).
Chrétien, M. 'Revue de la jurisprudence italienne', in *Clunet* (1886), p. 667.
Chrétien, M. *Principes de droit international public* (1893).
Clauss, I. *Die Lehre von der Staatsdienstbarkeiten* (1894).
Clement, W. H. P. *Law of the Canadian Constitution* (1892).
Clute, A. R. *The International Legal Status of Austria, 1938–1955* (1962).
Clute, R. E. 'Law and Practice in Commonwealth Extradition', in *A.J. Comp. L.* vol. VIII (1959), p. 15.
Cobbett, Pitt. *Leading Cases on International Law*, 4th ed. (1937).
Coccejus, S. von. *Introductio ad Henrici l.b. de Cocceji, Grotivm illustratvm.*
Cogordan, G. *La nationalité au point de vue des rapports internationaux* (1879).

Conac, G. and Feuer, G. 'Les conventions de coopération entre la République Malgache et la République Française', in *Annales Malgaches*, vol. I (1964), p. III.
Coret, A. 'L'independance du Samoa occidental', in *Rev. jur. et pol.* vol. XVI (1962), p. 135.
Crandall, S. B. *Treaties, their Making and Enforcement* (2nd ed. 1916).
Crisafulli, V. 'La continuità dello stato', in *Rivista di diritto internazionale*, vol. 47 (1964), p. 365.
Crusen, G. 'Les servitudes internationales', in Hague *Recueil*, vol. XXII (1928), p. 5.
Dahm, G. *Völkerrecht*, 3 vols. (1958).
Dambitsch, L. *Die Verfassung des Deutschen Reiches* (1910).
Davis, Chief H. O. In *African Independence* (1963).
Dawson, R. McG. *The Development of Dominion Status* (1937).
Deak, F. In *Proceedings of the Amer. Society of Int. Law* (1930).
Decottignies R. and Biéville M. de. *Les nationalités africaines* (1963).
Delbez, L. *Manuel de droit international public, droit general et droit particulier des Nations Unies*, 2nd ed. (1951).
De Louter, J. *Le droit international public positif*, 2 vols. (1920).
Descamps, P. 'La définition des droits acquis', in *Rev. gén. de droit int. pub.* vol. XV (1908), p. 385.
Despagnet, F. C. R. *Cours de droit international public*, 4th ed. (1910).
Develle, P. *La concession en droit international public* (1936).
De Visscher, F. 'La question des Îles d'Aland', in *Rev. de droit int. et de lég. comp.*, 3rd ser. vol. II (1921), p. 35.
Diena, G. 'Considerazioni critiche su alcune teorie di diritto internazionale', in *Studi Senesi* (1908).
Dölle, H., Deichert, F. and Zweigert, K. *Internationalrechtliche Betrachtungen zur Dekolonisierung* (1964).
Donati, D. *Stato e territorio* (1924).
Drysdale, J. *The Somali Dispute* (1963).
Dunn, F. S. 'International Law and Private property Rights', in *Columbia Law Review*, vol. XXVIII (1928), p. 166.
Dupuis, C. 'Règles générales du droit de la paix', in Hague *Recueil*, vol. XXXII (1930), p. 5.
Eagleton, C. *Responsibility of States in International Law* (1928).
Ehrlich, L. *Prawo miedzynarodowe* (1958).
Erhard, L. *Communauté ou Sécession* (1959).
Esgain, A. J. 'Military Servitudes and the New Nations', in *The New Nations in International Law and Diplomacy. The Yearbook of World Polity*: vol. III (1965), p. 42.
Everling, U. 'Die Neuregelung des Assoziations verhältnisse zwischen der Europäischen Wirtschaftsgemeinschaft und den afrikanischen Staaten und Madagascar sowie den überseeischen Ländern und Hoheitsgebieten', in *Z.f.a.ö.R.u.V.* vol. XXIV (1964), p. 472.
Fabunmi, L. A. *The Sudan in Anglo-Egyptian Relations* (1960).
Fauchille, P. *Traité de droit international public* (forming the 8th ed. of H. Bonfils's *Manuel de droit international public*), 3 vols. (1922).
Fawcett, J. E. S. *The British Commonwealth in International Law* (1963).
Feller, A. H. *The Mexican Claims Commissions. A Study in the Law and Procedure of International Tribunals* (1935).

Fenwick, C. G. *International Law* (3rd ed. 1948).
Feuer, G. 'Les conférences africaines et l'organisation de la Communauté africaine et malgache d'expression française', in *Annuaire français* (1961), p. 762.
Fiore, P. *International Law Codified and its Legal Sanction, or the Legal Organization of the Society of States*, trans. with introduction by E. M. Borchard (1918).
Fiore, P. *Nuovo diritto internazionale europeo* (1865); repub. under the title *Trattato di diritto internazionale público* (4th ed. 1904).
Fiore, M. P. 'Revue de la jurisprudence italienne', in Clunet, vol. x (1883), p. 73.
Fischer, G. *Un cas de décolonisation. Les États-Unis et Les Philippines* (1960).
Fischer, G. 'L'assistance technique de la France aux États nouveaux', in *Annuaire français* (1957), p. 92.
Fischer, O. *Das Problem der Identität und der Neuheit* (1892).
Fitzmaurice, G. C. 'The Juridical Clauses of the Peace Treaties', in Hague *Recueil*, vol. LXXIII (1948), p. 259.
Fleischmann, M. *Wörterbuch des deutschen Staats- und Verwaltungsrecht* (2nd ed. 1914).
Flory, M. 'Les bases militaires à l'étranger', in *Annuaire français* (1955), p. 3.
Forsyth, W. *Cases and Opinions on Constitutional Law* (1869).
Franck, T. M. *Race and Nationalism* (1960).
François, J. P. A. 'Règles générales du droit de la paix', in Hague *Recueil*, vol. LXVI (1938), p. 5.
Freeman, K. *The International Responsibility of States for Denial of Justice* (1938).
Freund, G. S. *Die Rechtsverhältnisse der öffentlichen Anleihen* (1907).
Freymond, J. *The Saar Conflict, 1945–1955.*
Fricker, K. V. *Vom Staatsgebiet, Gebiet und Gebietshoheit* (1867).
Friedrich, J. *Grundzüge des Völkerrechts* (1915).
Frisia. *Der Dawesweg*, vol. I (1927).
Fusinato, G. 'Annessione', in *Enciclopedia Giuridica Italiana*, vol. I, pt. 2, p. 2055.
Ganchit Inthachat. *La situation internationale du Mekong* (1955).
Gandolfi, M. A. 'Les accords de cooperation en matière de politique étrangère entre la France et les nouveaux Etats africains et malgache', in *Rev. jur. et pol.* vol. XVII (1963), p. 202.
Gandolfi, A. 'Naissance et mort sur le plan international d'un État éphémère: la Fédération du Mali', in *Annuaire français*, vol. VI (1960), p. 881.
Ganshof van der Meersch, W. J. *Fin de la souveraineté belge au Congo* (1963).
Gareis, C. *Institutionen des Volkerrechts* (1887).
Gautron, J. C. 'L'Evolution des rapports franco-sénégalais', in *Annuaire français*, vol. X (1964), p. 837.
Geilke, G. 'Rechtsprobleme Nordsiebenbürgens im Lichte des rumänischen Gesetzes', in *Jahrbuch für internationales Recht*, vol. IX (1961), p. 240.
Gémayl, P. *Un régime qui meurt: Les Capitulations en Egypte* (1938).
Genovskij, M. *Osnovi na meždunarodnoto prava* (1956).
Gentili, A. *De jure belli libri tres* (1612).
Gerbert, P. 'Les nouveaux États et les organisations internationales', in *Les nouveaux États dans les relations internationales*. Pub. of the Centre d'Étude des Relations Internationales, Paris (1962).
Gharsallah, M. 'Réflexions sur la decolonisation. Notions juridique, politique et economique', in *Rev. jur. et pol.* vol. XVII (1963), p. 235.
Ghosh, R. C. *Treaties and Federal Constitutions* (1961).

Gierke, O. von. *Die Genossenschaftstheorie und die deutsche Rechtsprechung* (1887) (Photographed reproduction of this edition issued in 1963).
Ginsburgs, G. 'Option of nationality in Soviet Treaty Practice, 1917-24', in *A.J.* vol. LV (1961), p. 919.
Ginsburgs, G. 'Option of Nationality in Soviet Treaty Law: The War-Time and Post-War Record', in *Iowa Law Review*, vol. XLIX (1964), p. 1130.
Gonidec, P. F. 'La Communauté', in *Public Law* (Summer, 1960), p. 177.
Gonidec, P. F. 'La nationalité et les citoyenntés dans la Communauté en 1958', in *Annuaire français* (1959), p. 748.
Gooch, G. P. and Temperley, H. W. V. *British Documents on the Origins of the War* (1898–1914), 2 vols. (1926–7).
Gould, W. L. *An introduction to International Law* (1957).
Gregory, C. N. 'The neutralization of the Aaland Islands', in *A.J.* vol. XVII (1923), p. 63.
Grotius, H. *De jure belli et pacis* (1625).
Guggenheim, P. *Traités internationaux III, Répartition des Compétences, Conféderation et Cantons*: Fiches juridiques Suisses, no. 488.
Guggenheim, P. *Traité de droit international public* (1953–4).
Gwyer, M. and Appadori, A. *Speeches and Documents on the Indian Constitution, 1921–47* (1957).
Hackworth, G. H. *Digest of International Law*, vol. I (1940); vol. II (1941); vols. III and IV (1942); vols. V, VI and VII (1943).
Haenel, A. *Deutsches Staatsrecht* (1892).
Hall, W. E. *International Law*, 8th ed.; revised by A. Pearce Higgins (1926).
Halleck, H. W. *Elements of International Law* (2nd ed. 1885).
Halleck, H. W. *International Law or Rules regulating the Intercourse of States in Peace and War*, 3rd ed., revised by Sir Sherston Baker, Bart. (1893).
Hamel, W. *Das Wesen des Staatsgebiets* (1938).
Hamel. 'Die Haftung des Deutschen Reiches für die Schulden der ehemaligen deutschen Schutzgebiete', in *Archiv für öffentl. Recht* (1924), p. 224.
Hatschek, J. *Deutsches und preussisches Staatsrecht* (1922).
Hatschek, J. *Völkerrecht als System rechtlich bedeutsamer Staatsakte* (1923).
Heffter, A. W. *Das europäisches Völkerrecht der Gegenwart auf den bisherigen Grundlagen* (1844).
Hendry, J. McL. *Treaties and Federal Constitutions* (1955).
Henrich, W. 'Kritik der Gebietstheorien', in *Zeitschrift für Völkerrecht*, vol. XIII (1926).
Henrich, W. *Theorie des Staatsgebiets* (1922).
Hershey, A. S. *The Essentials of International Public Law and Organization* (1929).
Hertslet, E. *The Map of Africa by Treaty* (3rd ed. 1909).
Herz, H. 'Beiträge zum Problem der Identität des Staates', in *Zeitschrift für öffentliches Recht*, vol. XV (1935), p. 271.
Heydte, F. A. von der. *Völkerrecht* (1958–60).
Hirsch, A. M. 'Utilization of International Rivers in the Middle East', in *A.J.* vol. L (1956), p. 81.
Hoijer, O. *Les traités internationaux* (1928).
Hold-Ferneck, A. *Lehrbuch des Völkerrechts* (1930).
Holtzendorff, F. J. W. Ph. von. *Handbuch des Völkerrechts* (1885–9).
Hourani, A. H. *Syria and Lebanon* (3rd ed. 1954).

Bibliography

Hoyt, E. C. *The Unanimity Rule in the Revision of Treaties* (1959).
Huang, T. T. F. 'Some International and Legal Aspects of the Suez Canal Question', in *A.J.* vol. LI (1957), p. 277.
Huber, M. 'Staatennachfolge', in *Zeitschrift für Völkerrecht und Bundesstaatsrecht*, vol. I (1907), p. 275.
Hughes, C. J. *The Federal Constitution of Switzerland* (1954).
L'Huillier, J. *Éléments de droit international public* (1950).
Hyde, C. C. *International Law chiefly as interpreted and applied by the United States*, 3 vols. 2nd ed. (1945).
Hyde, J. N. 'Permanent Sovereignty over Natural Wealth and Resources', in *A.J.* vol. L (1956), p. 854.
Jellinek, G. *Allgemeine Staatslehre* (1900). (Revised in 1905 and more considerably revised in 1914. 5th ed., 1929 reprinted 1960.)
Jenkyns, Sir H. *British Rule and Jurisdiction beyond the Seas* (1902).
Jennings, R. Y. 'The Commonwealth and International Law', in *B.Y.* vol. XXX (1953), p. 320.
Jennings, W. I. 'Dominion Legislation and Treaties', in *Canadian Bar Review*, vol. XV (1937), p. 455.
Jèze, G. In *Revue de science et législation financières* (1921).
Jones, F. Llewellyn. 'Upper Savoy and the Free Zones around Geneva, and Art. 435 of the Treaty of Versailles', in *Trans. Grot. Soc.* vol. X (1925), p. 173.
Jones, J. Mervyn. 'British Nationality Act, 1948', in *B.Y.* vol. XXV (1948), p. 158.
Jones, J. Mervyn. *British Nationality Law and Practice* (1947).
Kaeckenbeeck, G. 'The Protection of Vested Rights in International Law', in *B.Y.* vol. XVII (1936), p. 1.
Kaeckenbeeck, G. 'Le protection internationale des droit acquis', in Hague *Recueil*, vol. LIX (1937), p. 321.
Kaeckenbeeck, G. *The International Experiment of Upper Silesia* (1942).
Kamptz, H. von. *Beiträge zum Staats- und Völkerrecht* (1816).
Kaufmann, E. 'Regles générales du droit de la paix', in Hague *Recueil*, vol. LIV (1935), p. 313.
Kaufmann, E. 'Die Okkupationskosten und die Militärrenten des Memelgebietes', in *Z.f.a.ö.R.u.V.* vol. III (1932), p. 297.
Kaufmann, W. *Die Rechtskraft des internationalen Rechts* (1899).
Kaufmann, W. *Das Wesen des Völkerrechts und die clausula rebus sic stantibus* (1911).
Keith, A. B. *Responsible Government in the Dominions* (1912).
Keith, A. B. *Constitutional Law in British Dominions* (1933).
Keith, A. B. *Speeches and Documents on the British Dominions* (1918–31).
Kelsen, H. 'Théorie générale du droit international public', in Hague *Recueil*, vol. XLII (1932), p. 121.
Kelsen, H. *Allgemeine Staatslehre* (1925).
Kent, J. *Commentaries on American Law* (1826) (1860 ed. used).
Kirk, W. In Scottish *Geographical Magazine* (April 1960), p. 3.
Kirsch, M. 'L'évolution des tribunaux du travail outre-mer et de la procedure devant ces jurisdictions', *Rev. jur. et pol.* vol. XIV (1960).
Kiss, A. C. *Répertoire de la pratique française en matière de droit international public*, vol. I (1962).
Klein, F. *Die mittelbare Haftung im Völkerrecht* (1941).
Klüber, J. L. *Europäisches Völkerrecht* (1821).

Kohler, J. *Grundlagen des Völkerrechts* (1918).
Kondapi, C. *Indians Overseas 1868–1949*.
Korovin, E. A. *Měždunarodnoe pravo* (1951).
Koževnikov, F. I. *Měždunarodnoe pravo* (1964).
Krauss, H. 'Die Zuständigkeit der Länder der Bundesrepublik Deutschland zum Abschluss von Kulturabkommen mit auswärtigen Staaten nach dem Bonner Grundgesetz', in *Archiv des Völkerrechts*, vol. III (1951–2).
Krüger, H. 'Bundesrepublik Deutschland und Deutsches Reich', in *Süddeutsche Juristenzeitung*, vol. V (1950), p. 114.
Kunz, J. L. 'L'option de nationalité', In Hague *Recueil*, vol. XXXI (1930), p. 111.
Kunz, J. L. *Die Staatenverbindungen* (1929).
Laband, P. *Das Staatsrecht des Deutschen Reiches* (5th ed. 1911).
Lacharrière, R. de. 'L'evolution de la Communauté franco-africaine', in *Annuaire français* (1960), p. 9.
Lampué, P. 'Les groupments d'États africains', in *Rev. jur. et pol.* vol. XVIII (1964), p. 21.
Langer, L. *Seizure of Territory. The Stimson Doctrine and Related Principles in Legal Theory and Diplomatic Practice* (1947).
Lapidoth, R. 'De la valeur interne des traités internationaux dans le droit israelien', in *Rev. gén. de droit int. pub.* vol. LXIII (1959), p. 65.
Lapidoth, R. *La conclusion des traités internationaux en Israël* (1962).
Lapradelle, P. G. de and Politis, N. S. *Recueil des arbitrages internationaux*, vol. I, *1798–1855* (1932).
Latham, R. T. E. *The Law and the Commonwealth* (1937).
Lauterpacht, E. 'The Contemporary Practice of the United Kingdom in the Field of International Law', in *I.C.L.Q.* vol. VII (1958), pp. 92, 514.
Lauterpacht, E. 'State Succession and Agreements for the Inheritance of Treaties', in *I.C.L.Q.* vol. VII (1958), p. 524.
Lauterpacht, Sir H. *Private Law Sources and Analogies of International Law with special reference to International Arbitration* (1927).
Lauterpacht, Sir H. *The Development of International Law by the Permanent Court of International Justice* (1934).
Lauterpacht, Sir H. *The Function of Law in the International Community* (1933).
Lawrence, T. J. *A Handbook of Public International Law* (10th ed. 1925).
Lederle, A. *Das Recht der internationalen Gewässer* (1920).
Lehmann, R. 'The Field of Application of Nationality Laws in French Law', in Clunet, vol. LXXXII (1955), p. 5.
Lenz, H. *Untersuchung zur Frage der Identität der Republik Österreich mit der Monarchie der Habsburger* (1939).
Ligot, M. 'Vue générale sur les accords de coopération', in *Rev. jur. et pol.* vol. XVI (1962), p. 3.
Ligot, M. and Devernois, G. 'L'Union africaine et Malgache', in *Rev. jur. et pol.* vol. XVI (1962), p. 317.
Lindley, M. F. *Acquisition and Government of Backward Territory* (1926).
Lisovskiĭ, V. *Mezhdunarodnoe Pravo* (1955).
Liszt, F. *Le droit international. Traduction française* (9th ed. 1913).
Liszt, F. von and Fleischmann, M. *Das Völkerrecht* (12th ed. 1925).
Lucchini, L. 'Aspects juridiques de la frontière Sino-Indienne', in *Annuaire français*, 1963, p. 278.

Luchaire, F. *Manuel de droit d'outre-mer* (1949).
Luiking, H. F. W. *De Dienst van Scheepvaart in Indonesië* (1954).
Lumby, E. W. R. *The Transfer of Power in India, 1945–7* (1954).
McNair, A. D. (Lord). *Legal Effects of War* (3rd ed. 1948).
McNair, A. D. (Lord). 'The Effect of Peace Treaties upon Private Rights', in *Cambridge Law Journal*, vol. VII (1939–41), pp. 379–98.
McNair, A. D. (Lord). *The Law of Treaties* (1961).
McNair, A. D. (Lord). *International Law Opinions* (1956).
McNair, A. D. (Lord). 'Continuity of State Life', in *Maridakis Collection*, vol. III, p. 491.
Magoon, C. E. *Reports on the Law of Civil Government under Military Occupation* (1902).
Maillot, M. D. 'La politique marocaine de non-dépendance', in *Rev. jur. et pol.* vol. XVII (1963), p. 3.
Makarov, A. N. In *Annuaire de l'Institut de droit international*, vol. XLIII (1950).
Makarov, A. N. In *Annuaire de l'Institut de droit international*, vol. XLIV (1952).
Makarov, A. N. 'Bankroft-Vertrage', in Strupp-Schlochauer (A–H), 1960, p. 151.
Makarov, A. N. *Allgemeine Lehren des Staatsangehörigkeitsrechts* (1962).
Mancini, P. S. *Prelezioni* (1873).
Mangin, G. 'Les accords de coopération en matière de justice entre la France et les États africains et malgache', in *Rev. jur. et pol.* vol. XVI (1962), p. 339.
Mankiewicz, R. H. 'Les nouveaux États et les conventions de droit aérien', in *Annuaire français* (1961), p. 752.
Mann, F. A. 'The Liability for Debts of the former German Protectorates in Africa considered in the Light of Decisions of the German Supreme Court', in *Journal of Comparative Legislation and International Law*, 3rd ser. vol. XVI (1934), p. 281.
Manning, W. O. *Commentaries on the Law of Nations* (1839) (ed. by Sheldon Amos, 1875 used).
Mantellini, G. *Lo Stato e il codice civile* (1882).
Marchat, H. 'Le Conflit frontalier algéro-marocain', in *Rev. jur. et pol.* vol. XVIII (1963), p. 65.
Marek, K. *Identity and Continuity of States in Public International Law* (1954).
Marinoni, M. 'La natura giuridica del diritto internazionale privato', in *Rivista di diritto internazionale*, vol. VII (1912).
Marrès and Henri. *L'Etat belge responsable du désastre congolais* (1961).
Martens, F. de. *Traité de droit international*, translated from the Russian by A. Léo, 3 vols. (1883–7).
Martens, G. F. de. *Précis du droit des gens moderne de l'Europe* (1788).
Masouyé, C. *Decolonisation, indépendance et droit d'auteur* (B.I.R.P.I. pub. 1962).
Maung Maung. *Burma's Constitution* (1959).
Mercier, A. *Les servitudes internationales* (1939).
Mérignhac, A. *Traité de droit international public* (1907).
Meyer-Lindenberg, H. *Völkerrecht* (1957).
Monaco, R. *Manuale di diritto internazionale pubblico e privato* (1963).
Moore, Harrison, W. *Act of State in English Law* (1906).
Moore, J. B. *Digest of International Law. Issued by Presidents and Secretaries of State of the United States of America, Opinions and Decisions of Courts Federal and State*, 8 vols. (1906).
Moore, J. B. *History and Digest of the 'International Arbitrations', to which the United States has been a Party, etc.*, 4 vols. (1898).

Moos, X. von. *Zur Lehre von der Staatsservituten* (1933).
Mosler, H. 'Die völkerrechtliche Wirkung bundesstaatlicher Verfassungen', in *Festschrift für Richard Thoma* (1950).
Moussa, A. 'En marge de la position de l'Egypte dans la question des eaux de Nil', in *Revue égyptienne de droit international*, vol. XIV (1958), p. 43.
Münch, F. *Ist an dem Begriff der völkerrechtlichen Servitut festzuhalten?* (1931).
Münch, F. 'Zum Saarvertrag Vom 27 Oktober 1956', in *Z.f.a.ö.R.u.V.* vol. XVIII (1957), p. 1.
Muracciole, L. 'Loi fondamentale du 19 mai 1960 relative aux structures du Congo', in *Rev. jur. et pol.* vol. XVI (1962), p. 279.
Neyron, P. J. *De vi federum inter gentes* (1778).
Nguyen Quoc Dinh. 'L'internationalisation du Mékong', in *Annuaire français* (1962), p. 90.
Nguyen Quoc Dinh. 'La coopération internationale pour l'aménagement des eaux du Mékong', in *Rev. jur. et pol.* vol. XVIII (1964), p. 185.
Niboyet, J. P. 'La nationalité d'après les traités de paix qui ont mis fin a la grande guerre de 1914–1918', in *Rev. de droit int. et de lég. comp.* 3rd ser. vol. II (1921), p. 285.
Nielsen, F. K. *American and British Claims Arbitration. Under special Agreement between United States of America and Great Britain, 18 August 1810.* Report of F. K. Nielsen (1926).
Niemeyer, T. *Völkerrecht* (1923).
Noel-Baker, P. J. *The Present Juridical Status of the British Dominions in International Law* (1929).
Nolde, B. 'La monnaie en droit international public', in Hague *Recueil*, vol. XXVII (1929), p. 247.
Nys, E. *Le droit international* (2nd ed. 1904).
Nys, E. 'Les prétendues servitudes internationales', in *Rev. de droit int. de lég. comp.* 2nd ser. vol. XIII (1911), p. 314.
O'Connell, D. P. 'A Re-consideration of the Doctrine of International Servitude', in *The Canadian Bar Review*, p. 807.
O'Connell, D. P. *International Law* (1965).
O'Connell, D. P. 'The Crown in the British Commonwealth', in *I.C.L.Q.* vol. VI (1957), p. 103.
O'Connell, D. P. 'The Doctrine of Colonial Extra-Territorial Legislative Incompetence', in *L.Q.R.* vol. LXXV (1959), p. 318.
O'Higgins, P. 'Irish Extradition Law and Practice', in *B.Y.* vol. XXXIV (1958), p. 274.
Olivart, R. de D. y. *Tratado de derecho público* (1903).
Oppenheim, L. F. L. *International law, a treatise* (8th ed. by H. Lauterpacht, 2 vols. 1958).
Outrata, V. *Mezinárodní právo veřejoe* (1960).
Parry, C. *Nationality and Citizenship Laws of the Commonwealth* (1957).
Paul, V. *Studie z mezinárodního práva*.
Peritch, J. 'Conception du droit international privé d'aprés la doctrine et la pratique en Yougoslavie', in Hague *Recueil*, vol. XXVIII (1928), p. 299.
Peureux, M. G. 'Les conférences techniques de la Communauté en 1960 et 1961', in *Rev. jur. et pol.* vol. XV (1961), p. 557.
Pfeiffer, B. W. *Das Recht der Kriegsoberung in Bezug auf Staatscapitalien* (1823).
Phillimore, Sir R. *Commentaries upon International Law.* 4 vols. (1854).

Bibliography

Phillipson, C. *Termination of War and Treaties of Peace* (1916).
Piédelièvre. *Précis de droit international public ou droit des gens*, 2 vols.; vol. I, *Des États et de leurs relations en temps de paix* (1894).
Pierson-Mathy, P. 'L'Evolution politique de l'Afrique', in *Chronique de politique étrangère*, vol. XIV (1961), No. 1 à 3, p. 1.
Pillet, A. *Les conventions internationales relatives à la compétence judiciaire et à l'exécution des jugements* (1913).
Pilotti, M. 'Les Unions d'États', in Hague *Recueil*, vol. XXIV (1928), p. 445.
Pinto, R. 'Les conventions du 3 juin 1955 entre la France et la Tunisie', in *Annuaire français*, vol. I (1955), p. 53.
Piquemal, M. M. 'Le Sénat de la Communauté et le problème d'une assemblée centrale dans une Union d'États', in *Rev. jur. et pol.* vol. XV (1961), p. 394.
Plantey, A. A. 'Indépendance et coopération', in *Rev. jur. et pol.* vol. XVIII (1964), p. 6.
Podesta Costa, L. A. *Manual de derecho internacional público* (2nd ed. 1947).
Potter, P. B. 'The doctrine of servitudes in international law', in *A.J.* vol. IX (1915), p. 627.
Pradier-Fodéré, P. L. E. *Traité de droit international public européen et américain*, 6 vols. (1885–94).
Pufendorf, S. Freiherr von. *De jure naturae et gentium* (1672).
Quadri, R. *Diritto internazionale pubblico* (1960).
Quermonne, J. L. 'Les engagements internationaux des nouveaux Etats', in *Les nouveaux Etats dans les relations internationales*. Pub. of Centre d'Etude des Relations Internationales, Paris (1962).
Rauchhaupt, F. W. von. *Völkerrecht* (1936).
Reid, H. D. *International Servitudes in Law and Practice* (1932).
Reid, H. D. 'Les servitudes internationales', in Hague *Recueil*, vol. XLV (1935), p. 5.
Reinhardt, R. 'Identität und Rechtsnachfolge', in *Neue juristische Wochenschrift*, vol. V (1952), p. 441.
Reuter, P. *Droit international public* (1958).
Ripert, G. 'Les règles du droit civil applicables aux rapports internationaux', in Hague *Recueil*, vol. XLIV (1933), p. 569.
Rivier, A. P. O. *Principes du droit des gens*, 2 vols. (1896).
Romano, S. *Rivista di diritto internazionale*, vol. XX (1925).
Ross, A. *Textbook of International Law* (1947).
Rousseau, C. *Droit international public* (1953).
Roxburgh, R. F. *International Conventions and Third States* (1917).
Rudolf, W. 'Internationale Beziehungen der deutschen Länder', in *Archiv des Völkerrechts*, vol. XIII (1966), p. 53.
Rutherforth, T. *Institutes of International Law* (2nd ed. 1779).
Sack, A. N. In *Weltwirtschaftliches Archiv.* vol. II (1926).
Salvioli, G. 'La jurisprudence de la Cour permanente de Justice Internationale', in Hague *Recueil*, vol. XII (1926), p. 5.
Sampaio Doria. In *Revista da faculdado de direito*, vol. XXXII (1936).
Santos ,V. A. and Lennhoff, C. D. T. 'The Taganak Island Lighthouse Dispute', in *A.J.* vol. XLV (1951), p. 680.
Sauer, W. *System des Völkerrechts; eine Lehrbuchmässige Darstellung* (1952).
Sauser-Hall, G. 'La succession aux dettes publiques en cas d'annexion', in *Schweizerische Juristen-Zeitung*, vol. 35 (1938), p. 161.
Scelle, G. *Précis de droit des gens principes et systématique* (1932–4), p. 161.

Schachter, O. 'The Development of International Law through the Legal Opinions of the United Nations Secretariat', in *B.Y.* vol. XXV (1948), p. 91.
Schapiro, L. B. In *India Quarterly*, vol. XVIII (1962).
Schätzel, W. *Internationales Recht; Gesammelte Schriften und Vorlesungen*: vol. I, *Das Recht des völkerrechtlichen Gebietserwerbs*; vol. III, *Internationales Staatsangehörigkeitsrecht* (1959–63).
Schechtmann, J. B. 'The option clause in the Reich's treaties on the transfer of population', in *A.J.* vol. XXXVIII (1944), p. 356.
Scheuner, U. 'Völkerrechtliche Gesamtverantwortung des Bundes', in *der Konkordatsprozess* (1957).
Scheuner, U. 'Vom Bonner Grundgesetz zur gesamtdeutschen Verfassung', in *Festschrift für Hans Nawiasky* (1956).
Schiffner, E. 'Die Sopron-Köszeger Vizinalbahn A.G. Ein Beitrag zur Lehre von der Staatensukzession', in *Zeitschrift für öffentl. Recht.* vol. IX (1929–30), p. 161.
Schiffner, E. 'Die moderne Behandlung des Problems der Staatennachfolge', in *Zeitschrift für öffentl. Recht*, vol. XI (1931), p. 268.
Schmidt, B. *De servitutibus juris publici falso nomine sic appellatis* (1764).
Schnitzer, A. F. *Staat und Gebietshoheit* (1935).
Schönborn, W. 'La nature juridique du territoire', in Hague *Recueil*, vol. XXX (1928).
Schreiber, M. 'Vers un nouveau régime international du fleuve Niger', in *Annuaire français* (1963), p. 866.
Schrodt. *Systema juris gentium* (2nd ed. 1780).
Schuschnigg, K. von. *International Law* (1959).
Schwarzenberger, G. *Manual of International Law* (1952).
Seidl-Hohenveldern, J. 'Dekolonisierung, Politik und positives Recht', in *Juristenzeitung* (1964), p. 489.
Sereni, A. P. *Diritto internazionale*, 3 vols. (1956–60).
Sethi, L. R. 'India in the Community of Nations', in *Canadian Bar Review*, vol. XIV (1936), p. 39.
Sibert, M. *Traité de droit international public: le droit de la paix* (1951).
Smith, H. A. *Great Britain and the Law of Nations*, 2 vols. (1932).
Smith, Inez V. 'The Evolution of a New Nation: Problems of judicial reorganization', in *Southern California Law Review*, vol. XXXVII (1964), p. 21.
Soderhjelm, W. *Demilitarisation et neutralisation des Îles d'Aland en 1856 et 1921* (1921).
Spiropoulos, I. *Théorie générale du droit international* (1930).
Spiropoulos, I. *Traité théorique et pratique de droit international public* (1933).
Stael-Holsteni, L. de. 'La doctrine des servitudes internationales en Scandinavie', in *Rev. de droit int. et de lég. comp.* 3rd ser. vol. III (1922), p. 424.
Stengers, J. *Belgique et Congo; L'Elaboration de la Charte Coloniale* (1963).
Stewart, R. B. *Treaty Relations of the British Commonwealth* (1939).
Story, J. *Commentaries on the Constitution of the United States* (1891 ed.).
Strebel, H. 'Das Österreichergesetz vom Blickpunkt des Völkerrechts', in *Z.f.a.ö.R.u.V.* vol. XIX (1959), p. 483.
Strupp, K. 'Les régles générales du droit de la paix', in Hague *Recueil*, vol. XLVII (1934), p. 263.
Strupp, K. *Éléments du droit international, européen et américain*, 2 vols. (1930).
Strupp, K. *Grundzüge des positiven Völkerrechts* (1921).
Sulkowski, J. 'Questions juridiques soulevées dans les rapports internationaux par les variations de valeur des signes monétaires', in Hague *Recueil*, vol. IV (1929), p. 5.

Svarlein, O. *(An) Introduction to the Law of Nations* (1955).
Syatauw, J. J. G. *Some Newly Established Asian States and the Development of International Law* (1961).
Szlechter, E. *Les options conventionelles de nationalité* (1948).
Taylor, H. *A Treatise on International Public Law* (1901).
Taylor, A. McD. *Indonesian Independence and the United Nations* (1960).
Temperley. *A History of the Peace Conference of Paris*, edited by H. M. V. Temperley, 6 vols. (1920–2).
Thayer, L. E. 'The Capitulations of the Ottoman Empire and the Question of their abrogation', in *A.J.* vol. XVII (1923), p. 207.
Thieme, H. *Reichskonkordat und Länder* (1956).
Thierry, H. 'La cession à la Tunisie des terres des agricultures français', in *Annuaire français*, vol. IX (1963), p. 933.
Todd, A. *Parliamentary Government in the British Colonies* (1894).
Tregonning, K. G. 'The Claim for North Borneo by the Philippines', in *Australian Outlook*, vol. XVI (1962), p. 283.
Triepel, H. *Völkerrecht und Landesrecht* (1899) (reprinted 1958).
Twiss, T. *The Law of Nations* (1861) (2nd ed. 1884 used).
Ubertazzi, G. M. *Studi sui diritti reali nell'ordine internazionale* (1949).
Udina, M. In *Rassegna di diritto público*, vol. IX (1951).
Ullmann, E. *Völkerrecht* (1898).
Uren, C. K. 'The Succession of the Irish Free State', in *Michigan Law Review*, vol. XXX (1931), p. 70.
Váli, F. A. *Servitudes of international law: a study of rights in foreign territory* (2nd ed. 1958).
Vanselow, E. *Völkerrecht, Einführing in die Praxis der Staaten* (1931).
Varadachariar, N. D. *Indian States in the Federation* (1936).
Vattel, E. de. *Le droit des gens* (1758).
Verdross, A. *Die Verfassung der Völkerrechtsgemeinschaft* (1926).
Verdross, A. 'Règles générales du droit international de la paix', in Hague *Recueil*, vol. XXX (1929), p. 437.
Verdross, A. 'Staatsgebiet, Staatengemeinschaftsgebiet und Staatengebiet', in *Niemeyer's Zeitschrift für internationales Recht*, vol. XXXVII (1927), p. 293.
Verdross, A. 'Die Völkerrechtssubjektivität der Gliedstaaten der Sovjetunion', in *Österreichische Zeitschrift für öffentliches Recht*, Neue Folge, vol. I (1946–8), p. 212.
Verdross, A.–Zemanek, K. *Völkerrecht* (1959).
Vignes, D. 'Commission de Conciliation France-Italienne', in *Annuaire français*, 1962, p. 363.
Wade, E. E. S. 'Act of State in English Law: In Relation with International Law', in *B.Y.* vol. XV (1934), p. 98.
Wagnon, H. *Condordats et droit international* (1935).
Wahl, K. *Die deutscher Länder in der Aussenpolitik: Untersuchungen zu dem Staatsvertragskonkordats und Gesandtschaftsrechts der Einzelstaaten und ihrem Einfluss auf die auswärtige Verwaltung des Reiches* (1930).
Waldkirch, E. D. von. *Das Völkerrecht in seinen Grundzügen dargestellt* (1926).
Walz, G. A. *Völkerrecht und staatliches Recht* (1933).
Wehberg, H. 'Die Pflichten der Mandatormächte betreffend die deutschen schützgebietsanleihen', in *Weltwirtschaftliches Archiv*, vol. I (1927), p. 136.
Weis, P. *Nationality and Statelessness in International Law* (1956).

Wengler, W. *Völkerrecht*, 2 vols. (1963).
Werner, L. 'Die Eisenbahnen in der Rechtsordnung des neuen Österreich', in *Juristische Blätter*, vol. LXVIII, 1 (15de. 1945).
Westlake, J. *International Law*, part 1 (1904).
Westlake, J. 'Conquest, Nature of the Title by', in *The Law Quarterly Review*, vol. XVII (1901), p. 392.
Westlake, J. *Collected Papers* (1914).
Wharton, F. *A Digest of International Law of the United States, taken from Documents issued by Presidents and Secretaries of State and from Decisions of Federal Courts and Opinions of Attorneys-General*, 3 vols. (1887).
Wheaton, H. *Elements of International Law* (1836) (8th ed. by Dana 1866 used).
Whiteman, M. M. *Digest of International Law* (1963).
Wildman, R. *Institutes of International Law* (1849-50).
Wilson, R. R. and Clute, R. E. 'Commonwealth Citizenship and Common Status', in *A.J.* vol. LVII (1963), p. 566.
Winiarski, B. 'Principes généraux du droit fluvial international', in Hague *Recueil*, vol. XLV (1933), p. 79.
Wolff, C. *Jus gentium methodo scientifica pertactum* (1764).
Wolgast, E. *Völkerrecht* (1934).
Wright, O. *Mandates under the League of Nations* (1930).
Yadin, U. 'Reception and Rejection of English Law in Israel', in *I.C.L.Q.* vol. XI (1962), p. 59.
Young, R. 'Recent American Policy Concerning the Capitulations in the States of the Middle East', in *A.J.* vol. XLII (1948), p. 849.
Young, R. 'State of Syria: Old or New?' in *A.J.* vol. LVI (1962), p. 482.
Zachariä, H. A. *Deutsches Staat-und Bundesstaatsrecht* (1841).
Zachariä, H. A. *Ueber die Verpflichtung zur Aufrechthaltung der Handlungen der Regierung des Königreichs Westphalen* (1817).
Zacharova, N. V. 'States as Subjects of International Law and Social Revolution (Some Problems of Succession)', in *Sovětskij Ježegodnik měždunarodnogo prava* (1960).
Zatzépine, A. *Le droit de la nationalité des Républiques francophones d'Afrique et de Madagascar* (1963).
Zatzépine, A. 'La nationalité dans les Etats africains d'expression française et à Madagascar', in *Rev. jur. et pol.* vol. XVI (1962), p. 455.
Zorn, A. 'Das deutsche Gesandtschafts-Konsular- und Seerecht', in *Annalen* (1882).
Zorn, A. *Grundzüge des Völkerrechts* (2nd ed. 1903).

AUTHOR INDEX

Roman numerals I, II, indicate volume numbers

Abendroth, W., II, 22, 23
Accioly, H., I, 101; II, 13
Adam, II, 294
Agrewala, S. K., I, 146, 157, 493
Ahmed, with Shelvankar, II, 280
Alexandrowicz, C. H., II, 127
Andrassy, J., II, 246
Andreadès, G., I, 16
Antonucci, A., I, 4
Anzilotti, D., I, 16; II, 29
Appadorai, with Guyer, II, 75
Appleton, H., I, 12, 13, 16, 18, 244, 375, 395, 416
Audinet, II, 55, 57
Auer, P., I, 529
Aufricht, H., II, 74, 185, 190, 195
Avakov, M. M., I, 19; II, 2

Baddour, A. el-F. I. el-S., II, 244
Badr, G. M., II, 244
Balladore-Pallieri, G., I, 15; II, 212
Banerjee, A. C., II, 75, 76
Bar, C. L. von, I, 13, 30
Barbour, II, 244
Barclay, I, 273
Barckhausen, I, 201
Bardonnet, D., I, 521; II, 244, 245, 246
Barsegow, H. G., I, 19
Bartoš, V. M., I, 19; II, 2, 4, 89
Basdevant, J., II, 212
Bastid, Mme S., I, 22, 90
Batstone, R. K., II, 244
Baty, T., I, 5, 238
Baxter, R. R., II, 14
Beale, J. H., I, 107
Becker, L. E., II, 83
Beisswingert, R., II, 55, 59, 61, 79, 81, 82, 83, 86, 191
Bello, A., I, 18
Bentwich, N., I, 251
Berber, F. J., I, 15, 16, 22, 101, 239, 241; II, 13, 16, 18, 25, 26, 88, 166, 212, 341, 351
Bergbohm, C., II, 335
Bernhardt, R., II, 56, 57, 82
Biéville, de, I, 526

Binz, R., II, 313
Blix, H., II, 50, 53, 248
Bluntschli, J. K., I, 6, 199, 201, 455, 500; II, 1, 16, 21, 27
Boehmer, II, 342
Boratynski, S., I, 141
Borella, F., I, 58, 60
Boschan, S., II, 87, 344
Brandt, II, 383
Braütigam, H. O., II, 246
Brierly, J. L., I, 264, 353, 374; II, 18, 39
Broches, A., I, 371; II, 133
Brown, D. J. L., II, 18, 302
Brownlie, I., I, 508
Bruce, A. A., II, 62
Bulmerincq, A. von, I, 6; II, 1, 13
Bülow, G. P. von, I, 10
Burckhart, W., II, 239
Burda, A. and Klimowiecki, R., I, 134, 135
Burr, C. H., II, 62
Bustamante, Y. Sirven, A. S. de, I, 18, 101, 374, 388, 416, 463
Bynkershoek, C. van, I, 369

Cabouat, J., I, 12, 304, 345; II, 26
Caflisch, L., I, 3, 23, 31, 244; II, 352
Cahn, H. J., I, 18, 459
Calvo, C., I, 6, 24, 239, 373, 395, 529; II, 26
Cansacchi, G., I, 15, 101, 239, 241
Caponera, D., II, 244
Carlston, K. S., I, 304
Carolsfeld, von., II, 344
Castles, A. C., I, 37
Castren, E. J., I, 16, 18, 199, 244, 370, 375, 416, 454, 461; II, 1, 2, 4, 18, 55, 166, 212, 270, 374
Cavaglieri, A., I, 15, 16, 17, 18, 24, 25, 30, 31, 101, 199, 239, 241, 243, 303, 373, 374, 395, 416, 448, 459, 499; II, 1, 13, 16, 18, 21, 22, 26, 239, 255; 374
Cavaré, L., I, 200, 395, 482; II, 1, 2, 13, 26, 212
Chailley, P., II, 2, 15
Charpentier, J., I, 446, 473
Cheng, Bin, I, 268, 482; II, 330

Chevalier, II, 239
Chrétien, M., I, 11
Clauss, I., II, 18, 21, 22
Clement, W. H. P., II, 65
De Clercq, II, 45
Clute, R. E., I, 123, 380, 384, 435, 436, 508, 524; II, 323
Coccejus, S. von, I, 10
Cogordan, G., I, 500, 505, 536
Cohen, R., II, 170, 171, 198
Conac, G., I, 58, 69, 73
Coret, A., II, 362
Corsi, A., I, 12
Costes, I, 500
Cotran, E., I, 112, 159, 228, 279, 386, 527; II, 71, 72, 194, 358
Coursier, H., II, 212, 221
Crandall, S. B., II, 18, 39, 55
Crisafulli, I, 5
Crusen, G., II, 18, 21, 22, 255

Dahm, G., I, 18, 22, 33, 104, 199, 207, 239, 243, 369, 374, 387, 395, 417, 454, 461, 482, 484; II, 1, 14, 18, 25, 26, 27, 55, 57, 88, 212, 341
Dambitsch, L., II, 57
Davis, H. O., II, 140
Dawson, R. McG., II, 65
De Bandt, J. P., I, 163, 440
Decettignies, I, 526
Decoudu, J., I, 5, 401
De Louter, J., I, 370, 395, 408; II, 18, 26
Delbez, L., I, 104, 144, 152, 169, 199; II, 1, 14, 88
De Muralt, Jhr. R. W. G., I, 18; II, 1, 25, 40, 43, 44, 56, 96, 97, 137, 168, 191, 255, 267, 293, 340
Descamps, E., I, 242, 243, 248
Despagnet, F. C. R., I, 10, 106, 190, 199, 204, 205, 239, 243, 374, 395, 416, 454, 459, 465; II, 18, 21, 26, 98, 255, 374
Develle, P., I, 304, 306
Devernois, I, 70;
De Visscher, C., II, 19, 26, 268
De Visscher, P., I, 90, 91, 93, 94, 133, 163, 239, 297, 374, 395, 417, 440; II, 2, 14, 212
Dickinson, E. D., I, 209
Diena, G., II, 16
Dolski, A., I, 138
Donati, D., I, 22

Drost, P. N., I, 316, 374
Drysdale, J., II, 284
Duguit, L., I, 201
Dupuis, C., I, 266
Durieux, A., I, 91
Dybowski, K., I, 134

Eagleton, C., I, 353
Ehrlich, L., I, 19
Elias, T. O., II, 4, 310, 361
Erhard, L., I, 60; II, 20, 21, 22, 23, 26
Esgain, A. J., II, 16, 18, 239, 255, 257, 259, 260, 262
Everling, U., II, 309
Eysinga, W. J. M. van, II, 191, 270

Fabunmi, L. A., II, 244
Fachiri, A. P., I, 336
Farran, C. d'O., II, 244
Fauchille, P., I, 5, 104, 106, 108, 144, 145, 152, 153, 158, 172, 199, 201, 373, 377, 388, 420, 459, 500, 514; II, 18, 21, 48
Fawcett, J. E. S., II, 358
Feilchenfeld, E. H., I, 3, 4, 5, 9, 15, 16, 18, 24, 31, 101, 104, 244, 320, 369, 370, 375, 376, 385, 387, 396, 398, 411, 412, 419, 421, 449, 455, 458, 462, 464, 465, 467, 482, 499, 541; II, 18
Fenwick, C. G., I, 416; II, 18
Feller, A. H., I, 353
Feuer, G., I, 58, 69, 73, 239, 242, 243
Fiore P., I, 10, 11, 106, 145, 201, 306, 346, 373, 395, 454, 461; II, 26, 27, 39, 374
Fischer, G., I, 60, 187
Fischer, G., I, 433
Fischer, O., I, 24
Fitzgerald, P. J., II, 355
Fitzmaurice, Sir G. G., I, 263, 375, 395; II, 39, 374
Fleischmann, M., II, 55, 56, 57
Flory, M., I, 257; II, 22, 363
Focherini, A., I, 16
Focsaneanu, L., I, 210; II, 382
Forsyth, W., I, 514
Fouilloux, G., I, 210; II, 382
Francis, L. B., II, 261, 359
Franck, T. M., II, 172
Francois, J. P. A., I, 416; II, 18, 26
Freeman, K., I, 263, 266
Freund, G. S., I, 16

Author Index

Freymond, J., II, 14
Fricker, K. V., I, 22; II, 22
Friedrich, J., II, 1, 14, 26
Fuller, P., I, 320
Fusinato, G., I, 12, 239

Gabba, C. P., I, 11, 25; II, 29
Ganchit Inthachat, II, 252
Gandolfi, A., I, 58, 66, 69, 71; II, 170, 171, 198
Ganshof, van der Meersch, W. J., I, 93
Gareis, C., I, 15, 24, 200, 395, 448; II, 21, 22
Garner, J. W., I, 375, 377, 380, 381, 461; II, 18, 38
Garran, Sir R., II, 63
Gautron, J. C., I, 212, 228; II, 136, 330
Gémayl, P., II, 294
Genovskij, M., I, 19; II, 2
Gentili, A., I, 369
Gény, F., II, 2
Gerbet, P., II, 183
Gettys, L., I, 499, 529, 535
Gharsallah, M., I, 58
Ghosh, R. C., II, 60, 62, 63, 65
Gidel, G., I, 16, 18, 24, 25, 30, 31, 199, 200, 239, 242, 243, 244, 248, 250, 262, 263, 267, 304, 306, 319, 348, 358, 375, 379, 449
Gierke, O. von, I, 12
Ginsburgs, G., I, 530
Gonidec, P. F., I, 58, 523; II, 363
Gonzales Campos, J. D., II, 183, 191
Gould, W. L., I, 18, 101, 199, 239, 241, 374, 395, 416, 461, 482; II, 1, 26
Goupy, G., I, 242
Graupner, R., I, 502, 503, 504, 510, 514, 529, 536
Green, L. C., II, 277, 380
Grewe, W., I, 82
Grivaz, I, 242
Grotius, H., I, 5, 9, 369; II, 94
Guggenheim, P., I, 16, 18, 24, 25, 31, 101, 152, 177, 199, 200, 201, 205, 207, 239, 241, 262, 273, 304, 380, 395, 408, 448, 461, 465, 482; II, 1, 14, 16, 25, 26, 60, 351, 352
Guldberg, T., I, 304
Guyomar, G., I, 529
Gwiazdomorski, J., I, 137
Gwyer, M. with Appadori, A., II, 75

Haas, F. J., I, 10
Hackworth, G. H., I, 369, 380, 395, 416, 503
Haenal, A., II, 55, 57
Halecki, I, 135
Halewyck, I, 91
Hall, W. E., I, 3, 16, 17, 24, 199, 373, 395, 529; II, 1, 21, 26
Halleck, H. W., I, 17, 387, 395; II, 18, 57
Hamel, W., I, 22
Hartig, J., II, 80
Hatschek, J., I, 172, 395; II, 56, 57, 188, 313
Hecker, H., I, 15
Heffter, A. W., I, 6, 24, 199
Hendry, J. McL., II, 62
Henri and Marrès, I, 91
Henrich, W., I, 16, 22, 23
Herbst, L., I, 16; II, 4, 14, 15, 16, 20, 26, 40, 41, 43, 45, 46, 47, 104, 137, 158, 191, 239, 240, 248, 250, 252, 255, 259, 264, 268, 270, 294, 376
Hershey, A. S., I, 4, 104, 108, 199, 239, 348, 395, 416, 461; II, 2, 18, 26, 88
Herz, J. H., I, 5, 353
Heydte, F. A. Fr. von der, I, 199, 239, 304, 465; II, 1, 14, 16, 25, 83
Hirsch, A. M., II, 244, 249
Hobza, II, 2
Hoijer, O., I, 104, 239, 374; II, 1, 2, 18, 25, 26, 31, 55, 88
Hold von Ferneck, A. Freiherr, I, 200, 395, II, 1, 56
Holdich, II, 277
Holdsworth, Sir W., I, 255
Holtzendorff, F. J. W. P. von, I, 6, 15, 22, 199, 241, 482; II, 1, 14, 16, 18, 26, 27
Hourani, A. H., II, 158
Hoyt, E. C., I, 272
Huang, T. T. F., I, 304
Huber, M., I, 10, 13, 15, 24, 25, 31, 177, 191, 199, 200, 201, 205, 241, 232, 239, 304, 307, 387, 395, 407, 448, 449, 454, 463, 465; II, 1, 26, 55, 56, 57, 58
Hughes, C. J., II, 60
L'Huillier, J., II, 1, 14
Hurst, Sir C., I, 356, 482
Hyde, C. C., I, 5, 30, 107, 304, 347, 381, 396, 416, 459, 461
Hyde, J. N., II, 18, 19, 35

Isay, E., I, 535

Jellinek, H., I, 498, 499, 504, 507, 512, 517, 529
Jellinek, G., I, 14, 22, 31, 101, 241
Jenks, C. W., II, 1, 5, 14, 130, 203, 212
Jenkyns, Sir H., I, 37
Jennings, I., II, 65
Jennings, R. Y., I, 47
Jentgen, I, 90
Jèze, G., I, 30, 243, 370, 373, 375, 408, 416, 448, 456, 458, 461
Jones, F. Llewellyn, II, 239
Jones, J. Mervyn, I, 3, 4, 7, 24, 499, 529; II, 39, 40, 57, 112, 123, 374

Kaeckenbeeck, G., I, 104, 177, 178, 179, 181, 239, 244, 247, 251, 263, 265, 267, 275, 318, 345, 351, 512, 517, 534, 565
Kamal Hossain, II, 354, 355
Kamptz, H. von, I, 10
Kapur, J. L., I, 117, 146, 155, 172, 366
De Kat Angelino, I, 97, 98
Kaufmann, E., I, 273, 503
Kaufmann, W., I, 13; II, 21, 55
Keck, Z., I, 136, 138
Keith, A. B., I, 10, 24, 25, 31, 102, 142, 177, 178, 182, 199, 207, 347, 395, 466, 482, 499, 517, 535; II, 14, 18, 26, 39, 55, 58, 98, 374
Keith, K. J., II, 163
Kelsen, H., I, 23, 24, 26, 102, 199, 353, 374
Kennedy, W. P. M., II, 65
Kent, J., I, 5, 10; II, 94
Kiatibian, S., I, 12, 374; II, 1, 18, 21, 26, 27, 29, 39, 48, 55, 62, 91, 239, 241, 273, 374
Kierski, K., I, 140
Kirsch, M., I, 60
Kirk, W., II, 277
Kirsten, J., I, 19
Klein, F., II, 56
Klimowiecki, R. and Burda, A., I, 134, 135
Klüber, J. L., I, 5, 10; II, 239
Koch, T., I, 16, 448
Kohler, J., I, 13, 30
Kondapi, C., I, 287
Koodt, E., II, 4
Korovin, E. A., I, 19; II, 2
Koževnikov, F. I., I, 20; II, 2, 183
Kraus, H., II, 82

Krenz, F. E., II, 4
Kruger, H., II, 83
Kunugi, T., II, 210, 230
Kunz, J. L., I, 499, 514, 529, 535; II, 56, 57
Kutrzeba, S., I, 135

Laband, P., I, 448; II, 55, 56, 57
LaCharrière, R. de, I, 58
Lampué, P., I, 70, 73, 77, 81
Langer, L., II, 39
Lapidoth, R., II, 152, 155, 157, 326, 336
Lapradelle, P. G. de, I, 101, 106, 509
Larivière, L., I, 12, 18; II, 1, 2, 18, 26, 27, 31, 55, 88, 91, 96, 98, 103
Latham, R. T. E., I, 47
Lauterpacht, E., II, 248, 358
Lauterpacht, Sir H., I, 179, 275; II, 17, 18, 19, 22, 58
Lawrence, T. J., I, 199, 499
Lederle, II, 188, 270
Le Fur, L., I, 18, 30
Lehmann, R., I, 523
Lenz, H., I, 4
Lester, A. P., I, 16; II, 4, 14, 16, 26, 89, 132, 242, 244, 358
Ligot, M., I, 69, 70, 71
Lindley, M. F., II, 43, 76, 255, 288
Lisovskiĭ, V., I, 19
Liszt, F. von, I, 6, 408; II, 1, 14, 18, 21, 26, 30, 55, 56, 57
Litauer, J. J., I, 137
Louis-Lucas, P., II, 143
Lucchini, W., II, 280
Luchaire, F., I, 81, 523
Ludwiczak, W., I, 136
Luiking, H. F. W., II, 138
Lumby, E. W. R., II, 74, 129

Maillot, M. D., I, 257
Makarov, A. N., I, 504, 529; II, 59
Mallarmé, A., I, 304
Mancini, P. S., I, 11
Mangin, G., I, 73
Mangolt-Klein, H. von, II, 81, 82, 83
Mankiewicz, R. H., II, 325
Mann, F. A., I, 371, 421, 500, 514, 529
Manning, W. O., I, 5, 10
Mantellini, G., I, 11
Marchat, H., II, 291
Marek, K., I, 5; II, 28

Author Index

Marinoni, M., I, 16, 31
Marrès and Henri, I, 91
Martens, F. de, I, 6, 10, 199
Martens, G. F. von, I, 5, 10, 346, 373, 395, 463
Masouyé, C., II, 205
Maung Maung, I, 286, 287, 429; II, 130, 282
Maunz, T., II, 81, 82, 84
Meile, F., I, 13, 379
Menon, Krishna, II, 280
Mercier, A., II, 18, 239, 255
Merignac, A., I, 10
Merlin, I, 242
Meyer-Lindenberg, H. I, 199, 207, 374, 387, 416, 482; II, 1, 14, 25, 26
Meyrowitz, H., II, 221
Mitchell, J. D. B., I, 425
Monaco, R., I, 199, 416; II, 1
Monnier, J. P., I, 482, 539, 540
Moore, W. Harrison, I, 251; II, 63
Moore, J. B., I, 6
Moos, X. von, I, 15; II, 21, 23
Mosler, H., I, 15, 16, 18, 24, 30, 32, 101, 239, 242, 245, 250, 264, 267, 277, 304, 305, 306, 316, 319, 320, 332, 335, 347, 348, 349, 351, 354, 416, 461, 541; II, 54, 56, 57, 82, 83, 342
Moussa, A., II, 244
Müller, II, 344
Münch, I., I, 15; II, 14, 15, 16, 18, 20, 21, 22, 41
Muracciole, L., I, 73, 94
MacMichael, Sir H. A., II, 244, 245
McNair, A. D. Lord, I, 251, 269, 286, 500, 502, 506, 529; II, 15, 18, 19, 20, 21, 28, 40, 43, 44, 48, 49, 50, 55, 62, 64, 65, 99, 103, 123, 166, 168, 179, 182, 202, 233, 235, 236, 255, 297, 302, 313, 358, 371, 374, 375, 377, 378

Namitkiewicz, J., I, 140
Nawaz, M. K., II, 127
Neyron, P. J., I, 10
Nguyen Quoc Dinh, II, 252
Niboyet, J. P., I, 512
Nicholas, H. S., II, 63
Nielsen, F. K., I, 489, 490, 491
Niemeyer, T., II, 18
Noel-Baker, P. J., I, 47

Nolde, B., I, 191
Nys, E., I, 10, 239, 244, 529; II, 18, 22

O'Connell, D. P., I, 102, 192, 265, 268, 299, 305, 347, 371, 482, 524; II, 56, 58, 60, 62, 64, 74, 75, 81, 84, 85, 93, 229, 335, 368
O'Higgins, P., II, 124
Olivart, R. de D. y Olivart, Marqués de, I, 13
Olivi, A., I, 16
Oppenheim, L., I, 4, 13, 395, 499, 533; II, 17, 18, 21, 26, 55
Ordonneau, P., I, 60
Outrata, V., I, 19; II, 2

Paenson, I., I, 18, 191, 194, 214, 222, 226, 382, 383, 390, 403, 431, 451, 469; II, 158
Pahl, H., I, 19
Palandt, O., II, 344
Panhuys, Jhr. H. F. van, I, 14, 18; II, 372
Paone, P., I, 142
Parlavantzas, P. B., II, 55, 83
Parry, C., I, 519, 520, 524
Paul, V., I, 8; II, 4
Péritch, J., II, 378
Penson, J. H., I, 135
Peureux, M. G., I, 70
Pfeiffer, B. W., I, 10
Phillimore, Sir R. J., 5, 10, 387; II, 94
Phillips, O. H., I, 47
Phillipson, C., I, 104, 142, 152, 172, 177, 199, 205, 239, 387, 395, 463, 482, 499, 529; II, 18, 26, 48, 375
Pic, P., I, 298
Piédelièvre, I, 101, 104, 106, 144, 145, 152, 153, 169, 177, 182, 190, 199, 204, 247, 292, 373, 395, 416, 417, 454; II, 18, 21, 26, 27, 39, 212
Pierson-Mathy, P., I, 58
Pillet, A., II, 56, 57
Pilotti, M., II, 56
Piquemal, M. M., I, 72
Pitt Cobbett, I, 320
Planiol, M., I, 244
Plantey, A., I, 69
Podesta Costa, L. A., I, 395, 416, 529; II, 18, 26
Politis, N. S., II, 103
Pompe, C. A., II, 244

Pothier, I, 500
Potter, P. B., II, 18, 19
Pradier-Fodéré, P. L. E., I, 5, 6, 10, 24, 388, 395, 454; II, 21, 292
Pufendorf, S. Fr. von, I, 5, 10, 369

Quadri, R., I, 18; II, 25, 212
Quermonne, J. L., II, 132, 183

Raczynski, A., I, 140
Radnitzky, E., I, 23
Rama Rao, II, 280
Rao, K. Krishna, II, 278, 280
Rappard, W. E., II, 60
Rauchhaupt, F. W. von, I, 15, 102; II, 1
Rauschning, D., I, 5; II, 65, 119, 166
Reddaway, W. F., I, 135
Redslob, R., I, 416
Reid, H. D., II, 15, 17, 18, 21, 233, 234, 235, 239, 254, 257, 292
Repond, II, 255
Reuter, P., I, 18, 239, 243, 304, 395, 408, 416; II, 1, 14, 212
Ripert, G., I, 24
Rivier, A. P. O., I, 12, 373, 395, 514, 529; II, 18, 21, 26, 55, 57, 255, 374
Rogister, L. von, I, 16, 18, 31, 200; II, 1, 14, 18, 26, 57, 255
Rolin, H., 286
Romano, S., I, 12
Ronga, G., II, 205
Rosenne, S., I, 15, 31, 102, 103, 129, 214; II, 4, 156
Ross, A., I, 15, 16, 369, 387, 407, 417, 461; II, 14, 25, 26, 268
Rousseau, C. E., I, 18, 81, 153, 161, 177, 199, 239, 304, 374, 395, 461, 482; II, 1, 2, 27, 98, 136, 169, 198, 212, 245, 246
Roxburgh, R. F., II, 18
Rudolf, W., II, 82
Rutherford, T., I, 10

Sack, A. N., I, 18, 192, 370, 374, 375, 376, 377, 387, 388, 398, 408, 416, 454, 455, 456, 457, 458, 459, 462, 463, 464
Salem, E. R., I, 345
Salvioli, G., I, 275, 539
Sauer, W., I, 387, 395, 416; II, 88, 122
Sauser-Hall, G., I, 374
Savigny, O. von, I, 242

Sawer, G., II, 63
Sayre, F. B., I, 244, 247, 314
Scelle, G., I, 4
Schachter, O., I, 8; II, 128, 185
Schapiro, L. B., II, 280
Schätzel, W., I, 16, 512, 529; II, 35, 83
Schechtmann, J. B., I, 530
Scheuner, U., II, 54, 83
Schilling, K., I, 5
Schmidt, F. F., I, 16, 22
Schnitzer, A., I, 23, 177, 199, 201, 239, 241, 370, 407, 465; II, 2, 18, 22, 344
Schonborn, W., I, 11, 16, 17, 18, 22, 24, 25, 30, 31, 102, 104, 177, 199, 201, 232, 239, 244, 304, 307, 349, 374, 387, 395, 407, 416, 465, 482, 500, 529; II, 2, 16, 17, 18, 22, 25, 26, 55, 57, 98, 103, 191, 239, 271, 273, 314, 351, 374
Schreiber, M., II, 310
Schrodt, I, 10
Schuschnigg, K. von, I, 239, 374, 482
Schwartz, M. L., I, 15
Schwarzenberger, G., I, 104, 417, 482; II, 2, 14, 25
Scott, J. B., II, 58
Sedillot, I, 374
Segovia, I, 294
Selosse, R., I, 12, 30, 104, 106, 144, 152, 153, 169, 172, 177, 178, 190, 191, 199, 214, 243, 395, 417, 454, 461, 465, 500
Sen, Sirdar, D. K., I, 3, 5, 7, 8
Sereni, A. P., I, 15, 16, 26, 102, 199, 200, 207, 239, 241, 304, 307, 348, 349, 374, 395, 407, 417, 482; II, 2, 14, 16, 26, 273
Sethi, L. R., II, 127, 151
Shearer, I. A., II, 4, 132, 141, 151, 183, 358
Shelvankar, with Ahmed, II, 280
Sibert, M., I, 101, 144, 152, 158, 169, 199, 239, 304, 348, 395, 408, 454, 461; II, 2, 14, 18, 25, 26
Smith, Inez E., I, 133
Smith, H. A., II, 28, 92
Soderhjelm, W., II, 18
Spiropoulos, I., I, 102, 373; II, 18, 26
Stael-Holstein, L. de, II, 18, 254, 257
Stengers, J., I, 91
Stewart, R. B., I, 47
Stoerk, F., I, 500

Author Index

Strebel, H., I, 508
Strupp, K., I, 16, 102, 106, 144, 239, 374, 395, 499, 529; II, 15, 18, 21, 22, 26, 39, 56, 273, 299
Struycken, I, 273
Sulkowski, J., I, 192
Svarlien O., I, 239, 304, 482; II, 2, 14, 18, 26
Syatauw, J. J. G., II, 281
Szászy, I., I, 199, 247, 349, 395; II, 212
Szlechter, E., I, 506, 529, 532, 535

Taylor, H., I, 395
Taylor, A. McD., I, 437
Tekülve, II, 55
Temperley, H. W. V., I, 5, 400
Tervooren, E. P. M., I, 18, 98, 226, 437
Thayer, L. E., II, 292
Thieme, W., II, 83
Thompson, H., I, 141
Tixier, G., I, 210
Todd, A., I, 37
Tregonning, K. G., II, 289
Triepel, H., I, 25; II, 56, 57
Trotabas, I, 239
Twiss, Sir T., I, 7, 10

Ubertazzi, G. M., II, 18
Udina, M., I, 4, 5, 16, 18, 25, 31, 238, 275, 374, 395, 408, 416; II, 14, 17, 18, 212, 239, 255, 273, 298, 374
Ullmann, E., I, 239
Ullmer, II, 61
Uren, C. K., I, 209
Ursua, F. A., II, 2, 18

Váli, F. A., II, 17, 18, 19, 239, 242, 244, 257, 259, 262
Vallat, Sir F. A., I, 18; II, 365
Vanselow, E., I, 15, 102, 199, 408
Varadachariar, N. D., II, 75
Vareilles-Sommières, I, 242
Vattel, E. de, I, 5, 10, 369
Verdross, A., I, 23, 152, 199, 207, 239, 265, 286, 353, 374, 387, 395, 417, 482, 483, 499; II, 2, 14, 16, 25, 26, 56, 57, 212, 263, 268, 273, 351

Verosta, S., I, 23
Vitta, E., II, 212

Wade, E. C. S., I, 47, 253
Waelbroek, I, 91, 440
Wagnon, H., II, 30, 31, 97, 340, 341, 378, 380
Wahl, K., II, 55
Waldkirch, E. O. von, I, 15, 395, 416; II, 2, 14, 25, 26
Walz, G. A., II, 57
Weber, W., II, 83
Weis, P., I, 499, 512
Wengler, W., I, 416; II, 2, 4, 14, 16, 18, 56, 344, 351
Westlake, J., I, 13, 31, 199, 253, 318, 346, 348, 416, 461, 463, 505, 530; II, 14, 18, 21, 27, 55, 62
Wharton, F., I, 6, 496; II, 30
Wheaton, H., I, 5, 10, 374, 395, 454, 482; II, 2, 21
Wildman, R., I, 5, 10
Wilkinson, H. A., I, 30, 110, 152, 199, 385, 396; II, 40, 55, 98
Wilson, R. R., I, 524; II, 323
Winfield, P., I, 485
Winiarski, B., II, 18
Wolf, F., 203
Wolff, C., II, 22
Wolff, K., I, 408
Wolff, M., I, 137; II, 344
Wolgast, E., I, 15
Wright, Q., I, 151, 335
Wunsche, H., I, 19
Wynes, A., II, 63

Yadin, U., I, 132
Young, R., II, 154, 169, 191, 294, 296

Zachariä, H. A., I, 10
Zacharova, II, 2
Zatzépine, A., I, 523, 526
Zemanek, K., I, 152, 199, 207, 239, 374, 387, 395, 417, 482, 483, 499; II, 4, 25, 26, 116, 125, 132, 139, 141, 183, 212, 273, 355, 358
Zorn, A., I, 15, 24, 395, 448; II, 22, 59
Zucchelli, F., I, 16

GENERAL INDEX

Abolition of crown, effect on contracts, 367
Acquired rights, 32, 103, 297, 375, 538, 539
 definition of, 238, 244–50, 353
 expropriation of, 263–8
 history of, 239–44
 in Francophone States, 296
 theory of, 242
 to pensions, 465, 466
Act of State, doctrine of, 105, 183, 250–63, 280, 301
Addison, Viscount, 474
Aden
 currency of, 198
 Union of with South Arabian Federation, 119
 union of with South Arabia, effect on pending claims, 149
Administrative assistance, French, 187
Administrative debts, 465, 467, 468, 470, 488
Admiralty law, effect of independence on, 132
Africa, acquired rights in, 279–81
African Financial Community, 73
Ajmer, cession of, effect on acquired rights, 256
Akalkot, merger in Bombay, effect on judgments, 157
Alaska, cession of, effect on acquired rights, 247
Albania, restoration of, effect on concessions, 334
Alexandretta, Sandjak of, debts of, 403–4
 Sandjak of, cession of, effect on property, 223
Aleppo, incorporation of Alexandretta in, effect on debt, 403
Algeria
 Department of, status of, 78
 independence of, effect on acquired rights, 294–6
 independence of, effect on appeals, 162

 independence of, effect on civil service, 187
 independence of, effect on concessions, 344
 independence of, effect on criminal proceedings, 173
 independence of, effect on currency, 196
 independence of, effect on debts, 444–6
 independence of, effect on pending claims, 151
 independence of, effect on pensions, 473
 independence of, effect on property, 229
 treaty application to, 78
Alsace-Lorraine
 archives concerning, 233
 cession of to France, effect on acquired rights, 277
 cession of to France, effect on contracts, 354–5, 357
 cession of to France, effect on civil servants, 179
 cession of to France, effect on debt, 398, 400
 cession of to France, effect on judgments, 153
 cession of to France, effect on nationality, 500, 512, 515, 516
 cession of to France, effect on pensions, 469
 cession of to Germany, 167
 cession of to Germany, effect on concessions, 307
 cession of to Germany, effect on judgments, 152
 cession of to Germany, effect on judicial system, 145
 cession of to Germany, effect on legal system, 105, 106, 112
 cession of to Germany, effect on nationality, 500, 530
 cession of to Germany, effect on pensions, 467, 479

General Index

Alsace-Lorraine (*cont.*)
   cession of to Germany, effect on property, 207
American Civil War, effect on legal system, 118–19
Anglo-Iranian Oil Co., 337
Anglo-Palestine Bank, 194
Annexation, 3, 4
   effect of on legal system, 108–10
   effect of on nationality, 509–18
Anschluss, *see* Austria
Appeals, pending, effect of succession on, 158–69
Aquinas, St Thomas, 29
Arbitration in system of co-operation, 72
Archives, succession to, 232
Argentina, independence of, effect on debts, 419
Armed forces, effect of succession on, 181–2
Ashanti, 281, 282
Assam
   independence of, effect on judgments, 155
   independence of, effect on pending claims, 147
   partition of, effect on property, 220
Australia
   federation of, effect on debt, 386
   succession of to treaties, 42
   withdrawal of from treaties, 43
Australian colonies, treaty-making powers of, 39
Australian States, 48
Austria
   Anschluss of by Germany, effect on debts, 29, 380–4, 436–7
   Anschluss of by Germany, effect on legal system, 111
   Anschluss of by Germany, effect on nationality, 507–11
   Anschluss of by Germany, effect on property, 214
   restoration of, 435–7
   restoration of, effect on claims, 206
   restoration of, effect on contracts, 367
   restoration of, effect on pending claims, 145

Austria-Hungary, dismemberment of, 4
   dismemberment of, effect on currency, 192
   dismemberment of, effect on pensions, 467, 469, 479
   dismemberment of, effect on salaries, 480
Austrian-Hungarian Empire, dissolution of, effect on debts, 401–2, 420–1
Austrian Lloyd Company, 307
Austrian National Bank, 214
Auto-limitation, theory of, 14, 18, 25

Baghdad Railway, Co. 329
Bahamas, The, autonomy of, effect on pensions, 475, 477
Balfour Declaration, 47, 48
Baltic States, cession of, effect on property, 214
Bank of Naples, 218
Bank of Sicily, 218
Bank of Syria, 403
Bank of Syria and Lebanon, 222
Bankruptcy, effect of independence on, 130
Barbados, independence of, effect on pensions, 475, 477
Barbados, independence of, effect on pensions, 475, 477
Bavaria, cession of territory to, effect on pensions, 467
Bay Islands, cession of, effect on nationality, 502
Belgium
   independence of, 5
   independence of, effect on debt, 388, 448
   liability of for acts in Congo, 134
   union of with Netherlands, effect on delicts, 486
Bell, Sir Francis Dillon, 40
Bengal
   partition of, effect on judgments, 155
   partition of, effect on pending claims, 147, 148
   partition of, effect on property, 220, 221
Berlin, Congress of, 398
Berne Union, 124

Bessarabia, cession of, effect on nationality, 509, 530
Bikaner, merger of in Rajasthan, 259
Boer Republics
  annexation of, effect on acquired rights, 252
  annexation of, effect on concessions, 316–22
  annexation of, effect on contracts, 354, 360–2
  annexation of, effect on criminal proceedings, 169
  annexation of, effect on debt, 17, 378–9
  annexation of, effect on delicts, 483, 487–90
  annexation of, effect on nationality, 500–1, 505, 507, 511, 517, 531–2
  annexation of, effect on pending claims, 153
  annexation of, effect on pensions, 466
  annexation of, effect on precedent, 169
  annexation of, effect on property, 203
  annexation of, effect on salaries, 480–1
Bohemia and Moravia, Protectorate of, 212–13
Bombay, Union of, merger of Alkalkot in, effect on judgments, 157
Bondholding, 371
Bonds, succession to, 225
Bosnia, transfer of, effect on debt, 398
Brazil, independence of, effect on debt, 396
British nationality, 501, 502, 505–6, 514, 519–22, 530, 531
British possession, definition of, 56, 120–4
British protected persons, 519, 520, 521, 522, 528, 531
British ship, definition of, 121
British South Africa Co., 344
Buganda, federation of in Uganda, effect of on the legal system, 119
Bulgaria, cession of territory by, effect on pensions, 469
  independence of, effect on concessions, 307
  independence of, effect on debt, 398
Burdens and benefits theory, 30
Burma
  annexation of, effect on civil servants, 180
  annexation of, effect on contracts, 358–60
  annexation of, effect on debt, 378
  annexation of, effect on delicts, 486–7
  annexation of, effect on nationality, 507
  annexation of, effect on pensions, 466
  evolution of, 51, 52–3
  independence of, effect on civil service, 184
  independence of, effect on debt, 428–30
  independence of, effect on legal system, 126, 130
  independence of, effect on nationality, 520, 530
  independence of, effect on pending proceedings, 145
  independence of, effect on pensions, 471
  independence of, effect on property, 223
  nationalization of Indian property in, 286–7
Burundi
  independence of, effect on criminal proceedings, 173
  independence of, effect on debt, 391–2, 442
  independence of, effect on legal system, 114
  independence of, effect on pending claims, 152

California, cession of, effect on nationality, 504
Cambodia
  independence of, effect on civil service, 187
  independence of, effect of on copyright, 127
  independence of, effect on criminal proceedings, 172
  independence of, effect on debt, 434
  independence of, effect on judgments, 158
  independence of, effect on judicial system, 143
  independence of, effect on pending claims, 150

General Index

Cambodia (*cont.*)
  independence of, effect on pensions, 472
  independence of, effect on property, 226–7
Cameroon
  independence of, 67
  independence of, effect on appeals, 161
  independence of, effect on civil service, 188
  independence of, effect on nationality, 526–7
  judicial system of, 175
  mandate over, effect on debt, 423
  monetary union with, 70
Canada
  cession of, effect on nationality, 506
  federation of, effect on debt, 386
  signature by of International Cable Convention, 40
  tariff agreement of with Spain, 40
  tariff agreement of with United States, 40
Categorical imperative, 25
Cayenne, 61
Ceded colonies, 36–7
Central Africa, Union of Republics of, 66
Central African Airways Corporation, 230
Central African Power Corporation, 230
Central African Republic, 75
  currency of, 72, 73
  in system of cooperation, 71
  independence of, 66
  independence of, effect on appeals, 161
  independence of, effect on nationality, 525, 526
  independence of, effect on pending claims, 150
  independence of, effect on property, 211
  judicial system of, 175
  membership of in French Community, 67
  transitional measures of in matter of justice, 74

Central Bank of the States of Equatorial Africa and the Comores, 73
Central Bank of West Africa, 73
Cession, 3, 4, 23, 24
  effect of legal system, 108–10
  effect of on nationality, 509–18
Ceylon
  evolution of, 51, 52
  independence of, 55
  independence of, effect on appeals, 165
  independence of, effect on civil service, 184
  independence of, effect on debt, 427
  independence of, effect on legal system, 126, 129
  independence of, effect on pensions, 471, 475
  legal system of, 108
Chad, 59
  currency of, 72, 73
  establishment of, 75
  in system of cooperation, 71
  independence of, 66
  independence of, effect on appeals, 161
  independence of, effect on nationality, 525, 526
  independence of, effect on pending claims, 150
  independence of, effect on property, 211
  judicial system of, 175
  legal system of, 132
  membership of in French Community, 67
  transitional measures of in matter of justice, 74
  Vice-President of, 76
Chandernagore, cession of to India, effect on acquired rights, 258
Change of government, 6
Change of sovereignty, 6, 26
Characterization of acts, legal system governing, 144
Chetty, Shri R. K. Shammikham, 404
Chettyars, 287
Chile
  cession of territory to, effect on concessions, 308
  independence of, effect on debt, 6, 419

Chilean debt controversy, 12
Citizenship, see Nationality
Citizenship in French Community, 61–2
Civil service, effect of succession on, 177–81, 259
Claims against predecessor State, 237
Claims
  nationality of, effect of succession on, 537–42
  succession to, 205–7, 225, 482–93
  unliquidated, 485, 488
Colombia
  dissolution of, effect on debt, 388–9
  dissolution of, effect on delicts, 486
  succession of to delicts, 486
Colonial Conferences, 40, 42, 43
Colonial Development Loans, 426–7
Colonial divorces, 127–8, 149
Colonial Laws Validity Act, 1865, 37, 48
Colonial Stock Acts, 424–6
Colonies, see dependent territories
  ceded and settled, 36–7
  treaty-making by, 42–6
  withdrawal of from treaties, 42
'Colony', definition of for loan purposes, 424
Comité spécial du Katanga, 228
Commercial treaties
  application of to dependent territories, 78
  negotiation of by colonies, 41–6
Common Services Organization, see East Africa
Commonwealth, nature of the, 49, 52, 56
Communes of Savoy, separation of, effect on property, 216
Communist Manifesto, 20
Communist theory, 19
Community, French, see French Community
Comores Islands, 73
Comoro Archipelago, 59, 61
Compagnie du Katanga, 228
Compagnie du Port des Quais et des Entrepôts de Beyrouth, 340
Compagnie Générale de Telegraphie au Fil, 341
Companies, transfer of *situs of*, 130, 539–42

Compensation, assessment of, 263–8, 287–91, 345–62
Competence, sovereignty as, 16, 17, 23, 24, 26
Concessions
  effect of succession on, 304–52
  nature of, 304–5
Confederacy, succession to the, 208
Congo, 59
Congo, Belgian
  application of treaties to, 80
  monopoly in, 246
Congo (B)
  currency of, 72, 73
  establishment in, 75
  in system of cooperation, 71
  independence of, 66
  independence of, effect on appeals, 161
  independence of, effect on nationality, 525–6
  independence of, effect on pending claims, 150
  independence of, effect on property, 211
  independence of, effect on treaties, 76
  judicial system of, 175
  membership of in French Community, 67
  transitional measures of in matter of justice, 74
Congo (L)
  acquired rights in, 297
  devaluation of currency of, 193
  independence of, effect on appeals, 162–3
  independence of, effect on civil service, 188–9
  independence of, effect on concessions, 342–4
  independence of, effect on debt, 439–44
  independence of, effect on delicts, 483
  independence of, effect on legal system, 133–4
  independence of, effect on pending claims, 151–2
  independence of, effect on property, 228–9
  judicial system of, 151

General Index

Congo, Free State of, cession of, effect on debt, 380
Conscription, 182
Conseil d'Etat, appeals to, 73–4, 150, 159–62
Continuity of laws, *see* Independence
Continuity of States, 4, 12, 13, 26, 27
Contract
 breach of, responsibility for, succession to, see delict, frustration of, 117
 effect of succession on, 33, 117, 298–303, 353–68
Cooperation, *see* Justice
Cooperation, Francophone system of, 58, 68–75
Cooperation in matter of justice, 133, 143, 150, 157–8
Copyright law, effect on independence on, 124–6
Corporate association, 12
Costa Rica, independence of, effect on debt, 419
Cour de cassation, appeals to, 73–4, 150, 159–62
Court of Appeal of Eastern Africa, 163, 164, 165, 166, 167
Courts, jurisdiction of, 142–75
Creditors, rights of, 371–3, 417, 470
Crete
 cession of, effect on concessions, 302, 327
 cession of, effect on delicts, 484
Criminal proceedings, effect of succession on, 169–73
Croatia, separation of, effect on property, 214
Crown
 abolition of, 120
 abolition of, effect on contracts, 367
 abolition of, effect on property, 210
 and Parliament, 36
 cession of territory by, effect on nationality, 501, 502, 505–6, 514
 divisibility of, 38–9, 49
Crown Servants, 178, 185
Crown's dominions, definition of, 120–4
Cuba
 cession of, 29
 cession of, effect on concessions, 311–12
 cession of, effect on nationality, 500, 530
 independence of, effect on debt, 419
 Spanish, application of treaties to, 79
Cuba Telegraph Co., 313
Cuban debt controversy, 412–13
Currency
 effect of change of sovereignty on, 191, 193–8
 in Francophone States, 70, 72–3
Custodian of enemy alien property, 287–91
Cyprus
 annexation of, effect on nationality, 513, 530, 533
 independence of, 50, 53
 independence of, effect on debts, 425–6
 independence of, effect on legal system, 119
 independence of, effect on nationality, 521
 independence of, effect on pensions, 475, 477
 transfer of to Great Britain, effect on debt, 398
Cyrenaica, property in, 218
Czechoslovakia
 cession of territory by to Poland, 141
 dismemberment of, effect on archives, 233
 dismemberment of, effect on debt, 389
 dismemberment of, effect on property, 212–13
 independence of, effect on civil servants, 180–1
 independence of, effect on debt, 400, 420
 independence of, effect on legal system, 102
 independence of, effect on property, 203
 independence of, effect on salaries, 480
 independence of, effect on taxation, 191

Dahomey, 59
 conquest of, effect on acquired rights, 263
 independence of, 67

Dahomey (*cont.*)
  independence of, effect on appeals, 161
  independence of, effect on judicial system, 143
  judicial system of, 174
  membership of in Entente, 70
  membership of in West African Monetary Union, 70, 73
Dakar, 228
Danish West Indies
  cession of, effect on criminal proceedings, 172
  cession of, effect on pending claims, 146
Danzig
  annexation of, effect on debt, 384
  Free City of, pensions of, 468
Dead Sea concessions, 329
Deakin, A., 43
Debt, repartition of, 395
Delicts, succession to, 482–93
Demonetization, 196
Denial of Justice, 104, 482–93
Dependent territories, legal orders of, 75
Dettes hypothequées, 25, 467
Deutsche Reichsbahn, 214
Devaluation of currency, 192, 193–8
Devolution agreements, 66
Diplomatic representation, effect of succession on, 524, 537–42
Dismemberment
  effect on debt, 25, 387–94
  effect on legal system, 112–18
Divisibility of Crown, 38–9, 49
Divorce, colonial, 127–8, 149
Djebel Druze, incorporation of in Lebanon, effect on debt, 403
Djibouti-Addis Ababa Railway Co., 332–4
Dobroudja, cession of, 214
Dodecanese Islands, cession of to Italy, effect on debt, 398
Domicile, definition of, 512, 513, 515
Domicile of companies, 117, 539–42
Dominion Status, 46–9
Dominions, treaty-making powers of, 39, 46–8
Downer, Sir John, 40
Dresdener Bank, 487

East Africa Common Services Organization, 163, 166
  pensions of, 475
East African Currency Board, 195, 197–8
East Germany, status of, 19, 21
Eastern Africa Court of Appeal, 163–4, 165, 166, 167
Economic Commission for Africa, 76
Ecuador
  independence of, effect on debt, 419
  independence of, effect on delicts, 486
Egypt
  independence of, effect on nationality, 536
  membership of in U.A.R., 112
Eire, *see* Ireland
Enemy alien property, vesting of, 287–91
English law, applicability of to colonies, 36–7
Entente, Council of, 70
Equatorial Africa, Customs Union of, 70
Eritrea
  cession of, effect on appeals, 159
  cession of, effect on nationality, 514, 530
  cession of, effect on property, 215
  cession of, effect on pensions, 468
  federation of with Ethiopia, effect on concessions, 333–4
  incorporation in Ethiopia, effect on acquired rights, 278
  incorporation of in Ethiopia, effect on currency, 195
Establishment, right of in Francophone States, 74
Estonia
  incorporation of in Soviet Union, effect on debt, 386–7
  independence of, effect on claims, 539
  independence of, effect on debt, 404
Ethiopia
  archives of, 233
  annexation of, effect on criminal proceedings, 170
  annexation of, effect on judgments, 153
  annexation of, effect on property abroad, 209
  annexation of, effect on concessions, 311, 332–4

General Index

Ethiopia (*cont.*)
  conquest of, effect on debt, 29
  federation of with Eritrea, effect on concessions, 333–4
  restoration of, effect on concessions, 334
  restoration of, effect on debt, 435
  restoration of, effect on pensions, 468
  restoration of, effect on property, 215
European Communities, comparison of with French Community, 68
Exception de litispendance, 152
Exchange, rate of, 194, 223
Exchequer, effect of succession on, 204
Expropriation of acquired rights, 194, 203, 263–8, 283, 284–7, 292–6, 345–52
Extradition between Francophone States, 74
Extradition, *see also* Fugitive Offenders Act
Extradition treaties, territorial application of, 80
Extraterritorial legislative powers, 38

Federation of Mali, dissolution of, effect on property, 211, 228
Federation of Rhodesia and Nyasaland
  dissolution of, effect on appeals, 167
  dissolution of, effect on civil service, 185
  dissolution of, effect on contracts, 366
  dissolution of, effect on currency, 196–8
  dissolution of, effect on debt, 392–4
  dissolution of, effect on legal system, 114–15, 123
  dissolution of, effect on pensions, 474
  dissolution of, effect on property, 230–2
  evolution of, 50–1
Federation of South Arabia, formation of, effect on appeals, 165
Federation of West Indies
  dissolution of, effect on appeals, 164
  dissolution of, effect on property, 229
Fiji
  cession of, effect on acquired rights, 271
  cession of, effect on debt, 376
Finland
  independence of, 4

  independence of, effect on debt, 404
  independence of, effect on nationality, 530
Florida
  cession of, effect on acquired rights, 248
  cession of, effect on of legal system, 110
  cession of, effect on nationality, 529
Foreign Jurisdiction Act, 1890
Foreign laws, recognition of, 103
Formosa, annexation of, effect on nationality, 503, 516
Franc zone, 72–73, 195
France, membership of in French Community, 67
Francophone States, 58–85
  acquired rights in, 296
  civil servants in, 186
  independence of, effect on debt, 444
  independence of, effect on property, 210–12
  see also Cooperation
Frankfurt, annexation of, effect on pensions, 467
French citizenship, effect of succession on, 61, 67, 515–16, 523–7
French Community, 58–66, 65–8, 75–77, 105
  agreements to participate in, 69–70
  citizenship in, 61, 515–16, 523–7
  continuity of law in, 132
French Equatorial Africa, 66
French Establishments in India
  archives of, 233
  cession of, effect on acquired rights, 278–9
  cession of, effect on civil service, 188
  cession of, effect on debt, 435
  cession of, effect on judgments, 155
  cession of, effect on pending claims, 151
  cession of, effect on pensions, 472
French law, extension of to acquired territory, 106
French Polynesia, 61
French Revolution, property conception of, 200
French Union, 58–9
Frustration, doctrine of, 117

Frustration of contract, 298, 300, 302
Fugitive Offenders Act, 56, 116, 119, 120, 121, 122, 124

Gabon, 59
  currency of, 72
  establishment in, 75
  in system of cooperation, 71
  independence of, 66, 67
  independence of, effect on appeals, 161
  independence of, effect on nationality, 525, 526
  independence of, effect on pending claims, 150
  independence of, effect on property, 211
  judicial system of, 175
  membership of in French Community, 67, 69
  relations with Central African Union, 67
  transitional measures of in matter of justice, 74
Galicia, 135
  incorporation of in Poland, effect on acquired rights, 264
Gambia, The
  independence of, 55
  independence of, effect on legal system, 119
  independence of, effect on pensions, 475, 477
  independence of, effect on pending claims, 149
General principles of law, 30–1, 34
German colonies
  debts of, 421–3
  property of, 199
German property in Palestine, 287–91
Ghana
  abolition of monarchy in, 56
  acquired rights, 281–4
  becoming republic of, 124
  independence of, 55
  independence of, effect on legal system, 119
  independence of, effect on nationality, 521

  independence of, effect on pensions, 475, 476, 477
Gilbert Islands, acquisition of, effect on acquired rights, 272
Government, change of, 6
Great Britain, union of with Hanover, 49
Greece
  acquisition of Crete by, effect on concessions, 302
  cession of territory to, effect on acquired rights, 270
  cession of territory to, effect on delicts, 484
Guadaloupe, 61
Guatemala, independence of, effect on debt, 419
Guinea, 59
  independence of, 60, 64, 70
  independence of, effect on debt, 444
  independence of, effect on legal system, 133
  independence of, effect on nationality, 526
  independence of, effect on property, 212
  judicial system of, 174
  rights of lawyers in, 294
Gwalior State, retrocession of, effect of on legal system, 109

'Habitual residence', concept of, 512, 513, 514, 518
Hague Conventions on Private International Law, 78
Hanoi, 524
Hanover
  annexation of, effect on nationality, 514
  annexation of, effect on pensions, 467
  annexation of, effect on property, 202
  union of with Great Britain, 49
Hawaii
  annexation of, effect on debt, 377
  annexation of, effect on delicts, 490–1
  annexation of, effect of on legal system, 110, 111
Head of State treaties, 39, 46
Hegel, 29
Hegelian theory, 22

General Index

Heligoland, cession of, effect on nationality, 519, 530
Henri IV, 10
'Her Majesty's dominions', definition of, 56, 120–4
Hertslet, 45
Herzegovina, transfer of, effect on debt, 398
Hofmeyer, J. H., 40
Huguenot revolt, 4
Hungary, cession of territory to Roumaina by, effect on acquired rights, 266
Hyderabad, nationality of inhabitants of, 528

I.L.O., membership in of British India, 50
Idar State, merger of in Bombay, effect on acquired rights, 256
Imperative theory of law, 15, 28, 31, 102
Imperial conferences, 38
Independence
  grant of, effect on currency, 70, 72–3
  grant of, effect on legal system, 103, 118–41
  grant of, effect on nationality, 518–28
  technique of granting, 52–7
Independence of Francophone States, procedure adopted, 65–68
India, British, treaty-making by, 50–1
India
  evolution of, 49–50
  independence of, 52, 55
  independence of, effect on nationality, 520, 527
  merger of States in, effect on legal system, 109
  partition of, 7, 8, 55
  partition of, effect on acquired rights, 258–62
  partition of, effect on appeals, 168
  partition of, effect on archives, 234
  partition of, effect on civil service, 182–3
  partition of, effect on criminal proceedings, 171–2
  partition of, effect on contracts, 363–6
  partition of, effect on currency, 192
  partition of, effect on debt, 404–6
  partition of, effect on delicts, 493
  partition of, effect on divorces, 128
  partition of, effect on judgments, 153–5
  partition of, effect on legal system, 102, 116–17, 123, 125
  partition of, effect on pending claims, 146–8
  partition of, effect on pensions, 470–1, 474
  partition of, effect on property, 220–2
  partition of, effect on taxation, 191
Indian and Colonial divorces, 127–8
'Indian citizen', definition of, 171
Indian Establishments, cession of to India, effect on property, 222
Indies, Netherlands, evolution of, 97–8
Indigenat, concept of, 512
Indochina, application of treaties to, 79
  dismemberment of, effect on criminal proceedings, 172
  dismemberment of, effect on debt, 434
  dismemberment of, effect on judicial system, 142–3
  dismemberment of, effect on pending claims, 150
  dismemberment of, effect on pensions, 472
  dismemberment of, effect on property, 226
Indonesia, devaluation of currency of, 193
  expropriation in, 284–300
  independence of, 98
  independence of, effect on concessions, 335
  independence of, effect on debt, 437–8
  independence of, effect on judicial system, 142
  independence of, effect on legal system, 130
  independence of, effect on nationality, 532
  independence of, effect on pensions, 472–3
  independence of, effect on property, 226
  independence of, effect on salaries, 481
Industrial Property, Paris Convention for the Protection of, 78

Institute for the Colonization of Libya, 218
Instrumentalities, governmental, effect of succession on, 190
Intergovernmental agreements of colonies, 39
International Bank, *see* World Bank
International financial law, 374
International law
  creation of, 18, 29, 30–34
  protection of contracts by, 299
  relationship of with municipal law, 27, 32, 33, 82, 103, 371, 498–9
  role of in State succession, 17, 26, 28, 30–4
International Law Commission, 279
International Monetary Fund, 386
International Nickel Co. of Canada, 335
Ionian Islands
  cession of, effect on concessions, 307–8, 355–6
  cession of, effect on judgments, 153–4
  cession of, effect on nationality, 531
  cession of, effect on pensions, 470–3
Iraq Petroleum Co., 337
Ireland
  independence of, effect on debt, 404
  independence of, effect on funds abroad, 208–9
  independence of, effect on nationality, 502–3
Irian, *see* West New Guinea
Irish Free State, *see* Ireland
Israel
  archives of, 234
  devaluation of currency of, 193–4
  expropriation of German property by, 287–91
  independence of, effect on civil service, 184
  independence of, effect on concessions, 336–42
  independence of, effect on criminal proceedings, 170–1
  independence of, effect on debt, 431–3
  independence of, effect on legal instrumentalities, 190
  independence of, effect on legal system, 125, 128–9, 131–2

independence of, effect on nationality, 498
independence of, effect on pensions, 472
independence of, effect on precedent, 169
independence of, effect on property, 223–5
independence of, effect on taxation, 191
Italian court of cassation, 159
Italian Social Republic, 112, 153, 492
Italy
  unification of, 5, 11
  unification of, effect on contracts, 356
  unification of, effect on delicts, 483
Ivory Coast, 59
  independence of, 67
  independence of, effect on appeals, 161
  independence of, effect on judicial system, 143
  independence of, effect on legal system, 133
  judicial system of, 174
  nationality of, 523, 526
  membership of in Entente, 70
  membership of in West African Monetary Union, 70, 73

Jackson, Andrew, 110
Jaffa, 148
Jamaica
  independence of, 55
  independence of, effect on appeals, 165
  independence of, effect on nationality, 521
  independence of, effect on pending claims, 149
  independence of, effect on pensions, 475, 477, 479
  independence of, effect of on the legal system, 119
Java, cession of to Holland, effect on acquired rights, 270
Jind, accession of to India, effect on acquired rights, 260
Jordan, independence of, effect on pensions, 472

General Index

Judgments
  effect of succession upon, 152–5
  foreign, enforcement of, 153–6, 157–8
Judicial precedent, 168
Junagadh, nationality of inhabitants of, 528
Justice
  concept of, 18
  continuity of, 133, 143, 150, 157–8, 161–2
  cooperation in matter of, 73–4

Kamerun, see Cameroon
Kangra, annexation of, 259
Kashau-Oderberger Railway, 213
Kashmir, nationality of inhabitants of, 528
Katanga, 228
Kenya
  abolition of monarchy in, 56
  acquired rights in, 279, 296
  becoming republic of, 124
  becoming republic, effect on property, 210
  currency of, 197
  independence of, 55
  independence of, effect on appeals, 163, 164, 166
  independence of, effect on debts, 446
  independence of, effect on divorce, 128
  independence of, effect on legal system, 119
  independence of, effect on nationality, 521
  independence of, effect on pending claims, 149
  independence of, effect on pensions, 475, 476, 477
Korea
  annexation of, 380
  annexation of, effect on concessions, 322
  annexation of, effect on nationality, 504
  independence of, effect on nationality, 516

Land rights, see Acquired rights
Laos
  independence of, effect on civil service, 187
  independence of, effect of on copyright, 127
  independence of, effect on criminal proceedings, 172
  independence of, effect on debt, 434
  independence of, effect on judgments, 158
  independence of, effect on judicial system, 143
  independence of, effect on pending claims, 150
  independence of, effect on pensions, 472
  independence of, effect on property, 227
Latakieh, incorporation in Syria, effect on debt, 403
Latvia
  incorporation of in Soviet Union, effect on debt, 386–7
  independence of, effect on debt, 404
  independence of, effect on nationality, 530
Laurier, Sir W., 43
Laval, M., 332
Law, nature of, 30–2
Laws, see Legal system
Lease, international, effect on nationality, 500
Lebanon
  independence of, effect on concessions, 338–42
  independence of, effect on property, 222
  mandate over, effect on debt, 402–4
Legal system, effect of succession on, 30–1, 53–6, 73–4, 101–41, 237, 241, 337–8
  extension of to acquired territory, 106, 110, 111
  continuity of, 237, 241
Lenin, 20
Libya
  cession of, effect on debt, 398
  cession of, effect on pensions, 468

Libya (*cont.*)
  independence of, effect on contracts, 366
  independence of, effect on debt, 404, 435, 467
  independence of, effect on nationality, 514, 530
  independence of, effect on property, 202, 218–19
Limbay District, annexation of, effect on nationality, 501
limitation of actions, effect of changes on, 145
Lithuania
  incorporation of in Soviet Union, effect on debt, 386–7
  independence of, effect on debt, 404
  independence of, effect on judicial system, 142
  independence of, effect on nationality, 530
  seizure of railway by, 539
Loans, governing law of, 371
Local remedies, exhaustion of, effect of succession on rule concerning, 482, 539
Locus of cause of action, changes affecting, 144
Loi cadre, 1956, 78
Lombardy
  cession of, effect on debt, 397
  cession of, effect on nationality, 529
Louis XIII, 4
Louis Rwagasore, Crown Prince, 173
Louisiana
  cession of, effect on nationality, 504, 506
  cession of, effect on property, 204

Madagascar, 59
  annexation of, effect on concessions, 304, 308–10
  annexation of, effect on debt, 29, 377
Madras, dismissal of servants by, 183, 259
Maintenance orders, enforcement of, 127
Malagasy Institute of Issue, 73
Malagasy Republic, 58
  currency of, 72, 73
  in system of cooperation, 71, 72

  independence of, 74
  independence of, effect on appeals, 161
  independence of, effect on concessions, 344
  independence of, effect on judgments, 153
  independence of, effect on judicial system, 143
  independence of, effect on legal system, 133
  independence of, effect on nationality, 525, 526
  independence of, effect on pending claims, 150
  independence of, effect on property, 211
  independence of, effect on treaties, 76
  independence of, procedure adopted, 65
  Indians in, nationality of, 521
  judicial system of, 176
  membership of in French Community, 67
  transitional measures of in matter of justice, 74
Malawi
  becoming Crown dominion, 120
  independence of, 55, 57
  independence of, effect on appeals, 165
  independence of, effect on debt, 392–4
  independence of, effect on legal system, 119, 115, 123
  independence of, effect on nationality, 521, 522
  independence of, effect on pensions, 474, 475
  independence of, effect on property, 231
Malaya
  independence of, 53–4
  independence of, effect on legal system, 119
  independence of, effect on nationality, 522
  independence of, effect on pensions, 475, 477, 478
  independence of, effect on pending claims, 149

General Index

Malaya (cont.)
  independence of, effect on appeals, 165, 166
Malaysia
  formation of, 54
  formation of, effect on appeals, 163, 166
  formation of, effect on civil service, 186
  formation of, effect on legal system, 113, 119
  formation of, effect on pensions, 475, 477, 478
  formation of, effect on property, 232
  separation of Singapore from, effect on legal system, 118
Mali, 64
  independence of, effect on judicial system, 143
  independence of, effect on nationality, 525, 526
  independence of, procedure adopted, 65, 66
  judicial system of, 173
  membership of in West African Monetary Union, 73
Mali, Federation of
  currency of, 72
  dissolution of, 66
  establishment in, 74
  formation of, 76-7
  in system of cooperation, 72
  independence of, effect on concessions, 344
Malta
  independence of, 55
  independence of, effect on legal system, 119
  independence of, effect on nationality, 521
Manchukuo, debts of, 433
Mandate, consistency of laws with, 131
Mandated territories
  acquired rights in, 277
  concessions in, 335-6
  loans of, 430-1
Manila Railway Co., 313, 346
Martinique, 61
Mauritania, 59
  cession of, effect on nationality, 504

independence of, 67
independence of, effect on appeals, 161
independence of, effect on judicial system, 143
independence of, effect on nationality, 526
independence of, effect on property, 211
judicial system of, 174
membership of in West African Monetary Union, 73
Mauritius, legal system of, 108
Mayurbhanj State, merger of with Orissa, 257
Mentone, cession of, effect on pensions, 467
Metternich, Prince, 397
Mexico, independence of, effects on debt, 419
Military property, succession to, 204, 225
Milner, Lord, 487, 517
Minorca, cession of, effect on nationality, 506
Miquelon, treaty application to, 78
Mond Nickel Company, 335, 542
Monetary Union of Equatorial Africa and Cameroon, 70
Monetary Union of West Africa and Togo, 70, 73
Monopolies, 247
Montenegro
  debts of, 398
  separation of, effect on property, 214
Morocco
  acquired rights in, 292-4
  independence of, effect on appeals, 160
  independence of, effect on civil servants, 188
  independence of, effect on judicial system, 143
  independence of, effect on land titles, 292-4
  independence of, effect on legal system, 133
  independence of, effect on property, 212
  transportation in, 293

General Index

Municipal law, relationship of, with international law, 27, 82, 103, 371, 499
Mussolini, Duce B., 492
Muttra, conquest of, 258

Nabha
  cession of, effect on acquired rights, 256
  merger of with Patiala and East Punjab States Union, 259
Nassau, annexation of, effect on pensions, 467
National debt, definition of, 369
Nationalism, 11
Nationality, change of, effect on pensions, 468
  effect of succession on, 61, 67, 497–536
Nationality French, effect of independence on, 61, 67, 515–16, 523–7
'Nationality' linguistic use of, 498
Nationality of claims, effect of succession on, 537–542
Natural resources, permanent sovereignty, 279
Naturalized persons, effect of succession on nationality of, 517
Navarre, union of, with France, 4
Netherlands Indies, 97–8
Netherlands property in Indonesia, 284, 300
Netherlands–South Africa Railway Co., 541
New Caledonia, 61
  treaty application to, 78
Newfoundland, cession of to Canada, effect on legal system, 112
  transfer of to Canada, effect on debt, 427
  transfer of to Canada, effect on departments, 189
  transfer of to Canada, effect on pending claims, 146
  transfer of to Canada, effect on property, 225
New Granada, debts of, 389
New Guinea, mandate over, debts of, 430
New Zealand
  acquisition of, effect on acquired rights, 272
  tariff negotiations of with France, 40

Nicaragua, independence of, effect on debt, 419
Nice and Savoy
  cession of, effect on acquired rights, 242, 246
  cession of, effect on legal system, 108
  cession of, effect on nationality, 529
  cession of, effect on pensions, 467
Niger, 59
  independence of, 67
  independence of, effect on appeals, 161
  independence of, effect on judicial system, 143
  independence of, effect on nationality, 526
  judicial system of, 174
  membership of in Entente, 70
  membership of in West African Monetary Union, 73
Nigeria
  abolition of monarchy in, 56
  acquired rights in, 281
  independence of, effect on appeals, 165
  independence of, effect on legal system, 119
  independence of, effect on nationality, 521
  independence of, effect on pending claims, 149
  independence of, effect on pensions, 475, 476, 477, 479
Nisyros, cession of, effect on concessions, 325–6
Nitrate Railway Co., 346
Nkrumah, President, 281
North Borneo, union of with Malaysia, 113
Northern Cameroons, union of with Nigeria, 119
Northern Rhodesia, *see* Zambia
North Vietnam, acquired rights in, 291–2
Norway, cession of to Sweden, effect on debt, 396
Novation of debt, 375
Nyasaland, *see* Malawi

Oder-Neisse territories, taking of, effect on legal system, 111
Odious debts, 356

Olza District, cession of to Poland, effect on legal system, 40
Option of nationality, 529–36
Organic theory of the State, 12
Organization of African Unity, 70
Oriental Railway Co., 323
Orissa, merger of with Mayurbharj, 257
Ottawa Trade Agreement, 57
Ottoman Bank, 148
Ottoman Debt Arbitration, 5, 372, 402, 414, 420
Ottoman Empire
  dismemberment of, 5
  dismemberment of, effect on acquired rights, 277
  dismemberment of, effect on concessions, 307, 323–9
  dismemberment of, effect on nationality, 500, 515, 535–6
  dismemberment of, effect on pensions, 467
Ottoman public debt, 398, 399, 401–3
Overseas Territories, French, 75, 77, 79, 82

Pakistan
  independence of, effect on appeals, 168
  independence of, effect on civil service, 182–3
  independence of, effect on contracts, 363–6
  independence of, effect on criminal proceedings, 171
  independence of, effect on currency, 192
  independence of, effect on debt, 404–6
  independence of, effect on judgments, 153–5
  independence of, effect on legal system, 102, 116–17, 123, 125, 126
  independence of, effect on membership of U.N., 7, 8
  independence of, effect on nationality, 520, 527, 528
  independence of, effect on pending claims, 146–8
  independence of, effect on property, 220–2
  independence of, effect on treaties, 470–1, 474
Palazzo Venezia, 207
Palestine
  acquired rights in, 277
  archives of, 234
  mandate over, effect on concessions, 324–7
  mandate over, effect on jurisdiction, 145
  partition of, effect on acquired rights, 287–91
  partition of, effect on legal system, 128–9, 131–2
  partition of, effect on nationality, 498
  partition of, effect on pending claims, 148
  partition of, mandate over, effect on pensions, 472
  termination of mandate over, 431–3
  termination of mandate over, see Israel, Jordan
Palestine Currency Board, 193
Palestine Potash Ltd., 337
Panama, independence of, effect on debt, 398
Papal States
  annexation of, effect on treaties, 467
  debts of, 398
Paris, Convention of for Protection of Industrial Property, 78
Parliament and Crown, 36
Patiala and East Punjab States Union, 259
Patrimonio disponibile, 201, 219
Patrimonio indisponibile, 201, 215
Peaceful coexistence, 20, 21
Pending claims, 144–52
Pensions, succession to, 465–81
Permanent Mandates Commission, 430
Permanent Sovereignty over natural resources, 279
Personal obligations, 11
Personal union, 49
Personality, 3, 24
Peru, cession of territory by, effect on concessions, 308
Petsamo
  cession of, effect on claims, 542
  cession of, effect on concessions, 335

Philippines
- acquired rights in, 292
- cession of, effect on concessions, 311–12
- cession of, effect on nationality, 500, 504, 530
- cession of to United States, 29
- independence of, effect on contracts, 366
- independence of, effect on debt, 433–4
- independence of, effect on legal system, 129
- independence of, effect on pending claims, 146
- independence of, effect on property, 222

Phillimore, Sir R., 389
Pilsudski, Jozef, 135
Platen-Hallmund, Count, 514
Pledge, 374, 408–15
Poland
- cession of territory to by Czechoslovakia, 141
- expropriation of property by, 264–5, 272–7
- independence of, effect on acquired rights, 245
- independence of, effect on armed forces, 181
- independence of, effect on debt, 404
- independence of, effect on delicts, 493
- independence of, effect on judgments, 154
- independence of, effect on legal system, 134–41
- independence of, effect on nationality, 513
- independence of, effect on pensions, 469
- independence of, effect on property, 202, 203, 204
- restoration of, effect on contracts, 362

Porto Rico
- cession of, effect on legal system, 102
- cession of, effect on nationality, 503, 530
- cession of, effect on property, 204

Postal agreements, conclusion of by colonies, 39, 45
Potsdam Conference, 435

Poznan, 111
- cession of, effect on appeals, 168
- cession of, effect on criminal proceedings, 169
- cession of, effect on pending claims, 146

Practice of States, 18, 30
Precedent, 168–9
Prescription, effect of changes on, 145
President of France, office of, 69–70
Pretoria-Pietersburg Railway Co., 487, 488
Private law, 104–6, 107
Privy Council, appeals to, effect of succession on, 164–7
Procedural steps, effect of changes on, 145
Property, *see* acquired rights
Property located abroad, title to, 200, 207–10
Property rights, *see* acquired rights
Protectorate of Bohemia and Moravia, archives of, 233
Protectorates, Crown's powers in, 37
- ending of, 53–4
Public law, 104–6, 107
Public Officers' Agreements, 185, 186, 474–9
Punjab
- independence of, effect on judgments, 155
- partition of, effect on pending claims, 147
- partition of, effect on property, 220, 221

Quebec, legal system of, 108
Queensland, accession of to treaties, 42

Rajapramukh, accession of to India, 260
Rajasthan, merger of Bikaner in, 259
Ranjit Singh, Rajah, 259
Real obligations, 11
Recognition of foreign laws, 103
Repartition of debt, 395, 400, 414, 468
Republic
- becoming a, effect in Commonwealth, 55–7
- becoming a, effect on contracts, 367
- becoming a, effect on property, 210

Res judicata, effect of changes on, 145, 168
Reservation of bills, doctrine of, 38
Reserve Bank of India, 222
'Residence', concept of, 512, 513, 514
Responsibility, State, 134
Réunion, 61
Rhenish Confederation, formation of, effect on debt, 396
Rhodes, transfer of, effect on appeals, 158
Rhodesia, *see* Southern Rhodesia or Federation of Rhodesia and Nyasaland
Rhodesia Railways, 230
Risorgimento, 11
Roman law, succession doctrine in, 9
Roumania
 cession of territory to, effect on acquired rights, 266
 cession of territory by, effect on property, 214
Royal prerogative, 36, 37, 48, 49, 108, 120, 165–6
Royal Style and Titles, 48
Ruanda-Urundi, dismemberment of, effect on debt, 391–2
 dismemberment of, effect on legal system, 114
 partition of, effect on debt, 442
 partition of, effect on pending claims, 152
Rustchuk-Varna Railway, 307
Ruyuku Islands, administrative change over, effect on nationality, 518
Rwanda
 independence of, effect on criminal proceedings, 173
 independence of, effect on debt, 391–2, 442
 independence of, effect on legal system, 114
 independence of, effect on pending claims, 152

Saar
 occupation of, effect on civil servants, 179
 transfer of to France, effect on debt, 400

Sabah, 54
 civil servants in, 186
 incorporation of in Malaysia, effect on pensions, 475, 477
 property of, 232
Sahara, concessions in, 344
St Bartholomew, cession of, effect on pensions, 467
St Pierre, treaty application to, 78
St Pierre and Miquelon, 59, 61
Sainte-Marie Island, nationality in, 525
Salaries, effect of succession on, 480–1
Salonica, cession of, effect on appeals, 158
Samos
 cession of, effect on concessions, 327
 cession of, effect on delicts, 492
San Domingo
 annexation of by Spain, effect on acquired rights, 264
 Council of, 77
San Salvador, independence of, effect on debt, 419
Sarawak, 54
 incorporation of in Malaysia, effect on pensions, 475, 477
 civil servants in, 186
 annexation of territory to, effect on nationality, 501
 property of, 232
 union of with Malaysia, 113
Sardinia, incorporation of in Italy, 5
Savoy and Nice
 cession of, effect on contracts, 355
 cession of, effect on debt, 397
 cession of, effect on legal system, 108
 cession of, effect on pensions, 467
Savoy, communes of, effect on property, 216
Schleswig-Holstein
 cession of, effect on debt, 398
 cession of, effect on nationality, 535
 cession of, effect on pensions, 467
Secured debts, 407–15
Seizures, responsibility for, succession to, 486
Senegal, 59, 64
 independence of, 66
 independence of, effect on legal system, 133

General Index

Senegal (*cont.*)
  independence of, effect on nationality, 526
  independence of, effect on treaties, 76
  judicial system of, 173
  membership of in West African Monetary Union, 73
  President of, 70
  subrogation of in Mali's treaties, 66, 76–7
Serbia
  incorporation of in Yugoslavia, 5, 6
  independence of, effect on debt, 398
Settled colonies, 36–7
Shareholding, *situs* of, 117, 541–2
Ships, seizure of, responsibility for, succession to, 486
Sierra Leone
  acquired rights in, 281
  independence of, 55
  independence of, effect on appeals, 165
  independence of, effect on legal system, 119
  independence of, effect on nationality, 521
  independence of, effect on pending claims, 149
  independence of, effect on pensions, 477
Singapore
  civil servants in, 186
  independence of, effect on appeals, 163
  independence of, effect on pensions, 475, 477, 478
  participation of in Malaysia, 54
  secession of, effect on property, 232
  separation of from Malaysia, effect of on the legal system, 118
  union of with Malaysia, effect of on legal system, 113
Situs of property, changes of, 144
Slovakia
  creation of, effect of debt, 389
  state of, formation of, effect on pensions, 469
Société d'Electricité de Beyrouth, 339
Somalia
  formation of, effect on contracts, 366
  formation of, effect on property, 227

independence of, effect on appeals, 159
independence of, effect on nationality, 527
Somali Republic, independence of, effect on legal system, 112–13
Somaliland
  French, 59
  French, application of treaties to, 80
  government of British, 51
  independence of, 54
  independence of, effect on appeals, 165
  independence of, effect on contracts, 366
  independence of, effect on legal system, 112
  independence of, effect on pending claims, 149
  independence of, effect on pensions, 475–7
  independence of, effect on property, 227
  union of with Somali Republic, 112–13
Sopron-Köszeg Local Railway Co., 329
Soudan, 59
Soudanese Republic, *see* Mali
South Africa
  abolition of monarchy in, 56–7
  federation of, effect on debt, 386
  legal system of, 108
  withdrawal of from Commonwealth, effect on nationality, 522
South Arabia, Federation of, formation of, effect on appeals, 165
South Arabian Federation, 119
Southern Rhodesia
  member of Federation, 50–1
  pensions in, 474
  succession of to Federation, effect on property, 231
South West Africa, mandate over, effect on debt, 422
  mandate over, effect on treaties, 468
Sovereignty, change of, 6
  transmissibility of, 16, 17, 22, 23, 24, 26, 27, 28
Soviet, succession of to Tsarist Russia, 19, 20
Spain, cession of, effect on concessions, 311–12

State, organic theory of, 12
Statelessness, 503, 514, 517
States, successor, definition of, 8, 9
  continuity of, 4, 12, 13
Subrogation, 298, 327, 346, 372
Subrogation of Successor State, 239
Successor States, definition of, 8, 9
Sudetenland
  cession of, effect on nationality, 510, 521
  cession of, effect on pensions, 469
Sulu Islands, cession of to Spain, 270
Superannuation, effect of succession on, 479
Syria
  cession of to France, effect of on legal system, 112
  independence of, effect on property, 222
  mandate over, effect on debt, 402–4
  membership of in U.A.R., 112

Tahiti, annexation of, effect on debt, 377
Tanganyika
  abolition of monarchy in, 56
  becoming Crown dominion, 120
  becoming republic, effect on divorce, 128
  becoming republic, effect on property, 210
  independence of, 55, 57
  independence of, effect on appeals, 163, 164, 165, 166
  independence of, effect on divorces, 128
  independence of, effect on legal system, 119
  independence of, effect on nationality, 521, 522
  independence of, effect on pensions, 475, 477, 478
  union of with Zanzibar, 113–14
  union of with Zanzibar, effect on pending claims, 149
Tangier, return of to Morocco, effect on professions, 293
Tanzania
  currency of, 197
  formation of, effect of on legal system, 113–14
  union of, effect on pending claims, 149–50
Tarapaca
  cession of, effect on concessions, 308
  cession of, effect on debt, 409
Tax, right to, effect of succession on, 190
Taxation of acquired rights, 264
Taxation, effect of succession upon, 116–17
Taxes, arrears of, succession to, 214, 231
Templar Mediation, 194–5, 287–91
Territory
  relationship of debts to, 407–15
  theories of, 22–4, 27–8
Teschen, cession of, effect on nationality, 514–15
Texas
  incorporation of in U.S., effect on debt, 384–6, 412
  independence of, effect on acquired rights, 249
  independence of, effect on judgments, 152–3
  secession of, effect on debt, 397
Togo
  independence of, effect on nationality, 525, 526
  independence of, effect on property, 212
  judicial system of, 174
  monetary union with, 70
Torts, see delicts
Trans-Arabian Pipeline Co., 337
Transjordan, independence of, effect on concessions, 334
Transvaal
  annexation of, 466
  annexation of, effect on debt, 376
  see also Boer Republics
Transvaal Concessions Commission, 317–22, 356
Treaties
  application of to dependent territories, 77–8
  commercial, see commercial treaties
  devolution of on Francophone States, 66, 76
  effect on independence on, 42
  French, application of, 77–79

Treaties (*cont.*)
  internal implementation of, in French law, 80–2
  succession to, 42
Trieste
  archives of, 233
  Free Territory of, debts of, 404
  occupation of, effect on appeals, 159
  property in, 215
Trinidad and Tobago
  independence of, 55
  independence of, effect on appeals, 165
  independence of, effect on legal system, 119
  independence of, effect on nationality, 521
  independence of, effect on pending claims, 149
  independence of, effect on pensions, 475, 477
Trust Territories, Crown's powers in, 37
Tunis, protection over, effect on debt, 377
Tunisia
  acquired rights in, 292–4
  independence of, effect on appeals, 160
  independence of, effect on judicial system, 143
  independence of, effect on land titles, 292–4
  transportation in, 293
Turkey
  cession of territory by, effect on acquired rights, 270
  cession of territory by, effect on delicts, 484

Ubangi-Shari, 59
Uganda
  abolition of monarchy in, 56
  becoming Crown dominion, 120
  becoming republic, effect on property, 210
  currency of, 197
  independence of, 55, 57
  independence of, effect on appeals, 163, 164, 165, 166
  independence of, effect on debt, 426
  independence of, effect on legal system, 119
  independence of, effect on nationality, 521, 522
  independence of, effect on pending claims, 149
  independence of, effect on pensions, 475, 477
  independence of, effect on precedent, 169
Union, effect of on legal system, 112–13
Union Africaine et Malgache, 70
Union Minière du Haut-Katanga, 228, 343
United Arab Republic
  concessions in, 344
  formation of, effect on acquired rights, 279
  formation of, effect on debt, 386
  legal system of, 112
United Nations, attitude of towards succession, 7
United Nations declaration on permanent sovereignty over natural resources, 279
United Netherlands
  dissolution of, 5
  formation of, effect on delicts, 486
  see also Belgium, independence of
United States
  acquisition of territory by, effect on acquired rights, 265
  independence of, effect on debt, 396
  independence of, effect on legal system, 118
  independence of, effect on nationality, 519
Universal succession theory, 9, 10, 17, 24, 28, 373, 407, 492
Unjustified enrichment, 34, 104, 298, 375, 376, 483
Unjustified enrichment, doctrine of, 243–4, 266–7, 298, 303
Unneutral service, 319
Upper Silesia
  expropriation in, 266, 272–7
  cession of, effect on nationality, 534
  cession of, effect on pensions, 465, 466

General Index

Upper Volta
  independence of, 67
  independence of, effect on appeals, 161
  independence of, effect on judicial system, 150
  independence of, effect on nationality, 526
  judicial system of, 174
  legal system of, 133
  membership of in Entente, 70
  membership of in West African Monetary Union,
Uppington, Sir Thomas, 40
Uruguay, independence of, effect on debt, 419
Uttar Pradesh, merger of Vindhya Pradesh in, 259

Venezia
  cession of, effect on debt, 419
  cession of, effect on nationality, 530
  cession of, effect on pensions, 469
Venezuela
  independence of, effect on debt, 388, 419
  independence of, effect on delicts, 486
Vietnam
  acquired rights in, 291–2
  independence of, effect on civil service, 187
  independence of, effect of on copyright, 127
  independence of, effect on criminal proceedings, 172
  independence of, effect on debt, 434
  independence of, effect on judgments, 158
  independence of, effect on judicial system, 143
  independence of, effect on nationality, 524–5
  independence of, effect on pending claims, 150
  independence of, effect on pensions, 472
  independence of, effect on property, 227

Vindhya Pradesh, merger of in Uttar Pradesh, 259
Volta, 59

Warsaw Convention, 79
Wavell, Lord, 474
Weimar Constitution, 111
West Africa
  Customs Union of, 70
  Monetary Union of, 70, 73
West Indies
  evolution of, 51
  Federation of, dissolution of, effect on appeals, 164
  Federation of, dissolution of, effect on legal system, 114
  proposed tariff agreement of with United States, 40
Westminster, Statute of 1931, 38, 47, 48, 49, 51, 55
West New Guinea, cession of to Indonesia, effect on acquired rights, 278
Westphalia
  Kingdom of, formation of, effect on debt, 396
  Kingdom of, formation of, effect on pensions, 467
  Kingdom of, termination of, 10
Will of States, concept of, 15, 16, 33
World Bank, 371, 392
World Bank loans, 446–8

Yugoslavia
  dismemberment of, effect on debt, 390
  formation of, 5, 6
  partition of, effect on property, 214

Zambia
  exchange controls of, 197
  independence of, 50, 54
  independence of, effect on appeals, 165
  independence of, effect on concessions, 344–5
  independence of, effect on debt, 392–4
  independence of, effect on legal system, 115, 119, 123
  independence of, effect on pending claims, 149

Zambia (*cont.*)
  independence of, effect on pensions, 474, 475
  independence of, effect on property, 210, 231
  independence of, effect on nationality, 521
Zanzibar
  acquired rights in, 296
  independence of, effect on appeals, 164, 166
  independence of, effect on nationality, 521
  independence of, effect on pending claims, 149
  independence of, effect on pensions, 475, 477
  revolution in, 150
  union of with Tanganyika, 113
  union of with Tanganyika, effect on pending claims, 149
Zeltsweg-Wolfsberg und Unterdrauberg-Woellen Railway Co., 330

JX
4053
.O22
v.1